T0191533

Lecture Notes in Computer Science   12273

More information about this series at http://www.springer.com/series/7407

Donghyun Kim · R. N. Uma ·
Zhipeng Cai · Dong Hoon Lee (Eds.)

Computing and Combinatorics

26th International Conference, COCOON 2020
Atlanta, GA, USA, August 29–31, 2020
Proceedings

 Springer

Editors
Donghyun Kim
Georgia State University
Atlanta, USA

Zhipeng Cai
Computer Science
Georgia State University
Atlanta, GA, USA

R. N. Uma
Department of Mathematics and Physics
North Carolina Central University
Durham, NC, USA

Dong Hoon Lee
Korea University
Seoul, South Korea

ISSN 0302-9743   ISSN 1611-3349   (electronic)
Lecture Notes in Computer Science
ISBN 978-3-030-58149-7   ISBN 978-3-030-58150-3   (eBook)
https://doi.org/10.1007/978-3-030-58150-3

LNCS Sublibrary: SL1 – Theoretical Computer Science and General Issues

This Springer imprint is published by the registered company Springer Nature Switzerland AG
The registered company address is: Gewerbestrasse 11, 6330 Cham, Switzerland

Preface

The 26th International Computing and Combinatorics Conference (COCOON 2020) was held during August 29–31, 2020. This year, COCOON 2020 was organized as a fully online conference. COCOON 2020 provided an excellent venue for researchers working in the area of algorithms, theory of computation, computational complexity, and combinatorics related to computing. The technical program of the conference included 54 regular papers selected by the Program Committee from 126 full submissions received in response to the call for papers. Each submission was carefully reviewed by Program Committee members and/or external reviewers. Some of the papers were selected for publication in special issues of *Theoretical Computer Science* and the *Journal of Combinatorial Optimization*. It is expected that the journal version of the papers will appear in a more complete form.

We thank everyone who made this meeting possible: the authors for submitting papers, the Program Committee members, and external reviewers for volunteering their time to review conference papers. We also appreciate the financial sponsorship from Springer for the Best Paper Award. We would also like to extend special thanks to the chairs and conference Organizing Committee for their work in making COCOON 2020 a successful event.

August 2020

Donghyun Kim
R. N. Uma
Zhipeng Cai
Dong Hoon Lee

Organization

Steering Committee Members

Lian Li (Chair)	Hefei University of Technology, China
Zhipeng Cai	Georgia State University, USA
Xiaoming Sun	Chinese Academy of Sciences, China
My Thai	University of Florida, USA
Cong Tian	Xidian University, China
Jianping Yin	Dongguan University of Technology, China
Guochuan Zhang	Zhejiang University, China
Zhao Zhang	Zhejiang Normal University, China

General Chairs

Zhipeng Cai	Georgia State University, USA
Dong Hoon Lee	Korea University, South Korea

Program Chairs

Donghyun Kim	Georgia State University, USA
R. N. Uma	North Carolina Central University, USA

Publication Chairs

Yan Huang	Kennesaw State University, USA
Yingshu Li	Georgia State University, USA

Web/Submission System Chairs

Yongmin Ju	Georgia State University, USA
Yi Liang	Georgia State University, USA
Vannel Zeufack	Kennesaw State University, USA

Financial Chairs

Yongmin Ju	Georgia State University, USA
Daehee Seo	Sangmyung University, South Korea

Local Organization Chairs

Jeongsu Park	Korea University, South Korea
Daehee Seo	Sangmyung University, South Korea

Program Committee

Hans-Joachim Boeckenhauer	ETH Zurich, Switzerland
Zhi-Zhong Chen	Tokyo Denki University, Japan
Rajesh Chitnis	University of Birmingham, UK
Ovidiu Daescu	The University of Texas at Dallas, USA
Bhaskar Dasgupta	University of Illinois at Chicago, USA
Thang Dinh	Virginia Commonwealth University, USA
Stanley Fung	University of Leicester, UK
Xiaofeng Gao	Shanghai Jiao Tong University, China
Anirban Ghosh	University of North Florida, USA
Raffaele Giancarlo	Universita di Palermo, Italy
Yan Huang	Kennesaw State University, USA
Michael Khachay	Krasovsky Institute of Mathematics and Mechanics, Russia
Sung-Sik Kwon	North Carolina Central University, USA
Daniel Lee	Simon Fraser University, Canada
Joong-Lyul Lee	The University of North Carolina at Pembroke, USA
Shuai Cheng Li	City University of Hong Kong, Hong Kong
Wei Li	Georgia State University, USA
Xianyue Li	Lanzhou University, China
Bei Liu	Northwest University, USA
Bodo Manthey	University of Twente, The Netherlands
Manki Min	Louisiana Tech University, USA
Rashika Mishra	Lenovo, USA
N. S. Narayanaswamy	IIT Madras, India
Nam Nguyen	Towson University, USA
Pavel Skums	Georgia State University, USA
Xiaoming Sun	Institute of Computing Technology, Chinese Academy of Sciences, China
Ryuhei Uehara	Japan Advanced Institute of Science and Technology, Japan
Jianxin Wang	Central South University, China
Wei Wang	Xi'an Jiaotong University, China
Gerhard J. Woeginger	RWTH Aachen University, Germany
Wen Xu	Texas Woman's University, USA
Boting Yang	University of Regina, Canada
Chee Yap	New York University, USA

Peng Zhang	Shandong University, China
Zhao Zhang	Zhejiang Normal University, China
Yi Zhu	Hawaii Pacific University, USA
Yuqing Zhu	California State University Los Angeles, USA
Martin Ziegler	KAIST, South Korea

Contents

Subspace Approximation with Outliers

Amit Deshpande[1] and Rameshwar Pratap[2(✉)]

[1] Microsoft Research, Bengaluru, India
amitdesh@microsoft.com
[2] IIT Mandi, Mandi, India
rameshwar@iitmandi.ac.in

Abstract. The subspace approximation problem with outliers, for given n points in d dimensions $x_1, x_2, \ldots, x_n \in \mathbb{R}^d$, an integer $1 \leq k \leq d$, and an outlier parameter $0 \leq \alpha \leq 1$, is to find a k-dimensional linear subspace of $\mathbb{R}^d$ that minimizes the sum of squared distances to its nearest $(1-\alpha)n$ points. More generally, the ℓ_p subspace approximation problem with outliers minimizes the sum of p-th powers of distances instead of the sum of squared distances. Even the case of $p = 2$ or robust PCA is non-trivial, and previous work requires additional assumptions on the input or generative models for it. Any multiplicative approximation algorithm for the subspace approximation problem with outliers must solve the robust subspace recovery problem, a special case in which the $(1-\alpha)n$ inliers in the optimal solution are promised to lie exactly on a k-dimensional linear subspace. However, robust subspace recovery is Small Set Expansion (SSE)-hard, and known algorithmic results for robust subspace recovery require strong assumptions on the input, e.g., any d outliers must be linearly independent.

In this paper, we show how to extend dimension reduction techniques and bi-criteria approximations based on sampling and coresets to the problem of subspace approximation with outliers. To get around the SSE-hardness of robust subspace recovery, we assume that the squared distance error of the optimal k-dimensional subspace summed over the optimal $(1 - \alpha)n$ inliers is at least δ times its squared-error summed over all n points, for some $0 < \delta \leq 1 - \alpha$. Under this assumption, we give an efficient algorithm to find a *weak coreset* or a subset of $\mathrm{poly}(k/\epsilon) \log(1/\delta) \log\log(1/\delta)$ points whose span contains a k-dimensional subspace that gives a multiplicative $(1+\epsilon)$-approximation to the optimal solution. The running time of our algorithm is linear in n and d. Interestingly, our results hold even when the fraction of outliers α is large, as long as the obvious condition $0 < \delta \leq 1-\alpha$ is satisfied. We show similar results for subspace approximation with ℓ_p error or more general M-estimator loss functions, and also give an additive approximation for the affine subspace approximation problem.

Full version of paper is available here https://arxiv.org/pdf/2006.16573.pdf.

D. Kim et al. (Eds.): COCOON 2020, LNCS 12273, pp. 1–13, 2020.
https://doi.org/10.1007/978-3-030-58150-3_1

1   Introduction

Finding low-dimensional representations of large, high-dimensional input data is an important first step for several problems in computational geometry, data mining, machine learning, and statistics. For given input points $x_1, x_2, \ldots, x_n \in \mathbb{R}^d$, a positive integer $1 \leq k \leq d$ and $1 \leq p < \infty$, the ℓ_p subspace approximation problem asks to find a k-dimensional linear subspace V of $\mathbb{R}^d$ that essentially minimizes the sum of p-th powers of the distances of all the points to the subspace V, or to be precise, it minimizes the ℓ_p error

$$\left(\sum_{i=1}^n d(x_i, V)^p \right)^{1/p} \quad \text{or equivalently} \quad \sum_{i=1}^n d(x_i, V)^p.$$

For $p = 2$, the optimal subspace is spanned by the top k right singular vectors of the matrix $X \in \mathbb{R}^{n \times d}$ formed by $x_1, x_2, \ldots, x_n$ as its rows. The optimal solution for $p = 2$ can be computed efficiently by the Singular Value Decomposition (SVD) in time $O\left(\min\{nd^2, n^2d\} \right)$. Liberty's deterministic matrix sketching [15] and subsequent work [9] provide a faster, deterministic algorithm that runs in $O\left(nd \cdot \text{poly}(k/\epsilon) \right)$ time and gives a multiplicative $(1 + \epsilon)$-approximation to the optimum. There is also a long line of work on randomized algorithms [17,19] that sample a subset of points and output a subspace from their span, giving a multiplicative $(1 + \epsilon)$-approximation in running time $O(\text{nnz}(X)) + (n + d)\text{poly}(k/\epsilon)$, where $\text{nnz}(X)$ is the number of non-zero entries in X. These are especially useful on sparse data.

For $p \neq 2$, unlike the $p = 2$ case, we do not know any simple description of the optimal subspace. For any $p \geq 1$, Shyamalkumar and Varadarajan [18] give a $(1 + \epsilon)$-approximation algorithm that runs in time $O\left(nd \cdot \exp((k/\epsilon)^{O(p)}) \right)$. Building upon this, Deshpande and Varadarajan [4] give a bi-criteria $(1+\epsilon)$-approximation by finding a subset of $s = (k/\epsilon)^{O(p)}$ points in time $O\left(nd \cdot \text{poly}(k/\epsilon) \right)$ such that their s-dimensional linear span gives a $(1 + \epsilon)$-approximation to the optimal k-dimensional subspace. The subset they find is basically a *weak coreset*, and projecting onto its span also gives dimension-reduction result for subspace approximation. Feldman et al. [6] improve the running time to $nd \cdot \text{poly}(k/\epsilon) + (n + d) \cdot \exp(\text{poly}(k/\epsilon))$ for $p = 1$. Feldman and Langberg [5] extend this result to achieve a running time of $nd \cdot \text{poly}(k/\epsilon) + \exp((k/\epsilon)^{O(p)})$ for any $p \geq 1$. Clarkson and Woodruff [3] improve this running time to $O(\text{nnz}(X) + (n + d) \cdot \text{poly}(k/\epsilon) + \exp(\text{poly}(k/\epsilon)))$ for any $p \in [1, 2)$. The case $p \in [1, 2)$, especially $p = 1$, is important because the ℓ_1 error (i.e., the sum of distances) is more robust to outliers than the ℓ_2 error (i.e., the sum of squared distances).

We consider the following variant of ℓ_p subspace approximation in the presence of outliers. Given points $x_1, x_2, \ldots, x_n \in \mathbb{R}^d$, an integer $1 \leq k \leq d$, $1 \leq p < \infty$, and an outlier parameter $0 \leq \alpha \leq 1$, find a k-dimensional linear subspace V that minimizes the sum of p-th powers of distances of the $(1 - \alpha)n$ points nearest to it. In other words, let $N_\alpha(V) \subseteq [n]$ consist of the indices of the nearest $(1 - \alpha)n$ points to V among $x_1, x_2, \ldots, x_n$. We want to minimize $\sum_{i \in N_\alpha(V)} d(x_i, V)^p$.

The robust subspace recovery problem is a special case in which the optimal error for the subspace approximation problem with outliers is promised to be zero, that is, the optimal subspace V is promised to go through some $(1 - \alpha)n$ points among $x_1, x_2, \ldots, x_n$. Thus, any multiplicative approximation must also have zero error and recover the optimal subspace. Khachiyan [11] proved that it is NP-hard to find a $(d - 1)$-dimensional subspace that contains at least $(1 - \epsilon)(1 - 1/d)n$ points. Hardt and Moitra [10] study robust subspace recovery and define an (ϵ, δ)-Gap-Inlier problem of distinguishing between these two cases: (a) there exists a subspace of dimension δn containing $(1 - \epsilon)\delta n$ points and (b) every subspace of dimension δn contains at most $\epsilon \delta n$ points. They show a polynomial time reduction from the (ϵ, δ)-Gap-Small-Subset-Expansion problem to the (ϵ, δ)-Gap-Inlier problem. For more on Small Set Expansion conjecture and its connections to Unique Games, please see [16]. Under a strong assumption on the data (that requires any d or fewer outliers to be linearly independent), Hardt and Moitra give an efficient algorithms for finding k-dimensional subspace containing $(1 - k/d)n$ points. This naturally leaves open the question of finding other more reasonable approximations to the subspace approximation problem with outliers.

In recent independent work, Bhaskara and Kumar (see Theorem 12 in [1]) showed that if (ϵ, δ)-Gap-Small-Subset-Expansion problem is NP-hard, then there exists an instance of subspace approximation with outliers where the optimal inliers lie on a k-dimensional subspace but it is NP-hard to find even a subspace of dimension $O(k/\sqrt{\epsilon})$ that contains all but $(1 + \delta/4)$ times more points than the optimal number of outliers. This showed that even bi-criteria approximation for subspace recovery is a challenging problem. We compare and contrast our results with the result of Bhaskara and Kumar [1]. Their algorithm throws more outlier than the optimal solution, while we don't throw any extra outlier. Also, their bi-criteria approximation depends on the "rank-k condition" number which is a somewhat stronger assumption than ours.

The problem of clustering using points and lines in the presence of outliers has been studied in special cases of k-median and k-means clustering [2,13], and points and line clustering [7]. Krishnaswamy et al. [13] give a constant factor approximation for k-median and k-means clustering with outliers, whereas Feldman and Schulman give $(1 + \epsilon)$-approximations for k-median with outliers and k-line median with outliers that run in time linear in n and d.

Another recent line of research on robust regression considers data coming from an underlying distribution where a fraction of it is arbitrarily corrupted [12,14]. The problem we study is different as we do not assume any generative model for the input.

2   Our Contributions

– We assume that the ℓ_p error of the optimal subspace summed over the optimal $(1 - \alpha)n$ inliers is at least δ times its total ℓ_p error summed over all n points, for some $\delta > 0$. Under this assumption, we give an algorithm to efficiently find a subset of $\text{poly}(pk/\epsilon) \cdot \log(1/\delta) \log \log(1/\delta)$ points from $x_1, x_2, \ldots, x_n$ such that the span of this subset contains a k-dimensional linear subspace whose ℓ_p error over its nearest $(1 - \alpha)n$ points is within $(1 + \epsilon)$ of the optimum. The running time of our algorithm is linear in n and d. Note that even for δ as small as $1/\text{poly}(n)$, our algorithm outputs a fairly small subset of $\text{poly}(pk/\epsilon) \cdot \log n \log \log n$ points. The running time of our sampling-based algorithm is linear in n and d.

- Alternatively, the entire span of the above subset is a linear subspace of dimension $\text{poly}(pk/\epsilon) \cdot \log(1/\delta) \log \log(1/\delta)$ that gives a bi-criteria multiplicative $(1 + \epsilon)$-approximation to the optimal k-dimensional solution to the ℓ_p subspace approximation problem with outliers. Interestingly, this holds even when the fraction of outliers α is large, as long as the obvious condition $0 < \delta \leq 1 - \alpha$ is satisfied.

- Our assumption that the ℓ_p error of the optimal subspace summed over the optimal $(1 - \alpha)n$ inliers is at least δ times its total ℓ_p error summed over all n points, for some $\delta > 0$, is more reasonable and realistic than the assumptions used in previous work on subspace approximation with outliers. Without this assumption, our problem (even its special case of subspace recovery) is known to be Small Set Expansion (SSE)-hard [10].

- The technical contribution of our work is in showing that the sampling-based weak coreset constructions and dimension reduction results for the subspace approximation problem without outliers [4] also extend to its robust version for data with outliers. If we know the inlier-outlier partition of the data, then the result of [4] can easily be extended for the outlier version of the problem. However, if we don't know such a partitioning, then a brute-force approach has to go over all $\binom{n}{(1-\alpha)n}$ subsets and picks the best solution. This is certainly not an efficient approach as the number of such subsets is exponential in n. Further, on inputs that satisfy our assumption (stated above), it is easy to see that solving the subspace approximation problem without outliers gives a multiplicative $1/\delta$-approximation to the subspace approximation problem with outliers. Our contribution lies in showing that this approximation guarantee can be improved significantly in a small number of additional sampling steps.

- We show immediate extensions of our results to more general M-estimator loss functions as previously considered by [3].

- We show that our multiplicative approximation for the *linear* subspace approximation problem under ℓ_2 error implies an additive approximation for the *affine* subspace approximation problem under ℓ_2 error. The running time of this algorithm is also linear in n and d.

3   Warm-Up: Least Squared Error Line Approximation with Outliers

As a warm-up towards the main proof, we first consider the case $k = 1$ and $p = 2$, that is, for a given $0 < \alpha < 1$, we want to find the best line that minimizes the sum of squared distances summed over its nearest $(1 - \alpha)n$ points. Let $x_1, x_2, \ldots, x_n \in \mathbb{R}^d$ be the given points and let l^* be the optimal line. Let $I \subseteq [n]$ consist of the indices of the nearest $(1 - \alpha)n$ points to l^* among $x_1, x_2, \ldots, x_n$.

Our algorithm iteratively builds a subset $S \subseteq [n]$ by starting from $S = \emptyset$ and in each step samples with replacement $\text{poly}(k/\epsilon)$ i.i.d. points where each point x_i is picked with probability proportional to its squared distance to the span of the current subset $d(x_i, \text{span}\,(S))^2$. We abuse the notation as $\text{span}\,(S)$ to denote the linear subspace spanned by $\{x_i \; : \; i \in S\}$. These sampled points are added to S and the sampling algorithm is repeated $\text{poly}(k/\epsilon)$ times.

3.1   Additive Approximation

We are looking for a small subset $S \subseteq [n]$ of size $\text{poly}(1/\epsilon)$ that contains a close additive approximation to the optimal subspace over the optimal inliers, that is, for the projection of l^* onto $\text{span}\,(S)$ denoted by $P_S(l^*)$,

$$\sum_{i \in I} d(x_i, P_S(l^*))^2 \le \sum_{i \in I} d(x_i, l^*)^2 + \epsilon \sum_{i=1}^{n} \|x_i\|^2 \tag{1}$$

This immediately implies that there exists a line l_S in $\text{span}\,(S)$ such that

$$\sum_{i \in N_\alpha(l_S)} d(x_i, l_S)^2 \le \sum_{i \in I} d(x_i, l^*)^2 + \epsilon \sum_{i=1}^{n} \|x_i\|^2,$$

where $N_\alpha(l_S) \subseteq [n]$ consists of the indices of the nearest $(1 - \alpha)n$ points from $x_1, x_2, \ldots, x_n$ to l_S.

Given any subset $S \subseteq [n]$, define the set of *bad* points as a subset of inliers I whose error w.r.t. $P_S(l^*)$ is somewhat larger than their error w.r.t. the optimal line l^*, that is, $B(S) = \{i \in I \; : \; d(x_i, P_S(l^*))^2 > (1 + \epsilon/2)\,d(x_i, l^*)^2\}$ and *good* points as $G(S) = I \setminus B(S)$. The following lemma shows that sampling points with probability proportional to their squared lengths $\|x_i\|^2$ picks a bad point from $B(S)$ with probability at least $\epsilon/2$. Its proof is deferred to the full version.

Lemma 1. *If $S \subseteq [n]$ does not satisfy (1), then $\sum_{i \in B(S)} \|x_i\|^2 \ge \frac{\epsilon}{2} \sum_{i=1}^{n} \|x_i\|^2$.*

Below we show that a *bad* point sampled by squared-length sampling can be used to get another line closer to the optimal solution by a multiplicative factor, and repeat this. A proof of the following theorem is deferred to the full version.

Theorem 1. *For any given $x_1, x_2, \ldots, x_n \in \mathbb{R}^d$, let S be an i.i.d. sample of $O\left((1/\epsilon^2)\,\log(1/\epsilon)\right)$ points picked by squared-length sampling. Let $I \subseteq [n]$ be the set of optimal $(1 - \alpha)n$ inliers and l^* be the optimal line that minimizes their squared distance. Then*

$$\sum_{i \in I} d(x_i, P_S(l^*))^2 \le \sum_{i \in I} d(x_i, l^*)^2 + \epsilon \sum_{i=1}^{n} \|x_i\|^2, \quad \text{with a constant probability.}$$

3.2 Multiplicative Approximation

To turn this into a multiplicative $(1+\epsilon)$ guarantee, we need to use this adaptively by treating the projections of $x_1, x_2, \ldots, x_n$ orthogonal to span (S) as our new points, and repeating the squared length sampling on these new points. Here is the modified statement of the additive approximation that we need.

Theorem 2. *For any given points $x_1, x_2, \ldots, x_n \in \mathbb{R}^d$ and any initial subset S_0, let S be an i.i.d. sample of $O\left((1/\epsilon^2)\ \log(1/\epsilon)\right)$ points sampled with probability proportional to $d(x_i, \text{span}\,(S_0))^2$. Let $I \subseteq [n]$ be the set of optimal $(1-\alpha)n$ inliers and l^* be the optimal line that minimizes their squared distance. Then, with a constant probability, we have*

$$\sum_{i \in I} d(x_i, P_{S \cup S_0}(l^*))^2 \le \sum_{i \in I} d(x_i, l^*)^2 + \epsilon \sum_{i=1}^{n} d(x_i, \text{span}\,(S_0))^2.$$

Proof. Similar to the proof of Theorem 1 but using the projections of x_i's orthogonal to span (S_0) as the point set. In particular, we apply Lemma 1 to the projections of x_i's orthogonal span (S_0) instead of x_i's. Note that Theorem 1 is a special case with $S_0 = \emptyset$.

Repeating this squared-distance sampling adaptively for multiple rounds brings the additive approximation error down exponentially in the number of rounds. We defer a proof of the following theorem to the full version.

Theorem 3. *For any given points $x_1, x_2, \ldots, x_n \in \mathbb{R}^d$, any initial subset S_0 and positive integer T, let S_t be an i.i.d. sample of $O\left((1/\epsilon^2)\ \log(1/\epsilon)\ \log T\right)$ points sampled with probability proportional to $d(x_i, \text{span}\,(S_{t-1}))^2$, for $1 \le t \le T$. Let $I \subseteq [n]$ be the set of optimal $(1 - \alpha)n$ inliers and l^* be the optimal line that minimizes their squared distance. Then, with a constant probability,*

$$\sum_{i \in I} d(x_i, P_{S_0 \cup S_1 \cup \ldots \cup S_T}(l^*))^2 \le (1+\epsilon) \sum_{i \in I} d(x_i, l^*)^2 + \epsilon^T \sum_{i=1}^{n} d(x_i, \text{span}\,(S_0))^2.$$

Now assume that the optimal inlier error for l^* is at least δ times its error over the entire data, that is, $\sum_{i \in I} d(x_i, l^*)^2 \ge \delta \sum_{i=1}^{n} d(x_i, l^*)^2$. In that case, we can show a much stronger multiplicative $(1 + \epsilon)$-approximation instead of additive one using similar analysis as of [8]. We defer its proof to the full version of the paper.

Theorem 4. *For any given points $x_1, x_2, \ldots, x_n \in \mathbb{R}^d$, let $I \subseteq [n]$ be the set of optimal $(1 - \alpha)n$ inliers and l^* be the optimal line that minimizes their squared distance. Suppose $\sum_{i \in I} d(x_i, l^*)^2 \ge \delta \sum_{i=1}^{n} d(x_i, l^*)^2$. For any $0 < \epsilon < 1$, we can efficiently find a subset S of size $O\left((1/\epsilon^2) \log(1/\epsilon) \log(1/\delta) \log \log(1/\delta)\right)$ s.t.*

$$\sum_{i \in I} d(x_i, P_S(l^*))^2 \le (1+\epsilon) \sum_{i \in I} d(x_i, l^*)^2, \quad \text{with a constant probability.}$$

4 ℓ_p subspace approximation with outliers

Given an instance of k-dimensional subspace approximation with outliers as points $x_1, x_2, \ldots, x_n \in \mathbb{R}^d$, a positive integer $1 \le k \le d$, a real number $p \ge 1$, and an outlier parameter $0 < \alpha < 1$, let the optimal k-dimensional linear subspace be V^* that minimizes the ℓ_p error summed over its nearest $(1 - \alpha)n$ points from $x_1, x_2, \ldots, x_n$. Let $I \subseteq [n]$ denote the subset of indices of these nearest $(1 - \alpha)n$ points to V^*. In other words, $I = N_\alpha(V^*)$ consists of the indices of the optimal inliers. Given any subset $S \subseteq [n]$, let l_S be the line or direction in it that makes the smallest angle with V^*, and define the subspace W_S as the rotation of V^* along this angle so as to contain l_S. To be precise, let l^* be the projection of l_S onto V^* and let W^* be the orthogonal complement of l^* in V^*. Observe that W_S is the k-dimensional linear subspace spanned by l_S and W^*. We say that S contains a line l_S useful for *additive* approximation if

$$\sum_{i \in I} d(x_i, W_S)^p \le \sum_{i \in I} d(x_i, V^*)^p + \epsilon \sum_{i=1}^n \|x_i\|^p . \tag{2}$$

Define the set of *bad* points as the subset of inliers I whose error w.r.t. W_S is somewhat larger than their error w.r.t. the optimal subspace V^*, that is, $B(S) = \{i \in I : d(x_i, W_S)^p > (1 + \epsilon/2) \, d(x_i, V^*)^p\}$ and *good* points as $G(S) = I \setminus B(S)$. The following lemma shows that sampling i-th points with probability proportional to $\|x_i\|^p$ picks a *bad* point $i \in B(S)$ with probability at least $\epsilon/2$. A proof of the following lemma is deferred to the full version of the paper.

Lemma 2. *If $S \subseteq [n]$ does not satisfy (2), then $\sum_{i \in B(S)} \|x_i\|^p \ge \frac{\epsilon}{2} \sum_{i=1}^n \|x_i\|^p$.*

4.1 Additive Approximation: One Dimension at a Time

Below we show that a *bad* point $i \in B(S)$ can be used to improve W_S, or in other words, span $(S \cup \{i\})$ contains a line $l_{S \cup \{i\}}$ that is much closer to V^* than l_S. We defer a proof of the following theorem to the full version of the paper.

Theorem 5. *For any given points $x_1, x_2, \ldots, x_n \in \mathbb{R}^d$, let S be an i.i.d. sample of $O\left((p^2/\epsilon^2) \, \log(1/\epsilon)\right)$ points picked with probabilities proportional to $\|x_i\|^p$. Let $I \subseteq [n]$ be the set of optimal $(1 - \alpha)n$ inliers and V^* be the optimal subspace that minimizes the ℓ_p error over the inliers. Also let W_S be defined as in the beginning of Sect. 4. Then, with a constant probability, we have*

$$\sum_{i \in I} d(x_i, W_S)^p \le \sum_{i \in I} d(x_i, V^*)^p + \epsilon \sum_{i=1}^n \|x_i\|^p .$$

Note that we can start with any given initial subspace S_0 and prove a similar result for sampling points with probability proportional to $d(x_i, \text{span}(S_0))^p$.

Theorem 6. *For any given points* $x_1, x_2, \ldots, x_n \in \mathbb{R}^d$ *and an initial subspace* S_0, *let* S *be an i.i.d. sample of* $O\left((p^2/\epsilon^2) \log(1/\epsilon)\right)$ *points picked with probabilities proportional to* $d(x_i, \mathrm{span}\,(S_0))^p$. *Let* $I \subseteq [n]$ *be the set of optimal* $(1 - \alpha)n$ *inliers and* V^* *be the optimal subspace that minimizes the* ℓ_p *error over the inliers. Also let* W_S *be defined as in the beginning of Sect. 4. Then, with a constant probability, we have*

$$\sum_{i \in I} d(x_i, W_{S \cup S_0})^p \leq \sum_{i \in I} d(x_i, V^*)^p + \epsilon \sum_{i=1}^{n} d(x_i, \mathrm{span}\,(S_0))^p.$$

Proof. Similar to the proof of Theorem 5 above.

Once we have a line l_S that is close to V^*, we can project orthogonal to it and repeat the sampling again. The caveat is, we do not know l_S. One can get around this by projecting all the points $x_1, x_2, \ldots, x_n$ to $\mathrm{span}\,(S)$ of the current sample S, and repeat.

Theorem 7. *For any given points* $x_1, x_2, \ldots, x_n \in \mathbb{R}^d$, *let* $S = S_1 \cup S_2 \cup \ldots \cup S_k$ *be a sample of* $\tilde{O}\left(p^2 k^2 / \epsilon^2\right)$ *points picked as follows:* S_1 *be an i.i.d. sample of* $O\left((p^2 k/\epsilon^2) \log(k/\epsilon)\right)$ *points picked with probability proportional to* $\|x_i\|^p$, S_2 *be an i.i.d. sample of* $O\left((p^2 k/\epsilon^2) \log(k/\epsilon)\right)$ *points picked with probability proportional to* $d(x_i, \mathrm{span}\,(S_1))^p$, *and so on.*

Let $I \subseteq [n]$ *be the set of optimal* $(1 - \alpha)n$ *inliers and* V^* *be the optimal subspace that minimizes the* ℓ_p *error over the inliers. Then, with a constant probability,* $\mathrm{span}\,(S)$ *contains a* k-*dimensional subspace* V_S *such that*

$$\sum_{i \in I} d(x_i, V_S)^p \leq \sum_{i \in I} d(x_i, V^*)^p + \epsilon \sum_{i=1}^{n} \|x_i\|^p.$$

Proof. Similar to the proof of Theorem 5, Section 4.2 in [4].

4.2   Multiplicative Approximation

We can convert the above additive approximation into a multiplicative $(1 + \epsilon)$-approximation by using this adaptively, treating the projections of $x_1, x_2, \ldots, x_n$ orthogonal to $\mathrm{span}\,(S)$ as our new points, and repeating the sampling. To begin with, here is the modified statement of the additive approximation that we need.

Theorem 8. *For any given points* $x_1, x_2, \ldots, x_n \in \mathbb{R}^d$ *and any initial subset* S_0, *let* $S = S_0 \cup S_1 \cup \ldots \cup S_k$ *be a sample of* $|S| = \tilde{O}(p^2 k^2 / \epsilon^2)$ *points, where* S_1 *be an i.i.d. sample of* $O\left((p^2 k/\epsilon^2) \log(k/\epsilon)\right)$ *points picked with probability proportional to* $d(x_i, \mathrm{span}\,(S_0))^p$, S_2 *be an i.i.d. sample of* $O\left((p^2 k/\epsilon^2) \log(k/\epsilon)\right)$ *points picked with probability proportional to* $d(x_i, \mathrm{span}\,(S_0 \cup S_1))^p$, *and so on. Let* $I \subseteq [n]$ *be the set of optimal* $(1 - \alpha)n$ *inliers and* V^* *be the optimal* k-*dimensional linear* subspace that minimized the ℓ_p error over the inliers. Then, with a constant probability, S contains a k-dimensional subspace V_S such that

$$\sum_{i \in I} d(x_i, V_S)^p \leq \sum_{i \in I} d(x_i, V^*)^p + \epsilon \sum_{i=1}^{n} d(x_i, \operatorname{span}(S_0))^p.$$

Proof. Similar to the proof of Theorem 7 but using the projections of x_i orthogonal to $\operatorname{span}(S_0)$ as the point set. Theorem 7 is a special case with $S_0 = \emptyset$.

Repeating the result of Theorem 8 by sampling adaptively for multiple rounds brings the additive approximation error down exponentially in the number of rounds.

Theorem 9. *For any given points* $x_1, \ldots, x_n \in \mathbb{R}^d$ *and any initial subset* S_0, *let* S_t *be a subset sampled by Theorem 8 after projecting the points orthogonal to* $\operatorname{span}(S_0 \cup \ldots \cup S_{t-1})$, *for* $1 \leq t \leq T$. *Let* $I \subseteq [n]$ *be the set of optimal* $(1-\alpha)n$ *inliers and* V^* *be the optimal* k-*dimensional linear subspace that minimizes the* ℓ_p *error over the inliers. Then, with a constant probability,* $S = S_0 \cup S_1 \cup \ldots \cup S_T$ *of size* $|S| = \tilde{O}\left((p^2 k^2 T \log T)/\epsilon^2\right)$ *contains a* k-*dimensional linear subspace* V_S *s.t.*

$$\sum_{i \in I} d(x_i, V_S)^p \leq (1+\epsilon) \sum_{i \in I} d(x_i, V^*)^p + \epsilon^T \sum_{i=1}^{n} d(x_i, \operatorname{span}(S_0))^p.$$

Proof. By induction on the number of rounds T and using Theorem 8.

Now assume that the optimal ℓ_p error of V^* over the optimal inliers I is at least δ times its error over the entire data, that is, $\sum_{i \in I} d(x_i, V^*)^p \geq \delta \sum_{i=1}^{n} d(x_i, V^*)^p$. In that case, we can show a stronger multiplicative $(1+\epsilon)$-approximation instead of additive one. This can be thought of as a *weak coreset* extending the previous work on clustering given data using points and lines [7]. A proof of the following theorem is deferred to the full version of the paper.

Theorem 10. *For any given points* $x_1, x_2, \ldots, x_n \in \mathbb{R}^d$, *let* $I \subseteq [n]$ *be the set of optimal* $(1-\alpha)n$ *inliers and* V^* *be the optimal* k-*dimensional linear subspace that minimizes their* ℓ_p *error, for* $1 \leq p < \infty$. *Suppose* $\sum_{i \in I} d(x_i, V^*)^p \geq \delta \sum_{i=1}^{n} d(x_i, V^*)^p$. *Then, for any* $0 < \epsilon < 1$, *we can efficiently find a subset* S *of size* $|S| = \tilde{O}\left((p^2 k^2/\epsilon^2)\right) \log(1/\delta) \log\log(1/\delta))$ *that contains a* k-*dimensional linear subspace* V_S *such that*

$$\sum_{i \in I} d(x_i, V_S)^p \leq (1+\epsilon) \sum_{i \in I} d(x_i, V^*)^p, \quad \text{with a constant probability.}$$

5   M-estimator Subspace Approximation with Outliers

ℓ_p error or loss function is a special case of M-estimators used in statistics. General M-estimators as loss functions for subspace approximation or clustering have been previously studied in [7] for point and line median clustering and in [3] for robust regression. One way to define robust variants of the subspace approximation problem is to use more general loss functions that are more resilient to outliers. Here is one example of a popular M-estimator.

– Huber's loss function with threshold parameter t

$$L(x) = \begin{cases} x^2/2, & \text{if } |x| < t \\ t\,|x| - t^2/2, & \text{if } |x| \geq t. \end{cases}$$

The advantage of more general loss functions such as Huber loss is that they approximate squared-error for the nearer points but approximate ℓ_1-error for faraway points. They combine the smoothness of squared-error with the robustness of ℓ_1-error.

Clarkson and Woodruff [3] study the M-estimator variant of subspace approximation defined as follows. Given points $x_1, x_2, \ldots, x_n \in \mathbb{R}^d$, an integer $1 \leq k \leq d$, and an M-estimator loss function $M : \mathbb{R} \to \mathbb{R}$, find a k-dimensional linear subspace V that minimizes $\sum_{i=1}^{n} M\left(d(x_i, V)\right)$. Clarkson and Woodruff [3] show that the adaptive sampling for angle-drop lemma used by [4] to go from a large multiplicative approximation down to $(1+\epsilon)$-approximation can also be achieved by a non-adaptive *residual* sampling. Here we restate Theorem 45 from [3] using our notation of subspaces and distances instead of matrix norms.

Theorem 11. *(Theorem 45 of [3]) Given $x_1, x_2, \ldots, x_n \in \mathbb{R}^d$, an integer $1 \leq k \leq d$, and an M-estimator loss function $M(\cdot)$, let V_0 be any linear subspace such that $\sum_{i=1}^{n} M(d(x_i, V_0)) \leq C \sum_{i=1}^{n} M(d(x_i, V))$, where V is the k-dimensional linear subspace that minimizes the M-estimator error for its distances to $x_1, \ldots, x_n$ summed over all the points. Let $S \subseteq [n]$ be a sample of points, where each i gets picked independently with probability $\min\{1, C' \cdot M(d(x_i, V_0))/\sum_{i=1}^{n} M(d(x_i, V_0))\}$, for some constant $C' = O\left(Ck^3/\epsilon^2 \log(k/\epsilon)\right)$. Then, with a constant probability, we have the following, where $|S| = O\left(Ck^3/\epsilon^2 \log(k/\epsilon)\right)$.*

$$\sum_{i=1}^{n} M(d(x_i, \operatorname{span}(V_0 \cup S))) \leq (1 + \epsilon) \sum_{i=1}^{n} M(d(x_i, V)).$$

For general loss functions or M-estimators, one can define an analogous variant of the subspace approximation problem with outliers as follows. Given points $x_1, x_2, \ldots, x_n \in \mathbb{R}^d$, an integer $1 \leq k \leq d$, a monotone M-estimator loss function $M : \mathbb{R}_{\geq 0} \to \mathbb{R}_{\geq 0}$, and an outlier parameter $0 \leq \alpha \leq 1$, find a k-dimensional linear subspace V that minimizes the sum of M-estimator loss of distances to the nearest $(1 - \alpha)n$ points. In other words, let $N_\alpha(V) \subseteq [n]$ consist of the indices of the nearest $(1 - \alpha)n$ points to V among $x_1, x_2, \ldots, x_n$. We want to find a k-dimensional linear subspace V that minimizes $\sum_{i \in N_\alpha(V)} M\left(d(x_i, V)\right)$. This variant allows us to control the robustness in two ways: explicitly, using the outlier parameter in the definition, and implicitly, using an appropriate M-estimator loss function of our choice.

We observe that the proof of Theorem 45 in [3] is based on angle-drop lemma and our arguments in Sect. 4 for subspace approximation with outliers go through with very little or no change. Thus, we have the following theorem similar to their dimension reduction for subspace approximation, whose proof is similar to the proofs of Theorems 41 and 45 in [3].

Theorem 12. *For any given points $x_1, x_2, \ldots, x_n \in \mathbb{R}^d$, let $I \subseteq [n]$ be the set of optimal $(1 - \alpha)n$ inliers and V^* be the optimal k-dimensional linear subspace that minimizes their M-estimator error $\sum_{i \in I} M(d(x_i, V^*))$. Suppose $\sum_{i \in I} d(x_i, V^*)^p \geq \delta \sum_{i=1}^{n} d(x_i, V^*)^p$. Then, for any $0 < \epsilon < 1$, we can efficiently find a subspace V' of dimension $\tilde{O}\left(p^2 k^2 / \epsilon^2\right) \log(1/\delta)$ such that, with a constant probability, it contains a k-dimensional linear subspace $\tilde{V}$ satisfying*

$$\sum_{i \in I} d(x_i, \tilde{V})^p \leq (1 + \epsilon) \sum_{i \in I} d(x_i, V^*)^p.$$

6   Affine Subspace Approximation with Outliers

Given an input data set in a high-dimensional space, *affine subspace approximation* asks for an affine subspace that best fits this data. In other words, the subspace approximation problem with outliers, for a given outlier parameter $0 \leq \alpha \leq 1$, is to consider all partitions of $x_1, x_2, \ldots, x_n$ into $(1 - \alpha)n$ inliers and the remaining αn outliers, and find the affine subspace with the least squared error for the inliers over all such partitions. We present our result for affine subspace approximation problem with outliers, and defer the details to the full version.

Theorem 13. *For any given points $x_1, x_2, \ldots, x_n \in \mathbb{R}^d$, let $I \subseteq [n]$ be the set of optimal $(1 - \alpha)n$ inliers and V^* be the optimal k-dimensional affine subspace that minimizes their squared distance. Suppose $\sum_{i \in I} d(x_i, V^*)^2 \geq \delta \sum_{i=1}^{n} d(x_i, V^*)^2$. Then, for any $0 < \epsilon < 1$, we can efficiently find, in time linear in n and d, a k-dimensional linear subspace V' s.t.*

$$\sum_{i \in I} d(x_i, V')^2 \leq \sum_{i \in I} d(x_i, V^*)^2 + \epsilon \sum_{i \in I} \|x_i\|^2, \quad \text{with a constant probability.}$$

References

1. Bhaskara, A., Kumar, S.: Low rank approximation in the presence of outliers. In: Approximation, Randomization, and Combinatorial Optimization. Algorithms and Techniques, APPROX/RANDOM 2018, 20–22 August 2018 - Princeton, NJ, USA, pp. 4:1–4:16 (2018)
2. Chen, K.: A constant factor approximation algorithm for k-median clustering with outliers. In: Proceedings of the Nineteenth Annual ACM-SIAM Symposium on Discrete Algorithms, SODA 2008, San Francisco, California, USA, 20–22 January 2008, pp. 826–835 (2008)

3. Clarkson, K.L., Woodruff, D.P.: Input sparsity and hardness for robust subspace approximation. In: IEEE 56th Annual Symposium on Foundations of Computer Science, FOCS 2015, Berkeley, CA, USA, 17–20 October 2015, pp. 310–329 (2015)
4. Deshpande, A., Varadarajan, K.R.: Sampling-based dimension reduction for subspace approximation. In: Proceedings of the 39th Annual ACM Symposium on Theory of Computing, San Diego, California, USA, 11–13 June 2007, pp. 641–650 (2007)
5. Feldman, D., Langberg, M.: A unified framework for approximating and clustering data. In: Proceedings of the 43rd ACM Symposium on Theory of Computing, STOC 2011, San Jose, CA, USA, 6–8 June 2011, pp. 569–578 (2011)
6. Feldman, D., Monemizadeh, M., Sohler, C., Woodruff, D.P.: Coresets and sketches for high dimensional subspace approximation problems. In: Proceedings of the Twenty-First Annual ACM-SIAM Symposium on Discrete Algorithms, SODA 2010, Austin, Texas, USA, 17–19 January 2010, pp. 630–649 (2010)
7. Feldman, D., Schulman, L.J.: Data reduction for weighted and outlier-resistant clustering. In: Proceedings of the Twenty-Third Annual ACM-SIAM Symposium on Discrete Algorithms, SODA 2012, Kyoto, Japan, 17–19 January 2012, pp. 1343–1354 (2012)
8. Frieze, A.M., Kannan, R., Vempala, S.S.: Fast Monte-Carlo algorithms for finding low-rank approximations. J. ACM **51**(6), 1025–1041 (2004)
9. Ghashami, M., Phillips, J.M.: Relative errors for deterministic low-rank matrix approximations. In: Proceedings of the Twenty-Fifth Annual ACM-SIAM Symposium on Discrete Algorithms, SODA 2014, Portland, Oregon, USA, 5–7 January 2014, pp. 707–717 (2014)
10. Hardt, M., Moitra, A.: Algorithms and hardness for robust subspace recovery. In: COLT 2013 - The 26th Annual Conference on Learning Theory, 12–14 June 2013, Princeton University, NJ, USA, pp. 354–375 (2013)
11. Khachiyan, L.: On the complexity of approximating extremal determinants in matrices. J. Complex. **11**(1), 138–153 (1995)
12. Klivans, A., Kothari, P.K., Meka, R.: Efficient algorithms for outlier-robust regression. In Conference on Learning Theory, COLT 2018, Stockholm, Sweden, 6–9 July 2018, pp. 1420–1430 (2018)
13. Krishnaswamy, R., Li, S., Sandeep, S.: Constant approximation for k-median and k-means with outliers via iterative rounding. In: Proceedings of the 50th Annual ACM SIGACT Symposium on Theory of Computing, STOC 2018, Los Angeles, CA, USA, 25–29 June 2018, pp. 646–659 (2018)
14. Lai, K.A., Rao, A.B., Vempala, S.: Agnostic estimation of mean and covariance. In: IEEE 57th Annual Symposium on Foundations of Computer Science, FOCS 2016, 9–11 October 2016, Hyatt Regency, New Brunswick, New Jersey, USA, pp. 665–674 (2016)
15. Liberty, E.: Simple and deterministic matrix sketching. In: The 19th ACM SIGKDD International Conference on Knowledge Discovery and Data Mining, KDD 2013, Chicago, IL, USA, 11–14 August 2013, pp. 581–588 (2013)
16. Raghavendra, P., Steurer, D.: Graph expansion and the unique games conjecture. In: Proceedings of the 42nd ACM Symposium on Theory of Computing, STOC 2010, Cambridge, Massachusetts, USA, 5–8 June 2010, pp. 755–764 (2010)
17. Sarlós, T.: Improved approximation algorithms for large matrices via random projections. In: 47th Annual IEEE Symposium on Foundations of Computer Science (FOCS 2006), 21–24 October 2006, Berkeley, California, USA, Proceedings, pp. 143–152 (2006)

18. Shyamalkumar, N.D., Varadarajan, K.R.: Efficient subspace approximation algorithms. Discrete Comput. Geom. **47**(1), 44–63 (2012)
19. Woodruff, D.P.: Sketching as a tool for numerical linear algebra. Found. Trends® Theoret. Comput. Sci. **10**(1–2), 1–157 (2014)

Linear-Time Algorithms for Eliminating Claws in Graphs

Flavia Bonomo-Braberman[1], Julliano R. Nascimento[2(✉)], Fabiano S. Oliveira[3],
Uéverton S. Souza[4], and Jayme L. Szwarcfiter[3,5]

[1] Universidad de Buenos Aires. FCEyN. DC./CONICET-UBA. ICC,
Buenos Aires, Argentina
fbonomo@dc.uba.ar
[2] INF, Universidade Federal de Goiás, Goiânia, GO, Brazil
julliano@inf.ufg.br
[3] IME, Universidade do Estado do Rio de Janeiro, Rio de Janeiro, RJ, Brazil
fabiano.oliveira@ime.uerj.br
[4] IC, Universidade Federal Fluminense, Niterói, RJ, Brazil
ueverton@ic.uff.br
[5] IM, COPPE, and NCE, Universidade Federal do Rio de Janeiro,
Rio de Janeiro, RJ, Brazil
jayme@nce.ufrj.br

Abstract. Since many NP-complete graph problems have been shown polynomial-time solvable when restricted to claw-free graphs, we study the problem of determining the distance of a given graph to a claw-free graph, considering vertex elimination as measure. CLAW-FREE VERTEX DELETION (CFVD) consists of determining the minimum number of vertices to be removed from a graph such that the resulting graph is claw-free. Although CFVD is NP-complete in general and recognizing claw-free graphs is still a challenge, where the current best deterministic algorithm consists of performing $|V(G)|$ executions of the best algorithm for matrix multiplication, we present linear-time algorithms for CFVD on weighted block graphs and weighted graphs with bounded treewidth. Furthermore, we show that this problem can be solved in linear time by a simpler algorithm on forests, and we determine the exact values for full k-ary trees. On the other hand, we show that CLAW-FREE VERTEX DELETION is NP-complete even when the input graph is a split graph. We also show that the problem is hard to approximate within any constant factor better than 2, assuming the Unique Games Conjecture.

Keywords: Claw-free graph · Vertex deletion · Weighted vertex deletion

---

The authors would like to thank CAPES, FAPERJ, CNPq, ANPCyT, and UBACyT for the partial support.

D. Kim et al. (Eds.): COCOON 2020, LNCS 12273, pp. 14–26, 2020.
https://doi.org/10.1007/978-3-030-58150-3_2

1 Introduction

In 1968, Beineke [1] introduced claw-free graphs as a generalization of line graphs. Besides that generalization, the interest in studying the class of claw-free graphs also emerged due to the results showing that some NP-complete problems are polynomial time solvable in that class of graphs. For example, the maximum independent set problem is polynomially solvable for claw-free graphs, even on its weighted version [11].

A considerable amount of literature has been published on claw-free graphs. For instance, Chudnovsky and Seymour provide a series of seven papers describing a general structure theorem for that class of graphs, which are sketched in [5]. Some results on domination, Hamiltonian properties, and matchings are found in [16, 18, 29], respectively. In the context of parameterized complexity, Cygan et al. [10] show that finding a minimum dominating set in a claw-free graph is fixed-parameter tractable. For more on claw-free graphs, we refer to a survey by Faudree, Flandrin and Ryjáček [12] and references therein.

The aim of our work is to obtain a claw-free graph by a minimum number of vertex deletions. Given a graph G and a property Π, Lewis and Yannakakis [25] define a family of vertex deletion problems (Π-VERTEX DELETION) whose goal is finding the minimum number of vertices which must be deleted from G so that the resulting graph satisfies Π. Throughout this paper we consider the property Π as belonging to the class of claw-free graphs. For a set $S \subseteq V(G)$, we say that S is a *claw-deletion set* of G if $G \setminus S$ is a claw-free graph.

We say that a class of graphs $\mathcal{C}$ is *hereditary* if, for every graph $G \in \mathcal{C}$, every induced subgraph of G belongs to $\mathcal{C}$. If either the number of graphs in $\mathcal{C}$ or the number of graphs not in $\mathcal{C}$ is finite, then $\mathcal{C}$ is *trivial*. A celebrated result of Lewis and Yannakakis [25] shows that for any hereditary and nontrivial graph class $\mathcal{C}$, Π-VERTEX DELETION is NP-hard for Π being the property of belonging to $\mathcal{C}$. Therefore, Π-VERTEX DELETION is NP-hard when Π is the property of belonging to the class $\mathcal{C}$ of claw-free graphs. Cao et al. [4] obtain several results when Π is the property of belonging to some particular subclasses of chordal graphs. They show that transforming a split graph into a unit interval graph with the minimum number of vertex deletions can be solved in polynomial time. In contrast, they show that deciding whether a split graph can be transformed into an interval graph with at most k vertex deletions is NP-complete. Motivated by the works of Lewis and Yannakakis [25] and Cao et al. [4], since claw-free graphs is a natural superclass of unit interval graphs, we study vertex deletion problems associated with eliminating claws. The problems are formally stated below.

Problem 1. CLAW-FREE VERTEX DELETION (CFVD)
Instance: A graph G, and $k \in \mathbb{Z}^+$.
Question: Does there exist a claw-deletion set S of G with $|S| \le k$?

Problem 2. WEIGHTED CLAW-FREE VERTEX DELETION (WCFVD)
Instance: A graph G, a weight function $w : V(G) \to \mathbb{Z}^+$, and $k \in \mathbb{Z}^+$.
Question: Does there exist a claw-deletion set S of G with $\sum_{v \in S} w(v) \le k$?

By Roberts' characterization of unit interval graphs [27], CLAW-FREE VER-
TEX DELETION on interval graphs is equivalent to the vertex deletion problem
where the input is restricted to the class of interval graphs and the target class
is the class of unit interval graphs, a long standing open problem (see e.g. [4]).
Then, the results by Cao et al. [4] imply that CLAW-FREE VERTEX DELETION is
polynomial-time solvable when the input graph is in the class of interval $\cap$ split
graphs. Moreover, their algorithm could be also generalized to the weighted
version. In this paper, we show that CLAW-FREE VERTEX DELETION is NP-
complete when the input graph is in the class of split graphs.

The results by Lund and Yannakakis [26] imply that CLAW-FREE VERTEX
DELETION is APX-hard and admits a 4-approximating greedy algorithm. Even
for the weighted case, a pricing primal-dual 4-approximating algorithm is known
for the more general problem of 4-HITTING SET [17]. The CFVD problem is
NP-complete on bipartite graphs [33], and a 3-approximating algorithm is presented by Kumar et al. in [23] for weighted bipartite graphs. We prove that the
unweighted problem is hard to approximate within any constant factor better
than 2, assuming the Unique Games Conjecture, even for split graphs.

Regarding to parameterized complexity, CLAW-FREE VERTEX DELETION
is a particular case of H-FREE VERTEX DELETION, which can be solved in
$|V(H)|^k n^{\mathcal{O}(1)}$ time using the bounded search tree technique. In addition, it can
also be observed that CFVD is a particular case of 4-HITTING SET thus, by
Sunflower lemma, it admits a kernel of size $\mathcal{O}(k^4)$, and the complexity can be
slightly improved [13]. With respect to width parameterizations, it is well-known
that every optimization problem expressible in LinEMSOL$_1$ can be solved in linear time on graphs with bounded cliquewidth [6]. Since claws are induced subgraphs with constant size, it is easy to see that finding the minimum weighted S
such that $G \setminus S$ is claw-free is LinEMSOL$_1$-expressible. Therefore, WCFVD can
be solved in linear time on graphs with bounded cliquewidth, which includes
trees, block graphs and bounded treewidth graphs. However, the linear-time
algorithms based on the MSOL model-checking framework [7] typically do not
provide useful algorithms in practice since the dependence on the cliquewidth
involves huge multiplicative constants, even when the clique-width is bounded
by two (see [14]). In this work, we provide explicit discrete algorithms to effectively solve WCFVD in linear time in practice on block graphs and bounded
treewidth graphs. Even though forests are particular cases of bounded treewidth
graphs and block graphs, we describe a specialized simpler linear-time algorithm for CFVD on forests. This allows us to determine the exact values of
CFVD for a full k-ary tree T with n vertices. If $k = 2$, we show that a minimum claw-deletion set of T has cardinality $(n + 1 - 2^{(\log_2(n+1) \bmod 3)})/7$, and
$(nk - n + 1 - k^{(\log_k(nk-n+1) \bmod 2)})/(k^2 - 1)$, otherwise.

This paper is organized as follows. Section 2 is dedicated to show the hardness and inapproximability results. Sections 3, 4, and 5 present results on forests,
block graphs, and bounded treewidth graphs, respectively. Due to space constraints, some proofs were omitted.

Preliminaries. We consider simple and undirected graphs, and we use standard terminology and notation.

Let T be a tree rooted at $r \in V(T)$ and $v \in V(T)$. We denote by T_v the subtree of T rooted at v, and by $C_T(v)$ the set of children of v in T. For $v \neq r$, denote by $p_T(v)$ the parent of v in T, and by T_v^+ the subgraph of T induced by $V(T_v) \cup \{p_T(v)\}$. Let $T_r^+ = T$ and $p_T(r) = \emptyset$. When T is clear from the context, we simply write $p(v)$ and $C(v)$.

The *block-cutpoint-graph* of a graph G is the bipartite graph whose vertex set consists of the set of cutpoints of G and the set of blocks of G. A cutpoint is adjacent to a block whenever the cutpoint belongs to the block in G. The block-cutpoint-graph of a connected graph is a tree and can be computed in $\mathcal{O}(|V(G)| + |E(G)|)$ time [30].

Let G and H be two graphs. We say that G is *H-free* if G does not contain a graph isomorphic to H as an induced subgraph. A *claw* is the complete bipartite graph $K_{1,3}$. The class of *linear forests* is equivalent to that of claw-free forests. A vertex v in a claw C is a *center* if $d_C(v) = 3$. The cardinality $\mathrm{cdn}(G)$ of a minimum claw-deletion set in G is the *claw-deletion number* of G. For our proofs, it is enough to consider connected graphs, since a minimum (weight) claw-deletion set of a graph is the union of minimum (weight) claw-deletion sets of its connected components. For an n-vertex graph G, Williams et al. [32] show a randomized algorithm for detecting claws in $\mathcal{O}(n^\omega)$ time with high probability, where $\omega < 2.3728639$ is the matrix multiplication exponent [24]. As far as we know, the best deterministic algorithm for finding claws in a graph G takes $\mathcal{O}(n^{\omega+1})$ time [22].

2   Complexity and Approximability Results

The result of Lewis and Yannakakis [25] implies that CLAW-FREE VERTEX DELETION is NP-complete. In this section, we show that the same problem is NP-complete even when restricted to split graphs, a well known subclass of chordal graphs. Before the proof, let us recall that the VERTEX COVER (VC) problem consists of, given a graph G and a positive integer k as input, deciding whether there exists $X \subseteq V(G)$, with $|X| \leq k$, such that every edge of G is incident to a vertex in X.

Theorem 1. CLAW-FREE VERTEX DELETION *on split graphs is* NP-*complete.*

Proof. CLAW-FREE VERTEX DELETION is clearly in NP since claw-free graphs can be recognized in polynomial time [32]. To show NP-hardness, we employ a reduction from VERTEX COVER on general graphs [15].

Let (G, k) be an instance of vertex cover, where $V(G) = \{v_1, \ldots, v_n\}$, and $E(G) = \{e_1, \ldots, e_m\}$. Construct a split graph $G' = (C \cup I, E')$ as follows. The independent set is $I = \{v'_1, \ldots, v'_n\}$. The clique C is partitioned into sets C_i, $1 \leq i \leq m + 1$, each on $2n$ vertices. Given an enumeration $e_1, \ldots, e_m$ of $E(G)$, if $e_i = v_j v_\ell$, make v'_j and v'_ℓ adjacent to every vertex in C_i.

We prove that G has a vertex cover of size at most k if and only if G' has a claw-deletion set of size at most k. We present Claim 2 first.

Claim 2. *Every claw in G' contains exactly two vertices from I.*

Proof. Let C' be a claw in G'. Since $C' \cap C$ is a clique, $|C' \cap C| \leq 2$, thus $|C' \cap I| \geq 2$ and the center of the claw must be in C. On the other hand, by construction, $d_I(u) = 2$ for every $u \in \bigcup_{i=1}^{m} C_i$. This implies $|C' \cap I| \leq 2$.   ◇

Suppose that X is a vertex cover of size at most k in G. Then, every edge of G is incident with a vertex in X. Let $e_i \in E(G)$ and $X' = \{v' : v \in X\}$. By construction, every vertex in C_i is adjacent to a vertex in X', therefore $|N_{G' \setminus X'}(C_i) \cap I| \leq 1$. It follows by Claim 2 that $G' \setminus X'$ is claw-free.

Now, suppose that S' is a claw-deletion set of G' of size at most k. Recall that $|C_i| = 2n$, for every $1 \leq i \leq m+1$. Since $|S'| \leq k$, it follows that there exist $w_i \in C_i \setminus S'$, for every $1 \leq i \leq m+1$. Let $1 \leq i \leq m$ and $N_I(w_i) = \{u', v'\}$. Note that $\{u', v', w_i, w_{m+1}\}$ induces a claw in G'. Since S' is a claw-deletion set of G', we have that $S' \cap \{u', v'\} \neq \emptyset$. Let $S = \{v : v' \in S' \cap I\}$. By construction, every $uv \in E(G)$ is incident with a vertex in S, thus S is a vertex cover of G. □

Theorem 3 provides a lower bound for the approximation factor of CFVD. For terminology not defined here, we refer to Crescenzi [8].

Theorem 3. CLAW-FREE VERTEX DELETION *cannot be approximated with $2 - \varepsilon$ ratio for any $\varepsilon > 0$, even on split graphs, unless* Unique Games Conjecture *fails.*

Proof. The *Unique Games Conjecture* was introduced by Khot [19] in 2002. Some hardness results have been proved assuming that conjecture, for instance, see [20]. Given that VERTEX COVER is hard to approximate to within $2 - \varepsilon$ ratio for any $\varepsilon > 0$ assuming the Unique Games Conjecture [19], we perform an approximation-preserving reduction from VERTEX COVER. Let G be an instance of VERTEX COVER. Let $f(G) = G'$ where G' is the instance of CLAW-FREE VERTEX DELETION constructed from G according to the reduction of Theorem 1. From Theorem 1 we know that G has a vertex cover of size at most k if and only if G' has a claw-deletion set of size at most k. Recall that $k \leq n = |V(G)|$. Then, for every instance G of VERTEX COVER it holds that $\mathrm{opt}_{\mathrm{CFVD}}(G') = \mathrm{opt}_{\mathrm{VC}}(G)$. Now, suppose that S' is a $(2 - \varepsilon)$-approximate solution of G' for CFVD. Recall that $|C_i| = 2n$, for every $1 \leq i \leq m+1$. Since $\mathrm{opt}_{\mathrm{CFVD}}(G') = \mathrm{opt}_{\mathrm{VC}}(G) \leq n$, it follows that $|S'| < 2n$, thus, there exists $x \in C_{m+1} \setminus S'$, and $w \in C_i \setminus S'$, for every $1 \leq i \leq m$. Again, let $N_I(w) = \{u', v'\}$. Note that $\{u', v', w, x\}$ induces a claw in G'. Since S' is a claw-deletion set of G', we have that $S' \cap \{u', v'\} \neq \emptyset$. Let $S = \{v : v' \in S' \cap I\}$. By construction, every $uv \in E(G)$ is incident to a vertex in S, and therefore S is a vertex cover of G. Since $|S| \leq |S'|$ and S' is a $(2 - \varepsilon)$-approximate solution of G', then $|S| \leq |S'| \leq (2 - \varepsilon) \cdot \mathrm{opt}_{\mathrm{CFVD}}(G') = (2 - \varepsilon) \cdot \mathrm{opt}_{\mathrm{VC}}(G)$. Therefore, if CFVD admits a $(2 - \varepsilon)$-approximate algorithm then VERTEX COVER also admits a $(2 - \varepsilon)$-approximate algorithm, which implies that the Unique Games Conjecture fails [19].   □

3   Forests

We propose Algorithm 1 to compute a minimum claw-deletion set S of a rooted tree T.

Algorithm 1: CLAW-DELETION-SET(T, v, p)

    Input: A rooted tree T, a vertex v of T, and the parent p of v in T (possibly empty).

    Output: A minimum claw-deletion set S of T_v^+, such that: if
        $\mathrm{cdn}(T_v^+) = 1 + \mathrm{cdn}(T_v)$ then $p \in S$; if $\mathrm{cdn}(T_v^+) = \mathrm{cdn}(T_v)$ and
        $\mathrm{cdn}(T_v) = 1 + \mathrm{cdn}(T_v \setminus \{v\})$ then $v \in S$.

1 **if** $C(v) = \emptyset$ **then**
2   **return** $\emptyset$
3 **else**
4      $S := \emptyset$
5   **foreach** $u \in C(v)$ **do**
6          $S := S \cup \mathrm{CLAW\text{-}DELETION\text{-}SET}(T, u, v)$
7      $c := |C(v) \setminus S|$
8   **if** $c \geq 3$ **then**
9          $S := S \cup \{v\}$
10   **else if** $c = 2$ and $p \neq \emptyset$ and $v \notin S$ **then**
11        $S := S \cup \{p\}$
12   **return** S

Theorem 4. *Algorithm 1 is correct. Thus, given a forest F, and a positive integer k, the problem of deciding whether F can be transformed into a linear forest with at most k vertex deletions can be solved in linear time.*

Moreover, based on the algorithm, we have the following results.

Corollary 1. *Let T be a full binary tree with n vertices, and $t = \log_2(n + 1) \bmod 3$. Then $\mathrm{cdn}(T) = (n + 1 - 2^t)/7$.*

Corollary 2. *Let T be a full k-ary tree with n vertices, for $k \geq 3$, and $t = \log_k(nk - n + 1) \bmod 2$. Then $\mathrm{cdn}(T) = (nk - n + 1 - k^t)/(k^2 - 1)$.*

4   Block Graphs

We describe a dynamic programming algorithm to compute the minimum weight of a claw-deletion set in a weighted connected block graph G. The algorithm to be presented can be easily modified to compute also a set realizing the minimum.

If the block graph G has no cutpoint, the problem is trivial as G is already claw-free. Otherwise, let T be the block-cutpoint-tree of the block graph G. Consider T rooted at some cutpoint r of G, and let $v \in V(T)$. Let G_v the subgraph of G induced by the blocks in T_v. For $v \neq r$, let G_v^+ be the subgraph of G induced by the blocks in T_v^+. If b is a block, let $G_b^- = G_b \setminus \{p_T(b)\}$ (notice that $p_T(b)$ is a cutpoint of G, and it is always defined because r is not a block), and let $s(b)$ be the sum of weights of the vertices of b that are not cutpoints of G ($s(b) = 0$ if there is no such vertex).

We consider three functions to be computed for a vertex v of T that is a cutpoint of G:

- $f_1(v)$: the minimum weight of a claw-deletion set of G_v containing v.
- $f_2(v)$: the minimum weight of a claw-deletion set of G_v not containing v.
- For $v \neq r$, $f_3(v)$: the minimum weight of a claw-deletion set of G_v^+ containing neither v nor all the vertices of $p_T(v) \setminus \{v\}$ (notice that $p_T(v)$ is a block).

The parameter that solves the whole problem is $f(r) = \min\{f_1(r), f_2(r)\}$.

We define also three functions to be computed for a vertex b of T that is a block of G:

- $f_1(b)$: the minimum weight of a claw-deletion set of G_b^- containing $b \setminus \{p_T(b)\}$.
- $f_2(b)$: the minimum weight of a claw-deletion set of G_b^-.
- $f_3(b)$: the minimum weight of a claw-deletion set of G_b not containing $p_T(b)$.

Notice that $f_2(b) \leq f_3(b) \leq f_1(b)$. We compute the functions in a bottom-up order as follows, where v (resp. b) denotes a vertex of T that is a cutpoint (resp. block) of G. Notice that the leaves of T are blocks of G.

If $C(b) = \emptyset$, then $f_1(b) = s(b)$, $f_2(b) = 0$, and $f_3(b) = 0$. Otherwise,

- $f_1(v) = w(v) + \sum_{b \in C(v)} f_2(b)$; $f_1(b) = s(b) + \sum_{v \in C(b)} f_1(v)$;
- if $|C(v)| \leq 2$, then $f_2(v) = \sum_{b \in C(v)} f_3(b)$; if $|C(v)| \geq 3$, then $f_2(v) = \min_{b_1, b_2 \in C(v)} (\sum_{b \in \{b_1, b_2\}} f_3(b) + \sum_{b \in C(v) \setminus \{b_1, b_2\}} f_1(b))$;
- $f_2(b) = \min\{\sum_{v \in C(b)} \min\{f_1(v), f_3(v)\}, \min_{v_1 \in C(b)}(s(b) + f_2(v_1) + \sum_{v \in C(b) \setminus \{v_1\}} f_1(v))\}$;
- $f_3(b) = \sum_{v \in C(b)} \min\{f_1(v), f_3(v)\}$;
- if $C(v) = \{b\}$, then $f_3(v) = f_3(b)$;
  if $|C(v)| \geq 2$, then $f_3(v) = \min_{b_1 \in C(v)}(f_3(b_1) + \sum_{b \in C(v) \setminus \{b_1\}} f_1(b))$.

The explanation of the correctness of these formulas follows from Theorem 5.

Theorem 5. *Let G be a weighted connected block graph which is not complete. Let T be the block-cutpoint-tree of G, rooted at a cutpoint r. The previous function $f(r)$ computes correctly the minimum weight of a claw-deletion set of G.*

We obtain this result as a corollary.

Corollary 3. *Let G be a weighted block graph with n vertices and m edges. The minimum weight of a claw-deletion set of G can be determined in $\mathcal{O}(n+m)$ time.*

5   Graphs of Bounded Treewidth

Next, we present an algorithm able of solving WEIGHTED CLAW-FREE VERTEX DELETION in linear time on graphs with bounded treewidth, which also implies that we can recognize claw-free graphs in linear time when the input graph has treewidth bounded by a constant. For definitions of tree decompositions and treewidth, we refer the reader to [9,21,28].

Graphs of treewidth at most k are called *partial k-trees*. Some graph classes with bounded treewidth include: forests (treewidth 1); pseudoforests, cacti, outerplanar graphs, and series-parallel graphs (treewidth at most 2); Halin graphs and Apollonian networks (treewidth at most 3) [2]. In addition, control flow graphs arising in the compilation of structured programs also have bounded treewidth (at most 6) [31].

Based on the following results we can assume that we are given a nice tree decomposition of the input graph G.

Theorem 6. *[3] There exists an algorithm that, given a n-vertex graph G and an integer k, runs in time $2^{\mathcal{O}(k)} \cdot n$ and either outputs that the treewidth of G is larger than k, or constructs a tree decomposition of G of width at most $5k + 4$.*

Lemma 1. *[21] Given a tree decomposition $(T, \{X_t\}_{t \in V(T)})$ of G of width at most k, one can compute in time $\mathcal{O}(k^2 \cdot \max\{|V(T)|, |V(G)|\})$ a nice tree decomposition of G of width at most k that has at most $\mathcal{O}(k \cdot |V(G)|)$ nodes.*

Now we are ready to use a nice tree decomposition in order to obtain a linear-time algorithm for WEIGHTED CLAW-FREE VERTEX DELETION on graphs with bounded treewidth.

Theorem 7. WEIGHTED CLAW-FREE VERTEX DELETION *can be solved in linear time on graphs with bounded treewidth. More precisely, there is a $2^{\mathcal{O}(k^2)} \cdot n$-time algorithm to solve* WEIGHTED CLAW-FREE VERTEX DELETION *on n-vertex graphs G with treewidth at most k.*

Proof. Let G be a weighted n-vertex graph with $tw(G) \leq k$. Given a nice tree decomposition $\mathcal{T} = (T, \{X_t\}_{t \in V(T)})$ of G, we describe a procedure that computes the minimum weight of a claw-deletion set of G ($\mathrm{cdn}_w(G)$) using dynamic programming. For a node t of T, let $V_t = \bigcup_{t' \in T_t} X_{t'}$. First, we will describe what should be stored in order to index the table. Given a claw-deletion set $\hat{S}$ of G, for any bag X_t there is a partition of X_t into S_t, A_t, B_t and C_t where

- S_t is the set of vertices of X_t that are going to be removed ($S_t = \hat{S} \cap X_t$);
- $A_t = \{v \in X_t \setminus \hat{S} : |N_{V_t \setminus X_t}(v) \setminus \hat{S}| = 0\}$ is the set of non-removed vertices of X_t that are going to have no neighbor in $V_t \setminus X_t$ after the removal of $\hat{S}$;
- $B_t = \{v \in X_t \setminus \hat{S} : N_{V_t \setminus X_t}(v) \setminus \hat{S}$ induces a non-empty clique$\}$ is the set of non-removed vertices of X_t that, after the removal of $\hat{S}$, are going to have neighbors in $V_t \setminus X_t$, but no pair of non-adjacent neighbors;

– $C_t = \{v \in X_t \setminus \hat{S} : \text{ there exist } u, u' \in N_{V_t \setminus X_t}(v) \setminus \hat{S} \text{ with } uu' \notin E(G)\}$ is the set of non-removed vertices of X_t that, after the removal of $\hat{S}$, are going to have a pair of non-adjacent neighbors in $V_t \setminus X_t$.

In addition, the claw-deletion set $\hat{S}$ also provides the set $Z_t = \{(x, y) \in (X_t \setminus \hat{S}) \times (X_t \setminus \hat{S}) : \exists\, w \in V_t \setminus (X_t \cup \hat{S}) \text{ with } xy, wy \in E(G) \text{ and } wx \notin E(G)\}$ which consists of ordered pairs of vertices x, y of X_t that, after the removal of $\hat{S}$, are going to induce a $P_3 = x, y, w$ with some $w \in V_t \setminus X_t$.

Therefore, the recurrence relation of our dynamic programming has the signature $\mathrm{cdn}_w[t, S, A, B, C, Z]$, representing the minimum weight of a vertex set whose removal from $G[V_t]$ leaves a claw-free graph, such that S, A, B, C form a partition of X_t as previously described, and Z is as previously described too. The generated table has size $2^{\mathcal{O}(k^2)} \cdot n$.

Function cdn_w is computed for every node $t \in V(T)$, for every partition $S \cup A \cup B \cup C$ of X_t, and for every $Z \subseteq X_t \times X_t$. The algorithm performs the computations in a bottom-up manner. Let T rooted at $r \in V(T)$. Notice that $V_r = V(G)$, then $\mathrm{cdn}_w[r, \emptyset, \emptyset, \emptyset, \emptyset, \emptyset]$ is the weight of a minimum weight claw-deletion set of $G_r = G$, which solves the whole problem.

We present additional terminology. Let t be a node in T with children t' and t'', and $X \subseteq X_t$. To specify the sets S, A, B, C and Z on t' and t'', we employ the notation S', A', B', C', Z' and S'', A'', B'', C'', Z'', respectively.

We describe the recurrence formulas for the function cdn_w defined, based on the types of nodes in T. Recall that bags of leaves and root in T are empty.

– **Leaf node.** If t is a leaf node in T, then

$$\mathrm{cdn}_w[t, \emptyset, \emptyset, \emptyset, \emptyset, \emptyset] = 0. \tag{1}$$

– **Introduce node.** Let t be an introduce node with child t' such that $X_t = X_{t'} \cup \{v\}$ for some vertex $v \notin X_{t'}$. Let $S \cup A \cup B \cup C$ be a partition of X_t, and $Z \subseteq X_t \times X_t$. The recurrence is given by the following formulas.
  • If $v \in S$, then

$$\mathrm{cdn}_w[t, S, A, B, C, Z] = \mathrm{cdn}_w[t', S \setminus \{v\}, A, B, C, Z] + w(v). \tag{2.1}$$

  • If $v \in A$, and $N_{X_t \setminus S}(v)$ does not induce a $\overline{K}_3$, for every $(x, y) \in Z$, $vx \in E(G)$ or $vy \notin E(G)$, $N_{X_t}(v) \cap C = \emptyset$, then define Z' as $Z = Z' \cup \{(v, y) : y \in B \cup C \text{ and } vy \in E(G)\}$, and put

$$\mathrm{cdn}_w[t, S, A, B, C, Z] = \mathrm{cdn}_w[t', S, A \setminus \{v\}, B, C, Z'], \tag{2.2}$$

  Otherwise, put $\mathrm{cdn}_w[t, S, A, B, C, Z] = \infty$.
  • If $v \in B \cup C$, then

$$\mathrm{cdn}_w[t, S, A, B, C, Z] = \infty. \tag{2.3}$$

– **Forget node.** Consider t a forget node with child t' such that $X_t = X_{t'} \setminus \{v\}$ for some vertex $v \in X_{t'}$. Let $S \cup A \cup B \cup C$ be a partition of X_t, and $Z \subseteq X_t \times X_t$.

If $N_A(v) \neq \emptyset$, then

$$\mathrm{cdn}_w[t, S, A, B, C, Z] = \mathrm{cdn}_w[t', S \cup \{v\}, A, B, C, Z]. \tag{3.1}$$

Otherwise, $\mathrm{cdn}_w[t, S, A, B, C, Z] =$

$$\min \big\{ \mathrm{cdn}_w[t', S \cup \{v\}, A, B, C, Z], \mathrm{cdn}_w[t', S, A', B', C', Z'] \big\}, \tag{3.2}$$

among every (S, A', B', C', Z') such that:
$Z = (Z' \setminus \{(x, y) : x = v \text{ or } y = v\}) \cup \{(x, y) \in X_t \times X_t : xy, vy \in E(G) \text{ and } vx \notin E(G)\}$,
$A = A' \setminus N_G[v]$, $B = ((B' \setminus \{b \in B' : (v, b) \in Z'\}) \cup (A' \cap N_G(v))) \setminus \{v\}$,
$C = (C' \cup \{b \in B' : (v, b) \in Z'\}) \setminus \{v\}$.
– **Join node.** Consider t a join node with children t', t'' such that $X_t = X_{t'} = X_{t''}$. Let $S \cup A \cup B \cup C$ be a partition of X_t, and $Z \subseteq X_t \times X_t$. The recursive formula is given by

$\mathrm{cdn}_w[t, S, A, B, C, Z] =$
$\min \big\{ \mathrm{cdn}_w[t', S', A', B', C', Z'] + \mathrm{cdn}_w[t'', S'', A'', B'', C'', Z''] \big\} - w(S), \quad (4)$

among every (S', A', B', C', Z') and $(S'', A'', B'', C'', Z'')$ such that: $S = S' = S''$; $A = A' \cap A''$; $B = (A' \cap B'') \cup (A'' \cap B')$; $C = C' \cup C'' \cup (B' \cap B'')$; $Z = Z' \cup Z''$.

We explain the correctness of these formulas. The base case is when t is a leaf node. In this case $X_t = \emptyset$, then all the sets S, A, B, C, Z are empty. The set $X_t = \emptyset$ also implies that $G[V_t]$ is the empty graph, which is claw-free. Hence, $\mathrm{cdn}_w(G[V_t]) = 0$ and Formula (1) holds.

Let t be an introduce node with child t', and v the vertex introduced at t. First, suppose that $v \in S$. We assume by inductive hypothesis that $G[V_{t'} \setminus \hat{S}]$ is claw-free. Since $v \in S \subseteq \hat{S}$, we obtain that $G[V_t \setminus (\hat{S} \cup \{v\})]$ is claw-free. Then, the weight of a minimum weight claw-deletion set of $G[V_t]$ is increased by $w(v)$ from the one of $G[V_{t'}]$, stored at $\mathrm{cdn}_w[t', S', A', B', C', Z']$. Since $v \in S$, then $v \notin S'$ and the sets A', B', C', Z' in node t' are the same A, B, C, Z of t. Consequently Formula (2.1) holds.

Now, suppose that $v \in A \cup B \cup C$. By definition of tree decomposition, $v \notin N_{V_t \setminus X_t}(X_t)$. Then, if $v \in B \cup C$, the partition $S \cup A \cup B \cup C$ is not defined as required, and this justifies Formula (2.3). Thus, let $v \in A$. We have three cases in which $G[V_t \setminus \hat{S}]$ contains an induced claw: (i) $N_{X_t}(v)$ induces a $\overline{K}_3$, or (ii) there exists $(x, y) \in Z$, such that $vx \notin E(G)$ and $vy \in E(G)$, or (iii) there exists $c \in C$ such that $cv \in E(G)$. A set Z according to definition of cdn_w is obtained by Z' together with the pairs (x, y) such that $x = v$, $xy \in E(G)$ and y has at least one neighbor in $V_t \setminus (X_t \cup \hat{S})$. (Note that $v = y$ is never achieved, since v is an introduce node and $v \notin N_{V_t \setminus X_t}(X_t)$). Then, $Z = Z' \cup \{(v,y) : y \in B \cup C \text{ and } vy \in E(G)\}$. Hence, Formula (2.2) is justified by the negation of each of cases (i), (ii), (iii).

Next, let t be a forget node with child t'. Let v be the vertex forgotten at t. We consider $N_A(v) \neq \emptyset$ or not. Notice that if $N_G(v) \cap A \neq \emptyset$ and $v \notin \hat{S}$, then we have a contradiction to the definition of A, because some $a \in A$ is going to have a neighbor in $V_t \setminus (X_t \cup \hat{S})$. Therefore, if $N_A(v) \neq \emptyset$, v indeed must belong to $\hat{S}$, then Formula (3.1) holds.

Otherwise, consider that $N_A(v) = \emptyset$. In this case, either $v \in \hat{S}$ or $v \notin \hat{S}$. Then, we choose the minimum between these two possibilities. If $v \in \hat{S}$ we obtain the value stored at $\text{cdn}_w[t', S \cup \{v\}, A, B, C, Z]$. Otherwise, let $v \notin \hat{S}$. It follows that, for some $a \in A$, if $va \in E(G)$, then a must now belong to B. Consequently, A must be $A' \setminus N_G[v]$. Let $\mathcal{B} = \{b \in B' : (v,b) \in Z'\}$. Since $v \notin \hat{S}$, for every $x \in \mathcal{B}$, x must belong to C. Thus, the set B is given by $B' \setminus \mathcal{B}$ together with the vertices from A' that now belong to B. Recall that $v \notin X_t$, then $v \notin B$. Hence, $B = ((B' \setminus \mathcal{B}) \cup (A' \cap N_G(v))) \setminus \{v\}$. Finally, $C = (C' \cup \mathcal{B}) \setminus \{v\}$. Hence, Formula (3.2) holds.

To conclude, let t be a join node with children t' and t''. Note that the graphs induced by $V_{t'}$ and by $V_{t''}$ can be distinct. Then, we must sum the values of cdn_w in t' and in t'' to obtain cdn_w in t, and choose the minimum of all of these possible sums. Finally, we subtract $w(S)$ from the previous result, since $w(S)$ is counted twice.

By definition of join node, $X_t = X_{t'} = X_{t''}$, then $S = S' = S''$. Let $x \in X_t$. We have that $x \in A$ if and only if $|N_{V_{t'} \setminus X_{t'}}(x) \setminus \hat{S}| = |N_{V_{t''} \setminus X_{t''}}(x) \setminus \hat{S}| = 0$. Then, $A = A' \cap A''$.

Notice that $x \in B$ if and only if $(|N_{V_{t'} \setminus X_{t'}}(v) \setminus \hat{S}| = 0$ and $|N_{V_{t''} \setminus X_{t''}}(v) \setminus \hat{S}| > 1)$ or $(|N_{V_{t''} \setminus X_{t''}}(v) \setminus \hat{S}| = 0$ and $|N_{V_{t'} \setminus X_{t'}}(v) \setminus \hat{S}| > 1)$. Consequently $x \in B$ if and only if $x \in (A' \cap B'') \cup (A'' \cap B')$. This implies that $B = (A' \cap B'') \cup (A'' \cap B')$.

Now, $x \in C$ if and only if $x \in C'$ or $x \in C''$ or $(x \in B'$ and $x \in B'')$. (Note that by the definition of tree decomposition, the forgotten nodes in $G_{t'}$ and $G_{t''}$ are distinct and therefore the condition $x \in B'$ and $x \in B''$ is safe). Consequently, $C = C' \cup C'' \cup (B' \cap B'')$.

Finally, let $x, y \in X_t$. By definition of Z', if $(x,y) \in Z'$, then there exists $w \in V_{t'} \setminus (X_{t'} \cup \hat{S})$ with $xy, wy \in E(G)$ and $wx \notin E(G)$. This implies that $w \in V_t \setminus (X_t \cup \hat{S})$ and $xy, wy \in E(G)$ and $wx \notin E(G)$. Hence, $(x,y) \in Z$. By a similar argument, we conclude that if $(x,y) \in Z''$, then $(x,y) \in Z$. This gives $Z = Z' \cup Z''$, and completes Formula (4).

Since the time to compute each entry of the table is upper bounded by $2^{\mathcal{O}(k^2)}$ and the table has size $2^{\mathcal{O}(k^2)} \cdot n$, the algorithm can be performed in $2^{\mathcal{O}(k^2)} \cdot n$ time. This implies linear-time solvability for graphs with bounded treewidth. $\square$

References

1. Beineke, L.: Derived graphs of digraphs. In: Sachs, H., Voss, H.J., Walter, H.J. (eds.) Beiträge zur Graphentheorie, pp. 17–33. Teubner, Leipzig (1968)

2. Bodlaender, H.: A partial k-arboretum of graphs with bounded treewidth. Theoret. Comput. Sci. **209**(1–2), 1–45 (1998)
3. Bodlaender, H., Drange, P., Dregi, M., Fomin, F., Lokshtanov, D., Pilipczuk, M.: A $O(c^k n)$ 5-approximation algorithm for treewidth. SIAM J. Comput. **45**(2), 317–378 (2016)
4. Cao, Y., Ke, Y., Otachi, Y., You, J.: Vertex deletion problems on chordal graphs. Theoret. Comput. Sci. **745**, 75–86 (2018)
5. Chudnovsky, M., Seymour, P.: The structure of claw-free graphs. In: Webb, B. (ed.) Surveys in Combinatorics. London Mathematical Society Lecture Note Series, vol. 327, pp. 153–171. Cambridge University Press (2005)
6. Courcelle, B., Makowsky, J., Rotics, U.: Linear time solvable optimization problems on graphs of bounded clique-width. Theory Comput. Syst. **33**(2), 125–150 (2000)
7. Courcelle, B.: The monadic second-order logic of graphs. I. Recognizable sets of finite graphs. Inf. Comput. **85**(1), 12–75 (1990)
8. Crescenzi, P.: A short guide to approximation preserving reductions. In: Proceedings of the 12th Annual IEEE Conference on Computational Complexity, pp. 262–273 (1997)
9. Cygan, M., Nederlof, J., Pilipczuk, M., Pilipczuk, M., van Rooij, J., Wojtaszczyk, J.: Solving connectivity problems parameterized by treewidth in single exponential time. In: Proceedings of the 52nd IEEE Annual Symposium on Foundations of Computer Science, pp. 150–159 (2011)
10. Cygan, M., Philip, G., Pilipczuk, M., Pilipczuk, M., Wojtaszczyk, J.: Dominating set is fixed parameter tractable in claw-free graphs. Theoret. Comput. Sci. **412**(50), 6982–7000 (2011)
11. Faenza, Y., Oriolo, G., Stauffer, G.: Solving the weighted stable set problem in claw-free graphs via decomposition. J. ACM **61**(4), 20:1–20:41 (2014)
12. Faudree, R., Flandrin, E., Ryjáček, Z.: Claw-free graphs - a survey. Discrete Math. **164**(1), 87–147 (1997)
13. Fernau, H.: Parameterized algorithms for d-hitting set: the weighted case. Theoret. Comput. Sci. **411**(16–18), 1698–1713 (2010)
14. Flum, J., Grohe, M.: Parameterized Complexity Theory. Texts Theoretical Computer Science, EATCS Series (2006)
15. Garey, M., Johnson, D.: Computers and Intractability: A Guide to the Theory of NP-Completeness. Freeman and Company, San Francisco (1979)
16. Hedetniemi, S., Laskar, R.: Recent results and open problems in domination theory. In: Applications of Discrete Mathematics, pp. 205–218. SIAM Philadelphia (1988)
17. Hochbaum, D.: Approximation algorithms for the set covering and vertex cover problems. SIAM J. Comput. **11**, 555–556 (1982)
18. Flandrin, E., Fouquet, J.L., Li, H.: On Hamiltonian claw-free graphs. Discrete Mathemat. **111**(1–3), 221–229 (1993)
19. Khot, S.: On the power of unique 2-prover 1-round games. In: Proceedings of the Thirty-Fourth Annual ACM Symposium on Theory of Computing, pp. 767–775 (2002)
20. Khot, S., Vishnoi, N.: The unique games conjecture, integrality gap for cut problems and embeddability of negative-type metrics into ℓ_1. J. ACM **62**(1), 8 (2015)
21. Kloks, T. (ed.): Treewidth. LNCS, vol. 842. Springer, Heidelberg (1994). https://doi.org/10.1007/BFb0045375
22. Kloks, T., Kratsch, D., Müller, H.: Finding and counting small induced subgraphs efficiently. Inf. Process. Lett. **74**(3–4), 115–121 (2000)

23. Kumar, M., Mishra, S., Devi, N., Saurabh, S.: Approximation algorithms for node deletion problems on bipartite graphs with finite forbidden subgraph characterization. Theoret. Comput. Sci. **526**, 90–96 (2014)
24. Le Gall, F.: Powers of tensors and fast matrix multiplication. In: Proceedings of the 39th International Symposium on Symbolic and Algebraic Computation, pp. 296–303 (2014)
25. Lewis, J., Yannakakis, M.: The node-deletion problem for hereditary properties is NP-complete. J. Comput. Syst. Sci. **20**(2), 219–230 (1980)
26. Lund, C., Yannakakis, M.: The approximation of maximum subgraph problems. In: Lingas, A., Karlsson, R., Carlsson, S. (eds.) ICALP 1993. LNCS, vol. 700, pp. 40–51. Springer, Heidelberg (1993). https://doi.org/10.1007/3-540-56939-1_60
27. Roberts, F.: Indifference graphs. In: Harary, F. (ed.) Proof Techniques in Graph Theory, pp. 139–146. Academic Press (1969)
28. Robertson, N., Seymour, P.: Graph minors. III. Planar tree-width. J. Comb. Theory. Ser. B 36(1), 49–64 (1984)
29. Sumner, D.: Graphs with 1-factors. Proc. Am. Math. Soc. **42**(1), 8–12 (1974)
30. Tarjan, R.: Depth-first search and linear graph algorithms. SIAM J. Comput. **1**(2), 146–160 (1972)
31. Thorup, M.: All structured programs have small tree width and good register allocation. Inf. Comput. **142**(2), 159–181 (1998)
32. Williams, V.V., Wang, J.R., Williams, R., Yu, H.: Finding four-node subgraphs in triangle time. In: Proceedings of the Twenty-Sixth Annual ACM-SIAM Symposium on Discrete Algorithms, pp. 1671–1680. SIAM (2015)
33. Yannakakis, M.: Node deletion problems on bipartite graphs. SIAM J. Comput. **10**(2), 310–327 (1981)

A New Lower Bound for the Eternal Vertex Cover Number of Graphs

Jasine Babu$^{(\boxtimes)}$ and Veena Prabhakaran

Indian Institute of Technology Palakkad, Palakkad, India
jasine@iitpkd.ac.in, veenaprabhakaran7@gmail.com

Abstract. We obtain a new lower bound for the eternal vertex cover number of an arbitrary graph G, in terms of the cardinality of a vertex cover of minimum size in G containing all its cut vertices. The consequences of the lower bound include a quadratic time algorithm for computing the eternal vertex cover number of chordal graphs.

Keywords: Eternal vertex cover · Lower bound · Chordal graphs

1 Introduction

Eternal vertex cover problem is a dynamic variant of the classical minimum vertex cover problem [6,11]. It can be described in terms of a multi-round game played between an attacker and a defender who controls a fixed number of guards. The rules to play the game with k guards on a graph G are the following. Initially, the defender chooses an assignment of guards to vertices by placing the k guards on a subset of vertices of G. The positions of the guards define an *initial configuration*. In each round of the game, the attacker attacks an edge e of her choice. In response, the defender has to reconfigure the guards in such a way that each guard either moves from its current position to a neighboring vertex or remains its current position; however making sure that at least one guard is moved from one endpoint of the attacked edge e to its other endpoint. (All guards are assumed to move in parallel.) If the defender is not able to move guards according to these rules, the attacker wins. Otherwise, we say that the attack in the current round has been successfully defended and the game proceeds to the next round of attack-defense, considering the resultant positions of the guards as the new *configuration*. If the defender can keep on successfully defending any infinite sequence of attacks, we say that the defender has a defense strategy on this graph, with k guards. *Eternal vertex cover number* of a graph G, denoted by $\mathrm{evc}(G)$ is the minimum integer k such that the defender has a defense strategy on G, with k guards. It is well-known that eternal vertex cover number of a path on n vertices is $n-1$ and that of a cycle on n vertices is $\lceil \frac{n}{2} \rceil$ [11].

From the description of the game, it is clear that if both endpoints of an edge are without guards in some configuration, then an attack on that edge cannot

© Springer Nature Switzerland AG 2020
D. Kim et al. (Eds.): COCOON 2020, LNCS 12273, pp. 27–39, 2020.
https://doi.org/10.1007/978-3-030-58150-3_3

be defended. Hence, an implicit requirement is that the positions of guards in each round must be a vertex cover of the graph. When this game is played with k-guards, each configuration encountered in the game is equivalent to some function f from V to $\{0, 1, 2, \ldots, k\}$ such that $\sum_{v \in V} f(v) = k$ (where, for each $v \in V$, $f(v)$ will be the number of guards on v). A set of such configurations $\mathcal{C}$, such that the defender can start with any configuration in $\mathcal{C}$ as the initial configuration and keep moving between configurations in $\mathcal{C}$ for defending the attacks, is called an *evc class* of G and each configuration in $\mathcal{C}$ is an *eternal vertex cover configuration* of G. If $\mathcal{C}$ is an evc class of G such that the number of guards in the configurations in $\mathcal{C}$ is equal to $\text{evc}(G)$, then $\mathcal{C}$ is a *minimum evc class* of G.

Fomin et al. [6] showed that[1] given a graph G and an integer k, checking if the defender has a defense strategy on G using k guards is NP-hard. They gave an exact algorithm to compute eternal vertex cover number in $2^{O(n)}$ time complexity. The paper also gave an FPT algorithm to check if the defender has a defense strategy on a graph G using k guards when parameterized by k. The paper further showed that the problem is in PSPACE; however, it is not known if the problem is in NP or not for general graphs. It also remains unexplored if the problem is NP-hard or not, even for bipartite graphs.

Graph parameters like eternal total vertex cover number [1] and eternal domination number [7–9,12] are also defined in terms of multi-round attack-defense games on graphs. The way in which these parameters are related to eternal vertex cover number was explored by Anderson et al. [1] and Klostermeyer and Mynhardt [10]. An algorithm for computing eternal domination number of interval graphs was obtained by Rinemberg and Soulignac [13].

There are two popular versions of the eternal vertex cover problem: the former in which in any configuration, at most one guard is allowed on a vertex and the latter in which this restriction is not there. Since the main structural result in this paper is a lower bound for eternal vertex cover number, we will be assuming the version of the game in which there is no restriction on the number of guards allowed on a vertex. It can be easily verified that our proofs work the same way in the other model of the game as well.

Since any configuration encountered in the game is a vertex cover, it follows that $\text{mvc}(G) \leq \text{evc}(G)$, where $\text{mvc}(G)$ denotes the cardinality of a minimum vertex cover of G. This is the only general lower bound known for the parameter, so far in literature. The connected vertex cover number of a graph G, denoted by $\text{cvc}(G)$, is the minimum size of a vertex cover S such that the induced subgraph of G on S is connected. Klostermeyer and Mynhardt [11] showed that for any graph G, $\text{evc}(G) \leq \text{cvc}(G) + 1$. It follows from this result that for any graph G, $\text{evc}(G) \leq 2\,\text{mvc}(G)$. Fomin et al. [6] had improved this bound to show that twice the cardinality of a maximum matching in the graph is an upper bound to $\text{evc}(G)$. From this, a 2-factor approximation algorithm for computing eternal

---

[1] The results in Fomin et al. [6] are given for the variant of the problem in which more than one guard is allowed to be on a vertex in a configuration. But, the proof can be easily modified for to work for the other model as well.

vertex cover number follows. In order to come up with efficient algorithms for computing eternal vertex cover number of graphs that belong to graph families of interest, it is critical to improve the lower and upper bounds for the parameter.

In this work, we prove that the size of a minimum sized vertex cover of G that contains all the cut vertices of G is also a lower bound for $\mathrm{evc}(G)$. In Sect. 2, we show that the difference between the eternal vertex cover number and the new lower bound is at most one, for chordal graphs, internally triangulated planar graphs and in general for any graph whose 2-connected blocks are locally connected. The main structural property used to obtain this bound specifies a lower bound to the number of guards on each induced subgraph G' of G that join at a cut vertex of G, in any eternal vertex cover configuration of G. We refer to this property as the EVC-Cut-Property (see Definition 4). The improved lower bound for eternal vertex cover number has many algorithmic consequences, including a quadratic time algorithm for computing the eternal vertex cover number of chordal graphs and a PTAS for computing the eternal vertex cover number of internally triangulated planar graphs. Previously, such results were known only for biconnected graphs of the respective classes. The improved lower bound for eternal vertex cover number is obtained by a direct application of the EVC-Cut-Property. We believe that this property would be useful in general, for extending lower bound results for the eternal vertex cover number of biconnected graphs of a graph class of interest to lower bound results that are applicable for all graphs of the class.

2   A New Lower Bound

Definition 1 (x-components and x-extensions). *Let x be a cut vertex in a graph G and H be a component of $G \setminus x$. Let G' be the induced subgraph of G on the vertex set $V(H) \cup \{x\}$. Then G' is called an x-component of G and G is called an x-extension of G'.*

Let G' be a graph and G be an x-extension of G' for some $x \in V(G')$. It is easy to see that in every eternal vertex cover configuration of G at least $\mathrm{mvc}(G')$ guards are present on $V(G')$. However, it is interesting to note that it is possible to have less than $\mathrm{evc}(G')$ guards present on $V(G')$ in some eternal vertex cover configurations of G. We discuss an example of this below.

For the graph G' in Fig. 1(a), it is clear that $\mathrm{mvc}(G') = 2$. We will show that on G', the defender has no defense strategy with less than 4 guards. Suppose, we play the game on G' with less than 4 guards. Note that, any vertex cover of G' of size at most 3 must contain both v_2 and v_8. We also know that in any evc class of G', there must be a configuration in which v_1 is occupied. Further, $\{v_1, v_2, v_8\}$ is the only vertex cover of size at most 3 that contains v_1. But the configuration $\{v_1, v_2, v_8\}$ is not safe because, in order to defend an attack on an edge incident to v_8, the guard on v_8 must move and there is no other guard that can move to v_8. Therefore, $\mathrm{evc}(G') \geq 4$. It is not difficult to show that $\mathrm{evc}(G') = 4$ by maintaining in configurations with v_1, v_2 and v_8 along with one of the degree

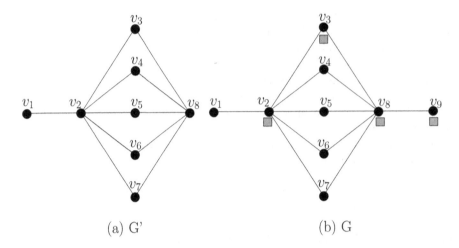

(a) G'   (b) G

Fig. 1. (a) A graph G' with evc$(G') = 4$. (b) G is a v_8- extension of G'. A valid eternal vertex cover configuration of G with less than evc(G') guards on $V(G')$ is indicated using gray squares.

two vertices. Similar to the case of G', we can see that evc$(G) \geq 4$. It is also easy to see that the defender has a defense strategy in G with four guards, by maintaining in configurations where v_2 and v_8 are occupied along with one of the degree one vertices and one of the degree two vertices. Thus, evc$(G) = 4$. It can be seen that, in the evc class of G that we just described, when v_9 is occupied, there exists less than evc(G') guards on $V(G')$ as shown in Fig. 1(b).

Let x be a cut vertex in a graph G. From the description above, it is clear that though a lower bound for evc(G) can be obtained in terms of the minimum vertex cover numbers of the x-components of G, it may not be possible to obtain a non-trivial lower bound for evc(G) in terms of the eternal vertex cover numbers of the x-components of G. Here, we introduce a new parameter and show that it is a lower bound for evc(G).

Definition 2. *Let G be a graph and $X \subseteq V(G)$. The smallest integer k, such that G has a vertex cover S of cardinality k with $X \subseteq S$, is denoted by* mvc$_X(G)$.

To simplify the expressions that appear later, we introduce the following notations. For any vertex $v \in V(G)$, mvc$_{\{v\}}(G)$ will be denoted by mvc$_v(G)$ and for any graph G and any set X, the notation $X(G)$ will be used to denote the set $X \cap V(G)$.

Definition 3. *Let X be the set of cut vertices of a graph G and let $x \in X$. The set of x-components of G will be denoted as $C_x(G)$. If B is any block of G, then the set of B-components of G is defined as*
$C_B(G) = \{G_i : G_i \in C_x(G)$ *for some $x \in X(B)$ and G_i edge disjoint with $B\}$.*

Definition 4 (EVC-Cut-Property). *Let G' be a graph and let X' be the set of cut vertices of G'. The graph G' is said to have the EVC-cut-property if for* *every graph G that is an x-extension of G' for some $x \in V(G')$, it is true that in each eternal vertex cover configuration of G, at least $\mathrm{mvc}_{X' \cup \{x\}}(G')$ guards are present on the vertices of G', out of which at least $\mathrm{mvc}_{X' \cup \{x\}}(G') - 1$ guards are present on $V(G') \setminus \{x\}$.*

Note 1. For a graph G' to satisfy the EVC-Cut-Property, it is not necessary that the vertex x is occupied by a guard in every eternal vertex cover configuration of an x-extension G of G'. All the $\mathrm{mvc}_{X' \cup \{x\}}(G')$ (or more) guards could be on vertices other than x.

Note 2. Definition 4 gives some lower bounds on the number of guards and not on the number of vertices with guards. Note that, if more than one guard is allowed on a vertex, then these two numbers could be different.

The following two lemmas are easy to obtain, using a straightforward counting argument.

Lemma 1. *Let G be a graph and X be the set of cut vertices of G. For any $x \in X$,*

$$\mathrm{mvc}_{X \cup \{x\}}(G) = \mathrm{mvc}_X(G) = 1 + \sum_{G_i \in \mathcal{C}_x(G)} \left[\mathrm{mvc}_{X(G_i)}(G_i) - 1 \right].$$

Lemma 2. *Let G be a graph and X be the set of cut vertices of G. If B is a block of G and v is any vertex of B such that $v \notin X(B)$, then*

$$\mathrm{mvc}_{X \cup \{v\}}(G) = \mathrm{mvc}_{X(B) \cup \{v\}}(B) + \sum_{G_i \in \mathcal{C}_B(G)} \left[\mathrm{mvc}_{X(G_i)}(G_i) - 1 \right].$$

Lemma 3. *Every graph satisfies EVC-cut-property.*

Proof. The proof is by induction on the number of blocks of the graph. First consider a graph G' with a single block. Let x be any vertex of G' and G be an x-extension of G'. Let C be an eternal vertex cover configuration of G and let S be the set of vertices of G on which guards are present in C. Since C is an eternal vertex cover configuration of G, S must be a vertex cover of G and $S \cap V(G')$ must be a vertex cover of G'. Therefore, $|S \cap V(G')| \geq \mathrm{mvc}(G')$. If $|S \cap V(G')| \geq \mathrm{mvc}_x(G')$, then there are at least $\mathrm{mvc}_x(G')$ guards on $V(G')$ and at least $\mathrm{mvc}_x(G') - 1$ guards on $V(G') \setminus \{x\}$, as we need to prove. Also, it is easy to see that $\mathrm{mvc}_x(G') \leq \mathrm{mvc}(G') + 1$. Therefore, we are left with the case when $\mathrm{mvc}(G') = |S \cap V(G')| < \mathrm{mvc}_x(G') = \mathrm{mvc}(G') + 1$. This implies that $x \notin S$. Thus, in the remaining case to be handled, the number of vertices on which guards are present is exactly $\mathrm{mvc}(G')$ and there is no guard on x.

From this point, let us focus on the number of guards on $V(G')$ and not just the number of vertices that are occupied. If there are more than $\mathrm{mvc}(G')$ guards in $V(G')$, then the conditions we need to prove are satisfied for the configuration C. In the remaining case, we have exactly $|S \cap V(G')| = \mathrm{mvc}(G')$ guards in $V(G')$, with $x \notin S$. In this case, we will derive a contradiction.

Consider an attack on an edge xv incident at x, where $v \in V(G')$. Let $\tilde{C}$ be the new configuration, after defending this attack and $\tilde{S}$ be the set of vertices on which guards are present in $\tilde{C}$. In the transition from C to $\tilde{C}$, a guard must have moved from v to x. Also, x being a cut vertex, no guard can move from $V(G) \setminus V(G')$ to $V(G') \setminus \{x\}$. Therefore, $|\tilde{S} \cap V(G')| = |S \cap V(G')| = \mathrm{mvc}(G')$. But, this is a contradiction because $\tilde{S} \cap V(G')$ is a minimum vertex cover of G' containing x, but we have $\mathrm{mvc}(G') < \mathrm{mvc}_x(G')$.

Thus, the lemma holds for all graphs with only one block. Now, as induction hypothesis, assume that the lemma holds for any graph G' with at most k blocks. We need to show that the lemma holds for any graph with $k + 1$ blocks.

Let G' be an arbitrary graph with $k+1$ blocks and let x be an arbitrary vertex of G'. Let X' be the set of cut vertices of G' and let G be an arbitrary x-extension of G'. Let C be an arbitrary eternal vertex cover configuration of G and let S be the set of vertices on which guards are present in C. Let $l = \mathrm{mvc}_{X' \cup \{x\}}(G')$. We need to show that there are at least l guards on $V(G')$ in C and at least $l - 1$ guards on $V(G') \setminus \{x\}$. Let t be the number of guards on $V(G')$ in C. We split our proof into two cases based on whether x is a cut vertex in G' or not.

Case 1. x is a cut vertex of G'

In this case, by our induction hypothesis, for each x-component G_i of G', at least $\mathrm{mvc}_{X'(G_i)}(G_i)$ guards are on $V(G_i)$ in the configuration C. There are two possible sub-cases.

(a) If x is not occupied by a guard in C, then by induction hypothesis, $t \geq \sum_{G_i \in \mathcal{C}_x(G')} \mathrm{mvc}_{X'(G_i)}(G_i)$. Since $\mathcal{C}_x(G')$ is non-empty, by Lemma 1, it follows that $t \geq \mathrm{mvc}_{X' \cup \{x\}}(G') = l$. Since x is not occupied, the number of guards on $V(G') \setminus \{x\}$ is t itself, where $t \geq l$, as shown.

(b) If x is occupied by a guard in C, still, in order to satisfy the induction hypothesis for all x-components of G', the number of guards on $V(G') \setminus \{x\}$ must be at least $\sum_{G_i \in \mathcal{C}_x(G')} \left(\mathrm{mvc}_{X'(G_i)}(G_i) - 1 \right)$. Therefore, by Lemma 1, it follows that the number of guards on $V(G') \setminus \{x\}$ is at least $l - 1$ and $t \geq l$.

Case 2. x is not a cut vertex of G':

Let B be the block of G' that contains x. By Lemma 2, we have:

$$l = \mathrm{mvc}_{X'(B) \cup \{x\}}(B) + \sum_{G_i \in \mathcal{C}_B(G')} \left(\mathrm{mvc}_{X'(G_i)}(G_i) - 1 \right) \tag{1}$$

Before proceeding with the proof, we establish the following claim.

Claim 1 *Suppose C' is an eternal vertex cover configuration of G. Then the number of guards on $V(G') \setminus \{x\}$ in configuration C' is at least $l - 1$.*

Proof. To count the number of guards on $V(G') \setminus \{x\}$, we count the total number of guards on the B-components of G' and the number of guards on the remaining vertices separately and add them up.

– First, we will count the total number of guards on the B-components of G'. For each B-component G_i of G', let $k_i = \mathrm{mvc}_{X'(G_i)}(G_i)$. For each cut vertex $v \in X'(B)$, let $\mathcal{C}_v$ denote the family of B-components of G' that intersect at the cut vertex v and let n_v denote $|\mathcal{C}_v|$. Consider a B-component G_i of G'. By our induction hypothesis, the number of guards on $V(G_i)$ is at least k_i in C'. Moreover, since G_i is connected to B by a single cut vertex, from the induction hypothesis it follows that the number of guards on $V(G_i) \setminus B$ is at least $k_i - 1$. Note that, for each cut vertex $v \in X'(B)$, the total number of guards on $\bigcup_{G_i \in \mathcal{C}_v} V(G_i)$ must be at least $1 + \sum_{i:G_i \in \mathcal{C}_v}(k_i - 1)$, to satisfy the above requirement. By summing this over all the cut vertices in $X'(B)$, the total number of guards on $\bigcup_{G_i \in \mathcal{C}_B(G')} V(G_i)$ must be at least $|X'(B)| + \sum_{G_i \in \mathcal{C}_B(G')} \left(\mathrm{mvc}_{X'(G_i)}(G_i) - 1 \right)$.

– Now, we will count the number of guards on the remaining vertices. To cover the edges inside the block B that are not incident at any vertex in $X'(B)$, at least $\mathrm{mvc}(B \setminus X'(B))$ vertices of $B \setminus X'(B)$ are to be occupied in C'. If x is occupied in C', then at least $\mathrm{mvc}_x(B \setminus X'(B))$ vertices of $B \setminus X'(B)$ are occupied in C'. Hence, irrespective of whether x is occupied in C' or not, the number of guards on $(V(B) \setminus X'(B)) \setminus \{x\}$ is at least $\mathrm{mvc}_x(B \setminus X'(B)) - 1$.

Therefore, the total number of guards on $V(G') \setminus \{x\}$ is at least $\mathrm{mvc}_x(B \setminus X'(B)) - 1 + |X'(B)| + \sum_{G_i \in \mathcal{C}_B(G')} \left(\mathrm{mvc}_{X'(G_i)}(G_i) - 1 \right)$. Since $\mathrm{mvc}_x(B \setminus X'(B)) + |X'(B)| = \mathrm{mvc}_{X'(B) \cup \{x\}}(B)$, we can conclude that the number of guards on $V(G') \setminus \{x\}$ is equal to $\mathrm{mvc}_{X'(B) \cup \{x\}}(B) - 1 + \sum_{G_i \in \mathcal{C}_B(G')} \left(\mathrm{mvc}_{X'(G_i)}(G_i) - 1 \right)$. Comparing this expression with Equation (1), we can see that the number of guards on $V(G') \setminus \{x\}$ is at least $l - 1$.   □

Now, we continue with the proof of Lemma 3. There are two possible subcases.

(a) If x is occupied by a guard in C, then by Claim 1, it follows that the number of guards on $V(G') \setminus \{x\}$ is at least $l - 1$ and the number of guards on $V(G')$ is at least l, as we require.

(b) If x is not occupied in C, then by Claim 1, $t \geq l - 1$. If $t \geq l$, we are done. If $t = l - 1$, then we will derive a contradiction. Consider an attack on an edge xu such that $u \in V(B)$. While defending this attack, a guard must move from u to x. Let $\tilde{C}$ be the new configuration in G and let $\tilde{S}$ be the set of vertices on which guards are present in $\tilde{C}$. Note that no guards from $V(G) \setminus V(G')$ can move to any vertex of $V(G') \setminus \{x\}$ in this transition from C to $\tilde{C}$, because x is a cut vertex in G. Therefore, in $\tilde{C}$, the total number of guards on $V(G') \setminus \{x\}$ is less than $l - 1$, contradicting Claim 1. Therefore, $t = l$ and the lemma holds for G'.

Thus, by induction, the lemma holds for every graph.   □

Remark 1. The above lemma holds for both the models of the eternal vertex cover problem; the first model in which the number of guards permitted on a vertex in any configuration is limited to one and the second model, where this restriction is not there. However, it is possible that, in the second model, the number of vertices on which guards are present could be smaller than $\mathrm{mvc}_{X \cup \{x\}}(G)$ in some valid configurations. An example illustrating this subtlety is shown in Fig. 2. In order to address this subtlety, the proof of Lemma 3 employs a careful interplay between the two quantities a) the number of guards in a configuration and b) the number of vertices on which guards are present in a configuration.

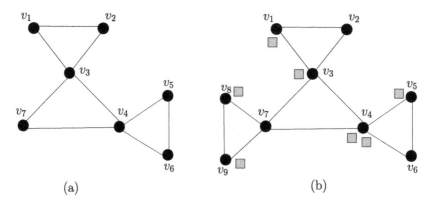

(a)   (b)

Fig. 2. Any vertex cover of the graph in (a) that contains vertex v_7 and both the cut vertices must be of size at least 5. The graph in (b) is a v_7-extension of the graph in (a). Positions of guards in an eternal vertex cover configuration of the graph in (b) are indicated using gray squares. This is a valid configuration. Note that, only four vertices of the graph in (a) are occupied in the configuration shown in (b).

Theorem 1. *For any connected graph G, $\mathrm{evc}(G) \geq \mathrm{mvc}_X(G)$, where X is the set of cut vertices of G.*

Proof. Let C be an eternal vertex cover configuration of G and S be the set of all vertices of G containing guards in C. Suppose $\mathrm{evc}(G) < \mathrm{mvc}_X(G)$. Then, there exists a vertex $x \in X$ such that $x \notin S$. Since every graph satisfies EVC-cut-property by Lemma 3, for each x-component G_i of G, exactly $\mathrm{mvc}_{X(G_i)}(G_i)$ guards are present on $V(G_i) \setminus \{x\}$. Therefore, the total number of guards is at least $\sum_{G_i \in \mathcal{C}_x(G)} \mathrm{mvc}_{X(G_i)}(G_i)$. Since there are at least two x-components, by comparing this expression with the RHS of the equation in Lemma 1, we can see that the total number of guards is more than $\mathrm{mvc}_X(G)$. This contradicts our initial assumption.   ☐

Observation 1 *Let G be a connected graph and let X be the set of cut vertices of G. If $\mathrm{evc}(G) = \mathrm{mvc}_X(G)$, then in every minimum eternal vertex cover configuration of G, there are guards on each vertex of X.*

Proof. For contradiction, assume that there exists a minimum eternal vertex cover configuration C of G with a cut vertex x unoccupied. Rest of the proof is exactly the same as in the proof of Theorem 1.   ☐

3   Algorithmic Implications

In this section, we first prove some general implications of Theorem 1, which are used for deriving algorithmic results for some well-known graph classes.

Definition 5 (Graph class[2] $\mathcal{F}$). $\mathcal{F}$ *is defined as the family of all connected graphs G satisfying the following property: if X is the set of cut vertices of G and S is any vertex cover of G with $X \subseteq S$ and $|S| = \mathrm{mvc}_X(G)$, then the induced subgraph $G[S]$ is connected.*

For any graph G and $S \subseteq V(G)$, let $\mathrm{evc}_s(G)$ denote the minimum number k such that G has an evc class $\mathcal{C}$ with k guards in which all vertices of S are occupied in every configuration of $\mathcal{C}$. For an example, let G be a path on three vertices u, v and w, in which v is the degree-two vertex. It can be easily seen that $\mathrm{evc}(G) = 2$. Since $\{\{u,v\}, \{v,w\}\}$ is an evc class of G in which each configuration has v occupied, $\mathrm{evc}_{\{v\}}(G) = 2$. Since G has no evc class in which each configuration contains u and has exactly two vertices, it follows that $\mathrm{evc}_{\{u\}}(G) = 3$. By Observation 1, we have the following generalization of Corollary 2 of [3].

Theorem 2. *Let G be a graph in $\mathcal{F}$ with at least two vertices and X be the set of cut vertices of G. If for every vertex $v \in V(G) \setminus X$, $\mathrm{mvc}_{X \cup \{v\}}(G) = \mathrm{mvc}_X(G)$, then $\mathrm{evc}(G) = \mathrm{evc}_X(G) = \mathrm{mvc}_X(G)$. Otherwise, $\mathrm{evc}(G) = \mathrm{evc}_X(G) = \mathrm{mvc}_X(G) + 1$.*

Proof. By Theorem 1, we have $\mathrm{mvc}_X(G) \leq \mathrm{evc}(G)$ and we have $\mathrm{evc}(G) \leq \mathrm{evc}_X(G)$.

- If for every vertex $v \in V(G) \setminus X$, $\mathrm{mvc}_{X \cup \{v\}}(G) = \mathrm{mvc}_X(G)$, then by Lemma 2 of [3], $\mathrm{evc}_X(G) = \mathrm{mvc}_X(G)$ and hence, $\mathrm{evc}(G) = \mathrm{evc}_X(G) = \mathrm{mvc}_X(G)$.
- If for some vertex $v \in V(G) \setminus X$, $\mathrm{mvc}_{X \cup \{v\}}(G) \neq \mathrm{mvc}_X(G)$, then by Theorem 1 of [3], $\mathrm{evc}_X(G) \neq \mathrm{mvc}_X(G)$. Let S be any minimum sized vertex cover of S that contains all vertices of X. Since S is a connected vertex cover of G, by a result by Klostermeyer and Mynhardt [11], $\mathrm{evc}(G) \leq \mathrm{evc}_X(G) \leq |S| + 1 = \mathrm{mvc}_X(G) + 1$. Thus, we have $\mathrm{mvc}_X(G) < \mathrm{evc}(G) = \mathrm{evc}_X(G) = \mathrm{mvc}_X(G) + 1$.   □

The following corollary is a generalization of Remark 3 of [2].

Corollary 1. *Let G be a graph in $\mathcal{F}$ with at least two vertices and X be the set of cut vertices of G. Then, $\mathrm{evc}(G) = \min\{k : \forall v \in V(G), G$ has a vertex cover S_v of size k such that $X \cup \{v\} \subseteq S_v\}$.*

The following result is a generalization of Corollary 3 of [2].

Observation 2 *Given a graph $G \in \mathcal{F}$ and an integer k, deciding whether $\mathrm{evc}(G) \leq k$ is in NP.*

---

[2] Note that the definition of this graph class is more general than the one in [2].

Proof. Consider any $G \in \mathcal{F}$ with at least two vertices and let X be the set of cut vertices of G. By Corollary 1, $\mathrm{evc}(G) = \min\{k : \forall v \in V(G), G$ has a vertex coverS_v of size k such that $X \cup \{v\} \subseteq S_v\}$. To check if $\mathrm{evc}(G) \leq k$, the polynomial time verifiable certificate consists of at most $|V|$ vertex covers of size at most k such that for each vertex $v \in V$, there exists a vertex cover in the certificate containing all vertices of $X \cup \{v\}$. $\square$

3.1   Graphs with Locally Connected Blocks

A graph G is *locally connected* if for every vertex v of G, its open neighborhood $N_G(v)$ induces a connected subgraph in G [5]. Biconnected chordal graphs and biconnected internally triangulated graphs are some well-known examples of locally connected graphs. If every block of a graph G is locally connected, then every vertex cover of G that contains all its cut vertices is connected. Hence, $G \in \mathcal{F}$ and by Theorem 2, we have:

Corollary 2. *Let G be a connected graph with at least two vertices, such that each block of G is locally connected and let X be the set of cut vertices of G. Then, $\mathrm{mvc}_X(G) \leq \mathrm{evc}(G) \leq \mathrm{mvc}_X(G) + 1$. Further, $\mathrm{evc}(G) = \mathrm{mvc}_X(G)$ if and only if for every vertex $v \in V(G) \setminus X$, $\mathrm{mvc}_{X \cup \{v\}}(G) = \mathrm{mvc}_X(G)$. In particular, these conclusions hold for chordal graphs and internally triangulated planar graphs that are connected and have at least two vertices.*

3.2   Hereditary Graph Classes

The following theorem is obtained by generalizing Theorem 3 of [3], by applying Theorem 2.

Theorem 3. *Let C be a hereditary graph class such that each biconnected graph in C is locally connected. If the vertex cover number of any graph in C can be computed in $O(f(n))$ time, then the eternal vertex cover number of any graph $G \in \mathsf{C}$ can be computed in $O(n.f(n))$ time.*

Proof. Let G be a graph in C. Since each block of G is locally connected, by Corollary 2, $\mathrm{mvc}_X(G) \leq \mathrm{evc}(G) \leq \mathrm{mvc}_X(G) + 1$. Further, by Corollary 2, to check whether $\mathrm{evc}(G) = \mathrm{mvc}_X(G)$, it is enough to decide if for every vertex $v \in V \setminus X$, $\mathrm{mvc}_{X \cup \{v\}}(G) = \mathrm{mvc}_X(G)$. Since minimum vertex cover computation can be done for graphs of C in $O(f(n))$ time, for a vertex v, checking whether $\mathrm{mvc}_{X \cup \{v\}}(G) = \mathrm{mvc}_X(G)$, takes only $O(f(n))$ time. Therefore, checking whether $\mathrm{evc}(G) = \mathrm{mvc}_X(G)$ can be done in $O(n.f(n))$ time. $\square$

3.3   Chordal Graphs

The following theorem is a special case of Theorem 3, using the fact that minimum vertex cover computation can be done for chordal graphs in $O(m+n)$ time [14], where m is the number of edges and n is the number of vertices of the input graph. This result is a generalization of a result for biconnected chordal graphs in [2].

Theorem 4. *Let G be a chordal graph and X be the set of cut vertices of G. Then, $\mathrm{mvc}_X(G) \leq \mathrm{evc}(G) \leq \mathrm{mvc}_X(G) + 1$ and the value of $\mathrm{evc}(G)$ can be determined in $O(n^2 + mn)$ time, where m is the number of edges and n is the number of vertices of the input graph.*

3.4 Internally Triangulated Planar Graphs

The following lemma is a generalization of a result in [2] for biconnected internally triangulated planar graphs.

Lemma 4. *Given an internally triangulated planar graph G and an integer k, deciding whether $\mathrm{evc}(G) \leq k$ is NP-complete.*

Proof. Since each block of an internally triangulated planar graph G is locally connected, every vertex cover S of G that contains all its cut vertices induces a connected subgraph. Therefore, by Observation 2, deciding whether $\mathrm{evc}(G) \leq k$ is in NP. Since this decision problem is known to be NP-hard for biconnected internally triangulated graphs [2], the lemma follows.   □

The existence of a polynomial time approximation scheme for computing the eternal vertex cover number of biconnected internally triangulated planar graphs, given in [2], is generalized by the following result.

Lemma 5. *There exists a polynomial time approximation scheme for computing the eternal vertex cover number of internally triangulated planar graphs.*

Proof. Let G be an internally triangulated planar graph. Let X be the set of cut vertices of G. It is possible to compute X in linear time, using a well-known depth first search based method. By Corollary 1, $\mathrm{evc}(G) = \max\{\mathrm{mvc}_{X \cup \{v\}}(G) : v \in V(G)\}$. It is easy to see that for a vertex $v \in V(G) \setminus X$, $\mathrm{mvc}_{X \cup \{v\}}(G) = |X| + 1 + \mathrm{mvc}(G \setminus (X \cup \{v\}))$. For $v \in V(G)$, $\mathrm{mvc}_{X \cup \{v\}}(G) = \mathrm{mvc}_X(G) = |X| + \mathrm{mvc}(G \setminus X)$. Using the PTAS designed by Baker et al. [4] for computing the vertex cover number of planar graphs, given any $\epsilon > 0$, it is possible to approximate $\mathrm{mvc}(G \setminus (X \cup \{v\}))$ within a $1 + \epsilon$ factor, in polynomial time. From this, a polynomial time approximation scheme for computing $\mathrm{evc}(G)$ follows.   □

4 Conclusion

The main structural property proven in this paper is the EVC-Cut-Property (Definition 4) which asserts that in any eternal vertex cover configuration of a graph G, each induced subgraph G' of G joining at a cut vertex x of G should have at least as many guards as the size of a minimum sized vertex cover of G' that contains x and all the cut vertices of G'. Using this property, we obtained a new lower bound for eternal vertex cover number. We showed that, for any graph G, $\mathrm{mvc}_X(G) \leq \mathrm{evc}(G)$, where $\mathrm{mvc}_X(G)$ is the size of a vertex cover of minimum cardinality that contains all the cut vertices of G. It was previously known that for any biconnected chordal graph G, $\mathrm{mvc}(G) \leq \mathrm{evc}(G) \leq \mathrm{mvc}(G) + 1$

and deciding the precise value of evc(G) from these two possible values can be done in polynomial time. Also, it was known that for any chordal graph G, evc(G) $\leq$ mvc$_x$(G)+1. From the new lower bound, it follows that for any chordal graph G, mvc$_x$(G) $\leq$ evc(G) $\leq$ mvc$_x$(G) + 1. Further, it follows that deciding the precise value of eternal vertex cover number of a chordal graph can be done in polynomial time. For graphs in which every block is locally connected, even though deciding whether $evc(G) \leq k$ is NP-hard in general, it holds true that the eternal vertex cover number can be at most one more than the new lower bound. In particular, this is true for internally triangulated planar graphs.

Since eternal vertex cover problem is only known to be in PSPACE in general [6], it is interesting to explore more classes of graphs for which eternal vertex cover number can be computed in polynomial time or can be approximated with a better approximation guarantee than the currently known 2-factor approximation algorithm. We believe that, EVC-Cut-Property is likely to be a useful tool for generalizing lower bounds obtained for the eternal vertex cover number of biconnected graphs of graph classes of interest, to obtain results that are applicable to all graphs that belong to the respective classes.

References

1. Anderson, M., Brigham, R., Carrington, J., Dutton, R., Vitray, R., Yellen, J.: Graphs simultaneously achieving three vertex cover numbers. J. Comb. Math. Comb. Comput. **91**, 275–290 (2014)
2. Babu, J., Chandran, L.S., Francis, M., Prabhakaran, V., Rajendraprasad, D., Warrier, J.N.: On graphs whose eternal vertex cover number and vertex cover number coincide. arxiv, https://arxiv.org/abs/1812.05125v2 (April 2019)
3. Babu, J., Chandran, L.S., Francis, M., Prabhakaran, V., Rajendraprasad, D., Warrier, J.N.: On graphs with minimal eternal vertex cover number. In: Pal, S.P., Vijayakumar, A. (eds.) CALDAM 2019. LNCS, vol. 11394, pp. 263–273. Springer, Cham (2019). https://doi.org/10.1007/978-3-030-11509-8_22
4. Baker, B.S.: Approximation algorithms for NP-complete problems on planar graphs. J. ACM **41**(1), 153–180 (1994)
5. Chartrand, G., Pippert, R.E.: Locally connected graphs. Časopis pro pěstování matematiky **99**(2), 158–163 (1974)
6. Fomin, F.V., Gaspers, S., Golovach, P.A., Kratsch, D., Saurabh, S.: Parameterized algorithm for eternal vertex cover. Inf. Process. Lett. **110**(16), 702–706 (2010)
7. Goddard, W., Hedetniemi, S.M., Hedetniemi, S.T.: Eternal security in graphs. J. Combin. Math. Combin. Comput. **52**, 169–180 (2005)
8. Goldwasser, J.L., Klostermeyer, W.F.: Tight bounds for eternal dominating sets in graphs. Discrete Math. **308**(12), 2589–2593 (2008)
9. Hartnell, B., Mynhardt, C.: Independent protection in graphs. Discrete Math. **335**, 100–109 (2014)
10. Klostermeyer, W.F., Mynhardt, C.M.: Graphs with equal eternal vertex cover and eternal domination numbers. Discrete Math. **311**, 1371–1379 (2011)
11. Klostermeyer, W., Mynhardt, C.: Edge protection in graphs. Austr. J. Comb. **45**, 235–250 (2009)
12. Klostermeyer, W.F., Mynhardt, C.: Vertex covers and eternal dominating sets. Discrete Appl. Math. **160**(7), 1183–1190 (2012)

13. Rinemberg, M., Soulignac, F.J.: The eternal dominating set problem for interval graphs. Inf. Process. Lett. **146**, 27–29 (2019)
14. Rose, D.J., Tarjan, R.E., Lueker, G.S.: Algorithmic aspects of vertex elimination on graphs. SIAM J. Comput. **5**(2), 266–283 (1976)

Bounded-Degree Spanners
in the Presence of Polygonal Obstacles

André van Renssen$^{(\boxtimes)}$ (ID) and Gladys Wong

University of Sydney, Sydney, Australia
andre.vanrenssen@sydney.edu.au, gwon6099@uni.sydney.edu.au

Abstract. Let V be a finite set of vertices in the plane and S be a finite set of polygonal obstacles. We show how to construct a plane 2-spanner of the visibility graph of V with respect to S. As this graph can have unbounded degree, we modify it in three easy-to-follow steps, in order to bound the degree to 7 at the cost of slightly increasing the spanning ratio to 6.

Keywords: Spanners · Bounded-degree · Polygonal obstacles

1 Introduction

A geometric graph G consists of a finite set of vertices $V \in \mathbb{R}^2$ and a finite set of edges $(p, q) \in E$ such that the endpoints $p, q \in V$. Every edge in E is weighted according to the Euclidean distance, $|pq|$, between its endpoints. For any two vertices x and y in G, their distance, $d_G(x, y)$ or $d(x, y)$ if the graph G is clear from the context, is defined as the sum of the Euclidean distance of each constituent edge in the shortest path between x and y. A t-spanner H of G is a subgraph of G where for all pairs of vertices in G, $d_H(x, y) \leq t \cdot d_G(x, y)$. The smallest $t \geq 1$ for which this property holds, is called the *stretch factor* or *spanning ratio* of H. For a comprehensive overview on spanners, see Bose and Smid's survey [9] and Narasimhan and Smid's book [12]. Since spanners are subgraphs where all original paths are preserved up to a factor of t, these graphs have applications in the context of geometric problems, including motion planning and optimizing network costs and delays. Another important factor considered when designing spanners is its maximum degree. If a spanner has a low maximum degree, each node needs to store only a few edges, making the spanner better suited for practical purposes.

Most research has focussed on designing spanners of the complete graph. This implicitly assumes that every edge can be used to construct the spanner. However, unfortunately, in many applications this is not the case. In motion planning we need to move around physical obstacles and in network design some connections may not be useable due to an area of high interference between the endpoints that corrupts the messages. This naturally gives rise to the concept of *obstacles* or *constraints*. Spanners have been studied for the case where these

© Springer Nature Switzerland AG 2020
D. Kim et al. (Eds.): COCOON 2020, LNCS 12273, pp. 40–51, 2020.
https://doi.org/10.1007/978-3-030-58150-3_4

obstacles form a plane set of line segments. It was shown that a number of graphs that are spanners without obstacles remain spanners in this setting [2,4,5,8]. In this paper we consider more complex obstacles, namely simple polygons.

Let S be a finite set of simple polygonal obstacles where each corner of each obstacle is a vertex in V, such that no two obstacles intersect. Throughout this paper, we assume that each vertex is part of at most one polygonal obstacle and occurs at most once along its boundary, i.e., the obstacles are vertex-disjoint simple polygons. Note that V can also contain vertices that do not lie on the corners of the obstacles. Two vertices are *visible* to each other if and only if the line segment connecting them does not properly intersect any obstacles (i.e., the line segment is allowed to touch obstacles at vertices or coincide with its boundary, but it is not allowed to intersect the interior). The line segment between two visible points is called a *visibility edge*. The *visibility graph* of a given point set V and a given set of polygonal obstacles S, denoted $Vis(V, S)$, is the complete graph on V excluding all the edges that properly intersect some obstacle. It is a well-known fact that the visibility graph is connected.

Clarkson [10] was one of the first to study this problem, showing how to construct a $(1 + \epsilon)$-spanner of $Vis(V, S)$. Modifying this result, Das [11] showed that it is also possible to construct a spanner of constant spanning ratio and constant degree. Recently, Bose *et al.* [4] constructed a 6-spanner of degree $6+c$, where c is the number of line segment obstacles incident to a vertex. In the process, they also show how to construct a 2-spanner of the visibility graph. We generalize these results and construct a 6-spanner of degree at most 7 in the presence of polygonal obstacles, simplifying some of the proofs in the process. Leading up to this main result, we first construct the polygon-constrained half-Θ_6-graph, denoted G_∞, a 2-spanner of the visibility graph of unbounded degree. We modify this graph in a sequence of three steps, each giving a 6-spanner of the visibility graph to bound the degree to 15, 10, and finally 7.

Each of these graphs may be of independent interest. Specifically, the graphs with degree 10 and 15 are constructed by solely removing edges from G_∞. Furthermore, in the graph of degree 15 the presence of an edge is determined by the vertices at its endpoints, whereas for the other two this involves the neighbors of these vertices. Hence, depending on the network model and communication cost, one graph may be more easily applicable than another.

2   Preliminaries

Next, we describe how to construct the polygon-constrained half-Θ_6-graph, G_∞. Before we can construct this graph, we first partition the plane around for each vertex $u \in V$ into six cones, each with angle $\theta = \frac{\pi}{3}$ and u as the apex. For ease of exposition, we assume that the bisector of one cone is a vertical ray going up from u. We refer to this cone as C_0^u or C_0 when the apex u is clear from the context. The cones are then numbered in counter-clockwise order $(C_0, \overline{C_2}, C_1, \overline{C_0}, C_2, \overline{C_1})$ (see Fig. 1). Cones of the form C_i are called *positive cones*, whereas cones of the form $\overline{C_i^u}$ are *negative cones*. For any two vertices u and v in V, we have the property that if $v \in C_i^u$ then $u \in \overline{C_i^v}$.

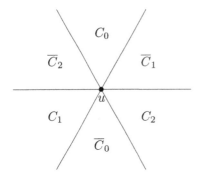

Fig. 1. The cones around u.

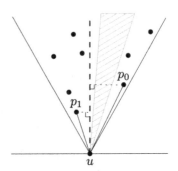

Fig. 2. The positive cone C_i^u is split into two subcones and an edge is added in each.

We are now ready to construct G_∞. For every vertex $u \in V$, we consider each of its positive cones and add a single edge in such a cone. More specifically, we consider all vertices visible to u that lie in this cone and add an undirected edge to the vertex whose projection on the bisector of the cone is closest to u. More precisely, the edge (u, v) is part of G_∞ when v is visible to u and $|uv'| < |uw'|$ for all $v \neq w$, where v' and w' are the projections of v and w on the bisector of the currently considered positive cone of u. For ease of exposition, we assume that no two vertices lie on a line parallel to one of the cone boundaries and no three vertices are collinear. This ensures that each vertex lies in a unique cone of each other vertex and their projected distances are distinct. If a point set is not in general position, one can rotate it by a small angle such that the resulting point set is in general position.

Since every vertex is part of at most one obstacle, obstacles can affect the construction in only a limited number of ways. Cones that are split in two (i.e., there are visible vertices on both sides of the obstacle) are considered to be two subcones of the original cone and we add an edge in each of the two subcones using the original bisector (see Fig. 2). If a cone is not split, the obstacle only changes the region of the cone that is visible from u. Since we only consider visible vertices when adding edges, this is already handled by the construction method.

We note that the construction described above is similar to that of the constrained half-Θ_6-graph as defined by Bose et al. [4] for line segment constraints. In their setting a cone can be split into multiple subcones and in each of the positive subcones an edge is added. This similarity will form a crucial part of the planarity proof in the next section.

Before we prove that G_∞ is a plane spanner, however, we first state a useful visibility property that will form a building block for a number of the following proofs. We note that this property holds for any three points, not just vertices of the input. Due to space constraints the proof of this and a number of other results are deferred to the appendix.

Lemma 1. *Let u, v, and w be three points where (w, u) and (u, v) are both visibility edges and u is not a vertex of any polygonal obstacle P where the open polygon P' intersects $\triangle wuv$. The area A, bounded by (w, u), (u, v), and a convex chain formed by visibility edges between w and v inside $\triangle wuv$, does not contain any vertices and is not intersected by any obstacles.*

For ease of notation, we define the canonical triangle of two vertices u and v with $v \in C_i^u$, denoted $\triangledown_u^v$, to be the equilateral triangle defined by the boundaries of C_i^u and the line through v perpendicular to the bisector of C_i^u.

3 The Polygon-Constrained-Half-Θ_6-Graph

In this section we show that graph G_∞ is a plane 2-spanner of the visibility graph. We first prove it is plane.

Lemma 2. G_∞ *is a plane graph.*

Proof. We prove this lemma by proving that G_∞ is a subgraph of the constrained half-Θ_6-graph introduced by Bose *et al.* [4]. Recall that in their graph the set of obstacles is a plane set of line segments.

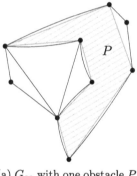

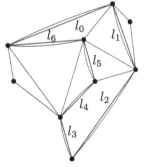

(a) G_∞ with one obstacle P.

(b) The constrained half-Θ_6-graph with constraints $l_0, l_1, ..., l_6$.

Fig. 3. G_∞ is a subgraph of the constrained half-Θ_6-graph. Edges coinciding with obstacle boundaries are drawn as slight arcs for clarity.

Given a set of polygonal obstacles, we convert them into line segments as follows: Each boundary edge on polygonal obstacle $P \in S$ forms a line segment obstacle l_i. Since these edges meet only at vertices and no two obstacles intersect, this gives a plane set of line segments. Recall that the constrained half-Θ_6-graph constructs subcones the same way as G_∞ does. This means that when considering the plane minus the interior of the obstacles in S, the constrained half-Θ_6-graphs adds the same edges as G_∞, while inside P the constrained half-Θ_6-graph may add additional edges (see Fig. 3). Hence, G_∞ is a subgraph of the constrained half-Θ_6-graph. Since Bose *et al.* showed that their graph is plane, it follows that G_∞ is plane as well.   □

Next, we show that G_∞ is a 2-spanner of the visibility graph.

Lemma 3. *Let u and v be vertices where (u, v) is a visibility edge and v lies in a positive cone of u. Let a and b be the two corners of $\triangledown_u^v$ opposite to u and let m be the midpoint of (a, b). There exists a path from u to v in G_∞ such that the path is at most $2 \cdot |uv| \geq (\sqrt{3} \cdot \cos \angle muv + \sin \angle muv) \cdot |uv|$ in length.*

These two lemmas imply the following theorem.

Theorem 1. *G_∞ is a plane 2-spanner of the visibility graph.*

We note that while every vertex in G_∞ has at most one edge in every positive subcone, it can have an unbounded number of edges in its negative subcones. In the following sections, we proceed to bound the degree of the spanner.

4   Bounding the Degree

In this section, we introduce G_{15}, a subgraph of the polygon-constrained half-Θ_6-graph of maximum degree 15. We obtain G_{15} from G_∞ by, for each vertex, removing all edges from its negative subcones except for the leftmost (clockwise extreme from u's perspective) edge, rightmost (counterclockwise) edge, and the edge to the closest vertex in that cone (see Fig. 4a). Note that the edge to the closest vertex may also be the leftmost and/or the rightmost edge.

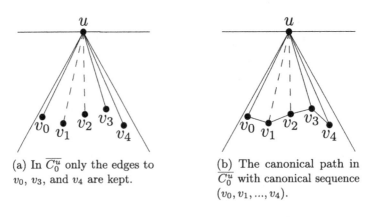

(a) In $\overline{C_0^u}$ only the edges to v_0, v_3, and v_4 are kept.

(b) The canonical path in $\overline{C_0^u}$ with canonical sequence $(v_0, v_1, ..., v_4)$.

Fig. 4. Transforming G_∞ into G_{15}.

By simply counting the number of subcones (three positive, three negative, and at most one additional subcone caused by an obstacle), we obtain the desired degree bound. Furthermore, since G_{15} is a subgraph of G_∞, it is also plane.

Lemma 4. *The degree of each vertex u in G_{15} is at most 15.*

Lemma 5. *G_{15} is plane.*

Finally, we look at the spanning ratio of G_{15}. We assume without loss of generality that we look at two vertices u and v such that $v \in \overline{C_0^u}$ and $u \in C_0^v$. Given vertex u and a negative subcone, we define the canonical sequence of this subcone as the vertices adjacent to u in G_∞ that lie in the subcone in counterclockwise order (see Fig. 4b). The canonical path of $\overline{C_0^u}$ refers to the path that connects the consecutive vertices in the canonical sequence of $\overline{C_0^u}$. This definition is not dissimilar to that of Bose *et al.* [4].

Lemma 6. *If v_i and v_{i+1} are consecutive vertices in the canonical sequence of the negative subcone $\overline{C_0^u}$, then $\triangle uv_iv_{i+1}$ is empty.*

Lemma 7. *G_{15} contains an edge between every pair of consecutive vertices on a canonical path.*

Proof. We first prove that the edges on the canonical path are in G_∞. Let v_1 and v_2 be a pair of consecutive vertices in the canonical sequence in $\overline{C_0^u}$. Assume, without loss of generality, that $v_2 \in \overline{C_2^{v_1}}$ and $v_1 \in C_2^{v_2}$. Let A be the area bounded by the positive subcones $C_0^{v_1}$ and $C_0^{v_2}$ that contain u (see Fig. 5a). Let A' be the set of vertices visible to v_1 or v_2 in A. We first show by contradiction that $A' = \emptyset$. According to Lemma 6, $\triangle uv_1v_2$ is empty and thus does not contain any vertices. We focus on the part of A to the left of uv_1. Consider vertex $x \in A$ to the left of uv_1 where x has the smallest interior angle $\angle xuv_1$. Since (u, v_1) is a visibility edge, the edge (u, x) is a visibility edge, as any obstacle blocking it implies the existence of a vertex with smaller angle. Applying Lemma 1 to xuv_1, there exists a convex chain from v_1 to x in $\triangle v_1xu$. The neighbor of v_1 in the convex chain is a closer visible vertex than u in $C_0^{v_1}$, contradicting that $(u, v_1) \in G_\infty$. An analogous argument for the region to the right of uv_2 contradicts that $(u, v_2) \in G_\infty$. Therefore, A does not contain any vertices visible to v_1 or v_2.

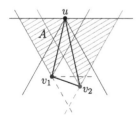

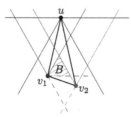

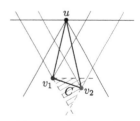

(a) Area A is bounded by $C_0^{v_1}$ and $C_0^{v_2}$.

(b) Triangle B is bounded by $\overline{C_1^{v_1}}$ and $C_0^{v_2}$.

(c) Triangle C is $\nabla_{v_1}^{v_2}$.

Fig. 5. A pair of consecutive vertices v_1 and v_2 along a canonical path and their surrounding empty areas.

Next, let B be the intersection of $\overline{C_1^{v_1}}$ and $\overline{C_2^{v_2}}$ (see Fig. 5b). Since (v_1, v_2) is part of the canonical path of $\overline{C_0^u}$, by Lemma 6, $\triangle uv_1v_2 = \emptyset$. Since B is contained in $\triangle uv_1v_2$, B is also empty.

Finally, let area C be the canonical triangle $\bigtriangledown_{v_1}^{v_2}$ (see Fig. 5c). Let C' be the set of visible vertices to v_1 and v_2 in C. We show that $C' = \emptyset$, by contradiction. Since both A and B are empty, the highest vertex $x \in C$ will have u as the closest visible vertex in C_0^x. This implies that x occurs between v_1 and v_2 in the canonical path, contradicting that they are consecutive vertices. Therefore, $C' = \emptyset$.

Since A, B, and C are all empty, v_2 is the closest vertex of v_1 in the subcone of $C_2^{v_1}$ that contains it. By Lemma 6 it is visible to v_1 and thus, (v_1, v_2) is an edge in G_∞.

It remains to show that (v_1, v_2) is preserved in G_{15}. Since $\triangle uv_1v_2$ is empty and G_{15} is plane (by Lemma 5), v_1 is the rightmost vertex in $\overline{C_2^{v_2}}$. Hence, it is not removed and thus, the canonical path in $\overline{C_0^u}$ exists in G_{15}.   □

Now that we know that these canonical paths exist in G_{15}, we can proceed to prove that it is a spanner.

Lemma 8. G_{15} *is a 3-spanner of* G_∞.

Since by Lemma 3, G_∞ is a 2-spanner of the visibility graph and by Lemma 8, G_{15} is a 3-spanner of G_∞, we obtain the main result of this section.

Theorem 2. G_{15} *is a plane 6-spanner of the visibility graph of degree at most 15.*

5   Improving the Analysis

Observing that we need to maintain only the canonical paths between vertices, along with the edge to the closest vertex in each negative subcone for the proof of Lemma 8 to hold, we reduce the degree as follows. Consider each negative subcone $\overline{C_i^u}$ of every vertex u and keep only the edge incident to the closest vertex (with respect to the projection onto the bisector of the cone) and the canonical path in $\overline{C_i^u}$. We show that the resulting graph, denoted G_{10}, has degree at most 10. Recall that at most one cone per vertex is split into two subcones and thus this cone can have two disjoint canonical paths, as we argue in Lemma 11.

As in the previous section, we proceed to prove that G_{10} is a plane 6-spanner of the visibility graph of degree 10. Since G_{10} is a subgraph of G_{15}, it is also plane. Furthermore, since the canonical path is maintained, the spanning property does not change.

Lemma 9. G_{10} *is a plane graph.*

Lemma 10. G_{10} *is a 3-spanner of* G_∞.

It remains to upper bound the maximum degree of G_{10}. We do this by charging the edges incident to a vertex to its cones. The four part charging scheme is described below (see Fig. 6). Scenarios A and B handle the edge to the closest vertex, while Scenarios C and D handle the edges along the canonical path. Hence, the total charge of a vertex is an upper bound on its degree.

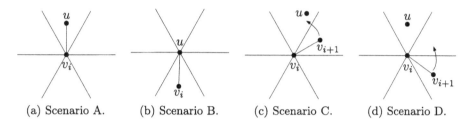

(a) Scenario A.   (b) Scenario B.   (c) Scenario C.   (d) Scenario D.

Fig. 6. The four scenarios of the charging scheme. The arrows in Scenarios C and D indicate the cone these edges are charged to.

Scenario A: Edge (u, v_i) lies in $C_j^{v_i}$ and v_i is the closest vertex of u in $\overline{C_j^u}$. Then (u, v_i) is charged to $C_j^{v_i}$.

Scenario B: Edge (u, v_i) lies in $\overline{C_j^u}$ and v_i is the closest vertex of u in $\overline{C_j^u}$. Then (u, v_i) is charged in $\overline{C_j^u}$.

Scenario C: Edge (v_i, v_{i+1}) lies on a canonical path of u, with $u \in C_j^{v_i}$, and $v_{i+1} \in \overline{C_{j+1}^{v_i}}$. Edge (v_i, v_{i+1}) is charged to $C_j^{v_i}$. Similarly, edge (v_i, v_{i-1}) on a canonical path of u, where $v_{i-1} \in \overline{C_{j-1}^{v_i}}$, is charged to $C_j^{v_i}$.

Scenario D: Edge (v_i, v_{i+1}) lies on a canonical path of u, with $u \in C_j^{v_i}$, and $v_{i+1} \in C_{j-1}^{v_i}$. Edge (v_i, v_{i+1}) is charged to $\overline{C_{j+1}^{v_i}}$. Similarly, edge (v_i, v_{i-1}) on a canonical path of u, where $v_{i-1} \in C_{j+1}^{v_i}$, is charged to $\overline{C_{j-1}^{v_i}}$.

Lemma 11. *The degree of every vertex in G_{10} is at most 10.*

Proof Sketch. Due to space constraints we only sketch this proof. The full proof can be found in the appendix.

Negative Subcones: Using Lemmas 6 and 7, it can be shown that Scenario B and D cannot both charge a negative subcone, leading to a total charge of 1 per negative subcone.

Positive Subcones: In this case, it can be shown that Scenario A and C cannot both charge a positive subcone. If a cone is not split by an obstacle, this implies a maximum charge of 2. In the remainder, we show that even when a cone is split, it still has charge at most 2. Let P be the obstacle that splits a positive cone $C_j^{v_i}$ into two subcones. Let u be the closest vertex of v_i in the right subcone of $C_j^{v_i}$ and let u' be the closest vertex in its left subcone (see Fig. 7).

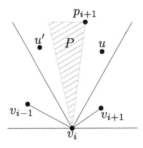

Fig. 7. Two positive subcones of v_i are each charged for one edge by Scenario C.

By construction, the maximum number of charges from edges fitting Scenario A stays the same, 1 per subcone. However, for edges from Scenario C, we show that the maximum charge per subcone reduces to 1. Let p_{i+1} be the vertex following v_i on the boundary of P on the side of u. Since (u, v_i) is an edge of G_∞, p_{i+1} is further from v_i than u is (or equal if $p_{i+1} = u$), as otherwise p_{i+1} would be a closer visible vertex than u, contradicting the existence of (u, v_i). For any vertex v_{i-1} in $\overline{C_2^{v_i}}$ or $C_1^{v_i}$, u is not visible since (v_i, p_{i+1}) blocks visibility and therefore (v_{i-1}, v_i) cannot be part of the canonical path in $\overline{C_0^u}$. We note that if $u = p_{i+1}$, v_{i-1} may be visible to u, but in this case it lies in a different subcone of u and hence would also not be part of this canonical path. Hence, v_i is the leftmost vertex of the canonical path of $\overline{C_0^u}$, and using an analogous argument, v_i is the rightmost vertex of the canonical path of $\overline{C_0^{u'}}$. Therefore, these positive subcones cannot be charged more than 1 each by Scenario C. Using the fact that Scenario A and C cannot occur at the same time, we conclude that each positive cone is charged at most 2, regardless of whether an obstacle splits it.

Thus, each positive cone is charged at most 2 and each negative subcone is charged at most 1. Since there are 3 positive cones and at most 4 negative subcones, the total degree bound is 10. $\square$

Putting the results presented in this section together, we obtain the following theorem.

Theorem 3. G_{10} *is a plane 6-spanner of the visibility graph of degree at most 10.*

6   Shortcutting to Degree 7

In order to reduce the degree bound from 10 to 7, we ensure that at most 1 edge is charged to each subcone. According to Lemma 11, the negative subcones and the positive subcones created by splitting a cone into two already have at most 1 charge. Hence, we only need to reduce the maximum charge of positive cones that are not split by an obstacle from 2 to 1. The two edges charged to a positive cone C_i^v come from edges in the adjacent negative subcones $\overline{C_{i-1}^v}$ and

$\overline{C^v_{i+1}}$ (Scenario C), whereas cone C^v_i itself does not contain any edges. Hence, in order to reduce the degree from 10 to 7, we need to resolve this situation whenever it occurs in G_{10}. We do so by performing a transformation described below when a positive cone is charged twice for Scenario C. The graph resulting from applying this transformation to every applicable vertex is referred to as G_7.

Let u be a vertex in G_{10} and let v be a vertex on its canonical path (in $\overline{C^u_i}$) whose positive cone is charged twice. Let (x, v) and (v, y) be the edges charged to $\overline{C^u_i}$ and assume without loss of generality that x occurs on the canonical path from u to y (see Fig. 8a). If neither x nor y is the closest vertex in the respective negative subcone of v that contains them, we remove (v, y) from the graph and add (x, y) (see Fig. 8b). This reduces the degree of v, but may cause a problem at x. In order to solve this, we consider the neighbor w of x on the canonical path of v. Since x is not the closest vertex in v's subcone, this neighbor exists. If $w \in \overline{C^x_i}$ and w is not the closest vertex of x in the subcone that contains it, we remove (x, w) (see Fig. 8c).

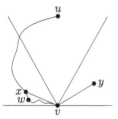
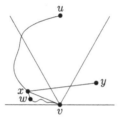
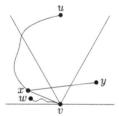

(a) The situation before the transformation.

(b) After (x, y) is added and (v, y) is removed.

(c) The situation after the transformation.

Fig. 8. Transforming G_{10} into G_7.

The reasons for these choices are as follows. If an edge (a, b) is part of a canonical path and b is the closest vertex to a in the negative subcone that contains it, then this edge is charged twice at a. It is charged once as the edge to the closest vertex (Scenario B) and once as part of the canonical path (Scenario C). Hence, we can reduce the charge to a by 1 without changing the graph.

In the case where we end up removing (v, y), we need to ensure that there still exists a spanning path between u and y (and any vertex following y on the canonical path). Therefore, we insert the edge (x, y). This comes at the price that we now need to ensure that the total charge of x does not increase. Fortunately, this is always possible.

Lemma 12. *The degree of every vertex in G_7 is at most 7.*

Lemma 13. *G_7 is a 3-spanner of G_∞.*

It remains to show that G_7 is a plane graph.

Lemma 14. *G_7 is a plane graph.*

Proof. By construction, each transformation performed when converting G_{10} to G_7 includes the addition of at most one edge (x, y) and the removal of at most two edges (v, y) and (x, w). By Lemma 9, G_{10} is a plane graph and thus the removal of (v, y) and (x, w) does not affect the planarity of G_7. It remains to consider the added edges. Specifically, we need to show that: (x, y) cannot intersect any edge from G_{10}, (x, y) cannot intersect an obstacle, and (x, y) cannot intersect another edge added during the construction of G_7.

We first prove that the edge (x, y) cannot intersect any edge from G_{10}. Since x, v, and y are consecutive vertices in the canonical sequence of a negative subcone of u, according to Lemma 6, $\triangle uxv$ and $\triangle uvy$ are empty. Furthermore, since the boundary edges of these triangles are edges in G_∞, which is plane by Lemma 2, no edges or obstacles can intersect these edges. Hence, since (x, y) lies inside the quadrilateral $uxvy$, edge (u, v) is the only edge that can intersect (x, y). However, since x and y lie in $\overline{C_{i-1}^v}$ and $\overline{C_{i+1}^v}$, both x and y are closer to u than v in $\overline{C_i^u}$, implying that (u, v) is not part of G_{10}. Therefore, (x, y) does not intersect any edge from G_{10}.

Next, we show that (x, y) cannot intersect any obstacles. Since by Lemma 6 no obstacles, vertices, or edges can pass through or exist within $\triangle uxv$ and $\triangle uvy$, the only obstacles we need to consider are $\triangle uxv$ and $\triangle uvy$ themselves and the line segment obstacle uv. We note that in all three cases the obstacle splits the negative cone $\overline{C_i^u}$ into two subcones, and x and y lie in different negative subcones and thus on different canonical paths (see Fig. 9). This implies that C_i^u is not charged twice by the same canonical path and thus, the transformation to G_7 would not add (x, y). Therefore, (x, y) cannot intersect any obstacles.

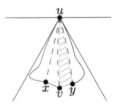

Fig. 9. The quadrilateral $uxvy$ in G_7 where $\triangle uvy$ is an obstacle itself. $\overline{C_0^u}$ is split into two subcones and x and y lie on two different canonical paths.

Finally, we show that the added edge (x, y) cannot intersect another edge added during the transformation from G_{10} to G_7. We prove this by contradiction. Let e be an added edge that intersects (x, y). Edge e cannot have x or y as an endpoint, as this would imply that it does not intersect (x, y). Furthermore, since by Lemma 6 $\triangle uxv$ and $\triangle uvy$ are empty and e cannot intersect edges (x, v) and (v, y), as shown above, v is one of the endpoints of e. By construction of G_7, e is added because either x or y has a positive cone charged by two edges from its adjacent negative subcones (one of which being the edge to v). However, this contradicts the fact that v lies in their positive cones (C_{i-1}^x and C_{i+1}^y) implied by the edge (x, y) being added during the transformation. Therefore, (x, y) cannot intersect any edge added while constructing G_7, completing the proof.   □

We summarize our main result in the following theorem.

Theorem 4. G_7 *is a plane 6-spanner of the visibility graph of degree at most 7.*

7 Conclusion

With the construction of these spanners, future work includes developing routing algorithms for them. There has been extensive research into routing algorithms, including routing on the visibility graph in the presence of line segment obstacles [3,6,7]. For polygonal obstacles, Banyassady *et al.* [1] developed a routing algorithm on the visibility graph with polygonal obstacles, though this work requires some additional information to be stored at the vertices.

References

1. Banyassady, B., et al.: Routing in polygonal domains. In: Proceedings of the 28th International Symposium on Algorithms and Computation. LIPIcs, vol. 92, pp. 10:1–10:13 (2017)
2. Bose, P., De Carufel, J.L., van Renssen, A.: Constrained generalized Delaunay graphs are plane spanners. Comput. Geom.: Theory Appl. **74**, 50–65 (2018)
3. Bose, P., Fagerberg, R., van Renssen, A., Verdonschot, S.: Competitive local routing with constraints. J. Comput. Geom. **8**(1), 125–152 (2017)
4. Bose, P., Fagerberg, R., van Renssen, A., Verdonschot, S.: On plane constrained bounded-degree spanners. Algorithmica **81**(4), 1392–1415 (2019)
5. Bose, P., Keil, J.M.: On the stretch factor of the constrained Delaunay triangulation. In: Proceedings of the 3rd International Symposium on Voronoi Diagrams in Science and Engineering, pp. 25–31 (2006)
6. Bose, P., Korman, M., van Renssen, A., Verdonschot, S.: Constrained routing between non-visible vertices. In: Cao, Y., Chen, J. (eds.) COCOON 2017. LNCS, vol. 10392, pp. 62–74. Springer, Cham (2017). https://doi.org/10.1007/978-3-319-62389-4_6
7. Bose, P., Korman, M., van Renssen, A., Verdonschot, S.: Routing on the visibility graph. J. Comput. Geom. **9**(1), 430–453 (2018)
8. Bose, P., van Renssen, A.: Spanning properties of Yao and θ-graphs in the presence of constraints. Int. J. Comput. Geom. Appl. **29**(02), 95–120 (2019)
9. Bose, P., Smid, M.: On plane geometric spanners: a survey and open problems. Comput. Geom.: Theory Appl. **46**(7), 818–830 (2013)
10. Clarkson, K.: Approximation algorithms for shortest path motion planning. In: Proceedings of the 19th Annual ACM Symposium on Theory of Computing, pp. 56–65 (1987)
11. Das, G.: The visibility graph contains a bounded-degree spanner. In: Proceedings of the 9th Canadian Conference on Computational Geometry, pp. 70–75 (1997)
12. Narasimhan, G., Smid, M.: Geometric Spanner Networks. Cambridge University Press, Cambridge (2007)

End-Vertices of AT-free Bigraphs

Jan Gorzny$^{1(\boxtimes)}$ (ID) and Jing Huang^2

^{1} University of Waterloo, Waterloo, ON, Canada
`jgorzny@uwaterloo.ca`
^{2} University of Victoria, Victoria, BC, Canada
`huangj@uvic.ca`

Abstract. The end-vertex problem for a search algorithm asks whether a vertex of the input graph is the last visited vertex of an execution of that search algorithm. We consider the end-vertex problem restricted to AT-free bigraphs for various search algorithms: Breadth-First Search (BFS), Lexicographic Breadth-First Search (LBFS), Depth-First Search (DFS), and Maximal Neighbourhood Search (MNS). Deciding whether a vertex of a graph is the end-vertex of any of these search algorithms is NP-complete in general. We show that we can decide whether a vertex is an end-vertex of BFS or MNS in polynomial time on AT-free bigraphs. Additionally, we show that we can decide whether a vertex is an end-vertex of DFS or LBFS in linear time on AT-free bigraphs; this improves the LBFS end-vertex complexity on this class of graphs.

Keywords: AT-free bigraph · End-vertex problem · Breadth-first search · Depth-first search · Lexicographic breadth-first search · Maximal neighbourhood search · Proper interval bigraph · Bipartite permutation graph

1 Introduction

Graph search algorithms are a way to systematically visit the vertices in a graph and have numerous applications. Well-known search algorithms like Breadth-First Search (BFS) and Depth-First Search (DFS) have been applied to a wide range of problems. For example, BFS can be used to check if a graph is bipartite and DFS can be used to find cut-vertices of a graph (see e.g. [4]). Lexicographic Breadth-First Search (LBFS), a variant of breadth-first search with a tie-breaking rule, is used for recognizing graph classes, computing graph parameters, and detecting certain graph structures (cf. [9]). Adding a similar tie-breaking rule to DFS yields Lexicographic Depth-First Search (LDFS), which was shown to be helpful for computing maximal cardinality matchings on cocomparability graphs [22]. Maximal Neighbhourhood Search (MNS) is a generalization of both LBFS and LDFS [12]. The relationship between these search algorithms and their descriptions are presented in [12].

Rose, Tarjan and Lueker [23] studied the end-vertices of search algorithms. They showed that if the input graph is chordal (i.e., containing no induced

© Springer Nature Switzerland AG 2020
D. Kim et al. (Eds.): COCOON 2020, LNCS 12273, pp. 52–63, 2020.
https://doi.org/10.1007/978-3-030-58150-3_5

Table 1. Known complexity results for the end-vertex problem. An entry "L" indicates that there is a linear time solution, and an entry "P" indicates that there is a polynomial time solution. An arrow → indicates that a result has been improved. Bold results are new.

Class	BFS	DFS	LBFS	LDFS	MNS	MCS
All Graphs	NPC	NPC	NPC	NPC	NPC [1]	NPC [1]
Weakly Chordal	NPC [8]	NPC	NPC [6,11]	NPC [8]	NPC [1]	NPC [6]
Chordal	?	NPC	?	L [6]	L [1]	P [6]
Interval	L [6]	L [1]	L [11]	L	L [1]	P
Unit Interval	L	L [1]	L [11]	L [1]	L [1]	L [1]
Split	P [8]	NPC [8]	L [1]	L [1]	L [1]	L [1]
Bipartite	NPC [8]	NPC [16]	NPC [17]	?	?	?
AT-Free Bipartite	**P**	**L**	P [17]→**L**	?	**P**	?

cycle of length ≥ 4) then the last visited vertex of an LBFS is simplicial (i.e., its neighbourhood induces a complete subgraph). This result has stimulated research on last visited vertices of LBFS of various classes of graphs (cf. [2,3, 11,15–17,19]). However, not all simplicial vertices of a chordal graph are LBFS end-vertices.

Research on end-vertices has expanded to study the complexity of determining if a vertex is a possible end-vertex of a search. The end-vertices of BFS, DFS, LBFS, LDFS, MNS, and Maximal Cardinality Search (MCS) have all been studied on various class graphs (cf. [1,6,8,11,17]). Table 1 shows the known complexity for the end-vertex problem, which is defined formally below.

Call the last visited vertex of a search S of a graph an *end-vertex* of S of the graph. We now formally define the *end-vertex problem* for a search S.

End-Vertex Problem for S:
Instance: A graph $G = (V, E)$, and a vertex t.
Question: Is there an ordering $\sigma : V(G) \rightarrow \{1, \ldots, n\}$ generated by S of V such that $\sigma(t) = n$?

The end-vertex problem is NP-complete in general for each of the aforementioned search algorithms (cf. [1,6,8,11]). On restricted graph classes, characterizations of end-vertices enable tractable algorithms for the end-vertex problem. For example, Corneil, Olariu and Stewart [14] proved that the end-vertices of LBFS of an interval graph are precisely the simplicial and admissible vertices after establishing that all LBFS end-vertices of AT-free graphs are admissible. Interval graphs are precisely the graphs which are both chordal and AT-free (defined in the next section), cf. [21]. End-vertices of LBFS of split graphs, HHD-free graphs and distance-hereditary graphs also have nice properties, cf. [8,15,19].

Recently, Gorzny and Huang [17] proved that the LBFS end-vertex problem remains NP-complete for bigraphs (see also [20]). For the subclass of AT-free bigraphs, they [17] obtained a characterization of end-vertices of LBFS using the notion of eccentricity, which appears in the next section. In this paper, we show that the BFS and MNS end-vertex problems have polynomial time solutions and that the DFS end-vertex problem has a linear time solution on AT-free bigraphs. We also provide a non-trivial linear-time algorithm to determine if a vertex of an AT-free bigraph is an LBFS end-vertex, which improves the result of [17].

2   Preliminaries

All graphs in this work are simple, finite, and undirected. A graph G is *bipartite* if $V(G)$ can be partitioned into two sets X and Y such that all edges of G have one end-point in X and the other in Y.

The *open neighbourhood* of a vertex v, denoted $N(v)$, is the set $\{u \in V \mid (u, v) \in E\}$ of vertices adjacent to v. The *closed neighbourhood* of a vertex, denoted $N[v]$, is the open neighbourhood of the vertex along with the vertex itself, i.e. $N[v] = N(v) \cup \{v\}$. If $X \subseteq V$, then the neighbourhood of the set X, denoted $N(X)$, is $\left(\cup_{v \in X} N(v) \right) \setminus X$.

We now define the class of AT-free (bipartite) graphs. Let G be a graph and x, y, z be three vertices of G. If P is a path on G, then $V(P)$ denotes the set of vertices of G in P. An (x, y)-path P *misses* (or *avoids*) z if $V(P) \cap N[z] = \emptyset$, that is, P contains neither z nor a neighbour of z; otherwise the vertex z is said to *intercept* (or *hit*) the path P. The vertex y is in the *middle of* x, z if some (x, y)-path misses z and some (y, z)-path misses x. A vertex is called *admissible* if it is not in the middle of any two vertices. If each of x, y, z is in the middle of the two others then x, y, z form an *asteroidal triple*. A graph which does not contain an asteroidal triple is called *asteroidal triple-free* (*AT-free*). A graph is an AT-free bigraph if it is bipartite and AT-free.

AT-free bigraphs are a popular class of bipartite graphs and they are exactly the bipartite permutation graphs [18]. This class is also equivalent to *proper interval bigraphs* (see e.g. [5,18]). A *strong ordering* (σ^A, σ^B) of a bipartite graph $G = (A, B, E)$ consists of an ordering σ^A of A and an ordering σ^B of B such that for all $ab, a'b' \in E$, where $a, a' \in A$ and $b, b' \in B$, $a <_{\sigma^A} a'$ and $b' <_{\sigma^B} b$ implies that $ab' \in E$ and $a'b \in E$. An ordering σ^A of A has the *adjacency property* if, for every $b \in B$, $N(b)$ consists of vertices that are consecutive in σ^A. The ordering σ^A has the *enclosure property* if, for every pair b, b' of vertices of B with $N(b) \subseteq N(b')$, the vertices of $N(b') \setminus N(b)$ appear consecutively in σ^A, implying that b is adjacent to the leftmost or rightmost neighbour of b' in σ^A. It was shown that every AT-free bigraph has a strong ordering [24], and moreover, that every such strong ordering has both the adjacency and enclosure properties [24]. A strong ordering can be computed in linear time [7].

We use $d(x, y)$ to denote the *distance* between vertices x, y. The *diameter* of G, denoted by diam(G), is the maximum distance of any two vertices. If $d(x, y) = $ diam(G), then we say that x, y are a *diametrical pair*. A pair of vertices (x, y) is said to be a *dominating pair* of a graph G if the set of all vertices that intercepts all (x, y)-paths is equal to $V(G)$. When x, y are both diametrical and dominating, they are called a *diametrical dominating pair*. For a vertex w, we use $L_\ell(w)$ to denote the set of all vertices u with $d(u,w) = \ell$. The maximum value ℓ for which $L_\ell(w) \neq \emptyset$ is called the *eccentricity* of w and is denoted by $\mathrm{ecc}_G(w)$ (we will drop the subscript when it is clear). When $\ell = \mathrm{ecc}(w)$, the vertices of $L_\ell(w)$ are called *eccentric vertices* of w.

Several propositions regarding end-vertices and the structure of AT-free bigraphs are necessary to simplify many of the proofs in this work.

Proposition 1 ([10,13]). *If v is the end-vertex of an LBFS of an AT-free graph G, then v is admissible and $\mathrm{ecc}(v) \geq \mathrm{diam}(G) - 1$.* □

Proposition 2 ([13]). *Let G be a connected AT-free graph and v be an admissible vertex in G. Suppose that there is an LBFS ordering which begins at v and ends at w. Then v, w are a dominating pair in G. Moreover, if $\mathrm{ecc}(v) = \mathrm{diam}(G)$, then v, w are a diametrical dominating pair.* □

Let z be a vertex in a graph G and ℓ be a natural number. Note that when G is bipartite $L_\ell(z)$ is an independent set for each ℓ. We shall use $N_\ell^z(a)$ to denote the set of all neighbours of a in $L_\ell(z)$, that is, $N_\ell^z(a) = N(a) \cap L_\ell(z)$. It is clear that if $a \in L_{\ell+1}(z)$ then $N_\ell^z(a) \neq \emptyset$.

Proposition 3 ([17]). *Let G be an AT-free bigraph and z be a vertex of G. Suppose that C is a connected component of $G - N[z]$ and that $a, b \in L_\ell(z)$ are two vertices in C. Then*

1. *$N_{\ell-1}^z(a) \subseteq N_{\ell-1}^z(b)$ or $N_{\ell-1}^z(a) \supseteq N_{\ell-1}^z(b)$;*
2. *$N_{\ell+1}^z(a) \subseteq N_{\ell+1}^z(b)$ or $N_{\ell+1}^z(a) \supseteq N_{\ell+1}^z(b)$;*
3. *if $N_{\ell-1}^z(a) \subsetneq N_{\ell-1}^z(b)$ then $N_{\ell+1}^z(a) \supseteq N_{\ell+1}^z(b)$;*
4. *if $N_{\ell+1}^z(a) \subsetneq N_{\ell+1}^z(b)$ then $N_{\ell-1}^z(a) \supseteq N_{\ell-1}^z(b)$.* □

Suppose that C is a component of $G - N[z]$ and $a, b \in N(z)$. It follows from statement 2 of Proposition 3 that either $N(a) \cap C \subseteq N(b) \cap C$ or $N(a) \cap C \supseteq N(b) \cap C$. In particular, if $c \in N(z)$ is a vertex adjacent to the maximum number of vertices in C, then for any $u \in L_\ell(z) \cap C$ with $\ell \geq 2$, $d(c, u) \leq \ell - 1$. We call C a *deep* component of $G - N[z]$ if it contains an eccentric vertex of z. Note that a deep component of $G - N[z]$ exists if and only if $\mathrm{ecc}(z) \geq 2$.

Proposition 4 ([17]). *Let G be a connected AT-free bigraph and z be a vertex of G. If $\mathrm{ecc}(z) \geq 3$, then $G - N[z]$ has at most two deep components.* □

Proposition 5 ([17]). *Let G be a connected AT-free bigraph and v be an admissible vertex with $\mathrm{ecc}(v) = \mathrm{diam}(G) - 1$. Suppose that x, y are a diametrical dominating pair. Then v is adjacent to one of x, y. Moreover, there is a shortest (x, y)-path containing v.* □

Finally, the LBFS end-vertex characterization on AT-free bigraphs obtained by [17] follows. It implies a polynomial time solution to the end-vertex problem for AT-free bigraphs: by testing all candidates for the vertex w, one can determine whether v is an LBFS end-vertex of G. However, this is not a linear time solution.

Theorem 1 ([17]). *Let G be a connected AT-free bigraph and v be a vertex of G. Then v is an end-vertex of an LBFS if and only if there exists a vertex w such that, for every eccentric vertex u of w, $N(u) \supseteq N(v)$.* □

3   The BFS End-Vertex Problem for AT-Free Bigraphs

In this section, we show that the BFS end-vertex problem is in P for AT-free bigraphs. We start by handling some easy cases: we observe that a necessary condition for BFS end-vertices shown in [8] is sometimes also sufficient for AT-free bigraphs, and we show that if hanging an AT-free bigraph by a vertex results in a single deep component, then any vertex in the last level can end the BFS.

Let $G = (V, E)$ be a graph, and let $v \in V$ be a vertex. We will define $height(v)$ to be the largest value h over all vertices $w \in V \setminus \{v\}$ such that $ecc(w) = d(w, v) = h$. If there are no vertices w such that $d(w, v) = ecc(w)$, define $height(v) = \infty$; in such a case, v is not a BFS end-vertex.

Definition 1 ([8]). *Let $G = (V, E)$ be a graph. We say that a vertex x dominates a vertex y if $N(y) \subsetneq N(x)$. For any $x \in V$ we denote by D_x the set of vertices dominated by x.* □

Theorem 2 ([8]). *Let $G = (V, E)$ be a graph, and let $t \in V$ be any vertex. A necessary condition for t to be the last vertex of some BFS ordering σ of G is that there exists a neighbour x of t such that $D_t \subseteq N(x)$.* □

Lemma 1 ($*^1$). *Let $G = (V, E)$ be an AT-free bigraph, and $v \in V$. If $height(v) \leq 2$, then the condition in Theorem 2 is also sufficient for v to be a BFS end-vertex.*

Lemma 2 ($*$). *Let $G = (V, E)$ be an AT-free bigraph, and $v \in V$ where $3 \leq height(v) < \infty$. If there is a vertex w such that $d(v, w) = ecc(w)$ and $G - N[w]$ has a single deep component, then v is a BFS end-vertex.*

We now prove the main result. Let $Z(v, w) = \{u \in L_{ecc(w)}(w) \mid N(v) \cap N(u) = \emptyset\}$ and let $Y(v, w) = \{u \in L_{ecc(w)}(w) \setminus \{v\} \mid N(v) \cap N(u) \neq \emptyset\}$. For a set $V' \subseteq V(G)$ and vertex $x \in V(G)$, we denote $d(V', x) = \min_{y \in V'} d(y, x)$.

Theorem 3. *Let $G = (V, E)$ be an AT-free bigraph, and $v \in V$ where $3 \leq height(v) < \infty$. Let $w \in V$ be such that $d(w, v) = ecc(w)$. The vertex v is a BFS end-vertex if and only if, either*

- *$G - N[w]$ has a single deep component; or*
- *$G - N[w]$ has two deep components C_1 and C_2, where without loss of generality $v \in C_1$, and there is a set $X \subseteq N(w) \cap N(C_2)$ such that for each $u \in Y(v, w)$, $d(X, v) \geq d(X, u)$ and $d(X, u') = ecc(w) - 1$ for all $u' \in Z(v, w)$.*

---

[1] Statements marked with a $*$ will be shown in the full version of the paper.

Proof. We first show necessity. Let v be a BFS end-vertex for some BFS ordering σ; if there are many, choose a BFS ordering ending at v for which $d(v, \sigma(1))$ is maximum. Let w be the first vertex of σ. Necessarily $d(w, v) = \mathrm{ecc}(w)$ and by assumption, $d(w, v) \geq 3$.

If v is an LBFS end-vertex, by Theorem 1, there must be an eccentric vertex u of w such that $N(u) \supseteq N(v)$; in such a case, every vertex of $L_{\mathrm{ecc}(w)}(w)$ has a common neighbour with v, and therefore $G - N[w]$ must have exactly one deep component and we are done. Therefore, we may assume that v is not an LBFS end-vertex. By Theorem 1, there must be an eccentric vertex u of w such that either $N(u) \subsetneq N(v)$ or $N(u)$ and $N(v)$ are incomparable. If all eccentric vertices of w are such that $N(u)$ and $N(v)$ are comparable, then it must be the case that $G - N[w]$ has a single connected component, and we are done.

We may therefore assume there is a vertex u of $L_{\mathrm{ecc}(w)}(w)$ such that $N(u)$ and $N(v)$ are incomparable; u and v must be in different components of $G - N[w]$ as otherwise we have a contradiction to Proposition 3. By Proposition 4, there are at most two deep components of $G - N[w]$. Let C_1, C_2 be the deep components of $G - N[w]$; without loss of generality, assume that $v \in C_1$. Necessarily, $N(C_2) \cap N(w)$ intersects every shortest (u, w)-path for every $u \in Z(v, w)$; therefore $d(X, u') = \mathrm{ecc}(w) - 1$ for all $u' \in Z(v, w)$. If $d(N(C_2), v) \geq d(N(C_2), u)$ for all $u \in Y(v, w)$, then we may take $X = N(C_2)$ and there is nothing left to prove.

Suppose to the contrary that for every $X \subseteq N(C_2)$ such that $d(X, u') = \mathrm{ecc}(w) - 1$ for all $u' \in Z(v, w)$, a shortest (v, w)-path is intersected, but $d(X, v) < d(X, v')$ for all $u \in Y(v, w)$ for some $v' \in Y(z, w)$. Let $X \subseteq N(C_2)$ be a smallest set that intersects some shortest (u, w)-path for every $u \in Z(v, w)$ and intersects some shortest (v, w)-path is intersected, but no shortest (v', w)-path is intersected for some $v' \in Y(z, w)$. Thus there must be a $v' \in Y(v, w)$ such that X does not separate w and v'. Let $p_i \in L_i(w) \cap P$ for any shortest (v, w)-path P; p_i is unique. Similarly, let $Q_i \in L_i(w) \cap Q$ for any shortest (v', w)-path Q; q_i is unique. There must also exist a shortest (v, w)-path P such that $N(q_{i+1}) \cap \{p_i\} = \emptyset$ as otherwise X intersects a shortest (v', w)-path (take any shortest (v, w)-path through X and choose q_{i+1} instead of p_{i+1} after the first i vertices), a contradiction. By Proposition 3, it must therefore be the case that $N(q_i) \cap L_{i-1}(w) \subsetneq N(p_i) \cap L_{i-1}(w)$, and in particular, $N(v') \subsetneq N(v)$.

Let P be a shortest (v, w)-path such that $P \cap X \neq \emptyset$, and let $b \in P \cap N(w)$. Among all choices for P, pick P so that the neighbour of $w \in P$ appears as left as possible in σ. Let Q be a shortest (v', w)-path such that $Q \cap X = \emptyset$, and let $a \in Q \cap N(w)$; at least one Q must exist since X does separate w and v'. Among all choices for Q, pick Q so that the neighbour of $w \in Q$ appears as left as possible in σ. There are two cases:

- $a <_\sigma b$. Then all vertices in $L_{\mathrm{ecc}(w)}(w)$ which are distance $\mathrm{ecc}(w) - 1$ away from a are reached before those at distance $\mathrm{ecc}(w) - 1$ away from b by the BFS. Since X was chosen to be as small as possible, there must be a $u \in Z(v, w)$ for which all shortest (u, w)-paths go through b. Therefore, u will appear after v in σ, a contradiction.

– $b <_\sigma a$. Then all vertices in $L_{\mathrm{ecc}(w)}(w)$ which are distance $\mathrm{ecc}(w) - 1$ away from b are reached before those at distance $\mathrm{ecc}(w) - 1$ away from a by the BFS. Since X intersects a shortest (v, w)-path, v' will appear after v in σ, a contradiction.

For sufficiency, suppose that $3 \leq height(v) < \infty$. If $G - N[w]$ has a single deep component, we are done by Lemma 2. Otherwise, $G - N[w]$ has two deep components by Proposition 4; assume without loss of generality that $v \in C_1$. If X does not intersect any shortest (v, w)-path, we can start BFS as follows: $w, X, w', N(w) \setminus (X \cup \{w'\})$, where w' is any neighbour of $c \in C_1 \cap L_2(w)$ where $N(c) \cap L_3(w) = L_3(w) \cap C_1$ (which must exist by Proposition 3). Then $L_{\mathrm{ecc}(w)}(w) \cap C_2$ will be visited before any vertices in $L_{\mathrm{ecc}(w)}(w) \cap C_1$, and those in $L_{\mathrm{ecc}(w)}(w) \cap C_1$ can be chosen so that v is last, using the techniques of the proof of Lemma 2 applied to only C_1. If instead X intersects some shortest (v, w)-path P, then it must intersect a shortest path to w for every vertex in $Y(v, w)$ as well. Let X be partitioned into disjoint sets $X_1 \cup X_2 \cup X_3$ such that X_1 consists of vertices which only intersect paths from w to $Z(v, w)$, X_2 consists of vertices that only intersect paths from w to $Z(v, w) \cup Y(v, w)$, and $X_3 = X \setminus (X_1 \cup X_2)$. Then w, X_1, X_2, X_3 is a valid BFS prefix, which can order $L_{\mathrm{ecc}(w)}(w)$ such that v is last: any vertex $v' \in C_1 \cap L_{\mathrm{ecc}(w)}(w)$ must be such that there is a largest index i where $P_i \cap P_i' \neq \emptyset$ for any shortest (v, w)-path P and any shortest (v', w)-path P'; indeed, $i = 2$ is such an index by definition of X_3. Therefore, we can always choose the vertex on the path P' before the vertex P when visiting level $i + 1$. □

Corollary 1. *The BFS end-vertex problem for AT-free bigraphs is in P.*

Proof. We can find a suitable w in polynomial time. We can also compute C_1, C_2, where without loss of generality $v \in C_1$. In polynomial time, we can see if $w' \in N(w) \cap N(C_2)$ is on a shortest (x, w)-path for all $x \in L_{\mathrm{ecc}(w)}(w)$ by computing $d_{G-\{w\}}(x, w')$ and comparing it to $d(w, v) - 1$. We can iterate over $W = N(w) \cap N(C_2)$ and add $w' \in W$ if w' is not on any shortest (v, w)-path.

Now the remaining vertices of W are all on some shortest (v, w)-path. We claim that we need at most one of these vertices. Suppose to the contrary that there are two vertices $w_1, w_2 \in W$ such that both w_1 and w_2 are on shortest (v, w)-paths P and P' respectively. If $P = P'$, then we only need to take whichever vertex in $\{w_1, w_2\}$ that intersects more (v', w)-paths for $v' \in Y(v, w)$. Suppose instead that $P \neq P'$. Consider $p_2 \in P \cap C_1 \cap L_2(w)$ and $p_2' \in P' \cap C_1 \cap L_2(w)$. By Proposition 3, $N_3^w(p_2) \subseteq N_3^w(p_2')$ or $N_3^w(p_2') \subseteq N_3^w(p_2)$; we can take P if we are in the former case or P' if we are in the latter to get all vertices in $C_1 \cap L_{\mathrm{ecc}(w)}(w)$ which can use either w_1 or w_2 for a shortest path to w. Therefore, we need only one additional vertex, which can be found by iterating over the set to see which covers the most paths to vertices in $Y(v, w)$. □

4 The LBFS End-Vertex Problem for AT-Free Bigraphs

Let G be an AT-free bigraph and let v be a vertex of G. Suppose that v is an end-vertex of LBFS of G. Then by Proposition 1 and Theorem 1, $\mathrm{ecc}(v) \geq \mathrm{diam}(G) - 1$

and there is a vertex w such that for every eccentric vertex u of w, $N(u) \supseteq N(v)$. When $\mathrm{ecc}(v) = \mathrm{diam}(G)$, such a vertex w can be chosen to be any vertex with $d(w, v) = \mathrm{ecc}(v)$ as shown in [17]. The following theorem explains how to find such a vertex w in the case when $\mathrm{ecc}(v) = \mathrm{diam}(G) - 1$.

Theorem 4. *Let G be a connected AT-free bigraph of $\mathrm{diam}(G) = k$. Suppose that v with $\mathrm{ecc}(v) = k - 1$ is an end-vertex of LBFS of G. If w is the first vertex of $L_r(v)$ where $r = \left\lceil \frac{\mathrm{ecc}(v)+3}{2} \right\rceil$ in an LBFS ordering of G that begins at v, then for every eccentric vertex u of w, $N(u) \supseteq N(v)$.*

Proof. Since v is an end-vertex of LBFS, there is an LBFS ordering σ of G with $\sigma(n) = v$ (i.e., v is the last vertex in σ). Denote $z = \sigma(1)$ and $s = \mathrm{ecc}(z)$. Clearly, $v \in L_s(z)$. We claim that $s \geq 3$. Indeed, the assumption $\mathrm{ecc}(v) = k - 1$ implies immediately that $s \geq 2$. Assume that $s = 2$. Then $N(v) \subseteq N(z)$ and $2 \leq \mathrm{ecc}(v) = k - 1 \leq 3$. If $\mathrm{ecc}(v) = 2$, then $N(v) = N(z)$ and hence for every eccentric vertex u of z, $N(u) \subseteq N(v)$. Since v is the last vertex in σ, we must have $N(u) = N(v)$ for every eccentric vertex u of z, which means G is a complete bigraph and $\mathrm{ecc}(v) = 2 = k$, a contradiction to the assumption $\mathrm{ecc}(v) = k - 1$.

Consider the case $\mathrm{ecc}(v) = 3$. If $N(w) \cap N(v) = \emptyset$ for some eccentric vertex w of z, then $d(v, w) \geq 4 > 3 = \mathrm{ecc}(v)$, a contradiction. Therefore, it must be the case that $N(u) \cap N(v) \neq \emptyset$ for every eccentric vertex u of z. Since $k = \mathrm{ecc}(v) + 1 = 4$, there are two eccentric vertices u, w of z with $N(u) \cap N(w) = \emptyset$. Since v is an LBFS end-vertex, by Theorem 1, $N(w) \supseteq N(v)$ and $N(u) \supseteq N(v)$. Pick $w' \in N(w) \setminus N(v)$ and $u' \in N(u) \setminus N(v)$, and (w', u', v) form an asteroidal triple in G, contradicting the assumption that G is AT-free. Hence we have $s = \mathrm{ecc}(z) \geq 3$.

Let $C_1, C_2, \ldots, C_q$ be the connected components of $G - N[z]$. Without loss of generality assume that $v \in C_q$. Let x, y be a diametrical dominating pair in G which exists according to Proposition 2. By Proposition 5, v is adjacent to one of x, y. Assume by symmetry that v is adjacent to y. Then y is also in C_q and $d(z, y) = d(z, v) - 1 = \mathrm{ecc}(z) - 1 = s - 1$.

Note that $d(x, y) = k = \mathrm{ecc}(v) + 1 \geq d(v, z) + 1 = s + 1$. Every vertex in $N[z] \cup C_q$ is at distance at most s from y and thus $x \notin N[z] \cup C_q$. Assume without loss of generality that $x \in C_1$. Denote $s_1 = d(x, z)$. The existence of an (x, y)-path of length $s_1 + s - 1$ (through the vertex z) implies that $k = d(x, y) \leq s_1 + s - 1$. On the other hand, any (x, y)-path through v is of length $\geq s_1 + s - 1$. Hence $k = d(x, y) = s_1 + s - 1$.

Consider a shortest (x, y)-path that contains v, which exists according to Proposition 5. Let $P : xx_1x_2 \ldots x_{k-2}vy$ be such a path. Then P contains a vertex in $N(z)$ as x and y belong to the different components of $G - N[z]$. Let $x_\alpha \in N(z)$ be the vertex in P with the smallest subscript and let Q be the subpath $x_\alpha x_{\alpha+1} \ldots vy$ of P. Since

$$s = \mathrm{ecc}(z) = d(z, v) \leq d(x_\alpha, v) + 1 = d(x_\alpha, y) \leq \mathrm{ecc}(z) = s,$$

we have $d(x_\alpha, y) = s$, i.e., the length of Q is s. It follows that P does not contain z and moreover, if Q is replaced by an (x_α, y)-path of length s through z then

---

Algorithm 1: Linear Time LBFS End-Vertex for AT-Free Bigraphs

---

Input: An AT-free graph G with vertex v.

Output: A vertex w such that $N(u) \supseteq N(v)$ for every eccentric vertex u of w in which case v is an end-vertex of G, or else v is not an end-vertex of LBFS of G.

1 Run LBFS begining at v to find an LBFS ordering τ. Let $w_1 = \tau(n)$ and w_2 be the first vertex of $L_r(v)$ in τ where $r = \left\lceil \frac{\text{ecc}(v)+3}{2} \right\rceil$

2 Run LBFS begining at w_1 to find all eccentric vertices of w_1. If $N(u) \supseteq N(v)$ for all eccentric vertices u of w_1, v is an end-vertex of LBFS of G.

3 Run LBFS begining at w_2 to find all eccentric vertices of w_2. If $N(u) \supseteq N(v)$ for all eccentric vertices u of w_2, v is an end-vertex of G; otherwise v is not an end-vertex of LBFS of G.

---

we obtain another shortest (x, y)-path P' containing z but not v. The existence of the shortest (x, y)-path P' (containing z) further implies every vertex in C_1 is at distance at most s_1 from z. Denote $P' : xx_1x_2 \ldots x_\alpha z y_1 y_2 \ldots y_{s-2}y$. Note that $x_{\alpha-1} \in N(x_\alpha) \setminus N(y_1)$ and $x_\alpha \in N(x_{\alpha+1}) \setminus N(y_2)$.

Clearly, $s_1 \leq s$. Suppose first that $s_1 = s$. Then

$$r = \left\lceil \frac{\text{ecc}(v) + 3}{2} \right\rceil = \left\lceil \frac{s_1 + s + 1}{2} \right\rceil = \left\lceil \frac{2s + 1}{2} \right\rceil = s + 1.$$

Let τ be an LBFS ordering of G that begins at v. Observe that $\{x_\alpha, y_1\} \subseteq L_{s-1}(v)$: by P, we know that $d(x_\alpha, v) = s - 1$, and $d(y_1, v) = d(y, v_1) + 1 = (d(z, y) - 1) + 1 = ((s-1) - 1) + 1) = s - 1$ as required by P'. Observe further that $L_{s-1}(v) \subseteq N(z) \cup C_q$: every vertex in C_q must be hit by P, and therefore can be distance at most $s - 2$ away from z; in order for such a vertex to exist, it must be a neighbour of x_α, which means in any case that it is not in C_q.

It follows that the first vertex w of $L_r(v)$ in τ must be in $N(z)$. Since $d(w, v) = s + 1$, w is not adjacent to $x_{\alpha+1}$ (and w is not adjacent to x_α as they are both neighbours of z) and hence is adjacent to $x_{\alpha-1}$ as P is a dominating path. Now it is easy to see that the eccentric vertices u of w are all in C_q (as $d(w, x) = s_1 - 2 = s - 2 < s + 1 = d(w, v)$) and satisfy the property that $N(u) \supseteq N(v)$.

Suppose now that $s_1 < s$. Then

$$r = \left\lceil \frac{\text{ecc}(v) + 3}{2} \right\rceil = \left\lceil \frac{s_1 + s + 1}{2} \right\rceil \leq \left\lceil \frac{2s}{2} \right\rceil = s.$$

In the case when $s_1 = s - 1$, w is a vertex adjacent to both x_α and y_1; note that $d(w, x) = s_1 = s - 1 < d(w, v) = s$. In the case when $s_1 \leq s - 2$, w is in C_q; note that $d(w, x) \leq s - 2 < s = d(w, v)$. In any case the eccentric vertices u of w are all in C_q and satisfy the property that $N(u) \supseteq N(v)$. □

Algorithm 1 solves the LBFS end-vertex problem for AT-free bigraphs. The correctness of the algorithm follows from Theorem 1, Theorem 4 and the remarks prior to Theorem 4. Recall that LBFS can be implemented in linear time [23]. Therefore a desired vertex w (as described in Theorem 1) can be found in linear time and verifying whether all eccentric vertices u of w satisfy the property that $N(u) \supseteq N(v)$ can also be done in linear time, the algorithm can be implemented to run in linear time. Therefore we have the following:

Theorem 5. *The LBFS end-vertex problem for AT-free bigraphs can be solved in linear time.* □

5   The DFS End-Vertex Problem for AT-Free Bigraphs

In this section we show that we can identify a DFS end-vertex in linear time on AT-free bigraphs. To do this, we refine the following characterization of (arbitrary) DFS end-vertices from [20]. Our refinement allows us to use a strong ordering to find the required set X.

Theorem 6 ([20]). *Let G be a connected graph, and let t be a vertex of G. Then t is a DFS end-vertex of G if and only if there is $X \subseteq V(G)$ such that $N_G[t] \subseteq X$ and $G[X]$ has a Hamiltonian path with endpoint t.* □

Corollary 2 (*). *Let (σ^A, σ^B) be a strong ordering of an AT-free bigraph. Without loss of generality, assume $v \in A$. Let $N(v) = \langle b_\alpha, \ldots, b_\beta \rangle$ in σ^B. Vertex v is a DFS-end vertex if and only if there is a set $A' \subseteq \langle a_i, \ldots, a_j \rangle$ such that $a_i \leq_{\sigma^A} v \leq_{\sigma^A} a_j$, and $G' = G[A' \cup N(v)]$ is an induced subgraph of G where $|A'| = |N(v)|$ and G' has a Hamiltonian path ending at v.*

Corollary 3 (*). *The DFS end-vertex problem can be solved in linear time for AT-free bigraphs.*

6   The MNS End-Vertex Problem for AT-free Bigraphs

In this section, we show that the MNS end-vertex problem for AT-free bigraphs is in P. The characterization of MNS end-vertices on AT-free bigraphs matches the characterization for MNS end-vertices on chordal graphs [2]. We therefore require one definition from [2] for the characterization for MNS end-vertices on AT-free bigraphs. Let $G = (V, E)$ be a graph and $x \in V$. Let $C_1, \ldots, C_k$ be the connected components of $G(V - N[x])$. The *substars* of x are the elements of $N_G(C_i)$ for each i.

Theorem 7 (*). *Let G be a connected AT-free bigraph and let x be a vertex of G. Then the following statements are equivalent: (1) the substars of x are totally ordered by inclusion; and (2) x is an MNS-end vertex.*

Corollary 4. *The MNS end-vertex problem for AT-free bigraphs is in P.*

7   Conclusion

We have shown that the end-vertex problem for BFS and MNS have polynomial time solutions for AT-free bigraphs. We have also demonstrated linear-time solutions for the DFS and LBFS end-vertex problem on AT-free bigraphs. It would be interesting to determine the complexity of the LDFS and MCS end-vertex problems on this class of graphs (and bipartite graphs in general). We conjecture that they can be solved in polynomial time on AT-free bigraphs.

References

1. Beisegel, J.: On the end-vertex problem of graph searches. Discret. Math. Theor. Comput. Sci. **21**(1) (2019). http://dmtcs.episciences.org/5572
2. Berry, A., Blair, J.R.S., Bordat, J.-P., Simonet, G.: Graph extremities defined by search algorithms. Algorithms **3**(2), 100–124 (2010)
3. Berry, A., Bordat, J.-P.: Local LexBFS properties in an arbitrary graph. In: Proceedings of Journées Informatiques Messines (JIM) (2000)
4. Bondy, J.A., Murty, U.S.R.: Graph Theory. Springer, Cham (2008)
5. Brandstädt, A., Spinard, J.P., Bang Le, V.: Graph Classes: A Survey, vol. 3. SIAM (1999)
6. Cao, Y., Wang, Z., Rong, G., Wang, J.: Graph searches and their end vertices. In: Lu, P., Zhang, G. (eds.) 30th International Symposium on Algorithms and Computation, (ISAAC), LIPIcs, vol. 149, pp. 1:1–1:18. Schloss Dagstuhl - Leibniz-Zentrum für Informatik (2019). https://doi.org/10.4230/LIPIcs.ISAAC.2019.1
7. Chang, J.-M., Ho, C.-W., Ko, M.-T.: LexBFS-ordering in asteroidal triple-free graphs. ISAAC 1999. LNCS, vol. 1741, pp. 163–172. Springer, Heidelberg (1999). https://doi.org/10.1007/3-540-46632-0_17
8. Charbit, P., Habib, M., Mamcarz, A.: Influence of the tie-break rule on the end-vertex problem (2014)
9. Corneil, D.G.: Lexicographic breadth first search – a survey. In: Hromkovič, J., Nagl, M., Westfechtel, B. (eds.) WG 2004. LNCS, vol. 3353, pp. 1–19. Springer, Heidelberg (2004). https://doi.org/10.1007/978-3-540-30559-0_1
10. Corneil, D.G., Dragan, F.F., Habib, M., Paul, C.: Diameter determination on restricted graph families. Discret. Appl. Math. **113**(2–3), 143–166 (2001)
11. Corneil, D.G., Köhler, E., Lanlignel, J.-M.: On end-vertices of lexicographic breadth first searches. Discret. Appl. Math. **158**(5), 434–443 (2010)
12. Corneil, D.G., Krueger, R.M.: A unified view of graph searching. SIAM J. Discret. Math. **22**(4), 1259–1276 (2008)
13. Corneil, D.G., Olariu, S., Stewart, L.: Linear time algorithms for dominating pairs in asteroidal triple-free graphs. SIAM J. Comput. **28**(4), 1284–1297 (1999)
14. Corneil, D.G., Olariu, S., Stewart, L.: The LBFS structure and recognition of interval graphs. SIAM J. Discret. Math. **23**(4), 1905–1953 (2009)
15. Dragan, F.F., Nicolai, F.: LexBFS orderings of distance hereditary graphs. UD, Fachbereich Mathematik (1995)
16. Gorzny, J.: On end vertices of search algorithms. Master's thesis, University of Victoria, Victoria, BC, Canada (2015)
17. Gorzny, J., Huang, J.: End-vertices of LBFS of (AT-free) bigraphs. Discret. Appl. Math. **225**, 87–94 (2017)

18. Hell, P., Huang, J.: Interval bigraphs and circular arc graphs. J. Graph Theory **46**(4), 313–327 (2004)
19. Jamison, B., Olariu, S.: On the semi-perfect elimination. Adv. Appl. Math. **9**(3), 364–376 (1988)
20. Kratsch, D., Liedloff, M., Meister, D.: End-vertices of graph search algorithms. In: Paschos, V.T., Widmayer, P. (eds.) CIAC 2015. LNCS, vol. 9079, pp. 300–312. Springer, Cham (2015). https://doi.org/10.1007/978-3-319-18173-8_22
21. Lekkerkerker, C., Boland, J.: Representation of a finite graph by a set of intervals on the real line. Fundamenta Mathematicae **51**(1), 45–64 (1962)
22. Mertzios, G.B., Nichterlein, A., Niedermeier, R.: A linear-time algorithm for maximum-cardinality matching on cocomparability graphs. SIAM J. Discret. Math. **32**(4), 2820–2835 (2018). https://doi.org/10.1137/17M1120920
23. Donald Rose, J., Endre Tarjan, R., Lueker, G.S.: Algorithmic aspects of vertex elimination on graphs. SIAM J. Comput. **5**(2), 266–283 (1976)
24. Spinrad, J., Brandstädt, A., Stewart, L.: Bipartite permutation graphs. Discret. Appl. Math. **18**(3), 279–292 (1987)

Approaching Optimal Duplicate Detection in a Sliding Window

Rémi Géraud-Stewart[1], Marius Lombard-Platet[1,2(✉)], and David Naccache[1]

[1] Département d'informatique de l'ENS, ENS, CNRS, PSL Research University,
Paris, France
{`remi.geraud,marius.lombard-platet,david.naccache`}@ens.fr
[2] Be-Studys, Be-Ys group, Châtelaine, Switzerland

Abstract. Duplicate detection is the problem of identifying whether a given item has previously appeared in a (possibly infinite) stream of data, when only a limited amount of memory is available.

Unfortunately the infinite stream setting is ill-posed, and error rates of duplicate detection filters turn out to be heavily constrained: consequently they appear to provide no advantage, asymptotically, over a biased coin toss [8].

In this paper we formalize the sliding window setting introduced by [12,15], and show that a perfect (zero error) solution can be used up to a maximal window size $w_{\max}$. Above this threshold we show that some existing duplicate detection filters (designed for the *non-windowed* setting) perform better that those targeting the windowed problem. Finally, we introduce a "queuing construction" that improves on the performance of some duplicate detection filters in the windowed setting.

We also analyse the security of our filters in an adversarial setting.

Keywords: Duplicate detection · Streaming algorithms · Sliding window

1 Introduction

1.1 Motivation

Throughout this paper, we are interested in the following problem:

Definition 1 (Duplicate detection problem over a sliding window, wDDP). *Given a stream $E_n = (e_1, e_2, \ldots, e_n)$, a sliding window size w and a "new" item $e^\star$, find whether $e^\star$ is also present in the last w elements of the stream, ie., whether $e^\star \in \{e_{n-w+1}, \ldots, e_n\}$. At every time increment, the new item is added to the stream, i.e., $E_{n+1} = E_n \mid e^\star$ where $\mid$ denotes concatenation.*

Note that for $w = \infty$, the problem becomes finding whether an element is a duplicate amongst all previous stream elements. For simplicity in the notation, when we refer to ∞DDP we instead write DDP.

© Springer Nature Switzerland AG 2020
D. Kim et al. (Eds.): COCOON 2020, LNCS 12273, pp. 64–84, 2020.
https://doi.org/10.1007/978-3-030-58150-3_6

Instances of the wDDP abound in computer science, with applications to file system indexation, database queries, network load balancing, network management [3], in credit card fraud detection [1], phone calls data mining [2], etc. A discussion about algorithms on large data streams can be found in [9].

In practice, additional constraints exist that we can capture with the following definition:

Definition 2 (wDDP with bounded memory). *At every time step n, given $e^\star$ and a current state (dependent on history) of at most M bits, solve the wDDP for E_n and $e^\star$.*

A filter attempting to solve the wDDP is called a duplicate detection filter (DDF). Perfect detection is however not always reachable and it might be more practical to work on a further relaxation of the problem, allowing for errors.

Approximate duplicate detection has many real-life use cases, and can sometimes play a critical role, for instance in cryptographic schemes where all security and secrecy fall apart as soon as a random nonce is used twice, such as the ElGamal [6] or ECDSA signatures. Other uses include improvements over caches [10], duplicate clicks [11], and others.

On a side note, it is clear that the input distribution plays a central role regarding how efficiently the wDDP can be solved. For instance, some deterministic streams may be expressed very compactly (such as the output of a PRNG with known seed) making the wDDP relatively easy. Information-theoretically, if the source has U bits of entropy then the situation is equivalent to having an U-bit, uniformly distributed input. This is the setting we consider here.

As said before, when the window size in wDDP grows infinitely large, it becomes the following problem: find whether $e^\star \in E_n$. Unfortunately any solution to this problem will necessary encounter a phenomenon called "saturation" on large enough data streams [8], and when it happens the algorithm performs no better than at random.

This is problematic on two grounds: it makes the comparison of several algorithms difficult (since they all asymptotically behave in that fashion), and the unavoidable saturation ruins any particular design's merits. As such, it is more interesting to focus on wDDP rather than DDP.

1.2   Contributions

In this paper, we start from a naïve solution for the wDDP to then derive bounds for when it can be solved within M memory bits, up to a window size $w_{\max}$, in constant time. We then introduce a generalization of the naïve solution, and study its error rate. We show that this construction, which we call Short Hash Filter (SHF), can push the value $w_{\max}$ further while operating in constant time— at the cost of some errors.

Unfortunately, for $w > w_{\max}$ the performance of SHF degrades very rapidly. We therefore turn our attention to existing data structures designed for the "non-windowed" setting. We show that some of them outperform dedicated data structures, including SHF, in the $w > w_{\max}$ regime. However, we exhibit a lower bound on the error rate of such filters.

We then introduce the "queuing construction", a black box transformation of non-windowed data structures into windowed ones, that improves their performance in the wDDP setting. Finally, we provide an analysis of our queueing construction's resistance to adversarial streams.

1.3 Related Work

The notion of sliding window was, as far as we know, first introduced in [11]. The wDDP formulation we rely on is due to [12,15], which also introduce algorithms for solving the wDDP approximately. To the best of our knowledge, the discrepancy between the wDDP and the DDP and the wDDP has not been studied. Similarly, the relation between w (the sliding window size), the error rate and M (the available memory) is not always present in similar papers, one exception being [12].

The notion of using subfilters, as in the queuing construction, can be found in the A2 filter's design [15] and a variation thereof can be found in [13] but in a different DDP formulation. The A2 is built from two Bloom filters, a construction which we generalize and analyse generically in this paper. Similarly, the construction in [13] only works with Bloom Filters. Literature review collects the following DDFs [4,5,7,8,12,15], which we will consider in this paper. The structure proposed in [11] is not designed for wDDP but a variant called 'landmark' sliding window, which consists of a zero-resetting of the memory at some user-defined epochs.

2   Notations and Basic Definitions

We consider an unbounded stream $E = (e_1, e_2, \ldots, e_n, \ldots)$ of elements from an alphabet Γ.

We usually consider the situations where the available memory is too small for perfect detection, i.e., $M \ll |\Gamma|$. Otherwise, if $M = |\Gamma|$ then the problem can be solved in constant time without errors [8].

An element e_j is a duplicate in E over the sliding window w, and we note $e_i \in_w E$ if there exists $j - w \leq i < j$ such that $e_i = e_j$. Otherwise we note $e_i \notin_w E$, and we say e_i is unseen over w. A false positive over w is an element $e \notin_w E$ which is classified as a duplicate, and a false negative is an element $e \in_w E$ which is classified as unseen.

The filter false positive probability (FP_i^w) is the probability that after i insertions, the *unseen* element $e_i \notin_w E$ is a false positive over w. The false positive rate FPR_i^w is the number of false positives divided by the number of unseen elements in E[1]. We similarly define the false negative probability FN_i^w, and the false negative rate FNR_i^w.

---

[1] We observe that $\mathrm{FPR}_n^w = \frac{1}{n} \sum_{i=1}^{n} \mathrm{FP}_i^w$, and similarly for FNR_n^w.

Remark. For benchmarking, we usually measure the error rate $ER^w = \text{FPR}^w + \text{FNR}^w$, as it allows a practical ranking of the solutions. An error rate of 0 means a perfect filter, while a filter answering randomly has an error rate of 1. A filter being always wrong has an error rate of 2.

3   Approximate Solution and SHF

3.1   Optimal and Approximate Optimal wDDF

Theorem 1. *For $M \geq w(\log_2(w) + 2\log_2(|\Gamma|))$, the wDDP can be solved exactly (with no errors) in constant time.*

Proof. Due to page limit restrictions, all proofs are in Appendix E.

However, this optimal filter requires that the size of Γ is known in advance. The dependence on $\log_2 |\Gamma|$ can be dropped, at the cost of allowing errors.

Theorem 2. *Let $w \in \mathbb{N}$. Let $M \simeq 2w \log_2 w$, then the wDDP can be solved with almost no error using M memory bits. More precisely, it is possible to create a filter of M bits with an FN of 0, an FP of $1 - (1 - \frac{1}{w^2})^w \sim \frac{1}{w}$, and a time complexity of $O(w)$.*

Using $M \simeq 5w \log_2 w$ bits of memory, a constant-time filter with the same error rate can be constructed.

Note that we only consider the false positive probability after the filter has inserted at least w elements, i.e., once the filter is full and has reached a stationary regime.

When $\log_2 |\Gamma| > 5 \log_2 w$ this DDF outperforms the naïve strategy[2], both in terms of time and memory, at the cost of a minimal error. When $\log_2 |\Gamma| > 2 \log_2 w$, it outperforms the exact solution described sooner in terms of memory.

3.2   Short Hash Filter Algorithm

The approximate filter we described uses hashes of size $2 \log_2(w)$ for a given sliding window w. However, this hash size is arbitrary, and while the current hash size guarantees a very low error rate, it can be changed. More importantly, in some practical cases the maximal amount of available memory is fixed beforehand. Fixing the memory is also more practical for benchmarking data structures, as it gives the guarantee that all filters operate under the same conditions.

This gives us the Short Hash Filter (SHF), described in Algorithm 1, in Appendix A. The implementation relies on a double-ended queue or a ring buffer, which allows pushing at beginning of a queue and popping at the end in constant time. A variant is described in Appendix D.

---

[2] The naïve strategy consisting of storing the w elements of the sliding window, requiring $w \log_2 |\Gamma|$ bits of memory.

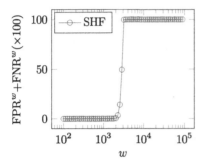
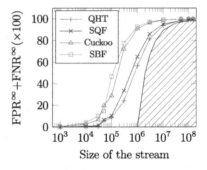

Fig. 1. Error rates of SHFs for $M = 10^5$ bits, for varying window sizes w.

Fig. 2. Error rate (times 100) of DDFs of 1Mb as a function of stream length. Hatched area represents over-optimal (impossible) values.

Error Probabilities. Let $w > 0$ be a window size and $M > 0$ the available memory.

Theorem 3. $\mathrm{FN}^w_{SHF} = 0$ and $\mathrm{FP}^w_{SHF} = 1 - \left(1 - \sqrt{w2^{-M/w}}\right)^w$.

Saturation. SHF has strictly increasing error probabilities, which reach a threshold of $1/2$ for some maximum window size $w_{\max}$. Beyond this value, these filters saturate extremely quickly: in other words, most SHF will either have an error rate of 0 or 1. An illustration of this phenomenon can be seen in Fig. 1, which shows the error rates for SHF with $M = 10^5$, against a uniformly random stream of 18-bit elements ($|\Gamma| = 2^{18}$). The benchmark used a finite stream of length 10^6.

The value $w_{\max}$ can be obtained by solving (numerically) for $\mathrm{FP}^{w_{\max}} = 1/2$ for a given M. Experiments (numerical resolution of $\mathrm{FP}^{\max} = 1/2$ for about 200 different values of M, uniformly distributed *on a log scale* between 10^2 and 10^6) indicate an approximately linear relationship between M and $w_{\max}$: $w^{SHF}_{\max} = 0.0233M + 186$ ($r^2 = 0.9977$).

4 Non-windowed DDFs in a wDDP Setting

4.1 Lower Bound on the Saturation Resistance

As said in the introduction, it has been proven [8] that all filters will reach saturation on the DDP setting. However, they sometimes prove to be efficient in some specific wDDP settings. This bound is useful for several reasons, notably it provides an estimation of how close to optimality existing filters are.

Theorem 4. *Let E be a stream of n elements uniformly selected from an alphabet of size $|\Gamma|$. For any DDF using M bits of memory, the error probability*
$$EP_n = \mathrm{FP}_n + \mathrm{FN}_n \text{ satisfies } EP_n \geq 1 - \frac{1-\left(1-\frac{1}{|\Gamma|}\right)^M}{1-\left(1-\frac{1}{|\Gamma|}\right)^n} \text{ for any } n > M.$$

The asymptotic error probability EP_∞ satisfies $EP_\infty \geq \left(1 - \frac{1}{|\Gamma|}\right)^M \approx 1 - M/|\Gamma|$.

Note, as highlighted in the proof, that this bound is *not tight*: better bounds may exist, the study of which we leave as an open question for future work.

4.2   Saturation Resistance of DDFs

We now evaluate the saturation rate for several DDFs, in the original DDP setting (without sliding window). Parameters are chosen to yield equivalent memory footprints and were taken from [8], namely:

– QHT [8], 1 bucket per row, 3 bits per fingerprint;
– SQF [5], 1 bucket per row, $r = 2$ and $r' = 1$;
– Cuckoo Filter [7], cells containing 1 element of 3 bits each;
– Stable Bloom Filter (SBF) [4], 2 bits per cell, 2 hashes, targeted FPR of 0.02.

These filters are run against a stream of uniformly sampled elements from an alphabet of 2^{26} elements. This results in around 8% duplicates amongst the 150 000 000 elements in the longest stream used. Results are plotted in Fig. 2.

The best results are given by the following filters, in order: QHT, SQF, Cuckoo and SBF. We also observe that QHT and SQF have error rates relatively close to the lower bound, hence suggesting that these filters are close to optimality, especially since the lower bound is not tight.

4.3   Performance in wDDP

We now consider the performance of the filters just discussed in the *windowed* setting, for which they were *not* designed. In particular, they cannot adjust their parameters as a function of w. Remarkably, some of these filters still outperform dedicated windowed filters for some window sizes at least, as shown in Fig. 3. In this benchmark, we used the following filters:

– block decaying Bloom Filter[3] (b_DBF) [12], sliding window of size w
– A2 filter [15], changing subfilter every $w/2$ insertions
– QHT [8], 1 bucket per row, 3 bits per fingerprint

Nevertheless, we will now discuss the queuing construction, which allow us to build windowed filters from the DDP filters.

5   Queuing Filters

We now describe the queuing construction, which produces a sliding window DDF from any DDF. We first give the description of the setup, before studying the theoretical error rates. A scheme describing our structure is detailed in Fig. 4.

---

[3] Note that by design, a b_DBF of 10^5 bits cannot operate for $w > 6000$.

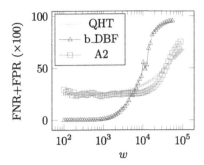

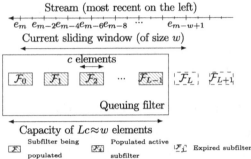

Fig. 3. Error rates for QHT, b_DBF, and A2. While A2 and b_DBF were designed and adjusted to the wDDP, this is not the case of QHT. Still, QHT outperforms these filters for some values of w.

Fig. 4. Architecture of the queuing filter, which consists of L subfilters $\mathcal{F}_i$, each containing up to c elements. Once the newest subfilter has inserted c elements in its structure, the oldest one expires. As such, the latter is dropped and a new one is created and put under population at the beginning of the queue. In this example, the sub-sliding window of $\mathcal{F}_1$ is $(e_{m-2}, e_{m-3}, e_{m-4})$.

5.1   The Queuing Construction

Principle of Operation. Let $\mathcal{F}$ be a DDF. Rather than allocating the whole memory to $\mathcal{F}$, we will create L copies of $\mathcal{F}$, each using a fraction of the available memory. Each of these *subfilters* has a limited timespan, and is allowed up to c insertions. The subfilters are organised in a queue. When inserting a new element in the queuing filter, it is inserted in the topmost subfilter of the queue. After c insertions, a new empty filter is added to the queue, and the oldest subfilter is popped and erased.

As such, we can consider that each subfilter operates on a sub-sliding window of size c, which makes the overall construction a DDF operating over a sliding window of size $w = cL$.

Insertion and Lookup. The filter returns DUPLICATE if and only if at least one subfilter does. Insertion is a simple insertion in the topmost subfilter.

Queue Update. After c insertions, the last filter of the queue is dropped, and a new (empty) filter is appended in front of the queue.

Pseudocode. We give a brief pseudocode for the queuing filter's functions Lookup and Insert, as well as a Setup function for initialisation, in Algorithm 2, in Appendix A. We introduced for simplicity a constructor $\mathcal{F}$.Setup that takes as input an integer M and outputs an initialized empty filter $\mathcal{F}$ of size at most M. Here subfilters is a FIFO that has a pop and push_first operations, which respectively removes the last element in the queue or inserts a new item in first position.

5.2 Error Rate Analysis

The queuing filter's properties can be derived from the subfilters'. False positive and false negative rates are of particular interest. In this section we consider a queuing filter $\mathcal{Q}$ with L subfilters of type $\mathcal{F}$ and capacity c (which means that the last subfilter is dropped after c insertions).

Remark. By definition, after c insertions the last subfilter is dropped. Information-theoretically, this means that all the information related to the elements inserted in that subfilter has been lost, and there are c such elements by design. Therefore, in the steady-state regime, the queuing filter holds information about at least $c(L-1)$ elements (immediately after deleting the last subfilter) and at most cL elements (immediately before this deletion).

If $w < cL$, the queuing filter can hold information about *more than* w *elements.*

False Positive Probability

Theorem 5. *Let* $\mathrm{FP}^w_{\mathcal{Q},m}$ *be the false positive probability of* $\mathcal{Q}$ *after* $m > w$ *insertions, over a sliding window of size* $w = cL$, *we have* $\mathrm{FP}^w_{\mathcal{Q},m} = 1 - (1 - \mathrm{FP}_{\mathcal{F},c})^{L-1} (1 - \mathrm{FP}_{\mathcal{F},m \bmod c})$ *where* $\mathrm{FP}_{\mathcal{F},m}$ *is the false positive probability of a subfilter* $\mathcal{F}$ *after* m *insertions.*

Remark. In the case $w < cL$, as mentioned previously, there is a non-zero probability that e^* is in the last subfilter's memory, despite not belonging to the sliding window.

Assuming a uniformly random input stream, and writing $\delta = cL - w$, the probability that e^* has occurred in $\{e_{m-cL}, \dots e_{m-w+1}\}$ is $1 - \left(1 - \frac{1}{|\Gamma|}\right)^{\delta}$. For large $|\Gamma|$ (as is expected to be the case in most applications), this probability is about $\frac{\delta}{|\Gamma|} \ll 1$. Hence, we can neglect the probability that e^* is present in the filter, and we consider the result of Theorem 5 to be a very good approximation even when $w < cL$.

False Negative Probability

Theorem 6. *Let* $\mathrm{FN}^w_{\mathcal{Q},m}$ *be the false negative probability of* $\mathcal{Q}$ *after* $m > w$ *insertions on a sliding window of size* $w = cL$, *we have* $\mathrm{FN}^w_{\mathcal{Q},m} = u_c^{L-1} u_{m \bmod c}$ *where we have introduced the short-hand notation* $u_\eta = p_\eta \mathrm{FN}_{\mathcal{F},\eta} + (1 - p_\eta)(1 - \mathrm{FP}_{\mathcal{F},\eta})$ *where* $\mathrm{FN}_{\mathcal{F},\eta}$ *(resp.* $\mathrm{FP}_{\mathcal{F},\eta}$*) is the false negative probability (resp. false positive) of the subfilter* $\mathcal{F}$ *after* η *insertions, and* $p_\eta = \frac{1 - \left(1 - \frac{1}{|\Gamma|}\right)^{\eta}}{1 - \left(1 - \frac{1}{|\Gamma|}\right)^{w}}$ $\approx \frac{\eta}{w}$.

Remark. As previously, the effect of $w < cL$ is negligible for all practical purposes and Theorem 6 is considered a good approximation in that regime.

5.3   FNR and FPR

From the above expressions we can derive relatively compact explicit formulas for the queuing filter's FPR and FNR when $m = cn$ for n a positive integer.

Theorem 7. *Let* $\mathrm{FPR}^w_{\mathcal{Q},m}$ *be the false positive rate of* $\mathcal{Q}$ *after* $m = cn > w$ *insertions on a sliding window of size* $w = cL$, *we have* $\mathrm{FPR}^w_{\mathcal{Q},cn} = 1 - \frac{(1-\mathrm{FP}_{\mathcal{F},c})^{L-1}}{c} \sum_{\ell=0}^{c-1}(1 - \mathrm{FP}_{\mathcal{F},\ell})$.

Theorem 8. *Let* $\mathrm{FNR}^w_{\mathcal{Q},m}$ *be the false negative rate of* $\mathcal{Q}$ *after* $m = cn > w$ *insertions on a sliding window of size* $w = cL$, *we have* $\mathrm{FNR}^w_{\mathcal{Q},cn} = \frac{u_c^{L-1}}{c} \sum_{\ell=0}^{c-1} u_\ell$.

As for the probabilities, the expressions derived above for the FNR and FNR are valid to first order in $(w - cL)/|\Gamma|$, i.e. they are good approximations even when $w \approx cL$.

5.4   Optimising Queuing Filters

Let us relax, temporarily, the a priori constraint that $w = cL$. The parameter L determines how many subfilters appear in the queuing construction. Summing up the false positive and false negative rates, we have a total error rate $\mathrm{ER}^w_{\mathcal{Q},cn} = 1 - \alpha\beta^{L-1} + \alpha'\beta'^{L-1}$, where $\beta = 1 - \mathrm{FP}_{\mathcal{F},c}$, $\beta' = u_c$, $\alpha = \frac{1}{c}\sum_{\ell=0}^{c-1} 1 - \mathrm{FP}_{\mathcal{F},\ell}$ and $\alpha' = \frac{1}{c}\sum_{\ell=0}^{c-1} u_\ell$ depend on w, c and the choice of subfilter type $\mathcal{F}$.

Because $u_\eta = p_\eta \mathrm{FN}_{\mathcal{F},\eta} + (1 - p_\eta)(1 - \mathrm{FP}_{\mathcal{F},\eta})$, differentiating with respect to L, knowing that $w = Lc$, and equating the derivative to 0, one can find the optimal value for L by solving for x, which has been obtained via Mathematica:

$$- \alpha\beta^{-1+x}\log(\beta) + (\beta + \mathrm{FN}_{\mathcal{F},c}(-1+x))^{-2+x} x^{-x}\Big[- \alpha\beta + \mathrm{FN}_{\mathcal{F},c}\left(-\beta(-2+x) + \mathrm{FN}_{\mathcal{F},c}(-1+x)\right)$$

$$+ (\alpha + \mathrm{FN}_{\mathcal{F},c}(-1+x)) \times (\beta + \mathrm{FN}_{\mathcal{F},c}(-1+x))(\log(\beta + \mathrm{FN}_{\mathcal{F},c}(-1+x)) - \log(x))\Big] = 0$$

If numerically solving the equation for individual cases is feasible, it seems unlikely that a closed-form formula exists.

5.5   Queuing Filters from Existing DDFs

Our queuing construction relies on a choice of subfilters. A first observation is that we may assume that all subfilters can be instances of a single DDF design (rather than a combination of different designs).

Indeed, a simple symmetry argument shows that a heterogenous selection of subfilters is always worse than a homogeneous one: the crux is that all subfilters play the same role in turn. Therefore we lose nothing by replacing atomically one subfilter by a more efficient one. Applying this to each subfilter we end with a homogenous selection.

It remains to decide which subfilter construction to choose. The results of an experimental comparison of different DDFs (details about the benchmark are given in Sect. 4.2) are summarized in Fig. 2. It appears that the most efficient filter (in terms of saturation rate) is the QHT, from [8].

6   Experiments and Benchmarks

This section provides details and additional information on the benchmarking experiments run to validate the above analysis. Our code is accessible online[4].

Benchmarking Queuing Filters. Applying the queuing construction to DDFs from the literature, we get new filters which are compared in the wDDP setting.

In Sect. 5.5 we suggested the heuristic that the DDFs with the least saturation rate in the DDP would yield the best (error-wise) queuing filter for the wDDP. This heuristic is supported by results, summarized in Fig. 5. For this benchmark we used the following parameters: uniform stream from an alphabet of size $|\Gamma| = 2^{18}$, memory size $M = 100,000$ bits, sliding window of size $w = 10,000$, and we measure the error rate (sum of FNR^w and FPR^w).

A surprising observation is that when Lw approaches the size of the stream, there is a drop in the error. This is an artifact due to the finite size of our simulations; the stream should be considered infinite, and this drop disappears as the simulation is run for longer (see Appendix B). This effect also alters the error rates for smaller window sizes, albeit much less, and we expect that filter designers care primarily about the small window regime. Nevertheless a complete understanding of this effect would be of theoretical interest, and we leave the study of this phenomenon for future work.

The Number of Subfilters. The number of subfilters L is an important parameter in the queuing construction, as it affects the filter's error rate in a nontrivial way. An illustration of this dependence is shown in Fig. 6 which plots the error rate of a queueing QHT on an uniform stream of alphabet size $\Gamma = 2^{16}$, with 10^5 elements in the stream, on various sliding window sizes.

We observe that the optimal value for L does indeed depend on the desired sliding window. However, other experiments on alphabets of other sizes yield very similar results, hence validating the observation made in Sect. 5.4 that the optimal number of subfilters does not depends on the alphabet, at least in first approximation.

Filters vs Queued Filters. Using the same stream as previously, we can build queued filters (with an optimal value L for each considered sliding window) and compare their performances to that of non-modified filters. Results on the QHT and SQF are shown in Fig. 7, results for the Cuckoo and SBF are shown in Appendix C.

We observe that queueing filters do not necessarily behave better than their 'vanilla' counterparts, especially on large sliding windows. This can be interpreted by the fact that the DDPs were optimised for infinite sliding windows, and as such operate better than their queueing equivalent on large sliding windows.

---

[4] https://github.com/mariuslp/duplicate_sliding_benchmark.

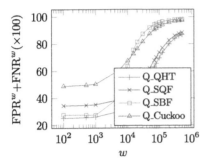
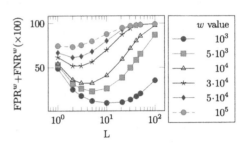

Fig. 5. Error rate (times 100) of queuing filters as a function of window size, $M = 10^5$, $L = 10$, $|\Gamma| = 2^{18}$, on a stream of size 10^7.

Fig. 6. Evolution of the error rate of a queueing QHT as a function of L, for several window sizes, with $M = 10^5$, $|\Gamma| = 2^{18}$, on a stream of size 10^6.

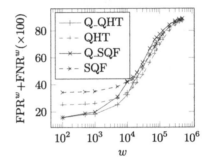

Fig. 7. Comparing performances of QHT and SQF filters, in 'vanilla' setting or when placed in our queueing structure.

7 Adversarial Resistance of Queueing Filters

As DDFs have numerous security applications, we now discuss the queuing construction from an adversarial standpoint. We consider an adversarial game in which the attacker wants to trigger false positives or false negatives over the sliding window. One motivation for doing so is causing cache saturation or denial of service by forcing cache misses, triggering false alarms or crafting fradulent transactions without triggering fraud detection systems.

To create a realistic adversary model, we assume like in [1] that the adversary does not have access to the filter's internal memory. Nonetheless, after every insertion she knows whether the inserted element was detected as a duplicate or not.

We first recall the definition of an adversarial game, adapted to our context.

Definition 3. *An adversary $\mathcal{A}$ feeds data to a sliding window DDF $\mathcal{Q}$, and for each inserted element, $\mathcal{A}$ knows whether $\mathcal{Q}$ answers DUPLICATE or UNSEEN, but has not access to $\mathcal{Q}$'s internal state $\mathcal{M}$. The game has two distinct parts.*

– In the first part, $\mathcal{A}$ can feed up to n elements to $\mathcal{Q}$ and learns $\mathcal{Q}$'s response for each insertion.
– In the second part, $\mathcal{A}$ sends a unique element $e^\star$.

$\mathcal{A}$ wins the n-false positive adversarial game (resp. n-false negative adversarial game) if and only if $e^\star$ is a false positive (resp. a false negative).

Variants of these games over a sliding window of size w are immediate.

Definition 4 (Adversarial False Positive Resistance). *We say that a DDF $\mathcal{F}$ is (p,n)-resistant to adversarial false positives if no polynomial-time probabilistic (PPT) adversary $\mathcal{A}$ can win the $n-$false positive adversarial game with probability greater than p.*

Note that if $\mathcal{F}$ is (p,n)-resistant, then it is (p,m)-resistant for all $m < n$.

We define similarly the notion of being *resistant to adversarial false negatives*. Finally, both definitions also make sense in a sliding window context.

Theorem 9 (Bound on false positive resistance). *Let $\mathcal{Q}$ be a filter of L subfilters $\mathcal{F}_i$, with c insertions maximum per subfilter, let w be a sliding window.*

If $\mathcal{F}$ is (p,c)-resistant to adversarial false positive attacks and $cL \leq w$, then $\mathcal{Q}$ is $(1 - (1 - p)^L, w)$-resistant to adversarial false positive attacks on a sliding window of size w.

If $cL > w$, the adversary has a success probability of at least $1 - (1-p)^L$.

Theorem 10 (Bounds on false negative resistance). *Let $\mathcal{Q}$ be a filter of L subfilters of kind $\mathcal{F}$, with c insertions maximum per subfilter, and let w be a sliding window. If $\mathcal{F}$ is (p,c)-resistant to adversarial false negative attacks, then $\mathcal{A}$ can win the adversarial game on the sliding window w with probability at least p^L.*

Furthermore, for q the lower bound on the false positive probability $\mathrm{FP}_{\mathcal{F},c}$ for a given stream, if $w \leq (L-1)c$ then $\mathcal{Q}$ is $(\min(1-q,p)^{L-1}p, w)$-resistant to false negative attacks on the sliding window w. On the other hand if $w > (L-1)c$ then $\mathcal{Q}$ is $(\max(1-q,p)^L, w)$-resistant to false negative attacks on the sliding window w.

A   SHF and Queueing Filter Algorithms

In this appendix, we give the pseudocode of our two structures, which we removed from the main part of the paper for page limit reasons.

Algorithm 1. SHF Setup, Lookup and Insert

1: **function** SETUP(M, w)   ▷ M is the available memory, w the size of the sliding window

2:     $h \leftarrow$ hash function of codomain size $\lfloor \frac{M}{2w} - \frac{1}{2}\log_2 w \rfloor$ bits

3:     $Q \leftarrow \emptyset$ ▷ Q is a queue of elements of size h

4:     $D \leftarrow \emptyset$ ▷ D is a dictionary $h \Rightarrow$ counter (of max value w)

1: **function** INSERT(e)

2:     Q.Push_Front($h(e)$)

3:     $D[h(e)]$++

4:     **if** Q.length() $> w$ **then**   1: **function** LOOKUP(e)

5:         $h' \leftarrow Q$.Pop_back()   2:   **if** $D[h(e)] > 0$ **then**

6:         $D[h']$--   3:   **return** DUPLICATE

7:         **if** $D[h'] = 0$ **then**   4:   **else**

8:             Erase key $D[h']$ 5:   **return** UNSEEN

Algorithm 2. Queuing Filter Setup, Lookup and Insert

1: **function** SETUP($\mathcal{F}, M, L, c$)   ▷ M is the available memory, $\mathcal{F}$ the subfilter structure, L the number of subfilters and c the number of insertions per subfilter

2:     subfilters $\leftarrow \emptyset$

3:     counter $\leftarrow 0$

4:     $m \leftarrow \lfloor M/L \rfloor$

5:     **for** i from 0 to $L - 1$ **do**

6:         subfilters.push_first($\mathcal{F}$.Setup(m))

7:     **store** (subfilters, L, m, counter)

1: **function** LOOKUP(e)   1: **function** INSERT(e)

2:     **for** i from 0 to $L - 1$ **do**   2:   subfilters[0].Insert(e)

3:         **if** subfilters[i].Lookup(e) **then**   3:   counter++

4:             **return** DUPLICATE   4:   **if** counter $== c$ **then**

5:     **return** UNSEEN   5:   subfilters.pop()

                                            6:         subfilters.push_first($\mathcal{F}$.Setup(m))

B   Effects of the Simulation's Finiteness

Theoretical results about the queuing construction apply in principle to an infinite stream. However, simulations are necessarily finite, and for very large windows (that are approximately the same size as the whole stream) this causes interesting artefacts in the error rates.

Note that these effects have very little impact on practical implementations of queuing filters, since almost all use cases assume a window size much smaller than the stream (or, equivalently, a very large stream). Nevertheless we illustrate the

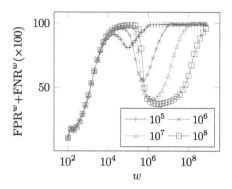 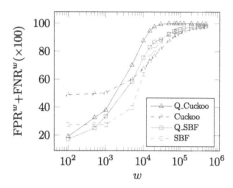

Fig. 8. Error rate for queuing QHT ($L = 10$, $M = 10^5$, $|\Gamma| = 2^{16}$) with streams of size 10^5 to 10^8.

Fig. 9. Comparing performances of the Cuckoo and SBF filters, in 'vanilla' setting or when placed in our queueing structure.

effect of the finite simulation and the parameters affecting it, if only to motivate a further analytical study of this phenomenon.

Figure 8 measures the error rate as a function of w, for different stream sizes N. A visible decrease in ER can be found around $w \approx N$. While we do not have any explanation for the difference in the peaks sizes and exact location, we give the hypothesis that it is related to the choice of $|\Gamma|$.

As can be seen on this simulation, there is only disagreement around $w \approx N/L$, and increasing N results in a later and smaller peak.

It is also possible to run simulations for different alphabet sizes Γ, which shows that the peak's position increases with $|\Gamma|$, although the relationship is not obvious to quantify.

C   Filters vs Queued Filters (Complement)

We here run a comparison of the Cuckoo Filter relative to the Queueing Cuckoo Filter, as well as the SBF relatively to the queueing SBF. The results are given in Fig. 9.

D   Compact Hash Short Filter

Removing the dictionary from the SHF construction yields a more memory-efficient, but less time-efficient construction, which we dub "compact" short hash filter (CSHF). The CSHF performs in linear time in w, and is a simple queue, the only point is that instead of storing e, the filter stores $h(e)$, where h is a hash function of codomain size $\lfloor \frac{M}{w} \rfloor$.

Error Rate. Let $w > 0$ be a window size and $M > 0$ the available memory.

Theorem 11. $\mathrm{FN}^w_{CSHF} = 0$ and $\mathrm{FP}^w_{CSHF} = 1 - \left(1 - 2^{-M/w}\right)^w$.

Proof. This is an immediate adaptation of the proof from Theorem 2. A CSHF has fingerprints of size $h' = \frac{M}{w}$.

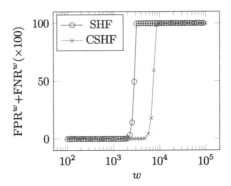

Fig. 10. Error rates of SHFs and CSHFs for $M = 10^5$ bits, for varying window sizes w.

Remark: A CSHF of size M on a sliding window w has the same error rate than an SHF of sliding window w and size $2M + w \log_2 w$.

Saturation. Similarly to SHF, CSHF saturates quickly over a certain $w_{\max}$. We compare SHF and CSHF saturations in Fig. 10.

Experimentally, we get $w_{\max}^{\text{CSHF}} = 0.0627M + 443$ $(r^2 = 0.9981)$.

E   Proofs

In this appendix, we give the proofs of all theorems stated in the paper. For the sake of convenience, each theorem is restated before giving its proof.

Theorem 1. *For $M \geq w(\log_2(w) + 2\log_2(|\Gamma|))$, the wDDP can be solved exactly (with no errors) in constant time.*

Proof. We explicitly construct a DDF that performs the detection. Storing all w elements in the sliding window takes $w \log_2(|\Gamma|)$ memory, using a FIFO queue Q; however lookup has a worst-time complexity of $O(w)$.

We therefore rely on an ancillary data structure for the sake of quickly answering lookup questions. Namely we use a dictionary D whose keys are elements from Γ and values are counters.

When an element e is inserted in the DDF, e is stored and $D[e]$ is incremented (if the key e did not exist in D, it is created first, and $D[e]$ is set to 1). In order to keep the number of stored elements to w, we discard the oldest element e_{last} in Q. As we do so, we also decrement $D[e_{\text{last}}]$, and if $D[e_{\text{last}}] = 0$ the key is deleted from D. The whole insertion procedure is therefore performed in constant time.

Lookup of an element $e^\star$ is simply done by looking whether the key $D[e^\star]$ exists, which is done in constant time.

The queue size is $w \log_2 |\Gamma|$, the dictionary size is $w(\log_2 |\Gamma| + \log_2 w)$ (as the dictionary cannot have more than w keys at the same time, a dictionary key occupies $\log_2 |\Gamma|$ bits and a counter cannot go over w, thus being less than $\log_2 w$ bits long). Thus a requirement of $w(\log_2(w) + 2\log_2(|\Gamma|))$ bits for this DDF to work.

Finally this filter does not make any mistake, as the dictionary D keeps an exact account of how many times each element is present in the sliding window.   □

Theorem 2. *Let* $w \in \mathbb{N}$. *Let* $M \simeq 2w \log_2 w$, *then the wDDP can be solved with almost no error using* M *memory bits. More precisely, it is possible to create a filter of* M *bits with an FN of* 0, *an FP of* $1 - (1 - \frac{1}{w^2})^w \sim \frac{1}{w}$, *and a time complexity of* $O(w)$.

Using $M \simeq 5w \log_2 w$ *bits of memory, a constant-time filter with the same error rate can be constructed.*

Proof. Here again we explicitly construct the filters that attain the theorem's bounds.

Let h be a hash function with codomain $\{0,1\}^{2\log_2 w}$. The birthday theorem [14] states that for a hash function h over a bits, one must on average collect $2^{a/2}$ input-output pairs before obtaining a collision. Therefore $2^{(2\log_2 w)/2} = w$ hash values $h(e_i)$ can be computed before having a 50% probability of a collision (here, a collision is when two distinct elements of the stream e_i, e_j with $i \neq j, e_i \neq e_j$ have the same hash, i.e. $h(e_i) = h(e_j)$). The 50% threshold we impose on h is arbitrary but nonetheless practical.

Let $\mathcal{F}$ be the following DDF: the filter's state consists in a queue of w hashes, and for each new element e, Detect(e) returns DUPLICATE if $h(e)$ is present in the queue, UNSEEN otherwise. Insert(e) appends $h(e)$ to the queue before popping the queue.

There is no false negative, and a false positive only happens if the new element to be inserted collides with at least one other element, which happens with probability $1 - (1 - \frac{1}{2^{2\log_2 w}})^w = 1 - (1 - \frac{1}{w^2})^w$, hence an FN of 0 and a FP of $1 - (1 - \frac{1}{w^2})^w$. The queue stores w hashes, and as such requires $w \cdot 2\log_2 w$ bits of memory.

Note that this solution has a time complexity of $O(w)$. Using an additional dictionary, as in the previous proof, but with keys of size $2\log_2(w)$, we get a filter with an error rate of about $\frac{1}{w}$ and constant time for insertion and lookup, using $w \cdot 2\log_2 w + w \cdot (2\log_2(w) + \log_2(w)) = 5w\log_2 w$ bits of memory.   □

Theorem 3. $\mathrm{FN}^w_{\mathrm{SHF}} = 0$ *and* $\mathrm{FP}^w_{\mathrm{SHF}} = 1 - \left(1 - \sqrt{w 2^{-M/w}}\right)^w$.

Proof. This is an immediate adaptation of the proof from Theorem 2. An SHF has fingerprints of size $h = \frac{M}{2w} - \frac{1}{2}\log_2 w$.   □

Theorem 4. *Let* E *be a stream of* n *elements uniformly selected from an alphabet of size* $|\Gamma|$. *For any DDF using* M *bits of memory, the error probability* $EP_n = \mathrm{FP}_n + \mathrm{FN}_n$ *satisfies* $EP_n \geq 1 - \frac{1 - (1 - \frac{1}{|\Gamma|})^M}{1 - (1 - \frac{1}{|\Gamma|})^n}$ *for any* $n > M$.

Proof. By definition, a perfect filter has the lowest possible error rate. With M bits of memory, a perfect filter can store at most M elements in memory [8, Theorem 2.1]. Up to reordering the stream, without loss of generality because it is random, we may assume that the filter stores the M last elements of the stream: any other strategy cannot yield a strictly lower error rate.

If an element is already stored in the filter, then the optimal filter will necessarily answer DUPLICATE. On the other hand, if the element is not in memory, a perfect filter can choose to answer randomly. Let p be the probability that a filter answers DUPLICATE when an element is not in memory. An optimal filter will lower the error rate of any filter using the same strategy with a different probability.

An unseen element, by definition, will be unseen in the M last elements of the stream, and hence will not be in the filter's memory, so the filter will return UNSEEN with probability $1-p$. For this reason, this filter has an FP probability of p.

On the other hand, a duplicate $e^\star \in E$ is classified as UNSEEN if and only if it was not seen in the last M elements of the stream, and the filter answers UNSEEN. Let D be the event *"There is at least one duplicate in the stream"* and C be the event *"There is a duplicate of $e^\star$ in the M previous elements of the stream"*. Then $e^\star$ triggers a false negative with probability

$$\mathrm{FN}_n = (1-\Pr[C|D])(1-p) = \left(1 - \frac{\Pr[C\cap D]}{\Pr[D]}\right)(1-p) = \left(1 - \frac{\Pr[C]}{\Pr[D]}\right)(1-p)$$

$$\mathrm{FN}_n = \left(1 - \frac{1-\Pr[\bar C]}{1-\Pr[\bar D]}\right)(1-p) = \left(1 - \frac{1-\left(1-\frac{1}{|\Gamma|}\right)^M}{1-\left(1-\frac{1}{|\Gamma|}\right)^n}\right)(1-p)$$

Hence, the error probability of the filter is

$$EP_n = \mathrm{FN}_n + p = \left(1 - \frac{1-\left(1-\frac{1}{|\Gamma|}\right)^M}{1-\left(1-\frac{1}{|\Gamma|}\right)^n}\right)(1-p) + p = 1 - \frac{1-\left(1-\frac{1}{|\Gamma|}\right)^M}{1-\left(1-\frac{1}{|\Gamma|}\right)^n}(1-p),$$

which is minimized when $p = 0$. □

Theorem 5. *Let* $\mathrm{FP}^w_{Q,m}$ *be the false positive probability of* Q *after* $m > w$ *insertions, over a sliding window of size* $w = cL$, *we have* $\mathrm{FP}^w_{Q,m} = 1 - (1-\mathrm{FP}_{\mathcal{F},c})^{L-1}(1-\mathrm{FP}_{\mathcal{F},m\bmod c})$ *where* $\mathrm{FP}_{\mathcal{F},m}$ *is the false positive probability of a subfilter* $\mathcal{F}$ *after* m *insertions.*

Proof. Let $E = (e_1,\ldots,e_m,\ldots)$ be a stream and $e^\star \notin_w E$.

Therefore, $e^\star$ is a false positive if and only if at least one subquery $\mathcal{F}_i.\mathsf{Lookup}(e^\star)$ returns DUPLICATE. Conversely, $e^\star$ is *not* a false positive when all subqueries $\mathcal{F}_i.\mathsf{Lookup}(e^\star)$ return UNSEEN, i.e., when $e^\star$ is not a false positive for each subfilter.

Each subfilter has undergone c insertions, except for the first subfilter which has only undergone $m \bmod c$, we immediately get Eq. (E). □

Theorem 6. *Let* $\mathrm{FN}^w_{\mathcal{Q},m}$ *be the false negative probability of* $\mathcal{Q}$ *after* $m > w$ *inser-tions on a sliding window of size* $w = cL$, *we have* $\mathrm{FN}^w_{\mathcal{Q},m} = u_c^{L-1} u_{m \bmod c}$ *where we have introduced the short-hand notation* $u_\eta = p_\eta \mathrm{FN}_{\mathcal{F},\eta} + (1 - p_\eta)(1 - \mathrm{FP}_{\mathcal{F},\eta})$ *where* $\mathrm{FN}_{\mathcal{F},\eta}$ *(resp.* $\mathrm{FP}_{\mathcal{F},\eta}$*) is the false negative probability (resp. false positive) of the subfilter* $\mathcal{F}$ *after* η *insertions, and* $p_\eta = \frac{1-\left(1-\frac{1}{|T|}\right)^\eta}{1-\left(1-\frac{1}{|T|}\right)^w} \approx \frac{\eta}{w}$.

Proof. Let $E = (e_1, \ldots, e_m, \ldots)$ be a stream, let w be a sliding window and let $e^\star \in_w E$.

Then $e^\star$ is a false negative if and only if all subfilters $\mathcal{F}_i$ answer $\mathcal{F}_i.\mathsf{Detect}(e^\star) = \mathsf{UNSEEN}$. There can be two cases:

- $e^\star$ is present in $\mathcal{F}_i$'s sub-sliding window;
- $e^\star$ is not present in $\mathcal{F}_i$'s sub-sliding window.

In the first case, $\mathcal{F}_i.\mathsf{Detect}(e^\star)$ returns UNSEEN if and only if $e^\star$ is a false negative for $\mathcal{F}_i$. This happens with probability $\mathrm{FN}_{\mathcal{F},c}$ by definition, except for $\mathcal{F}_0$, for which the probability is $\mathrm{FN}_{\mathcal{F},m \bmod c}$.

In the second case, $\mathcal{F}_i.\mathsf{Detect}(e^\star)$ returns UNSEEN if and only if $e^\star$ is not a false positive for $\mathcal{F}_i$, which happens with probability $1 - \mathrm{FP}_{\mathcal{F},c}$, execpt for $\mathcal{F}_0$, for which the probability is $1 - \mathrm{FP}_{\mathcal{F},m \bmod c}$.

Finally, each event is weighted by the probability p_c that $e^\star$ is in $\mathcal{F}_i$'s sub-sliding window:

$$p_c = \Pr[e^\star \text{ is in } \mathcal{F}_i \text{ sub-sliding window} - e^\star \in_w E] = \frac{\Pr[e^\star \text{ is in } \mathcal{F}_i \text{ sub-sliding window} \cap e^\star \in_w E]}{\Pr[e^\star \in_w E]}$$

$$= \frac{\Pr[e^\star \text{ is in } \mathcal{F}_i \text{ sub-sliding window}]}{\Pr[e^\star \in_w E]} = \frac{1 - \Pr[e^\star \text{ is not in } \mathcal{F}_i \text{ sub-sliding window}]}{1 - \Pr[e^\star \notin_w E]}$$

$$p_c = \frac{1 - \left(1 - \frac{1}{|T|}\right)^c}{1 - \left(1 - \frac{1}{|T|}\right)^w}$$

This concludes the proof.   □

Theorem 7. *Let* $\mathrm{FPR}^w_{\mathcal{Q},m}$ *be the false positive rate of* $\mathcal{Q}$ *after* $m = cn > w$ *insertions on a sliding window of size* $w = cL$, *we have* $\mathrm{FPR}^w_{\mathcal{Q},cn} = 1 - \frac{(1-\mathrm{FP}_{\mathcal{F},c})^{L-1}}{c} \sum_{\ell=0}^{c-1}(1 - \mathrm{FP}_{\mathcal{F},\ell})$.

Proof.

$$\mathrm{FPR}^w_{\mathcal{Q},cn} = \frac{1}{cn} \sum_{k=1}^{cn} \mathrm{FP}^w_{\mathcal{Q},k} = \frac{1}{cn} \sum_{k=1}^{n} \sum_{\ell=0}^{c-1} \mathrm{FP}^w_{\mathcal{Q},k+\ell} = \frac{1}{c} \sum_{\ell=0}^{c-1} \mathrm{FP}^w_{\mathcal{Q},\ell}$$

$$= \frac{1}{c} \sum_{\ell=0}^{c-1} 1 - (1 - \mathrm{FP}_{\mathcal{F},c})^{L-1}(1 - \mathrm{FP}_{\mathcal{F}},\ell)$$

$$= 1 - \frac{1}{c}(1 - \mathrm{FP}_{\mathcal{F},c})^{L-1} \sum_{\ell=0}^{c-1}(1 - \mathrm{FP}_{\mathcal{F},\ell})$$

□

Theorem 8. *Let* $\mathrm{FNR}_{\mathcal{Q},m}^w$ *be the false negative rate of* $\mathcal{Q}$ *after* $m = cn > w$ *insertions on a sliding window of size* $w = cL$, *we have* $\mathrm{FNR}_{\mathcal{Q},cn}^w = \frac{u_c^{L-1}}{c} \sum_{\ell=0}^{c-1} u_\ell$.

Proof.

$$\mathrm{FNR}_{\mathcal{Q},cn}^w = \frac{1}{cn} \sum_{k=1}^{cn} \mathrm{FN}_{\mathcal{Q},k}^w = \frac{1}{cn} \sum_{k=1}^{n} \sum_{\ell=0}^{c-1} \mathrm{FN}_{\mathcal{Q},k+\ell}^w = \frac{1}{c} \sum_{\ell=0}^{c-1} \mathrm{FN}_{\mathcal{Q},\ell}^w$$

$$= \frac{1}{c} \sum_{\ell=0}^{c-1} u_c^{L-1} u_\ell = \frac{u_c^{L-1}}{c} \sum_{\ell=0}^{c-1} u_\ell$$

□

Theorem 9 (Bound on false positive resistance). *Let* $\mathcal{Q}$ *be a filter of* L *subfilters* $\mathcal{F}_i$, *with* c *insertions maximum per subfilter, let* w *be a sliding window.*

If $\mathcal{F}$ *is* (p,c)-*resistant to adversarial false positive attacks and* $cL \le w$, *then* $\mathcal{Q}$ *is* $(1 - (1-p)^L, w)$-*resistant to adversarial false positive attacks on a sliding window of size* w.

If $cL > w$, *the adversary has a success probability of at least* $1 - (1-p)^L$.

Proof. If $cL \le w$, then information-theoretically the subfilters only have information on elements in the sliding window. The false positive probability for $\mathcal{Q}$ is $1 - (1 - \mathrm{FP}_{\mathcal{F},c})^L$, which is strictly increasing with $\mathrm{FP}_{\mathcal{F},c}$. Hence, the optimal solution is reached by to maximising the false positive probability in each subfilter $\mathcal{F}_i$. By hypothesis the latter is bounded above by p after c insertions.

On the other hand, if $cL > w$ then the oldest filter holds information about elements that are not in the sliding window anymore. Hence, a strategy for the attacker trying to trigger a false positive on $e^\star$ could be to make it so these oldest elements are all equal to $e^\star$. Let E be the optimal adversarial stream for triggering a false positive on the sliding window w with the element $e^\star$, when $cL \le w$. The adversary $\mathcal{A}$ can create a new stream $E' = e^\star | e^\star | \ldots | E$ where $e^\star$ is prepended $cL - w$ times to E.

After w insertions, the last subfilter will answer DUPLICATE with probability at least p, hence giving a lower bound on $\mathcal{A}'s$ success probability. If, for some reason, the last subfilter answers DUPLICATE with probability less than p, then the same reasoning as for when $cL \le w$ still applies, hence we get the corresponding lower bound (which is, in this case, an equality). □

Theorem 10 (Bounds on false negative resistance). *Let* $\mathcal{Q}$ *be a filter of* L *subfilters of kind* $\mathcal{F}$, *with* c *insertions maximum per subfilter, and let* w *be a sliding window. If* $\mathcal{F}$ *is* (p,c)-*resistant to adversarial false negative attacks, then* $\mathcal{A}$ *can win the adversarial game on the sliding window* w *with probability at least* p^L.

Furthermore, for q *the lower bound on the false positive probability* $\mathrm{FP}_{\mathcal{F},c}$ *for a given stream, if* $w \le (L-1)c$ *then* $\mathcal{Q}$ *is* $(\min(1-q,p)^{L-1}p, w)$-*resistant to false*

negative attacks on the sliding window w. *On the other hand if* $w > (L-1)c$
then Q *is* $(\max(1-q,p)^L, w)$-*resistant to false negative attacks on the sliding window* w.

Proof. Let us first prove that a PPT adversary $\mathcal{A}$ can win the game with probability at least p^L. For this, let us consider the adversarial game against the subfilter $\mathcal{F}$: after c insertions from an adversarial stream E_c, $\mathcal{A}$ choses a duplicate $e^\star$ which will be a false negative with probability p. Hence, if $\mathcal{A}$ crafts, for the filter Q, the following adversarial stream $E' = E_c \mid E_c \mid \cdots \mid E_c$ consisting of L concatenations of the stream E_c, then $e^\star$ is a false negative for Q if and only if it is a false negative for all subfilters $\mathcal{F}_i$, hence a success probability for $\mathcal{A}$ of p^L.

Now, Let us prove the case where $w \leq (L-1)c$. In this case, at any time, Q remembers all elements from inside the sliding window. As we have seen in the previous example, the success probability of $\mathcal{A}$ is strictly increasing with the probability of each subfilter to answer UNSEEN. The probability of a subfilter to answer UNSEEN is:

- $FN'_{\mathcal{F},c}$ if $e^\star$ is in the subfilter's sub-sliding window;
- $1 - FP'_{\mathcal{F},c}$ if $e^\star$ is not in the subfilter's sub-sliding window

where FN' and FP' are the probabilities of false negative and positives on the adversarial stream (which may be different from a random uniform stream).

However, since $e^\star$ is a duplicate, it is in at least one subfilter's sub-sliding window. As such, the optimal strategy for $\mathcal{A}$ is to maximise the probability of all subfilters to answer UNSEEN. Now, $FN'_{\mathcal{F},c}$ is bounded above by p and $1 - FP'_{\mathcal{F},c}$ is bounded above by $1-q$, so the best strategy is where as many filters as possible answer UNSEEN with probability $\max(p, 1-q)$, knowing that at least one filter must contain $e^\star$ and as such its probability for returning UNSEEN is at most p, hence the result.

Now, let us consider the case when $w > (L-1)c$. We have already introduce the element $e^\star$ in the last w elements, and we want to insert it again. It is possible, for the adversary, to create the following stream $E = (e_1, e_2, \ldots, e_{c-1}, e^\star, e_{c+1}, \ldots, e_{Lc}, e_{Lc+1})$, and to insert $e^\star$ afterwards.

When e_{Lc+1} is inserted, all elements $(e_1, \ldots, e_{c-1}, e^\star)$ are dropped as the oldest subfilter is popped. Hence, in this context $e^\star$ is not in any subfilter anymore, so by adapting the previous analysis, $\mathcal{A}$ can get a false negative with probability at most $\max(1-q, p)^L$. □

References

1. Carcillo, F., Pozzolo, A.D., Borgne, Y.L., Caelen, O., Mazzer, Y., Bontempi, G.: SCARFF: a scalable framework for streaming credit card fraud detection with spark. CoRR abs/1709.08920 (2017)

2. Cortes, C., Fisher, K., Pregibon, D., Rogers, A.: Hancock: a language for extracting signatures from data streams. In: Proceedings of the Sixth ACM SIGKDD International Conference on Knowledge Discovery and Data Mining. KDD 2000, Association for Computing Machinery (2000)
3. Demaine, E.D., López-Ortiz, A., Munro, J.I.: Frequency estimation of internet packet streams with limited space. In: Möhring, R., Raman, R. (eds.) ESA 2002. LNCS, vol. 2461, pp. 348–360. Springer, Heidelberg (2002). https://doi.org/10.1007/3-540-45749-6_33
4. Deng, F., Rafiei, D.: Approximately detecting duplicates for streaming data using stable Bloom filters. In: SIGMOD Conference, pp. 25–36. ACM (2006)
5. Dutta, S., Narang, A., Bera, S.K.: Streaming quotient filter: a near optimal approximate duplicate detection approach for data streams. Proc. VLDB Endow. **6**(8) (2013)
6. ElGamal, T.: A public key cryptosystem and a signature scheme based on discrete logarithms. In: Blakley, G.R., Chaum, D. (eds.) CRYPTO 1984. LNCS, vol. 196, pp. 10–18. Springer, Heidelberg (1985). https://doi.org/10.1007/3-540-39568-7_2
7. Fan, B., Andersen, D.G., Kaminsky, M., Mitzenmacher, M.D.: Cuckoo filter: practically better than bloom. In: Proceedings of the 10th ACM International on Conference on Emerging Networking Experiments and Technologies. CoNEXT 2014. ACM (2014)
8. Géraud, R., Lombard-Platet, M., Naccache, D.: Quotient hash tables: efficiently detecting duplicates in streaming data. In: Proceedings of the 34th ACM/SIGAPP Symposium on Applied Computing. SAC 2019, Association for Computing Machinery (2019)
9. Golab, L., Özsu, M.T.: Issues in data stream management. SIGMOD Rec. **32**(2) (2003)
10. Kleanthous, M., Sazeides, Y.: CATCH: a mechanism for dynamically detecting cache-content-duplication and its application to instruction caches. In: 2008 Design, Automation and Test in Europe, March 2008
11. Metwally, A., Agrawal, D., El Abbadi, A.: Duplicate detection in click streams. In: Proceedings of the 14th International Conference on World Wide Web. WWW 2005, Association for Computing Machinery (2005)
12. Shen, H., Zhang, Y.: Improved approximate detection of duplicates for data streams over sliding windows. J. Comput. Sci. Technol. **23**(6) (2008)
13. Shtul, A., Baquero, C., Almeida, P.S.: Age-partitioned bloom filters (2020)
14. Wagner, D.: A generalized birthday problem. In: Yung, M. (ed.) CRYPTO 2002. LNCS, vol. 2442, pp. 288–304. Springer, Heidelberg (2002). https://doi.org/10.1007/3-540-45708-9_19
15. Yoon, M.: Aging bloom filter with two active buffers for dynamic sets. IEEE Trans. Knowl. Data Eng. **22**(1) (2010)

Computational Complexity Characterization of Protecting Elections from Bribery

Lin Chen[1(✉)], Ahmed Sunny[1], Lei Xu[2], Shouhuai Xu[3], Zhimin Gao[4], Yang Lu[5], Weidong Shi[5], and Nolan Shah[6]

[1] Texas Tech University, 2500 Broadway, Lubbock, TX 79409, USA
{lin.chen,ahmed.sunny}@ttu.edu
[2] University of Texas Rio Grande Valley,
1201 W University Dr, Edinburg, TX 78539, USA
xuleimath@gmail.com
[3] University of Texas San Antonio, 1 UTSA Circle, San Antonio, TX 78249, USA
shouhuai.xu@utsa.edu
[4] Auburn University at Montgomery, 7430 East Dr, Montgomery, AL 36117, USA
mtion@masn.com
[5] University of Houston, 4800 Calhoun Rd, Houston, TX 77004, USA
ylu17@central.edu,wshi3@uh.edu
[6] Amazon Web Services, Seatle, USA
nolan@0x9b.com

Abstract. The bribery problem in election has received considerable attention in the literature, upon which various algorithmic and complexity results have been obtained. It is thus natural to ask whether we can protect an election from potential bribery. We assume that the protector can protect a voter with some cost (e.g., by isolating the voter from potential bribers). A protected voter cannot be bribed. Under this setting, we consider the following bi-level decision problem: Is it possible for the protector to protect a proper subset of voters such that no briber with a fixed budget on bribery can alter the election result? The goal of this paper is to give a full picture on the complexity of protection problems. We give an extensive study on the protection problem and provide algorithmic and complexity results. Comparing our results with that on the bribery problems, we observe that the protection problem is in general significantly harder. Indeed, it becomes Σ_2^p-complete even for very restricted special cases, while most bribery problems lie in NP. However, it is not necessarily the case that the protection problem is always harder. Some of the protection problems can still be solved in polynomial time, while some of them remain as hard as the bribery problem under the same setting.

Keywords: Voting · Complexity · NP-hardness · Σ_2^p-hardness

A 2 page extended abstract has been published at the Proceedings of the 17th International Conference on Autonomous Agents and MultiAgent Systems (AAMAS'18).

1   Introduction

In an election, there are a set of candidates and a set of voters. Each voter has a *preference list* of candidates. Given these preference lists, a winner is determined based on some voting rule, examples of which will be elaborated later.

In the context of election, the *bribery problem* has received considerable attention (see, for example, [1,8,9,13,14]). In this problem, there is an attacker who attempts to manipulate the election by bribing some voters, who will then report preference lists of the attacker's choice (rather than the voters' own preference lists). Each voter has a price for being bribed, and the attacker has an attack budget for bribing voters. There are two kinds of attackers: *constructive* vs. *destructive*. A *constructive* attacker attempts to make its designated candidate win an election, whereas the designated candidate would not win the election should there be no attacker. In contrast, a *destructive* attacker attempts to make its designated candidate lose the election, whereas the designated candidate would win the election should there be no attacker. The research question is: Given an attack budget for bribing, whether or not a (constructive or destructive) attacker can achieve its goal?

In this paper, we initiate the study of a new problem, called the *protection problem*, which extends the bribery problem as follows. There are also a set of candidates, a set of voters, and a bribery attacker. Each voter also has a *preference list* of candidates. There is also a voting rule according to which a winner is determined. Going beyond the bribery problem, the protection problem further considers a defender, who aims to protect elections from bribery. More specifically, the defender is given a defense budget and can use the defense budget to award some of the voters so that they cannot be bribed by the attacker anymore. This leads to an interesting problem: *Given a defense budget, is it possible to protect an election from an attacker with a given attack budget for bribing voters (i.e., assuring that the attacker cannot achieve its goal)?*

Our Contributions. We introduce the problem of protecting elections from bribery, namely the protection problem. Given a defense budget for rewarding some of the voters and an attack budget for bribing some of the rest voters, the protection problem asks whether or not the defender can protect the election. We investigate the protection problem against the aforementioned two kinds of bribery attackers: constructive vs. destructive.

We present a characterization on the computational complexity of the protection problem (summarized in Table 1 in Sect. 5). The characterization is primarily concerning the voting rule of r-approval, which will be elaborated in Sect. 2. At a high level, our results can be summarized as follows. (i) The *protection problem* is hard and might be much harder than the *bribery problem*. For example, the protection problem is Σ_2^p-complete in most cases, while the bribery problem is in NP under the same settings. (ii) The *destructive protection problem* (i.e., protecting elections against a destructive attacker) is *no* harder than the *constructive protection problem* (i.e., protecting elections against a constructive attacker) in all of the settings we considered. In particular, the destructive protection problem is Σ_2^p-hard only when the voters are weighted and have arbitrary prices, while the constructive protection problem is Σ_2^p-hard even when the voters are unweighted and have the unit price. (iii) Voter weights and prices have completely different effects on the computational complexity of the protection problem. For example, the constructive protection problem is coNP-hard in one case but is in P in another case.

Related Work. The problem of protecting elections from attacks seemingly has not received the due attention. Very recently, Yin et al. [19] considered the problem of defending elections against an attacker who can delete (groups of) voters. That is, the investigation is in the context of the *control problem*, where the attacker attempts to manipulate an election by adding or deleting some voters. The control problem has been extensively investigated (see, for example, [4,10–12,19]). Although the control problem is related to the bribery problem, the means used by the attacker in the control problem (i.e., attacker adding or deleting some voters) is different from the means used by the attacker in the bribery problem (i.e., attacker changing the preference lists of the bribed voters). We investigate the protection problem, which is defined in the context of the bribery problem rather than the control problem. That is, the problem we investigate is different from the problem investigated by Yin et al. [19].

The protection problem we study is inspired by the bribery problem. Faliszewski et al. [9] gave the first characterization on the complexity of the *bribery problem*, including some dichotomy theorems. In the bribery problem, the attacker can pay a fixed, but voter-dependent, price to arbitrarily manipulate the preference list of a bribed voter. The complexity of the bribery problem under the scoring rule of r-approval or r-veto for small values of r was addressed later by Lin [15] and Bredereck and Talmon [2]. There are also studies on measuring the bribery price in different ways (see, e.g., [1,7,13]).

Technically, the protection problem is related to the *bi-level optimization* problem, especially the *bi-level knapsack* problem [3,6,17,18]. In the bi-level knapsack problem, there is a leader and a follower. The leader makes a decision first (e.g., packing a subset of items into the knapsack), and then the follower solves an optimization problem given the leader's decision (e.g., finding the most profitable subset of items that have not been packed by the leader). The problem asks for the decision of the leader such that a certain objective function is optimized (e.g., minimizing the profit of the follower). The protection problem we study can be formulated as the bi-level problem by letting the defender award some voters who therefore cannot be bribed by the attacker anymore, and then the attacker bribes some of the remaining voters as an attempt to manipulate the election.

2   Problem Definition

Election Model. Consider a set of m candidates $\mathcal{C} = \{c_1, c_2, \ldots, c_m\}$ and a set of n voters $\mathcal{V} = \{v_1, v_2, \ldots, v_n\}$. Each voter v_j has a preference list of candidates, which is essentially a permutation of candidates, denoted as τ_j. The preference of v_j is denoted by $(c_{\tau_j(1)}, c_{\tau_j(2)}, \ldots, c_{\tau_j(m)})$, meaning that v_j prefers candidate $c_{\tau_j(z)}$ to $c_{\tau_j(z+1)}$, where $z = 1, 2, \ldots$. Since τ_j is a permutation over $\{1, 2, \ldots, m\}$, we denote by τ_j^{-1} the inverse of τ_j, meaning that $\tau_j^{-1}(i)$ is the position of candidate c_i in vector $(c_{\tau_j(1)}, c_{\tau_j(2)}, \ldots, c_{\tau_j(m)})$.

Voting Rules. In this paper, we focus on the scoring rule (or scoring protocol) that maps a preference list to a m-vector $\alpha = (\alpha_1, \alpha_2, \ldots, \alpha_m)$, where $\alpha_i \in \mathbb{N}$ is the score assigned to the i-th candidate on the preference list of voter v_j and $\alpha_1 \geq \alpha_2 \geq \ldots \geq \alpha_m$. Given that τ_j is the preference list of v_j, candidate $c_{\tau_j(i)}$ receives a score of α_i from v_j. The *total score* of a candidate is the summation of the scores it received from the voters. The winner is the candidate that receives the highest total score. We focus on a *single-winner* election, meaning that only one winner is selected. In the case of a tie, a random candidate with the highest total score is selected. However, our results remain valid for all-natural variation of selecting a single winner.

We say a scoring rule is *non-trivial*, if $\alpha_1 > \alpha_m$ (i.e., not all scores are the same). There are many (non-trivial) scoring rules, including the popular *r-approval, plurality, veto, Borda count* and so on. In the case of r-approval, $\alpha = (1, 1, \ldots, 1, 0, 0, \ldots, 0)$. In the case of plurality, $\alpha = (1, 0, \ldots, 0)$. In the case
$\underbrace{}_{r}\underbrace{}_{m-r}$
of veto, $\alpha = (1, 1, \ldots, 1, 0)$. It is clear that plurality and veto are special cases of the scoring rule of r-approval.

Weights of Voters. Voters can have different weights. Let $w_j \in \mathbb{N}$ be the weight of voter v_j. In a weighted election, the total score of a candidate is the *weighted sum* of the scores a candidate receives from the voters. For example, candidate c_i receives a score $w_j \cdot \alpha_{\tau_j^{-1}(i)}$ from voter v_j.

By re-indexing all of the candidates, we can set, without loss of generality, c_m as the winner in the absence of bribery.

Adversarial Models. We consider an attacker that does not belong to $\mathcal{C} \cup \mathcal{V}$ but attempts to manipulate the election by bribing some voters. Suppose voter v_j has a *bribing price* p_j^b, meaning that v_j, upon receiving a bribery of amount p_j^b from the attacker, will change its preference list to the list given by the attacker. The attacker has a total budget B. As in the bribery problem, we also consider two kinds of attackers:

– *Constructive attacker.* This attacker attempts to make a designated candidate win the election, meaning that the designated candidate is the only candidate who gets the highest score.
– *Destructive attacker.* This attacker attempts to make a designated candidate lose the election, meaning that there is another candidate that gets a strictly higher score than the designated candidate does.

Protection. In the protection problem, voter v_j, upon receiving an award of amount p_j^a (or *awarding price*) from the defender, will always report its preference list faithfully and cannot be bribed. Note that p_j^a may have multiple interpretations, such as monetary award, economic incentives or the cost of isolating voters from bribery. We say a voter v_j is *awarded* if v_j receives an award of p_j^a.

Problem Statement. We formalize our problem as follows.

The constructive protection problem (i.e., protecting elections against constructive attackers):

Input: A set $\mathcal{C}$ of m candidates. A set $\mathcal{V}$ of n voters, each with a weight $w_j \in \mathbb{Z}_{>0}$, a preference list τ_j, an awarding price of $p_j^a \in \mathbb{Z}_{>0}$ and a bribing price of $p_j^b \in \mathbb{Z}_{>0}$. A scoring rule for selecting a single winner. A defender with a defense budget $F \in \mathbb{Z}_{\geq 0}$. An attacker with an attack budget $B \in \mathbb{Z}_{\geq 0}$ attempting to make candidate c_m win the election.

Output: Decide whether there exists a $\mathcal{V}_F \subseteq \mathcal{V}$ such that

- $\sum_{j:v_j \in \mathcal{V}_F} p_j^a \leq F$; and
- for *any* subset $\mathcal{V}_B \subseteq \mathcal{V} \setminus \mathcal{V}_F$ with $\sum_{j:v_j \in \mathcal{V}_B} p_j^b \leq B$, c_m does not get a strictly higher score than any other candidate despite the attacker bribing the voters belonging to $\mathcal{V}_B$ (i.e., bribing $\mathcal{V}_B$).

The destructive protection problem (i.e., protecting elections against destructive attackers):

Input: A set $\mathcal{C}$ of m candidates. A set $\mathcal{V}$ of n voters, each with a weight $w_j \in \mathbb{Z}_{>0}$, a preference list τ_j, an awarding price of $p_j^a \in \mathbb{Z}_{>0}$ and a bribing price of $p_j^b \in \mathbb{Z}_{>0}$. A scoring rule for selecting a single winner. Suppose c_m is the winner if no voter is bribed. A defender with a defense budget $F \in \mathbb{Z}_{\geq 0}$. An attacker with an attack budget $B \in \mathbb{Z}_{\geq 0}$ attempting to make c_m lose the election by making $c \in \mathcal{C} \setminus \{c_m\}$ get a strictly higher score than c_m does.

Output: Decide if there exists a $\mathcal{V}_F \subseteq \mathcal{V}$ such that

- $\sum_{j:v_j \in \mathcal{V}_F} p_j^a \leq F$; and
- for *any* subset $\mathcal{V}_B \subseteq \mathcal{V} \setminus \mathcal{V}_F$ such that $\sum_{j:v_j \in \mathcal{V}_B} p_j^b \leq B$, no candidate $c \in \mathcal{C} \setminus \{c_m\}$ can get a strictly higher score than c_m does despite the attacker bribing $\mathcal{V}_B$.

Further Terminology and Notations. We denote by $W(c_i)$ the total score obtained by candidate c_i in the absence of bribery (i.e., no voter is bribed). If the defender can select $\mathcal{V}_F$ such that no constructive or destructive attacker can succeed, we say the defender succeeds. We call our problem as the (constructive or destructive) *weighted-\$-protection* problem, where "weighted" indicates that the voters are weighted and "\$" indicates that arbitrary awarding and bribing prices are involved. In addition to investigating the general *weighted-\$-protection* problem, we also investigate the following special cases of it:

- the *$-protection* problem with $w_j = 1$ for each j (i.e., the voters are not weighted);
- the *weighted-protection* problem with $p_j^a = p_j^b = 1$ for each j (i.e., voters are associated with the unit awarding price and the unit bribing price);
- the *unit-protection* problem with $w_j = p_j^a = p_j^b = 1$ for each j (i.e., voters are not weighted, and are associated with the unit awarding price and the unit bribing price).
- the *symmetric protection* problem with $p_j^a = p_j^b$ for each j (i.e., the awarding price and the bribing price are always the same), while noting that different voters may have different prices.

Please refer to the full version [5] of the paper for all the omitted proofs.

3 The Case of Constantly Many Candidates

3.1 The Weighted-$-Protection Problem

The goal of this subsection is to prove the following theorem.

Theorem 1. *For any non-trivial scoring rule, both the constructive and destructive weighted-$-protection problem, is Σ_2^p-complete.*

The theorem follows from Lemma 1 and Lemma 2 below, which shows the Σ_2^p membership and Σ_2^p-hardness, respectively. (see Appendix 7.3 of Chen et al. [5] for the full proof of Theorem 1).

Lemma 1. *For any non-trivial scoring rule, both the constructive and destructive weighted-$-protection problems are in Σ_2^p.*

Lemma 2. *For any non-trivial scoring rule, both the constructive and destructive weighted-$-protection problems are both Σ_2^p-hard even if there are only $m = 2$ candidates.*

Proof Sketch. The proof of Lemma 2 follows from De-Negre (DNeg) variant of bi-level knapsack problem, which is proved to be Σ_2^p-hard by Caprara et al. [3]. We give a brief explanation. In this De-Negre variant, there are an adversary and a packer. The adversary has a reserving budget $\bar{F}$ and the packer has a packing budget $\bar{B}$. There is a set of n items, each having a price $\bar{p}_j^a$ to the adversary, a price $\bar{p}_j^b$ to the packer, and a weight $\bar{w}_j = \bar{p}_j^b$ to both the adversary and the packer. The adversary first reserves a subset of items whose total price is no more than $\bar{F}$. Then the packer solves the knapsack problem with respect to the remaining items that are not reserved; i.e., the packer will select a subset of the remaining items whose total price is no more than $\bar{B}$ but their total weight is maximized. The De-Negre variant asks if the adversary can reserve a proper subset of items such that the total weight of the unreserved items that are selected by the packer is no more than some parameter W. The De-Negre variant is similar to the weighted-$-protection protection problem, because we can view the defender and attacker in the protection problem respectively as the adversary and packer in the bi-level knapsack problem. In the case of a single-winner election with $m = 2$ candidates, the goal of the defender is to assure that the constructive attacker cannot make the loser get a strictly higher score than the winner by bribing. This is essentially the same as ensuring that the constructive attacker cannot bribe a subset of non-awarded voters whose total weight is higher than a certain threshold, which is the same as the bi-level knapsack problem. □

3.2   The Weighted-Protection Problem

This is a special case of the weighted-$-protection problem when $p_j^a = p_j^b = 1$.

The following theorem used by Faliszewski et al. [9] was originally proved for another problem. In our context, $F = 0$ and thus $\mathcal{V}_F = \emptyset$, it is NP-hard to decide if the constructive attacker can succeed or, equivalently, if the defender *cannot* succeed. Hence, it is coNP-hard to decide if the defender can succeed and Theorem 2 follows.

Theorem 2 (By Faliszewski et al. [9]). *If m is a constant, the constructive weighted-protection problem is coNP-hard for any scoring rule that $\alpha_2, \alpha_3, \ldots, \alpha_m$ are not all equal (i.e., it does not hold that $\alpha_2 = \alpha_3 = \ldots = \alpha_m$).*

In contrast, the destructive version is easy. Using the fact that m, the number of candidates, is a constant, we can prove the following Theorem 3 through suitable enumerations. (see Appendix 7.4 of Chen et al. [5] for the proof of Theorem 3).

Theorem 3. *If m is a constant, then the destructive weighted-protection problem is in P for any scoring rule.*

3.3   The $-Protection Problem

This is the special case of the protection problem with $w_j = 1$ for every j. The following two theorems illustrate the significant difference (in terms of complexity) between the general problem and its special case with symmetricity (i.e., $p_j^a = p_j^b$). (see Appendix 7.5 of Chen et al. [5] for the full proof of Theorem 4).

Theorem 4. *For constant m and any non-trivial scoring rule, both the constructive and destructive $-protection problems are NP-complete.*

Theorem 5. *For constant m, both destructive and constructive symmetric $-protection problems are in P for any scoring rule.*

4 The Case of Arbitrarily Many Candidates

4.1 The Case of Constructive Attacker

The following Theorem 6 shows Σ_2^p-hardness for the most special cases of the constructive weighted-\$-protection problem, namely $w_j = p_j^a = p_j^b = 1$ (unit-protection). It thus implies readily the Σ_2^p-hardness for the more general constructive \$-protection and constructive weighted-protection.

Theorem 6. *For arbitrary m, the r-approval constructive unit-protection problem is Σ_2^p-complete.*

Membership in Σ_2^p follows directly from Lemma 1. To prove Theorem 6, it suffices to show the following.

Lemma 3. *For arbitrary m, the r-approval constructive unit-protection problem is Σ_2^p-hard even if $r = 4$.*

To prove Lemma 3, we reduce from a variant of the $\exists\forall$ 3 dimensional matching problem (or $\exists\forall$3DM), which is called $\exists\forall$3DM$'$ and defined below. The classical $\exists\forall$ 3DM is Σ_2^p-hard   proved by Mcloughlin [16]. By leveraging the proof by Mcloughlin [16], we can show the Σ_2^p-hardness of the $\exists\forall$3DM$'$ problem.

$\exists\forall$**3DM$'$:** Given a parameter t, three disjoint sets of elements W, X, Y of the same cardinality, and two disjoint subsets M_1 and M_2 of $W \times X \times Y$ such that M_1 contains each element of $W \cup X \cup Y$ at most once. Does there exist a subset $U_1 \subseteq M_1$ such that $|U_1| = t$ and for any $U_2 \subseteq M_2$, $U_1 \cup U_2$ is *not* a *perfect matching* (where a *perfect matching* is a subset of triples in which every element of $W \cup X \cup Y$ appears exactly once)?

Proof (Proof of Lemma 3). Given an arbitrary instance of $\exists\forall$ 3DM$'$, we construct an instance of the constructive unit-protection problem in r-approval election as follows. Recall that $r = 4$ and thus every voter votes for 4 candidates.

Suppose $|W| = |X| = |Y| = n$, $|M_1| = m_1$, $|M_2| = m_2$.

There are $3n + 2$ key candidates, including:

- $3n$ key candidates, each corresponding to one distinct element of $W \cup X \cup Y$ and we call them element candidates. The score of every element candidate is $n + \xi$;
- one key candidate called leading candidate, whose total score is $n + t + \xi - 1$;
- one key candidate called designated candidate, whose total score is ξ.

Here ξ is some sufficiently large integer, e.g., we can choose $\xi = (m_1 + m_2)n$. Besides key candidates, there are also many dummy candidates, each of score either 1 or $m_1 - t + 1$. The number of dummy candidates will be determined later.

There are $m_1 + m_2(m_1 - t + 1)$ key voters, including:

- m_1 key voters, each corresponding to a distinct triple in M_1 and we call them M_1-voters. For each $(w_i, x_j, y_k) \in M_1$, the corresponding voter votes for the 3 candidates corresponding to elements w_i, x_j, y_k together with the leading candidate;
- $m_2 \cdot (m_1 - t + 1)$ key voters, each distinct triple in M_2 corresponds to exactly $m_1 - t + 1$ voters and we call them M_2-voters. For every $(w_i, x_j, y_k) \in M_2$, each of its $m_1 - t + 1$ corresponding voters vote for the 3 candidates corresponding to elements w_i, x_j, y_k together with one distinct dummy candidate. Since the $m_1 - t + 1$ voters are identical, we can view them as $m_1 - t + 1$ copies, i.e., every M_2-voter has $m_1 - t + 1$ copies.

Besides key voters, there are also sufficiently many dummy voters. Each dummy voter votes for exactly one key candidate and 3 distinct dummy candidates. Dummy voters and dummy candidates are used to make sure that the score of key candidates are exactly as we have described. More precisely, if we only count the scores of key candidates contributed by key voters, then the element candidate corresponding to $z \in W \cup X \cup Y$ has a score of $d(z) = d_1(z) + (m_1 - t + 1)d_2(z)$ where $d_i(z)$ is the number of occurrences of z in the triple set M_i for $i = 1, 2$, and the leading candidate has a score of m_1. Hence, there are exactly $n + \xi - d(z)$ dummy voters who vote for the element candidate corresponding to z, and $n + t + \xi - 1 - m_1$ dummy voters who vote for the leading candidate.

Overall, we create $\sum_{z \in W \cup X \cup Y}(n + \xi - d(z)) + n + t + \xi - m_1 - 1$ dummy voters, and $3\sum_{z \in W \cup X \cup Y}(n + \xi - d(z)) + 3(n + t + \xi - m_1 - 1) + m_2$ dummy candidates.

As the leading candidate is the current winner, the constructive unit-protection problem asks whether the election can be protected against an attacker attempting to make the designated candidate win. The defense budget is $F = m_1 - t$ and the attack budget is $B = n$. In the following we show that the defender succeeds if and only if the given $\exists\forall$ 3DM$'$ instance admits a feasible solution U_1.

"Yes" Instance of $\exists\forall$ 3DM$'$ $\rightarrow$ "Yes" Instance of Constructive Unit-Protection. Suppose the instance of $\exists\forall$ 3DM$'$ admits a feasible solution U_1, we show that the answer for constructive unit-protection problem is "Yes".

Recall that each M_1-voter corresponds to a distinct triple (w_i, x_j, y_k) in M_1 and votes for 4 candidates – the leading candidate and the three candidates corresponding to w_i, x_j, y_k. We do *not* award M_1-voters corresponding to the triples in U_1, but award all of the remaining M_1-voters. The resulting cost is exactly $F = m_1 - t$. In what follows we show that after awarding voters this way, the attacker cannot make the designated candidate win.

Suppose on the contrary, the attacker can make the designated candidate win by bribing $\alpha \leq t$ voters among the M_1-voters, $\beta \leq m_2$ voters among the M_2-voters, and γ dummy voters. We claim that the following inequalities hold:

$$\alpha + \beta + \gamma \leq n \tag{1a}$$

$$4\alpha + 3\beta + \gamma \geq 3n + t \tag{1b}$$

Inequality (1a) follows from the fact that the attack budget is n and the attacker can bribe at most n voters. Inequality (1b) holds because of the following. Given that a candidate can get at most one score from each voter and that the attacker can bribe at most n voters, bribing voters can make the designated candidate obtain a score at most $n + \xi$. Hence, the score of each key candidate other than the designated one should be at most $n + \xi - 1$. Recall that without bribery, each of the $3n$ element candidate has a score of $n + \xi$ and the leading candidate has a score of $n + t + \xi - 1$. Hence, the attacker should decrease at least 1 score from each element candidate and t scores from the leading candidate, leading to a total score of $3n + t$. Note that an M_1-voter contributes 1 score to 4 key candidates, therefore it contributes in total a score of 4 to the key candidates. Similarly an M_2-voter contributes a score of 3, and a dummy voter contributes a score of 1 to the key candidates. Therefore, by bribing (for example) an M_1-voter, the total score of all the element candidates and the leading candidate can decrease by at most 4. Thus, inequality (1b) holds.

In the following we derive a contradiction based on Inequalities (1a) and (1b). By plugging $\gamma \le n - \alpha - \beta$ into Inequality (1b), we have $3\alpha + 2\beta \ge 2n + t$. Since $\beta \le n - \alpha$, we have $3\alpha + 2\beta \le \alpha + 2n \le 2n + t$. Hence, $3\alpha + 2\beta = \alpha + 2n = 2n + t$, and we have $\alpha = t$ and $\beta = n - t$. Note that the defender has awarded every M_1-voter except the ones corresponding to U_1, where $|U_1| = t$. Hence, every voter corresponding to the triples in U_1 is bribed. Furthermore, as Inequality (1b) is tight, bribing voters makes the designated candidate have a score of $n + \xi$, while making each of the other key candidates have a score of $n + \xi - 1$. This means that the score of each element candidate decreases exactly by 1. Hence, the attacker has selected a subset of M_2-voters such that together with the M_1-voters corresponding to triples in U_1, these voters contribute exactly a score of 1 to every element candidate. Let U_2 be the set of triples to which the bribed M_2-voters correspond, then $U_1 \cup U_2$ forms a 3-dimensional matching, which is a contradiction to the fact that U_1 is a feasible solution to the $\exists \forall$ 3DM' instance. Thus, the attacker cannot make the designated candidate win and the answer for the constructive unit-protection problem is "Yes".

"No" Instance of $\exists \forall$ 3DM' $\rightarrow$ "No" Instance of Constructive Unit-Protection. Suppose for any $U_1 \subseteq M_1$, $|U_1| = t$ there exists $U_2 \in M_2$ such that $U_1 \cup U_2$ is a perfect matching, we show that the answer to the constructive unit-protection problem is "No". Consider an arbitrary set of voters awarded by the defender. Among the awarded voters, let H be the set of triples that corresponds to the awarded M_1-voters. As $|H| \le m_1 - t$, $|M_1 \backslash H| \ge t$. We select an arbitrary subset $H_1 \subseteq M_1 \backslash H$ such that $|H_1| = t$. There exists some $H_2 \subseteq M_2$ such that $H_1 \cup H_2$ is a perfect matching, and we let the attacker bribe the set of voters corresponding to triples in $H_1 \cup H_2$. Note that this is always possible as every M_2-voter has $m_1 - t + 1$ copies, so no matter which M_2-voters are awarded the briber can always select one M_2-voter corresponding to each triple in H_2. It is easy to see that by bribing these voters, the score of every element candidate decreases by 1, and the score of the leading voter decreases by t. Meanwhile, let each bribed voter vote for the designated candidate and three distinct dummy candidates, then the designated candidate has a score of $n + \xi$ and becomes a winner, i.e., the answer to the constructive unit-protection problem is "No". □

Remark. The proof of Lemma 3 can be easily modified to prove the Σ_2^p-hardness of r-approval constructive unit-protection problem for any fixed $r \geq 4$. Specifically, we can make the same reduction, and add dummy candidates such that every voter additionally votes for exactly $r - 4$ distinct dummy candidates.

4.2   The Case of Destructive Attacker

Theorem 7. *Both r-approval destructive weighted-protection and r-approval (symmetric) \$-protection problems are NP-complete.*

The proof of Theorem 7 is based on a crucial observation of the equivalence between the destructive weighted-\$-protection problem (under an arbitrary scoring rule) and the *minmax vector addition problem* we introduce (see Appendix 7.1 in [5]). (See Appendix 7.6 of Chen et al. [5] for the full proof of Theorem 7).

5   Summary of Results

The preceding characterization of the computational complexity of the protection problem in various settings is summarized in Table 1.

Table 1. Summary of results for *single-winner* election under the *r-approval* scoring rule: "Symmetric" means $p_j^a = p_j^b$ for every j and "asymmetric" means otherwise; hardness results that are proved for the case with only two candidates (i.e., $m = 2$) are marked with a "◇" (Note that when $m = 2$, the 1-approval rule is the same as the plurality, veto or Borda scoring rule. It can be shown that with a slight modification, the hardness results hold for any *non-trivial* scoring rule); algorithmic results (marked with a "P") hold for arbitrary scoring rules; the complexity of the protection problem against a destructive attacker with $w_j = p_j^a = p_j^b = 1$ remains open; for most variants of the protection problem against a constructive attacker, we only provide hardness results and we do not know yet whether or not they belong to the class of coNP-complete or Σ_2^p-complete proble.

# of candidates	Model parameters	Destructive attacker	Constructive attacker
Constant	Weighted, priced, asymmetric	Σ_2^p-complete ◇ (Theorem 1)	Σ_2^p-complete ◇ (Theorem 1)
	Weighted, $p_j^a = p_j^b = 1$	P (Theorem 3)	coNP-hard (Theorem 2)
	$w_j = 1$, priced, asymmetric	NP-complete ◇ (Theorem 4)	NP-complete ◇ (Theorem 4)
	$w_j = 1$, priced, symmetric	P (Theorem 5)	P (Theorem 5)
	$w_j = 1$, $p_j^a = p_j^b = 1$	P (Theorem 5)	P (Theorem 5)
Arbitrary	Weighted, priced, asymmetric	Σ_2^p-complete ◇ (Theorem 1)	Σ_2^p-complete ◇ (Theorem 1)
	Weighted, $p_j^a = p_j^b = 1$	NP-complete (Theorem 7)	Σ_2^p-hard (Theorem 6)
	$w_j = 1$, priced, asymmetric	NP-complete (Theorem 7)	Σ_2^p-hard (Theorem 6)
	$w_j = 1$, priced, symmetric	NP-complete (Theorem 7)	Σ_2^p-hard (Theorem 6)
	$w_j = 1$, $p_j^a = p_j^b = 1$	?	Σ_2^p-hard (Theorem 6)

We remark three natural open problems for future research. One is the complexity of the destructive protection problem with $w_j = p_j^a = p_j^b = 1$. It is not clear whether the problem is in P or is NP-complete. Another is the constructive protection problem with $p_j^a = p_j^b = 1$ and arbitrary voter weights. We only show its coNP-hardness, it is not clear whether or not this problem is coNP-complete. The third problem is the complexity of r-approval constructive unit-protection problem when $r = \{1, 2, 3\}$ as our hardness proof only holds when $r \geq 4$.

6 Conclusion

We introduced the protection problem and characterized its computational complexity. We showed that the problem, in general, is Σ_2^p-complete, and identified settings in which the problem becomes easier. Moreover, we showed the protection problem in some parameter settings is polynomial-time solvable, suggesting that these parameter settings can be used for real-work election applications.

In addition to the open problems mentioned in Sect. 5, the following are also worth investigating. First, our hardness results would motivate the study of approximation or FPT (fixed parameter tractable) algorithms for the protection problem. Note that even polynomial time approximation schemes can exist for Σ_2^p-hard problems (see, e.g., By Caparara et al. [3]). It is thus desirable that a similar result can be obtained for some variants of the protection problem. Second, how effective is this approach when applied towards the problem of defending against other types of attackers that can, e.g., add or delete votes? Third, much research remains to be done in extending the protection problem to accommodate other scoring rules such as Borda and Copeland.

References

1. Bredereck, R., Chen, J., Faliszewski, P., Nichterlein, A., Niedermeier, R.: Prices matter for the parameterized complexity of shift bribery. Inf. Comput. **251**, 140–164 (2016)
2. Bredereck, R., Talmon, N.: NP-hardness of two edge cover generalizations with applications to control and bribery for approval voting. Inf. Process. Lett. **116**(2), 147–152 (2016)
3. Caprara, A., Carvalho, M., Lodi, A., Woeginger, G.J.: A study on the computational complexity of the bilevel knapsack problem. SIAM J. Optim. **24**(2), 823–838 (2014)
4. Chen, J., Faliszewski, P., Niedermeier, R., Talmon, N.: Elections with few voters: candidate control can be easy. J. Artif. Intell. Res. **60**, 937–1002 (2017)
5. Chen, L., et al.: Computational complexity characterization of protecting elections from bribery. arXiv preprint arXiv:2007.02533 (2020)
6. Chen, L., Zhang, G.: Approximation algorithms for a bi-level knapsack problem. Theor. Comput. Sci. **497**, 1–12 (2013)
7. Dey, P., Misra, N., Narahari, Y.: Frugal bribery in voting. Theor. Comput. Sci. **676**, 15–32 (2017)

8. Erdélyi, G., Reger, C., Yang, Y.: The complexity of bribery and control in group identification. Auton. Agent Multi-Agent Syst. **34**(1) (2019). Article number: 8. https://doi.org/10.1007/s10458-019-09427-9
9. Faliszewski, P., Hemaspaandra, E., Hemaspaandra, L.A.: How hard is bribery in elections? J. Artif. Intell. Res. **35**, 485–532 (2009)
10. Faliszewski, P., Hemaspaandra, E., Hemaspaandra, L.A.: Weighted electoral control. J. Artif. Intell. Res. **52**, 507–542 (2015)
11. Faliszewski, P., Rothe, J.: Control and bribery in voting. In: Brandt, F., Conitzer, V., Endriss, U., Lang, J., Procaccia, A.D. (eds.) Handbook of Computational Social Choice, pp. 146–168. Cambridge University Press, Cambridge (2016)
12. Hemaspaandra, E., Hemaspaandra, L.A., Schnoor, H.: A control dichotomy for pure scoring rules. In: Brodley, C.E., Stone, P. (eds.) Proceedings of the Twenty-Eighth AAAI Conference on Artificial Intelligence, Québec City, Québec, Canada, 27–31 July 2014, pp. 712–720. AAAI Press (2014)
13. Kaczmarczyk, A., Faliszewski, P.: Algorithms for destructive shift bribery. Auton. Agent. Multi-Agent Syst. **33**(3), 275–297 (2019). https://doi.org/10.1007/s10458-019-09403-3
14. Knop, D., Koutecký, M., Mnich, M.: Voting and bribing in single-exponential time. In: Vollmer, H., Vallée, B. (eds.) 34th STACS, STACS 2017. LIPIcs, Hannover, Germany, 8–11 March 2017, vol. 66, pp. 46:1–46:14. Schloss Dagstuhl - Leibniz-Zentrum für Informatik (2017)
15. Lin, A.: The complexity of manipulating k-approval elections. In: Filipe, J., Fred, A.L.N. (eds.) ICAART 2011 - Proceedings of the 3rd ICAART, Volume 2 - Agents, Rome, Italy, 28–30 January 2011, pp. 212–218. SciTePress (2011)
16. McLoughlin, A.M.: The complexity of computing the covering radius of a code. IEEE Trans. Inf. Theory **30**(6), 800–804 (1984)
17. Qiu, X., Kern, W.: Improved approximation algorithms for a bilevel knapsack problem. Theor. Comput. Sci. **595**, 120–129 (2015)
18. Wang, Z., Xing, W., Fang, S.: Two-group knapsack game. Theor. Comput. Sci. **411**(7–9), 1094–1103 (2010)
19. Yin, Y., Vorobeychik, Y., An, B., Hazon, N.: Optimally protecting elections. In: Kambhampati, S. (ed.) Proceedings of the 25th IJCAI, IJCAI 2016, New York, NY, USA, 9–15 July 2016, pp. 538–545. IJCAI/AAAI Press (2016)

Coding with Noiseless Feedback
over the Z-Channel

Christian Deppe[1], Vladimir Lebedev[2], Georg Maringer[1],
and Nikita Polyanskii[1(✉)]

[1] Institute for Communications Engineering, Technical University of Munich,
Munich, Germany
{christian.deppe,georg.maringer,nikita.polianskii}@tum.de
[2] Kharkevich Institute for Information Transmission Problems,
Russian Academy of Sciences, Moscow, Russia
lebedev37@mail.ru

Abstract. In this paper, we consider encoding strategies for the
Z-channel with noiseless feedback. We analyze the asymptotic case where
the maximal number of errors is proportional to the blocklength, which
goes to infinity. Without feedback, the asymptotic rate of error-correcting
codes for the error fraction $\tau \geq 1/4$ is known to be zero. It was also proved
that using the feedback a non-zero asymptotic rate can be achieved for
the error fraction $\tau < 1/2$. In this paper, we give an encoding strategy
that achieves the asymptotic rate $(1+\tau)(1 - h(\tau/(1+\tau)))$, which is positive for all $\tau < 1$. Additionally, we state an upper bound on the maximal
asymptotic rate of error-correcting codes for the Z-channel.

Keywords: Coding with feedback · Z channel · Encoding algorithm

1 Introduction

In optical communications and other digital transmission systems the ratio
between probability of errors of type $1 \to 0$ and $0 \to 1$ can be large [1]. Practically, one can assume that only one type of error can occur. These channels are
called asymmetric. This paper addresses the problem of finding coding strategies
for the Z-channel with feedback. The Z-channel depicted in Fig. 1 is of asymmetric nature because it permits an error $1 \to 0$, whereas it prohibits an error $0 \to 1$.
Transmission is referred to as being error-free if the output symbol matches the
input symbol of the respective symbol transmission.

We are considering a combinatorial setting in this paper. In this setting,
we limit the fraction of erroneous symbols by $\tau = t/n$, where n denotes the
blocklength and t the maximum number of errors within a block. This is in contrast to the probabilistic setting, in which the error probability of the channel
is fixed. Feedback codes achieving the capacity of the Z-channel in the probabilistic setting are considered in [2]. The figure of merit examined in this work
is the maximum asymptotic rate, written as $R(\tau)$ and also called capacity error

© Springer Nature Switzerland AG 2020
D. Kim et al. (Eds.): COCOON 2020, LNCS 12273, pp. 98–109, 2020.
https://doi.org/10.1007/978-3-030-58150-3_8

function [3], which we define to be the maximum rate at which information can be communicated over a channel error-free as the blocklength n goes to infinity in the aforementioned combinatorial setting.

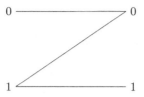

Fig. 1. Z-channel

The problem of finding encoding strategies for the Z-channel using noiseless feedback is equivalent to a variation of Ulam's game, the half-lie game. The first appearance of the half-lie game occurs in [4]. In this game for two players one player, referred to as Paul, tries to find an element $x \in \mathcal{M}$ by asking n yes-no questions which are of the form: Is $x \in A$ for some $A \subseteq \mathcal{M}$? The other player, the responder Carole, is allowed to lie at most t times if the correct answer to the question is yes. In comparison to the original Ulam game [5], Carole is not allowed to lie if the correct answer is no. Before Ulam proposed the game it was already described by Berlekamp [6] and by Renyi [7]. For a survey of results see [8]. It is known that for fixed t, the cardinality of the maximal set $\mathcal{M}$ is asymptotically $2^{n+t} t! n^{-t}$ for Paul to win the half-lie game. First this was shown for $t = 1$ in [9] and later generalized in [10,11] for arbitrary t. Due to the equivalence of the half-lie game and the coding problem with feedback for the Z-channel, the coding problem has been solved for an arbitrary but fixed number of errors for the asymptotic case when n goes to infinity.

For coding without feedback Bassalygo has shown in [12] that the maximal asymptotic rate for the Z-channel is equal to the one of the binary symmetric channel (BSC). Notably the results presented there show that the maximum asymptotic rate is zero for $\tau \geq 1/4$. It is worth noticing that the maximal asymptotic rate of error-correcting codes for the BSC with feedback was completely characterized by Berlekamp [6] and Zigangirov [13]. Their results show that the rate is positive for $\tau < 1/3$. For the construction of error correcting codes for asymmetric channels without feedback we refer to the work of Kløve [14].

By random arguments, it was proved in [15] that $R(\tau) > 0$ for $\tau < 1/2$. In [16] a feedback strategy based on the rubber method [3] was introduced to find an encoding strategy achieving a positive asymptotic rate for any $\tau < 1/2$. The corresponding lower bound on $R(\tau)$ is plotted in green on Fig. 2.

1.1 Our Contribution

In this paper, we develop new encoding algorithms for the Z-channel with feedback. In particular, we provide a family of error-correcting codes with the asymptotic rate $(1+\tau)(1 - h(\tau/(1+\tau)))$, which is positive for any $\tau < 1$ and improves the result from [16] in all but countable number of points. The corresponding lower bound on $R(\tau)$ is shown in blue in Fig. 2. Additionally, we prove an upper bound on $R(\tau)$, which is depicted as the dashed line.

1.2 Outline

The remainder of the paper is organized as follows. In Sect. 2, we formally define the problem of coding with feedback over the Z-channel and introduce some auxiliary terminology. In Sect. 3, we provide our encoding algorithm achieving a positive asymptotic rate for any fraction of errors $\tau < 1$, which gives rise to our main result, Theorem 1. An upper bound on the asymptotic rate is proposed in Sect. 4. Finally, Sect. 5 concludes the paper.

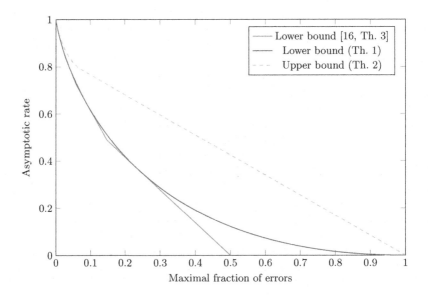

Fig. 2. Asymptotic rate of error-correcting codes for the Z-channel with noiseless feedback.

2 Coding with Feedback

A transmission scheme with feedback enables the sender to choose his encoding strategy in a way that makes use of the knowledge about previously received symbols at the receiver. This is shown in Fig. 3. Let $\mathcal{M}$ denote the set of possible messages. The sender chooses one of them, say m, which he wants to send to the receiver.

An encoding algorithm for a feedback channel of blocklength n is composed of a set of functions

$$c_i : \mathcal{M} \times \{0,1\}^{i-1} \to \{0,1\}, \quad i \in \{1,\ldots,n\}.$$

The encoding algorithm is then constructed as

$$c(m, y^{n-1}) = ((c_1(m), c_2(m, y_1), \ldots, c_n(m, y^{n-1}))), \tag{1}$$

where $y^k := (y_1, \ldots, y_k)$ with y_i being the ith received symbol. Moreover, the set of possible values for the received symbol y_i conditioned on c_i is defined by the channel, in our case the Z-channel depicted in Fig. 1.

Suppose that at most t errors occur within a block of length n. For $m \in \mathcal{M}$, we define the set of output sequences for an encoding strategy by

$$\mathcal{Y}_t^n(m) := \{y^n \in \{0,1\}^n : y_i \le c_i(m, y^{i-1}), \; d_H(y^n, c(m, y^{n-1})) \le t\} \;,$$

where $d_H(a, b)$ denotes the Hamming distance between the sequences a and b. Additionally, we denote the Hamming weight of a sequence a by $w_H(a)$.

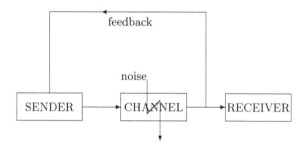

Fig. 3. Channel with feedback

Definition 1. *An encoding strategy (1) is called successful if*
$\mathcal{Y}_t^n(m_1) \cap \mathcal{Y}_t^n(m_2) = \emptyset$ *for all* $m_1, m_2 \in \mathcal{M}$ *with* $m_1 \ne m_2$.

Definition 2. *Let $M(n, t)$ denote the maximum number of messages in $\mathcal{M}$ for which there exists a successful encoding strategy. Such a strategy is said to be optimal.*

Definition 3. *For any τ with $0 \le \tau \le 1$, we define the maximal asymptotic rate of an optimal encoding strategy to be*

$$R(\tau) := \limsup_{n \to \infty} \frac{\log_2(M(n, \lceil \tau n \rceil))}{n}.$$

3 Lower Bound on $R(\tau)$

In this section we give a successful encoding strategy for the Z-channel, achieving an asymptotic rate $R(\tau)$ for any $\tau < 1$. This gives a lower bound on the maximal asymptotic rate of the Z-channel.

Theorem 1. *For any τ, $0 \leq \tau \leq 1$, we have*

$$R(\tau) \geq \underline{R}(\tau) := (1 + \tau) - (1 + \tau) \log(1 + \tau) + \tau \log \tau.$$

At the start of the message transmission the receiver only knows the set of possible messages $\mathcal{M}$. The sender chooses a message $m \in \mathcal{M}$. The goal of an encoding strategy is to reduce the number of possible messages from the receiver's viewpoint until only one message m is left. The encoding algorithm we provide divides the number of channel uses n into subblocks. Therefore, the encoding procedure is potentially divided into several steps. We denote the set of possible messages from the receiver's perspective after the ith step as $\mathcal{M}_{i+1}$ with $M_{i+1} = |\mathcal{M}_{i+1}|$, the number of remaining channel uses as n_{i+1} and the maximal number of possible errors t_{i+1}.

In the following the algorithm depicted in Fig. 4 is described. At every step, the sender (as well as the receiver) checks the following two properties

$$t_i = 0 \tag{2}$$

and

$$|\mathcal{M}_i| \leq n_i - t_i + 1. \tag{3}$$

Depending on which of them hold the sender chooses one out of three algorithms for encoding. If both conditions (2)–(3) do not hold, then the sender makes use of Partitioning Algorithm. This strategy tries to limit the set of possible messages by dividing the message space into subsets and sending the index of the subset containing the message. After this subblock transmission the sender and the receiver examine the conditions (2)–(3) and check whether the encoding and decoding strategies have to be adjusted for the remainder of the block.

If the property (2) is failed and the property (3) holds, then the sender uses the Weight Algorithm for information transmission in the remaining channel uses.

If the condition (2) is true, then the sender applies the Uncoded Algorithm for information transmission in the remaining channel uses. Below we describe the three algorithms required for our encoding strategy.

Partitioning Algorithm: This algorithm relies on the specific choice of positive integers δ and p with $\delta > p$. We partition the message space before the ith step $\mathcal{M}_i$ into $\binom{\delta}{p}$ subsets $\mathcal{M}_{i,k}$ of almost equal sizes

$$\mathcal{M}_i = \bigcup_{k=1}^{\binom{\delta}{p}} \mathcal{M}_{i,k}.$$

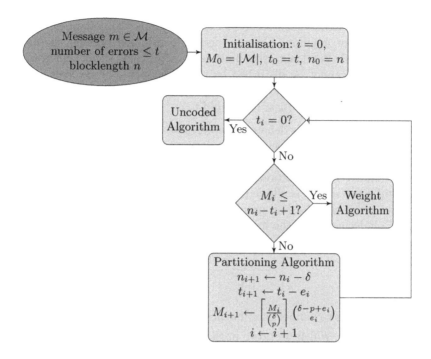

Fig. 4. Encoding algorithm for transmission over the Z-channel

The size of each group is either $\left\lceil M_i / \binom{\delta}{p} \right\rceil$, or $\left\lfloor M_i / \binom{\delta}{p} \right\rfloor$. The exact way in which the message space is to be partitioned is to be agreed between the sender and the receiver before the data transmission. Then the sender finds the index of the group containing the message and transmit this index using a subblock of length δ containing p ones. In this way the receiver can determine the number of errors inflicted by the channel within this subblock by counting the number of ones. There are $p + 1$ possible cases depending on the number of errors e_i within the respective subblock of the ith step.

If $e_i = p$ errors occur, the message space consistent with the outcome of the channel is not changed and the receiver obtains the information that $\mathcal{M}_{i+1} = \mathcal{M}_i$, $n_{i+1} = n_i - \delta$ and $t_{i+1} = t_i - p$.

When $e_i < p$ errors occur, there are $\binom{\delta-p+e_i}{e_i}$ subsets of messages $\mathcal{M}_{i,k}$ that are consistent with the outcome of the Z-channel. $\mathcal{M}_{i+1}$ is then equal to the union of these subsets. Therefore, the set of possible messages in accordance with the received δ symbols is reduced and we have $M_{i+1} \leq \left\lceil M_i / \binom{\delta}{p} \right\rceil \binom{\delta-p+e_i}{e_i}$. Moreover, the receiver and the sender obtain $n_{i+1} = n_i - \delta$ and $t_{i+1} = t_i - e_i$.

Weight Algorithm: The sender would like to transmit a message m' out of a given set $\mathcal{M}'$ using the channel n' times. We order the messages within this set by enumerating them: $\mathcal{M}' = \{m_0, m_1, \ldots, m_{|\mathcal{M}'|-1}\}$. The message m' then corresponds to one of the indices, say k. The sender transmits the symbol 1 over the channel until it has been received exactly k times. This happens at some point if a sufficient amount of channel uses is considered because the number of errors is limited. We denote this limit as t'. After that, the sender transmits 0-symbols which cannot be disturbed by the Z-channel. The receiver finds the Hamming weight w of the received sequence and outputs the message m_w. This strategy is successful, i.e., $m_k = m_w$, if $|\mathcal{M}'| \leq n' - t' + 1$.

Uncoded Algorithm: We denote the ordered set of possible messages as $\mathcal{M}' = \{m_0, m_1, \ldots, m_{|\mathcal{M}'|-1}\}$. The senders task is to send one of the messages, say m_k to the receiver by using the channel n' times. In order to do so, it sends the (standard) binary representation of the index k over the channel. This strategy is successful if the sender is allowed to use the channel at least $\lceil \log_2 \mathcal{M}' \rceil$ times.

Now we prove that for any proper choice of integers δ, p, k and t and real $\varepsilon > 0$, the sender can have the message set $\mathcal{M}$ of size at least

$$\left\lceil \frac{\binom{\delta}{p}}{\varepsilon} \right\rceil \frac{(1-\varepsilon)^k \binom{\delta}{p}^k}{\binom{\delta k - pk + t + p}{t+p}} - 1$$

for $n = \left\lceil \binom{\delta}{p}/\varepsilon \right\rceil + \delta k$ channel uses, having at most t errors. More formally, it is shown in Lemma 1, which we prove in the full version of the paper [17].

Lemma 1. *Let δ and p be positive integers such that $p < \delta$ and let $t \geq 0$. Let $\varepsilon > 0$ be fixed such that*

$$\gamma_e := (1-\varepsilon) \frac{\binom{\delta}{p}}{\binom{\delta-p+e}{e}} > 1, \quad \forall e \in \{0, \ldots, p-1\}.$$

We define $\gamma_p := 1$, $M_0 := \left\lceil \binom{\delta}{p}/\varepsilon \right\rceil$ and the set

$$\mathcal{S}_{(k,t,p)} := \left\{ (k_0, k_1, \ldots, k_p) \in \mathbb{N}_0^{p+1} : \sum_{i=0}^{p} k_i = k, \sum_{i=0}^{p} i k_i \leq t + p \right\}.$$

Then for any non-negative integers t and k such that $\delta k \geq t$, we have

$$M(M_0 + \delta k, t) \geq \left\lfloor M_0 \min_{\mathcal{S}_{(k,t,p)}} \prod_{e=0}^{p} \gamma_e^{k_e} \right\rfloor. \tag{4}$$

In particular, it follows that

$$M(M_0 + \delta k, t) \geq M_0 \frac{(1-\varepsilon)^k \binom{\delta}{p}^k}{\binom{\delta k - pk + t + p}{t+p}} - 1. \tag{5}$$

Remark 1. The set $\mathcal{S}_{(k,t,p)}$ includes $(k, 0, \ldots, 0)$. Thus, the minimization in (4) is well defined.

Proof of Theorem 1. Let us fix some positive $\tau < 1$. For any $\varepsilon_R > 0$ and small enough $\varepsilon_\tau > 0$, we shall prove the existence of a code of an arbitrary large blocklength and code rate at least $\underline{R}(\tau) - \varepsilon_R$ capable of correcting $\tau - \varepsilon_\tau$ fraction of errors.

In what follows, we vary positive integers k and δ with $k > \delta$. Define $t = \lceil \tau k \delta \rceil$, $p = \lfloor \delta(1/2 + \tau/2) \rfloor$, $M_0 = \lceil \binom{\delta}{p} / \varepsilon \rceil$ and $n = M_0 + \delta k$, where the real parameter ε is fixed and satisfies

$$0 < \varepsilon < \frac{1-\tau}{2} \le 1 - p/\delta,$$
$$0 < \underline{R}(\tau) + \log(1-\varepsilon) - 3\varepsilon_\tau. \tag{6}$$

Let δ_0 be such that for any $\delta \ge \delta_0(\varepsilon_\tau, \tau)$ and $k \ge \delta$, we have

$$\binom{\delta}{p} \ge 2^{\delta\left(h\left(\frac{1+\tau}{2}\right) - \varepsilon_\tau\right)} \tag{7}$$

and

$$\binom{\delta k - pk + t + p}{t + p} \le 2^{\delta k \frac{1+\tau}{2}\left(h\left(\frac{2\tau}{1+\tau}\right) + \varepsilon_\tau\right)}, \tag{8}$$

where the binary entropy function $h(x) := -x \log(x) - (1-x) \log(1-x)$. To prove the existence of such δ_0, we note that

$$\lim_{\delta \to \infty} \frac{p}{\delta} = \lim_{\delta \to \infty} \frac{\lfloor \delta(1/2 + \tau/2) \rfloor}{\delta} = \frac{1+\tau}{2},$$

and for $k \ge \delta$,

$$\lim_{\delta \to \infty} \frac{t + p}{\delta k - pk + t + p} = \frac{2\tau}{1+\tau},$$

and for any integers $u > v \ge 1$, the binomial coefficient $\binom{u}{v}$ satisfies

$$\sqrt{\frac{u}{8v(u-v)}} 2^{uh(v/u)} \le \binom{u}{v} \le \sqrt{\frac{u}{2\pi v(u-v)}} 2^{uh(v/u)}. \tag{9}$$

Then we take $k_0 = k_0(\delta, \tau, \varepsilon_\tau)$ such that for any $k \ge k_0$, the fraction of errors

$$\frac{t}{n} = \frac{t}{M_0 + \delta k} \ge \tau - \varepsilon_\tau$$

and the blocklength

$$n = M_0 + \delta k \le \delta k(1 + \varepsilon_\tau)$$

and

$$\frac{(1-\varepsilon)^k \binom{\delta}{p}^k}{\binom{\delta k - pk + t + p}{t + p}} \ge 2.$$

The latter can be achieved because of the choice of ε in (6) and large enough δ in (7)–(8). By Lemma 1, there exists a feedback error-correcting code of block-length $n = M_0 + \delta k$ and of size

$$M \geq M_0 \frac{(1-\varepsilon)^k \binom{\delta}{p}^k}{\binom{\delta k - pk + t + p}{t+p}} - 1 \geq \frac{(1-\varepsilon)^k \binom{\delta}{p}^k}{2\binom{\delta k - pk + t + p}{t+p}}, \qquad (10)$$

capable of correcting t errors when transmitted through the Z-channel. Thus, combining (7)–(10) yields

$$
\begin{aligned}
R(\tau - \varepsilon_\tau) &\geq \frac{\log M}{M_0 + \delta k} \\
&\geq \frac{k \log(1-\varepsilon) + \delta k \left(h\left(\frac{1+\tau}{2}\right) - \varepsilon_\tau - \frac{1+\tau}{2} h\left(\frac{2\tau}{1+\tau}\right) - \varepsilon_\tau \right) - 1}{\delta k (1 + \varepsilon_\tau)} \\
&= (1+\tau) \log\left(\frac{2}{1+\tau}\right) + \tau \log \tau - \varepsilon_R,
\end{aligned}
$$

where

$$\varepsilon_R \leq -\log(1-\varepsilon) + 3\varepsilon_\tau + \frac{1}{\delta k}.$$

As ε and ε_τ can be taken as small as needed and δ and k can be arbitrary large, the statement of Theorem 1 follows. $\blacksquare$

4   Upper Bound on $R(\tau)$

In this section we establish an upper bound on the rate $R(\tau)$. This upper bound is close to our lower bound for small values of τ. We make use of an approach similar to the one in [11]. We take an encoding strategy and consider only messages $m \in \mathcal{M}$ such that any output sequence in $\mathcal{Y}_t^n(m)$ has a relatively large Hamming weight. For those messages, it is possible to derive a good lower bound on the size of $\mathcal{Y}_t^n(m)$. The upper bound on the set of possible messages is then obtained by a sphere-packing argument.

Theorem 2. *For any τ, $0 < \tau < 1$, we have*

$$R(\tau) \leq \overline{R}(\tau) := \min_{\substack{0 \leq \tau' \leq \tau}} \max_{\substack{0 \leq r \leq 1, \\ h(v) \leq 1 - vh\left(\min\left(\frac{\tau - \tau'}{v(1-\tau')}, \frac{1}{2}\right)\right)}} r,$$

where $v = v(r, \tau')$ is a real number such that $0 \leq v \leq 1/2$ and $h(v)(1 - \tau') = r$.

Proof. We fix τ and τ' fulfilling the inequalities $0 \leq \tau' < \tau \leq 1$ and define $t := \tau n$ and $t' := \tau' n$. Denote $R(\tau)$ by $\overline{r}$. Next we fix some $\varepsilon > 0$. We define $\overline{v} \in [0, 1/2]$ as the unique real number that satisfies $h(\overline{v})(1 - \tau') = \overline{r} - \varepsilon$. We define the set of output sequences of the encoding strategy when the encoder would like to transmit the message m and the channel output is zero for the first t' symbols to be

$$\mathcal{Y}_{t,t'}^n(m) := \{y^n \in \mathcal{Y}_t^n(m) : \ y_i = 0 \text{ for } i \in [t']\}.$$

For any real v with $0 \leq v \leq 1$, let $W(n, t', v)$ denote the set of all binary words x^n that have $x_i = 0$ for all $i \leq t'$ and the Hamming weight at most $v(n - t')$. For $n \to \infty$, we have that the cardinality of $W(n, t', \overline{v} - \varepsilon)$ is

$$|W(n, t', \overline{v} - \varepsilon)| = \sum_{i=0}^{(\overline{v}-\varepsilon)(n-t')} \binom{n - t'}{i} \leq 2^{(n-t')(h(\overline{v}-\varepsilon)+o(1))},$$

where we make use of the inequality (9). Thus, there is a large enough n_0 so that $|W(n, t', \overline{v} - \varepsilon)|$ is at most $2^{(n-t')h(\overline{v})-1}$ for any $n \geq n_0$. By Definition 3, there exists a sufficiently large integer $n > n_0$ such that we have an encoding function (1) for a set of messages $\mathcal{M}$ with $|\mathcal{M}| \geq 2^{n(\overline{r}-\varepsilon)}$. For simplicity of notation, we assume that $(n - t')(\overline{v} - \varepsilon)$ is an integer and equal to n'. Define the set of *good* messages, written as $\mathcal{M}_{good}$, that consists of $m \in \mathcal{M}$ such that the Hamming weight of any $y^n \in \mathcal{Y}_{t,t'}^n(m)$ is at least n'. Since $n \geq n_0$, we obtain that $|\mathcal{M}_{good}| \geq |\mathcal{M}| - 2^{(n-t')h(\overline{v})-1} \geq 2^{(n-t')h(\overline{v})-1}$, where we used the fact $h(\overline{v})(1 - \tau') = \overline{r} - \varepsilon$. Now we prove that for any message $m \in \mathcal{M}_{good}$, the size of $\mathcal{Y}_{t,t'}^n(m)$ is uniformly bounded from below as follows

$$|\mathcal{Y}_{t,t'}^n(m)| \geq \max_{0 \leq \hat{t} \leq \min(t-t', n')} \binom{n'}{\hat{t}}.$$

Let $\binom{[a]}{b}$ denote the set of all possible subsets of $[a]$ of size b. To show the above inequality, take an arbitrary $\hat{t}$ with $0 \leq \hat{t} \leq \min(t - t', n')$ and define the mapping $\phi : \binom{[n']}{\hat{t}} \to \mathcal{Y}_{t,t'}^n(m)$ that takes an arbitrary subset $\{i_1, \ldots, i_{\hat{t}}\} \in \binom{[n']}{\hat{t}}$ with $1 \leq i_1 < i_2 < \ldots < i_{\hat{t}} \leq n'$ and outputs $y^n \in \{0,1\}^n$ defined as

$$y_i := \begin{cases} 0 & \text{for } i \in [t'], \\ c_i(m, y^{i-1}) & \text{for } i \in J, \\ 1 - c_i(m, y^{i-1}) & \text{o/w}, \end{cases}$$

where $J := \bigcup_{k=0}^{\hat{t}} [j_k + 1, j_{k+1} - 1]$, $j_0 := t'$, $j_{\hat{t}+1} := n + 1$ and for $k \in [\hat{t}]$, j_k is the smallest j so that the Hamming weight $w_H(y^{j-1}, c_j(m, y^{j-1})) = i_k$. One can easily see that this y^n belongs to $\mathcal{Y}_{t,t'}^n(m)$ and for distinct $\{i_1, \ldots, i_{\hat{t}}\} \neq \{s_1, \ldots, s_{\hat{t}}\}$, the outputs $\phi(\{i_1, \ldots, i_{\hat{t}}\})$ and $\phi(\{s_1, \ldots, s_{\hat{t}}\})$ are different. As the sets of output sequences are mutually disjoint, we conclude with

$$|\mathcal{M}_{good}| \max_{0 \leq \hat{t} \leq \min(t-t', n')} \binom{n'}{\hat{t}} \leq 2^{n-t'}.$$

As n can be taken arbitrary large, letting $n \to \infty$ yields

$$(n - t')h(\overline{v}) + n'h\left(\min\left(\frac{t - t'}{n'}, \frac{1}{2}\right)\right) + o(n) \leq n - t'.$$

Recall that $n' = (n - t')(\overline{v} - \varepsilon)$. Since the above inequality is true for any $\varepsilon > 0$, we have

$$h(\overline{v}) \leq 1 - \overline{v}h\left(\min\left(\frac{\tau - \tau'}{\overline{v}(1 - \tau')}, \frac{1}{2}\right)\right).$$

■

5   Conclusion

In this paper, we discussed a new family of error-correcting codes for the Z-channel with noiseless feedback in the combinatorial setting. By providing an explicit construction, we showed that the maximal asymptotic rate $R(\tau)$ is positive for any $\tau < 1$. We believe that the lower bound on $R(\tau)$ presented in Theorem 1 is tight for all τ. Another natural question to ask is whether the channel capacity (probabilistic setting) of the Z-channel can be achieved by the same encoding algorithm.

Acknowledgment. Christian Deppe was supported by the Bundesministerium für Bildung und Forschung (BMBF) through Grant 16KIS1005. Vladimir Lebedev's work was supported by the Russian Foundation for Basic Research (RFBR) under Grant No. 19-01-00364 and by RFBR and JSPS under Grant No. 20-51-50007. Georg Maringer's work was supported by the German Research Foundation (Deutsche Forschungsgemeinschaft, DFG) under Grant No. WA3907/4-1. Nikita Polyanskii's research was supported in part by a German Israeli Project Cooperation (DIP) grant under grant no. KR3517/9-1.

References

1. Blaum, M.: Codes for Detecting and Correcting Unidirectional Errors. IEEE Computer Society Press, Washington, D.C. (1994)
2. Tallini, L.G., Al-Bassam, S., Bose, B.: Feedback codes achieving the capacity of the Z-channel. IEEE Trans. Inf. Theory **54**(3), 1357–1362 (2008)
3. Ahlswede, R., Deppe, C., Lebedev, V.: Non-binary error correcting codes with noiseless feedback, localized errors, or both. Ann. Eur. Acad. Sci. **1**, 285–309 (2005)
4. Rivest, R.L., Meyer, A.R., Kleitman, D.J., Winklmann, K., Spencer, J.: Coping with errors in binary search procedures. J. Comput. Syst. Sci. **20**(3), 396–404 (1980)
5. Ulam, S.M.: Adventures of a Mathematician. University of California Press, Berkeley (1991)
6. Berlekamp, E.R.: Block coding for the binary symmetric channel with noiseless, delayless feedback. In: Proceedings of the Symposium on Error Correcting Codes (1968)

7. Renyi, A.: On a problem of information theory. MTA Mat. Kut. Int. Kozl. **6**(B), 505–516 (1961)
8. Cicalese, F.: Fault-Tolerant Search Algorithms - Reliable Computation with Unreliable Information. Monographs in Theoretical Computer Science, An EATCS Series. Springer, Heidelberg (2013). https://doi.org/10.1007/978-3-642-17327-1
9. Cicalese, F., Mundici, D.: Optimal coding with one asymmetric error: below the sphere packing bound. In: Du, D.-Z.-Z., Eades, P., Estivill-Castro, V., Lin, X., Sharma, A. (eds.) COCOON 2000. LNCS, vol. 1858, pp. 159–169. Springer, Heidelberg (2000). https://doi.org/10.1007/3-540-44968-X_16
10. Dumitriu, I., Spencer, J.: A halfliar's game. Theoret. Comput. Sci. **313**(3), 353–369 (2004)
11. Spencer, J., Yan, C.H.: The halflie problem. J. Comb. Theory, Ser. A **103**(1), 69–89 (2003)
12. Bassalygo, L.A.: New upper bounds for error correcting codes. Prob. Inf. Transm. **1**(4), 32–35 (1965)
13. Zigangirov, K.: On the number of correctable errors for transmission over a binary symmetrical channel with feedback. Prob. Inf. Transm. **12**(2), 85–97 (1976)
14. Kløve, T.: Error correcting codes for the asymmetric channel. Department of Pure Mathematics, University of Bergen (1981)
15. D'yachkov, A.G.: Upper bounds on the error probability for discrete memoryless channels with feedback. Probl. Peredachi Informatsii **11**(4), 13–28 (1975)
16. Deppe, C., Lebedev, V., Maringer, G.: Bounds for the capacity error function for unidirectional channels with noiseless feedback. In: Proceedings of the IEEE International Symposium on Information Theory (2020). https://arxiv.org/abs/2001.09030
17. Deppe, C., Lebedev, V., Maringer, G., Polyanskii, N.: Coding with noiseless feedback over the Z-channel. https://arxiv.org/abs/2007.04026

Path-Monotonic Upward Drawings
of Graphs

Seok-Hee Hong[1(✉)] and Hiroshi Nagamochi[2]

[1] University of Sydney, Sydney, Australia
seokhee.hong@sydney.edu.au
[2] Kyoto University, Kyoto, Japan
nag@amp.i.kyoto-u.ac.jp

Abstract. In this paper, we introduce a new problem of finding an upward drawing of a given plane graph γ with a set $\mathcal{P}$ of paths so that each path in the set is drawn as a poly-line that is monotone in the y-coordinate. We present a sufficient condition for an instance $(\gamma, \mathcal{P})$ to admit such an upward drawing. We also present a linear-time algorithm to construct such a drawing, which is straight-line for a simple graph, or poly-line otherwise. Our results imply that every 1-plane graph admits an upward drawing.

1 Introduction

Upward planar drawings of digraphs are well studied problem in Graph Drawing [3]. In an upward planar drawing of a directed graph, no two edges cross and each edge is a curve monotonically increasing in the vertical direction. It was shown that an upward planar graph (i.e., a graph that admits an upward planar drawing) is a subgraph of a planar st-graph and admits a straight-line upward planar drawing [4,13], although some digraphs may require exponential area [3]. Testing upward planarity of a digraph is NP-complete [10]; a polynomial-time algorithm is available for an embedded triconnected digraph [2].

Upward embeddings and orientations of undirected planar graphs were studied in [6]. Computing bimodal and acyclic orientations of *mixed graphs* (i.e., graphs with undirected and directed edges) is known to be NP-complete [14], and upward planarity testing for embedded mixed graph is NP-hard [5]. Upward planarity can be tested in cubic time for mixed outerplane graphs, and linear-time for special classes of mixed plane triangulations [8].

A *monotone drawing* is a straight-line drawing such that for every pair of vertices there exists a path that monotonically increases with respect to some direction. In an upward drawing, each directed path is monotone, and such paths are monotone with respect to the same (vertical) line, while in a monotone drawing, each monotone path is monotone with respect to a different line in general. Algorithms for constructing planar monotone drawings of trees and biconnected planar graphs are presented [1].

Research supported by ARC Discovery Project. For omitted proofs, see [12].

D. Kim et al. (Eds.): COCOON 2020, LNCS 12273, pp. 110–122, 2020.
https://doi.org/10.1007/978-3-030-58150-3_9

In this paper, we introduce a new problem of finding an upward drawing of a given plane graph γ together with a set $\mathcal{P}$ of paths so that each path in the set is drawn as a poly-line that is monotone in the y-coordinate. Let $\gamma = (V, E, F)$ be a plane graph and D be an upward drawing of γ. We call D *monotonic to a path* P of (V, E) if D is upward in the y-coordinate and the drawing induced by path P is y-monotone. We call D *monotonic to a set of paths* $\mathcal{P}$ if D is monotonic to each path in $\mathcal{P}$. More specifically, we initiate the following problem.

Path-monotonic Upward Drawing
Input: A connected plane graph γ, a set $\mathcal{P}$ of paths of length at least 2 and two outer vertices s and t.
Output: An (s, t)-upward drawing of γ that is monotonic to $\mathcal{P}$.

We present a sufficient condition for an instance $(\gamma, \mathcal{P})$ to admit an (s, t)-upward drawing of γ that is monotonic to $\mathcal{P}$ for any two outer vertices $s, t \notin V_{\mathrm{inl}}(\mathcal{P})$ (see Theorem 1). We also present a linear-time algorithm to construct such a drawing, which is straight-line for a simple graph, or poly-line otherwise.

Then we apply the result to a problem of finding an upward drawing of a non-planar embedding of a graph (Theorem 2), and prove that every 1-plane graph (i.e., a graph embedded with at most one crossing per edge) admits an (s, t)-upward poly-line drawing (Corollary 1). Note that there is a 1-plane graph that admits no straight-line drawing [17], and there is a 2-plane graph with three edges that admits no upward drawing.

Figure 1(a) shows an instance $(\gamma, \mathcal{P})$ with $\mathcal{P} = \{P_1 = (v_6, u_1, v_2), P_2 = (v_1, u_1, v_5), P_3 = (v_3, u_2, v_4), P_4 = (v_3, u_3, u_4, v_9), P_5 = (v_{11}, u_5, u_4, v_8), P_6 = (v_{10}, u_5, u_3, v_7), P_7 = (v_{10}, u_6, u_4, v_7), P_8 = (v_{12}, u_7, v_{14}), P_9 = (v_{10}, u_7, v_{13})\}$. Figure 1(b) shows an (s, t)-upward drawing monotonic to $\mathcal{P}$ such that each path is drawn as a poly-line monotone in the y-coordinate for $s = v_5$ and $t = v_8$.

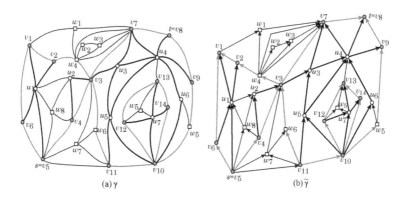

(a) γ (b) $\widetilde{\gamma}$

Fig. 1. (a) plane graph γ with a path set $\mathcal{P}$ and a cycle set $\mathcal{C}$, where the edges in paths in $\mathcal{P}$ (resp., cycles $\mathcal{C}$) are depicted with black thick lines (resp., gray thick lines), and the vertices in V_{inl} (resp., V_{end} and $V \setminus V_{\mathrm{inl}} \cup V_{\mathrm{end}}$) are depicted with white circles (resp., gray circles and white squares); (b) $(s = v_5, t = v_8)$-upward poly-line drawing monotonic to $\mathcal{P}$.

2   Preliminaries

Graphs. In this paper, a graph stands for an undirected multiple graph without self-loops. A graph with no multiple edges is called *simple*. Given a graph $G = (V, E)$, the vertex and edge sets are denoted by $V(G)$ and $E(G)$, respectively.

A path P that visits vertices $v_1, v_2, \ldots, v_{k+1}$ in this order is denoted by $P = (v_1, v_2, \ldots, v_{k+1})$, where vertices v_1 and v_{k+1} are called the *end-vertices*. Paths and cycles are simple unless otherwise stated.

A path with end-vertices $u, v \in V$ is called a u, v-path. A u, v-path that is a subpath of a path P is called the *sub-u, v-path* of P. Denote the set of end-vertices (resp., internal vertices) of all paths in a set $\mathcal{P}$ of paths by $V_{\mathrm{end}}(\mathcal{P})$ (resp., $V_{\mathrm{inl}}(\mathcal{P})$), which is written as $V_{\mathrm{end}}(P)$ (resp., $V_{\mathrm{inl}}(P)$) for $\mathcal{P} = \{P\}$.

Let G be a graph with a vertex set V with $n = |V|$ and an edge set E, and $N_G(v)$ denote the set of neighbors of a vertex v in G. Let X be a subset of V, and $G[X]$ denote the subgraph of G induced by the vertices in X. We denote by $N_G(X)$ the set of neighbors of X; i.e., $N_G(X) = \cup_{v \in X} N_G(v) \setminus X$. A connected component H of G may be denoted with the vertex subset $V(H)$ for simplicity.

For two distinct vertices $a, b \in V$, a bijection $\rho : V \to \{1, 2, \ldots, n\}$ is called an *st-numbering* if $\rho(a) = 1$, $\rho(b) = n$, and each vertex $v \in V \setminus \{a, b\}$ has a neighbor $v' \in N_G(v)$ with $\rho(v') < \rho(v)$ and a neighbor $v'' \in N_G(v)$ with $\rho(v) < \rho(v'')$. It is possible to find an *st*-numbering of a given graph with designated vertices a and b (if one exists) in linear time using depth-first search [7,16]. A biconnected graph admits an *st*-numbering for any specified vertices a and b.

Digraphs. Let $G = (V, E)$ be a digraph. The *indegree* (resp., *outdegree*) of a vertex $v \in V$ in G is defined to be the number of edges whose head is v (resp., whose tail is v). A *source* (resp., *sink*) is defined to be a vertex of indegree (resp., outdegree) 0. When G has no directed cycle, it is called *acyclic*. A digraph with n vertices is acyclic if and only if it admits a *topological ordering*, i.e., a bijection $\tau : V \to \{1, 2, \ldots, n\}$ such that $\tau(u) < \tau(v)$ for any directed edge (u, v).

We define an *orientation* of a graph $G = (V, E)$ to be a digraph $\widetilde{G} = (V, \widetilde{E})$ obtained from the graph by replacing each edge uv in G with one of the directed edge (u, v) or (v, u). A *bipolar orientation* (or *st-orientation*) of a graph is defined to be an acyclic digraph with a single source s and a single sink t [9,15], where we call such a bipolar orientation an (s, t)-*orientation*. A graph has a bipolar orientation if and only if it admits an *st*-numbering. Figure 1(b) illustrates an (s, t)-orientation for $s = v_5$ and $t = v_8$.

Lemma 1. *For any vertices s and t in a biconnected graph G possibly with multiple edges, an (s, t)-orientation $\widetilde{G}$ of G can be constructed in linear time.*

We call an orientation $\widetilde{G}$ of G *compatible* to a set $\mathcal{P}$ of paths in G if each path in $\mathcal{P}$ is directed from one end-vertex to the other in $\widetilde{G}$. The orientation in Fig. 1(b) is compatible to the path set $\mathcal{P}$.

Embeddings. An embedding Γ of a graph (or a digraph) $G = (V, E)$ is a representation of G (possibly with multiple edges) in the plane, where each vertex in V is a point and each edge $e \in E$ is a curve (a Jordan arc) between the points representing its end-vertices. We say that two edges *cross* if they have a point in common, called a *crossing*, other than their endpoints.

To avoid pathological cases, standard non-degeneracy conditions apply: (i) no edge contains any vertex other than its endpoints; (ii) no edge crosses itself; (iii) no two edges meet tangentially; and (iv) two edges cross at most one point, and two crossing edges share no end-vertex (where two edges may share the two end-vertices). In this paper, we allow three or more edges to share the same crossing. An edge that does not cross any other edge is called *crossing-free*.

Let Γ be an embedding of a graph (or digraph) $G = (V, E)$. We call Γ a *poly-line drawing* if each edge $e \in E$ is drawn as a sequence of line segments. The point where two consecutive line segments meet is called a *bend*. We call a poly-line drawing a *straight-line drawing* if it has no bend.

We call a curve in the xy-plane *y-monotone* if the y-coordinate of the points in the curve increases from one end of the curve to the other. We call Γ an *upward drawing* if (i) there is a direction d to be defined as the y-coordinate such that the curve for each edge $e \in E$ is y-monotone; and (ii) when G is a digraph, the head of e has a larger y-coordinate than that of the tail of e.

For two vertices $s, t \in V$, we call Γ an *(s, t)-upward drawing* if Γ is upward in the y-coordinate and the y-coordinate of s (resp., t) in Γ is uniquely minimum (resp., maximum) among the y-coordinates of vertices in Γ. Figure 1(b) shows an example of an (s, t)-upward poly-line drawing with $s = v_5$ and $t = v_8$.

Plane Graphs. An embedding of a graph G with no crossing is called a *plane graph* and is denoted by a tuple (V, E, F) of a set V of vertices, a set E of edges and a set F of faces. We call a plane graph *pseudo-simple* if it has no pair of multiple edges e and e' such that the cycle formed by e and e' encloses no vertex.

Let $\gamma = (V, E, F)$ be a plane graph. We say that two paths P and P' in γ *intersect* if they are edge-disjoint and share a common internal vertex w, and the edges uw and wv in P and $u'w$ and wv' in P' incident to w appear alternately around w (i.e., in one of the orderings u, u', v, v' and u, v', v, u').

Let C be a cycle in γ. Define $V_{\text{enc}}(C; \gamma)$, $E_{\text{enc}}(C; \gamma)$ and $F_{\text{enc}}(C; \gamma)$ to be the sets of vertices $v \in V \setminus V(C)$, edges $e \in E \setminus E(C)$ and inner faces $f \in F$ that are enclosed by C. The *interior subgraph* $\gamma[C]_{\text{enc}}$ induced from γ by C is defined to be the plane graph $(V(C) \cup V_{\text{enc}}(C; \gamma), E(C) \cup E_{\text{enc}}(C; \gamma), F_{\text{enc}}(C; \gamma) \cup \{f_C\})$, where f_C denotes the new outer face whose facial cycle is C. The *exterior subgraph* induced from γ by C is defined to be the plane graph $(V \setminus V_{\text{enc}}(C; \gamma), E \setminus E_{\text{enc}}(C; \gamma), F \cup \{f_C\} \setminus F_{\text{enc}}(C; \gamma))$, where f_C denotes the new inner face whose facial cycle is C. Note that when γ is biconnected, the graph $\gamma[C]_{\text{enc}}$ remains biconnected, since every two vertices $u, v \in V \setminus V_{\text{enc}}(C; \gamma)$ have two internally disjoint paths without using edges in $E_{\text{enc}}(C; \gamma)$.

We say that two cycles C and C' in γ *intersect* if $F_{\text{enc}}(C; \gamma) \setminus F_{\text{enc}}(C'; \gamma) \neq \emptyset \neq F_{\text{enc}}(C'; \gamma) \setminus F_{\text{enc}}(C; \gamma)$. Let $\mathcal{C}$ be a set of cycles in γ. We call $\mathcal{C}$ *inclusive* if no two cycles in $\mathcal{C}$ intersect. When $\mathcal{C}$ is inclusive, the *inclusion-forest* of $\mathcal{C}$ is defined to be a forest $\mathcal{I} = (\mathcal{C}, \mathcal{E})$ of a disjoint union of rooted trees such that (i) the cycles in $\mathcal{C}$ are regarded as the vertices of $\mathcal{I}$; and (ii) a cycle C is an ancestor of a cycle C' in $\mathcal{I}$ if and only if $F_{enc}(C'; \gamma) \subseteq F_{enc}(C; \gamma)$. Let $\mathcal{I}(\mathcal{C})$ denote the inclusion-forest of $\mathcal{C}$.

An *st-planar graph* is defined to be a bipolar orientation of a plane graph for which both the source and the sink of the orientation are on the outer face of the graph. A directed acyclic graph G has an upward planar drawing if and only if G is a subgraph of an *st*-planar graph [4,13]. Every *st*-planar graph can have a *dominance drawing* [3], in which for every two vertices u and v there exists a path from u to v if and only if both coordinates of u are smaller than the corresponding coordinates of v. The following result is known.

Lemma 2. [3] (i) *Every simple st-planar graph admits an upward straight-line drawing;*
(ii) *Every st-planar graph with multiple edges admits an upward poly-line drawing, where each multiple edge has at most one bend; and*
(iii) *Such a drawing in* (i) *and* (ii) *can be constructed in linear time.*

We see that (ii) follows from (i) by subdividing each multiple directed edge (u, v) into a directed path (u, w, v) with a new vertex w to obtain a simple *st*-planar graph. Figure 1(b) illustrates an example of an *st*-planar graph.

3   Path-Monotonic Upward Drawing

When a plane graph γ has a pair of multiple edges e and e' that encloses no vertex in the interior, we can ignore one of these edges (say e') to find an upward drawing of γ, because we can draw e' along the drawing of e in any upward drawing of the resulting plane graph. In what follows, we assume that a given plane graph is pseudo-simple.

We say that two paths P and P' in a plane graph γ are *1-independent* if they intersect at a common internal vertex and have no other common vertex; or they have no common vertex that is an internal vertex of one of them (where they may share at most two vertices that are end-vertices to both paths). We call a set $\mathcal{P}$ of paths in γ *1-independent* if any two paths in $\mathcal{P}$ are 1-independent.

In this paper, we present a sufficient condition for an instance $(\gamma, \mathcal{P})$ to admit an (s, t)-upward drawing of γ that is monotonic to $\mathcal{P}$ for any two outer vertices $s, t \notin V_{inl}(\mathcal{P})$. We also present a linear-time algorithm to construct such a drawing. The main contribution of this paper is summarized in the following main theorem.

Theorem 1. *Let $\gamma = (G = (V, E), F)$ be a pseudo-simple connected plane graph and $\mathcal{P}$ be a set of paths of length at least 2 in G, where V_{inl} denotes the set of internal vertices in paths in $\mathcal{P}$. If the following conditions hold, then any pair of outer vertices $s, t \notin V_{inl}$ admits an (s, t)-upward (straight-line, if γ is simple) drawing D monotonic to $\mathcal{P}$, which can be computed in linear time:*
(i) *$\mathcal{P}$ is 1-independent; and*
(ii) *There is no pair of a path $P \in \mathcal{P}$ and a cycle K with $|V(K) \setminus V_{inl}| \leq 1$ such that K encloses an end-vertex of P and the internal vertices of P and the*

vertices in $V(K) \cap V_{\mathrm{inl}}$ belong to the same component of the subgraph $G[V_{\mathrm{inl}}]$ induced from G by V_{inl}.

We assume that the boundary of γ forms a cycle C^o such that $V(C^o) \cap V_{\mathrm{inl}} = \emptyset$; if necessary, add two new outer edges $e_{s,t}$ and $e'_{s,t}$ joining the two outer vertices s and t to form a new outer facial cycle C^o of length 2. In what follows, we assume that the boundary of a given connected planar graph γ forms a cycle.

We prove Theorem 1 by showing that every instance satisfying the conditions of the theorem admits an (s,t)-orientation compatible to $\mathcal{P}$, which implies that the instance admits an (s,t)-upward straight-line (resp., poly-line) drawing monotonic to $\mathcal{P}$ by Lemma 2. To prove the existence of such an (s,t)-orientation compatible to $\mathcal{P}$, we show that Theorem 1 is reduced to the following case.

Lemma 3. *Let* $\gamma = (G = (V,E), F)$ *be a pseudo-simple connected plane graph and* $\mathcal{P}$ *be a set of paths of length at least 2 in* G, *where* V_{inl} *denotes the set of internal vertices in paths in* $\mathcal{P}$. *If the following conditions hold, then any pair of outer vertices* $s, t \notin V_{\mathrm{inl}}$ *admits an* (s,t)-*orientation* $\widetilde{\gamma}$ *of* γ *compatible to* $\mathcal{P}$, *which can be computed in linear time:*

(i) $\mathcal{P}$ *is 1-independent; and*

(ii) *For the set* $\{V_i \subseteq V_{\mathrm{inl}} \mid i = 1, 2, \ldots, p\}$ *of components in* $G[V_{\mathrm{inl}}]$ *and the partition* $\{\mathcal{P}_i \mid i = 1, 2, \ldots, p\}$ *of* $\mathcal{P}$ *such that* $V_{\mathrm{inl}}(\mathcal{P}_i) \subseteq V_i$, *there exists an inclusive set* $\mathcal{C} = \{C_1, C_2, \ldots, C_p\}$ *of edge-disjoint cycles such that, for each* $i = 1, 2, \ldots, p$, $V_i \subseteq V_{\mathrm{enc}}(C_i; \gamma)$ *and* $V_{\mathrm{end}}(\mathcal{P}_i) \subseteq V(C_i) \subseteq V \setminus V_{\mathrm{inl}}$.

The instance in Fig. 1(a) has three components $V_1 = \{u_1, u_2\}$, $V_2 = \{u_3, u_4, u_5, u_6\}$ and $V_3 = \{u_7\}$ in $G[V_{\mathrm{inl}}]$. The instance admits a cycle set $\mathcal{C} = \{C_1 = (v_1, v_2, w_4, v_3, v_4, v_5, v_6), C_2 = (v_3, v_7, v_8, v_9, w_5, v_{10}, v_{11}, w_6), C_3 = (v_{10}, v_{12}, v_{13}, v_{14})\}$, which satisfies the condition of Lemma 3. Figure 1(b) illustrates an (s,t)-orientation $\widetilde{\gamma}$ of γ in Fig. 1(a) that is compatible to $\mathcal{P}$.

We prove in Sect. 5 that a given instance of Theorem 1 can be augmented to a plane graph so that the condition of Lemma 3 is satisfied.

4   Bipolar Orientation on Plane Graphs

This section presents several properties on bipolar orientations in plane graphs, which will be the basis to our proof of Lemma 3. Let $g : V \to \mathbb{R}$ be a vertex-weight function in a graph $G = (V, E)$, where $\mathbb{R}$ denote the set of real numbers. We say that g is *bipolar* (or (a,b)-*bipolar*) to a subgraph $G' = (V', E')$ of G if (i) $g(u) \neq g(v)$ for the end-vertices u and v of each edge $e = uv \in E'$; (ii) V' contains a vertex pair (a, b) such that $g(a) < g(v) < g(b)$ for all vertices $v \in V' \setminus \{a, b\}$; and (iii) each vertex $v \in V' \setminus \{a, b\}$ has a neighbor $u \in N_{G'}(v)$ with $g(u) < g(v)$ and a neighbor $w \in N_{G'}(v)$ with $g(v) < g(w)$.

Observe that an (a, b)-bipolar function g to a graph G is essentially equivalent to an st-numbering of G in the sense that it admits an st-numbering $\sigma : V(G) \to \{1, 2, \ldots, |V(G)|\}$ of G such that $\sigma(a) = 1$, $\sigma(b) = |V(G)|$ and $\sigma(u) < \sigma(v)$ holds for any pair of vertices $u, v \in V$ with $g(u) < g(v)$. We observe that any bipolar function in a plane graph is bipolar to every cycle in the next lemma.

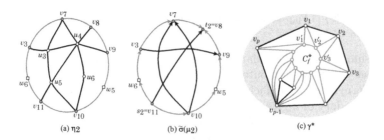

Fig. 2. (a) mesh graph $\eta_2 = (C_2, P_2)$ induced from the instance γ in Fig. 1(a) with cycle C_2; an instance satisfying the condition of Lemma 3: (b) $(s_2 = v_{11}, t_2 = v_8)$-orientation $\widetilde{\sigma}(\mu_2)$ of the split mesh graph $\sigma(\mu_2)$; (c) sun augmentation γ^*.

Lemma 4. *For a biconnected graph $G = (V, E)$, let $g : V \to \mathbb{R}$ be a function (s, t)-bipolar to G. If G admits a plane graph $\gamma = (V, E, F)$, then the boundary of each face $f \in F$ forms a cycle C_f and g is bipolar to C_f.*

The next lemma states that a bipolar orientation of a plane graph can be obtained from bipolar orientations of the interior and exterior subgraphs of a cycle.

Lemma 5. *For a biconnected plane graph $\gamma = (V, E, F)$ and a cycle C of the graph (V, E), let γ_C (resp., $\gamma_{\overline{C}}$) denote the interior (resp., exterior) subgraph of γ by C. For two outer vertices s and t of γ, let $\widetilde{\gamma_C}$ be an (s, t)-orientation of γ_C. Then the orientation $\widetilde{C}$ restricted from $\widetilde{\gamma_C}$ to C is an (a, b)-orientation of C for some $a, b \in V(C)$, and for any (a, b)-orientation $\widetilde{\gamma_{\overline{C}}}$ of $\gamma_{\overline{C}}$, the orientation $\widetilde{\gamma}$ of γ obtained by combining $\widetilde{\gamma_C}$ and $\widetilde{\gamma_{\overline{C}}}$ is an (s, t)-orientation of γ.*

We now examine a special type of instances of Lemma 3.

Mesh Graph. A *mesh graph* is defined to be a pair $\mu = (\gamma, \mathcal{P})$ of a biconnected plane graph $\gamma = (V, E, F)$ and a 1-independent set $\mathcal{P}$ of paths in the graph (V, E) such that (i) γ consists of an outer facial cycle C and the paths in $\mathcal{P}$; and (ii) each path $P \in \mathcal{P}$ ends with vertices in C and has no internal vertex from C, where $V = V(C) \cup \bigcup_{P \in \mathcal{P}} V(P)$ and $E = E(C) \cup \bigcup_{P \in \mathcal{P}} E(P)$. We may denote a mesh graph $(\gamma, \mathcal{P})$ with an outer facial cycle C by $\mu = (C, \mathcal{P})$. Figure 2(a) illustrates an example of a mesh graph.

Let $\mu = (\gamma = (V, E, F), \mathcal{P})$ be a mesh graph with an outer facial cycle C. To find an orientation of μ compatible to $\mathcal{P}$, we treat each u, v-path $P \in \mathcal{P}$ as a single edge $e_P = uv$, which we call the *split edge* of P. The *split mesh graph* is defined to be the graph $\sigma(\mu)$ obtained from μ by replacing each path $P \in \mathcal{P}$ with the split edge e_P; i.e., $\sigma(\mu) = (V(C), E(C) \cup \{e_P \mid P \in \mathcal{P}\})$.

Let $\widetilde{\sigma(\mu)}$ be an orientation of the split mesh graph $\sigma(\mu)$. We say that $\widetilde{\sigma(\mu)}$ *induces* an orientation $\widetilde{\mu}$ of μ if each u, v-path $P \in \mathcal{P}$ is directed from u to v in $\widetilde{\mu}$ when e_P is a directed edge (u, v) in $\widetilde{\sigma(\mu)}$. Clearly $\widetilde{\mu}$ is compatible to $\mathcal{P}$. Figure 2(b) illustrates an (s, t)-orientation of the split mesh graph.

The next lemma states that an (s,t)-orientation of a mesh graph compatible to $\mathcal{P}$ can be obtained by computing an (s,t)-orientation of the split mesh graph.

Lemma 6. *For a mesh graph μ and an (s,t)-orientation $\widetilde{\sigma(\mu)}$ of the split mesh graph $\sigma(\mu)$, the orientation $\widetilde{\mu}$ of μ induced by $\widetilde{\sigma(\mu)}$ is an (s,t)-orientation of μ.*

5 Coating and Confiner

To prove that Theorem 1 implies Lemma 3, this section gives a characterization of a plane graph that can be augmented to a plane graph such that specified vertices are contained in some cycles. Let $\gamma = (G = (V,E), F)$ be a plane graph.

We call an inclusive set $\mathcal{C} = \{C_1, C_2, \ldots, C_p\}$ of edge-disjoint cycles in γ a *coating* of a family $\mathcal{X} = \{X_1, X_2, \ldots, X_p\}$ of subsets of V if for each $i = 1, 2, \ldots, p$, $V(C_i) \cap X = \emptyset$ and $V_{\mathrm{enc}}(C_i; \gamma) \supseteq X_i$. We say that a coating $\mathcal{C} = \{C_1, C_2, \ldots, C_p\}$ of $\mathcal{X}$ *covers* a given family $\{Y_1, Y_2, \ldots, Y_p\}$ of vertices if $V(C_i) \supseteq Y_i$ for each $i = 1, 2, \ldots, p$.

For disjoint subsets $S, T \subseteq V$ in γ such that the subgraph $G[S]$ induced by S is connected, we call a cycle K of G an (S,T)-*confiner* if $|V(K) \setminus S| \leq 1$ and the interior vertex set $V_{\mathrm{enc}}(K; \gamma)$ of K contains some vertex $t \in T$.

A *plane augmentation* of a plane graph $\gamma = (V, E, F)$ is defined to be a plane embedding $\gamma^* = (V^*, E^*, F^*)$ of a supergraph (V^*, E^*) of (V, E) such that the embedding obtained from γ^* by removing the additional vertices in $V^* \setminus V$ and edges in $E^* \setminus E$ is equal to the original embedding γ.

Sun Augmentation. Let $\gamma = (V, E, F)$ be a pseudo-simple connected plane graph such that the outer boundary is a cycle. We introduce *sun augmentation*, a method of augmenting γ into a pseudo-simple biconnected plane graph by adding new vertices and edges in the interior of some inner faces of γ.

For an inner face $f \in F$, let $W_f = (v_1, v_2, \ldots, v_p)$ denote the sequence of vertices that appear along the boundary in the clockwise order, where $p \geq 3$ since γ is pseudo-simple. For each inner face $f \in F$:

(i) create a new cycle $C_f^* = (v_1', v_2', \ldots, v_p')$ with p new vertices v_i', $i = 1, 2, \ldots, p$ in the interior of f so that the facial cycle of f encloses C_f^*; and

(ii) join each vertex v_i, $i = 1, 2, \ldots, p$ with v_i' and v_{i+1}' with new edges $e_i' = v_i v_i'$ and $e_i'' = v_i v_{i+1}'$, where we regard v_{p+1}' as v_1'; We call the new face whose set consists of the p new edges e_i', $i = 1, 2, \ldots, p$ a *core face* and call a vertex along a core face a *core vertex*.

Figure 2(c) illustrates how the sun augmentation γ^* is constructed.

The next lemma characterizes when a plane graph with two vertex subsets X and Y can be augmented such that a set of cycles contains vertices in Y without visiting any vertex in X.

Lemma 7. *For a pseudo-simple connected plane graph $\gamma = (G = (V,E), F)$ such that the boundary forms a cycle C^o and a subset $X \subseteq V \setminus V(C^o)$, let $\{X_i \subseteq$*

$X \mid i = 1, 2, \ldots, p\}$ *denote the set of components in* $G[X]$ *and* $Y_i \subseteq N_G(X_i)$, $i = 1, 2, \ldots, p$ *be subsets of* V, *where possibly* $Y_i \cap Y_j \neq \emptyset$ *for some* $i \neq j$.

Then γ *contains no* (X_i, Y_i)*-confiner for any* $i = 1, 2, \ldots, p$ *if and only if the sun augmentation* $\gamma^* = (V^*, E^*, F^*)$ *of* γ *contains a coating* $\mathcal{C}$ *of* $\{X_1, X_2, \ldots, X_p\}$ *that covers* $\{Y_1, Y_2, \ldots, Y_p\}$. *Moreover the following can be computed in linear time:* (i) *Testing whether* γ *contains an* (X_i, Y_i)*-confiner for some* $i = 1, 2, \ldots, p$; *and* (ii) *Finding a coating* $\mathcal{C}$ *of* $\{X_1, X_2, \ldots, X_p\}$ *that covers* $\{Y_1, Y_2, \ldots, Y_p\}$ *in* γ^* *when* γ *contains no* (X_i, Y_i)*-confiner for any* $i = 1, 2, \ldots, p$.

We show how the assumption in Lemma 3 is derived from the assumption of Theorem 1 using Lemma 7. Let $\{V_i \subseteq V_{\text{inl}} \mid i = 1, 2, \ldots, p\}$ denote the set of components in $G[V_{\text{inl}}]$ and $\mathcal{P}_i$, $i = 1, 2, \ldots, p$ denote the partition of $\mathcal{P}$ such that $V_{\text{inl}}(\mathcal{P}_i) \subseteq V_i$. We apply Lemma 7 to the plane graph γ in Theorem 1 by setting $X := V_{\text{inl}}$, $X_i := V_i$ and $Y_i := V_{\text{end}}(\mathcal{P}_i)$, $i = 1, 2, \ldots, p$. Note that $X \subseteq V \setminus V(C^o)$. We show from the assumption in Theorem 1 that γ has no (X_i, Y_i)-confiner for any $i = 1, 2, \ldots, p$.

To derive a contradiction, assume that γ has an (X_i, Y_i)-confiner K for some $i \in \{1, 2, \ldots, p\}$, where $V_{\text{enc}}(K; \gamma)$ of K contains an end-vertex $y \in Y_i = V_{\text{end}}(\mathcal{P}_i)$ of some path $P \in \mathcal{P}_i$. Since $|K| \geq 2$ and $|K \setminus X_i| \leq 1$, K contains a vertex $v \in K \cap X_i$. Now vertex v and the internal vertices of P belong to the same component $G[X_i] = G[V_i]$ of $G[X]$ in γ. This contradicts the assumption in Theorem 1. Hence the condition of Lemma 7 holds and the sun augmentation γ^* of γ admits a coating $\mathcal{C} = \{C_1, C_2, \ldots, C_p\}$ of $\{X_i = V_i \mid i = 1, 2, \ldots, p\}$ that covers $\{Y_i = V_{\text{end}}(\mathcal{P}_i) \mid i = 1, 2, \ldots, p\}$. We see that such a set $\mathcal{C}$ of cycles satisfies the condition of Lemma 3.

6   Algorithmic Proof

This section presents an algorithmic proof to Lemma 3.

For a pseudo-simple biconnected plane graph $\gamma = (V, E, F)$ and a 1-independent set $\mathcal{P}$ of paths of length at least 2, we are given a partition $\{\mathcal{P}_i \mid i = 1, 2, \ldots, p\}$ of $\mathcal{P}$ and an inclusive set $\mathcal{C} = \{C_1, C_2, \ldots, C_p\}$ of edge-disjoint cycles that satisfy the condition of Lemma 3. For the instance $(\gamma, \mathcal{P}, \mathcal{C})$ in Fig. 1(a), we obtain $\mathcal{P}_1 = \{P_1, P_2, P_3\}$, $\mathcal{P}_2 = \{P_4, P_5, P_6, P_7\}$, $\mathcal{P}_3 = \{P_8, P_9\}$ and $\mathcal{C} = \{C_1 = (v_1, v_2, w_4, v_3, v_4, v_5, v_6), C_2 = (v_3, v_7, v_8, v_9, w_5, v_{10}, v_{11}, w_6), C_3 = (v_{10}, v_{12}, v_{13}, v_{14})\}$.

Let $\mathcal{I} = (\mathcal{C}, \mathcal{E})$ denote the inclusion-forest of $\mathcal{C}$, and $\text{Ch}(C)$ denote the set of child cycles C' of each cycle $C \in \mathcal{C}$ in $\mathcal{I}$, where the cycle C is called the *parent cycle* of each cycle $C' \in \text{Ch}(C)$. We call a cycle $C \in \mathcal{C}$ that has no parent cycle a *root cycle* in $\mathcal{C}$, and let $\mathcal{C}_{\text{rt}}$ denote the set of root cycles in $\mathcal{C}$. For a notational simplicity, we assume that the indexing of $C_1, C_2, \ldots, C_p$ satisfies $i < j$ when C_i is the parent cycle of C_j.

Based on the inclusion-forest $\mathcal{I}$, we first decompose the entire plane graph γ into plane subgraphs γ_i, $i = 0, 1, \ldots, p$ as follows. Define γ_0 to be the plane graph

$\gamma - \cup_{C \in \mathcal{C}_{\mathrm{rt}}}(V_{\mathrm{enc}}(C; \gamma) \cup E_{\mathrm{enc}}(C; \gamma))$ obtained from γ by removing the vertices and edges in the interior of root cycles $C \in \mathcal{C}_{\mathrm{rt}}$. For each $i = 1, 2, \ldots, p$, define γ_i to be the plane graph $\gamma[C_i]_{\mathrm{enc}} - \cup_{C \in \mathrm{Ch}(C_i)}(V_{\mathrm{enc}}(C; \gamma) \cup E_{\mathrm{enc}}(C; \gamma))$ obtained from the interior subgraph $\gamma[C_i]_{\mathrm{enc}}$ by removing the vertices and edges in the interior of child cycles C of C_i.

For each cycle C_i, $i = 1, 2, \ldots, p$, we consider the mesh graph $\mu_i = (C_i, \mathcal{P}_i)$, where μ_i is a plane subgraph of γ_i. For each inner face f of μ_i, we consider the interior subgraph $\gamma_i[C_f]_{\mathrm{enc}}$ of the facial cycle C_f of f in γ_i, where we call an inner face f of μ_i *trivial* if C_f encloses nothing in γ_i; i.e., $V_{\mathrm{enc}}(C_f; \gamma_i) \cup E_{\mathrm{enc}}(C_f; \gamma_i) = \emptyset$. Let $F(\mu_i)$ denote the set of non-trivial inner faces f of μ_i.

We determine orientations of subgraphs γ_i by an induction on $i = 0, 1, \ldots, p$. For specified outer vertices $s, t \in V(C^o) \setminus V_{\mathrm{inl}}$, compute an (s, t)-orientation $\widetilde{\gamma_0}$ of γ_0 using Lemma 1. Consider the plane subgraph γ_i with $i \geq 1$, where we assume that a bipolar orientation $\widetilde{\gamma_j}$ of γ_j has been obtained for all $j < i$. Let k denote the index of the parent cycle C_k of C_i or $k = 0$ if C_i is a root cycle, where a bipolar orientation $\widetilde{\gamma_k}$ of γ_k has been obtained. In $\widetilde{\gamma_k}$, cycle C_i forms an inner facial cycle and the orientation restricted to the facial cycle C_i is a bipolar orientation, which is an (s_i, t_i)-orientation $\widetilde{C_i}$ for some vertices $s_i, t_i \in V(C_i)$ by Lemma 4. We determine an (s_i, t_i)-orientation of γ_i as follows:

Step (a): Compute an (s_i, t_i)-orientation $\widetilde{\mu_i}$ of the mesh graph $\mu_i = (C_i, \mathcal{P}_i)$;
Step (b): Extend the orientation $\widetilde{\mu_i}$ to the interior subgraph $\gamma_i[C_f]_{\mathrm{enc}}$ of each non-trivial inner face $f \in F(\mu_i)$.

At Step (a), we compute an (s_i, t_i)-orientation $\sigma(\mu_i)$ of the split mesh graph $\sigma(\mu_i)$ to obtain an (s_i, t_i)-orientation $\widetilde{\mu_i}$ using Lemma 6. For Step (b), we observe that orientation $\widetilde{\mu_i}$ is (s_f, t_f)-bipolar to the facial cycle C_f of f for some vertices $s_f, t_f \in V(C_f)$ by Lemma 4. We compute an (s_f, t_f)-orientation $\widetilde{\gamma_i[C_f]}_{\mathrm{enc}}$ of the interior subgraph $\gamma_i[C_f]_{\mathrm{enc}}$ induced from γ_i by C_f using Lemma 1. An (s_i, t_i)-orientation of γ_i is obtained from the (s_i, t_i)-orientation $\widetilde{\mu_i}$ and (s_f, t_f)-orientations $\widetilde{\gamma_i[C_f]}_{\mathrm{enc}}$ for all inner faces $f \in F(\mu_i)$.

We repeat the above procedure until $i = p$. Finally construct an orientation $\widetilde{\gamma}$ of γ by combining bipolar orientations $\widetilde{\gamma_i}$ of γ_i, $i = 0, 1, \ldots, p$. By Lemma 5, $\widetilde{\gamma}$ is an (s, t)-orientation, which is compatible to $\mathcal{P}$ by the construction of $\widetilde{\gamma}$. This proves the correctness of our algorithm for computing an (s, t)-orientation $\widetilde{\gamma}$ compatible to $\mathcal{P}$.

The inclusion-forest of an inclusive set $\mathcal{C}$ of edge-disjoint cycles can be constructed in linear time [11]. Constructing all plane subgraphs γ_i and face sets $F(\mu_i)$, $i = 1, 2, \ldots, p$ can be done in linear time, since we can find them such that each edge in γ is scanned a constant number of times. We see that a bipolar orientation of mesh graph μ_i or subgraph γ_i can be computed in time linear to the size of the graph by Lemmas 1 and 6. The total size of these graphs μ_i, $i = 1, 2, \ldots, p$ and γ_i, $i = 0, 1, \ldots, p$ is bounded by the size of input graph γ. Therefore the algorithm can be executed in linear time. This proves Lemma 3.

Figure 3 shows an execution of the algorithm applied to the instance $(\gamma, \mathcal{P}, \mathcal{C})$ in Fig. 1(a). Figures 3(b), (c) and (f) show mesh graphs μ_1, μ_2 and μ_3,

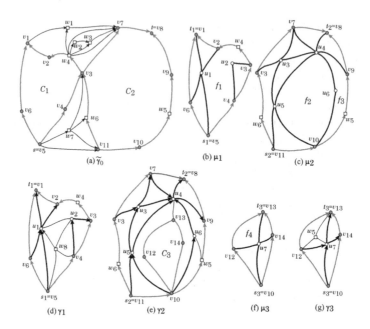

Fig. 3. (a) An $(s = v_5, t = v_7)$-orientation $\widetilde{\gamma}_0$ of γ_0; (b) Mesh graph $\mu_1 = (C_1, \mathcal{P}_1)$, where C_1 is directed as an $(s_1 = v_5, t_1 = v_1)$-orientation; (c) Mesh graph $\mu_2 = (C_2, \mathcal{P}_2)$, where C_2 is directed as an $(s_2 = v_{11}, t_2 = v_8)$-orientation; (d) Subgraph γ_1 with an (s_1, t_1)-orientation $\widetilde{\mu}_1$ of μ_1; (e) Subgraph γ_2 with an (s_2, t_2)-orientation $\widetilde{\mu}_2$ of μ_2; (f) Mesh graph $\mu_3 = (C_3, \mathcal{P}_3)$, where C_3 is directed as an $(s_3 = v_{10}, t_3 = v_{13})$-orientation; (e) Subgraph γ_3 with an (s_3, t_3)-orientation $\widetilde{\mu}_3$ of μ_3.

respectively for the instance in Fig. 1(a), where $\mathcal{C}_{rt} = \{C_1, C_2\}$, $\mathrm{Ch}(C_1) = \emptyset$, $\mathrm{Ch}(C_2) = \{C_3\}$, $F(\mu_1) = \{f_1\}$ ($C_{f_1} = (v_5, u_1, v_2, w_4, v_3, u_2, v_4)$), $F(\mu_2) = \{f_2, f_3\}$ ($C_{f_2} = (v_{10}, u_5, u_4, u_6)$, $C_{f_3} = (v_{10}, u_6, u_4, v_9, w_5)$), $F(\mu_3) = \{f_4\}$ ($C_{f_4} = (v_{12}, v_{13}, v_{14})$). Figures 3(a), (d), (e) and (g) show subgraphs γ_0, γ_1, γ_2 and γ_3, respectively for the instance in Fig. 1(a). Figure 1(b) shows an (s, t)-orientation of the instance γ in Fig. 1(a).

7   Upward Drawing of a Non-planar Embedding

Let Γ be a non-planar embedding of a graph G, and E^* denote the set of crossing edges. We define a *crossing-set* to be a maximal subset $E' \subseteq E^*$ such that every two edges $e, e' \in E'$ admit a sequence of edges $e_1, e_2, \ldots, e_p$, where $e_1 = e$, $e_p = e'$ and edges e_i and e_{i+1} cross for each $i = 1, 2, \ldots, p - 1$. Observe that E^* is partitioned into disjoint crossing-sets $E_1^*, E_2^*, \ldots, E_p^*$.

Let E_i^* be a crossing-set, and $\Gamma[E_i^*]$ denote the plane graph induced from Γ by the edges in E_i^*, where $\Gamma[E_i^*]$ is connected. We call E_i^* *outer* if the end-vertices of edges in E_i^* appear as outer vertices along the boundary of $\Gamma[E_i^*]$.

We apply Lemma 3 to the problem of finding an upward drawing of a non-planar embedding of a graph, and prove the following results.

Theorem 2. *Let Γ be a non-planar embedding of a graph G such that each crossing-set is outer, and let n_c denote the number of crossings in Γ. Then for any pair of outer vertices s and t in Γ, there is an (s,t)-upward drawing of Γ, and an upward poly-line drawing of Γ with $O(n + n_c)$ bends can be constructed in $O(n + n_c)$ time and space, where $n = |V(G)|$.*

Thomassen [17] showed that there are two forbidden subgraphs for a 1-plane graph (i.e., graph can be embedded at most one crossing per edge) to admit a straight-line drawing. Theorem 2 implies the following.

Corollary 1. *Every 1-plane graph admits an (s,t)-upward poly-line drawing for any outer vertices s and t, where each edge has at most one bend. Such a drawing can be constructed in linear time.*

References

1. Angelini, P., Colasante, E., Di Battista, G., Frati, F., Patrignani, M.: Monotone drawings of graphs. J. Graph Algorithms Appl. **16**(1), 5–35 (2012). https://doi.org/10.1007/978-3-642-18469-7_2
2. Bertolazzi, P., Di Battista, G., Liotta, G., Mannino, C.: Upward drawings of triconnected digraphs. Algorithmica **12**(6), 476–497 (1994). https://doi.org/10.1007/BF01188716
3. Di Battista, G., Eades, P., Tamassia, R., Tollis, I.G.: Graph Drawing: Algorithms for the Visualization of Graphs. Prentice Hall, Upper Saddle River (1998)
4. Di Battista, G., Tamassia, R.: Algorithms for plane representations of acyclic digraphs. Theoret. Comput. Sci. **61**, 175–198 (1988)
5. Binucci, C., Didimo, W., Patrignani, M.: Upward and quasi-upward planarity testing of embedded mixed graphs. Theor. Comput. Sci. **526**, 75–89 (2014)
6. Didimo, W., Pizzonia, M.: Upward embeddings and orientations of undirected planar graphs. J. Graph Algorithms Appl. **7**(2), 221–241 (2003)
7. Even, S., Tarjan, R.E.: Computing an st-numbering. Theoret. Comput. Sci. **2**(3), 339–344 (1976)
8. Frati, F., Kaufmann, M., Pach, J., Tóth, C., Wood, D.: On the upward planarity of mixed plane graphs. J. Graph Algorithms Appl. **18**(2), 253–279 (2014). https://doi.org/10.7155/jgaa.00322
9. de Fraysseix, H., Ossona de Mendez, P., Rosenstiehl, P.: Bipolar orientations revisited. Discr. Appl. Math. **56**(2–3), 157–179 (1995)
10. Garg, A., Tamassia, R.: On the computational complexity of upward and rectilinear planarity testing. SIAM J. Comput. **31**(2), 601–625 (1992)
11. Hong, S.-H., Nagamochi, H.: Re-embedding a 1-plane graph into a straight-line drawing in linear time. In: Hu, Y., Nöllenburg, M. (eds.) GD 2016. LNCS, vol. 9801, pp. 321–334. Springer, Cham (2016). https://doi.org/10.1007/978-3-319-50106-2_25
12. Hong, S., Nagamochi, H.: Path-monotonic upward drawings of plane graphs, Technical Report 2020–002. Kyoto University, Department of Applied Mathematics and Physics (2020)
13. Kelly, D.: Fundamentals of planar ordered sets. Discret. Math. **63**, 197–216 (1987)
14. Patrignani, M.: Finding bimodal and acyclic orientations of mixed planar graphs is NP-complete, RT-DIA-188-2011, August 2011

15. Rosenstiehl, P., Tarjan, R.E.: Rectilinear planar layouts and bipolar orientations of planar graphs. Discret. Comput. Geom. **1**(4), 343–353 (1986). https://doi.org/ 10.1007/BF02187706
16. Tarjan, R.E.: Two streamlined depth-first search algorithms. Fundamenta Informaticae **9**(1), 85–94 (1986)
17. Thomassen, C.: Rectilinear drawings of graphs. J. Graph Theory **12**(3), 335–341 (1988)

Seamless Interpolation Between Contraction Hierarchies and Hub Labels for Fast and Space-Efficient Shortest Path Queries in Road Networks

Stefan Funke[✉]

University of Stuttgart, Stuttgart, Germany
funke@fmi.uni-stuttgart.de

Abstract. We propose a conceptually simple, yet very effective extension of the highly popular Contraction Hierarchies (CH) speedup technique improving query times for shortest paths in road networks by one order of magnitude with very modest space overhead. Using our scheme we are able to answer queries on continental-sized road networks with more than half a billion edges in the microseconds range on standard workstation hardware. Previous approaches that are considerably faster than CH were only for shortest path *distance* queries (recovering the actual path required additional effort and space) or suffered from humongous space consumption hindering their practicality for large real-world road networks. Our approach can be interpreted as a seamless interpolation between Contraction Hierarchies and Hub Labels.

Keywords: Route planning · Contraction hierarchies · Hub labelling

1 Introduction

Computing the optimal path between given source and destination in a road network is not only the crucial primitive for well-known web-based or mobile navigation applications, but also the foundation of many more complex problems in transportation, logistics, or facility location. Without any preprocessing, Dijkstra's algorithm and slight variations of it are still considered state-of-the-art. Yet, with response times in the range of seconds on a country-sized network of around 20 million nodes, Dijkstra's variants are neither an option for web-services nor as subroutine in logistics applications.

This need for fast distance and shortest path queries in road networks has spurred astonishing progress in that area within the last 10–15 years. Here, the key idea is to first invest some time in a preprocessing phase computing auxiliary information about the network such that subsequent queries can be answered orders of magnitudes faster than plain Dijkstra's algorithm without compromising optimality of the result.

© Springer Nature Switzerland AG 2020
D. Kim et al. (Eds.): COCOON 2020, LNCS 12273, pp. 123–135, 2020.
https://doi.org/10.1007/978-3-030-58150-3_10

Amongst the first breakthrough results are techniques like *reach* [13], highway hierarchies [17] or arc flags [8]. All these techniques are based on a very aggressive pruning of the Dijkstra search space. Probably the most frequently used graph search pruning techniques in practice (e.g., used at Google or the Open Source Routing Machine OSRM [16]) are *contraction hierarchies (CH)* [12]. CH preprocessing on a country-sized network can typically be performed in few minutes and produces compact auxiliary information that allow path queries to be answered below one *millisecond* instead of seconds for Dijkstra's algorithm – an improvement of three orders of magnitude. But even faster techniques have been developed, if the main focus is on computing distances rather than the actual paths. Transit nodes [4,6,7] and hub-labels [2,3,14] allow for the exact answering of *distance* queries within few *microseconds* – another three orders of magnitudes faster. These methods abandon the paradigm of pruning the graph search and reduce the distance computation to few lookups in cleverly constructed distance arrays and tables – hence they are also sometimes called *distance oracles*. In practice, these approaches are often less attractive, though, due to their space consumption and their focus on *distance* queries. If the actual path is to be recovered, some additional time and space has to be invested.

The goal of this work is to bridge the gap between the ultrafast distance oracles and the slower pruned graph search based methods. In particular, we are interested in methods that have very small space overhead (compared to the size of the original network itself) and allow the easy retrieval of the optimal path like the methods based on pruned graph search. Yet, we want at least one order of magnitude speedup compared to approaches like CH.

1.1   Related Work

The idea of *reach* [13] is to associate with each edge e the length of the longest optimal path where e appears somewhere 'close to the middle'. Then during Dijkstra search from s to t edges of small reach can be discarded as long as source and target are far away from the current node under consideration. Combined with other ideas this allows for query times in the milliseconds range for country-sized road networks. Contraction Hierarchies [12] are created by repeated removal of nodes and inserting appropriate shortcut edges not to affect distances within the network. Which node to remove next is typically guided by some local heuristic (e.g. minimizing the number of inserted shortcuts), Making use of the shortcuts and the contraction order allows for query times around one millisecond. We will explain CH in more detail in Sect. 2. Highway Hierarchies [17] and Highway node routing [19] are based on similar ideas, but superseded by CH. CH has also been combined with other techniques, e.g., with arc flags in [9].

One of the first lookup based techniques was *transit node routing*. Here the idea is to identify a small set T of important nodes in the network, such that every 'long' optimal path contains at least one of these so-called *transit nodes*. In a preprocessing step, all pairwise distances between nodes in T are computed and stored, and for each node v in the network, all transit nodes encountered first on an optimal path starting from v are determined and stored (with their distance to v) as its *access nodes* $\mathcal{A}(v)$. For a query from s to t, one first has to decide whether the result will be a 'long' path. If so, the optimal distance can be determined by inspecting the (typically very small) access node sets $\mathcal{A}(s)$ and $\mathcal{A}(t)$ and their respective precomputed distances. If not, some backup scheme (e.g. CH) has to be used to determine the distance between s and t. Early incarnations of transit node routing like [7] employed a geometric notion of 'long', later, more efficient incarnations like [4] use more sophisticated notions which also required clever data structures (locality filters) to decide whether a query is 'long'. In any case, for 'long' paths it is not obvious at all how to not only return distances but actual paths without incurring a considerable overhead in time and space. Furthermore, there is the oddity that 'long' distances are typically returned much faster than 'short' distances via the local backup scheme. Nevertheless, for random source target queries, one can expect query times in the *microseconds range*. The other lookup based technique of hub labels (HL) [2] will be explained in more detail in Sect. 2. It also offers query times in the microseconds range but also at the cost of a very high space consumption and distance-only results. There has been considerable work on improving HL. For example, in [11], the authors have studied compression schemes to decrease the massive space requirements. In [15] different (hierarchical) HL construction schemes were discussed and evaluated (also on other graphs than road networks) and considerable improvements could be shown. Work along these lines is orthogonal to our results, though, as it could well be integrated with our scheme. See [5] for a comprehensive survey on the topic of route planning in transportation networks.

1.2 Contribution and Outline

In this paper we present a very simple and almost seamless interpolation between hub labels and contraction hierarchies. Depending on the additional space available, our scheme behaves more like hub labels (very fast, considerable space overhead) or more like contraction hierarchies (slower, little space overhead). Investing less space than that used by the original road network, we still obtain one order of magnitude of speedup compared to CH for continental-sized road networks with more than half a billion edges. Our scheme not only outputs distances but also paths in compressed CH representation. After recapitulating basics of CH as well as a CH-based HL, we show how to combine HL and CH to obtain a fast, space efficient, and extremely simple query scheme. We conclude with an experimental evaluation on continental-sized real-world road networks.

2 Preliminaries: Contraction Hierarchies and Hub Labels

Contraction Hierarchies. The contraction hierarchies approach [12] computes an overlay graph in which so-called shortcut edges span large sections of shortest paths. This reduces the hop length of optimal paths and therefore allows a variant of Dijkstra's algorithm to answer queries more efficiently.

The preprocessing is based on the so-called *node contraction* operation. Here, a node v as well as its adjacent edges are removed from the graph. In order not to affect shortest path distances between the remaining nodes, shortcut edges are inserted between neighbors u, w of v, if and only if uvw was a shortest path (which can easily be checked via a Dijkstra run). The cost of the new shortcut edge (u, w) is set to the summed costs of (u, v) and (v, w). During preprocessing all nodes are contracted in some order. The *level* of a node is the rank of a node in this order. In practice, simultaneous contraction of non-adjacent nodes is highly recommended, hence many nodes might have the same level.

Having contracted all nodes, the new graph $G^+(V, E^+)$ contains all original nodes and edges of G and additionally all shortcuts inserted during the contraction process. An edge $e = (v, w)$ – original or shortcut – is called *upward*, if the level of v is smaller than that of w, and downwards otherwise. By construction, the following holds: For every pair of nodes $s, t \in V$, there exists a shortest path in G^+ composed of a sequence of upward edges followed by a sequence of downwards edges. This property allows to search for the optimal path with a bidirectional Dijkstra only considering upward edges in the search starting at s, and only downwards edges in the reverse search starting in t. This reduces the search space significantly and allows for query answering within the *millisecond* range compared to *seconds* for Dijkstra. Note that bidirectional Dijkstra search immediately yields a compact, compressed representation of the optimal path, which can be easily decompressed to the desired level by recursively replacing shortcuts by the edges they replaced during the contraction phase.

CH-Based Hub Labels. Hub Labelling [10] is a scheme to answer shortest path *distance* queries which differs fundamentally from graph search based methods. Here the idea is to compute for every $v \in V$ a label $L(v)$ such that for given $s, t \in V$ the distance between s and t can be determined by just inspecting the labels $L(s)$ and $L(t)$. All the labels are constructed in a preprocessing step (based on the graph G), later on, G can even be thrown away. There are different approaches to compute such labels; we will be concerned with labels that work well for road networks and are based on CH, following the ideas in [3]. The labels we are constructing have the following form:

$$L(v) = \{(w, d(v, w)) : w \in H(v)\}$$

We call $H(v)$ a set of *hubs* – important nodes – for v. The hubs must be chosen such that for any s and t, the shortest path from s to t intersects $L(s) \cap L(t)$. If such labels have been computed, the computation of the shortest path distance between s and t boils down to determining the node $w \in L(s) \cap L(t)$ minimizing the distance sum. With the entries of a label stored in lexicographic order, this can be done very cache-efficiently in time $O(|L(s)| + |L(t)|)$.

Given a precomputed CH, there is an easy way of constructing such labels: run an upward Dijkstra from each node v and let the label $L(v)$ be the settled nodes with their respective distances. Clearly, this yields valid labels since CH answers queries exactly. The drawback is the space consumption; depending on the metric and the CH construction, one can expect labels consisting of several hundred node-distance pairs (even after a possible pruning step). Still, a distance query can then be answered in the *microseconds* range.

3 CH∼HL: Interpolating Between HL and CH

Starting point of our hybrid approach is a rather unclever way of answering source target queries when a CH is precomputed. For a query from s to t we proceed as follows: start an upward Dijkstra from s and construct a valid hub label $L(s)$ by collecting all nodes visited with their respective distances and sorting them lexicographically. Analogously, we construct the label $L(t)$. Then we use $L(s)$ and $L(t)$ to answer the shortest path distance query as usual. Clearly, nobody would use such an approach since it includes the same effort as a regular CH query answering (and even more). One important observation also made use of in the HL construction in [3] makes this unclever approach valuable, though: The hub label of a node v can also be constructed by considering all outgoing edges (v, w) to higher-level nodes w and taking the union of all their hub labels, where $d(v, w)$ is added to all distances in the hub label of w, and the obvious labels for v and its higher-level neighbors. See Fig. 1, left, for an example.

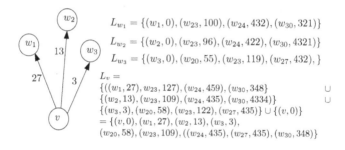

$$L_{w_1} = \{(w_1, 0), (w_{23}, 100), (w_{24}, 432), (w_{30}, 321)\}$$
$$L_{w_2} = \{(w_2, 0), (w_{23}, 96), (w_{24}, 422), (w_{30}, 4321)\}$$
$$L_{w_3} = \{(w_3, 0), (w_{20}, 55), (w_{23}, 119), (w_{27}, 432), \}$$
$$L_v =$$
$$\{((w_1, 27), w_{23}, 127), (w_{24}, 459), (w_{30}, 348\} \qquad \cup$$
$$\{(w_2, 13), (w_{23}, 109), (w_{24}, 435), (w_{30}, 4334)\} \qquad \cup$$
$$\{(w_3, 3), (w_{20}, 58), (w_{23}, 122), (w_{27}, 435)\} \cup \{(v, 0)\}$$
$$= \{(v, 0), (w_1, 27), (w_2, 13), (w_3, 3),$$
$$(w_{20}, 58), (w_{23}, 109), ((w_{24}, 435), (w_{27}, 435), (w_{30}, 348)\}$$

Fig. 1. $L(v)$ can be constructed from higher adjacent nodes w_1, w_2, w_3 by offsetting their labels and pruning.

So assuming we have – in a preprocessing stage – precomputed hub labels for all nodes of level L or higher, we modify our unclever approach by stopping the upward search as soon as we have reached nodes at level at least L. For sufficiently small L, the upward searches abort very quickly. Using the explored upward graphs we construct the hub labels for s and t in a top-down fashion using the above observation.

Why is there hope that this approach is efficient with respect to both query time as well as space consumption? In Fig. 2 we see a histogram of the CH level distribution for the European road network (see Table 2 for the characteristics of this dataset). The maximum CH level here is 485, but more than 50% of the nodes have level 0, 30% of all nodes have level 1, and less than 1% of all nodes have level more than 20. This means setting $L = 20$ would require computation of hub labels only for less than $1/100th$ of all nodes, which is beneficial in terms of space consumption as well as of preprocessing time. Still, the upward searches are limited up to level 20 instead of 485.

The choice of L can be interpreted as an interpolation parameter between CH and HL. For $L = 0$ (hub labels for all nodes) we have pure HL, for $L = \infty$ (no hub labels at all), we have pure CH. L hence can be chosen based on the available space for precomputed hub labels and desired query times.

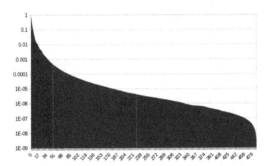

Fig. 2. Node level distribution for CH of Europe. y-coordinate (logarithmic scale!) denotes fraction of nodes having level $\geq$ x.

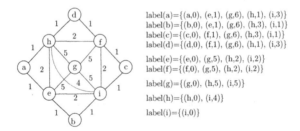

label(a)={(a,0), (e,1), (g,6), (h,1), (i,3)}
label(b)={(b,0), (e,1), (g,6), (h,3), (i,1)}
label(c)={(c,0), (f,1), (g,6), (h,3), (i,1)}
label(d)={(d,0), (f,1), (g,6), (h,1), (i,3)}

label(e)={(e,0), (g,5), (h,2), (i,2)}
label(f)={(f,0), (g,5), (h,2), (i,2)}

label(g)={(g,0), (h,5), (i,5)}

label(h)={(h,0), (i,4)}

label(i)={(i,0)}

Fig. 3. Toy graph with CH shortcuts and hub labels constructed

Our approach is best explained using an example. Consider the toy graph in Fig. 3, right, with all the original edges drawn in black. Contracting the nodes in their alphabetical order yields the shortcuts in blue and red with respective weights. Note, that one can simultaneously contract nodes a, b, c, d in a first round of contraction, assigning them a level of 1, then nodes e, f in the second round (assigning them a level of 2). The remaining nodes are contracted one by one, so we obtain level(g) $= 3$, level(h) $= 4$ and level(i) $= 5$. A CH search from d to b would explore in the upward search from node d the nodes h, f, g, i with distances 1, 1, 6, 3 and in the upward search from b the nodes e, i, g, h with distances 1, 1, 6, 3. Nodes h, g, i are settled from both sides with h and i having the smallest summed distances. Observe that neither of the two upward searches considers nodes a and c. On a larger scale this is what makes CH search considerably more effective than ordinary Dijkstra search. On the right of Fig. 3, we see hub labels constructed based on this CH. A HL query from c to h can be answered by inspecting the labels for c and h and determining the common hub with minimal added distances, which in this case would be h itself.

Already in this example it becomes obvious that storing labels for all nodes in the graph becomes quite space intensive. So in our CH$\sim$HLapproach we only store labels at nodes with a level at least L, e.g. only for nodes with level at least 2, that is for nodes e, f, g, h, and i. Then for a query, we first perform upward searches from both sides but only until reaching nodes of level at least 2. For a query from c to a, that would result in nodes f and i settled with distance 1 from c. The labels $\{(f,0),(g,5),(h,2),(i,2)\}$ for f and $\{(i,0)\}$ are combined with the respective distance offset of 1 to the label $\{(c,0),(f,1),(g,6),(h,3),(i,1)\}$ for c (which – no surprise is exactly the same label as if we had stored it as hub label right from the beginning). Similarly we combine the labels of nodes h and e that are at distance 1 from a to the label $\{(a,0),(e,1),(g,6),(h,1),(i,3)\}$ for a. We use these labels to answer the query from c to a. This hybrid approach can also be understood as deferring part of the label construction to query time hence saving a considerable amount of space and preprocessing time, yet still being faster than a CH search.

Augmenting Hub Labels for Path Recovery. Another, maybe even more serious disadvantage of lookup-based schemes like HL or transit node routing apart from excessive space consumption is the fact that as such they can only answer *distance* queries and recovering the actual optimal path requires additional effort. In case of CH-based hub labels, there is a very straightforward modification to allow also for easy path recovery, though, which might be folklore, but we were not able to find this simple idea stated or used explicitly in a paper, so we include it here for completeness.

If we construct the label of a node v as the (possibly pruned) search space of a CH upward search starting in v, we can augment each pair $(w, d_v(w))$ by a third component denoting the predecessor $pred_v(w)$ of w in the upward search from v, i.e., the label is now $(w, d_v(w), pred_v(w))$. If w was in the upward search space of v and hence in the label of v, $pred_v(w)$ is as well. Alternatively we can also store the predecessor edge $(pred_v(w), w)$. When answering a query using these augmented labels, we also immediately get a compressed path representation like in the CH scheme. The compressed representation can be collected by a linear scan over the two labels, decompression cost depends on the desired level of decompression, see [12].

4   Implementation and Experimental Evaluation

The implementation of CH, CH-based HL and our hybrid scheme CH$\sim$HLis in C++ (using g++ Version 8.3.0) and executed on Ubuntu 19.04. We used two machines, one *server* with an intel Xeon E5-2650v4/768 GB RAM, and a *workstation* with an AMD Threadripper 1950x/128 GB RAM. While the former has much more RAM and allows to compute also very space consuming acceleration structures, the latter can be considered commodity hardware (cost of less than 2,000 USD). Preprocessing was multithreaded but we always report CPU time multiplied with the number of used cores, since both HL as well as CH constructions scale extremely well with the number of cores. For benchmarking the road networks of all continents (except Australia and Antarctica as they are very small) as well as a smaller road network of Germany were extracted from OpenStreetMap [1]. We included all segments with the `highway` key and values as stated in Table 1 with their respective speeds to calculate travel times unless an explicit `maxspeed` tag was present.

Table 1. Road categories and respective speeds for reproducibility.

Type	Speed [km/h]	Type	Speed [km/h]
motorway	130	motorway_link	70
primary	100	primary_link	70
secondary	80	secondary_link	70
tertiary	70	tertiary_link	70
trunk	130	trunk_link	80
unclassified	50	residential	45
living_street	5	road	50
service	30	turning_circle	50

Table 2. Datasets used for benchmarking.

	Nodes	Edges	CH edges	RAM	Max CH
				RAM	Level
Germany	28M	57M	45M	5 GB	300
Africa	128M	264M	251M	24 GB	280
Asia	253M	517M	468M	47 GB	531
Europe	273M	547M	468M	49 GB	485
N.America	234M	476M	404M	42 GB	464
S.America	62M	129M	123M	12 GB	331

CH was built using the standard approach in [12], always contracting independent sets of nodes with low edge difference. The resulting augmented graph characteristics can be found in Table 2. For example, the road network of Europe consists of around 273 million nodes and 574 million edges. The CH construction adds 468 million shortcuts edges and yields a maximum CH level of 485. In RAM this graph uses 49 GB including additional information like longitude, latitude, road types, maximum speeds, etc. CH construction time never exceded one hour on either machine.

The important characteristics for our CH~HLscheme are space requirement and query time. Setting the level L determines how to interpolate between contraction hierarchy and hub labels. For $L = 0$, we essentially have pure HL, for $L = \infty$, we obtain the original CH scheme. In Table 3 we investigate the trade-off between query time and space consumption for South America, choosing values for L between 0 and 64. Query times are averaged over 1000 random source-target queries (for Dijkstra's algorithm only 100 queries).

Table 3. Detailed analysis; trade-off; up search, label construction, HL query, South America. *Server.*

	L							
	0	1	2	4	8	16	32	64
Space	221 GB	124 GB	74 GB	36 GB	12 GB	4 GB	0.8 GB	0.1 GB
# cores × time	685 m	456 m	290 m	186 m	97 m	48 m	17 m	3 m
Dijkstra (in μs)	11, 011, 372							
CH (in μs)	795							
HL (in μs)	4.5							
CHHL-L (in μs)	10.6	17.0	27.3	39.1	46.1	76.9	236.5	880.1
Up-search (in μs)	0.0	1.0	1.1	1.4	1.8	3.4	8.2	40.8
# labels collected	2	3	5	7	14	31	105	445

Plain Dijkstra on this network takes around 11 s, a CH query can be answered in less than a millisecond, about 4 orders of magnitude faster. HL can provide an answer in less than 5 ms, yet the space consumption of 221 GB is quite prohibitive (note that we did not apply any compression schemes as in [11]). Looking at our hybrid approach for varying values of L, we see that for $L = 0$ we have a query time overhead compared to pure HL of a factor of 2 due to initializing and managing the upward search and label merging (even though it never really comes into effect). With growing L the space consumption as well as preprocessing times naturally decrease rapidly, e.g. for $L = 8$ we only need 12 GB of additional space (compare that to 12 GB already necessary to store the graph including CH) and can complete the preprocessing in 1.5 core hours. The query time of 46 μs is about a factor of 10 worse than pure HL, yet more than 17 times faster than pure CH. Of these 46 μs, only a small fraction is required by the upward searches, most time is spent on the collection and merging of precomputed labels. Naturally, the further the upward search procedes, the more labels are there to collect. In this case, on average 14 labels (that is 7 times more than for the hub label scheme) have to be fetched. This alone already accounts for more than $30\,\mu s$, the remaining time is spent in the merging process. For $L = 64$, query times for our hybrid approach exceed those of pure CH, so larger choices for L are not considered.

South America was the smallest continental road network considered, for the larger ones, even our server hardware is not sufficient to compute the full hub label set. In Table 4 we compare our hybrid approach with other common speed-up techniques. Since the underlying road networks (in particular the edge weight generation) and the respective CH construction are not the same for the reported measurements, we normalized them according to the speedup compared to a pure CH query. This is along the lines of the comparison in [4] but focuses more on the comparison to CH, as this seems to be the currently most widely used technique in practice. Unfortunately we were not able to obtain permission to use the widely benchmarked PTV-DIMACS Europe graph. In Table 4 we state for each alternative speedup technique whether path recovery is easily possible, the preprocessing times (in work per node), the space overhead as well as the speedup compared to pure CH. For example, CH-based transit node routing mentioned in the related works section, has no easy way of recovering paths (for long distance queries), uses around $66\,\mu s$ of work per node and induces an overhead of 147 bytes/node. Query times are 75.2 faster than pure CH queries. For our approach we picked a few seemingly interesting choices for L and report the results for the network of Europe as well as that of Germany. For example, for the large Europe data set, when spending 159bytes/node (comparable to what CH-TNR requires), we can obtain a speedup of 47.7 compared to CH, yet have the ability to easily report compressed path representations. A possible sweetspot is $L = 22$, where only 33bytes/node are required as additional space (including predecessor information for path retrieval), and we still can achieve a speedup of 20. Choosing $L > 56$ does not seem to be worthwhile due to almost non-existant speedup. For the Germany network, (which is more comparable in size to the networks most other schemes were benchmarked for), the sweetspot could be seen around $L = 14$, where we still achieve a speedup of almost 15, while spending only 46bytes/node of additional space. Note that the absolute work/node numbers for preprocessing only indicate a magnitude since the preprocessing was conducted on vastly different machines.

Finally, in Table 5 we present results for all larger continents with – in our opinion sweetspot choices for L. For all of them, spending a fraction of the space necessary to store the network itself (see Table 2), we achieve query times of less or around $100\,\mu s$ even for continents having more than half a billion edges. CH queries are more in the milliseconds, Dijkstra queries almost in the minutes range for such large datasets. Preprocessing in any case could be performed in less than 2 h on the workstation, in fact extracting the respective graphs from OpenStreetMap took longer.

Table 4. Comparison of speed-up schemes in terms of path recovery capability, preprocessing time and space, and speedup vs. CH.

Method	From	Easy path recovery	Preprocessing		Query
			#cores × time/node	Bytes/node	Speed-up factor vs CH
CH	[12]	Yes		37	1.0
Grid-TNR	[7]	No	4,000 μs	21	3.9
HH-TNR-eco	[18]	No	83 μs	120	22.4
HH-TNR-gen	[18]	No	250 μs	247	57.2
TNR+AF	[9]	No	763 μs	321	129.4
HL local	[2]	No	320 μs	1221	223.6
HL global	[2]	No	560 μs	1269	464.1
HL-0 local	[3]	No	120 μs	1341	183.5
HL-i global	[3]	No	14,880 μs	1041	502.0
CH-TNR	[4]	No	66 μs	147	75.2
CHHL-EUR-10	NEW	Yes	73 μs	159	47.7
CHHL-EUR-14	NEW	Yes	52 μs	92	34.6
CHHL-EUR-22	NEW	Yes	31 μs	33	20.6
CHHL-EUR-32	NEW	Yes	19 μs	12	9.9
CHHL-EUR-40	NEW	Yes	14 μs	6	6.0
CHHL-EUR-56	NEW	Yes	8 μs	2	2.2
CHHL-GER-10	NEW	Yes	21 μs	99	21.0
CHHL-GER-14	NEW	Yes	13 μs	46	14.7
CHHL-GER-22	NEW	Yes	7 μs	15	8.2
CHHL-GER-32	NEW	Yes	4 μs	4	3.7

Table 5. Reasonable choices for L for different continental road networks. Space includes full graph information and CH. *Workstation.*

	L	Total space	Query Dijk	Query CH	Query CHHL
Germany	10	7.8 GB	9 s	585 μs	28 μs
Africa	9	35 GB	56 s	601 μs	49 μs
Asia	19	57 GB	35 s	1,546 μs	117 μs
Europe	18	58 GB	38 s	2,170 μs	82 μs
N.America	14	55 GB	31 s	1,644 μs	54 μs
S.America	12	18 GB	11 s	798 μs	52 μs

5   Discussion and Future Work

We have presented a conceptually very simple seamless interpolation between CH and HL allowing for speedup of CH depending on the available space. There are many avenues of future work in that direction. For example we have not considered more refined HL constructions as proposed, e.g., in [15] or applicability to non-road networks. In fact since we only perform CH for the lowest levels, our hybrid technique might be applicable also for cases where CH is not really competetive. Furthermore, we completely ignored existing work on hub label compression [11], mainly to keep the presentation as simple as possible. Both compression as well as HL tuning are orthogonal to our approach, though, and can be employed to lower L without increasing space consumption too much. Combinations of different speed-up technique have been explored before, our proposed scheme seems extremely organic and conceptually simple in comparison. Maybe its biggest advantage is simplicity: With implementations of CH and CH-based hub labels in place, we only require little extra code: the upward search can essentially be taken from the CH queries, the label merging from the hub label construction. Compared to maybe its closest competitor in terms of space/query-time tradeoff, CH-TNR, our scheme has a natural possibility to return (compressed) path representations and for larger networks does not exhibit the quadratic growth of the $|T| \times |T|$ distance table. Another important tuning measure could be to deliberately choose the memory layout such that fewer memory accesses are necessary to collect the precomputed labels.

References

1. OpenStreetMap (2020). https://www.openstreetmap.org/
2. Abraham, I., Delling, D., Goldberg, A.V., Werneck, R.F.: A hub-based labeling algorithm for shortest paths in road networks. In: Pardalos, P.M., Rebennack, S. (eds.) SEA 2011. LNCS, vol. 6630, pp. 230–241. Springer, Heidelberg (2011). https://doi.org/10.1007/978-3-642-20662-7_20
3. Abraham, I., Delling, D., Goldberg, A.V., Werneck, R.F.: Hierarchical hub labelings for shortest paths. In: Epstein, L., Ferragina, P. (eds.) ESA 2012. LNCS, vol. 7501, pp. 24–35. Springer, Heidelberg (2012). https://doi.org/10.1007/978-3-642-33090-2_4
4. Arz, J., Luxen, D., Sanders, P.: Transit node routing reconsidered. In: Bonifaci, V., Demetrescu, C., Marchetti-Spaccamela, A. (eds.) SEA 2013. LNCS, vol. 7933, pp. 55–66. Springer, Heidelberg (2013). https://doi.org/10.1007/978-3-642-38527-8_7
5. Bast, H., et al.: Route planning in transportation networks. CoRR, abs/1504.05140 (2015)
6. Bast, H., Funke, S., Matijevic, D., Sanders, P., Schultes, D.: In transit to constant time shortest-path queries in road networks. In: Proceedings of the ALENEX. SIAM (2007)
7. Bast, H., Funke, S., Sanders, P., Schultes, D.: Fast routing in road networks with transit nodes. Science **316**(5824), 566 (2007)

8. Bauer, R., Delling, D.: SHARC: fast and robust unidirectional routing. In: Proceedings of the ALENEX, pp. 13–26. SIAM (2008)
9. Bauer, R., Delling, D., Sanders, P., Schieferdecker, D., Schultes, D., Wagner, D.: Combining hierarchical and goal-directed speed-up techniques for Dijkstra's algorithm. ACM J. Exp. Algorithmics **15**, 2.1–2.31 (2010)
10. Cohen, E., Halperin, E., Kaplan, H., Zwick, U.: Reachability and distance queries via 2-hop labels. In: SODA, pp. 937–946. ACM/SIAM (2002)
11. Delling, D., Goldberg, A.V., Werneck, R.F.: Hub label compression. In: Bonifaci, V., Demetrescu, C., Marchetti-Spaccamela, A. (eds.) SEA 2013. LNCS, vol. 7933, pp. 18–29. Springer, Heidelberg (2013). https://doi.org/10.1007/978-3-642-38527-8_4
12. Geisberger, R., Sanders, P., Schultes, D., Vetter, C.: Exact routing in large road networks using contraction hierarchies. Transportation Science **46**(3), 388–404 (2012)
13. Gutman, R.J.: Reach-based routing: a new approach to shortest path algorithms optimized for road networks. In: Proceedings of the ALENEX/ANALCO, pp. 100–111. SIAM (2004)
14. Kosowski, A., Viennot, L.: Beyond highway dimension: small distance labels using tree skeletons. In: SODA, pp. 1462–1478. SIAM (2017)
15. Li, Y., Leong Hou, U., Yiu, M.L., Kou, N.M.: An experimental study on hub labeling based shortest path algorithms. Proc. VLDB Endow. **11**(4), 445–457 (2017)
16. Luxen, D., Vetter, C.: Real-time routing with OpenStreetMap data. In: Proceedings of the 19th ACM SIGSPATIAL International Conference on Advances in Geographic Information Systems, GIS 2011, pp. 513–516. ACM, New York (2011)
17. Sanders, P., Schultes, D.: Engineering highway hierarchies. ACM J. Exp. Algorithmics **17**(1), 1.1–1.40 (2012)
18. Schultes, D.: Route planning in road networks. Ph.D. thesis, Universität Karlsruhe (2008)
19. Schultes, D., Sanders, P.: Dynamic highway-node routing. In: Demetrescu, C. (ed.) WEA 2007. LNCS, vol. 4525, pp. 66–79. Springer, Heidelberg (2007). https://doi.org/10.1007/978-3-540-72845-0_6

Visibility Polygon Queries Among Dynamic Polygonal Obstacles in Plane

Sanjana Agrawal and R. Inkulu[✉]

Department of Computer Science and Engineering, IIT Guwahati, Guwahati, India
{sanjana18,rinkulu}@iitg.ac.in

Abstract. Given a polygonal domain, we devise a fully dynamic algorithm for maintaining the visibility polygon of any query point, i.e., as the polygonal domain is modified with vertex insertions and deletions to its obstacles, we update the visibility polygon of any query point. After preprocessing the initial input polygonal domain to build a few data structures, our dynamic algorithm takes $O(k(\lg |VP_{\mathcal{P}'}(q)|) + (\lg n')^2 + h)$ (resp. $O(k(\lg n')^2 + (\lg |VP_{\mathcal{P}'}(q)|) + h))$ worst-case time to update the visibility polygon $VP_{\mathcal{P}'}(q)$ of a query point q when any vertex v is inserted to (resp. deleted from) any obstacle of the current polygonal domain $\mathcal{P}'$. Here, n' is the number of vertices in $\mathcal{P}'$, h is the number of obstacles in $\mathcal{P}'$, $VP_{\mathcal{P}'}(q)$ is the visibility polygon of q in $\mathcal{P}'$ ($|VP_{\mathcal{P}'}(q)|$ is the number of vertices of $VP_{\mathcal{P}'}(q)$), and k is the number of combinatorial changes in $VP_{\mathcal{P}'}(q)$ due to the insertion (resp. deletion) of v.

1 Introduction

The polygonal domain comprises of a set of pairwise-disjoint simple polygons (obstacles) in the plane. We assume the obstacles in the polygonal domain are placed in a large bounding box. For any polygonal domain $\mathcal{P}$, the free space $\mathcal{F}(\mathcal{P})$ is the closure of the bounding box without the union of the interior of all the obstacles in $\mathcal{P}$. Any two points $p, q \in \mathcal{F}(\mathcal{P})$ are *visible* whenever the open line segment between p and q lies entirely in $\mathcal{F}(\mathcal{P})$. For a point $q \in \mathcal{F}(\mathcal{P})$, the *visibility polygon* of q, denoted by $VP_{\mathcal{P}}(q)$, is the maximal set of points in the plane visible to q among obstacles in $\mathcal{P}$. (When $\mathcal{P}$ is clear from the context, the visibility polygon of q is denoted by $VP(q)$.) The *visibility polygon query* problem seeks to preprocess the given polygonal domain $\mathcal{P}$ so that to efficiently compute $VP_{\mathcal{P}}(q)$ for any query point q located in $\mathcal{F}(\mathcal{P})$. Computing visibility polygons is a fundamental problem in computational geometry, and it is studied extensively.

1.1 Previous Work

In the following, n denotes the number of vertices defining the input simple polygon or polygonal domain, and h is the number of obstacles in the given

R. Inkulu's research is supported in part by SERB MATRICS grant MTR/2017/000474.

D. Kim et al. (Eds.): COCOON 2020, LNCS 12273, pp. 136–148, 2020.
https://doi.org/10.1007/978-3-030-58150-3_11

polygonal domain. The problem of computing the visibility polygon of a point in a simple polygon was first attempted by Davis and Benedikt in [11], and they presented an $O(n^2)$ time algorithm. Later, both ElGindy and Avis [12], and Lee [26], presented $O(n)$ time algorithms for the same problem. Joe and Simpson [21] corrected a flaw in [12,26], and devised an $O(n)$ time algorithm that correctly handles winding in the simple polygon. For a simple polygon with holes, both Suri and O' Rourke [31], and Asano [3] presented $O(n \lg n)$ time algorithms, and Heffernan and Mitchell [17] gave a $O(n + h \lg h)$ time solution. The visibility polygon computation among convex sets was considered by Ghosh in [13].

For both the simple polygon as well as the polygonal domain, the previous works considered the visibility polygon query problem. Bose et al. [6] gave an algorithm to preprocess the given simple polygon in $O(n^3 \lg n)$ time, build data structures of size $O(n^3)$, and answer any visibility polygon query in $O(\lg n + |VP(q)|)$ time. Later, Aronov et al. [2] devised an algorithm for the same problem with preprocessing time $O(n^2 \lg n)$, space $O(n^2)$, and query time $O(\lg^2 n + |VP(q)|)$. Zarei and Ghodsi [32] presents an algorithm that preprocesses the given polygonal domain in $O(n^3 \lg n)$ time to build data structures of size $O(n^3)$, and answers each visibility polygon query in $O((1 + h') \lg n + |VP(q)|)$ time, where $h' = min(h, |VP(q)|)$. The algorithm by Inkulu and Kapoor [18] preprocesses the input polygonal domain in $O(n^2 \lg n)$ time, builds data structures of size $O(n^2)$, and answers visibility polygon query in $O(\min(h, |VP(q)|)(\lg n)^2 + h + |VP(q)|)$ time. This paper also presented another algorithm with preprocessing time $O(T + |VG| + n \lg n)$, space $O(\min(|VG|, hn) + n)$, and query time $O(|VP(q)| \lg n + h)$. Here, $|VG|$ denotes the number of edges in the visibility graph, and T is the time to triangulate the free space of the given polygonal domain. Baygi and Ghodsi [5] constructed a data structure of size $O(n^2)$ in $O(n^2 \lg n)$ time, and their algorithm answers any visibility polygon query in $O(|VP(q)| + \lg n)$ time. Lu et al. [27] presented an algorithm to compute a data structure of size $O(n^2)$ in $O(n^2 \lg n)$ time, which helps in answering any visibility polygon query in $O(|VP(q)| + (\lg n)^2 + h \lg(n/h))$ time. Chen and Wang [8] gave an algorithm that preprocesses the polygonal domain in $O(n + h^2 \lg h)$ time to construct data structures of size $O(n + h^2)$, so that to answer any visibility polygon query in $O(|VP(q)| \lg n)$ time. The query version of visibility polygon computation in the polygonal domain comprising of convex obstacles was given by Pocchiola and Vegter [29]. Their algorithm computes the visibility polygon of any query point in $O(|VP(q)| \lg n)$ time by preprocessing the convex polygonal domain in $O(n \lg n)$ time and building data structures of size $O(n)$. Algorithms for computing visibility graphs were given in [15]. Ghosh [14] details a number of algorithms for visibility in plane.

In the context of visibility polygons, the main advantage in having dynamic algorithms is to update the visibility polygon efficiently (that is, with respect to update time) as compared to computing the entire visibility polygon from scratch using traditional algorithms. In doing this, the algorithm specifically exploits the recent changes that occurred to the polygonal domain; based on these changes, the current visibility polygon is locally modified. A dynamic algorithm is said to be *incremental* if it updates the visibility polygon of the given point efficiently whenever a new vertex is inserted to any of the obstacles of the current polygonal domain. Similarly, an algorithm is *decremental* if it efficiently updates the visibility polygon of the given point whenever a vertex of any of the obstacles of the current polygonal domain is deleted. If the dynamic algorithm is both incremental as well as decremental, then it is termed a *fully dynamic* algorithm. Both Inkulu and Nitish [19], and Inkulu et al. [20] devised fully dynamic algorithms for maintaining the visibility polygon of a query point in a dynamic simple polygon. Choudhury and Inkulu [9] devised a fully dynamic algorithm for maintaining the visibility graph of a dynamic simple polygon. The visibility in the context of a moving observer was studied in [1,7].

1.2   Our Results

In this paper, a fully dynamic algorithm for computing the visibility polygon of any query point q among a set of dynamic polygonal obstacles is proposed, i.e., the visibility polygon of q is updated whenever any vertex is inserted to any of the obstacles, or any vertex is deleted from any of the obstacles. Let $VP_{\mathcal{P}'}(q)$ be the visibility polygon of a query point q in the current polygonal domain $\mathcal{P}'$. Also, let n' be the number of vertices in $\mathcal{P}'$. When any vertex v is inserted to any of the obstacles of $\mathcal{P}'$, our algorithm takes $O(k(\lg |VP_{\mathcal{P}'}(q)|) + (\lg n')^2 + h)$ time to update the visibility polygon of q. Here, k is the number of combinatorial changes in $VP_{\mathcal{P}'}(q)$ due to the insertion of v. In the case of deletion of any vertex v of any of the obstacles of $\mathcal{P}'$, the $VP_{\mathcal{P}'}(q)$ is updated in $O(k(\lg n')^2 + (\lg |VP_{\mathcal{P}'}(q)|) + h)$ time. Here, k is the number of combinatorial changes in $VP_{\mathcal{P}'}(q)$ due to the deletion of v. Our output-sensitive visibility polygon query algorithm computes $VP_{\mathcal{P}'}(q)$ for any query point in $O(|VP_{\mathcal{P}'}(q)|(\lg n')^2 + h)$ time. The data structures constructed as part of answering the visibility polygon query algorithm facilitate in efficiently updating $VP_{\mathcal{P}'}(q)$ as the polygonal domain changes. We preprocess the initial input polygonal domain $\mathcal{P}$ in $O(n(\lg n)^2 + h(\lg h)^{1+\epsilon})$ time, and construct data structures of size $O(n)$. Here, n is the number of vertices of $\mathcal{P}$, h is the number of polygonal obstacles in $\mathcal{P}$, and $\epsilon > 0$ is a small positive constant (resulting from triangulating the free space of $\mathcal{P}$ using the algorithm in [4]). To our knowledge, this is the first algorithm for maintaining the visibility polygon of any given point in the dynamic polygonal domain. This algorithm obviates computing the visibility polygon of a given point from scratch whenever the polygon domain is modified with a vertex insertion or with a vertex deletion.

1.3   Terminology

We denote the initial input polygonal domain with $\mathcal{P}$, the number of vertices of $\mathcal{P}$ with n, and the number of obstacles in $\mathcal{P}$ with h. We use $\mathcal{P}'$ to denote the polygonal domain just before inserting (resp. deleting) a vertex, and $\mathcal{P}''$ to denote the polygonal domain just after inserting (resp. deleting) a vertex.

Also, n' denotes the number of $\mathcal{P}'$, and h is the number of obstacles in $\mathcal{P}$. It is assumed that every new vertex is added between two successive vertices of an obstacle. Whenever a new vertex v is inserted between two adjacent vertices v_i and v_{i+1} in polygonal domain $\mathcal{P}'$, it is assumed that two new edges are added to $\mathcal{P}'$: one between vertices v and v_i, and the other between vertices v and v_{i+1}. Similarly, in the case of deletion of a vertex v, it is assumed that after deleting v from $\mathcal{P}'$ which is adjacent to vertices v_i and v_{i+1} in $\mathcal{P}'$, a new edge is inserted between vertices v_i and v_{i+1}. After adding (resp. deleting) any vertex to (resp. from) any obstacle O in the current polygonal domain, our algorithm assumes O continues to be a simple polygon. Further, newly inserted vertex in $\mathcal{P}''$ is assumed to be contained in the bounding box of $\mathcal{P}$. The visibility polygon of q in any polygonal domain $\mathcal{P}'''$ is denoted by $VP_{\mathcal{P}'''}(q)$. For any simple polygon P, the boundary of P is denoted by $bd(P)$. Unless specified otherwise, the boundary of any simple polygon is assumed to be traversed in counter-clockwise order. It is assumed that all the angles are measured in counter-clockwise direction from the positive horizontal (x-)axis. A vertex v of the polygonal domain is said to be a *visible vertex* to q whenever v is visible from query point q. As in [22,23,25], we decompose the free space $\mathcal{F}(\mathcal{P})$ of the input polygonal domain $\mathcal{P}$ into corridors and junctions.

Let r' and r'' be two rays with origin at p. Let uv_1 and uv_2 be the unit vectors along the rays r' and r'' respectively. A *cone* $C_p(r', r'')$ is the set of points defined by rays r' and r'' such that a point $p' \in C_p(r', r'')$ if and only if p' can be expressed as a convex combination of the vectors uv_1 and uv_2 with positive coefficients. When the rays are evident from the context, we denote the cone with C_p. A cone C_p is called a *visibility cone* whenever C_p contains at least one point in $\mathcal{F}(\mathcal{P})$ that is visible from p. For any cone $C_p(r_i, r_j)$, among rays r_i and r_j, the ray that makes lesser angle with the positive x-axis at p is the *left ray* of C_p and the other ray is the *right ray* of C_p. For any cone, throughout the paper, we assume the counter-clockwise angle between the left ray of C_p and the right ray of C_p is less than π. We use *vertex* to denote any endpoint of any edge of the polygonal domain, and we use *node* to denote any tree node in data structures that we construct.

The preprocessing algorithm and the data structures are detailed in Sect. 2. Section 3 detail the dynamic algorithms. The output-sensitive visibility polygon query algorithm is given in Sect. 4.

2   Preprocessing Algorithm and Data Structures

We first preprocess the input polygonal domain $\mathcal{P}$. As described above, we partition the free space $\mathcal{F}(\mathcal{P})$ of $\mathcal{P}$ into $O(h)$ corridors and junctions, using algorithms in [22,23,25]. To efficiently compute tangents to dynamic sides of corridors, for each side S of every corridor, we construct a hull tree corresponding to S using the algorithm in [28,30]. For locating any vertex that is inserted to (resp. deleted from) any obstacle, and for locating query points, we compute a point location data structure for the corridor structure using the algorithm in [16]. In addition, as in [18], for every corridor C, we construct a set P_C of simple polygons corresponding to corridor C. One of the simple polygons in P_C, denoted with $P_4(C)$, is the corridor C itself. This polygon helps in determining vertices of C that are visible to q when q is located in C. If q is not located in C, the other three simple polygons in P_C, denoted by $P_1(S_1), P_2(S_1), P_3(S_2)$, each corresponding to a side of C, together help in determining vertices of C that are visible to q. In specific, two of these simple polygons $P_1(S_1), P_2(S_1)$ correspond to one side S_1 of C, and $P_3(S_2)$ correspond to the other side S_2 of C. As an obstacle in the polygonal domain gets modified, the corresponding corridor is also modified accordingly. Whenever a side S of any corridor C changes, we make the changes to $P_4(C)$ as well as to the simple polygons in P_C that correspond to side S. In the query phase, using the algorithm in [20], we compute visible vertices and constructed vertices (refer to [14]) in these dynamic simple polygons. As part of preprocessing required for the algorithm in [20], for every corridor C, each of the four simple polygons in P_C are further processed in linear time to construct data structures as required by the algorithm in [20].

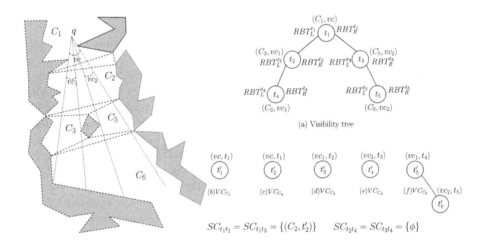

Fig. 1. Illustrating visibility tree, VC_{C_l}, and $SC_{t_i t_j}$ data structures.

Our query algorithm, detailed in Sect. 4, constructs visibility trees $TVIS^B_{\mathcal{P}'}(q)$ and $TVIS^U_{\mathcal{P}'}(q)$ for the input query point q. The visibility polygon of q is determined from the information stored at the nodes of these trees, and our dynamic algorithms update visibility trees as and when the current polygon domain is modified with vertex insertions and deletions. Our algorithms for updating the visibility polygon of a point $q \in \mathcal{F}(\mathcal{P}')$ assume the visibility trees $TVIS^B_{\mathcal{P}'}(q), TVIS^U_{\mathcal{P}'}(q)$ corresponding to q among obstacles in $\mathcal{P}'$ are accessible. The visibility trees were first defined in [24]. We modify visibility tree structures from [24] so that they are helpful in the dynamic polygonal domain. For every corridor C that has at least one point on the boundary of C that is visible to q, there exists at least one node in these trees that corresponds to C. Any node t in either of these trees corresponds to a corridor C^t. With t, we store a pointer to C^t, a visibility cone vc^t (with its apex at q), and two red-black balanced binary search trees (refer [10]), denoted with RBT_L^t, RBT_R^t. Refer to Fig. 1. The RBT_L^t (resp. RBT_R^t) at node t stores every (constructed) vertex v' of $VP_{\mathcal{P}'}(q)$ that belongs to the left (resp. right) side of corridor C whenever v' lies in vc^t. With each point p in both of these RBTs, we store the angle ray qp makes at q. If a point p is stored in $TVIS_{\mathcal{P}'}^B(q)$ (resp. $TVIS_{\mathcal{P}'}^U(q)$) then the line segment qp is guaranteed to intersect B (resp. U). For any point p located on the boundary of an obstacle, and for p visible to q, the sequence of corridors intersected by the line segment qp is said to be the *corridor sequence* of qp. We note that for any two points p', p'' in a corridor C, with both p' and p'' visible to q, the corridor sequence of qp' is not necessarily same as the corridor sequence of qp''. Hence, in any visibility tree of q, there could be more than one node that corresponds to any corridor. However, any (constructed) vertex of $VP_{\mathcal{P}'}(q)$ (or, any vertex of $\mathcal{P}'$) appears at most once in any of the RBTs stored at the nodes of these visibility trees. For any two nodes t', t'' of any visibility tree, for any point p' stored in either $RBT_L^{t'}$ or $RBT_R^{t'}$, and for any point p'' stored in either $RBT_L^{t''}$ or $RBT_R^{t''}$, the corridor sequence of qp' is not equal to the corridor sequence of qp''.

For every corridor C', the list of visibility cones that intersect C' are stored in a red-black tree, named $VC_{C'}$. In specific, the visibility cones in $VC_{C'}$ are stored in sorted order with respect to angle left bounding ray of each cone in $VC_{C'}$ makes at q. In addition, with each visibility cone vc in $VC_{C'}$, we store the pointer to a node in a visibility tree that saved a visible point belonging to $bd(C') \cap vc$. (Refer to Fig. 1.) If no such visible point exists, then the pointer to a node in the visibility tree that represents the corridor nearest to p along qp, where $p \in C' \cap vc$, is stored with vc. Whenever a vertex v is inserted (resp. deleted) to (resp. from) C', by searching in $VC_{C'}$, we determine the visibility cone in which we need to update the visibility polygon of q.

Let t' be any node in either of the visibility trees of q. And, let t'' be any child of t'. Also, let C', C'' be the corridors associated to t', t'' respectively. We note that it is not necessary for corridors C' and C'' to be adjacent in the corridor subdivision of $\mathcal{F}(\mathcal{P}')$. If C' and C'' are not adjacent, then there exists a unique sequence of corridors between C' and C'' and, this sequence of corridors is stored in a list $SC_{t't''}$. The list $SC_{t't''}$ is associated with the edge $t't''$ of the visibility tree. (Refer to Fig. 1.) Note that if C' and C'' are adjacent in the corridor subdivision of $\mathcal{F}(\mathcal{P}')$, then the list $SC_{tt'}$ would be empty. With every corridor $C \in SC_{t't''}$, we store a pointer to the node in visibility tree that corresponding to visibility cone $vc^{t'}$. In addition, the pointer stored with $vc^{t'}$ in VC_C points to the node t'.

3 Maintaining the Visibility Polygon of Any Query Point

Let $\mathcal{P}'$ be the polygonal domain just before inserting (resp. deleting) v to (resp. from) the boundary of an obstacle. Also, let v_i and v_{i+1} be the vertices between which v is located. We first describe parts that are common to both the insertion and deletion algorithms. Using point location data structure, we determine the corridor C in which v is located. If v is inserted to an obstacle in $\mathcal{P}'$, then we insert v at its corresponding position into at most three simple polygons in P_C. If v is deleted from an obstacle in $\mathcal{P}'$, then for every simple polygon $P \in P_C$, we delete v from P if $v \in P$. Then, for each simple polygon in P_C that got modified, we update the preprocessed data structures needed for determining visibility in dynamic simple polygons [20] Using the algorithm in [16] for ray-shooting in dynamic simple polygons, we determine whether v is visible to q among obstacles in $\mathcal{P}'$. This is accomplished using simple polygons in P_C: if $q \in C$, the ray-shooting query with ray qv is performed in $P_4(C)$; otherwise, if v belongs to a side S_1 (resp. S_2) of a corridor $C'(\neq C)$, we query with ray qv in each simple polygon in $P_{C'}$ that correspond to side S_1 (resp. S_2). From the correctness of characterizations in [18], it is immediate that we correctly determine whether v is visible to q. If v is found to be not visible to q, then $VP_{\mathcal{P}'}(q)$ does not change. In this case, we only update the preprocessed data structures for hull trees of sides of corridor C, as well as the data structures for dynamic point location. We note that all the updations of preprocessed data structures can be accomplished in $O((\lg n)^2)$ time.

Consider the case when v is visible to q. In this case, the insertion of v (resp. deletion of v) may cause the deletion of (resp. insertion of) some vertices from (resp. to) the current visibility polygon $VP_{\mathcal{P}'}(q)$. For every two vertices $v', v'' \in \{v, v_i, v_{i+1}\}$, we determine the (smaller) angle between rays qv' and qv''. Among these three possible cones, we find the cone vc_m with the maximum cone angle. The visible vertices belonging to vc_m are the potential candidates to be deleted (resp. inserted) from (resp. to) $VP_{\mathcal{P}'}(q)$ in the insertion (resp. deletion) algorithm. Let B_{C_q} be the lower bounding edge of corridor C_q containing q. Without loss of generality, suppose vc_m intersects B_{C_q}. Noting that $v \in C$, by searching in VC_C, we determine the visibility cone vc in which qv lies. Let t' be the node saved with vc in VC_C, and let C' be the corridor referred by t'. In the following subsections, we describe the insertion and deletion algorithms.

3.1   Insertion of a Vertex

If C' is same as C (to remind, v is in corridor C), then v is inserted to $RBT_L^{t'}$ (resp. $RBT_R^{t'}$) of node t' if v is located on the left (resp. right) side of C'. In the other sub-case, C' is not the same as C. This indicates there is no node present in $TVIS_{\mathcal{P}'}^B(q)$ that corresponds to C and vc, i.e., before the insertion of v, there was no point of $bd(C) \cap vc$ is visible to q. Let t_l', t_r' be the left and right children of t' respectively. A new node t'' is inserted as a left (resp. right) child of t', if v is located on the left (resp. right) side of C, and the parent of t_l' (resp. t_r') is changed to t''. The visibility cone vc' associated with t'' is same as the visibility cone vc associated with node t'. Without loss of generality, suppose t'' is inserted as the left child of t'. Let C'' be the corridor associated to node t_l'. The sequence of corridors $SC_{t't_l'}$ associated to edge $t't_l'$ is splitted into two sequences: the corridor sequence between C' to C along visibility cone vc is associated to edge $t't''$, and the corridor sequence between C and C'' along the visibility cone vc is saved with edge $t''t'_l$. In addition, for each corridor C'''' in $SC_{t''t'_l}$, the pointer stored with visibility cone vc in $VC_{C''''}$ is modified so that it points to node t''.

Suppose the rays bounding vc_m are qv_i and qv_{i+1}. Then, every vertex of $VP_{\mathcal{P}'}(q)$ continues to be visible to q. Hence, there is no vertex to be deleted from $VP_{\mathcal{P}'}(q)$. However, since v is visible to q, we need to insert v into a RBT of $TVIS_{\mathcal{P}'}^B(q)$. When v is located on the left (resp. right) side of C, if C' is same as C, then v will be inserted to $RBT_L^{t'}$ (resp. $RBT_R^{t'}$); otherwise, if C' is not same as C, then vertex v will be inserted to $RBT_L^{t''}$ (resp. $RBT_R^{t''}$).

Observation 1. *Let $\mathcal{P}'$ be the current polygonal domain. Let $VP_{\mathcal{P}'}(q)$ be the visibility polygon of a point $q \in \mathcal{P}'$. Whenever a new vertex v is inserted to an obstacle of $\mathcal{P}'$, the set of vertices of $VP_{\mathcal{P}'}(q)$ that get hidden due to the insertion of v are contiguous along the boundary of $VP_{\mathcal{P}'}(q)$. In specific, vertices stored in any red-black tree of any visibility tree hidden due to the insertion of v are contiguous at the leaves. (The proof is provided in the full version.)*

Suppose the rays bounding vc_m are qv_{i+1} and qv. In this case, due to the insertion of v, some vertices of $VP_{\mathcal{P}'}(q)$ may become not visible to q. To determine these vertices, we do the depth-first traversal of $TVIS_{\mathcal{P}'}^B(q)$, starting from t' if C' is same as C; otherwise, we do the depth-first traversal of $TVIS_{\mathcal{P}'}^B(q)$, starting from node t''. Let α_1 and α_2 be the angles made by rays qv_{i+1} and qv, respectively at q. Also, let $\alpha_1 < \alpha_2$. For every red-black tree T at every node t encountered in this traversal, we search in T to find the contiguous list of vertices such that each vertex in that list lies in the cone vc_m. By Observation 1, all the vertices belonging to this list are the ones that needed to be removed from T. Hence, we remove each vertex v' in this list from T, as v' is no more visible to q. Let C^t be the corridor referred by node t. During traversal, if visibility cone vc^t associated with node t is found to be lying completely inside vc_m, we delete the node corresponding to visibility cone vc^t in VC_{C^t}.

The handling of the last case in which the vc_m is bounded by rays qv_i and qv is analogous to the case in which vc_m is bounded by rays qv_{i+1} and qv.

3.2 Deletion of a Vertex

Suppose the rays bounding vc_m are qv_i and qv_{i+1}. The deletion of v does not change the visibility of any vertex belonging to $\mathcal{P}'$. Hence, there is no vertex needs to be added to $VP_{\mathcal{P}'}(q)$. However, since v is no more visible to q, we need to delete v from node t' of $TVIS_{\mathcal{P}'}^B(q)$. The vertex v will be deleted from $RBT_L^{t'}$ (resp. $RBT_R^{t'}$) if it is located on the left (resp. right) side of C. We determine whether vertices v_i and v_{i+1} are visible to q. If any of them is not visible to q, then using the algorithm in [20] for dynamic simple polygons, with cone vc_m, we determine the endpoints of constructed edges (refer to [14]) that incident to edge v_iv_{i+1}. In addition, we insert these endpoints into $RBTL^{t'}$ (resp. $RBT_R^{t'}$) if they are located on the left (resp. right) side of C.

Suppose the rays bounding vc_m are qv_{i+1} and qv. In this case, due to the deletion of v, some new vertices of $\mathcal{P}'$ may become visible to q. As in the above case, v is deleted from $RBT_L^{t'}$ (resp. $RBT_R^{t'}$) if it is located on the left (resp. right) side of C. Now, to determine vertices that become visible due to the deletion of v, we invoke the query algorithm described in Sect. 4 with $vc_m \cap vc$ as the visibility cone and q as the query point. Let vc' be the visibility cone $vc_m \cap vc$. Let vc_l' (resp. vc_r') be the left (resp. right) bounding ray of vc'. Also, let $\mathcal{C}$ be the set comprising of corridors such that the path in G_d from a node of G_d that corresponds to R to the node of G_d that corresponds to C_q. Given C and vc', our query algorithm determines all the vertices on the sides of corridors in $\mathcal{C}$ that are visible to q. (Refer to Sect. 4.)

Let T' be the tree returned by the query algorithm, and $T_{t'}$ be the subtree rooted at t' in $TVIS_{\mathcal{P}'}^B(q)$. (Note that t' is the node from which v is deleted.) For any corridor C_i, let VC_{C_i} (resp. VC_{C_i}') be the red-black tree storing the pointers to the nodes belonging to $T_{t'}$ (resp. T'). Without loss of generality, suppose vertex v is deleted from the left side of corridor C. Let rr_{vc} be the right bounding ray of visibility cone vc. For every node t'' in T', if the right bounding ray of its visibility cone is vc_r', we replace it with the ray rr_{vc}. In addition, we make similar changes in $VC_{C''}'$ corresponding to the corridor C'' referred by t''.

Further, every vertex belonging to T' is added to $TVIS_{\mathcal{P}'}^B(q)$. To accomplish this, we traverse the trees T' and $T_{t'}$ in the breadth-first order. For every node t'' that we encounter in the breadth-first traversal of T', we search in $VC_{C''t''}$ to find a visibility cone which is lying entirely inside the visibility cone $vc^{t''}$. If such a cone exists, it indicates that node t'' is present in $T_{t'}$. In this case, by traversing $T_{t'}$ in breadth-first order, we locate t'' in $T_{t'}$. Significantly, for every t'', breadth-first traversal of $T_{t'}$ starts from the node where the traversal in that tree was stopped in the previous search. The red-black trees stored at the node t'' in T' are merged with the red-black trees stored at the node found by the breadth-first traversal in $T_{t'}$.

In the other sub-case, if node t'' is not present in $T_{t'}$, it indicates that before deletion, the corridor represented by this node had no visible vertex on either of its sides in visibility cone vc. Due to the deletion of v, some portion of $bd(C_{t''})$ became visible. Hence, t'' is inserted in $T_{t'}$ such that the parent of t'' in $T_{t'}$ is same as the parent of t'' in T'. At the end, for every corridor C_i, we merge VC_{C_i}' with VC_{C_i}.

The handling of the last case in which the vc_m is bounded by rays qv_i and qv is analogous to the case in which vc_m is bounded by qv_{i+1} and qv.

4   Determining the Visibility Polygon of a Query Point

Let $\mathcal{P}'$ be the current polygonal domain. In the query phase, for any query point $q \in \mathcal{F}(\mathcal{P}')$, we compute $VP_{\mathcal{P}'}(q)$. We modify the algorithm for answering visibility polygon queries in [18], so that this algorithm accommodates dynamic obstacles. First, we determine all the sides of the corridors, each of which has at least one point visible from q. We store the (constructed) vertices of the visibility polygon in two visibility trees, denoted by $TVIS_{\mathcal{P}'}^{B}(q)$ and $TVIS_{\mathcal{P}'}^{U}(q)$. The visibility tree structures are described in Sect. 2. For convenience, in the query algorithm, at every node in both of these visibility trees, we save an additional cone, named *auxiliary visibility cone*. The auxiliary visibility cone vc_{aux}^{t} defined at a node t indicates that there is an obstacle $O \in \mathcal{P}'$ such that (i) $p \in bd(O) \cap vc_{aux}^{t}$, and (ii) p is visible to q. (The specific use of auxiliary visibility cones is described in the subsections below.) As in [18], for each such side S, the query algorithm computes all the vertices of S visible to q. To construct these trees, we use a stack. This stack contains objects which are yet to be processed by the algorithm. Each object obj in stack is represented by a tuple $[lr_{vc}, rr_{vc}, ptr_l, ptr_r, ptr_t]$. Here, lr_{vc} (resp. rr_{vc}) is the left (resp. right) bounding ray of the visibility cone vc; ptr_l (resp. ptr_r) is a pointer to the first unexplored corridor in the corridor sequence of line segment qp' (resp. qp''), where p' (resp. p'') is the point at which lr_{vc} (resp. rr_{vc}) strikes an obstacle $O \in \mathcal{P}'$ or the bounding box; and, ptr_t is a pointer to the node in a visibility tree that was created at the time of initialization of obj.

First, using the point location data structure, we determine the corridor C_q containing q. Let B_{C_q} (resp. U_{C_q}) be the lower (resp. upper) bounding edge of C_q. Using the hull trees, we find the points of tangency on both the sides of C_q. Note that there can be at most two points of tangency on each side. For any point of tangency p which is lying on the left (resp. right) side of C_q, if the ray qp intersects B_{C_q} then point p is known as p_l^B (resp. p_r^B), and if the ray qp intersects U_{C_q} then point p is known as p_l^U (resp. p_r^U).

If the visibility cone (p_l^B, p_r^B) (resp. (p_l^U, p_r^U)) exists, then we create a node t^B (resp. t^U) as root node of $TVIS_{\mathcal{P}'}^{B}(q)$ (resp. $TVIS_{\mathcal{P}'}^{U}(q)$). The node t^B (resp. t^U) refers to corridor C_q, and the visibility cone (p_l^B, p_r^B) (resp. (p_l^U, p_r^U)) is associated with t^B. Also we initialize obj^B (resp. obj^U) that corresponds to t^B (resp. t^U). And, obj^U, followed by obj^B, are pushed onto the stack.

The visible vertices in corridors other than corridor C_q are determined by processing objects in the stack. Let $obj = [lr_{vc}, rr_{vc}, ptr_l, ptr_r, ptr_t]$ be the object popped from the stack. Let CS_l and CS_r be the corridor sequences of line segments lr_{vc} and lr_{vc} respectively. When both ptr_l and ptr_r refer to the same corridor C', starting from C' in CS_l and CS_r, we find the last common corridor C'' that occurs in both CS_l and CS_r. For every corridor C_i between C' and C'' in CS_l (or, CS_r), a node t' associated with ptr_t and vc is inserted to VC_{C_i}, and C_i saves a pointer to t'. (This denotes the visibility of corridor C_i is hindered by the corridor corresponding to the node pointed by ptr_t.) Let C_l (resp. C_r) be the corridor after C'' in CS_l (resp. CS_r).

When the corridor C_l referred by ptr_l is different from the corridor C_r referred by ptr_r, it is immediate that there is an obstacle O that separates C_l from C_r. We find a tangent qp_r to the right side of C_l from q and a tangent qp_l to left side of C_r from q. We insert one node t_l as the left child of t which refers to C_l, and another node t_r as the right child of t which refers to C_r. For every corridor C''' in the sequence of corridors from C' to C'', C'''' together with a pointer to $VC_{C'''}$ is associated to both the edges tt_l and tt_r. We also associate visibility cone (lr_{vc}, qp_r) (resp. (qp_l, rr_{vc})) with t_l (resp. t_r). A node t' (resp. t'') with ptr_{t_l} (resp. ptr_{t_r}) and the visibility cone (lr_{vc}, qp_r) (resp. (qp_l, rr_{vc})) is inserted to VC_{C_l} (resp. VC_{C_r}). In addition, an auxiliary visibility cone (qp_r, qp_l) is stored at node t. We initialize obj_l (resp. obj_r) that corresponds to t_l (resp. t_r). And, obj_r is pushed onto the stack followed by obj_l.

If no corridor exists after C'' in CS_l, then we determine the point p at which ray lr_{vc} strikes an obstacle. Let C_p be the corridor in which p is located. We find the point of tangency p_l from q to the left side of C_p, using the hull tree corresponding to that side. One new node is inserted as left child t_l of t that correspond to C_p and vc. A node t' with ptr_{t_l} and vc is inserted to VC_{C_p}. We initialize an object obj that corresponds to t_l and push that object onto the stack. For every corridor C''' in the sequence of corridors from C' to C'', C''' together with a pointer to $VC_{C'''}$ is associated to edge tt_l. When tangent to the left side of C_p does not exist, no object is pushed onto the stack. The algorithm for handling when there is no corridor after C'' in CS_r is analogous.

As in [18], we traverse each of the visibility trees in depth-first order. At every node t, for each side S of C_t, we determine vertices of $VP_{P'}(q)$ that belong to $S \cap vc^t$, by applying the algorithm in [20] to each simple polygon in P_{C_t} that corresponds to S, with q and vc^t as the additional two parameters. In addition, we store visible vertices on the left side (resp. right side) of C_t in RBT_L^t (resp. RBT_R^t). We determine all the vertices of S_r (resp. S_l) that are visible from q and located in cone vc_{aux}^t, by applying the algorithm in [20] to each simple polygon in P_{C_t} that corresponds to S_r (resp. S_l), with q and vc_{aux}^t as the additional two parameters. In addition, we store these visible vertices in $RBT_R^{t_l}$ (resp. $RBT_L^{t_r}$).

To construct $VP_{P'}(q)$, we traverse both the visibility trees in depth-first order. First we traverse $TVIS_{P'}^B(q)$ followed by $TVIS_{P'}^U(q)$. At every node t encountered during the traversal, we traverse the leaf nodes of RBT_L^t in left to right order and output the respective points stored at them. Then, we recursively traverse the left subtree of t, followed by the right subtree of t. After that, we traverse the leaf nodes of RBT_R^t in the right to left order and output the respective points stored at them.

Theorem 1. *Given a polygonal domain $\mathcal{P}$ defined with h obstacles and n vertices, we preprocess $\mathcal{P}$ in $O(n(\lg n)^2 + h(\lg h)^{1+\epsilon})$ time to construct data structures of size $O(n)$ so that (i) whenever a vertex v is inserted to the current polygonal domain $\mathcal{P}'$, the algorithm updates the visibility polygon $VP_{P'}(q)$ of a query point q in $O(k(\lg |VP_{P'}(q)|) + (\lg n')^2 + h)$ time, (ii) whenever a vertex v is deleted from the current polygonal domain $\mathcal{P}'$, the algorithm updates the visibility polygon $VP_{P'}(q)$ of a query point q in $O(k(\lg n')^2 + (\lg |VP_{P'}(q)|) + h)$ time, and (iii) whenever a query point q is given, algorithm outputs the visibility polygon in the current polygonal domain in $O(|VP_{P'}(q)|(\lg n')^2 + h)$ time. Here ϵ is a small positive constant resulting from the triangulation of the free space $\mathcal{F}(\mathcal{P})$ using the algorithm in [4], k is the number of combinatorial changes in $VP_{P'}(q)$ due to the insertion or deletion of v, and n' is the number of vertices of $\mathcal{P}'$. (The proof is provided in the full version.)*

References

1. Akbari, K., Ghodsi, M.: Visibility maintenance of a moving segment observer inside polygons with holes. In: Proceedings of Canadian Conference on Computational Geometry, pp. 117–120 (2010)
2. Aronov, B., Guibas, L.J., Teichmann, M., Zhang, L.: Visibility queries and maintenance in simple polygons. Discrete Comput. Geom. **27**(4), 461–483 (2002). https://doi.org/10.1007/s00454-001-0089-9
3. Asano, T., Asano, T., Guibas, L.J., Hershberger, J., Imai, H.: Visibility of disjoint polygons. Algorithmica **1**(1), 49–63 (1986). https://doi.org/10.1007/BF01840436
4. Bar-Yehuda, R., Chazelle, B.: Triangulating disjoint Jordan chains. Int. J. Comput. Geom. Appl. **4**(4), 475–481 (1994)
5. Baygi, M.N., Ghodsi, M.: Space/query-time tradeoff for computing the visibility polygon. Comput. Geom. **46**, 371–381 (2013)
6. Bose, P., Lubiw, A., Munro, J.I.: Efficient visibility queries in simple polygons. Comput. Geom. **23**(3), 313–335 (2002)
7. Chen, D.Z., Daescu, O.: Maintaining visibility of a polygon with a moving point of view. Inf. Process. Lett. **65**(5), 269–275 (1998)
8. Chen, D.Z., Wang, H.: Visibility and ray shooting queries in polygonal domains. Comput. Geom. **48**(2), 31–41 (2015)
9. Choudhury, T., Inkulu, R.: Maintaining the visibility graph of a dynamic simple polygon. In: Pal, S.P., Vijayakumar, A. (eds.) CALDAM 2019. LNCS, vol. 11394, pp. 42–52. Springer, Cham (2019). https://doi.org/10.1007/978-3-030-11509-8_4
10. Cormen, T.H., Leiserson, C.E., Rivest, R.L., Stein, C.: Introduction to Algorithms. The MIT Press, Cambridge (2009)
11. Davis, L.S., Benedikt, M.L.: Computational models of space: isovists and isovist fields. Comput. Graph. Image Process. **11**(1), 49–72 (1979)
12. ElGindy, H.A., Avis, D.: A linear algorithm for computing the visibility polygon from a point. J. Algorithms **2**(2), 186–197 (1981)
13. Ghosh, S.K.: Computing the visibility polygon from a convex set and related problems. J. Algorithms **12**(1), 75–95 (1991)
14. Ghosh, S.K.: Visibility Algorithms in the Plane. Cambridge University Press, New York (2007)
15. Ghosh, S.K., Mount, D.M.: An output-sensitive algorithm for computing visibility graphs. SIAM J. Comput. **20**(5), 888–910 (1991)
16. Goodrich, M.T., Tamassia, R.: Dynamic ray shooting and shortest paths in planar subdivisions via balanced geodesic triangulations. J. Algorithms **23**(1), 51–73 (1997)
17. Heffernan, P.J., Mitchell, J.S.B.: An optimal algorithm for computing visibility in the plane. SIAM J. Comput. **24**(1), 184–201 (1995)
18. Inkulu, R., Kapoor, S.: Visibility queries in a polygonal region. Comput. Geom. **42**(9), 852–864 (2009)
19. Inkulu, R., Thakur, N.P.: Incremental algorithms to update visibility polygons. In: Gaur, D., Narayanaswamy, N.S. (eds.) CALDAM 2017. LNCS, vol. 10156, pp. 205–218. Springer, Cham (2017). https://doi.org/10.1007/978-3-319-53007-9_19
20. Inkulu, R., Sowmya, K., Thakur, N.P.: Dynamic algorithms for visibility polygons in simple polygons (CoRR 1704.08219) (2020). Accepted to Int. J. Comput. Geom. Appl
21. Joe, B., Simpson, R.: Corrections to Lee's visibility polygon algorithm. BIT Numer. Math. **27**(4), 458–473 (1987). https://doi.org/10.1007/BF01937271

22. Kapoor, S.: Efficient computation of geodesic shortest paths. In: Proceedings of Symposium on Theory of Computing, pp. 770–779 (1999)
23. Kapoor, S., Maheshwari, S.N.: Efficient algorithms for Euclidean shortest path and visibility problems with polygonal obstacles. In: Proceedings of Symposium on Computational Geometry, pp. 172–182 (1988)
24. Kapoor, S., Maheshwari, S.N.: Efficiently constructing the visibility graph of a simple polygon with obstacles. SIAM J. Comput. **30**(3), 847–871 (2000)
25. Kapoor, S., Maheshwari, S.N., Mitchell, J.S.B.: An efficient algorithm for Euclidean shortest paths among polygonal obstacles in the plane. Discrete Comput. Geom. **18**(4), 377–383 (1997). https://doi.org/10.1007/PL00009323
26. Lee, D.T.: Visibility of a simple polygon. Comput. Vis. Graph. Image Process. **22**(2), 207–221 (1983)
27. Lu, L., Yang, C., Wang, J.: Point visibility computing in polygons with holes. J. Inf. Comput. Sci. **16**(7), 4165–4173 (2011)
28. Overmars, M.H., van Leewen, J.: Maintenance of configurations in the plane. J. Comput. Syst. Sci. **23**(2), 166–204 (1981)
29. Pocchiola, M., Vegter, G.: Topologically sweeping visibility complexes via pseudo-triangulations. Discrete Comput. Geom. **16**(4), 419–453 (1996). https://doi.org/10.1007/BF02712876
30. Preparata, F.P., Shamos, M.I.: Computational Geometry: An Introduction. Springer, New York (1985). https://doi.org/10.1007/978-1-4612-1098-6
31. Suri, S., O'Rourke, J.: Worst-case optimal algorithms for constructing visibility polygons with holes. In: Proceedings of the Symposium on Computational Geometry, pp. 14–23 (1986)
32. Zarei, A., Ghodsi, M.: Efficient computation of query point visibility in polygons with holes. In: Proceedings of the Symposium on Computational Geometry, pp. 314–320 (2005)

How Hard Is Completeness Reasoning for Conjunctive Queries?

Xianmin Liu[1(⊠)], Jianzhong Li[1], and Yingshu Li[2]

[1] Harbin Institute of Technology, Harbin 150000, China
{liuxianmin,lijzh}@hit.edu.cn
[2] Georgia State University, Atlanta, USA
yili@gsu.edu

Abstract. Incomplete data has been wildly viewed in many real applications. In practical, data is often *partial complete*, it means that the whole part of data is incomplete but there exist special complete parts of data which can still support answering related queries. However, as far as we know, there are only few works focusing on managing partial complete data. Therefore, efficient methods for representing partial complete data and deciding which queries can be answered over the complete parts are seriously needed. The completeness reasoning problem, TC-QC (Table Completeness to Query Completeness), has been recognized as an important fundamental problem in managing partial complete data. Given completeness statements of data, the goal of the TC-QC problem is to determine whether the result of a special query Q is complete, that is to reason query completeness based on given data completeness. Previous works show that the TC-QC problem is NP-*hard* even for *conjunctive queries*, and a natural and interesting question is whether or not TC-QC can be solved efficiently by parameterized algorithms.

The paper investigates the parameterized complexity of completeness reasoning for conjunctive queries. We show that, if the query completeness size or the table completeness size is considered as a parameter, then the parameterized TC-QC problem for conjunctive queries is para-NP-*complete*. These results strongly indicate that no fixed-parameter tractable algorithms exist for the TC-QC problems parameterized by the above two parameters. Thus, more special cases of TC-QC defined by different constraints are studied. It is shown that, when the constraints about query structures like degree, tree-width and number of variables are considered, the parameterized TC-QC problems are still intractable. On the positive side, we show that, if each data completeness statement has a constant size bound, the parameterized TC-QC problem defined by the query completeness size can be solved by a fixed-parameter tractable algorithm.

1 Introduction

In many real applications, it usually suffers from the problem of owning only incomplete data and having no abilities of returning complete results required

© Springer Nature Switzerland AG 2020
D. Kim et al. (Eds.): COCOON 2020, LNCS 12273, pp. 149–161, 2020.
https://doi.org/10.1007/978-3-030-58150-3_12

by computing tasks (*e.g.* [3,5,8,10–12,15]). Therefore, research topics related with incomplete data are interesting and well motivated.

In fact, the study of incomplete data can be traced back to the times when the relational data model is proposed [4]. By the traditional works in the area of data and knowledge management, a popular and reasonable way is to utilize two kinds of assumptions for handling incomplete data, which are the *open world assumption* (OWA for short) and the *closed world assumption* (CWA for short). Within this framework, data in the applications should be clarified to be in the OWA or CWA beforehand. For the OWA, the owned data is assumed to be a subset (maybe proper subset) of the *truth* data, and those tuples in the truth data but not included in the owned data are missing; while, for the CWA, it is assumed that there are no missing tuples, but missing values in a tuple is allowed, which are usually represented by null values.

However, neither of them satisfies the requirements of describing incomplete data in real applications, since those two assumptions are only proper for the extreme cases like data is totally complete or any tuples can be missing. In practical, we are usually facing *partial complete* data, which means that the whole part of data maybe incomplete but there exist special complete parts of data which can still support answering related queries.

Example 1. Suppose we have the following database `weather`(city, year, temp) containing the average temperature records of two cities *Beijing* and *Shanghai* between 2011 and 2015.

⟨*true* `weather`⟩

city	year	temp
Shanghai	2011	15.7 °C
Shanghai	2012	15.3 °C
Shanghai	2013	15.6 °C
Shanghai	2014	15.1 °C
Shanghai	2015	15.5 °C
Beijing	2011	12.3 °C
Beijing	2012	12.7 °C
Beijing	2013	12.1 °C
Beijing	2014	11.9 °C
Beijing	2015	12.5 °C

⟨*owned* `weather`⟩

city	year	temp
Shanghai	2011	15.7 °C
Shanghai	2012	15.3 °C
Shanghai	2014	15.1 °C
Beijing	2011	12.3 °C
Beijing	2012	12.7 °C
Beijing	2013	12.1 °C
Beijing	2014	11.9 °C
Beijing	2015	12.5 °C

Let the database `weather` be obtained by integrating two databases `weatherBJ` and `weatherSH`. In addition, we know that `weatherBJ` includes the average temperature records of every year from 2011 to 2015, but `weatherSH` is incomplete. After integrating the two databases, the *owned* `weather` as shown above is obtained. Because of the incompleteness of `weatherSH`, compared with the *true* `weather`, there lacks two tuples for the city *Shanghai*. When utilizing the traditional method, it is obvious that we can only clarity `weather` is in OWA. Then, when requiring the average temperature of *Shanghai* of 2013, it will be warned that the result is *incomplete* base on the knowledge that `weather` is in OWA. However, in this case, the result of the query "*select the temperature record of*

Beijing in 2013" will be determined to be incomplete also. That is just the case of *partial complete* data, for which traditional methods lose the opportunities to answer queries over incomplete data. Obviously, more sophisticated solution should have the ability to confirm the completeness of the query when meeting the above cases.   □

To handle the above example, we need at least two kinds of mechanisms of managing partial incomplete data. One is to provide methods for expressing statements like *"the part of data related with* Beijing *is complete in* weather", and the other one is to support efficient reasoning the completeness of queries based on the completeness statements of data.

For the data completeness statements, since it does not work by using traditional methods, the concept of partial completeness is proposed in [9], and based on a more general and formal definition, in [14], *table completeness* and *query completeness* are introduced to satisfy the requirements of describe partial complete data. The *table* and *query completeness* statements can express the semantics like "some special parts of the data is complete" and "the result of some given query is complete" respectively. Then, for providing the ability of completeness reasoning, the TC-QC problem is formally defined in [14], whose intuitive aim is to determine *whether the result of some query is complete based on the fact that some parts of the data are complete*. Obviously, TC-QC is a fundamental problem of managing partial complete data.

In [14], the computational complexities of the TC-QC problem have been studied in the aspect of classical complexities. It has shown that the complexities of TC-QC ranges from PTIME to Π_2^p-complete when considering different query fragments. On the positive side, [13] shows that when considering only very simple table completeness statements, the TC-QC problem can be solved efficiently. Observing the above results, it is rather needed to provide more fine-grained complexity results for the TC-QC problem and seek for efficient algorithms for practical settings. Therefore, an interesting and natural research issue is to study the parameterized complexities of the TC-QC problem.

The paper investigates the parameterized complexity of completeness reasoning for conjunctive queries. We show that, if the query completeness size or the table completeness size is considered as a parameter, then the parameterized TC-QC problem for conjunctive queries is para-NP-*complete*. These results strongly indicate that the TC-QC problems parameterized by the above two parameters do not admit fixed-parameter tractable algorithms. Thus, more special cases of TC-QC defined by different constraints are studied. It is shown that, when the constraints about query structures like degree, tree-width and number of variables are considered, the parameterized TC-QC problems are still intractable. On the positive side, we show that, if each data completeness statement has a constant size bound, the parameterized TC-QC problem defined by the query completeness size can be solved by a fixed-parameter tractable algorithm.

The paper is organized as follows. Section 2 contains the necessary definitions. In Sect. 3, the complexities of two typical parameterized TC-QC problems are introduced. Section 4 introduces a deterministic algorithm for TC-QC and identified a tractable case by considering more constraints. Section 5 contains the complexity results of special parameterized TC-QC problems under several important constraints, and Sect. 6 is the conclusion.

2   Preliminaries

In this part, we will introduce the fundamental concepts and basic definitions about completeness reasoning and parameterized complexity.

The Relational Model. The relational database model assumes that the data are stored in *relations* or *tables*. The columns of a relation are *attributes*, and the rows are called *tuples*. For each attribute A, there is an associated domain $dom(A)$ of values. For each tuple t, let $t[A]$ represents the value of t in the column A, and we have $t[A] \in dom(A)$. A *database* D is composed of a set of relations, denoted by $D = \{R_1, \ldots, R_m\}$. The scheme of a relation R, denoted by $sch(R)$, is the set of attribute (or column) names, and the number of attributes (or the arity of R) is denoted by $arity(R)$.

Conjunctive Queries. A conjunctive query Q can be represented by

$$Q(x_1, \ldots, x_k) : -R_1(\bar{t}_1), R_2(\bar{t}_2), \ldots, R_l(\bar{t}_l).$$

Usually, the left-hand side of Q is called the *head*, and the right-hand side is called the *body*. Here, each $\bar{t}_i$ is a tuple of variables, every R_i is a relation in the database and is not necessarily distinct from the others, and each x_j in the head must occur in the body of Q. Assuming there are n variables totally in Q, the semantics of Q can be explained by the following expression.

$$Q(D) = \{(x_1, \ldots, x_k) \mid \exists y_1 \ldots \exists y_{n-k} \, R_1(\bar{t}_1) \wedge \cdots \wedge R_l(\bar{t}_l)\}$$

To be convenient, the above conjunctive query is also represented by

$$Q(\bar{t}) = Q(x_1, \ldots, x_k) = R_1(\bar{t}_1) \wedge R_2(\bar{t}_2) \wedge \cdots \wedge R_l(\bar{t}_l).$$

The Incomplete Data Model. The incomplete data (or incompleteness) is an old enough concept related to important issues such as data quality in database and knowledge management areas. Generally, it can be defined based on tuples and values. This paper only considers the tuple based incomplete data, and focuses on the *partial complete* data model. An *incomplete* (or *partial complete*) database, denoted by $\mathcal{D}$, is a pair of databases $\langle D^o, D^c \rangle$. Here, D^o and D^c have the same schemes, and $\mathcal{D}$ must satisfies $D^o \subseteq D^c$. Intuitively, D^c is the truth database which contains all tuples, and D^o is the database owned by users which may miss tuples from D^c. Usually, in real applications, users only own D^o which is incomplete, and the tuples in $D^c \setminus D^o$ are missed.

The Table Completeness. Intuitively, the table completeness statements are proposed for describing which part of tuples in the data are not missed (complete).

The following definitions are oriented from [14], and only conjunctive queries are considered here.

Let G be a *condition* expression represented by a set of *terms* like $R_i(\bar{t}_i)$, $x = y$ and $x = c$, where R_i is a relation, x and y are variables, and c is a constant. Given an incomplete database $\mathcal{D} = \langle D^o, D^c \rangle$, a table completeness statement $Compl(R(\bar{x}); G)$ is *satisfied* by $\mathcal{D}$, denoted by $\mathcal{D} \models Compl(R(\bar{x}); G)$, if and only if $Q_{R(\bar{x}); G}(D^c) \subseteq R(D^o)$, where $Q_{R(\bar{x}); G}$ is a conjunctive query defined by $Q(\bar{x}) :\text{--}R(\bar{x}), G$. Given a set Σ of table completeness statements, $\mathcal{D} \models \Sigma$ means that there is $\mathcal{D} \models \sigma$ for every $\sigma \in \Sigma$. In the following parts, we will use the TC to represent the table completeness for short, and q^σ to represent the associated query $Q_{R(\bar{x}; G)}$ of σ.

Example 2. Continued with Example 1, the completeness knowledge "*the records related with Beijing is complete*" about the data can be represented by the TC statement $\sigma = Compl(\texttt{whether}(x, y, z); x = \text{'Beijing'})$.   □

The Query Completeness. The *query completeness* (QC for short) statements are used to claim the query result is complete. According to [14], for a query Q, the QC statement $Compl(Q)$ is *satisfied* by an incomplete database $\mathcal{D}$, denoted by $\mathcal{D} \models Compl(Q)$, if and only if $Q(D^o) = Q(D^c)$. It means, even if D^c misses some unknown tuples from D^c, the query result $Q(D^o)$ is still complete and has quality guarantees. If $\varphi = Compl(Q)$ is a QC statement, we use q^φ to represent the associated query Q.

Completeness Reasoning. Based on TC and QC statements, we can define the TC-QC problem for reasoning query completeness from table completes. Assuming that Σ is a set of TC statements and φ is a QC statement, $\Sigma \models \varphi$ means that for any $\mathcal{D}$ satisfying $\mathcal{D} \models \Sigma$, there must be $\mathcal{D} \models \varphi$.

Definition 1 (The TC-QC Problem). *Given a set Σ of TC statements, and a QC statement φ, the TC-QC problem is to determine whether or not $\Sigma \models \varphi$.*

TC-QC is a fundamental and key problem in managing incompleteness. A typical usage can be explained by the following example.

Example 3. Continued with Example 1 and 2, let $\Sigma = \{\sigma\}$ where σ is defined in Example 2. Let us consider the query used in Example 1, it can be represented by $Q(x, y, z) : -\texttt{whether}(\text{'Beijing'}, 2013, z)$. In this case, solving the instance $\langle \Sigma, \varphi = Compl(Q) \rangle$ of TC-QC problem will determine that $\Sigma \models \varphi$, which suggest us that the result of query Q is complete.   □

Fundamental Parameterized Complexity. A parameterized problem can be represented by the form (I, k), where I is the input and k is an integer parameter. For example, a typical parameterized version of the classical Clique problem is represented by (G, k), where G is the graph and k is the clique size.

A parameterized problem is *fixed-parameter tractable* (*fpt* for short) if there is an algorithm that determines whether the answer of I is 'yes' within time $f(k) \cdot poly(n)$, where $f : \mathbb{N} \to \mathbb{N}$ is a computable function and n is the input size.

More details about the *fpt*-reduction and the parameterized complexity classes including para-NP, XP, W[1] and so on can be found in [7].

3   Parameterized Complexities by Limiting Input Sizes

First, we will consider the most restricted parameters, *input sizes*. Since most of other effective parameterization methods often choose parameters limited by the input sizes, constructing parameterized complexities and fpt-algorithms results for input sizes parameters will give further directions for them.

According to Definition 1, a TC-QC instance is composed of two inputs, the TC set Σ and the QC φ. Naturally, we consider two parameters, and formalize the following two parameterized problems. Here, $m = |\varphi|$ is the size of the input QC φ, and $n = |\Sigma|$ is the size of the input TC set Σ. Here, it should be noticed that $|\Sigma|$ is the size of information needed to represent all TCs in Σ, but not the number of TCs in Σ. For the later one, we will use $\#|\Sigma|$ instead.

The p-TC-QC-m Problem   *parameter:* $m = |\varphi|$
input: the TC set Σ, the QC φ.
problem: determine whether or not $\Sigma \models \varphi$.

The p-TC-QC-n Problem   *parameter:* $n = |\Sigma|$
input: the TC set Σ, the QC φ.
problem: determine whether or not $\Sigma \models \varphi$.

3.1   The p-TC-QC-m Problem

The following theorem shows that the p-TC-QC-m problem has high parameterized complexities, and is not fixed-parameter-tractable unless P = NP.

Theorem 1. *The p-TC-QC-m problem is* para-NP-*complete.*

Since p-TC-QC-m is hard, a possible and natural idea is to consider special cases that TC statements are limited. However, if the parameter $|\Sigma|$ is fixed, the problem will become trivial to be fixed-parameter-tractable which has a $O(m^m)$ time algorithm. The parameter $|\Sigma|$ is affected by both the number of TC statements and the size of single TC statement. If the number of TC statements $\#|\Sigma|$ is fixed, we have the following result.

Corollary 1. *Even if there are only fixed number of TC statements, that is $\#|TC|$ is a constant, the p-TC-QC-m problem is still* para-NP-*complete.*

When considering fixed database scheme, we have the following result.

Corollary 2. *Even if only fixed database scheme is considered, the p-TC-QC-m problem is still* para-NP-*complete. Even if there are only 6 tables and the maximum arity is bounded by 3, the p-TC-QC-m problem is still* para-NP-*complete.*

3.2   The p-TC-QC-n Problem

In this part, we will show that, when we have limited TC size, the p-TC-QC-n problem is also para-NP-*complete*, still fixed parameter intractable.

Theorem 2. *The p-TC-QC-n problem is* para-NP-*complete*.

Proof. The details are omitted.   □

Again, by observing the reduction used in the proof of Theorem 2 carefully, we can obtain parameterized complexity results for more special cases for which the reduction used in Theorem 2 still works.

Corollary 3. *Even if there are only fixed number of TC statements, that is* $\#|TC|$ *is a constant, the p-TC-QC-n problem is still* para-NP-*complete*.

When considering fixed database scheme, we have the following result.

Corollary 4. *Even if only fixed database scheme is considered, the p-TC-QC-n problem is still* para-NP-*complete. Even if there are only 6 tables and the maximum arity is bounded by 3, the p-TC-QC-n problem is still* para-NP-*complete*.

4   A Tractable Case by Limiting TC Length

In this part, based on introducing a deterministic algorithm for the TC-QC problem, a fixed-parameter tractable case for parameterized TC-QC with fixed TC length is identified.

4.1   A Deterministic Algorithm for the TC-QC Problem

In this part, after introducing some key concepts, a deterministic algorithm for the TC-QC problem will be introduced, which is the fundamental of understanding the tractable case.

Unfolding Queries. First, the concept of *unfolding queries* and an important lemma by [14] are introduced, which can be utilized to determine whether $\Sigma \models \varphi$ more conveniently by avoiding to check each possible model or build a minimal-model like theory for the TC-QC problem.

Given a conjunctive query $Q(\bar{t}) = R_1(\bar{t}_1) \wedge R_2(\bar{t}_2) \wedge \cdots \wedge R_l(\bar{t}_l)$, the *unfolding query* Q w.r.t. Σ, denoted by Q^{Σ}, is defined as follows:

$$Q^{\Sigma} = \bigwedge_{i \in [1,l]} \left(R_i(\bar{t}_i) \wedge \bigvee_{\sigma \in \Sigma, \sigma = Compl(R_i(\bar{t}_\sigma); G_\sigma)} \left(G_\sigma \wedge (\bar{t}_i = \bar{t}_\sigma) \right) \right).$$

Example 4. Let Q be the query $Q(x) = R(x, y) \land S(y, z)$, and the TC statements are as follows.

$$\sigma_1 = Compl(R(a, b);\ S(a, 1))$$
$$\sigma_2 = Compl(R(a, b);\ S(b, c))$$
$$\sigma_3 = Compl(S(a, b);\ R(a, c))$$

Then, the unfolding query Q^{Σ} is

$$Q^{\Sigma}(x) = \Big(R(x, y) \land \big(S(x, 1) \lor S(y, c^1) \big) \Big) \bigwedge \big(S(y, z) \land R(y, c^2) \big).$$

Then, we have the following useful result.

Lemma 1 [14]. *Given a set Σ of TC statements and a QC statement $\varphi = Compl(Q)$ satisfying that Q is a conjunctive query, $\Sigma \models \varphi$ if and only if $Q \subseteq Q^{\Sigma}$.*

Two Challenges of TC-QC. Based on Lemma 1, the idea of the proposed algorithm is naturally to design efficient algorithms for the TC-QC problem based on efficient query containment testing algorithms.

However, to achieve and implement such an idea, there are still two challenges. (1) It is well known that general conjunctive query containment is still NP-*complete*, but there are still opportunities based on the fact that many special tractable cases for the query containment problem have been developed. (2) The unfolding query Q^{Σ} is not a conjunctive query, and just a monotone query, even not a union of conjunctive queries.

Query Containment and Evaluation. To face the first challenge, we will reduce query containment to query evaluation problem. Given a conjunctive query q, there is an equivalent *tableau* expression. As shown in [1], a *tableau* representation is in the form $(\mathbf{T}, u)$, which is composed of the *tableau* $\mathbf{T}$ and the *summary* u of the query. Here, $\mathbf{T}$ is a set of tables whose values are constants in domain or variables, u is a tuple of constants and variables. The only constriction is that the variables in u must occur in $\mathbf{T}$.

Example 5. Let q be the conjunctive query

$$Q(x, y) : -R(x, z), S(z, 1), S(z, y).$$

$\mathbf{T}_S$	
z	1
z	y

$\mathbf{T}_R$	
x	z

The *tableau* form $(\mathbf{T}, u)$ can be represented by $\boxed{\begin{array}{c|c} x & z \end{array}}$, $\boxed{\begin{array}{c|c} z & 1 \\ z & y \end{array}}$ and $\boxed{u : (x, y)}$.

Then, we have the following celebrating result.

Lemma 2 [2]. *Given two conjunctive queries q and q', let $(\mathbf{T}, u)$ be the equivalent tableau query of q, then $q \subseteq q'$ iff $u \in q'(\mathbf{T})$.*

Disjunction-Eliminated Queries. To face the second challenge, an important concept utilized here is *disjunction-eliminated queries*. Observing the structure of Q^Σ, suppose for each $\bigvee$ operation used there is only one σ related with R_i, the query Q^Σ will become a conjunctive query which is easier to handle than a general Q^Σ. Thus, the intuitive idea of disjunction-eliminated queries is to build related conjunctive queries with Q^Σ by choosing one from all possible TC statements for each $\bigvee$ operation. The set of all possible disjunction-eliminated queries related with Q^Σ is represented by $[\![Q^\Sigma]\!]$.

Example 6. Continue with Example 4, the $[\![Q^\Sigma]\!]$ includes the following two queries.

$$q_1(x) = \big(R(x,y) \wedge S(x,1)\big) \bigwedge \big(S(y,z) \wedge R(y,c^2)\big)$$
$$q_2(x) = \big(R(x,y) \wedge S(y,c^1)\big) \bigwedge \big(S(y,z) \wedge R(y,c^2)\big)$$

Theorem 3. *Given Σ and conjunctive queries Q and q, $q \subseteq Q^\Sigma$ if and only if there is some $q' \in [\![Q^\Sigma]\!]$ satisfying $q \subseteq q'$.*

Algorithm CR-FixedTCS (Completeness Reasoning for Fixed TC Size)

Input: The TC set Σ, and a QC statement φ.
Output: true if $\Sigma \models \varphi$, otherwise false.

1. Let Q be the query q^φ;
2. build Q^Σ according to the definition of unfolding query;
3. $S_Q = \{Q^\Sigma\}$;
4. $L = $ the number of $\bigvee$ operations in Q^Σ;
   /**build $[\![Q^\Sigma]\!]$ by eliminating the $\bigvee$ operations**/
5. **for** i from 1 to L **do**
6.   Let $\bigvee_i$ be the ith operation in Q^Σ;
7.   Let U_i be the set of TC statements related with $\bigvee_i$;
8. $S'_Q = \emptyset$;
9.   **for** each item $q \in S_Q$ **do**
10.   **for** each TC statement $\sigma_{ij} \in U_i$ $(1 \le j \le |U_i|)$ **do**
11.   Let q' be the query obtained by replacing the subquery
                      of $\bigvee_i$ in q with $G_{\sigma_{ij}} \wedge (\bar{t}_i = \bar{t}_{\sigma_{ij}})$;
12.   insert q' into S'_Q;
13. $S_Q = S'_Q$;
    /**check whether $Q \subseteq Q^\Sigma$**/
14. Let $(\mathbf{T}, u)$ be the *tableau* representation of Q;
15. **for** each query $q \in S_Q$, **do**
16.   **if** $u \in q(\mathbf{T})$ **then**
17.   **return** true;
18. **return** false;

Fig. 1. The CR-FixedTCS Algorithm

The CR-FixedTCS Algorithm. Combining the techniques introduced above, the CR-FixedTCS (Completeness Reasoning for Fixed TC Size) algorithm is introduced, whose main idea is first making a reduction from TC-QC to query containment, and then utilizing the principles in Theorem 3 to determine the containment of queries. The details of CR-FixedTCS are shown in Fig. 1.

The main procedures of CR-FixedTCS can be summarized as follows.

(1) The unfolding query Q^{Σ} is built based on Σ and φ (line 1–2).
(2) Then, the query set $[\![Q^{\Sigma}]\!]$ is constructed by removing $\bigvee$ operations from Q^{Σ} (line 5–13). The queries in $[\![Q^{\Sigma}]\!]$ are generated in a bread-first way and maintained in S_Q. There are L rounds of generating quereis in total. Before the ith round, the queries in S_Q are obtained by removing all first $i-1$ $\bigvee$ operations from Q^{Σ}. In the ith round, for each query $q \in S_Q$, there are $|U_i|$ TC statements related with $\bigvee_i$, q will be transferred to $|U_i|$ queries obtained by replacing $\bigvee_i$ with all possible conditions related with TC statements in U_i (line 11).
(3) Finally, for each query $q \in [\![Q^{\Sigma}]\!]$, using the corresponding tableau $(\mathbf{T}, u)$ of Q, the answer of query containment can be determined by checking whether or not $u \in q'(\mathbf{T})$ (line 14–17).

The correctness of the CR-FixedTCS algorithm can be obtained easily by considering Theorem 3 and the definition of $[\![Q^{\Sigma}]\!]$. To be convenient, its time cost can be represented by $O(|[\![Q^{\Sigma}]\!]| \cdot \mathsf{cost}(Q, [\![Q^{\Sigma}]\!]))$, where $|[\![Q^{\Sigma}]\!]|$ is the size of $[\![Q^{\Sigma}]\!]$ and $\mathsf{cost}(Q, [\![Q^{\Sigma}]\!])$ is the evaluation cost of queries in $[\![Q^{\Sigma}]\!]$ on $\mathbf{T}_Q$.

4.2   Parameterzied Complexities of TC-QC with Fixed TC Length

In this part, the special cases of TC-QC problems with fixed TC length are considered. For the p-TC-QC-m problem, it is shown to be fixed-parameter tractable, that is in FPT, but the p-TC-QC-n problem is still para-NP-*complete*.

p-TC-QC-m with Fixed TC Length. Observing the CR-FixedTCS algorithm, a rough analysis can not guarantee that p-TC-QC-m with fixed TC length can be fixed-parameter tractable. Obviously, the set $[\![Q^{\Sigma}]\!]$ is dependent on all possible disjunction-eliminated operations. For each $\bigvee$ in Q^{Σ}, all related TC statements will be utilized, and the size $|[\![Q^{\Sigma}]\!]|$ can be bounded by $(\#|\Sigma|)^m$. Here, m is the QC statement size $|\varphi|$ which is an upper bound of $|Q|$, and $\#|TC|$ is the number of TC statements in Σ. Since the length of single TC statement is fixed, in the worst case, $\#|\Sigma|$ can be $\Theta(|x|)$. Therefore, the bound of $|[\![Q^{\Sigma}]\!]|$ can be $O(|x|^m)$ which is not allowed in the definition of fixed-parameter tractable algorithms.

However, two *isomorphic* TC statements should be considered as one same TC statement. Intuitively, they contain the same semantics and will produce equivalent queries in $[\![Q^{\Sigma}]\!]$.

Definition 2 (isomorphic TC statements). *Two TC statements σ_1 and σ_2 are* isomorphic, *if and only if there is an isomorphism between q^{σ_1} and q^{σ_2}.*

Here, an isomorphism is a bijection mapping f between the variables of q^{σ_1} and q^{σ_2} such that a query term $R_i(\overline{x})$ is in the body of q^{σ_1} iff the query term $R_i(f(\overline{x}))$ is in the body of q^{σ_2}, and the head part is also hold under f.

In fact, the fail of analysis discussed above is oriented from calculating many times for redundant TC statements. Based on a more careful analysis of the bound for non-redundant $|[\![Q^{\Sigma}]\!]|$ and a preprocessing algorithm for Σ, we can prove the following result.

Theorem 4 (Fixed TC Length). *If there is a constant c such that for each $\sigma \in \Sigma$ we have $|\sigma| \leq c$, the p-TC-QC-m problem is fixed-parameter tractable.*

p-TC-QC-n with Fixed TC Length. For the p-TC-QC-n problem, even if only TC statements with fixed length are allowed, it is still para-NP-*complete*. It should be noticed that even if the size of input TC statement sets is treated as the parameter, the constraint that each single TC has fixed length is still interesting, since the fact $\#|\Sigma|$ can also affect the parameter.

Corollary 5. *Even if only fixed-length TC statements are allowed, the p-TC-QC-n problem is still para-NP-complete.*

5 Parameterized Complexities by Constraints of Queries

In this part, several query related constraints are considered, and the parameterized complexity results of TC-QC are introduced.

p-TC-QC-m with Query Constraints. To consider more structural constraints of the associated queries further, a popular way is to focus on the *underlying graph* G_Q of Q. G_Q can be obtained by treating variables and constants appearing in Q as vertices and adding edges between two vertices when they appear in the same subquery in Q. Then, the constraints are defined on G_Q, which require G_Q to have bounded degree or bounded tree-width (see [6] for details). Intuitively, the above constraints do not allow Q to have complex structures. However, we obtain the following negative results.

Theorem 5. *Even when only QC statements satisfying that the underlying graphs of the queries are either of bounded degree or of bounded tree-width are allowed, the p-TC-QC-m problem is still para-NP-complete.*

Another interesting constraints is the number of variables used in the queries.

Theorem 6. *Suppose there exists a constant c, such that the number of variables used in q^{φ} is bounded by c, in this case, the p-TC-QC-m problem is still para-NP-complete.*

p-TC-QC-n with Query Constraints. For the p-TC-QC-n problem, when queries with degree constraints are considered, we have the following result.

Theorem 7. *Even when only QC statements satisfying that the underlying graphs of the queries are of bounded degree are allowed, the p-TC-QC-n problem is still* para-NP-*complete.*

Considering the constraint that only fixed number of variables are used in φ, we have the following result.

Theorem 8. *Suppose there exists a constant c, such that the number of variables used in $Q = q^\varphi$ is bounded by c, the p-TC-QC-n problem is* W[1]-*hard.*

6 Conclusion

In this paper, to exploit the idea of reasoning completeness for incomplete data, the TC-QC problem is studied from the parameterized complexity view. Moreover, we showed that the parameterized TC-QC problems defined by input sizes are para-NP-*complete*, even when considering several typical constraints, the special cases obtained are still para-NP-*complete*. By limiting the TC length, an important tractable case is identified and an *fpt*-algorithm is designed.

Acknowledgement. This work was supported in part by the Key Program of the National Natural Science Foundation of China under grant No. 61832003, the Major Program of the National Natural Science Foundation of China under grant No. U1811461, the General Program of the National Natural Science Foundation of China under grant No. 61772157, and the China Postdoctoral Science Foundation under grant 2016M590284.

References

1. Abiteboul, S., Hull, R., Vianu, V.: Foundations of Databases. Addison-Wesley, Boston (1995)
2. Aho, A.V., Sagiv, Y., Ullman, J.D.: Equivalences among relational expressions. SIAM J. Comput. **8**(2), 218–246 (1979)
3. Cai, Z., Miao, D., Li, Y.: Deletion propagation for multiple key preserving conjunctive queries: approximations and complexity. In: ICDE 2019, pp. 506–517 (2019)
4. Codd, E.F.: Understanding relations (installment #7). FDT - Bull. ACM SIGMOD **7**(3), 23–28 (1975)
5. Console, M., Guagliardo, P., Libkin, L.: On querying incomplete information in databases under bag semantics. In: IJCAI 2017, pp. 993–999 (2017)
6. Flum, J., Grohe, M.: Fixed-parameter tractability, definability, and model-checking. SIAM J. Comput. **31**(1), 113–145 (2001)
7. Flum, J., Grohe, M.: Parameterized Complexity Theory. Texts in Theoretical Computer Science. An EATCS Series. Springer, Heidelberg (2006). https://doi.org/10.1007/3-540-29953-X
8. Han, Y., Sun, G., Shen, Y., Zhang, X.: Multi-label learning with highly incomplete data via collaborative embedding. In: KDD 2018, pp. 1494–1503 (2018)

9. Levy,A.Y.: Obtaining complete answers from incomplete databases. In: VLDB 1996, Proceedings of 22th International Conference on Very Large Data Bases, 3–6 September 1996, pp. 402–412, Mumbai (1996)
10. Liu, X., Cai, Z., Miao, D., Li, J.: Tree size reduction with keeping distinguishability. Theor. Comput. Sci. **749**, 26–35 (2018)
11. Miao, D., Cai, Z., Li, J.: On the complexity of bounded view propagation for conjunctive queries. IEEE Trans. Knowl. Data Eng. **30**(1), 115–127 (2018)
12. Miao, D., Liu, X., Li, J.: On the complexity of sampling query feedback restricted database repair of functional dependency violations. Theor. Comput. Sci. **609**, 594–605 (2016)
13. Razniewski, S., Korn, F., Nutt, W., Srivastava, D.: Identifying the extent of completeness of query answers over partially complete databases. In: SIGMOD 2015, pp. 561–576 (2015)
14. Razniewski, S., Nutt, W.: Completeness of queries over incomplete databases. PVLDB **4**(11), 749–760 (2011)
15. Tang, X., et al.: Joint modeling of dense and incomplete trajectories for citywide traffic volume inference. In: WWW 2019, pp. 1806–1817 (2019)

Imbalance Parameterized by Twin Cover Revisited

Neeldhara Misra$^{(\boxtimes)}$ and Harshil Mittal

Indian Institute of Technology, Gandhinagar, Gandhinagar, India
{neeldhara.m,mittal_harshil}@iitgn.ac.in

Abstract. We study the problem of IMBALANCE parameterized by the twin cover of a graph. We show that IMBALANCE is XP parameterized by twin cover, and FPT when parameterized by the twin cover and the size of the largest clique outside the twin cover. In contrast, we introduce a notion of succinct representations of graphs in terms of their twin cover and demonstrate that IMBALANCE is NP-hard in the setting of succinct representations, even for graphs that have a twin cover of size one.

Keywords: Imbalance · Twin cover · FPT · XP · Succinct input

1 Introduction

Graph layout problems are combinatorial optimization problems where the objective is to find a permutation of the vertex set that optimizes some function of interest. In this paper we focus on the problem of determining the *imbalance* of a graph G. Given a permutation π of V, we define the left and right neighborhood of a vertex, $N_L(v)$ and $N_R(v)$, to be the set of vertices in the neighborhood of v that were placed before and after v in π. The imbalance of v is defined as the absolute difference between these quantities, that is, $\big| |N_L(v)| - |N_R(v)| \big|$ and the imbalance of the graph G with respect to π is simply the sum of the imbalances of the individual vertices. The imbalance of G is the minimum imbalance of G over all orderings of V, and an ordering yielding this imbalance is called an optimal ordering[1] The problem was introduced by [2], and finds several applications, especially in graph drawing [8,9,13–15].

IMBALANCE is known to be NP-complete for several special classes of graphs, including bipartite graphs of maximum degree six [2] and for graphs of degree at most four [10]. Further, the problem is known to be FPT when parameterized by imbalance [11], vertex cover [5], neighborhood diversity [1], and the combined parameter treewidth and maximum degree [11]. Recently, it was claimed that

---

[1] We refer the reader to the preliminaries for formal definitions of the terminology that we use in this section.

This work is supported by the SERB Early Career grant ECR/2018/002967.

D. Kim et al. (Eds.): COCOON 2020, LNCS 12273, pp. 162–173, 2020.
https://doi.org/10.1007/978-3-030-58150-3_13

imbalance is also FPT when parameterized by twin cover [7], which is a substantial improvement over the vertex cover parameter. We mention briefly here that a vertex cover of a graph G is a subset $S \subseteq V(G)$ such that $G \setminus S$ is an independent set, and a twin cover of a graph is a subset $T \subseteq V(G)$ such that the connected components of $G \setminus T$ consist of vertices which are true twins—in particular, note that each connected component induces a clique, and further, all vertices have the same neighborhood in the cover T. The method employed in [7] to obtain an FPT algorithm for IMBALANCE parameterized by twin cover relies on a structural lemma which, roughly speaking, states that there exist optimal orderings where any maximal collection of true twins appear together. Based on this, it is claimed that the cliques of $G \setminus S$ can be contracted into singleton vertices to obtain an equivalent instance H. By observing that the twin cover of G is a vertex cover of H, we may now use the FPT algorithm for IMBALANCE parameterized by vertex cover to obtain an imbalance-optimal ordering for H, and the contracted vertices can be "expanded back in place" to recover an optimal ordering for G.

Although the structural lemma is powerful, unfortunately, we are unable to verify the safety of the contraction step based on it. We note that the graph H has lost information about the sizes of the individual cliques from G, and the ILP formulation is blind to the distinctions between vertices that correspond to cliques of different sizes. Consider, for example, an instance with a twin cover of size one—the reduced instance is a star and any layout of H that distributes the leaves of the star almost equally around the center would have the same imbalance, and these are indeed all the optimal layouts of H. On the other hand, several of these layouts could have different imbalances when considered in the context of G. A natural fix to this issue is to mimic the ILP formulation directly for the graph H, and taking advantage of the structural lemma to come up with an appropriate set of variables that correspond to cliques of a fixed size. Unfortunately, this leads us to a situation where the number of variables is a function of the sizes of the cliques, and only yields an algorithm that is FPT in the size of the twin cover and the size of the largest clique outside the twin cover.

Our Contributions. With the premise that there is more to the twin cover parameterization for IMBALANCE, the focus of this paper is on the complexity of IMBALANCE parameterized by twin cover. We demonstrate that the problem is in XP when parameterized by twin cover (Theorem 2), and FPT when parameterized by the twin cover and the size of the largest clique. The first result is based on a slightly non-trivial dynamic programming algorithm, which can be thought of as a generalization of the classic dynamic programming routine for the Partition problem, in which we are given n numbers and the question is if they can be partitioned into two groups of equal sum. Indeed, the approach is inspired by the fact that the problem of finding the optimal layout for graphs that have a twin cover of size one is essentially equivalent to the Partition problem. However, generalizing to larger-sized twin covers involves accounting for several details and we also discuss why the natural brute-force approaches to an

XP algorithm end up failing. The second result is based on the ILP formulation that we alluded to earlier. We mention here that we rely crucially on the structural result of [7] for arguing the correctness of our algorithmic approaches.

We also propose a natural notion of a succinct representation for graphs with bounded twin covers. Note that such graphs can be specified completely by the adjacency matrix of the twin cover and for each clique outside the twin cover, its size and its neighborhood in the twin cover. In contrast to the algorithmic results above, the resemblance to Partition leads us to the interesting observation that the problem of IMBALANCE is NP-hard even for graphs that have a twin cover of size one in the succinct setting. This is formalized in Theorem 1. We find it particularly interesting that IMBALANCE is a problem for which the choice of representation leads to a stark difference in the complexity of the problem.

We note here that several FPT algorithms for other problems parameterized by twin cover remain FPT in a "strongly polynomial" sense and can be easily adapted to the setting of succinct input. For example, the algorithm for EQUITABLE COLORING [6] relies on reducing the problem to a maximum flow formulation where the sizes of the cliques outside the twin cover feature as capacities in the flow network, and this approach remains efficient for succinct input since the maximum flow can be found in strongly polynomial time. Similarly, the problems of PRECOLORING EXTENSION, CHROMATIC NUMBER, MAXCUT, and FEEDBACK VERTEX SET as proposed by Ganian [6] can be easily adapted to being strongly polynomial in our succinct representation.

This paper is organized as follows. We begin by describing the notation and terminology that is the most relevant to our discussions in the next section, and refer the reader to [3] for background on the parameterized complexity framework and to [4] for a survey of graph layout problems. We then establish the para-NP-hardness of IMBALANCE parameterized by twin cover in the setting of succinct representations in Sect. 3. The XP algorithm when parameterized by the twin cover is described in Sect. 4, respectively. Due to lack of space, we state some results without proof—these are marked by ⋆ and the proofs are provided in a full version [12] of this paper. The FPT algorithm in the combined parameter of twin cover and largest clique size is based on an ILP approach and is also defered to the full version.

2 Preliminaries

We use $G = (V, E)$ to denote an undirected, simple graph unless mentioned otherwise, and we will typically use n and m to denote $|V|$ and $|E|$, respectively. The *neighborhood* of a vertex $v \in V$ is given by $N(v) := \{u \mid (u, v) \in E\}$. The *closed neighborhood* of a vertex v is given by $N[v] := N(v) \cup \{v\}$. Likewise, the open and closed neighborhoods of a set $S \subseteq V$ are defined as: $N(S) := \{v \mid v \notin S$ and $\exists u \in S$ such that $(u, v) \in E\}$ and $N[S] := N(S) \cup S$, respectively. A subset $Y \subseteq V$ is said to be a set of true twins in G if for every pair of vertices u, v in Y, $N[u] = N[v]$.

Let $\mathcal{S}(V)$ denote the set of all orderings of $V(G)$, and let σ be an arbitrary but fixed ordering of $V(G)$. For $1 \leqslant i \leqslant n$, the ith vertex in the ordering is denoted by $\sigma(i)$. The relation $<_\sigma$ is defined as $u <_\sigma v$ if and only if u precedes v in the ordering σ. We also define the *left neighborhood* and *right neighborhood* of a vertex v in the natural way:

$$N_L(v, \sigma) = \{u \mid u \in N(v) \text{ and } u <_\sigma v\} \text{ and } N_R(v, \sigma) = \{u \mid u \in N(v) \text{ and } v <_\sigma u\}.$$

We also use $p(v, \sigma)$ and $q(v, \sigma)$ to denote the sizes of $N_L(v, \sigma)$ and $N_R(v, \sigma)$, respectively, and we refer to these numbers as the *predecessors* and the *successors* of v with respect to σ. If the permutation σ is clear from the context, we use the terms predecessors and successors without qualifying for σ.

An ordering σ of V is said to be a *clean ordering* if for every inclusion-wise maximal subset $Y \subseteq V$ that forms a set of true twins in G, the vertices of Y appear consecutively in σ, i.e., Y contains all vertices in V that lie between the smallest and largest elements of Y (with respect to $<_\sigma$).

Imbalance. The *imbalance* of a vertex v with respect to an ordering σ of V is denoted $\mathcal{I}(v, \sigma)$, and is defined as the absolute difference between the predecessors and the successors of v, that is, $\mathcal{I}(v, \sigma) = |p(v, \sigma) - q(v, \sigma)|$. The imbalance of an ordering σ, denoted $\mathcal{I}(\sigma)$, is the total imbalance of all the vertices with respect to σ, and the imbalance of the graph G is minimum imbalance over all permutations of V:

$$\mathcal{I}(G) = \min_{\sigma \in \mathcal{S}(V)} \mathcal{I}(\sigma), \text{ where } \mathcal{I}(\sigma) = \sum_{v \in V} \mathcal{I}(v, \sigma).$$

An ordering σ of V is said to be an *imbalance optimal ordering* if $\mathcal{I}(\sigma) = \mathcal{I}(G)$. We recall the following fact from [7].

Lemma 1 ([7]). *There exists a clean imbalance optimal ordering.*

Twin Cover. A subset $S \subseteq V$ is called a twin cover if for every component X of $G \setminus S$, the vertices of X form a set of true twins in G. In other words, for every component X of $G \setminus S$, the vertices of X form a clique such that for every pair of vertices u, v in $V(X)$, $N(u) \cap S = N(v) \cap S$. Henceforth, we will refer to the maximal cliques, or equivalently the components, of $G \setminus S$ as simply the 'cliques' of $G \setminus S$ for the sake of simplicity. We also say that $S \subseteq V$ is an ℓ-*bounded twin cover* if it is a twin cover such that every clique in $G \setminus S$ has at most ℓ vertices.

Note that the imbalance of a layout does not change if the positions of any pair of true twins are exchanged. Therefore, the following is an immediate consequence of Lemma 1.

Corollary 1. *Let G be a graph and let $S \subseteq V(G)$ be a twin cover of G. Then, there exists an imbalance optimal ordering of G where the vertices of every clique in $G \setminus S$ appear consecutively.*

For further discussion, a clean ordering in the context of a graph G given with a twin cover S is understood to be an ordering in which the vertices of every clique of $G \setminus S$ appear consecutively. Further, we also abuse language slightly and use the term "cliques" to always refer to the maximal cliques of $G \setminus S$, unless mentioned otherwise.

For a graph G with twin cover S, we define the *type* of a vertex v in $G \setminus S$ as $N(v) \cap S$, and the type of a clique C in $G \setminus S$ as the type of any arbitrarily chosen vertex in C. Observe that all vertices of any clique $C \in G \setminus S$ have the same type, and therefore the notion of the type of a clique is well-defined. Note that G is completely specified once the structure of a twin cover S and the sizes and types of all the cliques in $G \setminus S$ are given.

In particular, given $\mathcal{G} := (H, \{(\ell_i, S_i) \mid 1 \leqslant i \leqslant r\})$, where each S_i is a subset of $V(H)$, the graph G associated with $\mathcal{G}$ is defined in the following natural way. The vertex set of G is given by $V(G) := S \cup C_1 \cup \cdots C_i \cup \cdots \cup C_r$, where $|C_i| = \ell_i$ for all $i \in [r]$ and $|S| = |V(H)|$. Now, identify the vertices of S with $V(H)$ via an arbitrary but fixed mapping f, and define the set of edges as follows. For any pair of vertices $u, v \in S$, we have $(u, v) \in E(G)$ if and only if $(f(u), f(v)) \in E(H)$. Further, we induce a clique on each C_i, and finally, for any clique C_i and a vertex $v \in S$ we add edges between v and every vertex of C_i if and only if $f(v) \in S_i$. We say that $\mathcal{G}$ provides a *succinct representation based on a twin cover*. For brevity, we will usually refer to $\mathcal{G}$ as a succinct representation of G. For further discussion,we use the same notation to refer to both a vertex in $V(H)$ and its preimage (under the function f) in S, i.e., for any w in $V(H)$, we refer to $f^{-1}(w)$ in S as w for the sake of simplicity.

We now introduce the natural computational question associated with IMBALANCE. Given a graph $G = (V, E)$, a twin cover $S \subseteq V$ of size at most k, and a target t, determine if $\mathcal{I}(G) \leqslant t$. Unless mentioned otherwise[2], our focus will be on IMBALANCE parameterized by k, the size of the twin cover. For the most part, we assume that the input graph G is specified in the standard way, i.e, by its adjacency matrix or adjacency list. If, on the other hand, G is specified by a succinct representation in terms of its twin cover, then we say that the input is succinct, and if this is the scenario we are in, we state it explicitly.

3   Weak Para-NP-Hardness

In this section, we establish the NP-hardness of IMBALANCE when the input is succinct, even for graphs that have a twin cover of size one. This can be interpreted as a "weak" para-NP-hardness result for IMBALANCE when parameterized by twin cover.

Theorem 1 ($\star$). *For succinct input*, IMBALANCE *is NP-hard even for graphs that have a twin cover of size one.*

We establish this result by a reduction from the PARTITION problem, which is well-known to be weakly NP-hard. Recall that the input to PARTITION is a

---

[2] We also consider the parameter $(k + \ell)$ when we are given a ℓ-bounded twin cover.

set of positive integers $\{a_1, \ldots, a_r\}$, and the question is if there exists a subset $S \subset [r]$ such that $\sum_{i \in S} a_i = \sum_{i \notin S} a_i$. An intuitive visual for graphs that have a twin cover of size one is to imagine that we have balls suspended from a single point of varying weights, proportional to the sizes of the cliques, and a layout that optimizes the imbalance is faced with the task of distributing these balls on either side of the suspension point so that the total weight on either side is equally distributed.

To formalize this idea, we first argue a lower bound for the imbalance of any graph that has a twin cover of size one. To begin with, consider the function $\gamma(\ell) := \lfloor \ell^2/2 \rfloor$. We define the *intrinsic imbalance* of a clique C on ℓ vertices as $\gamma(\ell)$. For a graph G given by $\mathcal{G} := (H, \{(\ell_i, S_i) \mid 1 \leqslant i \leqslant r\})$, define $\iota(G) := \gamma(\ell_1) + \cdots + \gamma(\ell_r)$. Our first claim is the following.

Proposition 1 ($\star$). *Let G be given by $\mathcal{G} = (H, \{(\ell_i, S_i) \mid 1 \leqslant i \leqslant r\})$. Then, $\mathcal{I}(G) \geqslant \iota(G)$.*

The following observation is based on the fact that if a graph has a twin cover of size one, then in any layout, the imbalance of odd-sized cliques is one more than their intrinsic imbalance, and the imbalance of even-sized cliques is equal to their intrinsic imbalance, and this is true for any clean ordering, irrespective of where the cliques are placed in the layout relative to the twin cover vertex.

Proposition 2 ($\star$). *Let G be a connected graph given by $\mathcal{G} = (H, \{(\ell_i, S_i) \mid 1 \leqslant i \leqslant r\})$ where $H = \{v\}$. Then $\mathcal{I}(G) \geqslant \iota(G) + \sum_{i=1}^{r}(\ell_i \bmod 2)$.*

We have the following straightforward consequence of Proposition 2.

Corollary 2. *Let G be a connected graph given by $\mathcal{G} = (H, \{(\ell_i, S_i) \mid 1 \leqslant i \leqslant r\})$ where $H = \{v\}$. Then $\mathcal{I}(G) = \iota(G) + \sum_{i=1}^{r}(\ell_i \bmod 2) + \mathcal{I}(v)$.*

We are now ready to describe the reduction from PARTITION.

Proof (Proof of Theorem 1). Given an instance $\mathcal{P} := \{a_1, \ldots, a_r\}$ of PARTITION, let $G_{\mathcal{P}}$ be given by $\mathcal{G}(\mathcal{P}) = (H, \{(\ell_i, S_i) \mid 1 \leqslant i \leqslant r\})$, which in turn is defined as follows: $H = \{v\}, \ell_i = a_i$ for all $i \in [r]$, and $S_i = \{v\}$ for all $i \in [r]$. The instance of IMBALANCE is now given by $(G_{\mathcal{P}}, S = \{v\}, t)$, where $t = \iota(G_{\mathcal{P}}) + \sum_{i=1}^{r}(a_i \bmod 2)$. This completes the construction. We defer the proof of equivalence to the full version of this paper. □

4   An XP Algorithm

In this section, our goal is to demonstrate an XP algorithm for IMBALANCE parameterized by twin cover when the entire input is given explicitly in the standard form. Throughout, we use G to denote the graph given as input, $S \subseteq V(G)$ denotes a twin cover of size k, and the question is if G admits a layout whose imbalance is at most t. We denote the cliques of $G \setminus S$ by $C_1, \ldots, C_r$, and we let ℓ_i denote the number of vertices in C_i. We also use ℓ to denote $\max\{\ell_1, \ldots, \ell_r\}$.

To begin with, let us consider some natural brute-force approaches, described informally, that will eventually motivate the definitions that we will encounter later. Assuming we are dealing with a Yes-instance, let σ^* denote a clean ordering of $V(G)$ whose imbalance is at most t.

We briefly mention here that the natural brute-force approaches to the problem do not lead to XP running times. For example, guessing the relative order of the twin cover vertices and trying all possibilities of "final locations" for the cliques outside S requires examining $O((k + 1)^r)$ possibilities. Attempting to club together cliques that have the same neighborhood does not work because it fails to capture important information about clique sizes. Refining the notion of type to account for sizes again makes the approach too expensive. Attempting to threshold the sizes of the cliques at some function of k and working with a more nuanced notion of type[3] also turns out to be insufficient since we remain in the dark about the imbalance information of the twin cover vertices. For a more detailed discussion of each of these approaches and the motivation for our DP algorithm and it's relationship to the Subset Sum problem, we refer the reader to Sect. 3 in the full version of this paper.

Before describing our DP table and the associated recurrence, we first introduce some definitions. A clique C in $G \setminus S$ is said to be a *large* clique if $|V(C)| > k$, and is said to be a *small* clique otherwise. Further, a clique $C \in G \setminus S$ is *even* (respectively, *odd*) if it has an even (respectively, odd) number of vertices. Recall that the intrinsic imbalance of a clique on ℓ vertices is $\gamma(\ell)$. We now introduce two related notions. The *total imbalance* and *excess imbalance* of a clique C on ℓ vertices with respect to a layout σ is given by, respectively:

$$\gamma^*(C, \sigma) = \sum_{v \in C} \Im(v, \sigma) \text{ and } \gamma^+(C, \sigma) = \gamma^*(C, \sigma) - \gamma(\ell).$$

We now claim that the excess imbalance of any large clique is a function of its parity, type, and location in the layout σ, and in particular, it is independent of its size.

Lemma 2 ($\star$). *Let G be a graph and let $S \subseteq V(G)$ be a twin cover of G of size k. Further, let C be a large clique in $G \setminus S$ of type $T \subseteq S$. For any layout σ we have:*

$$\gamma^+(C, \sigma) = \begin{cases} \lfloor \frac{\delta(C,\sigma)^2}{2} \rfloor & \text{if C is an even clique,} \\ \lceil \frac{\delta(C,\sigma)^2}{2} \rceil & \text{if C is an odd clique,} \end{cases}$$

where $\delta(C, \sigma) = |N_L(v, \sigma) \cap S| - |N_R(v, \sigma) \cap S|$, for any $v \in C$.

Corollary 3. *Let G be a graph and let $S \subseteq V(G)$ be a twin cover of G of size k. Further, let C_i and C_j be large cliques in $G \setminus S$ that have the same parity and type. If σ is a layout that places C_i and C_j in the same location, then $\gamma^+(C_i) = \gamma^+(C_j)$.*

---

[3] i.e, using explicit sizes up to a threshold, and declaring all other cliques as large—an idea that we does play a role in our DP algorithm.

Proof. The claim follows from the fact that $\delta(C_i, \sigma) = \delta(C_j, \sigma)$ when C_i and C_j are large cliques with the same type and that share the same location in the layout σ. Further, $\gamma^+(C_i, \sigma) = \gamma^+(C_j, \sigma)$ since C_i and C_j have the same parity. □

Let us now formalize the notion of 'location' in an ordering of vertices in G. Let σ be an arbitrary but fixed ordering. We say that a vertex v in $G \setminus S$ is placed at the *location* $|\sigma_{<v} \cap S| + 1$, where $\sigma_{<v} := \{w \mid w <_\sigma v\}$. If σ is a clean ordering, we also say that a clique $C \in G \setminus S$ is placed at the *location* $|\sigma_{<v} \cap S| + 1$, where v is an arbitrarily chosen vertex of C. Note that since σ is a clean ordering, for any clique $C \in G \setminus S$, all its vertices are placed at the same location. Therefore the notion of the location of a clique is well-defined. Intuitively, the location of a clique tells us where it lies in the layout relative to the twin cover vertices. In particular, cliques that are placed at location $1 < i \leqslant k$ lie between the $(i-1)^{th}$ and the ith twin cover vertex; with cliques at locations 1 and $k + 1$ being placed to the left of the first twin cover vertex and to the right of the last twin cover vertex, respectively.

Let $\mathcal{C} := \left(2^S \times \{0\} \times [k]\right) \cup \left(2^S \times \{1\} \times \{e, o\}\right)$. A *class* is a triplet $(T, b, j) \in \mathcal{C}$. Recall that the type of a clique C is given by $N(C) \cap S$. Let $T \subseteq S$ be arbitrary but fixed, and let C be a clique of type T. Then, the class of the clique C is given by:

- $(T, 1, o)$ if C is a large odd clique.
- $(T, 1, e)$ if C is a large even clique.
- $(T, 0, j)$ if C is a small clique on j vertices.

We will typically use v to denote an element of $\mathcal{C}$.

We now turn to the notion of specifications, which capture the "demand" that we may make for the number and the total sizes of the cliques of a particular class at a particular location. Formally, a specification is a map from $\mathcal{C} \times [k + 1]$ to $[n] \cup \{0\}$. We relate specifications to layouts in the following definitions.

- Given a specification α, we say that a layout σ *respects* α *in count* if, for each location $j \in [k + 1]$ and for every class $v \in \mathcal{C}$, the number of cliques of class v in location j according to σ is $\alpha(v, j)$.
- Given a specification β, we say that a layout σ *respects* β *in size* if, for each location $j \in [k + 1]$ and for every class $v \in \mathcal{C}$, the total size of cliques of class v in location j according to σ is $\beta(v, j)$.

We say that two layouts σ and π are *similar with respect to* S if the layouts are identical when projected on the vertices of S. Our first observation is that the notion of specifications is sufficiently rich in the context of imbalance in the following sense: for an arbitrary but fixed pair of specifications (α, β), all similar layouts that respect α in size and β in count have the same imbalance. We formalize this claim below.

Lemma 3 ($\star$). *Let G be a graph and let S be a twin cover of G of size k. Also, let α and β be two specification functions for G and let σ and π be two clean layouts of G that are similar with respect to S. If σ and π both respect α in count and β in size, then $\Im(\sigma) = \Im(\pi)$.*

Based on the proof of Lemma 3, we have the following lemma.

Lemma 4 ($\star$). *Let G be a graph and let S be a twin cover of G of size k. Also, let α and β be two specification functions for G. Let π be an ordering of the vertices of S. For any layout σ of the vertices of G that respects α in count and β in size, and which is consistent with π when restricted to S, its imbalance can be computed in time $O(g(k) \cdot k \cdot n^{O(1)})$.*

Our next claim is that the number of specification functions is bounded by a function that is XP in k. More specifically, we have the following.

Proposition 3. *Let G be a graph and let S be a twin cover of G of size k. Then, the number of specification functions is bounded by $(n + 1)^{g(k)}$, where $g(k) = (2^k \cdot (k+2)) \times (k+1)$.*

Proof. This follows from the fact that the number of possible classes is at most $(2^k \cdot (k + 2))$, and that the number of functions from a domain with a elements to a range with b elements is b^a. □

We are now finally ready to present our dynamic programming algorithm. For any pair of specifications (α, β), we say that a layout respects (α, β) if it respects α in count and β in size. Recall that the cliques of $G \setminus S$ were denoted by $C_1, \ldots, C_r$. For $j \in [r]$, let H_j denote the graph $G[S \cup C_1 \cup \ldots \cup C_j]$. Now consider the following dynamic programming table, where α and β are specifications and $q \in [r]$:

$$\mathbb{T}(\alpha, \beta, q) = \begin{cases} 1 & \text{if there exists a layout } \sigma \text{ of } H_q \text{ that respects } (\alpha, \beta), \\ 0 & \text{otherwise.} \end{cases}$$

Before describing the recurrence for $\mathbb{T}_\pi(\alpha, \beta, q)$, we informally allude to why this is useful to compute. To check if G admits a layout of imbalance at most t, our algorithm proceeds as follows. For all specification pairs (α, β), we check if $\mathbb{T}(\alpha, \beta, r) = 1$. For all the instances where the entries are one, we compute the imbalance of any layout that respects (α, β) based on Lemma 3, by trying all possible choices for the ordering of twin cover vertices. If we ever encounter an imbalance value that is at most t then we abort and return YES, otherwise we return NO after all choices of π and the corresponding specification pairs have been exhaustively examined.

We now turn to the computation of the DP table $\mathbb{T}$. For the base case, we have $q = 1$, and it is easy to see that there are exactly $(k + 1)$ choices—one for each possible location—of pairs of specifications (α, β) for which $\mathbb{T}_\pi(\alpha, \beta, q) = 1$. For the sake of exposition, we explicitly describe these pairs. Recall that the size of C_1 is given by ℓ_1, suppose the class of C_1 is $\mathfrak{C}^\star$. Then consider the specification function pairs $(\alpha_i, \beta_i)_{i \in [k+1]}$ defined as follows:

$$\alpha_i(\mathfrak{C}, j) = \begin{cases} 1 & \text{if } j = i \text{ and } \mathfrak{C} = \mathfrak{C}^\star, \\ 0 & \text{otherwise}, \end{cases}$$

and

$$\beta_i(\mathfrak{C}, j) = \begin{cases} \ell_1 & \text{if } j = i \text{ and } \mathfrak{C} = \mathfrak{C}^\star, \\ 0 & \text{otherwise}. \end{cases}$$

This motivates the definition of $\mathbb{T}$ for the base case:

$$\mathbb{T}(\alpha, \beta, 1) = \begin{cases} 1 & \text{if there exists } i \in [k+1] \text{ such that} \\ & \quad \alpha = \alpha_i \text{ and } \beta = \beta_i \\ 0 & \text{otherwise}. \end{cases}$$

Before proceeding to the recurrence, let us introduce a definition that will make the recurrence simpler to describe. We say that a clique C of size ℓ whose class is $\mathfrak{C}$ is an *overfit* for a location $j \in [k+1]$ with respect to the pair of specifications (α, β) if:

- $\alpha(\mathfrak{C}, j) = 0$, i.e, there is no "demand" for a clique of class $\mathfrak{C}$ at location j; *or*
- $\beta(\mathfrak{C}, j) < \ell$, i.e, the total sizes of the cliques of class $\mathfrak{C}$ that are expected at location j is smaller than the size of C.

We now turn to the recurrence for $\mathbb{T}(\alpha, \beta, q)$ for some $q \in [r]$. Let the class of the clique C_q be $\mathfrak{C}^\star$. Define the following auxiliary specifications for $i \in [k+1]$, which, intuitively speaking, capture the subproblems of interest if the clique C_q were to be placed at location i:

$$\alpha_i(\mathfrak{C}, j) = \begin{cases} \alpha(\mathfrak{C}, j) - 1 & \text{if } j = i \text{ and } \mathfrak{C} = \mathfrak{C}^\star, \\ \alpha(\mathfrak{C}, j) & \text{otherwise}, \end{cases}$$

and

$$\beta_i(\mathfrak{C}, j) = \begin{cases} \beta_i(\mathfrak{C}, j) - \ell_q & \text{if } j = i \text{ and } \mathfrak{C} = \mathfrak{C}^\star, \\ \beta_i(\mathfrak{C}, j) & \text{otherwise}. \end{cases}$$

Let $B \subseteq [k+1]$ be the set of all locations for which C_q is *not* an overfit with respect to (α, β). Then, we have: $\mathbb{T}(\alpha, \beta, q) = \vee_{i \in B} \mathbb{T}(\alpha_i, \beta_i, q-1)$.

The discussions above lead us to the main result of this section.

Theorem 2 ($\star$). IMBALANCE *is in XP when parameterized by twin cover.*

5 Concluding Remarks

We investigated the complexity of IMBALANCE parameterized by twin cover. We demonstrated that that the problem is XP by a dynamic programming approach, and that it is FPT when parameterized by twin cover as well as the size of the largest clique in the graph when the twin cover is removed. It is also easy to see that the problem is FPT when parameterized by the twin cover and the *number* of cliques outside the twin cover, by simply restricting our attention to clean orderings and trying all possible permutations of the cliques and guessing where the twin cover vertices 'fit' among them. This leads us to conclude that the tractable cases are, roughly speaking, when there are a small number of large cliques or a large number of small cliques, and the interesting cases lie in the middle of this spectrum. The most evident open question that emerges from our discussions is the issue of whether IMBALANCE is FPT when parameterized by twin cover.

We also introduced a notion of succinct representations of graphs in terms of their twin cover. It would be interesting to revisit problems which are FPT in twin cover but with a "pseudo-polynomial" running time in the setting of succinct input as described here. In particular, from the work of Ganian [6], there are already some problems whose stated algorithms are not efficient in the succinct setting. For example, the algorithm for BOXICITY relies on the fact that the edges within the clique are irrelevant, based on which we may obtain an equivalent instance for which the twin cover becomes a vertex cover. It would be an interesting direction of future work to examine which of these problems remain FPT with a strongly polynomial running time when we work with succinct representations. Our work here demonstrates that IMBALANCE is already one problem for which the representation has a non-trivial influence on the complexity.

References

1. Bakken, O.R.: Arrangement problems parameterized neighbourhood diversity. Master's thesis, University of Bergen (2003)
2. Biedl, T.C., Chan, T.M., Ganjali, Y., Hajiaghayi, M.T., Wood, D.R.: Balanced vertex-orderings of graphs. Discret. Appl. Math. **148**(1), 27–48 (2005)
3. Cygan, M.: Parameterized Algorithms. Springer, Cham (2015). https://doi.org/10.1007/978-3-319-21275-3
4. Díaz, J., Petit, J., Serna, M.J.: A survey of graph layout problems. ACM Comput. Surv. **34**(3), 313–356 (2002)
5. Fellows, M.R., Lokshtanov, D., Misra, N., Rosamond, F.A., Saurabh, S.: Graph layout problems parameterized by vertex cover. In: Hong, S.-H., Nagamochi, H., Fukunaga, T. (eds.) ISAAC 2008. LNCS, vol. 5369, pp. 294–305. Springer, Heidelberg (2008). https://doi.org/10.1007/978-3-540-92182-0_28
6. Ganian, R.: Twin-cover: beyond vertex cover in parameterized algorithmics. In: Marx, D., Rossmanith, P. (eds.) IPEC 2011. LNCS, vol. 7112, pp. 259–271. Springer, Heidelberg (2012). https://doi.org/10.1007/978-3-642-28050-4_21

7. Gorzny, J., Buss, J.F.: Imbalance, cutwidth, and the structure of optimal orderings. In: Du, D.-Z., Duan, Z., Tian, C. (eds.) COCOON 2019. LNCS, vol. 11653, pp. 219–231. Springer, Cham (2019). https://doi.org/10.1007/978-3-030-26176-4_18

8. Kant, G.: Drawing planar graphs using the canonical ordering. Algorithmica **16**(1), 4–32 (1996). https://doi.org/10.1007/BF02086606

9. Kant, G., He, X.: Regular edge labeling of 4-connected plane graphs and its applications in graph drawing problems. Theoret. Comput. Sci. **172**(1–2), 175–193 (1997)

10. Kára, J., Kratochvíl, J., Wood, D.R.: On the complexity of the balanced vertex ordering problem. Discret. Math. Theoret. Comput. Sci. **9**(1) (2007)

11. Lokshtanov, D., Misra, N., Saurabh, S.: Imbalance is fixed parameter tractable. Inf. Process. Lett. **113**(19–21), 714–718 (2013)

12. Misra, N., Mittal, H.: Imbalance parameterized by twin cover revisited. CoRR abs/2005.03800 (2020). https://arxiv.org/abs/2005.03800

13. Papakostas, A., Tollis, I.G.: Algorithms for area-efficient orthogonal drawings. Comput. Geom. **9**(1–2), 83–110 (1998)

14. Wood, D.R.: Optimal three-dimensional orthogonal graph drawing in the general position model. Theor. Comput. Sci. **1–3**(299), 151–178 (2003)

15. Wood, D.R.: Minimising the number of bends and volume in 3-dimensional orthogonal graph drawings with a diagonal vertex layout. Algorithmica **39**(3), 235–253 (2004). https://doi.org/10.1007/s00453-004-1091-4

Local Routing in a Tree Metric 1-Spanner

Milutin Brankovic$^{(\boxtimes)}$, Joachim Gudmundsson(iD), and André van Renssen(iD)

University of Sydney, Sydney, Australia
mbra7655@uni.sydney.edu.au,
{joachim.gudmundsson,andre.vanrenssen}@sydney.edu.au

Abstract. Solomon and Elkin [10] constructed a shortcutting scheme for weighted trees which results in a 1-spanner for the tree metric induced by the input tree. The spanner has logarithmic lightness, logarithmic diameter, a linear number of edges and bounded degree (provided the input tree has bounded degree). This spanner has been applied in a series of papers devoted to designing bounded degree, low-diameter, low-weight $(1 + \epsilon)$-spanners in Euclidean and doubling metrics. In this paper, we present a simple local routing algorithm for this tree metric spanner. The algorithm has a routing ratio of 1, is guaranteed to terminate after $O(\log n)$ hops and requires $O(\Delta \log n)$ bits of storage per vertex where Δ is the maximum degree of the tree on which the spanner is constructed.

Keywords: Local routing · Spanners · Weighted trees · Doubling metrics

1 Introduction

Let T be a weighted tree. The tree metric induced by T, denoted M_T, is the complete graph on the vertices of T where the weight of each edge (u, v) is the weight of the path connecting u and v in T. For $t \geq 1$, a t-spanner for a metric (V, d) is a subgraph H of the complete graph on V such that every pair of distinct points $u, v \in V$ is connected by a path in H of total weight at most $t \cdot d(u, v)$. We refer to such paths as t-spanner paths. A t-spanner has diameter Λ if every pair of points is connected by a t-spanner path consisting of at most Λ edges. Typically, t-spanners are designed to be sparse, often with a linear number of edges. The lightness of a graph is the ratio of its weight to the weight of its minimum spanning tree. Solomon and Elkin [10] define a 1-spanner for tree metrics. Given an n vertex weighted tree of maximum degree Δ, the 1-spanner has $O(n)$ edges, $O(\log n)$ diameter, $O(\log n)$ lightness and maximum degree bounded by $\Delta + k$ (k is an adjustable parameter considered to be a constant for our purposes). While being an interesting construction in its own right, this tree metric 1-spanner has been used in a series of papers as a tool for reducing the diameter of various Euclidean and doubling metric spanner constructions [2,6,8,10,11].

Once a spanner has been constructed, it becomes important to find these short paths efficiently. A local routing algorithm for a weighted graph G is a

© Springer Nature Switzerland AG 2020
D. Kim et al. (Eds.): COCOON 2020, LNCS 12273, pp. 174–185, 2020.
https://doi.org/10.1007/978-3-030-58150-3_14

method by which a message can be sent from any vertex in G to a given destination vertex. The successor to each vertex u on the path traversed by the routing algorithm must be determined using only knowledge of the destination vertex, the neighbourhood of u and possibly some extra information stored at u. The efficiency of a routing algorithm is measured by the distance a message needs to travel through a network before reaching its destination as well as by the storage requirements for each vertex. There is a great deal of work on local routing algorithms in the literature. The difficulty of designing a good local routing algorithm clearly depends on properties of the underlying network. Some authors have designed algorithms for very general classes of networks. For example, the algorithm of Chan et al. [7] works in any network although its quality depends on the induced doubling dimension. Many authors have focused on highly efficient algorithms for specific classes of networks. For example, there has been a line of research into routing algorithms for various classes of planar graphs [4,5]. Support for efficient local routing algorithms is a desirable feature in a spanner and in some recent papers, researchers have designed spanners which simultaneously achieve support for efficient local routing with other properties. See, for example, the work of Ashvinkumar et al. [3].

There appears to be little work in the literature in designing spanners which achieve both support for local routing as well as low diameter. Given a spanner with diameter Λ, it is natural to require that a local routing algorithm on this spanner match this diameter, i.e., the algorithm should be guaranteed to terminate after at most Λ hops. Abraham and Malkhi [1] give a construction, for any $\epsilon > 0$, of a $(1 + \epsilon)$-spanner for points in two dimensional Euclidean space with an accompanying routing algorithm. The diameter of the routing algorithm is $O(D)$ with high probability where D is the quotient of the largest and smallest inter-point distances. The routing algorithm has routing ratio $O(\log n)$, with high probability, for n points on a uniform grid.

In this paper, we demonstrate that the 1-spanner construction of Solomon and Elkin [10] supports a local routing algorithm with $O(\log n)$ diameter in the worst case.

2   The Model

A local routing algorithm for a weighted graph G is a distributed algorithm in which each vertex is an independent processor. At the beginning of a round, a node may find that it has received a message. If a message is received, the algorithm decides to which neighbour the message should be forwarded. The following information is available to each vertex v in G:

1. A header contained in the message.
2. The label of v as well as labels of neighbouring vertices.

The message header stores the label of the destination vertex as well as other information if required by the routing algorithm. The labels are used not only as unique identifiers of vertices but may also store additional information if required. The labels of vertices are computed in a pre-processing step before the algorithm is run. Our model does not consider the running time of computation performed at each vertex in each round and so we do not specify the type of data structure used for headers and labels. The routing decision made at each vertex is deterministic. A routing algorithm is evaluated on the basis of the following quality measures.

- *Routing Ratio.* Given two vertices u, v of G, let $d_G(u,v)$ denote the shortest path distance from u to v and let $d_{route}(u,v)$ denote the total length of the path traversed by the routing algorithm when routing from u to v. The routing ratio is defined to be $\max_{u,v \in V} \left\{ \frac{d_{route}(u,v)}{d_G(u,v)} \right\}$.
- *Diameter.* A routing algorithm is said to have diameter Λ if a message is guaranteed to reach its destination after traversing at most Λ edges.
- *Storage.* A bound on the number of bits stored at vertices and in message headers.

3   Local Routing in Tree Metrics

3.1   The Spanner

In this subsection we describe the tree metric 1-spanner construction of Solomon and Elkin [10].

We first define some notation used in this section. T will denote a weighted, rooted tree and $wt(T)$ will denote its weight. Given a graph G, $V(G)$ and $E(G)$ denote its vertex and edge sets respectively. The root of T is denoted $rt(T)$ and $ch(v)$ denotes the number of children of v. As in the notation of [10], the children of a vertex v are denoted $c_1(v), ..., c_{ch(v)}(v)$ and $p(v)$ denotes the parent of a vertex v. The lowest common ancestor of two vertices $u, v \in V(T)$ will be denoted by $lca(u,v)$. Given $u, v \in V(T)$, $P(u,v)$ denotes the unique path from u to v in T. Given $v \in V(T)$, T_v will denote the subtree of T rooted at v.

The shortcutting procedure selects a constant number of cut vertices in the tree whose removal results in a forest of trees which are at most a constant fraction of the size of the input tree. The spanner is obtained by building the complete graph on these cut vertices and recursively applying the procedure to all subtrees obtained by removing the cut vertices. The original construction appearing due to Solomon and Elkin [10] actually builds a low diameter spanner on the cut vertices rather than the complete graph. Since we consider the number of cut vertices to be constant in the size of the input tree, we use the complete graph as it is easier to work with for the purposes of our routing algorithm.

We first outline the method by which the cut vertices are selected. We assume that among all subtrees rooted at children of a vertex v, the subtree rooted at the leftmost vertex is the largest. That is, $|T_{c_1(v)}| \geq |T_{c_i(v)}|$, for all $i > 1$.

For an integer d, we call a vertex v d-balanced if $|T_{c_1(v)}| \leq |T| - d$. We label an edge (u,v) of T as leftmost if $u = c_1(v)$ or $v = c_1(u)$. Let $P(v)$ denote the path of maximum length from v to some descendant of v which includes only leftmost edges. We say the last vertex on $P(v)$ is the leftmost vertex in T_v and we denote it by $l(v)$. We define $l(T) := l(rt(T))$. The construction we describe involves taking subtrees of an input tree. These subtrees inherit the 'leftmost' labelling of the input tree so it may be the case that $l(T) = rt(T)$. If there is a d-balanced vertex along $P(v)$, we denote the first such vertex by $b_d(v)$. Otherwise, $b_d(v) = NULL$.

Given a rooted tree T and a positive integer d, we define a set of vertices $CV(T, d)$ as follows. Set $v := rt(T)$. If $b_d(v) = NULL$, $CV(T, d)$ is defined to be $\emptyset$. Otherwise,

$$CV(T, d) := \{b_d(v)\} \cup \left(\bigcup_{i=1}^{ch(b_d(v))} CV(T_{c_i(b_d(v))}, d) \right).$$

Let k be a positive integer. We define a set of vertices

$$C_T := \begin{cases} V(T) \text{ if } k \geq n/2 - 1, \\ CV(T, d) \cup \{l(T), rt(T)\} \text{ otherwise.} \end{cases}$$

where $d := n/k$. (See Fig. 1 for an example.) The spanner is constructed via the following recursive procedure which takes as input a tree T and an integer parameter $k \geq 0$. Initialize the spanner as $G = T$. Compute the set C_T, with respect to k, and add the edges of the complete graph on C_T to G. Denote by $T \backslash C_T$ the forest obtained by removing the vertices in C_T, along with all incident edges, from T. Recursively run the algorithm on all trees in the forest $T \backslash C_T$ and add the resulting edges to G. Note that the parameter k is passed down to recursive calls of the algorithm while the parameter d is recomputed based on the size of the subtree on which the algorithm is called. The following lemmas are established by Solomon and Elkin [10]:

Lemma 1. *For $k > 2$, the set C_T contains at most $k + 1$ vertices.*

Lemma 2. *Each tree in the forest $T \backslash C_T$ has size at most $2n/k$.*

In particular, Lemma 2 implies that the recursion depth of the spanner construction algorithm is $O(\log n)$.

Solomon and Elkin [10] show that the graph resulting from a slightly more eloborate version of this shortcutting scheme has weight $O(\log n) \cdot wt(T)$. Their scheme differs from what we have presented in that instead of building the complete graph on the set of cut vertices C_T, they build a certain 1-spanner with $O(k)$ edges and diameter $O(\alpha(k))$ where α is the inverse Ackermann function. Since we consider the parameter k to be constant, this modification does not affect the weight bound of the construction.

Theorem 1. *Let T be a weighted rooted tree and let k be a positive integer, $k < n/2 - 1$. The graph G obtained by applying the algorithm described above to T using the parameter k is a 1-spanner for the tree metric induced by T. Moreover, G has diameter bounded by $O(\log n)$, weight bounded by $O(\log n) \cdot wt(T)$ and maximum degree bounded by $\Delta + O(k)$ where Δ is the maximum degree of T.*

T

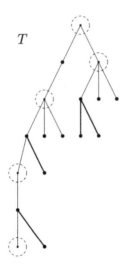

Fig. 1. A depiction of the set C_T for a tree with $n = 17$ vertices and the parameter k set to $k = 5$. The vertices of C_T are inside the dashed circles. The vertices and edges of the forest $T \setminus C_T$ are shown in bold.

Let G be the spanner resulting from running the algorithm described above on some tree T with respect to the parameter k. We define *canonical subtrees* of T with respect to k to be the subtrees computed during the course of the construction of G. Canonical subtrees are defined recursively as follows. As a base for the recursive definition, the input tree T is considered to be a canonical subtree with respect to T and k. Suppose T' is a canonical subtree with respect to T and k. Then each tree in the forest $T' \setminus C_{T'}$ is a canonical subtree with respect to T and k. We speak of canonical subtrees without reference to the parameters T and k when they are clear from context. Given a vertex v of T, we denote by T^v the canonical subtree for which $v \in C_{T^v}$. When a canonical subtree T' is small enough, $C_{T'} = V(T')$ and so it is clear that C_{T^v} is well defined for each $v \in V(T)$. We say that T^v is the canonical subtree of v and that v is a cut vertex of T^v.

We establish some technical properties of canonical subtrees which will be of use in the following section. We reword statement 4 in Corollary 2.17 from the paper of Solomon and Elkin [10] in Lemma 3.

Lemma 3. *Let T' be a canonical subtree of T and let T'' be the canonical subtree such that $T' \in T'' \setminus C_{T''}$. There are at most two edges in T with one endpoint in T' and the other outside T'. Moreover, any vertex of T' incident with a vertex outside T' must be $rt(T')$ or $l(T')$.*

In the spanner, a vertex u is connected to all vertices in C_{T^u}. The following lemmas ensure that in the routing algorithm described in the next section, under certain conditions, it is safe to make a 'greedy' choice from a subset of vertices in C_{T^u}.

Lemma 4. *Let T' and T'' be canonical subtrees such that $T'' \in T' \setminus C_{T'}$ and let v be some vertex of T''. Let X be the set of vertices in $C_{T'}$ which are ancestors of v. Let x be the element of X deepest in T and let x' be the child of x which is an ancestor of v. Then $x' = rt(T'')$ (See Fig. 2).*

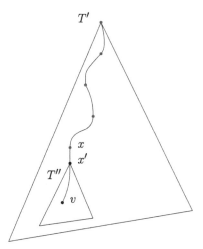

Fig. 2. Lemma 4. The set X consists of the red vertices. (Color figure online)

Lemma 5. *Let u and v be vertices in G such that v is not a vertex of T^u. Let X be the set of vertices in C_{T^u} which are ancestors of v. Suppose $X \neq \emptyset$ and let x be the last vertex on the path from u to v which is contained in T^u. Then $x \in X$. Moreover, x is the deepest vertex in X (See Fig. 3).*

Lemma 6. *Let u and v be vertices of T such that u is a descendant of v and T^v is contained in T^u. Let T' be the canonical subtree in the forest $T^u \setminus C_{T^u}$ which contains v and let X be the set of vertices in C_{T^u} which are descendants of v and ancestors of u. Let x be the element of X which is highest in T. Then either $rt(T')$ or $l(T')$ is the parent of x (See Fig. 4).*

3.2 Routing Algorithm

In this section, we describe a local routing algorithm for the spanner defined above. Throughout what follows, let G denote the graph obtained when the algorithm of the previous section is applied to a weighted, rooted tree T using a parameter $k \geq 2$. We first define the labels $label(v)$ for vertices $v \in V(G)$. We make use of the interval labelling scheme of Santaro and Khatib [9]. Let $rank(v)$ denote the rank of v in a post-order traversal of T. We define

$$L(v) := \min\{rank(w) : w \in V(T_v)\}.$$

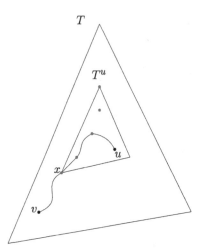

Fig. 3. Lemma 5. The set X consists of the red vertices. (Color figure online)

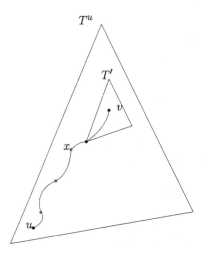

Fig. 4. Lemma 6. The set X consists of the red vertices. (Color figure online)

We define the label of v to be $label(v) = [L(v), rank(v)]$. The observation used in the routing algorithm of Santaro and Khatib [9] is that a vertex w is a descendant of v if and only if $rank(w) \in [L(v), rank(v)]$. Note that the label of each vertex can be computed in linear time in a single traversal of the tree.

Lemma 7. *In the labelling scheme outlined above, each vertex of G stores $O((\Delta + k)\log n)$ bits of information.*

Proof. Since G has n vertices, for each $v \in V(G)$, $rank(v)$ and $L(v)$ are both integers in the interval $[1, ..., n]$ and therefore require $O(\log n)$ bits to be represented. By Theorem 1, each vertex of G has at most $\Delta + O(1)$ neighbours in G.

Then, for any $v \in V(G)$, we require $O((\Delta + k) \log n)$ bits to store $rank(w)$ and $L(w)$ for each neighbour w of v. □

For this routing algorithm, no auxiliary data structure is required at each vertex and so the total storage requirement per vertex is $O((\Delta + k) \log n)$ bits.

For convenience of analysis, in each case we specify two routing steps. For ease of exposition, we consider a vertex u to be both a descendant and ancestor of itself.

Given a current vertex u and a destination vertex v, the algorithm executes the routing steps of one of the cases defined below:

Case 0: If v is a neighbour of u, route to v.

Case 1: u is an ancestor of v in T. Let X be the set of vertices in C_{T^u} which are ancestors of v. Let x be the deepest element of X. Route first to x and then to the child of x which is an ancestor of u.

Case 2: u is a descendant of v in T. Let X be the set of vertices in C_{T^u} which are descendants of v and ancestors of u. Let x be the highest vertex in X. Route first to X and then to its parent.

Case 3: u is not an ancestor or descendant of v. Let X be the set of vertices in C_{T^u} which are ancestors of v and not ancestors of u. If $X \neq \emptyset$, we define x to be the deepest vertex in X and define x' to be the child of x which is an ancestor of v. Let Y be the set of vertices in C_{T^u} which are ancestors of u but not ancestors of v. We define y to be the highest vertex in Y.

Case 3 a): X is empty. Route first to y and then to the parent of y.

Case 3 b): X is non-empty. Route first to x and then to x'.

The routing algorithm uses a greedy strategy. Given the destination vertex and neighbours due to tree edges and shortcuts, the algorithm simply selects the edge that appears to make the most progress. It is not obvious that this strategy gives the desired $O(\log n)$ diameter of the routing algorithm. Indeed, this bound would not hold if the shortcuts were arbitrary edges and hinges on the particular structure of the 1-spanner.

The arguments we make in our analysis will make use of certain integer sequences we assign to vertices of G. Note that these sequences are used only for the analysis of the algorithm and are not part of the labelling scheme. We define a unique integer sequence for each canonical subtree computed during the course of the spanner construction. Each vertex v will be assigned the sequence corresponding to the tree T^v.

The integer sequence for each canonical subtree is defined recursively as follows. The input tree T is given the empty sequence. Suppose T' is a canonical subtree which has already been associated with some sequence S. Consider the forest $T' \setminus C_{T'} = \{T_1, ..., T_p\}$. Each tree $T_j \in T' \setminus C_{T'}$ is associated with the sequence obtained by appending j to S. It is clear that every vertex of T appears in $C_{T'}$ for exactly one canonical subtree T'. Let S_v denote the sequence assigned to the vertex v. We refer to S_v as the canonical sequence of v.

Observe that if for two vertices $u, v \in V(G)$ we have that $S_u = S_v$, by definition of the spanner construction algorithm, u and v must be cut vertices of the same canonical subtree of T and are therefore connected by an edge in G. The routing algorithm works by choosing a successor vertex so as to incrementally transform the canonical sequence of the current vertex into the canonical sequence of the destination vertex.

Lemma 8. *Let u and v be vertices of G such that u is an ancestor of v. Consider the two vertices visited after executing the routing steps of Case 1 when routing from u to v. These vertices are on the path from u to v in T. Moreover, these vertices are visited in the order they appear on this path.*

Lemma 9. *Let u and v be vertices of G such that u is a descendant of v. Consider the two vertices visited after executing the routing steps of Case 2 when routing from u to v. These vertices are on the path from u to v in T. Moreover, these vertices are visited in the order they appear on this path.*

Lemma 8 and Lemma 9 are immediate from the definition of the routing steps.

Lemma 10. *Let u and v be vertices of G such that u is not an ancestor or a descendant of v. Suppose the set X, as defined in Case 3 of the routing algorithm, is empty. Consider the vertices visited after executing Case 3 a) of the routing algorithm. These vertices are on the path from u to the v. Moreover, these vertices are visited by the routing algorithm in the order they appear on this path.*

Proof. Let w_1 be the first vertex visited in Case 3 a) and let w_2 be the second. Then w_1 is the vertex y and w_2 is its parent. Since y is, by definition, not an ancestor of v, it lies on the path from u to $lca(u, v)$. Since w_2 is the parent of y, it is clearly the next vertex on $P(u, lca(u, v))$.   □

Lemma 11. *Let u and v be vertices of G such that u is not an ancestor or descendant of v. Suppose the set X, as defined in Case 3 of the routing algorithm, is non-empty. Consider the vertices visited after executing Case 3 b) of the routing algorithm. These vertices are on the path from $lca(u, v)$ to v. Moreover, these vertices are visited in the order they appear on this path.*

Proof. Let w_1 be the first vertex visited in Case 3 b) and let w_2 be the second. w_1 is an ancestor of v which is not an ancestor of u. It follows that w_1 is a descendant of $lca(u, v)$. By definition of Case 3 b), w_2 is the child of w_1 which is an ancestor of v. It is clear that w_2 is the successor to w_1 on the path $P(lca(u, v), v)$. The lemma follows.   □

Lemmas 8, 9, 10 and 11 imply the following:

Lemma 12. *Let u and v be vertices of G and let $P(u,v) = (u = x_1, ..., x_p = v)$. Suppose the routing steps of a single case of the routing algorithm are executed and vertices w_1 and w_2 are visited. Then there are indices $1 \leq i_1 \leq i_2 \leq p$ such that $w_1 = x_{i_1}$ and $w_2 = x_{i_2}$.*

Using Lemma 12, we can show the routing algorithm has a routing ratio of 1.

Theorem 2. *Let u and v be vertices of G. Let $\delta_T(u,v)$ denote the length of the path from u to v in T. The routing algorithm described above is guaranteed to terminate after a finite number of steps and the length of the path traversed is exactly $\delta_T(u,v)$.*

We now argue that the routing algorithm is guaranteed to terminate after traversing $O(\log n)$ edges. To that end, we prove the following lemma.

Lemma 13. *Let u and v be vertices of T such that u is either an ancestor or a descendant of v. Let u' be the vertex reached after executing the routing steps of either Case 1 or Case 2 when routing from u to v. Then the following statements hold:*

1. *If S_u is a prefix of S_v, then $|S_{u'}| > |S_u|$. Moreover, either $S_{u'} = S_v$ or S'_u is a prefix of S_v.*
2. *If S_v is a prefix of S_u, then $|S_{u'}| < |S_u|$. Moreover, either $S_{u'} = S_v$ or S_v is a prefix of $S_{u'}$.*
3. *Suppose S_u and S_v share a common prefix S of length $m < \min\{|S_u|, |S_v|\}$. Then $|S_{u'}| < |S_u|$. Moreover, either $S_{u'} = S$ or S is a prefix of $S_{u'}$*

Proof. We begin with the first statement. Suppose S_u is a prefix of S_v. Then T^u contains T^v. Let T' be the canonical subtree in the forest $T^u \setminus C_{T^u}$ which contains T^v. By definition, the canonical sequence of any cut vertex of T' can be obtained by appending some integer to S_u. Since T^v is contained in T', the canonical sequence associated to T' is a prefix of S_v. Then it is sufficient to show that $u' \in C_{T'}$. Suppose u is an ancestor of v so that the algorithm executes the routing steps of Case 1. Recall that in Case 1 the set X is defined as the set of vertices in C_{T^u} which are ancestors of v and the vertex x is defined as the deepest vertex in X. Then by definition of Case 1, u' is the child of x which is an ancestor of v. By Lemma 4, $u' = rt(T')$. Since $rt(T') \in C_{T'}$, the statement of the lemma follows in this case. Now suppose u is a descendant of v so that the algorithm executes the routing steps of Case 2. Recall that in Case 2, X is defined to be the set of vertices in C_{T^u} which are descendants of v and ancestors of u and x is defined to be the highest vertex in X. By definition of Case 2, the algorithm routes to x and then to the parent of x. Then u' is the parent of x. By Lemma 6, $u' \in \{l(T'), rt(T')\}$. Since $\{l(T'), rt(T')\} \subseteq C_{T'}$, the first statement of the lemma holds in this case.

We now address the second and third statements of the lemma. Suppose S_u is not a prefix of S_v. Let S be the longest common prefix of S_u and S_v. Then either $S = S_v$ or S is a prefix of S_v. Let T'' be the canonical subtree corresponding to the canonical sequence S. Observe that T'' contains T^u. Let T' be the canonical subtree such that $T^u \in T' \setminus C_{T'}$. Then either $T'' = T'$ or T'' contains T'. Note that the canonical sequence of any cut vertex of T' is a prefix of S_u. Moreover, for any canonical sequence S' of a cut vertex in T', either $S = S'$ or S is a prefix of S'. We claim that $u' \in C_{T'}$. When S_v is a prefix of S_u, we see this implies the second statement. When S_u and S_v share a prefix of length $m < \min\{|S_u|, |S_v|\}$, we see that our claim implies the third statement.

We now prove the claim. Suppose that u is an ancestor of v so that the algorithm executes the routing steps of Case 1. Let X and x be as defined in Case 1. Then u' is the child of x which is an ancestor of v. By Lemma 5, x is the last vertex on the path from u to v which is contained in T. Since x is an ancestor of v and u' is both a child of x and ancestor of v, it is clear that u' is the next vertex on $P(u, v)$. Since u is a vertex outside T' connected to a vertex in T^u, we see that $u' \in C_{T'}$ and so the claim holds in this case. Suppose now that u is a descendant of v so that the algorithm executes the routing steps of Case 2. Let X and x be as defined in Case 2. Note that since u is a descendant of v, $rt(T^u)$ must also be a descendant of v. Then $rt(T^u) \in X$. Since $rt(T^u)$ must be the highest vertex in X, we see that $x = rt(T^u)$. Since the parent of $rt(T^u)$ is clearly a member of $C_{T'}$, the claim holds. This completes the proof of the lemma. □

Note that if u is an ancestor (resp. descendant) of v, then by Lemma 12 the vertex reached after executing the steps of Case 1 (resp. Case 2) will also be an ancestor (resp. descendant) of v.

Lemma 14. *Suppose u and v in G are such that u is an ancestor or descendant of v in T. Then, when routing from u to v, the routing algorithm reaches v after traversing $O(\log n)$ edges.*

Consider the case where u is neither an ancestor nor a descendant of v. The following lemma shows that in this case, the algorithm either routes to a vertex on the path $P(lca(u, v), v)$ or it follows the routing steps that would be executed if the algorithm were routing from u to $lca(u, v)$.

Lemma 15. *Let u and v be vertices of G such that $lca(u, v) \notin \{u, v\}$. Suppose that the set X as defined in Case 3 is empty so that the algorithm executes the routing steps of Case 3 a) when routing from u to v. The same steps would be performed when routing from u to $lca(u, v)$.*

Using Lemmas 14 and 15, we establish our main result.

Theorem 3. *Let u and v be vertices in G. The routing algorithm reaches v when routing from u after traversing at most $O(\log n)$ edges.*

4   Conclusion

We have shown that a simplified version of the logarithmic diameter tree metric 1-spanner of Solomon and Elkin [10] supports a local routing algorithm of routing ratio 1 and logarithmic diameter. The shortcutting scheme of Solomon an Elkin has proven to be a powerful tool for the design of low weight, low diameter spanners. We believe our result will be of interest to researchers seeking to design high quality networks for the purpose of local routing.

References

1. Abraham, I., Malkhi, D.: Compact routing on Euclidian metrics. In: Proceedings of the 23rd Annual ACM Symposium on Principles of Distributed Computing, pp. 141–149 (2004)
2. Arya, S.K., Das, G., Mount, D.M., Salowe, J.S., Smid, M.H.M.: Euclidean spanners: short, thin, and lanky. In: Proceedings of the 27th Annual ACM Symposium on Theory of Computing (1995)
3. Ashvinkumar, V., Gudmundsson, J., Levcopoulos, C., Nilsson, B.J., van Renssen, A.: Local routing in sparse and lightweight geometric graphs. In: Proceedings of the 30th International Symposium on Algorithms and Computation. LIPIcs, vol. 149, pp. 30:1–30:13 (2019)
4. Bose, P., et al.: Online routing in convex subdivisions. Int. J. Comput. Geom. Appl. **12**(4), 283–296 (2002)
5. Bose, P., Fagerberg, R., Renssen, A., Verdonschot, S.: Optimal local routing on Delaunay triangulations defined by empty equilateral triangles. SIAM J. Comput. **44**(6), 1626–1649 (2015)
6. Chan, T., Li, M., Ning, L., Solomon, S.: New doubling spanners: better and simpler. SIAM J. Comput. **44**(1), 37–53 (2015)
7. Chan, T.H.H., Gupta, A., Maggs, B.M., Zhou, S.: On hierarchical routing in doubling metrics. ACM Trans. Algorithms **12**(4), 55:1–55:22 (2016)
8. Elkin, M., Solomon, S.: Optimal Euclidean spanners: really short, thin and lanky. In: Proceedings of the 45th Annual ACM Symposium on Theory of Computing, pp. 645–654 (2013)
9. Santoro, N., Khatib, R.: Labelling and implicit routing in networks. Comput. J. **28**(1), 5–8 (1985)
10. Solomon, S., Elkin, M.: Balancing degree, diameter, and weight in Euclidean spanners. SIAM J. Discrete Math. **28**(3), 1173–1198 (2014)
11. Solomon, S.: From hierarchical partitions to hierarchical covers: optimal fault-tolerant spanners for doubling metrics. In: Proceedings of the 46th Annual ACM Symposium on Theory of Computing, pp. 363–372 (2014)

Deep Specification Mining with Attention

Zhi Cao and Nan Zhang$^{(\boxtimes)}$

Institute of Computing Theory and Technology, and ISN Laboratory,
Xidian University, Xi'an 710071, China
zhicao@stu.xidian.edu.cn, nanzhang@xidian.edu.cn

Abstract. In this paper, we improve the method of specification mining based on deep learning proposed in [16]. In that neural network model, we find that if the length of a single trace exceeds 25 and the number of the tracking methods exceeds 15, the $F_{measure}$ output of the original model will decrease significantly. Accordingly, we propose a new model with attention mechanism to solve the forgetting problem of the original model for long sequence learning. First of all, test cases are used to generate as many as possible program traces, each of which covers a complete execution path. The trace set is then used for training a language model based on Recurrent Neural Networks (RNN) and attention mechanism. From these trajectories, a Prefix Tree Acceptor (PTA) is built and features are extracted using the new proposed model. Then, these features are used by clustering algorithms to merge similar states in the PTA to build multiple finite automata. Finally, a heuristic algorithm is used to evaluate the quality of these automata and select the one with the highest $F_{measure}$ as the final specification automaton.

Keywords: Specification mining · Deep learning · Trace · Attention · Finite state automata

1 Introduction

A system engineering activity requires a specification, which is a description of the goals to be achieved by the system. System specifications are at the core of all projects. As Brian Kerninghan puts it, "There are no errors without specifications, only 'surprise'." With software maintenance, specifications are also extremely important. Well-defined software specifications enable programmers to better understand software systems, thereby saving maintenance costs. However, many software lack software specifications for various reasons. Accordingly, Specification Mining was proposed and widely studied. Mined specifications can assist program debugging, and even developing verification tools to automatically find program errors to promote the correctness of systems.

Although software specification is very important, the cost of writing specifications is very high since it requires a lot of manpower and material resources. In

The research is supported by National Natural Science Foundation of China under Grant Nos. 61420106004, 61732013 and 61751207.

© Springer Nature Switzerland AG 2020
D. Kim et al. (Eds.): COCOON 2020, LNCS 12273, pp. 186–197, 2020.
https://doi.org/10.1007/978-3-030-58150-3_15

addition, there are special requirements for the professional skills of developers. And some legacy software does not have specification documents, which makes software reuse extremely difficult. Recently, many automated techniques have been proposed to mine a variety of specifications, such as finite state automata (FSA), temporal rules, sequence diagram, value-based invariants and so on. However, standard mining needs to further improve the accuracy of mining. The term specification mining first proposed by Ammons et al. "It is a machine learning method that specifies the formal specification of the protocol that code must follow when interacting with an application." Shoham et al. first tried using static analysis to mine client timing APIs [29]. They proposed a new method to implement client-side mining based on a static analysis of the time series API specification, providing inter-process analysis on a composite domain, which abstracts the aliasing and sequence of events for each object.

Traditional machine learning algorithms are dependent on the manual extraction of features [2]. Accordingly, there is a bottleneck of feature extraction in conventional-machine-learning-based image recognition, speech recognition [27] and natural language processing. The method based on fully connected neural network [9,30] also has drawbacks, such as too many parameters, inability to use time series information in the data and so on. As more effective recurrent neural network structures have been proposed, the ability of deep neural networks to express temporal and semantic information in data has been fully utilized, and has been used in machine learning, language recognition, language models, machine translation, and timing analysis. In terms of breakthrough, theoretically, the recurrent neural network can support sequences with arbitrary length. However, in a practical training process, if the sequence is too long, it will lead to gradient dissipation [31] and gradient explosion during optimization. Further, the expanded feed-forward neural network will take up too much memory, so a maximum length is generally specified in practice. When the sequence length exceeds the specified length, the sequence is truncated. Recurrent neural networks can make better use of information that traditional neural network structures cannot model, but at the same time, this also brings a grand challenge: the long-term dependence problem. In some circumstances, the model only needs short-term information to perform the current task. The RNN architecture of Long Short-Term Memory (LSTM) [11] is designed to solve this problem. A time-expanded view of LSTM is shown in Fig. 1. In many tasks, recurrent neural networks with LSTM structure perform better than standard recurrent neural networks.

In order to select only some key information for processing and improve the efficiency of the neural network [6], a technique named Attention Mechanism has been proposed to allow a model to focus only on important information and fully learn and absorb it. It is not a complete model and can be used in any sequence model. The Attention Mechanism is selective (selected by the calculated similarity weights) to focus on relevant contents of an input while ignoring other contents [18]. Many tasks are benefited from this technique. On one hand, it can make the results more accurate. On the other hand, it is able to solve the problem of excessive computational complexity. A general Attention structure

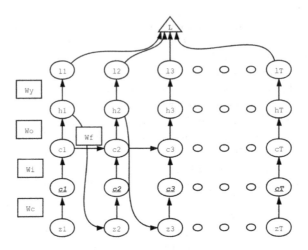

Fig. 1. A time-expanded view of LSTM

[1] has been designed in Tensorflow so that simple time series models can use the Attention Mechanism. The entire model can better focus on the step that contributes the most. To some extent it solves the problem of insufficient memory in the time series model. The Attention Mechanism is widely used in Natural Language Generation (NLG) [24], Question Answering System (QA) [13], Dialogue System [4,7], Multimedia Description (MD) [26], Text Classification [21], Recommendation Systems [15], Sentiment Analysis [23] and other tasks.

In this paper, we improve the Deep Specification Mining (DSM) method proposed in [16] and put forward a new model with Attention Mechanism to solve the forgetting problem of the original model for long sequence learning. The contributions of the paper are four-fold: (1) In the case where the length of a single trace exceeds 25 and the number of the tracking methods exceeds 15, the $F_{measure}$ output of the original model decreases significantly. We use the Attention Mechanism [5,28] to alleviate the poor performance of RNN in long sequences; (2) The DSM clustering algorithm is extended to optimize time and accuracy while the stability of the algorithm operation is also improved; (3) The method of extracting traces has been implemented in Python; (4) A new model is proposed, which is suitable to mine specifications from both long and short traces.

The rest of the paper is organized as follows: In the next section, our improved method of specification mining is elaborated, including test case generation, improvements in deep learning model and the procedure of specification mining. In Sect. 3, some relative experiments using our method are carried out and a comparison result is given in detail. In Sect. 4, conclusions are drawn.

2   Deep Specification Mining with Attention

In order to address the problem that the mining effect of the original model [16] on long traces is obviously reduced, we propose a new deep learning model. In our model, the improvement can be summarized as the following four points.

(1) We automatically generate test cases for considered methods. After input a test case, use a system method in Python to track and obtain a running trace of a program. Record all the running traces of target methods as subsequent training data set.

(2) We increase the number of types of clustering algorithms to make the model more stable and reliable. In our work, nine clustering algorithms are used while in the original method in [16] two clustering algorithms are employed, and then the best clustering result is chosen as the final result. Compared to the Kmeans algorithm, the MiniBatchKmeans [22] algorithm can significantly reduce the calculation time without affecting accuracy when the amount of data is too large.

(3) In order to solve the problem of the sudden decline in the mining effect of the original model in long traces, we employ the Attention Mechanism. After integrating the Attention Mechanism with the model, intermediate results of a certain step can be weighted and summed up, thereby alleviating the forgetting problem of the RNN language model.

(4) The model with the Attention Mechanism and the original model are integrated together so that the mined features are suitable for both short and long traces. We use two weighting methods for model fusion [17], and the final results are better than the original model.

2.1   Test Case Generation

We use the sys.settrace method in Python to track program execution, then use the frame.fcode.Coname method to filter the traces to make them only consist of the methods we concern. Since the method call tracking is global, we can add and delete the methods to be tracked according to our needs and concerns. We develop a lightweight program to track execution traces of programs, and record them as a data set required for training. Compared with other frameworks that generate traces, our method is light weight, high flexibility, and easy to achieve. However, the disadvantage is that some information on program execution cannot be obtained, such as changes of variable values, and invariants [25] during program running. But since our specification mining framework does not use information other than method call sequences during program running, the disadvantage can be ignored. Further, conventional methods of tracking objects are based on C, C++, Java and other programming languages while our lightweight framework first provides code tracking for Python language. An example of a code execution sequence is given as follows.

Example 1. ⟨START⟩ ZipOutputStream putNextEntry putNextEntry putNextEntry closeEntry closeEntry close ⟨END⟩.

2.2   Improvement in Deep Learning Models

We propose a char-rnn with Attention Mechanism learning model named ADSM on the basis of the predecessors. In 2014, Bahdanau etc. first proposed the Attention Mechanism [3]. They proposed the most classic Attention structure for machine translation, and visually showed the alignment effect of Attention with the target language, explaining what the deep model has learned. There are four main reasons why the Attention Mechanism has developed so rapidly:

(1) The use of Attention in tasks such as Question Answering (QA), Sentiment Analysis (SA), POS Tagging, Parsing and Dialogue, has achieved the results achieved by current SOTA models.
(2) Besides improving the effect, it can also improve the interpretability of neural networks [32], which is also one of the shortcomings of neural networks.
(3) It can overcome the loss of information and insufficient memory caused by RNN when the input is too long. Of course, you can also use the memory network and neural Turing machine to solve these two problems.
(4) It can reduce computation overhead because RNN is difficult to process in parallel, and selective focus based on attention can solve this problem to a certain extent.

2.3   Specification Mining

In this processing step, the input of our method is a group of execution traces used as a training data set, and the output is a specification expressed as a finite state automaton. The construction of an automaton includes several steps: Model Training, Trace Sampling, PTA Construction, Feature Extraction, State Merging, and Excellent Model Selection.

First of all, our proposed deep learning model is trained by the trace set obtained in the previous step, and then features are defined and specified for the trace set. Then, a heuristic method is used to select a subset of representative traces that can represent the total set of traces well. This subset can help us save computing time and computing power. Further, a prefix tree acceptor is built from this subset, and the trained model is then used to extract and calculate feature values of states in the prefix tree acceptor. Moreover, nine clustering algorithms in machine learning are employed to merge similar states in the prefix tree acceptor, and multiple Finite State Automata (FSA) [12] are generated by tuning parameter values. Finally, a heuristic method is used to evaluate these automaton and the one with the best evaluation result is selected as the final output.

The framework of our method is shown in Fig. 2, in which the technique of model fusion is employed. There are many ways to fuse models. In this paper, we adopt two modes of model fusion: mean value mode and square mode. Mean value method is that the probability of the next method to appear is predicted to be the average of the probability calculated by Char-rnn and the probability calculated by Char-rnn with Attention. Square method is that the probability of the next method to appear is predicted to be the square root of the sum of the squared probability calculated by Char-rnn and the squared probability calculated by Char-rnn with Attention.

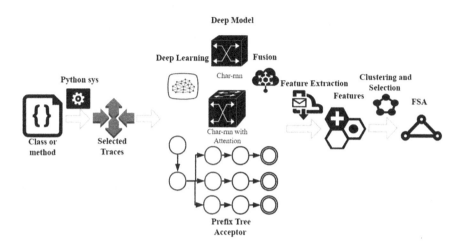

Fig. 2. The framework of specification mining based on model fusion

Model Training. The deep learning model based on a char-rnn[1] with Attention [5] we proposed is trained by a collection of traces. Our method can effectively alleviate the problem that the experimental effect becomes worse as the length of a trace increases. In general, the Attention Mechanism is to focus attention on important points and ignore other unimportant factors. According to different application scenarios, Attention is classified into Spatial Attention and Temporal Attention. The former is often used for image processing while the latter for natural language processing. The principle of the Attention Mechanism is to calculate the degree of matching between the current input sequence and the output vector. The higher the degree of matching is, the higher the relative score of the Attention point is.

Unfortunately, the current invocation of a program method is only related to some of the most recently called methods, and not to the methods that were called too long before the current method. Therefore, we propose a model fusion method. In the process of feature extraction, both the short trace segment feature information and the long trace segment feature information can be included.

Since the next execution of our program is only related to the previous program execution process, our approach is only to wrap an Attention structure outside the unidirectionally propagated Recurrent Neural Network neurons. The essence of the Attention Mechanism is a weighted sum operation of the output

---

[1] https://github.com/karpathy/char-rnn.

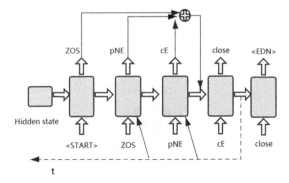

Fig. 3. Char-rnn model with Attention. (ZOS: ZipOutputStream, pNE: putNextEntry, cE: closeEntry)

of the previous Recurrent Neural Network neuron, so that the current step processing uses the output information of all previous steps (See Fig. 3). Recurrent Neural Network's poor memory has been alleviated to some extent.

Trace Sampling. Our trace set contains a large number of training samples, which contains a lot of redundant data. This redundant data can cause expensive computational costs. And data redundancy can easily result in an imbalance of training data [19], and a serious shadow on the impact of results. We select a subset that can represent the entire training set according to the same heuristic algorithm in [16].

PTA Construction. We build a Prefix Tree Acceptor (PTA) [8] from the sampled subset of traces. A PTA is a tree-like finite state automaton as shown in Fig. 4. Each path in the PTA from the initial state to a final state (double-circled node) denotes a sampled trace. After building the PTA, we calculate and predict values of two kinds of features given in the step of Feature Extraction using the trained language model.

Feature Extraction. The aim of training model is to extract features. During feature extraction, we care about two kinds of data features: (1) State calling

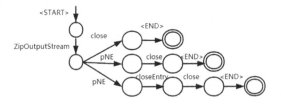

Fig. 4. An example of prefix tree acceptor

sequence contained before reaching the current state: it captures sequence information before the current state. Set the value of the method that has appeared before to 1, and the value that has not appeared to 0; (2) Probability of the next possible method call after reaching the current state: it uses the trained Recurrent Neural Network model to predict the probability of the next upcoming state, and take the state with the highest probability as the next upcoming method.

State Merging. In our method, nine clustering algorithms from the Sklearn library [14] are employed: (1) kmeans (2) hierarchical (3) hierarchicalComplete (4) affinityPropagation (5) hierarchicalAverage (6) Birch (7) hierarchicalSingle (8) MeanShift (9) MiniBatchKMeans. In order to select the best performing model, we set the number of clusters as a model parameter. The number of clusters for each algorithm is set to $numCluster-1$, with a total of $9\times(numCluster-1)$ FSA. In our experiment, the value of $numCluster$ is set to 20, so there will be totally 9×19 FSA generated. Then, we use a heuristic algorithm to pick the best FSA.

Excellent Model Selection. We select the optimal FSA according to a heuristic algorithm. This algorithm uses an index named $F_{measure}$ to evaluate the quality of a model. The value of $F_{measure}$ index for an FSA can be calculated by means of Eq. (1), which is the harmonic mean of prediction accuracy (Precision) and acceptance rate of the automaton (Recall). Precision of an inferred FSA is the percentage of sentences accepted by its corresponding ground truth model among the ones that are generated by that FSA. Recall of an inferred FSA is the percentage of sentences accepted by itself among the ones that are generated by the corresponding ground truth model [20]. Figure 5 shows the final result of model selection of AVL Tree.

$$F_{measure} = \frac{2 \times (Precision \times Recall)}{Precision + Recall} \tag{1}$$

3   Experimental Results

3.1   DataSet

In our experiments, we select 11 target library classes as the benchmark to evaluate the effectiveness of our proposed approach on short traces. Table 1 shows further details of the selected library classes execution traces. In addition, we have added two datasets of long traces: AVL Tree and RedBlackTree. These datasets are created using Pyhton programs. These datasets perform poorly on the original model [16]. We improve the model by adding Attention Mechanism in it. The overall prediction accuracy based on long traces has been greatly improved. Then we adopt the idea of model fusion to make our model have a good performance on both long and short trace datasets. The length of single traces in AVL Tree and RedBlackTree datasets is larger than 200.

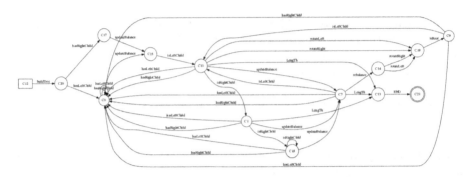

Fig. 5. AVL Tree specification

Table 1. The detailed description of DataSets

Target library class	Nums	Generated test cases	Recorded method calls
ArrayList	18	42865	22996
HashMap	11	53396	67942
Hashtable	8	79403	89811
LinkedList	7	13731	4847
NFST	5	158998	95149
Signatrue	5	79096	205386
Socket	21	80035	130876
StringTokenizer	5	148648	336924
StackAr	7	549648	132826
ZipOutputStream	5	162971	43626
AVL	19	1000	314899
MyStack	5	1000	19714
RedBlackTree	16	1000	210188

3.2   Experimental Settings

We set the number of test inputs to 1000. The average length of the traces generated is larger than 200.

Dropout settings. The dropout deep learning model was proposed by Hinton to prevent overfitting in 2012 [10]. When a complex feed-forward neural network is trained on a small data set, it is easy to cause overfitting. In order to prevent overfitting, the performance of the neural network can be improved by preventing the cooperation of feature detectors. We add Dropout between every two layers of LSTM [18] in the deep learning model with a ratio of 0.5.

Attention needs to look back several steps. Parameter attnlength denotes the maximum look-back length. If the sequence is not long, the value of attnlength is the sequence length. But the training target in our method is a set of program

Table 2. The comparison between DSM model and ADSM* model (F: $F_{measure}$, P: Precision, R: Recall)

Library class	DSM	ADSM			ADSM-mean			ADSM-Sqrt		
	F(%)	P(%)	R(%)	F(%)	P(%)	R(%)	F(%)	P(%)	R(%)	F(%)
HashMap	86.71	100	100	100	100	100	100	100	100	100
ArrayList	22.21	72.72	95	82.38	77.19	95.21	85.26	81.11	95.49	87.71
RedBlackTree	89.2	96.77	100	98.36	96.77	100	98.36	93.75	100	96.77
Hashtable	79.92	100	99.49	99.74	100	99.49	99.74	100	99.49	99.75
LinkedList	30.98	95.23	100	97.56	95.23	100	97.56	95.24	99.76	97.45
MyStack	100	100	100	100	100	100	100	100	100	100
NFST	77.52	92.31	96.33	94.27	92.31	97.15	94.67	94.12	98.5	96.26
Signature	100	100	100	100	100	100	100	100	100	100
Socket	54.24	94.38	100	97.1	96.55	99.61	98.05	96.27	100	98.1
StackAr	74.38	96.05	99.98	97.98	98.64	99.98	99.31	96.28	100	97.99
StringTokenizer	100	93.33	100	97.11	100	100	100	100	100	100
ZOS	88.82	100	100	100	100	100	100	100	100	100
AVL	90.41	100	100	100	97.06	100	98.51	94.29	100	97.06

execution traces and a large value of attnlength will worsen the final result, so we need to set the value of attnlength to an experimental value.

3.3   ADSM* Versus DSM

In the experiments, we compare the effectiveness of our proposed model with the previous Deep Specification Mining (DSM) [16] work proposed by David Lo et al. The comparison result is shown in Table 2.

4   Conclusions and Future Work

Specification helps people develop, understand and maintain software. In this paper, we propose the ADSM* models. Compared with the previous DSM [16] model, our model employs the Attention Mechanism to solve the forgetting problem of the original model for long sequence learning. Then combined with the previous method, the technique of model fusion is used to improve the experimental results on the basis of the original model. In our method, we add more clustering algorithms and expand from the original two algorithms to nine algorithms to improve the stability and robustness of the model operation. We use Python language to write a lightweight method to track code execution traces. In order to cover execution paths of the target code as many as possible, we have written a large number of test cases. Then a representative trace subset is selected to build a Prefix Tree Acceptor (PTA), and clustering algorithms are used to merge similar state nodes in the PTA to construct multiple FSAs. The optimal FSA is selected according to $F_{measure}$ and outputted as the final model. The results of the ADSM are on average greater than 0.95.

In the future, it is planned to add invariants [25] and parameters to the model in our method to further improve the effectiveness of the model. We can also use adversarial text generation techniques [33] to further improve the anti-interference and ability to prevent attacks of the model.

References

1. Abadi, M., et al.: TensorFlow: a system for large-scale machine learning. In: Proceedings of 12th USENIX Symposium on Operating Systems Design and Implementation, pp. 265–283 (2016)
2. Ashton, E.A., Molinelli, L., Totterman, S., Parker, K.J.: Evaluation of reproducibility for manual and semi-automated feature extraction in CT and MR images. In: Proceedings of International Conference on Image Processing, vol. 3, p. III (2002)
3. Bahdanau, D., Cho, K., Bengio, Y.: Neural machine translation by jointly learning to align and translate. arXiv:1409.0473 [cs.CL] (2014)
4. Black, E., Hunter, A.: An inquiry dialogue system. Auton. Agent. Multi-Agent Syst. **19**(2), 173–209 (2009)
5. Chaudhari, S., Polatkan, G., Ramanath, R., Mithal, V.: An attentive survey of attention models. arXiv:1904.02874 (2019)
6. Chorowski, J., Bahdanau, D., Serdyuk, D., Cho, K., Bengio, Y.: Attention-based models for speech recognition. Comput. Sci. **10**(4), 429–439 (2015)
7. Eckert, W., Levin, E., Pieraccini, R.: User modeling for spoken dialogue system evaluation. In: Proceedings of IEEE Workshop on Automatic Speech Recognition and Understanding, pp. 80–87 (1997)
8. García, P., de Parga, M., López, D., Ruiz, J.: Learning automata teams. In Proceedings of International Colloquium on Grammatical Inference, pp. 52–65 (2010)
9. Hansen, L.K., Salamon, P.: Neural network ensembles. IEEE Trans. Pattern Anal. Mach. Intell. **12**(10), 993–1001 (1990)
10. Hinton, G.E., Srivastava, N., Krizhevsky, A., Sutskever, I., Salakhutdinov, R.R.: Improving neural networks by preventing co-adaptation of feature detectors. arXiv:1207.0580 (2012)
11. Hochreiter, S., Schmidhuber, J.: Long short-term memory. Neural Comput. **9**(8), 1735–1780 (1997)
12. Hopcroft, J.: An n log n algorithm for minimizing states in a finite automaton. In: Theory of Machines and Computations, pp. 189–196 (1971)
13. Hovy, E., Ravichandran, D.: Learning surface text patterns for a question answering system. In: Proceedings of the 40th Annual Meeting on Association for Computational Linguistics, pp. 41–47 (2002)
14. Komer, B., Bergstra, J., Eliasmith, C.: Hyperopt-Sklearn: automatic hyperparameter configuration for Scikit-learn. In: Proceedings of the 13th Python in Science Conference, pp. 32–37 (2014)
15. Kumar, R., Raghavan, P., Rajagopalan, S., Tomkins, A.: Recommendation systems. J. Comput. Syst. Sci. **40**(1), 42–61 (1997)
16. Le, T.-D.B., Lo, D.: Deep specification mining. In Proceedings of the 27th ACM SIGSOFT International Symposium on Software Testing and Analysis, pp. 106–117 (2018)

17. Li, Y., Zhao, H., Zhang, W., Jin, Z., Mei, H.: Research on the merging of feature models. Chin. J. Comput. **36**(1), 1–9 (2013)
18. Liu, J., Wang, G., Hu, P., Duan, L., Kot, A.C.: Global context-aware attention LSTM networks for 3D action recognition. In: Proceedings of 2017 IEEE Conference on Computer Vision and Pattern Recognition (CVPR), pp. 3671–3680 (2017)
19. Liu, X.-Y., Wu, J., Zhou, Z.-H.: Exploratory undersampling for class-imbalance learning. IEEE Trans. Syst. Man Cybern. Part B (Cybern.) **39**(2), 539–550 (2008)
20. Lo, D., Khoo, S.: QUARK: empirical assessment of automaton-based specification miners. In: Proceedings of 13th Working Conference on Reverse Engineering. pp. 51–60 (2006)
21. Lodhi, H., Saunders, C., Shawe-Taylor, J., Cristianini, N., Watkins, C.: Text classification using string kernels. J. Mach. Learn. Res. **2**(3), 419–444 (2002)
22. Newling, J., Fleuret, F.: Nested mini-batch k-means. arXiv:1602.02934 (2016)
23. Prabowo, R., Thelwall, M.: Sentiment analysis: a combined approach. J. Informetr. **3**(2), 143–157 (2013)
24. Reiter, E., Dale, R.: Building natural language generation systems. Comput. Linguist. **27**(2), 298–300 (1996)
25. Leino, K.R.M., Müller, P.: Object invariants in dynamic contexts. In: Odersky, M. (ed.) ECOOP 2004. LNCS, vol. 3086, pp. 491–515. Springer, Heidelberg (2004). https://doi.org/10.1007/978-3-540-24851-4_22
26. Salembier, P., Smith, J.R.: MPEG-7 multimedia description schemes. IEEE Trans. Circ. Syst. Video Technol. **11**(6), 748–759 (2001)
27. Shannon, R.V., Zeng, F.G., Kamath, V., Wygonski, J., Ekelid, M.: Speech recognition with primarily temporal cues. Science **270**(5234), 303–304 (1995)
28. Shiba, T., Tsuchiya, T., Kikuno, T.: Using artificial life techniques to generate test cases for combinatorial testing. In: Proceedings of the 28th Annual International Computer Software and Applications Conference, vol. 1, pp. 72–77 (2004)
29. Shoham, S., Yahav, E., Fink, S.J., Pistoia, M.: Static specification mining using automata-based abstractions. IEEE Trans. Softw. Eng. **34**(5), 651–666 (2008)
30. Specht, D.F.: A general regression neural network. IEEE Trans. Neural Netw. **2**(6), 568–576 (2002)
31. Stewart, A.K., Boyd, C.A.R., Vaughan-Jones, R.D.: A novel role for carbonic anhydrase: cytoplasmic PH gradient dissipation in mouse small intestinal enterocytes. J. Physiol. **516**(1), 209–217 (1999)
32. Tan, S., Sim, K.C., Gales, M.: Improving the interpretability of deep neural networks with stimulated learning. In: Proceedings of 2015 IEEE Workshop on Automatic Speech Recognition and Understanding (ASRU), pp. 617–623 (2015)
33. Wang, K., Wan, X.: SentiGAN: generating sentimental texts via mixture adversarial networks. In: Proceedings of the 27th International Joint Conference on Artificial Intelligence (IJCAI 2018), pp. 4446–4452 (2018)

Constructing Independent Spanning Trees in Alternating Group Networks

Jie-Fu Huang[1] and Sun-Yuan Hsieh[2(✉)]

[1] Department of Computer Science and Information Engineering,
National Cheng Kung University, No. 1, University Road, Tainan 701, Taiwan
p78001099@mail.ncku.edu.tw
[2] Department of Computer Science and Information Engineering,
Institute of Medical Informatics, and the Center for Innovative
FinTech Business Models, National Cheng Kung University,
No. 1, University Road, Tainan 701, Taiwan
hsiehsy@mail.ncku.edu.tw

Abstract. In a graph G, two spanning trees T_1 and T_2 are rooted at the same vertex r. If for every $v \in V(G)$ the paths from v to the root r in T_1 and T_2 are internally vertex-disjoint, they are independent spanning trees (ISTs). ISTs have numerous applications, such as secure message distribution and fault-tolerant broadcasting. The alternating group network AN_n (n stands for the dimension) is a subclass of Cayley graphs, and the approach of constructing ISTs in AN_n has not been proposed until now. In this paper, we propose a recursive algorithm for constructing ISTs in AN_n. The algorithm is a top-down approach, and the parent of one node in an IST is not determined by any rule. The correctness of the algorithm is verified, and the time complexity is analyzed. We use PHP to implement the algorithm and test cases from AN_3 to AN_{10}. The testing results show that all trees are ISTs in all cases. We conclude that our algorithm is not only correct but also efficient.

Keywords: Independent spanning trees · Alternating group networks · Triangle breadth-first search · Interconnection networks · Cayley graph

1 Introduction

In a graph G, two spanning trees T_1 and T_2 are rooted at the same vertex r. If for every $v \in V(G)$ the paths from v to the root r in T_1 and T_2 are internally vertex-disjoint, they are independent spanning trees (ISTs). The ISTs problem is appealing and has attracted considerable attention. It can be applied in many research fields, such as secure message distribution [2,15], fault-tolerant broadcasting [2], and pattern derivation in mitochondrial DNA sequences [14].

Accordingly, how to construct ISTs in graphs is worth studying. For a k-connected graph, Zehavi and Itai have presented how to construct k ISTs [20]. The conjecture is correct in k-connected graphs with $k \leq 4$ [5,6,9], but it has not

© Springer Nature Switzerland AG 2020
D. Kim et al. (Eds.): COCOON 2020, LNCS 12273, pp. 198–209, 2020.
https://doi.org/10.1007/978-3-030-58150-3_16

been solved for $k \geq 5$. However, it is so difficult to find ISTs in arbitrary graphs that researchers have changed to study the ISTs problems on interconnection networks over the past decade.

The IST problem has been solved on several interconnection networks, including locally twisted cubes [3,8,13], hypercubes [16,17], folded hypercubes [18], and bubble-sort networks [10,11]. However, the algorithm for constructing ISTs in alternating group networks has not been proposed up to now. In this paper, we focus on alternating group networks.

A class of graphs called group graphs or Cayley graphs are crucial for the design and analysis of interconnection networks for parallel and distributed computing. [1,4,7,12]. The alternating group network AN_n (n stands for the dimension) were proposed by Youhu in 1998 [19]. The alternating group networks are Cayley graphs and vertex symmetric. According to [21], $n-1$ vertex-disjoint paths exist between any two vertices of AN_n. In this paper, we propose a recursive algorithm for constructing $n-1$ ISTs in AN_n. The remainder of this paper is arranged as follows: Sect. 2 preliminaries; Sect. 3 algorithm; Sect. 4 testing and analysis; and Sect. 5 conclusion.

2   Preliminaries

An alternating group network AN_n is defined to be a Cayley graph $G = G(V, E)$ in an alternating group A_n, where V is the set of all even permutations of $\langle n \rangle = \{1, 2, \ldots, n\}$ and E consists of symmetric edges (u, v) such that any two distinct permutations u and v are linked through an edge if and only if one can be reached from the other by three operations such as left child, right child, and friend. Suppose that $n \geq 3$, the alternating group network AN_n has the vertex set of even permutations from $\{1, 2, \ldots, n\}$; two vertices $[a_1, a_2, a_3, \ldots, a_n]$ and $[b_1, b_2, b_3, \ldots, b_n]$ are adjacent if one of the following three conditions is satisfied.

- The first condition is $a_1 = b_3$, $a_2 = b_1$, $a_3 = b_2$ and $a_j = b_j$ for $4 \leq j \leq n$. As illustrated in Fig. 1(a), node b is the left child of node a.
- The second condition is $a_1 = b_2$, $a_2 = b_3$, $a_3 = b_1$ and $a_j = b_j$ for $4 \leq j \leq n$. As presented in Fig. 1(b), node b is the right child of node a.
- The third condition is that there exists $i \in \{4, 5, \ldots, n\}$ such that $a_1 = b_2, a_2 = b_1, a_3 = b_i, a_i = b_3$, and $a_j = b_j$ for $j \in \{4, 5, \ldots, n\} \backslash \{i\}$. As shown in Fig. 1(c), node b is friend i of node a.

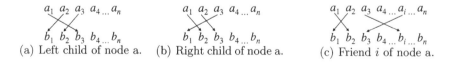

(a) Left child of node a.   (b) Right child of node a.   (c) Friend i of node a.

Fig. 1. Three operations in alternating group networks.

AN_3 and AN_4 are shown in Fig. 2 and Fig. 3.

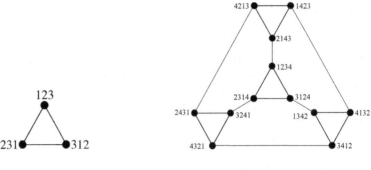

123

Fig. 2. AN_3.   **Fig. 3.** AN_4.

3   Algorithm

Firstly, we introduce basic notations:

- the root: node $123456\ldots n$ is chosen as the root of all ISTs;
- cluster A: a set of nodes, and their last symbol is A;
- the root cluster: the set of nodes, and their last symbol is the same with the root's last symbol. In AN_n, the root cluster is cluster n;
- trunk: a set of nodes with the same last symbols created by createTrunk function;
- the origin: the starting node of a trunk;
- T_j^n: the jth IST of AN_n, and the last symbol of its trunk whose is j;
- tid: the last symbol of the origin, and it is j in T_j^n.

We can divide AN_n into n objects of AN_{n-1}, and classify every node into a cluster by its last symbol. Thus, there are n clusters in AN_n. For example, we can divide AN_4 into four objects of AN_3. There are four clusters in AN_4, as shown in Fig. 4.

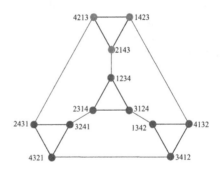

Fig. 4. Four clusters of AN_4.

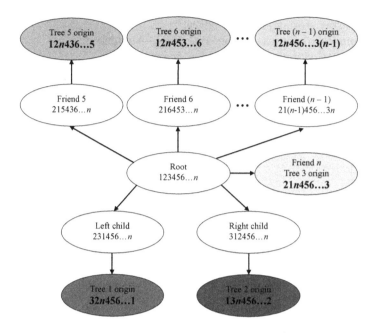

Fig. 5. Origins.

We can transform every node in AN_{n-1} into a node in AN_n if we append one symbol n in the nth position. We can use the property to construct the ISTs of AN_n from AN_{n-1}. There are $n-1$ edges and $n-1$ nodes adjacent to the root in AN_n. Of the $n-1$ nodes, $n-2$ nodes can be transformed from AN_{n-1} if we append one symbol n in the nth position, but the friend n is a new node. The $n-2$ nodes use their new edge incident to a node, namely an **origin** and the friend n itself is an origin, too. The origins are used to create trunks to traverse other clusters. The idea is presented in Fig. 5. The white nodes in the center are transformed from some node in AN_{n-1} if we append a symbol n in the last position. The root's child 1 in AN_n takes its new edge to create the origin of T_1^n. The root's child 2 in AN_n takes its new edges to create the origin of T_2^n. The root in AN_n takes its new edge to create the origin of T_3^n. The root's friends 5 to $n-1$ in AN_n take their new edges to create the origins of T_5^n to T_{n-1}^n. T_4^n does not execute any createTrunk function; hence, it has no origin.

3.1 Recursive Algorithm

Algorithm 1 use the following global variables.

- *tary*: a two-dimensional array storing the trees in this iteration; $tary[tid][node]$ is *node*'s parent. Every tree includes all nodes. If the node is not traversed, its value is 0, namely $tary[tid][node] = 0$;
- *ptary*: an array storing the trees in the previous iteration;

- *edge*: an array storing all direct edges.
  $edge[from][to]=1$ represents the edge $from{\rightarrow}to$ unused;
  $edge[from][to]=0$ represents the edge $from{\rightarrow}to$ used.

Construct the ISTs of AN_3 by Hands. AN_3 is a triangle, where there are two ISTs. We can construct those ISTs by hand as illustrated in Fig. 6.

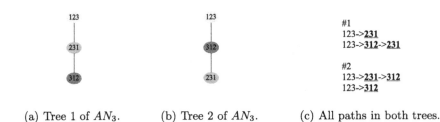

(a) Tree 1 of AN_3.   (b) Tree 2 of AN_3.   (c) All paths in both trees.

Fig. 6. ISTs in AN_3 and all paths.

Duplicate Previous Trees. *tary* is stored in *ptary* at the end in each iteration so that the ISTs in this iteration can be reused in the next iteration. In the starting of each iteration, the algorithm will duplicate the previous ISTs to *tary*. Table 1 displays the relation of a tree in this iteration and the mapping tree in the previous iteration. Accordingly, T_1^n comes from T_1^{n-1} and T_{n-1}^n comes from T_3^{n-1}. T_3^n is a totally new tree, and it does not duplicate any previous tree.

Create an OriginSet. An *OriginSet* is an array storing the origins. We create the origins from the root. In AN_4, we create three origins, namely 3241, 1342, and 2143 to create trunks, as presented in Fig. 7.

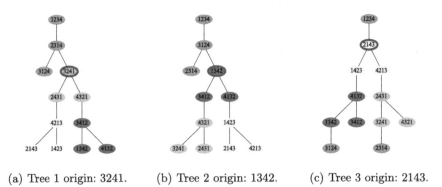

(a) Tree 1 origin: 3241.   (b) Tree 2 origin: 1342.   (c) Tree 3 origin: 2143.

Fig. 7. Origins (nodes with dark brown outlines) in AN_4.

Algorithm 1: RECURSIVE ALGORITHM

Input : n ▷ the dimension n of AN_n

Output: the ISTs from AN_3 to AN_n

1   **for** $dim = 3; dim \leq n; dim = dim + 1$ **do**

2   **if** $dim == 3$ **then**

3          $\lfloor$ Construct the ISTs of AN_3 by hand;

4   **else if** $dim \geq 4$ **then**

5   Duplicate previous trees in the previous iteration to the trees in this iteration;

6   Create an $OriginSet$;   ▷ an array storing origins

7   **for** $every\ origin\ in\ the\ OriginSet$ **do**

8             $\lfloor$ Execute CreateTrunk function;   ▷ (1)

9   // Create branches

10   **if** $dim == 4$ **then**

11   // AN_4 executes createBranch function three times.

12   **for** $i = 0; i < 3; i = i + 1$ **do**

13   **for** $j = 1; j \leq dim - 1; j = j + 1$ **do**

14   **if** $i == 0$ **then**

15                     $\lfloor$ createBranch($tary$, j, $edge$, true, n);

16   **else**

17                     $\lfloor$ createBranch($tary$, j, $edge$, false, n);

18   **else if** $dim \geq 5$ **then**

19   // Every tree executes createBranch function four times.

20   **for** $i = 0; i < 4; i = i + 1$ **do**

21   **for** $j = 1; j \leq dim - 1; j = j + 1$ **do**

22   **if** $i == 0$ **then**

23                     $\lfloor$ createBranch($tary$, j, $edge$, true, n);

24   **else**

25                     $\lfloor$ createBranch($tary$, j, $edge$, false, n);

26   createBranch($tary$, 3, $edge$, true, n);   ▷ (2)

27      $ptary = tary$;   ▷ $tary$ must be stored to use in next iteration.

28   /* Comments:

29   (1) T_4 executes a createBranch function to produce neighbors along the root cluster, T_4 first appears in AN_5, and it duplicates T_3^4 to $tary[4]$.

30   (2) Compared with other trees, T_3 executes createBranch function one more time to traverse the root cluster. */

Table 1. The mapping of tid in this iteration and tid in the previous iteration.

Tree id	1	2	3	4	5	6	...	$n-1$
Previous tree id	1	2	No previous tid, a new tree	4	5	6	...	3

3.2   CreatTrunk Function

We create a trunk from an origin through a triangle breadth-first search (TBFS) traversal. However, the TBFS traversal just only traverses nodes whose the last symbol is the same with that of the origin.

BFS Order. In the createTrunk function, each node in *tkQue* will traverse all unvisited nodes adjacent to it in this order:
    1. left child; 2. right child; 3. friends 4, 5, 6 ..., $n - 1$.

MBFS Traversal. Because AN_n is symmetric, some child c of one node v may be traversed by another node w earlier. In such case, we should transfer c's parent from w to v. For instance, the graph presented in Fig. 8(a) occurs. We set the edge (marked blue X) from used to unused and use another edge (marked blue arrow) to traverse c. Hence, the triangle shape is retained. Figure 8(b) illustrates this idea.

(a) BFS   (b) TBFS

Fig. 8. BFS and TBFS processes. (Color figure online)

Basic functions:

-   function leftchild(*parent*): returns the left child of *parent*;
-   function rightchild(*parent*): returns the right child of *parent*;
-   function getFriend(*parent*, *p*): returns the friend *p* of *parent* by swapping first and second symbols, as well as the third and the *p*th ($p \neq 1, 2, 3$) symbols of *parent*.

In Fig. 9, the trunk nodes of T_1^5 are indicated by ellipses with blue borders.

3.3   createBranch Function

The createBranch function is used to traverse all unvisited nodes in one step each time from a tree after the createTrunk function. For instance, the branch nodes of T_1^5 in the first, second, and third executions of createBranch functions are indicated by ellipses with brown, gold, and gray borders in Fig. 9.

Function createTrunk($tary$, tid, $edge$, $origin$)

    Input   : $tary$, tid, $seed$, $origin$
    Output: the trunk of $tary[tid]$

1 $tkQue = \text{array}(origin)$;   ▷ Put $origin$ into $tkQue$.

2 **for** $j = 0;\ j < |tkQue|;\ j = j + 1$ **do**

3       $v = tkQue[j]$;   ▷ $tkQue$'s $(j+1)$th element

4       $lch = \text{leftchild}(v)$; $rch = \text{rightchild}(v)$;

5   // **left or right children unvisited**

6   **if** *($tary[tid][lch] == 0$ and $edge[v][lch] == 1$) or ($tary[tid][rch] == 0$ and $edge[v][rch] == 1$)* **then**

7   **if** *lch has been visited* **then**

8   remove *lch* from $tkQue$; $edge[tree[tid][lch]][lch] = 1$;   ▷ (4)

9   **if** *rch has been visited* **then**

10   remove *rch* from $tkQue$; $edge[tree[tid][rch]][rch] = 1$;   ▷ (4)

11   // visit left child

12           $tary[tid][lch] = v$; $tkQue[] = lch$; $edge[v][lch] = 0$;   ▷ (1)(2)(3)

13   // visit right child

14           $tary[tid][rch] = v$; $tkQue[] = rch$; $edge[v][rch] = 0$;   ▷ (1)(2)(3)

15   // **traverse friend 4 to** $|origin| - 1$

16   **for** $i = 4;\ i \le |origin| - 1;\ i = i + 1$ **do**

17           $fd = \text{getFriend}(v, i)$;

18   **if** $tary[tid][fd] == 0$ and $edge[v][fd] == 1$ **then**

19               $tary[tid][fd] = v$;   ▷ (1)

20               $edge[v][fd] = 0$;   ▷ (2)

21               $tkQue[] = fd$;   ▷ (3)

22 // (1) Set its the parent.

23 // (2) Set the edge used (from 1 to 0).

24 // (3) Put it into $tkQue$.

25 // (4) Set the edge from its parent to itself unused (from 0 to 1).

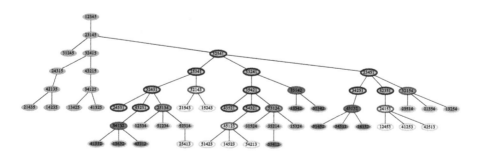

Fig. 9. Trunk nodes (blue border) of T_1^5 after createTrunk function. Branch nodes (brown, gold, and gray border) of T_1^5 after createBranch function. (Color figure online)

Function createBranch($tary$, tid, $edge$, $first$, n)

Input : $tary$, tid, $edge$, $first$, n

Output: nodes can be visited by $tary[tid]$ in a step

1 // global represents global variable

2 global bQ;   ▷ a two-dimensional array storing nodes traversed by T_{tid} not to

3   ▷ traverse all nodes in it next time

4 global $bQIx$;   ▷ the starting position in $bQ[tid]$ each time

5 **if** $first == true$ **then**

6   // first execution

7   **for** each node v in $tary[tid]$ **do**

8   // Only T_4^n is permitted to traverse from the root cluster.

9   **if** v has parent and (($tid \neq 4$ and v's last symbol $\neq n$) or $tid == 4$) **then**

10   // visit the left child

11   **if** $tary[tid][lch] == 0$ and $edge[v][lch] == 1$ **then**

12                $tary[tid][lch] = v$; $bQ[tid][] = lch$; $edge[v][lch] = 0$;   ▷ (1)(2)(3)

13   // visit the right child

14   **if** $tary[tid][rch] == 0$ and $edge[v][rch] == 1$ **then**

15                $tary[tid][rch] = v$; $bQ[tid][] = rch$; $edge[v][rch] = 0$;   ▷ (1)(2)(3)

16   // traverse friend 4 to n

17   **for** $i = 4$; $i \leq n$; $i = i + 1$ **do**

18                $fd = \text{getFriend}(v, i)$;

19   **if** $tary[tid][fd] == 0$ and $edge[v][fd] == 1$ **then**

20                    $tary[tid][fd]=v$; $edge[v][fd]=0$; $bQ[tid][] = fd$;   ▷ (1)(2)(3)

21 **else**

22      $qsize = \text{count}(bQ[tid])$;   ▷ current size of $bQ[tid]$

23   // New element will be put into $bQ[tid]$, but will be utilized in next execution.

24   **for** $y = bQIx[tid]$; $y < qsize$; $y = y + 1$ **do**

25          $v = bQ[tid][y]$;

26   // visit the left child

27   **if** $tary[tid][lch] == 0$ and $edge[v][lch] == 1$ **then**

28             $tary[tid][lch] = v$; $bQ[tid][] = lch$; $edge[v][lch] = 0$;   ▷ (1)(2)(3)

29   // visit the right child

30   **if** $tary[tid][rch] == 0$ and $edge[v][rch] == 1$ **then**

31             $tary[tid][rch] = v$; $bQ[tid][] = rch$; $edge[v][rch] = 0$;   ▷ (1)(2)(3)

32   **for** $i = 4$; $i \leq n$; $i = i + 1$ **do**

33             $fd = \text{getFriend}(v, i)$;

34   **if** $tary[tid][fd] == 0$ and $edge[v][fd] == 1$ **then**

35                $tary[tid][fd] = v$; $edge[v][fd] = 0$; $bQ[tid][] = fd$;   ▷ (1)(2)(3)

36      $bQIx[tid] = y$;   ▷ the position for next execution

37 // (1) Set its parent.

38 // (2) Set the edge used (from 1 to 0).

39 // (3) Put it into $bQ[tid]$.

3.4 Path Composition

Finally, the outcome paths from the root to other nodes produced by the algorithm contain the trunk part and the branch part, as illustrated in Fig. 10. There are origins in trunks of trees except for T_4. Because T_4 done not execute any createTrunk function, it appends the last symbol of the root to its previous tree as its trunk.

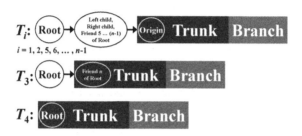

Fig. 10. Path composition.

4   Testing and Analysis

We use PHP to implement the algorithm and draw ISTs in Graphviz. The cases tested are AN_3 to AN_{10}. We test whether all paths in all trees are inner vertex-disjoint. The results prove that all paths in all trees are internally vertex-disjoint in all cases. The algorithm is correct. Since the algorithm traverse every node and every directed edge once, we summarize the numbers of nodes and directed edges from AN_3 to AN_n to get the time complexity of AN_n. The number of nodes in AN_n is $\frac{n!}{2}$ and the number of directed edges in AN_n is $\frac{n!}{2} \times (n-1)$. The time complexity is $O(n \times (\frac{n!}{2} + \frac{n!}{2} \times (n-1))) = O(n^2 \times n!)$.

5   Conclusion

In this paper, we propose a recursive algorithm for constructing ISTs in alternating group networks. The algorithm is a top-down approach, and the parent of one node in an IST is not determined by any rule. The correctness of the algorithm is verified, and the time complexity is analyzed. We use PHP to implement the algorithm and test different cases from AN_3 to $AN_{1}0$. The results prove that all trees of all cases are ISTs. We conclude that our algorithm is not only correct but also efficient. We hope the algorithm can bring some new ideas to the IST problem domain.

References

1. Akers, S.B., Krishnamurthy, B.: A group-theoretic model for symmetric interconnection networks. IEEE Trans. Comput. **38**, 555–566 (1989)
2. Bao, F., Funyu, Y., Hamada, Y., Igarashi, Y.: Reliable broadcasting and secure distributing in channel networks. IEICE Trans. Fundam. Electron. Commun. Comput. Sci. **81**(5), 796–806 (1998)
3. Chang, Y.-H., Yang, J.-S., Hsieh, S.-Y., Chang, J.-M., Wang, Y.-L.: Construction independent spanning trees on locally twisted cubes in parallel. J. Comb. Optim. **33**(3), 956–967 (2016). https://doi.org/10.1007/s10878-016-0018-8
4. Chen, B., Xiao, W., Parhami, B.: Internode distance and optimal routing in a class of alternating group networks. IEEE Trans. Comput. **55**(12), 1645–1648 (2006)
5. Cheriyan, J., Maheshwari, S.N.: Finding nonseparating induced cycles and independent spanning trees in 3-connected graphs. J. Algorithms **9**(4), 507–537 (1988)
6. Curran, S., Lee, O., Yu, X.X.: Finding four independent trees. SIAM J. Comput. **35**(5), 1023–1058 (2006)
7. Hamidoune, Y.O., Llado, A.S., Serra, O.: The connectivity of hierarchical Cayley digraphs. Discrete Appl. Math. **37–38**, 275–280 (1992)
8. Hsieh, S.Y., Tu, C.J.: Constructing edge-disjoint spanning trees in locally twisted cubes. Theor. Comput. Sci. **410**, 926–932 (2009)
9. Itai, A., Rodeh, M.: The multi-tree approach to reliability in distributed networks. Inf. Comput. **79**(1), 43–59 (1988)
10. Kao, S.-S., Chang, J.-M., Pai, K.-J., Wu, R.-Y.: Constructing independent spanning trees on bubble-sort networks. In: Wang, L., Zhu, D. (eds.) COCOON 2018. LNCS, vol. 10976, pp. 1–13. Springer, Cham (2018). https://doi.org/10.1007/978-3-319-94776-1_1
11. Kao, S.-S., Pai, K.-J., Hsieh, S.-Y., Wu, R.-Y., Chang, J.-M.: Amortized efficiency of constructing multiple independent spanning trees on bubble-sort networks. J. Comb. Optim. **38**(3), 972–986 (2019). https://doi.org/10.1007/s10878-019-00430-0
12. Lakshmivarahan, S., Jwo, J.S., Dhall, S.K.: Symmetry in interconnection networks based on Cayley graphs of permutations: a survey. Parallel Comput. **19**, 361–407 (1993)
13. Liu, Y.J., Lan, J.K., Chou, W.Y., Chen, C.: Constructing independent spanning trees for locally twisted cubes. Theor. Comput. Sci. **412**, 2237–2252 (2011)
14. Silva, E., Pedrini, H.: Inferring patterns in mitochondrial DNA sequences through hypercube independent spanning trees. Comput. Biol. Med. **70**, 51–57 (2016)
15. Rescigno, A.A.: Vertex-disjoint spanning trees of the star network with applications to fault-tolerance and security. Inf. Sci. **137**, 259–276 (2001)
16. Werapun, J., Intakosum, S., Boonjing, V.: An efficient parallel construction of optimal independent spanning trees on hypercubes. J. Parallel Distrib. Comput. **72**(12), 1713–1724 (2012)
17. Yang, J.S., Chang, J.M., Tang, S.M., Wang, Y.L.: Parallel construction of optimal independent spanning trees on hypercubes. Parallel Comput. **33**, 73–79 (2007)
18. Yang, J.S., Chan, H.C., Chang, J.M.: Broadcasting secure messages via optimal independent spanning trees in folded hypercubes. Discrete Appl. Math. **159**(12), 1254–1263 (2011)

19. Youhu, J.: A new class of Cayley networks based on the alternating groups. Appl. Math.-JCU **14A**(2), 235–239 (1998). in Chinese
20. Zehavi, A., Itai, A.: Three tree-paths. J. Graph Theory **13**(2), 175–188 (1989)
21. Zhou, S., Xiao, W., Parhami, B.: Construction of vertex-disjoint paths in alternating group networks. Supercomputing **54**(2), 206–228 (2010)

W[1]-Hardness of the k-Center Problem Parameterized by the Skeleton Dimension

Johannes Blum$^{(\boxtimes)}$ (iD)

University of Konstanz, Konstanz, Germany
johannes.blum@uni-konstanz.de

Abstract. In the k-CENTER problem, we are given a graph $G = (V, E)$ with positive edge weights and an integer k and the goal is to select k center vertices $C \subseteq V$ such that the maximum distance from any vertex to the closest center vertex is minimized. On general graphs, the problem is NP-hard and cannot be approximated within a factor less than 2.

Typical applications of the k-CENTER problem can be found in logistics or urban planning and hence, it is natural to study the problem on transportation networks. Such networks are often characterized as graphs that are (almost) planar or have low doubling dimension, highway dimension or skeleton dimension. It was shown by Feldmann and Marx that k-CENTER is W[1]-hard on planar graphs of constant doubling dimension when parameterized by the number of centers k, the highway dimension hd and the pathwidth pw [11]. We extend their result and show that even if we additionally parameterize by the skeleton dimension κ, the k-CENTER problem remains W[1]-hard. Moreover, we prove that under the Exponential Time Hypothesis there is no exact algorithm for k-CENTER that has runtime $f(k, hd, pw, \kappa) \cdot |V|^{o(pw+\kappa+\sqrt{k+hd})}$ for any computable function f.

Keywords: k-Center · Skeleton dimension · Parameterized complexity

1 Introduction

The k-CENTER problem consists of the following task: Given a graph $G = (V, E)$ with positive edge weights $\ell : E \to \mathbb{Q}^+$ and some $k \in \mathbb{N}$, choose k center vertices $C \subseteq V$ that minimize the maximum distance from any vertex of the graph to the closest center. Formally, if the shortest path distances in G are given by $\text{dist} : V^2 \to \mathbb{Q}^+$ and $B_r(v) = \{w \in V \mid \text{dist}(v, w) \leq r\}$ denotes the ball of radius r around v, we aim for a solution $C \subseteq V$ of size $|C| \leq k$ that has minimum cost, which is the smallest radius $r \geq 0$ such that $V = \bigcup_{v \in C} B_r(v)$.

On general graphs, the k-CENTER problem is NP-complete [15], as well as on planar graphs [14] and geometric graphs using L_1-, L_2- or L_∞-distances [9]. On the positive side there is a general 2-approximation algorithm by Hochbaum and Shmoys [12], i.e. an efficient algorithm that computes a solution which deviates from the optimum at most by a factor of 2. This factor is tight, as for any $\epsilon > 0$,

© Springer Nature Switzerland AG 2020
D. Kim et al. (Eds.): COCOON 2020, LNCS 12273, pp. 210–221, 2020.
https://doi.org/10.1007/978-3-030-58150-3_17

it is NP-hard to compute a $(2 - \epsilon)$-approximation, even when considering planar graphs [14] or graphs with L_1- or L_∞-distances [9].

However, common applications of the k-CENTER problem arise in domains like logistics or urban planning. For instance, one might want to place a limited number of warehouses, hospitals or police stations on a map such that the distance from any point to the closest facility is minimized. Hence, it is natural to study the problem on transportation networks. Common characterizations of such networks are graphs that are planar or have low doubling dimension, highway dimension or skeleton dimension. For formal definitions of these parameters, see Sect. 2. Usually, it is assumed that in transportation networks the mentioned parameters are bounded by $\mathcal{O}(\mathrm{polylog}|V|)$ or $\mathcal{O}(\sqrt{|V|})$. It was shown that on graphs of maximum degree Δ and highway dimension hd, the skeleton dimension is at most $(\Delta + 1) \cdot hd$ [13]. The relationship between highway dimension hd and skeleton dimension κ was also evaluated experimentally on several real-world road networks and it turned out that $\kappa \ll hd$ [5]. Moreover, it was conjectured that on road networks the skeleton dimension is a constant whereas the highway dimension grows faster than $\mathcal{O}(\mathrm{polylog}|V|)$.

Still, a low highway dimension or skeleton dimension does not suffice to overcome the general inapproximability bound of k-CENTER. In particular, it was shown that for any $\epsilon > 0$, there is no $(2 - \epsilon)$-approximation algorithm for graphs of highway dimension $hd \in \mathcal{O}(\log^2 |V|)$ [10] or skeleton dimension $\kappa \in \mathcal{O}(\log^2 |V|)$ [4], unless $P = NP$.

Apart from approximation, a common way of dealing with NP-hard problems is the use of fixed-parameter algorithms. Such an algorithm computes an exact solution in time $f(p) \cdot n^{\mathcal{O}(1)}$, where f is a computable function and p a parameter of the problem instance which is independent of the problem size n. In other words, if a problem admits a fixed-parameter algorithm, the complexity of the problem can be captured through some parameter p. If this is the case, we call the problem fixed-parameter tractable (FPT). A natural parameter for k-CENTER is the number of center vertices k. However, it was shown that in general, k-CENTER is W[2]-hard for parameter k, and hence it is not fixed-parameter tractable unless W[2] = FPT [8]. Feldmann and Marx studied the fixed-parameter tractability of k-CENTER on transportation networks [11]. They showed that k-CENTER is W[1]-hard even if the input is restricted to planar graphs of constant doubling dimension and the parameter is a combination of k, the highway dimension hd and the pathwidth pw. Moreover, they proved that under the Exponential Time Hypothesis (ETH) there is no exact algorithm with runtime $f(k, pw, hd) \cdot |V|^{o(pw + \sqrt{k + hd})}$. In the present paper we extend their result and show that one can additionally parameterize by the skeleton dimension κ without affecting W[1]-hardness. Formally, we show the following theorem.

Theorem 1. *On planar graphs of constant doubling dimension, the k-CENTER problem is W[1]-hard for the combined parameter (k, pw, hd, κ) where pw is the pathwidth, hd the highway dimension and κ the skeleton dimension of the input* *graph. Assuming ETH there is no $f(k, pw, hd, \kappa) \cdot |V|^{o(pw+\kappa+\sqrt{k+hd})}$ time algorithm[1] for any computable function f.*

The reduction of Feldmann and Marx produces a graph where the maximum degree Δ can be quadratic in the input size. As we have $\Delta \leq \kappa$, it does not imply any hardness for the skeleton dimension. Our new construction yields a graph of constant maximum degree, which enables us to bound the skeleton dimension as well as the highway dimension and the pathwidth.

The results reported by Blum and Storandt [5] indicate that in real-world road networks, the skeleton dimension κ is significantly smaller than the highway dimension, which motivates the use of κ as a parameter. Note that in general, the parameters pw, hd and κ are incomparable [4]. Still, our main result shows that combining all these parameters and the number of centers k does not allow a fixed-parameter algorithm unless $\mathrm{FPT} = \mathrm{W}[1]$. However, for the combined parameters (k, hd) [10] and (k, κ) [11], the existence of a fixed-parameter approximation algorithm was shown, i.e. an approximation algorithm with runtime $f(p) \cdot n^{\mathcal{O}(1)}$ for parameter p. Theorem 1 indicates that apart from approximation there is not much hope for efficient algorithms.

2   Preliminaries

For $n \in \mathbb{N}$, let $[n] = \{1, \ldots, n\}$. Addition modulo 4 is denoted by $\boxplus$. For $(a, b), (a', b') \in \mathbb{N}$ let $(a, b) \leq (a', b')$ iff $a < a'$ or $a = a'$ and $b \leq b'$.

In a graph $G = (V, E)$ we denote the shortest s-t path by $\pi(s, t)$ and the length of a path P by $|P|$. The concatenation of two paths P and P' is denoted by $P \circ P'$.

A graph G is planar if it can be embedded into the plane without crossing edges, and d-doubling if for any $r > 0$, any ball $B_{2r}(v)$ of radius $2r$ in G is contained in the union of d balls of radius r. If d is the smallest integer such that G is d-doubling, the graph G has doubling dimension $\log_2 d$.

For the highway dimension several slightly different definitions can be found in the literature [1–3]. Here we use the one given in [3].

Definition 1. *The highway dimension of a graph G is the smallest integer hd such that for any radius r and any vertex v there is a hitting set $S \subseteq B_{4r}(v)$ of size hd for the set of all shortest paths π satisfying $|\pi| > r$ and $\pi \subseteq B_{4r}(v)$.*

To define the skeleton dimension, which was introduced in [13], we need to consider the geometric realization $\tilde{G}$ of a graph G. Intuitively, $\tilde{G}$ is a continuous version of G where every edge is subdivided into infinitely many infinitely short edges. For a vertex $s \in V$, let T_s be the shortest path tree of s. We assume that in G every shortest path is unique, which can be achieved e.g. by slightly perturbing the edge weights, and it follows that T_s is also unique. The skeleton T_s^* is defined as the subtree of $\tilde{T}_s$ induced by all $v \in \tilde{V}$, for which there is some vertex w such that v is contained in $\pi(s, w)$ and moreover, we have $\mathrm{dist}(s, v) \leq 2 \cdot \mathrm{dist}(v, w)$.

---

[1] Here $o(pw + \kappa + \sqrt{k + hd})$ stands for $g(pw + \kappa + \sqrt{k + hd})$ where g is a function with $g(x) \in o(x)$.

Definition 2. *For a skeleton* $T_s^* = (V^*, E^*)$ *and a radius* $r > 0$, *let* $\text{Cut}_s^r = \{v \in V^* \mid \text{dist}(s, v) = r\}$. *The skeleton dimension of a graph* G *is* $\kappa = \max_{s,r} |\text{Cut}_s^r|$.

We assume that the reader is familiar with the notion of pathwidth. A formal definition can be found, e.g. in [6].

3 The Reduction

Following the idea of Feldmann and Marx [11], who showed that on planar graphs of constant doubling dimension, k-CENTER is $W[1]$-hard for parameter (k, pw, hd), we present a reduction from the GRID TILING WITH INEQUALITY (GT$_\leq$) problem. This problem asks the following question: Given χ^2 sets $S_{i,j} \subseteq [n]^2$ of pairs of integers, where $(i, j) \in [\chi]^2$, is it possible to choose one pair $s_{i,j} \in S_{i,j}$ from every set, such that

- if $s_{i,j} = (a, b)$ and $s_{i+1,j} = (a', b')$ we have $a \leq a'$, and
- if $s_{i,j} = (a, b)$ and $s_{i,j+1} = (a', b')$ we have $b \leq b'$.

It is known that the GT$_\leq$ problem is $W[1]$-hard for parameter χ and, unless the Exponential Time Hypothesis (ETH) fails, it has no $f(\chi) \cdot n^{o(\chi)}$ time algorithm for any computable f [7].

3.1 The Reduction of Feldmann and Marx

In [11] the following graph $H_{\mathcal{I}}$ is constructed from an instance $\mathcal{I}$ of GT$_\leq$. For any of the χ^2 sets $S_{i,j}$, the graph $H_{\mathcal{I}}$ contains a gadget $H_{i,j}$ that consists of a cycle $O_{i,j} = v_1 v_2 \ldots v_{16n^2+4} v_1$ and five additional vertices $x_{i,j}^1, x_{i,j}^2, x_{i,j}^3, x_{i,j}^4$ and $y_{i,j}$. Every edge contained in some cycle $O_{i,j}$ has unit length and every vertex $y_{i,j}$ is connected to $O_{i,j}$ via edges to $v_1, v_{4n^2+2}, v_{8n^2+3}$ and v_{12n^2+4}, which all have length $2n^2 + 1$. Moreover, for every pair $(a, b) \in S_{i,j}$ and $\tau = (a - 1) \cdot n + b$, the gadget $H_{i,j}$ contains the four edges

- $\{x_{i,j}^1, v_\tau\}$ of length $2n^2 - \frac{a}{n+1}$,
- $\{x_{i,j}^2, v_{\tau+4n^2+1}\}$ of length $2n^2 + \frac{b}{n+1} - 1$,
- $\{x_{i,j}^3, v_{\tau+8n^2+2}\}$ of length $2n^2 + \frac{a}{n+1} - 1$, and
- $\{x_{i,j}^4, v_{\tau+12n^2+3}\}$ of length $2n^2 - \frac{b}{n+1}$.

Finally, the individual gadgets are connected in a grid-like fashion, which means that there is a path from $x_{i,j}^2$ to $x_{i,j+1}^4$ and from $x_{i,j}^3$ to $x_{i+1,j}^1$. Each of these paths has length 1 and consists of $n + 2$ edges of length $\frac{1}{n+2}$.

Feldmann and Marx showed that the given GT$_\leq$ instance $\mathcal{I}$ has a solution if and only if the k-CENTER problem in the graph $H_{\mathcal{I}}$ has a solution of cost $2n^2$ using $k = 5\chi^2$ centers. Moreover, the graph $H_{\mathcal{I}}$ is planar and has doubling dimension $\mathcal{O}(1)$, highway dimension $\mathcal{O}(\chi^2)$ and pathwidth $\mathcal{O}(\chi)$. Observe that the degree of any vertex $x_{i,j}^h$ is $|S_{i,j}|$. This means that the skeleton dimension of $H_{\mathcal{I}}$ might be as large as $\Omega(n^2)$, as the maximum degree of $H_{\mathcal{I}}$ is a lower bound on its skeleton dimension. We show now how to construct a graph $G_{\mathcal{I}}$ that resembles $H_{\mathcal{I}}$, but has skeleton dimension $\mathcal{O}(\chi)$ and fulfills the other mentioned properties.

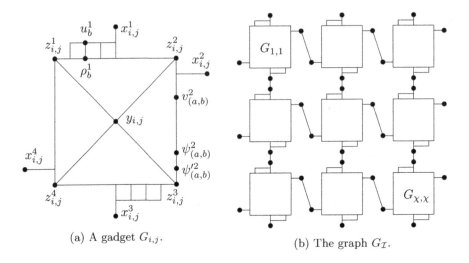

(a) A gadget $G_{i,j}$.

(b) The graph $G_{\mathcal{I}}$.

Fig. 1. A single gadget $G_{i,j}$ and the whole graph $G_{\mathcal{I}}$.

3.2   Our Construction

We assume that in the given $\mathrm{GT}_{\leq}$-instance, for all $(i,j) \in [\chi]^2$ and every $b \in [n]$, there is some $a \in [n]$ such that $(a,b) \in S_{i,j}$. This is a valid assumption, as from an instance $\mathcal{I}$ of ordinary $\mathrm{GT}_{\leq}$, we can construct the following instance $\mathcal{I}'$. For $i \in [\chi-1]$ and $j \in [\chi]$ we add the pairs $\{(n + \chi - i, b) \mid b \in [n]\}$ to $S_{i,j}$. Moreover, we add the pairs $\{(0, b) \mid b \in [n]\}$ to every $S_{\chi,j}$. It can be easily verified that $\mathcal{I}$ has a solution if and only if $\mathcal{I}'$ has a solution.

Given a $\mathrm{GT}_{\leq}$-instance $\mathcal{I}$ we construct the following graph $G_{\mathcal{I}}$ (cf. Fig. 1). Like in [11], we create a gadget $G_{i,j}$ for every set $S_{i,j}$. Any $G_{i,j}$ contains a cycle $O_{i,j}$, which initially consists of four edges that have length $2^{n+2} + 1/n$. Denote the four vertices of the cycle $O_{i,j}$ by $z_{i,j}^1, \ldots, z_{i,j}^4$ and for $h \in [4]$ let $O_{i,j}^h = \pi\left(z_{i,j}^h, z_{i,j}^{h \boxplus 1}\right)$. Now, for any pair $(a,b) \in S_{i,j}$ and any $h \in [4]$ we insert a vertex $v_{(a,b)}^h$ into the path $O_{i,j}^h$ and place it such that its distance to $z_{i,j}^h$ is $d_{(a,b)} = 2^b - 1 + \frac{a}{n}$.

It follows that the distance between $v_{(a,b)}^h$ and $v_{(a,b)}^{h \boxplus 1}$ is $2^{n+2} + 1/n$. Moreover, for $(a',b') \leq (a,b)$, the distance from $v_{(a',b')}^h$ to $v_{(a,b)}^h$ is $2^b - 2^{b'} + (a-a')/n$.

Additionally, for any pair $(a,b) \in S_{i,j}$ and any $h \in [4]$,, we insert two vertices $\psi_{(a,b)}^h$ and $\psi_{(a,b)}'^h$ into the path $O_{i,j}^h$ such that their distance from $v_{(a,b)}^h$ is 2^{n+1} and $2^{n+1} + 1/n$, respectively. This implies that $\mathrm{dist}\left(\psi_{(a,b)}'^h, v_{(a,b)}^{h \boxplus 1}\right) = 2^{n+1}$ and $\mathrm{dist}\left(\psi_{(a,b)}^h, v_{(a,b)}^{h \boxplus 1}\right) = 2^{n+1} + 1/n$.

Any gadget $G_{i,j}$ also contains a central vertex $y_{i,j}$ that is connected to each $z_{i,j}^h$ through an edge of length $2^{n+1}+1$. Finally, we add four vertices $x_{i,j}^1, \ldots, x_{i,j}^4$ to every gadget $G_{i,j}$, through which we will connect the individual gadgets. For $(a,b) \in S_{i,j}$ and $h \in [4]$ denote the distance between $v_{(a,b)}^h$ and $x_{i,j}^h$ by $d_{(a,b)}^h$. The idea of our reduction is that we attach every $x_{i,j}^h$ to the cycle $O_{i,j}$ such that for every pair $(a,b) \in S_{i,j}$ and $h \in \{1,3\}$, the distance $d_{(a,b)}^h$ reflects the value of b, whereas for $h \in \{2,4\}$, the distance $d_{(a,b)}^h$ reflects the value of a.

For the latter, we simply add an edge between $x_{i,j}^2$ and the vertex $v_{(a^*,b^*)}^2$ where $(a^*,b^*) = \min S_{i,j}$.[2] The length of this edge is chosen as

$$d_{(a^*,b^*)}^2 = 2^n + 1 + d_{(a^*,b^*)} = 2^n + 2^{b^*} + \frac{a^*}{n}.$$

Similarly we add an edge between $x_{i,j}^4$ and $v_{(a^*,b^*)}^4$ and set its length to

$$d_{(a^*,b^*)}^4 = 2^{n+1} - d_{(a^*,b^*)} = 2^{n+1} + 1 - 2^{b^*} - \frac{a^*}{n}.$$

It follows that for all $(a,b) \in S_{i,j}$ we have

$$d_{(a,b)}^2 = d_{(a^*,b^*)}^2 + d_{(a,b)} - d_{(a^*,b^*)} = 2^n + 2^b + \frac{a}{n} \quad \text{and}$$

$$d_{(a,b)}^4 = d_{(a^*,b^*)}^4 + d_{(a^*,b^*)} - d_{(a,b)} = 2^{n+1} + 1 - 2^b - \frac{a}{n}.$$

Attaching $x_{i,j}^1$ and $x_{i,j}^3$ to $G_{i,j}$ is slightly more elaborate. We want to ensure that for any two pairs $(a,b), (a,b') \in S_{i,j}$ that agree on the first component, we have $d_{(a,b)}^1 = d_{(a,b')}^1$. For that purpose, we add a path $U_{i,j}^1 = u_1^1 \ldots u_n^1$ and set the length of every edge $\{u_\lambda^1, u_{\lambda+1}^1\}$ to 2^λ. Moreover, we add the edge $\{u_n^1, x_{i,j}^1\}$ of length 2^n. For every $b \in [n]$, consider the vertex $v_{(a^*,b)}^1$ that is furthest from $z_{i,j}^1$. We call it also the b-portal ρ_b^1. We attach it to u_b^1 through an edge of length $2^b - a^*/n$, the so called b-portal edge. It follows that for $(a,b) \in S_{i,j}$ we have $\mathrm{dist}(v_{(a,b)}^1, u_b^1) = 2^b - a^*/n + d_{(a^*,b)} - d_{(a,b)} = 2^b - a/n$ and $\mathrm{dist}(u_b^1, x_{i,j}^1) = \sum_{\lambda=b}^{n} 2^\lambda = 2^{n+1} - 2^b$, and hence we have

$$d_{(a,b)}^1 = 2^{n+1} - \frac{a}{n}.$$

Similarly we proceed with the vertices contained in $O_{i,j}^3$. We add a path $U_{i,j}^3 = u_1^3 \ldots u_n^3$, set the length of every edge $\{u_\lambda^3, u_{\lambda+1}^3\}$ to 2^λ and add the edge $\{u_n^3, x_{i,j}^3\}$ of length 2^n. For $b \in [n]$ we use the vertex $v_{(a^*,b)}^3$ that is closest to $z_{i,j}^3$ as the b-portal ρ_b^3 and attach it to u_b^3 trough a portal edge of length $2^b - 1 + a^*/n$. It follows that

$$d_{(a,b)}^3 = 2^{n+1} - 1 + \frac{a}{n}.$$

To complete the construction, we connect the individual gadgets in a grid-like fashion. For $i \in [n-1]$ we connect $x_{i,j}^3$ and $x_{i+1,j}^1$ through a path $P_{i,j}$ of length 1 that consists of $(n+1)$ edges of length $1/(n+1)$ each. Moreover, for $j \in [n-1]$ we connect $x_{i,j}^2$ and $x_{i,j+1}^4$ through a path $P_{i,j}' = w_1 \ldots w_n$ where $w_1 = x_{i,j+1}^4$ and $w_n = x_{i,j}^4$. We set the length of every edge $\{w_{\lambda+1}, w_\lambda\}$ to 2^λ which implies that $|P_{i,j}'| = 2^n - 2$. The resulting graph $G_\mathcal{I}$ can be constructed in polynomial time from the given $\mathrm{GT}_\leq$-instance $\mathcal{I}$.

---

[2] here the minimum is taken w.r.t the lexical order as defined in the preliminaries.

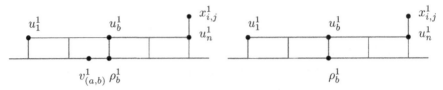

(a) The shortest path tree of a vertex $v^1_{(a,b)}$. (b) The shortest path tree of a vertex u^1_b.

Fig. 2. Illustration of the shortest path structure as shown in Lemma 1.

3.3 Graph Properties

We now formulate some basic properties of $G_{\mathcal{I}}$ that will be useful to prove the correctness of our reduction and to obtain bounds on several graph parameters. We first observe that all shortest paths between the cycle $O_{i,j}$ and a path $U^h_{i,j}$ have a certain structure (cf. Fig. 2).

Lemma 1. *Let* $a, b, b' \in [n]$ *and* $h \in \{1, 3\}$. *For* $\beta \in [n]$ *denote the path*
$$\pi \left(v^h_{(a,b)}, \rho^h_\beta \right) \circ \left\{ \rho^h_\beta, u^h_\beta \right\} \circ \pi \left(u^h_\beta, u^h_{b'} \right) \text{ by } P_\beta.$$

(a) If $b' \geq b$, *the shortest path from* $v^h_{(a,b)}$ *to* $u^h_{b'}$ *is* P_b.
(b) If $b' < b$, *the shortest path from* $v^h_{(a,b)}$ *to* $u^h_{b'}$ *is* $P_{b'}$.

Moreover, it holds that for any vertex v of the graph $G_{\mathcal{I}}$, there is some central vertex $y_{i,j}$ not too far away.

Lemma 2. *For every vertex* $v \in V$, *we have* $\min_{(i,j)} \mathrm{dist}(v, y_{i,j}) \leq 2^{n+2} + 2^{n+1}$.

3.4 Correctness of the Reduction

We show now that the $\mathrm{GT}_\leq$-instance $\mathcal{I}$ has a solution if and only if the k-CENTER instance $G_{\mathcal{I}}$ has a solution of cost at most 2^{n+1} for $k = 5\chi^2$ centers.

Lemma 3. *A solution for the* $\mathrm{GT}_\leq$-*instance* $\mathcal{I}$ *implies a solution for the* k-CENTER *instance* $G_{\mathcal{I}}$ *of cost at most* 2^{n+1}.

Proof (Proof sketch). For $(i, j) \in [n]^2$ let $s_{i,j}$ be the pair from $S_{i,j}$ that is chosen in a solution of $\mathcal{I}$. For the k-CENTER instance $G_{\mathcal{I}}$, we choose a center set C of size $5\chi^2$ by selecting from every gadget $G_{i,j}$ the central vertex $y_{i,j}$ and the four vertices $v^1_{s_{i,j}}, \ldots, v^4_{s_{i,j}}$. It can be shown that every gadget $G_{i,j}$ is contained in the balls of radius 2^{n+1} around $y_{i,j}$ and $v^1_{s_{i,j}}, \ldots, v^4_{s_{i,j}}$.

Consider now a path $P_{i,j}$, which connects $x^3_{i,j}$ and $x^1_{i+1,j}$, and let $s_{i,j} = (a, b)$ and $s_{i+1,j} = (a', b')$. It holds that $a \leq a'$. From $G_{i,j}$ and $G_{i+1,j}$ we have chosen a center $v^3_{(a,b)}$ and $v^1_{(a',b')}$, respectively, which have distance

$$d^3_{(a,b)} + |P_{i,j}| + d^1_{(a',b')} = 2^{n+1} - 1 + \frac{a}{n} + 1 + 2^{n+1} - \frac{a'}{n} = 2^{n+2} + \frac{a - a'}{n} \leq 2^{n+2}$$

from each other. Hence, $P_{i,j}$ can be covered with two balls of radius 2^{n+1} around $v^3_{(a,b)}$ and $v^1_{(a',b')}$. Similarly one can show that every path $P'_{i,j}$ is also covered through the chosen center set. $\qquad\square$

It can also be shown that every solution for $G_{\mathcal{I}}$ of cost at most 2^{n+1} contains four equidistant vertices $v^1_{(a,b)}, \dots, v^4_{(a,b)}$ from every $G_{i,j}$, which yield a solution for $\mathcal{I}$. We obtain the following lemma, and hence, our reduction is correct.

Lemma 4. *A solution for the k-CENTER instance $G_{\mathcal{I}}$ of cost at most 2^{n+1} implies a solution for the $GT_\le$-instance $\mathcal{I}$.*

4   Bounds on Graph Parameters

In this section we show bounds on the doubling dimension, the highway dimension, the skeleton dimension and the pathwidth of the graph $G_{\mathcal{I}}$, which imply Theorem 1. We first observe that $G_{\mathcal{I}}$ is planar and has constant doubling dimension. We omit a formal proof, but one can proceed similarly to [11].

Lemma 5. *The graph $G_{\mathcal{I}}$ is planar and has constant doubling dimension.*

We next bound the highway dimension of $G_{\mathcal{I}}$.

Lemma 6. *The graph $G_{\mathcal{I}}$ has highway dimension $hd \in \mathcal{O}(\chi^2)$.*

Proof. For any radius $r > 0$ we specify a set H_r such that every shortest path π satisfying $|\pi| > r$ intersects H_r and moreover, for every vertex $v \in V$ we have $|H_r \cap B_{4r}(v)| \in \mathcal{O}(\chi^2)$. Let $X = \{y_{i,j}, x^h_{i,j}, z^h_{i,j} \mid (i,j) \in [\chi]^2, h \in [4]\}$. For $r \ge 2^{n+2}$ we choose $H_r = X$. We have $|H_r| = 9\chi^2$ and hence for every vertex $v \in V$ we have $|H_r \cap B_{4r}(v)| \in \mathcal{O}(\chi^2)$. We show now that any shortest path of length more than r intersects H_r. Clearly, all shortest paths that are not completely contained within one single gadget are hit by H_r as all $x^h_{i,j}$ are contained in H_r and the paths $P_{i,j}$ and $P'_{i,j}$ between the individual gadgets have length at most $2^n - 2$. Consider some gadget $G_{i,j}$. All edges of the cycle $O_{i,j}$ have length at least $1/n$ and for any $h \in [4]$ we have $\text{dist}(z^h_{i,j}, z^{h\boxplus 1}_{i,j}) = 2^{n+2} + 1/n$. Hence, any subpath of $O_{i,j}$ that has length at least 2^{n+2} intersects H_r. Moreover, for $h \in \{1,3\}$, the path $U^h_{i,j}$ has length $2^n - 2$.

It remains to consider some shortest path $\pi(s,t)$ where $s \in O_{i,j}$ and $t \in U^h_{i,j}$. Let $t = u^h_b$. According to Lemma 1, the shortest path $\pi(s,t)$ traverses exactly one portal edge $\{\rho^h_\beta, u^h_\beta\}$ where $\beta \in [b]$. This means that $\text{dist}(s,t) = \text{dist}(s, \rho^h_\beta) + \text{dist}(\rho^h_\beta, u^h_\beta) \le \text{dist}(s, \rho^h_\beta) + 2^b$. The vertex s is contained in the shortest path $\pi(z^h_{i,j}, \rho^h_\beta)$ or in $\pi(\rho^h_\beta, z^{h\boxplus 1}_{i,j})$. In the first case we have $\text{dist}(s, \rho^h_\beta) < \text{dist}(z^h_{i,j}, \rho^h_\beta) \le 2^\beta$. This implies that $\text{dist}(s,t) < 2^\beta + 2^b \le 2^{n+1}$. In the second case we have $\text{dist}(s, \rho^h_\beta) \le 2^{n+2} - 2^\beta$ and moreover Lemma 1 implies that $\beta = b$. Hence we obtain $\text{dist}(s,t) \le 2^{n+2} - 2^\beta + 2^\beta = 2^{n+2}$. This means that every shortest path of length more than $r \ge 2^{n+2}$ is hit by H_r.

Let now $r < 2^{n+2}$. For a shortest path $p = v_1 \ldots v_\nu$ and $q > 0$ let $p^{\langle q \rangle}$ be a q-cover of p, i.e. we have $p^{\langle q \rangle} \subseteq \{v_1, \ldots, v_\nu\}$ such that any subpath of p that has length at least q contains some node from $p^{\langle q \rangle}$. We consider q-covers $p^{\langle q \rangle}$ that are constructed greedily, i.e. we start with $p^{\langle q \rangle} = \{v_1\}$ and iteratively add the closest vertex that has distance at least q. For $(i,j) \in [\chi]^2$ let

$$X_{i,j} = \bigcup_{h \in [4]} O_{i,j}^h \,^{\langle r/4 \rangle} \cup \bigcup_{h \in \{1,3\}} U_{i,j}^h \,^{\langle r/4 \rangle} \cup \{u_n^1, u_n^3\} \cup P_{i,j}^{\langle r/4 \rangle} \cup P_{i,j}' \,^{\langle r/4 \rangle}$$

and choose $H_r = X \cup \bigcup_{(i,j) \in [\chi]^2} X_{i,j}$. Consider some shortest path $\pi(s,t)$ that has length more than r. Clearly, $\pi(s,t)$ is hit by H_r if it contains some node from X or it is a subpath of some cycle $O_{i,j}$, some path $U_{i,j}^h$ or some path $P_{i,j}$ or $P_{i,j}'$. It remains to be shown that $\pi(s,t)$ is also hit by H_r if $s \in O_{i,j}$ and $t \in U_{i,j}^h$. Let $t = u_b^h$. Lemma 1 implies that $\pi(s,t)$ consists of a subpath p of $O_{i,j}$, a portal edge $\{\rho_\beta^h, u_\beta^h\}$ and a subpath p' of $U_{i,j}^h$. Assume that $\pi(s,t)$ is not hit by H_r. By the choice of $X_{i,j}$ we have $|p| < r/4$ and $|p'| < r/4$. This means that $\mathrm{dist}(\rho_\beta^h, u_\beta^h) > r/2$. By construction of the graph $G_\mathcal{I}$ we have $\mathrm{dist}(\rho_\beta^h, u_\beta^h) \leq 2^\beta$ and hence $2^\beta > r/2$. As we have $u_\beta^h \notin X_{i,j}$, it holds that $\beta \notin \{1, n\}$ and moreover it follows from the choice of $U_{i,j}^h \,^{\langle r/4 \rangle}$, that $\mathrm{dist}(u_{\beta-1}^h, u_\beta^h) \leq r/4$. However, by construction of $G_\mathcal{I}$ we have $\mathrm{dist}(u_{\beta-1}^h, u_\beta^h) = 2^{\beta-1}$, which implies $2^\beta \leq r/2$, a contradiction to $2^\beta > r/2$. This means that every shortest path of length more than r is hit by H_r.

Finally we have to show that for every vertex $v \in V$ we have $|H_r \cap B_{4r}(v)| \in \mathcal{O}(\chi^2)$. As for the $r/4$-cover of some shortest path p we have $|B_{4r}(v) \cap p^{\langle r/4 \rangle}| \in \mathcal{O}(1)$, it follows that for every $(i,j) \in [\chi]^2$ we have $|B_{4r}(v) \cap X_{i,j}| \in \mathcal{O}(1)$. Moreover there are χ^2 different sets $X_{i,j}$ and we have $|X| = 9\chi^2$, which implies $|H_r \cap B_{4r}(v)| \in \mathcal{O}(\chi^2)$.   □

Observe, that for any graph G of highway dimension hd and maximum degree Δ, an upper bound of $(\Delta+1)hd$ on the skeleton dimension of G follows [13]. As the graph $G_\mathcal{I}$ has maximum degree $\Delta = 4$, it follows that the skeleton dimension of $G_\mathcal{I}$ is bounded by $\mathcal{O}(\chi^2)$.

However, with some more effort, we can show a stronger bound of $\mathcal{O}(\chi)$. To this end we can bound the size of a skeleton within a single gadget. For simplicity, in the following we confuse a graph G and its geometric realization $\tilde{G}$.

Lemma 7. *For any* $(i,j) \in [\chi]^2$ *and any vertex* s *contained in* $G_{i,j}$, *the subtree of the skeleton* T_s^* *induced by the vertices of* $G_{i,j}$ *is the union of a constant number of paths.*

We will also use the following lemma, which was shown in [5].

Lemma 8. *Consider vertices* $u, v, w \in V$ *such that* v *is contained in* $\pi(u, w)$. *If* w *is contained in the skeleton of* u, *it is also contained in the skeleton of* v.

Moreover we can show that every cut in any skeleton of $G_\mathcal{I}$ intersects at most $\mathcal{O}(\chi)$ different gadgets and connecting paths between two gadgets.

Lemma 9. *For every vertex* $s \in V$ *and every radius* $r > 0$, Cut_s^r *intersects* $\mathcal{O}(\chi)$ *gadgets* $G_{i,j}$ *and* $\mathcal{O}(\chi)$ *paths* $P_{i,j}$ *and* $P'_{i,j}$.

Proof. It can be shown that for any $(i,j) \in [\chi]^2$, we have $\mathrm{dist}(y_{i,j}, y_{i+1,j}) = 2^{n+3} + 4 + 2/n$ and $\mathrm{dist}(y_{i,j}, y_{i,j+1}) = 2^{n+3} + 3 + 2/n$. This means that for any $(i,j),(i',j') \in [\chi]^2$ we have

$$\mathrm{dist}(y_{i,j}, y_{i',j'}) = |i - i'| \cdot (2^{n+3} + 4 + 2/n) + |j - j'| \cdot (2^{n+3} + 3 + 2/n). \quad (1)$$

Let $r > 0, s \in V$ and consider a vertex $v \in \mathrm{Cut}_s^r$. It holds that $\mathrm{dist}(s, v) = r$. According to Lemma 2 there are two central vertices $y_{i,j}$ and $y_{i',j'}$ satisfying $\mathrm{dist}(s, y_{i,j}) \leq 2^{n+2} + 2^{n+1}$ and $\mathrm{dist}(v, y_{i',j'}) \leq 2^{n+2} + 2^{n+1}$. Using the triangle inequality we obtain that $\mathrm{dist}(y_{i,j}, y_{i',j'}) \in [r^-, r^+]$ where $r^- = r - (2^{n+3} + 2^{n+2})$ and $r^+ = r + 2^{n+3} + 2^{n+2}$. Moreover, the ball around $y_{i',j'}$ of radius $2^{n+2} + 2^{n+1}$ intersects $\mathcal{O}(1)$ gadgets $G_{i'',j''}$ and $\mathcal{O}(1)$ paths $P_{i'',j''}$ and $P'_{i'',j''}$. This means that any bound on the size of the set $Y = \{y_{i',j'} \mid \mathrm{dist}(y_{i,j}, y_{i',j'}) \in [r^-, r^+]\}$ yields a bound on the number of gadgets and paths intersecting Cut_s^r.

Consider now a vertex $y_{i',j'} \in Y$. Assume that $i' \geq i$ and consider some $i^* \geq i' + 4$. It follows from Eq. (1) and $\mathrm{dist}(y_{i,j}, y_{i',j'}) \geq r^-$ that

$$\mathrm{dist}(y_{i,j}, y_{i^*,j'}) \geq \mathrm{dist}(y_{i,j}, y_{i',j'}) + 4 \cdot (2^{n+3} + 4 + 2/n) > r^+.$$

This means that $y_{i^*,j'} \notin Y$ and it follows that for any $j' \in [\chi]$ we have $|\{i^* \geq i \mid y_{i^*,j'} \in Y\}| \leq 3$. Similarly we can show that $|\{i^* \leq i \mid y_{i^*,j'} \in Y\}| \leq 3$ for any $j' \in [\chi]$. This implies $|Y| \in \mathcal{O}(\chi)$, which completes the proof. □

Combining Lemmas 7 to 9, we obtain that the skeleton dimension of $G_\mathcal{I}$ is bounded by $\mathcal{O}(\chi)$.

Lemma 10. *The graph* $G_\mathcal{I}$ *has skeleton dimension* $\kappa \in \mathcal{O}(\chi)$.

Proof. Let $s \in V, r > 0$ and consider Cut_s^r. Any vertex $v \in \mathrm{Cut}_s^r$ is either contained in some gadget $G_{i,j}$ or some connecting path $P_{i,j}$ or $P'_{i,j}$.

We start with bounding the number of vertices that are contained in Cut_s^r and some $P_{i,j}$ or $P'_{i,j}$. For any $(i,j) \in [\chi]^2$ we have $|\mathrm{Cut}_s^r \cap P_{i,j}| \leq 2$ as $P_{i,j}$ contains at most two distinct vertices that have the same distance from s. For the same reason we have $|\mathrm{Cut}_s^r \cap P'_{i,j}| \leq 2$. Hence Lemma 9 implies that the size of $\mathrm{Cut}_s^r \cap \{P_{i,j}, P'_{i,j} \mid (i,j) \in [\chi]^2\}$ is bounded by $\mathcal{O}(\chi)$.

Consider now some gadget $G_{i,j}$. We show that $|\mathrm{Cut}_s^r \cap G_{i,j}| \in \mathcal{O}(1)$. If s is contained in $G_{i,j}$ this follows immediately from Lemma 7, as Cut_s^r intersects any path in T_s^* at most twice. If s is not contained in $G_{i,j}$, Lemma 8 implies that $\mathrm{Cut}_s^r \cap G_{i,j}$ is a subset of $\left\{ \mathrm{Cut}_{x_{i,j}^h}^{r(h)} \mid h \in [4] \text{ and } r(h) = r - \mathrm{dist}(s, x_{i,j}^h) \right\} \cap G_{i,j}$. Observe that every $x_{i,j}^h$ is contained in $G_{i,j}$, which means that $|\mathrm{Cut}_{x_{i,j}^h}^{r(h)} \cap G_{i,j}| \in \mathcal{O}(1)$. This means that the size of $\mathrm{Cut}_s^r \cap \{G_{i,j} \mid (i,j) \in [\chi]^2\}$ is bounded by $\mathcal{O}(\chi)$. Hence we have $|\mathrm{Cut}_s^r| \in \mathcal{O}(\chi)$ and it follows that $G_\mathcal{I}$ has skeleton dimension $\kappa \in \mathcal{O}(\chi)$. □

Finally we bound the pathwidth of the graph $G_\mathcal{I}$.

Lemma 11. *The graph $G_\mathcal{I}$ has pathwidth $pw \in \mathcal{O}(\chi)$.*

Proof. Consider the graph $\hat{G}_\mathcal{I}$ that arises when we contract all vertices of degree 2 except the vertices $x_{i,j}^h$. It suffices to show that $\hat{G}_\mathcal{I}$ has pathwidth at most $\mathcal{O}(\chi)$. For $(i,j) \in [\chi]^2$ denote the gadget $G_{i,j}$ and the cycle $O_{i,j}$ after the contraction by $\hat{G}_{i,j}$ and $\hat{O}_{i,j}$, respectively. We first construct a path decomposition of constant width for every $\hat{G}_{i,j}$. To this end, consider the cycle $\hat{O}_{i,j}$, which (as every cycle) has a path decomposition where every bag has size at most 3. For $h \in \{1,3\}$ and $b \in [n]$, add u_b^h to every bag containing the portal ρ_b^h. Finally, add $y_{i,j}$ and $x_{i,j}^1, \ldots, x_{i,j}^4$ to every bag. This yields a tree decomposition of $\hat{G}_{i,j}$ which has constant width.

We now combine the path decompositions of the gadgets $\hat{G}_{i,j}$ to a path decomposition of $\hat{G}_\mathcal{I}$. For $(i,j) \in [\chi]^2$, consider the path decomposition of $\hat{G}_{i,j}$ and add the vertices $\{x_{i',j'}^1, \ldots x_{i',j'}^4 \mid 1 \le (i'-i) \cdot \chi + (j'-j) \le \chi\}$ to every bag. According to Fig. 1, these are the vertices $x_{i',j'}^h$ of the χ gadgets after $\hat{G}_{i,j}$ when considering the gadgets row-wise from left to right. Denote the resulting path decomposition by $\mathcal{P}_{(i-1)\cdot\chi+j}$. We can observe, that its width is bounded $\mathcal{O}(1) + 4\chi$. Concatenating all these path decompositions as $\mathcal{P}_1 \mathcal{P}_2 \ldots \mathcal{P}_{\chi^2}$ then yields a path decomposition of $\hat{G}_\mathcal{I}$ of width $\mathcal{O}(1) + 4\chi$, which concludes the proof. $\square$

5   Conclusion

The properties shown in the previous section now imply Theorem 1. As the GT$_\le$ problem is $W[1]$-hard for parameter χ and we have $k = 5\chi^2, hd \in \mathcal{O}(\chi^2), \kappa \in \mathcal{O}(\chi)$ and $pw \in \mathcal{O}(\chi)$, it follows that on planar graphs of constant doubling dimension, k-CENTER is $W[1]$-hard for parameter (k, pw, hd, κ). Assuming ETH there is no $f(\chi) \cdot n^{o(\chi)}$ time algorithm for GT$_\le$ and hence, k-CENTER has no $f(k, hd, pw, \kappa) \cdot |V|^{o(pw+\kappa+\sqrt{k+h})}$ time algorithm unless ETH fails.

It follows that on planar graphs of constant doubling dimension, k-CENTER has no fixed-parameter algorithm for parameter (k, pw, hd, κ) unless FPT = W[1]. Moreover, it was shown that k-CENTER has no efficient $(2 - \epsilon)$-approximation algorithm for graphs of highway dimension $hd \in \mathcal{O}(\log^2 |V|)$ [10] or skeleton dimension $\kappa \in \mathcal{O}(\log^2 |V|)$ [4].

Still, combining the paradigms of approximation and fixed-parameter algorithms allows one to compute a $(2 - \epsilon)$ approximation for k-CENTER on transportation networks. For instance, there is a 3/2-approximation algorithm that has runtime $2^{\mathcal{O}(k \cdot hd \log hd)} \cdot n^{\mathcal{O}(1)}$ for highway dimension hd [10] and a $(1 + \epsilon)$-approximation algorithm with runtime $(k^k / \epsilon^{\mathcal{O}(k \cdot d)}) \cdot n^{\mathcal{O}(1)}$ for doubling dimension d [11]. As the doubling dimension is bounded by $\mathcal{O}(\kappa)$, the latter result implies a $(1 + \epsilon)$-approximation algorithm that has runtime $(k^k / \epsilon^{\mathcal{O}(k \cdot \kappa)}) \cdot n^{\mathcal{O}(1)}$.

On the negative side, there is no $(2 - \epsilon)$-approximation algorithm with runtime $f(k) \cdot n^{\mathcal{O}(1)}$ for any $\epsilon > 0$ and computable f unless W[2] = FPT [11]. It remains open, to what extent the previously mentioned algorithms can be improved.

References

1. Abraham, I., Delling, D., Fiat, A., Goldberg, A.V., Werneck, R.F.: Highway dimension and provably efficient shortest path algorithms. J. ACM **63**(5), 41–41:26 (2016). https://doi.org/10.1145/2985473
2. Abraham, I., Delling, D., Fiat, A., Goldberg, A.V., Werneck, R.F.: VC-dimension and shortest path algorithms. In: Aceto, L., Henzinger, M., Sgall, J. (eds.) ICALP 2011. LNCS, vol. 6755, pp. 690–699. Springer, Heidelberg (2011). https://doi.org/10.1007/978-3-642-22006-7_58
3. Abraham, I., Fiat, A., Goldberg, A.V., Werneck, R.F.F.: Highway dimension, shortest paths, and provably efficient algorithms. In: Proceedings of the 21st Annual ACM-SIAM Symposium on Discrete Algorithms (SODA), pp. 782–793 (2010). https://doi.org/10.1137/1.9781611973075.64
4. Blum, J.: Hierarchy of transportation network parameters and hardness results. In: Proceedings of the 14th International Symposium on Parameterized and Exact Computation (IPEC). LIPIcs, vol. 148, pp. 4:1–4:15. Schloss Dagstuhl - Leibniz-Zentrum für Informatik (2019). https://doi.org/10.4230/LIPIcs.IPEC.2019.4
5. Blum, J., Storandt, S.: Computation and growth of road network dimensions. In: Wang, L., Zhu, D. (eds.) COCOON 2018. LNCS, vol. 10976, pp. 230–241. Springer, Cham (2018). https://doi.org/10.1007/978-3-319-94776-1_20
6. Bodlaender, H.L.: A partial k-arboretum of graphs with bounded treewidth. Theor. Comput. Sci. **209**(1–2), 1–45 (1998). https://doi.org/10.1016/S0304-3975(97)00228-4
7. Cygan, M., et al.: Parameterized Algorithms. Springer, Cham (2015). https://doi.org/10.1007/978-3-319-21275-3
8. Demaine, E.D., Fomin, F.V., Hajiaghayi, M.T., Thilikos, D.M.: Fixed-parameter algorithms for (k,r)-center in planar graphs and map graphs. ACM Trans. Algorithms **1**(1), 33–47 (2005). https://doi.org/10.1145/1077464.1077468
9. Feder, T., Greene, D.H.: Optimal algorithms for approximate clustering. In: Simon, J. (ed.) Proceedings of the 20th Annual ACM Symposium on Theory of Computing (STOC), pp. 434–444. ACM (1988). https://doi.org/10.1145/62212.62255
10. Feldmann, A.E.: Fixed-parameter approximations for k-center problems in low highway dimension graphs. Algorithmica **81**(3), 1031–1052 (2018). https://doi.org/10.1007/s00453-018-0455-0
11. Feldmann, A.E., Marx, D.: The parameterized hardness of the k-center problem in transportation networks. Algorithmica **82**(7), 1989–2005 (2020). https://doi.org/10.1007/s00453-020-00683-w
12. Hochbaum, D.S., Shmoys, D.B.: A unified approach to approximation algorithms for bottleneck problems. J. ACM **33**(3), 533–550 (1986). https://doi.org/10.1145/5925.5933
13. Kosowski, A., Viennot, L.: Beyond highway dimension: small distance labels using tree skeletons. In: Proceedings of the 28th Annual ACM-SIAM Symposium on Discrete Algorithms (SODA), pp. 1462–1478. SIAM (2017)
14. Plesník, J.: On the computational complexity of centers locating in a graph. Aplikace matematiky, **25**(6), 445–452 (1980). https://dml.cz/bitstream/handle/10338.dmlcz/103883/AplMat_25-1980-6_8.pdf
15. Vazirani, V.V.: Approximation Algorithms. Springer, Heidelberg (2001). https://doi.org/10.1007/978-3-662-04565-7. http://www.springer.com/computer/theoretical+computer+science/book/978-3-540-65367-7

An Optimal Lower Bound for Hierarchical Universal Solutions for TSP on the Plane

Patrick Eades$^{(\boxtimes)}$ (ID) and Julián Mestre (ID)

University of Sydney, Sydney, Australia
patrick.eades@sydney.edu.au

Abstract. A Universal TSP tour on a metric space is a total order defined over all points in the space, such that an approximate traveling salesman tour on any finite subset can be found by visiting each point of the subset in the induced order. The performance of a UTSP tour is evaluated by comparing the worst-case ratio of the length of the induced tour to the length of the optimal TSP tour over all subsets of size n. This problem has attracted significant interest over the past thirty years, especially in the case where the locations are points in the Euclidean plane.

For points in the plane Platzman and Bartholdi [*J. ACM*, 36(4):719–737, 1989] achieved a competitive ratio of $O(\log n)$ using an ordering derived from the Sierpinski curve. We introduce the notion of hierarchical orderings which captures all the commonly discussed orderings for the UTSP, including those derived from the Sierpinski, Hilbert, Lebesgue and Peano curves.

Our main result is a lower bound of $\Omega(\log n)$ on the competitive ratio of any Universal TSP tour using hierachical orderings. This is an improvement for this setting on the best known lower bound for Universal TSP on the plane for arbitrary orderings of $\Omega\left(\sqrt[6]{\frac{\log n}{\log\log n}}\right)$ due to Hajiaghayi *et al.* [*Proc. of SODA*, 649–658, 2006].

1 Introduction

The *traveling salesman problem* (TSP) is one of the most studied problems in theoretical computer science. For a given set of locations and their pairwise distances the TSP is to find the shortest tour visiting all locations. In the case when the locations are points in $\mathbb{R}^2$ with their Euclidean distances this problem is known as the *Planar TSP*.

The *universal traveling salesman problem* (UTSP) is to define a total order over a metric space, such that an approximate traveling salesman tour on any finite subset can be found by visiting each point of the subset in the induced order. Such a total order is known as a UTSP tour. In the plane the total order is generally chosen according to some space-filling curve, such as the Hilbert curve (for an example see Fig. 1). The primary advantage of the UTSP as a TSP heuristic is its simplicity and speed, once a total order has been chosen, employing it only requires sorting. The performance of a UTSP tour on a set

© Springer Nature Switzerland AG 2020
D. Kim et al. (Eds.): COCOON 2020, LNCS 12273, pp. 222–233, 2020.
https://doi.org/10.1007/978-3-030-58150-3_18

of points is given by the ratio between the length of the tour produced by the UTSP and length of the optimal TSP solution on those points. The *competitive ratio* of a UTSP tour is the worst case ratio on any set of size n. It is convenient to consider the unit square $[0,1]^2$ rather than the entire plane $\mathbb{R}^2$, a convention we will follow.

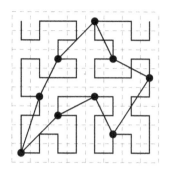

Fig. 1. The UTSP tour induced by the Hilbert space-filling curve.

It is known in the planar case there exist orderings of the unit square such that the competitive ratio is bounded by $O(\log n)$, where n is the size of the set of points we are to visit with the tour [16]. The known orderings are all of the type we call *hierarchical*. At a very high level, a hierarchical ordering divides the plane into "fat" convex regions of equal measure, orders the regions to provide a partial ordering on the points, and then recurses on each piece until the ordering is total. We show for *any* such hierarchical ordering and all large n, there exists a set of points of size n such that the competitive ratio is $\Omega(\log n)$.

Our approach employs the probabilistic method. We draw a random line through the unit square and show there is a high probability that some points spaced (approximately) evenly along the line will be ordered by the UTSP substantially differently to the order they appear along the line. Hence the UTSP tour will backtrack over itself many times, while the TSP tour will not.

While our restriction to hierarchical orderings initially seems very restrictive it covers all the orderings typically used in the UTSP and similar applications. Non-hierarchical orderings (such as the lexographical ordering) have very poor locality, making them unsuitable for the UTSP. This is discussed further in the conclusion.

1.1   Prior Work

The TSP is known to be NP-complete [13], even when restricted to the Euclidean plane [15]. A celebrated algorithm of Christofides [6] gives a 1.5-approximate solution to the TSP for general metric spaces, which remains the best upper bound in this setting. When restricted to a Euclidean metric Arora [1] gives a polynomial time approximation scheme (PTAS). Interestingly, the metric TSP cannot be approximated within a factor of $\frac{123}{122}$ unless $P = NP$ [14]; in contrast to the PTAS available for the Euclidean TSP this suggests the metric TSP is a fundamentally more difficult problem.

The UTSP problem was formally introduced by Platzman and Bartholdi [16] in 1989, in response to a need for faster performing TSP algorithms. The motivating application involved a food delivery service whose subset of clients requiring delivery changed every day, requiring the delivery tour to be efficiently re-calculated. Platzman and Bartholdi used the ordering induced by the Sierpinski space-filling curve, and proved the competitive ratio for this ordering was $O(\log n)$. They further conjectured that the bound could be tightened to $O(1)$ by improving the analysis.

This was refuted later the same year in a note by Bertsimas and Grigni [3], who provided $\Omega(\log n)$ examples for the orderings induced by the Sierpinksi, Hilbert and zig-zag curves. In their lower bound examples Bertsimas and Grigni carefully place a line across the unit square, and points evenly along the line, such that the UTSP must backtrack repeatedly over itself. They demonstrate this pattern can be found recursively on any section of the line so long as there are enough points on that section to form a backtrack, which leads to a $\Omega(\log n)$ sum. This approach has inspired Hajiaghayi et al. [11] and our own lower bound.

The first general lower bound for all total orderings of the plane was provided by Hajiaghayi et al. [11] who considered points on a grid-graph to show a lower bound of $\Omega\left(\sqrt[6]{\frac{\log n}{\log \log n}}\right)$. Hajiaghayi et al. adapt the method of Bertsimas and Grigni and place points along a line. To overcome not knowing the ordering in advance they employ the probabilistic method and show the expected backtracks along a random line are logarithmic. However the increased complexity of bounding the expectation in this setting results in losing some tightness in the lower bound. Hajiaghayi et al. further conjecture their method could be improved to provide a tight lower bound of $\Omega(\log n)$.

The UTSP has also been defined on a finite metric space with m elements, instead of Euclidean space. In this setting the UTSP problem is to find a *master tour* of the m elements, which induces a total order. Competitive ratios in this model are generally described in terms of m, the size of the metric space, rather than n, the number of points in the tour, which can be significant if $n \ll m$, as in the case of the Euclidean plane.

The first upper bound in the finite metric space setting is due to Jia et al. [12], who showed a competitive ratio of $O\left(\frac{\log^4 m}{\log \log m}\right)$. An elegant construction of Schalekamp and Schmoys [17] shows the UTSP has $O(1)$ competitive ratio on tree metrics and therefore, using Bartal's tree embedding [2,8], an expected $O(\log m)$ performance on finite metric spaces. The current best known deterministic upper bound in this setting is $O(\log^2 m)$, which follows from the *well-padded tree cover* of Gupta et al. [10].

For lower bounds in finite metric spaces Gorodezky et al. [9] construct a set with competitive ratio $\Omega(\log m)$ by taking points from a random walk on a Ramanujan graph. Bhalgat *et al.* [4] show the same bound with a simpler construction using two random walks; their construction has some nice additional properties.

A recent result of Christodoulou and Sgouritsa [5] provides an ordering of the $m \times m$ grid-graph with competitive ratio $O\left(\frac{\log m}{\log \log m}\right)$, disproving a conjecture of Bertsimas and Grigni [3]. Their result is interesting in the context of the UTSP on finite metric spaces, but as their bound depends on m it cannot be extended to the Euclidean plane. The *generalized Lebesgue orderings* used by Christodoulou and Sgouritsa are a grid-specific version of a hierarchical ordering.

2   Preliminaries and Notation

Given $\preceq$, a total ordering of $[0,1]^2$, and $S = \{s_1, \ldots, s_n\} \subset [0,1]^2$ labeled such that $s_1 \preceq \cdots \preceq s_n$, we define the performance of $\preceq$ on S and the optimal TSP value for S to be:

- UTSP$_\preceq(S) = \sum_{i=1}^n d(s_i, s_{i+1})$,
- TSP$(S) = \min_{\pi \in \mathcal{S}_n} \sum_{i=1}^n d(s_{\pi(i)}, s_{\pi(i+1)})$,

where $s_{n+1} = s_1$, and $\mathcal{S}_n$ is the symmetric group of order n. Namely, UTSP$_\preceq(S)$ is the cost of visiting S in the order dictated by $\preceq$, while TSP(S) is the optimal cost of visiting S.

The competitive ratio of $\preceq$, as function of the number of points we are to visit, is

$$\rho_\preceq(n) = \sup_{\substack{S \subset [0,1]^2 \\ |S| \leq n}} \frac{\text{UTSP}_\preceq(S)}{\text{TSP}(S)}.$$

Throughout this paper we will be working with decompositions into nicely behaved pieces. To quantify niceness we adapt the concept of α-fatness commonly used in computational geometry (for example by [7]).

Definition 1. *Let R be a convex region in $\mathbb{R}^2$, r_{in} be the radius of the largest ball contained by R and r_{out} be the radius of the smallest ball containing R. We say R is α-fat if $\frac{r_{in}}{r_{out}} \geq \alpha$.*

Our result concerns the performance of a certain class of total orderings that we call *hierarchical*. These are orderings that can be constructed by partitioning the unit square into k nice regions, recursively ordering each region and then concatenating these partial orderings to get a total ordering of the whole unit square.

Such a construction leads to a natural hierarchical decomposition of the unit square: Level 0 is made up of a single region, the whole unit square; whereas in general level i in the decomposition is made up of k^i regions. Let us denote the regions in level i with $\mathcal{Q}_i$. Figure 1 shows the order of the third level regions of the decomposition associated with Hilbert's space filling curve.

Definition 2. *An ordering $\preceq$ is hierarchical if, for some fixed constants k and α, it can be constructed by recursively partitioning into regions such that for all regions $R \in Q_j$ at level j we have:*

1. *R is convex,*
2. *area$(R) = 1/k^j$, and*
3. *R is α-fat*

It is worth noting that while seemingly restrictive at first sight, most classical orderings of the unit square such as the Hilbert, Peano, Sierpinski and Lebesgue space filling curves fall within this framework.

Our main result is a lower bound argument that shows that for any ordering constructed in this fashion there is a family of point sets for which the approximation ratio is at least logarithmic on the number of points.

Throughout the paper we will make use of some properties of the perimeter of the regions in the decomposition that stem from our convexity and α-fatness assumptions. Our first observation is that the perimeter is a polygon.

Observation 1. *For any $Q \in Q_i$, the perimeter of Q is polygon made up of straight edges, one of each region neighboring Q.*

Proof. Let T be a region neighboring Q. Since both T and Q are convex, it follows that T and Q meet along a straight line segment.

Our second observation roughly states that up to α factors, the perimeter of such a region is similar to the perimeter of a ball with equal measure.

Observation 2. *For any region $Q \in Q_i$, its perimeter P must be proportional to $k^{-\frac{i}{2}}$; more precisely,*

$$2\alpha\sqrt{\pi}k^{-\frac{i}{2}} \leq P \leq 2\alpha^{-1}\sqrt{\pi}k^{-\frac{i}{2}}. \tag{1}$$

Proof. Let r_{in} be the radius of the largest ball enclosed in Q and r_{out} be the radius of the smallest ball enclosing Q. By α-fatness we have $r_{\text{in}} \geq \alpha r_{\text{out}}$.

The inner ball must have area no greater than Q, hence $\pi r_{\text{in}}^2 \leq k^{-i}$ and so $r_{\text{in}} \leq (\pi k^i)^{-\frac{1}{2}}$. Similarly the outer ball must have area no less than Q and so $r_{\text{out}} \geq (\pi k^i)^{-\frac{1}{2}}$.

The circumference of the inner ball is $2\pi r_{\text{in}} \geq 2\pi(\alpha r_{\text{out}}) \geq \alpha(2\sqrt{\pi}k^{-\frac{i}{2}})$. The circumference of the outer ball is $2\pi r_{\text{out}} \leq 2\pi(\alpha^{-1}r_{\text{in}}) \leq \alpha^{-1}(2\sqrt{\pi}k^{-\frac{i}{2}})$. The perimeter of Q is, by convexity, bounded by the perimeters of the inner and outer balls, and hence must be between $2\alpha\sqrt{\pi}k^{-\frac{i}{2}}$ and $2\alpha^{-1}\sqrt{\pi}k^{-\frac{i}{2}}$.

We say $Q \in Q_i$ is an *inner region* if it does not touch the boundary of its parent; namely, if all its neighbors are siblings regions in the decomposition. The following lemma shows that for large enough k, every region has a child that is an inner region.

Lemma 1. *If $k > \frac{16}{\alpha^4}$ then every region T in the decomposition has at least one child region Q that is an inner region.*

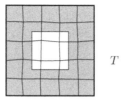

T

Fig. 2. All the non-inner children of T must fit inside a strip (denoted in gray) of width $\frac{2}{\alpha\sqrt{\pi}}\sqrt{\frac{1}{k^{j+1}}}$ around the border of T which is not large enough to accommodate all the children of T. Hence T have an inner child.

Proof. Let T $\in$ $\mathcal{Q}_j$ and $\mathcal{R} = \left\{R \in \mathcal{Q}_{j+1} \mid R \text{ is a child of } T \text{ and } R \text{ touches the boundary of } T\right\}$. Recall that each $R \in \mathcal{R}$ has $\text{area}(R) = \frac{1}{k^{j+1}}$ and, because the region is fat, there exists a ball of area $\frac{1}{\alpha^2 k^{j+1}}$ enclosing R. Therefore, as exemplified in Fig. 2, there must be a strip of width $\frac{2}{\alpha\sqrt{\pi}}\sqrt{\frac{1}{k^{j+1}}}$ around the boundary of T that contains all the regions in $\mathcal{R}$.

Now by Observation 2, T's perimeter cannot be larger than $2\sqrt{\pi}\alpha^{-1}k^{-\frac{j}{2}}$. Hence all of $\mathcal{R}$ must be contained in a strip of area less than $\frac{4}{\alpha^2}\frac{1}{k^j\sqrt{k}}$. It follows that $|\mathcal{R}| \leq \frac{4\sqrt{k}}{\alpha^2}$, and thus if $k > \frac{16}{\alpha^4}$ then $|\mathcal{R}| < k$ and so there must exist at least one child of T that does not touch its boundary.

Notice that the requirement that k is large is not a restrictive one. Given a decomposition with $k \leq \frac{16}{\alpha^4}$ we can instead take a decomposition which has a single level for multiple levels of our original decomposition. For example a decomposition with $k = 4$ could be turned into one with $k = 256$ by merging four levels, which would accommodate $\alpha = 0.5$. Since k and α are constants, this is always achievable by merging a constant number of levels, so it does not impact our argument.

Our lower bound construction makes use of some properties of random lines intersecting the unit square. Let us denote with $\mathcal{L}$ the set of all lines which intersect the unit square. As Fig. 3 shows, a line $\ell \in \mathcal{L}$ is uniquely determined by the angle it makes with respect to the x-axis, and its x-intercept or similarly its y-intercept. We define a procedure Λ for sampling a line $\ell \in \mathcal{L}$ as follows: Pick uniformly at random $\beta \in [0, \pi)$, consider the β-angled projection of $[0, 1]$ on the x and y axes and pick an intercept uniformly at random within the shorter projection of the two; in other words, if $\beta \in \left[\frac{\pi}{4}, \frac{3\pi}{4}\right]$ then we pick an intercept along the x-axis, and if $\beta \notin \left[\frac{\pi}{4}, \frac{3\pi}{4}\right]$ then we pick an intercept along the y-axis. Note that even though the probability distribution over lines is not uniform, the probability densities of any two lines in $\mathcal{L}$ differ by at most a factor of 2 since the length of the smaller projection is always in the range $[1, 2]$.

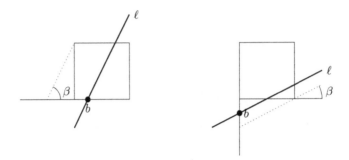

Fig. 3. The space $\mathcal{L}$ of lines intersecting the unit square is sampled by uniformly picking an angle $\beta \in [0, \pi)$ and an x-axis (or y-axis) intercept b in the β-angle projection of the square to the x-axis (y-axis).

3   Logarithmic Lower Bound

In this section we prove that any hierarchical ordering as in Definition 2 must have asymptotic approximation ratio that grows logarithmically with the cardinality of the set we are to visit.

Theorem 1. *For any hierarchical ordering $\preceq$ of $[0,1]^2$, we have $\rho_\preceq(n) = \Omega(\log n)$.*

The key ingredient in our proof of this Theorem is the existence of a probability distribution over families of subsets $S_1, S_2, \ldots \subset [0,1]^2$ of size k^i such that:

1. $\text{TSP}(S_i) = O(1)$, and
2. $\text{E}[\text{UTSP}_\preceq(S_i)] = \Omega(i)$.

Defining this distribution is exceedingly simple: Pick a random line ℓ accordingly to the sampling procedure Λ, and construct S_i by picking one representative point on ℓ from each region in $\mathcal{Q}_i$ that ℓ intersects; that is, one point from each region in the ith level of the hierarchical decomposition associated with $\preceq$.

Our goal for the rest of the section is to prove the two properties stated above.

Lemma 2. *For any $\preceq$ and any line $\ell \in \mathcal{L}$, $\text{E}[\text{TSP}(S_i) \mid \ell] = O(1)$.*

Proof. The cost of the optimal travelling salesman tour of any number of points in one dimension is upper bounded by twice the distance between the smallest and largest points, since there is a tour that visits each point in ascending order, then returns to the start.

Since the points of S_i lie on the intersection of ℓ and $[0,1]^2$, $\text{TSP}(S_i) \leq 2\sqrt{2}$.

In order to prove the second property we need to first establish a few key facts and definitions about the random process for constructing the S_i sets. Let $A, B, C \in \mathcal{Q}_j$ be regions at level $j \leq i$ of the decomposition. We say these regions form an *out-of-order triplet* with respect to a line $\ell \in \mathcal{L}$ if:

1. A, B, and C have the same parent region in the decomposition,
2. ℓ cuts through A, B, and C in that order (or the reverse order), and
3. either $B \preceq A, C$ or $A, C \preceq B$

If B is the central part of some out-of-order triplet (A, B, C), we define its *share* $\chi(B)$ to be $\|\ell \cap B\|$, otherwise, $\chi(B) = 0$. Figure 4 provides a pictorial representation of the share of a region.

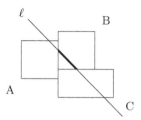

Fig. 4. An out-of-order triplet (A, B, C) induces a share $\chi(B)$ shown by the thick line segment.

Our first observation is that these shares provide a lower bound on the cost of the universal tour on S_i.

Lemma 3. *For any given $\ell \in \mathcal{L}$ and its associated set S_i we have*

$$\text{UTSP}_{\preceq}(S_i) \geq \sum_{j \leq i} \sum_{Q \in \mathcal{Q}_j} \chi(Q).$$

Proof. Let (A, B, C) be an out-of-order triplet at level $j \leq i$ whose parent is T. Assume without loss of generality that $B \preceq A, C$ (the case $A, C \preceq B$ is symmetric). Thus there must exist $a \in S_i \cap A$, $b \in S_i \cap B$, and $c \in S_i \cap C$ such that $b \preceq a, c$. This in turn means that we must have two points $u, v \in S_i \cap (T \setminus B)$ that are consecutive in $\preceq$ such that $\ell[u, v]$ cuts through B. We charge $\chi(B)$ to the segment $\ell[u, v]$ of the UTSP$_{\preceq}$ solution.

Note that the segment $\ell[u, v]$ can only be charged by other children of T, which by definition are all disjoint, so the total charge to the segment cannot exceed $\|\ell[u, v]\|$. Thus the lemma follows.

We will show that, under expectation, ℓ cuts through a substantial number of out-of-order triplets, each with a substantial share. But first, we need to introduce a few concepts.

Let Q be a region at level j that does not touch the boundary of its parent region; by Lemma 1 we can assume without loss of generality that there are at least k^{j-1} such regions. Recall that by Observation 1, Q can only meet its neighbours along straight line segments. Call these the *edges* of Q. Note that Q can have at most $k - 1$ edges, since Q shares edges only with its siblings. Let P

be the perimeter of Q. Call an edge *short* if its length is less than $\frac{\alpha}{10k}P$ and *long* otherwise. It follows that the total length of short edges is at most $\frac{\alpha}{10}P$. Call the angle[1] between a pair of edges *wide* if it is greater than $\pi - \delta$, where $\delta = \frac{\alpha}{5}$ and *narrow* otherwise; recall that since $\alpha \leq 1$, this means that $\delta \leq 1/5$.

We will now introduce the concept of a *meta-edge* of Q. Let e be an edge of Q. The meta-edge $\hat{e}$ induced by e consists of all the edges that form a wide angle with e and e itself. Note that the edges in $\hat{e}$ form a contiguous section of the Q's boundary about e.

Define $W(\hat{e})$, the *width* of $\hat{e}$, to be the distance between the first and last endpoints in $\hat{e}$. Define $H(\hat{e})$, the *height* of $\hat{e}$, to be the maximum distance between a point on any edge in $\hat{e}$ and the line connecting the first and last endpoints of $\hat{e}$. Define $\theta(\hat{e})$, the *angle* of $\hat{e}$, to be the angle between the first and last edges in $\hat{e}$. Finally, define $L(\hat{e})$, the *length* of $\hat{e}$, to be the sum of the lengths of the edges in $\hat{e}$. Figure 5 exemplifies these concepts.

Observe that because all edges that make up $\hat{e}$ form a wide angle with e, it must be the case that $\theta \geq \pi - 2\delta$. Note that for a meta-edge with a given length, its height is maximized and its width minimized when it forms an isosceles triangle. Therefore,

$$H \leq \frac{L}{2}\sin\left(\frac{\pi - \theta}{2}\right) \leq \frac{L}{2}\sin\delta \leq \frac{L\delta}{2}, \text{ and} \tag{2}$$

$$W \geq L\sin\left(\frac{\theta}{2}\right) \geq L\sin\left(\frac{\pi}{2} - \delta\right) \geq L\sin\left(\frac{\pi}{6}\right) \geq \frac{L}{2}. \tag{3}$$

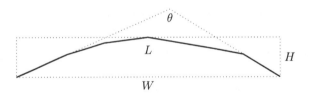

Fig. 5. A meta-edge with height H, width W and angle θ and L the length of the solid chain.

Call a set of three edges of Q a *fat triad* for Q if each edge is long and the angle between any pair of the edges is narrow. First we will show that every inner region admits a fat triad and then we will show that this leads to having a large share value. Due to space constraints the proofs of Lemmas 4 and 5 are deferred to the Appendix.

Lemma 4. *Every inner region $Q \in \mathcal{Q}_i$ has a fat triad.*

Lemma 5. *If $Q \in \mathcal{Q}_j$ is an inner region, then $\mathrm{E}[\chi(Q)] = \Omega(k^{-j})$.*

---

[1] The angle between a pair of edges is the angle at which the lines going through them meet.

We have all the tools to show that the expected value of the universal TSP tour on S_i is at least $\Omega(i)$.

Lemma 6. *For any* $\preceq$, $\mathrm{E}[\mathrm{UTSP}_{\preceq}(S_i)] = \Omega(i)$.

Proof. By Lemma 3 we know that the sum of the χ-values are a lower bound:

$$\mathrm{E}[\mathrm{UTSP}_{\preceq}(S_i)] \geq \sum_{j \leq i} \sum_{Q \in \mathcal{Q}_j} \mathrm{E}[\chi(Q)].$$

By Lemma 5, we know that every inner region $Q \in \mathcal{Q}_j$ has $\mathrm{E}[\chi(Q)] = \Omega(k^{-j})$. If $k > \frac{16}{\alpha^4}$ then, by Lemma 1, every region in the previous level of the decomposition has at least one child that is an inner region. Therefore, we must have k^{j-1} inner regions in $\mathcal{Q}_j$, so $\sum_{Q \in \mathcal{Q}_j} \mathrm{E}[\chi(Q)] = \Omega(1)$, and the lemma follows.

Everything is in place to give the proof of Theorem 1.

Proof (Proof of Theorem 1). Let $\hat{S}_i$ be a S_i such that $\mathrm{UTSP}_{\preceq}(\hat{S}_i) \geq \mathrm{E}[\mathrm{UTSP}_{\preceq}(S_i)]$. By Lemma 6, it follows that $\mathrm{UTSP}_{\preceq}(\hat{S}_i) = \Omega(i)$. On the other hand, by Lemma 2, we know that $\mathrm{TSP}(\hat{S}_i) = O(1)$. Finally, the cardinality of $\hat{S}_i$ is trivially bounded by k^i, so

$$\rho_{\preceq}(k^i) \geq \frac{\mathrm{UTSP}_{\preceq}(\hat{S}_i)}{\mathrm{TSP}(\hat{S}_i)} = \Omega(i).$$

Since this holds for all i, in general we have

$$\rho_{\preceq}(n) = \Omega(\log n).$$

4   Conclusion

We have demonstrated that hierarchical orderings of the plane cannot achieve a competitive ratio better than the $O(\log n)$ proved by Platzman and Bartholdi when they introduced the UTSP problem. Included in our definition of hierarchical are the requirements that the regions are of equal measure, are convex and are α-fat. While these restrictions initially appear restrictive they cover all the orderings typically used for the UTSP. We conclude by examining examine each of these assumptions in more detail and discuss how they could potentially be relaxed.

The requirement that the regions are of equal measure is used to simplify the presentation of our arguments and could be relaxed to require regions of measure within some constant factor. The only change this would make to our proofs is to include the constant factor in various expressions, which would not change the asymptotic bound.

Similarly, the requirement that the regions are convex does not seem to be integral to our methods. Since each region is α-fat it must contain a disk which

covers most of its area, and must fit within an outer disk. Hence it must consist
of a fat, convex core (which can create the jumps required for the lower bound)
and a non-convex border area. Intuitievely, having a non-convex border area
can only increase the cost, since a line can intersect a region multiple times. By
placing a point on the line each time the line intersects a region, that region can
create additional jumps with itself, as in Fig. 6.

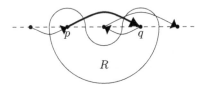

Fig. 6. If ℓ intersects a region R more than once, it will cause a jump by itself from p
to q.

The requirement that the regions are α-fat, however, is integral to our concep-
tion of a hierarchical ordering and new ideas are needed to lift this requirement.

References

1. Arora, S.: Polynomial time approximation schemes for Euclidean traveling salesman and other geometric problems. J. ACM **45**(5), 753–782 (1998)
2. Bartal, Y.: Probabilistic approximations of metric spaces and its algorithmic applications. In: Proceedings of the 37th Annual IEEE Symposium on Foundations of
   Computer Science, pp. 184–193 (1996)
3. Bertsimas, D., Grigni, M.: Worst-case examples for the spacefilling curve heuristic for the Euclidean traveling salesman problem. Oper. Res. Lett. **8**(5), 241–244
   (1989)
4. Bhalgat, A., Chakrabarty, D., Khanna, S.: Optimal lower bounds for universal and
   differentially private steiner trees and TSPs. In: Goldberg, L.A., Jansen, K., Ravi,
   R., Rolim, J.D.P. (eds.) APPROX/RANDOM -2011. LNCS, vol. 6845, pp. 75–86.
   Springer, Heidelberg (2011). https://doi.org/10.1007/978-3-642-22935-0_7
5. Christodoulou, G., Sgouritsa, A.: An improved upper bound for the universal TSP
   on the grid. In: Proceedings of the 28th Annual ACM-SIAM Symposium on Discrete Algorithms, pp. 1006–1021 (2017)
6. Christofides, N.: Worst-case analysis of a new heuristic for the travelling salesman
   problem. Technical report, CMU Technical Report (1976)
7. Efrat, A., Katz, M.J., Nielsen, F., Sharir, M.: Dynamic data structures for fat
   objects and their applications. Comput. Geom. **15**(4), 215–227 (2000)
8. Fakcharoenphol, J., Rao, S., Talwar, K.: A tight bound on approximating arbitrary
   metrics by tree metrics. J. Comput. Syst. Sci. **69**(3), 485–497 (2004)
9. Gorodezky, I., Kleinberg, R.D., Shmoys, D.B., Spencer, G.: Improved lower bounds
   for the universal and a priori TSP. In: Serna, M., Shaltiel, R., Jansen, K., Rolim,
   J. (eds.) APPROX/RANDOM -2010. LNCS, vol. 6302, pp. 178–191. Springer,
   Heidelberg (2010). https://doi.org/10.1007/978-3-642-15369-3_14

10. Gupta, A., Hajiaghayi, M.T., Räcke, H.: Oblivious network design. In: Proceedings of the 17th Annual ACM-SIAM Symposium on Discrete Algorithms, pp. 970–979 (2006)
11. Hajiaghayi, M.T., Kleinberg, R.D., Leighton, F.T.: Improved lower and upper bounds for universal TSP in planar metrics. In: Proceedings of the 17th Annual ACM-SIAM Symposium on Discrete Algorithms, pp. 649–658 (2006)
12. Jia, L., Lin, G., Noubir, G., Rajaraman, R., Sundaram, R.: Universal approximations for TSP, Steiner tree, and set cover. In: Proceedings of the 37th Annual ACM Symposium on Theory of Computing, pp. 386–395 (2005)
13. Karp, R.M.: Reducibility among combinatorial problems. In: Miller, R.E., Thatcher, J.W., Bohlinger, J.D. (eds.) Complexity of Computer Computations, pp. 85–103. The IBM Research Symposia Series. Springer, Boston (1972). https://doi.org/10.1007/978-1-4684-2001-2_9
14. Karpinski, M., Lampis, M., Schmied, R.: New inapproximability bounds for TSP. J. Comput. Syst. Sci. **81**(8), 1665–1677 (2015)
15. Papadimitriou, C.H.: The Euclidean traveling salesman problem is NP-complete. Theor. Comput. Sci. **4**(3), 237–244 (1977)
16. Platzman, L.K., Bartholdi III, J.J.: Spacefilling curves and the planar travelling salesman problem. J. ACM **36**(4), 719–737 (1989)
17. Schalekamp, F., Shmoys, D.B.: Algorithms for the universal and a priori TSP. Oper. Res. Lett. **36**(1), 1–3 (2008)

Quantum Speedup for the Minimum Steiner Tree Problem

Masayuki Miyamoto[1]([✉]), Masakazu Iwamura[2], Koichi Kise[2],
and François Le Gall[3]

[1] Kyoto University, Kyoto, Japan
miyamoto.masayuki.46s@st.kyoto-u.ac.jp
[2] Osaka Prefecture University, Sakai, Japan
[3] Nagoya University, Nagoya, Japan

Abstract. A recent breakthrough by Ambainis, Balodis, Iraids, Kokainis, Prūsis and Vihrovs (SODA'19) showed how to construct faster quantum algorithms for the Traveling Salesman Problem and a few other NP-hard problems by combining in a novel way quantum search with classical dynamic programming. In this paper, we show how to apply this approach to the minimum Steiner tree problem, a well-known NP-hard problem, and construct the first quantum algorithm that solves this problem faster than the best known classical algorithms. More precisely, the complexity of our quantum algorithm is $\mathcal{O}(1.812^k \text{poly}(n))$, where n denotes the number of vertices in the graph and k denotes the number of terminals. In comparison, the best known classical algorithm has complexity $\mathcal{O}(2^k \text{poly}(n))$.

1 Introduction

Background: Quantum Speedup of Dynamic Programming Algorithms. The celebrated quantum algorithm by Grover [10] for quantum search (Grover search) gives a quadratic speed up over classical algorithms for the unstructured search problem [3,10]. Its generalization, quantum amplitude amplification [4,15], is also useful to speed up classical algorithms. For many problems, however, Grover search or quantum amplitude amplification does not immediately give a speedup. A simple example is the Traveling Salesman Problem (TSP). The trivial brute-force algorithm for the TSP has running time $\mathcal{O}(n!)$, where n denote the number of vertices of the graph. While Grover search can be applied to improve this complexity to $\mathcal{O}(\sqrt{n!})$, the well-known classical algorithm by Held and Karp [11], based on dynamic programming, already solves the TSP in $\mathcal{O}^*(2^n)$ time,[1] which is significantly better than that quantum speedup.

Recently, Ambainis, Balodis, Iraids, Kokainis, Prūsis and Vihrovs [1] developed a breakthrough approach to achieve quantum speedups for several fundamental NP-hard problems, by combining in a clever way Grover search and (classical) dynamic programming. For the TSP, in particular, they obtained a

---

[1] In this paper the $\mathcal{O}^*$ notation hides polynomial factors in n.

© Springer Nature Switzerland AG 2020
D. Kim et al. (Eds.): COCOON 2020, LNCS 12273, pp. 234–245, 2020.
https://doi.org/10.1007/978-3-030-58150-3_19

$\mathcal{O}^*(1.728^n)$-time quantum algorithm, which outperforms the $\mathcal{O}^*(2^n)$-time classical algorithm mentioned above. They also constructed similar quantum algorithms, faster than the best known classical algorithms, for a few other NP-hard problems: checking the existence of a path in an hypercube (and several similar vertex ordering problems), computing the graph bandwidth, the minimum set cover problem and the feedback arc set problem.

While the approach from [1] has the potential to lead to speed-ups for other hard problems, it cannot be applied to any computational problem. The approach (currently) works only for computational problems that can be expressed with dynamic programming using a recurrence relation of a simple form. An important question is to identify which other problems can be sped-up in the quantum setting by this approach, i.e., identify which other problems admit this formulation.

In this paper we show that another fundamental NP-hard problem, the Minimum Steiner Tree Problem, can be sped up by such a combination of Grover search and dynamic programming.

The Minimum Steiner Tree Problem. Given an undirected weighted graph $G = (V, E, w)$ and a subset of terminals $K \subseteq V$, a Steiner tree is a subtree of G that connects all vertices in K. Below, we will write $n = |V|$ and $k = |K|$. The task of finding a Steiner tree of minimum total weight is called the Minimum Steiner Tree problem (MST problem). This problem is NP-hard [13]. Note that for fixed constant k, this problem can be solved in polynomial time, which means that the MST problem is fixed parameter tractable [5,8].

The MST problem has applications to solve problems such as power supply network, communication network and facility location problem [12]. Since all these problems need to be solved in practice, designing algorithms as fast as possible for the MST problem is of fundamental importance.

A naive way to solve the MST problem is to compute all possible trees. Since the number of all trees in the graph $G = (V, E)$ can be as large as $\mathcal{O}(2^{|E|})$, this is extremely inefficient. The Dreyfus-Wagner algorithm [6] is a well-known algorithm based on dynamic programming for solving the MST problem in time $\mathcal{O}^*(3^k)$. This algorithm has been the fastest algorithm for decades. Fuchs, Kern and Wang [9] finally improved this complexity to $\mathcal{O}^*(2.684^k)$, and Mölle, Richter and Rossmanith [14] further improved it to $\mathcal{O}((2 + \delta)^k n^{f(\delta^{-1})})$ for any constant $\delta > 0$. For a graph with a restricted weight range, Björklund, Husfeldt, Kaski and Koivisto have proposed an $\mathcal{O}^*(2^k)$ algorithm using subset convolution and Möbius inversion [2]. The main tool in all these algorithms [2,9,14] is dynamic programming.

Our Results. Our main result is the following theorem (see also Table 1).

Theorem 1. *There exists a quantum algorithm that solves with high probability the Minimum Steiner Tree problem in time $\mathcal{O}^*(1.812^k)$, where k denotes the size of the terminal set.*

The quantum algorithm of Theorem 1 is the first quantum algorithm that solves the MST problem faster than the best known classical algorithms.

Our approach is conceptually similar to the approach introduced in [1]: we combine Grover search and (classical) dynamic programming. All the difficulty is to find the appropriate dynamic programming formulation of the MST problem. The dynamic programming formulation used in the Dreyfus and Wagner algorithm [6] cannot be used since that characterisation of minimum Steiner trees is not suitable for Grover search. Instead, we rely on another characterization introduced by Fuchs, Kern and Wang [9]. More precisely, Ref. [9] introduced, for any $r \geq 2$ the concept of "r-split" of a graph and showed how to use it to derive a dynamic programming formulation that decomposes the computation of a minimum Steiner trees into several parts. By considering the case $r = 3$, i.e., decomposing trees into three parts, they obtained their $\mathcal{O}^*(2.684^k)$-time algorithm. In Sect. 3.2 we show how to derive another recurrence relation (Eq. (2)). Interestingly, we use a 2-split to derive this relation, and not a 3-split as in [9] (it seems that a 3-split only gives worse complexity in the quantum setting). We then show in Sect. 4 how to use Grover search to compute efficiently a minimum Steiner tree using Eq. (2). This is done by applying Grover search recursively several times with different size parameters.

Table 1. Comparison of the algorithms for the Minimum Steiner Tree problem. Here n denotes the number of nodes in the graph and k denotes the size of the terminal set.

Algorithm	Complexity	Classical or quantum
Dreyfus and Wagner [6]	$\mathcal{O}^*(3^k)$	Classical
Fuchs et al. [9]	$\mathcal{O}^*(2.684^k)$	Classical
Mölle et al. [14]	$\mathcal{O}((2+\delta)^k n^{f(\delta^{-1})})$	Classical
Björklund et al. [2]	$\mathcal{O}^*(2^k)$ [for restricted weights]	Classical
This paper	$\mathcal{O}^*(1.812^k)$	**Quantum**

2 Preliminaries

General Notation. We denote H the binary entropy function, defined as $H(\alpha) = -\alpha \log \alpha - (1 - \alpha) \log(1 - \alpha)$ for any $\alpha \in [0, 1]$.

Graph-Theoretic Notation. In this paper we consider undirected weighted graphs $G = (V, E, w)$ with weight function $w : E \to \mathbb{R}^+$, where $\mathbb{R}^+$ denotes the set of positive real numbers. Given a subset $E' \subseteq E$ of edges, we write $V(E') \subseteq V$ the set of vertices induced by E', and write $w(E') = \sum_{e \in E'} w(e)$. Given a tree T of G, i.e., a subgraph of G isomorphic to a tree, we often identify T with its edge set. In particular, we write its total weight $w(T)$.

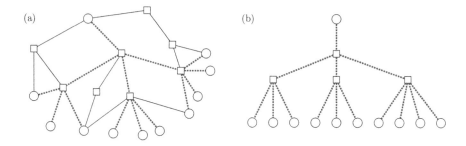

Fig. 1. (a) An example of a graph $G = (V, E, w)$. The graph is unweighted, i.e., $w(e) = 1$ for all $e \in E$. Circled nodes represent the nodes in the terminal set K and rectangular nodes represent the nodes in $V \setminus K$. The red dotted edges show the minimum Steiner tree T. In this case we have $W_G(K) = 14$. (b) The tree T extracted from (a). (Color figure online)

Minimum Steiner Trees. Given an undirected weighted graph $G = (V, E, w)$ and a subset of vertices $K \subseteq V$, usually referred to as terminals, a Steiner tree is a tree of G that spans K (i.e., connects all vertices in K). A Steiner tree T is a minimum Steiner tree (MST) if its total edge weight $w(T)$ is the minimum among all Steiner trees for K. Note that all leaves of a Steiner tree T are necessarily vertices in K. We denote $W_G(K)$ the weight of an MST. Figure 1 shows an example. The Minimum Steiner Tree Problem (MST problem) asks, given G and K, to compute $W_G(K)$ and output an MST. In this paper we write $n = |V|$ and $k = |K|$. When describing algorithms for the MST problem, we often describe explicitly only the computation of $W_G(K)$. For all the (classical and quantum) algorithms for the MST problem described in this paper, which are all based on dynamic programming, an MST can be obtained from the computation of $W_G(K)$ simply by keeping record of the intermediate steps of the computation.

Graph Contraction. For a graph $G = (V, E, w)$ and a subset of vertices $A \subseteq V$, a graph contraction G/A is a graph which is obtained by removing all edges between vertices in A, replacing all vertices in A with one new vertex v_A, and replacing each edge $e \in E$ with one endpoint u outside A and the other endpoint in A by an edge between u and v_A of weight $w(e)$. If a vertex $u \in V$ is incident to multiple edges $e_1, e_2, ..., e_s \in E$ with the other endpoint in A, then the graph G/A has an edge (u, v_A) with a weight $\min_{i=1}^{s} w(e_i)$ instead of having s edges between u and v_A.

Quantum Algorithm for Minimum Finding. The quantum algorithm for minimum finding by Dürr and Høyer [7], referred to as "D-H algorithm" in this paper, is a quantum algorithm for finding the minimum in an (unsorted) database that is based on Grover's quantum search algorithm [10]. More precisely, the D-H algorithm is given as input quantum access to N elements $a_1, ..., a_N$ from an ordered set, i.e., the algorithm has access to a quantum oracle that maps the quantum state $|i\rangle|0\rangle$ to the quantum state $|i\rangle|a_i\rangle$, for any $i \in \{1, \ldots, N\}$. The algorithm outputs with high probability (i.e., probability at least $1 - 1/\text{poly}(N)$) the value $\min\{a_i | i = 1, ..., N\}$ using only $\mathcal{O}(\sqrt{N})$ calls to the oracle. This gives a quadratic speedup with respect to classical algorithms for minimum finding.

3   Building Blocks from Prior Work

In this section we describe results from prior works that will be used to build our quantum algorithm.

3.1   The Dreyfus-Wagner Algorithm

The Dreyfus-Wagner algorithm [6], referred to as "D-W algorithm" in this paper, solves the MST problem in time $\mathcal{O}^*(3^k)$ by using dynamic programming. The result from [6] that we will need in this paper is not the final algorithm, but rather the following technical result.

Theorem 2 ([6]). *For any value* $\alpha \in (0, 1/2]$, *all the weights* $W_G(X)$ *for all the sets* $X \subseteq K$ *such that* $|X| \leq \alpha|K|$ *can be computed in time* $\mathcal{O}^* \left(2^{(H(\alpha)+\alpha)k} \right)$.

For completeness we give below an overview of the proof of Theorem 2. The key observation is as follows. Assume that we have an MST T for $X \cup \{q\}$ where $X \subseteq K, q \in K\backslash X$. If q is a leaf of T, then there is a vertex $p \in V(T)$ such that there is a shortest path P_{qp} that connects q and p in T, and p has more than two neighbors in T (otherwise, T is a path and we decompose T into two paths). Hence, we have $T = P_{qp} \cup T'$ where T' is an MST for $X \cup \{p\}$. Note that p might not be a terminal, i.e., possibly $p \notin K$. After removing P_{qp} from T, p splits the remaining component T' into two edge disjoint subtrees, i.e., for some nontrivial subset $X' \subseteq X$, MSTs T'_1 for $X' \cup \{p\}$ and T'_2 for $(X\backslash X') \cup \{p\}$, we have the decomposition $T' = T'_1 \cup T'_2$. This holds in both cases $p \in K$ and $p \notin K$, and even when q is not a leaf of T (in this case, we take $p = q$ and $P_{qp} = \emptyset$). This implies that an MST T for $X \cup \{q\}$ can be computed from the MSTs T' for $X' \cup \{p\}$ and the shortest paths P_{pq} for all $p \in V$ and $X' \subseteq X$.

We thus obtain the following recursion:

$$W_G(X \cup \{q\}) = \min_{\substack{p \in V \\ X' \subset X}} \{d_G(q, p) + W_G(X' \cup \{p\}) + W_G((X\backslash X') \cup \{p\})\} \quad (1)$$

where $d_G(q, p)$ is the weight of a shortest path P_{qp} (shortest paths of all pairs of vertices can be computed in $\text{poly}(n)$ time). See Fig. 2 for an illustration of the decomposition.

Using this recursion, weights of MSTs for all subsets of terminals $X \subseteq K$ with size $|X| \leq \alpha k$ can be computed in time

$$\mathcal{O}^* \left(\sum_{i=0}^{\alpha k} \binom{k}{i} 2^i \right),$$

where $\binom{k}{i}$ represents the number of sets $X \subset K$ with $|X| = i$ and 2^i represents the number of sets $X' \subset X$. As claimed in Theorem 2, for $\alpha \leq 1/2$, this complexity is upper bounded by $\mathcal{O}^* \left(2^{(H(\alpha)+\alpha)k} \right)$ where H is the binary entropy function.

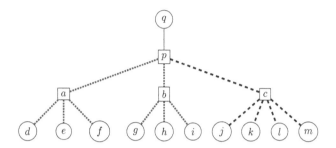

Fig. 2. An illustration for Dreyfus-Wagner decomposition for the tree in Fig. 1. The MST T for $X \cup \{q\}$ is decomposed into three parts: a black solid path P_{qp}, an MST T_1' for $X' \cup \{p\}$ with blue dashed edges, an MST T_2' for $(X\backslash X') \cup \{p\}$ with red dotted edges. In this case we have $X = \{d, e, f, g, h, i, j, k, l, m\}$ and $X' = \{j, k, l, m\}$. (Color figure online)

3.2 The Algorithm by Fuchs, Kern and Wang

Fuchs, Kern and Wang [9] have improved the D-W algorithm by dividing the algorithm into two parts: a dynamic programming part and a part which merges subtrees. In this paper we will not use directly this improved algorithm. Instead, we will use the main technique introduced in [9] to obtain another recurrence relation on which our quantum algorithm will be based.

The central idea that we need is the concept of "r-split" of an MST. This concept was introduced in [9] for any value $r \geq 2$ and used with $r = 3$ to construct their $\mathcal{O}^*(2.684^k)$-time algorithm for the MST problem. For our purpose, on the other hand, we will need the version with $r = 2$, which we define below.

Definition 1. *Let T be an MST for the terminal set K. A 2-split of T is an edge disjoint partition $T = T_1 \cup E'$ such that T_1 is a subtree of T and the subgraph induced by the edge subset E' is a subforest of T. We also use the following notation.*

$$A := V(T_1) \cap V(E')$$
$$K_1 := K \cap V(T_1)\backslash A$$
$$K_2 := K \cap V(E')\backslash A$$

We call A the set of split nodes. When T and E' are both nonempty, we have $A \neq \emptyset$ since T is a tree.

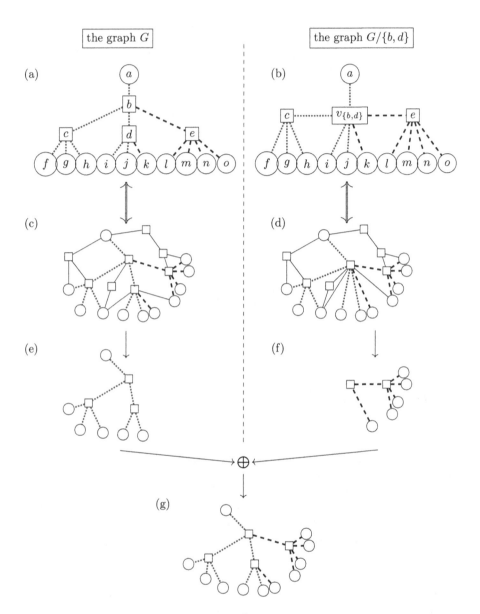

Fig. 3. An example of 2-split $T = T_1 \cup E'$. In this graph we have the terminal set $K = \{a, f, g, h, i, j, k, l, m, n, o\}$, $K_1 = \{f, g, h, i, j\}$, and $A = \{b, d\}$. (a): The red dotted edges show the tree T_1 and the blue dashed edges show the forest E'. (b): The contracted graph $G/\{b, d\}$. (c): Graph G containing the tree of (a). (d): Graph $G/\{b, d\}$ containing the tree of (b). (e): The tree induced by red dotted edges in graph G. (f): The tree induced by blue dashed edges in graph $G/\{b, d\}$. (g): The minimum Steiner tree. This is obtained by merging the tree with red dotted edges of (e) extracted from G and the tree with blue dashed edges of (f) extracted from $G/\{b, d\}$. (Color figure online)

We use the following two results from [9] (see also Fig. 3 for an illustration).

Lemma 1 ([9]). *Let T be an MST for the terminal set K. For any 2-split $T = T_1 \cup E'$, the following two properties hold:*

- *In the graph G, the tree T_1 is an MST for $K_1 \cup A$;*
- *In the graph G/A, the subgraph E'/A (i.e., the result of contracting A in the subgraph of G induced by E') is an MST for $K_2 \cup \{v_A\}$ where v_A denotes the added vertex introduced in G/A during the contraction.*

Theorem 3 ([9]). *Let T be an MST for the terminal set K. For any $\eta > 0$ and any $0 < \alpha \leq \frac{1}{2}$, there exists a 2-split $T = T_1 \cup E'$ such that the following two conditions hold:*

- $(\alpha - \eta)k \leq |K_1| \leq (\alpha + \eta)k$;
- *and* $|A| \leq \lceil \log(1/\eta) \rceil$.

By Lemma 1 and Theorem 3, we obtain the following recursion for any $\eta > 0$ and any $0 < \alpha \leq \frac{1}{2}$:

$$W_G(K) = \min_{\substack{K_1 \subseteq K \\ |K_1| = (\alpha \pm \eta)k}} \min_{\substack{A \subseteq V \\ |A| \leq \lceil \log(1/\eta) \rceil}} \left\{ W_G(K_1 \cup A) + W_{G/A}(K_2 \cup \{v_A\}) \right\}, \quad (2)$$

where K_2 is defined from K and A as $K_2 = K \setminus (K_1 \cup A)$. In Eq. (2) the shorthand "$|K_1| = (\alpha \pm \eta)k$" means $(\alpha - \eta)k \leq |K_1| \leq (\alpha + \eta)k$ and $W_{G/A}(K_2 \cup \{v_A\})$ is the weight of an MST for $K_2 \cup \{v_A\}$ in the graph G/A.

4 Quantum Algorithm for the MST

In this section we present our quantum algorithm for the MST. The main idea is to recursively apply the D-H algorithm on Eq. (2).

4.1 Our Quantum Algorithm

Algorithm 1 shows our quantum algorithm, which consists of a classical part (Step 1) and a quantum part (Step 2). It uses two parameters $\beta \in (0, 1/2]$ and $\varepsilon \in (0, 1)$. The value of β will be set in the analysis of Sect. 4.2, and ε will be a very small constant.

At Step 1, the algorithm computes the values of $W_G(X \cup A)$ and $W_{G/A}(X \cup \{v_A\})$ for all $X \subseteq K$ such that $|X| \leq ((1-\beta)/4 + 15\varepsilon)k$ and all $A \subseteq V$ such that $|A| \leq \lceil \log(1/\varepsilon) \rceil$. (Remember the definition of v_A in Lemma 1). This is done classically, using the D-W algorithm.

At Step 2, we use D-H algorithm on Eq. (2), three times recursively, to compute a minimum Steiner tree for K. Let us now describe more precisely how Step 2 is implemented. The three levels of application of the D-H algorithm in our algorithm use Eq. (2) in a slightly different way:

Algorithm 1. Quantum algorithm for THE MINIMUM STEINER TREE

---

input: a graph $G = (V, E, w)$ and a subset of vertices $K \subseteq V$
parameters: two constants $\beta \in (0, 1/2]$ and $\varepsilon \in (0, 1)$
output: a minimum Steiner tree for K in G.

1. For all $X \subseteq K$ such that $|X| \leq ((1 - \beta)/4 + 15\varepsilon)k$ and all $A \subseteq V$ such that $|A| \leq \lceil \log(1/\varepsilon) \rceil$, compute the values of $W_G(X \cup A)$ and $W_{G/A}(X \cup \{v_A\})$ classically using the D-W algorithm.
2. Apply the D-H algorithm to Eq. (2) three times recursively. In the last recursive call, directly use the values computed at Step 1.

- Level 1: D-H algorithm over Eq. (2) with parameters $\alpha = 1/2$ and $\eta = \varepsilon$. This implements a search over all $K_1 \subset K$ such that $|K_1| = (\frac{1}{2} \pm \varepsilon)k$ and all $A \subseteq V$ such that $|A| \leq \lceil \log(1/\varepsilon) \rceil$. This requires procedures computing $W_G(K_1 \cup A)$ and $W_{G/A}(K_2 \cup \{v_A\})$, where $K_2 = K \backslash (K_1 \cup A)$. These two procedures are implemented at Level 2.
- Level 2: D-H algorithm over each of the following two formulas, which are obtained using Eq. (2) with parameters $\alpha = 1/2$ and $\eta = \varepsilon$.

$$W_G(K_1 \cup A) =$$

$$\min_{\substack{K_2 \subseteq K_1 \cup A \\ |K_2| = (\frac{1}{4} \pm O(\varepsilon))k}} \min_{\substack{A' \subseteq V \\ |A'| \leq \lceil \log(1/\varepsilon) \rceil}} \Big\{ W_G(K_2 \cup A') + W_{G/A'}(K_3 \cup \{v_{A'}\}) \Big\},$$

where $K_3 = (K_1 \cup A) \backslash (K_2 \cup A')$.

$$W_{G/A}(K_2 \cup \{v_A\}) =$$

$$\min_{\substack{K_4 \subseteq K_2 \cup \{v_A\} \\ |K_4| = (\frac{1}{4} \pm O(\varepsilon))k}} \min_{\substack{A' \subseteq V \\ |A'| \leq \lceil \log(1/\varepsilon) \rceil}} \Big\{ W_{G/A}(K_4 \cup A') + W_{(G/A)/A'}(K_5 \cup \{v_{A'}\}) \Big\},$$

where $K_5 = (K_2 \cup \{v_A\}) \backslash (K_4 \cup A')$. This requires procedures computing the four quantities

$$W_G(K_2 \cup A'), \ W_{G/A'}(K_3 \cup \{v_{A'}\}), \ W_{G/A}(K_4 \cup A'), \ W_{(G/A)/A'}(K_5 \cup \{v_{A'}\}).$$

These four procedures are implemented at Level 3.
- Level 3: D-H algorithm over each of the four corresponding formulas, which are obtained from Eq. (2), with parameter $\alpha = \beta$, $\alpha = (1 - \beta)$, $\alpha = \beta$ and $\alpha = (1 - \beta)$, respectively, for some $\beta \in (0, 1/2]$, and parameter $\eta = \varepsilon$. For example, the first formula, which corresponds to the computation of the term $W_G(K_2 \cup A')$, is:

$$W_G(K_2 \cup A') =$$

$$\min_{\substack{K_6 \subseteq K_2 \cup A' \\ |K_6| = (\frac{\beta}{4} \pm O(\varepsilon))k}} \min_{\substack{A'' \subseteq V \\ |A''| \leq \lceil \log(1/\varepsilon) \rceil}} \Big\{ W_G(K_6 \cup A'') + W_{G/A''}(K_7 \cup \{v_{A''}\}) \Big\},$$

$$W_G(K_2 \cup A') =$$

$$\min_{\substack{K_6 \subseteq K_2 \cup A' \\ |K_6| = (\frac{\beta}{4} \pm O(\varepsilon))k}} \min_{\substack{A'' \subseteq V \\ |A''| \leq \lceil \log(1/\varepsilon) \rceil}} \left\{ W_G(K_6 \cup A'') + W_{G/A''}(K_7 \cup \{v_{A''}\}) \right\},$$

where $K_7 = (K_2 \cup A') \setminus (K_6 \cup A'')$. This time, the quantities $W_G(K_6 \cup A'')$ and $W_{G/A''}(K_7 \cup \{v_{A''}\})$ in this formula (and similarly for the other three formulas) can be obtained directly from the values computed at Step 1 of the algorithm.[2]

4.2   Running Time

The parameter ε is a small constant. To simplify the analysis below we introduce the following notation: the symbol $\hat{O}$ hides all factors that are polynomial in n and also all factors of the form $2^{O(\varepsilon k)}$.

Analysis of the Classical Part. Note that constructing the contracted graphs G/A can be done in polynomial time.

By using Theorem 2, the complexity of the classical part of the algorithm is

$$\hat{O}\left(\binom{k}{(1-\beta)k/4} 2^{(1-\beta)k/4} \right) = \hat{O}\left(2^{(H(\frac{1-\beta}{4}) + \frac{1-\beta}{4})k} \right). \tag{3}$$

The Quantum Part. At step 2 of our algorithm, we apply the D-H algorithm in three levels. The size of the search space of the D-H algorithm executed at Level 1 is

$$\hat{O}\left(\binom{k}{k/2} \right). \tag{4}$$

The size of the search space of each of the two executions of the D-H algorithm at Level 2 is

$$\hat{O}\left(\binom{k/2}{k/4} \right). \tag{5}$$

The size of the search space of each of the four executions of the D-H algorithm at Level 3 is

$$\hat{O}\left(\binom{k/4}{\beta k/4} \right), \tag{6}$$

respectively. The complexity of the quantum part of this algorithm is thus

$$\hat{O}\left(\sqrt{\binom{k}{k/2}\binom{k/2}{k/4}\binom{k/4}{\beta k/4}} \right). \tag{7}$$

---

[2] Indeed, it is easy to check that all the $O(\varepsilon)$ terms in the above analysis are actually upper bounded by 15ε.

Analysis of the Parameter β. Using Stirling's Formula, the classical and quantum parts of the complexity (Eqs. (3) and (7)) can be respectively expressed as

$$\hat{\mathcal{O}}\left(2^{\left(H\left(\frac{1-\beta}{4}\right)+\frac{1-\beta}{4}\right)k}\right) \text{ and } \hat{\mathcal{O}}\left(2^{\frac{1}{2}\left(\frac{3}{2}+\frac{H(\beta)}{4}\right)k}\right). \tag{8}$$

Since the complexity is minimized when the complexities of the classical and quantum parts equal, we can optimize the parameter β by solving the following equation:

$$H\left(\frac{1-\beta}{4}\right) + \frac{1-\beta}{4} = \frac{1}{2}\left(\frac{3}{2} + \frac{H(\beta)}{4}\right). \tag{9}$$

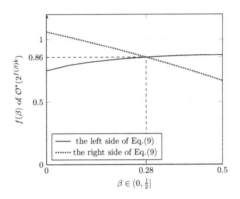

Fig. 4. Running time of our algorithm.

Numerical calculation show that the solution of this equation is $\beta \approx 0.28325$, which gives total running time $\hat{\mathcal{O}}(c^k)$ for $c = 1.8118...$ (see also Fig. 4). By taking an appropriately small choice of ε, we thus obtain running time $\mathcal{O}^*(1.812^k)$, as claimed in Theorem 1.

Remark 1. Introducing additional parameters in level 1 or level 2 of Step 2 (instead of using $\alpha = 1/2$) does not improve the running time. Modifying the number of levels (e.g., using two levels, or four levels) also leads to a worse complexity.

Acknowledgements. The authors are grateful to Shin-ichi Minato for his support. FLG was supported by JSPS KAKENHI grants Nos. JP16H01705, JP19H04066, JP20H00579, JP20H04139 and by the MEXT Quantum Leap Flagship Program (MEXT Q-LEAP) grant No. JPMXS0118067394.

References

1. Ambainis, A., Balodis, K., Iraids, J., Kokainis, M., Prūsis, K., Vihrovs, J.: Quantum speedups for exponential-time dynamic programming algorithms. In: Proceedings of the Thirtieth Annual ACM-SIAM Symposium on Discrete Algorithms, pp. 1783–1793. SIAM (2019)

2. Björklund, A., Husfeldt, T., Kaski, P., Koivisto, M.: Fourier meets Möbius: fast subset convolution. In: Proceedings of the Thirty-Ninth Annual ACM Symposium on Theory of Computing, pp. 67–74 (2007)
3. Boyer, M., Brassard, G., Høyer, P., Tapp, A.: Tight bounds on quantum searching. Fortschritte der Physik: Prog. Phys. **46**(4–5), 493–505 (1998)
4. Brassard, G., Hoyer, P., Mosca, M., Tapp, A.: Quantum amplitude amplification and estimation. Contemp. Math. **305**, 53–74 (2002)
5. Downey, R.G., Fellows, M.R.: Parameterized Complexity. Springer, Heidelberg (2012)
6. Dreyfus, S.E., Wagner, R.A.: The Steiner problem in graphs. Networks **1**(3), 195–207 (1971)
7. Durr, C., Hoyer, P.: A quantum algorithm for finding the minimum. arXiv preprint quant-ph/9607014 (1996)
8. Flum, J., Grohe, M.: Parameterized Complexity Theory. Springer, Heidelberg (2006)
9. Fuchs, B., Kern, W., Wang, X.: Speeding up the Dreyfus-Wagner algorithm for minimum Steiner trees. Math. Methods Oper. Res. **66**(1), 117–125 (2007)
10. Grover, L.K.: A fast quantum mechanical algorithm for database search. In: Proceedings of the Twenty-Eighth Annual ACM Symposium on Theory of Computing, pp. 212–219 (1996)
11. Held, M., Karp, R.M.: A dynamic programming approach to sequencing problems. J. Soc. Ind. Appl. Math. **10**(1), 196–210 (1962)
12. Hwang, F.K., Richards, D.S.: Steiner tree problems. Networks **22**(1), 55–89 (1992)
13. Karp, R.M.: Reducibility among combinatorial problems. In: Miller, R.E., Thatcher, J.W., Bohlinger, J.D. (eds.) Complexity of Computer Computations. The IBM Research Symposia Series, pp. 85–103. Springer, Boston (1972). https://doi.org/10.1007/978-1-4684-2001-2_9
14. Mölle, D., Richter, S., Rossmanith, P.: A faster algorithm for the Steiner Tree problem. In: Durand, B., Thomas, W. (eds.) STACS 2006. LNCS, vol. 3884, pp. 561–570. Springer, Heidelberg (2006). https://doi.org/10.1007/11672142_46
15. Mosca, M.: Quantum searching, counting and amplitude amplification by eigenvector analysis. In: MFCS 1998 Workshop on Randomized Algorithms, pp. 90–100 (1998)

Access Structure Hiding Secret Sharing from Novel Set Systems and Vector Families

Vipin Singh Sehrawat[1(✉)] and Yvo Desmedt[2,3]

[1] Seagate Technology, Singapore, Singapore
vipin.sehrawat.cs@gmail.com
[2] The University of Texas at Dallas, Richardson, USA
[3] University College London, London, UK

Abstract. Secret sharing provides a means to distribute shares of a secret such that any authorized subset of shares, specified by an access structure, can be pooled together to recompute the secret. The standard secret sharing model requires public access structures, which violates privacy and facilitates the adversary by revealing the high-value targets. In this paper, we address this shortcoming by introducing *hidden access structures*, which remain secret until some authorized subset of parties collaborate. The central piece of this work is the construction of a set-system $\mathcal{H}$ with strictly greater than $\exp\left(c\dfrac{1.5(\log h)^2}{\log\log h}\right)$ subsets of a set of h elements. Our set-system $\mathcal{H}$ is defined over $\mathbb{Z}_m$, where m is a non-prime-power, such that the size of each set in $\mathcal{H}$ is divisible by m but the sizes of their pairwise intersections are not divisible by m, unless one set is a subset of another. We derive a vector family $\mathcal{V}$ from $\mathcal{H}$ such that superset-subset relationships in $\mathcal{H}$ are represented by inner products in $\mathcal{V}$. We use $\mathcal{V}$ to "encode" *any* access structure and thereby develop the first *access structure hiding secret sharing* scheme. The information rate (secret-size/maximum-share-size) of our scheme is $1/2$. For a setting with ℓ parties, our scheme supports 2^{ℓ} out of the $2^{2^{\ell-O(\log\ell)}}$ possible access structures. The scheme assumes semi-honest polynomial-time parties, and its security relies on the Generalized Diffie-Hellman assumption.

Keywords: Computational secret sharing · Hidden access structures · Computational hiding · Computational secrecy · Extremal set theory.

1 Introduction

A secret sharing scheme [4,9,13] is a method by which a dealer, holding a secret string, distributes strings, called shares, to parties such that authorized subsets

V. S. Sehrawat—This work was done while the author was a PhD candidate at institute[2].

V. S. Sehrawat and Y. Desmedt—Research partially supported by NPRP award NPRP8-2158-1-423 from the Qatar National Research Fund (a member of The Qatar Foundation). The statements made herein are solely the responsibility of the authors.

© Springer Nature Switzerland AG 2020
D. Kim et al. (Eds.): COCOON 2020, LNCS 12273, pp. 246–261, 2020.
https://doi.org/10.1007/978-3-030-58150-3_20

of parties, specified by a public access structure, can reconstruct the secret. Secret sharing is a foundational tool with many applications in cryptography, distributed computing and secure storage. The extensive survey by Beimel [2] gives a review of the notable results in the area.

Motivation. Existing secret sharing model requires the access structure to be known to the parties. Since secret reconstruction requires shares of any authorized subset, from the access structure, having a public access structure reveals the high-value targets, which can lead to compromised security in the presence of malicious parties. Having a public access structure also implies that some parties must publicly consent to the fact that they themselves are not trusted.

Need for Hidden Access Structures: Consider a scenario where Alice calls her lawyer to dictate her will/testament. She instructs that each of her 15 family members should receive a valid "share" of the will. In addition, the shares should be indistinguishable from each other in terms of size and entropy. She also insists that in order to reconstruct her will, {Bob, Tom, Catherine} or {Bob, Cristine, Keri, Roger} or {Rob, Eve} must be part of the collaborating set. But, Alice does not want to be in the bad books of her other, less trusted family members. So, she demands that the shares of her will and the procedure to reconstruct it back from the shares must not reveal her "trust structures", until after the will is successfully reconstructed. This problem can be generalized to secret sharing, but with *hidden access structures*, which remain secret until some authorized subset of parties collaborate.

Superpolynomial Size Set-Systems and Efficient Cryptography: In this paper, we demonstrate that set-systems with specific intersections can be used to enhance existing cryptographic protocols, particularly the ones meant for distributed security. In order to minimize the computational cost of cryptographic protocols, it is desirable that parameters such as exponents, moduli and dimensions do not grow too big. For a set-system whose size is superpolynomial in the number of elements over which it is defined, achieving a large enough size requires smaller modulus and fewer number of elements, which translates into smaller dimensions, exponents and moduli for its cryptographic applications.

Our Contributions. We bolster the privacy guarantees of secret sharing by introducing *hidden access structures*, which remain unknown until some authorized subset of parties collaborate. We develop the first access structure hiding (computational) secret sharing scheme. As the basis of our scheme, we construct a novel set-system, which is defined by the following theorem.

Theorem 1. *Let $\{\alpha_i\}_{i=1}^r$, be $r > 1$ positive integers, and $m = \prod_{i=1}^r p_i^{\alpha_i}$ be a positive integer with r different prime divisors: $p_1, \ldots, p_r$. Then there exists $c = c(m) > 0$, such that for every integer $h > 0$, there exists an explicitly constructible non-uniform[1] set-system $\mathcal{H}$ over a universe of h elements such that the following conditions hold:*

---

[1] all member sets do not have equal size.

1. $|\mathcal{H}| > \exp\left(c\dfrac{1.5(\log h)^r}{(\log\log h)^{r-1}}\right),$

2. $\forall H \in \mathcal{H} : |H| = 0 \bmod m,$

3. $\forall G, H \in \mathcal{H},$ where $G \neq H$: if $H \subset G$ or $G \subset H,$ then $|G \cap H| = 0 \bmod m,$
   else $|G \cap H| \neq 0 \bmod m,$

4. $\forall G, H \in \mathcal{H},$ where $G \neq H$ and $\forall i \in \{1, \ldots, r\} : |G \cap H| \in \{0, 1\} \bmod p_i^{\alpha_i}.$

(Recall that $a \bmod m$ denotes the smallest non-negative $b = a \bmod m$.) In secret sharing, the family of minimal authorized subsets $\Gamma_0 \in \Gamma,$ corresponding to an access structure $\Gamma,$ is defined as the collection of the minimal sets in $\Gamma.$ Therefore, Γ_0 forms the *basis* of $\Gamma.$ Note that Conditions 2 and 3 of Theorem 1 define the superset-subset relations in the set-system $\mathcal{H}.$ We derive a family of vectors $\mathcal{V} \in (\mathbb{Z}_m)^h$ from our set-system $\mathcal{H},$ that captures the superset-subset relations in $\mathcal{H}$ as (vector) inner products in $\mathcal{V}.$ This capability allows us to capture "information" about any minimal authorized subset $\mathcal{A} \in \Gamma_0$ in the form of an inner product, enabling efficient testing of whether a given subset of parties $\mathcal{B}$ is a superset of $\mathcal{A}$ or not. Since Γ is monotone, $\mathcal{B} \supseteq \mathcal{A},$ for some $\mathcal{A} \in \Gamma_0,$ implies that $\mathcal{B} \in \Gamma,$ i.e., $\mathcal{B}$ is an authorized subset of parties. Similarly, $\mathcal{B} \not\supseteq \mathcal{A},$ for all $\mathcal{A} \in \Gamma_0,$ implies that $\mathcal{B} \notin \Gamma,$ i.e., $\mathcal{B}$ is not an authorized subset of parties. We use our novel set-system and vector family to construct the first access structure hiding (computational) secret sharing scheme. We assume semi-honest polynomial-time parties, and reduce the security and privacy guarantees of our scheme to the Generalized Diffie-Hellman assumption [14]. The maximum share size for our scheme is $\approx 2|k|,$ where $|k|$ is the length of the secret.

Organization. The rest of this paper is organized as follows: we recall the pertinent background and results in Sect. 2. Section 3 formally defines access structure hiding computational secret sharing. We present the construction of our set-systems and vector families in Sect. 4, and use them to develop the first access structure hiding computational secret sharing scheme in Sect. 5. We finish by describing two open problems.

2 Preliminaries

We begin by recalling an informal definition of the Generalized Diffie-Hellman (GDH) assumption [14]. For a formal definition, see [3]. For a positive integer $n,$ we define $[n] := \{1, \ldots, n\}.$

Definition 1 (GDH Assumption: Informal). Let $\{a_1, a_2, \ldots, a_n\}$ be a set of n different integers. Given a group G and an element $g \in G,$ it is hard to compute $g^{\prod_{i \in [n]} a_i}$ for an algorithm that can query $g^{\prod_{i \in I} a_i}$ for any proper subset $I \subsetneq [n].$

Definition 2 (Dirichlet's Theorem (1837)). For all coprime integers a and $q,$ there are infinitely many primes, $p,$ of the form $p = a \bmod q.$

Definition 3 (Euler's Theorem). Let y be a positive integer and $\mathbb{Z}_y^*$ denote the multiplicative group mod $y.$ Then for every integer c that is coprime to $y,$ it holds that: $c^{\varphi(y)} = 1 \bmod y,$ where $\varphi(y) = |\mathbb{Z}_y^*|$ denotes Euler's totient function.

Definition 4 (Hadamard/Schur product). For any two vectors $\mathbf{u}, \mathbf{v} \in \mathcal{R}^n$, their Hadamard/Schur product, denoted by $\mathbf{u} \circ \mathbf{v}$, is a vector in the same linear space whose i-th element is defined as: $(\mathbf{u} \circ \mathbf{v})[i] = \mathbf{u}[i] \cdot \mathbf{v}[i]$, for all $i \in [n]$.

Definition 5 (Negligible Function). For security parameter ω, a function $\epsilon(\omega)$ is called *negligible* if for all $c > 0$ there exists a ω_0 such that $\epsilon(\omega) < 1/\omega^c$ for all $\omega > \omega_0$.

Definition 6 (Computational Indistinguishability [6]). Let $X = \{X_\omega\}_{\omega \in \mathbb{N}}$ and $Y = \{Y_\omega\}_{\omega \in \mathbb{N}}$ be ensembles, where X_ω's and Y_ω's are probability distributions over $\{0,1\}^{\kappa(\omega)}$ for some polynomial $\kappa(\omega)$. We say that $\{X_\omega\}_{\omega \in \mathbb{N}}$ and $\{Y_\omega\}_{\omega \in \mathbb{N}}$ are polynomially/computationally indistinguishable if the following holds for every (probabilistic) polynomial-time algorithm $\mathcal{D}$ and all $\omega \in \mathbb{N}$:

$$\Big| \Pr[t \leftarrow X_\omega : \mathcal{D}(t) = 1] - \Pr[t \leftarrow Y_\omega : \mathcal{D}(t) = 1] \Big| \leq \epsilon(\omega),$$

where ϵ is a negligible function.

Definition 7 (Access Structure). Let $\mathcal{P} = \{P_1, \ldots, P_\ell\}$ be a set of parties. A collection $\Gamma \subseteq 2^\mathcal{P}$ is monotone if $\mathcal{A} \in \Gamma$ and $\mathcal{A} \subseteq \mathcal{B}$ imply that $\mathcal{B} \in \Gamma$. An access structure $\Gamma \subseteq 2^\mathcal{P}$ is a monotone collection of non-empty subsets of $\mathcal{P}$. Sets in Γ are called authorized, and sets not in Γ are called unauthorized.

If Γ consists of all subsets of $\mathcal{P}$ with size greater than or equal to a fixed threshold t ($1 \leq t \leq \ell$), then Γ is called a t-threshold access structure.

Definition 8 (Minimal Authorized Subset). For an access structure Γ, a family of minimal authorized subsets $\Gamma_0 \in \Gamma$ is defined as:

$$\Gamma_0 = \{\mathcal{A} \in \Gamma : \mathcal{B} \not\subset \mathcal{A} \text{ for all } \mathcal{B} \in \Gamma \setminus \{\mathcal{A}\}\}.$$

Definition 9 (Computational Secret Sharing [11]). A computational secret sharing scheme with respect to an access structure Γ, a security parameter ω, a set of ℓ polynomial-time parties $\mathcal{P} = \{P_1, \ldots, P_\ell\}$, and a set of secrets $\mathcal{K}$, consists of a pair of polynomial-time algorithms, (Share, Recon), where:

- Share is a randomized algorithm that gets a secret $k \in \mathcal{K}$ and access structure Γ as inputs, and outputs ℓ shares, $\{\Pi_1^{(k)}, \ldots, \Pi_\ell^{(k)}\}$, of k,
- Recon is a deterministic algorithm that gets as input the shares of a subset $\mathcal{A} \subseteq \mathcal{P}$, denoted by $\{\Pi_i^{(k)}\}_{i \in \mathcal{A}}$, and outputs a string in $\mathcal{K}$,

such that, the following two requirements are satisfied:

1. *Perfect Correctness:* for all secrets $k \in \mathcal{K}$ and every authorized subset $\mathcal{A} \in \Gamma$, it holds that: $\Pr[\text{Recon}(\{\Pi_i^{(k)}\}_{i \in \mathcal{A}}, \mathcal{A}) = k] = 1$,
2. *Computational Secrecy:* for every unauthorized subset $\mathcal{B} \notin \Gamma$ and all different secrets $k_1, k_2 \in \mathcal{K}$, it holds that the distributions $\{\Pi_i^{(k_1)}\}_{i \in \mathcal{B}}$ and $\{\Pi_i^{(k_2)}\}_{i \in \mathcal{B}}$ are computationally indistinguishable (with respect to ω).

Remark 1 (Perfect Secrecy). If $\forall k_1, k_2 \in \mathcal{K}$ with $k_1 \neq k_2$, the distributions $\{\Pi_i^{(k_1)}\}_{i \in \mathcal{B}}$ and $\{\Pi_i^{(k_2)}\}_{i \in \mathcal{B}}$ are identical, then the scheme is called a perfect secret sharing scheme.

2.1 Set Systems with Restricted Intersections

The problem of constructing set systems under certain intersection restrictions and bounding their size has a central place in Extremal Set Theory. We shall not give a full account of such problems, but only touch upon the results that are particularly relevant to our set-system and its construction. For a broader account, we refer the interested reader to the survey by Frankl and Tokushige [5].

Lemma 1 ([8]). *Let $m = \prod_{i=1}^{r} p_i^{\alpha_i}$ be a positive integer with $r > 1$ different prime divisors. Then there exists an explicitly constructible polynomial Q with n variables and degree $O(n^{1/r})$, which is equal to 0 on $z = (1, 1, \ldots, 1) \in \{0,1\}^n$ but is nonzero mod m on all other $z \in \{0,1\}^n$. Furthermore, $\forall z \in \{0,1\}^n$ and $\forall i \in \{1, \ldots, r\}$, it holds that: $Q(z) \in \{0,1\}$ mod $p_i^{\alpha_i}$.*

Theorem 2 ([8]). *Let m be a positive integer, and suppose that m has $r > 1$ different prime divisors: $m = \prod_{i=1}^{r} p_i^{\alpha_i}$. Then there exists $c = c(m) > 0$, such that for every integer $h > 0$, there exists an explicitly constructible uniform set-system $\mathcal{H}$ over a universe of h elements such that:*

1. $|\mathcal{H}| \geq exp\left(c\dfrac{(\log h)^r}{(\log \log h)^{r-1}}\right)$,
2. $\forall H \in \mathcal{H} : |H| = 0 \bmod m$,
3. $\forall G, H \in \mathcal{H}, G \neq H : |G \cap H| \neq 0 \bmod m$.

3 Access Structure Hiding Computational Secret Sharing

In this section, we give a formal definition of an access structure hiding computational secret sharing scheme.

Definition 10. An access structure hiding computational secret sharing scheme with respect to an access structure Γ, a set of ℓ polynomial-time parties $\mathcal{P} = \{P_1, \ldots, P_\ell\}$, a set of secrets $\mathcal{K}$ and a security parameter ω, consists of two pairs of polynomial-time algorithms, (HsGen, HsVer) and (Share, Recon), where (Share, Recon) are the same as defined in the definition of computational secret sharing (see Definition 9), and (HsGen, HsVer) are defined as:

- HsGen is a randomized algorithm that gets $\mathcal{P}$ and Γ as inputs, and outputs ℓ *access structure tokens* $\{\mho_1^{(\Gamma)}, \ldots, \mho_\ell^{(\Gamma)}\}$,
- HsVer is a deterministic algorithm that gets as input the *access structure tokens* of a subset $\mathcal{A} \subseteq \mathcal{P}$, denoted by $\{\mho_i^{(\Gamma)}\}_{i \in \mathcal{A}}$, and outputs $b \in \{0,1\}$,

such that, the following three requirements are satisfied:

1. *Perfect Completeness:* every authorized subset of parties $\mathcal{A} \in \Gamma$ can identify itself to be a member of the access structure Γ, i.e., formally, it holds that:
   $Pr[\text{HsVer}(\{\mho_i^{(\Gamma)}\}_{i \in \mathcal{A}}) = 1] = 1$,

2. *Perfect Soundness:* every unauthorized subset of parties $\mathcal{B} \notin \Gamma$ can identify itself to be outside of the access structure Γ, i.e., formally, it holds that:
$Pr[\text{HsVer}(\{\mho_i^{(\Gamma)}\}_{i \in \mathcal{B}}) = 0] = 1$,

3. *Computational Hiding:* for all access structures $\Gamma, \Gamma' \subseteq 2^\mathcal{P}$, where $\Gamma \neq \Gamma'$, and each subset of parties $\mathcal{B} \notin \Gamma, \Gamma'$ that is unauthorized in both Γ and Γ', it holds that:

$$\left| Pr[\Gamma \mid \{\mho_i^{(\Gamma)}\}_{i \in \mathcal{B}}, \{\Pi_i^{(k)}\}_{i \in \mathcal{B}}] - Pr[\Gamma' \mid \{\mho_i^{(\Gamma)}\}_{i \in \mathcal{B}}, \{\Pi_i^{(k)}\}_{i \in \mathcal{B}}] \right| \leq \epsilon(\omega),$$

where ϵ is a negligible function and $\{\Pi_i^{(k)}\}_{i \in \mathcal{B}}$ denotes the subset of shares of a secret k, that belong to the parties in $\mathcal{B}$, and are generated by Share with respect to the access structure Γ.

4   Novel Set-Systems and Vector Families

In this section, we construct our novel set-systems and vector families. The following notations are frequently used throughout this section.

- We denote the coefficient of x^k in the power series for $f(x)$ by $[x^k] : f(x)$,
- Let L be an ordered list of a finite number of different symbols, and $u \in L^e$ be a string comprised of $e \in \mathbb{N}$ different symbols from L. We define $\rhd$ to represent *string membership*, i.e., $j \rhd u$ denotes that the string u contains the jth symbol from the ordered list L.

4.1   Set System Construction

In this section, we provide the proof for Theorem 1 by giving an explicit construction of the set-system $\mathcal{H}$ defined in it.

Proof (Theorem 1). We use the polynomial Q defined in Lemma 1 to construct our set-system. We begin by recalling the following property of Q:

$$Q(z) = 0 \bmod m \iff z_1 = z_2 = \cdots = z_n = 1, \tag{4.1}$$

where $z = (z_1, z_2, \ldots z_n) \in \{0,1\}^n$. We know from Lemma 1 that Q has degree $d = O(n^{1/r})$, and can be written as:

$$Q(z_1, z_2, \ldots, z_n) = \sum_{i_1, i_2, \ldots, i_l} a_{i_1, i_2, \ldots, i_l} z_{i_1} z_{i_2} \ldots z_{i_l},$$

where $0 \leq l \leq d$, and $a_{i_1, i_2, \ldots, i_l} \in \mathbb{Z}$ with $1 \leq i_1 < i_2 < \cdots < i_l \leq n$. Reducing that modulo m, we get:

$$\tilde{Q}(z_1, z_2, \ldots, z_n) = \sum_{i_1, i_2, \ldots, i_l} \tilde{a}_{i_1, i_2, \ldots, i_l} z_{i_1} z_{i_2} \ldots z_{i_l}, \tag{4.2}$$

where $\tilde{a}_{i_1,i_2,\ldots,i_l} = a_{i_1,i_2,\ldots,i_l} \bmod m$. Let $L = (0,1,\ldots,n-1)$ be an ordered list of n symbols. Define a characteristic function $\psi : \{0,1,\ldots,n-1\}^n \to \{0,1\}^n$ as:

$$\psi(u)[j] := \begin{cases} 1 & \text{if } j \rhd u \\ 0 & \text{otherwise,} \end{cases} \tag{4.3}$$

where $1 \le j \le n$ and $\psi(u)[j]$ denotes the jth bit of $\psi(u) \in \{0,1\}^n$. If a string $u \in \{0,1,\ldots,n-1\}^n$, defined over the symbols in L, contains the jth symbol from the ordered list L, then $\psi(u)[j] = 1$, else $\psi(u)[j] = 0$. Define a comparison function $\delta(x,y) : \{0,1\} \times \{0,1\} \to \{0,1\}$ as:

$$\delta(u,v) := \neg(u \oplus v), \tag{4.4}$$

where $\neg$ and $\oplus$ denote negation and XOR, respectively. Hence, $\delta(u,v) = 1$ if $u = v$, else $\delta(u,v) = 0$. Let $\mathbf{A} = (a_{x,y})$ be a $n^n \times n^n$ matrix ($x,y \in \{0,1,\ldots,n-1\}^n$). For $x' = \psi(x)$ and $y' = \psi(y)$, define each entry $a_{x,y}$ as:

$$a_{x,y} = \tilde{Q}(\delta(x_1',y_1'),\delta(x_2',y_2'),\ldots,\delta(x_n',y_n')) \bmod m, \tag{4.5}$$

where $\tilde{Q}(\cdot)$ is the polynomial defined in Eq. 4.2, and x_j', y_j' denote the jth bit of the binary bit strings $x', y' \in \{0,1\}^n$. It follows from Eq. 4.3, Eq. 4.4 and Eq. 4.5 that if $a_{x,y} = \tilde{Q}(1,1,\ldots,1) = 0 \bmod m$, then either $x = y$ or $\forall j \in [n]$ it holds that $y_j' = x_j'$, i.e., x and y are comprised of the same symbols. In both cases, we say that x and y "cover" each other, and denote it by $x \Upsilon y$. We know from Eq. 4.2 that the polynomial $\tilde{Q}(z)$ can be defined as a sum of monomials $z_{i_1} z_{i_2} \ldots z_{i_l}$ ($l \le d$), where each monomial $z_{i_1} z_{i_2} \ldots z_{i_l}$ occurs with multiplicity $\tilde{a}_{i_1,i_2,\ldots,i_l}$ in the sum. Therefore, since matrix $\mathbf{A}$ is generated via $\tilde{Q}$, it follows from Eq. 4.2 that $\mathbf{A}$ can be defined as the sum of matrices $\mathbf{B}_{i_1,i_2,\ldots,i_l}$, whose entries are defined as:

$$b_{x,y}^{i_1,i_2,\ldots,i_l} = \delta(x_{i_1}',y_{i_1}')\delta(x_{i_2}',y_{i_2}')\ldots\delta(x_{i_l}',y_{i_l}'). \tag{4.6}$$

Hence, it follows from Eq. 4.2, Eq. 4.5 and Eq. 4.6, that $\mathbf{A}$ can be written as:

$$\mathbf{A} = \sum_{i_1,i_2,\ldots,i_l} \tilde{a}_{i_1,i_2,\ldots,i_l} \mathbf{B}_{i_1,i_2,\ldots,i_l}, \tag{4.7}$$

where $\tilde{a}_{i_1,i_2,\ldots,i_l}$ is the multiplicity with which the matrix $\mathbf{B}_{i_1,i_2,\ldots,i_l}$ occurs in the sum. Next, we analyze the matrices $\mathbf{A}$ and $\mathbf{B}_{i_1,i_2,\ldots,i_l}$. In particular, we count the number of 0 entries in $\mathbf{A}$ and the number of 1 entries in $\mathbf{B}_{i_1,i_2,\ldots,i_l}$.

Analysis of the Matrices. We begin by counting the total number of entries $a_{x,y} \in \mathbf{A}$ that are equal to 0, which translates into counting the number of $x,y \in \{0,1,\ldots,n-1\}^n$ such that $x \Upsilon y$.

Let S be a set of n different symbols. Let *unique symbol weight* (USW) denote the number of different symbols in a string, i.e., $\text{USW}(x) = \text{w}(\psi(x))$, where $\text{w}(\cdot)$ denotes the Hamming weight. To form a string x of length n such that $USW(x) = k$, for a fixed $k \leq n$, the first step is to select k distinct symbols $s_{i_1}, s_{i_2} \ldots, s_{i_k}$ from $\mathcal{S}$. We know from Rosen [12] (Section 2.4.2), that the number of onto functions from a set of n elements to a set of k elements is given by $k! \{ {n \atop k} \}$, where $\{ {n \atop k} \}$ denotes Stirling number of the second kind (see Graham et al. [7], p. 257). Hence, $k! \{ {n \atop k} \}$ is the total number of strings of length n, that contain exactly the selected k-out-of-n symbols: $s_{i_1}, s_{i_2} \ldots, s_{i_k}$.

Let N_k denote the total number of different $x \in \{0, 1, \ldots, n-1\}^n$ such that $USW(x) = k$. We know that for a fixed set of k-out-of-n symbols, the number strings $x \in \{0, 1, \ldots, n-1\}^n$ satisfying $USW(x) = k$ is $k! \{ {n \atop k} \}$. Accounting for the number of ways one can choose k-out-of-n symbols, we get: $N_k = \binom{n}{k} k! \{ {n \atop k} \}$.

We know that for each k, there are N_k rows in matrix $\mathbf{A}$ that "cover" exactly $k! \{ {n \atop k} \}$ entries. Hence, from Eq. 4.5, the number of $a_{x,y} = 0 \bmod m$ entries in $\mathbf{A}$ is:

$$S(n) = \sum_{k=1}^{n} N_k \cdot k! \left\{ {n \atop k} \right\} = \sum_{k=1}^{n} \binom{n}{k} k! \left\{ {n \atop k} \right\} k! \left\{ {n \atop k} \right\}. \tag{4.8}$$

We recall the following well known identities involving the first-order Eulerian numbers (see Graham et al. [7], p. 267) and Stirling numbers of the second kind:

$$\ell! \left\{ {n \atop \ell} \right\} = \sum_{k=0}^{n} \left\langle {n \atop k} \right\rangle \binom{k}{n-\ell}; \qquad (n-\ell)! \left\{ {n \atop n-\ell} \right\} = \sum_{k=0}^{n} \left\langle {n \atop k} \right\rangle \binom{k}{\ell},$$

where $\left\langle {n \atop k} \right\rangle$ denotes the first-order Eulerian number, which gives the total number of permutations $\pi_1, \pi_2, \ldots, \pi_n$ with k ascents, i.e., k places where $\pi_t < \pi_{t+1}$. Therefore, Eq. 4.8 can be rewritten as:

$$S(n) = \sum_{k=0}^{n} \binom{n}{k} k! \left\{ {n \atop k} \right\} k! \left\{ {n \atop k} \right\}$$

$$= \sum_{k=0}^{n} \binom{n}{k} k! \left\{ {n \atop k} \right\} \sum_{j=0}^{n} \left\langle {n \atop j} \right\rangle \binom{j}{n-k}$$

$$= n! \sum_{k=0}^{n} \left\{ {n \atop k} \right\} \left(\sum_{j=0}^{n} \left\langle {n \atop j} \right\rangle \binom{j}{n-k} \right) \frac{1}{(n-k)!}.$$

Thus, the exponential generating function for $S(n)$ comes out to be:

$$\sum_{n \geq 0} S(n) \frac{x^n}{n!} = \sum_{n \geq 0} \sum_{k=0}^{n} \left\{ {n \atop k} \right\} x^k \left(\sum_{j=0}^{n} \left\langle {n \atop j} \right\rangle \binom{j}{n-k} \right) \frac{x^{n-k}}{(n-k)!}.$$

Recall the following definition of Touchard polynomial (Jacques Touchard (1939)):

$$T_n(x) = \sum_{k=0}^{n} \left\{ {n \atop k} \right\} x^k.$$

We write $S(n)$ as:

$$S(n) = n![x^n] : (T_n(x)P_n(x)), \tag{4.9}$$

where the second polynomial, $P_n(x)$, is defined via convolution as:

$$P_n(x) = \sum_{k=0}^{n} \left(\sum_{j=0}^{n} \left\langle \binom{n}{j} \right\rangle \binom{j}{k} \right) \frac{x^k}{k!} = \sum_{k=0}^{n} \frac{(n-k)!}{k!} \left\{ \begin{matrix} n \\ n-k \end{matrix} \right\} x^k.$$

Observe that all diagonal entries $a_{x,x}$ in matrix $\mathbf{A}$ are 0, and $\mathbf{A}$ is symmetric across its diagonal.

Lemma 2. *Let the term* B-entries *denote the entries* $b_{x,y}^{i_1,i_2,\ldots,i_l} \in \mathbf{B}_{i_1,i_2,\ldots,i_l}$ *that are equal to 1. Then the following holds for* B-entries:

1. $\forall x \in \{0,1,\ldots,n-1\}^n$, *each entry* $a_{x,x} \in \mathbf{A}$ *has the same number of* B-entries, $b_{x,x}^{i_1,i_2,\ldots,i_l} = 1$, *and this number is divisible by* m,
2. *for each pair* x,y $(x,y \in \{0,1,\ldots,n-1\}^n)$, *the total number of* B-entries, $b_{x,y}^{i_1,i_2,\ldots,i_l} = 1$, *corresponding to* $a_{x,y} \in \mathbf{A}$, *is divisible by* m *iff* $x \Upsilon y$, *else not.*

Proof. We know from Eq. 4.6 that except for the B-entries, all other entries in matrices $\mathbf{B}_{i_1,i_2,\ldots,i_l}$ are equal to 0. Hence, it follows from Eq. 4.7 that each entry $a_{x,y} \in \mathbf{A}$ is simply the total number of B-entries, $b_{x,y}^{i_1,i_2,\ldots,i_l} = 1$. It further follows from Eq. 4.5 and Eq. 4.1 that for all x, we get $a_{x,x} = \tilde{Q}(1,1,\ldots,1) = 0 \bmod m$, i.e., for all x, the total number of B-entries, $b_{x,x}^{i_1,i_2,\ldots,i_l} = 1$, is divisible by m. Furthermore, it follows from Eq. 4.6 that because $x = x$, all entries $b_{x,x}^{i_1,i_2,\ldots,i_l}$ are indeed B-entries and all cells $a_{x,x}$ have the same number of corresponding B-entries, $b_{x,x}^{i_1,i_2,\ldots,i_l} = 1$. Finally, it follows from Eq. 4.5 and Eq. 4.1 that for all pairs (x,y), where $x \neq y$, the total number of B-entries, $b_{x,y}^{i_1,i_2,\ldots,i_l} = 1$, is: $a_{x,y} = \tilde{Q}(1,1,\ldots,1) = 0 \bmod m$ if $x \Upsilon y$, and $a_{x,y} \neq 0 \bmod m$ otherwise. ∎

By taking all $a_{x,y} = 0 \bmod m$ $(\forall x,y \in \{0,1,\ldots,n-1\}^n)$ entries of $\mathbf{A}$ to denote sets with the corresponding B-entries, $b_{x,y}^{i_1,i_2,\ldots,i_l} = 1$, as the elements in those sets leads to a set-system $\mathcal{H}$, that satisfies Conditions 2 and 3 of Theorem 1. The number of elements, h, over which $\mathcal{H}$ is defined is:

$$h = \tilde{Q}(n,n,\ldots,n) = \sum_{l \leq d} \sum \tilde{a}_{i_1,i_2,\ldots,i_l} n^l \leq (m-1) \sum_{l \leq d} \binom{n}{l} n^l$$

$$< (m-1) \sum_{l \leq d} n^{2l}/l! < 2(m-1)n^{2d}/d!,$$

assuming $n \geq 2d$. For the sake of convenience, we assume $n > 2$. From Eq. 4.9, it is easy to verify that the following holds for $n > 2$:

$$|\mathcal{H}| = S(n) > n^{1.5n}. \tag{4.10}$$

We know from [8] that for $r > 1, m = \prod_{i=1}^{r} p_i^{\alpha_i}, d = O(n^{1/r}), c = c(m) > 0$ and $h < 2(m-1)n^{2d}/d!$, the following relation holds:

$$n^n \geq \exp\left(c\frac{(\log h)^r}{(\log \log h)^{r-1}}\right).$$

Therefore, the following can be derived from Eq. 4.10 and elementary estimations for binomial coefficients:

$$|\mathcal{H}| > \exp\left(c\frac{1.5(\log h)^r}{(\log \log h)^{r-1}}\right).$$

Since $m \geq 6$ and $r \geq 2$, the size of our set-system $\mathcal{H}$ is strictly greater than $\exp\left(c\frac{1.5(\log h)^2}{\log \log h}\right)$. Condition 4 of Theorem 1 follows directly from Lemma 1. It is easy to verify that the total number of B-entries corresponding to each cell (x, y), where $x \neq y$ and for which $a_{x,y} = 0 \bmod m$, is not same. Moreover, since all $b_{x,x}^{i_1,i_2,\ldots,i_l}$ entries are indeed B-entries, it holds that $a_{x,y} < a_{x,x}$ for all $x \neq y$. Hence, the sets in $\mathcal{H}$ do not have the same size, making $\mathcal{H}$ a non-uniform set-system. This completes the proof of Theorem 1. ∎

4.2 Covering Vector Families

Definition 11 (Covering Vectors). Let $m, h > 0$ be positive integers, $S \subseteq \mathbb{Z}_m \setminus \{0\}$, and $w(\cdot)$ and $\langle \cdot, \cdot \rangle$ denote Hamming weight and inner product, respectively. We say that a subset $\mathcal{V} = \{\mathbf{v}_i\}_{i=1}^{N}$ of vectors in $(\mathbb{Z}_m)^h$ forms an S-covering family of vectors if the following two conditions are satisfied:

- $\forall i \in [N]$, it holds that: $\langle \mathbf{v}_i, \mathbf{v}_i \rangle = 0 \bmod m$,
- $\forall i, j \in [N]$, where $i \neq j$, it holds that:

$$\langle \mathbf{v}_i, \mathbf{v}_j \rangle \bmod m = \begin{cases} 0 & \text{if } w(\mathbf{v}_i \circ \mathbf{v}_j \bmod m) = 0 \bmod m \\ \in S & \text{otherwise,} \end{cases}$$

where $\circ$ denotes Hadamard/Schur product (see Definition 4).

Recall from Theorem 1 that h, m are positive integers, with $m = \prod_{i=1}^{r} p_i^{\alpha_i}$ having $r > 1$ different prime divisors. Further, recall Condition 4 of Theorem 1, which implies that the sizes of the pairwise intersections of the sets in $\mathcal{H}$ occupy at most $2^r - 1$ residue classes modulo m. If each set $H_i \in \mathcal{H}$ is represented by a representative vector $\mathbf{v}_i \in (\mathbb{Z}_m)^h$, then for the resulting subset $\mathcal{V}$ of vectors in $(\mathbb{Z}_m)^h$, the following result follows from Theorem 1.

Corollary 1 (to Theorem 1) *For the set-system $\mathcal{H}$ defined in Theorem 1, if each set $H_i \in \mathcal{H}$ is represented by a unique representative vector $\mathbf{v}_i \in (\mathbb{Z}_m)^h$, then for a set S of size $2^r - 1$, the set of vectors $\mathcal{V} = \{\mathbf{v}_i\}_{i=1}^{N}$, formed by the representative vectors of all sets in $\mathcal{H}$, forms an S-covering family such that $N > \exp\left(c\frac{1.5(\log h)^r}{(\log \log h)^{r-1}}\right)$ and $\forall i, j \in [N]$ it holds that $\langle \mathbf{v}_i, \mathbf{v}_j \rangle = |H_i \cap H_j|(\bmod m)$.*

5 Our Scheme

In Sect. 5.1, we introduce an algorithm to encode and identify hidden access structures, that remain unknown unless some authorized subset of parties collaborate. Followed by that, in Sect. 5.2, we extend that algorithm into an access structure hiding computational secret sharing scheme. We assume semi-honest polynomial-time parties, which try to gain additional information while correctly following the protocols. The following notations are frequently used from hereon.

- If each party P_i holds a value x_i, then for any subset of parties $\mathcal{A}$, $\{x_i\}_{i \in \mathcal{A}}$ denotes the set of all x_i values that belong to the parties $P_i \in \mathcal{A}$,
- $\prod_{i \in \mathcal{A}} x_i$ and $\sum_{i \in \mathcal{A}} x_i$ respectively denote the product and sum of all values from the set $\{x_i\}_{i \in \mathcal{A}}$,
- *large prime* refers to a prime number of size equal to or greater than the minimum size recommended by NIST for primes [1].

5.1 Access Structure Encoding Scheme (ASES)

In this section, we describe our scheme to encode and identify hidden access structures. Let $\mathcal{P} = \{P_1, \ldots, P_\ell\}$ be a set of ℓ polynomial-time parties and $\Omega \in \Gamma_0$ be any minimal authorized subset (see Definition 8). Hence, each party $P_i \in \mathcal{P}$ can be identified as $P_i \in \Omega$ or $P_i \in \mathcal{P} \setminus \Omega$. We divide the scheme into two parts: *setup* and *encoding*.

Setup. The scheme is initialized as follows:

1. For $\eta \gg \ell$, generate a set of distinct large primes, $\{p_1, p_2, \ldots, p_\eta\}$. Generate a prime $q = u \prod_{i=1}^{\eta} p_i + 1$, where u is an integer. We know from Dirichlet's Theorem (see Definition 2) that there are infinitely many such primes q. Generating q in this manner ensures hardness of the discrete log problem in $\mathbb{Z}_q$ [10], which, by extension translates into hardness of the Generalized Diffie-Hellman assumption in $\mathbb{Z}_q$.
2. Let $w = \prod_{i=1}^{\eta} p_i$ and $m = \varphi(q)$. Then, it follows from $q = u \prod_{i=1}^{\eta} p_i + 1$ that $w \mid \varphi(q)$, where φ denotes Euler's totient function (see Definition 3). Hence, the following holds for primes β_d and positive integers α_d:

$$m = w \cdot \prod_{d \geq 1} \beta_d^{\alpha_d} = \prod_{i=1}^{\eta} p_i \cdot \prod_{d \geq 1} \beta_d^{\alpha_d}.$$

   Let $r = d + \eta$ denote the total number of prime factors of m.
3. Construct a set-system $\mathcal{H}$ modulo m (as defined by Theorem 1). Let $\mathcal{V} \in (\mathbb{Z}_m)^h$ denote the covering vectors family (as defined by Corollary 1) representing $\mathcal{H}$ such that each vector $\mathbf{v}_i \in \mathcal{V}$ represents a unique set $H_i \in \mathcal{H}$.
4. Randomly sample $H \in \mathcal{H}$. Let $\mathbf{v} \in \mathcal{V}$ be the representative vector for H. We call $\mathbf{v}$ and H the *access structure vector* and *access structure set*, respectively.

Distributing Access Structures. Following procedure "encodes" the access structure Γ that originates from Ω, and outputs ℓ *access structure tokens*.

1. For each party $P_i \in \Omega$, randomly select a unique vector $\mathbf{v}_i \xleftarrow{\$} \mathcal{V}$, such that, $\langle \mathbf{v}, \mathbf{v}_i \rangle \neq 0 \bmod m$ (i.e., $H \nsubseteq H_i$ and $H_i \nsubseteq H$) and $\mathbf{v} = \sum_{i \in \Omega} \mathbf{v}_i \bmod m$. Compute the identifier for party P_i as: $x_i = \langle \mathbf{v}, \mathbf{v}_i \rangle \bmod m$.
2. For each party $P_e \in \mathcal{P} \setminus \Omega$, select a unique *covering party* $P_i \in \Omega$. Let $H_i \in \mathcal{H}$ be the set represented by P_i's covering vector, $\mathbf{v}_i \in \mathcal{V}$. Randomly sample $H_j \in \mathcal{H}$, such that, $H_i \subset H_j$. Let $\mathbf{v}_j \in \mathcal{V}$ be the covering vector representing H_j.
3. Compute $\mathbf{v}_e \in \mathcal{V}$ such that: $\mathbf{v}_e + \mathbf{v}_i = \mathbf{v}_j \bmod m$. Verify that $\langle \mathbf{v}, \mathbf{v}_e \rangle \neq 0 \bmod m$, which translates into $H \nsubseteq H_e, H_e \nsubseteq H$, for $H_e \in \mathcal{H}$ represented by $\mathbf{v}_e$. If these requirements do not hold, go back to Step 2.
4. Compute the identifier for party P_e as: $x_e = \langle \mathbf{v}, \mathbf{v}_e \rangle \bmod m$. Generating identifiers in this manner for parties $P_e \in \mathcal{P} \setminus \Omega$ ensures that they are "covered" by the identifiers of parties in Ω. Since each party $P_i \in \Omega$ can "cover" at most one party $P_e \in \mathcal{P} \setminus \Omega$, our scheme requires that $|\mathcal{P}| \leq 2 \cdot |\Omega|$.
5. Each party $P_z \in \mathcal{P}$ receives an *access structure token* $t_z^{(\Gamma)} = \mu^{x_z} \bmod q$, where $\mu \xleftarrow{\$} \mathbb{Z}_q^* \setminus \{1\}$.

In case of an identifier collision, i.e., $x_i = x_j$, where x_j is the identifier of another party $P_j \in \mathcal{P}$, re-generate the identifier for either P_i or P_j. Recall from Corollary 1 that $\langle \mathbf{v}, \mathbf{v}_i \rangle$ occupies $\leq 2^r - 1$ residue classes $\bmod m$. Therefore, the probability of an identifier collision is $\approx 1/(2^r - 1)^2$, which may be non-negligible. The set of parameters $\{m, q, \mathcal{H}, \mathcal{V}, \mu\}$ defines an ASES instance. Since our scheme works with a minimal authorized subset, the set of identifiers, $\{x_z\}_{z \in \mathcal{P}}$, represents 2^ℓ out of the $2^{2^{\ell - O(\log \ell)}}$ possible access structures.

Access Structure Identification. Theorem 3 proves that any authorized subset of parties $\mathcal{A} \in \Gamma$ can use its set of access structure tokens, $\{t_i^{(\Gamma)}\}_{i \in \mathcal{A}}$, to identify itself as a member of the access structure Γ.

Theorem 3. *Every authorized subset $\mathcal{A} \in \Gamma$ can identify itself as a member of the access structure Γ by verifying that:* $\prod_{i \in \mathcal{A}} t_i^{(\Gamma)} = 1 \bmod q$.

Proof. Recall that for any authorized subset $\mathcal{A} \in \Gamma$, it holds that the set $H_\mathcal{A} \in \mathcal{H}$, represented by $\sum_{i \in \mathcal{A}} \mathbf{v}_i = \mathbf{v}_\mathcal{A}$, is a superset of the *access structure set* $H \in \mathcal{H}$, i.e., $H \subseteq H_\mathcal{A}$. Hence, from Theorem 1 and Corollary 1, it follows that: $\langle \mathbf{v}, \mathbf{v}_\mathcal{A} \rangle = 0 \bmod m = y \cdot m = y \cdot \varphi(q)$, where y is a positive integer. This translates into $\mu^{\langle \mathbf{v}, \mathbf{v}_\mathcal{A} \rangle} = 1 \bmod q$ (using Euler's theorem). Hence, the following holds for all authorized subsets $\mathcal{A} \in \Gamma$:

$$\prod_{i \in \mathcal{A}} t_i^{(\Gamma)} = \prod_{i \in \mathcal{A}} \mu^{x_i} = \mu^{\left\langle \mathbf{v}, \sum_{i \in \mathcal{A}} \mathbf{v}_i \right\rangle} = \mu^{\langle \mathbf{v}, \mathbf{v}_\mathcal{A} \rangle} = \mu^{y \cdot \varphi(q)} = 1 \bmod q.$$

■

Perfect Soundness and Computational Hiding.

Theorem 4. *Every unauthorized subset $\mathcal{B} \notin \Gamma$ can identify itself to be outside Γ by using its set of access structure tokens, $\{t_i^{(\Gamma)}\}_{i \in \mathcal{B}}$, to verify that: $\prod_{i \in \mathcal{B}} t_i^{(\Gamma)} \neq 1 \bmod q$. Given that the Generalized Diffie-Hellman problem is hard, the following holds for all unauthorized subsets $\mathcal{B} \notin \Gamma$ and all access structures $\Gamma' \subseteq 2^{\mathcal{P}}$, where $\Gamma \neq \Gamma'$ and $\mathcal{B} \notin \Gamma'$:*

$$\left| Pr[\Gamma \mid \{t_i^{(\Gamma)}\}_{i \in \mathcal{B}}] - Pr[\Gamma' \mid \{t_i^{(\Gamma)}\}_{i \in \mathcal{B}}] \right| \leq \epsilon(\omega),$$

where $\omega = |\mathcal{P} \setminus \mathcal{B}|$ is the security parameter and ϵ is a negligible function.

Proof. It follows from the ASES procedure that for all unauthorized subsets $\mathcal{B} \notin \Gamma$, it holds that the set $H_{\mathcal{B}} \in \mathcal{H}$, represented by $\sum_{i \in \mathcal{B}} \mathbf{v}_i = \mathbf{v}_{\mathcal{B}}$, cannot be a superset or subset of the *access structure set* $H \in \mathcal{H}$. Hence, it follows from Theorem 1 and Corollary 1 that: $\langle \mathbf{v}, \mathbf{v}_{\mathcal{B}} \rangle \neq 0 \bmod m$, which translates into the following relation by Euler's theorem (since $m = \varphi(q)$ and $\mu \xleftarrow{\$} \mathbb{Z}_q^* \setminus \{1\}$) :

$$\prod_{i \in \mathcal{B}} t_i^{(\Gamma)} = \prod_{i \in \mathcal{B}} \mu^{x_i} = \mu^{\left\langle \mathbf{v}, \sum\limits_{i \in \mathcal{B}} \mathbf{v}_i \right\rangle} = \mu^{\langle \mathbf{v}, \mathbf{v}_{\mathcal{B}} \rangle} \neq 1 \bmod q.$$

Hence, any unauthorized subset $\mathcal{B} \notin \Gamma$ can identify itself as not being a part of the access structure Γ by simply multiplying its *access structure tokens*, $\{t_i^{(\Gamma)}\}_{i \in \mathcal{B}}$. The security parameter $\omega = |\mathcal{P} \setminus \mathcal{B}|$ accounts for this minimum information that is available to any unauthorized subset $\mathcal{B} \notin \Gamma$.

If some unauthorized subset $\mathcal{B} \notin \Gamma$ has non-negligible advantage in distinguishing access structure Γ from any other $\Gamma' \subseteq 2^{\mathcal{P}}$, where $\Gamma \neq \Gamma'$ and $\mathcal{B} \notin \Gamma'$, then the following must hold for some non-negligible function χ:

$$\left| Pr[\Gamma \mid \{t_i^{(\Gamma)}\}_{i \in \mathcal{B}}] - Pr[\Gamma' \mid \{t_i^{(\Gamma)}\}_{i \in \mathcal{B}}] \right| \geq \chi(\omega), \tag{5.1}$$

Let $g \in \mathbb{Z}_q^*$ be a generator of $\mathbb{Z}_q^*$ (recall that $\mathbb{Z}_q^*$ is a cyclic group). We know that the setup procedure used to generate q ensures that: $|\mathbb{Z}_q^*| = \varphi(q) \gg |\mathcal{P}|$. Hence, given that g is a generator of $\mathbb{Z}_q^*$, it follows that for each identifier x_i, there exists some $a_i \in \mathbb{Z}$ such that: $\mu^{x_i} = g^{a_i} \bmod q$. Therefore, by extension, it follows that for all sets $\mathcal{B}$, there exists set(s) of n different integers $I_{\mathcal{B}} = \{a_1, \ldots, a_n\}$, where $n = |\mathcal{B}|$, such that $\mu^{\sum_{i \in \mathcal{B}} x_i} = g^{\prod_{i=1}^{n} a_i} \bmod q$. Hence, it holds that: $\prod_{i \in \mathcal{B}} \mu^{x_i} = g^{\prod_{i=1}^{n} a_i} \bmod q$.

We know that each unauthorized subset $\mathcal{B} \notin \Gamma$ has at least one proper superset $\mathcal{A} \supsetneq \mathcal{B}$, such that $\mathcal{A} \in \Gamma$. Since g is a generator of $\mathbb{Z}_q^*$, there exists set(s) of n' different integers $I_{\mathcal{A}} = I_{\mathcal{B}} \cup \{a_{n+1}, \ldots, a_{n'}\}$, where $n' = |\mathcal{A}|$, such that the following holds: $\prod_{i \in \mathcal{A}} \mu^{x_i} = g^{\prod_{i=1}^{n'} a_i} \bmod q$.

We know that in order to satisfy Eq. 5.1, $\mathcal{B}$ must gain some non-negligible information about $g^{\prod_{i=1}^{n'} a_i}$ in $\mathbb{Z}_q^*$. We also know that $\mathcal{B}$ can compute $g^{\prod_{i=1}^{n} a_i} \bmod q$. Hence, it follows directly from Definition 1 that gaining any non-negligible information about $g^{\prod_{i=1}^{n'} a_i}$ from $g^{\prod_{i=1}^{n} a_i}$ in $\mathbb{Z}_q^*$ requires solving the Generalized Diffie-Hellman (GDH) problem. Therefore, Eq. 5.1 cannot hold given that the GDH assumption holds. Hence, the advantage of $\mathcal{B} \notin \Gamma$ must be negligible in the security parameter ω. ∎

5.2 Building the Full Scheme

The following procedure allows an honest dealer to employ the ASES scheme and realize an access structure hiding computational secret sharing scheme.

1. Perform ASES to generate *access structure tokens* $t_z^{(\Gamma)} = \mu^{x_z} \bmod q$, for each party $P_z \in \mathcal{P}$.
2. Follow Step 1 of the setup procedure of ASES to generate a suitable prime q'.
3. Generate a set-system $\mathcal{H}'$ modulo m' (as defined by Theorem 1), where $m' = \varphi(q')$. Let $\mathcal{V}'$ denote the covering vector family (as defined by Corollary 1) that is formed by the representative vectors $\mathbf{v}_i \in \mathcal{V}$ for the sets $H_i \in \mathcal{H}$.
4. Generate the secret that needs to be shared: $k \xleftarrow{\$} \mathbb{Z}_{q'}^*$, and randomly sample $|\Omega|$ integers, $\{b_i\}_{i=1}^{|\Omega|}$, such that: $\prod_{i=1}^{|\Omega|} b_i = k \bmod q'$.
5. Generate $\gamma \xleftarrow{\$} \mathbb{Z}_{q'}^* \backslash \{1\}$. For each party $P_j \in \mathcal{P} \backslash \Omega$, employ ASES with parameters $\{m', q', \mathcal{H}', \mathcal{V}', \gamma\}$ to generate identifier $y_j \in \mathbb{Z}_m$, and access structure token: $s_j^{(k)} = \gamma^{y_j} \bmod q'$. Party P_j receives $s_j^{(k)}$ as its share.
6. The share for each party $P_i \in \Omega$ is generated as: $s_i^{(k)} = (b_i \cdot \gamma^{y_i}) \bmod q'$. Each party $P_z \in \mathcal{P}$ receives < access structure token, share > pair: $(t_z^{(\Gamma)}, s_z^{(k)})$.

Completeness, Soundness, Correctness, Secrecy and Hiding: We prove that our access structure hiding computational secret sharing scheme satisfies the completeness, soundness, correctness, hiding and secrecy requirements outlined by the definition of Access Structure Hiding Computational Secret Sharing (see Definition 10). Since independent iterations of ASES are used to generate the access structure tokens and shares, perfect completeness follows directly from Theorem 3. Similarly, perfect soundness and computational hiding follow directly from Theorem 4. Hence, we move on to proving perfect correctness and computational secrecy.

Perfect Correctness: It follows directly from Theorem 3 that for all authorized subsets $\mathcal{A} \in \Gamma$, it holds that: $\prod_{i \in \mathcal{A}} \gamma^{y_i} = 1 \bmod q'$. Hence, any $\mathcal{A} \in \Gamma$ can reconstruct the secret, k, by combining its shares as:

$$\prod_{i \in \mathcal{A}} s_i^{(k)} \bmod q' = 1 \cdot \prod_{y \in \Omega} b_y \bmod q' = k, \qquad (\text{using } \prod_{i \in \mathcal{A}} \gamma^{y_i} = 1 \bmod q').$$

Since each party $P_z \in \mathcal{P}$ receives two elements, $s_i^{(k)}$ and $t_i^{(\Gamma)}$, both of which have (almost) the same size as the secret, the information rate of our scheme is $\approx 1/2$.

Computational Secrecy: Since independent iterations of ASES are used to generate the sets $\{t_z^{(\Gamma)}\}_{z \in \mathcal{P}}$ and $\{s_z^{(k)}\}_{z \in \mathcal{P}}$, computational indistinguishability (w.r.t. security parameter $\omega = |\mathcal{P} \setminus \mathcal{B}|$) of all different access structures $\Gamma, \Gamma' \subseteq 2^{\mathcal{P}}$, for all unauthorized subsets $\mathcal{B} \notin \Gamma, \Gamma'$ follows directly from Theorem 4, i.e., it holds that: $\left| Pr[\Gamma \mid \{t_i^{(\Gamma)}\}_{i \in \mathcal{B}}, \{s_i^{(k)}\}_{i \in \mathcal{B}}] - Pr[\Gamma' \mid \{t_i^{(\Gamma)}\}_{i \in \mathcal{B}}, \{s_i^{(k)}\}_{i \in \mathcal{B}}] \right| \leq \epsilon(\omega)$.

Theorem 5. *Given that GDH problem is hard, it holds for every unauthorized subset $\mathcal{B} \notin \Gamma$ and all different secrets $k_1, k_2 \in \mathcal{K}$ that the distributions $\{s_i^{(k_1)}\}_{i \in \mathcal{B}}$ and $\{s_i^{(k_2)}\}_{i \in \mathcal{B}}$ are computationally indistinguishable w.r.t. the security parameter $\omega = |\mathcal{P} \setminus \mathcal{B}|$.*

Proof. Since the set $\{b_i\}_{i=1}^{|\Omega|}$ is generated randomly, secrecy of the b_i values follows from one-time pad. Moving on to the secrecy of γ^{y_i} values: since $\gamma(\neq 1)$ is a random element from $\mathbb{Z}_{q'}^*$, there exists a generator g of $\mathbb{Z}_{q'}^*$ (note that $\mathbb{Z}_{q'}^*$ is a cyclic group) such that for each identifier, y_i, generated by the ASES procedure, there exists an $a_i \in \mathbb{Z}$ such that: $\gamma^{y_i} = g^{a_i} \bmod q'$. By extension, there exists set(s) of n different integers $I_\mathcal{B} = \{a_1, \ldots, a_n\}$, where $n = |\mathcal{B}|$, such that: $\prod_{i \in \mathcal{B}} \gamma^{y_i} = g^{\prod_{i=1}^n a_i} \bmod q'$. We know that each unauthorized subset $\mathcal{B} \notin \Gamma$ has at least one proper superset $\mathcal{A} \supsetneq \mathcal{B}$, such that $\mathcal{A} \in \Gamma$. Since g is a generator of $\mathbb{Z}_{q'}^*$, there exists set(s) of n' different integers $I_\mathcal{A} = I_\mathcal{B} \cup \{a_{n+1}, \ldots, a_{n'}\}$, where $n' = |\mathcal{A}|$, such that: $\prod_{i \in \mathcal{A}} \gamma^{y_i} = g^{\prod_{i=1}^{n'} a_i} \bmod q'$. It follows from Definition 1 that in order to gain any non-negligible information about $g^{\prod_{i=1}^{n'} a_i}$ from $g^{\prod_{i=1}^{n} a_i}$, in $\mathbb{Z}_{q'}^*$, $\mathcal{B}$ must solve the GDH problem. Therefore, for every unauthorized subset $\mathcal{B} \notin \Gamma$, computational indistinguishability of $\{s_i^{(k_1)}\}_{i \in \mathcal{B}}$ and $\{s_i^{(k_2)}\}_{i \in \mathcal{B}}$ w.r.t. the security parameter ω follows directly from the GDH assumption. ∎

Open Problems. Our access structure hiding secret sharing scheme requires that $|\mathcal{P}| \leq 2|\Omega|$, where $\Omega \in \Gamma_0$ is any minimal authorized subset. It is worth exploring whether this restriction can be further relaxed, or removed. Another interesting problem is defining and constructing set-systems and vector families that can support simultaneous encoding of multiple minimal authorized subsets.

References

1. Barker, E.B., Chen, L., Roginsky, A.L., Vassilev, A.T., Davis, R.: Recommendation for Pair-Wise Key-Establishment Schemes Using Discrete Logarithm Cryptography. Special Publication (NIST SP)- 800–56Ar3 (2018)
2. Beimel, A.: Secret-sharing schemes: a survey. In: Chee, Y.M., et al. (eds.) IWCC 2011. LNCS, vol. 6639, pp. 11–46. Springer, Heidelberg (2011). https://doi.org/10.1007/978-3-642-20901-7_2
3. Biham, E., Boneh, D., Reingold, O.: Breaking generalized Diffie-Hellman modulo a composite is no easier than factoring. Inf. Process. Lett. **70**(2), 83–87 (1999)
4. Blakley, G.: Safeguarding cryptographic keys. In: American Federation of Information Processing, vol. 48 (1979)

5. Frankl, P., Tokushige, N.: Invitation to intersection problems for finite sets. J. Combin. Theor. Ser. A **144**, 157–211 (2016)
6. Goldwasser, S., Micali, S.M.: Probabilistic encryption & how to play mental poker keeping secret all partial information. In: STOC (1982)
7. Graham, R.L., Knuth, D.E., Patashnik, O.: Concrete Mathematics, 2nd edn. Addison-Wesley Professional, Boston (1994)
8. Grolmusz, V.: Superpolynomial size set-systems with restricted intersections mod 6 and explicit ramsey graphs. Combinatorica **20**, 71–86 (2000)
9. Ito, M., Saito, A., Nishizeki, T.: Secret sharing scheme realizing general access structure. Electron. Commun. Jpn. (Part III: Fundam. Electron. Sci.) **72**(9), 56–64 (1989)
10. Joux, A., Odlyzko, A., Pierrot, C.: The past, evolving present, and future of the discrete logarithm. In: Koç, Ç.K. (ed.) Open Problems in Mathematics and Computational Science, pp. 5–36. Springer, Cham (2014). https://doi.org/10.1007/978-3-319-10683-0_2
11. Krawczyk, H.: Secret sharing made short. In: Stinson, D.R. (ed.) CRYPTO 1993. LNCS, vol. 773, pp. 136–146. Springer, Heidelberg (1994). https://doi.org/10.1007/3-540-48329-2_12
12. Rosen, K.H.: Handbook of Discrete and Combinatorial Mathematics, 2nd (edn.). Chapman & Hall/CRC, London (2010)
13. Shamir, A.: How to share a secret. Commun. ACM **22**, 612–613 (1979)
14. Steiner, M., Tsudik, G., Waidner, M.: Diffie-Hellman key distribution extended to group communication. In: ACM Conference on Computer and Communications Security (1996)

Approximation Algorithms for Car-Sharing Problems

Kelin Luo$^{(\boxtimes)}$ and Frits C. R. Spieksma

Department of Mathematics and Computer Science,
Eindhoven University of Technology, Eindhoven, The Netherlands
{k.luo,f.c.r.spieksma}@tue.nl

Abstract. We consider several variants of a car-sharing problem. Given are a number of requests each consisting of a pick-up location and a drop-off location, a number of cars, and nonnegative, symmetric travel times that satisfy the triangle inequality. Each request needs to be served by a car, which means that a car must first visit the pick-up location of the request, and then visit the drop-off location of the request. Each car can serve two requests. One problem is to serve all requests with the minimum total travel time (called CS_{sum}), and the other problem is to serve all requests with the minimum total latency (called CS_{lat}). We also study the special case where the pick-up and drop-off location of a request coincide. We propose two basic algorithms, called the match and assign algorithm and the transportation algorithm. We show that the best of the resulting two solutions is a 2-approximation for CS_{sum} (and a 7/5-approximation for its special case), and a 5/3-approximation for CS_{lat} (and a 3/2-approximation for its special case); these ratios are better than the ratios of the individual algorithms. Finally, we indicate how our algorithms can be applied to more general settings where each car can serve more than two requests, or where cars have distinct speeds.

Keywords: Car-sharing · Approximation algorithms · Matching

1 Introduction

We investigate the following car-sharing problem: there are n cars (or servers), with car k stationed at location d_k ($1 \le k \le n$), and there are $2n$ requests, each request i consisting of a pick-up location s_i and a drop-off location t_i ($1 \le i \le 2n$). Between every pair of locations x and y, a number $w(x, y)$ is given; these numbers can be interpreted as the distance between locations x and y or the time needed to travel between x and y. These distances, or times, are non-negative, symmetric, and satisfy the triangle inequality. Each request needs to be served by a car, which means that a car must first visit the pick-up location, and then

This project has received funding from the European Union's Horizon 2020 research and innovation programme under the Marie Skłodowska-Curie grant agreement number 754462, and NWO Gravitation Project NETWORKS, Grant Number 024.002.003.

visit the drop-off location. The car sharing problem is to assign all requests to the cars such that each car serves exactly two requests while minimizing total travel time, and/or while minimizing total waiting time (called total latency), incurred by customers that submitted the requests. Let us elaborate on these two objectives.

- **Minimize total travel time.** The total travel time is the travel time each car drives to serve its requests, summed over the cars. From the company or drivers' perspective, this is important since this objective reflects minimizing costs while serving all requests. From a societal point of view, this objective also helps to reduce emissions. We use CS_{sum} to refer to the car-sharing problem with the objective to minimize total travel time. The special case of CS_{sum} where the pick-up and drop-off location is identical for each request, is denoted by $CS_{sum,s=t}$.
- **Minimize total latency.** The total latency represents the sum of the travel times needed for each individual customer to arrive at her/his drop-off location, summed over the customers. From the customers' perspective, this is important because it helps customers to reach their destinations as soon as possible. We use CS_{lat} to refer to the car-sharing problem with the objective to minimize total latency. The special case of CS_{lat} where the pick-up and drop-off location is identical for each request, is denoted by $CS_{lat,s=t}$.

Motivation. Consider a working day morning. A large number of requests, each consisting of a pick-up and a drop-off location has been submitted by the customers. The car-sharing company has to assign these requests to available cars. In many practical situations, each request is allowed to occupy at most two seats in a car (see Uber [1]). Thus, in a regular car where at most four seats are available, at most two requests can be combined. Since the company knows the location of the available cars, an instance of our problem arises.

Another application can be found in the area of collective transport for specific groups of people. For instance, the company Transvision [2] organizes collective transport by collecting all requests in a particular region of the Netherlands, combines them, and offers them to regular transport companies. In their setting customers must make their request the evening before the day of the actual transport; the number of requests for a day often exceeds 5.000. However, in this application, it is true that a car may pick up more than two requests (we come back to this issue in Sect. 5).

The problems $CS_{sum,s=t}$ and $CS_{lat,s=t}$ are natural special cases of CS_{sum} and CS_{lat} respectively, and can be used to model situations where items have to be delivered to clients (whose location is known and fixed). For instance, one can imagine a retailer sending out trucks to satisfy clients' demand where each truck is used to satisfy two clients.

Related Work. In the literature, car-sharing systems are increasingly studied. Agatz et al. [3] consider the problem of matching cars and customers in real-time with the aim to minimize the total number of vehicle-miles driven.

Stiglic et al. [9] show that a small increase in the flexibility of either the cars or the customers can significantly increase the performance of a dynamic car-sharing system. Furthermore, Wang et al. [10] introduce the notion of stability for a car sharing system and they present methods to establish stable or nearly stable solutions. More recently, Ashlagi et al. [4] study the problem of matching requests to cars that arrive online and need to be assigned after at most a pre-specified number of time periods. Every pair of requests that is matched yields a profit and the goal of the car sharing system is to match requests with maximum total profit.

Bei and Zhang [5] introduce CS_{sum}, and give a 2.5-approximation algorithm for it. In fact, both CS_{sum} and CS_{lat} are a special case of the so-called two-to-one assignment problem (2-1-AP) investigated by Goossens et al. [7]. Given a set G of n green elements, and a set R of $2n$ red elements, we call a *triple* a set of three elements that consist of a single green element and two red elements; further, there is a cost-coefficient for each triple. The 2-1-AP problem is to find a collection of triples covering each element exactly once, while the sum of the corresponding cost-coefficients is minimized. In the context of our car sharing problem, the green elements represent the cars, and the red elements represent the requests. For the special case of 2-1-AP where the cost of each triple (i, j, k) is defined as the sum of the three corresponding distances, i.e., $cost(i, j, k) = d_{ij} + d_{jk} + d_{ki}$, that satisfy the triangle inequality, Goossens et al. [7] give an algorithm with approximation ratio 4/3. The definition of the cost-coefficients in CS_{sum}, as well as in CS_{lat} differs from this expression; we refer to Sect. 2 for a precise definition.

Our Results. We formulate and analyze three polynomial-time approximation algorithms for our car-sharing problems: a match and assign algorithm MA, a transportation algorithm TA, and a combined algorithm CA which runs MA and TA, and then outputs the best of the two solutions. These algorithms are extended versions of algorithms in [7] using as additional input a parameter $\alpha \in \{1, 2\}$ and a vector $v \in \{u, \mu\}$; for their precise description, we refer to Sect. 3. All of them run in time $O(n^3)$. Here, we establish their worst-case ratio's (see Williamson and Shmoys [11] for appropriate terminology).

Table 1. Overview of our results

Problem	MA$(1, u)$	MA$(2, \mu)$	TA(1)	TA(2)	CA$(1, u)$	CA$(2, \mu)$
CS_{sum}	2^* (Lemma 5)	3	3^* (Lemma 6)	4	2^* (Theorem 1)	3
$CS_{sum,s=t}$	$3/2^*$	$3/2$	3^*	4	$7/5^*$	$10/7$
CS_{lat}	4	2^*	3	2^*	3	$5/3$ (Theorem 2)
$CS_{lat,s=t}$	2	2^*	2	2^*	$8/5$	$3/2^*$

For all four problems, we show how the above mentioned algorithms behave with respect to their worst-case ratios. Notice that for $CS_{sum,s=t}$, CS_{lat} and $CS_{lat,s=t}$, the worst-case ratio of the combined algorithm CA is strictly better than each of the two worst-case ratios of the algorithms CA consists of. An overview of all our results is shown in Table 1; u and μ are defined in Sect. 2; an "*" means that the corresponding worst-case ratio is tight; results not attributed to a specific Lemma or Theorem are proven in [8].

The two problems CS_{sum} and CS_{lat} only differ in their objectives, i.e., anything that is a feasible solution in CS_{sum} is also a feasible solution in CS_{lat} and vice versa. A similar statement can be made for $CS_{sum,s=t}$ and $CS_{lat,s=t}$. Hence, we can use a two-criteria approach to judge a solution; more concretely, we call an algorithm a (ρ, φ)-approximation algorithm if the cost of its solution is at most ρ times the cost of an optimal solution to CS_{sum}, and at most φ times the cost of an optimal solution of CS_{lat}. Therefore, $CA(1, u)$ is a $(2, 3)$-approximation (resp. $(\frac{7}{5}, \frac{8}{5})$-approximation) algorithm and $CA(2, \mu)$ is a $(4, \frac{5}{3})$-approximation (resp. $(\frac{10}{7}, \frac{3}{2})$-approximation) algorithm. Notice that, from a worst-case perspective, none of these two algorithms dominates the other.

2   Preliminaries

Notation. We consider a setting with n cars, denoted by $D = \{1, 2, ..., n\}$, with car k at location d_k $(k \in D)$. There are $2n$ requests $R = \{1, 2, ..., 2n\}$, where request i is specified by the pick-up location s_i and the drop-off location t_i $(i \in R)$. The distance (or cost, or travel time) between location x_1 and x_2 is denoted by $w(x_1, x_2)$. We assume here that distances $w(x_1, x_2)$ are non-negative, symmetric, and satisfy the triangle inequality. Furthermore, we extend the notation of distance between two locations to the distance of a path: $w(x_1, x_2, ..., x_k) = \sum_{i=1}^{k-1} w(x_i, x_{i+1})$. We want to find an *allocation* $M = \{(k, R_k) : k \in D, R_k \subseteq R\}$, where $|R_k| = 2$ and $R_1, R_2, .., R_n$ are pairwise disjoint; the set R_k contains the two requests that are assigned to car k. For each car $k \in D$ and $(k, R_k) \in M$ where R_k contains request i and request j, i.e., $R_k = \{i, j\}$, we denote the *travel time* of serving the requests in R_k by:

$$cost(k, \{i, j\}) \equiv \min\{w(d_k, s_i, s_j, t_i, t_j), w(d_k, s_i, s_j, t_j, t_i), w(d_k, s_i, t_i, s_j, t_j),$$
$$w(d_k, s_j, s_i, t_i, t_j), w(d_k, s_j, s_i, t_j, t_i), w(d_k, s_j, t_j, s_i, t_i)\}. \tag{1}$$

Notice that the six terms in (1) correspond to all distinct ways of visiting the locations s_i, s_j, t_i and t_j where s_i is visited before t_i and s_j is visited before t_j. We view $cost(k, \{i, j\})$ as consisting of two parts: one term expressing the travel time between d_k and the first pick-up location s_i or s_j; and another term capturing the travel time from the first pick-up location to the last drop-off location. For convenience, we give a definition of the latter quantity.

$$u_{ij} \equiv \min\{w(s_i, s_j, t_i, t_j), w(s_i, s_j, t_j, t_i), w(s_i, t_i, s_j, t_j)\}$$
$$\text{for each } i, j \in R \times R, i \neq j. \tag{2}$$

Notice that the u_{ij}'s are not necessarily symmetric. For $CS_{sum,s=t}$, $u_{ij} \equiv w(s_i, s_j)$. Using (1) and (2), the travel time needed to serve requests in $R_k = \{i, j\}$ $(k \in D)$ is then given by:

$$cost(k, \{i, j\}) = \min\{w(d_k, s_i) + u_{ij}, w(d_k, s_j) + u_{ji}\}. \tag{3}$$

We denote the travel time of an allocation M by:

$$cost(M) = \sum_{(k, R_k) \in M} cost(k, R_k). \tag{4}$$

In CS_{sum} and $CS_{sum, s=t}$, the goal is to find an allocation M that minimizes $cost(M)$.

Let us now consider CS_{lat}. Here, we focus on the waiting time as perceived by an individual customer, from the moment the car leaves its location until the moment the customer reaches its drop-off location. More formally, we denote the *latency* of serving requests in $R_k = \{i, j\}$ by:

$$
\begin{aligned}
wait(k, \{i, j\}) \equiv \min \\
\{w(d_k, s_i, s_j, t_i) + w(d_k, s_i, s_j, t_i, t_j), w(d_k, s_i, s_j, t_j) + w(d_k, s_i, s_j, t_j, t_i), \\
w(d_k, s_i, t_i) + w(d_k, s_i, t_i, s_j, t_j), w(d_k, s_j, s_i, t_i) + w(d_k, s_j, s_i, t_i, t_j), \\
w(d_k, s_j, s_i, t_j) + w(d_k, s_j, s_i, t_j, t_i), w(d_k, s_j, t_j) + w(d_k, s_j, t_j, s_i, t_i)\}.
\end{aligned}
\tag{5}
$$

Again, the six terms in (5) correspond to all distinct ways of visiting the locations s_i, s_j, t_i and t_j where s_i is visited before t_i and s_j is visited before t_j. We view $wait(k, R_k)$ as consisting of two parts: one term expressing the waiting time between d_k and the first pick-up location s_i or s_j; and another term capturing the waiting time from the first pick-up location to the last drop-off location. For convenience, we give a definition of the latter quantity.

$$
\begin{aligned}
\mu_{ij} \equiv \min\{w(s_i, s_j, t_i) + w(s_i, s_j, t_i, t_j), w(s_i, s_j, t_j) + w(s_i, s_j, t_j, t_i), \\
w(s_i, t_i) + w(s_i, t_i, s_j, t_j)\} \text{ for each } i, j \in R \times R, i \neq j.
\end{aligned}
\tag{6}
$$

Notice that the μ_{ij}'s are not necessarily symmetric. For $CS_{lat, s=t}$, $\mu_{ij} \equiv w(s_i, s_j)$. Using (5) and (6), the latency needed to serve requests in $R_k = \{i, j\}$ ($k \in D$) is then given by:

$$wait(k, \{i, j\}) = \min\{2w(d_k, s_i) + \mu_{ij}, 2w(d_k, s_j) + \mu_{ji}\}. \tag{7}$$

We denote the latency of an allocation M by:

$$wait(M) = \sum_{(k, R_k) \in M} wait(k, R_k). \tag{8}$$

Thus, in CS_{lat} and $CS_{lat, s=t}$, the goal is to find an allocation M that minimizes $wait(M)$.

A natural variant of the latency objective is one where the latency is counted with respect to the pick-up location as opposed to the drop-off location in CS_{lat}. Clearly, then the drop-off location becomes irrelevant, and in fact our approximation results for $CS_{lat, s=t}$ become valid for this variant.

Remark. Bei and Zhang [5] prove that the special car-sharing problem, i.e., $CS_{sum,s=t}$ is NP-hard. Their proof can also be used to prove that $CS_{lat,s=t}$ is NP-hard. In fact, we point out that the arguments presented in Goossens et al. [7] allow to establish the APX-hardness of these two problems.

Paper Outline. In Sect. 3, we present two kinds of algorithms, i.e., the match and assignment algorithm and the transportation algorithm. In Sect. 4, we prove the approximation ratios. Section 5 concludes the paper.

3   Algorithms

We give three polynomial-time approximation algorithms for our car-sharing problems. In Sect. 3.1 we describe the match and assign algorithm $MA(\alpha, v)$, and in Sect. 3.2 we describe the transportation algorithm $TA(\alpha)$. As described before, the third algorithm, $CA(\alpha, v)$, simply runs $MA(\alpha, v)$ and $TA(\alpha)$, and then outputs the best of the two solutions. Let $\alpha \in \{1, 2\}$ be the coefficient that weighs the travel time between the car location and the first pick-up location, and let $v \in \{u, \mu\}$ (where u is defined in (2), and μ is defined in (6)).

3.1   The Match and Assign Algorithm

The match-and-assign algorithm $MA(\alpha, v)$ goes through two steps: in the first step, the algorithm pairs the requests based on their combined serving cost, and in the second step, the algorithm assigns the request-pairs to the cars.

Algorithm 1. Match-and-assign algorithm $(MA(\alpha, v))$

1: *Input*: non-negative weighted graph $G = (V, E, w)$, requests $R = \{i = (s_i, t_i) : 1 \leq i \leq m, s_i, t_i \in V\}$, cars $D = \{k : 1 \leq k \leq n, d_k \in V\}$, $\alpha \in \{1, 2\}$ and $v \in \{u, \mu\}$.
2: *Output*: An allocation $MA = \{(k, \{i, j\}) : k \in D, i, j \in R\}$.
3: For $i, j \in R$ do
4:      $v_1(\{i, j\}) \equiv \frac{v_{ij} + v_{ji}}{2}$
5: end for
6: Let $G_1 \equiv (R, v_1)$ be the complete weighted graph where an edge between vertex $i \in R$ and vertex $j \in R$ has weight $v_1(i, j)$.
7: Find a minimum weight perfect matching M_1 in $G_1 \equiv (R, v_1)$ with weight $v_1(M_1)$.
8: For $k \in D$ and $\{i, j\} \in M_1$ with $v_{ij} \geq v_{ji}$ do
9:      $v_2(k, \{i, j\}) \equiv \min\{\alpha w(d_k, s_i) + \frac{v_{ij} - v_{ji}}{2}, \alpha w(d_k, s_j) - \frac{v_{ij} - v_{ji}}{2}\}$
10: end for
11: Let $G_2 \equiv (D \cup M_1, v_2)$ be the complete bipartite graph with *left* vertex-set D, *right* vertex-set M_1 and edges with weight $v_2(k, \{i, j\})$ for $k \in D$, and $\{i, j\} \in M_1$.
12: Find a minimum weight perfect matching M_2 in $G_2 \equiv (D \cup M_1, v_2)$ with weight $v_2(M_2)$.
13: Output allocation $MA = M_2$.

The key characteristics of algorithm $MA(\alpha, v)$ are found in lines 4 and 9 where the costs of the first and second step are defined. A resulting quantity is

$v_1(M_1) + v_2(M_2)$; we now prove two lemma's concerning this quantity, which will be of use in Sect. 4.

Lemma 1. *For each $\alpha \in \{1,2\}$ and $v \in \{u, \mu\}$, we have:*

$$v_1(M_1) + v_2(M_2) = \sum_{(k,\{i,j\}) \in M_2} \min\{\alpha w(d_k, s_i) + v_{ij}, \alpha w(d_k, s_j) + v_{ji}\}.$$

The proof can be found in [8].

Lemma 2. *For $\alpha \in \{1,2\}$, $v \in \{u, \mu\}$, and for each allocation M, we have:*

$$v_1(M_1) + v_2(M_2) \le \frac{1}{2} \sum_{(k,\{i,j\}) \in M} (\alpha(w(d_k, s_i) + w(d_k, s_j)) + v_{ij} + v_{ji}).$$

Proof. For an allocation M, let $M_R = \{R_k : (k, R_k) \in M\}$. Observe that

$$v_1(M_1) \le \sum_{\{i,j\} \in M_R} \frac{v_{ij} + v_{ji}}{2}, \tag{9}$$

since M_1 is a minimum weight perfect matching in $G_1 \equiv (R, v_1)$.

We claim that

$$v_2(M_2) \le \frac{1}{2} \sum_{(k,\{i,j\}) \in M} \alpha(w(d_k, s_i) + w(d_k, s_j)). \tag{10}$$

When summing (9) and (10), the lemma follows.

Hence, it remains to prove (10). Consider an allocation M, and consider the matching M_1 found in the first step of MA. Based on M and M_1, we construct the graph $G' = (R \cup D, M_1 \cup \{(\{i, k\}, \{j, k\}) : (k, \{i, j\}) \in M\})$. Note that every vertex in graph G' has degree 2. Thus, we can partition G' into a set of disjoint cycles called C; each cycle $c \in C$ can be written as $c = (i_1, j_1, k_1, i_2, j_2, k_2, \ldots, k_h, i_1)$, where $\{i_s, j_s\} \in M_1$, $(k_s, \{j_s, i_{s+1}\}) \in M$ for $1 \le s < h$ and $(k_h, \{j_h, i_1\}) \in M$. Consider now, for each cycle $c \in C$, the following two matchings called M_ℓ^c and M_r^c:

- $M_\ell^c = \{(\{i_1, j_1\}, k_1), (\{i_2, j_2\}, k_2), \ldots, (\{i_h, j_h\}, k_h)\}$,
- $M_r^c = \{(k_1, \{i_2, j_2\}), (k_2, \{i_3, j_3\}), \ldots, (k_h, \{i_1, j_1\})\}$.

Obviously, both $M_\ell \equiv \bigcup_{c \in C} M_\ell^c$, and $M_r \equiv \bigcup_{c \in C} M_r^c$ are a perfect matching in $G_2 = (D \cup M_1, v_2)$. Given the definition of $v_2(k, \{i, j\})$ (see line 9 of Algorithm MA), we derive for each pair of requests $\{i, j\}$ and two cars a, b: $v_2(a, \{i, j\}) + v_2(b, \{i, j\}) \le \alpha w(d_a, s_i) + \frac{v_{ij} - v_{ji}}{2} + \alpha w(d_b, s_j) - \frac{v_{ij} - v_{ji}}{2} = \alpha(w(d_a, s_i) + w(d_b, s_j))$. Similarly, it follows that: $v_2(a, \{i, j\}) + v_2(b, \{i, j\}) \le \alpha(w(d_a, s_j) + w(d_b, s_i))$. Thus, for each $c \in C$:

$$\sum_{(k,\{i,j\}) \in M_\ell^c} v_2(k, \{i, j\}) + \sum_{(k,\{i,j\}) \in M_r^c} v_2(k, \{i, j\}) \le \sum_{\substack{\{i,k\},\{j,k\} \in c \\ (k,\{i,j\}) \in M}} \alpha(w(d_k, s_i) + w(d_k, s_j)). \tag{11}$$

Note that M_2 is a minimum weight perfect matching in $G_2 = (D \cup M_1, v_2)$, and both M_ℓ and M_r are a perfect matching in $G_2 = (D \cup M_1, v_2)$. Thus:

$$v_2(M_2) \leq \sum_{c \in C} \min\{v_2(M_\ell^c), v_2(M_r^c)\}$$

$$\leq \frac{1}{2} \sum_{c \in C} (\sum_{(k,\{i,j\}) \in M_\ell^c} v_2(k, \{i,j\}) + \sum_{(k,\{i,j\}) \in M_r^c} v_2(k, \{i,j\}))$$

$$\leq \frac{1}{2} \sum_{(k,\{i,j\}) \in M} \alpha(w(d_k, s_i) + w(d_k, s_j)).$$

The last inequality follows from (11), and hence (10) is proven.   □

3.2   The Transportation Algorithm

In this section, we present the transportation algorithm. The idea of the algorithm is to replace each car $k \in D$ by 2 virtual cars called $\gamma(k)$ and $\delta(k)$, resulting in two car sets $\Gamma = \{\gamma(1), ..., \gamma(n)\}$ and $\Delta = \{\delta(1), ..., \delta(n)\}$. Next we assign the requests to the $2n$ cars using a particular definition of the costs; a solution is found by letting car $k \in D$ serve the requests assigned to car $\gamma(k)$ and $\delta(k)$.

Algorithm 2. Transportation algorithm (TA(α))

1: *Input*: non-negative weighted graph $G = (V, E, w)$, requests $R = \{i = (s_i, t_i) : 1 \leq i \leq m, s_i, t_i \in V\}$, cars $D = \{k : 1 \leq k \leq n, d_k \in V\}$, two virtual car sets $\Gamma = \{\gamma(1), ..., \gamma(n)\}$, and $\Delta = \{\delta(1), ..., \delta(n)\}$, and $\alpha \in \{1, 2\}$.
2: *Output*: An allocation TA $= \{(k, \{i,j\}) : k \in D, i, j \in R\}$.
3: For $k \in D, i \in R$ do
4:         $v_3(\gamma(k), i) = \alpha w(d_k, s_i, t_i) + w(t_i, d_k)$
5:         $v_3(\delta(k), i) = w(d_k, s_i, t_i)$
6: end for
7: Let $G_3 \equiv (\Gamma \cup \Delta \cup R, v_3)$ be the complete bipartite graph with *left* vertex-set $\Gamma \cup \Delta$, *right* vertex-set R, and edges with weight $v_3(x, i)$ for $x \in \Gamma \cup \Delta$ and $i \in R$.
8: Find a minimum weight perfect matching M_3 in $G_3 \equiv (\Gamma \cup \Delta \cup R, v_3)$ with weight $v_3(M_3)$.
9: Output allocation TA $= M_4 \equiv \{(k, \{i,j\}) : (\gamma(k), i), (\delta(k), j) \in M_3, k \in D\}$.

The crucial points of algorithm TA(α) are found in lines 4 and 5 where the costs of assigning a request are defined; a resulting quantity is $v_3(M_3)$. We now prove two lemma's concerning this quantity $v_3(M_3)$, which will be of use in Sect. 4.

Lemma 3. *For each $\alpha \in \{1, 2\}$, we have:*

$$v_3(M_3) = \sum_{(k,\{i,j\}) \in M_4} \min\{\alpha w(d_k, s_i, t_i) + w(t_i, d_k, s_j, t_j), \alpha w(d_k, s_j, t_j) + w(t_j, d_k, s_i, t_i)\}.$$

This lemma follows directly from the definition of the costs in lines 4 and 5 of TA.

Lemma 4. *For $\alpha \in \{1, 2\}$ and for each allocation M, we have:*

$$v_3(M_3) \leq \sum_{(k,\{i,j\}) \in M} \min\{\alpha w(d_k, s_i, t_i) + w(t_i, d_k, s_j, t_j), \alpha w(d_k, s_j, t_j) + w(t_j, d_k, s_i, t_i)\}.$$

This lemma is obvious since M_3 is a minimum weight perfect matching.

Remark. Both MA(α, v) and TA(α) runs in time $O(n^3)$ since a minimum matching M in a weighted graph of n vertices can be found in time $O(n^3)$ [6].

4   Approximation Results

In this section, we analyze the combined algorithm CA(α, v), i.e., the best of the two algorithms MA(α, v) and TA(α), for CS$_{sum}$ and CS$_{lat}$. We denote the allocation by the match and assign algorithm MA(α, v) (resp. the transportation algorithm TA(α)) by MA (resp. TA). We denote an optimal allocation of a specific problem by $M^* = \{(k, R_k^*) : k \in D\}$ with $R_k^* = \{i, j\}$ $(i, j \in R)$. Let $M_R^* = \{R_k^* : (k, R_k^*) \in M^*\}$ denote the pairs of requests in M^*. With a slight abuse of notation, we use CA(I) to denote the allocation found by CA for instance I.

4.1   Approximation Results for CS$_{sum}$

We first establish the worst-case ratios of MA$(1, u)$ and TA(1), and next prove that CA$(1, u)$ is a 2-approximation algorithm.

Lemma 5. MA$(1, u)$ *is a 2-approximation algorithm for* CS$_{sum}$.

Proof. We assume wlog that, for each $(k, \{i, j\}) \in M^*$, $cost(k, \{i, j\}) = w(d_k, s_i) + u_{ij}$. We have:

$$cost(\mathrm{MA}(1, u)) = v_1(M_1) + v_2(M_2) \quad \text{(by (3), (4)) and Lemma 1)}$$

$$\leq \frac{1}{2} \sum_{(k,\{i,j\}) \in M^*} (w(d_k, s_i) + w(d_k, s_j) + u_{ij} + u_{ji}) \quad \text{(by Lemma 2)}$$

$$\leq \frac{1}{2} \sum_{(k,\{i,j\}) \in M^*} (2w(d_k, s_i) + 4u_{ij}) \tag{12}$$

$$\leq \frac{1}{2} \sum_{(k,\{i,j\}) \in M^*} 4cost(k, \{i, j\}) \quad \text{(by } cost(k, \{i, j\}) = w(d_k, s_i) + u_{ij})$$

$$= 2\, cost(M^*).$$

The second inequality follows from the triangle inequality, $w(s_i, s_j) \leq u_{ij}$, and $u_{ji} \leq 2u_{ij}$ for each request pair $\{i, j\} \in R^2$; the corresponding proof can be found in [8]. □

Notice that the statement in Lemma 5 is actually tight by the instance depicted in Fig. 1.

Lemma 6. $TA(1)$ *is a 3-approximation algorithm for* CS_{sum}.

The proof can be found in [8].

Theorem 1. $CA(1, u)$ *is a 2-approximation algorithm for* CS_{sum}. *Moreover, there exists an instance I for which* $cost(CA(I)) = 2\ cost(M^*(I))$.

Proof. It is obvious that, as $cost(CA(1, u)) = \min\{cost(MA(1, u)), cost(TA(1))\}$, Lemma's 5 and 6 imply that $CA(1, u)$ is a 2-approximation algorithm for CS_{sum}. We now provide an instance for which this ratio is achieved. Consider the instance I depicted in Fig. 1. This instance has $n = 2$ with $D = \{1, 2\}$ and $R = \{1, 2, 3, 4\}$. Locations corresponding to distinct vertices in Fig. 1 are at distance 1. Observe that an optimal solution is $M^*(I) = \{(k_1, \{1, 3\}), (k_2, \{2, 4\})\}$ with $cost(M^*(I)) = 2$. Note that $M_R^* = \{\{1, 3\}, \{2, 4\}\}$. Let us now analyse the performance of $MA(1, u)$ and $TA(1)$ on instance I.

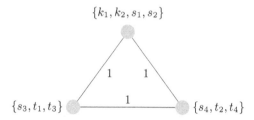

Fig. 1. A worst-case instance for the combined algorithm $CA(1, u)$ of CS_{sum}.

Based on the u_{ij} values as defined in (3), $MA(1, u)$ can find, in the first step, matching $M_1 = \{\{1, 2\}, \{3, 4\}\}$ with $v_1(M_1) = 3$. Then, no matter how the second step matches the pairs to cars (since two cars stay at the same location), the total cost of $MA(1, u)$ will be 4. $TA(1)$ can assign request 1 to car $\gamma(1)$, and request 2 to car $\delta(1)$, and similarly, request 3 to car $\gamma(2)$, and request 4 to car $\delta(2)$. Note that $v_3(\{(k_1, 1), (k_1, 2), (k_2, 3), (k_2, 4)\}) = v_3(\{(k_1, 1), (k_1, 3), (k_2, 2), (k_2, 4)\}) = 6$. Thus the total cost of $TA(1)$ is 4.

To summarize, the instance in Fig. 1 is a worst-case instance for the combined algorithm $CA(1, u)$. □

4.2 Approximation Results for CS_{lat}

For CS_{lat}, we analyze algorithm $CA(2, \mu)$, which outputs the best of the two solutions, $MA(2, \mu)$ and $TA(2)$.

Lemma 7. *For each* $(k, \{i, j\}) \in D \times R^2$, $2w(d_k, s_i) + 2w(d_k, s_j) + \mu_{ij} + \mu_{ji} + \min\{2w(d_k, s_i, t_i) + w(t_i, d_k, s_j, t_j), 2w(d_k, s_j, t_j) + w(t_j, d_k, s_i, t_i)\} \leq \min\{8w(d_k, s_i) + 5\mu_{ij}, 8w(d_k, s_j) + 5\mu_{ji}\}$.

The proof can be found in [8].

Theorem 2. $CA(2, \mu)$ *is a 5/3-approximation algorithm for* CS_{lat}.

Proof. Based on Lemma 2 and Lemma 4, we have $2(v_1(M_1) + v_2(M_2)) + v_3(M_3) \leq \sum_{(k,\{i,j\})\in M^*}(2w(d_k, s_i) + 2w(d_k, s_j) + \mu_{ij} + \mu_{ji} + \min\{2w(d_k, s_i, t_i) + w(t_i, d_k, s_j, t_j), 2w(d_k, s_j, t_j) + w(t_j, d_k, s_i, t_i)\})$. By Lemma 7, $2(v_1(M_1) + v_2(M_2)) + v_3(M_3) \leq \sum_{(k,\{i,j\})\in M^*} \min\{8w(d_k, s_i) + 5\mu_{ij}, 8w(d_k, s_j) + 5\mu_{ji}\}$. Hence we have:

$$
\begin{aligned}
3wait(CA(2, \mu)) &\leq 2wait(MA(2, \mu)) + wait(TA(2)) \\
&\leq 2(v_1(M_1) + v_2(M_2)) + v_3(M_3) \quad \text{(by lemma 1 and 3)} \\
&\leq \sum_{(k,\{i,j\})\in M^*} \min\{8w(d_k, s_i) + 5\mu_{ij}, 8w(d_k, s_j) + 5\mu_{ji}\} \\
&\leq \sum_{(k,\{i,j\})\in M^*} 5\min\{2w(d_k, s_i) + \mu_{ij}, 2w(d_k, s_j) + \mu_{ji}\} \\
&= 5\ wait(M^*).
\end{aligned}
$$

$\square$

5 Conclusions

We have analyzed two algorithms for four different versions of a car sharing problem. One algorithm, called match and assign, first matches the requests into pairs, and then assigns the pairs to the cars. Another algorithm, called transportation assigns two requests to each car. These two algorithms emphasize different ingredients of the total cost and the total latency. Accordingly, we have proved that (for most problem variants) the worst-case ratio of the algorithm defined by the best of the two corresponding solutions is strictly better than the worst-case ratios of the individual algorithms.

We point out that the algorithms can be generalized to handle a variety of situations. We now list these situations, and shortly comment on the corresponding worst-case behavior.

Generalized car-sharing problem: $|R| = a \cdot n$. In this situation, $a \cdot n$ requests are given, and each car can serve a requests, $a \geq 2$. We can extend algorithm TA for the resulting problem by replacing a single car by a cars, and use an appropriately defined cost between a request in R and a car. We obtain that the extended TA algorithm is a $(2a - 1)$-approximation for CS_{sum} and an a-approximation for CS_{lat}, generalizing our results for $a = 2$. We refer to [8] for the proofs.

Related car-sharing problem: different speed. In this situation, we allow that cars have different speeds. Indeed, let car k have speed p_k for each $k \in D$. We denote the travel time of serving requests in R_k by $cost(k, R_k)/p_k$ and the travel time of an allocation M by $\sum_{(k,R_k) \in M} cost(k, R_k)/p_k$. Analogously, we can adapt the latency of serving requests in R_k and the latency of an allocation M. Although it is unclear how to generalize algorithm MA, we can still use algorithm TA(α) in this situation. By defining $v_3(k, i)$ in terms of the cost above, we get the worst-case ratios of TA(α) as shown in Table 1.

Car redundancy or deficiency: $2|D| > |R|$ or $2|D| < |R|$. We shortly sketch how to modify TA(α) for this situation. For the problem with $2|D| > |R|$, by adding a number of dummy requests R_d with $|R_d| = 2n - |R|$, where the distance between any two requests in R_d is 0, the distance between a request in R_d and R is a large constant, and the distance between a request in R_d and a car in D is 0, an instance of our problem arises. For the problem with $2|D| < |R|$, by adding a number of dummy cars D_d with $|D_d| = \lceil |R|/2 \rceil - n$, where the distance between a car in D_d and a request in R is 0, an instance of our problem arises. We claim that minor modifications of the proofs for TA imply that TA(1) is a 3-approximation algorithm for CS_{sum}, and TA(2) is a 2-approximation algorithm for CS_{lat}, On the other hand, it is not clear how to generalize MA(α, v) for this situation.

References

1. How uberpool works. https://www.uber.com/nl/en/ride/uberpool/. Accessed 20 Jan 2020
2. Transvision. https://www.transvision.nl/. Accessed 23 Jan 2020
3. Agatz, N., Campbell, A., Fleischmann, M., Savelsbergh, M.: Time slot management in attended home delivery. Transp. Sci. **45**(3), 435–449 (2011)
4. Ashlagi, I., Burq, M., Dutta, C., Jaillet, P., Saberi, A., Sholley, C.: Edge weighted online windowed matching. In: Proceedings of the 2019 ACM Conference on Economics and Computation, pp. 729–742 (2019)
5. Bei, X., Zhang, S.: Algorithms for trip-vehicle assignment in ride-sharing. In: Thirty-Second AAAI Conference on Artificial Intelligence (2018)
6. Gabow, H.N.: Data structures for weighted matching and nearest common ancestors with linking. In: Proceedings of the First Annual ACM-SIAM Symposium on Discrete Algorithms, pp. 434–443 (1990)
7. Goossens, D., Polyakovskiy, S., Spieksma, F.C., Woeginger, G.J.: Between a rock and a hard place: the two-to-one assignment problem. Math. Methods Oper. Res. **76**(2), 223–237 (2012)
8. Luo, K., Spieksma, F.C.R.: Approximation algorithms for car-sharing problems (2020)
9. Stiglic, M., Agatz, N., Savelsbergh, M., Gradisar, M.: Making dynamic ride-sharing work: The impact of driver and rider flexibility. Transp. Res. Part E: Logist. Transp. Rev. **91**, 190–207 (2016)
10. Wang, X., Agatz, N., Erera, A.: Stable matching for dynamic ride-sharing systems. Transp. Sci. **52**(4), 850–867 (2018)
11. Williamson, D.P., Shmoys, D.B.: The Design of Approximation Algorithms. Cambridge University Press, Cambridge (2011)

Realization Problems on Reachability Sequences

Matthew Dippel, Ravi Sundaram, and Akshar Varma$^{(\boxtimes)}$

Northeastern University, Boston, USA
{mdippel,akshar}@ccs.neu.edu,
r.sundaram@northeastern.edu

Abstract. The classical Erdös-Gallai theorem kicked off the study of graph realizability by characterizing degree sequences. We extend this line of research by investigating realizability of directed acyclic graphs (DAGs) given both a local constraint via degree sequences and a global constraint via a sequence of reachability values (number of nodes reachable from a given node). We show that, without degree constraints, DAG reachability realization is solvable in linear time, whereas it is strongly NP-complete given upper bounds on in-degree or out-degree. After defining a suitable notion of bicriteria approximation based on consistency, we give two approximation algorithms achieving $O(\log n)$-reachability consistency and $O(\log n)$-degree consistency; the first, randomized, uses LP (Linear Program) rounding, while the second, deterministic, employs a k-set packing heuristic. We end with two conjectures that we hope motivate further study of realizability with reachability constraints.

Keywords: Reachability sequences · Graph realization · Bicriteria approximation · Strong NP-completeness

1 Introduction

Given a property P, the Graph Realization problem asks whether there exists a graph that satisfies the property P. Starting with the Erdös-Gallai paper [10] on degree sequences [18,21] many other properties have been considered in the literature ranging from eccentricities [6,25] to connectivity and flow [11,12]. The best studied among these remain extensions of realization given degree sequences [1,4] and variants focusing on different subclasses of graphs [7,8,19,20,26]. In addition to their theoretical significance, realization questions occur naturally in numerous application contexts, including network design [12], social networks [5,28], DNA sequencing [29], enumerating chemical compounds [2], and phylogeny and evolutionary tree reconstruction [17,30].

A. Varma—This work was supported by the NSF-CNS-1718286 and NSF-CCF-1535929 grants.

D. Kim et al. (Eds.): COCOON 2020, LNCS 12273, pp. 274–286, 2020.
https://doi.org/10.1007/978-3-030-58150-3_22

We consider the realization problem on digraphs: we are given as input a sequence of tuples $(r_i, I(i), O(i))$, where r_i is the reachability value[1], $I(i)$ the in-degree and $O(i)$ the out-degree of each node $i, 1 \leq i \leq n$; and we wish to determine the existence of a digraph such that each node has the prescribed reachability value and the prescribed in-degree and out-degree. This formulation extends the local properties considered by degree sequences to global properties captured by the reachability sequence. Like all realization problems this has connections [1] to the graph isomorphism problem and graph canonization.

The study of reachability sequences has applications in several contexts. In the scientific context, reachability and degree constraints can reflect measurements obtained from naturally occurring networks with the aim being to generate a model that explains the measurements. Alternatively, from an engineering perspective, the goal may be to find an implementation satisfying the desired properties as specified by the reachability sequences. As an example scenario, consider the spread of a malicious virus in a network. Perhaps the first step to preventing the spread of this disease may be to understand the reach of infected nodes (using reachability values) before controlling the spread by disconnecting infected nodes from neighbors (using degree information). Alternatively, the goal may be to construct resilient networks that restrict the spread of the virus.

1.1 Our Contributions

We characterize the complexity of the realizability of acyclic digraphs as summarized in Table 1. Instead of referring to bounded vs. unbounded in-degree, we simply talk about trees vs. DAGs since trees are DAGs with in-degree bounded by one and they capture the essential behavior of bounded in-degree digraphs. This usage makes the exposition of the hardness results more natural.

Table 1. Reachability realization for unbounded out-degree DAGs is linear time. The other three cases are strongly NP-complete with bicriteria approximation algorithms achieving an approximation factor of $(O(\log n), O(\log n))$.

		Out-degree bounded	Out-degree unbounded
In-Degree	Bounded (Trees)	$(O(\log n), O(\log n))$	$(O(\log n), O(\log n))$
	Unbounded (DAGs)	$(O(\log n), O(\log n))$	Linear-time

- In Sect. 3 we give linear time verifiable, necessary and sufficient conditions, for realizing unbounded out-degree DAGs (Theorem 1).
- We define a notion of bicriteria approximation in Sect. 2 and give two algorithms in Sect. 4 to solve the reachability realization problem, both achieving an $(O(\log n), O(\log n))$-approximation.

---

[1] The reachability value of a node is the number of nodes reachable from that node.

- Theorem 3: Randomized LP rounding algorithm that runs in time $O(n^{\frac{37}{18}})$ if that the matrix multiplication exponent $\omega \approx 2$ and its dual $\alpha \approx 1$ [23].
- Theorem 5: Deterministic algorithm using k-set packing heuristics [13,22] that runs in $n^{O(k^3)}$ time.

- In Sect. 5 we prove the strong NP-completeness of reachability realization when there are degree constraints. This includes one of our most technically involved results, a reduction from a generalized version of 3-PARTITION to show the strong NP-completeness of reachability realization when both in-degree and out-degree are bounded (Theorem 6). We also give simpler reductions from 3-PARTITION for reachability realization when only one of in-degree or out-degree is bounded (Theorems 7, 8).

Both approximation algorithms work in the presence of non-uniform degree bounds, that is, each degree might be a different value. On the other hand, our hardness results, except Theorem 8, prove that reachability realization problems are strongly NP-complete even when the degree bounds are uniform. In particular, we note that the Theorems 6 and 7 which have uniform degree bounds rely on having the in-degree bounded while in Theorem 8, where only the out-degree is bounded, we are only able to show hardness in the non-uniform case.

2   Preliminaries

Let n denote the length of the given reachability sequence and V the set of nodes in the corresponding graph, so that $|V| = n$. For node i in graph G we let $C(i)$ denote the set of children of i, i.e., $C(i) = \{j | (i,j) \in G\}$. The **out-degree** of i, $O_G(i)$ is the number of its children, i.e., $|C(i)|$; the **in-degree** of node i in graph G, $I_G(i)$ is the number of nodes with arcs directed into i. The reachability value of node u is the number of nodes it can reach: $r_u = |\{v : \exists \text{ path from } u \text{ to } v \in G\}|$. If the graph is a tree the reachability value r_i can be recursively defined as $1 + \sum_{j \in C(i)} r_j$. A rooted tree with out-degree upper bounded by k is called a k-**ary tree** otherwise they are **general trees**. **Full trees** are k-ary trees where every out-degree is either k or 0. A **complete k-ary tree** is a k-ary tree with every level except possibly the last filled and all nodes in the last level filled from the left. The unique reachability sequence of such trees is denoted by $T_k^c(n)$.

We now define the appropriate notions for the purpose of approximation. We say that a graph G is δ-**in-degree consistent** with graph H if they have the same set of nodes and if for all nodes i the following holds: $I_H(i) \leq I_G(i) \leq \delta \cdot I_H(i)$. Here in-degree can be replaced with out-degree to get δ-**out-degree consistency**. If a graph G is both in-degree and out-degree consistent with graph H, then we say it is δ-**degree-consistent**. For ρ-**reachability consistency** we generalize the idea of reachability to get a similar notion of approximation as degree consistency. Given a tree we say that it is ρ-reachability consistent if for all nodes i the following holds: $a_i \leq 1 + \sum_{j \in C(i)} a_j \leq \rho \cdot a_i$, where a_i is the reachability label on node i in the approximate solution. The above notion of approximation can be extended to DAGs by replacing the inequality constraint with $a_i \leq O_G(i) + \max_{j \in C(i)} a_j \leq \rho \cdot a_i$. Finally, we utilize the language of bicriteria optimization (see [9,27]) to say that G (ρ, δ)-**approximates** graph H if it is ρ-reachability consistent with the reachability sequence of H and it is δ-degree consistent with H. This captures the intuition that G approximately matches both the structure of G and its reachability sequence.

3 Linear Time Algorithm for DAGs

We show that there exist polynomial-time verifiable, necessary and sufficient conditions that characterize reachability sequences of unbounded out-degree DAGs. This is reminiscent of conditions for the reconstruction of graphs given degree sequences (see [10]). However it is in contrast to the hardness result of degree realization for DAGs [8,20]. The inequalities in this section are deceptively simple considering the hardness results we prove in Sect. 5. Readers fond of puzzles are invited to prove the inequalities in Theorem 1 themselves before reading on.

Theorem 1 (DAG reachability). *Given a sequence of natural numbers* $\{r_1, r_2, \ldots, r_n\}$ *in non-decreasing order there exists a DAG for which the given sequence is the sequence of the reachability sizes of the DAG iff* $r_i \leq i$ *for all* i.

Proof. In a DAG, nodes can only reach nodes with a strictly lower reachability otherwise its reachability would increase to a higher value causing a contradiction. Since there are at most $i - 1$ nodes of lower reachability than r_i, it can reach at most i nodes including itself. Hence $r_i \leq i$ is a necessary condition. Next, for all i, connect i to the first $r_i - 1$ nodes. Observe that, excluding itself, i cannot reach more than $r_i - 1$ nodes since every node j it connects to can only connect to a node k with $k < j$ but i is already connected to k. Hence it can reach exactly r_i nodes and the inequality is also a sufficient condition. $\square$

4 Approximation Algorithms

We present two approximation algorithms that are ρ-reachability consistent and δ-degree consistent with $\rho = \delta = O(\log n)$ given the reachability sequence along with the degree sequence. Thus the (ρ, δ)-approximation factor for our algorithms comes out to be $(O(\log n), O(\log n))$. The randomized algorithm runs in $O(n^{\omega + \max\{\frac{1}{18}, \omega - 2, \frac{1-\alpha}{2}\}})$ time as detailed in Sect. 4.1 while the deterministic algorithm runs in $n^{O(k^3)}$ time as we detail in Sect. 4.2. We compare further trade-offs between the two algorithms in Sect. 4.3 including the motivation for the more technically involved deterministic algorithm. While the exposition for both the algorithms addresses details using the full k-ary tree case, the results extend to all acyclic digraph cases in a straightforward manner by replacing reachability and degree consistency conditions for trees with that of DAGs.

4.1   LP Based Randomized Rounding (LPRR) Algorithm

The intuition behind the LPRR algorithm is to model the desired graph G as a collection of flows. Between every pair of nodes r_i and r_j with $r_i > r_j$ we assume a flow f_{ij} on each edge out of i and into j. We have three constraints for each node: the sum of flows into it is $l(i)$ (in-degree requirement), the sum of flows out of it is $O_G(i)$ (out-degree requirement), and that the reachability consistency conditions are satisfied. Further, there cannot be an edge (f_{ij} must be 0) from node i to node j if node i has a smaller reachability value than node j.

The existence of G guarantees that the LP is feasible. After solving for a feasible set of f_{ij} values we round each edge ij to 1 with probability f_{ij} independently $24 \ln n$ times. Each time an edge is rounded to 1 it is added to the solution (initialized to a graph with all nodes in V but no edges). We then argue that the resulting structure satisfies the approximate reachability and degree consistency requirements with high probability using concentration bounds.

$$
\begin{aligned}
\min \quad & 1 \\
\text{s. t.} \quad & \sum_j f_{ji} = l(i) \ \forall i, && \text{In-degree requirement} \\
& \sum_j f_{ij} = O_G(i) \ \forall i, && \text{Out-degree requirement} \\
& r_i = 1 + \sum_j f_{ij} \cdot r_j \ \forall i, && \text{Reachability consistency} \\
& f_{ij} = 0 \ \forall i,j \text{ s.t. } r_i \le r_j && \text{Acyclicity}
\end{aligned}
$$

In particular, the following multiplicative form of the Chernoff bound is used.

Theorem 2. *Let $X = \sum_{i=1}^n X_i$, where X_i are independent Bernoulli trials with $\Pr[X_i = 1] = p_i \ \forall \ 1 \le i \le n$ and let $\mu = \mathbb{E}[X] = \sum_{i=1}^n p_i$. Then, for $0 < \epsilon < 1$*

$$
\Pr[|X - \mu| \ge \epsilon] \le 2e^{-\mu \epsilon^2 / 3} \tag{1}
$$

Theorem 3 (LPRR). *Given a reachability sequence for a full k-ary tree, T, there exists a randomized $O(n^{\omega + \max\{\frac{1}{18}, \omega - 2, \frac{1-\alpha}{2}\}})$-time algorithm that constructs a DAG that is an $(O(\log n), O(\log n))$-approximation to T.*

Proof. **Analysis of running time:** Clearly the bottleneck here is the LP solver and the state of the art solver runs in $O(n^{\omega + \max\{\frac{1}{18}, \omega - 2, \frac{1-\alpha}{2}\}})$ time [23] where ω is the best known matrix multiplication exponent [24] and α is its dual. Further, under the common belief that $\omega \approx 2$ and $\alpha \approx 1$, our algorithm runs in $O(n^{\frac{37}{18}})$.

Proof of Correctness: First, observe that vertex i has a total flow of $l(i)$ coming into it. So in one rounding the expected in-degree will be $l(i)$ and after $24 \ln n$ roundings the expected in-degree value will be $\mu_1 = 24 \ln n \cdot l(i)$. Invoking Chernoff bound with $\epsilon = 1/2$ we get that the probability that the node's in-degree lies outside the range $[\mu_1/2, 3\mu_1/2]$ is at most $2/n^2$. Similarly, we get the expected out-degree to be $\mu_2 = 24 \ln n \cdot O_G(i)$ and the probability that the out-degree of any node lies outside the range $[\mu_2/2, 3\mu_2/2]$ is at most $2/n^2$. Further for any node i, the reachability $1 + \sum_j f_{ij} \cdot r_j$ will have expected value $\mu_3 = 24 \ln n \cdot r_i$ and the probability that it lies outside the range $[\mu_3/2, 3\mu_3/2]$ is at most $2/n^2$. Applying the union bound over the $3n$ constraints in the LP, the probability that any of them lies outside their prescribed range is at most $3n \cdot \frac{2}{n^2} = o(1)$ as n goes to infinity. Thus with high probability after rounding, all of the quantities are within their prescribed ranges, i.e., the degree and reachability consistency are guaranteed to be within a logarithmic factor giving us the required (ρ, δ)-approximation. $\square$

4.2 k-set Packing Based Deterministic Algorithm

We give the intuition behind the algorithm, DSHS (Deterministic Sieving using Hurkens-Schrijver) before presenting the technical details. DSHS runs in two (essentially independent) sieving phases, each phase taking $O(\log n)$ rounds: The MatchChildren phase matches each node (other than the leaves) with a (valid) set of children. The MatchParent phase matches each node (other than the root) with a parent.[2] Each phase starts with the entire set of candidate nodes and in each round sets up a $(k+1)$-set packing problem. The problem of k-set packing is to find the largest *disjoint* sub-collection of a given collection of sets each of cardinality k. The (approximate) solution to this problem sieves or reduces the candidate set by a constant factor, allowing each phase to finish in $O(\log n)$ rounds. Putting the results from the two phases together we get the desired (ρ, δ)-approximation factor. We use the following improvement of Hurkens-Schrijver's algorithm [22]. Note that a smaller ϵ can improve the approximation but comes at the cost of a worse running time.

Theorem 4 (Theorem 5, Furer-Yu [13]; with $\epsilon = \frac{1}{3}$). *The $(k+1)$-Set Packing problem can be approximated to a factor $\frac{3}{k+3}$ in deterministic time $n^{O(k^3)}$.*

Theorem 5 (DSHS). *Given a reachability sequence $\{r_1, r_2, \ldots, r_n\}$ for a full k-ary tree, T, there exists a deterministic $n^{O(k^3)}$-time algorithm that constructs a DAG that is an $(O(\log n), O(\log n))$-approximation to T.*

Proof. **DSHS (Deterministic Sieving using Hurkens-Schrijver):** We initialize using an empty DAG with all the n nodes and no edges.

Phase MatchChildren: Initialize C_1 to be the set of all candidate nodes: nodes other than leaves (which have value 1). In round t the universe consists of C_t along with an entire set of V. Note that this has cardinality $|C_t| + |V|$ and is not the same as $C_t \cup V$. We create a collection of all possible $(k+1)$-sets with each set consisting of an element i from C_t and k elements, $j_1, j_2, \ldots, j_k$ from V such that $r_i = 1 + r_{j_1} + r_{j_2} + \ldots + r_{j_k}$. Note that each $(k+1)$-set is a possible match for i to its children. The existence of T guarantees that the optimal solution to this $(k+1)$-Set Packing problem has size $|C_t|$ – namely the sub-collection

---

[2] The root will have value n and leaves will have value 1.

consisting of each candidate node and its k children in T. Invoking the Hurkens-Schrijver approximation algorithm from the above theorem we are guaranteed to find a collection of sets that is at least $(3/(k+2)) \cdot |C_t|$. We use this sub-collection of sets to augment our solution DAG with the corresponding arcs from the node i to each of its children $(j_1, j_2, \ldots, j_k)$ for each set. We also remove the corresponding candidate nodes i from C_t to get C_{t+1}. Phase MatchChildren ends when the candidate set C_t becomes empty.

Phase MatchParent: Initialize P_1 to be the set of all candidate nodes: nodes other than leaves. In round t the universe consists of P_t along with an entire set of V. Note that this has cardinality $|P_t| + |V|$ and is not the same as $P_t \cup V$. We create a collection of all possible $(k+1)$-sets with each set consisting of one element, i from P_t and k elements from V, of which one, j is the parent and the remaining $k - 1$ nodes $j_1, j_2, \ldots, j_{k-1}$ are siblings of i such that $r_j = 1 + r_i + r_{j_1} + r_{j_2} + \ldots + r_{j_{k-1}}$. Note that each $(k+1)$-set is a possible match for i to its parent j. The existence of T guarantees that the optimal solution to this $(k+1)$-Set Packing problem has size $|P_t|$ – namely the sub-collection consisting of each candidate node and its parent and siblings in T. Invoking the Hurkens-Schrijver approximation algorithm from the above theorem we are guaranteed to find a collection of sets that is at least $(3/(k+2)) \cdot |P_t|$. We use this sub-collection of sets to augment our solution DAG with the corresponding arcs from the node j to i and to each of its $k-1$ siblings for each set. We also remove the corresponding candidate nodes, i from P_t to get P_{t+1}. Phase MatchParent ends when the candidate set P_t becomes empty.

Analysis of Running Time: The bottleneck step is running the Hurkens-Schrijver approximation algorithm for set-packing which takes $n^{O(k^3)}$ time. Each of the two phases takes a logarithmic number of rounds, $\log_{\frac{k+2}{k-1}} n$ to be precise, which is absorbed into the total $n^{O(k^3)}$-time since the big-O is in the exponent.

Proof of Correctness: Note that after phase MatchChildren every eligible node is matched to exactly k children satisfying the reachability consistency condition exactly. However, some nodes may not have parents and some may have too many parents. Still every node is guaranteed to get at most one parent per round and so no node has more than $O(\log n)$ parents at the end of Phase MatchChildren. Similarly, after phase MatchParent every eligible node has at least one parent. However some parents may get too many children. Yet, in each round a parent gets at most k children and so no node gets more than $O(k \log n)$ children. Thus at the end of the two phases we are guaranteed $O(\log n)$-degree consistency. Now observe that in each round of either phase, each node i either gets a valid set of k children, that is children $j_1, j_2, \ldots j_k$ such that $r_i = 1 + r_{j_1} + r_{j_2} + \ldots + r_{j_k}$, or no children at all; and we know that at the end of Phase MatchChildren every node other than leaves gets at least one valid set of children. Hence, we are guaranteed an $O(\log n)$-reachability consistent solution. Thus the solution DAG at the end of both phases is an (ρ, δ)-approximation to T. $\square$

4.3   Trade-Offs Between the Two Approximation Algorithms

The major trade-off between the DSHS and LPRR algorithms is the running time; while DSHS runs in $n^{O(k^3)}$, the LPRR algorithm is independent of k and runs in $O(n^\omega)$. Hence, unlike the deterministic algorithm, the randomized algorithm can be used even when k is a function of n. We also note that LPRR can be derandomized using the method of conditional probability [3]. While these might suggest that the more complex and technically involved DSHS algorithm is inferior, that is not the case. The LPRR algorithm results in more complex solutions, in particular, LPRR may return digraphs with multi-edges while DSHS is guaranteed to return simple digraphs. Also, the multi-edges provide a tighter concentration of reachability consistency, albeit away from the reachability values, which may be a desirable property in applications where certainty is more important than consistency. While that is an important application, it is more common to require simple digraphs which the randomized algorithm cannot guarantee. This motivates the more technically involved DSHS algorithm.

5   Strong NP-completeness Results

When the in-degrees and/or the out-degrees are constrained by the degree sequence we prove strong NP-completeness [15] using pseudo-polynomial transformations [16]. The reductions embed an instance of problems like 3-PARTITION between two consecutive levels of a tree. We first present the proof for the full k-ary tree realization problem (all in-degrees 1 or 0 and all out-degrees k or 0) in Sect. 5.1 which illustrates all the technicalities involved. We give a simpler reduction (in Sect. 5.2) to prove that realization of general trees (no out-degree bound) is also strongly NP-complete. In Sect. 5.3 we give a reduction to prove strong NP-completeness when there is only an out-degree bound.

5.1   Hardness of Realization for Full k-ary Trees

We prove hardness of the realization problem for full k-ary trees by reduction from the K-PwT problem, which we show to be strongly NP-complete via an involved series of reductions in the full version. Since K-PwT is strongly NP-complete we can reduce from a subclass, Π_p, such that the largest number in the instance is polynomially bounded, formally, $\text{MAX}[I] \leq p(\text{LENGTH}[I])$, $\forall I \in \Pi_p$.

Problem 1 (K-PwT). Given a set X with $|X| = Km$, $K \geq 2$, sizes $s : X \mapsto \mathbb{Z}^+$ and a target vector $B = (b_1, \ldots, b_m) \in \mathbb{N}^m$, can X be partitioned into m disjoint sets $A_1, A_2, \ldots, A_m$, such that, $|A_i| = k$ and $\sum_{a \in A_i} s(a) = b_i$, for $1 \leq i \leq m$?

Theorem 6 (Full k-ary tree). *It is strongly NP-complete to determine the existence of a full k-ary tree whose reachability sequence equals a given sequence.*

Proof. The problem is clearly in NP since a tree acts as a certificate. Set $k = K$ and define a number M which is a power of K, is much greater in magnitude than any of the other numbers in the problem, and is polynomially bounded by the maximum integer in the K-PwT instance (Eq. 2). We also define m' and m'' such that $m + m'$ and $m + m''$ are powers of K (Eq. 3).

$$M_1 = \max\left(\{s(x_i)|x_i \in X\} \cup \{b_i|b_i \in B\}\right); M_2 = KmM_1; M = K^{\lceil \log_k M_2 \rceil} \quad (2)$$

$$m' = K^d - Km, \ m'' = K^{d-1} - m = m'/K, \text{ where } d = \lceil \log_K(Km) \rceil \quad (3)$$

We make the sequence $S = C \cup P \cup G \cup D$ using four "component" sequences: the "child component" $C = C' \cup C''$, the "parent component" $P = P' \cup P''$, the "ancestor component" G and the "descendant component" D.

The "child component" C is the union of the C' and C'' while the "parent component" P is the union of the P' and P''. C' is in one-to-one correspondence with the set X, using the sizes of elements from X with M added to them while P' is in one-to-one-correspondence with B with changes to accommodate those made to sizes of elements of X while making C'. The sets C'' and P'' ensure that the cardinality of C and P respectively are a power of K.

We construct the "ancestor component" in "levels". The lowest level l_{d-2} is constructed from P, by arbitrarily taking blocks of K elements, adding them all up and incrementing the result by one. Formally, order the elements in P arbitrarily as $P_1, P_2, \ldots, P_{K^{d-1}}$ and let $l_{d-2} = \{l_{d-2,i} \mid l_{d-2,i} = 1 + \sum_{j=1}^K P_{(i-1)K+j}, 1 \leq i \leq K^{d-2}\}$. Other levels l_{d-i} are constructed in a similarly from levels l_{d-i+1}. This is continued until l_0 which has only one element since $|P|$ is a power of K and the size of each level above reduces by a factor of K. The element in l_0 would be the largest number in the final instance. The "descendant component" is constructed using reachability sequences of complete trees on the elements $c_i \in C$. For each such c_i, we make a complete k-ary tree on c_i nodes and use its reachability sequence $T_k^c(c_i)$. The descendant component is then $D = \bigcup_i T_k^c(c_i)$. Since each $c_i \in C$ has the form $Kx + 1$, $T_k^c(c_i)$ will also be full trees.

$$C' = \left\{K(s(x) + M) + 1 \Big| x \in X\right\}, \ C'' = \{\overbrace{KM + 1, \ldots, KM + 1}^{m' \text{ times}}\} \quad (4)$$

$$P' = \left\{K(b_i + KM + 1) \Big| b_i \in B\right\}, \ P'' = \{\overbrace{K^2M + K, \ldots, K^2M + K)}^{m'' \text{ times}}\} \quad (5)$$

$$G = \bigcup_{i=0}^{d-2} l_i, \text{ where "levels" } l_i \text{ are defined in text}; \ D = \bigcup_{i=1}^{K^d} T_k^c(c_i), \ \forall c_i \in C \quad (6)$$

Constructing S takes polynomial time as elements in P and C are derived directly from the K-PwT instance, there are a logarithmic number of levels each computed in polynomial time, and the polynomial number of trees in D each be computed in linear time. All that remains is to prove that the reduction is valid.

By construction, elements in G and P will form a partial full k-ary tree with the elements in P as the "leaves", elements in C and D will make a forest with elements from C as roots of the trees in the forest, and C'' can be arbitrarily partitioned to connect to P'' elements. If there is a partition of X, we can partition C' accordingly to complete the tree.

To prove that a full k-ary tree implies a partition it is sufficient to prove that in any tree the set of children of P' is equal to C', that is, the nodes of P' and C' occur in consecutive levels in any tree. The node in l_0 is the largest and will necessarily have to be the root. This will be followed by the nodes from l_1 since no other nodes are large enough to reach those in l_0 (given the out-degree bound of k). Continuing the argument, $l_i \in G$ will always appear in consecutive levels in any tree and that P will follow below G. Since the in-degree is 1 no node from $p \in P$ will be a child of any $p' \in P$. Further, nodes in D will all be less than M/K in value and hence k of them will not be enough to reach nodes in P thus necessitating that all children of nodes of P come from C. We note that nodes from C' can not be children of nodes from P'' and so the set of children of P'' have to be C''. Since a value of the order of KM has to be reached for nodes in P' and all nodes in C' are of the order of M, all the nodes from C' will be used. Thus any tree will have nodes from P' and C' in consecutive levels and therefore have a partition. This proves NP-completeness and as the maximum integer used is polynomially bounded it also proves strong NP-completeness. □

5.2 Hardness of Realization for General Trees

Theorem 7 (General Trees). *It is strongly NP-complete to realize a general tree given a reachability sequence.*

Proof. This problem is in NP as a tree acts as a certificate and all that remains is give a reduction from 3-PARTITION.

Problem 2 (3-PARTITION). Given a set A, a target B and a size function $s : A \to Z^+$ such that $|A| = 3m$ and $B/4 < s(a_i) < B/2 \ \forall a_i \in A$, can A be partitioned into m disjoint sets $A_1, A_2, \dots, A_m$, such that for $1 \leq i \leq m$, $\sum_{a \in A_i} s(a) = B$?

Since this problem is strongly NP-complete [14], for the reduction, we use an instance of 3-PARTITION wherein the numbers are polynomially bounded in the input length. The notation $[n]$ is used for the set consisting of the first n natural numbers. The constructed instance is as follows:

$$S = \{m(B+1)+1\} \cup \{B+1, \dots \ m \text{ times } \dots, B+1\} \cup \left(\bigcup_{i=1}^{m} [s(a_i)] \right)$$

This construction is clearly polynomial time, all that remains is to show that this is valid reduction. In an abuse of notation the reachability size is often used to refer to the node with that reachability size.

In any potential tree, then the $m(B+1)+1$ node is forced to be the root as it cannot be the child of any node. Further, it will have m children, all the $B+1$ nodes as they cannot be the children of any other node. Considering the remaining nodes in a bottom up fashion, we see that a fixed structure is enforced on all these nodes due to the in-degree constraint in rooted trees. Any 2 node can only have a 1 as it's child, exhausting all 1's and leaving only 2's to be single children of 3's and only 3's as children for 4's and so on. By construction, there are exactly as many nodes of size $s - 1$ as there are nodes of size s for all $s < B + 1$ and hence they all get exhausted. This enforces that each node labelled $s(a_i)$ is a root of a path consisting of nodes with sub-tree sizes $[s(a_i)]$.

These restrictions are always present and a tree can be realized iff the paths rooted at $s(a_i)$ can be correctly made children of the $B + 1$ nodes. This happens iff there is a partition of the 3-PARTITION instance; if there is no partition then the paths cannot be joined to the partial tree above it to form a single tree. □

5.3   Hardness of Realization with Out-Degree Constraints

Theorem 8 (Bounded out-degree). *It is strongly NP-complete to realize an acyclic graph given a reachability sequence and out-degree constraints.*

Proof. We reduce from 3-PARTITION, again using an instance with the maximum number polynomially bounded in the length of the problem. Let $s_i := s(a_i)$ and $M := mB^2$ and note that M is much bigger than every number in the 3-PARTITION instance and that the $\sum_i s_i = mB$. Let the reachability sequence $S := S_s \cup S_b \cup S_a$ where $S_s = \{Ms_i\}$, S_b be a multiset with m copies of $MB + 1$, and S_1 be a multiset of $mB - |A|$ copies of 1. Let the out-degree constraint for $MB + 1$ nodes be equal to three and for the s_i nodes be equal to s_i.

To achieve out-degree constraints, each of the s_i nodes will need to pick up $s_i - 1$ ones exhausting nodes in S_1. For the $MB + 1$ nodes to achieve their degree requirement they'll have to pick up exactly three nodes from S_s set which will be possible iff there is a valid partition of the 3-PARTITION instance. □

6   Conclusion

In this paper we initiate the study of the realization problem for DAGs and rooted directed trees given a reachability sequence. We provide a linear time algorithm for DAGs with unbounded out-degrees and show hardness results for variants when we are also given a degree sequence bounding the in-degree and/or out-degree. We define a notion of bicriteria approximation based on reachability and degree consistency and give two $(O(\log n), O(\log n))$-approximation algorithms for all of these problems. We conclude with two intriguing conjectures:

- Given a uniform out-degree bound and a reachability sequence the DAG realizability problem is solvable in poly-time.
- The general digraph realizability problem given a reachability sequence (with or without degree sequences) is strongly NP-complete.

References

1. Aigner, M., Triesch, E.: Realizability and uniqueness in graphs. Disc. Math. **136**(1–3), 3–20 (1994)
2. Akutsu, T., Nagamochi, H.: Comparison and enumeration of chemical graphs. Comput. Struct. Biotechnol. J. **5**(6), e201302004 (2013)
3. Alon, N., Spencer, J.H.: The Probabilistic Method, 4th edn. Wiley Publishing, Hoboken (2016)
4. Bar-Noy, A., Choudhary, K., Peleg, D., Rawitz, D.: Realizability of graph specifications: characterizations and algorithms. In: Lotker, Z., Patt-Shamir, B. (eds.) SIROCCO 2018. LNCS, vol. 11085, pp. 3–13. Springer, Cham (2018). https://doi.org/10.1007/978-3-030-01325-7_1
5. Bar-Noy, A., Choudhary, K., Peleg, D., Rawitz, D.: Graph profile realizations and applications to social networks. In: Das, G.K., Mandal, P.S., Mukhopadhyaya, K., Nakano, S. (eds.) WALCOM 2019. LNCS, vol. 11355, pp. 3–14. Springer, Cham (2019). https://doi.org/10.1007/978-3-030-10564-8_1
6. Behzad, M., Simpson, J.E.: Eccentric sequences and eccentric sets in graphs. Disc. Math. **16**(3), 187–193 (1976)
7. Berger, A.: A note on the characterization of digraphic sequences. Disc. Math. **314**, 38–41 (2014)
8. Berger, A., Müller-Hannemann, M.: How to attack the NP-complete dag realization problem in practice. In: Klasing, R. (ed.) SEA 2012. LNCS, vol. 7276, pp. 51–62. Springer, Heidelberg (2012). https://doi.org/10.1007/978-3-642-30850-5_6
9. Ehrgott, M., Gandibleux, X.: A survey and annotated bibliography of multiobjective combinatorial optimization. OR-Spektrum **22**(4), 425–460 (2000)
10. Erdos, P., Gallai, T.: Graphs with points of prescribed degrees. Mat. Lapok **11**(264–274), 132 (1960)
11. Frank, A.: Augmenting graphs to meet edge-connectivity requirements. SIAM J. Disc. Math. **5**(1), 25–53 (1992)
12. Frank, H., Chou, W.: Connectivity considerations in the design of survivable networks. IEEE Trans. Circ. Theory **17**(4), 486–490 (1970)
13. Fürer, M., Yu, H.: Approximating the k-set packing problem by local improvements. In: Fouilhoux, P., Gouveia, L.E.N., Mahjoub, A.R., Paschos, V.T. (eds.) ISCO 2014. LNCS, vol. 8596, pp. 408–420. Springer, Cham (2014). https://doi.org/10.1007/978-3-319-09174-7_35
14. Garey, M.R., Johnson, D.S.: Complexity results for multiprocessor scheduling under resource constraints. SIAM J. Comput. **4**(4), 397–411 (1975)
15. Garey, M.R., Johnson, D.S.: "Strong"NP-completeness results: motivation, examples, and implications. J. ACM (JACM) **25**(3), 499–508 (1978)
16. Garey, M.R., Johnson, D.S.: Computers and Intractability: A Guide to the Theory of NP-Completeness. WH Freeman and Company, San Francisco (1979)
17. Guindon, S., Gascuel, O.: A simple, fast, and accurate algorithm to estimate large phylogenies by maximum likelihood. Syst. Biol. **52**(5), 696–704 (2003)
18. Hakimi, S.L.: On realizability of a set of integers as degrees of the vertices of a linear graph I. J. Soc. Ind. Appl. Math. **10**(3), 496–506 (1962)
19. Harary, F.: A survey of the reconstruction conjecture. In: Graphs and Combinatorics, pp. 18–28. Springer (1974). https://doi.org/10.1007/BFb0066431
20. Hartung, S., Nichterlein, A.: NP-Hardness and fixed-parameter tractability of realizing degree sequences with directed acyclic graphs. In: Cooper, S.B., Dawar, A., Löwe, B. (eds.) CiE 2012. LNCS, vol. 7318, pp. 283–292. Springer, Heidelberg (2012). https://doi.org/10.1007/978-3-642-30870-3_29

21. Havel, V.: A remark on the existence of finite graphs. Casopis Pest. Mat. **80**(477–480), 1253 (1955)
22. Hurkens, C.A.J., Schrijver, A.: On the size of systems of sets every t of which have an SDR, with an application to the worst-case ratio of heuristics for packing problems. SIAM J. Disc. Math. **2**(1), 68–72 (1989)
23. Jiang, S., Song, Z., Weinstein, O., Zhang, H.: Faster Dynamic Matrix Inverse for Faster LPs. arXiv preprint arXiv:2004.07470 (2020)
24. Le Gall, F.: Powers of tensors and fast matrix multiplication. In: Proceedings of the 39th International Symposium on Symbolic and Algebraic Computation, pp. 296–303. ACM (2014)
25. Lesniak, L.: Eccentric sequences in graphs. Periodica Math. Hungarica **6**(4), 287–293 (1975)
26. Lovász, L.: A note on the line reconstruction problem. In: Classic Papers in Combinatorics, pp. 451–452. Springer (2009). https://doi.org/10.1007/978-0-8176-4842-8_35
27. Marathe, M.V., Ravi, R., Sundaram, R., Ravi, S., Rosenkrantz, D.J., Hunt III, H.B.: Bicriteria network design problems. J. Algorithms **28**(1), 142–171 (1998)
28. Mihail, M., Vishnoi, N.K.: On generating graphs with prescribed vertex degrees for complex network modeling. In: Position Paper, Approx. and Randomized Algorithms for Communication Networks (ARACNE) 142 (2002)
29. Mossel, E., Ross, N.: Shotgun assembly of labeled graphs. IEEE Trans. Netw. Sci. Eng. **6**(2), 145–157 (2017)
30. Ng, M.P., Wormald, N.C.: Reconstruction of rooted trees from subtrees. Disc. Appl. Math. **69**(1–2), 19–31 (1996)

Power of Decision Trees with Monotone Queries

Prashanth Amireddy, Sai Jayasurya, and Jayalal Sarma[✉]

Indian Institute of Technology Madras, Chennai, India
jayalal@cse.iitm.ac.in

Abstract. In this paper we initiate study of the computational power of adaptive and non-adaptive monotone decision trees - decision trees where each query is a monotone function on the input bits. In the most general setting, the monotone decision tree height (or size) can be viewed as a *measure of non-monotonicity* of a given Boolean function. We also study the restriction of the model by restricting (in terms of circuit complexity) the monotone functions that can be queried at each node. This naturally leads to complexity classes of the form $\mathsf{DT}(mon\text{-}\mathcal{C})$ for any circuit complexity class $\mathcal{C}$, where the height of the tree is $\mathcal{O}(\log n)$, and the query functions can be computed by monotone circuits in class $\mathcal{C}$. In the above context, we prove the following characterizations and bounds.

– We show that the decision tree height can be exactly characterized (both in the adaptive and non-adaptive versions of the model) in terms of the *alternation* $(\mathsf{alt}(f))$ of a function (defined as the maximum number of times that the function value changes, in any chain in the Boolean lattice). We also characterize the non-adaptive decision tree height with a natural generalization of certification complexity of a function. We also show upper bounds and characterizations for non-deterministic and randomized variants of the monotone decision trees in terms of $\mathsf{alt}(f)$.
– We show that $\mathsf{DT}(mon\text{-}\mathcal{C}) = \mathcal{C}$ when $\mathcal{C}$ contains monotone circuits for the threshold functions. For AC^0, we show that any function in AC^0 can be computed by a sub-linear height monotone decision tree with queries having monotone AC^0 circuits.
– To explore the logarithmic height case - $\mathsf{DT}(mon\text{-}\mathsf{AC}^0)$ - we show that for any f (on n bits) in $\mathsf{DT}(mon\text{-}\mathsf{AC}^0)$, and for any constant $0 < \epsilon \leq 1$, there is an AC^0 circuit for f with $\mathcal{O}(n^\epsilon)$ negation gates. In contrast, it can be derived from [14] that for every $f \in \mathsf{AC}^0$ with $\mathsf{alt}(f) = \Omega(n)$, and for every $\epsilon > 0$, any AC^0 circuit computing it with $\mathcal{O}(n^\epsilon)$ negations will need at least $\frac{1}{\epsilon}$ depth.

En route the main results, as a tool, we study the monotone variant of the decision list model, and prove corresponding characterizations in terms of $\mathsf{alt}(f)$ and also derive as a consequence that $\mathsf{DT}(mon\text{-}\mathcal{C}) = \mathsf{DL}(mon\text{-}\mathcal{C})$ if $\mathcal{C}$ has appropriate closure properties (where $\mathsf{DL}(mon\text{-}\mathcal{C})$ is defined similar to $\mathsf{DT}(mon\text{-}\mathcal{C})$ but for decision lists).

© Springer Nature Switzerland AG 2020
D. Kim et al. (Eds.): COCOON 2020, LNCS 12273, pp. 287–298, 2020.
https://doi.org/10.1007/978-3-030-58150-3_23

1   Introduction

The decision tree model is a fundamental abstraction that captures computation appearing in various scenarios - ranging from query based decision making procedures to learning algorithms for Boolean functions. The model represents the algorithmic steps in order to compute a Boolean function $f : \{0,1\}^n \to \{0,1\}$, as a sequence of branching operations based on queries to the input bits and the branching depends on the result of the query. It is quite natural to view the branching as a rooted tree where the leaves of the tree are labelled with 0 or 1 to represent value of the function if the computation reaches that leaf.

The simplest form studied is when the queries are directly to bits of the input [7,11] - and hence the nodes of a decision tree (except for leaves) are labelled with input variables which it queries. For a Boolean function f, the (deterministic) decision tree complexity, $\mathsf{DT}(f)$, is the minimum height of any decision tree computing f. By *height*, we always refer to the maximum number of internal nodes in a path from root to a leaf. The size of the decision tree, which is defined as the number of leaves in the tree is an independently interesting measure of complexity of f, and indeed, since the tree is binary, the size cannot be more than exponential in $\mathsf{DT}(f)$. Generalizations of the model of decision trees in the algorithmic setting have been studied - like randomized and quantum decision trees (see [7]). Decision trees can be adaptive and non-adaptive depending on whether, in the algorithm, the next query depends on the Boolean result of the previous queries or not. In the interpretation of the tree, this translates to whether the tree queries the same variable at all nodes in the same level.

The (adaptive) decision tree height, $\mathsf{DT}(f)$ is related to many fundamental complexity measures of Boolean functions. It is known to be polynomially related to degree of f over $\mathbb{R}$, block sensitivity, certificate complexity (see survey [7]) and with the recent resolution of sensitivity conjecture, even to sensitivity of the Boolean function f. Non-adaptive decision trees are not as powerful.

An important generalization of the decision tree model is by allowing stronger queries than the individual bit queries. One of the well-studied models in this direction is that of parity decision trees where each query is a parity of a subset of input bits [12]. Each node in the tree is associated with a subset $S \subseteq [n]^1$ and the query to the input at the node is the function $\oplus_{i \in S} x_i$, where x_i stands for the ith bit of x. The model of parity decision trees received a lot of attention due to its connection to a special case of log-rank conjecture known as the XOR-log-rank conjecture [19]. The conjecture, in particular, implies that the non-adaptive $(\mathsf{DT}_\oplus^{na}(f))$ and adaptive $(\mathsf{DT}_\oplus(f))$ parity decision complexity measures of functions are not polynomially related in general[2].

Other well-studied generalizations of the standard decision tree model include *linear decision trees* [8,16,18] (where each node queries a linear function of the

---

[1] We denote the set $\{1, 2, \ldots n\}$ by $[n]$.

[2] If $\mathsf{supp}(f) = \{S \subseteq [n] \mid \hat{f}(S) \neq 0\}$, $\mathsf{sps}(f) = |\mathsf{supp}(f)|$ and $\mathsf{fdim}(f) = \dim(\mathsf{supp}(f))$, then by [19], $\log \mathsf{sps}(f)/2 \leq \mathsf{DT}_\oplus(f) \leq \mathsf{fdim}(f) = \mathsf{DT}_\oplus^{na}(f)$ [9,15]. The XOR-logrank conjecture [19] states that $\mathsf{DT}_\oplus(f) \leq \mathsf{poly}\,(\log \mathsf{sps}(f))$, and $\exists f$ for which $\mathsf{fdim}(f)$ and $\log(\mathsf{sps}(f))$ are exponentially far apart.

form $\sum_i \alpha_i x_i + \beta > 0$) and *algebraic decision trees* [2,3,17] (where each node queries the sign of a polynomial evaluation of degree at most d in terms of the input variable). Polynomial size linear decision trees can compute knapsack problem which is NP-complete and the above studies prove exponential size lower bounds for explicit languages. Ben-Asher and Newman [1], studied the decision trees when conjunction and disjunction of variables are allowed as queries on the internal nodes and showed lower bounds for the height of such decision trees required to compute the threshold function (Th_n^k).

Our Results: We initiate the study of a new generalization of the decision tree model based on allowing more general queries. The most general version of our model allows the algorithm to query arbitrary monotone functions[3] on the input. We define the deterministic monotone decision tree complexity of a function f, denoted by $\mathsf{DT}_m(f)$ to be the minimum height of any decision tree with monotone queries at each node, that computes f. When the decision tree is non-adaptive we denote it by $\mathsf{DT}_m^{na}(f)$.

DT_m and DT_m^{na} as Measures of Non-monotonicity: Monotone decision tree complexity measures can also be interpreted as a measure of non-monotonicity of the function f. Our first result is an exact characterization of this measure in terms of a well-studied measure of non-monotonicity called *alternation*. For $x \neq y \in \{0,1\}^n$, we say $x \prec y$ if $\forall i \in [n]$, $x_i \leq y_i$. A *chain* $\mathcal{X}$ on $\{0,1\}^n$ is a sequence $\langle x^{(1)}, x^{(2)}, \ldots, x^{(\ell-1)}, x^{(\ell)} \rangle$ such that $\forall i \in [\ell], x^{(i)} \in \{0,1\}^n$ and $x^{(1)} \prec x^{(2)} \prec \ldots \prec x^{(\ell)}$. Alternation of f for a chain $\mathcal{X}$, denoted as $alt(f, \mathcal{X})$ is the number of times the value of f changes in the chain. We define *alternation* of a function f as: $\mathsf{alt}(f) := \max_{\text{chain}\mathcal{X}} alt(f, \mathcal{X})$. Our first main result is the following connection between the monotone decision tree height and the alternation of the function in the case of adaptive and non-adaptive setting. They are exponentially far apart similar to what is conjectured in the case of parity decision trees.

Theorem 1. *For any Boolean function* f, $\mathsf{DT}_m(f) = \lceil \log(\mathsf{alt}(f) + 1) \rceil$, *and* $\mathsf{DT}_m^{na}(f) = \mathsf{alt}(f)$.

En route to proving the above theorem, we also relate a similar generalization of a well-studied computational model called decision lists (see Sect. 2 for a definition). If $\mathsf{DL}_m(f)$ stands for the minimum length of any monotone decision list computing a Boolean function f, then we show that, $\mathsf{DL}_m(f) = \mathsf{alt}(f) + 1$. We also provide a natural generalization of certificate complexity of a Boolean function, denoted by C_m (and its non-adaptive version denoted by C_m^{na}) and show that for every function f, $\mathsf{C}_m^{na}(f) = \mathsf{DT}_m^{na}(f)$ (proof deferred to the full version of this paper).

Non-deterministic & Randomized Monotone Decision Trees: We study non-deterministic & randomized monotone decision trees (see Sect. 5) and consider variants of the definitions, and show equivalences and bounds. In particular, we show constant upper bounds for the height of non-deterministic monotone

---

[3] Indeed, even though the queries are restricted to monotone functions on inputs, the model is universal, since in normal decision trees, the queries are already monotone.

decision trees (Theorem 7) and show characterizations for the height of the randomized version in terms of deterministic monotone decision trees (Theorem 8).

Power of Restricted Query Functions: While the above models provide a measure of non-monotonicity, one of the main drawbacks of the above decision tree model is that, the computational model is not succinctly representable. It is natural to see if we can restrict the query functions to circuit complexity classes which allow succinct representation for functions. An immediate direction is to understand the power of the model if the query functions are restricted to circuit complexity classes; studied in Sect. 6. More formally, we define $\mathsf{DT}(mon\text{-}\mathcal{C})$ to be the class of functions that can be computed by monotone decision trees of height $\mathcal{O}(\log n)$ where each query function has a monotone circuit in $\mathcal{C}$, or equivalently all the queries belong to $mon\text{-}\mathcal{C}$.

To justify the bound of $\mathcal{O}(\log n)$ on the height of monotone decision trees, we show that if we allow the upper bound on height to be asymptotically different from $\Theta(\log n)$, then the class of functions computed by the model will be different from $\mathcal{C}$[4]. More precisely, if $\mathsf{DT}^{d(n)}$ denotes the class of functions computed by monotone decision trees of height at most $d(n)$ (thus $\mathsf{DT}(mon\text{-}\mathcal{C}) \equiv \mathsf{DT}^{\mathcal{O}(\log n)}(mon\text{-}\mathcal{C})$), then we show that, for any $g(n) = o(\log n)$, and $h(n) = \omega(\log n)$, $\mathsf{DT}^{g(n)}(mon\text{-}\mathcal{C}) \subsetneq \mathcal{C}$ and $\mathsf{DT}^{h(n)}(mon\text{-}\mathcal{C}) \not\subseteq \mathcal{C}$. This justifies the question of $\mathsf{DT}(mon\text{-}\mathcal{C})$ vs $\mathcal{C}$. We prove:

Theorem 2. *For any circuit complexity class* $\mathcal{C}$ *such that* $mon\text{-}\mathsf{TC}^0 \subseteq mon\text{-}\mathcal{C}$, $\mathsf{DT}(mon\text{-}\mathcal{C}) = \mathcal{C}$.

Hence, in particular, $\mathsf{DT}(mon\text{-}\mathsf{TC}^0) = \mathsf{TC}^0$. The situation when $\mathcal{C}$ does not contain TC^0 is less understood. We start by arguing that all functions in AC^0 can be computed by monotone decision trees in sub-linear height. More specifically; For any constant r, $\mathsf{AC}^0 \subseteq \mathsf{DT}^{d(n)}(mon\text{-}\mathsf{AC}^0)$ where $d(n) = \Omega\left(\frac{n}{\log^r n}\right)$ (see Theorem 10). It is natural to ask whether the sub-linear height can be improved further. In particular, whether $\mathsf{DT}(mon\text{-}\mathsf{AC}^0)$ is equal to AC^0 or not. Towards this, by using a technique from [14], we first show a negation limited circuit for functions in $\mathsf{DT}(mon\text{-}\mathsf{AC}^0)$:

Theorem 3. *If a Boolean function* f *on* n *variables is in* $\mathsf{DT}(mon\text{-}\mathsf{AC}^0)$, *then for a constant* $\epsilon \in (0, 1]$, *there is an* AC^0 *circuit for* f *with* $\mathcal{O}(n^\epsilon)$ *negation gates.*

In a tight contrast, it can be derived using [14] that if $f \in \mathsf{AC}^0$ with $\mathsf{alt}(f) = \Omega(n)$, then any AC^0 circuit computing it with $\mathcal{O}(n^\epsilon)$ negations will have depth at least $\frac{1}{\epsilon}$ (see Theorem 11). Thus, an asymptotic improvement to this, with respect to the number of negations, will imply $\mathsf{DT}(mon\text{-}\mathsf{AC}^0) \neq \mathsf{AC}^0$.

En route these main results, we also note that the analogously defined class of functions $\mathsf{DL}(mon\text{-}\mathcal{C})$ for decision lists (defined in Sect. 2) is exactly equal

---

[4] It is assumed that in $\mathcal{C}$, all the circuits are polynomial sized, and that there is atleast one function with $\Omega(n)$ alternation.

to $\mathsf{DT}(mon\text{-}\mathcal{C})$. Defining $\mathsf{RDT}(mon\text{-}\mathcal{C})$ similar to $\mathsf{DT}(mon\text{-}\mathcal{C})$ but for randomized decision trees, we show $\mathsf{RDT}(mon\text{-}\mathcal{C}) = \mathsf{DT}(mon\text{-}\mathcal{C}) = \mathsf{DL}(mon\text{-}\mathcal{C}) = \mathcal{C}$ if $mon\text{-}\mathsf{TC}^0 \subseteq mon\text{-}\mathcal{C}$, and $\mathsf{DL}(mon\text{-}\mathsf{AC}^0) = \mathsf{DT}(mon\text{-}\mathsf{AC}^0) \subseteq \mathsf{RDT}(mon\text{-}\mathsf{AC}^0) \subseteq \mathsf{AC}^0$.

2 Preliminaries

In this section, we define the basic terms and notation. Unless mentioned otherwise, Boolean functions discussed in this paper are from $\{0,1\}^n$ to $\{0,1\}$. For definitions of circuits, circuit complexity classes and monotone functions, we refer the reader to [11]. For any circuit complexity class $\mathcal{C}$, we define $mon\text{-}\mathcal{C}$ as the class of functions which can be computed by using monotone circuits in $\mathcal{C}$.

A *monotone decision tree* T is a rooted directed binary tree. Each of its leaves is labelled by a 0 or 1, each internal vertex/node v is labelled by a monotone function $f_v : \{0,1\}^n \to \{0,1\}$. Each internal node has two outgoing edges, one labelled by 0 and another by 1. A computation of T on input $x \in \{0,1\}^n$ is the path from the root to one of the leaves L that in each of the internal vertices v follows the edge that has label equal to the value of $f_v(x)$. Label of the leaf that is reached by the path is the output of the computation. The tree T computes the function $f : \{0,1\}^n \to \{0,1\}$ if and only if on each input $x \in \{0,1\}^n$ the output of T is equal to $f(x)$. Monotone decision tree complexity of f is the minimum height (max. no. of internal nodes in path from root to any leaf) of such a tree computing f. We denote this value by $\mathsf{DT}_m(f)$.

The *monotone decision list* model, denoted by $L = (f_1, c_1)(f_2, c_2) \ldots (f_k, c_k)$ is a series of tuples (f_i, c_i) where each f_i is a monotone function on n variables, and each c_i is a Boolean constant 0 or 1. Here, each (f_i, c_i) is called as a node; f_i the query function of that node and c_i the value of the node. The last query f_k may be often assumed to be the constant function $\mathbf{1}$ w.l.o.g. An input $x \in \{0,1\}^n$ is said to *activate* the node (f_i, c_i) if $f_i(x) = 1$ and $\forall j < i, \; f_j(x) = 0$. Here L is said to represent/compute the following Boolean function f_L defined as: $f_L(x) = c_i$, where x activates the ith node of L. The monotone decision list complexity of a Boolean function f, denote by $\mathsf{DL}_m(f)$, is the minimum size/length (i.e, number of nodes) of a monotone decision list computing it. By simple modifications, we can derive that the monotone decision lists can be assumed to have certain properties : (1) **Alternating Constants**: We can convert a decision list L to an L' computing the same function where the constants c_i's are alternating between 0 and 1. (2) **Forward Firing**: By forward firing, we mean that on any input $x \in \{0,1\}^n$, if certain query of a decision list passes (evaluates to 1), then so do all the queries that follow it. We denote $\mathsf{DL}(mon\text{-}\mathcal{C})$ as the class of functions which can be computed by a decision list of polynomial length where all the query functions belong to $mon\text{-}\mathcal{C}$.

A version of decision list that has been considered in the literature is when we allow the query functions to be just $\wedge$ of variables; called *monotone term decision lists* [10]. When the query functions are allowed to be general (non-monotone) terms, then they are called *term decision lists* [6] and the class of functions computed by TDLs of size at most $\mathsf{poly}(n)$ is denoted by TDL.

Recalling the definition of *alternation* of a function from the introduction, we state the following characterization of Boolean functions originally proved in [4]. *For any* $f : \{0,1\}^n \to \{0,1\}$ *there exists* $k = \mathsf{alt}(f)$ *monotone functions* $f_1, \ldots, f_k$ *each from* $\{0,1\}^n$ *to* $\{0,1\}$ *such that* $f(x) = \oplus_{i=1}^{k} f_i$ *if* $f(0^n) = 0$ *and* $f(x) = \neg \oplus_{i=1}^{k} f_i$ *if* $f(0^n) = 1$.

3   Monotone Decomposition of Boolean Functions

Motivated by the characterization stated in previous section we define a monotone decomposition of a Boolean function as follows: For any Boolean function $f : \{0,1\}^n \to \{0,1\}$, the monotone decomposition of f is a minimal set of monotone functions $M = \{f_1, f_2, \ldots f_k\}$ such that $f = \oplus_{i \in [k]} f_i$ where k is said to be the size/length of the decomposition. We call each f_i to be the monotone components in the decomposition. We define two constraints on the such monotone decompositions: (1) Implication property: There exists an ordering of M such that $\forall i \in [k-1]$, $f_i \implies f_{i+1}$ holds. In this case, the decompositions are called *boundary decompositions* and the f_is are called *boundary functions*. (2) Optimality Property: If the set M is also of minimum size monotone decomposition of f then we term it as *alternation decomposition* of the function f.

For a given function, even the alternation decomposition of f need not be unique. When all chains in the Boolean hypercube have the same alternation, then the decomposition can be proved to be unique.

We now state this as the following lemma (from [4]) bringing out the extra properties that we need - the proof follows easily from the proof in [4].

Lemma 1. *For any Boolean function* $f : \{0,1\}^n \to \{0,1\}$ *there is a monotone decomposition with implication and optimality properties of length* $\mathsf{alt}(f)$ *(if* $f(0^n) = 0$*) and length* $\mathsf{alt}(f) + 1$ *(if* $f(0^n) = 1$*).*

Constraints on Monotone Components: We continue the study in this section by imposing complexity constraints on the function f. A natural question to ask is if the monotone components of f in its monotone decomposition are necessarily harder than f in terms of circuit complexity classes. We first answer this question for classes that contain monotone circuits for the threshold functions. In this case, we show that we can always find a monotone decomposition where the component functions are in *mon-C*. The proof details are deferred to full version.

Lemma 2. *If mon-*$\mathsf{TC}^0 \subseteq$ *mon-C, then for any* f *computed by a circuit in the class* $\mathcal{C}$, *there is a monotone decomposition* $f_1 \oplus f_2 \oplus \ldots \oplus f_{2n+1}$ *with implication property such that each* f_i *is in mon-C.*

By the above Lemma, for any $f \in \mathsf{TC}^0$ we have given a decomposition into $2n + 1$ monotone TC^0 functions. However, the monotone decomposition can be far from having the optimality property. If the function has uniform alternation among all chains of length $n+1$, then this can be improved to $\mathsf{alt}(f)$ keeping the complexity of the monotone components to be within TC^0 (See full version).

4   Adaptive & Non-adaptive Monotone Decision Trees

In this section, we prove the characterization for adaptive and non-adaptive monotone decision tree heights in terms of alternation of the function.

Adaptive Decision Trees: We will now prove the main theorem of this section which characterizes $\mathsf{DT}_m(f)$ (and en route $\mathsf{DL}_m(f)$ too) in terms of $\mathsf{alt}(f)$.

Theorem 4. *For any Boolean function f, $\mathsf{DT}_m(f) = \lceil \log(\mathsf{alt}(f) + 1) \rceil$.*

Proof. We first establish a relation between $\mathsf{DL}_m(f)$ and $\mathsf{DT}_m(f)$.

Lemma 3. $\mathsf{DT}_m(f) = \lceil \log \mathsf{DL}_m(f) \rceil$.

We only outline the idea[5] here: To go from a decision list to a decision tree - it is easy to convert the decision list into normal form such that $\exists i$ such that for every $x \in \{0,1\}^n$, $f_j(x) = 1$ if $j \geq i$ and 0 otherwise. The monotone decision tree then is designed to find this i by a binary search by querying the monotone functions. The other direction $\mathsf{DL}_m(f) \leq 2^{\mathsf{DT}_m(f)}$ uses an idea due to [5] which was introduced for converting general decision trees to term decision lists. Observe that if all the queries of the decision tree pass on an input, the output will be the label of the rightmost leaf, say c. Thus, we would have (A, c), where A is the $\wedge$ of all queries that lead to the rightmost leaf. Extending this, we construct a monotone decision list with number of nodes same as the no. of leaves in the decision tree.

Thus, it suffices to prove that $\mathsf{DL}_m(f) = \mathsf{alt}(f) + 1$, which we do below:

$\mathsf{DL}_m(f) \leq \mathsf{alt}(f) + 1$: First suppose $f(0^n) = 0$. Then by Lemma 1 there are $k = \mathsf{alt}(f)$ many monotone functions such that $f = f_1 \oplus f_2 \oplus \cdots \oplus f_k$, and $\forall i, f_i \implies f_{i+1}$. It can be shown easily that the monotone decision list $(f_1, 0)(f_2, 1)(f_3, 0)(f_4, 1) \ldots (\mathbf{1}, 0)$ or $(f_1, 1)(f_2, 0)(f_3, 1)(f_4, 0) \ldots (\mathbf{1}, 0)$ computes f, when k is even or odd respectively. On the other hand, if $f(0^n) = 1$, we have $f = f_1 \oplus f_2 \oplus \cdots \oplus f_k \oplus 1$, which gives the monotone decision lists $(f_1, 1)(f_2, 0) \ldots (\mathbf{1}, 1)$ or $(f_1, 0)(f_2, 1) \ldots (\mathbf{1}, 1)$ computing f depending on whether k is even or odd respectively.

$\mathsf{DL}_m(f) \geq \mathsf{alt}(f) + 1$: We claim that if a Boolean function f on n variables can be computed by a monotone decision list $L = (f_1, c_1)(f_2, c_2) \ldots (f_\ell, c_\ell)$ of length ℓ, we have $\mathsf{alt}(f) \leq \ell - 1$. To show this, it suffices to argue that for any chain $\langle x^{(1)}, x^{(2)}, \ldots, x^{(s)} \rangle$ in the Boolean hypercube, where $1 \leq s \leq n+1$; the number of alternations of the function f along the chain is at most $\ell - 1$. Consider the sequence S of length s where for $1 \leq i \leq s$, the integer $S[i]$ is the index of the node activated on inputting $x^{(i)}$ to L. So note that $1 \leq S[i] \leq \ell$ for every i. By definition of the activated node, observe that for any $1 \leq i < s$, $f_{S[i]}(x^{(i)}) = 1$, which implies $f_{S[i]}(x^{(i+1)}) = 1$ too, since $x^{(i)} \prec x^{(i+1)}$. So, the node that $x^{(i+1)}$ activates cannot be after $f_{S[i]}$. That is, $S[i+1] \leq S[i]$ for

---

[5] Using the same constructions, we also observe that $\mathsf{DT}(mon\text{-}\mathcal{C}) = \mathsf{DL}(mon\text{-}\mathcal{C})$ for any circuit complexity class $\mathcal{C}$ with appropriate closure properties.

all $1 \leq i < s$. If two consecutive elements in chain activate the same node, L outputs the same value on these assignments and hence there is no alternation at that point of the chain. So the number of alternations is upper bounded by the number pairs $S[i], S[i+1]$ such that $S[i] \neq S[i+1]$. Since $1 \leq S[i] \leq \ell$ and $S[i] \geq S[i+1]$ for all i, we get $\mathsf{alt}(f) \leq \ell - 1$.

Constructing Adaptive MDTs from Negation Limited Circuits: The above theorem provides a characterization for decision tree height in terms of alternation $\mathsf{alt}(f)$ of the Boolean function. A classical result by Markov [13], implies that any Boolean function can be computed by Boolean circuits that use at most $\lceil \log(\mathsf{alt}(f)+1) \rceil$ many negation gates. Since the number of negation gates in the circuit can be logarithmically smaller, this can give shallow decision trees. By a bottom-up query based evaluations of monotone sub-circuits of the given circuit, we derive the following theorem (details deferred to full version).

Theorem 5. *Let f be a Boolean function computed by a circuit C using k negations. Then there is a monotone decision tree of height $k + 1$ computing f.*

Non-Adaptive Monotone Decision Trees: We first establish a relation between the non-adaptive monotone decision tree and alternation:

Theorem 6. *For any Boolean function, $\mathsf{alt}(f) = k$ if and only if f can be computed by a non-adaptive monotone decision tree of height k.*

We refer the reader to the full version of this paper for a detailed argument. To outline the idea used there; for the forward implication we use Lemma 1 to design the decision tree. For the reverse implication, since the tree is non-adaptive, the query function at each level of the decision tree will be the same. Using this fact, we argue that any chain must have alternation at most k with respect to f.

We now discuss a characterization of non-adaptive monotone decision tree complexity through a generalization of certificate complexity of the function.

Definition 1 (Monotone Certificate Complexity). *For an input $x \in \{0,1\}^n$ of a Boolean function f, we call a set $S_x = \{f_1, f_2 \ldots f_k\}$ of monotone Boolean functions on n variables as a monotone certificate (set) if for any input $y \in \{0,1\}^n$, we have that $[\bigvee_{i=1}^{k} f_i(y) = f_i(x)] \Rightarrow [f(y) = f(x)]$. The monotone certificate complexity of x, denoted $\mathsf{C}_m(f, x)$ is defined as the minimum size $|S_x|$ of a monotone certificate S_x of x. The monotone certificate complexity of the function f itself is defined as $\mathsf{C}_m(f) := max_x\{\mathsf{C}_m(f, x)\}$.*

Interestingly, there is a constant upper bound of the size monotone certificate set for any function f. We show that, $\mathsf{C}_m(f) \leq 2$ (proof given only in full version). If the monotone certificate sets are restrained to be the same for all inputs, we call such a measure as the non-adaptive monotone certificate complexity of the function f, denoted by $\mathsf{C}_m^{na}(f)$. We show that $\mathsf{C}_m^{na}(f) = \mathsf{DT}_m^{na}(f)$ by using the above definition and defer these easy details to the full version of the paper.

5   Non-deterministic and Randomized MDTs

Inspired by the definitions of a non-deterministic decision tree and certificate complexity of a Boolean function, we study a non-deterministic variants of monotone decision trees as well. We define[6] a non-deterministic monotone decision tree as a tree where there can be single or multiple outgoing edges at each internal node, and each edge in the tree is labelled by a monotone function or the negation of a monotone function, and the leaves are labelled 0 or 1. An input is said to be accepted if there is at least one path from the root to a leaf labelled 1 along which all the functions appearing as labels on the edges evaluate to 1. Analogous to the normal monotone decision trees, we prove (details in full version) a bound on the height and the size as the complexity measures of the non-deterministic monotone decision tree (height denoted by $\mathsf{DT}_m^n(f)$).

Theorem 7. *For any Boolean function f, $\mathsf{DT}_m^n(f) \leq 2$ and size of the optimal non-deterministic monotone decision tree is $\lceil \frac{\mathsf{alt}(f)}{2} \rceil$.*

We also study randomized monotone decision trees. In this model, monotone query nodes in the decision tree, random bit choices are also allowed at the internal nodes of the tree and each of the random choice nodes also has two outgoing edges to children one with labelled 0 and the other labelled 1. We say the tree computes a Boolean function f if for any input x, the probability (over the choice of the settings for the random bit choices in the tree) of the computation reaching a leaf with label $f(x)$ is atleast $\frac{2}{3}$. By $\mathsf{DT}_m^r(f)$, we denote the minimum height of a RMDT computing a Boolean function f. The following theorem implies that randomization does not help when the monotone queries are unrestricted. The proof is deferred to the full version due to space constraints.

Theorem 8. *For any Boolean function f, $\mathsf{DT}_m^r(f) = \mathsf{DT}_m(f)$.*

We also study a more powerful variant of the randomized model where each node is allowed to have a multi-set of w monotone functions associated with it (which we call the query set) and on an input x to the decision tree, at each node, one of the query functions is chosen uniformly at random from the corresponding query set. Again, we say that the tree computes a Boolean function f if for any input x, the probability of the computation reaching a leaf with label $f(x)$ is atleast $\frac{2}{3}$. We denote by $\mathsf{DT}_m^{R,w}(f)$, the minimum height of such a randomized decision tree that computes f. It can be observed that any RMDT can be implemented in this model as well with query sets of size 2 at each node: a monotone query f_i being replaced with the query set $\{f_i, f_i\}$, and a node with a random bit choice by the query set $\{\mathbf{0}, \mathbf{1}\}$. This gives $\mathsf{DT}_m^{R,w}(f) \leq \mathsf{DT}_m^r(f)$, $\forall w \geq 2$. For the other direction, the following is shown (details in full version).

Theorem 9. *For any function f, $\mathsf{DT}_m^r(f) \leq (1 + k).\mathsf{DT}_m^{R,w}(f)$, where $w = 2^k$.*

---

[6] In the full version of this paper, we define another natural variant of non-determinism, and show its equivalence to this model.

6   Monotone Decision Trees with Query Restrictions

In this section, we study the power of monotone decision trees under restricted query functions. Recall that $\mathsf{DT}(mon\text{-}\mathcal{C})$ is the class of functions that admit decision trees of height $\mathcal{O}(\log n)$, where n is the number of variables and the query functions are from $mon\text{-}\mathcal{C}$. We first justify our reason to consider the height $\mathcal{O}(\log n)$. By a counting argument, we can derive that for any $h = \omega(\log n)$, there is a function f on n variables that has a decision tree of height h with query functions computed by monotone polynomial sized circuits, but f cannot be computed by a polynomial size circuit. In contrast, for any $h = o(\log n)$, if a function $f \in \mathcal{C}$ on n variables has alternation $\Omega(n)$, then f does not have a decision tree of height h, with query functions computable by monotone circuits in $\mathcal{C}$. With this background, we study $\mathsf{DT}(mon\text{-}\mathcal{C})$ as defined above.

Deterministic MDTs with Query Restrictions: $\mathsf{DT}(mon\text{-}\mathcal{C})$ **vs** $\mathcal{C}$: As mentioned in the introduction, we ask : How much can monotone decision tree computation, with query functions computable by monotone circuits in the class $\mathcal{C}$, simulate general computation in the class $\mathcal{C}$. In this direction, we first show that $\mathsf{DT}(mon\text{-}\mathcal{C}) \subseteq \mathcal{C}$ when $\mathcal{C}$ has reasonable closure properties.

Lemma 4. *For a circuit complexity class $\mathcal{C}$ closed under $\neg, \wedge, \vee$, $\mathsf{DT}(mon\text{-}\mathcal{C}) \subseteq \mathcal{C}$.*

Proof. As we have already established that $\mathsf{DT}(mon\text{-}\mathcal{C}) = \mathsf{DL}(mon\text{-}\mathcal{C})$ in the construction in Lemma 3, it suffices to show that $\mathsf{DL}(mon\text{-}\mathcal{C}) \subseteq \mathcal{C}$. Let the Boolean function f belong to $\mathsf{DL}(mon\text{-}\mathcal{C})$ via the decision list $L = (f_1, c_1)(f_2, c_2) \ldots (f_k, c_k)$ where $k = \mathsf{poly}(n)$; and each query function f_i has a (monotone) circuit C_i from the class $\mathcal{C}$. Using the normal form for the decision lists (see full version) for circuit classes with the above property, we will assume that the c_i's are alternating; and the query functions f_i are forward firing, i.e $f_1 \Rightarrow f_2 \Rightarrow \cdots \Rightarrow f_k$. As we can always (choose to) prepend a $(\mathbf{0}, 0)$ node at the beginning, or append a $(\mathbf{1}, 1)$ node at the end of L while still maintaining the normal form and the function it computes; w.l.o.g we may assume that k is even and $c_1 = 0$. Due to the alternating constants property, this means $c_{2i} = 1$ and $c_{2i-1} = 0$.

We will now show that the Boolean function $g := \overline{f_1} f_2 \vee \overline{f_3} f_4 \cdots \vee \overline{f_{k-1}} f_k$ is equivalent to f. To observe this, we will argue that for any input x, $g(x)$ is equal to the output of L on x. Suppose x activates an even indexed node, say (f_{2i}, c_{2i}). By definition of activated node, it means that $f_{2i}(x) = 1$ and $f_{2i-1}(x) = 0$, which means that the term $\overline{f_{2i-1}} f_{2i}$ in g evaluates to 1 for x. Thus, $g(x) = 1 = c_{2i} = f(x)$. A similar argument can be made when x activates an odd indexed node (say $(2i-1)^{th}$) in L to show that $g(x) = 0 = c_{2i-1} = f(x)$. Finally, we note that because of the closure properties of $\mathcal{C}$, the expression g (equivalent to f) can be converted to a circuit in $\mathcal{C}$. $\qquad\square$

If the class $\mathcal{C}$ is rich enough to include monotone circuits for the threshold functions, for example say the class TC^0 itself, then we can actually prove equality: Note that the Monotone Decomposition given in Lemma 2 can be easily transformed into a MDL with the same functions being queries. Thus, we get $\mathcal{C} \subseteq$ $\mathsf{DL}(mon\text{-}\mathcal{C})$, which when combined with the fact that $\mathsf{DT}(mon\text{-}\mathcal{C}) = \mathsf{DL}(mon\text{-}\mathcal{C})$ (see proof of Lemma 3) and Lemma 4 completes the proof of Theorem 2.

Monotone Decision Trees and AC^0: We now address the question AC^0 vs $\mathsf{DT}(mon\text{-}\mathsf{AC}^0)$. We know that $\mathsf{DT}(mon\text{-}\mathsf{AC}^0) = \mathsf{DL}(mon\text{-}\mathsf{AC}^0)$ is contained in AC^0 by Lemma 4. An interesting challenge is to prove or disprove the reverse containment. It is easy to show that $\mathsf{DT}(mon\text{-}\mathsf{AC}^0)$ is indeed more powerful than polynomial sized term decision lists, which is a strict subset of AC^0 (proof deferred to full version). Towards comparing the class with AC^0, using the above discussion, for any $g(n) = o(\log n)$, and $h(n) = \omega(\log n)$, $\mathsf{DT}^{g(n)}(mon\text{-}\mathsf{AC}^0) \subsetneq$ AC^0 and $\mathsf{DT}^{h(n)}(mon\text{-}\mathsf{AC}^0) \not\subseteq \mathsf{AC}^0$. In contrast to this, we show that the whole of AC^0 can be computed by monotone decision trees with sub-linear height. By using a theorem due to Santha and Wilson (See Theorem 4.1 of [14]), which reduces the number of negations in the circuit to $\frac{n}{\log^r n}$, and then applying Theorem 5, we show:

Theorem 10. $\forall$ constant r, $\mathsf{AC}^0 \subseteq \mathsf{DT}^{d(n)}(mon\text{-}\mathsf{AC}^0)$ where $d(n) = \Omega\left(\frac{n}{\log^r n}\right)$.

We now prove Theorem 3 from the introduction. That is, for any $f : \{0,1\}^n \to \{0,1\}$ in $\mathsf{DT}(mon\text{-}\mathsf{AC}^0)$, and for any constant $0 < \epsilon \leq 1$, there is an AC^0 circuit for f with $\mathcal{O}(n^\epsilon)$ negation gates.

Proof of Theorem 3 (Towards $\mathsf{DL}(mon\text{-}\mathsf{AC}^0) \not\subseteq \mathsf{AC}^0$): Supposing $f \in$ $\mathsf{DL}(mon\text{-}\mathsf{AC}^0)$, by the construction given in the proof of Lemma 4, we can write $f = \overline{f_1}f_2 \vee \overline{f_3}f_4 \vee \ldots \overline{f_{\ell-1}}f_\ell$, where $\ell = \mathcal{O}(n^k)$ for some constant k. In addition, all the f_i's have monotone AC^0 circuits and $\forall i \in [\ell - 1], f_i \implies f_{i+1}$. Thus, it suffices to produce $\overline{f_i}$ for every $i \in [\ell]$ which is odd, from $f_1, \ldots f_n$, using a constant depth polynomial size circuit that uses $\mathcal{O}(n^\epsilon)$ negations. Indeed, the trivial circuit uses $\ell = \mathcal{O}(n^k)$ negations.

The main observation is that the bits (the outputs of f_i where i is odd) we need to invert are already in sorted order, since $\forall i, f_i \implies f_{i+1}$. Let this bit-string be $s = 0^j 1^{m-j}$, where $m := \lceil \ell/2 \rceil$. We need to output $\overline{s} = 1^j 0^{m-j}$.

We now use a construction due to [14] where we divide s into $t = n^\epsilon$ contiguous blocks $B_1 B_2 \ldots B_t$ each of length $p := m/n^\epsilon = \mathcal{O}(n^{k-\epsilon})$. Observe that the negation of block B_i is of the form 1^p or 0^p or $1^j 0^{p-j}$ for some $0 \leq j \leq p$, based on whether B_i witnesses switching from 0s to 1s in s. As proved in [14] (Theorem 3.6 in [14]), this can be implemented using an iterative construction which uses only $\mathcal{O}(n^\epsilon)$ negations. In the proof of Theorem 3.6 in [14], the authors also observe, this part of their construction uses only unbounded $\wedge$ and $\vee$ gates and hence works for AC^0. In contrast, we show a depth lower bound for circuits that use $\mathcal{O}(n^\epsilon)$ negations, and computes functions in AC^0 with high alternation.

Theorem 11. For every $f \in \mathsf{AC}^0$ with $\mathsf{alt}(f) = \Omega(n)$, and for every $\epsilon > 0$, any AC^0 circuit computing it with $\mathcal{O}(n^\epsilon)$ negations will have depth at least $\frac{1}{\epsilon}$

The above Theorem can be derived from the results of [14] (Theorem 3.2 of [14], and verifying that their proof works for single bit output functions also).

Randomized MDTs with Query Restrictions: Similar to the deterministic case, when the height is restricted to $\mathcal{O}(\log n)$, we can define $\mathsf{RDT}(mon\text{-}\mathcal{C})$ for a circuit complexity class $\mathcal{C}$. We show, by carefully using threshold to compute the probability bounds, $\mathsf{RDT}(mon\text{-}\mathcal{C}) = \mathcal{C}$, if $mon\text{-}\mathsf{TC}^0 \subseteq mon\text{-}\mathcal{C}$. By using a carefully constructed normal form for randomized monotone decision trees we also show $\mathsf{RDT}(mon\text{-}\mathsf{AC}^0) \subseteq \mathsf{AC}^0$.

References

1. Ben-Asher, Y., Newman, I.: Decision trees with and or queries. In Proceedings of 10th Annual Conference on Structure in Complexity Theory, pp. 74–81 (1995)
2. Ben-Or, M.: Lower bounds for algebraic computation trees. In: Proceedings of the 15th ACM Symposium on Theory of Computing, pp. 80–86 (1983)
3. Björner, A., Lovász, L., Yao, A.C.C.: Linear decision trees: volume estimates and topological bounds. In Proceedings of the 24th ACM Symposium on Theory of Computing, pp. 170–177 (1992)
4. Blais, E., Canonne, C.L., Oliveira, I.C., Servedio, R.A., Tan, L.-Y.: Learning circuits with few negations. Approx. Random. Comb. Opti. **40**, 512–527 (2015)
5. Blum, A.: Rank-r decision trees are a subclass of r-decision lists. Inf. Process. Lett. **42**(4), 183–185 (1992)
6. Bshouty, N.H.: A subexponential exact learning algorithm for DNF using equivalence queries. Inf. Process. Lett. **59**, 37–39 (1996)
7. Buhrman, H., de Wolf, R.: Complexity measures and decision tree complexity: a survey. Theor. Comput. Sci. **288**(1), 21–43 (2002)
8. Dobkin, D., Lipton, R.J.: A lower bound of n on linear search programs for the knapsack problem. J. Comput. Syst. Sci. **16**, 413–417 (1978)
9. Gopalan, P., O'Donnell, R., Servedio, R.A., Shpilka, A., Wimmer, K.: Testing Fourier dimensionality and sparsity. SIAM J. Comput. **40**(4), 1075–1100 (2011)
10. Guijarro, D., Lavin, V., Raghavan, V.: Monotone term decision lists. Theoret. Comput. Sci. **259**(1), 549–575 (2001)
11. Jukna, S.: Boolean Function Complexity: Advances and Frontiers. Springer, Heidelberg (2012). https://doi.org/10.1007/978-3-642-24508-4
12. Kushilevitz, E., Mansour, Y.: Learning decision trees using the Fourier spectrum. SIAM J. Comput. **22**(6), 1331–1348 (1993)
13. Markov, A.A.: On the inversion complexity of a system of functions. J. ACM **5**(4), 331–334 (1958)
14. Santha, M., Wilson, C.: Limiting negations in constant depth circuits. SIAM J. Comput. **22**(2), 294–302 (1993)
15. Sanyal, S.: Fourier sparsity and dimension. Theory Comput. **15**(11), 1–13 (2019)
16. Snir, M.: Proving lower bounds for linear decision trees. In: Even, S., Kariv, O. (eds.) ICALP 1981. LNCS, vol. 115, pp. 305–315. Springer, Heidelberg (1981). https://doi.org/10.1007/3-540-10843-2_25
17. Steele, J.M., Yao, A.C.: Lower bounds for algebraic decision trees. Technical report, Department of Computer Science, Stanford University (1980)
18. Yao, A.C., Rivest, R.L.: On the polyhedral decision problem. SIAM J. Comput. **9**(2), 343–347 (1980)
19. Zhang, Z., Shi, Y.: On the parity complexity measures of Boolean functions. Theoret. Comput. Sci. **411**(26), 2612–2618 (2010)

Computing a Maximum Clique in Geometric Superclasses of Disk Graphs

Nicolas Grelier$^{(\boxtimes)}$

Department of Computer Science, ETH Zürich, Zürich, Switzerland
nicolas.grelier@inf.ethz.ch

Abstract. In the 90's Clark, Colbourn and Johnson wrote a seminal paper, where they proved that maximum clique can be solved in polynomial time in unit disk graphs. Since then, the complexity of maximum clique in intersection graphs of (unit) d-dimensional balls has been investigated. For ball graphs, the problem is NP-hard, as shown by Bonamy *et al.* (FOCS '18). They also gave an efficient polynomial time approximation scheme (EPTAS) for disk graphs, however the complexity of maximum clique in this setting remains unknown. In this paper, we show the existence of a polynomial time algorithm for solving maximum clique in a geometric superclass of unit disk graphs. Moreover, we give partial results toward obtaining an EPTAS for intersection graphs of convex pseudo-disks.

Keywords: Pseudo-disks · Line transversals · Intersection graphs

1 Introduction

In an *intersection graph*, every vertex can be represented as a set, such that two vertices are adjacent if and only if the corresponding sets intersect. In most settings, those sets are geometric objects, lying in a Euclidean space of dimension d. Due to their interesting structural properties, the intersection graphs of d-dimensional balls, called d-ball graphs, have been extensively studied. For dimensions 1, 2 and 3, the d-ball graphs are called *interval graphs*, *disk graphs* and *ball graphs*, respectively. If all d-balls have the same radius, their intersection graphs are referred to as *unit d-ball graphs*. The study of these classes has many applications ranging from resource allocation to telecommunications [1,8,14].

Many problems that are NP-hard for general graphs remain NP-hard for d-ball graphs, with fixed $d \geq 2$. Even for unit disk graphs, most problems are still NP-hard. A famous exception to this rule is the problem of computing a maximum clique, which can be done in polynomial time in unit disk graphs

---

N. Grelier—The author wants to thank Michael Hoffmann for his advice and his help concerning the writing of the paper. Research supported by the Swiss National Science Foundation within the collaborative DACH project Arrangements and Drawings as SNSF Project 200021E-171681.

© Springer Nature Switzerland AG 2020
D. Kim et al. (Eds.): COCOON 2020, LNCS 12273, pp. 299–310, 2020.
https://doi.org/10.1007/978-3-030-58150-3_24

as proved by Clark, Colbourn and Johnson [6]. Their algorithm requires the position of the unit disks to be given, but a robust version of their algorithm, which does not require this condition, was found by Raghavan and Spinrad [13]. This is a nontrivial matter as Kang and Müller have shown that the recognition of unit d-ball graphs is NP-hard, and even $\exists\mathbb{R}$-hard, for any fixed $d \geq 2$ [12].

Finding the complexity of computing a maximum clique in general disk graphs (with arbitrary radii) is a longstanding open problem. However in 2017, Bonnet et al. found a subexponential algorithm and a quasi polynomial time approximation scheme (QPTAS) for maximum clique on disk graphs [4]. The following year, Bonamy et al. extended the result to unit ball graphs, and gave a randomised EPTAS for both settings [3]. The current state-of-the-art about the complexity of computing a maximum clique in d-ball graphs is summarised in Table 1.

Table 1. Complexity of computing a maximum clique on d-ball graphs

	unit d-ball graphs	general d-ball graphs
$d = 1$	linear [2]	polynomial [10]
$d = 2$	polynomial [6]	Unknown but EPTAS [3,4]
$d = 3$	Unknown but EPTAS [3]	NP-hard [3]
$d = 4$	NP-hard [3]	NP-hard [3]

Bonamy et al. show that the existence of an EPTAS follows from the fact that: For any graph G that is a disk graph or a unit ball graph, the disjoint union of two odd cycles is a forbidden induced subgraph in the complement of G. Surprisingly, the proofs for disk graphs on one hand and unit ball graphs on the other hand are not related. Bonamy et al. ask whether there is a natural explanation of this common property. They say that such an explanation could be to show the existence of a geometric superclass of disk graphs and unit ball graphs, for which there exists an EPTAS for solving maximum clique.

By looking at Table 1, a pattern seems to emerge: The complexity of computing a maximum clique on $(d-1)$-ball graphs and unit d-ball graphs might be related. We extend the question of Bonamy et al. and ask for a geometric intersection graphs class that contains all interval graphs and all unit disk graphs, for which maximum clique can be solved in polynomial time. Recall that finding the complexity of maximum clique in disk graphs is still open. Therefore a second motivation for our question is that showing the existence of polynomial time algorithms for geometric superclasses of unit disk graphs, may help to determine the complexity of maximum clique in disk graphs.

We introduce a class of geometric intersection graphs which contains all interval graphs and all unit disk graphs, for which we show that maximum clique can be solved efficiently. Furthermore, the definition of our class generalises to any dimension, i.e. for any fixed $d \geq 2$ we give a class of geometric intersection graphs that contains all $(d-1)$-ball graphs and all unit d-ball graphs. We conjecture that for $d = 3$, there exists an EPTAS for computing a maximum clique in the corresponding class. It is necessary that these superclasses be defined as classes of geometric intersection graphs. Indeed, it must be if we want to understand better the reason why efficient algorithms exist for both settings. For instance, taking the union of interval graphs and unit disk graphs would not give any insight, since it is a priori not defined by intersection graphs of some geometric objects.

In order to define the class, we first introduce the concept of d-*pancakes*. A 2-pancake is defined as the union of all unit disks whose centres lie on a line segment s, with s itself lying on the x-axis. An example is depicted in Fig. 1. This is definition is equivalent to the Minkowski sum of a unit disk centred at the origin and a line segment on the x-axis, where the Minkowski sum of two sets A, B is equal to $\{a + b \mid a \in A, b \in B\}$. Similarly a 3-pancake is the union of all unit balls whose centres lie on a disk $\mathcal{D}$, with $\mathcal{D}$ lying on the xy-plane. More generally, we have:

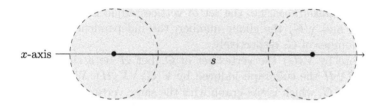

Fig. 1. The union of the unit disks centred at points of s is a 2-pancake.

Definition 1. A d-*pancake* is a d-dimensional geometric object. Let us denote by $\{\xi_1, \xi_2, \ldots, \xi_d\}$ the canonical basis of $\mathbb{R}^d$. A d-pancake is defined as the Minkowski sum of the unit d-ball centred at the origin and a $(d-1)$-ball in the hyperspace induced by $\{\xi_1, \xi_2, \ldots, \xi_{d-1}\}$.

We denote by Π^d the class of intersection graphs of some finite collection of d-pancakes and unit d-balls. In this paper, we give a polynomial time algorithm for solving maximum clique in Π^2: the intersection graphs class of unit disks and 2-pancakes. This is to put in contrast with the fact that computing a maximum clique in intersection graphs of unit disks and axis-parallel rectangles (instead of 2-pancakes) is NP-hard and even APX-hard, as shown together with Bonnet and Miltzow [5], even though maximum clique can be solved in polynomial time in axis-parallel rectangle graphs [11].

Relatedly, it would be interesting to generalise the existence of an EPTAS for maximum clique to superclasses of disk graphs. This was achieved with Bonnet and Miltzow for intersection graphs of homothets of a fixed bounded centrally symmetric convex set [5]. In this paper, we aim at generalising further to intersection graphs of convex pseudo-disks, for which we conjecture the existence of an EPTAS, and give partial results towards proving it. The proof of these partial results relies on geometric permutations of line transversals. We do a case analysis on the existence of certain geometric permutations, and show that some convex pseudo-disks must intersect. Holmsen and Wenger have written a survey on geometric transversals [15]. The results that are related to line transversals are either of Hadwiger-type, concerned with the conditions of existence of line transversals, or about the maximum number of geometric permutations of line transversals. To the best of our knowledge, we do not know of any result that uses geometric permutations of line transversals to show something else. We consider this tool, together with the polynomial time algorithm for computing a maximum clique in Π^2, to be our main contributions.

2   Preliminaries

2.1   Graph Notations

Let G be a simple graph. We say that two vertices are *adjacent* if there is an edge between them, otherwise they are *independent*. For a vertex v, $\mathcal{N}(v)$ denotes its *neighbourhood*, i.e. the set of vertices adjacent to v. We denote by $\omega(G)$, $\alpha(G)$, and $\chi(G)$ the clique number, the independence number and the chromatic number of G, respectively.

We denote by $V(G)$ the vertex set of G. Let H be a subgraph of G. We denote by $G \setminus H$ the subgraph induced by $V(G) \setminus V(H)$. We denote by $\overline{G}$ the *complement* of G, which is the graph with the same vertex set, but where edges and non-edges are interchanged. A *bipartite graph* is graph whose vertex set can be partitioned into two independent sets. A graph is *cobipartite* if its complement is a bipartite graph.

We denote by iocp(G) the *induced odd cycle packing number* of G, i.e. the maximum number of vertex-disjoint induced odd cycles (for each cycle the only edges are the ones making the cycle), such that there is no edge between two vertices of different cycles.

2.2   Geometric Notations

Throughout the paper we only consider Euclidean spaces with the Euclidean distance. Let p and p' be two points in $\mathbb{R}^d$. We denote by (p, p') the line going through them, and by $[p, p']$ the line segment with endpoints p and p'. We denote by $d(p, p')$ the distance between them. For any fixed d, we denote by O the origin in $\mathbb{R}^d$. When $d = 2$, we denote by Ox and Oy the x and y-axis, respectively. For $d = 3$, we denote by xOy the xy-plane. We usually denote a d-pancake by P^d. As a reminder, a 2-pancake is the Minkowski sum of the unit disk centred at the origin O and a line segment lying on the axis Ox.

Definition 2. Let $\{S_i\}_{1 \leq i \leq n}$ be a family of subsets of $\mathbb{R}^d$. We denote the *intersection graph* of $\{S_i\}$ by $G(\{S_i\})$. It is the graph whose vertex set is $\{S_i \mid 1 \leq i \leq n\}$ and where there is an edge between two vertices if and only if the corresponding sets intersect.

Definition 3. In $\mathbb{R}^2$ we denote by $\mathcal{D}(c, \rho)$ a closed disk centred at c with radius ρ. Let $\mathcal{D} = \mathcal{D}(c, \rho)$ and $\mathcal{D}' = \mathcal{D}(c', \rho')$ be two intersecting disks. We call *lens induced by* $\mathcal{D}$ *and* $\mathcal{D}'$ the surface $\mathcal{D} \cap \mathcal{D}'$. We call *half-lenses* the two closed regions obtained by dividing the lens along the line (c, c').

For any $x_1 \leq x_2$, we denote by $P^2(x_1, x_2)$ the 2-pancake that is the Minkowski sum of the unit disk centred at O and the line segment with endpoints x_1 and x_2. Therefore we have $P^2(x_1, x_2) = \bigcup_{x_1 \leq x' \leq x_2} \mathcal{D}((x', 0), 1)$. Behind the definition of the d-pancakes is the idea that they should be the most similar possible to unit d-balls. In particular 2-pancakes should behave as much as possible like unit disks. This is perfectly illustrated when the intersection of a 2-pancake and a unit disk is a lens, as the intersection of two unit disks would be.

Definition 4. Let $\{P_j^2\}_{1 \leq j \leq n}$ be a set of 2-pancakes. For any unit disk $\mathcal{D}$, we denote by $L(\mathcal{D}, \{P_j^2\})$, or simply by $L(\mathcal{D})$ when there is no risk of confusion, the set of 2-pancakes in $\{P_j^2\}$ whose intersection with $\mathcal{D}$ is a lens.

Let $\mathcal{D}$ denote $\mathcal{D}(c, 1)$ for some point c. Remark that if a 2-pancake $P^2(x_1, x_2)$ for some $x_1 \leq x_2$ is in $L(\mathcal{D})$, then the intersection between $\mathcal{D}$ and $P^2(x_1, x_2)$ is equal to $\mathcal{D} \cap \mathcal{D}((x_1, 0), 1)$ or $\mathcal{D} \cap \mathcal{D}((x_2, 0), 1)$. We make an abuse of notation and denote by $d(\mathcal{D}, P^2(x_1, x_2))$ the smallest distance between c and a point in the line segment $[x_1, x_2]$. Observe that if the intersection between $\mathcal{D}$ and $P^2(x_1, x_2)$ is equal to $\mathcal{D} \cap \mathcal{D}((x_1, 0), 1)$, then $d(\mathcal{D}, P^2(x_1, x_2)) = d(c, (x_1, 0))$, and otherwise $d(\mathcal{D}, P^2(x_1, x_2)) = d(c, (x_2, 0))$. The following observation gives a characterisation of when the intersection between a unit disk and a 2-pancake is a lens.

Observation 1. *Let* $\mathcal{D}((c_x, c_y), 1)$ *be a unit disk intersecting with a 2-pancake* $P^2(x_1, x_2)$. *Their intersection is a lens if and only if* $(c_x \leq x_1$ *or* $c_x \geq x_2)$ *and the interior of* $\mathcal{D}((c_x, c_y), 1)$ *does not contain any point in* $\{(x_1, \pm 1), (x_2, \pm 1)\}$.

The observation follows immediately from the fact that the intersection is a lens if and only if $\mathcal{D}((c_x, c_y), 1)$ does not contain a point in the open line segment between the points $(x_1, -1)$ and $(x_2, -1)$, nor in the open line segment between the points $(x_1, 1)$ and $(x_2, 1)$.

3   Results

We answer in Sect. 4 the 2-dimensional version of the question asked by Bonamy *et al.* [3]: We present a polynomial time algorithm for computing a maximum clique in a geometric superclass of interval graphs and unit disk graphs.

Theorem 1. *There exists a polynomial time algorithm for computing a maximum clique on* Π^2, *even without a representation.*

Kang and Müller have shown that for any fixed $d \geq 2$, the recognition of unit d-ball graphs is NP-hard, and even $\exists \mathbb{R}$-hard [12]. We conjecture that it is also hard to test whether a graph is in Π^d for any fixed $d \geq 3$, and prove it for $d = 2$.

Theorem 2. *Testing whether a graph is in Π^2 is NP-hard, and even $\exists\mathbb{R}$-hard.*

The proof of Theorem 2 figures in the full version of the paper [9]. It immediately implies that given a graph G in Π^2, finding a representation of G with 2-pancakes and unit disks is NP-hard. Therefore having a robust algorithm as defined in [13] is of interest. The algorithm of Theorem 1 takes any abstract graph as input, and outputs a maximum clique or a certificate that the graph is not in Π^2.

For $d = 3$, we conjecture the following:

Conjecture 1. There exists an integer K such that for any graph G in Π^3, we have iocp($\overline{G}$) $\leq K$.

We show in the full version of the paper [9] that this would be sufficient to obtain an EPTAS.

Theorem 3. *If Conjecture 1 holds, there exists a randomised EPTAS for computing a maximum clique in Π^3, even without a representation.*

By construction the class Π^d contains all $(d - 1)$-ball graphs and all unit d-ball graphs. Indeed a $(d - 1)$-ball graph can be realised by replacing in a representation each $(d-1)$-ball by a d-pancake. In addition to this property, we want fast algorithms for maximum clique on Π^d. The definition of Π^d may seem unnecessarily complicated. The most surprising part of the definition is probably the fact that we use d-pancakes instead of simply using $(d - 1)$-balls restricted to be in the same hyperspace of $\mathbb{R}^d$. However, we show in the full version of the paper [9] that our arguments for proving fast algorithms would not hold with this definition.

We give partial results toward showing the existence of an EPTAS for maximum clique on intersection graphs of *convex pseudo-disks*. We say that a graph is a *convex pseudo-disk graph* if it is the intersection graph of convex sets in the plane such that the boundaries of every pair intersect at most twice. We denote by $\mathcal{G}$ the intersection class of convex pseudo-disk graphs. A structural property used to show the existence of an EPTAS for disk graphs is that for any disk graph G, iocp($\overline{G}$) ≤ 1. The proof of Bonnet *et al.* relies heavily on the fact that disks have centres [4]. However, convex pseudo-disks do not, therefore adapting the proof in this new setting does not seem easy. While we were not able to extend this structural result to the class $\mathcal{G}$, we show a weaker property: The complement of a triangle and an odd cycle is a forbidden induced subgraph in $\mathcal{G}$. We write "complement of a triangle" to make the connection with *iocp* clear, but remark that actually the complement of a triangle is an independent set of three vertices. Below we state this property more explicitly.

Theorem 4. *Let G be in $\mathcal{G}$. If there exists an independent set of size 3, denoted by H, in G, and if for any $u \in H$ and $v \in G \setminus H$, $\{u, v\}$ is an edge of G, then $G \setminus H$ is cobipartite.*

Note that a cobipartite graph is not the complement of an odd cycle. Given the three pairwise non-intersecting convex pseudo-disks in H, we give a geometric characterisation of the two independent sets in the complement of $G \setminus H$. We conjecture that Theorem 4 is true even when H is the complement of any odd-cycle, which implies:

Conjecture 2. For any convex pseudo-disk graph G, we have $\mathrm{iocp}(\overline{G}) \leq 1$.

If Conjecture 2 holds, it is straightforward to obtain an EPTAS for maximum clique in convex pseudo-disks graphs, by using the techniques of Bonamy *et al.* [3].

4 Computing a Maximum Clique on Π^2 in Polynomial Time

In this section we prove Theorem 1. Due to space constraint, we only give here a polynomial algorithm that needs a representation of the graph. The additional lemmas giving a robust version of the algorithm are in the full version of the paper [9]. The idea of the algorithm is similar to the one of Clark, Colbourn and Johnson [6]. We prove that if u and v are the most distant vertices in a maximum clique, then $\mathcal{N}(u) \cap \mathcal{N}(v)$ is cobipartite.

In their proof, Clark, Colbourn and Johnson use the following fact: if c and c' are two points at distance ρ, then the diameter of the half-lenses induced by $\mathcal{D}(c,\rho)$ and $\mathcal{D}(c',\rho)$ is equal to ρ. We prove here a similar result.

Lemma 1. *Let c and c' be two points at distance ρ, and let be $\rho' \geq \rho$. Then the diameter of the half-lenses induced by $\mathcal{D}(c,\rho)$ and $\mathcal{D}(c',\rho')$ is at most ρ'.*

Proof. First note that if $\rho' > 2\rho$ then the half-lenses are half-disks of $\mathcal{D}(c,\rho)$. The diameter of these half-disks is equal to 2ρ, which is smaller than ρ'. Let us now assume that we have $\rho' \leq 2\rho$. The boundary of the lens induced by $\mathcal{D}(c,\rho)$ and $\mathcal{D}(c',\rho')$ consists of two arcs. The line (c,c') intersects exactly once with each arc. One of these two intersections is c', we denote by c'' the other. Let us consider the disk $\mathcal{D}(c'',\rho')$. Note that it contains the disk $\mathcal{D}(c,\rho)$. Therefore the lens induced by $\mathcal{D}(c,\rho)$ and $\mathcal{D}(c',\rho')$ is contained in the lens induced by $\mathcal{D}(c'',\rho')$ and $\mathcal{D}(c',\rho')$, whose half-lenses have diameter ρ'. The claim follows from the fact that the half-lenses of the first lens are contained in the ones of the second lens. $\square$

Before stating the next lemma, we introduce the following definition:

Definition 5. *Let $\{S_i\}_{1 \leq i \leq n}$ and $\{S'_j\}_{1 \leq j \leq n'}$ be two families of sets in $\mathbb{R}^2$. We say that $\{S_i\}$ and $\{S'_j\}$ fully intersect if for all $i \leq n$ and $j \leq n$ the intersection between S_i and S'_j is not empty.*

Lemma 2. *Let $\mathcal{D} := \mathcal{D}(c,1)$ be a unit disk and let $P^2 := P^2(x_1,x_2)$ be in $L(\mathcal{D})$. Let $\{\mathcal{D}_i\}$ be a set of unit disks that fully intersect with $\{\mathcal{D},P^2\}$, such that for any $\mathcal{D}_i$ we have $d(\mathcal{D},\mathcal{D}_i) \leq d(\mathcal{D},P^2)$. Moreover if P^2 is in $L(\mathcal{D}_i)$ we require $d(\mathcal{D}_i,P^2) \leq d(\mathcal{D},P^2)$. Also let $\{P^2_j\}$ be a set of 2-pancakes that fully intersect with $\{\mathcal{D},P^2\}$, such that for any P^2_j in $\{P^2_j\} \cap L(\mathcal{D})$, we have $d(\mathcal{D},P^2_j) \leq d(\mathcal{D},P^2)$. Then $G(\{\mathcal{D}_i\} \cup \{P^2_j\})$ is cobipartite.*

Proof. The proof is illustrated in Fig. 2. Without loss of generality, let us assume that the intersection between $\mathcal{D}$ and P^2 is equal to $\mathcal{D} \cap \mathcal{D}((x_1, 0), 1)$. Remember that by definition we have $x_1 \leq x_2$. Let $P^2(x_1', x_2')$ be a 2-pancake in $\{P_j^2\}$. As it is intersecting with P^2, we have $x_2' \geq x_1 - 2$. Assume by contradiction that we have $x_1' > x_1$. Then with Observation 1, we have that $P^2(x_1', x_2')$ is in $L(\mathcal{D})$ and $d(\mathcal{D}, P^2(x_1', x_2')) > d(\mathcal{D}, P^2)$, which is impossible. Therefore we have $x_1' \leq x_1$, and so $P^2(x_1', x_2')$ must contain $\mathcal{D}((x', 0), 1)$ for some x' satisfying $x_1 - 2 \leq x' \leq x_1$. As the line segment $[(x_1 - 2, 0), (x_1, 0)]$ has length 2, the 2-pancakes in $\{P_j^2\}$ pairwise intersect.

We denote by ρ the distance $d(\mathcal{D}, P^2)$. Let $\mathcal{D}(c_i, 1)$ be a unit disk in $\{\mathcal{D}_i\}$. By assumption, c_i is in $\mathcal{D}(c, \rho) \cap \mathcal{D}((x_1, 0), 2)$. We then denote by R the lens that is induced by $\mathcal{D}(c, \rho)$ and $\mathcal{D}((x_1, 0), 2)$. We cut the lens into two parts with the line $(c, (x_1, 0))$, and denote by R_1 the half-lens that is not below this line, and by R_2 the half-lens that is not above it. With Lemma 1, we obtain that the diameter of R_1 and R_2 is at most 2. Let us assume without loss of generality that c is not below Ox. We denote by X_1 the set of unit disks in $\{\mathcal{D}_i\}$ whose centre is in R_1. We denote by X_2 the union of $\{P_j^2\}$ and of the set of unit disks in $\{\mathcal{D}_i\}$ whose centre is in R_2. Since the diameter of R_1 is 2, any pair of unit disks in X_1 intersect, therefore $G(X_1)$ is a complete graph. To show that $G(X_2)$ is a complete graph too, it remains to show that any unit disk $\mathcal{D}(c_i, 1)$ in X_2 and any 2-pancake $P^2(x_1', x_2')$ in $\{P_j^2\}$ intersect. We denote by P_+^2 the following convex shape: $\cup_{x_1' \leq x \leq x_2'} \mathcal{D}((x, 0), 2)$. Note that the fact that $\mathcal{D}(c_i, 1)$ and $P^2(x_1', x_2')$ intersect is equivalent to having c_i in P_+^2. Let us consider the horizontal line going through c, and let us denote by c' the left intersection with the circle centred at $(x_1, 0)$ with radius 2. We also denote by r_2 the extremity of R that is in R_2.

Let us assume by contradiction that c_i is above the line segment $[c, c']$. As by assumption c_i is in R_2, it implies that the x-coordinate of c_i is smaller than the one of c. Therefore P^2 is in $L(\mathcal{D}_i)$ and $d(\mathcal{D}_i, P^2) > d(\mathcal{D}, P^2)$, which is impossible by assumption. Let us denote by $R_{2,-}$ the subset of R_2 that is not above the line segment $[c, c']$. To prove that $\mathcal{D}(c_i, 1)$ and $P^2(x_1', x_2')$ intersect, it suffices to show that P_+^2 contains $R_{2,-}$. As shown above, $P^2(x_1', x_2')$ contains $\mathcal{D}((x', 0), 1)$ for some x' satisfying $x_1 - 2 \leq x' \leq x_1$. This implies that P_+^2 contains $\mathcal{D}((x_1 - 2, 0), 2) \cap \mathcal{D}((x_1, 0), 2)$, and in particular contains x_1. Moreover as c is not below Ox, r_2 is also in $\mathcal{D}((x_1 - 2, 0), 2) \cap \mathcal{D}((x_1, 0), 2)$. As P^2 intersects $\mathcal{D}$, P_+^2 contains c. Let us assume by contradiction that P_+^2 does not contain c'. Then x_2' must be smaller than the x-coordinate of c', because otherwise the distance $d((x_2', 0), c')$ would be at most $d((x_1, 0), c')$, which is equal to 2. But then if P_+^2 does not contain c', then it does not contain c either, which is a contradiction. We have proved that P_+^2 contains the points x_1, c, c' and r_2. By convexity, and using the fact that two circles intersect at most twice, we obtain that $R_{2,-}$ is contained in P_+^2. This shows that any two elements in X_2 intersect, which implies that $G(X_2)$ is a complete graph. Finally, as $X_1 \cup X_2 = \{\mathcal{D}_i\} \cup \{P_j^2\}$, we obtain that $G(\{\mathcal{D}_i\} \cup \{P_j^2\})$ can be partitioned into two cliques, i.e. it is cobipartite. $\square$

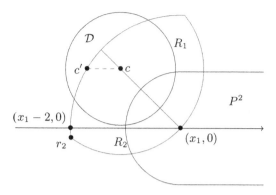

Fig. 2. Illustration of the proof of Lemma 2

Lemma 3. *Let* $\mathcal{D} := \mathcal{D}(c, 1)$ *and* $\mathcal{D}' := \mathcal{D}(c', 1)$ *be two intersecting unit disks. Let* $\{\mathcal{D}_i\}$ *be a set of unit disks that fully intersect with* $\{\mathcal{D}, \mathcal{D}'\}$, *such that for each unit disk* $\mathcal{D}_i$ *we have* $d(\mathcal{D}, \mathcal{D}_i) \leq d(\mathcal{D}, \mathcal{D}')$ *and* $d(\mathcal{D}', \mathcal{D}_i) \leq d(\mathcal{D}, \mathcal{D}')$. *Also let* $\{P_j^2\}$ *be a set of 2-pancakes that fully intersect with* $\{\mathcal{D}, \mathcal{D}'\}$, *such that for any* P_j^2 *in* $\{P_j^2\} \cap L(\mathcal{D})$, *we have* $d(\mathcal{D}, P_j^2) \leq d(\mathcal{D}, \mathcal{D}')$, *and for any* P_j^2 *in* $\{P_j^2\} \cap L(\mathcal{D}')$, *we have* $d(\mathcal{D}', P_j^2) \leq d(\mathcal{D}, \mathcal{D}')$. *Then* $G(\{\mathcal{D}_i\} \cup \{P_j^2\})$ *is cobipartite.*

The proof of Lemma 3 figures in the full version of the paper [9]. Note that Lemma 2 and Lemma 3 give a polynomial time algorithm for maximum clique on Π^2 when a representation is given. First compute a maximum clique that contains only 2-pancakes, which can be done in polynomial time since the intersection graph of a set of 2-pancakes is an interval graph [10]. Then for each unit disk $\mathcal{D}$, compute a maximum clique which contains exactly one unit disk, $\mathcal{D}$, and an arbitrary number of 2-pancakes. Because finding out whether a unit disk and a 2-pancake intersect takes constant time, computing such a maximum clique can be done in polynomial time. Note that if a maximum clique contains at least two unit disks, then in quadratic time we can find in this maximum clique either a pair of unit disks or a unit disk and a 2-pancake whose intersection is a lens, such that the conditions of Lemma 2 or of Lemma 3 are satisfied. By applying the corresponding lemma, we know that we are computing a maximum clique in a cobipartite graph, which is the same as computing a maximum independent set in a bipartite graph. As this can be done in polynomial time [7], we can compute a maximum clique on Π^2 in polynomial time when the representation is given.

5   Intersection Graphs of Convex Pseudo-disks

In this section we are interested in computing a maximum clique in intersection graphs of convex pseudo-disks. Due to space constraint, some of the lemmas that imply Theorem 4 are proven only in the full version of the paper [9]. Our proof relies on line transversal and their geometric permutations on the three convex pseudo-disks that form a triangle in the complement, denoted by $\mathcal{D}_1$, $\mathcal{D}_2$ and $\mathcal{D}_3$. As there are only three sets, the geometric permutation of a line transversal is given simply by stating which set is the second one intersected.

Definition 6. A *line transversal* ℓ is a line that goes through the three convex pseudo-disks $\mathcal{D}_1$, $\mathcal{D}_2$ and $\mathcal{D}_3$. We call *(convex pseudo-)disk in the middle* of a line transversal the convex pseudo-disk it intersects in second position.

For sake of readability, we from now on omit to mention that a disk in the middle is a convex pseudo-disk, and simply refer to it as disk in the middle. We are going to conduct a case analysis depending on the number of convex pseudo-disks being the disk in the middle for some line transversal. When there exists no line transversal, we can prove a stronger statement.

Lemma 4. *If there is no line transversal through a family of convex sets F, then for any pair of convex sets $\{C_1, C_2\}$ that fully intersects with F, C_1 and C_2 intersect.*

Proof. Let us prove the contrapositive. Assume that C_1 and C_2 do not intersect, therefore there exists a separating line. As all sets in F intersect C_1 and C_2, they also intersect the separating line, which is thus a line transversal of F. $\square$

Using the notation of Theorem 4, Lemma 4 immediately implies that if there is no line transversal through the sets representing H, then $G \setminus H$ is a clique, which is an even stronger statement than required.

The following lemma is the key-tool used in our proofs. It is illustrated in Fig. 3. Let $\mathcal{D}_1$, $\mathcal{D}_2$ and $\mathcal{D}_3$ be three convex pseudo-disks that do not pairwise intersect.

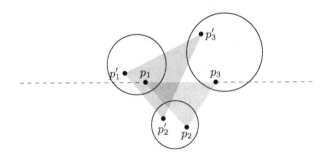

Fig. 3. Illustration of Lemma 5. The triangles $p_1 p_2 p_3$ and $p'_1 p'_2 p'_3$ intersect.

Lemma 5. *Assume that $\mathcal{D}_1$ nor $\mathcal{D}_3$ is the disk in the middle of a line transversal. Let p_i and p'_i be in $\mathcal{D}_i$, $1 \leq i \leq 3$. For sake of simplicity, assume that the line (p_1, p_3) is horizontal. If at least one of p'_1, p'_3 is above this line, and $\mathcal{D}_2$ is below it, then the triangles $p_1 p_2 p_3$ and $p'_1 p'_2 p'_3$ intersect.*

Proof. Suppose by contradiction that the two triangles do not intersect. Thus there is a separating line ℓ. The separating line intersects with $[p_i, p_i']$, $1 \leq i \leq 3$, and by convexity it is a line transversal of $\{\mathcal{D}_1, \mathcal{D}_2, \mathcal{D}_3\}$. By assumption, its intersection with $\mathcal{D}_2$ is below the line (p_1, p_3). However, as one of p_1', p_3' is above (p_1, p_3), the part of ℓ between $\mathcal{D}_1$ and $\mathcal{D}_3$ is also above (p_1, p_3). This implies that either $\mathcal{D}_1$ or $\mathcal{D}_3$ is the disk in the middle of ℓ, which is a contradiction. Remark the lemma can be generalised to any convex set $\{\mathcal{D}_1, \mathcal{D}_2, \mathcal{D}_3\}$, since we did not use the fact that they are pseudo-disks.   □

Let $\{\mathcal{D}_j'\}$ be a set of convex pseudo-disks that fully intersect with $\{\mathcal{D}_1, \mathcal{D}_2, \mathcal{D}_3\}$.

Lemma 6. *If there exists one convex pseudo-disk $\mathcal{D}_i \in \{\mathcal{D}_1, \mathcal{D}_2, \mathcal{D}_3\}$ such that the disk in the middle of all line transversals of $\{\mathcal{D}_1, \mathcal{D}_2, \mathcal{D}_3\}$ is $\mathcal{D}_i$, then $G(\{\mathcal{D}_j'\})$ is cobipartite.*

Proof. Without loss of generality, let us assume that the disk in the middle of all line transversals is $\mathcal{D}_2$. Let ℓ be a line transversal, that we will assume to be horizontal. Let $\mathcal{D}'$ be a convex pseudo-disk intersecting pairwise with $\mathcal{D}_1$, $\mathcal{D}_2$ and $\mathcal{D}_3$. We denote by p_1' a point in $\mathcal{D}' \cap \mathcal{D}_1$ and by p_3' a point in $\mathcal{D}' \cap \mathcal{D}_3$. If the line segment $[p_1', p_3']$ intersect $\mathcal{D}_2$, we have the following: Since $\mathcal{D}'$ and $\mathcal{D}_2$ are pseudo-disks, then $\mathcal{D}'$ must either contain all the part of $\mathcal{D}_2$ that is above or the one that is below the line (p_1', p_3'). We will partition the convex pseudo-disks in $\{\mathcal{D}_j'\}$ in four sets depending on the line segment $[p_1', p_3']$.

1. $[p_1', p_3']$ is above $\mathcal{D}_2$,
2. $[p_1', p_3']$ intersects $\mathcal{D}_2$ and $\mathcal{D}'$ contains all the part of $\mathcal{D}_2$ above it,
3. $[p_1', p_3']$ is below $\mathcal{D}_2$,
4. $[p_1', p_3']$ intersects $\mathcal{D}_2$ and $\mathcal{D}'$ contains all the part of $\mathcal{D}_2$ below it.

We are going to show that the set $X_1 \subseteq \{\mathcal{D}_j'\}$ of convex pseudo-disks in case 1 or 2 all pairwise intersect. By symmetry, the same holds for the set $X_2 \subseteq \{\mathcal{D}_j'\}$ of convex pseudo-disks in cases 3 and 4, and thus the claim will follow.

Let us suppose that we have two convex pseudo-disks $\mathcal{D}'$ and $\mathcal{D}''$ in case 1. Let us suppose by contradiction that they do not intersect. Without loss of generality, let us assume that p_1' is above $[p_1'', p_3'']$. We can then apply Lemma 5 to show that $\mathcal{D}'$ and $\mathcal{D}''$ intersect, which is a contradiction.

Let us assume that $\mathcal{D}'$ and $\mathcal{D}''$ are in case 2. If the line segments $[p_1', p_3']$ and $[p_1'', p_3'']$ intersect then it is done by convexity. Therefore we can assume without loss of generality that $[p_1', p_3'] \cap \mathcal{D}_2$ is above $[p_1'', p_3''] \cap \mathcal{D}_2$. Hence both $\mathcal{D}'$ and $\mathcal{D}''$ contain $[p_1', p_3'] \cap \mathcal{D}_2$, which shows that they intersect.

Finally, let us assume without loss of generality that $\mathcal{D}'$ is in case 1 and $\mathcal{D}''$ is in case 2. Suppose by contradiction that $\mathcal{D}'$ and $\mathcal{D}''$ do not intersect. Therefore by convexity the line segments $[p_1', p_3']$ and $[p_1'', p_3'']$ do not intersect. We deduce that $[p_1', p_3']$ is above $[p_1'', p_3''] \cap \mathcal{D}_2$. Let p_2' be a point in $\mathcal{D}' \cap \mathcal{D}_2$. By assumption p_2' cannot be above $[p_1'', p_3'']$, otherwise it would also be in $\mathcal{D}''$. As there is no line transversal having $\mathcal{D}_1$ or $\mathcal{D}_3$ as disk in the middle, we apply Lemma 5 to show that $\mathcal{D}'$ and $\mathcal{D}''$ intersect, which concludes the proof.   □

Notice that Lemma 6 implies Theorem 4 when it is assumed that in a representation of H, there is only one geometric permutation of the line transversals. The cases when there are two or three geometric permutations are more technical, and are proven in the full version of the paper [9].

References

1. Bar-Noy, A., Bar-Yehuda, R., Freund, A., Naor, J., Schieber, B.: A unified approach to approximating resource allocation and scheduling. J. ACM (JACM) **48**(5), 1069–1090 (2001)
2. Bhattacharya, B., Hell, P., Huang, J.: A linear algorithm for maximum weight cliques in proper circular arc graphs. SIAM J. Discrete Math. **9**(2), 274–289 (1996)
3. Bonamy, M., Bonnet, E., Bousquet, N., Charbit, P., Thomassé, S.: EPTAS for max clique on disks and unit balls. In 2018 IEEE 59th Annual Symposium on Foundations of Computer Science (FOCS), pp. 568–579. IEEE (2018)
4. Bonnet, E., Giannopoulos, P., Kim, E.J., Rzążewski, P., Sikora, F.: QPTAS and subexponential algorithm for maximum clique on disk graphs. In 34th International Symposiumon Computational Geometry (SoCG), pp. 12:1–12:15 (2018)
5. Bonnet, É., Grelier, N., Miltzow, T.: Maximum clique in disk-like intersection graphs (2020). arXiv preprint arXiv:2003.02583
6. Clark, B.N., Colbourn, C.J., Johnson, D.S.: Unit disk graphs. Discrete Math. **86**(1–3), 165–177 (1990)
7. Edmonds, J., Karp, R.M.: Theoretical improvements in algorithmic efficiency for network flow problems. J. ACM (JACM) **19**(2), 248–264 (1972)
8. Fishkin, A.V.: Disk graphs: a short survey. In: Solis-Oba, R., Jansen, K. (eds.) WAOA 2003. LNCS, vol. 2909, pp. 260–264. Springer, Heidelberg (2004). https://doi.org/10.1007/978-3-540-24592-6_23
9. Grelier, N.: Computing a maximum clique in geometric superclasses of disk graphs (2020). arXiv preprint arXiv:2007.03492
10. Gupta, U.I., Lee, D.T., Leung, J.Y.-T.: Efficient algorithms for interval graphs and circular-arc graphs. Networks **12**(4), 459–467 (1982)
11. Imai, H., Asano, T.: Finding the connected components and a maximum clique of an intersection graph of rectangles in the plane. J. Algorithms **4**(4), 310–323 (1983)
12. Kang, R.J., Müller, T.: Sphere and dot product representations of graphs. Discrete Comput. Geom. **47**(3), 548–568 (2012). https://doi.org/10.1007/s00454-012-9394-8
13. Raghavan, V., Spinrad, J.: Robust algorithms for restricted domains. In Proceedings of the Twelfth Annual ACM-SIAM Symposium on Discrete Algorithms, pp. 460–467. Society for Industrial and Applied Mathematics (2001)
14. van Leeuwen, E.J.: Optimization and approximation on systems of geometric objects. Universiteit van Amsterdam [Host] (2009)
15. Wenger, R., Holmsen, A.: Helly-type theorems and geometric transversals. In: Handbook of Discrete and Computational Geometry, 3rd edn., pp. 91–123. Chapman and Hall/CRC (2017)

Shortest Watchman Tours in Simple Polygons Under Rotated Monotone Visibility

Bengt J. Nilsson[1]([✉]) [ID], David Orden[2] [ID], Leonidas Palios[3], Carlos Seara[4] [ID], and Paweł Żyliński[5] [ID]

[1] Malmö University, Malmö, Sweden
`bengt.nilsson.TS@mau.se`
[2] Universidad de Alcalá, Alcalá de Henares, Spain
`david.orden@uah.es`
[3] University of Ioannina, Ioannina, Greece
`palios@cs.uoi.gr`
[4] Universitat Politècnica de Catalunya, Barcelona, Spain
`carlos.seara@upc.edu`
[5] University of Gdańsk, Gdańsk, Poland
`pawel.zylinski@ug.edu.pl`

Abstract. We present an $O(nrG)$ time algorithm for computing and maintaining a minimum length shortest watchman tour that sees a simple polygon under monotone visibility in direction θ, while θ varies in $[0, 180°)$, obtaining the directions for the tour to be the shortest one over all tours, where n is the number of vertices, r is the number of reflex vertices, and $G \leq r$ is the maximum number of gates of the polygon used at any time in the algorithm.

Keywords: Visibility · Polygons · Watchman tours

1 Introduction

Arguably, problems concerning visibility and motion planning in polygonal environments are among the most well-studied in computational geometry. A problem that encompasses both the visibility and motion planing aspects is that of computing a *shortest watchman tour* in an environment, i.e., the shortest closed tour that sees the complete free-space of the environment. This problem has been shown NP-hard [6,9] and even $\Omega(\log n)$-inapproximable [18] for polygons

Bengt J. Nilsson is supported by grant 2018-04001 from the Swedish Research Council, David Orden by H2020-MSCA-RISE project 734922-CONNECT and project MTM2017-83750-P of the Spanish Ministry of Science (AEI/FEDER, UE), Carlos Seara by H2020-MSCA-RISE project 734922-CONNECT, projects MTM2015-63791-R MINECO/FEDER and Gen. Cat. DGR 2017SGR1640, and Paweł Żyliński by grant 2015/17/B/ST6/01887 from the National Science Centre, Poland.

© Springer Nature Switzerland AG 2020
D. Kim et al. (Eds.): COCOON 2020, LNCS 12273, pp. 311–323, 2020.
https://doi.org/10.1007/978-3-030-58150-3_25

with holes having a total of n segments. Chin and Ntafos [6] showed a linear time algorithm to compute a shortest watchman tour in a simple rectilinear polygon. Then, after a few false starts [7,12,28,29], Tan et al. [30] proved an $O(n^4)$ time algorithm for computing a shortest watchman tour through a given boundary point in an arbitrary simple polygon, the so-called *fixed* watchman tour. Carlsson et al. [4] showed how to generalize algorithms for a shortest fixed watchman tour to compute a shortest watchman tour in a simple polygon without any pre-specified point to pass through, a *floating* watchman tour, using quadratic factor overhead. Tan [27] improved this to a linear factor overhead, thus establishing an $O(n^5)$ time algorithm for this case. Dror et al. [8] improved this to $O(n^3 \log n)$ time for the fixed case and thus $O(n^4 \log n)$ time for the floating case.

As for visibility, many different definitions have been considered [3]. Standard visibility means that two points see each other if the line segment connecting them does not intersect the exterior of the environment free space. *R*-visibility requires the axis parallel rectangle spanning the two points not to intersect the exterior of the environment free space. In this work, we consider *monotone visibility*, where two points θ-see each other if there is a path Π connecting the two points such that Π is monotone w.r.t. direction θ and Π does not intersect the exterior of the environment free space.

Visibility plays a central role in diverse advanced application areas, for example, in surveillance, computer graphics, sensor placement, and motion planning as well as in wireless communication. Our particular monotone visibility model has practical applications in material processing and manufacturing.

1.1   Our Results and Background

We present an $O(nrG)$ time algorithm for computing and maintaining a shortest (floating) watchman tour that sees a simple polygon under monotone visibility in direction θ, while θ varies in $[0, 180°)$, obtaining the directions for the tour to be the shortest one over all tours, where n is the number of vertices, r is the number of reflex vertices, and G is the maximum number of gates of the polygon used at any time in the algorithm; see Sect. 2 for a formal definition. In particular, we have $G \leq r$ in all cases.

The problem of computing a shortest watchman tour for a given polygon, under rotated monotone visibility, is related to a variety of problems concerning the concept of "oriented" kernels in polygons, which has already attracted attention in the literature. In particular, for a given set $\mathcal{O}$ of predefined directions, Schuierer et al. [24] provided an algorithm to compute the $\mathcal{O}$-Kernel of a simple polygon. Next, Schuierer and Wood [25] introduced the concept of the *external* $\mathcal{O}$-Kernel of a polygon, in order to compute the $\mathcal{O}$-Kernel of a simple polygon with holes. In addition, when restricted to $\mathcal{O} = \{0°, 90°\}$, Gewali [10] described a linear-time algorithm for orthogonal polygons without holes, and a quadratic one for orthogonal polygons with holes, whereas Palios [23] gave an output-sensitive algorithm for that problem in orthogonal polygons with holes. More recently, Orden et al. [22] presented algorithms for computing the orientations θ (in $[-90°, 90°)$) such that the $\{0°\}$-Kernel$_\theta(\mathbf{P})$ of a simple (or orthogonal) polygon $\mathbf{P}$: is not empty, has maximum/minimum area or maximum/minimum perimeter. Finally, the issue of computing the orientation θ that minimizes some parameter for a given problem instance has been recently studied in [1,2,21].

Section 2 contains preliminary results and an overview of the linear-time algorithm for computing a shortest watchman tour in rectilinear polygons, being the basis for our approach. In Sect. 3, we present our algorithm and prove its correctness. Finally, in Sect. 4, we analyze the running time of the algorithm and conclude the presentation in Sect. 5.

2   Preliminaries

Let θ be a direction, specified using its angle to the x-axis, and let $\mathbf{P}$ be a simple polygon having n edges. A path Π inside $\mathbf{P}$ is *monotone w.r.t.@ direction θ* or θ-*monotone* if and only if the intersection between any line parallel to direction θ and Π is a connected set. In standard visibility, two points p and q in $\mathbf{P}$ see each other if and only if the line segment between p and q does not intersect the exterior of $\mathbf{P}$. In θ-monotone visibility, two points p and q θ-*see* each other if and only if there is a θ-monotone path between p and q not intersecting the exterior of $\mathbf{P}$.

Let v be a reflex vertex of $\mathbf{P}$ incident to the boundary edge e. If we extend e maximally inside $\mathbf{P}$, we obtain a line segment $\bar{e}$ collinear with e, and we can associate the direction to $\bar{e}$ being the same as that of e as we traverse the boundary of $\mathbf{P}$ in counterclockwise order; see Fig. 1(a). Thus, any reflex vertex is adjacent to two extensions in $\mathbf{P}$. Any directed segment in $\mathbf{P}$ intersecting the interior of $\mathbf{P}$ and connecting two boundary points of $\mathbf{P}$ is called a *cut* of $\mathbf{P}$. Thus, an extension $\bar{e}$ is a cut in $\mathbf{P}$. A cut c partitions $\mathbf{P}$ into two components, $\mathbf{L}(c)$, the component locally to the left of c according to its direction, and $\mathbf{R}(c)$, the component locally to the right of c according to its direction.

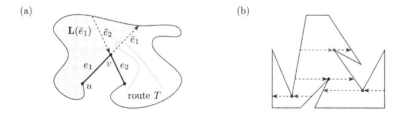

(a)

(b)

Fig. 1. (a) T must have a point in $\mathbf{L}(\bar{e}_1)$ (marked gray) to see u. (b) Dominant extensions (gates) are marked with blue and red, the remaining extensions are black. (Color figure online)

Consider a closed tour T inside $\mathbf{P}$. Chin and Ntafos [6,7] argue for standard visibility that in order for T to see the whole polygon $\mathbf{P}$, it is sufficient for T to see the vertices of $\mathbf{P}$, and therefore, it is sufficient for T to have a point in $\mathbf{L}(\bar{e})$

for every extension $\bar{e}$ in $\mathbf{P}$, i.e., to intersect the left of any extension in $\mathbf{P}$; see again Fig. 1(a).

For monotone visibility in direction θ, we introduce the following definitions. Consider a reflex vertex v of $\mathbf{P}$ and let l be the directed line with angle θ to the x-axis passing through v. If the two boundary edges incident to v lie on the same side of l, let s be the maximal segment collinear to l inside $\mathbf{P}$ that passes through v. The segment s passes through v and partitions $\mathbf{P}$ into three components incident to v. Two components $\mathbf{P_L}$ and $\mathbf{P_R}$ have v as a convex vertex and the third component has s as a boundary edge; $\mathbf{P_R}$ is the first subpolygon traversed by the counterclockwise traversal of $\mathbf{P}$ starting at v, whereas $\mathbf{P_L}$ is the other component having v as convex vertex. The problem thus reduces to obtaining the shortest tour that intersect the left of a given set of cuts.

Now, we can argue similarly for monotone visibility in direction θ as in the standard visibility case. Assume the tour T has points in $\mathbf{P_R}$. Unless T intersects s, T cannot see any points in $\mathbf{P_L}$. Similarly, if T has points in $\mathbf{P_L}$, then T cannot see any points in $\mathbf{P_R}$, unless it intersects s. To mimic the standard visibility situation, we introduce two cuts c_f and c_b incident to v, where c_f is the portion of s bounding $\mathbf{P_R}$, and c_b is the portion of s bounding $\mathbf{P_L}$. Specifically, the cut c_f is directed away from v and we call it a *forward θ-cut*, and symmetrically, the cut c_b is directed towards v and we call it a *backward θ-cut*; see Fig. 1(b).

We also color the θ-cuts and their associated reflex vertices. A θ-cut is *red*, if the boundary edges incident to the associated vertex v both lie locally to the right of the directed line l defined above. The vertex v is thus called a *red* vertex. Analogously, a θ-cut is *blue*, if the boundary edges incident to the associated vertex v both lie locally to the left of the directed line l, and v is called a *blue* vertex. Other reflex vertices are not colored as they do not break monotonicity w.r.t.@ direction θ and are therefore not used; see Fig. 1(b).

Similarly to the standard visibility case, we define the region $\mathbf{L}(c)$ for a θ-cut c to be the part of the polygon $\mathbf{P}$ locally to the left of c according to its direction, and $\mathbf{R}(c)$ to be the part of the polygon $\mathbf{P}$ locally to the right of c. We claim the following lemma that corresponds to the standard visibility case [7]; its correctness follows from the definition of the θ-cut.

Lemma 1. *A tour T in $\mathbf{P}$ is a watchman tour under monotone visibility in direction θ if and only if it intersects the region $\mathbf{L}(c)$, for every θ-cut c in $\mathbf{P}$.*

The lemma allows us to use the algorithm of Chin and Ntafos [6] for computing the shortest watchman tour under θ-monotone visibility, since it computes the shortest tour that intersect the left of a set of cuts. The algorithm works roughly as follows. First, it identifies the proper set of cuts inside the polygon. Second, it reduces the shortest tour problem to a shortest path problem in a triangulated two-manifold, computes the shortest path, and transforms the path to a tour in the original polygon. Since all θ-cuts are parallel line segments, we can do the first step in $O(n)$ time using the algorithm by Chazelle [5] that partitions a simple polygon into $O(n)$ visibility trapezoids by introducing parallel line segments at reflex vertices in the polygon.

Similarly as for standard visibility, we define *domination* between cuts. Given two θ-cuts c and c', we say that c *dominates* c' if $\mathbf{L}(c) \subset \mathbf{L}(c')$. We call c a *dominating* θ-*cut* or *gate*, if c is not dominated by any other θ-cut in $\mathbf{P}$. We refer to the issuing reflex vertex of a gate as the *gate vertex*, whereas the edge touched by the other endpoint of the gate is called the *gate edge*. Carlsson *et al.* [4] show how to compute the dominating cuts in $\mathbf{P}$ in linear time, given the complete set of cuts ordered along the boundary, in standard visibility. Their method transfers directly to the case of monotone visibility in direction θ, since given the trapezoidation of the polygon, the ordering can be obtained by a traversal of the boundary, ordering the forward θ-cuts and the backward θ-cuts separately, and then merging these two sets of θ-cuts. The process thus takes linear time.

In the algorithm, we establish *gates* as explained above and remove the portions of the polygon that lie locally to the left of them, resulting in the polygon $\mathbf{P}'(\theta)$; see Fig. 2(a). The optimal tour will only reflect on the gates in $\mathbf{P}$ to see everything on the other side of them, so it is completely contained in $\mathbf{P}'(\theta)$. We then triangulate $\mathbf{P}'(\theta)$ and establish a constant-size subset $\mathcal{V}$ of vertices such that the optimum tour must pass through at least one of them; see Sect. 4. In the next step, we compute for each vertex v in $\mathcal{V}$, a triangulated two-manifold $\mathbf{H}_v(\theta)$ (see Sect. 2.1) such that the shortest path from v to its image v' in $\mathbf{H}_v(\theta)$ corresponds to the shortest watchman tour in $\mathbf{P}$ that passes through v. We then establish the shortest path $S(v, v')$ in $\mathbf{H}_v(\theta)$, for each v in $\mathcal{V}$, pick the shortest of these paths, and finally transform it back to the polygon $\mathbf{P}'(\theta)$. The whole computation can be done in $O(n)$ time [6].

2.1   The Two-Manifold

In our approach, we extensively exploit the concept of the two-manifold used in the algorithm by Chin and Ntafos [6]. We therefore provide some more details.

Without loss of generality assume that $\theta = 0°$. Consider the dominant extensions (or gates in our case) in $\mathbf{P}$. Chin and Ntafos [6,7] prove that an optimal watchman tour will never intersect the interior of any region $\mathbf{L}(c)$ for any dominant extension c. Thus, we define $\mathbf{P}' = \mathbf{P}'(0°) \stackrel{\text{def}}{=} (\mathbf{P} \setminus \bigcup_{c \in \mathcal{G}} \mathbf{L}(c))^*$, where $\mathcal{G}$ is the set of dominant extensions and $\mathcal{S}^*$ denotes the closure of a set $\mathcal{S}$. (We take the closure to include the boundary points of $\mathbf{P}'$.) The dominant extensions (gates) of $\mathbf{P}$ are now part of the boundary of $\mathbf{P}'$, and so we refer to them as the *essential edges* of $\mathbf{P}'$. The polygon $\mathbf{P}'$ is triangulated and, given a vertex v, $\mathbf{P}'$ is then *unrolled* from v to v' using the essential edges as mirrors giving $\mathbf{H}_v$ $(= \mathbf{H}_v(0°))$, where v' is the image of v, as follows. The counterclockwise traversal of the boundary of $\mathbf{P}'$ starting at v encounters the incident triangles from the triangulation in order along the edges and vertices of the traversal. When reaching an essential edge, we reflect all subsequent triangles using the essential edge as mirror. As the traversal continues, we repeat this step until the traversal reaches the vertex v again. In the two-manifold, the second instance of the vertex v is called the *image* of v and denoted v'. Between the vertex v and the first essential edge, subsequent consecutive pairs of essential edges, and between the final essential edge and v', we perform a standard breadth-first-search to keep those triangles of the triangulation that form a path between the mirroring segments in $\mathbf{H}_v$ (see Fig. 2), as this will aid the shortest path finding algorithm in later steps [11,17]. The size of $\mathbf{H}_v$ is linear, because each triangle from the triangulation of $\mathbf{P}'$ is used at most six times in the construction of $\mathbf{H}_v$, once for each side of the triangle and once for each vertex of the triangle, since each boundary edge and vertex is passed only once as we perform the traversal of $\mathbf{P}'$.

From Heron [13], we know that the shortest path between two points that also touches a line (with both points on the same side of the line) makes perfect reflection on the line; see Fig. 2(b, c). Thus, the shortest path in $\mathbf{H}_v$ between v and its image v' corresponds exactly to the shortest watchman tour in $\mathbf{P}$ that passes through v as the path is folded back along the gates in $\mathbf{P}$. Computing the shortest path in a triangulated simple polygon can be done in linear time [11,17], and since $\mathbf{H}_v$ consists of a linear number of connected triangles, computing the path takes $O(n)$ time. Folding back the path to obtain the tour also takes $O(n)$ time by traversing the path and computing the points of intersection between the path and the triangle sides corresponding to gates in $\mathbf{P}$.

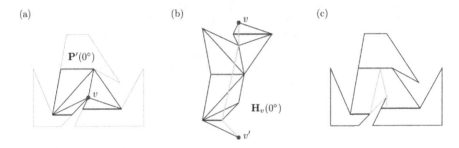

Fig. 2. (a, b) The polygon $\mathbf{P}'(0°)$ with the distinguished vertex v that acts as starting point for the unrolling process resulting in the two-manifold $\mathbf{H}_v(0°)$. (c) The resulting shortest watchman tour in $\mathbf{P}$.

3   The Algorithm

Given that we can compute the shortest watchman tour under monotone visibility in a specific direction θ in linear time, our objective is to find the direction θ for which the length of a shortest watchman tour under monotone visibility in this direction is minimal. Let $T(\theta)$ denote a shortest watchman tour under monotone visibility in direction θ. The idea of the algorithm is to compute the tour $T(0°)$, and then rotate the direction θ from $0°$ to $180°$, updating $T(\theta)$ as the rotation proceeds.

Consider the tour $T(\theta)$ for a fixed direction θ and let $\mathcal{G}(\theta)$ be the set of gates visited by $T(\theta)$. Treat $T(\theta)$ as a (weakly simple) polygon and divide the vertex set of $T(\theta)$ into two types. The *stable vertices* of $T(\theta)$ coincide with reflex vertices of $\mathbf{P}$, even if they sometimes correspond to convex vertices in $T(\theta)$; see Fig. 2(c). The *moving vertices* of $T(\theta)$ are the reflections on the gates in $\mathcal{G}(\theta)$.

We partition $T(\theta)$ into subpaths going from one stable vertex to the next one in counterclockwise order along $T(\theta)$. Any such path is either a line segment between stable vertices of $T(\theta)$ or it is a path that starts at a stable vertex, passes a consecutive sequence of moving vertices, and finishes then again at a stable vertex. We call such a subpath a *maximal moving subpath of* $T(\theta)$. Any maximal moving subpath of $T(\theta)$ has the following property.

Lemma 2. *A maximal moving subpath $C(\theta)$ of $T(\theta)$ has at most three moving vertices and they touch gates in order having alternating colors.*

Proof. Let v be the stable vertex at the first endpoint of $C(\theta)$. Let $S(v, v')$ be the shortest path between v and its image v' in the two-manifold $\mathbf{H}_v(\theta)$. The moving vertices of $C(\theta)$ correspond to consecutive crossings of gates by $S(v, v')$ in $\mathbf{H}_v(\theta)$ without touching a stable vertex. Since all gates are parallel, when following $S(v, v')$, no two consecutive gates in $\mathbf{H}_v(\theta)$ can have the same color without $S(v, v')$ (and thus $T(\theta)$) touching a stable vertex, otherwise one of them dominates the other, contradicting that they are both gates. Thus, the sequence of consecutive gates in $\mathbf{H}_v(\theta)$ is color alternating. Next, it is clear that the sequence of gates cannot consist of more than three gates, since four or more would mean that $T(\theta)$ is self intersecting and thus could be shortened [6,7]. $\square$

Given $T(\theta)$ and the set of gates $\mathcal{G}(\theta)$, assume we increase the rotation to $\theta + \varepsilon$ to obtain the tour $T(\theta + \varepsilon)$ and the set of gates $\mathcal{G}(\theta + \varepsilon)$; we refer to such a rotation as an *ε-rotation*. We say that $T(\theta)$ and $T(\theta + \varepsilon)$ are *close* if each of the following properties hold:

1. The stable vertices of $T(\theta)$ and $T(\theta + \varepsilon)$ are the same.
2. The gate vertices for the gates in $\mathcal{G}(\theta)$ and $\mathcal{G}(\theta + \varepsilon)$ in $\mathbf{P}$ are the same.
3. For any pair of gates $>\in \mathcal{G}(\theta)$ and $g_\varepsilon \in \mathcal{G}(\theta + \varepsilon)$ with the same gate vertex, they also have the same gate edge.
4. For any pair of gates $>\in \mathcal{G}(\theta)$ and $g_\varepsilon \in \mathcal{G}(\theta+\varepsilon)$ with the same gate vertex $v_>$, if $T(\theta)$ touches $v_>$, then $T(\theta + \varepsilon)$ also touches $v_>$, and if $T(\theta)$ touches the other endpoint of $¿$, then $T(\theta + \varepsilon)$ also touches the other end point of g_ε.

We claim the following lemma. Its proof basically makes an analysis of the cases based on the number of moving vertices, at most three, in a maximal moving subpath; each case leads to a trigonometric formula.

Lemma 3. *If $T(\theta)$ and $T(\theta + \varepsilon)$ are close, then $\|T(\theta + \varepsilon)\| = \|T(\theta)\| + \sum_{k=1}^{|\mathcal{G}(\theta)|} f_k(\varepsilon)$, where*

$$
f_k(\varepsilon) = \sqrt{\frac{a_{k,0}^2 + a_{k,1} \tan \varepsilon + a_{k,2} \tan^2 \varepsilon}{1 + a_{k,3} \tan \varepsilon + a_{k,4} \tan^2 \varepsilon}} - a_{k,0} + \sqrt{\frac{a_{k,5}^2 + a_{k,6} \tan \varepsilon + a_{k,7} \tan^2 \varepsilon}{1 + a_{k,8} \tan \varepsilon + a_{k,9} \tan^2 \varepsilon}} - a_{k,5}
$$

$$
+ \sqrt{\frac{a_{k,10}^2 + a_{k,11} \tan \varepsilon + a_{k,12} \tan^2 \varepsilon + a_{k,13} \tan^3 \varepsilon + a_{k,14} \tan^4 \varepsilon}{1 + a_{k,15} \tan \varepsilon + a_{k,16} \tan^2 \varepsilon + a_{k,17} \tan^3 \varepsilon + a_{k,18} \tan^4 \varepsilon}} - a_{k,10}
$$

$$
+ \sqrt{\frac{a_{k,19}^2 + \sum_{i=1}^{14} a_{k,19+i} \tan^i \varepsilon}{1 + \sum_{i=1}^{14} a_{k,33+i} \tan^i \varepsilon}} - a_{k,19},
$$

for some constants $a_{k,0}, \ldots, a_{k,47}$, $1 \le k \le |\mathcal{G}(\theta)|$, *only depending on the stable vertices, the gate vertices, the gate edges, and the angle* θ.

By Lemma 3, as long as $T(\theta)$ maintains the closeness properties in a small neighborhood, $\theta + \varepsilon$ of θ, with $\varepsilon > 0$, the length function $\|T(\theta)\|$ is smooth (continuous and differentiable), and we can obtain the angles of minima for $\|T(\theta)\|$ using standard analytic methods. The function consists of $O(|\mathcal{G}(\theta)|)$ terms, requiring us to test $O(|\mathcal{G}(\theta)|)$ potential solutions, thus taking $O(|\mathcal{G}(\theta)|)$ time.

However, when the closeness properties do not hold, at least one of the following changes occur: the current set of stable vertices of $T(\theta)$ changes, the current set of gate vertices changes, some gate in the current set $\mathcal{G}(\theta)$ changes its gate edge, or the tour $T(\theta)$ reaches or leaves an endpoint of a gate. We call the angles where such changes occur *events* and present them in further detail next.

3.1 Events

In general, we have two types of events: those defined by the vertices of the polygon (or pairs of them), and those defined by the stable and moving vertices of the current tour. We further subdivide them into the following six types.

Validity event: a new gate arises or an old gate disappears. This happens when the gate becomes collinear to a polygon edge adjacent to the gate vertex.

Domination event: a gate "changes gate vertex", i.e., a cut c issued from a vertex v, previously dominated by a gate g with gate vertex v', becomes collinear to g, v and v' have the same color, and as the rotation proceeds, v becomes the new gate vertex.

Jumping event: the endpoint of a gate g on the gate edge, reaches a reflex vertex of **P** issuing a cut of different color to that of g.

Passing event: the endpoint of a gate on the gate edge, reaches an uncolored reflex vertex or a convex vertex of **P**.

Bending event: a maximal moving subpath of $T(\theta)$ reaches or leaves a reflex vertex of $\mathbf{P}'(\theta)$.

Cuddle event: a moving vertex of the tour reaches or leaves a gate endpoint.

Lemma 4. *The set of events is complete.*

Proof. Consider the four properties necessary for two tours $T(\theta)$ and $T(\theta + \varepsilon)$ to be close. We take the contrapositive for each property and show that the only cases when these can occur is if one of the listed events occurs for $T(\theta)$.

The Current Set of Stable Vertices of $T(\theta)$ *Changes.* Since the only part of $T(\theta)$ that changes under ε-rotation are the maximal moving subpaths, a stable vertex can never be directly exchanged for another vertex. Therefore, the only other possibilities are that a stable vertex is either added to or removed from $T(\theta)$, but these are exactly the *bending events*.

The Current Set of Gate Vertices Changes. There are three possibilities that this can happen. First, a gate vertex is exchanged for another gate vertex. In order for this to happen, there must be some angle when a gate is collinear to a θ-cut of some other reflex vertex with the same color. These are exactly the *domination events*. The two other possibilities are that a gate is either added to or removed from $\mathcal{G}(\theta)$, but these are exactly the *validity events*.

Some Gate in the Current Set $\mathcal{G}(\theta)$ Changes Gate Edge. For this to happen, the endpoint of the gate opposite the gate vertex must lie at a vertex of the polygon. If this vertex is reflex and has the same color as the current gate, we have a *domination event*. If the vertex is reflex but has the opposite color of the gate, by definition, we have a *jumping event*. If the vertex is either reflex but uncolored or convex, then we have exactly a *passing event*. Since vertices can be of no other types, these three event types cover this case.

The Tour $T(\theta)$ Reaches or Leaves an Endpoint of a Gate. This is exactly the definition of the *cuddle events*.

Thus, the six event types completely cover all the cases.   □

The reason for defining six types of events is that our algorithm will handle each of them slightly differently, as is explained in the next section.

3.2   Handling Events

The algorithm maintains, for a given angle θ, the following information: $T(\theta)$, $\mathcal{G}(\theta)$, $\mathbf{H}_v(\theta)$ for a reflex vertex v coinciding with a stable vertex of $T(\theta)$, the change function $\|T(\theta + \varepsilon)\| = \|T(\theta)\| + \sum_{1 \leq k \leq |\mathcal{G}(\theta)|} f_k(\varepsilon)$ (a function of ε), for each gate in $\mathcal{G}(\theta)$, the visibility polygon of the gate vertex (for standard visibility, not monotone visibility), and a priority queue $\mathcal{Q}$ maintaining $O(|\mathcal{G}(\theta)|)$ angles of future potential events, a constant number for each gate. We next present how each event is handled during the running of the algorithm as the direction θ rotates from $0°$ to $180°$.

ALGORITHM

Let $T_{\mathrm{opt}} \leftarrow T(0°)$, $\theta \leftarrow 0°$, compute the event angles (c.f. validity event routine below), insert them in $\mathcal{Q}$, and repeat the following steps while $\theta < 180°$.

Step 1. Get the next event angle θ from the priority queue $\mathcal{Q}$.

Step 2. Depending on the event type, perform one of the following routines.

Validity event routine. For each such event:

1. Compute the gates $\mathcal{G}(\theta)$ and the optimal tour $T(\theta)$ for direction θ in $O(n)$ time as explained in Sect. 2.1.
2. Empty the priority queue $\mathcal{Q}$.
3. For each segment s of the shortest path in $\mathbf{H}_v(\theta)$ that crosses a gate, we establish the shortest path from the endpoints of the gate to the endpoints of s, and associate the reflex vertices on those paths that are closest to the endpoints of s (at most four). We can quickly test (in $O(|\mathcal{G}(\theta)|)$ total time) whether any such vertex crosses s during the subsequent rotation and establish at what rotation angle this happens, i.e., the potential next bending and cuddle events. Insert each of the two events per gate in $\mathcal{Q}$.

4. For each of the gates in $\mathcal{G}(\theta)$, compute the standard visibility polygon for the gate vertex and obtain the next passing event, jumping event, domination event, and validity event (if they exist) by traversing the boundary of the visibility polygon starting from the angle θ from the gate vertex. This takes $O(n)$ time per gate. Insert each of the four events per gate in $\mathcal{Q}$. This takes a total of $O(n|\mathcal{G}(\theta)|)$ time for all the gates.

5. Look at the next angle θ' in $\mathcal{Q}$. Compute the change function $\|T(\theta + \varepsilon)\|$ and the best local angle $\theta + \varepsilon$, for $\varepsilon > 0$, such that $\theta < \theta + \varepsilon \leq \theta'$. If $\|T(\theta + \varepsilon)\| < T_{\mathrm{opt}}$, then update T_{opt}. This takes $O(|\mathcal{G}(\theta)|)$ time, since the change function has $O(|\mathcal{G}(\theta)|)$ terms, each being the square root of rational polynomials of degree at most 14; see Lemma 3.

The time complexity is $O(n|\mathcal{G}(\theta)|)$ for this case.

Domination event routine. For each such event:

1. Update the set of gates in $\mathcal{G}(\theta)$ by exchanging one gate for a collinear gate with different gate vertex. This takes constant time.
2. Remove the events in $\mathcal{Q}$ associated to the old gate. This takes $O(|\mathcal{G}(\theta)|)$ time by a traversal of $\mathcal{Q}$.
3. For the new gate vertex, compute the visibility polygon around the gate vertex, and obtain the next passing event, jumping event domination event, and validity event (if they exist) by traversing the boundary of the visibility polygon starting from the angle θ from the gate vertex. Insert each of the four events in $\mathcal{Q}$. This takes $O(n)$ time.
4. Perform Step 5 as for validity events.

The time complexity is $O(n)$ for this case.

Jumping event routine. For each such event:

1. Since the set of gate vertices does not change, only update the gate edge and then recompute the tour obtaining the next jump event by continuing the traversal of the boundary of the visibility polygon starting from the angle θ from the gate vertex. Add it to $\mathcal{Q}$. This takes $O(n)$ time.
2. Perform Step 5 as for validity events.

Passing event routine. For each such event:

1. Update the change function $\|T(\theta + \varepsilon)\|$ with the appropriate term consisting of the square root of rational polynomials of degree at most 14. This takes $O(|\mathcal{G}(\theta)|)$ time.
2. Perform Step 5 as for validity events.

Bending event routine. Here, neither the set of gate vertices nor the set of gate edges change, so we proceed as in Steps 3 and 5 for validity events. The time complexity is $O(|\mathcal{G}(\theta)|)$.

Cuddle event routine. Handled as bending events.

4   Analysis

The correctness of our algorithm follows directly from Lemmas 3 and 4. To analyze the time complexity, define $G \stackrel{\text{def}}{=} \max_{0° \leq \theta < 180°} |\mathcal{G}(\theta)|$. We note that the number of validity events is $2r$ and take $O(nG)$ time each, the number of domination and jumping events is $O(rG)$ and take $O(n)$ time each, and the number of passing, bending, and cuddling events is $O(nr)$ (since they each associate a vertex, either of the tour or of the polygon, with a reflex vertex of the polygon) and take $O(G)$ time each. Thus, the complexity of our algorithm is $O(nrG)$.

It remains to prove that for a fixed angle θ, we can quickly, in linear time, obtain a constant sized set $\mathcal{V}$ of polygon vertices so that $S(v, v')$ from v to its image v' in $\mathbf{H}_v(\theta)$ corresponds to a shortest watchman tour in $\mathbf{P}$, for some $v \in \mathcal{V}$. If $\mathbf{P}'(\theta)$ has two essential edges (corresponding to gates in $\mathbf{P}$) with the same color, we know from the proof of Lemma 2 that the highest reflex vertex along a path between the gates in a coordinate system where the gates are parallel to the x-axis must be touched by the tour, otherwise it is not shortest. Since there are two paths between those gates, we obtain a set $\mathcal{V}$ of two vertices in this case. If $\mathbf{P}'(\theta)$ has one red and one blue essential edge, a shortest tour either touches one of the edge endpoints or it can be slid along the essential edge until it touches a reflex vertex in the polygon. We obtain such a reflex vertex by computing $S(p, p')$ for each essential edge endpoint p and following $S(p, p')$ to the last vertex before it intersects the first gate in $\mathbf{H}_p(\theta)$. We thus obtain a set $\mathcal{V}$ of at most eight vertices, four essential edge endpoints and four vertices obtained from $\mathbf{H}_p(\theta)$. We have shown the following theorem.

Theorem 1. *The presented algorithm computes the minimum length shortest (floating) watchman tour under monotone visibility in direction θ over all $0° \leq \theta < 180°$ in a simple polygon in $O(nrG)$ time and $O(nG)$ storage, where n is the number of vertices, r is the number of reflex vertices, and $G \leq r$ is the maximum number of gates of the polygon used at any time in the algorithm.*

5   Conclusions

Observe that our approach can also be used to obtain optimal tours for other parameters which are dependent on the rotation angle θ, e.g., the longest of all shortest watchman tours, the one with smallest or largest area, etc. All we need is to adapt Lemma 3 for the specific problem.

An interesting extension of our problem is to minimize the longest out of multiple tours that together see a polygon under rotated monotone visibility. For standard visibility the problem is known to be NP-hard even for two tours [19] and efficient constant factor approximation algorithms also exist for this case [20].

References

1. Alegría-Galicia, C., Orden, D., Palios, L., Seara, C., Urrutia, J.: Capturing points with a rotating polygon (and a 3D extension). Theory Comput. Syst. **63**(3), 543–566 (2019)
2. Alegría-Galicia, C., Orden, D., Seara, C., Urrutia, J.: Efficient computation of minimum-area rectilinear convex hull under rotation and generalizations. arXiv:1710.10888v2 (2019)
3. Asano, T., Ghosh, S.K., Shermer, T.: Chapter 19. Visibility in the plane. In: Sack, J.R., Urrutia, J. (eds.) Handbook on Computational Geometry. Elsevier Science Publishers (1999)
4. Carlsson, S., Jonsson, H., Nilsson, B.J.: Finding the shortest watchman route in a simple polygon. Discrete Comp. Geom. **22**, 377–402 (1999)
5. Chazelle, B.: Triangulating a simple polygon in linear time. Discrete Comp. Geom. **6**(3), 485–524 (1991)
6. Chin, W., Ntafos, S.: Optimum watchman routes
7. Chin, W., Ntafos, S.: Shortest watchman routes in simple polygons. Discrete Comp. Geom. **6**(1), 9–31 (1991)
8. Dror, M., Efrat, A., Lubiw, A., Mitchell, J.S.B.: Touring a sequence of polygons. In: 35th STOC 2003, pp. 473–482 (2003)
9. Dumitrescu, A., Tóth, C.D.: Watchman tours for polygons with holes. Comput. Geom. **45**(7), 326–333 (2012)
10. Gewali, L.P.: Recognizing *s*-star polygons. Patt. Rec. **28**(7), 1019–1032 (1995)
11. Guibas, L., Hershberger, J., Leven, D., Sharir, M., Tarjan, R.: Linear time algorithms for visibility and shortest path problems inside triangulated simple polygons. Algorithmica **2**, 209–233 (1987)
12. Hammar, M., Nilsson, B.J.: Concerning the time bounds of existing shortest watchman route algorithms. In: Chlebus, B.S., Czaja, L. (eds.) FCT 1997. LNCS, vol. 1279, pp. 210–221. Springer, Heidelberg (1997). https://doi.org/10.1007/BFb0036185
13. Heron of Alexandria. Catoptrica (On Reflection). ∼62
14. Hershberger, J., Suri, S.: A pedestrian approach to ray shooting: shoot a ray, take a walk. J. Algorithms **18**(3), 403–431 (1995)
15. Huskić, G., Buck, S., Zell, A.: GeRoNa: generic robot navigation. J. Intell. Robot. Syst. **95**(2), 419–442 (2019)
16. Icking, C., Klein, R.: Searching for the kernel of a polygon: a competitive strategy. In: 11th SoCG 1995, pp. 258–266 (1995)
17. Lee, D.T., Preparata, F.P.: Euclidean shortest paths in the presence of rectilinear barriers. Networks **14**, 393–410 (1984)
18. Mitchell, J.S.B.: Approximating watchman routes. In: 24th SODA 2013, pp. 844–855 (2013)
19. Mitchell, J.S.B.,Wynters, E.L.: Watchman routes for multiple guards. In: 3rd CCCG 1991, pp. 126–129 (1991)
20. Nilsson, B.J., Packer, E.: An approximation algorithm for the two-watchman route in a simple polygon. In: 32nd EuroCG 2016, pp. 111–114 (2016)
21. Orden, D., Palios, L., Seara, C., Urrutia, J., Żyliński, P.: On the width of the monotone-visibility kernel of a simple polygon. In: 36th EuroCG 2020, pp. 13:1–13:8 (2020)
22. Orden, D., Palios, L., Seara, C., Żyliński, P.: Generalized kernels of polygons under rotation. In: 34th EuroCG 2018, pp. 74:1–74:6 (2018)

23. Palios, L.: An output-sensitive algorithm for computing the s-kernel. In: 27th CCCG 2015, pp. 199–204 (2015)
24. Schuierer, S., Rawlins, G.J.E., Wood, D.: A generalization of staircase visibility. In: 3rd CCCG 1991, pp. 96–99 (1991)
25. Schuierer, S., Wood, D.: Generalized kernels of polygons with holes. In: 5th CCCG 1993, pp. 222–227 (1993)
26. Schuierer, S., Wood, D.: Multiple-guards kernels of simple polygons. Theoretical Computer Science Center Research Report HKUST-TCSC-98-06 (1998)
27. Tan, X.-H.: Fast computation of shortest watchman routes in simple polygons. Inf. Process. Lett. **77**(1), 27–33 (2001)
28. Tan, X., Hirata, T.: Constructing shortest watchman routes by divide-and-conquer. In: Ng, K.W., Raghavan, P., Balasubramanian, N.V., Chin, F.Y.L. (eds.) ISAAC 1993. LNCS, vol. 762, pp. 68–77. Springer, Heidelberg (1993). https://doi.org/10.1007/3-540-57568-5_236
29. Tan, X.-H., Hirata, T., Inagaki, Y.: An incremental algorithm for constructing shortest watchman routes. Int. J. Comput. Geom. Appl. **3**(4), 351–365 (1993)
30. Tan, X.-H., Hirata, T., Inagaki, Y.: Corrigendum to "An incremental Algorithm for constructing shortest watchman routes". Int. J. Comput. Geom. Appl. **9**(3), 319–324 (1999)

Tight Approximation for the Minimum Bottleneck Generalized Matching Problem

Julián Mestre[1]([⊠]) and Nicolás E. Stier Moses[2]

[1] School of Computer Science, University of Sydney, Sydney, Australia
julian.mestre@sydney.edu.au
[2] Facebook Inc., Menlo Park, USA

Abstract. We study a problem arising in statistical analysis called the *minimum bottleneck generalized matching problem* that involves breaking up a population into blocks in order to carry out generalizable statistical analyses of randomized experiments. At a high level the problem is to find a clustering of the population such that each part is at least a given size and has at least a given number of elements from each treatment class (so that the experiments are statistically significant), and that all elements within a block are as similar as possible (to improve the accuracy of the analysis).

More formally, given a metric space (V, d), a treatment partition $\mathcal{T} = \{T_1, \ldots, T_k\}$ of V, and a target cardinality vector $(b_0, b_1, \ldots, b_k) \in Z_+^{k+1}$ such that $b_0 \geq \sum_{j=1}^{k} b_j$. The objective is to find a partition $M_1, \ldots, M_\ell$ of V minimizing the maximum diameter of any part such that for each part we have $|M_i| \geq b_0$ and $|M_i \cap T_j| \geq b_j$ for all $j = 1, \ldots, k$.

Our main contribution is to provide a tight 2-approximation for the problem. We also show how to modify the algorithm to get the same approximation ratio for the more general problem of finding a partition where each part spans a given matroid.

1 Introduction

In Social Science and related fields, designing experiments on a sample of the population so that the insights obtained from the experiments can be generalized to the whole population is a major challenge. Statistical techniques such as blocking, are used for designing sound experiments. Given a population the objective is to break it up into homogeneous *blocks* of at least a given minimum size and then randomly assign elements within blocks to treatment and control groups. It is important that these blocks are large enough (so that the results are statistically significant) and homogeneous (so that there are no hidden variables that could explain variabilities between treatment and control outcomes). While the concept of blocking and randomized experiments goes back to the seminal work of Fischer [5], the design of efficient algorithms for blocking has attracted the attention of the Statistics community [7,8,18] in more recent times. Indeed,

© Springer Nature Switzerland AG 2020
D. Kim et al. (Eds.): COCOON 2020, LNCS 12273, pp. 324–334, 2020.
https://doi.org/10.1007/978-3-030-58150-3_26

the efficiency of the blocking algorithm used and the quality of the blockings found are crucial in the context of A/B testing in online advertising platforms where treatment effects on advertisers are typically small [13] yet very economically relevant due to the large scale of these platforms.

The work of Higgins *et al.* [8] is particularly relevant to our paper. The authors cast the problem of finding a good blocking as an optimization problem, which they call *minimum threshold blocking*: Given a metric space (V, d) and a cardinality lower bound b, the objective is to partition V so that each part has cardinality at least b and the maximum diameter of any one part is minimized. Here V is the population that we want to block and d a distance function capturing how similar any two elements in V are (low distance implying similarity). They showed that the problem admits a 4-approximation and that it is NP-hard to approximate within $2 - \epsilon$.

While designing experiments that use a good blocking structure is highly desirable, sometimes the treatment partition is already given to us, either because someone else performed the experiment, because the sample size is small, or because the dissimilarity function was not fully available at the time the experiment was run. In these situations, when analyzing the experimental results, we still want to partition our population so that each part is as homogeneous as possible, and each part gets enough representatives from each treatment class. Sävje *et al.* call this problem the *minimum bottleneck generalized matching*[1] and show how to generalize the 4-approximation of Higgins *et al.* [8] to get a 4-approximation for this more general problem.

In the Computer Science community, the problem of clustering points to minimize the maximum radius of the clusters such that each cluster has at least a given number of points has been studied by Aggarwal *et al.* [1] in the context of anonymity preserving clustering. This is identical to the minimum threshold blocking problem except that we need to minimize the maximum cluster radius rather than the maximum cluster diameter. The authors call this problem *r-gather* and they give an optimal 2-approximation algorithm that in term generalizes the classical 2-approximation for k-center of Hochbaum and Shmoys [9]. Although the radius and diameter objectives are not equivalent, it is known how to modify the algorithm for r-gather to minimize the diameters of the clusters rather than the radii [11]. Enforcing the treatment partition constraints on the clusters, however, cannot be reduced to the r-gather problem.

Our main contribution is a 2-approximation algorithm for the minimum bottleneck generalized matching problem, which matches the hardness of approximation of Higgins *et al.* [8] for the special case of minimum threshold blocking. We also extend our 2-approximation algorithm to handle more complex constraints that go beyond the treatment partition constraints and involve finding a partition whose parts span a given matroid [17].

---

[1] Matching here refers to the concept in Statistics. It should not be confused with the traditional concept from Graph Theory.

1.1   Related Work

The problem of clustering points in a metric space has been studied extensively in Algorithm Theory. Many objectives have been proposed such as k-center [6,9] where we want to minimize the maximum radius of the clusters, k-median [15] where we want to minimize the sum of the cluster radii, and k-means [16] where we want to minimize the total intra-cluster variance.

In addition to different objectives, researchers have proposed side constraints to the clustering problem such as allowing the algorithm to leave a small set of outliers unclustered [3], imposing capacity constraints [12] or anonymity constraints [1] on the clusters, or a matroid constraint on the set of centers we can pick [20].

To the best of our knowledge, none of these works deals with the bottleneck generalized matching problem of Sävje et al. [19]. The most closely related work that we are aware is the work of Li et al. [14] on ℓ-diversity clustering: Here they want a clustering such that each cluster has at least ℓ points, and all of its points come from different treatment classes and the goal is to minimize the maximum radius of any cluster. Our cluster constraints are in a sense complementary; namely, instead of upper bounding how many points we need from a treatment class, we want to get at least a prescribed number.

2   Formal Problem Definition and Notation

The input of the *minimum bottleneck generalized matching* problem is a metric space (V, d), a treatment partition $\mathcal{T} = \{T_1, T_2, \ldots, T_k\}$ of V, and a target cardinality vector $(b_0, b_1, b_2, \ldots, b_k) \in Z_+^{k+1}$ such that $b_i \leq |T_i|$ for all i and $b_0 \geq \sum_{j=1}^{k} b_j$. The distance function $d : V \times V \to R$ is non-negative, symmetric, and obeys the triangle inequality.

Our ultimate goal is to compute a partition $\mathcal{M} = \{M_1, M_2, \ldots\}$ of V. A partition is said to be feasible if for all $M \in \mathcal{M}$ we have $|M| \geq b_0$ and $|M \cap T_j| \geq b_j$ for all $j \in [k]$. Here $[k]$ is a short hand notation for the set $\{1, \ldots, k\}$. Later we will use $[0, \ldots, k]$ to denote the set $\{0, 1, \ldots, k\}$.

We define the cost of a partition $\mathcal{M}$ to be the maximum diameter[2] among parts $M \in \mathcal{M}$:

$$cost(\mathcal{M}) = \max_{M \in \mathcal{M}} \max_{u,v \in M} d(u, v).$$

The goal of the minimum bottleneck generalized matching problem is to find a feasible partition $\mathcal{M}$ with minimum cost. Our main result is a 2-approximation algorithm for this problem. The approach is based on ideas from an algorithm of Aggarwal et al. [1] for the r-gather problem, where they only have a lower bound on the size of the cluster, but no treatment partition constraints.

---

[2] The diameter is defined as the maximum distance between nodes in a set.

3 Minimum Bottleneck Generalized Matching

In this section we prove that there is a 2-approximation for our problem.

Theorem 1. *There is a polynomial time 2-approximation algorithm for the minimum bottleneck generalized matching problem.*

Let opt be the cost of the optimal solution. Suppose that we had a polynomial time routine parametrized by a scalar g such that:

- if $g \geq$ opt the routine returns a solution with cost $\leq 2g$, and
- if $g <$ opt the routine either reports "failure" or returns a solution with cost $\leq 2g$.

We can use this parametrized routine to design a polynomial time 2-approximation algorithm as follows. For each pair $u, v \in V$, run the routine with $g = d(u, v)$ and return the best solution found.

Note that one of these choices of g must equal opt, so for that choice we are guaranteed a solution with cost 2opt. Returning the best solution found can only yield a better result. Therefore, the correctness of the 2-approximation hinges on the existence of the parametrized routine. The rest of this section is devoted to developing this routine.

3.1 Description of the Parametrized routine

Our routine attempts to build a feasible solution of cost at most $2g$ in three steps. First we pick a set of centers. Second, we build, if possible, a partial cluster around each of the centers that fulfills the treatment partition cardinality constraints. Third, we augment this partial solution by assigning the remaining points to a nearby cluster. Only the second step may not be possible to be carried out, in which case we declare "failure".

Finding centers. The first step of the parametrized routine is to select a set of centers $c_1, \ldots, c_\ell$ such that every element in V has a center at distance at most g and the distance between two centers is greater than g. More formally, the centers have the following two properties

1. $\min_{i \in [\ell]} d(u, c_i) \leq g$ for all $u \in V$, and
2. $d(c_i, c_{i'}) > g$ for all $i, i' \in [\ell]$ where $i \neq i'$.

We can compute such a set of centers using the iterative approach of Hochbaum and Shmoys [9]: Iteratively pick an arbitrary element v of V, declare v to be a center and remove from V all elements at distance at most g from v. The process ends when all elements of V have been removed.

Finding a partial solution. The second step is to construct a partial partition[3] $\{M_1, \ldots, M_\ell\}$ of V such that for each $i \in [\ell]$ we have the following three properties:

1. $|M_i| = b_0$,
2. $|M_i \cap T_j| \geq b_j$ for each $j \in [k]$, and
3. $d(v, c_i) \leq g$ for all $v \in M_i$.

We can find such a partial partition, if one exists, by solving a maximum flow problem in a layered directed graph depicted in Fig. 1 and described below. The vertex set of the network flow instance is as follows:

- In the first layer, we have the source s by itself.
- In the second layer, we have $k + 1$ dummy vertices for each center; namely, we have a vertex a_i^j for each $i \in [\ell]$ and $j \in [0, \ldots, k]$.
- The third layer contains the ground set V.
- Finally, in the fourth layer, we only have the sink t.

The layers are connected as follows:

- For all $i \in [\ell]$, the source s is connected to a_i^0 with an edge with capacity $b_0 - \sum_{j=1}^{k} b_j$.
- For all $i \in [\ell]$ and $j \in [k]$, the source s is connected a_i^j with an edge with capacity b_j.
- Each a_i^0 is connected to each $v \in V$ with an edge without capacity if $d(c_i, v) \leq g$.
- Each a_i^j is connected to each $v \in T_j$ with an edge without capacity if $d(c_i, v) \leq g$.
- Finally, each $v \in V$ is connected to t with an edge with capacity 1.

We solve this problem using any of the traditional combinatorial algorithms [2] for maximum s-t flow. These algorithms return an integral flow that obeys the capacity constraints and sends the maximum amount of flow from s to t. If the value of the maximum flow is less that $b_0 \cdot \ell$ then the parametrized routine declares "failure". Otherwise, we create a partial partition by setting M_i to be the set of nodes $v \in V$ such that there exists a unit of flow going from some a_i^j to v.

Augmenting the Partial Solution. The third and final step is to augment our partial solution by adding every vertex v not assigned so far to one of the parts M_i such that $d(v, c_i) \leq g$. Notice that because of the way the centers were constructed in the first step, we are always able to identify such a center.

If the algorithm does not declare failure in the second step, it returns the augmented solution from the third step that forms a full partition of V.

---

[3] A partial partition of V is a partition of a subset of V.

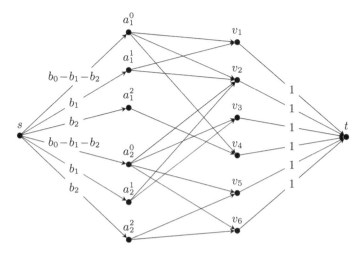

Fig. 1. Maximum flow instance for step two of the parametrized routine. In this example $\ell = 2$, $k = 2$, $T_1 = \{v_1, v_2, v_3\}$, and $T_2 = \{v_4, v_5, v_6\}$.

3.2 Correctness of the Parametrized Routine

If the routine does not fail, it returns a feasible partition $\{M_1, \ldots, M_\ell\}$ where $c_i \in M_i$ for each $i \in [\ell]$. This is because the centers are more than g apart from one another and we only assign to M_i that are at distance at most g to c_i. Furthermore, for any two vertices $u, v \in M_i$ we have $d(u, v) \le d(u, c_i) + d(c_i, v) \le 2g$, so the solution has cost at most $2g$ as desired.

If the routine fails, we need to argue that $g <$ opt. We prove the contrapositive: If $g \ge$ opt then the routine does not fail. This boils down to arguing that the network flow problem defined in the second step of the routine is feasible. To that end, consider an optimal solution $\mathcal{O} = \{O_1, O_2, \ldots\}$. Recall that any two centers in $c_1, \ldots, c_\ell$ are at distance strictly greater than $g \ge$ opt from one another. It follows that they must lie in different sets in the optimal solution. Assume, without loss of generality, that $c_i \in O_i$. We build a flow as follows. For each $j = 1, \ldots, k$, pick b_j elements $v \in O_i \cap T_j$ and push one unit of flow along the path $\langle s, a_i^j, v, t \rangle$; finally pick any $b_0 - \sum_{j=1}^{k} b_j$ elements $v \in O_i$ that were not chosen so far and push one unit of flow along the path $\langle s, a_i^0, v, t \rangle$. (The existence of the elements is guaranteed by the feasibility of $\mathcal{O}$.) The resulting flow is feasible and has value $b_0 \cdot \ell$ as needed.

3.3 Time Complexity and Implementation Details

The most expensive step of the parametrized routine is the computation of the maximum flow. An alternative to computing a flow would be build a bipartite graph where s and t are removed and the a_i^j vertex is replaced with b_j copies for $j \in [k]$ and $b_0 - \sum_{j=1}^{k} b_j$ copies for $j = 0$. The objective in this new graph is to find a maximum cardinality matching (matching in the standard Graph-theoretic sense). Using the Hopcroft-Karp algorithm [10], this can be done in $O(n^{2.5})$ time where $n = |V|$.

In principle this would have to be repeated for each possible choice of g of which there are $O(n^2)$ many. However, one can perform binary search on the candidate values of g until we find the smallest value of g for which the parametrized routine does not fail, which only adds a $O(\log n)$ factor to the $O(n^{2.5})$ running time.

4   Generalization to Matroid Constraints

In this section we explore a generalization of the basic setting that involves a richer set of constraints on each part that involves matroids.

Before we proceed any further, it is worth recalling some basic terminology from Matroid Theory [17]. A subset system is a pair (V, E) where E is a collection subsets of V such that for all $A \in E$ and $A' \subset A$ we have $A' \in E$. A subset system is a matroid if for all $A, B \in E$ such that $|A| < |B|$, there exists $x \in B \setminus A$ such that $A + x \in E$. The rank function associated with an independence system E is $\operatorname{rank} A = \max_{B \subseteq A : B \in E} |B|$, that is, the rank of A is the cardinality of the largest independent subset of A. Finally, a set A is said to span the matroid if $\operatorname{rank}(A) = \operatorname{rank}(E)$.

For our generalization, instead of a target partition and a cardinality vector like we had before, we are given a matroid (V, E) defined by the ground set V that we are to partition and an independence system E.

The objective is to compute a partition $\mathcal{M} = \{M_1, M_2, \ldots\}$ of V such that M_i spans (V, E) for all $i \in [\ell]$ and the maximum diameter of any one part is minimized:

$$cost(\mathcal{M}) = \max_{M \in \mathcal{M}} \max_{u,v \in M} d(u,v).$$

As we shall see in Lemma 1, the constraints of the standard bottleneck generalized matching problem can be achieved with a carefully designed matroid system, so this new problem is a strict generalization of the former. For example, if each element in the ground set is associated with an edge in some auxiliary graph, then we could ask that each cluster forms a connect subgraph using a graphic matroid. We call this new problem the *minimum bottleneck generalized matching problem with a matroid constraint*.

Lemma 1. *Let (V, E) be a subset system where $A \in E$ if and only if $\sum_i \max(|A \cap T_i| - b_i, 0) \leq b_0 - \sum_i b_i$. Then (V, E) is a matroid and $A \in E$ is maximal if and only if $|A| = b_0$ and $|A \cap T_i| \geq b_i$ for all i.*

Proof. For any $A \in E$, we have

$$
\begin{aligned}
|A| &= \sum_i |A \cap T_i| \\
&= \sum_i (|A \cap T_i| - b_i) + \sum_i b_i \\
&\leq \sum_i \max(|A \cap T_i| - b_i, 0) + \sum_i b_i \\
&\leq b_0 - \sum_i b_i + \sum_i b_i \\
&= b_0
\end{aligned}
$$

Thus, $|A| \leq b_0$ for all $A \in E$. Furthermore, for any $A \in E$ if $|A| = b_0$ all inequalities are strict, so $b_i \geq |A \cap T_i|$ for all i. On the other hand, for any $A \in E$ if $|A| < b_0$ then the subset is clearly not maximal.

To see why the system is a matroid, let $A, B \in E$ such that $|A| < |B|$. If $\sum_i \max(|A \cap T_i| - b_i, 0) < b_0 - \sum_i b_i$ then for any $x \in B \setminus A$ we have $A + x \in E$. Otherwise, since $|A| < |B|$, there must exist i such that $|A \cap T_i| < b_i$ and $|A \cap T_i| < |B \cap T_i|$ in which case for any $x \in B \cap T_i \setminus A$ we have $A + x \in E$. $\square$

To solve the problem we proceed as before, by designing a routine that is parametrized by a scalar g. If $g \geq \text{opt}$, the routine returns a feasible solution with cost $2g$, or if $g < \text{opt}$ either returns a "failure" message or a solution with cost $2g$.

We can use this routine in the same way as we did in the previous problem to get a 2-approximation by guessing the value of opt and running the routine on each choice.

4.1 Parametrized Routine

The first and third steps remain the same as before: In the first step we compute a set of centers $c_1, \ldots, c_\ell$ such that every element in V has a center at distance at most g and the distance between centers is strictly greater than g; while in the third step we augment the partial partition found in the modified second step. The key difference is how we find the partial solution that satisfies the matroid constraints in the second step.

Modified second step. The new second step involves solving a matroid intersection problem defined by two matroids (V', E'_1) and (V', E'_2).

The ground set of the matroids V' contains ℓ copies of each element in V, more formally,

$$
V' = \{ v^i : \text{ for all } v \in V, i \in [\ell] \}.
$$

The independence system of the first matroid enforces that the i-th copy of the element chosen is independent in the input matroid

$$
E'_1 = \{ X \subseteq V' : \{ v : v^i \in X \} \in E \text{ for all } i \in [\ell] \}.
$$

The independence system of the second matroid enforces that we select at most one copy of each element

$$E_2' = \left\{ X \subseteq V' : \left| \{v^i : i \in [\ell]\} \cap X \right| \leq 1 \text{ for all } v \in V \right\}$$

We use a matroid intersection algorithm to find a maximum cardinality set X in $E_1' \cap E_2'$. If $|X| < \text{rank}(V, E) \cdot \ell$, then we declare "failure". Otherwise, we create a partial partition with parts $M_i = \{v \in V : v^i \in X\}$ for each $i \in [\ell]$. At this point each part spans the input matroid (V, E), however, there are elements that may not have been assigned. We assign each of these remaining elements $v \in V$ to a part M_j such that $d(v, c_j) \leq g$. Such a center is guaranteed to exist due to the way the centers are selected.

4.2   Correctness

The correctness of the new parametrized routine is similar to that of the old routine. If the routine returns a partition $\{M_1, \ldots, M_\ell\}$ then it satisfies the matroid spanning requirements; indeed, the partial partition $\{M_1', \ldots, M_\ell'\}$ already has the spanning property, namely $M_i' \in E$ and $|M_i'| = \text{rank}(V, E)$, so M_i' spans (V, E), and therefore so does M_i. Furthermore, the diameter of any part is at most $2g$ since for any two $u, v \in M_i$ we have $d(u, v) \leq d(u, c_i) + d(c_i, v) \leq 2g$.

Finally, we argue that if $g \geq$ opt then the parametrized routine never fails. Let $\mathcal{O} = \{O_1, O_2, \ldots\}$ be an optimal solution. Recall that any two centers indeed $c_1, \ldots, c_\ell$ are at distance strictly greater than $g \geq$ opt from one another. It follows that they must lie in different parts in the optimal solution. Assume, without loss of generality, that $c_i \in O_i$. Let $M_i' \subseteq O_i$ be a maximum cardinality independent set. Because O_i spans (V, E), it must be the case that $|M_i'| = \text{rank}(V, E)$. Let $X = \cup_{i \in [\ell]} \{v^i : v \in M_i'\}$ be a subset of the ground set of the matroid intersection instance $(V', E_1' \cap E_2')$ defined in step two of the parametrized routine. Notice that $X \in E_1'$ because each $M_i' \in E$ and $X \in E_2'$ because the sets $\{M_1', \ldots, M_\ell'\}$ are disjoint.

4.3   Time Complexity

Using the matroid intersection algorithm of Cunningham [4] we can find the needed maximum cardinality in $(V', E_1' \cap E_2')$ in $O(r^{1.5}n')$ calls to an independence oracle for the underlying matroids, where r is the maximum size of the common independent set and $n' = |V'|$. In our case, $r = O(n)$, $n' = O(\ell n) = O(n^2)$, and we can test independence in the matroids by using an oracle for the input matroid (V, E). Therefore, the running time is $O(n^{3.5}Q)$, where Q is the time it takes to test independence in (V, E).

As described in the previous section, we can implement the 2-approximation algorithm so as to perform $O(\log n)$ calls to the parametrized routine. Therefore, the overall running time is $O(n^{3.5}Q \log n)$.

5 Conclusion

In this paper we developed a tight 2-approximation algorithm for the minimum threshold generalized matching problem and showed that our approach can be generalized to tackle a more general version of the problem involving finding a partition whose parts span a given matroid. Our hope is that better approximations can lead to better statistical analyses.

Acknowledgement. We would like to thank Jasjeet Sekhon for early discussions on minimum bottleneck generalized matching.

References

1. Aggarwal, G., et al.: Achieving anonymity via clustering. ACM Trans. Algorithms **6**(3), 49:1–49:19 (2010)
2. Ahuja, R.K., Magnanti, T.L., Orlin, J.B.: Network Flows: Theory, Algorithms, and Applications. Prentice Hall, Upper Saddle River (1993)
3. Charikar, M., Khuller, S., Mount, D.M., Narasimhan, G.: Algorithms for facility location problems with outliers. In: Proceedings of the 12th Annual Symposium on Discrete Algorithms, pp. 642–651 (2001)
4. Cunningham, W.H.: Improved bounds for matroid partition and intersection algorithms. SIAM J. Comput. **15**(4), 948–957 (1986)
5. Fisher, R.A.: The arrangement of field experiments. J. Ministry Agric. Great Br. **33**, 503–513 (1926)
6. Gonzalez, T.F.: Clustering to minimize the maximum intercluster distance. Theor. Comput. Sci. **38**, 293–306 (1985)
7. Greevy, R., Lu, B., Silber, J.H., Rosenbaum, P.: Optimal multivariate matching before randomization. Biostatistics **5**(2), 263–275 (2004)
8. Higgins, M.J., Sävje, F., Sekhon, J.S.: Improving massive experiments with threshold blocking. Proc. Natl. Acad. Sci. **113**(27), 7369–7376 (2016)
9. Hochbaum, D.S., Shmoys, D.B.: A best possible heuristic for the k-center problem. Math. Oper. Res. **10**(2), 180–184 (1985)
10. Hopcroft, J.E., Karp, R.M.: An $n^{5/2}$ algorithm for maximum matchings in bipartite graphs. SIAM J. Comput. **2**(4), 225–231 (1973)
11. Khuller, S..: Personal communication (2019)
12. Khuller, S., Sussmann, Y.J.: The capacitated K-center problem. SIAM J. Discrete Math. **13**(3), 403–418 (2000)
13. Lewis, R.A., Rao, J.M.: The unfavorable economics of measuring the returns to advertising. Q. J. Econ. **130**(4), 1941–1973 (2015)
14. Li, J., Yi, K., Zhang, Q.: Clustering with diversity. In: Proceedings of the 37th International Colloquium on Automata, Languages and Programming, pp. 188–200 (2010)
15. Li, S., Svensson, O.: Approximating k-median via pseudo-approximation. SIAM J. Comput. **45**(2), 530–547 (2016)
16. Lloyd, S.: Least squares quantization in PCM. IEEE Trans. Inf. Theory **28**(2), 129–137 (1982)
17. Oxley, J.G.: Matroid Theory. Oxford University Press, Oxford (1992)

18. Rosenbaum, P.R.: Optimal matching for observational studies. J. Am. Stat. Assoc. **84**(408), 1024–1032 (1989)
19. Sävje, F., Higgins, M.J., Sekhon, J.S.: Generalized full matching. CoRR, abs/1703.03882 (2019)
20. Swamy, C.: Improved approximation algorithms for matroid and knapsack median problems and applications. ACM Trans. Algorithms **12**(4), 49:1–49:22 (2016)

Graph Classes and Approximability
of the Happy Set Problem

Yuichi Asahiro[1], Hiroshi Eto[2], Tesshu Hanaka[3], Guohui Lin[4], Eiji Miyano[5(⊠)],
and Ippei Terabaru[5]

[1] Kyushu Sangyo University, Fukuoka, Japan
[2] Kyushu University, Fukuoka, Japan
[3] Chuo University, Tokyo, Japan
[4] University of Alberta, Edmonton, Canada
[5] Kyushu Institute of Technology, Iizuka, Japan
miyano@ces.kyutech.ac.jp

Abstract. In this paper we study the approximability of the MAXI-
MUM HAPPY SET problem (MaxHS) and the computational complexity
of MaxHS on graph classes: For an undirected graph $G = (V, E)$ and a
subset $S \subseteq V$ of vertices, a vertex v is *happy* if v and all its neighbors are
in S; otherwise *unhappy*. Given an undirected graph $G = (V, E)$ and an
integer k, the goal of MaxHS is to find a subset $S \subseteq V$ of k vertices such
that the number of happy vertices is maximized. MaxHS is known to be
NP-hard. In this paper, we design a $(2\Delta + 1)$-approximation algorithm
for MaxHS on graphs with maximum degree Δ. Next, we show that the
approximation ratio can be improved to Δ if the input is a connected
graph and its maximum degree Δ is a constant. Then, we show that
MaxHS can be solved in polynomial time if the input graph is restricted
to proper interval graphs, or block graphs. We prove nevertheless that
MaxHS remains NP-hard even for bipartite graphs or for cubic graphs.

1 Introduction

Homophily is the principle that in social networks people are more likely to
connect with people sharing similar interests with them. Easley and Kleinberg [15] mentioned that homophily is one of the most basic laws governing
the structure of social networks and it provides us with a first, fundamental
illustration of how a network's surrounding contexts can drive the formation of
its links. Then, motivated by a study of algorithmic aspects of the homophily
laws in social networks, Zhang and Li [28] introduced an optimization problem in terms of *graph coloring*, called the MAXIMUM HAPPY VERTICES problem
(MaxHV). MaxHV has attracted growing attention and thus there is a large literature [1–3, 13, 21, 27–29].

1.1 Our Problem and Contributions

Very recently, we formulated the happy problem motivated by the homophily
laws as a "vertex-subset" problem [4]: For an undirected graph $G = (V, E)$

© Springer Nature Switzerland AG 2020
D. Kim et al. (Eds.): COCOON 2020, LNCS 12273, pp. 335–346, 2020.
https://doi.org/10.1007/978-3-030-58150-3_27

and a subset $S \subseteq V$ of vertices, a vertex v is *happy* if v and all its neighbors are in S. Given an undirected graph $G = (V, E)$ and an integer k, the goal of the MAXIMUM HAPPY SET problem (MaxHS) is to find a subset $S \subseteq V$ of k vertices such that the number of happy vertices is maximized. In [4] we showed that there are fixed-parameter algorithms for MaxHS when parameterized by the *tree-width*, the *clique-width* plus k, the *neighborhood diversity*, or the *twin-cover number*. On the other hand, MaxHS is W[1]-hard when parameterized by k even for split graphs.

In this paper we focus on the approximability of MaxHS and the computational complexity of MaxHS on several graph classes such as proper interval graphs, block graphs, bipartite graphs, and graphs with bounded degrees. Our main results are summarized as follows:

1. There is a simple $(2\Delta + 1)$-approximation algorithm for MaxHS on graphs with maximum degree Δ.
2. There is a Δ-approximation algorithm for MaxHS on connected graphs with maximum degree Δ if Δ is a constant.
3. MaxHS can be solved in polynomial time if the input graph is restricted to proper interval graphs, or block graphs (while MaxHS is NP-hard for chordal graphs).
4. MaxHS is NP-hard even for bipartite graphs.
5. MaxHS is NP-hard even for cubic (i.e., 3-regular) graphs.

We remark that split graphs, proper interval graphs, and block graphs are important subclasses of chordal graphs and the third positive result is in contrast to the W[1]-hardness of MaxHS on split graphs. Also, remark that the treewidth of any graph with maximum degree two is at most two and thus MaxHS can be solved in polynomial time for graphs of the maximum degree two [4]. Due to space constraints, some results and proofs are omitted.

1.2 Related Work

In [28], an "edge-variant" of MaxHS is also considered: For an undirected graph $G = (V, E)$ and a subset $S \subseteq V$ of vertices, an edge is *happy* if its both endpoints are in S; otherwise *unhappy*. Given an undirected graph and an integer k, the goal of MAXIMUM EDGE HAPPY SET problem (MaxEHS) is to find a subset $S \subseteq V$ of k vertices such that the number of happy edges is maximized. Actually, however, MaxEHS is identical to the DENSEST k-SUBGRAPH problem (DkS), which is defined as a problem of finding a subgraph of the given graph with exactly k vertices such that the number of edges in the subgraph is maximized. Therefore, MaxEHS is generally NP-hard since it is a generalization of the MAXIMUM CLIQUE problem [18]. Moreover, it is NP-complete even to decide if there exists a solution with at least $k^{1+\varepsilon}$ happy edges for any positive constant ε [5]. In [17] it is shown that MaxEHS is NP-hard for graphs whose maximum degree is three. The problem MaxEHS is NP-hard even for very restricted classes of graphs, such as chordal graphs, comparability graphs, triangle-free graphs and bipartite graphs

with maximum degree three [14,17]. Fortunately, MaxEHS is solvable in polynomial time on graphs whose maximum degree is two, cographs, split graphs, and
k-trees [14]. Interestingly, the complexity of MaxEHS on (proper) interval graphs
and on planar graphs remains open. Still, it is known that there is a PTAS for
MaxEHS on interval graphs [23].

Kortsarz and Peleg proposed an $O(n^{0.3885})$-approximation algorithm for Max-
EHS on n-vertex graphs [20]. Then, Feige, Kortsarz, and Peleg gave an $O(n^\delta)$-
approximation algorithm for some $\delta < 1/3$ [16]. Bhaskara et al. proposed an
$O(n^{1/4+\epsilon})$-approximation $n^{O(1/\epsilon)}$-time algorithm for any $\epsilon > 0$ [6]. On the other
hand, there are inapproximability results of MaxEHS under several assumptions
[11,19,22]. However, it remains open whether there is a constant factor approximation algorithm for MaxEHS.

In [9], Broersma, Golovach, and Patel proved that for an n-vertex graph G
with the clique-width $cw(G)$, MaxEHS can be solved in time $k^{O(cw(G))} \times n$, but
it cannot be solved in time $2^{o(cw(G) \log k)} \times n^{O(1)}$ unless the ETH fails. Bourgeois
et al. gave FPT algorithms for MaxEHS parameterized by treewidth and vertex
cover number, respectively [8]. Moreover, several exact algorithms are proposed
[7,12]. So far many researchers have investigated the edge variant MaxEHS, while
there are few previous results for MaxHS.

2   Preliminaries

Let $G = (V, E)$ be an undirected graph, where V and E denote the set of vertices
and the set of edges, respectively. $V(G)$ and $E(G)$ also denote the vertex set and
the edge set of G, respectively. Throughout the paper, let $n = |V|$ and $m = |E|$
for any given graph. We denote an edge with endpoints u and v by $\{u, v\}$.
The set of vertices adjacent to a vertex v in G, i.e., the open neighborhood of
v is denoted by $N(v) = \{u \in V \mid \{u, v\} \in E\}$. Similarly, let $N(S) = \{u \in
V \setminus S \mid v \in S, \{u, v\} \in E\}$ be the open neighborhood of a subset S of vertices.
The closed neighborhood of v (S, resp.) is denoted by $N[v]$ ($N[S]$, resp.), i.e.,
$N[v] = \{v\} \cup N(v)$ ($N[S] = S \cup N(S)$, resp.). The degree of v is denoted by
$deg(v) = |N(v)|$. Let $\Delta(G)$ and $\delta(G)$ (or simply Δ and δ) be the maximum and
the minimum degrees of G, respectively.

A graph H is a subgraph of a graph $G = (V, E)$ if $V(H) \subseteq V$ and $E(H) \subseteq E$.
For a subset of vertices $U \subseteq V$, let $G[U]$ be the subgraph of G induced by U.
For a subset C of $V(G)$, if every pair of two vertices in C is adjacent in $G[C]$,
then $G[C]$ is called a *clique* and also C is called a *clique set*. In the following we
often use C and $G[C]$ (i.e., clique set and clique) without distinction. A *complete
bipartite graph* $(V \cup U, E)$ is a bipartite graph such that for every two vertices
$v \in V$ and $u \in U$ $\{v, u\}$ is an edge in E.

A graph is r-*regular* if the degree $deg(v)$ of every vertex v is exactly $r \geq 0$.
A 3-regular graph is often called a *cubic* graph. A *chord* of a cycle is an edge
between two vertices of the cycle that is not an edge of the cycle. A graph G is
chordal if each cycle in G of length at least 4 has at least one chord. A graph
$G = (V, E)$ is an *interval graph* if the following two conditions are satisfied for

a collection $\mathcal{I}$ of intervals on the real line, and $\mathcal{I}$ is called *interval model* of G: (i) There is a one-to-one correspondence between V and $\mathcal{I}$, and (ii) for a pair of vertices $u, v \in V$ and their corresponding two intervals $I_u, I_v \in \mathcal{I}$, $I_u \cap I_v \neq \emptyset$ if and only if $\{u, v\} \in E$. A *proper interval graph* is an interval graph that has an interval model in which no interval properly contains another. A *block* in a graph is a maximal connected subgraph with no *cut-vertex*, i.e., a maximal 2-connected subgraph. A graph is called a *block graph* if every block is a clique.

For a subset $S \subset V$ of the vertices, the *cut* $(S, V \setminus S)$ is the set of all edges in G with one endpoint in S and the other in $V \setminus S$; these edges are said to be cut by $(S, V \setminus S)$. A cut $(S, V \setminus S)$ is called a *bisection* of G if $|S| - |V \setminus S| \leq 1$. A *minimum bisection* of G is a bisection with minimum cardinality. The cardinality of the minimum bisection is also known as a *bisection width* of G.

For an undirected graph $G = (V, E)$ and the subset $S \subseteq V$ of vertices, a vertex v is *happy* if $N[v] \subseteq S$; otherwise, i.e., if $N[v] \not\subseteq S$, then v is *unhappy*. Let $\#h(S)$ and $\#u(S)$ denote the number of happy and unhappy vertices in a subset S of vertices, respectively. From the definitions, $|S| = \#h(S) + \#u(S)$ holds. The MAXIMUM HAPPY SET problem (MaxHS) is formally defined as follows:

MAXIMUM HAPPY SET problem (MaxHS)
Input: An undirected graph $G = (V, E)$ and an integer k.
Goal: Find a subset $S \subseteq V$ of k vertices such that the number $\#h(S)$ of happy vertices is maximized.

An algorithm ALG is called a σ-approximation algorithm and ALG's approximation ratio is σ if $OPT(G)/ALG(G) \leq \sigma$ holds for every input G, where $ALG(G)$ and $OPT(G)$ are the numbers of happy vertices in subsets of vertices obtained by ALG and an optimal algorithm, respectively.

In [4], the following tractability and intractability are shown for MaxHS:

Theorem 1 ([4]). *The problem MaxHS can be solved in polynomial time for graphs with constant-bounded treewidth such as trees, cactus graphs, series-parallel graphs, outerplanar graphs, and graphs with the maximum degree two.*

Theorem 2 ([4]). *The problem MaxHS is W[1]-hard when parameterized by k even for split graphs.*

3   Approximation Algorithm

In this section, we study the approximability of MaxHS and propose a Δ-approximation algorithm if the input is a connected graph and its maximum degree Δ is a constant. Before describing our Δ-approximation algorithm, however, we will take a look at the most natural greedy strategy as a warm-up. Then, we show that the approximation ratio of the greedy algorithm is $2\Delta + 1$, and the analysis of the approximation ratio is asymptotically tight in Sect. 3.1. The Δ-approximation algorithm is provided in Sect. 3.2.

3.1 Greedy $(2\Delta + 1)$-Approximation Algorithm for General Graphs

Consider a graph G with maximum degree Δ, an arbitrary vertex v, and its (at most) Δ neighbor vertices. If we select v and all its neighbors into a solution set S, then those $1 + \Delta$ vertices make at least one vertex happy. This observation develops the following algorithm, named Greedy-Pick: (**Step 1**) Pick a vertex v such that the number of its neighbors which are not yet in S is minimum among all the vertices. (**Step 2(i)**) If $|N[v] \setminus S| \leq k - |S|$, then add $N[v]$ to S (i.e., update $S = S \cup N[v]$) and go back to **Step 1**. (**Step 2(ii)**) Otherwise, add an arbitrary set of $k-|S|$ vertices to $|S|$, and finally output S. Note that the running time of Greedy-Pick is clearly polynomial. We can show that the approximation ratio of Greedy-Pick is $2\Delta + 1$, and the analysis of the approximation ratio is asymptotically tight.

Theorem 3. *The approximation ratio of* Greedy-Pick *is* $2\Delta+1$ *for graphs with maximum degree* Δ.

Remark 1. There exists a bad example for which the number of happy vertices by an optimal algorithm is $2\Delta - 4$ times of the one by Greedy-Pick, where Δ is the maximum degree of an input graph although details are omitted here.

3.2 Δ-Approximation Algorithm for Connected Graphs

In this subsection, we assume that the input is restricted to connected graphs whose maximum degree is a constant. Then, we propose a more sophisticated algorithm than Greedy-Pick, named ALG_p, where p is a prescribed parameter integer and it is given later. The basic strategy of ALG_p is as follows: ALG_p first enumerates all the vertex-sets of size exactly p. Let $\mathcal{U}_p = \{U \mid U \subseteq V, |U| = p\}$. Then, consider a subset $U \in \mathcal{U}_p$ and its closed neighborhood $N[U]$. ALG_p handles the following two cases. (i) First suppose that $|N[U]| > k$ holds for every $U \in \mathcal{U}_p$. This implies that the number $\#h(S^*)$ of happy vertices in an optimal solution S^* is less than p. Therefore, ALG_p tries to find a solution of size less than p. From the assumption that p is a constant, ALG_p could output an optimal solution in polynomial time. (ii) Next suppose that $|N[U']| \leq k$ holds for some $U' \in \mathcal{U}_p$. Then, ALG_p works almost the same way as Greedy-Pick.

Here is a detailed description of ALG_p.

Algorithm ALG_p

Input: A connected graph $G = (V, E)$ and an integer $k < |V|$.

Output: A subset $S \subset V$ of k vertices.

Step 1. Construct $\mathcal{U}_p = \{U \mid U \subseteq V, |U| = p\}$ and $\mathcal{W}_{<p} = \{W \mid W \subseteq V, |W| \leq p - 1\}$.

Step 2. (i) If $|N[U]| > k$ holds for every subset $U \in \mathcal{U}_p$, then find $S_1 = N[\text{argmax}_{W \in \mathcal{W}_{<p}, |N[W]| \leq k} \#h(W)]$, set $k' = k - |S_1|$, and goto Step 4.
(ii) Otherwise, find $S_1 = N[\text{argmin}_{U \in \mathcal{U}_p} |N[U]|]$, set $k' = k - |S_1|$, and goto Step 3.

Step 3. If there exists a vertex $v \in S_1$ satisfying $k' \geq |N[v] \setminus S_1|$, then update $S_1 = S_1 \cup N[v]$ and $k' = k' - |N[v] \setminus S_1|$. Repeat this step if such a vertex exists.

Step 4. Pick an arbitrary set S_2 of k' vertices from $V \setminus S_1$ and output $S = S_1 \cup S_2$.

On the performance of $\mathtt{ALG}_p$, we show the next theorem.

Theorem 4. *For a connected graph $G = (V, E)$ with the maximum degree Δ, $\mathtt{ALG}_p$ is a $((1+\frac{1}{p})\Delta - 1)$-approximation algorithm which runs in $O(p\Delta|V|^p)$ time.*

Proof. We first bound the running time of $\mathtt{ALG}_p$. **Step 1** takes $O(|V|^p)$ time. In **Step 2**, for each set U in $\mathcal{U}_p \cup \mathcal{W}_{<p}$, we need to obtain $N[U]$ which takes $O(p\Delta)$ time. While obtaining $N[U]$, we can also calculate $\#h(U)$. Since the number of vertex subsets in $\mathcal{U}_p \cup \mathcal{W}_{<p}$ is $O(|V|^p)$, the total time needed for **Step 2** is $O(p\Delta|V|^p)$. As for **Step 3**, we obtain $N[v] \setminus S_1$ for every $v \in S_1$ in $O(|V| + |E|)$ time at the first iteration of this step. At the second and the later iteration, we can maintain these information by removing one vertex and adding its adjacent vertices, taking $O(|V| + |E|)$ time during this step in an amortized sense. In addition, at each execution of **Step 3**, $O(|V|)$-time is needed to find a vertex satisfying the condition. Since the number of iterations of **Step 3** is at most $O(|V|)$, the total time of **Step 3** is $O(|V|^2)$. Clearly **Step 4** can be done in $O(|V|)$ time. In summary, the total running time of $\mathtt{ALG}_p$ is $O(p\Delta|V|^p)$ since $p \geq 2$.

In the following, we analyze the approximation ratio of $\mathtt{ALG}_p$. For **Step 2**, we first consider the case that $|N[U]| > k$ holds for every $U \in \mathcal{U}_p$. This condition implies that the number $\#h(S^*)$ of happy vertices in an optimal solution S^* is less than p. Assume that $\{v_1, v_2, \ldots, v_q\}$ for some $q < p$ are happy in S^*. Since $S^* \supseteq N[\{v_1, v_2, \ldots, v_q\}]$, it holds that $|N[\{v_1, v_2, \ldots, v_q\}]| \leq k$. The set $\{v_1, v_2, \ldots, v_q\}$ clearly belongs to $\mathcal{W}_{<p}$, so that this set is tested when obtaining S_1. Hence $\mathtt{ALG}_p$ outputs it or another subset of vertices having the same number of happy vertices, i.e., $\mathtt{ALG}_p$ outputs an optimal solution in this case.

Let us proceed to the case that it holds $|N[U']| \leq k$ for some $U' \in \mathcal{U}_p$ in **Step 2(ii)**. The following arguments give the approximation ratio of $\mathtt{ALG}_p$:

- $\mathtt{ALG}_p$ selects at most $(p+i)(\Delta - 1) + \Delta$ vertices to make $p+i$ vertices happy among them in the output for an integer i;
- the integer i is maximized by repeating **Step 3**;
- $\mathtt{ALG}_p$ wastes at most $\Delta - 2$ vertices in **Step 4**, i.e., they are all unhappy; and hence
- the number k of the output (solution) size is bounded above by $(p + i)(\Delta - 1) + \Delta$, which is an upper bound of the optimal number of happy vertices.

In this case, $\#h(S_1) \geq p$ holds since $\mathtt{ALG}_p$ finds $N[U']$ or a better set of smaller size than k as S_1 in **Step 2**. Here we observe that $|S_1| \leq (\Delta - 1)p + 2$ holds as follows. Consider a set P of p vertices $v_1, v_2, \ldots, v_p$, which forms a path $\langle v_1, v_2, \ldots, v_p \rangle$ in G, where this path must not be simple here. Since $P \in \mathcal{U}_p$,

$N[P]$ is a candidate of S_1. It holds that $|N[P]| \leq p + (\Delta - 1) \cdot 2 + (\Delta - 2)(p - 2)$, where the second term $(\Delta - 1) \cdot 2$ of the right-hand side represents an upper bound of $|(N[v_1] \cup N[v_p]) \setminus \{v_2, v_{p-1}\}|$, and the third term $(\Delta - 2)(p - 2)$ is also an upper bound of $|N[\{v_2, \ldots, v_{p-1}\}] \setminus P|$. Since S_1 has the minimum size among $N[U]$'s for $U \in \mathcal{U}_p$, the following inequality holds:

$$|S_1| \leq |N[P]| \leq p + (\Delta - 1) \cdot 2 + (\Delta - 2)(p - 2) = (\Delta - 1)p + 2$$

Note that an optimal solution need not be connected, while $\mathtt{ALG}_p$ has a vertex subset which includes a connected subgraph in its output.

In **Step 3**, if $v \in S_1$ and $|N[v] \setminus S_1| \geq \Delta$ implying $|N[v] \setminus S_1| = |N(v)| = \Delta$ since Δ is the maximum degree of a vertex, then v is not happy in S_1 and $N(v) \cap S_1 = \emptyset$. Thus, removing v from S_1 does not decrease the number of happy vertices in S_1, that is, $\#h(S_1 \setminus \{v\}) = \#h(S_1)$, contradicting the choice of S_1 which must have the minimum size among $N[U]$'s for $U \in \mathcal{U}_p$. Note that the condition $|N[v] \setminus S_1| = \Delta + 1$ means that $v \notin S_1$, which contradicts the assumption $v \in S_1$. Hence, the number of vertices $N[v] \setminus S_1$ added to S_1 is at most $\Delta - 1$ for one execution of this step. Thus, in total, at most $i(\Delta - 1)$ vertices are added to S_1 in this step, where i is the number of the iterations of this step. In other words, i is (at least) the number of happy vertices newly added to S_1. So far, the number $\#h(S_1)$ of happy vertices in S_1 has increased to (at least) $p + i$ from p obtained in **Step 2**.

Step 4 does not make any vertex happy. However, we know that $|S_2| \leq \Delta - 2$ by the terminating condition of **Step 3**.

Finally, we analyze the approximation ratio. The number of happy vertices by $\mathtt{ALG}_p$ is at least $p + i$. On the other hand, the total number k of vertices is represented by $k_2 + k_3 + k_4$, where k_2, k_3, and k_4 are the numbers of vertices added to the solution in **Steps 2, 3**, and **4**, respectively. By the above argument, it hold $k_2 \leq (\Delta - 1)p + 2$, $k_3 \leq i(\Delta - 1)$, and $k_4 \leq \Delta - 2$, which yields that

$$k = k_2 + k_3 + k_4$$
$$\leq ((\Delta - 1)p + 2) + i(\Delta - 1) + (\Delta - 2) = (p + i)(\Delta - 1) + \Delta.$$

Since k is a trivial upper bound of the size of happy vertices, the approximation ratio of $\mathtt{ALG}_p$ is at most

$$\frac{k}{p + i} \leq \frac{(p + i)(\Delta - 1) + \Delta}{p + i} \leq \left(1 + \frac{1}{p}\right)\Delta - 1.$$

$\square$

By the above theorem, one can see that there is a trade-off between the approximation ratio and the running time of $\mathtt{ALG}_p$. In particular, $\mathtt{ALG}_p$ is an $O(\Delta^2 |V|^\Delta)$-time Δ-approximation algorithm by setting $p = \Delta$.

Corollary 1. *If the maximum degree Δ of the input connected graph $G = (V, E)$ is a constant, then $\mathtt{ALG}_{\Delta-1}$ runs in $O(\Delta^2 |V|^\Delta)$-time, i.e., polynomial time and the approximation ratio of $\mathtt{ALG}_{\Delta-1}$ is Δ.*

4   Complexity for Graph Classes

4.1   Block Graphs

In this subsection we show that MaxHS can be solved in polynomial time if the input graph is restricted to block graphs. Recall that a block is a maximal connected subgraph without a cut-vertex and a block graph is a graph whose blocks are all cliques. Note that by the maximality of blocks, two different blocks of a graph overlap in at most one vertex, which is thus a cut-vertex of G. Also, note that the class of block graphs is equivalent to the class of *diamond-free* chordal graphs and thus block graphs include no induced cycle of length more than three. The interaction between blocks and cut-vertices can be represented by a special graph [26]: Suppose that a graph $G = (V, E)$ consists of β blocks, B_1 through B_β and also G has γ cut-vertices, c_1 through c_γ. The *block-cutpoint graph* of a graph G is a bipartite graph T in which one partite set consists of the cut-vertices c_i's of G, $1 \leq i \leq \gamma$, and the other has a vertex b_j for each block B_j of G, $1 \leq j \leq \beta$. The block-cutpoint graph T includes $\{c_i, b_j\}$ as an edge of T if and only if the cut-vertex c_j is in B_i.

If G is a connected block graph, then its block-cutpoint graph T is a tree, whose leaves are blocks of G. In the following, a cut-vertex c_i and a vertex b_j in T are called a *cut-node* and a *block-node*, respectively. Note that blocks can be found using the depth-first search, and thus the block-cutpoint tree T can be computed in $O(|V| + |E|)$ time [24]. For the tree T, we distinguish one arbitrary block-node as a *root* of T. This introduces a parent-child relation in T.

Algorithm. The following is an outline of our algorithm, which is based on the dynamic programming (DP) approach: **(Step 1)** Given a block graph $G = (V, E)$ as input, we first compute the *weighted* block-cutpoint tree $T = (V_T, E_T, w)$ where V_T, E_T, and w are the node set, the edge set, and a node-weight function such that $w : V_T \to \mathbf{Z}^+$, respectively. **(Step 2)** Next, to simplify the DP-based algorithm, we remove every 0-weight node from T by contracting the 0-weight node and one of its neighbors and obtain the *modified* block-cutpoint tree, say, T'. **(Step 3)** Then, we find an optimal solution by using the tree representation T'. As an example, see Fig. 1. If the block-cutpoint tree of G is given as input, then the DP-based algorithm gives us the following theorem:

Theorem 5. *The problem MaxHS on block graphs can be solved in time $O(k^2|V|)$ for the input graph $G = (V, E)$ and the integer k.*

4.2   Proper Interval Graphs

As shown in [4], MaxHS remains NP-hard even for split graphs, which immediately implies that MaxHS is NP-hard even for chordal graphs. In this subsection we show that MaxHS can be solved in polynomial time if the input graph is restricted to proper interval graphs, one of the important subclasses of chordal graphs. Note that the treewidth (or pathwidth) of a proper interval graph is

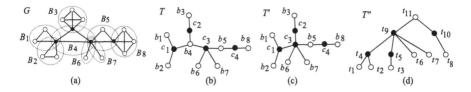

Fig. 1. (a) Block graph G given as input, (b) weighted block-cutpoint tree T of G, (c) modified block-cutpoint tree T', and (d) relabeled tree T'' with root t_{11} (which is originally b_5 in T')

equal to the size of the maximum clique in the graph, and thus generally the treewidth is not constant-bounded.

The following is an outline of our algorithm, which is based on the DP approach again: **(Step 1)** Given a proper interval graph $G = (V, E)$ as input, we first compute the path representation of the proper interval graph in polynomial time by using a modification of Maximum Cardinality Search [25] and, for example, Prime's algorithm. **(Step 2)** Then we find an optimal solution by following the path representation of G computed in **Step 1**. We can show the following theorem if the path representation of G is given as input:

Theorem 6. *The problem* MaxHS *on proper interval graphs can be solved in time* $O(k|V|)$ *for the input graph* $G = (V, E)$ *and the integer* k.

4.3 Bipartite Graphs

In this subsection we show the NP-hardness of MaxHS on bipartite graphs:

Theorem 7. *The problem* MaxHS *on bipartite graphs is NP-hard.*

Proof (sketch). We will reduce the general MaxHS to MaxHS on bipartite graphs; given a graph $G = (V, E)$ and an integer k, we transform G to a bipartite graph $G' = (V', E')$ and an integer k', respectively. Assume that $|V| = n$ and n is even. Let $V = \{v_1, v_2, \ldots, v_n\}$ be n vertices in the original graph G. Then, for each $i = 1, 2, \ldots, n$, we construct a complete bipartite graph $G'_i = (V'_i, E'_i)$ of $4n$ vertices, one partite set has $2n$ vertices, $a_{i,1}$ through $a_{i,2n}$, and the other partite set has $2n$ vertices, $b_{i,1}$ through $b_{i,2n}$. Moreover, the constructed graph G' has two edges $\{a_{i,2n}, b_{j,1}\}$ and $\{b_{i,1}, a_{j,2n}\}$ if and only if the original graph G has an edge $\{v_i, v_j\}$. Figure 2 illustrates $G'_i = (V'_i, E'_i)$ and $G'_j = (V'_j, E'_j)$. The total number of vertices in the reduced graph G' is $4n^2$. Finally, we set $k' = 4kn$. This completes the reduction, which can be done in polynomial time. One can see that the constructed graph G' is bipartite.

We can show that the original G has a subset $S \subseteq V$ of k vertices such that the number of *unhappy* vertices in S is at most ℓ (or equivalently the number of happy vertices is at least $k - \ell$) if and only if the constructed graph G' has a subset $S' \subseteq V'$ of $4kn$ vertices such that the number of *unhappy* vertices in S' is at most 2ℓ (or equivalently the number of happy vertices is at least $4kn - 2\ell$). We can assume that $\ell \leq k \leq n - 1$ is satisfied and thus $2\ell \leq 2n - 2$. □

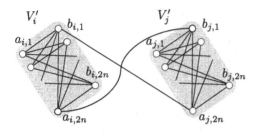

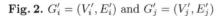

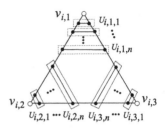

Fig. 2. $G'_i = (V'_i, E'_i)$ and $G'_j = (V'_j, E'_j)$ **Fig. 3.** ith vertex gadget G'_i

4.4 Cubic Graphs

In this subsection, we show the intractability of MaxHS on cubic graphs; while MaxHS can be solved in polynomial time for graphs of the maximum degree two [4]. We prove its NP-hardness by reducing the following MINIMUM BISECTION problem (MinBis) on cubic (i.e., 3-regular) graphs to MaxHS on cubic graphs: Given an undirected graph $G = (V, E)$ such that $|V|$ is even, the goal of MinBis is to find a minimum bisection $(S, V \setminus S)$ of G, i.e., a cut $(S, V \setminus S)$ with $|S| = |V \setminus S|$ and the bisection width. It is known [10] that MinBis is NP-hard for r-regular graphs having the even number of vertices, $r \geq 3$.

Theorem 8. *The problem MaxHS on cubic graphs is NP-hard.*

Proof (sketch). Consider an input cubic graph $G = (V, E)$ of MinBis with $|V| = n$ vertices. Suppose that n is even. Also, suppose that the bisection width of G is b. Then, we construct an instance pair, a cubic graph $G' = (V', E')$ and an integer k, of MaxHS. Let $V = \{v_1, v_2, \ldots, v_n\}$ and $E = \{e_1, e_2, \ldots, e_m\}$. Since G is a cubic graphs, $m = 3n/2$ holds. The graph G' consists of n subgraphs $G'_1 = (V'_1, E'_1)$ through $G'_n = (V'_n, E'_n)$, which are associated with n vertices, v_1 through v_n. We call G'_i the ith *vertex gadget*, which is illustrated in Fig. 3. For each $i \in \{1, \ldots, n\}$, the ith vertex gadget G'_i has $6n + 3$ vertices, i.e., $V'_i = \{v_{i,1}, v_{i,2}, v_{i,3}\} \cup \bigcup_{j=1}^{n} (U_{i,1,j} \cup U_{i,2,j} \cup U_{i,3,j})$, where every $U_{i,1,j}$ ($U_{i,2,j}$ or $U_{i,3,j}$) consists of two vertices for each j. We call three vertices $\{v_{i,1}, v_{i,2}, v_{i,3}\}$ *outer vertices*, and the remaining $6n$ vertices *inner vertices* in the ith vertex gadget. Also, G'_i has $9n + 3$ edges, called *new edges*. Then, three edges incident to v_i in the original cubic graph G are replaced with three edges, called *old edges*, where exactly one edge is incident to one vertex of $\{v_{i,1}, v_{i,2}, v_{i,3}\}$ in the ith vertex gadget. This completes the construction from G to G'. One sees that the total number of vertices is $6n^2 + 3n$. Finally, we set $k = (6n^2 + 3n)/2$. This reduction can be done in polynomial time.

It can be shown that the bisection width of G is (at most) b if and only if G' has a subset $S' \subseteq V'$ of $k = (6n^2 + 3n)/2$ vertices such that the number of happy vertices is (at least) $\#h(S') = (6n^2 + 3n)/2 - b$, or equivalently, the number of unhappy vertices in S is at most $\#u(S') = b$ in the selected subset S' as the solution of MaxHS.   □

5   Conclusion

We studied the approximability and the computational complexity of MaxHS. To this end, we designed approximation algorithms and DP-based exact algorithms for several subclasses of chordal graphs. Furthermore, we showed NP-hardness for restricted graph classes. One of the further researches is to design a good approximation algorithm for disconnected graphs, since the proposed Δ-approximation algorithm works only for connected graphs. Extending the algorithm for proper interval graphs to cope with interval graphs is another interesting topic.

Acknowledgments. We would like to thank the anonymous referees for their helpful comments, especially pointing out small errors in the proof of Theorem 4. This work was partially supported by the Natural Sciences and Engineering Research Council of Canada, the Grants-in-Aid for Scientific Research of Japan (KAKENHI) Grant Numbers JP17K00016 and JP17K00024, JP19K21537, and JST CREST JPMJR1402.

References

1. Agrawal, A.: On the parameterized complexity of happy vertex coloring. In: Brankovic, L., Ryan, J., Smyth, W.F. (eds.) IWOCA 2017. LNCS, vol. 10765, pp. 103–115. Springer, Cham (2018). https://doi.org/10.1007/978-3-319-78825-8_9
2. Aravind, N.R., Kalyanasundaram, S., Kare, A.S.: Linear time algorithms for happy vertex coloring problems for trees. In: Mäkinen, V., Puglisi, S.J., Salmela, L. (eds.) IWOCA 2016. LNCS, vol. 9843, pp. 281–292. Springer, Cham (2016). https://doi.org/10.1007/978-3-319-44543-4_22
3. Aravind, N., Kalyanasundaram, S., Kare, A., Lauri, J.: Algorithms and hardness results for happy coloring problems. arXiv preprint arXiv:1705.08282 (2017)
4. Asahiro, Y., Eto, H., Hanaka, T., Lin, G., Miyano, E., Terabaru, I.: Parameterized algorithms for the happy set problem. In: Rahman, M.S., Sadakane, K., Sung, W.-K. (eds.) WALCOM 2020. LNCS, vol. 12049, pp. 323–328. Springer, Cham (2020). https://doi.org/10.1007/978-3-030-39881-1_27
5. Asahiro, Y., Hassin, R., Iwama, K.: Complexity of finding dense subgraphs. Discrete Appl. Math. **121**, 15–26 (2002)
6. Bhaskara, A., Charikar, M., Chlamtac, E., Feige, U., Vijayaraghavan, A.: Detecting high log-densities: an $o(n^{\frac{1}{4}})$ approximation for densest k-subgraph. In: STOC 2010, pp. 201–210 (2010)
7. Bourgeois, N., Giannakos, A., Lucarelli, G., Milis, I., Paschos, V.T.: Exact and superpolynomial approximation algorithms for the densest k-subgraph problem. Eur. J. Oper. Res. **262**(3), 894–903 (2017)
8. Bourgeois, N., Giannakos, A., Lucarelli, G., Milis, I., Paschos, V.T.: Exact and approximation algorithms for densest k-subgraph. In: Ghosh, S.K., Tokuyama, T. (eds.) WALCOM 2013. LNCS, vol. 7748, pp. 114–125. Springer, Heidelberg (2013). https://doi.org/10.1007/978-3-642-36065-7_12
9. Broersma, H., Golovach, P., Patel, V.: Tight complexity bounds for FPT subgraph problems parameterized by the clique-width. Theoret. Comput. Sci. **485**, 69–84 (2013)
10. Bui, T.N., Chaudhuri, S., Leighton, F.T., Sipser, M.: Graph bisection algorithms with good average case behavior. Combinatorica **7**(2), 171–191 (1987)

11. Chalermsook, P., et al.: From gap-ETH to FPT-inapproximability: clique, dominating set, and more. In: FOCS 2017, pp. 743–754 (2017)

12. Chang, M.S., Chen, L.H., Hung, L.J., Rossmanith, P., Wu, G.H.: Exact algorithms for problems related to the densest k-set problem. Inf. Process. Lett. **114**(9), 510–513 (2014)

13. Choudhari, J., Reddy, I.V.: On structural parameterizations of happy coloring, empire coloring and boxicity. In: Rahman, M.S., Sung, W.-K., Uehara, R. (eds.) WALCOM 2018. LNCS, vol. 10755, pp. 228–239. Springer, Cham (2018). https://doi.org/10.1007/978-3-319-75172-6_20

14. Corneil, D., Perl, Y.: Clustering and domination in perfect graphs. Discrete Appl. Math. **9**(1), 27–39 (1984)

15. Easley, D., Kleinberg, J.: Networks, Crowds, and Markets: Reasoning About a Highly Connected World. Cambridge University Press, Cambridge (2010)

16. Feige, U., Peleg, D., Kortsarz, G.: The dense k-subgraph problem. Algorithmica **29**(3), 410–421 (2001)

17. Feige, U., Seltser, M.: On the densest k-subgraph problem. Technical report CS97-16, Weizmann Institute, Rehovot (1997). http://www.wisdom.weizmann.ac.il

18. Garey, M.R., Johnson, D.S.: Computers and Intractability: A Guide to the Theory of NP-Completeness. W. H. Freeman & Co., New York (1979)

19. Khot, S.: Ruling out PTAS for graph min bisection, dense k subgraph, and bipartite clique. SIAM J. Comput. **36**(4), 1025–1071 (2006)

20. Kortsarz, G., Peleg, D.: On choosing a dense subgraph. In: FOCS 1993, pp. 692–701 (1993)

21. Lewis, R., Thiruvady, D., Morgan, K.: Finding happiness: an analysis of the maximum happy vertices problem. Comput. Oper. Res. **103**, 265–276 (2019)

22. Manurangsi, P.: Almost-polynomial ratio ETH-hardness of approximating densest k-subgraph. In: STOC 2017, pp. 954–961 (2017)

23. Nonner, T.: PTAS for densest k-subgraph in interval graphs. Algorithmica **74**(1), 528–539 (2016)

24. Tarjan, R.: Depth first search and linear graph algorithms. SIAM J. Comput. **1**(2), 146–160 (1972)

25. Tarjan, R., Yannakakis, M.: Simple linear-time algorithms to test chordality of graphs, test acyclicity of hypergraphs, and selectively reduce acyclic hypergraphs. SIAM J. Comput. **13**, 566–579 (1984)

26. West, D.: Introduction to Graph Theory. Prentice-Hall Inc, Englewood Cliffs (2000)

27. Zhang, P., Jiang, T., Li, A.: Improved approximation algorithms for the maximum happy vertices and edges problems. In: Xu, D., Du, D., Du, D. (eds.) COCOON 2015. LNCS, vol. 9198, pp. 159–170. Springer, Cham (2015). https://doi.org/10.1007/978-3-319-21398-9_13

28. Zhang, P., Li, A.: Algorithmic aspects of homophyly of networks. Theoret. Comput. Sci. **593**, 117–131 (2015)

29. Zhang, P., Xu, Y., Jiang, T., Li, A., Lin, G., Miyano, E.: Improved approximation algorithms for the maximum happy vertices and edges problems. Algorithmica **80**(5), 1412–1438 (2018)

A Simple Primal-Dual Approximation Algorithm for 2-Edge-Connected Spanning Subgraphs

Stephan Beyer[1], Markus Chimani[1], and Joachim Spoerhase[2]([✉])

[1] Theoretical Computer Science, Osnabrück University, Osnabrück, Germany
{stephan.beyer,markus.chimani}@uni-osnabrueck.de
[2] Department of Computer Science, Aalto University, Espoo, Finland
joachim.spoerhase@aalto.fi

Abstract. Our paper is motivated by the search for *combinatorial* and, in particular, *primal-dual* approximation algorithms for higher-connectivity survivable network design problems (SND). The best known approximation algorithm for SND is Jain's powerful but "non-combinatorial" iterative LP-rounding technique, which yields factor 2. In contrast, known combinatorial algorithms are based on *multi-phase primal-dual* approaches that increase the connectivity in each phase, thereby naturally leading to a factor depending (logarithmically) on the maximum connectivity requirement. Williamson raised the question if there are *single-phase* primal-dual algorithms for such problems. A single-phase primal-dual algorithm could potentially be key to a primal-dual *constant-factor* approximation algorithm for SND. Whether such an algorithm exists is an important open problem (Shmoys and Williamson).

In this paper, we make a first, small step related to these questions. We show that there is a primal-dual algorithm for the *minimum 2-edge-connected spanning subgraph problem* (2ECSS) that requires only a single growing phase and that is therefore the first such algorithm for any higher-connectivity problem. The algorithm yields approximation factor 3, which matches the factor of the best known (two-phase) primal-dual approximation algorithms for 2ECSS. Moreover, we believe that our algorithm is *more natural and conceptually simpler* than the known primal-dual algorithms for 2ECSS. It can be implemented without data structures more sophisticated than binary heaps and graphs, and without graph algorithms beyond depth-first search.

1 Introduction

An undirected multigraph $G = (V, E)$ with $n := |V|, m := |E|, m \geq n$, is *2-edge-connected* if for every edge $e \in E$ the graph $G - e := (V, E \setminus \{e\})$ is

The first two authors are supported by the German Research Foundation (DFG), grant CH 897/3-1. The third author is supported by the European Research Council (ERC) under the European Union's Horizon 2020 research and innovation programme, grant 759557, and by the Academy of Finland, grant 310415.

D. Kim et al. (Eds.): COCOON 2020, LNCS 12273, pp. 347–359, 2020.
https://doi.org/10.1007/978-3-030-58150-3_28

connected. The *minimum 2-edge-connected spanning subgraph* problem (2ECSS) is defined as follows: Given a 2-edge-connected undirected multigraph $G = (V, E)$ with edge costs $c: E \to \mathbb{R}_{\geq 0}$, find an edge subset $E' \subseteq E$ of minimum cost $c(E') := \sum_{e \in E'} c(e)$ such that $G' = (V, E')$ is 2-edge-connected. Any edge of G may only be used once in G'. 2ECSS is a fundamental NP-hard network design problem that arises naturally in the planning of infrastructure where one wants to guarantee a basic fault tolerance.

2ECSS belongs to the general class of survivable network design problems (SND) where we demand certain edge-connectivity requirements for subsets of nodes. The *k-survivable network design problem* (kSND) is a special case where k represents the *maximum* requirement. The problem kECSS is a special case of kSND where all node subsets have an *identical* requirement of k.

Motivation for This Work. Jain's powerful iterative LP-rounding technique [6] gives a 2-approximation for general SND. While this is a very strong result when we aim at optimizing the approximation factor, it requires to iteratively solve the underlying LP relaxation. It is therefore often desirable to design *combinatorial* approximation algorithms when we take into account not only the worst-case approximation factor but also simplicity, implementability, and running time. In particular, *primal-dual* algorithms have the advantage of being combinatorial and additionally providing a *per-instance* factor (beyond the worst-case factor) by comparing the approximate (primal) solution to the computed dual solution. The known combinatorial algorithms for kSND are based on the primal-dual paradigm and achieve a factor of $\mathcal{O}(\log k)$. Obtaining a constant-factor (in particular, matching Jain's factor 2) primal-dual approximation algorithm for a survivable network design problem is an important open problem in approximation algorithms (see, e.g., open problem no. 4 in the text book by Shmoys and Williamson [14]). The logarithmic factor of the primal-dual algorithms for kSND is closely related to the fact that these algorithms require k phases to gradually satisfy these connectivity requirements: in phase i, we lose a factor of $\mathcal{O}(1/(k-i+1))$ in the approximation factor. It is therefore a natural attempt to attack the above open problem by designing a *single-phase* algorithm, that is, an algorithm that requires only a single growing phase instead of k many. Yet, even the various known primal-dual algorithms for the special case of 2ECSS require two growing phases. A related open question by Williamson [12] is if it is possible "to design a single-phase algorithm for some class of edge-covering problems". This work is therefore motivated by the following research question.

Is there a single-phase primal-dual approximation algorithm for kSND?

We remark that there is a combinatorial 2-approximation algorithm for kECSS [8] and a *simple* combinatorial 3-approximation algorithm for 2ECSS [7]. However, these algorithms are not primal-dual. Moreover, the 2-approximation [8] is based on weighted matroid intersection, which is intimately related to the uniform connectivity requirements in kECSS. It therefore seems hard to generalize it to kSND. The second algorithm for 2ECSS follows a two-phase approach. To the best of our knowledge, the primal-dual paradigm is the only known combinatorial approach for kSND.

Our Contribution. In this paper, we make a (small) first step addressing the above open questions. We provide the first example of a primal-dual algorithm for some higher-connectivity network design problem, namely 2ECSS, that grows the solution in a *single* phase. Our algorithm has an approximation factor of 3. While this does not match the best known factor of 2 in general, it does match the factor of the best known (two-phase) primal-dual approximation algorithms. We hope that our work helps to obtain single-phase or even constant-factor primal-dual approximation algorithms for more general connectivity requirements. For example, it is straight-forward to obtain a single-phase primal-dual algorithm for 2SND that generalizes both our 3-approximation algorithm for 2ECSS as well as the 2-approximation algorithm for constrained forest problems by Goemans and Williamson [5]. However, we know neither the factor of this algorithm nor if it can be generalized to kSND.

Besides requiring only a single growing phase, our algorithm is also arguably *simpler and more natural* than other primal-dual algorithms for 2ECSS. It maintains a spanning forest starting with an empty edge set. In each iteration, a new edge incident to a leaf is selected in a natural greedy manner and added to the forest. If this produces a cycle, this cycle is contracted. This growing phase ends when the graph has been contracted into a single node. A subsequent cleanup step removes redundant edges in reverse order of their addition.

From an algorithmic perspective the (to our best knowledge) new conceptual idea is to create cycles already in the first (and only) growing phase. We contract these cycles on the fly to maintain a forest structure. From a technical viewpoint, this requires to grow the solution only at the leaves of the current solution.

Our algorithm requires only trivial data structures (arrays, lists, graphs, and optionally binary heaps) and no graph algorithms beyond depth-first search. It runs in $\mathcal{O}(\min\{nm, m + n^2 \log n\})$ time (which is slightly slower than the fastest two-phase primal-dual algorithm) while requiring only $\mathcal{O}(m)$ space.

Related Work. In contrast to our paper, most existing work focuses on the classical goals of improving the approximation factor or the running time. Below, we give an overview over the quite extensive results. Although some algorithms mentioned below are designed for kECSS or kSND, we describe the results when restricting to 2ECSS.

The first approximation algorithms [1,7] for 2ECSS compute a minimum spanning tree in G and augment it to become 2-edge-connected. Their factor 3 is based on a 2-approximation for the latter (weighted tree augmentation) problem. The algorithm of [1] runs in $\mathcal{O}(n^2)$ time and that of [7] in $\mathcal{O}(m + n \log n)$.

In [8], a 2-approximation algorithm for kECSS is obtained by reducing the problem to a weighted matroid intersection problem that can be solved in time $\mathcal{O}(n(m + n \log n) \log n)$ [2]. The 2-approximation algorithm for SND in [6] is based on iterative rounding of solutions to a linear programming formulation that we will see in a later section. On the negative side, no algorithm with factor less than 2 is known, and, unless $P = NP$, there cannot be a polynomial-time approximation with factor better than roughly $1 + \frac{1}{300}$ [10].

Besides the algorithms mentioned above, there is a separate history of applying the primal-dual method. The basic idea of a primal-dual algorithm is that a feasible solution to the dual of the aforementioned linear program is computed and is exploited to compute an approximate primal solution. There are several primal-dual 3-approximation algorithms [3,4,9,11,13] with the best running time being $\mathcal{O}(n^2 + n\sqrt{m}\log\log n)$. All algorithms grow a solution in two phases: they first obtain a spanning tree, and then augment that tree to be 2-edge-connected. In the end, unnecessary edges are deleted in a cleanup phase to obtain minimality.

Preliminaries. A *graph* G is a pair (V, E) with node set V and edge set E. We always consider graphs to be undirected multigraphs. As we allow parallel edges, we identify edges by their names, not by their incident nodes. For each $e \in E$, let $V(e) := \{v, w\} \subseteq V$ be the two nodes incident to e. We may describe subgraphs of G simply by their (inducing) edge subset $H \subseteq E$. By $V(H) := \bigcup_{e \in H} V(e)$ we denote the set of nodes spanned by the edges of H. For each $v \in V(H)$, let $\delta_H(v) := \{e \in H \mid v \in V(e)\}$ be the edges incident to v. For any $S \subsetneq V(H)$, let $\delta_H(S) := \{e \in H \mid V(e) = \{u, v\}, u \in S, v \notin S\}$. The *degree* $\deg_H(v) := |\delta_H(v)|$ of $v \in V$ in H is the number of incident edges of v in H.

A *path* P of length $k \geq 0$ is a subgraph with $P = \{e_1, \ldots, e_k\}$ such that there is an orientation of its edges where the head of e_i coincides with the tail of e_{i+1} for $i < k$. In such an orientation, let u be the tail of e_1 and v the head of e_k. We call u and v the *endpoints* of P, and P a *u-v-path* (or, equivalently, a *path between u and v*). Observe that our definition of paths allows nodes but not edges to repeat (due to set notation). A path P is *simple* if and only if $\deg_P(v) \leq 2$ for all $v \in P$. For a simple u-v-path P, we call $V(P) \setminus \{u, v\}$ the *inner nodes* of P. We call a path *closed* if both endpoints coincide (i.e., if it is a u-v-path with $u = v$), and *open* otherwise. A *cycle* is a closed path of length at least 2. We say two paths P_1, P_2 are *disjoint* if and only if $P_1 \cap P_2 = \varnothing$, i.e., they do not share a common edge (they may share nodes). A *forest* is a graph without cycles.

Let $G' = (V', E')$ be a 2-edge-connected graph. An edge $e \in E'$ is *essential in* G' if and only if $G' - e = (V', E' \setminus \{e\})$ is not 2-edge-connected; it is *nonessential* otherwise. G' is *minimal 2-edge-connected* if and only if all $e \in E'$ are essential. An *ear* is a simple path P of length at least 1 such that $E' \setminus P$ is 2-edge-connected.

For any function $f: A \to B$ and any $A' \subseteq A$, we denote by $f(A') := \{f(a) \mid a \in A'\}$ the image of A' under f (unless otherwise stated). We also define $f^{-1}(b) := \{a \in A \mid f(a) = b\}$.

Organization of the Paper. In Sect. 2, we will describe the algorithm combinatorially and state our main theorem. We will then analyse the algorithm (in particular, show the approximation factor) in Sect. 3.

2   Algorithm

Let $G' = (V', E')$ be a graph and let $F = (V', E_F)$ be a (spanning) subforest in G'. For $e \in E' \setminus E_F$, let $\ell_e \in \{0, 1, 2\}$ denote the number of leaves v in F (that is, $\deg_F(v) \leq 1$) incident to e.

Algorithm 1: Approximation algorithm for 2ECSS

---

1 graph $G' = (V', E')$ with edge costs $c' := c$ as a copy of $G = (V, E)$
2 solution $T := \varnothing$
3 forest $F := (V', \varnothing)$

4 **while** *F is not a single node* **do**   // grow phase
5 $\quad$ Simultaneously decrease the cost $c'(e)$ for each edge $e \in E' \setminus E_F$ at speed
$\quad\quad$ ℓ_e until some edge, say $\tilde{e}$, gets cost 0
6 $\quad$ Add $\tilde{e}$ to F and to T
7 $\quad$ **if** *$\tilde{e}$ closes a cycle Q in F* **then** contract Q in F and in G'

8 **forall** *$e \in T$ in reverse order of addition* **do**   // cleanup phase
9 $\quad$ **if** *$T - e$ is 2-edge-connected* **then** remove e from T

Our algorithm is outlined in Algorithm 1. Given a graph $G = (V, E)$ with cost function $c \colon E \to \mathbb{R}_{\geq 0}$, the main *grow phase* selects edges $T \subseteq E$ such that T is spanning and 2-edge-connected, but not necessarily minimal. The central idea of the grow phase is to maintain a forest F and, in contrast to several other primal-dual approaches, to only grow the solution with edges that are currently attached to nodes of degree ≤ 1 in F.[1] (Note that $\ell_e = 0$ for any edge e not incident on a leaf in F and thus the cost of e is not decreased in the current iteration.) Afterwards, a *cleanup phase* removes nonessential edges from T, checking them in reverse order of their addition, to obtain the final solution. This is analogous to the clean-up phase in known primal-dual algorithms for network design problems.

Theorem 1. *There is a single-phase primal-dual 3-approximation algorithm for 2ECSS that runs in $\mathcal{O}(\min\{nm, m + n^2 \log n\})$ time and $\mathcal{O}(m)$ space.*

3   Analysis

In this section, we provide a proof of our main result stated in Theorem 1. The analysis of the time and space requirements is deferred to the full version. In what follows, we prove the approximation factor 3.

---

[1] This is a key difference to the *second* phase suggested in [9], which on first sight looks somewhat similar (but leads to very different proof strategies).

Outline of the Analysis. On a high level, our analysis follows the standard steps for analyzing primal-dual algorithms. A key step in the analysis of [5] is to prove a purely graph-theoretical property concerning the average degree of certain node subsets in a forest. In contrast, our purely graph-theoretical property (of partial solutions constructed during the algorithm) is the *leaf-degree property*: it bounds the *sum of degrees* (w.r.t. the final solution computed by the algorithm) of leaves in the current forest F by a multiple of the *number* of certain leaves in F.

Let us describe the main steps in more detail. Algorithm 1 computes an approximate solution without any reference to a linear program. Section 3.1 consists in re-interpreting the algorithm as a primal-dual algorithm: we state the standard ILP formulation for 2ECSS along with its dual relaxation, and describe how Algorithm 1 can be seen as an algorithm computing an integral primal solution to this LP along with an implicit fractional dual feasible solution.

As common in the analysis of primal-dual algorithms, we bound the primal solution value by a multiple of the dual solution value. Section 3.2 consists in reducing this task to proving our leaf-degree property.

Section 3.3 is dedicated to prove the leaf-degree property. We restate this property independent of the algorithm, that is, as a general property of sub-forests in minimal 2-edge-connected graphs. Its proof is inductive over the ear decomposition of the 2-edge-connected graph and employs a careful charging scheme over the sequence of ears. Unfortunately, the charging scheme is quite technical and the specific leaf-degree property that we prove, is somewhat tailored to our algorithm. However, we expect that more general variants of this property would arise in potential generalizations of our algorithm. We feel that, regarding potential generalizations to higher connectivity requirements, it would be crucial to substantially simplify this proof and remove its reliance on ear decompositions, which would not be directly applicable to more general connectivity requirements. We therefore believe that proving this and related generalized degree properties might be of independent algorithmic or graph-theoretical interest.

Terminology and Basic Properties. We call the iterations within the phases of Algorithm 1 *grow steps* and *cleanup steps*, respectively. In a grow step, a cycle may be contracted and some edges become incident to the contracted node. As we identify edges by their names, the names of these edges are retained although their incident nodes change.

Let E' and E_F be the edge set of G' and F, respectively. During the algorithm we have the following invariants: both G' and F use the common node set V' that describes a partition of V; we consider T to form a subgraph of G; each edge in E_F represents an edge of T that is not part of a cycle in G; we have $E_F \subseteq E' \subseteq E$.

Initially, each node of V forms an individual partition set, i.e., $|V'| = |V|$, and $E_F = \varnothing$. We merge partition sets (nodes of V', cf. line 7) when we contract a cycle, i.e., when the corresponding nodes in V induce a 2-edge-connected sub-graph in T. Arising self-loops are removed both from G' and F. The grow phase terminates once $|V'| = 1$, i.e., all nodes of V are in a common 2-edge-connected component.

Observe that for an edge $e \in E'$, we naturally define $V(e) \subseteq V$ as its incident nodes in original G, and $V'(e) \subseteq V'$ as its incident nodes in G' and F.

Let $L := \{v \in V' \mid \deg_F(v) \leq 1\}$ be the set of *leaves* (including isolated nodes) in F. For any edge $e \in E'$, let $\ell_e := |V'(e) \cap L| \in \{0, 1, 2\}$ be the number of incident nodes of e that are leaves in F. An edge $e \in E'$ is *eligible* if $e \notin E_F$ and $\ell_e \geq 1$. Let $\Delta(e) := \frac{c'(e)}{\ell_e}$ for eligible edges $e \in E'$. Now line 5 can be described as: (1) find the minimum (w.r.t. Δ) eligible edge $\tilde{e} \in E$, (2) for each eligible edge e, decrease $c'(e)$ by $\ell_e \Delta(\tilde{e})$. For convenience, we denote $\Delta(\tilde{e})$ by $\tilde{\Delta}$.

3.1 Reformulation as Primal-Dual Algorithm

Let $\mathcal{S} := 2^V \setminus \{\varnothing, V\}$ and $\mathcal{S}_e := \{S \in \mathcal{S} \mid e \in \delta_G(S)\}$ for any $e \in E$. We analyze the approximation factor using the primal-dual method. Hence consider the basic integer program for 2ECSS:

$$\text{minimize} \quad \sum_{e \in E} c(e) x_e \tag{1}$$

$$\sum_{e \in \delta_G(S)} x_e \geq 2 \qquad\qquad \forall S \in \mathcal{S} \tag{2}$$

$$x_e \in \{0, 1\} \qquad\qquad \forall e \in E. \tag{3}$$

For its linear relaxation, (3) is substituted by $0 \leq x_e \leq 1$ for every $e \in E$. The bound $x_e \leq 1$ is important since edge duplications are forbidden. Its dual is

$$\text{maximize} \quad 2 \sum_{S \in \mathcal{S}} y_S - \sum_{e \in E} z_e \tag{4}$$

$$\sum_{S \in \mathcal{S}_e} y_S - z_e \leq c(e) \qquad\qquad \forall e \in E \tag{5}$$

$$y_S \geq 0 \qquad\qquad \forall S \in \mathcal{S} \tag{6}$$

$$z_e \geq 0 \qquad\qquad \forall e \in E. \tag{7}$$

We show that Algorithm 1 implicitly constructs a solution $(\bar{y}, \bar{z})$ to the dual program. Let $(\bar{y}^i, \bar{z}^i)$ denote this dual solution computed after the i-th grow step. Initially, we have the dual solution $(\bar{y}^0, \bar{z}^0) = 0$. Following this notion, let $F^i = (V^i, E_{F^i})$ be the forest after the i-th grow step, $L^i := \{v \in V^i \mid \deg_{F^i}(v) \leq 1\}$, and $\ell_e^i := |V^i(e) \cap L^i|$ for each $e \in E'$. For any node $v \in V^i$, let $S^i(v)$ be the corresponding node subset of V after the i-th grow step.

Lemma 1. *The grow phase constructs a feasible solution to the dual problem implicitly as follows. We have, for each $i \geq 0$ and $v \in V^i$,*

$$\bar{y}_{S^i(v)}^{i+1} := \begin{cases} \bar{y}_{S^i(v)}^i + \tilde{\Delta} & \text{if } v \in L^i \\ \bar{y}_{S^i(v)}^i & \text{otherwise,} \end{cases} \qquad \bar{z}_e^{i+1} := \begin{cases} \bar{z}_e^i + \tilde{\Delta} & \text{if } v \in L^i \text{ and } e \in \delta_{F^i}(v) \\ \bar{z}_e^i & \text{otherwise.} \end{cases}$$

Before giving the detailed proof, we want to emphasize two facts in the above lemma that may not be evident on first sight: Firstly, the node subset for the update of $\bar{y}$ does not change: we set $\bar{y}_{S^i(v)}^{i+1}$, not $\bar{y}_{S^{i+1}(v)}^{i+1}$. Consequently, a possible contraction does not have any influence on this value. Secondly, $\bar{z}$ changes only if v is a leaf and e is already in the forest.

Proof (Lemma 1). Let $\bar{c}^i$ be c' after the i-th grow step. We show for each $i \geq 0$ that $(\bar{y}^i, \bar{z}^i)$ satisfies (a) $\bar{c}^i(e) = c(e) - \sum_{S \in \mathcal{S}_e} \bar{y}_S^i + \bar{z}_e^i$ and (b) $\bar{c}^i(e) \geq 0$. This proves the claim since (a) connects the algorithm values $\bar{c}^i(e)$ to a variable assignment of (5), in particular, $\bar{c}^i(e)$ matches the right-hand side minus the left-hand side of (5), and (b) shows that this variable assignment is a feasible solution to (5). For $i = 0$, (a) and (b) hold, since $(\bar{y}^0, \bar{z}^0) = 0$ matches the initialization $\bar{c}^0 := c$. Now consider any $i > 0$. Note that this is trivial for the cases with $\bar{c}^{i+1}(e) = \bar{c}^i(e)$.

(a) Consider $v \in L^i$ and any $e \in \delta_G(S^i(v))$. By $\bar{y}_{S^i(v)}^{i+1} = \bar{y}_{S^i(v)}^i + \tilde{\Delta}$, the left-hand side of (5) becomes $\sum_{S \in \mathcal{S}_e} \bar{y}_S^i - \bar{z}_e^i = \sum_{S \in \mathcal{S}_e} \bar{y}_S^{i+1} - \bar{z}_e^i - \tilde{\Delta}$. By the definition of $\bar{z}_e^{i+1}$, this coincides with $\sum_{S \in \mathcal{S}_e} \bar{y}_S^{i+1} - \bar{z}_e^{i+1}$ if $e \in \delta_F(v)$, and with $\sum_{S \in \mathcal{S}_e} \bar{y}_S^{i+1} - \bar{z}_e^{i+1} - \tilde{\Delta}$ otherwise. This change is reflected exactly by $\bar{c}^{i+1}(e) := \bar{c}^i(e) - \ell_e^i \tilde{\Delta}$ (that is, decreasing c' by $\tilde{\Delta}$ for each leaf incident to e in F) if and only if e is eligible.

(b) Assume by contradiction that there is an $e \in E$ with $\bar{c}^i(e) \geq 0$ and $\bar{c}^{i+1}(e) < 0$. Note that $\bar{c}^i(\tilde{e}) = \ell_{\tilde{e}}^i \tilde{\Delta}$. By $\bar{c}^{i+1}(e) := \bar{c}^i(e) - \ell_e^i \tilde{\Delta} < 0$ we get $\bar{c}^i(e) < \ell_e^i \tilde{\Delta}$, which contradicts the choice of $\tilde{e}$. □

3.2   Reducing a Primal-Dual Relation to the Leaf-Degree Property

Before we state the leaf-degree property in Lemma 3, we observe (in Lemma 2) a necessary prerequisite that explains why the cleanup phase has to remove nonessential edges in reverse order. Then, under the assumption the leaf-degree property has been proven, we can show the approximation factor in Lemma 4.

Let $\bar{T}$ be the solution edges remaining after the cleanup phase. Let $(V^i, \bar{T}^i)$ be the graph on nodes V^i that consists of all edges in $\bar{T}$ without self-loops. In other words, $\bar{T}^i \subseteq \bar{T}$ are the edges corresponding to $\bar{T}$ when mapped into the node partition defined by F^i.

Lemma 2. *For each i, every edge $e \in \bar{T}^i \setminus E_{F^i}$ is essential in $(V^i, \bar{T}^i \cup E_{F^i})$.*

Proof. First observe that for a cycle Q in a 2-edge-connected graph H, an edge $e \notin Q$ is essential in H if and only if e is essential in H after contracting Q. The claim holds trivially for the single-node forest (i.e., after the last grow step). Assume by contradiction that there is an i with an edge $e \in \bar{T}^i \setminus E_{F^i}$ that is nonessential in $(V^i, \bar{T}^i \cup E_{F^i})$.

First consider the case that $\tilde{e}$ with $\tilde{e} \neq e$ is chosen in the $(i+1)$-th grow step. Obviously, e is still nonessential in $(V^i, \bar{T}^i \cup E_{F^i} \cup \{\tilde{e}\})$. If $\tilde{e}$ does not close a cycle, we have $V^{i+1} = V^i$, $\bar{T}^{i+1} = \bar{T}^i$, and $E_{F^{i+1}} = E_{F^i} \cup \{\tilde{e}\}$. If $\tilde{e}$ closes a cycle, the edge e is not affected by the contraction (otherwise it would never become part of the solution). In both cases, the edge e remains nonessential in $(V^{i+1}, \bar{T}^{i+1} \cup E_{F^{i+1}})$. Overall, edge e will remain nonessential until it is chosen in a grow step.

Now consider the case that e itself is chosen in the $(i+1)$-th grow step. Since e is nonessential in $(V^i, \bar{T}^i \cup E_{F^i} \cup \{e\})$, it is nonessential in the corresponding cleanup step and removed in the cleanup phase. In other words, $e \notin \bar{T}$, thus $e \notin \bar{T}^i$, a contradiction. □

We partition L^i into the set $L_0^i := \{v \in L^i \mid \deg_{F^i}(v) = 0\}$ of isolated nodes in F^i, the set $L_1^i := \{v \in L^i \mid \deg_{F^i}(v) = 1, \delta_{F^i}(v) \subseteq \bar{T}^i\}$ of degree-1 nodes in F^i incident to an edge in the contracted solution $\bar{T}^i$, and the set $L_2^i := \{v \in L^i \mid \deg_{F^i}(v) = 1, \delta_{F^i}(v) \cap \bar{T}^i = \varnothing\}$ of the degree-1 nodes in F^i incident to an edge in $E^i \setminus \bar{T}^i$, i.e., not being in the contracted solution.

Lemma 3 (Leaf-Degree Property). *We have* $\sum_{v \in L^i} \deg_{\bar{T}^i}(v) \leq 3(|L^i| + |L_0^i|) + |L_1^i|$.

Lemma 4. *The solution obtained by Algorithm 1 costs at most three times the optimum cost.*

This result is *tight*, as can be seen in Fig. 1.

Proof. Let $(\bar{y}, \bar{z})$ be the *dual* solution Algorithm 1 produces implicitly, as described by Lemma 1, with dual solution value B. On the other hand, $\bar{T}$ is called our *primal* solution. Note that for all edges $e \in \bar{T}$, we have $c'(e) = 0$, i.e., their constraints (5) are tight. Hence we can rewrite our primal solution value

$$c(\bar{T}) = \sum_{e \in \bar{T}} c(e) = \sum_{e \in \bar{T}} \left(\sum_{S \in S_e} \bar{y}_S - \bar{z}_e \right) = \sum_{S \in \mathcal{S}} \deg_{\bar{T}}(S) \bar{y}_S - \sum_{e \in \bar{T}} \bar{z}_e.$$

We prove a 3-approximation by showing that $c(\bar{T}) \leq 3B$, i.e.,

$$\sum_{S \in \mathcal{S}} \deg_{\bar{T}}(S) \bar{y}_S - \sum_{e \in \bar{T}} \bar{z}_e \leq 3 \left(\sum_{S \in \mathcal{S}} 2\bar{y}_S - \sum_{e \in E} \bar{z}_e \right),$$

or equivalently

$$\sum_{S \in \mathcal{S}} \deg_{\bar{T}}(S) \bar{y}_S \leq 6 \sum_{S \in \mathcal{S}} \bar{y}_S - 2 \sum_{e \in \bar{T}} \bar{z}_e - 3 \sum_{e \in E \setminus \bar{T}} \bar{z}_e. \tag{8}$$

Observe that (8) trivially holds initially since all values $(\bar{y}^0, \bar{z}^0)$ are zero. We show that (8) holds after each grow step. Assume it holds for $(\bar{y}^i, \bar{z}^i)$. We look at the increase of the left-hand side and right-hand side of (8) when adding an edge to F^i. By Lemma 1, we have $\bar{y}_{S^i(v)}^{i+1} = \bar{y}_{S^i(v)}^i + \tilde{\Delta}$ for all $v \in L^i$ and $\bar{z}_e^{i+1} = \bar{z}_e^i + \tilde{\Delta}$ for all $e \in \delta_F(L_1^i \cup L_2^i)$. Hence it remains to show that

$$\sum_{v \in L^i} \deg_{\bar{T}^i}(v) \tilde{\Delta} \leq 6 \sum_{v \in L^i} \tilde{\Delta} - 2 \sum_{v \in L_1^i} \tilde{\Delta} - 3 \sum_{v \in L_2^i} \tilde{\Delta}$$

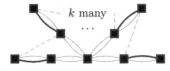

$$\sum_{v \in L} \deg_{E'}(v) = 8k$$
$$|L_0| = 1, \ |L_1| = 2k, \ |L_2| = 0$$
$$3\left(|L| + |L_0|\right) + |L_1| = 8k + 6$$

Fig. 1. An example showing tightness for the approximation factor as well as for the leaf-degree property. For the approximation factor, consider all thick edges' costs to be 0, all solid thin edges' costs 1, and all dashed edges' costs $1 + \varepsilon$ for an arbitrary small $\varepsilon > 0$. The algorithm's solution consists of all solid edges of total cost $3k$. The optimum solution is the Hamiltonian cycle consisting of all dashed edges, all thick edges, and two solid thin edges to connect the center node. Its total cost is $k + 1 + (k - 1)\varepsilon$. The factor $\frac{3k}{k+1+(k-1)\varepsilon}$ approaches 3 for $k \to \infty$. For the leaf-degree property, all edges are in E, thick edges in $F \subsetneq E$, solid edges in $E' \subsetneq E$.

holds. After dividing by $\tilde{\Delta}$ and since $|L^i| = |L_0^i| + |L_1^i| + |L_2^i|$, the right-hand side simplifies to $6|L^i| - 2|L_1^i| - 3|L_2^i| = 6|L_0^i| + 4|L_1^i| + 3|L_2^i| = 3(|L^i| + |L_0^i|) + |L_1^i|$, i.e., we have Lemma 3. □

3.3 Proof of the Leaf-Degree Property

This section is dedicated to show the following theorem. The theorem is a reformulation of Lemma 3 in terms that are totally independent of the setting and notation used in the previous section.

Theorem 2 (Reformulation of Lemma 3). *Let $G = (V, E)$ be a 2-edge-connected graph and E' a minimal 2-edge-connected spanning subgraph in G. Let $F \subseteq E$ be an edge set describing a (not necessarily spanning) forest in G such that each edge $e \in E' \setminus F$ is essential in $E' \cup F$. Let $L_0 := V \setminus V(F)$, $L_1 := \{v \in V(F) \mid \deg_F(v) = 1, \delta_F(v) \subseteq E'\}$, $L_2 := \{v \in V(F) \mid \deg_F(v) = 1, \delta_F(v) \cap E' = \varnothing\}$, and $L := L_0 \cup L_1 \cup L_2$. Then we have $\sum_{v \in L} \deg_{E'}(v) \le 3(|L| + |L_0|) + |L_1|$.*

Figure 1 illustrates an asymptotically tight example. Throughout this section, we will use the following convention: We call the nodes in L *leaves*; they are either $L_1 \cup L_2$, degree-1 nodes in F, or L_0, isolated nodes w.r.t. F. This is quite natural since E and E' do not contain any degree-1 nodes. For any subforest $F' \subseteq F$, let $L(F') := L \cap V(F')$. We use the term *component* for a connected component in F since E and E' consist of one connected component only. Hence these two terms are reasonable only in the context of F.

We consider an *ear decomposition* of E', that is, we consider an ordered partition of E' into disjoint edge sets $O_0, O_1, \ldots$ where O_0 is a simple cycle and where O_t for $t \ge 1$ is a simple u-v-path with $V(O_t) \cap \bigcup_{i=0}^{t-1} V(O_i) = \{u, v\}$. Such an ear decomposition exists since E' is 2-edge-connected. Note that every ear O_t has at least one inner node since it would otherwise only consist of a single

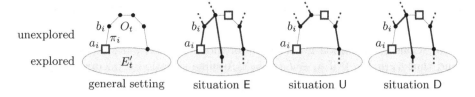

Fig. 2. Illustration of the general setting for an ear O_t and a $\pi_i \in \Pi$ with $\theta(b_i) = t$, and examples of situations E, U, and D. Thick edges are in F, rectangular nodes in L.

edge which would be nonessential in E'. Let $E'_t := \bigcup_{i=0}^{t-1} O_i$ be the subgraph of E' that contains of the first t ears of the ear sequence.

We interpret the ear decomposition as a sequential procedure. We say O_t is added to E'_t at *time* t. For $t_2 > t_1 \geq 1$, the ear O_{t_1} appears *earlier* than O_{t_2}, and O_{t_2} appears *later* than O_{t_1}. At any time t, we call a node v *explored* if $v \in V(E'_t)$, otherwise it is *unexplored*; we call a component *discovered* if it contains an explored node, otherwise it is *undiscovered*. Observe that the inner nodes v of O_t are not yet explored at time t. We define $\theta(v) := t$ as the time when v will become explored. Clearly, we have $\theta(v) := 0$ for all nodes $v \in O_0$.

The basic idea of our proof is to use the ear sequence to keep track (over time t) of $\deg_{E'_t}(v)$ for $v \in L$ via a charging argument. Consider any $t \geq 1$. An inner (and thus unexplored) node of O_t might be in L. Every such leaf has a degree of 2 in E'_{t+1}. However, the endpoints of O_t may be explored leaves whose degrees increase in E'_{t+1}. We tackle this problem by assigning this increase to other leaves and making sure that the total assignment to each leaf is bounded.

Let Π be the set of all edges in E' that are incident to a leaf that is simultaneously an endpoint of some ear O_t. We denote the edges in Π by $\pi_1, \ldots, \pi_{|\Pi|}$ in increasing time of their ears, i.e., for $\pi_i \in O_t, \pi_j \in O_{t'}$ with $i < j$ we have $t \leq t'$. We say i is the *index* of edge $\pi_i \in \Pi$. To be able to refer to the nodes $V(\pi_i) =: \{a_i, b_i\}$ by index, we define a_i as the endpoint and b_i as the inner node of the ear containing π_i. Note that there might be distinct $\pi_i, \pi_j \in \Pi$ with $\theta(b_i) = \theta(b_j)$ if both a_i and a_j are leaves (with possibly even $b_i = b_j$). By C_i we denote the component that contains b_i.

For any index i, we may have: *situation* E if π_i is an element of F, *situation* U if $\pi_i \notin F$ and C_i is undiscovered, and *situation* D if $\pi_i \notin F$ and C_i is discovered, c.f. Fig. 2.

We will assign the degree increments of a_i to other leaves by some charging scheme χ, which is the sum of several distinct charging schemes. The precise definition of these (sub)schemes is subtle and necessarily intertwined with the analysis of the schemes' central properties. Thus we will concisely define them only within the proofs of Lemmata 5 and 6 below. We call a leaf *charged* due to a specific situation if that situation applied at the time when the increment was assigned to the leaf. Let $\chi_E, \chi_U, \chi_D \colon L \to \mathbb{N}$ be the overall charges (on a leaf) due to situation E, U, D, respectively. The leaf-degree property will follow by observing that no leaf is charged too often by these different chargings.

S. Beyer et al.

Lemma 5. *We can establish a charging scheme* χ_E *such that we guarantee* $\chi_E(v) \leq 1$ *if* $v \in L_1$ *and* $\chi_E(v) = 0$ *if* $v \in L_0 \cup L_2$.

Proof. Consider situation E occurring for index i. By $\pi_i \in F$, we have $a_i \in L_1$ (and thus $\chi_E(a_i) = 0$ if $a_i \in L_0 \cup L_2$). Assume situation E occurs for another index $j \neq i$ such that $a_i = a_j$. This yields $\pi_i, \pi_j \in F$ which contradicts that a_i is a leaf. Hence the claim follows by setting $\chi_E(a_i) = 1$. $\qquad\qquad\square$

Lemma 6. *We can establish charging schemes* χ_U, χ_D *such that we guarantee* $\chi_U(v) + \chi_D(v) \leq 2$ *if* $v \in L_0$ *and* $\chi_U(v) + \chi_D(v) \leq 1$ *if* $v \in L_1 \cup L_2$.

Proof (Sketch). The proof of this lemma is rather technical and can be found in the full version. It mainly exploits the finding of contradictions to the fact that each edge $e \in E' \setminus F$ is essential in $E' \cup F$. Two mappings can be established: first an injective mapping (based on induction) from edges π_i in situation D to leaves, and second an 'almost injective' (relaxing the mappings to L_0 nodes slightly) mapping from edges π_i in situation U to remaining leaves. For the latter, we establish an algorithm that hops through components. We show that this algorithm identifies suitable distinct leaves. The charging schemes χ_U, χ_D with the desired properties follow from these mappings. $\qquad\qquad\square$

Proof (Theorem 2). Let $v \in L$ be any leaf. The charging of v during the whole process is $\chi(v) := 2 + \chi_E(v) + \chi_U(v) + \chi_D(v)$ where the 2 comes from an implicit charging of the degree of v when v is discovered. By Lemmata 5 and 6, we obtain $\chi(v) \leq 4$ for $v \in L_0$, $\chi(v) \leq 4$ for $v \in L_1$, and $\chi(v) \leq 3$ for $v \in L_2$. This yields $\sum_{v \in L} \deg_{E'}(v) \leq 4|L_0| + 4|L_1| + 3|L_2| \leq 3(|L| + |L_0|) + |L_1|$. $\qquad\square$

References

1. Frederickson, G.N., JáJá, J.: Approximation algorithms for several graph augmentation problems. SIAM J. Comput. **10**(2), 270–283 (1981)
2. Gabow, H.N.: A matroid approach to finding edge connectivity and packing arborescences. J. Comput. Syst. Sci. **50**(2), 259–273 (1995)
3. Gabow, H.N., Goemans, M.X., Williamson, D.P.: An efficient approximation algorithm for the survivable network design problem. Math. Program. **82**, 13–40 (1998)
4. Goemans, M.X., Goldberg, A.V., Plotkin, S.A., Shmoys, D.B., Tardos, É., Williamson, D.P.: Improved approximation algorithms for network design problems. In: Proceedings of SODA 1994, pp. 223–232 (1994)
5. Goemans, M.X., Williamson, D.P.: A general approximation technique for constrained forest problems. SIAM J. Comput. **24**(2), 296–317 (1995)
6. Jain, K.: A factor 2 approximation algorithm for the generalized Steiner network problem. Combinatorica **21**(1), 39–60 (2001)
7. Khuller, S., Thurimella, R.: Approximation algorithms for graph augmentation. J. Algorithms **14**(2), 214–225 (1993)
8. Khuller, S., Vishkin, U.: Biconnectivity approximations and graph carvings. J. ACM **41**(2), 214–235 (1994)
9. Klein, P.N., Ravi, R.: When cycles collapse: a general approximation technique for constrained two-connectivity problems. In: Proceedings of IPCO 1993, pp. 39–55 (1993)

10. Pritchard, D.: k-Edge-connectivity: approximation and LP relaxation. In: Jansen, K., Solis-Oba, R. (eds.) WAOA 2010. LNCS, vol. 6534, pp. 225–236. Springer, Heidelberg (2011). https://doi.org/10.1007/978-3-642-18318-8_20
11. Saran, H., Vazirani, V., Young, N.: A primal-dual approach to approximation algorithms for network Steiner problems. In: Proceedings of the Indo-US workshop on Cooperative Research in Computer Science, pp. 166–168 (1992)
12. Williamson, D.P.: On the design of approximation algorithms for a class of graph problems. Ph.D. thesis, Massachusetts Institute of Technology (1993)
13. Williamson, D.P., Goemans, M.X., Mihail, M., Vazirani, V.: A primal-dual approximation algorithm for generalized Steiner network problems. Combinatorica **15**(3), 435–454 (1995)
14. Williamson, D.P., Shmoys, D.B.: The Design of Approximation Algorithms. Cambridge University Press, Cambridge (2011)

Uniqueness of DP-Nash Subgraphs and D-sets in Weighted Graphs of Netflix Games

Gregory Gutin[1]([⊠]), Philip R. Neary[2], and Anders Yeo[3,4]

[1] Department of Computer Science, Royal Holloway, University of London, Egham, UK
g.gutin@rhul.ac.uk
[2] Department of Economics, Royal Holloway, University of London, Egham, UK
philip.neary@rhul.ac.uk
[3] Department of Mathematics and Computer Science, University of Southern Denmark, Odense, Denmark
andersyeo@gmail.com
[4] Department of Pure and Applied Mathematics, University of Johannesburg, Johannesburg, South Africa

Abstract. Gerke et al. (2019) introduced Netflix Games and proved that every such game has a pure strategy Nash equilibrium. In this paper, we explore the uniqueness of pure strategy Nash equilibria in Netflix Games. Let $G = (V, E)$ be a graph and $\kappa : V \to \mathbb{Z}_{\geq 0}$ a function, and call the pair (G, κ) a *weighted graph*. A spanning subgraph H of (G, κ) is called a DP-*Nash subgraph* if H is bipartite with partite sets D, P called the D-*set* and P-*set* of H, respectively, such that no vertex of P is isolated and for every $x \in D$, $d_H(x) = \min\{d_G(x), \kappa(x)\}$. We prove that whether (G, κ) has a unique DP-Nash subgraph can be decided in polynomial time. We also show that when $\kappa(v) = k \in \mathbb{Z}_{\geq 0}$ for every $v \in V$, the problem of deciding whether (G, κ) has a unique D-set is polynomial time solvable for $k = 0$ and 1, and co-NP-complete for $k \geq 2$.

1 Introduction

In this paper, all graphs are undirected, finite, without loops or parallel edges. Let $G = (V, E)$ be a graph and $\kappa : V \to \mathbb{Z}_{\geq 0}$ a function. For $v \in V$, we will call $\kappa(v)$ the *weight* of v and the pair (G, κ) a *weighted graph*. A spanning subgraph H of (G, κ) is called a DP-*Nash subgraph* if H is bipartite with partite sets D and P called the D-*set* and P-*set* of H, respectively, such that no vertex of P is isolated and for every $x \in D$, $d_H(x) = \min\{d_G(x), \kappa(x)\}$, where $d_H(x)$ and $d_G(x)$ are the degrees of x in H and G, respectively. Since H is a bipartite graph, we will write it as the triple $(D, P; E')$, where D, P are D-set and P-set of H, respectively, and E' is the edge set of H. A vertex set B is a D-*set* of (G, κ) if (G, κ) has a DP-Nash subgraph in which B is the D-set. Gerke et al. [6] proved the following:

© Springer Nature Switzerland AG 2020
D. Kim et al. (Eds.): COCOON 2020, LNCS 12273, pp. 360–371, 2020.
https://doi.org/10.1007/978-3-030-58150-3_29

Theorem 1. *Every weighted graph (G, κ) has a DP-Nash subgraph.*

Theorem 1 implies that every weighted graph has a D-set.

Let us consider a few examples of DP-Nash subgraphs and D-sets. If $\kappa(x) = 0$ for every $x \in V$ then there is only one DP-Nash subgraph with D-set V and empty P-set. If $\kappa(x) = 1$ for every $x \in V$ then every DP-Nash subgraph is a spanning vertex-disjoint collection of stars, each with at least two vertices. If $\kappa(x) = d_G(x)$ for every $x \in V$ then the D-set of each DP-Nash subgraph of (G, κ) is a maximal independent set of G. It is well-known that a vertex set is maximal independent if and only if it is independent dominating. Since finding both maximum size independent set and minimum size independent dominating set are both NP-hard [2], so are the problems of finding a D-set of maximum and minimum size. For more information on complexity of independent domination, see [7].

The notion of a D-set is not directly related to the CAPACITATED DOMINATION problem where the number of vertices which a vertex can dominate does not exceed its weight (capacity) [3,10]. D-sets provide what one can call *exact* capacitated domination, not studied in the literature yet, as far as we know.

Theorem 1 means that all Netflix Games introduced in [6] have pure strategy Nash equilibria; see Sect. 2 for a brief discussion of Netflix Games and their relation to DP-Nash subgraphs and D-sets in weighted graphs. As explained in Sect. 2, there are two natural problems of interest in economics.

DP-NASH SUBGRAPH UNIQUENESS: *decide whether a weighted graph has a unique DP-Nash subgraph,* and

D-SET UNIQUENESS: *decide whether a weighted graph has a unique D-set.*

While the problems are clearly related, we show that their time complexities are not unless P=co-NP: DP-NASH SUBGRAPH UNIQUENESS is polynomial-time solvable and D-SET UNIQUENESS is co-NP-complete. In fact, for D-SET UNIQUENESS we prove the following complexity dichotomy when $\kappa(x) = k$ for every vertex $x \in V$, where k is a non-negative integer. If $k \geq 2$ then D-SET UNIQUENESS is co-NP-complete and if $k \in \{0, 1\}$ then D-SET UNIQUENESS is in P. We note that the proof of Theorem 1 in [6] implies that constructing a DP-Nash subgraph and, thus, a D-set in every weighted graph is polynomial-time solvable.

Preliminaries are given in Sect. 3. To obtain the above polynomial-time complexity results for DP-NASH SUBGRAPH UNIQUENESS and D-SET UNIQUENESS, we first prove in Sect. 4 a charaterization of weighted graphs with unique D-sets, which we believe is of interest in its own right. In Sect. 5, we show that DP-NASH SUBGRAPH UNIQUENESS is in P. In Sect. 6 we prove the above-mentioned complexity dichotomy for D-SET UNIQUENESS.[1] We conclude the paper in Sect. 7.

2   Motivation

There are many economic situations that are collectively referred to as *combinatorial assignment problems*. The first systematic approach to issues of this type

---

[1] It is somewhat interesting that despite the characterization for D-SET UNIQUENESS, the problem is co-NP-complete.

was by Gale and Shapley [4] who studied 'matching' in marriage markets. They imagined a group of n women and another group of n men, where everyone wants to be matched with one member of the opposite sex. The problem of finding an assignment that leaves everyone 'content' is difficult since there are $n!$ possible assignments and individuals have preferences. Gale and Shapley proposed a solution. They called an assignment between women and men *stable* if there does not exist a woman-man pair (call them Ann and Barry) such that: 1) Ann is not paired with Barry, 2) Ann prefers Barry to her match, and 3) Barry prefers Ann to his match. Gale and Shapley's 'deferred acceptance algorithm' confirms that a stable match always exists. Variants and extensions of the algorithm have been applied to a wide variety of assignment problems in economics including college admissions, the market for kidney donors, and refugee resettlement (see [15] for a survey).[2]

The assignment problem that motivates our study arises in the provision of local public goods. The story is as follows. There is a society of individuals arranged in a social network modelled as a graph where vertices represent individuals and edges capture friendships. There is a desirable product, say access to Netflix or Microsoft Office, that is available for purchase. While the product can be shared upon purchase, an owner may only share access with a limited number of friends. Individual preferences are such that it is always better to have access than not, but, since access is costly each individual prefers that a friend purchases and shares their access than vice versa. This describes the Netflix Games of Gerke et al. [6].[3] For a given Netflix game, a D-set lists those who purchase the product in equilibrium, while a DP-Nash subgraph lists those who purchase (the D-set), those who free-ride (the P-set), and exactly who in D each individual in P receives an offer of access from (the edge set).[4] Netflix Games generalise the models of local public goods without weight constraints, see [1,5], for which the stable outcomes correspond to maximal independent sets.

The rationale for a detailed focus on what weighted graphs (G, κ) admit a unique DP-Nash subgraph and/or a unique D-set is that economic models with a unique equilibrium are as rare as they are useful. Uniqueness is rare due to the mathematical structure of economic models (formally, the best-response map of Nash [13,14] rarely admits only one fixed point). Uniqueness is useful as (i) it saves the analyst from an 'equilibrium selection' headache - justifying why

---

[2] Lloyd Shapley and Alvin Roth received the 2012 Nobel Memorial Prize in Economics for their work in this area. (David Gale died in 2007.)

[3] Vertices being constrained in the number of neighbours they may share with seems well-suited to applications. In Netflix Games sharing bestows a benefit on neighbours, but this need not be the case. Gutin et al. [8] add constrained sharing to the Susceptible-Infected-Removed (SIR) model of disease transmission of Kermack and McKendrick [11]. Gutin et al. interpret constrained sharing as 'social distancing' restrictions imposed on a population and document how the reach of an epidemic is curtailed when such measures are in place.

[4] One example from Gerke et al. was of a group of individuals who each want to attend an event and can ride-share to get to it. Every individual will be assigned as either a *D*river or a *P*assenger, hence the labels D and P.

one equilibrium is more likely to emerge than another, and (ii) allows those who study *game-design* to be confident in generating a particular outcome (since only one outcome is stable). It is for this reason that models with unique equilibria are so highly coveted (see for example the model of currency attacks in [12]), and why we believe the study of conditions under which unique DP-Nash subgraphs and D-sets exist will be of great interest to the economics community.

3   Preliminaries

In the rest of the paper, we will often write G instead of (G, κ) when the weight function κ is clear from the context. We will often omit the subscript G in $N_G(x)$ and $d_G(x)$ when the graph G under consideration is clear from the context. We will often shorten the term DP-Nash subgraph to Nash subgraph.

In the rest of this section, we provide two simple assumptions for the rest of the paper which will allow us to simplify some of our proofs. In both assumptions, (G, κ) is a weighted graph.

Assumption 1: *For all $u \in V$ we have $\kappa(u) \le d(u)$.*

Assumption 1 does not change the set of DP-Nash subgraphs of any weighted graph as if $\kappa(u) > d(u)$ we may let $\kappa(u) = d(u)$ without changing $\min\{\kappa(u), d(u)\}$. Due to this assumption, we can simplify the definition of a DP-Nash subgraph of a weighted graph (G, κ). A spanning subgraph H of G is called a *DP-Nash subgraph* if H is bipartite with partite sets D, P called the *D-set* and *P-set* of H, respectively, such that no vertex of P is isolated and for every $x \in D$, $d_H(x) = \kappa(x)$. Note that Assumption 1 may not hold for a subgraph of (G, κ) if the subgraph uses the same weight function κ restricted to its vertices.

Assumption 2: *If uv is an edge in G, then $\kappa(u) > 0$ or $\kappa(v) > 0$.*

This assumption does not change our problem due to the following:

Proposition 1. *Let G^* be obtained from G by deleting all edges uv with $\kappa(u) = \kappa(v) = 0$. Then $(D, P; E')$ is a Nash subgraph of (G, κ) if and only if $(D, P; E')$ is a Nash subgraph of (G^*, κ).*

Proof. Let uv be any edge in G with $\kappa(u) = \kappa(v) = 0$ and let $(D, P; E')$ be a Nash subgraph of (G, κ). Note that $uv \notin E'$ as if $u \in D$ then E' contains no edge incident with u and if $v \in D$ then E' contains no edge incident with v and if $u, v \in P$ then E' does not contain the edge uv. This implies $(D, P; E')$ is a Nash subgraph of (G^*, κ).

Conversely if $(D, P; E')$ is a Nash subgraph of (G^*, κ) then $(D, P; E')$ is a Nash subgraph of (G, κ) as both graphs have the same weight function and G^* is a spanning subgraph of G. □

4   Characterisation of Weighted Graphs with Unique D-set

We begin this section by introducing some definitions and additional notation. For a set F of edges of a graph H and a vertex x of H, $N_F(x) =$

$\{y \in V(H)|xy \in F\}$ and $d_F(x) = |N_F(x)|$. For a vertex set Q of a graph H, $N_H(Q) = \bigcup_{x \in Q} N_H(x)$. Define $X(G, \kappa)$, $Y(G, \kappa)$ and $Z(G, \kappa)$ as follows. If (G, κ) is clear from the context these sets will be denoted by X, Y and Z, respectively.

$$X = X(G, \kappa) := \{x \mid \kappa(x) = d(x)\}$$
$$Y = Y(G, \kappa) := N(X) \setminus X$$
$$Z = Z(G, \kappa) := V(G) \setminus (X \cup Y)$$

Lemma 1. *Let $u \in V(G)$ and let $X = X(G, \kappa)$. If $|N_G(u) \cap X| \le \kappa(u)$ then there exists a Nash subgraph $(D, P; E)$ of (G, κ) where $u \in D$ and $N_G(u) \cap X \subseteq P$. Furthermore, if $|N_G(u) \cap X| < \kappa(u)$ and $w \in N_G(u) \setminus X$ then there exists a Nash subgraph $(D, P; E)$ of (G, κ) where $u \in D$ and $\{w\} \cup (N_G(u) \cap X) \subseteq P$.*

Proof. Let $u \in V(G)$ such that $|N_G(u) \cap X| \le \kappa(u)$. Recall that by Assumption 1 we have $\kappa(v) \le d_G(v)$ for all $v \in V(G)$. Let E^* denote an arbitrary set of $\kappa(u)$ edges incident with u, such that $N_G(u) \cap X \subseteq N_{E^*}(u)$. Let $T' = N_{E^*}(u)$, $G' = G \setminus (\{u\} \cup T')$ and $(P', D'; E')$ a Nash subgraph of G', which exists by Theorem 1. Let $P = P' \cup T'$ and let $D = D' \cup \{u\}$.

Initially let $\hat{E} = E' \cup E^*$. Clearly every vertex in P has at least one edge into D. Now let $v \in D$ be arbitrary. If $d_{\hat{E}}(v) \ne \kappa(v)$ (recall that $\kappa(v) \le d_G(v)$) then we observe that $v \in D'$ and

$$d_{\hat{E}}(v) = d_{E'}(v) = \min\{d_{G'}(v), \kappa(v)\} < \kappa(v).$$

Since v either has no edge to u or does not lie in X, observe that we can add $\kappa(v) - d_{G'}(v)$ edges to $\hat{E}$ between v and T' resulting in $d_{\hat{E}}(v) = \kappa(v)$. After doing the above for every $x \in D$ we obtain a Nash subgraph $(D, P; \hat{E})$ of G with the desired properties. This completes our proof of the case $|N_G(u) \cap X| \le \kappa(u)$. The same proof can be used for the case $|N_G(u) \cap X| < \kappa(u)$ if we choose E^* such that $w \in T'$. $\qquad\square$

Lemma 2. *If $X \cup Z$ is not an independent set in (G, κ), then there exist DP-Nash subgraphs of G with different D-sets. If $X \cup Z$ is an independent set in G then there exists a DP-Nash subgraph $(D, P; E')$ of (G, κ) where $D = X \cup Z$ and $P = Y$.*

Proof. First assume that $X \cup Z$ is not independent in G and that uv is an edge where $u, v \in X \cup Z$. By the definition of Z we have that $u, v \in X$ or $u, v \in Z$.

First consider the case when $u, v \in X$. Note that $|N_G(u) \cap X| \le d(u) = \kappa(u)$, which by Lemma 1 implies that there is a Nash subgraph $(D', P'; E')$ in G where $u \in D'$ and $v \in P'$. Analogously, we can obtain a Nash subgraph $(D'', P''; E'')$ in G where $v \in D''$ and $u \in P''$, which implies that there exist Nash subgraphs of G with different D-sets, as desired.

We now consider the case when $u, v \in Z$. As uv is an edge in G we may without loss of generality assume that $\kappa(v) \ge 1$ (by Assumption 2). As $|N_G(v) \cap X| = 0 < \kappa(v)$, Lemma 1 implies that there is a Nash subgraph $(D', P'; E')$ in

G where $v \in D'$ and $u \in P'$. As $|N_G(u) \cap X| = 0 \leq \kappa(u)$, Lemma 1 implies that there is a Nash subgraph $(D'', P''; E'')$ in G where $u \in D''$. As there exist Nash subgraphs where $u \in P'$ and where $u \in D''$, we are done in this case.

Now let $X \cup Z$ be independent in G and let $P = Y$ and $D = X \cup Z$. Let E' contain all edges between X and Y as well as any $\kappa(z)$ edges from z to P for all $z \in Z$. As $Y = N(X) \setminus X$ we conclude that $(D, P; E')$ is a Nash subgraph of (G, κ). $\qquad\qquad\qquad\qquad\qquad\qquad\qquad\qquad\qquad\qquad\qquad\qquad\qquad\square$

To state our characterisation result for weighted graphs possessing a unique D-set, we need some additional definitions and two properties.

Given a weight κ on a graph G, for any subset $U \subseteq V(G)$ let U^κ denote a set of vertices obtained from U by replacing each vertex, $u \in U$, by its $\kappa(u)$ copies. Note that if $\kappa(u) = 0$ then the vertex u is not in U^κ and $|U^\kappa| = \sum_{u \in U} \kappa(u)$.

Given a weighted graph (G, κ), let G^{aux} be a bipartite graph with partite sets $R' = X \cup Z$ and $Y' = Y^\kappa$. For a vertex $y \in Y$, there is an edge from a copy of y to $r \in R'$ in G^{aux} if and only if there is an edge from y to r in G.

Let $Y^{\kappa > 0} \subseteq Y$ consist of all vertices $y \in Y$ with $\kappa(y) > 0$. For every set $\emptyset \neq W \subseteq Y^{\kappa > 0}$ let

$$L(W) = \{x \in X \cup Z \mid |N(x) \cap W| > d(x) - \kappa(x)\}.$$

We now define the properties $M^*(G, \kappa)$ and $O^*(G, \kappa)$:

$M^*(G, \kappa)$ holds if for every set $\emptyset \neq W \subseteq Y^{\kappa > 0}$ there is no matching from $L(W)$ to W^κ of size $|L(W)|$ in G^{aux}.

$O^*(G, \kappa)$ holds if for every set $\emptyset \neq W \subseteq Y^{\kappa > 0}$ we have $|L(W)| > |W^\kappa|$.

Theorem 2. *If $X \cup Z$ is not independent in G then (G, κ) has at least two different D-sets. If $X \cup Z$ is independent in G then the following three statements are equivalent:*

(a) G has a unique D-set;
(b) $M^*(G, \kappa)$ holds;
(c) $O^*(G, \kappa)$ holds.

Proof. The case of $X \cup Z$ being not independent follows from Lemma 2. We will therefore assume that $X \cup Z$ is independent in G and prove the rest of the theorem by showing that (a) $\Rightarrow$ (b) $\Rightarrow$ (c) $\Rightarrow$ (a). The following three claims complete the proof.

Claim A: (a) $\Rightarrow$ (b).

Proof of Claim A: Suppose that (a) holds but (b) does not. As (b) is false, $M^*(G, \kappa)$ does not hold, which implies that there exists a $\emptyset \neq W \subseteq Y^{\kappa > 0}$ such that there is a matching, M, from $L(W)$ to W^κ of size $|L(W)|$ in G^{aux}.

Let $D_1 = W$, $P_1 = L(W)$ and $G_2 = G - (P_1 \cup D_1)$. Let $(D_2, P_2; E_2')$ be a DP-Nash subgraph of G_2, which exists by Theorem 1. We will now prove the following six subclaims.

Subclaim A.1: For every $y \in Y$, we have $|N(y) \cap X| \geq \kappa(y) + 1$.

Proof of Subclaim A.1: Assume that Subclaim A.1 is false and there exists a vertex $y \in Y$ such that $|N(y) \cap X| \leq \kappa(y)$. By Lemma 1, there exists a Nash subgraph $(D', P'; E')$ in G where $y \in D'$. By Lemma 2, there exists a Nash subgraph $(D'', P''; E'')$ in G where $y \in P''$ (as $P'' = Y$). Therefore (a) is false, a contradiction.   ⋄

Sublaim A.2: If $u \in D_1 = W$ then $N(u) \cap X \subseteq P_1$. Furthermore, $|N(u) \cap P_1| \geq \kappa(u) + 1$.

Proof of Subclaim A.2: Let $u \in D_1$ (and therefore $u \in W$) be arbitrary and let $r \in N(u) \cap X$ be arbitrary. We will show that $r \in P_1$, which will prove the first part of the claim. As $r \in X$ we have $d_G(r) = \kappa(r)$. This implies that $|N(r) \cap W| \geq 1 > 0 = d_G(r) - \kappa(r)$. Hence, $r \in L(W) = P_1$ as desired.

We now prove the second part of Subclaim A.2. Since $u \in Y$, Subclaim A.1 implies that $|N(u) \cap X| \geq \kappa(u) + 1$. As every vertex in $N(u) \cap X$ also belongs to P_1, we have $|N(u) \cap P_1| \geq \kappa(u) + 1$.   ⋄

Subclaim A.3: There exists a Nash subgraph $(D_1, P_1; E_1')$ of $G[D_1 \cup P_1]$.

Proof of Subclaim A.3: P_1 and D_1 were defined earlier so we will now define E_1'. Let all edges of the matching M belong to E_1'. That is if $u'v \in M$ and $u' \in V(G^{\mathrm{aux}})$ is a copy of $u \in V(G)$, then add the edge uv to E_1'. We note that every vertex in P_1 is incident to exactly one of the edges added so far and every vertex $u \in D_1$ is incident to at most $\kappa(u)$ such edges. By Subclaim A.2 we can add further edges between P_1 and D_1 such that every vertex $u \in D_1$ is incident with exactly $\kappa(u)$ edges from E_1'.   ⋄

Subclaim A.4: Every $u \in (X \cup Z) \setminus L(W)$ has at least $\kappa(u)$ neighbours in $Y \setminus W$.

Proof of Subclaim A.4: As $u \notin L(W)$ we have that $|N_G(u) \cap W| \leq d(u) - \kappa(u)$. This implies that $|N_G(u) \setminus W| \geq \kappa(u)$. As $X \cup Z$ is independent this implies that u has at least $\kappa(u)$ neighbours in $Y \setminus W$, as desired.   ⋄

Recall that $(D_2, P_2; E_2')$ is a Nash subgraph of G_2 and by Subclaim A.3, $(D_1, P_1; E_1')$ is a DP-Nash subgraph of $G[D_1 \cup P_1]$.

Subclaim A.5: There exists a Nash subgraph $(P_1 \cup P_2, D_1 \cup D_2, E_1' \cup E_2' \cup E^*)$ of G for some E^*.

Proof of Subclaim A.5: Let $P = P_1 \cup P_2$, $D = D_1 \cup D_2$ and $E' = E_1' \cup E_2'$. Clearly every vertex in P is incident with an edge in E'.

First consider a vertex $u \in D_1$. By Subclaim A.2, u has at least $\kappa(u) + 1$ neighbours in P_1 in G. Therefore, by Subclaim A.3, u is incident with exactly $\kappa(u)$ edges of E_1' and so also with $\kappa(u)$ edges of E'.

Now consider $u \in D_2$. Note that u is incident with $\min\{\kappa(u), d_{G_2}(u)\}$ edges of E_2'. If $u \in X \cup Z \setminus L(W)$ then by Subclaim A.4, $\min\{\kappa(u), d_{G_2}(u)\} = \kappa(u)$ implying that u is incident with exactly $\kappa(u)$ edges of E' as desired. We may therefore assume that $u \notin X \cup Z \setminus L(W)$, which implies that $u \in Y \setminus W$. By Subclaim A.1, u has at least $\kappa(u) + 1$ neighbours in X in G. Therefore, $d_{G_2}(u) + |N(u) \cap P_1| \geq \kappa(u) + 1$ (as every edge from u to X is counted in the sum on the left hand side of the inequality). Thus, if $\min\{\kappa(u), d_{G_2}(u)\} < \kappa(u)$, then we can add edges from u to P_1 to E' until u is incident with exactly $\kappa(u)$

edges of E'. Continuing the above process for all u and letting E^* be the added edges, we obtain the claimed result. ◇

Subclaim A.6: Claim A holds.

Proof of Subclaim A.6: By Lemma 2 there exists a DP-Nash subgraph, (D, P, E'), with $D = X \cup Z$ and $P = Y$. By Subclaim A.5, there exists a DP-Nash subgraph of G where some vertices of Y belong to D, contradicting the fact that (a) holds. This completes the proof of Subclaim A.6, and therefore also of Claim A. ◇

Claim B: (b) $\Rightarrow$ (c).

Proof of Claim B: Suppose that (b) holds but (c) does not. As (c) does not hold there exists a $\emptyset \neq W \subseteq Y^{\kappa > 0}$ such that $|L(W)| \leq |W|$. Assume that W is chosen such that $|W|$ is minimum possible with this property. As (b) holds there is no matching between W^κ and $L(W)$ in G^{aux} saturating every vertex of $L(W)$. By Hall's Theorem, this implies that there exists a set $S \subseteq L(W)$ such that $|N_{G^{\mathrm{aux}}}(S)| < |S|$. Note that $N_G(S) \subseteq W$ such that $N_{G^{\mathrm{aux}}}(S)$ contains exactly the copies of $N_G(S)$. Note that $|N_G(S)| \leq |N_{G^{\mathrm{aux}}}(S)| < |S|$ as $W \subseteq Y^{\kappa > 0}$. Let $W' = W \setminus N_G(S)$.

By definition we have

$$L(W') = \{x \in X \cup Z \mid |N_G(x) \cap W'| > d(x) - \kappa(x)\}.$$

We will now prove the following subclaim.

Subclaim B.1: $L(W') \subseteq L(W) \setminus S$.

Proof of Subclaim B.1: Let $u \in L(W')$ be arbitrary and note that $|N_G(u) \cap W| \geq |N_G(u) \cap W'| > d(u) - \kappa(u)$. This implies that $u \in L(W)$.

We will now show that $u \notin S$. If $u \in S$, then $N(u) \subseteq N(S)$, so u has no neighbours in $W' = W \setminus N(S)$. Therefore, $|N_G(u) \cap W'| = 0$, and as we assumed that $d(v) \geq \kappa(v)$ for all $v \in V(G)$, the following holds

$$|N_G(u) \cap W'| = 0 \leq d(u) - \kappa(u).$$

Therefore, $u \notin L(W')$, a contradiction. This implies that $u \notin S$ and therefore $L(W') \subseteq L(W) \setminus S$. ◇

By Subclaim B.1, we have that $|L(W')| \leq |L(W)| - |S| < |L(W)| - |N_G(S)| = |W'|$. This contradicts the minimality of $|W|$, and therefore completes the proof of Claim B.

Claim C: (c) $\Rightarrow$ (a).

Proof of Claim C: Suppose that (c) holds but (a) does not. By Lemma 2 and the fact that (a) does not hold, there exists a Nash subgraph $(D, P; E')$ of G such that $D \neq X \cup Z$.

If $Y^{\kappa > 0} \subseteq P$, then no vertex of $X \cup Z$ can belong to P as it would have no edge to D (as $X \cup Z$ is independent). Therefore, $X \cup Z \subseteq D$ in this case. Due to the definition of X (and Y) and the fact that $X \subseteq D$, we have that $Y \subseteq P$, which implies that $D = X \cup Z$ and $Y = P$, which is a contradiction to our assumption that $D \neq X \cup Z$.

So we may assume that $Y^{\kappa > 0} \not\subseteq P$. This implies that $Y^{\kappa > 0} \cap D \neq \emptyset$. Let $W = Y^{\kappa > 0} \cap D$. We now prove the following subclaim.

Subclaim C.1: $L(W) \subseteq P$.

Proof of Subclaim C.1: Let $w \in L(W)$ be arbitrary. Hence, $|N_G(w) \cap W| > d(w) - \kappa(w)$. If $w \in D$, then w has at least $\kappa(w)$ neighbours in P in G. By the above it has at least $d(w) - \kappa(w) + 1$ neighbours in $W \subseteq D$, contradicting the fact that w has $d(w)$ neighbours. This implies that $w \notin D$. Therefore, $w \in P$ and as $w \in L(W)$ is arbitrary, we must have $L(W) \subseteq P$.   ◇

We now return to the proof of Claim C. Recall that $X \cup Z$ is independent and $L(W) \subseteq X \cup W$ and every vertex in P has at least one edge to D in E'. By Subclaim C.1, $L(W) \subseteq P$, which implies that there are at least $|L(W)|$ edges from $L(W)$ to W, as $W = Y^{\kappa > 0} \cap D$. As there are at most $\theta = \sum_{w \in W} \kappa(w)$ edges from W to $L(W)$ we must have $|L(W)| \leq \theta = \sum_{w \in W} \kappa(w) = |W^\kappa|$.

The above is a contradiction to (c). This completes the proof of Claim C and therefore also of the theorem.   □

We immediately have the following:

Corollary 1. *All Nash subgraphs of (G, κ) have the same D-set if and only if $X \cup Z$ is independent in G and $O^*(G, \kappa)$ holds.*

Note that if $\kappa(x) = 0$ for all $x \in G$ then $X = V(G)$ and $Y = \emptyset$. In this case $O^*(G, \kappa)$ vacuously holds and there is a unique Nash subgraph of (G, κ) with D-set V and empty P-set.

5   Complexity of Uniqueness of Nash Subgraph

Theorem 3. *DP-NASH SUBGRAPH UNIQUENESS is in P.*

Proof. Let (G, κ) be a weighted graph, and let $X = X(G, \kappa)$, $Y = Y(G, \kappa)$ and $Z = Z(G, \kappa)$ be as defined in the previous section. If $X \cup Z$ is not independent then there exist distinct Nash subgraphs in (G, κ) by Lemma 2. So we may assume that $X \cup Z$ is independent. By Lemma 2 there exists a Nash subgraph $(D, P; E')$ in G where $D = X \cup Z$ and $P = Y$.

If $Z \neq \emptyset$, then let $z \in Z$ be arbitrary. In E' we may pick any $\kappa(z)$ edges out of z, as every vertex in Y has an edge to X in E'. As $d(z) > \kappa(z)$ we note that by picking different edges incident with z we get distinct Nash subgraphs of G. We may therefore assume that $Z = \emptyset$.

Recall the definition of G^{aux}, which has partite sets $R' = X$ and $Y' = Y^\kappa$ (as $Z = \emptyset$).

We will now prove the following two claims which complete the proof of the theorem since the existence of a matching in $G^{\text{aux}} - x$ saturating its partite set Y' can be decided in polynomial time for every $x \in X$.

Claim A: *If for every $x \in X$ there exists a matching in $G^{\text{aux}} - x$ saturating Y' then there is only one Nash subgraph in G.*

Proof of Claim A: We will first show that if the statement of Claim A holds then $O^*(G, \kappa)$ holds. Suppose that $O^*(G, \kappa)$ does not hold. This implies that there is a set $\emptyset \neq W \subseteq Y^{\kappa > 0}$ such that $|L(W)| \leq |W^\kappa|$. Note that, as $Z = \emptyset$, we have $L(W) = N_G(W) \cap X$. As $W \neq \emptyset$ and $W \subseteq Y$, we have that $N_G(W) \cap X \neq \emptyset$. Let $x \in N_G(W) \cap X$ be arbitrary. Now the following holds.

$$|(N_G(W) \cap X) \setminus \{x\}| = |L(W)| - 1 \leq |W^\kappa| - 1 < |W^\kappa|$$

This implies that there cannot be a matching in $G^{\text{aux}} - x$ saturating Y', a contradiction. Thus, $O^*(G, \kappa)$ must hold. By Corollary 1 we have that all Nash subgraphs must therefore have the same D-set. By Lemma 2 we have that all Nash subgraphs $(D, P; E')$ must therefore have $D = X$ and $P = Y$. By the definition of X we note that E' must contain exactly the edges between X and Y, and therefore there is a unique Nash subgraph in G.   ◇

Claim B: *If for some $x \in X$ there is no matching in $G^{\text{aux}} - x$ saturating Y', then there are at least two distinct Nash subgraphs in G.*

Proof of Claim B: Let $x \in X$ be defined as in the statement of Claim B. By Hall's Theorem there exists a set $S' \subseteq Y'$ such that $|N_{G^{\text{aux}}}(S') \setminus \{x\}| < |S'|$. Let $S \subseteq Y$ be the set of vertices for which there is a copy in S'. Note that $(N_G(S) \cap X) \setminus \{x\} = N_{G^{\text{aux}}}(S') \setminus \{x\}$ and $|S'| \leq |S^\kappa|$, which implies the following.

$$|N_G(S) \cap X| \leq |(N_G(S) \cap X) \setminus \{x\}| + 1 = |N_{G^{\text{aux}}}(S') \setminus \{x\}| + 1$$
$$< |S'| + 1 \leq |S^\kappa| + 1.$$

As all terms above are integers, this implies that $|N_G(S) \cap X| \leq |S^\kappa|$. As $L(S) = N_G(S) \cap X$ by the definition of $L(S)$, we note that $|L(S)| \leq |S^\kappa|$ and therefore $O^*(G, \kappa)$ does not hold, which by Corollary 1 implies that there are distinct Nash subgraphs in G (even with distinct D-sets). This completes the proof of Claim B and therefore also of the theorem.   □

6 Complexity of Uniqueness of D-set

If $Z = \emptyset$ then G has a unique D-set if and only if D has a unique Nash subgraph (this follows from the proof of Theorem 3). Thus, if $Z = \emptyset$ then by Theorem 3 it is polynomial to decide whether G has a unique D-set.

However, as we can see below, in general, it is co-NP-complete to decide whether a weighted graph (G, κ) has a unique D-set (the D-SET UNIQUENESS problem). To refine this result, we consider the case when $\kappa(v) = k$ for every $v \in V(G)$. We observed in Sect. 1 that if $k = 0$ then $V(G)$ is the only D-set in G. The next theorem shows that D-SET UNIQUENESS remains in P when $k = 1$. However, Theorem 5 shows that for $k \geq 2$, D-SET UNIQUENESS is co-NP-complete.

Theorem 4. *Let (G, κ) be a weighted graph and let $\kappa(x) = 1$ for all $x \in V(G)$. Let $X = \{x \mid d_G(x) = 1\}$, $Y = N(X)$ and $Z = V(G) \setminus (X \cup Y)$. Then all DP-Nash subgraphs have the same D-set if and only if $X \cup Z$ is independent and $|N_G(y) \cap X| \geq 2$ for all $y \in Y$. In particular, D-SET UNIQUENESS is in P in this case.*

Proof. If $X \cup Z$ is not independent then we are done by Lemma 2, so assume that $X \cup Z$ is independent. By Lemma 2, there exists a DP-Nash subgraph, $(D, P; E')$, such that $Y = P$. If $|N_G(y) \cap X| < 2$ for some $y \in Y$, then by Lemma 1 there exists a DP-Nash subgraph, $(D', P'; E'')$, of G, where $y \in D'$. This implies that there exists DP-Nash subgraphs where y belongs to its D-set and where y belongs to its P-set, as desired.

We now assume that $X \cup Z$ is independent and $|N_G(y) \cap X| \geq 2$ for all $y \in Y$. We will prove that all DP-Nash subgraphs have the same D-set in (G, κ) and we will do this by proving that $O^*(G, \kappa)$ holds, which by Corollary 1 implies the desired result.

Recall that $O^*(G, \kappa)$ holds if for every set $\emptyset \neq W \subseteq Y$ we have $|L(W)| > |W|$ (as $Y^{\kappa > 0} = Y$ and $W^\kappa = W$). Let W be arbitrary such that $\emptyset \neq W \subseteq Y$. By the definition of $L(W)$, we have that $|L(W)| \geq |N(W) \cap X|$. As no vertex in X has edges to more than one vertex in Y (as $d_G(x) = 1$) we have that $|N(W) \cap X| = \sum_{w \in W} |N(w) \cap X| \geq 2|W|$. Therefore, we have

$$|L(W)| \geq |N(W) \cap X| \geq 2|W| > |W|.$$

implying that $O^*(G, \kappa)$ holds, as desired.   □

The following result is proved by reductions from 3-SAT. This reduction is direct for the case of $k = 2$, where for an instance I of 3-SAT formula, we can construct a weighted graph (G, κ) such that $\kappa(x) = 2$ for every vertex x of G and (G, κ) at least two D-sets if and only if I is satisfiable. In the case of $k \geq 3$, we first trivially reduce from 3-SAT to k-OUT-OF-$(k + 2)$-SAT, where a CNF formula F has $k + 2$ literals in every clause and F is satisfied if and only if there is a truth assignment which satisfies at least k literals in every clause. Then we reduce from k-OUT-OF-$(k + 2)$-SAT to the complement of D-SET UNIQUENESS. While the main proof structure is similar in both cases, the constructions of (G, κ) are different. The full proof can be found in [9].

Theorem 5. *Let $k \geq 2$ be an integer. D-SET UNIQUENESS is co-NP-complete for weighted graphs (G, κ) with $\kappa(x) = k$ for all $x \in V(G)$.*

7   Conclusions

We have proved that UNIQUENESS D-SET is co-NP-complete. It is not hard to solve this problem in time $\mathcal{O}^*(2^n)$, where $\mathcal{O}^*$ hides not only coefficients, but also polynomials in n. Indeed, we can consider every non-empty subset S of $V(G)$ in turn and check whether S is the D-set of a Nash subgraph of (G, κ) using network flows. Conditional on the Strong Exponential Time Hypothesis holding, one can show that there exists a $\delta > 0$ such that UNIQUENESS D-SET cannot be solved in time-$\mathcal{O}^*(2^{n\delta})$. A natural open question is to compute a maximum such value δ.

Consider a weighted graph (K_{3n}, κ), where $n \geq 1$ and $\kappa(v) = 2$ for every $v \in V(K_{3n})$. Observe that every p-size subset of $V(K_{3n})$ for $n \leq p \leq 3n - 2$ is a D-set. Thus, a weighted graph can have an exponential number of D-sets and hence of Nash subgraphs. This leads to the following open questions: (a) What is the complexity of counting all Nash subgraphs of a weighted graph? (b) Is there an $O^*(\mathrm{dp}(G,\kappa))$-time algorithm to generate all Nash subgraphs of (G,κ), where $\mathrm{dp}(G,\kappa)$ is the number of Nash subgraphs in (G,κ)?

Acknowledgement. Anders Yeo's research was partially supported by grant DFF-7014-00037B of Independent Research Fund Denmark.

References

1. Bramoullé, Y., Kranton, R.: Public goods in networks. J. Econ. Theory **135**(1), 478–494 (2007)
2. Corneil, D., Perl, Y.: Clustering and domination in perfect graphs. Discrete Appl. Math. **9**, 27–39 (1984)
3. Cygan, M., Pilipczuk, M., Wojtaszczyk, J.O.: Capacitated domination faster than $O(2^n)$. Inf. Process. Lett. **111**(23–24), 1099–1103 (2011)
4. Gale, D., Shapley, L.S.: College admissions and the stability of marriage. Am. Math. Mon. **69**(1), 9–15 (1962)
5. Galeotti, A., Goyal, S., Jackson, M.O., Vega-Redondo, F., Yariv, L.: Network games. Rev. Econ. Stud. **77**(1), 218–244 (2010)
6. Gerke, S., Gutin, G., Hwang, S.H., Neary, P.R.: Netflix games: local public goods with capacity constraints (2019). arXiv:1905.01693
7. Goddard, W., Henning, M.A.: Independent domination in graphs: a survey and recent results. Discrete Math. **313**(7), 839–854 (2013)
8. Gutin, G., Hirano, T., Hwang, S.H., Neary, P.R., Toda, A.A.: The effect of social distancing on the reach of an epidemic in social networks (2020). arXiv:2005.03067
9. Gutin, G., Neary, P.R., Yeo, A.: Uniqueness of DP-Nash subgraphs and D-sets in capacitated graphs of netflix games. arXiv:2003.07106 (2020)
10. Kao, M., Chen, H., Lee, D.: Capacitated domination: problem complexity and approximation algorithms. Algorithmica **72**(1), 1–43 (2015)
11. Kermack, W.O., McKendrick, A.G.: A contribution to the mathematical theory of epidemics. Proc. R. Soc. London. A **115**(772), 700–721 (1927). Containing Papers of a Mathematical and Physical Character. http://www.jstor.org/stable/94815
12. Morris, S., Shin, H.S.: Unique equilibrium in a model of self-fulfilling currency attacks. Am. Econ. Rev. **88**(3), 587–597 (1998)
13. Nash, J.: Non-cooperative games. Ann. Math. **54**(2), 286–295 (1951)
14. Nash, J.F.: Equilibrium points in n-person games. Proc. Natl. Acad. Sci. U.S.A. **36**(1), 48–49 (1950)
15. Roth, A.E.: Deferred acceptance algorithms: history, theory, practice, and open questions. Int. J. Game Theory **36**(3), 537–569 (2008)

On the Enumeration of Minimal Non-pairwise Compatibility Graphs

Naveed Ahmed Azam$^{(\boxtimes)}$ ⓘ, Aleksandar Shurbevskiⓘ, and Hiroshi Nagamochi

Department of Applied Mathematics, Kyoto University, Kyoto, Japan
{azam,shurbevski,nag}@amp.i.kyoto-u.ac.jp

Abstract. A graph is a pairwise compatibility graph (PCG) if it can be represented by an edge weighted tree whose set of leaves is the set of vertices of the graph, and there is an edge between two vertices in the graph if and only if the distance between them in the tree is within a given interval. Enumerating all minimal non-PCGs (each of whose induced subgraphs is a PCG) with a given number of vertices is a challenging task, since it involves a large number of "configurations" that need to be inspected, an infinite search space of weights, and the construction of finite size evidence that a graph is not a PCG. We handle the problem of a large number of configurations by first screening graphs that are PCGs by using a heuristic PCG generator, and then constructing configurations that show some graphs to be PCGs. Finally, we generated configurations by excluding those configurations which cannot be used to show that a given graph is a PCG. To deal with the difficulty of infinite search space and construction of finite size evidence, we use linear programming (LP) formulations whose solutions serve as finite size evidence. We enumerated all minimal non-PCGs with nine vertices, the smallest integer for which minimal non-PCGs are unknown. We prove that there are exactly 1,494 minimal non-PCGs with nine vertices and provide evidence for each of them.

Keywords: Pairwise compatibility graph · Branch-and-bound algorithm · Linear programming

1 Introduction

A graph is called a *pairwise compatibility graph* (PCG) if there exists an edge weighted tree called a *witness tree*, whose set of leaves is the set of vertices of the graph, such that there is an edge between two vertices in the graph if and only if the distance between them in the tree is within a given interval. PCGs are an interesting class of graphs that have applications in the field of computational biology. For example, Kearney et al. [10] pointed out that PCGs are useful in studying the evolutionary relationship between a set of organisms. Durocher

Partially supported by JSPS KAKENHI Grant no. 18J23484.

et al. [8] noted that the results of Kearney et al. [10] imply that a polynomial-time algorithm that can determine if a given graph is a PCG or not leads to a polynomial-time algorithm for solving the well-known maximum clique problem for certain graph classes. It is believed that the problem of confirming if a graph is a PCG or not is NP-hard [7,8].

Related Work: Kearney et al. [10] conjectured that every graph with $n \geq 1$ vertices is a PCG, however, Yanhaona et al. [14] and Durocher et al. [8] independently refuted the conjecture by proving that there are some graphs that are non-PCG, and Baiocchi et al. [3] uncovered several classes of graphs that are not PCG, in particular, the wheel graphs with $n \geq 9$ vertices. Calamoneri et al. [5] showed that every graph with $n \leq 7$ vertices is a PCG and Calamoneri et al. [4] proved that any induced subgraph of a PCG is a PCG. For each PCG there exists a witness tree each of whose non-leaf vertices are of degree, [5,6]. Xiao and Nagamochi [13] proved that a graph is a PCG if and only if every biconnected component of the graph is a PCG. Calamoneri et al. [6] showed that a graph G with a pair of non-adjacent vertices u and v that have the same set of neighbors is a PCG if and only if the subgraph of G induced by $V(G) \setminus \{u\}$ is a PCG. Azam et al. [1] proved that there are exactly seven non-PCGs with eight vertices. Note that all non-PCGs with eight vertices are minimal non-PCGs i.e., a non-PCG each of whose induced subgraphs is a PCG, since every graph with at most seven vertices is known to be a PCG [5].

Difficulties: For a graph with $n \geq 1$ vertices, a *configuration* is defined to be a tuple that consists of the graph, a tree with n leaves, a correspondence between the vertices in the graph and the leaves in the tree, and a bi-partition of all pairs of non-adjacent vertices in the graph. We call a configuration *plausible* if there exist a weight function and a closed interval such that the tree in the configuration is a witness of the graph, and one bi-partition class contains the pairs of non-adjacent vertices in the graph whose distance in the tree is to the left of the interval, and the other bi-partition class to the right. Observe that to show that a graph with $n \geq 1$ vertices is not a PCG it is necessary to exclude all configurations with the graph and real valued weight functions. This leads to the following three difficulties in enumerating all PCGs with a given number of vertices:

(i) Large number of configurations: Although the numbers of graphs, trees, correspondences, and bi-partitions are finite, the total number of configurations increases exponentially with the increase in n. For instance, when n is $7, 8$ and 9 there are approximately 2×10^{11}, 4×10^{14}, and 3×10^{18} configurations, respectively.

(ii) Infinite search space: There exists an infinite space of possible assignments of weights that needs to be excluded to confirm that a graph is not a PCG for a fixed configuration.

(iii) Finite size evidence: When a graph is a PCG then its witness tree is evidence to this. However, when a graph is not a PCG, then due to the infinite search space of edge weights it is a challenging task to construct finite size evidence that shows that a given graph is not a PCG.

These difficulties eventually necessitate a non-trivial method that can efficiently handle the problem of large number of configurations, infinite search space, and construction of finite size evidence to prove that a graph is not a PCG.

Our Contribution: In this paper, we propose a method to enumerate all minimal non-PCGs with a given number of vertices. Our method consists of two main phases: (I) Graph screening; and (II) Constructing evidence based on linear programming (LP). The aim of (I) is to remove some graphs for which we do not need to further inspect configurations, to handle the difficulty (i), the large number of configurations. To achieve this, in phase (I) we use two methods: (I-1) A PCG generator; and (I-2) Constructing plausible configurations. In (I-1), we heuristically generate all PCGs for a given weighted tree taking into account the tree symmetries to avoid repeatedly generating the same PCGs. In (I-2), we try to construct a plausible configuration with weights bounded from above, using a set of linear inequalities.

In phase (II), for each graph that is left after phase (I), we construct finite size evidence whether the graph is a PCG or not. Recall that a large number of configurations poses a difficulty, and therefore we only consider those configurations that satisfy a certain necessary condition to be plausible, detailed in Sect. 4.1. We call such configurations *essential*. This phase consists of two sub-phases: (II-1) Enumerating essential configurations; and (II-2) Solving configuration-based linear programs (LPs). In (II-1), we design a branch-and-bound algorithm to enumerate all essential configurations. In (II-2) to handle difficulties (ii) and (iii), we test each of the enumerated essential configurations in (II-1) by means of solving a linear program which is feasible if and only if the given configuration is plausible. As a definite proof to the infeasibility of the linear program, we use another linear program based on Gale's theorem [9, Theorem 2.8] which is feasible if and only if the first one is not. Thus, we get finite size evidence as proof that the graph is a PCG or not.

The rest of the paper is organized as follows: We discuss some basic notions in Sect. 2. We give a detailed explanation of phases (I) and (II) of our method in Sects. 3 and 4, respectively. Experimental results are given in Sect. 5, and we conclude the paper and discuss future directions in Sect. 6.

2 Basic Notions

For a non-empty set S and an integer $h \in [0, |S|]$, we denote by $\binom{S}{h}$ the family of all subsets of S of size h. Let S be a set and $K = \{0, 1, \ldots, k\}$ for some $k \leq |S| - 1$, we define a *k-coloring* of S to be a function $\lambda : S \to K$. Let $\Lambda_k(S)$ denote the set of k-colorings of a set S.

Let G be a graph with $n \geq 1$ vertices. We denote by $V(G)$ the vertex set of G, by $E(G)$ the edge set of G and by $\overline{E}(G)$ the set $\binom{V(G)}{2} \setminus E(G)$ of pairs of non-adjacent vertices. We denote by $G[X]$ the induced subgraph of G defined by the subset $X \subseteq V(G)$.

Let T be a tree. We denote by $L(T)$ the set of leaves in T. We define a *leaf-edge* in T to be an edge incident to a leaf in T. For any two distinct vertices

$u, v \in V(T)$, let $P_T(u, v)$ denote the unique simple path between them in T and denote by $E_T(u, v)$ the set of edges in $P_T(u, v)$. For a subset $X \subseteq L(T)$, we define the *tree contraction* $T\langle X \rangle$ of T due to X to be the tree with leaf set X obtained by: removing those vertices in T that are not contained in any path connecting two vertices in X; and contracting all degree 2 vertices then created. We define a *binary tree* to be a tree whose all non-leaf vertices have degree exactly 3. For an integer $n \geq 1$, we denote by $\mathcal{T}_n$ a maximal set of mutually non-isomorphic binary trees with n leaves.

For an edge weighted tree T with weight w and vertices $u, v \in V(T)$, we define the *distance* $d_{T,w}(u, v)$ between u and v in T to be $\sum_{e \in E_T(u,v)} w(e)$. For two integers $d_{\min}, d_{\max} \in \mathbb{R}_+$, we define $\mathrm{PCG}(T, w, d_{\min}, d_{\max})$ to be the graph G with vertex set $L(T)$ and edge set $\{uv \mid d_{\min} \leq d_{T,w}(u, v) \leq d_{\max}\}$, in which case we denote $G = \mathrm{PCG}(T, w, d_{\min}, d_{\max})$, and call T a *witness tree* of G. We define a *minimal non-pairwise compatibility graph* (MNPCG for short) to be a non-PCG each of whose induced proper subgraphs is a PCG.

For an integer $n \geq 1$, we denote by $\mathcal{G}_n$ a maximal set of mutually non-isomorphic connected graphs with n vertices. For a graph $G \in \mathcal{G}_n$ and a binary tree $T \in \mathcal{T}_n$, we denote by $\Sigma(G, T)$ the set of bijections from $V(G)$ to $L(T)$. For $G \in \mathcal{G}_n$, $T \in \mathcal{T}_n$, $\sigma \in \Sigma(G, T)$, weight w and reals $d_{\min}, d_{\max} \in \mathbb{R}_+$, observe that there exists a bi-partition of $\overline{E}(G)$ such that the pairs of leaves corresponding to one partition class have distance strictly less than $d_{\min}$, while the others have distance strictly greater than $d_{\max}$. Therefore there exists a 2-coloring $\lambda \in \Lambda_2(\overline{E}(G))$ such that for each pair $uv \in \overline{E}(G)$ it holds that $\lambda(uv) = 0$ if $d_{T,w}(\sigma(u), \sigma(v)) < d_{\min}$ and $\lambda(uv) = 1$ if $d_{T,w}(\sigma(u), \sigma(v)) > d_{\max}$. For a graph $G \in \mathcal{G}_n$, we define a *configuration* of G to be a tuple (G, T, σ, λ) for some binary tree $T \in \mathcal{T}_n$, bijection $\sigma \in \Sigma(G, T)$ and 2-coloring $\lambda \in \Lambda_2(\overline{E}(G))$. Note that for a given graph $G \in \mathcal{G}_n$, there are $n! 2^{|\overline{E}(G)|} |\mathcal{T}_n|$ configurations. For a graph G, we define a *plausible* configuration to be a configuration (G, T, σ, λ) such that:

(i) G is isomorphic to $\mathrm{PCG}(T, w, d_{\min}, d_{\max})$, for some $w, d_{\min}$ and $d_{\max}$, with isomorphism σ; and

(ii) for each pair $uv \in \overline{E}(G)$ it holds that $d_{T,w}(\sigma(u), \sigma(v)) < d_{\min}$ if $\lambda(uv) = 0$ and $d_{T,w}(\sigma(u), \sigma(v)) > d_{\max}$ if $\lambda(uv) = 1$.

Clearly it holds that a graph G is a PCG if and only if there exists a plausible configuration (G, T, σ, λ), and we say that G is a PCG due to the configuration (G, T, σ, λ).

Let (G, T, σ, λ) be a configuration, $Z \subsetneq V(G)$ and $R = \{\sigma(z) \mid z \in Z\}$. For the restriction σ' of σ on Z, and the restriction λ' of λ on the set $\overline{E}(G[Z])$, we define a *subconfiguration* of (G, T, σ, λ) induced by Z to be the configuration $(G[Z], T\langle R \rangle, \sigma', \lambda')$. By the known fact that a graph is a PCG if and only if each of its induced subgraphs is a PCG [4], it follows that a configuration is plausible if and only if all of its subconfigurations are plausible. We call an implausible configuration a *minimal implausible configuration* (MIC for short) each of whose subconfigurations is plausible, where we denote an MIC with a graph of four vertices by MIC4. We define an *MIC4-free configuration* to be a configuration with no subconfiguration that is MIC4.

3   Graph Screening

In this section, we describe phase (I) of our enumeration approach, where in order to reduce our computational effort, we try to collect as many as possible graphs that are PCGs. In Sect. 3.1, we describe (I-1) a PCG generator that for a fixed tree randomly assigns edge weights and generates PCGs for which the tree is a witness tree, but takes into account certain symmetries on the tree so as to avoid unnecessary duplication. In Sect. 3.2, we describe (I-2) where we try to construct a plausible configuration to show that a given graph is a PCG by solving a system of linear inequalities.

3.1   PCG Generator

We present a PCG generator to heuristically generate as many as possible PCGs with $n \geq 3$ vertices for which a given binary tree T is a witness tree. This PCG generator is based on two main ideas which are discussed below.

First, to avoid the repeated generation of the same PCGs, for a given binary tree T with n leaves, we assign edge-weights w by restricting the weights of some leaf-edges that can be mapped to each other under some tree automorphism. More precisely, for two leaf-edges e and e' incident with leaves u and u', respectively, such that there exists an automorphism that maps u' to u, we add the constraint $w(e') \leq w(e)$.

The second idea is to efficiently generate all PCGs with a fixed witness tree and weight assignment. By Calamoneri et al. [6], it is sufficient to consider positive integer weights w instead of real. Thus we have the following observation.

Observation 1. *For each* $\mathrm{PCG}(T, w, d_{\min}, d_{\max})$ *with positive integer valued* w, *it holds that* $\mathrm{PCG}(T, w, d_{\min}, d_{\max}) = \mathrm{PCG}(T, w, x - 0.5, y + 0.5)$ *such that* $x = \min\{d_{T,w}(a, b) \mid a, b \in L(T), d_{\min} \leq d_{T,w}(a, b) \leq d_{\max}\}$ *and* $y = \max\{d_{T,w}(a, b) \mid a, b \in L(T), d_{\min} \leq d_{T,w}(a, b) \leq d_{\max}\}$.

From Observation 1 it follows that for a binary tree T and a positive integer valued weight assignment w, it is sufficient to use only a finite number of pairs $(d_{\min}, d_{\max})$ to generate all PCGs with witness tree T and weight w as $\mathrm{PCG}(T, w, d_{\min}, d_{\max})$. Thus, in our PCG generator, based on Observation 1 we generate all PCGs with witness tree T and a positive integer weight assignment w by fixing x and y from the set $\{d_{T,w}(a, b) \mid a, b \in L(T)\}$.

For a tree $T \in \mathcal{T}_n$ and a leaf-edge $e = uv \in E(T)$ with leaf u, we define *equivalent edge class* $C(e; T)$ to be the set of leaf-edges such that for each $u'v' \in C(e; T)$ with leaf u' there exists an automorphism ψ of T such that $\psi(u') = u$ holds. We next give the main steps of our PCG generator to generate PCGs for each tree $T \in \mathcal{T}_n$:

(i)   Randomly assign weights from a closed interval to the non-leaf-edges;
(ii) For each leaf-edge $e \in E(T)$ and a given subset $S \subseteq C(e; T)$, randomly assign weight w in a closed interval to e such that $w(e') \leq w(e)$ holds for each $e' \in S$; and

(iii) For each pair of integers $x, y \in \{d_{T,w}(a,b) \mid a, b \in L(T)\}$ with $x \leq y$, construct the PCG graph $\mathrm{PCG}(T, w, x - 0.5, y + 0.5)$. Observe that the number of edges in $\mathrm{PCG}(T, w, x - 0.5, y + 0.5)$ is equal to the size of $\{a, b \in L(T) \mid d_{T,w}(a, b) \in [x, y]\}$, that is known before the generation of $\mathrm{PCG}(T, w, x - 0.5, y + 0.5)$. By using this observation, we do not generate PCGs of m edges if we know that we have already enumerated all PCGs with m edges in $\mathcal{G}_n$ to avoid the generation of unnecessary PCGs.

3.2 Constructing Plausible Configurations

For a graph and a tree, in method (I-2) we try to calculate an edge weight assignment and two reals bounded above by some value, such that the graph is isomorphic to the PCG due to the tree, weight assignment and interval bounded by reals. In other words, we try to construct a configuration with the given graph and tree such that the graph is a PCG due to the configuration, i.e., the configuration is plausible. More precisely, for a graph G, a tree T and a real $\alpha \geq 0$, we construct a $\mathrm{PCG}(T, w, d_{\min}, d_{\max})$ with $w, d_{\min}, d_{\max}$ bounded above by α, and try to confirm if there exist a bijection σ between vertex set of G and the leaf set of T and a 2-coloring λ over the set of non-adjacent pairs in G such that:

(i) for each edge in G it holds that the distance between their corresponding leaves under σ is in the interval $[d_{\min}, d_{\max}]$; and
(ii) the pairs of leaves corresponding to the pairs of non-adjacent vertices under σ with color 0 have distance strictly less than $d_{\min}$ and the others have distance strictly greater than $d_{\max}$.

To achieve this, for G, T, and α, we use an integer linear program, $\mathrm{ILP}_{\mathrm{suff}}(G, T, \alpha)$ proposed by Azam et al. [2]. For a graph G with n vertices and a binary tree T with n leaves, $\mathrm{ILP}_{\mathrm{suff}}(G, T, \alpha)$ has $\mathcal{O}(n^2)$ binary variables, $\mathcal{O}(n)$ continuous variables, and $\mathcal{O}(n^4)$ constraints. In addition to a weight w, reals $d_{\min}$ and $d_{\max}$ that are bounded above by α, $\mathrm{ILP}_{\mathrm{suff}}(G, T, \alpha)$ tries to find a mapping σ and a 2-coloring λ that satisfy (i) and (ii). This linear program $\mathrm{ILP}_{\mathrm{suff}}(G, T, \alpha)$ is always feasible and the mapping σ is an isomorphism between G and $\mathrm{PCG}(T, w, d_{\min}, d_{\max})$ if σ is a bijection. The mapping σ is a bijection if the objective value of $\mathrm{ILP}_{\mathrm{suff}}(G, T, \alpha)$ is 0, and hence we get a configuration (G, T, σ, λ) due to which G is a PCG. However, if the objective value of $\mathrm{ILP}_{\mathrm{suff}}(G, T, \alpha)$ is greater than 0, then we cannot draw any conclusion as to whether G is a PCG or not. Therefore, having a solution to $\mathrm{ILP}_{\mathrm{suff}}(G, T, \alpha)$ with objective value 0 is a sufficient condition for G to be a PCG.

4 Constructing Evidence Based on LP

In this section, we give details on phase (II), namely, how to prove that a graph is a PCG if it has not been so detected by the methods in phase (I), and constructing finite evidence if it is not a PCG by using essential configurations.

In Sect. 4.1, we give a branch-and-bound algorithm to phase (II-1) enumerating essential configurations for a given graph, and in Sect. 4.2 we describe our configuration-based linear programs used in phase (II-2) to provide finite size evidence to the fact of a given graph being a PCG or not.

4.1   Enumerating Essential Configurations

In phase (II-1), for a fixed graph, we generate a set of configurations that satisfy a necessary condition to be plausible. As a necessary condition, we use the absence of an MIC4 subconfiguration, since MIC4 configurations can be recognized efficiently [2]. Hence, we enumerate all MIC4-free configurations with a fixed bijection, since by relying on vertex labeling of the graph and trees, we can always fix a bijection. To achieve this, for a given graph, we propose a branch-and-bound algorithm to enumerate all pairs of trees and 2-colorings that correspond to MIC4-free configurations with a fixed bijection. We call such a pair of tree and 2-coloring a *feasible* pair.

We first give an informal intuition of our branch-and-bound algorithm. To search all pairs recursively, we start with a binary tree with two leaves and a 2-coloring such that no color has been assigned to non-adjacent pairs. If all non-adjacent pairs that are leaves in the current tree have been assigned a color, then for each edge xy in the current tree, we extend the current tree by adding a new vertex z subdividing xy, and a new leaf ℓ adjacent to z. Otherwise, for a non-adjacent pair that has not been assigned a color, we extend the current 2-coloring into two colorings that have color 0 or 1 for this uncolored pair. We call these extension operations the *tree extension operation* and the *coloring extension operation*.

We bound the current branch if the current pair of tree and 2-coloring cannot be extended to a feasible pair. To efficiently perform this procedure, we use a characterization by Azam et al. [2], to test the existence of an MIC4.

To perform our algorithm systematically, we fix the vertex set of a graph G with n vertices to be $\{v_1, v_2, \ldots, v_n\}$ and generate feasible pairs that correspond to MIC4-free configurations with a fixed identity bijection. As the root of our branching procedure, we start with $X = \{v_1, v_2\}$, the unique tree with a single edge $\{v_1 v_2\}$ and a 2-coloring that is currently not defined on any pair of non-adjacent vertices that are in X. Next, we discuss the tree extension and the coloring extension operations in more detail below.

Tree Extension Operation: Assume that all pairs of non-adjacent vertices that are in X with $|X| = k$ are colored. Then we perform the tree extension operation for each edge xy in the current tree in increasing order of the label of y, by adding a new degree-three vertex $z = v_{n+k-2+1}$ that subdivides the edge xy, and a new leaf $\ell = v_{k+1}$ incident to z. Note that at any stage of the algorithm it holds that $X = \{v_1, v_2, \ldots, v_k\}$ for some $k \in [2, n]$. As a result of the tree extension operation on the current tree, we get a unique tree with leaf set $X \cup \{v_{k+1}\}$. We call such a tree an *extended tree* of the current tree. An illustration of the tree extension operation is given in Fig. 1(a)-(b). We argue

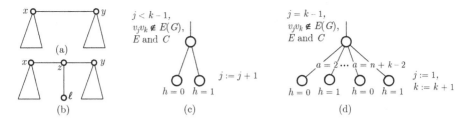

Fig. 1. (a)-(b) An example of the tree extension operation. (a) A tree T; (b) The extended tree T' of T obtained by adding a new vertex z and a new leaf ℓ by subdividing edge $xy \in E(T)$; (c)-(d) An illustration of the branching procedure for a subproblem $S(E; C, j, k)$ with $v_j v_k \in \overline{E}(G)$, edge set E and coloring C; (c) Two branches obtained when $j < k - 1$ by applying the coloring extension operation; and (d) The branches obtained when $j = k - 1$ by applying the tree extension and coloring extension operations for each edge $x v_a \in E, a \in [2, k] \cup [n + 1, n + k - 2]$.

that our branching procedure generates all trees that have the leaf set $V(G)$ by the following lemma.

Lemma 1. *For any binary tree T with $|L(T)| \geq 3$ there exists a tree H with $L(H) \subsetneq L(T)$ and $|L(T)| = |L(H)| + 1$ such that T is an extended tree of H.*

Proof. Let $z\ell \in E(T)$ be a leaf-edge such that z and ℓ are non-leaf and leaf vertices, respectively. There always exists such an edge $z\ell$ since $|L(T)| \geq 3$. Let x and y denote the neighbors of z other than ℓ. Then by applying the tree extension operation on the tree H such that $V(H) = V(T) \setminus \{z, \ell\}$ and $E(H) = (E(T) \setminus \{z\ell, yz, xz\}) \cup \{xy\}$, we get T, from which the claim follows. $\square$

Coloring Extension Operation: Notice that, for an integer $k \in [2, n]$, due to the systematic selection of vertices it follows that the set of uncolored pairs are $v_j v_k$, $j \leq k - 1$. After assigning a color to the vertex pair $v_j v_k$, $j < k$, we consider the next pair uv to color to be the pair $v_{j+1} v_k$ if $j < k - 1$ and $v_1 v_{k+1}$ otherwise (if $j = k - 1$). For any pair j, k with $j < k$, we define $A_{j,k}$ to be the set consisting of all those pairs that are already considered for coloring. Thus it holds that $v_c v_d \in A_{j,k}$ for all c, d such that $c < d \leq k - 1$, and j is the smallest integer for which we have $v_{j+1} v_k \in A_{j,k}$. This implies that for any pair j, k with $j < k$, we can uniquely determine the set of colored vertex pairs as the pair of non-adjacent vertices that are in $A_{j,k}$.

Subproblem and Recursion: Let $k \in [2, n]$ be an integer. We formalize a subproblem and recursive relations for our algorithm to enumerate MIC4-free configurations. For a pair of integers j and k with $j < k$ and the set $Y = \overline{E}(G) \cap A_{j,k}$ of colored pairs, we represent a 2-coloring $\lambda : Y \to \{0, 1\}$ by a set $C = \{(c, d; \lambda(v_c v_d)) \mid v_c v_d \in Y\} \cup \{(c, d; 2) \mid v_c v_d \in E(G)\}$. Thus, we represent a pair (T, λ) of a tree T with edge set E and a current coloring λ by the pair (E, C)

of sets. Finally, we define a subproblem $\mathcal{S}(E; C, i, j)$ to be the set of all possible feasible pairs that can be extended from the current pair (E, C). Observe that $\mathcal{S}(\{v_1, v_2\}; \emptyset, 1, 2)$ is the required set of all feasible pairs of trees and 2-colorings. Furthermore, for $j < k$ with $k \in [3, n]$, $z = v_{n+k+2-1}$ and $\ell = v_{k+1}$, we have the following recursion

$$\mathcal{S}(E; C, j, k) =$$
$$\begin{cases} \mathcal{S}(E; C, j+1, k), & j < k-1, v_j v_k \in E(G), \\ \bigcup_{xv_a \in E} \mathcal{S}((E \setminus \{xv_a\}) \cup \{xz, v_a z, \ell z\}; C, 1, k+1), & j = k-1, v_j v_k \in E(G), \\ \bigcup_{h=0,1} \mathcal{S}(E; C \cup \{(j, k; h)\}, j+1, k), & j < k-1, v_j v_k \in \overline{E}(G), \\ \bigcup_{xv_a \in E, h=0,1} \mathcal{S}((E \setminus \{xv_a\}) \cup \{xz, v_a z, \ell z\}; C \cup \{(j, k; h)\}, 1, k+1), & j = k-1, v_j v_k \in \overline{E}(G). \end{cases}$$
$$(1)$$

An illustration of the recursion for the case when $v_j v_k \in \overline{E}(G)$ in Eq. (1) is given in Fig. 1(c)-(d).

Bounding Procedure: Let $k \geq 4$ be an integer. We bound a subproblem $\mathcal{S}(P; C, j, k)$ if the current pair of tree T and coloring λ cannot be extended to a feasible pair. To perform this bounding operation, we need to check if there exists a subset $Z \subseteq \{v_1, v_2, \ldots, v_k\}$ of size 4 such that for each pair of non-adjacent vertices that are in Z, the current coloring λ is defined and the configuration induced by Z is implausible. To efficiently verify this, we use a characterization of MIC4 given by Azam et al. [2]. However, to use this method, for each subset $Z = \{v_h, v_k, v_i, v_j\}$ such that $h < i \leq j - 1$, we need to find two pairs of vertices in Z such that each pair has a common neighbor in the tree contraction $T\langle Z \rangle$. For this purpose we use Lemma 2.

Lemma 2. Let T be a tree with $|L(T)| \geq 4$ and $Z \subseteq L(T)$ be with $|Z| = 4$. Let $a_1, b_1, a_2, b_2 \in Z$ be such that the vertex sets of $P_T(a_1, b_1)$ and $P_T(a_2, b_2)$ are disjoint. Then for each $i = 1, 2$, the pair a_i and b_i have a common neighbor in $T\langle Z \rangle$.

Proof. Since $P_T(a_1, b_1)$ and $P_T(a_2, b_2)$ are disjoint, there exist two unique non-leaf vertices $c, d \in V(T)$ such that $c \in V(P_T(a_1, b_1))$, $d \in V(P_T(a_2, b_2))$ and $V(P_T(c, d)) \subsetneq V(P_T(a_1, b_2))$. Then to obtain the tree contraction $T\langle Z \rangle$, we first remove those vertices in T that are not contained in any path connecting two vertices in Z. That is, we recursively remove all leaves from $L(T) \setminus Z$. This implies that all non-leaf vertices in $V(T)$ except c and d are of degree 2 after the removal of all leaves. Thus, by removing all those vertices of degree 2 to get $T\langle Z \rangle$, we can see that c is the common neighbor of a_1, b_1 and d is the common neighbor of a_2, b_2, from which the claim follows. □

4.2 Configuration-Based LPs

We use linear programming formulations to handle the difficulty of the infinite search space, and the construction of finite size evidence. For a configuration (G, T, σ, λ) we solve the formulation $\mathcal{L}(G, T, \sigma, \lambda)$ proposed by Azam et al. [1]. For a graph with n vertices and a binary tree T with n leaves, the formulation $\mathcal{L}(G, T, \sigma, \lambda)$ has $\mathcal{O}(n)$ variables and $\mathcal{O}(n^2)$ constraints. The formulation has a solution w, $d_{\min}$ and $d_{\max}$ if and only if the configuration is plausible. Note that instead of trying all possible real weights to confirm if a graph is a PCG or not due to the given configuration, it suffices to solve this single formulation. Finally, to get a definite proof for the implausibility of a configuration (G, T, σ, λ), Azam et al. [1] introduced another formulation, $\mathcal{D}(G, T, \sigma, \lambda)$. For a graph with n vertices and a binary tree T with n leaves, $\mathcal{D}(G, T, \sigma, \lambda)$ has $\mathcal{O}(n^2)$ variables and $\mathcal{O}(n)$ constraints. The linear program $\mathcal{D}(G, T, \sigma, \lambda)$ is formulated in such a way that it admits a solution if and only if $\mathcal{L}(G, T, \sigma, \lambda)$ does not, based on the following theorem due to Gale [9].

Theorem 1 ([9, Theorem 2.8]). *For $A \in \mathbb{R}^{m \times n}$, $b \in \mathbb{R}^m$, let $x \in \mathbb{R}^n$ and $y \in \mathbb{R}^m$ be variables. Then either "$Ax \leq b$" or "$A^\top y \geq 0$, $b^\top y < 0$" has a non-negative solution.*

Hence, the solution of $\mathcal{D}(G, T, \sigma, \lambda)$ will serve as a finite size evidence to show that G is not a PCG due to (G, T, σ, λ).

5 Experimental Results and Discussion

We present experimental results of our proposed enumeration method to enumerate all MNPCGs with nine vertices executed in phases (I) and (II). We performed all experiments on a PC with Intel(R) Xeon(R) E5-1600v3 processor running at 3.00 GHz, 64 GB of memory, and Windows 7. We solved the ILP$_{\mathrm{suff}}$ and configuration-based LPs $\mathcal{L}$ and $\mathcal{D}$ by using the IBM ILOG CPLEX 12.8 solver as integer linear programming (ILP) to avoid any possible numerical errors in solving the formulations by the solver.

There are 261,080 non-isomorphic connected graphs with nine vertices, available at [12], and six binary trees with nine leaves, which are not difficult to obtain by pen and paper. We used the NAUTY [11] software to generate canonical forms of graphs for easy comparison during the generation of PCGs. As a preprocessing step, we removed all graphs that are non-biconnected or contain a pair of non-adjacent vertices that have the same set of neighbors, since known results described in Sect. 1 tell us that any such graph cannot be an MNPCG [4,13], as well as those graphs that are a supergraph of a known MNPCG [1].

We ran the graph generation phase (I-1) for ten days, after which we were left with 7,108 graphs. Next, for each of these graphs we checked the sufficient condition for a graph to be a PCG in phase (I-2) by setting an upper limit on edge weights to be $\alpha = 300$ and limiting the execution time of the CPLEX solver to 60 s, which identified 4,603 graphs to be PCGs in 18 days, and then setting the

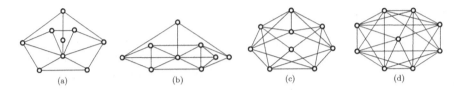

Fig. 2. An illustration of three MNPCGs with nine vertices. (a) An MNPCG with the minimum number of 16 edges; (b) An MNPCG with 19 edges; (c) An MNPCGs with 22 edges; and (d) An MNPCG with maximum number of 27 edges.

time limit to 300 s, which identified another 583 graphs to be PCGs in 14 days. Therefore, after finishing phase (I) in 42 days, we were left with 1,922 graphs for which we sought definite proof in phase (II).

Finally, we executed phase (II) to get definite proof for each of the 1,922 graphs left after our preprocessing step and phase (I). Phase (II) took 46 days of computation to complete, and it detected that 428 graphs among the 1,922 graphs were PCGs. Hence, we conclude that there are 1,494 MNPCGs with nine vertices, and we were able to enumerate all PCGs with nine vertices in 88 days. An illustration of four of the graphs proven to be MNPCGs is given in Fig. 2. We summarize our findings in the following Theorem.

Theorem 2. *For nine vertices and β edges, there are exactly 4, 35, 152, 289, 371, 337, 192, 85, 23, 5 and 1 MNPCGs if $\beta = 16, 17, \ldots, 25$, and 27, respectively, and no MNPCG otherwise.*

We give a computational proof of Theorem 2 by providing for each graph G the solution of linear program $\mathcal{D}(G, T, I, \lambda)$ from phase (II-2) for each MIC4-free configuration (G, T, I, λ), obtained in phase (II-1), if any exists, at https://www-or.amp.i.kyoto-u.ac.jp/~azam/MNPCG_9.

6   Conclusion

We proposed a two-phase method to enumerate all MNPCGs with a given number of vertices. In phase (I), we handled the difficulty of a large number of configurations by designing a PCG generator taking into account tree automorphisms and then constructing plausible configurations to prove a graph to be a PCG. In phase (II), we enumerated all MIC4-free configurations by designing a branch-and-bound algorithm and used linear programming formulations to handle the difficulty of infinite search space of weight assignment and construction of finite size evidence. By using this method we proved that there are exactly 1,494 MNPCGs with nine vertices.

Open Problems and Future Directions: The wheel graph, known to be an MNPCG on $n \geq 9$ vertices [3] is one of the sparsest graphs verified by our algorithm. It is an interesting question what is the minimum and maximum number of edges in an MNPCG with n vertices.

In addition, sample illustrations in Fig. 2 of the MNPCGs discovered through this work, as well as those shown by Azam et al. [1] on eight vertices, Durocher et al. [8] and Baiocchi et al. [3] indicate that MNPCGs tend to be symmetric. It would be interesting to uncover a relationship between the symmetry of a graph and its membership in the class of PCG graphs.

Finally, since there are 11,716,571 connected graphs on ten vertices [12], it would be very interesting to either devise a different enumeration approach, or improve the individual phases of our method, in order to efficiently enumerate all MNPCGs with ten vertices.

References

1. Azam, N.A., Ito, M., Shurbevski, A., Nagamochi, H.: Enumerating all pairwise compatibility graphs with a given number of vertices based on linear programming. In: 2nd International Workshop on Enumeration Problems and Applications (WEPA), paper 6c (2018)
2. Azam, N.A., Shurbevski, A., Nagamochi, H.: A method for enumerating all pairwise compatibility graphs with a given number of vertices. Discrete Appl. Math. (To appear)
3. Baiocchi, P., Calamoneri, T., Monti, A., Petreschi, R.: Some classes of graphs that are not PCGs. Theor. Comput. Sci. **791**, 62–75 (2019). https://doi.org/10.1016/j.tcs.2019.05.017
4. Calamoneri, T., Frangioni, A., Sinaimeri, B.: Pairwise compatibility graphs of caterpillars. Comput. J. **57**(11), 1616–1623 (2014)
5. Calamoneri, T., Frascaria, D., Sinaimeri, B.: All graphs with at most seven vertices are pairwise compatibility graphs. Comput. J. **56**(7), 882–886 (2013)
6. Calamoneri, T., Montefusco, E., Petreschi, R., Sinaimeri, B.: Exploring pairwise compatibility graphs. Theor. Comput. Sci. **468**, 23–36 (2013)
7. Calamoneri, T., Sinaimeri, B.: Pairwise compatibility graphs: a survey. SIAM Rev. **58**(3), 445–460 (2016)
8. Durocher, S., Mondal, D., Rahman, M.S.: On graphs that are not PCGs. Theor. Comput. Sci. **571**, 78–87 (2015)
9. Gale, D.: The Theory of Linear Economic Models. University of Chicago Press, Chicago (1989)
10. Kearney, P., Munro, J.I., Phillips, D.: Efficient generation of uniform samples from phylogenetic trees. In: Benson, G., Page, R.D.M. (eds.) WABI 2003. LNCS, vol. 2812, pp. 177–189. Springer, Heidelberg (2003). https://doi.org/10.1007/978-3-540-39763-2_14
11. McKay, B.D., Piperno, A.: Practical graph isomorphism, II. J. Symbolic Comput. **60**, 94–112 (2014)
12. http://users.cecs.anu.edu.au/~bdm/data/graphs.html. Accessed June 2019
13. Xiao, M., Nagamochi, H.: Some reduction operations to pairwise compatibility graphs. Inf. Process. Lett. **153**, 105875 (2020). https://doi.org/10.1016/j.ipl.2019.105875
14. Yanhaona, M.N., Bayzid, M.S., Rahman, M.S.: Discovering pairwise compatibility graphs. Discrete Math. Algorithms Appl. **2**(04), 607–623 (2010)

Constructing Tree Decompositions of Graphs with Bounded Gonality

Hans L. Bodlaender[1]([⊠]), Josse van Dobben de Bruyn[2], Dion Gijswijt[2], and Harry Smit[3]

[1] Department of Information and Computing Sciences, Utrecht University, P.O. Box 80.089, 3508 YB Utrecht, The Netherlands
h.l.bodlaender@uu.nl
[2] Delft Institute of Applied Mathematics, Delft University of Technology, Delft, The Netherlands
{j.vandobbendebruyn,d.c.gijswijt}@tudelft.nl
[3] Department of Mathematics, Utrecht University, P.O. Box 80.010, 3508 TA Utrecht, The Netherlands
h.j.smit@uu.nl

Abstract. In this paper, we give a constructive proof of the fact that the treewidth of a graph is at most its divisorial gonality. The proof gives a polynomial time algorithm to construct a tree decomposition of width at most k, when an effective divisor of degree k that reaches all vertices is given. We also give a similar result for two related notions: stable divisorial gonality and stable gonality.

1 Introduction

In this paper, we investigate the relation between well-studied graph parameters: treewidth and divisorial gonality. In particular, we give a constructive proof that the treewidth of a graph is at most its divisorial gonality.

Treewidth is a graph parameter with a long history. Its first appearance was under the name of *dimension*, in 1972, by Bertele and Briochi [4]. It was rediscovered several times since, under different names (see e.g. [5]). Robertson and Seymour introduced the notions of *treewidth* and *tree decompositions* in their fundamental work on graph minors; these notions became the dominant terminology.

The notion of divisorial gonality finds its origin in algebraic geometry. Baker and Norine [2] developed a divisor theory on graphs in analogy with divisor theory on curves, proving a Riemann–Roch theorem for graphs. The graph analog of gonality for curves was introduced by Baker [1]. To distinguish it from other notions of gonality (which we discuss briefly in Sect. 5), we denote the version we study by *divisorial gonality*. Divisorial gonality can be described in terms of a

This research was initiated at the Sandpiles and Chip Firing Workshop, held November 25–26, 2019 at the Centre for Complex Systems Studies, Utrecht University.
J. van Dobben de Bruyn—Supported by NWO grant 613.009.127.

D. Kim et al. (Eds.): COCOON 2020, LNCS 12273, pp. 384–396, 2020.
https://doi.org/10.1007/978-3-030-58150-3_31

chip firing game. A placement of k chips on the vertices of a graph (where vertices can have 0 or more chips) is called an *effective divisor* of *degree k*. Under certain rules (see Sect. 2), sets of vertices can *fire*, causing some of the chips to move to different vertices. The divisorial gonality of a graph is the minimum degree of an effective divisor such that for each vertex v, there is a firing sequence ending with a configuration with at least one chip at v.

The treewidth of a graph is never larger than its divisorial gonality[1]. A non-constructive proof of this fact was given by van Dobben de Bruyn and Gijswijt [10]. Their proof is based on the characterization of treewidth in terms of brambles, due to Seymour and Thomas [13]. In this paper, we give a constructive proof of the same fact. We formulate our proof in terms of a search game characterization of treewidth, but with small modifications, we can also obtain a corresponding tree decomposition. The proof also yields a polynomial time algorithm that, when given an effective divisor of degree k, constructs a search strategy with at most $k + 1$ searchers and a tree decomposition of width at most k of the input graph.

This paper is organized as follows. Some preliminaries are given in Sect. 2. In Sect. 3, we prove the main result with help of a characterization of treewidth in terms of a search game and discuss that we also can obtain a tree decomposition of width equal to the degree of a given effective divisor that reaches all vertices. An example is given in Sect. 4. In Sect. 5, we give constructive proofs that bound the treewidth of a graph in terms of two related other notions of gonality.

2   Preliminaries

2.1   Graphs

In this paper, all graphs are assumed to be finite. We allow multiple edges, but no loops. Let $G = (V, E)$ be a graph. For disjoint $U, W \subseteq V$ we denote by $E(U, W)$ the set of edges with one end in U and one end in W, and use the shorthand $\delta(U) = E(U, V \setminus U)$. The *degree* of a vertex $v \in V$ is $\deg(v) = |\delta(\{v\})|$, and given $v \in U \subseteq V$ we denote by $\text{outdeg}_U(v) = |E(\{v\}, V \setminus U)|$ the number of edges from v to $V \setminus U$. By $N(U)$ we denote the set of vertices in $V \setminus U$ that have a neighbor in U. The *Laplacian* of G is the matrix $Q(G) \in \mathbb{R}^{V \times V}$ given by

$$Q_{uv} = \begin{cases} \deg(u) & \text{if } u = v, \\ -|E(\{u\}, \{v\})| & \text{otherwise.} \end{cases}$$

2.2   Divisors and Gonality

Let $G = (V, E)$ be a connected graph with Laplacian matrix $Q = Q(G)$. A *divisor* on G is an integer vector $D \in \mathbb{Z}^V$. The *degree* of D is $\deg(D) = \sum_{v \in V} D(v)$. We say that a divisor D is *effective* if $D \geq 0$, i.e., $D(v) \geq 0$ for all $v \in V$.

---

[1] Conversely, graphs of treewidth 2 can have arbitrarily high divisorial gonality, which can be seen by considering 'chains of circuits'. See for instance [7,11].

The divisorial gonality can be defined in a number of equivalent ways. Most intuitive is the definition in terms of a chip firing game. An effective divisor D can be viewed as a chip configuration with $D(v)$ chips on vertex v. If $U \subset V$ is such that $\mathrm{outdeg}_U(v) \le D(v)$ for every $v \in U$ (i.e., each vertex has at least as many chips as it has edges to vertices outside U), then we say that U *can be fired*. If this is the case, then *firing* U means that every vertex in U gives chips to each of its neighbors outside U, one chip for every edge connecting to that neighbor. The resulting chip configuration is the divisor $D' = D - Q\mathbf{1}_U$. The assumption $\mathrm{outdeg}_U(v) \le D(v)$ guarantees that the number of chips on each vertex remains nonnegative, i.e. that D' is effective. Now, the divisorial gonality of a graph is the minimum number k such that there is a starting configuration (divisor) with k chips, such that for each vertex $x \in V$ there is a sequence of sets we can fire such that x receives a chip.

We now give the more formal definition, that is needed in our proofs. Two divisors D and D' are *equivalent* (notation: $D \sim D'$) if $D' = D - Qx$ for some $x \in \mathbb{Z}^V$. Note that equivalent divisors have the same degree since $Q^T \mathbf{1} = 0$. If D and D' are equivalent, then, since the null space of Q consists of all scalar multiples of $\mathbf{1}$, $D' = D - Qx$ has a unique solution $x \in \mathbb{Z}^V$ that is nonnegative and has $x_v = 0$ for at least one vertex v. We denote this x by $\mathrm{script}(D, D')$ and write $\mathrm{dist}(D, D') = \max\{x_v : v \in V\}$. Note that if $t = \mathrm{dist}(D, D')$, then $\mathrm{script}(D', D) = t\mathbf{1} - x$ and thus $\mathrm{dist}(D', D) = \mathrm{dist}(D, D')$. If D, D', D'' are pairwise equivalent, then we have the triangle inequality $\mathrm{dist}(D, D'') \le \mathrm{dist}(D, D') + \mathrm{dist}(D', D'')$ as $\mathrm{script}(D, D'') = \mathrm{script}(D, D') + \mathrm{script}(D', D'') - c\mathbf{1}$ for some nonnegative integer c.

Let D be a divisor. If D is equivalent to an effective divisor, then we define

$$\mathrm{rank}(D) = \max\{k \in \mathbb{Z}_{\ge 0} : D - E \text{ is equivalent to an effective divisor}$$
$$\text{for every effective divisor } E \text{ of degree at most } k\}.$$

If D is not equivalent to an effective divisor, we set $\mathrm{rank}(D) = -1$. The *divisorial gonality* of a graph G is defined as

$$\mathrm{dgon}(G) = \min\{\deg(D) : \mathrm{rank}(D) \ge 1\}.$$

In the remainder of the paper, we will only consider effective divisors. If we can go from D to D' by sequentially firing a number of subsets, then clearly $D \sim D'$. The converse is also true (part (i) of the next lemma) as was shown in [10, Lemma 1.3]. (The proof can also be found in [6].).

Lemma 1. *Let D and D' be equivalent effective divisors.*

(i) *There is a unique increasing chain $\emptyset \subsetneq U_1 \subseteq U_2 \subseteq \cdots \subseteq U_t \subsetneq V$ of subsets on which we can fire in sequence to obtain D' from D. That is, setting $D_0 = D$ and $D_i = D_{i-1} - Q\mathbf{1}_{U_i}$ for $i = 1, \ldots, t$ we have $D_t = D'$ and D_i is effective for all $i = 0, \ldots, t$.*

(ii) *We have $t = \mathrm{dist}(D, D') \le \deg(D) \cdot |V|$.*

We see that the two definitions of divisiorial gonality are equivalent. Lemma 1 shows that we even can require the sets of vertices that are fired to be increasing.

For a given vertex q, a divisor $D \geq 0$ is called q-reduced if there is no nonempty set $U \subseteq V \setminus \{q\}$ such that $D - Q\mathbf{1}_U \geq 0$.

Lemma 2 ([2, Proposition 3.1]). *Let D be an effective divisor and let q be a vertex. There is a unique q-reduced divisor equivalent to D.*

Let D be an effective divisor and let D_q be the q-reduced divisor equivalent to D. Suppose that $D \neq D_q$. By Lemma 1 we obtain D_q from D by firing on a chain of sets $U_1 \subseteq \cdots \subseteq U_t$ and, conversely, we obtain D from D_q by firing on the complements of $U_t, \ldots, U_1$. Since D_q is q-reduced, it follows that q is in the complement of U_t, and hence $q \notin U_1$. It follows that $x = \mathrm{script}(D, D_q)$ satisfies $x_q = 0$ and $D_q(q) \geq D(q)$. In particular, a divisor D has positive rank if and only if for every $q \in V$ the q-reduced divisor equivalent to D has at least one chip on vertex q.

Given an effective divisor D and a vertex q, Dhar's algorithm [9] finds in polynomial time a nonempty subset $U \subseteq V \setminus \{q\}$ on which we can fire, or concludes that D is q-reduced.

Algorithm 1: Dhar's burning algorithm

Input   : Divisor $D \geq 0$ on G and vertex q.
Output: Nonempty subset $U \subseteq V(G) \setminus \{q\}$ s.t. $D - Q\mathbf{1}_U \geq 0$ or $U = \emptyset$ if none exists.

$U \leftarrow V \setminus \{q\}$;
while $\mathrm{outdeg}_U(v) > D(v)$ *for some* $v \in U$ **do**
    $U \leftarrow U \setminus \{v\}$
end
return U

Lemma 3. *Dhar's algorithm is correct, and the output is the unique inclusion-wise maximal subset $U \subseteq V \setminus \{q\}$ that can be fired.*

Proof. The set returned by Algorithm 1 can be fired, as it satisfies the requirement $\mathrm{outdeg}_U(v) \leq D(v)$ for every $v \in U$. To complete the proof it therefore suffices to show that U contains every subset $W \subseteq V \setminus \{q\}$ that can be fired.

Let $W \subseteq V \setminus \{q\}$ be any such subset. At the start of the algorithm $U = V \setminus \{q\}$ contains W. While $U \supseteq W$, we have $\mathrm{outdeg}_U(v) \leq \mathrm{outdeg}_W(v) \leq D(v)$ for any $v \in W$, so the algorithm never removes a vertex $v \in W$ from U.   □

Note: in particular, Lemma 3 shows that the output of Algorithm 1 does not depend on the order in which vertices are selected for removal.

If throughout the algorithm we keep for every vertex v the number $\mathrm{outdeg}_U(v)$ and a list of vertices for which $\mathrm{outdeg}_U(v) > D(v)$, then we need only $O(|E|)$ updates, and we can implement the algorithm to run in time $O(|E|)$.

Lemma 4. *Let D be an effective divisor on the graph $G = (V, E)$, let $q \in V$, and let D_q be the q-reduced divisor equivalent to D. Let U be the set returned by Dhar's algorithm when applied to D and q, and suppose that $U \neq \emptyset$. Let $D' = D - Q\mathbf{1}_U$. Then $\mathrm{dist}(D', D_q) = \mathrm{dist}(D, D_q) - 1$.*

Proof. Let $x = \mathrm{script}(D, D_q)$. Since D_q is q-reduced, we have $x_q = 0$. On the other hand, since $D \neq D_q$ (as we can fire on U), the number $t = \max\{x_v : v \in V\}$ is positive. Let $W = \{v \in V : x_v = t\}$. By Lemma 1, we can fire on W, so by Lemma 3 we have $W \subseteq U$.

Let $x' = \mathrm{script}(D', D_q)$ and let $t' = \max\{x'_v : v \in V\}$. As D_q is q-reduced, we have $x'_q = 0$. Since there is a unique nonnegative $y \in \mathbb{Z}^V$ with $y_q = 0$ and $D_q = D - Qy$, and we have $D - Qx = D_q = (D - Q\mathbf{1}_U) - Qx'$, it follows that $x = x' + \mathbf{1}_U$. Since $U \supseteq W$, it follows that $x - \mathbf{1}_W \geq x'$, and hence $t - 1 \geq t'$. We find that $\mathrm{dist}(D', D_q) \leq \mathrm{dist}(D, D_q) - 1$. Since $\mathrm{dist}(D, D') = 1$, equality follows by the triangle inequality. $\qquad\square$

Since $\mathrm{dist}(D, D_q) \leq \deg(D) \cdot |V(G)|$, we can find a q-reduced divisor equivalent to D using no more than $\deg(D) \cdot |V|$ applications of Dhar's algorithm.

2.3   Treewidth and Tree Decompositions

The notions of treewidth and tree decomposition were introduced by Robertson and Seymour [12] in their fundamental work on graph minors.

Let $G = (V, E)$ be a graph, let $T = (I, F)$ be a tree, and let $X_i \subseteq V$ be a set of vertices (called *bags*) associated to i for every node $i \in I$. The pair $(T, (X_i)_{i \in I})$ is a *tree decomposition* of G if it satisfies the following conditions:

1. $\bigcup_{i \in I} X_i = V$;
2. for all $e = vw \in E$, there is an $i \in I$ with $v, w \in X_i$;
3. for all $v \in V$, the set of nodes $I_v = \{i \in I \mid v \in X_i\}$ is connected (it induces a subtree of T).

The *width* of the tree decomposition is $\max_{i \in I} |X_i| - 1$. The *treewidth* of a G is the minimum width of a tree decomposition of G. Note that the treewidth of a multigraph is equal to the treewidth of the underlying simple graph.

There are several notions that are equivalent to treewidth. We will use a notion that is based on a Cops and Robbers game, introduced by Seymour and Thomas [13]. Here, a number of searchers need to catch a fugitive. Searchers can move from a vertex in the graph to a 'helicopter', or from a helicopter to any vertex in the graph. Between moves of searchers, the fugitive can move with infinite speed in the graph, but may not move over or to vertices with a searcher. The fugitive is captured when a searcher moves to the vertex with the fugitive, and there is no other vertex without a searcher that the fugitive can move to. The location of the fugitive is known to the searchers at all times. We say that k searchers can capture a fugitive in a graph G, if there is a strategy for k searchers on G that guarantees that the fugitive is captured. In the initial configuration, the fugitive can choose a vertex, and all searchers are in a helicopter. A search strategy is *monotone* if it is never possible for the fugitive to move to a vertex that had been unreachable before. In particular, in a monotone search strategy, there is never a path without searchers from the location of the fugitive to a vertex previously occupied by a searcher.

Theorem 1 (Seymour and Thomas [13]**).** *Let G be a graph and k a positive integer. The following statements are equivalent.*

1. *The treewidth of G is at most k.*
2. *$k+1$ searchers can capture a fugitive in G.*
3. *$k+1$ searchers can capture a fugitive in G with a monotone search strategy.*

3   Construction of a Search Strategy

In this section, we present a polynomial time algorithm that, given an effective divisor D of degree k as input, constructs a monotone search strategy with $k+1$ searchers to capture the fugitive.

We start by providing a way to encode monotone search strategies. Let G be a graph. For $X \subseteq V(G)$, the vertex set of a component of $G - X$ is called an *X-flap*. A *position* is a pair (X, R), where $X \subseteq V(G)$ and R is a union² of X-flaps (we allow $R = \emptyset$). The set X represents the vertices occupied by searchers, and the fugitive can move freely within some X-flap contained in R (if $R = \emptyset$, then the fugitive has been captured). In a monotone search strategy, the fugitive will remain confined to R, so placing searchers on vertices other than R is of no use. Therefore, it suffices to consider three types of moves for the searchers: (a) remove searchers that are not necessary to confine the fugitive to R; (b) add searchers to R; (c) if R consists of more than one X-flap, restrict attention to the X-flap $R_i \subset R$ containing the fugitive. This leads us to the following definition.

Definition 1. *Let G be a graph and let k be a positive integer. A* monotone search strategy *(MSS) with k searchers for G is a directed tree $T = (\mathcal{P}, F)$ where $\mathcal{P}$ is a set of positions with $|X| \leq k$ for every $(X, R) \in \mathcal{P}$, and the following hold:*

(i) *The root of T is $(\emptyset, V)$.*
(ii) *If (X, R) is a leaf of T, then $R = \emptyset$.*
(iii) *Let (X, R) be a non-leaf of T. Then $R \neq \emptyset$ and there is a set $X' \subseteq X \cup R$ such that exactly one of the following applies:*
   (a) *$X' \subset X$ and position (X', R) is the unique out-neighbor of (X, R).*
   (b) *$X' \supset X$ and position (X', R') is the unique out-neighbor of (X, R), where $R' = R \setminus X'$.*
   (c) *$X' = X$ and the out-neighbors of (X, R) are the positions $(X, R_1), \ldots, (X, R_t)$ where $t \geq 2$ and $R_1, \ldots, R_t$ are the X-flaps contained in R.*

---

² Here we deviate from the definition of position as stated in [13] in that we allow R to consist of zero X-flaps or more than one X-flap.

If condition (ii) *does not necessarily hold, we say that* T *is a* partial *MSS. Note that we do not consider the root node to be a leaf even if it has degree* 1.

It is clear that if T is an MSS for k searchers, then, as the name suggests, k searchers can capture the fugitive, the fugitive can never reach a vertex that it could not reach before, and a searcher is never placed on a vertex from which a searcher was previously removed.

Lemma 5. *Let* G *be a graph on* n *vertices and let* T *be a (partial) MSS with* k *searchers for* G. *Then* T *has no more than* $n^2 + 1$ *nodes.*

Proof. For any position (X, R), define $f(X, R) = |R|(|X| + |R|)$. For any leaf node (X, R) we have $f(X, R) \geq 0$. For any non-leaf node (X, R), the value $f(X, R)$ is at least the sum of the values of its children plus the number of children. Indeed, in case (a) and (b) we have $f(X, R) \geq f(X', R') + 1$, and in case (c) we have $f(X, R) \geq f(X, R_1) + \cdots + f(X, R_k) + k$ as can be easily verified. It follows that $f(X, R)$ is an upper bound on the number of descendants of (X, R) in T. Since every non-root node is a descendant of the root, it follows that the total number of nodes is at most $1 + f(\emptyset, V) = 1 + n^2$. $\qquad\square$

In the construction of an MSS we will use the following lemma.

Lemma 6. *Let* R *be an* X*-flap. Let* D *be a positive rank effective divisor such that* $X \subseteq \mathrm{supp}(D)$ *and* $R \cap \mathrm{supp}(D) = \emptyset$. *Then we can find in polynomial time an effective divisor* $D' \sim D$ *such that* $X \subseteq \mathrm{supp}(D')$, $R \cap \mathrm{supp}(D') = \emptyset$, *and such that from* D' *we can fire a subset* U *with* $U \cap R = \emptyset$ *and* $U \cap X \neq \emptyset$.

Proof. Let $q \in R$. Let U be the set found by Dhar's algorithm. Since R is connected and U does not contain R, it follows that $U \cap R = \emptyset$ (otherwise $\mathrm{outdeg}_U(r) \geq 1 > D(r)$ for some $r \in U \cap R$). If $U \cap X$ is nonempty, we set $D' = D$ and we are done. Otherwise, we set $D \leftarrow D - 1_U$. Then $X \subseteq \mathrm{supp}(D)$, $R \cap \mathrm{supp}(D) = \emptyset$ and we iterate. We must finish in no more than $\deg(D) \cdot |V|$ iterations by Lemma 1 and Lemma 4. Hence, we can find the required D' and U in time $|E(G)| \cdot |V(G)| \deg(D)$. $\qquad\square$

Construction of a Monotone Search Strategy. Let G be a connected graph and let D be an effective divisor on G of positive rank. Let $k = \deg(D)$. We will construct an MSS for $k+1$ searchers on G. We do this by keeping a partial MSS, starting with only the root node $(\emptyset, V)$ and an edge to the node $(X, V \setminus X)$, where $X = \mathrm{supp}(D)$. Then, we iteratively grow T at the leaves (X, R) with $R \neq \emptyset$ until T is an MSS. At each step, we also keep, for every leaf (X, R) of T, an effective divisor $D' \sim D$ such that $X \subseteq \mathrm{supp}(D')$ and $R \cap \mathrm{supp}(D') = \emptyset$. We now describe the iterative procedure.

While T has a leaf (X, R) with $R \neq \emptyset$, let D' be the divisor associated to (X, R) and perform one of the following steps.

  I. If R consists of multiple X-flaps $R_1, \ldots, R_t$, then we add nodes $(X, R_1), \ldots, (X, R_t)$ as children of (X, R) and associate D' to each. Iterate.

II. If $X' = N(R)$ is a strict subset of X, then add the node (X', R) as a child of (X, R), associate D' to this node and iterate.

III. The remaining case is that $N(R) = X$ and R is a single X-flap. By Lemma 6 we can find an effective divisor $D'' \sim D'$ such that $X \subseteq \mathrm{supp}(D'')$, $R \cap \mathrm{supp}(D'') = \emptyset$ and from D'' we can fire on a set U such that $U \cap R = \emptyset$ and $U \cap X \neq \emptyset$. We set $U \cap X = \{s_1, s_2, \ldots, s_t\}$. That we can fire on U implies that

$$D''(s_i) \geq |N(s_i) \cap R| \quad \text{for } i = 1, \ldots, t. \tag{1}$$

For $i = 1, \ldots, t$ we define positions (X_i, R_i) and (X'_i, R_i) as follows:

$$X_i = X'_{i-1} \cup (N(s_i) \cap R), \quad R_i = R \setminus X_i, \quad \text{and} \quad X'_i = X_i \setminus \{s_i\},$$

where we set $X'_0 = X$. Using (1) and the fact that $X'_0 \subseteq \mathrm{supp}(D'')$, it is easy to check that $|X'_i| \leq k$ and $|X_i| \leq k + 1$ for every i. Since every edge in $\delta(R)$ has at least one endpoint in every X'_i, it follows that indeed R_i is a union of X'_i-flaps (and of X_i-flaps). We add the path $(X, R) \to (X_1, R_1) \to (X'_1, R_1) \to \cdots \to (X'_t, R_t)$ to T (it may happen that $(X_i, R_i) = (X'_{i-1}, R_{i-1})$ in which case we leave out one of the two). We associate $D'' - Q1_U$ to the leaf (X'_t, R_t).

By Lemma 5, we are done in at most $|V(G)|^2$ steps. This completes the construction. By combining the construction described above with that of the lemma below, we obtain Theorem 2. Note that so far only a non-constructive proof that the divisorial gonality of a graph is an upper bound for the treewidth was known [10]. See [6] for the proof of the next lemma.

Lemma 7. *Let $T' = (\mathcal{P}, F)$ be a monotone search strategy for k searchers in the connected graph G and let T be the undirected tree obtained by ignoring the orientation of edges in T'. Then $(T, \{X\}_{(X,R) \in \mathcal{P}})$ is a tree decomposition of G of width at most $k - 1$.*

Theorem 2. *There is a polynomial time algorithm that, when given a graph G and an effective divisor of degree k, finds a tree decomposition of G of width at most k.*

4   An Example

We apply the constructions of the previous section to a relatively small example. Let G be the graph as in Fig. 1. Let D be the divisor on G that has value 3 on vertex a and value 0 elsewhere. If we follow the construction of Sect. 3, we will end up with the monotone search strategy found in Fig. 2. We start with the root node (X, R) with $X = \emptyset$ and $R = V$ and connect it to the node $(\mathrm{supp}(D), V \setminus \mathrm{supp}(D))$. The three ways of growing the tree (steps I, II, III) are indicated in the picture. The four occurrences of step III are explained below.

For compactness of notation, we write the divisors as a formal sum. For instance, if D' has 2 chips on b and 1 chip on g, we write $D' = 2b + g$.

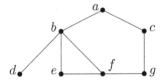

Fig. 1. An example graph G. It has divisorial gonality equal to 3.

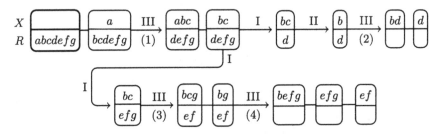

Fig. 2. The monotone search strategy obtained from G with divisor $D = 3a$. Each node shows the corresponding pair (X, R) with the root being $(\emptyset, \{a, b, c, d, e, f, g\})$. The labels I–III refer to the steps in the construction.

(1) Divisor D' is equal to $3a$. We fire the set $\{a\}$ and obtain the new divisor $a + b + c$.

(2) Divisor D' is equal to $a + b + c$. We fire the set $\{a, b, c, e, f, g\}$ and obtain the new divisor $a + c + d$.

(3) Divisor D' is equal to $a + b + c$. We fire the set $\{a, c\}$ and obtain the new divisor $2b + g$.

(4) Divisor D' is equal to $2b + g$. We fire the set $\{a, b, c, d, g\}$ and obtain the new divisor $e + 2f$.

5   Other Notions of Gonality

5.1   Stable Divisorial Gonality

The *stable divisorial gonality* of a graph G is the minimum of dgon(H) over all subdivisions H of G (i.e., graphs H that can be obtained by subdividing zero or more edges of G). The bound for divisorial gonality can easily be transferred to one for stable divisorial gonality. If G is simple, then the treewidth of G equals the treewidth of any of its subdivisions. (This is well known.) If G is not simple, then either the treewidth of G equals the treewidth of all its subdivisions, or G is obtained by adding parallel edges to a forest (i.e., the treewidth of G equals 1), and we subdivide at least one of these parallel edges (thus creating a graph with a cycle; the treewidth will be equal to 2 in this case.) In the latter case, the (stable) divisorial gonality will be at least two. Thus, we have the following easy corollary.

Corollary 1. *The treewidth of a graph G is at most the stable divisorial gonality of G.*

Standard treewidth techniques allow us to transform a tree decomposition of a subdivision of G into a tree decomposition of G of the same width. (For each subdivided edge $\{v, w\}$ replace each occurrence of a vertex representing a subdivision of this edge by v in each bag.)

5.2   Stable Gonality

Related to (stable) divisiorial gonality is the notion of *stable gonality*; see [8]. This notion is defined using finite harmonic morphisms to trees.

Let G and H be undirected nonempty graphs. We allow G and H to have parallel edges but not loops. A graph homomorphism from G to H is a map $f : V(G) \cup E(G) \rightarrow V(H) \cup E(H)$ that maps vertices to vertices, edges to edges, and preserves incidences of vertices and edges:

- $f(V(G)) \subseteq V(H)$,
- if e is an edge between vertices u and v, then $f(e)$ is an edge between $f(u)$ and $f(v)$.

A *finite morphism* from G to H (notation: $f : G \rightarrow H$) is graph homomorphism f from G to H together with an *index function* $r_f : E(G) \rightarrow \mathbb{Z}_{>0}$.

A finite morphism $f : G \rightarrow H$ with index function r_f is *harmonic* if for every vertex $v \in V(G)$, there is a constant $m_f(v)$ such that for each edge $e \in E(H)$ incident to $f(v)$, we have

$$\sum_{e' \text{ incident to } v; f(e')=e} r_f(e') = m_f(v)$$

If H is connected and $|E(G)| \geq 1$, then there is a positive integer $\deg(f)$, the *degree* of f, such that for all vertices $w \in V(H)$ and edges $e \in E(H)$, we have

$$\deg(f) = \sum_{v \in V(G); f(v)=w} m_f(v) = \sum_{e' \in E(G); f(e')=e} r_f(e');$$

see [14, Lemma 2.12] and [3, Lemma 2.3]. In particular, f is surjective in this case.

A *refinement* of a graph G is a graph G' that can be obtained from G by zero or more of the following two operations: subdivide an edge; add a leaf (i.e., add one new vertex and an edge from that vertex to an existing vertex).

The *stable gonality* of a connected non-empty graph G is the minimum degree of a finite harmonic morphism of a refinement of G to a tree.

Lemma 8. *Let G be an undirected connected graph without loops and at least one edge. Given a tree T and a finite harmonic morphism $f : G \rightarrow T$ of degree k, a tree decomposition of G of width at most k can be constructed in $O(k^2|V(G)|)$ time.*

Before proving the lemma, we make some simple observations. Recall that indices $r_f(e)$ are positive integers. We thus have for each edge $e \in E(T)$:

$$|\{e' \in E(G) \mid f(e') = e\}| \leq \sum_{e' \in E(G); f(e')=e} r_f(e') = \deg(f).$$

Since G is connected and has at least one edge, it follows that $m_f(v) \geq 1$ for every $v \in V(G)$. Hence, for each vertex $i \in V(T)$:

$$|\{v \in V(G) \mid f(v) = i\}| \leq \sum_{v \in V(G); f(v)=i} m_f(v) = \deg(f).$$

Proof (of Lemma 8). We build a tree decomposition of G in the following way. For each edge $e \in E(T)$, we have that $|\{e' \in E(G) \mid f(e') = e\}| \leq k$. Call this number $\ell(e)$. We subdivide e precisely $\ell(e)$ times; that is, we add $\ell(e)$ new vertices on this edge. Let T' be the tree that is obtained in this way.

To the nodes i of T', we associate sets X_i in the following way. If i is a node of T (i.e., not a node resulting from the subdivisions), then $X_i = f^{-1}(i)$, i.e., all vertices mapped by the morphism to i. By the observation above, we have that $|X_i| \leq \deg(f) = k$.

Consider an edge $\{i, j\}$ in T. Write $k' = \ell(\{i, j\})$. Recall that there are $k' \leq k$ edges of G that are mapped to $\{i, j\}$. Suppose these are $e_1 = \{v_1, w_1\}, \ldots, e_{k'} = \{v_{k'}, w_{k'}\}$ with $f(v_1) = f(v_2) = \cdots = f(v_{k'}) = i$ and $f(w_1) = f(w_2) = \cdots = f(w_{k'}) = j$. Let $i_1, i_2, \ldots, i_{k'}$ be the subdivision nodes of the edge $\{i, j\}$, with i_1 incident to i and $i_{k'}$ incident to j. Set $X_{i_r} = \{v_s \mid r \leq s \leq k'\} \cup \{w_t \mid 1 \leq t \leq r\}$ for $r \in \{1, \ldots, k'\}$. The construction is illustrated in Fig. 3. We claim that this yields a tree decomposition of G of width at most k.

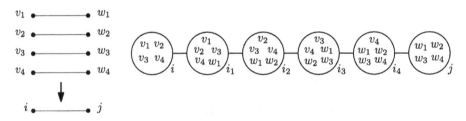

Fig. 3. Example of a step in the proof of Lemma 8. Here $k' = 4$. Left: four edges are mapped to the edge $\{i, j\}$ by the finite harmonic morphism. Right: the corresponding bags in the tree decomposition.

For all edges $\{v, w\} \in E(G)$, we have $\{f(v), f(w)\} \in E(T)$. Suppose without loss of generality that $f(v)$ has the role of i, $f(v)$ the role of j, $v = v_r$ and $w = w_r$ in the construction above. Then $v, w \in X_{i_r}$.

Finally, for all $v \in V$, the sets X_i to which v belongs are the following: v is in $X_{f(v)}$, and for each edge incident to $f(v) \in T$, v is in zero or more successive bags of subdivision nodes of this edge, with the first one (if existing), incident to $f(v)$. Thus, the bags to which v belongs form a connected subtree.

The first condition of tree decompositions follows from the second and the fact that G is connected. Hence T', with bags as defined above, yields a tree decomposition of G.

Finally, note that each set X_i is of size at most $k + 1$: vertices in T have a bag of size k and subdivision vertices have a bag of size $k' + 1 \leq k + 1$. So, we have a tree decomposition of G of width at most k.

It is straightforward to see that the construction in the proof can be carried out in $O(k^2|V(G)|)$ time. (Use that $|V(T)| \leq |V(G)|$, since f is surjective.)   □

Theorem 3. *Let G be an undirected connected graph without loops. Suppose that G has stable gonality k. Then G has treewidth at most k. Given a refinement G' of G and a finite harmonic morphism $f : G' \to T$ of degree k, a tree decomposition of G of width at most k can be constructed in $O(k^2|V(G')|)$ time.*

Proof. The degenerate case that G has no edges must be handled separately; here we have that the treewidth of G is 0, which is equal to its stable gonality.

Suppose G has at least one edge. By Lemma 8, we obtain a tree-decomposition of G' of width k in $O(k^2|V(G')|)$ time. Standard treewidth techniques allow us to transform a tree decomposition of a refinement of G into a tree decomposition of G of the same or smaller width. Added leaves can just be removed from all bags where they occur. For each subdivided edge $\{v, w\}$, replace each occurrence of a vertex representing a subdivision of this edge by v in each bag.   □

Acknowledgements. We thank Gunther Cornelissen, Bart Jansen, Erik Jan van Leeuwen, Marieke van der Wegen, and Tom van der Zanden for helpful discussions.

References

1. Baker, M.: Specialization of linear systems from curves to graphs. Algebra Number Theor. **2**(6), 613–653 (2008)
2. Baker, M., Norine, S.: Riemann-Roch and Abel-Jacobi theory on a finite graph. Adv. Math. **215**(2), 766–788 (2007)
3. Baker, M., Norine, S.: Harmonic morphisms and hyperelliptic graphs. Int. Math. Res. Not. **2009**(15), 2914–2955 (2009)
4. Bertele, U., Brioschi, F.: Nonserial Dynamic Programming. Academic Press, New York (1972)
5. Bodlaender, H.L.: A partial k-arboretum of graphs with bounded treewidth. Theor. Comput. Sci. **209**, 1–45 (1998)
6. Bodlaender, H.L., van Dobben de Bruyn, J., Gijswijt, D., Smit, H.: Constructing tree decompositions of graphs with bounded gonality . ArXiV e-prints, arXiv:2005.05569 (2020)
7. Cools, F., Draisma, J., Payne, S., Robeva, E.: A tropical proof of the Brill-Noether theorem. Adv. Math. **230**(2), 759–776 (2012)
8. Cornelissen, G., Kato, F., Kool, J.: A combinatorial Li-Yau inequality and rational points on curves. Math. Ann. **361**(1–2), 211–258 (2015)

9. Dhar, D.: Self-organized critical state of sandpile automaton models. Phys. Rev. Lett. **64**(14), 1613 (1990)
10. van Dobben de Bruyn, J., Gijswijt, D.: Treewidth is a lower bound on graph gonality . ArXiV e-prints, arXiv:1407.7055v2 (2014)
11. Hendrey, K.: Sparse graphs of high gonality. SIAM J. Discrete Math. **32**(2), 1400–1407 (2018)
12. Robertson, N., Seymour, P.D.: Graph minors. II. Algorithmic aspects of tree-width. J. Algorithms **7**(3), 309–322 (1986)
13. Seymour, P.D., Thomas, R.: Graph searching and a minimax theorem for tree-width. J. Comb. Theor. Ser. B **58**, 239–257 (1993)
14. Urakawa, H.: A discrete analogue of the harmonic morphism and Green kernel comparison theorems. Glasgow Math. J. **42**(3), 319–334 (2000)

Election Control Through Social Influence with Unknown Preferences

Mohammad Abouei Mehrizi[1]([✉]), Federico Corò[2], Emilio Cruciani[3],
and Gianlorenzo D'Angelo[1]

[1] Gran Sasso Science Institute, L'Aquila, Italy
{mohammad.aboueimehrizi,gianlorenzo.dangelo}@gssi.it
[2] Sapienza University of Rome, Rome, Italy
federico.coro@uniroma1.it
[3] Inria, I3S, UCA, CNRS, Sophia Antipolis, France
emilio.cruciani@inria.fr

Abstract. The election control problem through social influence asks to find a set of nodes in a social network of voters to be the starters of a political campaign aiming at supporting a given target candidate. Voters reached by the campaign change their opinions on the candidates. The goal is to shape the diffusion of the campaign in such a way that the chances of victory of the target candidate are maximized. Previous work shows that the problem can be approximated within a constant factor in several models of information diffusion and voting systems, assuming that the controller, i.e., the external agent that starts the campaign, has full knowledge of the preferences of voters. However this information is not always available since some voters might not reveal it. Herein we relax this assumption by considering that each voter is associated with a probability distribution over the candidates. We propose two models in which, when an electoral campaign reaches a voter, this latter modifies its probability distribution according to the amount of influence it received from its neighbors in the network. We then study the election control problem through social influence on the new models: In the first model, under the Gap-ETH, election control cannot be approximated within a factor better than $1/n^{o(1)}$, where n is the number of voters; in the second model, which is a slight relaxation of the first one, the problem admits a constant factor approximation algorithm.

Keywords: Computational social choice · Election control · Influence Maximization · Social influence

1 Introduction

Social media play a fundamental role in everyone's life providing information, entertainment, and learning. Many social media users prefer to access social

This work has been partially supported by the Italian MIUR PRIN 2017 Project ALGADIMAR "Algorithms, Games, and Digital Markets."

network platforms such as Facebook or Twitter before news websites as they provide faster means for information diffusion [15]. As a consequence, online social networks are also exploited as a tool to alter users' opinions. The extent to which the opinions of an individual are conditioned by social interactions is called social influence. It has been observed that social influence starting from a small set of individuals may generate a cascade effect that allows to reach a large part of the network. Recently, this capability has been used to affect the outcome of political elections. There exists evidence of political intervention which shows the effect of social media manipulation on the elections outcome, e.g., by spreading fake news [17]. A real-life example is in the 2016 US election where a study showed that on average 92% of people remembered pro-Trump fake news and 23% of them remembered pro-Clinton fake news [2]. Several other cases have been studied [4, 10, 12, 19].

There exists a wide literature about manipulation of voting systems; we point the reader to a recent survey [9]. Despite that, only few studies focus on the problem of controlling the outcome of political elections through the spread of information in social networks. The *election control* problem [20] consists in selecting a set of nodes of a network to be the starters of a diffusion with the aim of maximizing the chances for a target candidate to win an election. In particular, in the *constructive* election control problem, the goal is to maximize the *Margin of Victory* (MoV) of the target candidate on its most critical opponent, i.e., the difference of votes (or score, depending on the voting system) between the two candidates after the effect of social influence. A variation of the problem, known as *destructive* election control, aims at making a target candidate lose. Both problems have been originally analyzed under the Independent Cascade Model (ICM) [11], and considering *plurality voting*; approximation and hardness-of-approximation results are provided [20]. Corò et al. [6, 7] analyzed the problem in arbitrary scoring rules voting systems under the Linear Threshold Model (LTM) [11], providing constant factor approximation algorithms. It has been later shown that it is NP-hard to find any constant factor approximation in the multi-winner scenario [1].

Faliszewski et al. [8] examine bribery in an opinion diffusion process with voter clusters: each node is a cluster of voters, represented as a weight, with a specific list of candidates; there is an edge between two nodes if they differ by the ordering of a single pair of adjacent candidates. The authors show that making a specific candidate win in their model is NP-hard and fixed-parameter tractable with respect to the number of candidates. Bredereck et al. [5] studied the problem of manipulating diffusion on social networks, though not specifically in the context of elections. They show that identifying successful manipulation via bribing, adding/deleting edges, or controlling the order of asynchronous updates are all computationally hard problems. A similar approach is taken by Apt et al. [3], where the authors introduce a threshold model for social networks in order to characterize the role of social influence in the global adoption of a commercial product.

In all previous works it is assumed that the controller knows the preference list of each voter. However, this assumption is not always satisfied in realistic scenarios as voters may not reveal their preferences to the controller. Herein, in Sect. 2, we introduce two new models, *Probabilistic Linear Threshold Ranking* (PLTR) and *Relaxed-PLTR* (R-PLTR), that encompass scenarios where the preference lists of the voters are not fully revealed. Specifically, we use an uncertain model in which the controller only knows, for each voter, a probability distribution over the candidates. In fact, in applied scenarios, the probability distribution could be inferred by analyzing previous social activity of the voters, e.g., re-tweets or likes of politically oriented posts. We envision that some given focused news about a target candidate spread through the network as a message. We model such a diffusion via the LTM [11]. The message will have an impact on the opinions of voters who received it from their neighbors, leading to a potential change of their vote if the neighbors exercise a strong influence on them. With this intuition in mind, in our models, the probability distribution of the voters reached by the message is updated as a function of the degree of influence that the senders of the message have on them. The rationale is that the controller, without knowing the exact preference list which is kept hidden, can just update its estimation on it by considering the mutual degree of influence among voters. We acknowledge that our models do not cover all scenarios that can arise in election control, e.g., messages about multiple candidates. However they represent a first step towards modeling uncertainty.

We study on our models both the constructive and destructive election control problems. We show in Sect. 3 that the election control problem in PLTR is at least as hard to approximate as the Densest-k-Subgraph problem. In Sect. 4, instead, we provide an algorithm that guarantees a constant factor approximation to the election control problem in R-PLTR. In the relaxed model, R-PLTR, also "partially-influenced" nodes change their probability distribution. Although this simple modification is enough to make the problem substantially easier, preliminary experimental results (available in the full version) show that the hardness of approximation for PLTR is purely theoretical and is due to hard instances in the reduction.

2 Influence Models and Problem Statement

Background. Influence Maximization is the problem of finding a subset of the most influential users in a social network with the aim of maximizing the spread of information given a particular diffusion model. In this work, we focus on the diffusion model known as *Linear Threshold Model* (LTM) [11]. Given a graph $G = (V, E)$, each edge $(u, v) \in E$ has a weight $b_{uv} \in [0, 1]$, each node $v \in V$ has a threshold $t_v \in [0, 1]$ sampled uniformly at random and independently from the others, and the sum of the weights of the incoming edges of v is $\sum_{(u,v) \in E} b_{uv} \leq 1$. Each node can be either *active* or *inactive*. Let A_0 be a set of initially active nodes and A_t be the set of nodes active at time t. A node v becomes active if the sum of the incoming active weights at time $t - 1$ is greater than or equal to its threshold t_v, i.e., $v \in A_t$ if and only if $v \in A_{t-1}$ or $\sum_{u \in A_{t-1}:(u,v) \in E} b_{uv} \geq t_v$. The process terminates at the first time $\tilde{t}$ in which the set of active nodes would not change in the next round, i.e., $A_{\tilde{t}} = A_{\tilde{t}+1}$. We define the eventual set of active nodes as $A := A_{\tilde{t}}$ and the expected size of A as $\sigma(A_0)$. Given a budget B, the influence maximization problem consists in finding a set of nodes A_0 of size B, called *seeds*, in such a way that $\sigma(A_0)$ is maximum.

Kempe et al. [11] showed that the distribution of active nodes A, for any set A_0, is equal to the distribution of the sets of nodes that are *reachable* from A_0 in the set of random graphs called *live-edge graphs*. A live-edge graph is a subgraph in which each node has at most one incoming edge. Even if the number of live-edge graphs is exponential, by using standard Chernoff-Hoeffding bounds, it is possible to compute a $(1 \pm \epsilon)$-approximation of $\sigma(A_0)$, for a given A_0, with high probability by sampling a polynomial number of live-edge graphs. Moreover, $\sigma(A_0)$ is monotone and submodular w.r.t. to the initial set A_0; hence, an optimal solution can be approximated to a factor of $1 - 1/e$ using a simple greedy algorithm [16]. There has been intensive research on the problem in the last decade. We point the reader to a recent survey on the topic [13].

Notation. Let $G = (V, E)$ be a directed graph representing a social network of voters and their interactions. We denote the set of m candidates running for the election as $C = \{c_1, c_2, \ldots, c_m\}$ and the target candidate as $c_* \in C$. Each node $v \in V$ has a probability distribution over the candidates π_v, where $\pi_v(c_i)$ is the probability that v votes for candidate c_i; then for each $v \in V$ we have that $\pi_v(c_i) \geq 0$ for each candidate c_i and $\sum_{i=1}^{m} \pi_v(c_i) = 1$. Moreover, we denote by N_v^- and N_v^+, respectively, the sets of incoming and outgoing neighbors for each node $v \in V$. For each candidate c_i, we assume that $\pi_v(c_i)$ is at least a polynomial fraction of the number of voters, i.e., $\pi_v(c_i) = \Omega(1/|V|^\gamma)$ for some constant $\gamma > 0$.[1] Let $X_v(c_i)$ be an indicator random variable, where $X_v(c_i) = 1$ if v votes for c_i, with probability $\pi_v(c_i)$, and $X_v(c_i) = 0$ otherwise. We define the expected *score* of a candidate c_i as the expected number of votes that c_i obtains from the voters $F(c_i, \emptyset) := \mathbf{E}\left[\sum_{v \in V} X_v(c_i)\right] = \sum_{v \in V} \pi_v(c_i)$.

PLTR Model. As in LTM, each node v has a threshold $t_v \in [0,1]$; each edge $(u,v) \in E$ has a weight b_{uv}, that models the influence of node u on v, with the constraint that, for each node v, $\sum_{u:(u,v) \in E} b_{uv} \leq 1$. We assume the weight of each existing edge (u,v) not to be too small, i.e., $b_{uv} = \Omega(1/|V|^\gamma)$ for some constant $\gamma > 0$ (see footnote 1).

Given an initial set of seed nodes S, the diffusion process proceeds as in LTM: Inactive nodes become active if the sum of the weights of incoming edges from active neighbors is greater than or equal to their threshold. Mainly, we are modeling the spread of some ads/news about the target candidate: Active nodes

---

[1] The assumption is used in the approximation results, since Influence Maximization problem with exponential (or exponentially small) weights on nodes is an open problem. However, the assumption is realistic: Current techniques to estimate such parameters generate values linear in the number of messages shared by a node.

receive the message and spread it to their neighbors. Moreover, in PLTR, active nodes are influenced by the message, increasing their probability of voting for the target candidate. In particular, an active node v increases the probability of voting for $c_\star$ by an amount equal to the sum of the weights of its edges incoming from other active nodes, i.e., it adds $\sum_{u \in A \cap N_v^-} b_{uv}$ to the initial probability $\pi_v(c_\star)$. Then it normalizes to maintain π_v as a probability distribution. Formally, for each node $v \in A$, where A is the set of active nodes at the end of LTM, the preference list of v is denoted as $\tilde{\pi}_v$ and it is equal to:

$$\tilde{\pi}_v(c_\star) = \frac{\pi_v(c_\star) + \sum_{u \in A \cap N_v^-} b_{uv}}{1 + \sum_{u \in A \cap N_v^-} b_{uv}} \quad \text{and} \quad \tilde{\pi}_v(c_i) = \frac{\pi_v(c_i)}{1 + \sum_{u \in A \cap N_v^-} b_{uv}}, \quad (1)$$

for each $c_i \neq c_\star$. All inactive nodes $v \in V \setminus A$ will have $\tilde{\pi}_v(c_i) = \pi_v(c_i)$ for all candidates, including $c_\star$. As for the expected score before the process, we can compute the expected final score of a candidate c_i as $F(c_i, S) := \mathbf{E}\left[\sum_{v \in V} X_v(c_i, S)\right] = \sum_{v \in V} \tilde{\pi}_v(c_i)$, where $X_v(c_i, S)$ is the indicator random variable after the process, i.e., $X_v(c_i, S) = 1$ if v votes for c_i, with probability $\tilde{\pi}_v(c_i)$, and $X_v(c_i, S) = 0$ otherwise.

Let us denote by $\mathcal{G}$ the set of all possible live-edge graphs sampled from G. We can also compute $F(c_i, S)$ by means of live-edge graphs used in the LTM model as

$$F(c_i, S) = \sum_{G' \in \mathcal{G}} F_{G'}(c_i, S) \cdot \mathbf{P}(G'), \quad (2)$$

where $F_{G'}(c_i, S)$ is the score of c_i in $G' \in \mathcal{G}$ and $\mathbf{P}(G')$ is the probability of sampling live-edge G'. More precisely, for the target candidate we have

$$F_{G'}(c_\star, S) = \sum_{v \in R_{G'}(S)} \frac{\pi_v(c_\star) + \sum_{u \in R_{G'}(S) \cap N_v^-} b_{uv}}{1 + \sum_{u \in R_{G'}(S) \cap N_v^-} b_{uv}} + \sum_{v \in V \setminus R_{G'}(S)} \pi_v(c_\star),$$

where $R_{G'}(S)$ is the set of nodes reachable from S in G'. A similar formulation can be derived for $c_i \neq c_\star$.

R-PLTR Model. In the next section we prove that the election control problem in PLTR is hard to approximate to within a polynomial fraction of the optimum (Theorem 1). However, we show that a small relaxation of the model allows us to approximate it to within a constant factor. In the relaxed model, that we call *Relaxed Probabilistic Linear Threshold Ranking* (R-PLTR), the probability distribution of a node is updated if it has at least an active incoming neighbor (also if the node is not active itself). More formally, every node $v \in V$ (and not just every node $v \in A$ as in PLTR) changes its preference by updating its probability distribution via Eq. (1); thus also nodes that have at least an active incoming neighbor can change. The rationale is that a voter might slightly change its opinion about the target candidate if it receives some influence from its active incoming neighbors even if the received influence is not enough to activate it (thus making it propagate the information to its outgoing neighbors). Therefore, we include this small amount of influence in the objective function.

In the next section, we show that election control in R-PLTR is still NP-hard, and then we give an algorithm that guarantees a constant approximation ratio in this setting.

Problem Statement. In the *constructive election control* problem we maximize the expected Margin of Victory (MoV) of the target candidate w.r.t. its most voted opponent, akin to [6,20]. We define the MoV(S) obtained starting from S as the expected increase, w.r.t. the value before the process, of the difference between the score of $c_\star$ and that of the most voted opponent.[2] Formally, if c and $\hat{c}$ are respectively the candidates different from $c_\star$ with the highest score before and after the diffusion process

$$\text{MoV}(S) := F(c, \emptyset) - F(c_\star, \emptyset) - (F(\hat{c}, S) - F(c_\star, S)). \tag{3}$$

Given a budget B, the *constructive election control problem* asks to find a set of seed nodes S, of size at most B, that maximizes MoV(S). It is worth noting that MoV can also be expressed as a function of the score gained by candidate $c_\star$ and the score lost by its most voted opponent $\hat{c}$ at the end of the process. We define the score gained and lost by a candidate c_i as

$$g^+(c_i, S) := F(c_i, S) - F(c_i, \emptyset), g^-(c_i, S) := F(c_i, \emptyset) - F(c_i, S).$$

Therefore, we can rewrite MoV(S) as

$$\text{MoV}(S) = g^+(c_\star, S) + g^-(\hat{c}, S) - F(\hat{c}, \emptyset) + F(c, \emptyset). \tag{4}$$

The *destructive election control problem*, instead, aims at making the target candidate lose by minimizing its MoV. In this dual scenario, the probability distributions of the voters are updated slightly differently in our models, i.e., influenced voters have a lower probability of voting for the target candidate $c_\star$ mimicking the spread of "negative" news about $c_\star$.

In our model the controller can send to the seed nodes a message in support of only one single candidate, e.g., latest news about the candidate. We prove that the best strategy is that of sending messages in support of the target candidate $c_\star$, i.e., if the controller wants $c_\star$ to win, then, according to our models, the direct strategy of targeting voters with news about $c_\star$ is more effective than the alternative strategy of distracting the same voters with news about other candidates. The proof of this observation, as well as other proofs, are omitted due to space limitations and deferred to the full version.

3   Hardness Results

In this section we provide two hardness results related to election control in PLTR and R-PLTR. In Theorem 1 we show that maximizing the MoV in PLTR

---

[2] The increment in margin of victory, instead of just the margin, cannot be negative and gives well defined approximation ratios.

is at least as hard to approximate as the Densest-k-subgraph problem. This implies several conditional hardness of approximation bounds for the election control problem. Indeed, it has been shown that the Densest-k-subgraph problem is hard to approximate: to within any constant bound under the Unique Games with Small Set Expansion conjecture [18]; to within $n^{-1/(\log \log n)^c}$, for some constant c, under the exponential time hypothesis (ETH) [14]; to $n^{-f(n)}$ for any function $f \in o(1)$, under the Gap-ETH assumption [14]. Then, in Theorem 2, we show that maximizing the MoV in R-PLTR is still NP-hard.

Theorem 1. *An α-approximation to the election control problem in PLTR gives an $\alpha\beta$-approximation to the Densest k-Subgraph problem, for a positive constant $\beta < 1$.*

Proof. Given an undirected graph $G = (V, E)$ and an integer k, Densest k-Subgraph (DkS) is the problem of finding the subgraph induced by a subset of V of size k with the highest number of edges.

The reduction works as follows: Consider the PLTR problem on G with budget $B = k$, where each undirected edge $\{u, v\}$ is replaced with two directed edges (u, v) and (v, u). Let us consider m candidates and let us assume that $\pi_v(\hat{c}) = 1$ for a $\hat{c} \neq c_\star$ and $\pi_v(c_i) = \pi_v(c_\star) = 0$ for each $c_i \neq \hat{c}$ and for each $v \in V$. Assign to each edge $(u, v) \in E$ a weight $b_{uv} = \frac{1}{n^\gamma}$, for any fixed constant $\gamma \geq 4$ and $n = |V|$.

We show the reduction considering the problem of maximizing the score, because in the instance considered in the reduction the MoV is exactly equal to twice the score. Indeed, the score of $\hat{c}$ after PLTR starting from any initial set S is $F(\hat{c}, S) = |V| - F(c_\star, S)$. Thus, according to the definition of MoV in Eq. (4), we get that

$$\text{MoV}(S) = |V| - (|V| - F(c_\star, S) - F(c_\star, S)) = 2F(c_\star, S).$$

To compute the expected final score of the target candidate, we average its score in all live-edge graphs in $\mathcal{G}$, according to Eq. (2). In our reduction, though, the empty live-edge graph $G'_\emptyset = (V, \emptyset)$ is sampled *with high probability*, i.e., with probability at least $1 - n^{-\Theta(1)}$. In fact, for any $\gamma \geq 2$, it is possible to show that $\mathbf{P}\left(G'_\emptyset\right) = \prod_{v \in V}\left(1 - \sum_{u \in N_v^-} b_{uv}\right) \geq 1 - \frac{1}{n^{\gamma-2}}$, using a binomial expansion argument.

The score obtained by $c_\star$ in any live-edge graph G' starting from any seed set S is

$$F_{G'}(c_\star, S) = \sum_{v \in R_{G'}(S)} \frac{\pi_v(c_\star) + \sum_{u \in R_{G'}(S) \cap N_v^-} \frac{1}{n^\gamma}}{1 + \sum_{u \in R_{G'}(S) \cap N_v^-} \frac{1}{n^\gamma}} = \Theta\left(\sum_{v \in R_{G'}(S)} \frac{|R_{G'}(S) \cap N_v^-|}{n^\gamma}\right),$$

since $1 \leq 1 + \sum_{u \in R_{G'}(S) \cap N_v^-} \frac{1}{n^\gamma} \leq 2$ for each $v \in R_{G'}(S)$. Note that the sum in the previous approximation of $F_{G'}(c_\star, S)$, namely $\sum_{v \in R_{G'}(S)} |R_{G'}(S) \cap N_v^-|$, is equal to the number of edges of the subgraph induced by the set $R_{G'}(S)$ of nodes reachable from S in G', which is not greater than n^2, and thus $F_{G'}(c_\star, S) = \mathcal{O}\left(\frac{1}{n^{\gamma-2}}\right)$.

In the empty live-edge graph $G'_\emptyset$ the set $R_{G'_\emptyset}(S)$ at the end of LTM is equal to S, since the graph has no edges. Thus $F_{G'_\emptyset}(c_\star, S) = \frac{1}{n^\gamma} \cdot \sum_{v \in S} \frac{|S \cap N_v^-|}{1 + \sum_{u \in S \cap N_v^-} \frac{1}{n^\gamma}}$ and since the denominator is, again, bounded by two constants we have that

$$F_{G'_\emptyset}(c_\star, S) = \Theta\left(\frac{\sum_{v \in S} |S \cap N_v^-|}{n^\gamma}\right) = \Theta\left(\frac{\mathrm{SOL}_{DkS}(S)}{n^\gamma}\right),$$

where $\mathrm{SOL}_{DkS}(S) := \sum_{v \in S} |S \cap N_v^-|$ is the number of edges of the subgraph induced by S, i.e., the value of the objective function of DkS for solution S.

Thus, the expected final score of the target candidate is

$$F(c_\star, S) = F_{G'_\emptyset}(c_\star, S) \cdot \mathbf{P}(G'_\emptyset) + \sum_{G' \neq G'_\emptyset} F_{G'}(c_\star, S) \cdot \mathbf{P}(G').$$

Since $F_{G'}(c_\star, S)$ and $\sum_{G' \neq G'_\emptyset} \mathbf{P}(G')$ are in $\mathcal{O}\left(\frac{1}{n^{\gamma-2}}\right)$, then

$$\sum_{G' \neq G'_\emptyset} F_{G'}(c_\star, S) \cdot \mathbf{P}(G') = \mathcal{O}\left(\frac{1}{n^{2(\gamma-2)}}\right) = \mathcal{O}\left(\frac{\mathrm{SOL}_{DkS}(S)}{n^\gamma}\right),$$

for any $\gamma \geq 4$. Thus $F(c_\star, S) = \Theta\left(\frac{\mathrm{SOL}_{DkS}(S)}{n^\gamma}\right) \cdot \Theta(1) + \mathcal{O}\left(\frac{\mathrm{SOL}_{DkS}(S)}{n^\gamma}\right)$, which means $F(c_\star, S) = \Theta\left(\frac{\mathrm{SOL}_{DkS}(S)}{n^\gamma}\right)$. We apply the Bachmann-Landau definition of Θ notation: There exist positive constants n_0, β_1, and β_2 such that, for all $n > n_0$,

$$\beta_1 \frac{\mathrm{SOL}_{DkS}(S)}{n^\gamma} \leq F(c_\star, S) \leq \beta_2 \frac{\mathrm{SOL}_{DkS}(S)}{n^\gamma}.$$

In this case, the constants n_0, β_1, and β_2 do not depend on the specific instance.

Since the previous bounds hold for any set S we also have that $\beta_1 \frac{\mathrm{OPT}_{DkS}}{n^\gamma} \leq$ OPT, where OPT is the value of an optimal solution for PLTR and OPT_{DkS} is the value of an optimal solution for DkS.

Suppose there exists an α-approximation algorithm for PLTR, i.e., an algorithm that finds a set S s.t. the value of its solution is $\mathrm{MoV}(S) = 2F(c_\star, S) \geq \alpha \cdot$ OPT. Then,

$$\frac{\alpha}{2} \cdot \beta_1 \frac{\mathrm{OPT}_{DkS}}{n^\gamma} \leq \frac{\alpha}{2} \cdot \mathrm{OPT} \leq F(c_\star, S) \leq \beta_2 \frac{\mathrm{SOL}_{DkS}(S)}{n^\gamma}.$$

Thus $\mathrm{SOL}_{DkS}(S) \geq \frac{\alpha}{2} \frac{\beta_1}{\beta_2} \mathrm{OPT}_{DkS}$, i.e., it is an $\frac{\alpha\beta_1}{2\beta_2}$-approximation to DkS. $\square$

Theorem 2. *Election control in R-PLTR is NP-hard.*

Proof. We prove the hardness by reduction from Influence Maximization under LTM, which is known to be *NP*-hard [11].

Consider an instance $\mathcal{I}_{\text{LTM}} = (G, B)$ of Influence Maximization under LTM. $\mathcal{I}_{\text{LTM}}$ is defined by a weighted graph $G = (V, E, w)$ with weight function $w : E \rightarrow [0, 1]$ and by a budget B. Let $\mathcal{I}_{\text{R-PLTR}} := (G', B)$ be the instance that corresponds to $\mathcal{I}_{\text{LTM}}$ on R-PLTR, defined by the same budget B and by a graph $G' = (V', E', w')$ that can be built as follows:

1. Duplicate each vertex in the graph, i.e., we define the new set of nodes as $V' := V \cup \{v_{|V|+1}, \dots, v_{2|V|}\}$.
2. Add an edge between each vertex $v \in V$ to its copy in V', i.e., we define the new set of edges as $E' := E \cup \{(v_1, v_{|V|+1}), \dots, (v_{|V|}, v_{2|V|})\}$.
3. Keep the same weight for each edge in E and we set the weights of all new edges to 1, i.e., $w'(e) = w(e)$ for each $e \in E$ and $w'(e) = 1$ for each $e \in E' \setminus E$. Note that the constraint on incoming weights required by LTM is not violated by w'.
4. Consider m candidates $c_\star, c_1, \dots, c_{m-1}$. For each $v \in V$ we set $\pi_v(c_\star) = 1$ and $\pi_v(c_i) = 0$ for any other candidate $i \in \{1, \dots, m-1\}$. For each $v \in V' \setminus V$ we set $\pi_v(c_\star) = 0$, $\pi_v(c_1) = 1$ and $\pi_v(c_i) = 0$ for any other candidate $i \in \{2, \dots, m-1\}$.

Let S be the initial set of seed nodes of size B that maximizes $\mathcal{I}_{\text{LTM}}$ and let A be the set of active nodes at the end of the process. The value of the MoV obtained by S in $\mathcal{I}_{\text{R-PLTR}}$ is $\text{MoV}(S) = |V| - |V \setminus A|$. Indeed, each node $v \in V$ in G' has $\tilde{\pi}_v(c_\star) = \pi_v(c_\star) = 1$, because the probability of voting for the target candidate remains the same after the normalization. Moreover, each node $v_i \in V \cap A$ influences its duplicate $v_{|V|+i}$ with probability 1 and therefore $\tilde{\pi}_{v_{|V|+i}}(c_\star) = (\pi_{v_{|V|+i}}(c_\star) + 1)/2 = \frac{1}{2}$. Therefore, $F(c_\star, \emptyset) = F(c_1, \emptyset) = |V|$, $F(c_\star, S) = |V| + \frac{1}{2}|A|$, and $F(c_1, S) = |V \setminus A| + \frac{1}{2}|A|$.

Let S be the initial set of seed nodes of size B that achieves the maximum in $\mathcal{I}_{\text{R-PLTR}}$. Without loss of generality, we can assume that $S \subseteq V$, since we can replace any seed node $v_{|V|+i}$ in $V' \setminus V$ with its corresponding node v_i in V without decreasing the objective function. If A is the set of active nodes at the end of the process, then by using similar arguments as before, we can prove that $\text{MoV}(S) = |V| - |V \setminus A|$. Let us assume that S does not maximize $\mathcal{I}_{\text{LTM}}$, then, S would also not maximize $\mathcal{I}_{\text{R-PLTR}}$, which is a contradiction since S is an optimal solution for $\mathcal{I}_{\text{R-PLTR}}$.

We can prove the NP-hardness for the case of maximizing the score by using the same arguments. In fact, notice that maximizing the score of $c_\star$, i.e., $F(c_\star, S) = |V| + \frac{1}{2}|A|$, is exactly equivalent to maximize the cardinality of the active nodes in LTM. □

4   Approximation Results

In this section we first show that we can approximate the optimal MoV to within a constant factor by optimizing the increment in the score of $c_\star$. In detail we show that, given two solutions S^* and S^{**} such that $g^+(c_\star, S^*)$ and $\text{MoV}(S^{**})$ are maximum, then $\text{MoV}(S^*) \geq \frac{1}{3}\text{MoV}(S^{**})$. Indeed, we show a more general statement that is: If a solution S approximates $g^+(c_\star, S^*)$ within a factor α, then $\text{MoV}(S) \geq \frac{\alpha}{3}\text{MoV}(S^{**})$.

Then we show that a simple greedy hill-climbing approach (Algorithm 1) gives a constant factor approximation to the problem of maximizing $g^+(c_\star, S)$, where the constant is $\frac{1}{2}(1 - \frac{1}{e})$. By combining the two results, we get a $\frac{1}{6}(1 - \frac{1}{e})$-approximation algorithm for the election control problem in R-PLTR. The next theorem generalizes [20, Theorem 5.2] as it holds for any scoring rule and for any model in which we have the ability to change only the position of $c_\star$ in the lists of a subset of voters and the increment in score of $c_\star$ is at least equal to the decrement in scoring of the other candidates.

Theorem 3. *An α-approximation algorithm for maximizing the increment in score of a target candidate gives an $\frac{\alpha}{3}$-approximation to the election control problem.*

Proof. Let us consider two solutions S and S^* for the problem of maximizing the MoV for candidate $c_\star$, with S^* as the optimal solution to this problem. These solutions arbitrarily select a subset of voters and modify their preference list changing the score of $c_\star$. Let us fix c and $\hat{c}$, respectively, as the candidates different from $c_\star$ with the highest score before and after the solution S is applied. Assume there exists an α-approximation to the problem of maximizing the increment in score of the target candidate; if we do not consider the gain given by the score lost by the most voted opponent, we have that

$$\text{MoV}(S) = g^+(c_\star, S) + g^-(\hat{c}, S) - F(\hat{c}) + F(c) \geq \alpha g^+(c_\star, S^*) - F(\hat{c}) + F(c)$$

$$\geq \frac{\alpha}{3}[g^+(c_\star, S^*) + g^-(\bar{c}, S^*) + g^-(\hat{c}, S^*)] - F(\hat{c}) + F(c),$$

where the last inequality holds because $g^+(c_\star, S) \geq g^-(c_i, S)$ for any solution S and candidate c_i since S modifies only the score of $c_\star$, increasing it, while the score of all the other candidates is decreased, and the increment in score to c^* is equal to the sum of the decrement in score of all the other candidates. Since $F(\hat{c}) \leq F(c)$, we have that

$$\text{MoV}(S) \geq \frac{\alpha}{3}[g^+(c_\star, S^*) + g^-(\bar{c}, S^*) + F(c) + g^-(\hat{c}, S^*) - F(\hat{c}) + F(\bar{c}) - F(\bar{c})]$$

$$= \frac{\alpha}{3}[\text{MoV}(S^*) + g^-(\hat{c}, S^*) - F(\hat{c}) + F(\bar{c})],$$

where $\bar{c}$ is the candidate with the highest score after the solution S^* is applied. By definition of $\bar{c}$ we have that $F(\bar{c}, S^*) \geq F(\hat{c}, S^*)$, which implies that

$$g^-(\bar{c}, S^*) - g^-(\hat{c}, S^*) = F(\bar{c}) - F(\bar{c}, S^*) - F(\hat{c}) + F(\hat{c}, S^*) \leq F(\bar{c}) - F(\hat{c}).$$

Thus, $g^-(\hat{c}, S^*) - F(\hat{c}) + F(\bar{c}) \geq 0$ and we conclude that $\text{MoV}(S) \geq \frac{\alpha}{3}\text{MoV}(S^*)$. $\qquad\square$

Constructive Election Control in R-PLTR. Next theorem shows how to get a constant factor approximation to the problem of maximizing the MoV in R-PLTR by reducing the problem to an instance of the weighted version of the influence maximization problem with LTM [11]. This extension of the LTM, associates to each node a non-negative weight that captures the importance of activating that node. The goal is to find the initial seed set in order to maximize the sum of the weights of the active nodes at the end of the process, i.e., finding $\arg\max_S \sigma_w(S) = \mathbf{E}\left[\sum_{v \in A} w(v)\right]$, where w is a weight function over the node set.

Algorithm 1. GREEDY R-PLTR

Require: Social graph $G = (V, E)$; Budget B
1: $S = \emptyset$; $\hat{G} = (G, w)$ ▷ Weighted graph $\hat{G}$
2: **while** $|S| \leq B$ **do**
3:     $v = \arg\max_{u \in V \setminus S} \sigma_w(S \cup \{u\}) - \sigma_w(S)$
4:     $S = S \cup \{v\}$
5: **return** S

A simple hill-climbing greedy algorithm achieves a $(1 - 1/e)$-approximation if the weights are polynomial (or polynomially small) in the number of nodes of the graph and the number of live-edge graph samples is polynomially large in the weights [11].[3] We exploit this result to approximate the MoV via Algorithm 1, reducing the problem of maximizing the score to that of maximizing $\sigma_w(S)$ in the weighted LTM. We define a new graph $\hat{G}$ with the same sets of nodes and edges of G. Then, we assign a weight to each node $v \in V$ equal to $w(v) := \sum_{u \in N_v^+} b_{vu}(1 - \pi_u(c_\star))$. Note that we are able to correctly approximate the value of $\sigma_w(S)$ using such weights since by hypothesis on the model $b_{uv} \geq \frac{1}{|V|^{\gamma_1}}$, for each $(u, v) \in E$ and for some constant $\gamma_1 > 0$, and since $\pi_v(c_i) \geq \frac{1}{|V|^{\gamma_2}}$, for each $v \in V$ for some constant $\gamma_2 > 0$. By applying a multiplicative form of the Chernoff bound we can get a $1 \pm \epsilon$ approximation of $\sigma_w(S)$, with high probability [11, Proposition 4.1].

Thus, we can use Algorithm 1 to maximize the influence on $\hat{G}$. The algorithm starts with an empty set S and adds to it, in each of B rounds, the node v with maximal marginal gain w.r.t. the solution computed so far.

Theorem 4. *Algorithm 1 guarantees a $\frac{1}{6}(1 - \frac{1}{e})$-approximation factor to constructive election control in R-PLTR.*

Proof. We first prove that Algorithm 1 gives an $\frac{1}{2}(1 - \frac{1}{e})$-approximation to the problem of maximizing the increment in score of the target candidate $c_\star$ in

---

[3] It is still an open question how well the value of $\sigma_w(S)$ can be approximated for an influence model with arbitrary node weights.

R-PLTR. Let S and $S^\star$ respectively be the set of initial seed nodes found by the greedy algorithm and the optimal one. We have that

$$g^+(c_\star, S) = \sum_{v \in V} \frac{(1 - \pi_v(c_\star)) \sum_{u \in A \cap N_v^-} b_{uv}}{1 + \sum_{u \in A \cap N_v^-} b_{uv}}$$

and, since the denominator is at most 2, that

$$g^+(c_\star, S) \geq \frac{1}{2} \sum_{v \in V} (1 - \pi_v(c_\star)) \sum_{u \in A \cap N_v^-} b_{uv} = \frac{1}{2} \sum_{u \in A} \sum_{v \in N_u^+} b_{uv}(1 - \pi_v(c_\star)),$$

where A is the set of active nodes at the end of the process.

Note that $\sum_{u \in A} \sum_{v \in N_u^+} b_{uv}(1 - \pi_v(c_\star))$ is exactly the objective function that the greedy algorithm maximizes. Hence, we know that

$$\sum_{u \in A} \sum_{v \in N_u^+} b_{uv}(1 - \pi_v(c_\star)) \geq (1 - 1/e) \sum_{u \in A^\star} \sum_{v \in N_u^+} b_{uv}(1 - \pi_v(c_\star)),$$

where $A^\star$ is the set of active nodes at the end of the process starting from $S^\star$.

Therefore $g^+(c_\star, S) \geq \frac{1}{2}(1 - 1/e)\, g^+(c_\star, S^\star)$ since

$$g^+(c_\star, S^\star) = \sum_{v \in V} \frac{(1 - \pi_v(c_\star)) \sum_{u \in A^\star \cap N_v^-} b_{uv}}{1 + \sum_{u \in A^\star \cap N_v^-} b_{uv}} \leq \sum_{u \in A^\star} \sum_{v \in N_u^+} b_{uv}(1 - \pi_v(c_\star)),$$

where the inequality holds since all the denominators in $g^+(c_\star, S^\star)$ are at least 1. Thus, Algorithm 1 achieves a $\frac{1}{2}\left(1 - \frac{1}{e}\right)$-approximation to the maximum increment in score. Using Theorem 3 we get a $\frac{1}{6}\left(1 - \frac{1}{e}\right)$-approximation for the MoV. $\square$

Destructive Election Control in R-PLTR. The *destructive election control* problem is similar to the constructive problem, but in this scenario, in our models, the probability that a voter v votes for $c_\star$ *decreases* depending on the amount of influence received by v and the loss of probability of $c_\star$ is evenly split over all the other candidates. In this way, we avoid negative values and values that do not sum to 1. In detail, if A is the set of active nodes at the end of LTM, then, for each $v \in V$, the preference list π_v changes as follows:

$$\tilde{\pi}_v(c_\star) = \frac{\pi_v(c_\star)}{1 + \sum_{u \in A \cap N_v^-} b_{uv}} \quad \text{and} \quad \tilde{\pi}_v(c_i) = \frac{\pi_v(c_i) + \frac{1}{m-1} \sum_{u \in A \cap N_v^-} b_{uv}}{1 + \sum_{u \in A \cap N_v^-} b_{uv}}$$

for each $c_i \neq c_\star$. We define MoV_D, i.e., what we want to maximize, as

$$\text{MoV}_D(S) := F(\hat{c}, S) - F(c_\star, S) - (F(c, \emptyset) - F(c_\star, \emptyset)) = g^-(c_\star, S) + g^+(\hat{c}, S) + \Delta,$$

where S is the initial set of seed nodes and $\Delta = F(\hat{c}, \emptyset) - F(c, \emptyset)$ is the sum of constant terms that are not modified by the process. Note that maximizing MoV_D is NP-hard (it can be proved with a similar argument to that of Theorem 2).

Similarly to the constructive case, we define a new graph $\hat{G}$ with the same sets of nodes and edges of G. Then, we assign a weight to each node $v \in V$ equal to $w(v) := \sum_{u \in N_v^+} b_{vu} \pi_u(c_\star)$ and we run Algorithm 1 to find a seed set that approximates the maximum expected weight of active nodes.

Theorem 5. *Algorithm 1 guarantees a $\frac{1}{4}(1 - \frac{1}{e})$-approximation factor to the destructive election control in R-PLTR.*

References

1. Abouei Mehrizi, M., D'Angelo, G.: Multi-winner election control via social influence. In: Richa, A., Scheideler, C. (eds.) SIROCCO 2020. LNCS, vol. 12156, pp. 331–348. Springer, Cham (2020). https://doi.org/10.1007/978-3-030-54921-3_19
2. Allcott, H., Gentzkow, M.: Social media and fake news in the 2016 election. J. Econ. Perspect. **31**(2), 211–36 (2017)
3. Apt, K.R., Markakis, E.: Social networks with competing products. Fundam. Inform. **129**(3), 225–250 (2014). https://doi.org/10.3233/FI-2014-970
4. Bond, R.M., et al.: A 61-million-person experiment in social influence and political mobilization. Nature **489**, 295 (2012). https://doi.org/10.1038/nature11421
5. Bredereck, R., Elkind, E.: Manipulating opinion diffusion in social networks. In: IJCAI, pp. 894–900 (2017). https://doi.org/10.24963/ijcai.2017/124
6. Corò, F., Cruciani, E., D'Angelo, G., Ponziani, S.: Exploiting social influence to control elections based on scoring rules. In: IJCAI, pp. 201–207, July 2019. https://doi.org/10.24963/ijcai.2019/29
7. Corò, F., Cruciani, E., D'Angelo, G., Ponziani, S.: Vote for me! Election control via social influence in arbitrary scoring rule voting systems. In: AAMAS, pp. 1895–1897 (2019). http://dl.acm.org/citation.cfm?id=3306127.3331955
8. Faliszewski, P., Gonen, R., Koutecký, M., Talmon, N.: Opinion diffusion and campaigning on society graphs. In: IJCAI, pp. 219–225 (2018). https://doi.org/10.24963/ijcai.2018/30
9. Faliszewski, P., Rothe, J.: Control and bribery in voting. In: Handbook of Computational Social Choice, pp. 146–168. Cambridge University Press (2016). https://doi.org/10.1017/CBO9781107446984.008
10. Ferrara, E.: Disinformation and social bot operations in the run up to the 2017 french presidential election. First Monday **22**(8) (2017). http://firstmonday.org/ojs/index.php/fm/article/view/8005
11. Kempe, D., Kleinberg, J.M., Tardos, É.: Maximizing the spread of influence through a social network. Theory Comput. **11**, 105–147 (2015)
12. Kreiss, D.: Seizing the moment: the presidential campaigns' use of twitter during the 2012 electoral cycle. New Media Soc. **18**(8), 1473–1490 (2016)
13. Li, Y., Fan, J., Wang, Y., Tan, K.L.: Influence maximization on social graphs: a survey. IEEE Trans. Knowl. Data Eng. **30**(10), 1852–1872 (2018)
14. Manurangsi, P.: Almost-polynomial ratio ETH-hardness of approximating densest k-subgraph. In: STOC, pp. 954–961 (2017). https://doi.org/10.1145/3055399.3055412

15. Matsa, K.E., Shearer, E.: News use across social media platforms 2018. Pew Research Center (2018). http://www.journalism.org/2018/09/10/news-use-across-social-media-platforms-2018/. Accessed 9 Feb 2019

16. Nemhauser, G.L., Wolsey, L.A., Fisher, M.L.: An analysis of approximations for maximizing submodular set functions–I. Math. Program. **14**(1), 265–294 (1978). https://doi.org/10.1007/BF01588971

17. Pennycook, G., Cannon, T., Rand, D.G.: Prior exposure increases perceived accuracy of fake news. J. Exp. Psychol. Gen. **147**(12), 1865–1880 (2018)

18. Raghavendra, P., Steurer, D.: Graph expansion and the unique games conjecture. In: STOC, pp. 755–764 (2010). https://doi.org/10.1145/1806689.1806792

19. Stier, S., Bleier, A., Lietz, H., Strohmaier, M.: Election campaigning on social media: politicians, audiences, and the mediation of political communication on facebook and twitter. Polit. Commun. **35**(1), 50–74 (2018). https://doi.org/10.1080/10584609.2017.1334728

20. Wilder, B., Vorobeychik, Y.: Controlling elections through social influence. In: AAMAS, pp. 265–273 (2018). http://dl.acm.org/citation.cfm?id=3237428

k-Critical Graphs in P_5-Free Graphs

Kathie Cameron[1], Jan Goedgebeur[2,3], Shenwei Huang[4(✉)], and Yongtang Shi[5]

[1] Department of Mathematics, Wilfrid Laurier University,
Waterloo, ON N2L 3C5, Canada
kcameron@wlu.ca
[2] Department of Applied Mathematics,
Computer Science and Statistics,
Ghent University, 9000 Ghent, Belgium
[3] Computer Science Department,
University of Mons, 7000 Mons, Belgium
Jan.Goedgebeur@UGent.be
[4] College of Computer Science,
Nankai University, Tianjin 300350, China
shenweihuang@nankai.edu.cn
[5] Center for Combinatorics and LPMC,
Nankai University, Tianjin 300071, China
shi@nankai.edu.cn

Abstract. Given two graphs H_1 and H_2, a graph G is (H_1, H_2)-free if it contains no induced subgraph isomorphic to H_1 or H_2. Let P_t be the path on t vertices. A graph G is k-vertex-critical if G has chromatic number k but every proper induced subgraph of G has chromatic number less than k. The study of k-vertex-critical graphs for graph classes is an important topic in algorithmic graph theory because if the number of such graphs that are in a given hereditary graph class is finite, then there is a polynomial-time algorithm to decide if a graph in the class is $(k-1)$-colorable. In this paper, we initiate a systematic study of the finiteness of k-vertex-critical graphs in subclasses of P_5-free graphs. Our main result is a complete classification of the finiteness of k-vertex-critical graphs in the class of (P_5, H)-free graphs for all graphs H on 4 vertices. To obtain the complete dichotomy, we prove the finiteness for four new graphs H using various techniques – such as Ramsey-type arguments and the dual of Dilworth's Theorem – that may be of independent interest.

1 Introduction

All graphs in this paper are finite and simple. We say that a graph G *contains* a graph H if H is isomorphic to an induced subgraph of G. A graph G is *H-free* if it does not contain H. For a family of graphs $\mathcal{H}$, G is $\mathcal{H}$-free if G is H-free for every $H \in \mathcal{H}$. When $\mathcal{H}$ consists of two graphs, we write (H_1, H_2)-free instead of $\{H_1, H_2\}$-free. As usual, P_t and C_s denote the path on t vertices and the cycle on s vertices, respectively. The complete graph on n vertices is denoted by K_n. The graph K_3 is also referred to as the *triangle*. For two graphs G and H, we

© Springer Nature Switzerland AG 2020
D. Kim et al. (Eds.): COCOON 2020, LNCS 12273, pp. 411–422, 2020.
https://doi.org/10.1007/978-3-030-58150-3_33

use $G + H$ to denote the *disjoint union* of G and H. For a positive integer r, we use rG to denote the disjoint union of r copies of G. The *complement* of G is denoted by $\overline{G}$. A *clique* (resp. *independent set*) in a graph is a set of pairwise adjacent (resp. nonadjacent) vertices. If a graph G can be partitioned into k independent sets $S_1, \ldots, S_k$ such that there is an edge between every vertex in S_i and every vertex in S_j for all $1 \leq i < j \leq k$, G is called a *complete k-partite graph*; each S_i is called a *part* of G. If we do not specify the number of parts in G, we simply say that G is a *complete multipartite graph*. We denote by $K_{n_1, \ldots, n_k}$ the complete k-partite graph such that the ith part S_i has size n_i, for each $1 \leq i \leq k$. A *q-coloring* of a graph G is a function $\phi : V(G) \longrightarrow \{1, \ldots, q\}$ such that $\phi(u) \neq \phi(v)$ whenever u and v are adjacent in G. Equivalently, a q-coloring of G is a partition of $V(G)$ into q independent sets. A graph is *q-colorable* if it admits a q-coloring. The *chromatic number* of a graph G, denoted by $\chi(G)$, is the minimum number q for which G is q-colorable. The *clique number* of G, denoted by $\omega(G)$, is the size of a largest clique in G.

A graph G is *k-chromatic* if $\chi(G) = k$. We say that G is *k-critical* if it is k-chromatic and $\chi(G - e) < \chi(G)$ for any edge $e \in E(G)$. For instance, K_2 is the only 2-critical graph and odd cycles are the only 3-critical graphs. A graph is *critical* if it is k-critical for some integer $k \geq 1$. Critical graphs were first defined and studied by Dirac [11–13] in the early 1950s, and then by Gallai and Ore [15,16,29] among many others, and more recently by Kostochka and Yancey [24]. A weaker notion of criticality is the so-called vertex-criticality. A graph G is *k-vertex-critical* if $\chi(G) = k$ and $\chi(G - v) < k$ for any $v \in V(G)$. For a set $\mathcal{H}$ of graphs and a graph G, we say that G is *k-vertex-critical $\mathcal{H}$-free* if it is k-vertex-critical and $\mathcal{H}$-free. We are mainly interested in the following question.

The meta question. Given a set $\mathcal{H}$ of graphs and an integer $k \geq 1$, are there only finitely many k-vertex-critical $\mathcal{H}$-free graphs?

This question is important in the study of algorithmic graph theory because of the following theorem.

Theorem 1 (Folklore). *Given a set $\mathcal{H}$ of graphs and an integer $k \geq 1$, if the set of all k-vertex-critical $\mathcal{H}$-free graphs is finite, then there is a polynomial-time algorithm to determine whether an $\mathcal{H}$-free graph is $(k-1)$-colorable.*

In this paper, we study k-vertex-critical graphs in the class of P_5-free graphs. Our research is mainly motivated by the following two results.

Theorem 2 ([21]). *For any fixed $k \geq 5$, there are infinitely many k-vertex-critical P_5-free graphs.*

Theorem 3 ([3,26]). *There are exactly 12 4-vertex-critical P_5-free graphs.*

In light of Theorem 2 and Theorem 3, it is natural to ask which subclasses of P_5-free graphs have finitely many k-vertex-critical graphs for $k \geq 5$. For example, it was known that there are exactly 13 5-vertex-critical (P_5, C_5)-free graphs [21], and that there are finitely many 5-vertex-critical (P_5, banner)-free graphs [4,22], and finitely many k-vertex-critical $(P_5, \overline{P_5})$-free graphs for every fixed k [9]. Hell and Huang proved that there are finitely many k-vertex-critical (P_6, C_4)-free graphs [19]. This was later generalized to $(P_t, K_{r,s})$-free graphs in the context of H-coloring [23]. Apart from these, there seem to be very few results on the finiteness of k-vertex-critical graphs for $k \geq 5$. The reason for this, we think, is largely because of the lack of a good characterization of k-vertex-critical graphs. In this paper, we introduce new techniques into the problem and prove some new results beyond 5-vertex-criticality.

1.1   Our Contributions

We initiate a systematic study on the subclasses of P_5-free graphs. In particular, we focus on (P_5, H)-free graphs when H has small number of vertices. If H has at most three vertices, the answer is either trivial or can be easily deduced from known results. So we study the problem for graphs H when H has four vertices. There are 11 graphs on four vertices up to isomorphism:

- K_4 and $\overline{K_4} = 4P_1$;
- $P_2 + 2P_1$ and $\overline{P_2 + 2P_1}$;
- C_4 and $\overline{C_4} = 2P_2$;
- $P_1 + P_3$ and $\overline{P_1 + P_3}$;
- $K_{1,3}$ and $\overline{K_{1,3}} = P_1 + K_3$;
- $P_4 = \overline{P_4}$.

The graphs $\overline{P_2 + 2P_1}$, $\overline{P_1 + P_3}$ and $K_{1,3}$ are usually called *diamond*, *paw* and *claw*, respectively.

One can easily answer our meta question for some graphs H using known results, e.g., Ramsey's Theorem for $4P_1$-free graphs: any k-vertex-critical $(P_5, 4P_1)$-free graph is either K_k or has at most $R(k, 4) - 1$ vertices, where $R(s, t)$ is the Ramsey number, namely the minimum positive integer n such that every graph of order n contains either a clique of size s or an independent set of size t. However, the answer for certain graphs H cannot be directly deduced from known results. In this paper, we prove that there are only finitely many k-vertex-critical (P_5, H)-free graphs for every fixed $k \geq 1$ when H is K_4, or $\overline{P_2 + 2P_1}$, or $P_2 + 2P_1$, or $P_1 + P_3$. (Note that these results do not follow from the finiteness of k-vertex-critical $(P_5, \overline{P_5})$-free graphs proved in [9].) By combining our new results with known results, we obtain a complete classification of the finiteness of k-vertex-critical (P_5, H)-free graphs when H has 4 vertices.

Theorem 4. *Let H be a graph of order 4 and $k \geq 5$ be a fixed integer. Then there are infinitely many k-vertex-critical (P_5, H)-free graphs if and only if H is $2P_2$ or $P_1 + K_3$.*

To obtain the complete classification, we employ various techniques, some of which have not been used before to the best of our knowledge. For $H = K_4$, we use a hybrid approach combining the power of a computer algorithm and mathematical analysis. For $P_1 + P_3$ and $P_2 + 2P_1$, we use the idea of fixed sets (that was first used in [20] to give a polynomial-time algorithm for k-coloring

P_5-free graphs for every fixed k) combined with Ramsey-type arguments and the dual of Dilworth's Theorem. We hope that these techniques could be helpful for attacking other related problems. The remainder of the paper is organized as follows. We present some preliminaries in Sect. 2 and prove our new results in Sect. 3. Finally, we give the proof of Theorem 4 in Sect. 4.

2   Preliminaries

For general graph theory notation we follow [1]. Let $G = (V, E)$ be a graph. If $uv \in E$, we say that u and v are *neighbors* or *adjacent*; otherwise u and v are *nonneighbors* or *nonadjacent*. The *neighborhood* of a vertex v, denoted by $N_G(v)$, is the set of neighbors of v. For a set $X \subseteq V(G)$, let $N_G(X) = \bigcup_{v \in X} N_G(v) \setminus X$. We shall omit the subscript whenever the context is clear. For $X, Y \subseteq V$, we say that X is *complete* (resp. *anticomplete*) to Y if every vertex in X is adjacent (resp. nonadjacent) to every vertex in Y. If $X = \{x\}$, we write "x is complete (resp. anticomplete) to Y" instead of "$\{x\}$ is complete (resp. anticomplete) to Y". If a vertex v is neither complete nor anticomplete to a set S, we say that v is *mixed* on S. We say that H is a *homogeneous set* if no vertex in $V - H$ is mixed on H. A vertex is *universal* in G if it is adjacent to all other vertices. A vertex subset $K \subseteq V$ is a *clique cutset* if $G - K$ has more components than G and K induces a clique. For $S \subseteq V$, the subgraph *induced* by S, is denoted by $G[S]$. A *k-hole* in a graph is an induced cycle H of length $k \geq 4$. If k is odd, we say that H is an *odd hole*. A *k-antihole* in G is a k-hole in $\overline{G}$. Odd antiholes are defined analogously. The graph obtained from C_k by adding a universal vertex, denoted by W_k, is called the *k-wheel*.

List Coloring. Let $[k]$ denote the set $\{1, 2, \ldots, k\}$. A *k-list assignment* of a graph G is a function $L : V(G) \to 2^{[k]}$. The set $L(v)$, for a vertex v in G, is called the *list* of v. In the *list k-coloring* problem, we are given a graph G with a k-list assignment L and asked whether G has an *L-coloring*, i.e., a k-coloring of G such that every vertex is assigned a color from its list. We say that G is *L-colorable* if G has an L-coloring. If the list of every vertex is $[k]$, then the list k-coloring problem is precisely the k-coloring problem.

A common technique in the study of graph coloring is called *propagation*. If a vertex v has its color forced to be $i \in [k]$, then no neighbor of v can be colored with color i. This motivates the following definition. Let (G, L) be an instance of the list k-coloring problem. The color of a vertex v is said to be *forced* if $|L(v)| = 1$. A *propagation from a vertex v with $L(v) = \{i\}$* is the procedure of removing i from the list of every neighbor of v. If we denote the resulting k-list assignment by L', then G is L-colorable if and only if $G - v$ is L'-colorable. A propagation from v could make the color of other vertices forced; if we continue to propagate from those vertices until no propagation is possible, we call the procedure "*exhaustive propagation from v*". It is worth mentioning that the idea of propagation is featured in many recent studies on coloring P_t-free graphs and related problems, see [2,5] for example.

An Example of Propagation. Let G be a 4-vertex path w, x, y, z with $L(w) = \{1\}$, $L(x) = \{1, 2\}$, $L(y) = \{2, 3\}$, and $L(z) = \{1, 2\}$. Then propagation from w results in the new list assignment L' where $L'(x) = \{2\}$ and $L'(v) = L(v)$ for $v \neq x$. On the other hand, exhaustive propagation from w results in the new list assignment L'' where $L''(w) = \{1\}$, $L''(x) = \{2\}$, $L''(y) = \{3\}$, $L''(z) = \{1, 2\}$.

Lemma 1 (Folklore). *Any k-vertex-critical graph cannot contain clique cut-sets.*

Another folklore property of vertex-critical graphs is that such graph cannot contain two nonadjacent vertices u, v such that $N(v) \subseteq N(u)$. We generalize this property to anticomplete subsets.

Lemma 2. *Let G be a k-vertex-critical graph. Then G has no two nonempty disjoint subsets X and Y of $V(G)$ that satisfy all the following conditions.*

- *X and Y are anticomplete to each other.*
- *$\chi(G[X]) \leq \chi(G[Y])$.*
- *Y is complete to $N(X)$.*

Proof. Suppose that G has a pair of nonempty subsets X and Y that satisfy all three conditions. Since G is k-vertex-critical, $G - X$ has a $(k-1)$-coloring ϕ. Let $t = \chi(G[Y])$. Since Y is complete to $N(X)$, at least t colors do not appear on any vertex in $N(X)$ under ϕ. So we can obtain a $(k-1)$-coloring of G by coloring $G[X]$ with those t colors. This contradicts that G is k-chromatic. □

A graph G is *perfect* if $\chi(H) = \omega(H)$ for each induced subgraph H of G. An *imperfect* graph is a graph that is not perfect. A classical theorem of Dilworth [10] states that the largest size of an antichain in a partially ordered set is equal to the minimum number of chains that partition the set. We will use the dual of Dilworth's Theorem which says that the largest size of a chain in a partially ordered set is equal to the minimum number of antichains that partition the set. This was first proved by Mirsky [27] and it has an equivalent graph-theoretic interpretation via comparability graphs. A graph is a *comparability graph* if the vertices of the graph are elements of a partially ordered set and two vertices are connected by an edge if and only if the corresponding elements are comparable.

Theorem 5 (Dual Dilworth Theorem [27]). *Every comparability graph is perfect.*

Theorem 6 (Strong Perfect Graph Theorem [7]). *A graph is perfect if and only if it contains no odd holes or odd antiholes.*

3   New Results

In this section, we prove four new results: there are finitely many k-vertex-critical (P_5, H)-free graphs when $H \in \{K_4, \overline{P_2 + 2P_1}, P_2 + 2P_1, P_1 + P_3\}$.

3.1 $P_1 + P_3$-Free Graphs

Theorem 7. *For every fixed integer $k \geq 1$, there are finitely many k-vertex-critical $P_1 + P_3$-free graphs.*

Proof. Let G be a k-vertex-critical $P_1 + P_3$-free graph. If G contains a K_k, then G is isomorphic to K_k. So we assume in the following that G is K_k-free. Let $K = \{v_1, \ldots, v_t\}$ be a maximal clique, where $1 \leq t < k$. Since K is maximal, every vertex in $V \setminus K$ is not adjacent to at least one vertex in K. We partition $V \setminus K$ into the following subsets.

- F_1 is the set of nonneighbors of v_1.
- For $2 \leq i \leq t$, F_i is the set of nonneighbors of v_i that are not in $F_1 \cup \cdots \cup F_{i-1}$.

By the definition, v_i is complete to F_j if $i < j$. Since G is $P_1 + P_3$-free, each F_i is P_3-free, and so is a disjoint union of cliques.

Claim 1. If F_i has at least two components, then every neighbor of v_i is either complete or anticomplete to F_i.

Proof. Let v be a neighbor of v_i. Suppose that v has a neighbor f in F_i. Let K be the component of F_i containing f. If v is not adjacent to some vertex $f' \in F_i \setminus K$, then $\{f', f, v, v_i\}$ induces a $P_1 + P_3$, a contradiction. So v is complete to $F_i \setminus K$. Since F_i has at least two components, v has a neighbor in a component other than K. It follows from the same argument that v is complete to K. This completes the proof. □

Claim 2. For every nonneighbor v of v_i and every component K of F_i, v is either complete or anticomplete to K.

Proof. If v is mixed on an edge xy in K, then $\{v, v_i, x, y\}$ induces a $P_1 + P_3$, a contradiction. □

By Claim 1 and Claim 2, if F_i has at least two components, every component of F_i is a homogeneous set of G. Moreover, since v_i is complete to F_j for $i < j$, no vertex in $\{v_j\} \cup F_j$ with $j > i$ is mixed on two components of F_i. We next show that each F_i has bounded size.

Claim 3. $|F_1| \leq k$.

Proof. We show that F_1 is connected. Suppose not. Let K and K' be two component of F_1 with $|K| \leq |K'|$. Then $N(K) = N(K')$. By Lemma 2, G is not k-vertex-critical. This is a contradiction. Therefore, F_1 is a clique and so has at most k vertices. □

Claim 4. For each $1 \leq i \leq t$, F_i has bounded size.

Proof. We prove this by induction on i. By Claim 3, the statement is true for $i = 1$. Now assume that $i \geq 2$ and F_j has bounded size for each $1 \leq j < i$. If F_i is connected, then $|F_i| \leq k$ and we are done. So we assume that F_i has at least two components. We will show that the number of components in F_i is bounded and this will complete the proof. For this purpose, we construct a graph X as follows.

- $V(X)$ is the set of all components of F_i.
- Two components K and K' of F_i are connected by an edge in X if and only if $N(K) \subseteq N(K')$ or $N(K') \subseteq N(K)$.

Note that X is a comparability graph. Next we show that $\omega(X) \leq k$. Suppose that $K_1, \ldots, K_t$ is a maximum clique in X with $t > k$. We may assume that $N(K_1) \subseteq N(K_2) \subseteq \cdots \subseteq N(K_t)$. It follows from Lemma 2 that $|K_i| > |K_j|$ for $i < j$, i.e., $|K_1| > |K_2| > \cdots > |K_t| \geq 1$. So $|K_1| \geq k$. This is a contradiction, since G is K_k-free. This proves that $\omega(X) \leq k$. Since X is perfect by Theorem 5, $V(X)$ can be partitioned into at most k independent sets $S_1, \ldots, S_k$. We show that each S_p has bounded size. Let K and K' be two components in S_p. Then there are vertices x and x' such that $x \in N(K) \setminus N(K')$ and $x' \in N(K') \setminus N(K)$. Note that $x, x' \in T_i = \bigcup_{1 \leq j < i} F_j \cup \{v_j\}$. If $|S_p| > 2|T_i|^2$, by the pigeonhole principle, there are two pairs $\{K, K'\}$ and $\{L, L'\}$ of components that correspond to the same pair $\{x, x'\}$ in T_i. Then $\{K, x, L, K'\}$ induces a $P_1 + P_3$. This shows that each S_p has size at most $2|T_i|^2$, which is a constant by the inductive hypothesis. Therefore, X has constant number of vertices, i.e., F_i has constant number of components. This completes the proof. □

By Claim 3 and Claim 4, each $|F_i| \leq M$ for some constant M (depending only on k). Therefore, G has bounded size. □

3.2 $P_2 + 2P_1$-Free and Diamond-Free Graphs

Theorem 8. *For every fixed integer $k \geq 1$, there are finitely many k-vertex-critical (P_5, P_2+2P_1)-free graphs and k-vertex-critical $(P_5$, diamond$)$-free graphs.*

Due to page limits we omit the proof of Theorem 8.

3.3 K_4-Free Graphs

Let G_1 be the 13-vertex graph with vertex set $\{0, 1, \ldots, 12\}$ and the following edges: $\{3, 4, 5, 6, 7\}$ and $\{0, 1, 2, 8, 9\}$ induce two disjoint 5-holes Q and Q'; 12 is complete to $Q \cup Q'$; 11 is complete to Q and 10 is complete to Q' with 10 and 11 being connected by an edge. Let G_2 be the 14-vertex graph with vertex set $\{0, 1, \ldots, 13\}$ and the following edges: $\{12, 13\}$ is a cutset of G_2 such that 12 and 13 are not adjacent and $G_2 - \{12, 13\}$ has exactly two components; one component of $G_2 - \{12, 13\}$ is a 5-hole induced by $\{0, 1, 2, 3, 4\}$, and this 5-hole is complete to $\{12, 13\}$; the other component, induced by $\{5, 6, 7, 8, 9, 10, 11\}$, is the graph in Fig. 1, and 12 is complete to $\{5, 8, 9, 10, 11\}$ and 13 is complete to $\{6, 7, 9, 10, 11\}$.

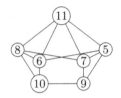

Fig. 1. One component of $G_2 - \{12, 13\}$.

It is routine to verify that G_1 and G_2 are 5-vertex-critical (P_5, K_4)-free graphs. The main result in this subsection is that they are the only 5-vertex-critical (P_5, K_4)-free graphs.

Theorem 9. *Let G be a 5-vertex-critical (P_5, K_4)-free graph. Then G is isomorphic to either G_1 or G_2.*

The next two lemmas are based on a computer generation approach to exhaustively generate all k-vertex-critical graphs in a given class of $\mathcal{H}$-free graphs via a recursive algorithm. The idea of computer generation was first used in [21], and later developed extensively by Goedgebeur and Schaudt [18] and Chudnovsky et al. [6].

We say that G' is a *1-vertex extension* of G if G can be obtained from G' by deleting a vertex in G'. Roughly speaking, the generation algorithm starts with some small substructure which must occur in any k-vertex-critical graph, and then exhaustively searches for all 1-vertex extensions of the substructure. The algorithm stores those extensions that are k-vertex-critical and $\mathcal{H}$-free in the output list $\mathcal{F}$. Then it recursively repeats the procedure for all $(k-1)$-colorable substructures found in the previous iterations. The pseudocode of the generation algorithm is given in Algorithm 1 and Algorithm 2.

Algorithm 1: Generate(k, $\mathcal{H}$, S)

Input: An integer k, a set $\mathcal{H}$ of forbidden induced subgraphs, and a
      graph S.
Output: A list $\mathcal{F}$ of all k-vertex-critical $\mathcal{H}$-free graphs containing S.
1 Let $\mathcal{F}$ be an empty list.
2 Extend(S).
3 Return $\mathcal{F}$.

Algorithm 2: Extend(G)

---

1   **if** G is $\mathcal{H}$-free and is not generated before **then**
2   **if** $\chi(G) \geq k$ **then**
3   **if** G is k-vertex-critical **then**
4 | add G to $\mathcal{F}$
5   **end**
6   **end**
7   **else**
8   **for** each valid 1-vertex extension G' of G **do**
9 | Extend(G')
10   **end**
11   **end**
12 **end**

It should be noted that with a naive implementation the algorithm may not terminate. For instance, if we extend a graph G by repeatedly adding vertices that have the same neighborhood as some vertex in G, the program will never terminate. So one has to design certain pruning rules to make the algorithm terminate. For instance, if G contains two nonadjacent vertices u, v such that $N(u) \subseteq N(v)$, then we only need to consider all 1-vertex extensions G' such that the unique vertex in $V(G') \setminus V(G)$ is adjacent to u but not adjacent to v (by Lemma 2). In [21], the authors designed two pruning rules like this so that the algorithm terminates with 13 5-vertex-critical (P_5, C_5)-free graphs. Later, the technique was extensively developed by Goedgebeur and Schaudt [18] who introduced many more useful pruning rules that are essential for generating all critical graphs in certain classes of graphs, e.g., 4-vertex-critical (P_7, C_4)-free graphs and 4-vertex-critical (P_8, C_4)-free graphs. The word "valid" in Algorithm 2 is used precisely to quantify those extensions that survive a specific set of pruning rules.

The algorithm we use in this paper is exactly the one developed in [18]. Hence, the valid extensions on line 8 in Extend(G) are with respect to all pruning rules given in Algorithm 2 in [18] (since we only use those rules as a black box, we do not define them here [17]).

Theorem 10 ([18]). *If Algorithm 1 terminates and returns the list $\mathcal{F}$, then $\mathcal{F}$ is exactly the set of all k-vertex-critical $\mathcal{H}$-free graphs containing S.*

Let F be the graph obtained from a 5-hole by adding a new vertex and making it adjacent to four vertices on the hole.

Lemma 3. *Let G be a 5-vertex-critical (P_5, K_4)-free graph. If G contains an induced W_5 or F, then G is isomorphic to either G_1 or G_2.*

Proof. We run Algorithm 1 with the following inputs: $k = 5$, $\mathcal{H} = \{P_5, K_4\}$ and $S = W_5$ or $S = F$. If $S = W_5$, then the algorithm terminates with the graphs G_1 and G_2, and if $S = F$, then it terminates with only the graph G_2. The correctness of the algorithm follows from Theorem 10.   □

Lemma 4. *Let G be a 5-vertex-critical (P_5, K_4)-free graph. If G is 7-antihole-free, then G is isomorphic to G_1.*

Proof. It was proved in [8] that G must contain a 5-hole. We run Algorithm 1 with the following inputs: $k = 5$, $\mathcal{H} = \{P_5, K_4, \overline{C_7}\}$ and $S = C_5$. The algorithm terminates and outputs G_1 as the only critical graph. The correctness of the algorithm follows from Theorem 10.   □

Lemma 5. *Let G be a (P_5, K_4, W_5, F)-free graph. If G contains an 7-antihole, then G is 4-colorable.*

Due to page limits we omit the proof of Lemma 5. We are now ready to prove Theorem 9.

Proof (Proof of Theorem 9). Let G be a 5-vertex-critical (P_5, K_4)-free graph. If G contains an induced W_5 or F, then G is either G_1 or G_2 by Lemma 3. So we can assume that G is (W_5, F)-free as well. By Lemma 5, G must be 7-antihole-free, and so is G_1 by Lemma 4.   □

4   A Complete Classification

Proof (Proof of Theorem 4). An infinite family of 5-vertex-critical $2P_2$-free graphs is constructed in [21]. It can be easily checked that these graphs are $P_1 + K_3$-free. Since $2P_2$ and $P_1 + K_3$ do not contain any universal vertices, for every fixed $k \geq 6$ one can obtain an infinite family of k-vertex-critical $2P_2$-free graphs and $(P_5, P_1 + K_3)$-free graphs by adding $k - 5$ universal vertices to the 5-vertex-critical family in [21].

Now assume that H is not $2P_2$ or $P_1 + K_3$. Let G be a k-vertex-critical (P_5, H)-free graph. We may assume that G is K_k-free for otherwise G is K_k. If $H = 4P_1$, then Ramsey's theorem [30] shows that $|G| \leq R(4, k) - 1$. If $H = K_4$, then there are no k-vertex-critical (P_5, K_4)-free graphs for any $k \geq 6$ [14]. Moreover, there are only two 5-vertex-critical (P_5, K_4)-free graphs by Theorem 9. If H is a diamond or $P_2 + 2P_1$, then the finiteness follows from Theorem 8. If $H = C_4$, then the finiteness follows from [19]. If $H = P_4$, then G is perfect and so $(k - 1)$-colorable, a contradiction. If H is a claw, then the finiteness follows from [25]. If H is $P_1 + P_3$, then the finiteness follows from Theorem 7. If H is a paw, then G is either triangle-free or a complete multipartite graph by a result of Olariu [28]. In either case, G is $(k - 1)$-colorable, a contradiction.   □

In view of Theorem 4, it is natural to ask the following question, which we leave as a possible future direction.

Problem. Which five-vertex graphs H could lead to finitely many k-vertex-critical (P_5, H)-free graphs?

As mentioned in the introduction, it was shown in [9] that $H = \overline{P_5}$ is one such graph.

Acknowledgment. Kathie Cameron is supported by the Natural Sciences and Engineering Research Council of Canada (NSERC) grant RGPIN-2016-06517. Jan Goedgebeur is supported by a Postdoctoral Fellowship of the Research Foundation Flanders (FWO). Shenwei Huang is partially supported by the National Natural Science Foundation of China (11801284) and the Fundamental Research Funds for the Central Universities, Nankai University. Yongtang Shi is partially supported by the National Natural Science Foundation of China (Nos. 11771221, 11922112) and the Fundamental Research Funds for the Central Universities, Nankai University.

References

1. Bondy, J.A., Murty, U.S.R.: Graph Theory. Springer, Cham (2018)
2. Bonomo, F., Chudnovsky, M., Maceli, P., Schaudt, O., Stein, M., Zhong, M.: Three-coloring and list three-coloring of graphs without induced paths on seven vertices. Combinatorica **38**, 779–801 (2018)
3. Bruce, D., Hoàng, C.T., Sawada, J.: A certifying algorithm for 3-colorability of P_5-free graphs. In: Dong, Y., Du, D.-Z., Ibarra, O. (eds.) ISAAC 2009. LNCS, vol. 5878, pp. 594–604. Springer, Heidelberg (2009). https://doi.org/10.1007/978-3-642-10631-6_61
4. Cai, Q., Huang, S., Li, T., Shi, Y.: Vertex-critical (P_5, banner)-free graphs. In: Frontiers in Algorithmics-13th International Workshop. LNCS, vol. 11458, pp. 111–120 (2019)
5. Chudnovsky, M., Goedgebeur, J., Schaudt, O., Zhong, M.: Obstructions for three-coloring and list three-coloring H-free graphs. SIAM J. Discrete Math. **34**, 431–469 (2020)
6. Chudnovsky, M., Goedgebeur, J., Schaudt, O., Zhong, M.: Obstructions for three-coloring graphs without induced paths on six vertices. J. Combin. Theory, Ser. B **140**, 45–83 (2020)
7. Chudnovsky, M., Robertson, N., Seymour, P., Thomas, R.: The strong perfect graph theorem. Ann. Math. **164**, 51–229 (2006)
8. Chudnovsky, M., Robertson, N., Seymour, P., Thomas, R.: K_4-free graphs with no odd holes. J. Combin. Theory Ser. B **100**, 313–331 (2010)
9. Dhaliwal, H.S., Hamel, A.M., Hoàng, C.T., Maffray, F., McConnell, T.J.D., Panait, S.A.: On color-critical (P_5, co-P_5)-free graphs. Discrete Appl. Math. **216**, 142–148 (2017)
10. Dilworth, R.P.: A decomposition theorem for partially ordered sets. Ann. Math. **51**, 161–166 (1950)
11. Dirac, G.A.: Note on the colouring of graphs. Mathematische Zeitschrift **54**, 347–353 (1951)
12. Dirac, G.A.: A property of 4-chromatic graphs and some remarks on critical graphs. J. London Math. Soc. **27**, 85–92 (1952)
13. Dirac, G.A.: Some theorems on abstract graphs. Proc. London Math. Soc. **2**, 69–81 (1952)
14. Esperet, L., Lemoine, L., Maffray, F., Morel, G.: The chromatic number of $\{P_5, K_4\}$-free graphs. Discrete Math. **313**, 743–754 (2013)
15. Gallai, T.: Kritische graphen I. Publ. Math. Inst. Hungar. Acad. Sci. **8**, 165–92 (1963)
16. Gallai, T.: Kritische graphen II. Publ. Math. Inst. Hungar. Acad. Sci. **8**, 373–395 (1963)

17. Goedgebeur, J.: Homepage of generator for k-critical $\mathcal{H}$-free graphs. https://caagt. ugent.be/criticalpfree/

18. Goedgebeur, J., Schaudt, O.: Exhaustive generation of k-critical $\mathcal{H}$-free graphs. J. Graph Theory **87**, 188–207 (2018)

19. Hell, P., Huang, S.: Complexity of coloring graphs without paths and cycles. Discrete Appl. Math. **216**, 211–232 (2017)

20. Hoàng, C.T., Kamiński, M., Lozin, V.V., Sawada, J., Shu, X.: Deciding k-colorability of P_5-free graphs in polynomial time. Algorithmica **57**, 74–81 (2010)

21. Hoàng, C.T., Moore, B., Recoskiez, D., Sawada, J., Vatshelle, M.: Constructions of k-critical P_5-free graphs. Discrete Appl. Math. **182**, 91–98 (2015)

22. Huang, S., Li, T., Shi, Y.: Critical (P_6, *banner*)-free graphs. Discrete Appl. Math. **258**, 143–151 (2019)

23. Kamiński, M., Pstrucha, A.: Certifying coloring algorithms for graphs without long induced paths. Discrete Appl. Math. **261**, 258–267 (2019)

24. Kostochka, A.V., Yancey, M.: Ore's conjecture on color-critical graphs is almost true. J. Combin. Theory Ser B **109**, 73–101 (2014)

25. Lozin, V.V., Rautenbach, D.: Some results on graphs without long induced paths. Inform. Process. Lett. **88**, 167–171 (2003)

26. Maffray, F., Morel, G.: On 3-colorable P_5-free graphs. SIAM J. Discrete Math. **26**, 1682–1708 (2012)

27. Mirsky, L.: A dual of Dilworth's decomposition theorem. Am. Math. Monthly **78**, 876–877 (1971)

28. Olariu, S.: Paw-free graphs. Inform. Process. Lett. **28**, 53–54 (1988)

29. Ore, O.: The Four Color Problem. Academic Press, Cambridge (1967)

30. Ramsey, F.P.: On a problem of formal logic. Proc. London Math. Soc. **s2–30**, 264–286 (1930)

New Symmetry-less ILP Formulation for the Classical One Dimensional Bin-Packing Problem

Khadija Hadj Salem[1]([✉])[iD] and Yann Kieffer[2]

[1] Université de Tours, LIFAT EA 6300, CNRS, ROOT ERL CNRS 7002,
64 Avenue Jean Portalis, 37200 Tours, France
`khadija.hadj-salem@univ-tours.fr`
[2] Univ. Grenoble Alpes, Grenoble INP, LCIS, 26000 Valence, France
`yann.kieffer@lcis.grenoble-inp.fr`

Abstract. In this article, we address the classical *One-Dimensional Bin Packing Problem* (1D-BPP), an $\mathcal{NP}$-hard combinatorial optimization problem. We propose a new formulation of integer linear programming for the problem, which reduces the search space compared to those described in the literature, as well as two families of cutting planes. Computational experiments are conducted on the data-set found in BPPLib and the results show that it is possible to solve more instances and to decrease the computation time by using our new formulation.

Keywords: Bin packing · Integer linear programming · Cutting plane

1 Introduction

The *one-dimensional Bin Packing Problem*, noted 1D-BPP from here on, is a well studied combinatorial optimization problem, with a rich literature detailing different approaches for its solution. It can be informally defined as follows: n items have to be packed each into one of n available bins. Each item i has a non-negative weight w_i $(i = 1, \ldots, n)$ and all bins have the same positive integer capacity C. The objective is to find a packing with a minimum number of bins such that the total weights of the items in each bin does not exceed the capacity C.

We consider the following example, using a set of bins with capacity $C = 6$, a set of items $i = 1, 2, \ldots, 8$, with weights w_i (given in Table 1). A feasible solution as well as an optimal solution, respectively, with 8 bins and 4 bins, are given in Fig. 1.

A central theme for this study is the computational effect of the removal of symmetric solutions. To the best of our knowledge, no numerical studies have been published to ascertain the performance gain of symmetry breaking constraints for 1D-BPP.

© Springer Nature Switzerland AG 2020
D. Kim et al. (Eds.): COCOON 2020, LNCS 12273, pp. 423–434, 2020.
https://doi.org/10.1007/978-3-030-58150-3_34

Table 1. An example of data, with 8 items

Items i	1	2	3	4	5	6	7	8
Weights w_i	2	2	5	1	2	3	2	4

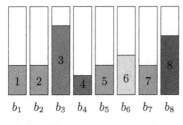

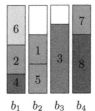

A feasible solution, with 8 bins   An optimal solution, with 4 bins

Fig. 1. Solutions for the 1D-BPP

This article presents our study of a new symmetry-less formulation for 1D-BPP without and with adding cutting planes, and a comparative study of the performances of these two kinds of approaches.

The remainder of this paper is structured as follows. In the next section, we briefly review the exact solution methods for 1D-BPP which rely on integer linear programming. In Sect. 3, we present the new symmetry-less ILP formulation. Sect. 4 is devoted to cutting planes for that formulation. Finally, in Sect. 5, we present computational results obtained by running the proposed formulations on a number of benchmark instances for the 1D-BPP and discuss their performances. Conclusion and perspectives follow in Sect. 6.

2   Previous Work on ILP Formulations for 1D-BPP

2.1   Assignment-Based Models

The compact ILP formulation for 1D-BPP, which Martello and Toth attribute to Kantorovich (see [8]), is the following. Let y_j be a decision variable equal to 1 if bin j is used in the packing, and 0 otherwise, for all $j \in \{1, \ldots, n\}$. Similarly, let x_{ij} be a decision variable equal to 1 if item i is packed into bin j, and 0 otherwise, for all $i \in \{1, \ldots, n\}$ and $j \in \{1, \ldots, n\}$.

The full model, hereafter denoted as ILP-0, is:

$$\text{ILP} - 0: \quad \min \sum_{j=1}^{n} y_j \tag{1}$$

$$
s.t. \begin{cases}
\displaystyle\sum_{j=1}^{n} x_{ij} = 1 & \forall\, i \in \{1, \dots, n\} & (2) \\[3ex]
\displaystyle\sum_{i=1}^{n} w_i * x_{ij} \leq C * y_j & \forall\, j \in \{1, \dots, n\} & (3) \\[3ex]
x_{ij} \in \{0,1\} & \forall\, i \in \{1, \dots, n\},\ j \in \{1, \dots, n\} & (4) \\[1ex]
y_j \in \{0,1\} & \forall\, j \in \{1, \dots, n\} & (5)
\end{cases}
$$

In this formulation, constraints (2) ensure that each item is packed into exactly one bin, constraints (3) impose that the capacity of any used bin is not exceeded and both constraints (4) and (5) define the variable domains.

An obvious lower bound for the 1D-BPP, computable in $\mathcal{O}(n)$ time, is the optimal value of the *continuous relaxation* of ILP-0. This lower bound, usually denoted L_1 in the literature, can be computed by:

$$
L_1 = \left\lceil \sum_{j=1}^{n} w_i / C \right\rceil \tag{6}
$$

It is easily seen that the *worst-case performance ratio* of L_1 is equal to $\frac{1}{2}$ (see, e.g., [9]).

2.2 Other Methods for Optimally Solving the 1D-BPP

Among other methods for solving 1D-BPP exactly, we can find the pseudo-polynomial ILP formulations coming from a graph representation of the solution space and the branching algorithms. An overview of these methods is given in Table 2. More detailed information is provided below.

Table 2. An overview of exact solutions for the 1D-BPP: pseudo-polynomial models & branching algorithms

Methods	Type	Reference	Supported ILP solver
MTP	B&B	Martello and Toth (1990)	Not required
BISON	B&B	Scholl et al. (1997)	Not required
CVRPSEP	B&B	Lysgaard et al. (2004)	Not required
SCIP-BP	B&P	Ryan and Foster (1981)	SCIP[a]
ONECUT	ILP	Dyckhoff (1981)	CPLEX[b]
DPFLOW	ILP	Cambazard and O'Sullivan (2010)	CPLEX, SCIP
SchedILP	ILP	Arbib et al. (2017)	CPLEX

[a]SCIP: Solving Constraint Integer Programs
[b]CPLEX: https://www.ibm.com/analytics/cplex-optimizer

As shown in Table 2, the first four rows describe a set of four enumeration algorithms. Three of them are branch-and-bound algorithms proposed by [8,11] and [7], respectively. The last one is a branch-and-price algorithm in [10]. In the same way, the last two rows give the two algorithms based on a pseudo-polynomial formulations solved through an ILP solver (like CPLEX, SCIP, GUROBI). The first one uses the model proposed by [5]. The second one uses the model proposed by [2]. The third one uses the model proposed by [1]. According to the results discussed in [3], among the approaches based on pseudo-polynomial models, the **DPFLOW** has mainly theoretical interest, but has the advantage of being easily understandable. In the same way, among the enumeration algorithms, the **SCIP-BP** is effective only on small-size instances ($n \leq 100$).

Computer codes of these methods can be found in the BPPLIB, a library dedicated to Bin Packing and Cutting Stock Problems, available at http://or.dei.unibo.it/library/bpplib [4].

3   A Symmetry-less ILP for the 1D-BPP

The study of the topic of symmetry breaking constraints for the classical formulation ILP-0 has led us to the consideration of an alternative encoding, and thus an alternate formulation for the 1D-BPP.

Instead of having variables encoding the membership of *items* in *bins*, this alternate encoding directly encodes a partition of the set of items. Indeed, a solution with k bins to an instance of the 1D-BPP can be seen as a partition of the n items into k parts. The actual parts of the partition are referenced by their smallest-indexed item. Only one set of doubly-indexed variables is necessary for this: in contrast to the ILP-0 formulation, no variable is used to represent the bins.

More precisely, the variable z_{ij} is set to 1 if the lowest-indexed item sharing the same bin as item i is item j, and 0 otherwise, for all $i \in \{1, \ldots, n\}$ and $j \in \{1, \ldots, i\}$. Then $z_{ii} = 1$ if and only if i is the smallest-indexed item in its bin. One can think of bins as labeled by their smallest-indexed item. Hence, counting bins can be achieved by summing the diagonal variables z_{jj}. The set of constraints for this formulation includes all constraints of the classical formulation; only y_j has to be replaced by z_{jj}. We denote by ILP-1 the resulting formulation.

$$\text{ILP} - 1: \quad \min \sum_{j=1}^{n} z_{jj} \tag{7}$$

$$s.t. \begin{cases} \sum_{j=1}^{i} z_{ij} = 1 & \forall\, i \in \{1, \ldots, n\} & (8) \\[2mm] \sum_{i=j}^{n} w_i * z_{ij} \leq C * z_{jj} & \forall\, j \in \{1, \ldots, n\} & (9) \\[2mm] z_{ij} \in \{0, 1\} & \forall\, i \in \{1, \ldots, n\},\, j \in \{1, \ldots, i\} & (10) \end{cases}$$

We now argue that this formulation admits no symmetry at all.

Theorem 1. *There is a one-to-one correspondence between the encodings of feasible solutions for* ILP-1, *and partitions of the items.*

Proof. Given an encoding $z = (z_{ij})_{i,j}$ of a feasible solution, we can recover the parts of the associated partition in this manner: there are as many parts as indices j for which $z_{jj} = 1$ and the set of these parts is $S_j = \{i \in \{j, \ldots, n\} \mid z_{ij} = 1\}$.

Given a partition $\mathcal{P} = (S_j)_{j \in I}$ of $\{1, \ldots, n\}$, the associated encoding is the one described in an earlier part of this section. $\square$

Using the same example given in Sect. 1, the optimal solution to ILP-0 given in Fig. 1 can be encoded as a solution to the formulation ILP-1, as shown in Fig. 2. In this solution, items 5 and 1 are packed in bin 1; items 2, 4 and 6 are packed in bin 2; item 3 is packed in bin 3 and finally items 7 and 8 are packed in bin 7.

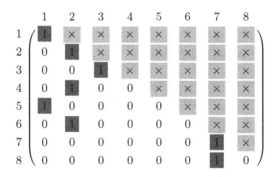

Fig. 2. A corresponding encoding for the optimal solution to ILP-0 using ILP-1

Since the ILP-1 admits no symmetry, one can expect that the solution of ILP-1 instances has better performance than equivalent ILP-0 instances of 1D-BPP. An empirical evaluation of that statement is actually part of the study that we report on in Sect. 5.

Another quality of formulation ILP-1 is that it is a strict ILP formulation, and it is compact. Hence, wherever an ILP formulation P includes a BPP-like set of constraints, akin to those found in ILP-0, these constraints can be replaced by those in ILP-1 while retaining other constraints, resulting in a new formation P'. Wherever ILP-1 improves upon ILP-0, such a reformulated P' may supposedly improve upon the original P.

This quality is not shared by other 1D-BPP reformulations as ILP such as are the state of the art today, since they depart further from the original encoding ILP-0, and also have a number of inequalities that is not polynomially bounded in the number of items.

4   Cutting Plane Constraints for the ILP-1 Formulation

We now introduce two families of constraints:

$$z_{jk} + z_{ij} \leq 1 \quad \forall \, i \in \{1,\ldots,n\}, \; j \in \{1,\ldots,i-1\}, \; k \in \{1,\ldots,j-1\} \quad \text{(C1)}$$

$$\sum_{k=1}^{j-1} z_{jk} + z_{ij} \leq 1 \qquad\qquad \forall \, i \in \{1,\ldots,n\}, \; j \in \{1,\ldots,i-1\} \quad \text{(C2)}$$

We will now prove in several steps that these two sets of inequalities are actually cutting planes for the ILP-1 formulation.

Proposition 1. *The inequalities (C2) are valid for the ILP-1 formulation.*

Proof. Consider a feasible solution x for ILP-1, and let i in $\{1,\ldots,n\}$, and k in $\{i+1,\ldots,n\}$. We distinguish two cases according to the value of z_{ij}.

- First we consider the case $z_{ij} = 0$. Then $\sum_{k=1}^{j-1} z_{jk} \leq \sum_{k=1}^{j} z_{jk} = 1$, as a consequence of constraint (8). So $\sum_{k=1}^{j-1} z_{jk} \leq 1$, and also $\sum_{k=1}^{j-1} z_{jk} + z_{ij} \leq 1$.
- In the case where $z_{ij} = 1$, we will first prove that $z_{jk} = 0$ for all $k < j$. Since $z_{ij} = 1$, the constraint (10) forces z_{jj} to equal 1. But then, according to constraint (9), all the z_{jk} for $k < j$ must equal 0. So $\sum_{k=1}^{j-1} z_{jk} = 0$, and hence $\sum_{k=1}^{j-1} z_{jk} + z_{ij} \leq 1$.

$\square$

Proposition 2. *Let i be in $\{1,\ldots,n\}$, j be in $\{1,\ldots,i-1\}$, and k be in $\{1,\ldots,j-1\}$. The inequality (C2) is stronger than the inequality (C1), when considered as reinforcements to the formulation ILP-1.*

Proof. In order to prove the statement, we will derive inequality (C1) from (C2). Assume (C2) holds, then:

$$z_{jk} + z_{ij} \leq \sum_{l=1}^{j-1} z_{jl} + z_{ij} \leq 1$$

where the first inequality holds, because in ILP-1, all variables are assumed to be positive. $\square$

Proposition 3. *The inequality (C1) is a valid inequality for the ILP-1 formulation.*

Proof. This is the consequence of Propositions 1 and 2. $\square$

Proposition 4. *There exist fractional solutions of* ILP-1 *that are separated by inequalities (C1) and (C2).*

Proof. We need to consider an instance of 1D-BPP such that there exists α with $1/2 < \alpha < 1$ and $w_1 + \alpha w_2 \leq C$.

Then the following is a feasible solution of the relaxation of ILP-1: set $z_{21} = z_{32} = \alpha$; $z_{22} = z_{33} = 1 - \alpha$; $z_{ii} = 1$ for all i in $\{1, 4, 5, \ldots, n\}$; and $z_{ij} = 0$ for all other variables of the formulation.

This solution is represented in Fig. 3. Please note that the meaningful values all lie in the first three rows.

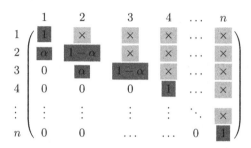

Fig. 3. A feasible solution to the relaxation of ILP-1 that is cut by (C1)

Equations (8) are obviously satisfied by z. The inequality (8) holds because of the hypothesis we made for the case $j = 1$; because $(1 - \alpha)w_2 + \alpha w_3 \leq max(w_2, w_3) \leq C$ for the case $j = 2$; and trivially holds for all the other cases.

But the inequalities (C1) will cut that point, namely z does not satisfy $z_{21} + z_{32} \leq 1$, since $\alpha + \alpha = 2\alpha > 1$.

Since the inequalities (C2) are stronger than (C1), these too are cuts for ILP-1. □

The number of inequalities in (C1) is $O(n^3)$, while it is $O(n^2)$ for (C2). Since (C2) inequalities are both much fewer and stronger than (C1), it seems that their use for performance improvement should be favored over (C1). In Section 5, we study empirically the performance benefits of adding one or the other of these families of inequalities.

5   Computational Experiments and Discussion

In this section, we analyze the performance of the new formulation ILP-1 without and with adding cutting planes. Our experiments were motivated by the following goals: comparing the number of optimally solved instances and the run-time performances of our formulation ILP-1 with the standard formulation ILP-0 and determining the benefits obtained by including the cutting plane inequalities described in Sect. 4.

5.1 Setup

We implemented formulations ILP-0, ILP-1 and all its variants in Gurobi Optimizer 7.5.2 using Python 3.6 (https://www.gurobi.com/), running on a PC running Linux Debian 8.0 ("Jessy"). It has a Core 2 Duo CPU running at 3 GHz, and 4 GB of RAM. All executions where run within a single thread; only one core of the CPU was used.

5.2 Data-Sets

In order to test the performances of formulations ILP-0, ILP-1 and ILP-1+Ck ($k \in \{1, 2\}$), we considered the data-sets from the literature of the 1D-BPP, referred to in the following as the BPPLIB and described in [4]. All instances are downloaded from the web page http://or.dei.unibo.it/library/bpplib. The main characteristics of the used data-sets are summarized in Table 3. Each data-set contains a number of tested instances (column #) of the 1D-BPP, characterized by having the same number of items (column **n**) and the same bin capacity (column **C**). Detailed information about the structure of each of these benchmarks can be found in [4] or in the BPPLIB web page.

Table 3. Main characteristics of the 9 used data-sets from the literature of the 1D-BPP (provided by the BPPLIB) considered in the experiments

Data-set	Ref.	Parameters of the instances		
		#inst.	n	C
Falkenauer T	[6]	40	$\{60, 120\}$	1000
Falkenauer U	[6]	40	$\{120, 250\}$	150
Scholl 1	[11]	360	$\{50, 100\}$	$\{100, 120, 150\}$
Scholl 2	[11]	240	$\{50, 100\}$	1000
Scholl 3	[11]	10	200	100 000
Schwerin 1	[12]	100	100	1000
Schwerin 2	[12]	100	120	1000
Wascher	[13]	17	$[57 - 239]$	10 000
Randomly generated	[3]	240	$\{50, 100\}$	$\{50, 75, 100, 120, 125, 150, 200, 300, 400, 500, 750, 1000\}$

5.3   Comparison of the ILP Models

In order to evaluate the formulations, ILP-0, ILP-1 and ILP-1+Ck for k in $\{1, 2\}$, we first compare its size complexity, which indicates how large a problem is in terms of binary variables and constraints as a function of n (the number of bins as well as of items). We note that in these formulations no Big-M constraints are considered.

The ILP-1 and ILP-1+Ck for k in $\{1, 2\}$ formulations have a smaller number of binary variables (n^2) than the ILP-0 ($n^2 + n$). On the other hand, both ILP-0 and ILP-1 are generally equivalent. They have the same order of number of constraints: $\mathcal{O}(n)$. In contrast, formulation ILP-1+C1 has the largest number of constraint with an order of $\mathcal{O}(n^3)$. Hence, the strengthening of formulation ILP-1 by cutting plane constraints seems to be more favorable for effectively reducing the search tree.

5.4   Computational Results: Analysis of the Gap and the Solution Times

In this section, we analyze our results under two main axes:

- **Axis 1: ILP-1vs. ILP-0:** our goal is to assess the performance of the new symmetry-less ILP-1 against the standard ILP-0.
- **Axis 2: ILP-1+Ck for** k**in** $\{1, 2\}$**vs. ILP-1:** our goal is to evaluate, with respect to ILP-1, the benefits obtained by including cutting plane inequalities.

Axis 1: ILP-1 vs. ILP-0. Table 4 gives the number of instances optimally solved in one CPU minute by the formulation ILP-0, respectively the formulation ILP-1. From these results, we can make the following observations:

- Formulation ILP-1 generally performs better than the formulation ILP-0, both when activating and deactivating the Gurobi Optimizer proprietary cuts. It was able to optimally solve within the time limit (60 s) in total 804 and 908 instances (in 5.7 and 4.5 s on average), respectively. Yet, the formulation ILP-0 was able to optimally solve within the time limit and in total only 597 and 584 instances (in 11 and 7.6 seconds on average), respectively.
- Formulation ILP-1 was able to solve within the time limit all the instances in the data-sets FalkT$_{(60,1000)}$, **FalkT**$_{(120,150)}$ and **Scho1**$_{(50,150)}$, either when activating or deactivating Gurobi proprietary cuts (see Table 4). In contrast, the formulation ILP-0 was unable to solve any instance in the data-set **FalkT**$_{(60,1000)}$ and able to optimally solve only 8 instances in the data-set **FalkT**$_{(120,150)}$ and 47 instances in the data-set **Scho1**$_{(50,150)}$ (in 30 or 16.8 and 1.7 or 1 s on average, respectively) when activating or deactivating the Gurobi proprietary cuts.
- Formulation ILP-0 provides the highest number of optimally solved instances only in both **Scho2**$_{(100,1000)}$ and **Schw1**$_{(100,1000)}$ data-sets (when

activating and deactivating the Gurobi proprietary cuts) and in the data-set $\mathbf{Schw2}_{(120,1000)}$ (when deactivating the Gurobi proprietary cuts). In addition, it was able to optimally solve a single instance in the data-set $\mathbf{Wae}_{([57-239],10000)}$.

Table 4. Number of instances solved in less than one minute (average CPU time in seconds), for formulations ILP-0 and ILP-1

Data-set	#inst.	ILP-0		ILP-1	
		No GC	With GC	No GC	With GC
$\mathbf{FalkT}_{(60,1000)}$	20	0 (60.0)	0 (60.0)	**20** (0.9)	**20** (1.3)
$\mathbf{FalkT}_{(120,1000)}$	20	0 (60.0)	0 (60.0)	0 (60.0)	0 (60.0)
$\mathbf{FalkU}_{(120,150)}$	20	8 (30.0)	8 (16.8)	**16** (8.3)	**20** (6.8)
$\mathbf{FalkU}_{(250,150)}$	20	0 (60.0)	- (60.0)	**9** (12.7)	- (60.0)
$\mathbf{Scho1}_{(50,100)}$	60	18 (1.3)	19 (0.8)	**48** (0.2)	**59** (0.04)
$\mathbf{Scho1}_{(50,120)}$	60	17 (2.2)	19 (2.9)	**45** (0.1)	**59** (0.1)
$\mathbf{Scho1}_{(50,150)}$	60	47 (1.7)	47 (1.0)	**54** (0.7)	**60** (0.1)
$\mathbf{Scho1}_{(100,100)}$	60	8 (12.9)	7 (4.3)	**42** (0.3)	**59** (0.3)
$\mathbf{Scho1}_{(100,120)}$	60	3 (15.0)	6 (23.4)	**42** (2.8)	**55** (1.4)
$\mathbf{Scho1}_{(100,150)}$	60	29 (11.5)	17 (11.3)	**50** (6.7)	**56** (2.7)
$\mathbf{Scho2}_{(50,1000)}$	120	111 (0.7)	113 (0.9)	**112** (1.0)	**118** (1.2)
$\mathbf{Scho2}_{(100,1000)}$	120	**103** (1.5)	**101** (1.7)	94 (3.0)	97 (4.6)
$\mathbf{Scho3}_{(200,100000)}$	10	0 (60.0)	0 (60.0)	0 (60.0)	0 (60.0)
$\mathbf{Schw1}_{(100,1000)}$	100	**52** (8.4)	**48** (10.3)	39 (18.8)	32 (16.9)
$\mathbf{Schw2}_{(120,1000)}$	100	**49** (8.8)	38 (9.8)	40 (20.3)	**39** (20.9)
$\mathbf{Wae}_{([57-239],10000)}$	10	1 (40.6)	- (60.0)	0 (60.0)	- (60.0)
RG	240	151 (8.1)	161 (8.1)	**193** (4.4)	**234** (2.0)
Total (average)	1140	597 (11.0)	584 (7.6)	**804** (5.7)	**908** (4.5)

Table 4 confirms the clear superiority of the formulation ILP-1 over the formulation ILP-0. This means that the new symmetry-less ILP for the 1D-BPP performs better.

Axis 2: ILP-1+Ck for k in $\{1,2\}$ vs. ILP-1. Table 5 gives the number of instances solved in one CPU minute, by, respectively, the ILP-1 and ILP-1+Ck for k in $\{1,2\}$ formulations. From these results, we can see that both formulations ILP-1+Ck for k in $\{1,2\}$ generally have a similar performance, in particular they perform better than the formulation ILP-1, both when activating and deactivating the Gurobi Optimizer proprietary cuts. They were able to optimally solve within the time limit and when activating the Gurobi proprietary cuts in total 928 and 927 instances (in 6.5 and 5.1 s on average), respectively. Yet, the formulation ILP-1 was able to optimally solve within the time limit and in total only 908 instances in 4.5 s on average.

In contrast, the formulation ILP-1+C2 performs clearly better, when deactivating the Gurobi proprietary cuts, than the other two ILPs. In fact, it was able to solve within the time limit in total 860 instances (in 5 s on average). Yet, both formulations ILP-1 and ILP-1+C1 were able to optimally solve within the time limit and in total only 804 and 835 instances (in 5.7 and 4.2 s on average), respectively. This means that the formulation ILP-1+C1 performs also better than the formulation ILP-1.

Table 5. Number of instances solved in less than one minute (average CPU time in seconds), for formulations ILP-1 and ILP-1+Ck for k in $\{1, 2\}$

Data-set	#inst.	ILP-1		ILP-1+C1		ILP-1+C2	
		No GC	With GC	No GC	With GC	No GC	With GC
FalkT$_{(60,1000)}$	20	**20** (0.9)	**20** (1.3)	**20** (2.0)	**20** (2.7)	**20** (1.9)	**20** (2.5)
FalkT$_{(120,1000)}$	20	0 (60.0)	0 (60.0)	0 (60.0)	1 (37.9)	0 (60.0)	0 (60.0)
FalkU$_{(120,150)}$	20	16 (8.3)	**20** (6.8)	19 (9.4)	**20** (7.6)	18 (9.2)	**20** (6.8)
FalkU$_{(250,150)}$	20	**9** (12.7)	- (60.0)	- (60.0)	- (60.0)	- (60.0)	- (60.0)
Scho1$_{(50,100)}$	60	48 (0.2)	59 (0.04)	54 (0.6)	**60** (0.1)	**55** (0.5)	**60** (0.07)
Scho1$_{(50,120)}$	60	45 (0.1)	59 (0.1)	50 (0.1)	**60** (0.2)	**54** (0.2)	**60** (0.1)
Scho1$_{(50,150)}$	60	54 (0.7)	**60** (0.1)	56 (1.2)	**60** (0.6)	**57** (0.6)	**60** (0.7)
Scho1$_{(100,100)}$	60	42 (0.3)	**59** (0.3)	45 (0.6)	**59** (0.8)	**47** (0.7)	**59** (0.8)
Scho1$_{(100,120)}$	60	42 (2.8)	55 (1.4)	43 (1.3)	**57** (1.7)	**45** (1.8)	56 (1.0)
Scho1$_{(100,150)}$	60	50 (6.7)	56 (2.7)	50 (4.0)	**57** (4.2)	**52** (4.5)	55 (2.3)
Scho2$_{(50,1000)}$	120	112 (1.0)	**118** (1.2)	113 (1.0)	**118** (0.4)	**116** (1.6)	**118** (0.6)
Scho2$_{(100,1000)}$	120	94 (3.0)	97 (4.6)	**96** (3.2)	99 (3.6)	95 (3.3)	**104** (2.9)
Scho3$_{(200,100000)}$	10	0 (60.0)	0 (60.0)	0 (60.0)	0 (60.0)	0 (60.0)	0 (60.0)
Schw1$_{(100,1000)}$	100	39 (18.8)	32 (16.9)	40 (12.4)	40 (13.2)	**48** (18.4)	**43** (21.7)
Schw2$_{(120,1000)}$	100	**40** (20.3)	39 (20.9)	36 (13.9)	**40** (16.8)	37 (18.2)	34 (24.7)
Wae$_{([57-239],10000)}$	10	0 (60.0)	- (60.0)	- (60.0)	- (60.0)	- (60.0)	- (60.0)
RG	240	193 (4.4)	234 (2.0)	213 (4.5)	237 (1.8)	**216** (3.8)	238 (1.8)
Total (average)	1140	804 (5.7)	908 (4.5)	835 (4.2)	**928** (6.5)	**860** (5.0)	927 (5.1)

Table 5 clearly confirms the benefits obtained by including cutting plane inequalities to the new symmetry-less ILP formulation ILP-1. This means that formulations ILP-1+Ck for k in $\{1, 2\}$ were slightly better than the new symmetry-less ILP formulation ILP-1.

6 Conclusion and Future Work

We have presented a study of how a new symmetry-less formulation can improve the resolution performance of Integer Linear Formulations for the 1-dimensional bin packing problem. Our study includes a folklore symmetry-less formulation and 2 series of cuts for this formulation. This folklore formulation encodes partitions directly, removing the need for variables to encode the use of bins.

One exciting perspective of this work would be to investigate the impact of reusing the concept of that folklore formulation, i.e. encoding partitions of sets, on the solution of other optimization problem ILP formulations, i.e. Bin Packing with Conflicts, Cutting Stock Problem, etc.

References

1. Arbib, C., Marinelli, F.: Maximum lateness minimization in one-dimensional bin packing. Omega **68**, 76–84 (2017)
2. Cambazard, H., O'Sullivan, B.: Propagating the bin packing constraint using linear programming. In: Cohen, D. (ed.) CP 2010. LNCS, vol. 6308, pp. 129–136. Springer, Heidelberg (2010). https://doi.org/10.1007/978-3-642-15396-9_13
3. Delorme, M., Iori, M., Martello, S.: Bin packing and cutting stock problems: Mathematical models and exact algorithms. Eur. J. Oper. Res. **255**(1), 1–20 (2016)
4. Delorme, M., Iori, M., Martello, S.: BPPLIB: a library for bin packing and cutting stock problems. Optim. Lett. **12**(2), 235–250 (2018)
5. Dyckhoff, H.: A new linear programming approach to the cutting stock problem. Oper. Res. **29**(6), 1092–1104 (1981)
6. Falkenauer, E.: A hybrid grouping genetic algorithm for bin packing. J. Heuristics **2**(1), 5–30 (1996)
7. Lysgaard, J., Letchford, A.N., Eglese, R.W.: A new branch-and-cut algorithm for the capacitated vehicle routing problem. Math. Program. **100**(2), 423–445 (2004)
8. Martello, S., Toth, P.: Knapsack problems: algorithms and computer implementations (1990)
9. Martello, S., Toth, P.: Lower bounds and reduction procedures for the bin packing problem. Discrete Appl. Math. **28**(1), 59–70 (1990)
10. Ryan, D., Foster, E.: An integer programming approach to scheduling. Computer scheduling of public transport urban passenger vehicle and crew scheduling, pp. 269–280 (1981)
11. Scholl, A., Klein, R., Jürgens, C.: Bison: a fast hybrid procedure for exactly solving the one-dimensional bin packing problem. Comput. Oper. Res. **24**(7), 627–645 (1997)
12. Schwerin, P., Wäscher, G.: The bin-packing problem: A problem generator and some numerical experiments with FFD packing and MTP. Int. Trans. Oper. Res. **4**(5–6), 377–389 (1997)
13. Wäscher, G., Gau, T.: Heuristics for the integer one-dimensional cutting stock problem: a computational study. Oper.-Res.-Spectr. **18**(3), 131–144 (1996)

On the Area Requirements of Planar Greedy Drawings of Triconnected Planar Graphs

Giordano Da Lozzo[1]($\boxtimes$), Anthony D'Angelo[2], and Fabrizio Frati[1]

[1] Roma Tre University, Rome, Italy
{giordano.dalozzo,fabrizio.frati}@uniroma3.it
[2] Carleton University, Ottawa, Canada
anthonydangelo@cmail.carleton.ca

Abstract. In this paper we study the area requirements of planar greedy drawings of triconnected planar graphs. Cao, Strelzoff, and Sun exhibited a family $\mathcal{H}$ of subdivisions of triconnected plane graphs and claimed that every planar greedy drawing of the graphs in $\mathcal{H}$ respecting the prescribed plane embedding requires exponential area. However, we show that every n-vertex graph in $\mathcal{H}$ actually has a planar greedy drawing respecting the prescribed plane embedding on an $O(n) \times O(n)$ grid. This reopens the question whether triconnected planar graphs admit planar greedy drawings on a polynomial-size grid. Further, we provide evidence for a positive answer to the above question by proving that every n-vertex Halin graph admits a planar greedy drawing on an $O(n) \times O(n)$ grid. Both such results are obtained by actually constructing drawings that are convex and angle-monotone. Finally, we consider α-Schnyder drawings, which are angle-monotone and hence greedy if $\alpha \leq 30°$, and show that there exist planar triangulations for which every α-Schnyder drawing with a fixed $\alpha < 60°$ requires exponential area for any resolution rule.

1 Introduction

Let (M, d) be a metric space, where M is a set of points and d is a metric on M. A *greedy embedding* of a graph G into (M, d) is a function ϕ that maps each vertex v of G to a point $\phi(v)$ in M in such a way that, for every ordered pair (u, v) of vertices of G, there is a distance-decreasing path from u to v in G, i.e., a path $(u = w_1, w_2, \ldots, w_k = v)$ such that $d\big(\phi(w_i), \phi(v)\big) > d\big(\phi(w_{i+1}), \phi(v)\big)$, for $i = 1, \ldots, k - 1$. Greedy embeddings, introduced by Rao et al. [23], can be used as a data structure to support a simple and local routing scheme, called *greedy routing*, in which a vertex forwards a packet to any neighbor that is closer to the packet's destination than itself. In order for greedy routing to be efficient, a greedy embedding should be *succinct*, i.e., a polylogarithmic number of bits should be used to store the coordinates of each vertex. A number of algorithms

Partially supported by the MSCA-RISE project "CONNECT", N° 734922, by the NSERC of Canada, and by the MIUR-PRIN project "AHeAD", N° 20174LF3T8.

D. Kim et al. (Eds.): COCOON 2020, LNCS 12273, pp. 435–447, 2020.
https://doi.org/10.1007/978-3-030-58150-3_35

have been proposed to construct succinct greedy embeddings of graphs [4, 11, 13, 14, 18, 25, 26]. A natural choice is the one of considering M to be the Euclidean plane $\mathbb{R}^2$ and d to be the Euclidean distance ℓ_2. Within this setting, not every graph [21, 22], and not even every binary tree [15, 20], admits a greedy embedding; further, there exist trees whose every greedy embedding requires a polynomial number of bits to store the coordinates of some of the vertices [2].

From a theoretical point of view, most research efforts have revolved around two conjectures posed by Papadimitriou and Ratajczak [21, 22]. The first one asserts that every 3-connected planar graph admits a *greedy drawing*, i.e., a straight-line drawing in $\mathbb{R}^2$ that induces a greedy embedding into $(\mathbb{R}^2, \ell_2)$. This conjecture has been confirmed independently by Leighton and Moitra [15] and by Angelini et al. [3]. The second conjecture, which strengthens the first one, asserts that every 3-connected planar graph admits a greedy drawing that is also convex. While this is still open, it has been recently proved by the authors of this paper that every 3-connected planar graph admits a *planar* greedy drawing [8].

An interesting question is whether succinctness and planarity can be achieved simultaneously. That is, does every 3-connected planar graph admit a planar, and possibly convex, greedy drawing on a polynomial-size grid? Cao, Strelzoff, and Sun [7] claimed a negative answer by exhibiting a family $\mathcal{H}$ of subdivisions of 3-connected plane graphs and by showing that, for any n-vertex graph in $\mathcal{H}$, any planar greedy drawing that respects the prescribed plane embedding requires $2^{\Omega(n)}$ area and hence $\Omega(n)$ bits for representing the coordinates of some vertices.

Subsequently to the definition of greedy drawings, several more constrained graph drawing standards have been introduced. Analogously to greedy drawings, they all concern straight-line drawings in $\mathbb{R}^2$. In a *self-approaching* drawing [1, 9, 19], for every pair of vertices u and v, there is a self-approaching path from u to v, i.e., a path P such that $\ell_2(a, c) > \ell_2(b, c)$, for any three points a, b, and c in this order along P. In an *increasing-chord* drawing [1, 9, 19], for every pair of vertices, there is a path between them which is self-approaching in both directions. In an *angle-monotone* drawing [5, 9, 16, 17], for every pair of vertices u and v, there is a β-monotone path from u to v for some angle β, i.e., a path $(w_1 = u, w_2, \ldots, w_k = v)$ such that each edge (w_i, w_{i+1}) lies in the closed 90°-wedge centered at w_i and bisected by the ray originating at w_i with slope β. Note that an angle-monotone drawing is increasing-chord, an increasing-chord drawing is self-approaching, and a self-approaching drawing is greedy. The first implication was proved in [9], while the other two descend from the definitions. Finally, a notable class of straight-line drawings are α-*Schnyder* drawings [19], which are angle-monotone if $\alpha \leq 30°$ and will be formally defined later.

Our Contributions. We show that every n-vertex graph in the family $\mathcal{H}$ defined by Cao et al. [7] actually admits a convex angle-monotone drawing that respects the prescribed plane embedding and lies on an $O(n) \times O(n)$ grid. This reopens the question about the existence of succinct planar greedy drawings of 3-connected planar graphs. Further, we provide an indication that this question might have a positive answer by proving that the n-vertex Halin graphs, a notable family of triconnected planar graphs, admit convex angle-monotone drawings on an

$O(n) \times O(n)$ grid. Finally, we construct bounded-degree planar triangulations whose α-Schnyder drawings all require exponential area, for any fixed $\alpha < 60°$. This result was rather surprising to us, as any planar triangulation admits a $60°$-Schnyder drawing on an $O(n) \times O(n)$ grid [24]; further, although $30°$-Schnyder drawings have been proved to exist for all stacked triangulations, our result shows that they are not the right tool to obtain succinct planar greedy drawings.

2 Definitions and Preliminaries

A *straight-line drawing* of a graph maps each vertex to a point in the plane and each edge to a straight-line segment. A *planar drawing*, i.e., one with no crossings, partitions the plane into connected regions, called *faces*. The unbounded face is the *outer face*; the other faces are *internal*. Two planar drawings of a connected planar graph are *equivalent* if they determine the same circular order of the edges incident to each vertex. A *planar embedding* is an equivalence class of planar drawings. A *plane graph* is a planar graph equipped with a planar embedding and a designated outer face. A straight-line drawing is *convex* if it is planar and every face is delimited by a convex polygon. A *grid drawing* is such that each vertex is mapped to a point with integer coordinates. The *width* (resp. *height*) of a grid drawing is the number of grid columns (rows) intersecting it. A drawing *lies on a $W \times H$ grid* if it is a grid drawing with width W and height H. The *area* of a graph drawing is defined as the area of the smallest axis-parallel rectangle enclosing the drawing (when proving upper bounds) or as the area of the smallest convex polygon enclosing the drawing (when proving lower bounds). Any constraint implying a finite minimum area for a graph drawing (e.g., requiring vertices to have distance at least 1 or to lie at grid points) is called a *resolution rule*. We measure angles in radians. In a straight-line drawing of a graph, the *slope* of an edge (u, v) is the angle spanned by a counter-clockwise rotation around u of a ray originating at u and directed rightwards bringing the ray to overlap with (u, v); hence, the edge slopes are in the range $[0, 2\pi)$. We let $(x(v), y(v))$ be the point in the plane representing a vertex v in a graph drawing.

A *planar triangulation* G is a plane graph whose every face is bounded by a 3-cycle. Denote by (a_1, a_2, a_3) the 3-cycle bounding the outer face of G. A *Schnyder wood* $(\mathcal{T}_1, \mathcal{T}_2, \mathcal{T}_3)$ of G is an assignment of directions and colors 1, 2 and 3 to the internal edges of G such that the following two properties hold; see the figure below and refer to [24]. Let $i - 1 = 3$, if $i = 1$, and let $i + 1 = 1$, if $i = 3$.

Property (1) Each internal vertex v has one outgoing edge e_i of each color i, with $i = 1, 2, 3$. The outgoing edges e_1, e_2, and e_3 appear in this clockwise order at v. Further, all the incoming edges of color i appear in the clockwise sector between the edges e_{i+1} and e_{i-1}. **Property (2)** At the external vertex a_i, all the internal edges are incoming and of color i.

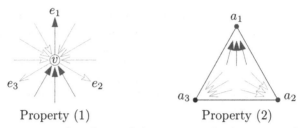

Property (1)   Property (2)

A *planar 3-tree* can be obtained from a 3-cycle, by repeatedly inserting a vertex into any internal face and connecting it to the vertices of the face. The planar triangulations with a unique Schnyder wood are the planar 3-trees [6,12].

For $0 < \alpha \leq \frac{\pi}{3}$, a planar straight-line drawing of a planar triangulation G with Schnyder wood $(\mathcal{T}_1, \mathcal{T}_2, \mathcal{T}_3)$ is an α-*Schnyder drawing* if, for each internal vertex v of G, its outgoing edge in $\mathcal{T}_1$ has direction in $[\frac{\pi}{2} - \frac{\alpha}{2}, \frac{\pi}{2} + \frac{\alpha}{2}]$, its outgoing edge in $\mathcal{T}_2$ has direction in $[\frac{11\pi}{6} - \frac{\alpha}{2}, \frac{11\pi}{6} + \frac{\alpha}{2}]$, and its outgoing edge in $\mathcal{T}_3$ has direction in $[\frac{7\pi}{6} - \frac{\alpha}{2}, \frac{7\pi}{6} + \frac{\alpha}{2}]$. Note that, by definition, in an α-Schnyder drawing, for each internal vertex v of G, its incoming edges in $\mathcal{T}_1$, $\mathcal{T}_2$, and $\mathcal{T}_3$, if any, have direction in $[\frac{3\pi}{2} - \frac{\alpha}{2}, \frac{3\pi}{2} + \frac{\alpha}{2}]$, $[\frac{5\pi}{6} - \frac{\alpha}{2}, \frac{5\pi}{6} + \frac{\alpha}{2}]$, and $[\frac{\pi}{6} - \frac{\alpha}{2}, \frac{\pi}{6} + \frac{\alpha}{2}]$, respectively. Figure 3b shows the angular widths of an α-Schnyder drawing. "Usual" Schnyder drawings [24] are 60°-Schnyder drawings; see, e.g., [10].

3   Angle-Monotone Drawings of Cao-Strelzoff-Sun Graphs

Cao et al. [7] defined the following family $\mathcal{H}$ of plane graphs. For $i = 1, 2, \ldots$, the plane graph $\mathfrak{H}_i \in \mathcal{H}$ on $3i + 4$ vertices is inductively defined as follows: The plane graph $\mathfrak{H}_1$ consists of a cycle $(x_2, z_1, y_2, x_1, z_2, y_1)$ and a vertex x_0 inside such a cycle and adjacent to x_1, y_1, and z_1; see the left part of the figure. For $i \geq 2$, the plane graph $\mathfrak{H}_i$ is obtained by embedding in the outer face of $\mathfrak{H}_{i-1}$ the vertices x_{i+1}, y_{i+1}, and z_{i+1}, and the edges of the cycle $(x_{i+1}, z_i, y_{i+1}, x_i, z_{i+1}, y_i)$, which bounds the outer face of $\mathfrak{H}_i$; see the right part of the figure. In contrast to the result in [7], we prove the following.

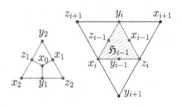

Theorem 1. Every n-vertex plane graph in $\mathcal{H}$ admits a planar angle-monotone drawing on an $O(n) \times O(n)$ grid that respects the plane embedding.

Proof sketch. We construct, for every $i \geq 1$, a planar straight-line drawing Γ_i of $\mathfrak{H}_i = (V_i, E_i)$ satisfying the following properties:

i. the vertices of $\mathfrak{H}_i$ lie on a $(2i + 3) \times (2i + 3)$ grid;
ii. there exist paths $p_i(\alpha)$, with $\alpha \in \{\frac{\pi}{2}, \frac{5\pi}{4}, \frac{7\pi}{4}\}$, originating at x_0 and each terminating at a distinct vertex in $\{x_{i+1}, y_{i+1}, z_{i+1}\}$, that are vertex-disjoint except at x_0, that together span all the vertices in V_i, and such that all the edges in $p_i(\alpha)$ have slope α.

Property ii implies that Γ_i is angle-monotone. Namely, consider any two vertices u and v of $\mathfrak{H}_i$. If both u and v belong to the same path $p_i(\alpha)$, then the subpath of $p_i(\alpha)$ from u to v is either α-monotone or $(\pi + \alpha)$-monotone. If $u \in p_i(\alpha)$ and $v \in p_i(\beta)$, with $\alpha \neq \beta$, then the path p^* consisting of the subpath of $p_i(\alpha)$ from u to x_0 and of the subpath of $p_i(\beta)$ from x_0 to v is $\frac{\pi}{2}$-monotone (if $\beta = \frac{\pi}{2}$), or $\frac{3\pi}{2}$-monotone (if $\alpha = \frac{\pi}{2}$), or π-monotone (if $\alpha = \frac{7\pi}{4}$ and $\beta = \frac{5\pi}{4}$), or 0-monotone (if $\alpha = \frac{5\pi}{4}$ and $\beta = \frac{7\pi}{4}$).

Our proof is by induction on i. In the base case $i = 1$ and a drawing Γ_1 of $\mathfrak{H}_1$ satisfying Properties i and ii is constructed as in Fig. 1a.

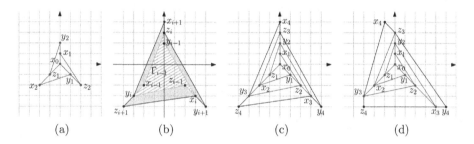

(a)　　　　　(b)　　　　　(c)　　　　　(d)

Fig. 1. Illustrations for the proof of Theorem 1: (a) The drawing Γ_1 of $\mathfrak{H}_1$; (b) The drawing Γ_i of $\mathfrak{H}_i$ obtained from the drawing Γ_{i-1} of $\mathfrak{H}_{i-1}$, with $i > 1$. (d) The convex angle-monotone drawing Γ_3' of $\mathfrak{H}_3$ obtained from (c) Γ_3.

If $i > 1$, suppose we have inductively constructed a drawing Γ_{i-1} of $\mathfrak{H}_{i-1}$ satisfying Properties i and ii. Assume, as in Fig. 1b, that z_i is in $p_{i-1}(\frac{\pi}{2})$, y_i is in $p_{i-1}(\frac{5\pi}{4})$, and x_i is in $p_{i-1}(\frac{7\pi}{4})$; the other cases can be treated analogously.

We obtain Γ_i from Γ_{i-1} by placing x_{i+1} at $(\mathrm{x}(z_i), \mathrm{y}(z_i) + 1)$, y_{i+1} at $(\mathrm{x}(x_i) + 1, \mathrm{y}(x_i) - 1)$, and z_{i+1} at $(\mathrm{x}(y_i) - 1, \mathrm{y}(y_i) - 1)$, and by drawing the edges incident to these vertices as straight-line segments. We have the following.

Claim 1. Γ_i satisfies Properties i and ii.

Proof sketch. Clearly, Γ_{i-1} is a planar drawing on the $(2i + 3) \times (2i + 3)$ grid (implying Property i). Property ii is satisfied with $p_i(\frac{\pi}{2}) = p_{i-1}(\frac{\pi}{2}) \cup (z_i, x_{i+1})$, $p_i(\frac{5\pi}{4}) = p_{i-1}(\frac{5\pi}{4}) \cup (y_i, z_{i+1})$, and $p_i(\frac{7\pi}{4}) = p_{i-1}(\frac{7\pi}{4}) \cup (x_i, y_{i+1})$. □

Claim 1 concludes the induction and the proof of the theorem. □

We note that, for $i \geq 1$, the graph $\mathfrak{H}_i$ even admits a *convex* angle-monotone drawing Γ_i' on a $(2i + 3) \times (2i + 3)$ grid; indeed, Γ_i' can be obtained from the planar angle-monotone drawing Γ_i of $\mathfrak{H}_i$ described in the proof of Theorem 1 by moving x_i one unit to the right and one unit down, y_{i+1} and z_{i+1} one unit to the right, and x_{i+1} one unit to the left; see Figs. 1c and 1d. We have the following.

Claim 2. The straight-line drawing Γ_i' of $\mathfrak{H}_i$ is convex, angle-monotone and lies on a $(2i + 3) \times (2i + 3)$ grid.

Proof. It is easy to see that Γ_i' is a convex drawing of $\mathfrak{H}_i$ on an $(2i+3) \times (2i+3)$ grid. We prove that Γ_i' is angle-monotone. Consider the following three paths: (1) $P_1 = p_i(\frac{\pi}{2}) \cup p_i(\frac{5\pi}{4})$; (2) $P_2 = p_i(\frac{\pi}{2}) \cup p_i(\frac{7\pi}{4})$; and (3) $P_3 = p_{i-1}(\frac{5\pi}{4}) \cup p_i(\frac{7\pi}{4})$.

If u and v both belong to P_1, P_2, or P_3, then the subpath of such a path from u to v is (1) $\frac{\pi}{2}$- or $\frac{3\pi}{2}$-monotone, (2) $\frac{3\pi}{4}$- or $\frac{7\pi}{4}$-monotone, or (3) 0- or π-monotone, respectively. Note that u and v both belong to one of P_1, P_2, or P_3, unless one of them, say u, is z_{i+1} and the other one, say v, belongs to $p_i(\frac{7\pi}{4})$. In such a case, a β-monotone path P from u to v can be defined as follows. If $v = x_i$, then P coincides with the edge (z_{i+1}, x_i); if $v = y_{i+1}$, then P coincides with the path (z_{i+1}, x_i, y_{i+1}); in both cases, P is 0-monotone. Finally, if v belongs to $p_{i-2}(\frac{7\pi}{4})$, then P is defined as the subpath of $p_i(\frac{5\pi}{4})$ from u to the only neighbor of v in $p_i(\frac{5\pi}{4})$, and from that neighbor to v; then P is $\frac{\pi}{4}$-monotone.   □

He and Zhang [14] pointed out that, although the graphs $\mathfrak{H}_i$'s are not 3-connected, they can be made so by adding the three additional edges (x_{i+1}, y_{i+1}), (y_{i+1}, z_{i+1}), and (z_{i+1}, x_{i+1}). Let $\mathfrak{H}_i^+$ be the resulting graph. We note here that the drawing Γ_i of $\mathfrak{H}_i$ whose construction is described in the proof of Theorem 1 can be turned into a convex angle-monotone drawing Γ_i^+ of $\mathfrak{H}_i^+$ simply by drawing the edges (x_{i+1}, y_{i+1}), (y_{i+1}, z_{i+1}), and (z_{i+1}, x_{i+1}) as straight-line segments.

4   Angle-Monotone Drawings of Halin Graphs

In this section, we show how to construct convex angle-monotone drawings of Halin graphs on a polynomial-size grid.

We denote the number of leaves of a tree T by $\ell(T)$. A tree all whose vertices but one are leaves is a *star*. A *rooted tree* T is a tree with one distinguished vertex, called *root* and denoted by $r(T)$. The *height* of a rooted tree is the maximum number of edges in any path from the root to a leaf. In a rooted tree T, we denote by $T(v)$ the subtree of T rooted at a vertex v. An *ordered rooted tree* is a rooted tree in which the children of each internal vertex u are assigned a left-to-right order $u_1, \ldots, u_k$; the vertices u_1 and u_k are the *leftmost* and the *rightmost child* of u, respectively. The *leftmost path* of an ordered rooted tree T is the path $(v_1, \ldots, v_h)$ in T such that v_1 is the root of T, v_{i+1} is the leftmost child of v_i, for $i = 1, \ldots, h-1$, and v_h is a leaf, which is called the *leftmost leaf* of T. The *rightmost path* and the *rightmost leaf* of T can be defined analogously.

A *Halin graph* G is a planar graph that admits a plane embedding $\mathcal{E}$ such that, by removing all the edges incident to the outer face $f_{\mathcal{E}}$ of $\mathcal{E}$, one gets a tree T_G whose internal vertices have degree at least 3. Note that G is 3-connected and its leaves are incident to $f_{\mathcal{E}}$.

Theorem 2. *Every n-vertex Halin graph G admits a convex angle-monotone drawing on an $O(n) \times O(n)$ grid.*

If T_G contains one internal vertex, then G is a wheel and a convex angle-monotone drawing on a $3 \times (n-1)$ grid can easily be computed; see Fig. 2a(top). In the following, we assume that T_G contains at least two internal vertices.

Let ξ be an internal vertex of T_G whose every neighbor is a leaf, except for one, which we denote by ρ; see Fig. 2b. Such a vertex exists by the above assumption. Further, let $T \subset T_G$ be the tree obtained from T_G by removing ξ and all its adjacent leaves and by rooting the resulting tree at ρ. Also, let $S \subset T_G$ be the star obtained from T_G by removing the vertices of T and by rooting the resulting tree at ξ. We regard T and S as ordered rooted trees such that the left-to-right order of the children of each vertex is the one induced by the plane embedding $\mathcal{E}$ of G. For any subtree $T' \subseteq T_G$, let $G[T']$ be the subgraph of G induced by the vertices of T'. In Lemma 1, we show how to construct a drawing Γ of $G[T]$. Then, we will exploit Lemma 1 in order to prove Theorem 2.

Lemma 1. The graph $G[T]$ has a drawing Γ satisfying the following properties:

(i) Γ is angle-monotone and convex;
(ii) Γ lies on a $W_\Gamma \times H_\Gamma$ grid, where $W_\Gamma = 2\ell(T) - 1$ and $H_\Gamma = \ell(T)$;
(iii) the leaves of T lie at $(0,0), (2,0), \ldots, (2\ell(T) - 2, 0)$, where the i-th leaf of T lies at $(2i - 2, 0)$, for $i = 1, \ldots, \ell(T)$; and
(iv) for each vertex v of T, the edges of the leftmost path (resp., of the rightmost path) of $T(v)$ have slope $\frac{5\pi}{4}$ (resp., slope $\frac{7\pi}{4}$).

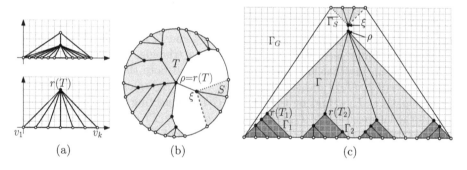

(a)   (b)   (c)

Fig. 2. (a) A convex angle-monotone drawing of a wheel on the grid (top) and the base case for the proof of Lemma 1 (bottom). (b) The trees T and S for the proof of Theorem 2. (c) The convex angle-monotone drawing Γ_G of G constructed from the drawings Γ of $G[T]$ and $\overline{\Gamma_S}$ of $G[S]$.

Proof sketch. Our proof is by induction on the height h of T. In the base case we have $h = 1$, hence T is a star and a straight-line drawing Γ of $G[T]$ satisfying Properties i to iv is constructed as in Fig. 2a(bottom).

Suppose now that $h > 1$; see Fig. 2c. Let $T_1, \ldots, T_k$ be the left-to-right order of the subtrees of T rooted at the children of $r(T)$, where $k \geq 2$. For each T_i which is not a single vertex, assume to have inductively constructed a drawing Γ_i of $G[T_i]$ satisfying Properties i to iv. For each T_i which is a single vertex, let Γ_i consist of the point $(0,0)$. For $i = 1, \ldots, k$, let W_i be the width of Γ_i. Place the drawings $\Gamma_1, \ldots, \Gamma_k$ side by side, so that all their leaves lie on the x-axis, so that the leftmost leaf of T_1 is at $(0,0)$, and so that, for $i = 1, \ldots, k-1$, the rightmost leaf of T_i is two units to the left of the leftmost leaf of T_{i+1}. We conclude the construction of Γ by placing $r(T)$ at $(\ell(T) - 1, \ell(T) - 1)$. We have the following.

Claim 3. Γ satisfies Properties i to iv.

Proof sketch. Property iii holds true since it is inductively satisfied by each drawing Γ_i and since, by construction, the rightmost leaf of T_i is two units to the left of the leftmost leaf of T_{i+1}, for $i = 1, \ldots, k-1$.

Concerning Property ii, we have that $W_\Gamma = \sum_{i=1}^{k} W_{\Gamma_i} + (k-1) = \sum_{i=1}^{k}(2\ell(T_i)-1)+(k-1) = 2\ell(T)-1$, where we exploited $W_{\Gamma_i} = 2\ell(T_i)-1$, which is true by induction. Further, by construction and by induction, each vertex of T_i has a y-coordinate between 0 and $\ell(T_i) - 1$. Since $\ell(T_i) < \ell(T)$, the maximum y-coordinate of any vertex of T in Γ is the one of $r(T)$, hence $H_\Gamma = \ell(T)$.

Property iv holds true for each vertex different from $r(T)$ since it is inductively satisfied by each drawing Γ_i. Further, since $W_\Gamma = 2\ell(T) - 1$, since $r(T)$ lies at $(\ell(T) - 1, \ell(T) - 1)$, and since the leftmost and rightmost leaves of T lie at $(0,0)$ and $(2\ell(T) - 2, 0)$, respectively, the slopes of the segments from $r(T)$ to such leaves are $\frac{5\pi}{4}$ and $\frac{7\pi}{4}$, respectively. Hence, the edges of the leftmost (resp., rightmost) path of T have slope $\frac{5\pi}{4}$ (resp., $\frac{7\pi}{4}$), given that the edges of the leftmost (resp., rightmost) path of T_1 have slope $\frac{5\pi}{4}$ (resp., $\frac{7\pi}{4}$), by induction.

Finally, we prove Property i. We first prove that Γ is convex. By induction, each internal face of Γ which is also a face of some Γ_i is delimited by a convex polygon. The outer face of Γ is delimited by a triangle, by Properties iii and iv. Let f be an internal face incident to $r(T)$ and note that f is delimited by two edges $(r(T), r(T_i))$ and $(r(T), r(T_{i+1}))$, by the rightmost path of T_i, by the leftmost path of T_{i+1}, and by the edge of $G[T]$ connecting the rightmost leaf of T_i with the leftmost leaf of T_{i+1}. The angles of f at $r(T)$, at the internal vertices of the rightmost path of T_i or of the leftmost path of T_{i+1}, at the rightmost leaf of T_i, and at the leftmost leaf of T_{i+1} are at most π by Properties iii and iv. The angle of f at $r(T_i)$ is larger than or equal to $\frac{\pi}{2}$ and smaller than π; namely, the slope of the edge $(r(T), r(T_i))$ is in the interval $[\frac{5\pi}{4}, \frac{7\pi}{4})$, by Property iv and by $i < k$; further, the slope of the edge of the rightmost path of T_i incident to $r(T_i)$ is $\frac{7\pi}{4}$, by Property iv. The argument for the angle of f at $r(T_{i+1})$ is symmetric.

We now prove that Γ is angle-monotone. Let u and v be any two vertices of T. If u and v both belong to a subtree T_i of T, then a β-monotone path between u and v exists in Γ since it exists in Γ_i, by induction. Otherwise, either u and v belong to distinct subtrees T_i and T_j of T, or one of u and v is $r(T)$. In the former case, suppose w.l.o.g. that $i < j$. Let P be the path from u to v consisting of: **(1)** the rightmost path P_u of $T_i(u)$; **(2)** the path P_{uv} in $G[T]$ from the rightmost leaf of $T_i(u)$ to the leftmost leaf of $T_j(v)$ that only passes through leaves of T; and **(3)** the leftmost path P_v of $T_j(v)$. Since the edges of P_u (which are traversed in the direction of P_u) and those of P_v (which are traversed in the direction opposite to the one of P_v) have slope $\frac{7\pi}{4}$ and $\frac{\pi}{4}$, by Property iv, and the edges of P_{uv} have slope 0, Property iii, we have that P is 0-monotone.

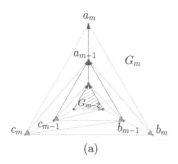
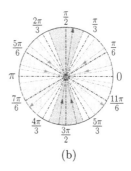

(a)   (b)

Fig. 3. Illustrations for the proof of Theorem 3: (a) The graph G_m. (b) The different angular widths of an α-Schnyder drawing, with $\alpha < \frac{\pi}{3}$.

In the latter case, suppose w.l.o.g. that $v = r(T)$ and that $u \in V(T_i)$, for some $i \in \{1, \ldots, k\}$. By Property iv, all the edges of the path from u to v in T have slope in the closed interval $[\frac{\pi}{4}, \frac{3\pi}{4}]$, hence such a path is $\frac{\pi}{2}$-monotone. □

Claim 3 concludes the proof of the lemma. □

We now prove Theorem 2. We construct a drawing Γ_G of G as follows; see Fig. 2c. We initialize Γ_G to the drawing Γ of $G[T]$ obtained by Lemma 1. Further, we apply Lemma 1 a second time in order to construct a drawing Γ_S of $G[S]$. Let $\overline{\Gamma_S}$ be the drawing of $G[S]$ obtained by rotating Γ_S by π radians. We translate $\overline{\Gamma_S}$ so that ξ lies one unit above ρ. Further, we draw the edge (ρ, ξ) as a vertical straight-line segment. Finally, we draw the edge between the leftmost (rightmost) leaf of S and the rightmost (leftmost) leaf of T as a straight-line segment.

We have the following claim, which concludes the proof of Theorem 2.

Claim 4. Γ_G is a convex angle-monotone drawing of G on an $O(n) \times O(n)$ grid.

Proof sketch. By Properties ii and iv of Lemma 1, the width of Γ_G is $\max(2\ell(T) - 1, 2\ell(S) - 1)$ and the height of Γ_G is $\ell(T) + \ell(S)$. Both such values are in $O(n)$.

Properties i,iii and iv imply that the faces of Γ_G which are also faces of Γ or $\overline{\Gamma_S}$, as well as the outer face of Γ_G, are delimited by convex polygons. Consider any face f incident to the edge (ρ, ξ). By Property iv of Lemma 1, the angles of f incident to the internal vertices of the leftmost and rightmost paths of T are equal to π, hence f is delimited by a quadrilateral Q; the angles of f incident to ρ and to ξ are $\frac{3\pi}{4}$, again by Property iv of Lemma 1 and since (ρ, ξ) is vertical, hence the remaining two angles of Q sum up to $\frac{\pi}{2}$ and Q is convex.

We now prove that Γ_G is angle-monotone. Let u and v be any two vertices of G. If u and v both belong to T or both belong to S, then a β-monotone path between u and v exists in Γ_G since it exists in Γ or in $\overline{\Gamma_S}$, respectively, by Lemma 1. Otherwise, we can assume that u belongs to S and that v belongs to T. Then the path P from u to v in T_G is $\frac{3\pi}{2}$-monotone. Namely, by Property iv of Lemma 1, the edge of P in S, if any, has slope in the interval $[\frac{5\pi}{4}, \frac{7\pi}{4}]$; further, by construction, the edge (ξ, ρ) has slope $\frac{3\pi}{2}$; finally, again by Property iv of Lemma 1, all the edges of P in T, if any, have slope in the interval $[\frac{5\pi}{4}, \frac{7\pi}{4}]$. □

5 α-Schnyder Drawings of Plane Triangulations

For a function $f(n)$ and a parameter $\varepsilon > 0$, we write $f(n) \in \Omega_\varepsilon(n)$ if $f(n) \geq c_\varepsilon n$ for a constant $c_\varepsilon > 0$ only depending on ε. Next, we prove the following theorem.

Theorem 3. There exists an infinite family $\mathcal{F}$ of bounded-degree planar 3-trees such that, for any resolution rule, any n-vertex graph in $\mathcal{F}$ requires $2^{\Omega_\varepsilon(n)}$ area in any $(\frac{\pi}{3}-\varepsilon)$-Schnyder drawing, for any fixed $0 < \varepsilon < \frac{\pi}{3}$.

Proof sketch. We define a $3m$-vertex plane 3-tree G_m; see Fig. 3a. The plane 3-tree G_1 is a cycle (a_1, b_1, c_1). For any integer $m > 1$, G_m is obtained from G_{m-1} by embedding a cycle (a_m, b_m, c_m) in the outer face of G_{m-1}, so that it contains G_{m-1} in its interior, and by inserting the edges (a_m, a_{m-1}), (b_m, a_{m-1}), (b_m, b_{m-1}), (c_m, a_{m-1}), (c_m, b_{m-1}), and (c_m, c_{m-1}). Since G_m is a plane 3-tree, it has a unique Schnyder wood $(\mathcal{T}_1, \mathcal{T}_2, \mathcal{T}_3)$; see [6,12]. Assume, w.l.o.g., that all the internal edges incident to a_m, b_m, and c_m belong to $\mathcal{T}_1$, $\mathcal{T}_2$, and $\mathcal{T}_3$, respectively.

Claim 5. For $1 \leq k < m$, the edges (a_k, b_k) and (a_k, c_k) belong to $\mathcal{T}_1$ and are directed towards a_k, the edge (a_k, a_{k+1}) belongs to $\mathcal{T}_1$ and is directed towards a_{k+1}, the edge (b_k, c_k) belongs to $\mathcal{T}_2$ and is directed towards b_k, the edges (b_{k+1}, a_k) and (b_{k+1}, b_k) belong to $\mathcal{T}_2$ and are directed towards b_{k+1}, and the edges (c_{k+1}, a_k), (c_{k+1}, b_k), and (c_{k+1}, c_k) belong to $\mathcal{T}_3$ and are directed towards c_{k+1}.

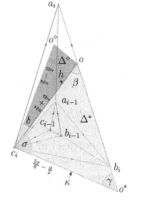

We now prove that, for any fixed $\alpha = \frac{\pi}{3} - \varepsilon$ with $\varepsilon > 0$, any α-Schnyder drawing Γ of G_m (respecting the plane embedding of G_m and corresponding to the unique Schnyder wood of G_m) requires $2^{\Omega_\varepsilon(m)}$ area. We exploit the next claim. For $i = 1, \ldots, m$, let Δ_i be the triangle (a_i, b_i, c_i) in Γ.

Claim 6. For any $i = 2, \ldots, m-1$, the area A_i of Δ_i is at least k_ε times the area A_{i-1} of Δ_{i-1}, where $k_\varepsilon > 1$ is a constant only depending on ε.

Proof sketch. Refer to the figure on the right. For two elements x and y, each representing a point or a vertex in Γ, let $\ell(x, y)$ be the line through x and y. Let o (resp. o^*) be the intersection point between $\ell(a_i, b_i)$ and the line with slope $\frac{\pi}{6} + \frac{\alpha}{2}$ (resp. $\frac{5\pi}{6} - \frac{\alpha}{2}$) through c_i and let $o^\diamond$ be the intersection point between the line with slope $\frac{\pi}{2} - \frac{\alpha}{2}$ through c_i and the line through o perpendicular to $\ell(c_i, o)$. Let A^* and $A^\diamond$ denote the areas of the triangles $\Delta^* = (c_i, o, o^*)$ and $\Delta^\diamond = (c_i, o^\diamond, o)$, respectively. By Claim 5 and since Γ is an α-Schnyder drawing, we have that the slopes of the edges (b_i, a_i), (c_i, a_i), (b_{i-1}, a_{i-1}), and (c_{i-1}, a_{i-1}) are in the range $[\frac{\pi}{2} - \frac{\alpha}{2}, \frac{\pi}{2} + \frac{\alpha}{2}]$, the slope of (b_i, c_i) is in the range $[\frac{5\pi}{6} - \frac{\alpha}{2}, \frac{5\pi}{6} + \frac{\alpha}{2}]$, and the slope of (c_i, a_{i-1}) is in the range $[\frac{\pi}{6} - \frac{\alpha}{2}, \frac{\pi}{6} + \frac{\alpha}{2}]$. Thus, Δ_{i-1} is enclosed in Δ^* and $\Delta^\diamond$ is enclosed in the region $\Delta_i - \Delta_{i-1}$, hence $A_{i-1} \leq A^*$ and $A_i \geq A^\diamond + A_{i-1}$. Therefore, $\frac{A_i}{A_{i-1}} \geq k_\varepsilon$ is implied by $\frac{A^\diamond}{A^*} \geq k_\varepsilon - 1$.

Let h be the length of the segment $\overline{c_i o}$, let δ be the internal angle of $\Delta^\diamond$ at c_i, and let σ, β, and γ be the internal angles of Δ^* at c_i, o, and o^*, respectively. By construction, the slope of the segments $\overline{c_i o^\diamond}$ and $\overline{c_i o}$ are $\frac{\pi}{2} - \frac{\alpha}{2}$ and $\frac{\pi}{6} + \frac{\alpha}{2}$, respectively, hence $\delta = \frac{\pi}{3}$. Therefore, we have **(Eq. 1)** $A^\diamond = \frac{h^2 \tan(\delta)}{2} = \frac{\sqrt{3}}{2} h^2$.

Simple geometric arguments prove that $\sigma = \frac{\pi}{3} + \alpha$, $\beta \leq \frac{\pi}{3}$, and $\gamma \geq \frac{\pi}{3} - \alpha$. Let κ denote the length of the segment $\overline{c_i o^*}$. By the *law of sines* applied to Δ^*, we have $\kappa = h \sin(\beta)/\sin(\gamma)$. By $\beta \leq \frac{\pi}{3}$ and $\gamma \geq \frac{\pi}{3} - \alpha$, we get $\kappa \leq h \sin(\frac{\pi}{3})/\sin(\frac{\pi}{3} - \alpha) = h\sqrt{3}/(2\sin(\frac{\pi}{3} - \alpha))$. Further, since the segments $\overline{c_i o}$ and $\overline{c_i o^*}$ are two sides of Δ^*, whose angle at c_i is σ, we have $A^* = h\kappa \sin(\sigma)/2$. Using the upper bound for κ and $\sigma = \frac{\pi}{3} + \alpha$, we get **(Eq. 2)** $A^* \leq \frac{h^2 \sqrt{3}}{4} \frac{\sin(\frac{\pi}{3} + \alpha)}{\sin(\frac{\pi}{3} - \alpha)}$.

By **Eqs. 1** and **2**, we get $\frac{A^\diamond}{A^*} \geq \frac{2\sin(\frac{\pi}{3} - \alpha)}{\sin(\frac{\pi}{3} + \alpha)}$. Since $\frac{\pi}{3} - \alpha = \varepsilon$ and $\frac{\pi}{3} + \alpha = \frac{2\pi}{3} - \varepsilon$, we have that $\frac{A^\diamond}{A^*} \geq k_\varepsilon - 1$ is satisfied with $k_\varepsilon = 1 + 2\sin(\varepsilon)/\sin(\frac{2\pi}{3} - \varepsilon)$. Since $0 < \varepsilon < \frac{\pi}{3}$ is fixed, we have that k_ε is a constant greater than 1.   □

Claim 6 immediately implies that the area of the triangle $(a_{m-1}, b_{m-1}, c_{m-1})$ is at least k_ε^{m-2} times the area of the triangle (a_1, b_1, c_1). Since the area of the triangle (a_1, b_1, c_1) is greater than some constant depending on the adopted resolution rule, we get that the area of Γ is in $2^{\Omega_\varepsilon(m)}$.

We now define the family $\mathcal{F}$ of the statement. For any positive integer m and any $n = 6m - 2$, we construct the graph $F_n \in \mathcal{F}$ from the complete graph K_4, by taking two copies G'_m and G''_m of G_m and by identifying the vertices incident to the outer face of each copy with the three vertices incident to two distinct triangular faces of the K_4. Observe that F_n is a bounded-degree planar 3-tree. In any α-Schnyder drawing Γ of F_n (in fact in planar drawing of F_n), at least one of the two copies of G_m, say G'_m, is drawn so that its outer face is delimited by the triangle (a_m, b_m, c_m). Since F_n has a unique Schnyder wood [6,12], the restriction of such a Schnyder wood to the internal edges of G'_m satisfies the properties of Claim 5. It follows that the restriction of Γ to G'_m is an α-Schnyder drawing of G'_m (respecting the plane embedding of G'_m), and therefore it requires $2^{\Omega_\varepsilon(m)}$ area. The proof is concluded by observing that $m \in \Omega(n)$.   □

6   Conclusions and Open Problems

In this paper, we refuted a claim by Cao et al. [7] and re-opened the question of whether 3-connected planar graphs admit planar, and possibly convex, greedy drawings on a polynomial-size grid. We provided some evidence for a positive answer by showing that n-vertex Halin graphs admit convex greedy drawings on an $O(n) \times O(n)$ grid; in fact, our drawings are angle-monotone, a stronger property than greediness. Moreover, we proved that α-Schnyder drawings, which are even more constrained, might require exponential area for any fixed $\alpha < \frac{\pi}{3}$. Several questions remain open in this topic. We mention two of them. **(Q1)** Does every 2-outerplanar graph admit a planar, and possibly convex, greedy drawing on a polynomial-size grid? Note that the class of 2-outerplanar graphs is strictly larger than the one of Halin graphs. **(Q2)** Does every plane 3-tree admit a planar greedy drawing on a polynomial-size grid? We indeed proved a negative answer if "greedy drawing" is replaced by "α-Schnyder drawing", for any fixed $\alpha < \frac{\pi}{3}$.

References

1. Alamdari, S., Chan, T.M., Grant, E., Lubiw, A., Pathak, V.: Self-approaching Graphs. In: Didimo, W., Patrignani, M. (eds.) GD 2012. LNCS, vol. 7704, pp. 260–271. Springer, Heidelberg (2013). https://doi.org/10.1007/978-3-642-36763-2_23
2. Angelini, P., Di Battista, G., Frati, F.: Succinct greedy drawings do not always exist. Networks **59**(3), 267–274 (2012)
3. Angelini, P., Frati, F., Grilli, L.: An algorithm to construct greedy drawings of triangulations. J. Graph Alg. Appl. **14**(1), 19–51 (2010)
4. Bläsius, T., Friedrich, T., Katzmann, M., Krohmer, A.: Hyperbolic embeddings for near-optimal greedy routing. ALENEX **2018**, 199–208 (2018)
5. Bonichon, N., Bose, P., Carmi, P., Kostitsyna, I., Lubiw, A., Verdonschot, S.: Gabriel triangulations and angle-monotone graphs: local routing and recognition. In: Hu, Y., Nöllenburg, M. (eds.) GD 2016. LNCS, vol. 9801, pp. 519–531. Springer, Cham (2016). https://doi.org/10.1007/978-3-319-50106-2_40
6. Brehm, E.: 3-orientations and Schnyder 3-tree decompositions. Ph.D. thesis, Freie Universität Berlin (2000)
7. Cao, L., Strelzoff, A., Sun, J.Z.: On succinctness of geometric greedy routing in Euclidean plane. In: ISPAN 2009, pp. 326–331. IEEE Computer Society (2009)
8. Da Lozzo, G., D'Angelo, A., Frati, F.: On planar greedy drawings of 3-connected planar graphs. Discret. Comput. Geom. **63**(1), 114–157 (2020)
9. Dehkordi, H.R., Frati, F., Gudmundsson, J.: Increasing-chord graphs on point sets. J. Graph Alg. Appl. **19**(2), 761–778 (2015)
10. Dhandapani, R.: Greedy drawings of triangulations. Discrete Comput. Geom. **43**(2), 375–392 (2010)
11. Eppstein, D., Goodrich, M.T.: Succinct greedy geometric routing using hyperbolic geometry. IEEE Trans. Comput. **60**(11), 1571–1580 (2011)
12. Felsner, S., Zickfeld, F.: On the number of planar orientations with prescribed degrees. Electr. J. Comb. **15**(1) (2008)
13. Goodrich, M.T., Strash, D.: Succinct greedy geometric routing in the Euclidean plane. In: Dong, Y., Du, D.-Z., Ibarra, O. (eds.) ISAAC 2009. LNCS, vol. 5878, pp. 781–791. Springer, Heidelberg (2009). https://doi.org/10.1007/978-3-642-10631-6_79
14. He, X., Zhang, H.: On succinct greedy drawings of plane triangulations and 3-connected plane graphs. Algorithmica **68**(2), 531–544 (2014)
15. Leighton, T., Moitra, A.: Some results on greedy embeddings in metric spaces. Discrete Comput. Geom. **44**(3), 686–705 (2010)
16. Lubiw, A., Mondal, D.: Construction and local routing for angle-monotone graphs. J. Graph Alg. Appl. **23**(2), 345–369 (2019)
17. Lubiw, A., O'Rourke, J.: Angle-monotone paths in non-obtuse triangulations. In: CCCG 2017, pp. 25–30 (2017)
18. Muhammad, R.: A distributed geometric routing algorithm for ad hoc wireless networks. In: ITNG 2007, pp. 961–963. IEEE (2007)
19. Nöllenburg, M., Prutkin, R., Rutter, I.: On self-approaching and increasing-chord drawings of 3-connected planar graphs. J. Comput. Geom. **7**(1), 47–69 (2016)

20. Nöllenburg, M., Prutkin, R.: Euclidean greedy drawings of trees. Discrete Comput. Geom. **58**(3), 543–579 (2017)
21. Papadimitriou, C.H., Ratajczak, D.: On a conjecture related to geometric routing. Theoret. Comput. Sci. **344**(1), 3–14 (2005)
22. Papadimitriou, C.H., Ratajczak, D.: On a conjecture related to geometric routing. In: Nikoletseas, S.E., Rolim, J.D.P. (eds.) ALGOSENSORS 2004. LNCS, vol. 3121, pp. 9–17. Springer, Heidelberg (2004). https://doi.org/10.1007/978-3-540-27820-7_3
23. Rao, A., Papadimitriou, C.H., Shenker, S., Stoica, I.: Geographic routing without location information. In: MOBICOM 2003, pp. 96–108. ACM (2003)
24. Schnyder, W.: Embedding planar graphs on the grid. In: SODA 1990, pp. 138–148. SIAM (1990)
25. Sun, Y., Zhang, Y., Fang, B., Zhang, H.: Succinct and practical greedy embedding for geometric routing. Comput. Commun. **114**, 51–61 (2017)
26. Wang, J.J., He, X.: Succinct strictly convex greedy drawing of 3-connected plane graphs. Theoret. Comput. Sci. **532**, 80–90 (2014)

On the Restricted 1-Steiner Tree Problem

Prosenjit Bose[1], Anthony D'Angelo[1](✉), and Stephane Durocher[2]

[1] Carleton University, Ottawa, ON K1S-5B6, Canada
jit@scs.carleton.ca, anthony.dangelo@carleton.ca
[2] University of Manitoba, Winnipeg, MB R3T-2N2, Canada
durocher@cs.umanitoba.ca
http://www.scs.carleton.ca/~jit

Abstract. Given a set P of n points in $\mathbb{R}^2$ and an input line γ, we present an algorithm that runs in optimal $\Theta(n \log n)$ time and $\Theta(n)$ space to solve a restricted version of the 1-Steiner tree problem. Our algorithm returns a minimum-weight tree interconnecting P using at most one Steiner point $s \in \gamma$ where edges are weighted by the Euclidean distance between their endpoints.

Keywords: Minimum k-Steiner tree · Steiner point restrictions

1 Introduction

Finding the shortest interconnecting network for a given set of points is an interesting problem for anyone concerned with conserving resources. Sometimes, we are able to add new points in addition to the given input points to reduce the total length of the edges in the interconnecting network. These extra points are called Steiner points. However, finding where to place these Steiner points and how many to place is NP-hard [11,12,23,33], and so a natural question is: *What is the shortest spanning network that can be constructed by adding only k Steiner points to the given set of points?* This is the k-Steiner point problem.

Consider a set P of n points in the 2-D Euclidean plane, which are also called *terminals* in the Steiner tree literature. The **Minimum Spanning Tree (MST)** problem is to find the minimum-weight tree interconnecting P where edges are weighted by the Euclidean distance between their endpoints. Let $\mathrm{MST}(P)$ be a Euclidean minimum spanning tree on P and let $|\mathrm{MST}(P)|$ be the sum of its edge-weights (also called the *length* of the tree). Imagine we are given another set S of points in the 2-D Euclidean plane. The set S is the set of *Steiner points* that we may use as intermediate nodes in addition to the points of P to compute the minimum-weight interconnection of P. An MST on the union of the terminals P with some subset of Steiner points $S' \subseteq S$, i.e., $\{P \cup S'\}$, is a Steiner tree. In the Euclidean **Minimum Steiner Tree (MStT)** problem, the goal is to find a subset $S' \subseteq S$ such that $|\mathrm{MST}(\{P \cup S'\})|$ is no longer than $|\mathrm{MST}(\{P \cup X\})|$

Funded in part by the Natural Sciences and Engineering Research Council of Canada (NSERC).

D. Kim et al. (Eds.): COCOON 2020, LNCS 12273, pp. 448–459, 2020.
https://doi.org/10.1007/978-3-030-58150-3_36

for any $X \subseteq S$. Such a minimum-weight tree is a MStT. For our restricted k-Steiner tree problem, we are given an input line γ in $\mathbb{R}^2$; the line $\gamma = S$ and the cardinality of S' is at most k.

As 3-D printing enters the mainstream, material-saving and time-saving printing algorithms are becoming more relevant. Drawing on the study of MStTs, Vanek et al. [36] presented a geometric heuristic to create support-trees for 3-D printed objects where the forking points in these trees are solutions to a constrained Steiner point problem. Inspired by the work of Vanek et al. as well as the solutions for the 1-Steiner and k-Steiner point problems in the 2-D Euclidean plane [8,12,24], we present an efficient algorithm to compute an exact solution for the 1-Steiner point problem where the placement of the Steiner point is constrained to lie on an input line. We present another motivating example. Imagine we have a set V of wireless nodes that must communicate by radio transmission. To transmit a longer distance to reach more distant nodes requires transmitting at a higher power. The MST of V can be used to model a connected network that spans the nodes of V while minimizing total power consumption. Suppose that an additional wireless node is available to be added to V, but that the new node's position is restricted to lie on a road γ on which it will be delivered on a vehicle. Where on γ should the additional node be positioned to minimize the total transmission power of the new network?

We refer to our problem as a 1-*Steiner tree problem restricted to a line*. For our purposes, let an ***optimal Steiner point*** be a point $s \in \gamma$ such that $|\operatorname{MST}(P \cup \{s\})| \leq |\operatorname{MST}(P \cup \{u\})|$ for all $u \in \gamma$.

Problem. Given a set of n points P in $\mathbb{R}^2$ and a line γ in $\mathbb{R}^2$, compute the MStT of P using at most 1 optimal Steiner point $s \in \gamma$.

A restricted version of our problem has been studied for the case when the input point set P lies to one side of the given input line and a point from the line *must* be chosen. Chen and Zhang gave an $O(n^2)$-time algorithm to solve this problem [15]. Similar problems have also been studied by Li et al. [29] building on the research of Holby [28]. The two settings they study are: (a) the points of P lie anywhere and *must* connect to the input line using any number of Steiner points, and any part of the input line used in a spanning tree does not count towards its length; and (b) the same problem, but the optimal line to minimize the network length is not given and must be computed. Li et al. provide 1.214-approximation[1] algorithms for both (a) and (b) in $O(n \log n)$ and $O(n^3 \log n)$ time respectively. The problems of Chen and Zhang, Li et al., and Holby are different than our problem since we are not required to connect to our input line, we have no restriction on the placement of the points of P with respect to the line, and travel in our network has the same cost ***on*** the input line as ***off*** of it. For example, one can imagine if the points of the point set were close to the line but far from each other, in which case the solution of Li et al. [29]

---

[1] This means the length of their tree is at most 1.214 times the length of the optimal solution. Here they take advantage of the result of Chung and Graham [18] showing that the MST is a 1.214-approximation (to three decimals) of the MStT.

would connect the points to the line and get a tree with much less weight/length than even the MStT. Such an example is shown in Fig. 1. In Fig. 1 the MStT of points $\{a, b, c, d\}$ is the same as its MST since all triples form angles larger than $\frac{2\pi}{3}$ [12,25]. In our setting, the MST is the best solution for this point set, whereas in the setting of Holby [28] and Li et al. [29], the best solution connects each input point directly to γ to form a spanning tree between the points using pieces of γ. The length of the MST is significantly larger than the length of the other solution since in their setting, only the edges connecting the points to γ contribute to the length of the spanning tree.

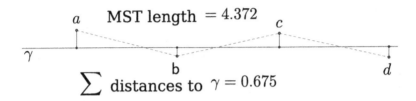

Fig. 1. Here we have γ as the x-axis, $a = (0.489, 0.237)$, $b = (1.865, -0.114)$, $c = (3.26, 0.184)$, and $d = (4.75, -0.141)$. The MST of $\{a, b, c, d\}$ in red dashed line segments and its length, the input line γ, a spanning tree of $\{a, b, c, d\}$ connecting each point to γ, and the length of this spanning tree for the setting of Holby [28] and Li et al. [29]. (Color figure online)

We use a type of Voronoi diagram in our algorithm whose regions are bounded by rays and segments. We make a general position assumption that γ is not collinear with any ray or segment in the Voronoi diagrams. In other words, the intersection of the rays and segments of these Voronoi diagrams with γ is either empty or a single point. We also assume that the edges of MST(P) have distinct weights. In this paper we show the following.

Theorem 1. *Given a set P of n points in the Euclidean plane and a line γ, there is an algorithm that computes in optimal $\Theta(n \log n)$ time and optimal $\Theta(n)$ space a minimum-weight tree connecting all points in P using at most one point of γ.*

Section 2 reviews the tools and properties we will need for our algorithm, and Sect. 3 presents our algorithm and the proof of Theorem 1.

2   Relevant Results

There has been a lot of research on Steiner trees in various dimensions, metrics, norms, and under various constraints. See the surveys by Brazil et al. [7] and Brazil and Zachariasen [12] for a good introduction. In the general Euclidean case it has been shown that Steiner points that reduce the length of the MST have degree 3 or 4 [32]. There are results for building Steiner trees when the *terminal set* is restricted to *zig-zags* [4,20], *curves* [33], *ladders* [19], and *checkerboards* [6,9,10]; for when the angles between edges are constrained [11,12]; for obstacle-avoiding Steiner trees [37–41] (which include geodesic versions where the terminals, Steiner points, and tree are contained in polygons); and for k-Steiner trees with k as a fixed constant where you can use at most k Steiner points (for terminals and Steiner points in various normed planes including the 2-D Euclidean plane, there is an $O(n^{2k})$-time algorithm) [8,12,24].

2.1 Tools

Without loss of generality, we consider the positive x-axis to be the basis for measuring angles, so that 0 radians is the positive x-axis, $\frac{\pi}{3}$ radians is a counterclockwise rotation of the positive x-axis about the origin by $\frac{\pi}{3}$ radians, etc.

Observation 2. *Given a point set $V \subset \mathbb{R}^2$, if we build $\mathrm{MST}(V)$, each point $v \in V$ will have at most 6 neighbours in the MST. This is because, due to the sine law, for any two neighbours w and z of v in $\mathrm{MST}(V)$ the angle $\angle wvz$ must be at least $\frac{\pi}{3}$ radians. These potential neighbours can be found by dividing the plane up into 6 interior-disjoint cones of angle $\frac{\pi}{3}$ all apexed on v. The closest point of V to v in each cone is the potential neighbour of v in the MST in that cone.*

Consider our input line γ as being the real number line, represented by the x-axis in the Euclidean plane. This line can be parametrized by x-coordinates. Let an ***interval*** on γ be the set of points on γ in between and including two fixed x-coordinates, called the endpoints of the interval. Our approach will be to divide the input line into $O(n)$ intervals using a special kind of Voronoi diagram outlined below. The intervals have the property that for any given interval I, if we compute $\mathrm{MST}(P \cup \{s\})$ for any $s \in I$, the subset of possible neighbours of s in the MST is constant. For example, Fig. 2 shows a set V of input points with the blue points labelled p_i for $1 \leq i \leq 6$, the input line γ, and a green interval I. The plane is divided into 6 cones of 60 degrees, all apexed on the red point $x \in I$. In $\mathrm{MST}(V \cup \{x\})$, if x connects to a point in cone i, it connects to p_i. The green interval I has the property that this is true anywhere we slide x and its cones in I.

Oriented Voronoi Diagrams. The 1-Steiner point algorithm of Georgakopoulos and Papadimitriou (we refer to this algorithm as *GPA*) [24] works by subdividing the plane into $O(n^2)$ regions defined by the cells of the *Overlaid Oriented Voronoi Diagram* (overlaid **OVD**).[2] Refer to the cone $\mathbb{K}$ defining an OVD as an *OVD-cone*. Let $\mathbb{K}_v$ be a copy of the OVD-cone whose apex coincides with point $v \in \mathbb{R}^2$. OVDs are a type of Voronoi diagram made up of oriented Voronoi

---

[2] In the Georgakopoulos and Papadimitriou paper [24] this is referred to as *Overlaid Oriented Dirichlet Cells*.

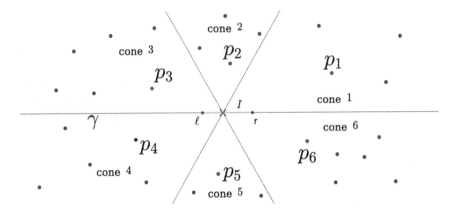

Fig. 2. Every point along the green interval I of γ (i.e., between the ℓ endpoint and the r endpoint) has the same potential MST neighbour (the blue points) in the same cone. (Color figure online)

regions (**OVRs**) where the OVR of a site $p \in P$ is the set of points $w \in \mathbb{R}^2$ for which p is the closest site in $\mathbb{K}_w \cap P$. If $\mathbb{K}_w \cap P = \emptyset$ we say w belongs to an OVR whose site is the empty set. These notions are illustrated in Fig. 3.

Chang et al. [13] show us that the OVD for a given OVD-cone of angle $\frac{\pi}{3}$ (e.g., the OVD in Fig. 3) can be built in $O(n \log n)$ time using $O(n)$ space. The OVD is comprised of segments and rays that are subsets of bisectors and cone boundaries which bound the OVRs. The size of the OVD is $O(n)$.

Since by Observation 2 a vertex of the MST has a maximum degree of 6, by overlaying the 6 OVDs for the 6 cones of angle $\frac{\pi}{3}$ that subdivide the Euclidean plane (i.e., each of the six cones defines an orientation for a different OVD) the GPA creates $O(n^2)$ regions. Each of these regions has the property that if we place a Steiner point s in the region, the points of P associated with this region (up to 6 possible points) are the only possible neighbours of s in the MStT (similar to the example in Fig. 2). The GPA then iterates over each of these regions. In region R, the GPA considers each subset of possible neighbours associated with R. For each such subset it then computes the optimal location for a Steiner point whose neighbours are the elements of the subset, and then computes the length of the MStT using that Steiner point, keeping track of the best solution seen. The generalized algorithm for placing k Steiner points [8,12] essentially does the same thing k times (by checking the topologies of the MStT for all possible placements of k points), but is more complicated (checking the effects that multiple Steiner points have on the MStT is more complex).

Updating Minimum Spanning Trees. In order to avoid actually computing each of the candidate MSTs on the set of P with the addition of our candidate Steiner points, we instead compute the *differences in length* between MST(P) and the candidate MStTs. Georgakopoulos and Papadimitriou similarly avoid

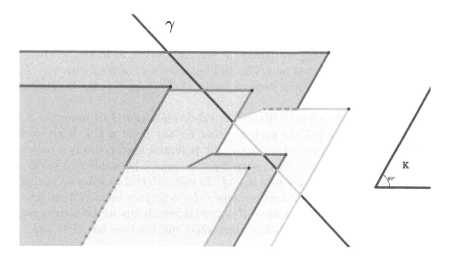

Fig. 3. An example of an OVD for 6 points defined by the OVD-cone $\mathbb{K}$ with bounding rays oriented towards 0 and $\frac{\pi}{3}$. The 6 sites (i.e., the points) are the blue top-right points of the coloured OVRs. When intersected with γ, the OVD creates intervals along γ. Each interval corresponds to exactly one OVR, but an OVR may create multiple intervals (for example, the light-blue OVR creates the two orange intervals). The site corresponding to an interval outside of a coloured OVR is a special site represented by the empty set. (Color figure online)

repeated MST computations by performing $O(n^2)$ preprocessing to allow them to answer queries of the following type in constant time: given that the edges $ab_1, ab_2, \ldots, ab_j$ are decreased by $\delta_1, \delta_2, \ldots, \delta_j$ for constant j, what is the new MST? They then use these queries to find the length of the MStT for each candidate Steiner point. Refer to [24] for details. Brazil et al. also perform some preprocessing in time between $O(n^2)$ and $O(n^3)$ [8]. However, using an approach involving an auxiliary tree and lowest common ancestor (LCA) queries, we can compute what we need in $o(n^2)$ time. We first compute $\mathrm{MST}(P)$ and build an auxiliary tree in $O(n \log n)$ time and process the auxiliary tree in $O(n)$ time [27] to support LCA queries in $O(1)$ time [5,30].

3   Algorithm

In this section we present our algorithm and prove Theorem 1. The algorithm computes OVDs for the 6 cones of angle $\frac{\pi}{3}$ that divide up the Euclidean plane (i.e., each of the 6 cones defines an orientation for a different OVD). Though they can be overlaid in $O(n^2)$ time, we do not need to overlay them. As mentioned in Sect. 2.1, each OVD has $O(n)$ size and is therefore comprised of $O(n)$ rays and segments. As illustrated in Fig. 3, intersecting any given OVD with a line γ carves γ up into $O(n)$ intervals since we have $O(n)$ rays and segments, each of which intersect a line $O(1)$ times.[3] Each interval corresponds to an intersection of γ with exactly one OVR of the OVD since OVDs are planar, but multiple non-adjacent intervals may be defined by the same OVR, as in Fig. 3. Therefore each interval I is a subset of an OVR, and for every pair of points $u_1, u_2 \in I$ the closest point in $\mathbb{K}_{u_1} \cap P$ is the same as in $\mathbb{K}_{u_2} \cap P$, where $\mathbb{K}$ is the OVD-cone of the OVD being considered.

If we do this with all six OVDs, γ is subdivided into $O(n)$ intervals. As in Fig. 2, each interval I has the property that for any point $u \in I$, if we were to build $\mathrm{MST}(P \cup \{u\})$, the ordered set of six potential neighbours is a constant-sized set.[4] Each element of this ordered set is defined by a different OVD and corresponds to the closest point in $\mathbb{K}_u \cap P$. In each interval we solve an optimization problem to find the optimal placement for a Steiner point in that interval (i.e., minimize the sum of distances of potential neighbours to the Steiner point) which takes $O(1)$ time since each of these $O(1)$ subproblems has $O(1)$ size.

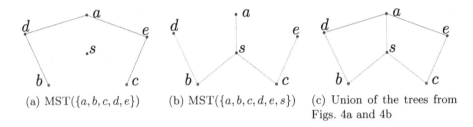

(a) MST($\{a, b, c, d, e\}$)   (b) MST($\{a, b, c, d, e, s\}$)   (c) Union of the trees from Figs. 4a and 4b

Fig. 4. The union of the trees in (a) and (b) gives the graph in (c) with cycles (s, b, d, a), (s, a, e, c), and (s, b, d, a, e, c) whose longest edges excluding s are (d, a) and (a, e).

Once we have computed an optimal placement for a Steiner point for each computed interval of our input line γ, we want to compute which one of these $O(n)$ candidates produces the MStT, i.e., the candidate s that produces the smallest length of the $\mathrm{MST}(P \cup \{s\})$. Let T^* be the union of $\mathrm{MST}(P)$ and $\mathrm{MST}(P \cup \{s\})$, as in Fig. 4. For a candidate s, the savings are calculated by summing the length of the longest edge on each cycle of T^* excluding the edges incident to s minus the sum of the lengths of the edges incident to s in $\mathrm{MST}(P \cup \{s\})$. For example, in Fig. 4c, the candidate edges on the left cycle are (b, d) and (d, a), and on the right cycle they are (a, e) and (e, c); we sum the lengths of the longest candidate edge from each cycle, i.e., (d, a) and (a, e), and subtract the sum of the lengths of edges (s, a), (s, b), and (s, c) to calculate the savings we get from choosing s as the solution Steiner point. Note that the longest edge on the cycle (s, b, d, a, e, c) is either (d, a) or (a, e). As will be seen in the proof of Theorem 1, the sum of the lengths of the edges incident to s are computed when determining s. What remains to find are the lengths of the longest edges

---

[3] This follows from the zone theorem [3,14,21].

[4] In other words, each $u \in I$ has the same constant-sized set of fixed candidate topologies that could be the result of $\mathrm{MST}(P \cup \{u\})$.

of MST(P) on the cycles of T^*. The following theorem from Bose et al. [5] tells us that with $O(n \log n)$ preprocessing of MST(P), we can compute the sum in which we are interested in $O(1)$ time for each candidate Steiner point.[5] First an auxiliary binary tree is computed whose nodes correspond to edge lengths and leaves correspond to points of P. This tree has the property that the LCA of two leaves is the longest edge on the path between them in MST(P). They then take advantage of a result that uses $O(n)$ preprocessing on the auxiliary tree enabling them to perform $O(1)$-time LCA queries (either Harel and Tarjan [27], Schieber and Vishkin [34], or Bender and Farach-Colton [2]).

Lemma 1 (Bose et al. 2004 [5, paraphrased Theorem 2]**).** *We can preprocess a set of n points in $\mathbb{R}^2$ in $O(n \log n)$ time into a data structure of size $O(n)$ such that the longest edge on the path between any two points in the MST can be computed in $O(1)$ time.*

We are now ready to finish proving Theorem 1.

Theorem 1. *Given a set P of n points in the Euclidean plane and a line γ, there is an algorithm that computes in optimal $\Theta(n \log n)$ time and optimal $\Theta(n)$ space a minimum-weight tree connecting all points in P using at most one point of γ.*

Proof. The tree $T = \text{MST}(P)$ and its length are computed in $O(n \log n)$ time and $O(n)$ space by computing the Voronoi diagram in those bounds [1,3,22,26], walking over the Voronoi diagram creating the dual and weighting the edges in $O(n)$ time and space (the reasoning for which follows from Shamos [35]), and computing the MST from the Delaunay triangulation in $O(n)$ time and space [16,31]. By Lemma 1, in $O(n \log n)$ time and $O(n)$ space we compute the longest edge auxiliary tree T' and preprocess it to answer LCA queries in $O(1)$ time. Each of the 6 OVDs is then computed in $O(n \log n)$ time and $O(n)$ space [8,13,17]. In $O(n)$ time and space we extract $\mathbb{L}$, the set of rays and segments defining each OVR of each OVD. While computing the OVDs, in $O(n)$ time we add labels to the boundary rays and segments describing which OVD-cone defined them and the two sites corresponding to the two OVRs they border.

Since γ is a line, it intersects any element of $\mathbb{L}$ $O(1)$ times and we can compute each of these intersections in $O(1)$ time. Therefore, computing the intersections of γ with $\mathbb{L}$ takes $O(n)$ time and space. Assume without loss of generality that γ is the x-axis. Given our $O(n)$ intersection points, we can make a list of the $O(n)$ intervals they create along γ in $O(n \log n)$ time and $O(n)$ space by sorting the intersection points by x-coordinate and then walking along γ. During this process we also use the labels of the elements of $\mathbb{L}$ to label each interval with its six potential neighbours described above in $O(1)$ time per interval.

By the triangle inequality, an optimal Steiner point has degree more than 2. In [32] it was shown to have degree no more than 4. Therefore an optimal Steiner point has degree 3 or 4. We then loop over each interval looking for the solution by finding the optimal placement of a Steiner point in the interval for $O(1)$ fixed

---

[5] A similar result was shown in Monma and Suri [30, Lemma 4.1, pg. 277].

topologies. Consider an interval I and its set of potential neighbours $P' \subset P$ of size at most 6. For each subset $\mathbb{P}$ of P' of size 3 and 4 (of which there are $O(1)$), we compute $O(1)$ candidate optimal Steiner points in γ. Note that γ is actually a polynomial function, $\gamma(x)$. Our computation is done using the following distance function $d(x)$, where a_x and a_y are the x and y coordinates of point a respectively, and $\gamma(x)$ is the evaluation of γ at x: $d_{\mathbb{P}}(x) = \sum_{a \in \mathbb{P}}^{|\mathbb{P}|} \sqrt{(a_x - x)^2 + (a_y - \gamma(x))^2}$. We then take the derivative of this distance function and solve for the global minima by finding the roots within the domain specified by the endpoints of I. Since the size of $\mathbb{P}$ is bounded by a constant and since the degree of the polynomial γ is a constant, this computation takes $O(1)$ time and $O(1)$ space and the number of global minima is $O(1)$. Note that the value of the distance function at a particular x for a particular $\mathbb{P}$ tells us the sum of edge lengths from the point $u = (x, \gamma(x))$ to the points in $\mathbb{P}$. We associate this value with u. Out of the $O(1)$ candidate points, we choose the one for which $d_{\mathbb{P}}(x)$ is minimum. We can break ties arbitrarily, since a tie means the points offer the same amount of savings to the MST since they both have the same topology in the MST (meaning they have the same cycles in $\mathrm{MST}(P) \cup \mathrm{MST}(P \cup \{u\})$), and since the value of $d_{\mathbb{P}}(x)$ being the same means that the sum of adjacent edges is the same.

Once we have our $O(1)$ candidate optimal Steiner points for I, we need to compare each one against our current best solution s. In other words, for each candidate u we need to compare $|\mathrm{MST}(P \cup \{u\})|$ with $|\mathrm{MST}(P \cup \{s\})|$. We take advantage of the following: if we compute the union of $\mathrm{MST}(P)$ and $\mathrm{MST}(P \cup \{u\})$ we get at most $\binom{4}{2} = 6$ simple cycles[6] through u. Let this connected set of cycles be Q. If $\mathbb{P}_u$ is the set of neighbours associated with the candidate u, we have $|\mathrm{MST}(P \cup \{u\})| = |\mathrm{MST}(P)| + d_{\mathbb{P}_u}(u) - \Delta$, where Δ is the sum of the longest edge in each cycle of Q excluding from consideration the edges incident to u. By Lemma 1, we can compute Δ in $O(1)$ time using T'. Due to space constraints, we omit the proof that removing the longest edge from each cycle of Q results in a tree. If $|\mathrm{MST}(P \cup \{u\})| < |\mathrm{MST}(P \cup \{s\})|$ we set $s = u$.

Finally, we check if $|\mathrm{MST}(P \cup \{s\})| < |T|$. If so, we return $\mathrm{MST}(P \cup \{s\})$. Otherwise we return T.

Now we show the space and time optimality. The $\Omega(n)$-space lower-bound comes from the fact that we have to read in the input. The $\Omega(n \log n)$-time lower-bound comes from a reduction from the *closest pair* problem (CPP). The CPP is where we are given n points in $\mathbb{R}^2$ and we are supposed to return a closest pair with respect to Euclidean distance. The CPP has an $\Omega(n \log n)$ lower-bound [31, Theorem 5.2]. Indeed, given an instance of CPP we can turn it into our problem in $O(n)$ time by using the points as the input points P and choosing an arbitrary γ.

Given the solution to our problem, we can find a closest pair in $O(n)$ time by walking over the resulting tree. First, remove the Steiner point (if any) and its incident edges to break our tree up into $O(1)$ connected components. Consider one of these components $\mathbb{C}$. $\mathbb{C}$ may contain both points of multiple closest pairs, or none. Imagine $\mathbb{C}$ contained both points for exactly one closest pair. Then the

---

[6] In a simple cycle the only vertex seen twice is the first/last vertex.

edge connecting them will be in $\mathbb{C}$ and it will be the edge with minimum-weight in $\mathbb{C}$; otherwise it contradicts that we had a minimum-weight tree. Imagine $\mathbb{C}$ contained both points for multiple closest pairs. Pick one of the closest pairs. If $\mathbb{C}$ does not contain the edge e connecting the two points of the pair, then there is a path between them in $\mathbb{C}$ consisting of minimum-weight edges (whose weights match e) connecting other closest pairs; otherwise we contradict the minimality of our tree or that both points were in the same connected component. If no component contains both points of a closest pair, then the path between a closest pair goes through the Steiner point. Once again, choose a closest pair (a, b) and let the edge connecting this closest pair be e. Due to the minimality of our tree, the weight of every edge on the path between a and b is no more than that of e. However, since no component contains a closest pair, that means that a and b are incident to the Steiner point. Therefore, we get a solution to the CPP by walking over our resulting tree and returning the minimum among a minimum-weight edge connecting neighbours of the Steiner point and a minimum-weight edge seen walking through our tree excluding edges incident to the Steiner point. □

Corollary 1. *Given a set P of n points in the Euclidean plane and j lines $\Gamma = \{\gamma_1, \ldots \gamma_j\}$, by running the algorithm of Theorem 1 for each $\gamma \in \Gamma$, in $O(jn \log n)$ time and $O(n+j)$ space we compute a minimum-weight tree connecting all points in P using at most one point from $\gamma_1, \ldots \gamma_j$.*

Acknowledgements. The authors thank Jean-Lou De Carufel for helpful discussions.

References

1. Aurenhammer, F., Klein, R., Lee, D.: Voronoi Diagrams and Delaunay Triangulations. World Scientific (2013)
2. Bender, M.A., Farach-Colton, M.: The LCA problem revisited. In: Gonnet, G.H., Viola, A. (eds.) LATIN 2000. LNCS, vol. 1776, pp. 88–94. Springer, Heidelberg (2000). https://doi.org/10.1007/10719839_9
3. de Berg, M., Cheong, O., van Kreveld, M.J., Overmars, M.H.: Computational Geometry: Algorithms and Applications, 3rd edn. Springer, Heidelberg (2008). https://doi.org/10.1007/978-3-540-77974-2
4. Booth, R.S., Weng, J.F.: Steiner minimal trees for a class of zigzag lines. Algorithmica **7**(2&3), 231–246 (1992)
5. Bose, P., Maheshwari, A., Narasimhan, G., Smid, M.H.M., Zeh, N.: Approximating geometric bottleneck shortest paths. Comput. Geom. **29**(3), 233–249 (2004)
6. Brazil, M., Cole, T., Rubinstein, J.H., Thomas, D.A., Weng, J.F., Wormald, N.C.: Minimal Steiner trees for $2^k \times 2^k$ square lattices. J. Comb. Theory Ser. A **73**(1), 91–110 (1996)
7. Brazil, M., Graham, R.L., Thomas, D.A., Zachariasen, M.: On the history of the Euclidean Steiner tree problem. Arch. Hist. Exact Sci. **68**(3), 327–354 (2014)
8. Brazil, M., Ras, C.J., Swanepoel, K.J., Thomas, D.A.: Generalised k-Steiner tree problems in normed planes. Algorithmica **71**(1), 66–86 (2015)
9. Brazil, M., Rubinstein, J.H., Thomas, D.A., Weng, J.F., Wormald, N.C.: Full minimal Steiner trees on lattice sets. J. Comb. Theory Ser. A **78**(1), 51–91 (1997)

10. Brazil, M., Rubinstein, J.H., Thomas, D.A., Weng, J.F., Wormald, N.C.: Minimal Steiner trees for rectangular arrays of lattice points. J. Comb. Theory Ser. A **79**(2), 181–208 (1997)
11. Brazil, M., Thomas, D.A., Weng, J.F.: On the complexity of the Steiner problem. J. Comb. Optim. **4**(2), 187–195 (2000)
12. Brazil, M., Zachariasen, M.: Optimal Interconnection Trees in the Plane: Theory, Algorithms and Applications, vol. 29. Springer, Heidelberg (2015). https://doi.org/10.1007/978-3-319-13915-910.1007/978-3-319-13915-9
13. Chang, M., Huang, N., Tang, C.Y.: An optimal algorithm for constructing oriented Voronoi diagrams and geographic neighborhood graphs. Inf. Process. Lett. **35**(5), 255–260 (1990)
14. Chazelle, B., Guibas, L.J., Lee, D.T.: The power of geometric duality. BIT Comput. Sci. Sect. **25**(1), 76–90 (1985)
15. Chen, G., Zhang, G.: A constrained minimum spanning tree problem. Comput. Oper. Res. **27**(9), 867–875 (2000)
16. Cheriton, D.R., Tarjan, R.E.: Finding minimum spanning trees. SIAM J. Comput. **5**(4), 724–742 (1976)
17. Chew, L.P., Dyrsdale III, R.L.: Voronoi diagrams based on convex distance functions. In: Symposium on Computational Geometry, pp. 235–244. ACM (1985)
18. Chung, F.R.K., Graham, R.L.: A new bound for Euclidean Steiner minimal trees. Ann. N. Y. Acad. Sci. **440**(1), 328–346 (1985)
19. Chung, F., Graham, R.: Steiner trees for ladders. Ann. Discret. Math. **2**, 173–200 (1978)
20. Du, D., Hwang, F., Weng, J.: Steiner minimal trees on zig-zag lines. Trans. Am. Math. Soc. **278**(1), 149–156 (1983)
21. Edelsbrunner, H., Seidel, R., Sharir, M.: On the zone theorem for hyperplane arrangements. SIAM J. Comput. **22**(2), 418–429 (1993)
22. Fortune, S.: A sweepline algorithm for Voronoi diagrams. Algorithmica **2**, 153–174 (1987)
23. Garey, M.R., Graham, R.L., Johnson, D.S.: The complexity of computing Steiner minimal trees. SIAM J. Appl. Math. **32**(4), 835–859 (1977)
24. Georgakopoulos, G.K., Papadimitriou, C.H.: The 1-Steiner tree problem. J. Algorithms **8**(1), 122–130 (1987)
25. Gilbert, E., Pollak, H.: Steiner minimal trees. SIAM J. Appl. Math. **16**(1), 1–29 (1968)
26. Guibas, L.J., Stolfi, J.: Ruler, compass and computer. In: Earnshaw, R.A. (ed.) Theoretical Foundations of Computer Graphics and CAD, pp. 111–165. Springer, Heidelberg (1988). https://doi.org/10.1007/978-3-642-83539-1_4
27. Harel, D., Tarjan, R.E.: Fast algorithms for finding nearest common ancestors. SIAM J. Comput. **13**(2), 338–355 (1984)
28. Holby, J.: Variations on the Euclidean Steiner tree problem and algorithms. Rose-Hulman Undergraduate Math. J. **18**(1), 7 (2017)
29. Li, J., Liu, S., Lichen, J., Wang, W., Zheng, Y.: Approximation algorithms for solving the 1-line Euclidean minimum Steiner tree problem. J. Comb. Optim. **39**(2), 492–508 (2020)
30. Monma, C.L., Suri, S.: Transitions in geometric minimum spanning trees. Discret. Comput. Geom. **8**, 265–293 (1992)
31. Preparata, F.P., Shamos, M.I.: Computational Geometry - An Introduction. Texts and Monographs in Computer Science. Springer, Heidelberg (1985). https://doi.org/10.1007/978-1-4612-1098-6

32. Rubinstein, J.H., Thomas, D.A., Weng, J.F.: Degree-five Steiner points cannot reduce network costs for planar sets. Networks **22**(6), 531–537 (1992)
33. Rubinstein, J.H., Thomas, D.A., Wormald, N.C.: Steiner trees for terminals constrained to curves. SIAM J. Discret. Math. **10**(1), 1–17 (1997)
34. Schieber, B., Vishkin, U.: On finding lowest common ancestors: simplification and parallelization. SIAM J. Comput. **17**(6), 1253–1262 (1988)
35. Shamos, M.: Computational geometry, Ph.D. thesis (1978)
36. Vanek, J., Galicia, J.A.G., Benes, B.: Clever support: efficient support structure generation for digital fabrication. Comput. Graph. Forum **33**(5), 117–125 (2014)
37. Winter, P.: Euclidean Steiner minimal trees with obstacles and Steiner visibility graphs. Discret. Appl. Math. **47**(2), 187–206 (1993)
38. Winter, P.: Euclidean Steiner minimum trees for 3 terminals in a simple polygon. In: Proceedings of the Seventh Canadian Conference on Computational Geometry, Univ. Laval, Quebec, Canada, pp. 247–255 (1995)
39. Winter, P.: Steiner minimum trees in simple polygons. DIMACS Technical Report 95-43 (1995)
40. Winter, P., Zachariasen, M., Nielsen, J.: Short trees in polygons. Discret. Appl. Math. **118**(1–2), 55–72 (2002)
41. Zachariasen, M., Winter, P.: Obstacle-avoiding Euclidean Steiner trees in the plane: an exact algorithm. In: Goodrich, M.T., McGeoch, C.C. (eds.) ALENEX 1999. LNCS, vol. 1619, pp. 282–295. Springer, Heidelberg (1999). https://doi.org/10.1007/3-540-48518-X_17

Computational Complexity of Synchronization Under Regular Commutative Constraints

Stefan Hoffmann$^{(\boxtimes)}$ (iD)

Informatikwissenschaften, FB IV, Universität Trier,
Universitätsring 15, 54296 Trier, Germany
hoffmanns@informatik.uni-trier.de

Abstract. Here we study the computational complexity of the constrained synchronization problem for the class of regular commutative constraint languages. Utilizing a vector representation of regular commutative constraint languages, we give a full classification of the computational complexity of the constrained synchronization problem. Depending on the constraint language, our problem becomes PSPACE-complete, NP-complete or polynomial time solvable. In addition, we derive a polynomial time decision procedure for the complexity of the constrained synchronization problem, given a constraint automaton accepting a commutative language as input.

Keywords: Constrained synchronization · Computational complexity · Automata theory · Commutative language

1 Introduction

A deterministic semi-automaton is synchronizing if it admits a reset word, i.e., a word which leads to a definite state, regardless of the starting state. This notion has a wide range of applications, from software testing, circuit synthesis, communication engineering and the like, see [10,11]. The famous Černý conjecture [1] states that a minimal synchronizing word has at most quadratic length. We refer to the mentioned survey articles for details. Due to its importance, the notion of synchronization has undergone a range of generalizations and variations for other automata models. It was noted in [9] that in some generalizations only certain paths, or input words, are allowed (namely those for which the input automaton is defined). In [5] the notion of constrained synchronization was introduced in connection with a reduction procedure for synchronizing automata. The paper [2] introduced the computational problem of constrained synchronization. In this problem, we search for a synchronizing word coming from a specific subset of allowed input sequences. For further motivation and applications we refer to the aforementioned paper [2]. In this paper, a complete analysis of the complexity landscape when the constraint language is given by small partial automata was

© Springer Nature Switzerland AG 2020
D. Kim et al. (Eds.): COCOON 2020, LNCS 12273, pp. 460–471, 2020.
https://doi.org/10.1007/978-3-030-58150-3_37

done. It is natural to extend this result to other language classes, or even to give a complete classification of all the complexity classes that could arise. Our work is in this vein, we will look at the complexity landscape for commutative regular constraint languages.

2 Prerequisites

2.1 General Notions and Problems Related to Automata and Synchronization

By $\mathbb{N}_0 = \{0, 1, 2, \ldots\}$ we denote the natural numbers with zero. Setting $n < \infty$ for all $n \in \mathbb{N}_0$, we will use the symbol ∞ in connection with $\mathbb{N}_0$. Hence we regard $\mathbb{N}_0 \cup \{\infty\}$ as an ordered set with top element ∞. Throughout the paper, we consider deterministic finite automata (DFAs). Recall that a DFA $\mathcal{A}$ is a tuple $\mathcal{A} = (\Sigma, Q, \delta, q_0, F)$, where the alphabet Σ is a finite set of input symbols, Q is the finite state set, with start state $q_0 \in Q$, and final state set $F \subseteq Q$. The transition function $\delta : Q \times \Sigma \to Q$ extends to words from Σ^* in the usual way. The function δ can be further extended to sets of states in the following way. For every set $S \subseteq Q$ with $S \neq \varnothing$ and $w \in \Sigma^*$, we set $\delta(S, w) := \{\delta(q, w) \mid q \in S\}$. We call $\mathcal{A}$ *complete* if δ is defined for every $(q, a) \in Q \times \Sigma$; if δ is undefined for some (q, a), the automaton $\mathcal{A}$ is called *partial*. If $|\Sigma| = 1$, we call $\mathcal{A}$ a *unary* automaton. The set $L(\mathcal{A}) = \{w \in \Sigma^* \mid \delta(q_0, w) \in F\}$ denotes the language accepted by $\mathcal{A}$. A semi-automaton is a finite automaton without a specified start state and with no specified set of final states. The properties of being *deterministic*, *partial*, and *complete* for semi-automata are defined as for DFAs. When the context is clear, we call both deterministic finite automata and semi-automata simply *automata*. An automaton $\mathcal{A}$ is called *synchronizing* if there exists a word $w \in \Sigma^*$ with $|\delta(Q, w)| = 1$. In this case, we call w a *synchronizing word* for $\mathcal{A}$. We call a state $q \in Q$ with $\delta(Q, w) = \{q\}$ for some $w \in \Sigma^*$ a *synchronizing state*.

Theorem 1 [11]. *For any deterministic complete semi-automaton, we can decide if it is synchronizing in polynomial time $O(|\Sigma||Q|^2)$. Additionally, if we want to compute a synchronizing word w, then we need time $O(|Q|^3 + |Q|^2|\Sigma|)$ and the length of w will be $O(|Q|^3)$.*

The following obvious remark, stating that the set of synchronizing words is a two-sided ideal, will be used frequently without further mentioning.

Lemma 1. *Let $\mathcal{A} = (\Sigma, Q, \delta)$ be a deterministic and complete semi-automaton and $w \in \Sigma^*$ be a synchronizing word for $\mathcal{A}$. Then for every $u, v \in \Sigma^*$, the word uwv is also synchronizing for $\mathcal{A}$.*

We assume the reader to have some basic knowledge in computational complexity theory and formal language theory, as contained, e.g., in [8]. For instance, we make use of regular expressions to describe languages. For a word $w \in \Sigma^*$ we denote by $|w|$ its length, and for a symbol $x \in \Sigma$ we write $|w|_x$ to denote the number of occurences of x in the word. We denote the empty word, i.e., the word of length zero, by ε. We also make use of complexity classes like P, NP, or PSPACE. With $\leqslant_m^{\log}$ we denote a logspace many-one reduction. If for two problems L_1, L_2 it holds that $L_1 \leqslant_m^{\log} L_2$ and $L_2 \leqslant_m^{\log} L_1$, then we write $L_1 \equiv_m^{\log} L_2$. In [2] the *constrained synchronization problem* was defined for a fixed partial deterministic automaton $\mathcal{B} = (\Sigma, P, \mu, p_0, F)$.

Decision Problem 1: [2] $L(\mathcal{B})$-CONSTR-SYNC
Input: Deterministic complete semi-automaton $\mathcal{A} = (\Sigma, Q, \delta)$.
Question: Is there a synchronizing word $w \in \Sigma^*$ for $\mathcal{A}$ with $w \in L(\mathcal{B})$?

The automaton $\mathcal{B}$ will be called the *constraint automaton*. If an automaton $\mathcal{A}$ is a yes-instance of $L(\mathcal{B})$-CONSTR-SYNC we call $\mathcal{A}$ *synchronizing with respect to $\mathcal{B}$*. Occasionally, we do not specify $\mathcal{B}$ and rather talk about L-CONSTR-SYNC.

A language $L \subseteq \Sigma^*$ is called *commutative* if with $w \in L$, every word arising out of w by permuting its letters is also in L. Essentially, a commutative language is defined by conditions that say how often a letter is allowed to appear in its words, but not by the actual position of that letter. For this class of languages it was noted that it is structurally simple [6,7]. Also in terms of synchronizing words this class yields quite simple automata [3], but nevertheless may give algorithmic hard problems, as this class is sufficient for many reductions [3]. Here, we are concerned with L-CONSTR-SYNC for the case that the constraint language L is a commutative regular language. We will use the shuffle operation in connection with unary languages frequently to write commutative languages.

Definition 1. *The* shuffle operation, *denoted by* $\sqcup\!\sqcup$, *is defined as*

$$u \sqcup\!\sqcup v := \left\{ x_1 y_1 x_2 y_2 \cdots x_n y_n \;\middle|\; \begin{array}{l} u = x_1 x_2 \cdots x_n, v = y_1 y_2 \cdots y_n, \\ x_i, y_i \in \Sigma^*, 1 \leqslant i \leqslant n, n \geqslant 1 \end{array} \right\},$$

for $u, v \in \Sigma^*$ and $L_1 \sqcup\!\sqcup L_2 := \bigcup_{x \in L_1, y \in L_2} (x \sqcup\!\sqcup y)$ for $L_1, L_2 \subseteq \Sigma^*$.

2.2 Unary Languages

Let $\Sigma = \{a\}$ be a unary alphabet. Suppose $L \subseteq \Sigma^*$ is regular with an accepting complete deterministic automaton $\mathcal{A} = (\Sigma, S, \delta, s_0, F)$. Then by considering the sequence of states $\delta(s_0, a^1), \delta(s_0, a^2), \delta(s_0, a^3), \ldots$ we find numbers $i \geqslant 0, p > 0$ with $i + p$ minimal such that $\delta(s_0, a^i) = \delta(s_0, a^{i+p})$. We call these numbers the index i and the period p of the automaton $\mathcal{A}$. If $Q = \{\delta(s_0, a^m) \mid m \geqslant 0\}$, then $i + p = |S|$. In our discussion unary languages that are accepted by automata with a single final state appear.

Lemma 2 [7]. *Let $L \subseteq \{a\}^*$ be a unary language that is accepted by an automaton with a single final state, index i and period p. Then either $L = \{u\}$ with $|u| < i$ (and if the automaton is minimal we would have $p = 1$), or L is infinite with $L = a^{i+m}(a^p)^*$ and $0 \leqslant m < p$. Hence two words u, v with $\min\{|u|, |v|\} \geqslant i$ are both in L or not if and only if $|u| \equiv |v| \pmod{p}$.*

2.3 Known Result on Constrained Synchronization and Commutative Languages

Here we collect results from [2,7], and some consequences that will be used later. First a mild extension of a lemma from [2], where it was formulated only for the class P, but it also holds for NP and PSPACE.

Lemma 3. *Let* $\mathcal{X}$ *denote any of the complexity classes* P, NP *or* PSPACE. *If* $L(\mathcal{B})$ *is a finite union of languages* $L(\mathcal{B}_1), L(\mathcal{B}_2), \ldots, L(\mathcal{B}_n)$ *such that for each* $1 \leqslant i \leqslant n$ *the problem* $L(\mathcal{B}_i)$-CONSTR-SYNC $\in \mathcal{X}$, *then* $L(\mathcal{B})$-CONSTR-SYNC $\in \mathcal{X}$.

The next result from [2] states that the computational complexity is always in PSPACE.

Theorem 2 [2]. *For any constraint automaton* $\mathcal{B} = (\Sigma, P, \mu, p_0, F)$ *the problem* $L(\mathcal{B})$-CONSTR-SYNC *is in* PSACE.

If $|L(\mathcal{B})| = 1$, then $L(\mathcal{B})$-CONSTR-SYNC is obviously in P. Simply feed this single word into the input semi-automaton for every state and check if a unique state results. Hence by Lemma 3 the next is implied.

Lemma 4. *Let* $\mathcal{B} = (\Sigma, P, \mu, p_0, F)$ *be a constraint automaton such that* $L(\mathcal{B})$ *is finite, then* $L(\mathcal{B})$-CONSTR-SYNC $\in$ P.

The following result from [2] gives a criterion for containment in NP.

Theorem 3 [2]. *Let* $\mathcal{B} = (\Sigma, P, \mu, p_0, F)$ *be a partial deterministic finite automaton. Then,* $L(\mathcal{B})$-CONSTR-SYNC $\in$ NP *if there is a* $\sigma \in \Sigma$ *such that for all states* $p \in P$, *if* $L(\mathcal{B}_{p,\{p\}})$ *is infinite, then* $L(\mathcal{B}_{p,\{p\}}) \subseteq \{\sigma\}^*$.

With this we can deduce another sufficient condition for containment in NP, which is more suited for commutative languages.

Lemma 5. *Let* Σ *be our alphabet and suppose* $a \in \Sigma$. *If*

$$L = \{a\}^* \sqcup\!\sqcup F_1 \sqcup\!\sqcup \ldots \sqcup\!\sqcup F_k$$

for finite languages $F_1, \ldots, F_k$, *then* L-CONSTR-SYNC $\in$ NP.

The next result from [2] will be useful in making several simplifying assumptions about the constraint language later in Sect. 3.1.

Theorem 4 [2]. *Let* $L \subseteq L' \subseteq \Sigma^*$. *If* $L' \subseteq \{v \in \Sigma^* \mid \exists u, w \in \Sigma^* : uvw \in L\}$, *then* L-CONSTR-SYNC $\equiv_m^{\log} L'$-CONSTR-SYNC.

The following Theorem 5 is taken from [7] and will be crucial in deriving our vector representation form for the constraint language later in Sect. 3.1.

Theorem 5. *Let* $\Sigma = \{a_1, \ldots, a_k\}$ *be our alphabet. A commutative language* $L \subseteq \Sigma^*$ *is regular if and only if it could be written in the form*

$$L = \bigcup_{i=1}^{n} U_1^{(i)} \sqcup \ldots \sqcup U_k^{(i)}$$

with non-empty unary regular languages $U_j^{(i)} \subseteq \{a_j\}^*$ *for* $i \in \{1, \ldots, n\}$ *and* $j \in \{1, \ldots k\}$ *that could be accepted by a unary automaton with a single final state.*

With respect to the Constrained Synchronization Problem 1, for commutative constraint languages $L(\mathcal{B})$, we will refer more to the form given by Theorem 5 than to the specific automaton $\mathcal{B} = (\Sigma, P, \mu, p_0, F)$ underlying it. In Sect. 3.6 we will give some details how to compute such a form for a given automaton accepting a commutative language.

3   Results

Our main result, Theorem 6, gives a complete classification of the computational complexity of L-CONSTR-SYNC, for different regular commutative constraint languages. In the following sections, we will prove various simplifications, propositions, corollaries and lemmata that ultimately will all be used in proving Theorem 6. First, we will give criteria that allow certain simplification of the constraint language, and derive a mechanism to describe a given constraint language by a set of vectors, which gives all the essential information with regard to our problem. This notion will be used repeatedly in all the following arguments. In Sect. 3.2 we will give sufficient conditions for containment in P. Then we single out those instances that give hardness results for the complexity classes NP and PSPACE in Sect. 3.3 and Sect. 3.4. Finally, in Sect. 3.5, we combine all these results to prove Theorem 6. From Theorem 6, in the last Sect. 3.6, a decision procedure is derived to decide the complexity of $L(\mathcal{B})$-CONSTR-SYNC, if we allow $\mathcal{B}$ to be part of our input.

3.1   Simplifications of the Constraint Language

Our first Proposition 1 follows from Theorem 4. Very roughly, it says that for the letters that are allowed infinitely often, the exact way in which they appear is not that important, but only that we can find arbitrary long sequences of them. We then use this result to derive a more compact description, in terms of vectors over $\mathbb{N}_0 \cup \{\infty\}$, to capture the essential part of a commutative constraint language L with respect to the problem L-CONSTR-SYNC.

Proposition 1. *(infinite language simplification) Let* $\Sigma = \{a_1, \ldots, a_k\}$ *be our alphabet. Consider the Constrained Synchronization Problem 1 with commutative constraint language* L. *Suppose*

$$L = \bigcup_{i=1}^{n} U_1^{(i)} \sqcup \ldots \sqcup U_k^{(i)}$$

with unary languages $U_j^{(i)} \subseteq \{a_j\}^*$ for $i \in \{1,\dots,n\}$ and $j \in \{1,\dots k\}$. If for some $i_0 \in \{1,\dots,n\}$ and $j_0 \in \{1,\dots k\}$ the unary language $U_{j_0}^{(i_0)}$ is infinite, then construct the new language

$$L' = \bigcup_{i=1}^{n} V_1^{(i)} \sqcup \dots \sqcup V_k^{(i)}$$

with

$$V_j^{(i)} = \begin{cases} \{a_j\}^* & \text{if } i = i_0 \text{ and } j = j_0 \\ U_j^{(i)} & \text{otherwise.} \end{cases}$$

We simply change the single language $U_{j_0}^{(i_0)}$ for the language $\{a_j\}^*$. Then a complete and deterministic input semi-automaton $\mathcal{A} = (\Sigma, Q, \delta)$ has a synchronizing word in L if and only if it has one in L' and L-CONSTR-SYNC $\equiv_m^{\log}$ L'-CONSTR-SYNC.

Suppose L is a constraint language with

$$L = \bigcup_{i=1}^{n} U_1^{(i)} \sqcup \dots \sqcup U_k^{(i)}$$

according to Theorem 5. By Proposition 1, for our purposes we can assume that if $U_j^{(i)}$ is infinite, then it has the form $U_j^{(i)} = \{a_j\}^*$. The unary languages $U_j^{(i)}$ for $j \in \{1,\dots,k\}$ and $i \in \{1,\dots,n\}$ are accepted by some unary automaton with a single final state. By Lemma 2, if such a language is non-empty and finite it contains only a single word. Hence, the only relevant information is whether such a unary language part is infinite or what length has the single unary word it contains. This is captured by the next definition.

Definition 2. *(vector representation of L) Let $\Sigma = \{a_1,\dots,a_k\}$ be our alphabet. Consider the Constrained Synchronization Problem 1 with commutative regular constraint language L. Suppose*

$$L = \bigcup_{i=1}^{n} U_1^{(i)} \sqcup \dots \sqcup U_k^{(i)} \tag{1}$$

with non-empty unary languages $U_j^{(i)} \subseteq \{a_j\}^*$ for $i \in \{1,\dots,n\}$ and $j \in \{1,\dots k\}$ that are acceptable by unary automata with a single final state. Then we say that a set of vectors $N \subseteq (\mathbb{N}_0 \cup \{\infty\})^k$ corresponds to L, according to Eq. (1), if $N = \{(n_1^{(i)},\dots,n_k^{(i)}) \mid i \in \{1,\dots,n\}\}$ with[1]

$$n_j^{(i)} = \begin{cases} \infty & \text{if } U_j^{(i)} \text{ is infinite }, \\ |u| & \text{if } U_j^{(i)} = \{u\} \end{cases}$$

---

[1] Note that, as by assumption, the languages $U_j^{(i)}$ for $i \in \{1,\dots,n\}$ and $j \in \{1,\dots,k\}$ are accepted by unary automata with a single final state, by Lemma 2, they only contain a single word if they are finite and non-empty.

for $i \in \{1, \ldots, n\}$ *and* $j \in \{1, \ldots, k\}$. *By Theorem 5, every regular commutative constraint language has at least one vector representation.*

Example 1. Let $\Sigma = \{a, b, c\}$ with $a = a_1, b = a_2, c = a_3$. For the language $L = \{aa\} \sqcup b^* \cup \{a\} \sqcup \{bb\} \sqcup c(cc)^*$ we have $N = \{(2, \infty, 0), (1, 2, \infty)\}$. Please see Example 3 for other languages.

The language L is infinite precisely if for some vector at least one entry equals ∞. Another important observation, quite similar to Proposition 1, allows us to make further assumptions about the constraint language, or the vectors corresponding to it. It will be used in the proofs of Proposition 5 and Proposition 6.

Proposition 2. *(comparable vectors simplification) Let* $\Sigma = \{a_1, \ldots, a_k\}$. *Consider* L-CONSTR-SYNC. *Suppose* L *has the form stated in Theorem 5,*

$$L = \bigcup_{i=1}^{n} U_1^{(i)} \sqcup \ldots \sqcup U_k^{(i)} \tag{2}$$

with unary languages $U_j^{(i)} \subseteq \{a_j\}^*$ *for* $i \in \{1, \ldots, n\}$ *and* $j \in \{1, \ldots k\}$. *Let* N *be the vector set, corresponding to Eq. (2) and according to Definition 2. Suppose* $x, y \in N$ *with* $x \leqslant y$ *and* $x = (x_1^{(i_0)}, \ldots, x_k^{(i_0)})$ *for* $i_0 \in \{1, \ldots, n\}$, *i.e., the vector* x *arises out of the part* $U_1^{(i_0)} \sqcup \ldots \sqcup U_k^{(i_0)}$ *in the above union for* L. *Construct the new language*

$$L' = \bigcup_{i \in \{1, \ldots n\} \setminus \{i_0\}} U_1^{(i)} \sqcup \ldots \sqcup U_k^{(i)}$$

without the part $U_1^{(i_0)} \sqcup \ldots \sqcup U_k^{(i_0)}$. *Then a complete and deterministic input semi-automaton* $\mathcal{A} = (\Sigma, Q, \delta)$ *has a synchronizing word in* L *if and only if it has one in* L' *and* L-CONSTR-SYNC $\equiv_m^{\log}$ L'-CONSTR-SYNC.

Example 2. Let $\Sigma = \{a, b, c\}$ with $a = a_1, b = a_2, c = a_3$. If $L = aaa^* \sqcup \{b\} \cup a^* \sqcup \{bb\} \sqcup \{c\} \cup \{a\}$, then $N = \{(\infty, 1, 0), (\infty, 2, 1), (1, 0, 0)\}$. After simplification by Proposition 2 and Proposition 1, we get a computationally equivalent constrained synchronization problem, with constraint language $L' = a^* \sqcup \{bb\} \sqcup \{c\}$ and vector representation $N' = \{(\infty, 2, 1)\}$. In this case N' contains precisely the maximal vector in N.

Hence, by taking the maximal vectors, which does not change the complexity, we can assume that the vectors associated with any regular commutative constraint language are pairwise incomparable.

3.2 The Polynomial Time Solvable Variants of the Problem

If in the sets $U_1^{(i)} \sqcup \ldots \sqcup U_k^{(i)}$ each $U_j^{(i)}$ is either infinite or $U_j^{(i)} = \{\varepsilon\}$, then L-CONSTR-SYNC $\in$ P.

Proposition 3. *Let $\Sigma = \{a_1, \ldots, a_k\}$ be our alphabet. Consider the Constrained Synchronization Problem 1. Suppose the commutative constraint language L is decomposed as stated in Theorem 5,*

$$L = \bigcup_{i=1}^{n} U_1^{(i)} \sqcup \ldots \sqcup U_k^{(i)}. \tag{3}$$

Denote by $N = \{(n_1^{(i)}, \ldots, n_k^{(i)}) \mid i = 1, \ldots, n\}$ the vector representation, according to Definition 2 and corresponding to Eq. (3). If for all $i \in \{1, \ldots, n\}$ and all $j \in \{1, \ldots, k\}$ we have $n_j^{(i)} \in \{0, \infty\}$, then the problem is in P.

Interestingly, because of Lemma 6 stated next, if in the sets $U_1^{(i)} \sqcup \ldots \sqcup U_k^{(i)}$, we have at most one $j_0 \in \{1, \ldots, k\}$ such that $U_{j_0}^{(i)} = \{a_{j_0}\}$, and at most one other $j_1 \in \{1, \ldots, k\}$ such that $U_{j_1}^{(i)}$ is infinite, and $U_j^{(i)} = \{\varepsilon\}$ for all $j \in \{1, \ldots, k\} \backslash \{j_0, j_1\}$, then also L-CONSTR-SYNC $\in P$. Later, we will see that only a slight relaxation of this condition, for example, if instead $U_{j_0}^{(i)} = \{a_{j_0} a_{j_0}\}$ in the above, then the problem becomes NP-complete.

Lemma 6. *Let $\mathcal{A} = (\Sigma, Q, \delta)$ be a unary semi-automaton with $\Sigma = \{a\}$ and $S \subseteq Q$. Then $|\delta(S, a^k)| = 1$ for some $k \geqslant 0$ if and only if $|\delta(S, a^{|Q|-1})| = 1$.*

Proposition 4. *Let $\Sigma = \{a_1, \ldots, a_k\}$ be our alphabet. Consider the Constrained Synchronization Problem 1. Suppose the commutative constraint language L is decomposed as stated in Theorem 5,*

$$L = \bigcup_{i=1}^{n} U_1^{(i)} \sqcup \ldots \sqcup U_k^{(i)}. \tag{4}$$

Denote by $N = \{(n_1^{(i)}, \ldots, n_k^{(i)}) \mid i = 1, \ldots, n\}$ the vector representation, according to Definition 2 and corresponding to Eq. (4). If for all $i \in \{1, \ldots, n\}$ in the vector $(n_1^{(i)}, \ldots, n_k^{(i)})$, at most one entry equals ∞ and at most one entry is non-zero, and if so it equals one, then the problem is solvable in polynomial time.

3.3   The NP-complete Variants of the Problem

In this section, we state a criterion, in terms of the constraint language, which gives NP-hardness. Surprisingly, in contrast to Proposition 4, if some letter, whose appearance is bounded in an infinite language of the form $U_1^{(i)} \sqcup \ldots \sqcup U_k^{(i)}$, is allowed to appear more than once, then we get NP-hardness.

Proposition 5. *Let $\Sigma = \{a_1, \ldots, a_k\}$ be our alphabet. Consider the Constrained Synchronization Problem 1. Suppose the commutative constraint language L is decomposed as stated in Theorem 5,*

$$L = \bigcup_{i=1}^{n} U_1^{(i)} \sqcup \ldots \sqcup U_k^{(i)}. \tag{5}$$

*Denote by N the vector representation, according to Definition 2 and correspond-
ing to Eq. (5). Suppose we find $i_0 \in \{1, \ldots, k\}$ with $(n_1^{(i_0)}, \ldots, n_k^{(i_0)}) \in N$ such
that at least one of the following conditions is true:*

(i) $n_{j_0}^{(i_0)} = \infty$ and $2 \leqslant n_{j_1}^{(i_0)} < \infty$ for distinct $j_0, j_1 \in \{1, \ldots, k\}$, or

(ii) $n_{j_0}^{(i_0)} = \infty$ and $1 \leqslant n_{j_1}^{(i_0)}, n_{j_2}^{(i_0)} < \infty$ for distinct $j_0, j_1, j_2 \in \{1, \ldots, k\}$.

Then the problem is NP-hard.

3.4   The **PSPACE**-complete Variants of the Problem

Proposition 6. *Let $\Sigma = \{a_1, \ldots, a_k\}$ be our alphabet. Consider the Constrained
Synchronization Problem 1. Suppose the commutative constraint language L is
decomposed as stated in Theorem 5,*

$$L = \bigcup_{i=1}^{n} U_1^{(i)} ⊔ \ldots ⊔ U_k^{(i)}. \tag{6}$$

*Denote by N the vector representation, according to Definition 2 and correspond-
ing to Eq. (6). Suppose we find $i_0 \in \{1, \ldots, n\}$ and distinct $j_0, j_1, j_2 \in \{1, \ldots, k\}$
with $(n_1^{(i_0)}, \ldots, n_k^{(i_0)}) \in N$ such that $n_{j_0}^{(i_0)} = n_{j_1}^{(i_0)} = \infty$ and $1 \leqslant n_{j_2}^{(i_0)} < \infty$. Then
the problem is PSPACE-hard.*

3.5   Main Theorem

Combining everything up to now gives our main computational complexity classification result for $L(\mathcal{B})$-CONSTR-SYNC.

Theorem 6. *Let $\Sigma = \{a_1, \ldots, a_k\}$ be our alphabet. Consider the Constrained
Synchronization Problem 1. Suppose the commutative constraint language L is
decomposed as stated in Theorem 5,*

$$L = \bigcup_{i=1}^{n} U_1^{(i)} ⊔ \ldots ⊔ U_k^{(i)}. \tag{7}$$

*Denote by $N = \{(n_1^{(i)}, \ldots, n_k^{(i)}) \mid i = 1, \ldots, n\}$ the vector representation, accord-
ing to Definition 2 and corresponding to Eq. (7).*

*(i) Suppose for all $i \in \{1, \ldots, n\}$, if we have distinct $j_0, j_1 \in \{1, \ldots, k\}$ with
$n_{j_0}^{(i)} = n_{j_1}^{(i)} = \infty$, then $n_j^{(i)} \in \{0, \infty\}$ for all other $j \in \{1, \ldots, k\} \backslash \{j_0, j_1\}$.
More formally,*

$$\forall i \in \{1, \ldots, n\} : (\exists j_0, j_1 \in \{1, \ldots, k\} : j_0 \neq j_1 \wedge n_{j_0}^{(i)} = n_{j_1}^{(i)} = \infty)$$

$$\rightarrow (\forall j \in \{1, \ldots, k\} : n_j^{(i)} \in \{0, \infty\}).$$

*Furthermore, suppose N fulfills the condition mentioned in Proposition 5,
then it is NP-complete.*

(ii) If the set N fulfills the condition imposed by Proposition 6, then it is
   PSPACE-*complete.*
(iii) In all other cases the problem is in P.

We give some examples for all cases in Example 3.

Example 3. Let $\Sigma = \{a, b, c\}$ with $a = a_1, b = a_2, c = a_3$.

– If $L = \{aa\} \sqcup b(bb)^*$ with $N = \{(2, \infty, 0)\}$, then L-Constr-Sync is NP-complete.
– If $L = \{a\} \sqcup b(bb)^* \sqcup \{c\}$ with $N = \{(1, \infty, 1)\}$, then L-Constr-Sync is NP-complete.
– The constraint language from Example 1 gives a NP-complete problem.
– If $L = \{aa\} \sqcup b(bb)^* \cup (aaa)^* \sqcup b \sqcup c^*$ with $N = \{(2, \infty, 0), (\infty, 1, \infty)\}$, then L-Constr-Sync is PSPACE-complete.
– If $L = \{a\} \sqcup b(bb)^*$ with $N = \{(1, \infty, 0)\}$, then L-Constr-Sync $\in$ P.
– If $L = (aa)^* \sqcup c(ccc)^*$ with $N = (\infty, 0, \infty)$, then L-Constr-Sync $\in$ P.

3.6   Deciding the Computational Complexity of the Constrained Synchronization Problem

This section addresses the issue of deciding the computational complexity of $L(\mathcal{B})$-Constr-Sync, for a constraint automaton such that $L(\mathcal{B})$ is commutative. The next definition is a mild generalization of a definition first given in [4], and used for state complexity questions in [6,7].

Definition 3. *Let* $\Sigma = \{a_1, \ldots, a_k\}$ *and suppose* $\mathcal{A} = (\Sigma, Q, \delta, s_0, F)$ *is a complete and deterministic automaton accepting a commutative language. Set* $Q_j = \{\delta(s_0, a_j^i) : i \geqslant 0\}$ *for* $j \in \{1, \ldots, k\}$. *The automaton* $\mathcal{C}_\mathcal{A} = (\Sigma, Q_1 \times \ldots \times Q_k, \mu, t_0, E)$ *with* $t_0 = (s_0, \ldots, s_0)$,

$$\mu(w, (s_1, \ldots, s_k)) = (\delta(s_1, a_1^{|w|_{a_1}}), \ldots, \delta(s_k, a_k^{|w|_{a_k}}))$$

and $E = \{(\delta(t_0, a_1^{|w|_{a_1}}), \ldots, \delta(t_0, a_k^{|w|_{a_k}})) : w \in L(\mathcal{A})\}$ *is called the* commutative automaton *constructed from* $\mathcal{A}$.

If $\mathcal{A}$ is the minimal automaton of a commutative language, it is exactly the definition from [4,6,7]. In that case, also in [4,6,7], it was shown that $L(\mathcal{C}_\mathcal{A}) = L(\mathcal{A})$, and that $L(\mathcal{A})$ is a union of certain shuffled languages. Both statements still hold for any automaton $\mathcal{A}$ such that $L(\mathcal{A})$ is commutative.

Theorem 7. *Let* $\Sigma = \{a_1, \ldots, a_k\}$ *and suppose* $\mathcal{A} = (\Sigma, Q, \delta, s_0, F)$ *is a complete and deterministic automaton accepting a commutative language. Denote by* $\mathcal{C}_\mathcal{A} = (\Sigma, Q_1 \times \ldots \times Q_k, \mu, t_0, E)$ *the commutative automaton from Definition 3. Then* $L(\mathcal{C}_\mathcal{A}) = L(\mathcal{A})$.

The set of words that lead into a single state of the commutative automaton has a simple form.

Lemma 7. *Let* $\Sigma = \{a_1, \ldots, a_k\}$ *and suppose* $\mathcal{A} = (\Sigma, Q, \delta, s_0, F)$ *is a complete and deterministic automaton accepting a commutative language. Denote by* $\mathcal{C}_{\mathcal{A}} = (\Sigma, Q_1 \times \ldots \times Q_k, \mu, t_0, E)$ *the commutative automaton from Definition 3. Let* $s = (s_1, \ldots, s_k) \in Q_1 \times \ldots \times Q_k$ *and set* $U_j = \{u \in \{a_j\}^* \mid \delta(s_0, u) = s_j\}$. *Then*

$$\{w \in \Sigma^* \mid \mu(t_0, w) = (s_1, \ldots, s_k)\} = U_1 \,\sqcup\ldots\sqcup\, U_k.$$

Example 4. Note that the form from Lemma 7 need not hold for some arbitrary automaton. For example, let $\Sigma = \{a, b\}$ and $L = \Sigma^+$. Then a minimal automaton has two states with a single accepting state, and the commutative automaton derived from it has four states, with three accepting states. We have $L = a^+ \cup b^+ \cup a^+ \sqcup b^+$.

As the language of any deterministic automaton could be written as a disjoint union of languages which lead into a single final state, the next is implied.

Corollary 1. *Let* $\Sigma = \{a_1, \ldots, a_k\}$ *and suppose* $\mathcal{A} = (\Sigma, Q, \delta, s_0, F)$ *is a complete and deterministic automaton accepting a commutative language. Denote by* $\mathcal{C}_{\mathcal{A}} = (\Sigma, Q_1 \times \ldots \times Q_k, \mu, t_0, E)$ *the commutative automaton from Definition 3. Suppose* $E = \{(s_1^{(l)}, \ldots, s_k^{(l)}) \mid l \in \{1, \ldots, m\}\}$ *for some* $m \geqslant 0$. *Set*[2] $U_j^{(l)} = \{u \in \{a_j\}^* \mid \delta(s_0, u) = s_j^{(l)}\}$ *for* $l \in \{1, \ldots, m\}$ *and* $j \in \{1, \ldots, k\}$. *Then*

$$L(\mathcal{A}) = \bigcup_{l=1}^{m} U_1^{(l)} \,\sqcup\ldots\sqcup\, U_k^{(l)}. \tag{8}$$

With these notions, we can derive a decision procedure. First construct the commutative automaton. Then derive a representation as given in Eq. (8). Use this representation to compute a vector representation according to Definition 2. With the help of Theorem 6, from such a vector representation the computational complexity could be read off.

Theorem 8. *Let* $\Sigma = \{a_1, \ldots, a_k\}$ *be a fixed alphabet. For a given (partial) automaton* $\mathcal{B} = (\Sigma, P, \mu, p_0, F)$ *accepting a commutative language, the computational complexity of* $L(\mathcal{B})$-CONSTR-SYNC *could be decided in polynomial time.*

4 Conclusion

We have looked at the Constrained Synchronization Problem 1 for commutative regular constraint languages, thereby continuing the investigation started in [2]. The complexity landscape for regular commutative constraint languages is completely understood. Only the complexity classes P, NP and PSPACE arise, and we have given conditions for P, NP-complete and PSPACE-complete problems. In [2] the questions was raised if we can find constraint languages that give

---

[2] If we start with the minimal automaton, then these are the same sets $U_j^{(l)}$ as introduced in [6].

other levels of the polynomial time hierarchy. At least for commutative regular languages this is not the case. Lastly, we have given a procedure to decide the computational complexity of $L(\mathcal{B})$-CONSTR-SYNC, for a given automaton $\mathcal{B}$ accepting a commutative language.

Acknowledgement. I thank Prof. Dr. Mikhail V. Volkov for suggesting the problem of constrained synchronization during the workshop 'Modern Complexity Aspects of Formal Languages' that took place at Trier University 11.–15. February, 2019. The financial support of this workshop by the DFG-funded project FE560/9-1 is gratefully acknowledged. I thank my supervisor, Prof. Dr. Henning Fernau, for accepting me as I am, do not judge me on, and always listening to, my sometimes dumb musings; and for giving valuable feedback, discussions and research suggestions concerning the content of this article.

References

1. Černý, J.: Poznámka k homogénnym experimentom s konečnými automatmi. Matematicko-fyzikálny časopis **14**(3), 208–216 (1964)
2. Fernau, H., Gusev, V.V., Hoffmann, S., Holzer, M., Volkov, M.V., Wolf, P.: Computational complexity of synchronization under regular constraints. In: Rossmanith, P., Heggernes, P., Katoen, J. (eds.) 44th International Symposium on Mathematical Foundations of Computer Science, MFCS 2019. LIPIcs, Aachen, Germany, 26–30 August 2019, vol. 138, pp. 63:1–63:14. Schloss Dagstuhl - Leibniz-Zentrum für Informatik (2019). http://www.dagstuhl.de/dagpub/978-3-95977-117-7
3. Fernau, H., Hoffmann, S.: Extensions to minimal synchronizing words. J. Automata Lang. Comb. **24**(2–4), 287–307 (2019). https://doi.org/10.25596/jalc-2019-287
4. Gómez, A.C., Álvarez, G.I.: Learning commutative regular languages. In: Clark, A., Coste, F., Miclet, L. (eds.) ICGI 2008. LNCS (LNAI), vol. 5278, pp. 71–83. Springer, Heidelberg (2008). https://doi.org/10.1007/978-3-540-88009-7_6
5. Gusev, V.V.: Synchronizing automata of bounded rank. In: Moreira, N., Reis, R. (eds.) CIAA 2012. LNCS, vol. 7381, pp. 171–179. Springer, Heidelberg (2012). https://doi.org/10.1007/978-3-642-31606-7_15
6. Hoffmann, S.: State complexity, properties and generalizations of commutative regular languages. Information and Computation (to appear)
7. Hoffmann, S.: Commutative regular languages – properties and state complexity. In: Ćirić, M., Droste, M., Pin, J.É. (eds.) CAI 2019. LNCS, vol. 11545, pp. 151–163. Springer, Cham (2019). https://doi.org/10.1007/978-3-030-21363-3_13
8. Hopcroft, J.E., Motwani, R., Ullman, J.D.: Introduction to Automata Theory, Languages, and Computation, 2nd edn. Addison-Wesley, Boston (2001)
9. Martyugin, P.V.: Synchronization of automata with one undefined or ambiguous transition. In: Moreira, N., Reis, R. (eds.) CIAA 2012. LNCS, vol. 7381, pp. 278–288. Springer, Heidelberg (2012). https://doi.org/10.1007/978-3-642-31606-7_24
10. Sandberg, S.: 1 Homing and synchronizing sequences. In: Broy, M., Jonsson, B., Katoen, J.-P., Leucker, M., Pretschner, A. (eds.) Model-Based Testing of Reactive Systems. LNCS, vol. 3472, pp. 5–33. Springer, Heidelberg (2005). https://doi.org/10.1007/11498490_2
11. Volkov, M.V.: Synchronizing automata and the Černý conjecture. In: Martín-Vide, C., Otto, F., Fernau, H. (eds.) LATA 2008. LNCS, vol. 5196, pp. 11–27. Springer, Heidelberg (2008). https://doi.org/10.1007/978-3-540-88282-4_4

Approximation Algorithms for General Cluster Routing Problem

Xiaoyan Zhang[1], Donglei Du[2], Gregory Gutin[3], Qiaoxia Ming[1],
and Jian Sun[1(✉)]

[1] School of Mathematical Science and Institute of Mathematics,
Nanjing Normal University, Jiangsu 210023, People's Republic of China
sunjian199203@126.com
[2] Faculty of Management, University of New Brunswick,
Fredericton, New Brunswick E3B 5A3, Canada
ddu@unb.ca
[3] Department of Computer Science Royal Holloway,
University of London Egham, Surrey TW20 0EX, UK
g.gutin@rhul.ac.uk

Abstract. Graph routing problems have been investigated extensively
in operations research, computer science and engineering due to their
ubiquity and vast applications. In this paper, we study constant approximation algorithms for some variations of the cluster general routing
problem. In this problem, we are given an edge-weighted complete undirected graph $G = (V, E, c)$, whose vertex set is partitioned into clusters
$C_1, \ldots, C_k$. We are also given a subset $V^{'}$ of V and a subset $E^{'}$ of E.
The weight function c satisfies the triangle inequality. The goal is to find
a minimum cost walk T that visits each vertex in V' only once, traverses
every edge in E' at least once and for every $i \in [k]$ all vertices of C_i are
traversed consecutively.

Keywords: Routing problem · Approximation algorithm · General
routing problem

1 Introduction

Graph routing problems have been studied extensively since the early 1970s.
Most of there problems are NP-hard, and hence no polynomial-time exact algorithms exist for most of them unless P=NP. In a typical routing problem, a
salesman starts from a home location, visits a set of prescribed cities exactly

---

J. Sun—This research is supported or partially supported by the National Natural
Science Foundation of China (Grant Nos. 11871280, 11371001, 11771386 and 11728104),
the Natural Sciences and Engineering Re-search Council of Canada (NSERC) Grant
06446 and Qinglan Project.

© Springer Nature Switzerland AG 2020
D. Kim et al. (Eds.): COCOON 2020, LNCS 12273, pp. 472–483, 2020.
https://doi.org/10.1007/978-3-030-58150-3_38

once, and returns to the original location with minimum total distance travelled.

Arguably the most well-known routing problem is the *travelling salesman problem (TSP)* (see [6] for a compendium of results on the problem). We are given a weighted graph $G = (V, E, c)$ (directed or undirected) with vertex set V, edge set E, and cost $c(e)$ for each edge $e \in E$. The TSP's goal is to find a Hamiltonian cycle with minimum total cost. Without loss of generality, we may assume that G is a complete graph (digraph); otherwise, we could replace the missing edges with edges of very large cost.

Unfortunately, the TSP is NP-hard even for metric arc costs [10]. Therefore, one approach for solving the TSP (and other NP-hard problems) is using (polynomial-time) approximative algorithm whose performance is measured by the *approximation ratio*, which is the maximum ratio of the approximative solution value to the optimum value among all problem instances. The best known approximation algorithm for the TSP with triangle inequality is by Christofides [3] with ratio 1.5. For the general TSP where the triangle inequality does not hold, there is no (polynomial-time) approximation algorithm with a constant approximation ratio, unless P=NP [11]. TSP along with its variations have been extensively investigated in the literature. Here are two generalizations of TSP studied in the literature.

The *general routing problem (GRP)*: Let $G = (V, E, c)$ be an edge-weighted complete undirected graph such that the triangle inequality holds for the weight function c. The goal is to find a minimum cost walk that visits each vertex in a required subset $V' \subseteq V$ exactly once and traverses every edge in a required subset $E' \subseteq E$ at least once. For this problem, Jansen [9] gave a 1.5-approximation algorithm.

The *cluster travelling salesman problem (CTSP)*: Let $G = (V, E, c)$ be an edge-weighted complete undirected graph such that the triangle inequality holds for the weight function c. The vertex set V is partitioned into clusters $C_1, \ldots, C_k$. The goal is to compute a minimum cost Hamiltonian cycle T that visits all vertices of each cluster consecutively (and thus for each cluster we have starting and finishing vertices on T). Arkin et al. [1] designed a 3.5-approximation algorithm for the problem with given starting vertices in each cluster. Guttmann-Beck et al. [7] proposed a 1.9091-approximation algorithm for the problem in which the starting and ending vertices of each cluster are specified and gave a 1.8-approximation algorithm if for each cluster two vertices are given such that one of the them can be a starting vertex and the other the finishing vertex.

In this paper, we introduced and studied the *general cluster routing problem* (GCRP) which generalizes both GRP and CTSP. We provide approximation algorithms of constant approximation ratio for variations of this problem. In GCRP, we are given an edge-weighted undirected graph $G = (V, E, c)$ such that the triangle inequality holds for the weight function c. The vertex set V is partitioned into clusters $C_1, \ldots, C_k$. For any given vertex subset $V' \subseteq V$ and edge subset $E' \subseteq E$, the aim is to find a minimum cost walk T (hereafter a walk will be called a *tour*) that visits each vertex in V' exactly once and traverses each edge in E' at least once such that for every $i \in [k]$ all vertices of T belonging to C_i are visited consecutively in T. Depending on whether or not the starting and finishing vertices of a cluster are specified or not, we consider two cases. When every cluster has a pair of specified starting and finishing vertices, we offer a 2.4-approximation combinatorial algorithm. When every cluster has unspecified starting and finishing vertices, depending on whether the *required* edges (i.e., those in E') are incident with different clusters or not, we further consider two subcases. If all required edges are only distributed in the clusters, we get a 3.25-approximation combinatorial algorithm. On the other hand, if there exist edges from E' incident with two different clusters, we get a 2.25-approximation combinatorial algorithm.

The remainder of this paper is organized as follows. We provide some preliminaries in Sect. 2. We study algorithms for the GCRP in Sect. 3. We conclude in Sect. 4.

2   Preliminaries

In this section, we recall some algorithms for three problems along with some preliminary results, which will be used as subroutines in our algorithms later.

2.1   The Travelling Salesman Path Problem

The *traveling salesman path problem (TSPP)* [5,7,8,12–14] is a generalization of the TSP, but received much less attention than TSP in the literature. In TSPP, given an edge-weighted undirected graph $G = (V, E, c)$ and two vertices $s, t \in V$, the aim is to find a minimum cost Hamiltonian path from s to t. Note that vertices s and t need not be distinct. However, when $s = t$ TSPP is equivalent to the TSP. Let $MST(G)$ be a minimum spanning tree of G. For simplicity, $MST(G)$ will also denote the cost of this tree.

Hoogeveen [8] considered three variations of the travelling salesman path problem (TSPP), where as part of the inputs, the following constraints are placed on the end vertices of the resulting Hamiltonian path:

(1) both the source and the destination are specified;
(2) one of the source and the destination is specified;
(3) neither the source nor the destination are specified.

Property 1. For Cases (2) and (3), it was shown in [8] that a straightforward adaptation of Christofide's algorithm can yield an algorithm with a performance ratio of $\frac{3}{2}$.

However, Case (1) is more difficult, for which many results exist in the literature. On the positive side, a $\frac{5}{3}$-approximation algorithm is proposed in [8], followed by an improved $\frac{8}{5}$-approximation in [13]. Sebo [12] gave a strongly polynomial algorithm and improved the analysis of the metric $s - t$ path TSP. He found a tour of cost less than 1.53 times the optimum of the subtour elimination

LP. On the negative side, the usual integer linear programming formulation has an integrality gap at least 1.5.

Let $c(P)$ be the sum of all the edge costs of a given path or tour P. The following result from [8] will be used later.

Theorem 1 [8]. *There exists a polynomial-time algorithm for travelling salesman path problem with given end vertices s and t, and we can find two solutions S_1 and S_2 for the problem which satisfy the following inequalities:*

$$c(S_1) \leq 2MST(G) - c(s,t) \leq 2OPT - c(s,t),$$
$$c(S_2) \leq MST(G) + \frac{1}{2}(OPT + c(s,t)) \leq \frac{3}{2}OPT + \frac{1}{2}c(s,t).$$

Corollary 1 [8]. *The shorter of the tours S_1 and S_2 is at most $\frac{5}{3}OPT$.*

Proof. By Theorem 1, if $c(s,t) \geq \frac{1}{3}OPT$, then $c(S_1) \leq \frac{5}{3}OPT$. Otherwise (i.e. $c(s,t) \leq \frac{1}{3}OPT$) we have $c(S_2) \leq \frac{5}{3}OPT$. □

Below, we consider a more general problem, called the *travelling general path problem (TGPP)*. Let $G = (V, E, c)$ be a weighted connected graph with two specified ending vertices $s, t \in V$. For any given vertex subset $V' \subseteq V$ and edge subset $E' \subseteq E$, the objective is to find a minimum cost path from s to t in G that visits all vertices in V' exactly once and traverses all edges in E'. Note that when $s = t$, this problem becomes the general routing problem introduced in [2] which was discussed earlier. We focus on the case $s \neq t$ in the reminder of this paper.

Note that this is a minimum cost problem and the edge costs satisfy the triangle inequality. Thus, we can reduce the visits of vertices and edges not in V' and E'. Namely, we can create a new reduced graph as follow in the problem:

$$G' = (\{v|v \in e, e \in E'\} \cup \{s\} \cup \{t\} \cup V', E').$$

We assume that s and t are two different vertices in the new graph G'. First, we compute the connected components of G' via depth-first search in polynomial time. Then, contracting each component to a vertex, we construct a new complete graph G^*, where each edge cost between vertices is the longest edge cost between each pair of components, which is defined as the distance of each pair of component. This can be done in polynomial time. But we only consider those edges between the vertices with degree $d(v) \in \{0, 1\}$. Finally from the graph G^*, we create a feasible solution as described in Algorithm 1.

Theorem 2. *(⋆) Let S be the path output by Algorithm 1. Then we have*

$$c(S) \leq \min\left\{3OPT - c(s,t), \frac{3}{2}OPT + \frac{1}{2}c(s,t)\right\}.$$

Corollary 2. *The length of the tour output by Algorithm 1 is at most $2OPT$.*

Proof. By Theorem 2, if $c(s,t) \geq OPT$, then $c(S) \leq 3OPT - c(s,t) \leq 2OPT$. Otherwise, if $c(s,t) \leq OPT$, we have $c(S) \leq \frac{3}{2}OPT + \frac{1}{2}c(s,t) \leq 2OPT$. □

Algorithm 1. Algorithm of TGPP with specified vertice

Input:
  1: An edge-weighted undirected graph $G = (V, E, c)$.
  2: Starting vertex s and ending vertex t of G.
  3: $V' \subseteq V$, $E' \subseteq E$ are required vertex subset and edge subset, respectively.
Output: A travelling general salesman path.
     begin:
  4: Construct a new graph $G' = (\{v | v \in e, e \in E'\} \cup \{s\} \cup \{t\} \cup V', E')$.
  5: Compute the connected components $K_1, \ldots, K_k$ of G'.
  6: Let U be the set of vertices v with degree $d(v) \in \{0, 1\}$. Define a complete graph
     $G_k = ([k], E_k)$ with the cost $c(e)$ of edge $e = (i, j)$ with $i \neq j$ equal to the longest
     link between a vertex in $K_i \cap U$ and a vertex in $K_j \cap U$.
  7: Copy the edges of $MST(G^*)$ except for those on s-t path.
  8: Find an Eulerian walk between s and t.
  9: Turn the Eulerian walk into a Hamilton path S.
 10: **output** S.
     end

2.2   The Stacker Crane Problem

Given a weighted graph $G = (V, E, c)$ whose edge costs satisfy the triangle inequality. Let $D = \{(s_i, t_i) : i = 1, \ldots, k\}$ be a given set of special directed arcs, each with length l_i. The arc $\overrightarrow{(s_i, t_i)}$ denotes an object that is at vertex s_i and needs to be moved to vertex t_i using a vehicle (called the stacker crane). The problem is to compute a shortest walk that traverses each directed arc $\overrightarrow{(s_i, t_i)}$ at least once in the specified direction (from s_i to t_i). Let $D = \sum_i l_i$ and $A = OPT - D$.

This problem is a generalization of the TSP, which can be viewed as an instance of this problem where each vertex is replaced by an arc of zero-length. Frederickson et al. presented a 1.8-approximation algorithm for this problem [4]. This algorithm applies two subroutines and then selects the better of the two solutions generated. The main ideas of these two subroutines are summarized below for convenience (see [4,7] for details):

- Algorithm Short-Arcs 1: Shrink the directed arcs and reduce the problem to an instance of TSP. Use an approximation algorithm for the TSP instance, and then recover a solution for the original problem. This algorithm works well when $D \leq \frac{3}{5}OPT$.
- Algorithm Long-Arcs 1: Complete the set of directed arcs into a directed cycle cover. Then find a set of edges of minimum total weight to connect the cycles together. Add two copies of each one of these edges, and orient the copies in opposite directions to each other. The resulted graph is Eulerian, and the algorithm outputs an Euler walk of this solution. The algorithm performs well when $D > \frac{3}{5}OPT$.

The following theorem can be derived from [4].

Theorem 3 [4]. *Consider an instance of the Stacker Crane Problem where the sum of the lengths of the special directed arcs is D. Let OPT be an optimal solution, and let $A = OPT - D$. The walk returned by Algorithm Short-Arcs 1 has length at most $\frac{3}{2}A + 2D$. The walk returned by Algorithm Long-Arcs 1 has length at most $3A + D$.*

2.3 The Rural Postman Problem

Let $E' \subseteq E$ be a specified subset of special edges. We use $c(e)$ to denote the edge cost of e. The rural postman problem (RPP) is to compute a shortest walk that visits all the edges in E'. The Chinese Postman Problem is a special case of RPP in which $E' = E$, i.e., the walk must include all the edges. The Chinese Postman Problem is solvable in polynomial time by reducing it to weighted matching, whereas RPP is NP-hard. Let $D = \sum_i l_i$ be the total length of the paths in all clusters. We recall the algorithms in [4,7].

- Algorithm Short-Arcs 2: Consider the line graph $c(G)$ of original graph G. This algorithm works well when $D \le \frac{3}{5}OPT$.
- Algorithm Long-Arcs 2: Complete the set of undirected arcs into a cycle cover. Then find a set of edges of minimum total weight to connect the cycles together. Add two copies of each one of these edges. The resulting graph is Eulerian, and the algorithm outputs an Euler walk of this solution. The algorithm performs well when D is large. Note that Algorithm Long-Arcs 2 is similar to Long-Arcs 1, but in this case, D is a set of undirected edges. The algorithm performs well when $D > \frac{3}{5}OPT$.

The two algorithms defined above for SCP can be modified to solve RPP. It is easy to see that the second part of Theorem 3 holds for this case as well, i.e. the walk returned by Algorithm Long-Arcs 2 has length at most $3A + D$.

Remark 1. As indicated by Frederickson et al. [4], it is easy to show that the above algorithms produce a $\frac{3}{2}$ performance ratio for RPP.

3 The General Cluster Routing Problem

3.1 The General Cluster Routing Problem with Pre-specified Starting and Ending Vertices

Note that there may exist two subcases in this case. First, each edge in E' is fully contained in its cluster. Second, some edges may be incident with more than one cluster.

Let s_i and t_i be pre-specified starting and ending vertices of cluster $C_i, i \in [k]$. Since the goal is to find a minimal total edge cost and the edge costs satisfy the triangle inequality, we can ignore the vertices not in V' and edges not in E' from graph G to consider a new graph instead. Namely, for every cluster C_i, $i \in [k]$, consider the GCRP in the following new graph $\overline{G} = \cup \overline{C_i}$, where

$$\overline{C_i} = (\overline{V_i}, \overline{E_i}) = \left(\{ v | v \in e, e \in E'_i \} \cup V'_i \cup \{ s_i \} \cup \{ t_i \}, E'_i \right).$$

Our algorithm is based on the following idea. First, within each cluster $\overline{C_i}$, we find a path p_i, starting with s_i and ending at t_i, visits all the vertices in V' and edges of each cluster $\overline{C_i}$. This can be done by Algorithm 1. Second, we need to connect the paths by adding some edges to make the resulting graph into a single cycle.

Let $G = (V, E)$ be a complete graph with vertex set V and edge set E, the vertex set is partitioned into clusters $C_1, \ldots, C_k$. The starting and ending vertices in each cluster are specified. Let $\overline{C_i} = (\overline{V_i}, \overline{E_i})$ be the new graph as described above. Clearly, the desired tour in G does not always exist, e.g., when there exists a required edge $e \in E'$ between cluster C_i and cluster C_j, $i \neq j$, and this required edge is not a (t_i, s_j) edge (in such a case, at least one of the clusters must be visited more than one time). Henceforth, we will assume that the desired tour does exist.

Algorithm 2. Algorithm of given starting and ending vertices
___

Input:
1: An edge-weighted graph $G = (V, E, c)$.
2: A partition of V into clusters $C_1, \ldots, C_k$.
3: Each cluster C_i with starting and ending vertices s_i and t_i, respectively, $i = 1, \ldots, k$.
Output: A general cluster routing tour.
    begin:
4: Construct a new graph $\overline{G} = \cup_{i=1}^{k} \overline{C_i}$.
5: For $i = 1, \ldots, k$, apply Algorithm 1 to get a path p_i and orient the (s_i, t_i) edge a direction, from s_i to t_i, to obtain the arc $\overrightarrow{(s_i, t_i)}$.
6: Apply Algorithm Short-Arcs 1 and Algorithm Long-Arcs 1 for SCP on special arc $\overrightarrow{(s_i, t_i)}$, $i = 1, \ldots, k$, and output the shorter solution T.
7: In T, replace the special directed arc (s_i, t_i) by the path p_i, for $i = 1, \ldots, k$.
8: **Output** the resulting tour T_s.
    end

The main idea of Algorithm 2 is illustrated as follows:

In Step 1, we first consider the number of connected components of $\overline{C_i}$. If the number is 1, it means that there exists a path from s_i to t_i that visits all the required edges in E' and vertices in V'. When the number is more than 2, shrinking the connected components to be vertices and finding a path to connect all these vertices lead to a feasible solution.

In Step 2, by applying Algorithm 1, we can get a path from the starting vertex s_i to ending vertex t_i.

In Step 3, we only need to connect these clusters to form a tour. In this progress, we can shrink the directed arc $\overrightarrow{(s_i, t_i)}$ and reduce the problem to an instance of TSP. Use Christofides' algorithm [3] for the TSP instance.

In Step 4 by replacing the special directed arc (s_i, t_i) by path p_i, we obtain a solution to the original graph.

Our algorithm is a combinational algorithm, which deals with the condition of the pre-specified starting and ending vertices carefully. Let OPT be the cost of the optimal solution. Let L be the sum of lengths of the paths of OPT through each cluster and let A be the length of the other edges of OPT that are not in L. Let D be the total length of the directed arcs $(s_i, t_i), i = 1, \ldots, k$. Then, we have the following theorem:

Theorem 4. $(\star)$ *Let T be the tour output by Algorithm 2. Then*

$$c(T_s) \leq 2.4\, OPT.$$

For the second case, there exists required edges in E' between different clusters. If there exist required edges incident with two different clusters, they must be (t_i, s_j) edges. First, we need to compute the number of (t_i, s_j) edges. Suppose the number is k. If $k = 0$, it is just Case 1. If $k \geq 2$, we then get $k+1$ components and we can shrink the components and go back to Case 1 again.

According to Theorem 4, for the general cluster routing problem with pre-specified vertices, we now get a 2.4-approximation combinatorial algorithm.

3.2   The General Cluster Routing Problem Without Specifying Starting and Ending Vertices

In this section, we consider the version of GCRP where, for each cluster C_i we are free to choose the starting and ending vertices. We consider the two cases again. In the first case, all required edges in E' are only distributed within the clusters. In the second case, there exist some required edges incident with some different clusters.

For every cluster C_i, $i \in [k]$, we consider GCRP on the new graph $\overline{G} = \cup \overline{C_i}$ defined as before:

$$\overline{C_i} = (\overline{V_i}, \overline{E_i}) = (\{v | v \in e \in E_i'\} \cup V_i', E_i').$$

We first consider the connected components of $\overline{C_i}$. In order to obtain the resulted tour, the degree of every vertex of the tour must be even. Therefore, there also exist some cases that the tour cannot exist, i.e., there exists a vertex $v \in \overline{V_i}$ with degree $d(v) > 2$ (in such a case, at least one of the clusters must be visited more than once). Henceforth, we will assume that the desired tour exists.

To solve the first case when all required edges in E' are only distributed within the clusters, we propose an algorithm which computes two different solutions. Then we select the shorter one of these two tours. To get the first solution, by using Algorithm 1 with unspecified ends, we can find paths within each cluster. Then we can view this as a Rural Postman Problem instance. To get the second solution, for each cluster, we select two vertices s_i and t_i such that $c(s_i, t_i)$ is maximized. Let them be the end vertices of each cluster. Then we can apply Algorithm 2 to get the second tour. Finally, we select the shorter tour.

The algorithm for the case when the tour exists can be described as follows:

Algorithm 3. Algorithm of unspecified ending vertices

Input:

1: An edge-weighted graph $G = (V, E, c)$, $V' \subseteq V$, $E' \subseteq E$.

2: A partition of V into clusters $C_1, \ldots, C_k$.

Output: A cluster general routing tour.

   begin:

3: Consider the new graph $\overline{C_i}$, for $i \in [k]$.

4: Apply Algorithm 1 with unspecified end vertices in each cluster $\overline{C_1}, \ldots, \overline{C_k}$. Let path p_i be the resulting path on $\overline{C_i}$, and denote its end vertices by a_i and b_i. Apply Algorithm Long-Arc 2 and Algorithm Short-Arc 2 to output the shorter solution for RPP with special edges (a_i, b_i) and let T_1 be the tour obtained by replacing special edge (a_i, b_i) by path p_i, for $i \in [k]$.

5: In each cluster find vertices s_i and t_i that maximize $c(s_i, t_i)$, for $i \in [k]$. Apply Algorithm 2 with the end vertices $\{s_i, t_i\}$ to output a tour T_2

6: **Output** the shorter of T_1 and T_2.

   end

We will analyze the approximation ratio of Algorithm 3. We first introduce some notations. As in the previous section, let L denote the sum of the lengths of the Hamiltonian paths within the clusters in OPT, and let A denote the sum of the lengths of the remaining edges of OPT. Let $D = \sum_{i=1}^{k} c(s_i, t_i)$ denote the sum cost of required edges. The first algorithm works well when D is small, and the second works well when D is large.

Theorem 5. ($\star$) *Let T_1 be the tour computed in Step 2 of Algorithm 3. Then we have*

$$c(T_1) \leq \frac{3}{2}OPT + \frac{1}{2}L + 2D.$$

Theorem 6. ($\star$) *Let T_2 be the tour computed in Step 3 of Algorithm 3. Then we have*

$$c(T_2) \leq \frac{3}{2}OPT + 3L - 2D.$$

Now we can get the following theorem:

Theorem 7. *Let T be the tour returned by Algorithm 3, then*

$$c(T) \leq \frac{13}{4}OPT.$$

Proof. Note that $L \leq OPT$. If $2D \leq \frac{5}{4}L$, Theorem 5 implies that

$$c(T_1) \leq \frac{3}{2}OPT + \frac{7}{4}L \leq \frac{13}{4}OPT.$$

Otherwise, when $2D \geq \frac{5}{4}L$, Theorem 6 implies that

$$c(T_2) \leq \frac{13}{4}OPT.$$

Since the algorithm chooses the shorter one between the tours T_1 and T_2, the proof is completed.   □

Next, we will consider Case 2 when there exist required edges between clusters.

We consider the problem in three different cases. In the first case, the number of required edges incident with different clusters is k. In the second case, some clusters have two required edges incident with other clusters. In the third case, the number of clusters with required edges incident with other cluster is 0.

In the first case, we only need to find paths between each specified vertices. This can be seen as an instance of Travelling Salesman Path Problem as we described before. So the performance ratio of this case is 1.5.

In the second case, for the clusters which have two required edges incident with other clusters, we find paths in them and it becomes the third case.

Without loss of generality, we consider the third case: the number of clusters with required edges incident to other cluster is 0. For every cluster C_i, we denote the specified vertex as a_i. First, in each cluster, by computing the distance between each component, we select the longest one; that is, we find the vertex b_i such that $c(a_i, b_i)$ is maximum. This can be done in polynomial time, because the number of vertices in each cluster is no more than n. Then we can find the

---

Algorithm 4. Algorithm of existing required edges between clusters

---

Input:
1: An edge-weighted graph $G = (V, E, c)$, $V' \subseteq V$, $E' \subseteq E$.
2: A partition of V into clusters $C_1, \ldots, C_k$.
Output: A general cluster routing tour.
   begin:
3: Let the vertex adjacent to required edges between different cluster C_i be a_i. Find a vertex that maximize $c(a_i, b_i)$, for $i = 1, \ldots, k$.
4: For each $\overline{C_i}$, compute a path p_i, a Hamiltonian path with end vertices a_i and b_i, for $i = 1, \ldots, k$.
5: Apply Algorithm Long-Arc 2 and Algorithm Short-Arc 2 to output the shorter solution for RPP with the special edges $\{(a_i, b_i) | i = 1, \ldots, k\}$ to obtain tour S, for $i = 1, \ldots, k$.
6: In T, replace the special edge (a_i, b_i) by the path p_i, for $i = 1, \ldots, k$.
7: **return** the resulting tour T.
   end

---

path p_i in each cluster C_i by Algorithm 1. Since this problem has no direction, we apply Algorithm Long-Arc 2 and Algorithm Short-Arc 2 to output the shorter solution for RPP and find the tour with the edge (a_i, b_i). At last, we replace the edge(a_i, b_i) by path p_i. The whole algorithm can be described as follows:

Theorem 8. $(\star)$ *Let T be the tour output by Algorithm 4. Then $c(T) \leq \frac{9}{4} OPT$.*

Algorithm 4 is a 2.25-approximation algorithm for the general cluster routing problem with unspecified end vertices, in which some required edges may be incident with different clusters. Therefore, the performance ratio of approximation algorithm for the problem with unspecified vertices is 3.25.

4   Conclusion

In this paper, we present constant approximation algorithms for two variations of the general cluster routing problem. However, the two presented algorithms have different approximation ratio, and in our future work we will consider whether we can design approximation algorithms with the same approximation ratio for these two problems.

References

1. Arkin, E., Hassin, R., Klein, L.: Restricted delivery problems on a network. Networks **29**, 205–216 (1997)
2. Bienstock, D., Goemans, M.-X., Simchi, D., Williamson, D.-P.: A note on the prize-collecting traveling salesman problem. Math. Program. **59**, 413–420 (1991)
3. Christofides, N.: Worst-case analysis of a new heuristic for the traveling salesman problem. Carnegie-Mellon Univ Pittsburgh Pa Management Sciences Research Group (1976)
4. Frederickson, G.-N., Hecht, M.-S., Kim, C.-E.: Approximation algorithms for some routing problems. SIAM J. Comput. **7**, 178–193 (1978)
5. Fumei, L., Alantha, N.: Traveling salesman path problems. Math. Program. **13**, 39–59 (2008)
6. Gutin, G., Punnen, A.: The Traveling Salesman Problem and its Variations. Kluwer, Dordrecht (2002)
7. Guttmann-Beck, N., Hassin, R., Khuller, S., Raghavachari, B.: Approximation algorithms with bounded performance guarantees for the clustered traveling salesman problem. Algorithmica **28**, 422–437 (2000)
8. Hoogeveen, J.-A.: Analysis of Christofides' heuristic: some paths are more difficult than cycles. Oper. Res. Lett. **10**, 291–295 (1991)
9. Jansen, K.: An approximation algorithm for the general routing problem. Inf. Process. Lett. **41**, 333–339 (1992)
10. Karp, R.-M.: Reducibility among combinatorial problems. Complex. Comput. Comput. **2**, 85–103 (1972)
11. Sahni, S., Gonzales, T.: P-complete approximation problems. J. ACM **23**, 555–565 (1976)
12. Sebö, A., Van Zuylen, A.: The salesman's improved paths through forests. J. ACM **66**(4), 1–16 (2019)

13. Sebő, A.: Eight-fifth approximation for the path TSP. In: Goemans, M., Correa, J. (eds.) IPCO 2013. LNCS, vol. 7801, pp. 362–374. Springer, Heidelberg (2013). https://doi.org/10.1007/978-3-642-36694-9_31
14. Traub, V., Vygen, J.: Approaching $\frac{3}{2}$ for the s-t path TSP. J. ACM **66**(2), 1–17 (2019)

Hardness of Sparse Sets and Minimal Circuit Size Problem

Bin Fu[✉][iD]

Department of Computer Science, University of Texas Rio Grande Valley,
Edinburg, TX 78539, USA
bin.fu@utrgv.edu

Abstract. We study the magnification of hardness of sparse sets in nondeterministic time complexity classes on a randomized streaming model. One of our results shows that if there exists a $2^{n^{o(1)}}$-sparse set in NDTIME($2^{n^{o(1)}}$) that does not have any randomized streaming algorithm with $n^{o(1)}$ updating time, and $n^{o(1)}$ space, then NEXP $\neq$ BPP, where a $f(n)$-sparse set is a language that has at most $f(n)$ strings of length n. We also show that if MCSP is ZPP-hard under polynomial time truth-table reductions, then EXP $\neq$ ZPP.

Keywords: MCSP · Sparse sets · Magnification · Reductions

1 Introduction

Hardness magnification has been intensively studied in the recent years [4,10, 12,13]. A small lower bound such as $\Omega(n^{1+\epsilon})$ for one problem may bring a large lower bound such as super-polynomial lower bound for another problem. This research is closely related to Minimum Circuit Size Problem (MCSP) that is to determine if a given string of length $n = 2^m$ with integer m can be generated by a circuit of size k. For a function $s(n) : \mathbb{N} \to \mathbb{N}$, MCSP$[s(n)]$ is that given a string x of length $n = 2^m$, determine if there is a circuit of size at most $s(n)$ to generate x. This problem has received much attention in the recent years [2–8,10–13].

Hardness magnification results are shown in a series of recent papers about MCSP [4,10,12,13]. Oliveira and Santhanam [13] show that $n^{1+\epsilon}$-size lower bounds for approximating MKtP$[n^\beta]$ with an additive error $O(\log n)$ implies EXP $\not\subseteq$ P/poly. Oliveira, Pich and Santhanam [12] show that for all small $\beta > 0$, $n^{1+\epsilon}$-size lower bounds for approximating MCSP$[n^{\beta m}]$ with factor $O(m)$ error implies NP $\not\subseteq$ P/poly. McKay, Murray, and Williams [10] show that an $\Omega(n\text{poly}(\log n))$ lower bound on poly$(\log n)$ space deterministic streaming model for MCSP$[\text{poly}(\log n)]$ implies separation of P from NP.

The hardness magnification of non-uniform complexity for sparse sets is recently developed by Chen et al. [4]. Since MCSP$[s(n)]$ are of sub-exponential density for $s(n) = n^{o(1)}$, the hardness magnification for sub-exponential density sets is more general than the hardness magnification for MCSP. They show that

D. Kim et al. (Eds.): COCOON 2020, LNCS 12273, pp. 484–495, 2020.
https://doi.org/10.1007/978-3-030-58150-3_39

if there is an $\epsilon > 0$ and a family of languages $\{L_b\}$ (indexed over $b \in (0,1)$) such that each L_b is a 2^{n^b}-sparse language in NP, and $L_b \notin \mathrm{Circuit}[n^{1+\epsilon}]$, then NP $\not\subseteq \mathrm{Circuit}[n^k]$ for all k, where $\mathrm{Circuit}[f(n)]$ is the class of languages with nonuniform circuits of size bounded by function $f(n)$. Their result also holds for all complexity classes C with $\exists C = C$.

On the other hand, it is unknown if MCSP is NP-hard. Murray and Williams [11] show that NP-completeness of MCSP implies the separation of EXP from ZPP, a long standing unsolved problem in computational complexity theory. Hitchcock and Pavan [8,11] if MCSP is NP-hard under polynomial time truth-table reductions, then EXP$\not\subseteq$ NP $\cap$ P/poly.

Separating NEXP from BPP, and EXP from ZPP are two of major open problems in the computational complexity theory. We are motivated by further relationship about sparse sets and MCSP, and the two separations NEXP $\neq$ BPP and EXP $\neq$ ZPP. We develop a polynomial method on finite fields to magnify the hardness of sparse sets in nondeterministic time complexity classes over a randomized streaming model. One of our results show that if there exists a $2^{n^{o(1)}}$-sparse set in NDTIME($2^{n^{o(1)}}$) that does not have a randomized streaming algorithm with $n^{o(1)}$ updating time, and $n^{o(1)}$ space, then NEXP $\neq$ BPP, where a $f(n)$-sparse set is a language that has at most $f(n)$ strings of length n. Our magnification result has a flexible trade off between the spareness and time complexity.

We use two functions $d(n)$ and $g(n)$ to control the sparseness of a tally set T. Function $d(n)$ gives an upper bound for the number of elements of in T and $g(n)$ is the gap lower bound between a string 1^n and the next string 1^m in T, which satisfy $g(n) < m$. The class $\mathrm{TALLY}(d(n), g(n))$ defines the class of all those tally sets. By choosing $d(n) = \log \log n$, and $g(n) = 2^{2^{2n}}$, we prove that if MCSP is ZPP $\cap$ TALLY$(d(n), g(n))$-hard under polynomial time truth-table reductions, then EXP $\neq$ ZPP.

1.1   Comparison with the Existing Results

Comparing with some existing results about sparse sets hardness magnification in this line [4], there are some new advancements in this paper.

1. Our magnification of sparse set is based on a uniform streaming model. A class of results in [4] are based on nonuniform models. In [10], they show that if there is $A \in$ PH, and a function $s(n) \geq \log n$, search-MCSP$^A[s(n)]$ does not have $s(n)^c$ updating time in deterministic streaming model for all positive, then P $\neq$ NP. MCSP$[s(n)]$ is a $s(n)^{O(s(n))}$-sparse set.
2. Our method is conceptually simple, and easy to understand. It is a polynomial algebraic approach on finite fields.
3. A flexible trade off between sparseness and time complexity is given in our paper.

Proving NP-hardness for MCSP implies EXP $\neq$ ZPP [8,11]. We consider the implication of ZPP-hardness for MCSP, and show that if MCSP is ZPP $\cap$

TALLY$(d(n), g(n))$-hard for a function pair such as $d(n) = \log \log n$ and $g(n) = 2^{2^{2^n}}$, then EXP $\neq$ ZPP. It seems that proving MCSP is ZPP-hard is much easier than proving MCSP is NP-hard since ZPP $\subseteq$ (NP $\cap$ coNP) $\subseteq$ NP. According to the low-high hierarchy theory developed by Schöning [14], the class NP $\cap$ coNP is the low class L_1. Although MCSP may not be in the class ZPP, it is possible to be ZPP-hard.

2 Notations

Minimum Circuit Size Problem (MCSP) is that given an integer k, and a binary string T of length $n = 2^m$ for some integer $m \geq 0$, determine if T can be generated by a circuit of size k. Let $\mathbb{N} = \{1, 2, \cdots\}$ be the set of all natural numbers. For a language L, L^n is the set of strings in L of length n, and $L^{\leq n}$ is the set of strings in L of length at most n. For a finite set A, denote $|A|$ to be the number of elements in A. For a string s, denote $|s|$ to be its length. If x, y, z are not empty strings, we have a coding method that converts a x, y into a string $\langle x, y \rangle$ with $|x| + |y| \leq |\langle x, y \rangle| \leq 3(|x| + |y|)$ and converts x, y, z into $\langle x, y, z \rangle$ with $|x| + |y| + |z| \leq |\langle x, y, z \rangle| \leq 3(|x| + |y| + |z|)$. For example, for $x = x_1 \cdots x_{n_1}, y = y_1 \cdots y_{n_2}, z = z_1 \cdots z_{n_3}$, let $\langle x, y, z \rangle = 1x_1 \cdots 1x_{n_1} 001 y_1 \cdots 1 y_{n_2} 00 z_1 \cdots z_{n_3}$.

Let DTIME$(t(n))$ be the class of languages accepted by deterministic Turing machines in time $O(t(n))$. Let NDTIME$(t(n))$ be the class of languages accepted by nondeterministic Turing machines in time $O(t(n))$. Define EXP $= \cup_{c=1}^{\infty} $DTIME$(2^{n^c})$ and NEXP $= \cup_{c=1}^{\infty}$NDTIME(2^{n^c}). P/poly, which is also called PSIZE, is the class of languages that have polynomial-size circuits.

We use a polynomial method on a finite field F. It is classical theory that each finite field is of size p^k for some prime number p and integer $k \geq 1$ (see [9]). For a finite field F, we denote $R(F) = (p, t_F(u))$ to represent F, where $t_F(u)$ is a irreducible polynomial over field GF(p) for the prime number p and its degree is $\deg(t_F(.)) = k$. The polynomial $t_F(u)$ is equal to u if F is of size p, which is a prime number. Each element of F with $R(F) = (p, t_F(u))$ is a polynomial $q(u)$ with degree less than the degree of $t_F(u)$. For two elements $q_1(u)$ and $q_2(u)$ in F, their addition is defined by $(q_1(u) + q_2(u))(\mod t_F(u))$, and their multiplication is defined by $(q_1(u) \cdot q_2(u))(\mod t_F(u))$ (see [9]). Each element in GF(2^k) is a polynomial $\sum_{i=0}^{k-1} b_i u^i$ ($b_i \in \{0, 1\}$), which is represented by a binary string $b_{k-1} \cdots b_0$ of length k.

We use GF(2^k) field in our randomized streaming algorithm for hardness magnification . Let F be a GF(2^k) field (a field of size $q = 2^k$) and has its $R(F) = (2, t_F(u))$. Let $s = a_0 \cdots a_{m-1}$ be a binary string of length m with $m \leq k$, and u be a variable. Define $w(s, u)$ to be the element $\sum_{i=0}^{m-1} a_i u^i$ in GF(2^k). Let x be a string in $\{0, 1\}^*$ and k be an integer at least 1. Let $x = s_{r-1} s_{t-2} \cdots s_1 s_0$ such that each s_i is a substring of x of length k for $i = 1, 2, \cdots, r - 1$, and the substring s_0 has its length $|s_0| \leq k$. Each s_i is called a k-segment of x for $i = 0, 1, \cdots, r - 1$. Define the polynomial $d_x(z) = z^r + \sum_{i=0}^{r-1} w(s_i, u) z^i$, which converts a binary string into a polynomial in GF(2^k).

We develop a streaming algorithm that converts an input string into an element in a finite field. We give the definition to characterize the properties of the streaming algorithm developed in this paper. Our streaming algorithm is to convert an input stream x into an element $d_x(a) \in F = \mathrm{GF}(2^k)$ by selecting a random element a from F.

Definition 1. *Let* $r_0(n), r_1(n), r_2(n), s(n), u(n)$ *be nondecreasing functions from* $\mathbb{N}$ *to* $\mathbb{N}$*. Define* Streaming$(r_0(n), r_1(n), s(n), u(n), r_2(n))$ *to be the class of languages* L *that have one-pass streaming algorithms that has input* (n, x) *with* $n = |x|$ *(x is a string and read by streaming), it satisfies*

1. *It takes* $r_0(n)$ *time to generate a field* $F = \mathrm{GF}(2^k)$*, which is represented by* $(2, t_F(.))$ *with a irreducible polynomial* $t_f(.)$ *over* $\mathrm{GF}(2)$ *of degree* k*.*
2. *It takes* $O(r_1(n))$ *random steps before reading the first bit from the input stream* x*.*
3. *It uses* $O(s(n))$ *space that includes the space to hold the field representation generated by the algorithm. The space for a field representation is* $\Omega((\deg(t_F(.)) + 1))$ *and* $O((\deg(t_F(.)) + 1))$ *for the irreducible polynomial* $t_F(.)$ *over* $\mathrm{GF}(2)$*.*
4. *It takes* $O(u(n))$ *field conversions to elements in* F *and* $O(u(n))$ *field operations in* F *after reading each bit.*
5. *It runs* $O(r_2(n))$ *randomized steps after reading the entire input.*

3 Overview of Our Methods

In this section, we give a brief description about our methods used in this paper. Our first result is based on a polynomial method on a finite field whose size affects the hardness of magnification. The second result is a translational method for zero-error probabilistic complexity classes.

3.1 Magnify the Hardness of Sparse Sets

We have a polynomial method over finite fields. Let L be $f(n)$-sparse language in NDTIME$(t_1(n))$. In order to handle an input string of size n, a finite field $F = \mathrm{GF}(q)$ with $q = 2^k$ for some integer k is selected, and is represented by $R(F) = (2, t_F(z))$, where $t_F(z)$ is a irreducible polynomial over $\mathrm{GF}(2)$. An input $y = a_1 a_2 \cdots a_n$ is partitioned into k-segments $s_{r-1} \cdots s_1 s_0$ such that each s_i is converted into an element $w(s_i, u)$ in F, and y is transformed into an polynomial $d_y(z) = z^r + \sum_{i=0}^{r-1} w(s_i, u) z^i$. A random element $a \in F$ is chosen in the beginning of streaming algorithm before processing the input stream. The value $d_y(a)$ is evaluated with the procession of input stream. The finite F is large enough such that for different y_1 and y_2 of the same length, $d_{y_1}(.)$ and $d_{y_2}(.)$ are different polynomials due to their different coefficients derived from y_1 and y_2, respectively. Let $H(y)$ be the set of all $\langle n, a, d_y(a) \rangle$ with $a \in F$ and $n = |y|$. Set $A(n)$ is the union of all $H(y)$ with $y \in L^n$. The set of A is $\cup_{i=1}^{\infty} A(n)$. A small lower bound for the language A is magnified to large lower bound for L.

The size of field F depends on the density of set L and is $O(f(n)n)$. By the construction of A, if $y \in L$, there are q tuples $\langle n, a, d_y(a) \rangle$ in A that are generated by y via all a in F. For two different y_1 and y_2 of length n, the intersection $H(y_1) \cap H(y_2)$ is bounded by the degree of $d_{y_1}(.)$. If $y \notin L$, the number of items $\langle n, a, d_y(a) \rangle$ generated by y is at most $\frac{q}{4}$ in A. If $y \in L$, the number of items $\langle n, a, d_y(a) \rangle$ generated by y is q in A. This enables us to convert a string x of length n in L into some strings in A of length much smaller than n, make the hardness magnification possible.

3.2 Separation by ZPP-**Hardness of** MCSP

Our another result shows that ZPP-hardness for MCSP implies EXP $\neq$ ZPP. We identify a class of functions that are padding stable, which has the property if $T \in \text{TALLY}(d(n), g(n))$, then $\{1^{n+2^n} : 1^n \in T\} \in \text{TALLY}(d(n), g(n))$. The function pair $d(n) = \log \log n$ and $g(n) = 2^{2^{2n}}$ has this property. We construct a very sparse tally set $L \in \text{EXP} \cap \text{TALLY}(d(n), g(n))$ that separates ZPEXP from ZPP, where ZPEXP is the zero error exponential time probabilistic class. It is based on a diagonal method that is combined with a padding design. A tally language L has a zero-error 2^{2^n}-time probabilistic algorithm implies $L' = \{1^{n+2^n} : 1^n \in L\}$ has a zero-error 2^n-time probabilistic algorithm. Adapting to the method of [11], we prove that if MCSP is ZPP $\cap$ TALLY$(d(n), g(n))$-hard under polynomial time truth-table reductions, then EXP $\neq$ ZPP.

4 Hardness Magnification via Streaming

In this section, we show a hardness magnification of sparse sets via a streaming algorithm. A classical algorithm to find irreducible polynomial [15] is used to construct a field that is large enough for our algorithm.

Theorem 1. *[15] There is a deterministic algorithm that constructs a irreducible polynomial of degree n in $O(p^{\frac{1}{2}}(\log p)^3 n^{3+\epsilon} + (\log p)^2 n^{4+\epsilon})$ operations in F, where F is a finite field $\text{GF}(p)$ with prime number p.*

Definition 2. *Let $f(n)$ be a function from N to N. For a language $A \subseteq \{0,1\}^*$, we say A is $f(n)$-sparse if $|A^n| \leq f(n)$ for all large integer n.*

4.1 Streaming Algorithm

The algorithm Streaming(.) is based on a language L that is $f(n)$-sparse. It generates a field $F = \text{GF}(2^k)$ and evaluates $d_x(a)$ with a random element a in F. A polynomial $z^r + \sum_{i=0}^{r-1} b_i z^i = z^r + b_{r-1} z^{r-1} + b_{r-2} z^{r-2} + \cdots + b_0$ can be evaluated by $(\cdots ((z + b_{r-1})z + b_{r-2})z + \ldots)z + b_0$ according to the classical Horner's algorithm. For example, $z^2 + z + 1 = (z+1)z + 1$.

Algorithm

Streaming(n, x)

Input: an integer n, and string $x = a_1 \cdots a_n$ of the length n;

Steps:

1. Select a field size $q = 2^k$ such that $8f(n)n < q \leq 16f(n)n$.
2. Generate an irreducible polynomial $t_F(u)$ of degree k over GF(2) such that $(2, t_F(u))$ represents finite $F = \mathrm{GF}(q)$ (by Theorem 1 with $p = 2$);
3. Let a be a random element in F;
4. Let $r = \lceil \frac{n}{k} \rceil$; (Note that r is the number of k-segments of x. See Sect. 2)
5. Let $j = r - 1$;
6. Let $v = 1$;
7. Repeat
8. {
9.   Receive the next k-segment s_j from the input stream x;
10.   Convert s_j into an element $b_j = w(s_j, u)$ in GF(q);
11.   Let $v = v \cdot a + b_j$;
12.   Let $j = j - 1$;
13. }
14. Until $j < 0$ (the end of the stream);
15. Output $\langle n, a, v \rangle$;

End of Algorithm

Now we have our magnification algorithm. Let $M(.)$ be a randomized Turing machine to accept a language A that contains all $\langle |x|, a, d_x(a) \rangle$ with $a \in F$ and $x \in L$. We have the following randomized streaming algorithm to accept L via the randomized algorithm $M(.)$ for A.

Algorithm
Magnification(n, x)
Input integer n and $x = a_1 \cdots a_n$ as a stream;
Steps: Let $y =$ Streaming(n, x); Accept if $M(y)$ accepts;
End of Algorithm

4.2   Hardness Magnification

In this section, we derive some results about hardness magnification via sparse set. Our results show a trade off between the hardness magnification and sparseness via the streaming model.

Definition 3. *For a nondecreasing function $t(.) : \mathbb{N} \to \mathbb{N}$, define* BTIME($t(n)$) *the class of languages L that have two-side bounded error probabilistic algorithms with time complexity $O(t(n))$. Define* BPP $= \cup_{c=1}^{\infty}$ BTIME(n^c).

Theorem 2. *Assume that $u_1(m)$ be nondecreasing function for the time to generate an irreducible polynomial of degree m in GF(2), and $u_2(m)$ be the nondecreasing function of a time upper bound for the operations $(+, .)$ in GF(2^m). Let $f(.), t_1(.), t_2(.), t_3(n)$ be nondecreasing functions $\mathbb{N} \to \mathbb{N}$ with $f(n) \leq 2^{\frac{n}{2}}$, $v(n) = (\log n + \log f(n))$, and $10v(n) + t_1(n) + u_1(10v(n)) + n \cdot u_2(10v(n)) \leq t_2(v(n))$ for all large n. If there is a $f(n)$-sparse set L with $L \in$ NDTIME($t_1(n)$) and $L \notin$ Streaming($u_1(10v(n)), v(n), v(n), 1, t_3(10v(n))$), then there is a language A such that $A \in$ NDTIME($t_2(n)$) and $A \notin$ BTIME($t_3(n)$).*

Proof. Select a finite field $GF(q)$ with $q = 2^k$ for an integer k by line 1 of the algorithm streaming(.). For each $x \in L^n$, let x be partitioned into k-segments: $s_{r-1}s_{r-2}\cdots s_0$. Let $w(s_i, u)$ convert s_i into an element of $GF(q)$ (See Sect. 2). Define polynomial $d_x(z) = z^r + \sum_{i=0}^{r-1} w(q, s_i)z^i$. For each x, let $H(x)$ be the set $\{\langle n, a, d_x(a)\rangle | a \in GF(q)\}$, where $n = |x|$. Define set $A(n) = \cup_{y \in L^n} H(y)$ for $n = 1, 2 \cdots$, and language $A = \cup_{n=1}^{+\infty} A(n)$.

Claim 1. For any $x \notin L^n$ with $n = |x|$, we have $|H(x) \cap A(n)| < \frac{q}{4}$.

Proof. Assume that for some $x \notin L^n$ with $n = |x|$, $|H(x) \cap A(n)| \geq \frac{q}{4}$. It is easy to see that $r \leq n$ and $k \leq n$ for all large n by the algorithm Streaming(.) and the condition of $f(.)$ in the theorem. Assume that $|H(x) \cap H(y)| < r + 1$ for every $y \in L^n$. Since $A(n)$ is the union $H(y)$ with $y \in L^n$ and $|L^n| \leq f(n)$, there are at most $rf(n) \leq nf(n) < \frac{q}{8}$ elements in $H(x) \cap A(n)$ by line 1 of the algorithm Streaming(.). Thus, $|H(x) \cap A(n)| < \frac{q}{8}$. This brings a contradiction. Therefore, there is a $y \in L^n$ to have $|H(x) \cap H(y)| \geq r + 1$. Since the polynomials $d_x(.)$ and $d_y(.)$ are of degrees at most r, we have $d_x(z) = d_y(z)$ (two polynomials are equal). Thus, $x = y$. This brings a contradiction because $x \notin L^n$ and $y \in L^n$.

Claim 2. If $x \in L$, then Streaming$(|x|, x) \in A$. Otherwise, with probability at most $\frac{1}{4}$, Streaming$(|x|, x) \in A$.

Proof. For each x, it generates $\langle n, a, d_x(a)\rangle$ for a random $a \in GF(q)$. Each $a \in GF(q)$ determines a random path. We have that if $x \in L$, then $\langle n, a, d_x(a)\rangle \in A$, and if $x \notin L$, then $\langle n, a, d_x(a)\rangle \in A$ with probability at most $\frac{1}{4}$ by Claim 1.

Claim 3. $A \in \text{NDTIME}(t_2(m))$.

Proof. Let $z = 10v(n) = 10(\log n + \log f(n))$. Each element in field $F = GF(2^k)$ is of length k. For each $u = \langle n, a, b\rangle$ $(a, b \in F)$, we need to guess a string $x \in L^n$ such that $b = d_x(a)$. It is easy to see that $v(n) \leq |\langle n, a, b\rangle| \leq 10v(n)$ for all large n if $\langle n, a, b\rangle \in A$ (See Sect. 2 about coding). Let $m = |\langle n, a, b\rangle|$. It takes at most $u_1(z)$ steps to generate a irreducible polynomial $t_F(.)$ for the field F by our assumption.

   Since $L \in \text{NDTIME}(t_1(n))$, checking if $u \in A$ takes nondeterministic $t_1(n)$ steps to guess a string $x \in L^n$, $u_1(z)$ deterministic steps to generate $t_F(u)$ for the field F, $O(z)$ nondeterministic steps to generate a random element $a \in F$, and additional $O(n \cdot u_2(z))$ steps to evaluate $d_x(a)$ in by following algorithm Streaming(.) and check $b = d_x(a)$. The polynomial $t_F(u)$ in the $GF(2)$ has degree at most z. Each polynomial operation ($+$ or .) in F takes at most $u_2(z)$ steps. Since $z + t_1(n) + u_1(z) + n \cdot u_2(z) \leq t_2(m)$ time by the condition of this theorem, we have $A \in \text{NDTIME}(t_2(m))$.

Claim 4. If $A \in \text{BTIME}(t_3(m))$, then $L \in$ Streaming$(u_1(10v(n)), v(n), v(n), 1, t_3(10v(n)))$.

Proof. The field generated at line 2 in algorithm Streaming(.) takes $u_1(10(\log n + \log f(n)))$ time. Let $x = a_1 \cdots a_n$ be the input string. The string x partitioned into k-segments $s_{r-1} \cdots s_0$. Transform each s_i into an element $b_i = w(s_i, u)$ in GF(q) in the streaming algorithm. We generate a polynomial $d_x(z) = z^r + \sum_{i=0}^{r-1} b_i z^i = z^r + b_{r-1} z^{r-1} + b_{r-2} z^{r-2} + \cdots + b_0$. Given a random element $a \in$ GF(q), we evaluate $d_x(a) = (\cdots ((a + b_{r-1})a + b_{r-2})a + \ldots)a + b_0$ according to the classical algorithm. Therefore, $d_x(a)$ is evaluated in Streaming(.) with input $(|x|, x)$.

If $A \in$ BTIME($t_3(m)$), then L has a randomized streaming algorithm that has at most $t_3(10v(n))$ random steps after reading the input, and at most O($v(n)$) space. After reading one substring s_i from x, it takes one conversion from a substring of the input to an element of field F by line 10, and at most two field operations by line 11 in the algorithm Streaming(.).

Claim 4 brings a contradiction to our assumption about the complexity of L in the theorem. This proves the theorem.

Proposition 1. *Let $f(n) : \mathbb{N} \to \mathbb{N}$ be a nondecreasing function. If for each fixed $\epsilon \in (0, 1)$, $f(n) \leq n^\epsilon$ for all large n, then there is a nondecreasing unbounded function $g(n) : \mathbb{N} \to \mathbb{N}$ with $f(n) \leq n^{\frac{1}{g(n)}}$.*

Proof. Let $n_0 = 1$. For each $k \geq 1$, let n_k be the least integer such that $n_k \geq n_{k-1}$ and $f(n) \leq n^{\frac{1}{k}}$ for all $n \geq n_k$. Clearly, we have the infinite list $n_1 \leq n_2 \cdots \leq n_k \leq \cdots$ such that $\lim_{k \to +\infty} n_k = +\infty$. Define function $g(k) : \mathbb{N} \to \mathbb{N}$ such that $g(n) = k$ for all $n \in [n_{k-1}, n_k)$. For each $n \geq n_k$, we have $f(n) \leq n^{\frac{1}{k}}$.

Our Definition 4 is based Proposition 1. It can simplify the proof when we handle a function that is $n^{o(1)}$.

Definition 4. *A function $f(n) : \mathbb{N} \to \mathbb{N}$ is $n^{o(1)}$ if there is a nondecreasing function $g(n) : \mathbb{N} \to \mathbb{N}$ such that $\lim_{n \to +\infty} g(n) = +\infty$ and $f(n) \leq n^{\frac{1}{g(n)}}$ for all large n. A function $f(n) : \mathbb{N} \to \mathbb{N}$ is $2^{n^{o(1)}}$ if there is a nondecreasing function $g(n) : \mathbb{N} \to \mathbb{N}$ such that $\lim_{n \to +\infty} g(n) = +\infty$ and $f(n) \leq 2^{n^{\frac{1}{g(n)}}}$ for all large n.*

Corollary 1. *If there exists a $2^{n^{o(1)}}$-sparse language L in NDTIME($2^{n^{o(1)}}$) such that L does not have any randomized streaming algorithm with $n^{o(1)}$ updating time, and $n^{o(1)}$ space, then NEXP $\neq$ BPP.*

Proof. Let $g(n) : \mathbb{N} \to \mathbb{N}$ be an arbitrary unbounded nondecreasing function that satisfies $\lim_{n \to +\infty} g(n) = +\infty$ and $g(n) \leq \log \log n$. Let $t_1(n) = f(n) = 2^{n^{\frac{1}{g(n)}}}$ and Let $t_2(n) = 2^{2n}$, $t_3(n) = n^{\sqrt{g(n)}}$, and $v(n) = (\log n + \log f(n))$.

It is easy to see that $v(n) = n^{o(1)}$, and both $u_1(n)$ and $u_2(n)$ are $n^{O(1)}$ (see Theorem 1). For any fixed $c_0 > 0$, we have $t_2(v(n)) > t_2(\log f(n)) \geq t_2(n^{\frac{1}{g(n)}}) > t_1(n) + n^{c_0}$ for all large n. For all large n, we have

$$t_3(10v(n)) \leq t_3(20 \log f(n)) = t_3(20 n^{\frac{1}{g(n)}}) \tag{1}$$

$$\leq (20 n^{\frac{1}{g(n)}})^{\sqrt{g(20 n^{\frac{1}{g(n)}})}} \leq (n^{\frac{2}{g(n)}})^{\sqrt{g(n)}} = n^{o(1)}. \tag{2}$$

Clearly, these functions satisfy the inequality of the precondition in Theorem 2. Assume $L \in$ Streaming$(\text{poly}(v(n)), v(n), v(n), 1, t_3(10v(n)))$. With $O(v(n)) = n^{o(1)}$ space, we have a field representation $(2, t_F(.))$ with $\deg(t_F(.)) = n^{o(1)}$. Thus, each field operation takes $n^{o(1)}$ time by the brute force method for polynomial addition and multiplication. We have $t_3(10v(n)) = n^{o(1)}$ by inequality (2). Thus, the streaming algorithm updating time is $n^{o(1)}$. Therefore, we have that L has a randomized streaming algorithm with $n^{o(1)}$ updating time, and $n^{o(1)}$ space. This gives a contradiction. So, $L \notin$ Streaming$(\text{poly}(v(n)), v(n), v(n), 1, t_3(10v(n)))$. By Theorem 2, there is $A \in$ NDTIME$(t_2(n))$ such that $A \notin$ BTIME$(t_3(n))$. Therefore, $A \notin$ BPP. Thus, NEXP $\neq$ BPP.

5   Implication of ZPP-Hardness Of MCSP

In this section, we show that if MCSP is ZPP$\cap$TALLY-hard, then EXP $\neq$ ZPP. The conclusion still holds if TALLY is replaced by a very sparse subclass of TALLY languages.

Definition 5. *For a nondecreasing function $t(.) : \mathbb{N} \to \mathbb{N}$, define ZTIME$(t(n))$ the class of languages L that have zero-error probabilistic algorithms with time complexity $O(t(n))$. Define ZPP $= \cup_{c=1}^{\infty}$ZTIME(n^c), and ZPEXP $= \cup_{c=1}^{\infty}$ZTIME(2^{n^c}).*

Definition 6. *For an nondecreasing function $f(n) : \mathbb{N} \to \mathbb{N}$, define TALLY$[f(k)]$ to be the class of tally set $A \subseteq \{1\}^*$ such that for each $1^m \in A$, there is an integer $i \in \mathbb{N}$ with $m = f(i)$. For a tally language $T \subseteq \{1\}^*$, define Pad$(T) = \{1^{2^n+n}|1^n \in T\}$.*

Definition 7. *For two languages A and B, a polynomial time truth-table reduction from A to B is a polynomial time computable function $f(.)$ such that for each instance x for A, $f(x) = (y_1, \cdots, y_m, C(.))$ to satisfy $x \in A$ if and only if $C(B(y_1), \cdots, B(y_m)) = 1$, where $C(.)$ is circuit of m input bits and $B(.)$ is the characteristic function of B.*

Let $\leq_r^P$ be a type of polynomial time reductions ($\leq_{tt}^P$ represents polynomial time truth-table reductions), and C be a class of languages. A language A is C-hard under $\leq_r^P$ reductions if for each $B \in C$, $B \leq_r^P A$.

Definition 8. *Let k be an integer. Define two classes of functions with recursions: (1) $\log^{(1)}(n) = \log_2 n$, and $\log^{(k+1)}(n) = \log_2(\log^{(k)}(n))$. (2) $\exp^{(1)}(n) = 2^n$, and $\exp^{(k+1)}(n) = 2^{\exp^{(k)}(n)}$.*

Definition 9. *For two nondecreasing functions $d(n), g(n) : \mathbb{N} \to \mathbb{N}$, the pair $(d(n), g(n))$ is time constructible if $(d(n), g(n))$ can be computed in time $d(n) + g(n)$ steps.*

Definition 10. *Define TALLY$(d(n), g(n))$ to be the class of tally sets T such that $|T^{\leq n}| \leq d(n)$ and for any two strings $1^n, 1^m \in T$ with $n < m$, they satisfy $g(n) < m$. We call $d(n)$ to be the density function and $g(n)$ to be the gap function. A gap function $g(n)$ is padding stable if $g(2^n + n) < 2^{g(n)} + g(n)$ for all $n > 1$.*

Lemma 1.

1. *Assume the gap function $g(n)$ is padding stable. If $T \in \text{TALLY}(d(n), g(n))$, then $\text{Pad}(T) \in \text{TALLY}(d(n), g(n))$.*
2. *For each integer $k > 0$, $g(n) = \exp^{(k)}(2n)$ is padding stable.*

Proof. Part 1. Let 1^n be a string in T. The next shortest string $1^m \in T$ with $n < m$ satisfies $g(n) < m$. We have $1^{2^n + n}$ and $1^{2^m + m}$ are two consecutive neighbor strings in $\text{Pad}(T)$ such that there is no other string $1^k \in \text{Pad}(T)$ with $2^n + n < k < 2^m + m$. We have $g(2^n + n) < 2^{g(n)} + g(n) < 2^m + m$. Since the strings in $\text{Pad}(T)^{\leq n}$ are one-one mapped from the strings in T with length less than n, $|\text{Pad}(T)^{\leq n}| \leq |T^{\leq n}| \leq d(n)$, we have $\text{Pad}(T) \in \text{TALLY}(d(n), g(n))$. This proves Part (1).

Part 2. We have inequality $g(2^n + n) = \exp^{(k)}(2(2^n + n)) < \exp^{(k)}(4 \cdot 2^n) = \exp^{(k)}(2^{n+2}) \leq \exp^{(k)}(2^{2n}) = 2^{g(n)} < 2^{g(n)} + g(n)$. Therefore, gap function $g(n)$ is padding stable. This proves Part 2.

Lemma 2. *Let $d(n)$ and $g(n)$ be nondecreasing unbounded functions from N to N, and $(d(n), g(n))$ is time constructible. Then there exists a time constructible increasing unbounded function $f(n) : \mathbb{N} \to \mathbb{N}$ such that $\text{TALLY}[f(n)] \subseteq \text{TALLY}(d(n), g(n))$.*

Proof. Compute the least integer n_1 with $d(n_1) > 0$. Let s_1 be the number of steps for the computation. Define $f(1) = \max(s_1, n_1)$. Assume that $f(k-1)$ has been defined. We determine the function value $f(k)$ below.

For an integer $k > 0$, compute $g(f(k-1))$ and the least k numbers $n_1 < n_2 < \cdots < n_k$ such that $0 < d(n_1) < d(n_2) < \cdots < d(n_k)$. Assume the computation above takes s steps. Define $f(k)$ to be the $\max(2s, n_k, g(f(k-1)) + 1)$. For each language $T \in \text{TALLY}[f(n)]$, there are at most k strings in T with length at most $f(k)$. On the other hand, $d(n_k) \geq k$ by the increasing list $0 < d(n_1) < d(n_2) < \cdots < d(n_k)$. Therefore, we have $|T^{\leq n_k}| \leq k \leq d(n_k)$. Furthermore, we also have $g(f(k-1)) < f(k)$. Since s is the number of steps to determine the values s, n_k, and $g(f(k-1)) + 1$. We have $2s \leq f(k)$. Thus, $f(k)$ can be computed in $f(k)$ steps by spending some idle steps. Therefore, the function $f(.)$ is time constructible.

We will use the notion $\text{TALLY}[f(k)]$ to characterize extremely sparse tally sets with fast growing function such as $f(k) = 2^{2^{2^k}}$. It is easy to see that $\text{TALLY} = \text{TALLY}[I(.)]$, where $I(.)$ is the identity function $I(k) = k$.

Lemma 3. *Let $d(n)$ and $g(n)$ be nondecreasing unbounded functions. If function $g(n))$ is padding stable, then there is a language A such that $A \in \text{ZTIME}(2^{O(n)}) \cap \text{TALLY}(d(n), g(n))$ and $A \notin \text{ZPP}$.*

Proof. It is based on the classical translational method. Assume $\text{ZTIME}(2^{O(n)}) \cap \text{TALLY}(d(n), g(n)) \subseteq \text{ZPP}$. Let $f(.)$ be a time constructible increasing unbounded function via Lemma 2 such that $\text{TALLY}[f(n)] \subseteq \text{TALLY}(d(n), g(n))$. Let $t_1(n) = 2^{2^n}$ and $t_2(n) = 2^{2^{n-1}}$. Let L be a tally language in $\text{DTIME}(t_1(n)) \cap \text{TALLY}[f(n)]$, but it is not in $\text{DTIME}(t_2(n))$. Such a language L can be constructed via a standard diagonal method. Let $M_1, \cdots, M_2$ be the list of Turing machines such that each M_i has time upper bound by function $t_2(n)$. Define language $L \in \text{TALLY}[f(n)]$ such that for each k, $1^{f(k)} \in L$ if and only if $M_k(1^{f(k)})$ rejects in $t_2(f(k))$ steps. We have $L \in \text{TALLY}(d(n), g(n))$ by Lemma 2.

Let $L_1 = \text{Pad}(L)$. We have $L_1 \in \text{TALLY}(d(n), g(n))$ by Lemma 1. We have $L_1 \in \text{DTIME}(2^{O(n)}) \subseteq \text{ZTIME}(2^{O(n)})$. Thus, $L_1 \in \text{ZPP}$. So, $L \in \text{ZTIME}(2^{O(n)})$. Therefore, $L \in \text{ZTIME}(2^{O(n)}) \cap \text{TALLY}(d(n), g(n))$. We have $L \in \text{ZPP}$. Thus, $L \in \text{DTIME}(2^{n^{O(1)}}) \subseteq \text{DTIME}(2^{2^{n-1}})$. This brings a contradiction.

Theorem 3. *Let $d(n)$ and $g(n)$ be nondecreasing unbounded functions from $\mathbb{N}$ to $\mathbb{N}$. Assume that $g(n)$ is padding stable. If MCSP is $\text{ZPP} \cap \text{TALLY}(d(n), g(n))$-hard under polynomial time truth-table reductions, then $\text{EXP} \neq \text{ZPP}$.*

Proof. Assume that MCSP is $(\text{ZPP} \cap \text{TALLY}(d(n), g(n))$-hard under polynomial time truth-table reductions, and $\text{EXP} = \text{ZPP}$.

Let L be a language in $\text{ZTIME}(2^{O(n)}) \cap \text{TALLY}[d(.), g(.)]$, but $L \notin \text{ZPP}$ by Lemma 3. Let $L' = \text{Pad}(L)$. Clearly, every string 1^y in L' has the property that $y = 2^n + n$ for some integer n. This property is easy to check and we reject all strings without this property in linear time. We have $L' \in \text{ZPP}$. Therefore, there is a polynomial time truth-table reduction from L' to MCSP via a polynomial time truth-table reduction $M(.)$. Let polynomial $p(n) = n^c$ be the running time for $M(.)$ for a fixed c and $n \geq 2$.

Define the language $R = \{(1^n, i, j),$ the i-th bit of j-th query of $M(1^{n+2^n})$ is equal to 1, and $i, j \leq p(n + 2^n)\}$. We can easily prove that R is in EXP. Therefore, $R \in \text{ZPP} \subseteq \text{P/poly}$ (See [1]).

Therefore, there is a class of polynomial size circuits $\{C_n\}_{n=1}^{\infty}$ to recognize R such that $C_n(.)$ recognize all $(1^n, i, j)$ with $i, j \leq p(n + 2^n)$ in R. Assume that the size of C_n is of size at most $q(n) = n^{t_0} + t_0$ for a fixed t_0. For an instance $x = 1^n$ for L, consider the instance $y = 1^{n+2^n}$ for L'. We can compute all non-adaptive queries $\langle T, s(n) \rangle$ to MCSP in $2^{n^{O(1)}}$ time via $M(y)$. If $s(n) \geq q(n)$, the answer from MCSP for the query $\langle T, s(n) \rangle$ is yes since $\langle T, s(n) \rangle$ can be generated as one of the instances via the circuit $C_n(.)$. If $s(n) < q(n)$, we can use a brute force method to check if there exists a circuit of size at most $q(n)$ to generate T. It takes $2^{n^{O(1)}}$ time. Therefore, $L \in \text{EXP}$. Thus, $L \in \text{ZPP}$. This bring a contradiction as we already assume $L \notin \text{ZPP}$.

Corollary 2. *For any integer $k \geq 1$, if MCSP is $\text{ZPP} \cap \text{TALLY}(\log^{(k)}(n), \exp^{(k)}(2n))$-hard under polynomial time truth-table reductions, then $\text{EXP} \neq \text{ZPP}$.*

Corollary 3. *If MCSP is ZPP-hard under polynomial time truth-table reductions, then $\text{EXP} \neq \text{ZPP}$.*

Acknowledgements. This research was supported in part by National Science Foundation Early Career Award 0845376, and Bensten Fellowship of the University of Texas Rio Grande Valley. Part of this research was conducted while the author was visiting the School of Computer Science and Technology of Hengyang Normal University in the summer of 2019 and was supported by National Natural Science Foundation of China 61772179.

References

1. Adleman, L.: Two theorems on random polynomial time. In: Proceedings of the 19th Annual IEEE Symposium on Foundations of Computer Science, pp. 75–83 (1978)
2. Allender, E., Hirahara, S.: New insights on the (non-)hardness of circuit minimization and related problems. In: 42nd International Symposium on Mathematical Foundations of Computer Science, MFCS 2017, Aalborg, Denmark, August 21–25, 2017, pp. 54:1–54:14 (2017)
3. Allender, E., Holden, D., Kabanets, V.: The minimum oracle circuit size problem. Comput. Complex. **26**(2), 469–496 (2017)
4. Chen, L., Jin, C., Williams, R.: Hardness magnification for all sparse NP languages. Electron. Colloq. Comput. Complex. **26**, 118 (2019)
5. Hirahara, S., Oliveira, I.C., Santhanam, R.: NP-hardness of minimum circuit size problem for OR-AND-MOD circuits. In: 33rd Computational Complexity Conference, CCC 2018, San Diego, CA, USA, June 22–24, 2018, pp. 5:1–5:31 (2018)
6. Hirahara, S., Santhanam, R.: On the average-case complexity of MCSP and its variants. In: 32nd Computational Complexity Conference, CCC 2017, Riga, Latvia, July 6–9, 2017, pp. 7:1–7:20 (2017)
7. Hirahara, S., Watanabe, O.: Limits of minimum circuit size problem as oracle. In: 31st Conference on Computational Complexity, CCC 2016, Tokyo, Japan, May 29–June 1, 2016, pp. 18:1–18:20 (2016)
8. Hitchcock, J.M., Pavan, A.: On the NP-completeness of the minimum circuit size problem. In: 35th IARCS Annual Conference on Foundation of Software Technology and Theoretical Computer Science, FSTTCS 2015, Bangalore, India, December 16–18, 2015, pp. 236–245 (2015)
9. Bosch, S.: Transzendente erweiterungen. Algebra, pp. 377–429. Springer, Heidelberg (2020). https://doi.org/10.1007/978-3-662-61649-9_8
10. McKay, D.M., Murray, C.D., Williams, R.R.: Weak lower bounds on resource-bounded compression imply strong separations of complexity classes. In: Proceedings of the 51st Annual ACM SIGACT Symposium on Theory of Computing, STOC 2019, Phoenix, AZ, USA, June 23–26, 2019, pp. 1215–1225 (2019)
11. Murray, C.D., Williams, R.R.: On the (non) np-hardness of computing circuit complexity. Theor. Comput. **13**(1), 1–22 (2017)
12. Oliveira, I.C., Pich, J., Santhanam, R.: Hardness magnification near state-of-the-art lower bounds. In: 34th Computational Complexity Conference, CCC 2019, New Brunswick, NJ, USA, July 18–20, 2019, pp. 27:1–27:29 (2019)
13. Oliveira, I.C., Santhanam, R.: Hardness magnification for natural problems. In: 59th IEEE Annual Symposium on Foundations of Computer Science, FOCS 2018, Paris, France, October 7–9, 2018, pp. 65–76 (2018)
14. Schöning, U.: A low and a high hierarchy within NP. JCSS **27**, 14–28 (1983)
15. Shoup, V.: New algorithms for finding irreducible polynomials over finite fields. In: 29th Annual Symposium on Foundations of Computer Science, White Plains, New York, USA, October 24–26, 1988, pp. 283–290 (1988)

Succinct Monotone Circuit Certification: Planarity and Parameterized Complexity

Mateus Rodrigues Alves[1], Mateus de Oliveira Oliveira[2],
Janio Carlos Nascimento Silva[1,3], and Uéverton dos Santos Souza[1(✉)]

[1] Instituto de Computação, Universidade Federal Fluminense, Niterói, Brazil
matheusra@id.uff.br, janio.carlos@ifto.edu.br, ueverton@ic.uff.br
[2] Department of Informatics, University of Bergen, Bergen, Norway
mateus.oliveira@uib.no
[3] Instituto Federal do Tocantins, Campus Porto Nacional, Porto Nacional, Brazil

Abstract. Monotone Boolean circuits are circuits where each gate is either an AND gate or an OR gate. In other words, negation gates are not allowed in monotone circuits. This class of circuits has sparked the attention of researchers working in several subfields of combinatorics and complexity theory. In this work, we introduce the notion of *certification-width* of a monotone Boolean circuit, a complexity measure that intuitively quantifies the minimum number of edges that need to be traversed by a minimal set of positive weight inputs in order to certify that C is satisfied. We call the problem of computing this new invariant, the SUCCINCT MONOTONE CIRCUIT CERTIFICATION (SMCC) problem. We prove that SMCC is NP-complete even when the input monotone circuit is planar. Subsequently, we show that the problem is W[1]-hard, but still in W[P], when parameterized by the size of the solution. We also show that SMCC is fixed-parameter tractable when restricted to monotone circuits of bounded genus. In contrast, we show that SMCC on planar circuits does not admit a polynomial kernel, unless NP $\subseteq$ coNP/poly.

Keywords: Monotone circuits · Planarity · Genus · FPT · Treewidth

1 Introduction

Boolean circuits are one of the earliest combinatorial formalisms for the representation of Boolean functions. Besides being a fundamental object of study in classical complexity theory, Boolean circuits also play a central role in the field of parameterized complexity [5]. More specifically, while the satisfiability problem for general Boolean circuits can be used to define the class NP, the satisfiability problem for Boolean circuits of bounded weft can be used to define the levels of the W-hierarchy [5]. An important, and well-studied, subclass of

This work was supported by CAPES (Finance Code: 001), CNPq (Grant Number: 303726/2017-2), FAPERJ (Grant Number: E-26/203.272/2017), Bergen Research Foundation, and by the Research Council of Norway (Grant Number: 288761).

© Springer Nature Switzerland AG 2020
D. Kim et al. (Eds.): COCOON 2020, LNCS 12273, pp. 496–507, 2020.
https://doi.org/10.1007/978-3-030-58150-3_40

Boolean circuits is the class of monotone Boolean circuits, i.e., circuits where only AND and OR gates are allowed. While the standard satisfiability problem for monotone Boolean circuits is trivial, since the all-ones vector is always a satisfying truth assignment, some weighted versions of satisfiability problems are still interesting in this setting. One of these problems is the WEIGHTED MONOTONE CIRCUIT SATISFIABILITY (WMCS) problem, where we are given a monotone Boolean circuit C as input, and the goal is to find a minimum-weight satisfying assignment for the inputs of C [3,10,13]. The WMCS is particularly relevant in the field of circuit design, since the minimum number of inputs necessary to make a monotone circuit evaluate to true is a parameter that is often taken into consideration [12].

In this work, we introduce the notion of a *succinct certificate* for a monotone Boolean circuit. Given a monotone circuit C, a succinct certificate for C is a connected sub-circuit of C with a minimal set of edges that is sufficient to ensure that C is satisfiable. Just like circuit size and circuit depth, the minimum size of a succinct certificate is an interesting complexity measure. Additionally, a succinct certificate may be seen as a minimal map to be followed by a satisfying truth assignment. This map may find applications in the field of circuit design and may be used as a way of representing solutions to problems modeled through monotone circuits.

We study the complexity of computing the size of a minimum succinct certificate of a given monotone circuit C. We call this invariant the *certification-width* of C, and name the problem of computing the value of this invariant as the SUCCINCT MONOTONE CIRCUIT CERTIFICATION (SMCC) problem. The problem under consideration is both of theoretical and practical relevance. From a theoretic perspective, the minimum size of a succinct certificate naturally gives information about the complexity of a circuit. Therefore, determining the underlying structure that makes SMCC (fixed-parameter) tractable is interesting from the perspective of complexity theory. From a practical perspective, SMCC can be applied in many problem-reduction representations [14,18,19].

The notion of planarity is well-explored in graph theory and has significant relevance in the field of circuit analysis. In particular VLSI (Very Large-Scale Integration) circuits, which are widely applied in electronics and engineering, are typically modeled by planar graphs. In addition, there are several studies on circuits and satisfiability problems defined on certain structures that are planar or that satisfy certain structural properties (see [1,2,10–13,17,20,21]).

We show that SMCC is NP-hard even when the input monotone circuit is planar, and that SMCC is W[1]-hard, but in W[P], when parameterized by solution size. Subsequently, we present a polynomial-time algorithm that takes a monotone circuit as input and either solves the instance or bounds the diameter of the input; then using the notion of contraction obstructions for treewidth we are able to conclude that the treewidth of the resulting circuit is bounded by $k+g$, where k is the solution size and g is the genus of the input circuit. Thus, by using such a win/win approach and applying a dynamic programming algorithm we solve SMCC in FPT time when parameterized by $k + g$. This result also implies that SMCC can be solved in time $2^{O(k)} \cdot n^{O(1)}$ on planar circuits.

Due to space constraints, some proofs were omitted.

1.1 Preliminaries

We use standard graph-theoretic and parameterized complexity notation, and we refer the reader to [4,5] for any undefined notation.

A Boolean circuit is a combinatorial model for the representation of Boolean functions. We formalize the notion of a Boolean circuit according to Definition 1. In general, a circuit can have multiples outputs. Nevertheless, for convenience, we will adopt the following definition.

Definition 1. *A Boolean circuit is a directed acyclic graph $C(V, E)$ having only one sink, where the set of vertices V is partitioned into $(I, G, \{v_{out}\})$: (i) a set of inputs $I = \{i_1, i_2, \dots\}$ composed of the vertices of in-degree 0; (ii) a set of gates $G = \{g_1, g_2, \dots\}$, which are vertices labeled with Boolean operators; (iii) and the single output (sink) vertex v_{out} with out-degree equal to 0 and also labeled with a Boolean operator. The input vertices represent Boolean variables that can take values from $\{0, 1\}$ (\{false, true\}, depending on the conventions), and the label/operator of a gate or output vertex w is given by $f(w)$. A monotone circuit is a Boolean circuit where the Boolean operators allowed are in \{AND, OR\}.*

Note that we are considering general circuits with no restrictions on the number of in-neighbors and out-neighbors. Besides, in this work, we only deal with monotone circuits.

Definition 2. *An assignment of C is a vector $X = [x_1, x_2, \dots, x_{|I|}]$ of values for the set of inputs I, where for each j, $x_j \in \{0, 1\}$ is the value assigned to input i_j. We say that X is a satisfying truth assignment if the circuit C evaluates to 1 (true) when given x as input.*

In Fig. 1a, we have an example of a circuit C with six inputs $i_1, i_2, \dots, i_6$, four gates g_1, g_2, g_3, g_4 and the output vertex v_{out}. Figure 1b shows an example of the results of an assignment $X = [0, 1, 1, 1, 1, 0]$ to the circuit presented in Fig. 1a. In this example, the function AND of v_{out} returns 1, thus, X is a satisfying truth assignment according to Definition 2.

We denote by $X \to C$ the adapted directed graph in which the values of X were assigned to I, and the label of the gates are replaced by the returned values of their respective functions (see Fig. 1b).

The directions of the edges represent inputs to functions of the gates. When all in-edges of a gate g_j have a value assigned to it, then the gate will be assigned with a value computed according to the operator $f(g_j)$. We note that the signal of an input may not reach v_{out}, for example, in Fig. 1b, the assignment sets i_5 to 1. However, this signal cannot reach v_{out} because $f(g_2)$ was not satisfied. This situation brings us another important definition: the critical edges.

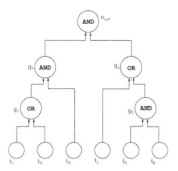

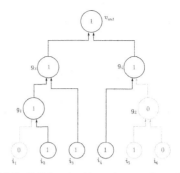

(a) Graph representation of circuit C.   (b) Satisfying truth assignment on C.

Fig. 1. Graph representation of a circuit and a satisfying truth assignment for it.

Definition 3. *Given a monotone circuit C with a satisfying truth assignment X, an edge (v_j, v_k) is considered critical to $X \to C$ if the signal output by v_j is positive and can reach the vertex v_{out} through the gate v_k.*

According to Definition 3, in Fig. 1 the edge (i_5, g_2) is not critical while (i_2, g_1), (i_3, g_3), (i_4, g_4), (g_1, g_3), (g_3, v_{out}) and (g_4, v_{out}) are critical edges in $X \to C$. This motivates the notion of *positive certificate* stated in Definition 4.

Definition 4. *Given a monotone circuit C, and a satisfying truth assignment X of C, a positive certificate for $X \to C$ is a connected subgraph of C formed by the critical edges and their respective vertices.*

Notice that a positive certificate may have redundant edges. Next, we define the notion of *succinct certificate*; and *certification-width* of C.

Definition 5. *Given a monotone circuit C, and a satisfying truth assignment X of C, a succinct certificate for $X \to C$, is a connected subgraph $SC_{X \to C}$ of its positive certificate such that:*

- v_{out} *is a vertex of $SC_{X \to C}$; and*
- *for every vertex v of $SC_{X \to C}$ holds that*
  - *if $f(v) = \text{AND}$, then every in-edge of v is in $SC_{X \to C}$;*
  - *if $f(v) = \text{OR}$, then exactly one in-edge of v is in $SC_{X \to C}$.*

The size of a succinct certificate $SC_{X \to C}$ is the number of edges of $SC_{X \to C}$.

Definition 6. *The certification-width of a monotone circuit C is the minimum size among all possible succinct certificates on all satisfying truth assignments of C.*

We remark that the notion of certification-width is closely related to the notion of *energy complexity* of a circuit C, which is defined as the maximum number of gates outputting "1" over all assignments to C (see [22]).

Now, we have all elements to describe our main problem.

SUCCINCT MONOTONE CIRCUIT CERTIFICATION (SMCC)
Instance: A monotone circuit C; a positive integer k.
Goal: Determine whether the certification-width of C is at most k.

We denote by $\text{SMCC}(k)$ the parameterized version of SUCCINCT MONO-TONE CIRCUIT CERTIFICATION where k is the parameter.

2   NP-Completeness on Planar Circuits

Now, we dedicate our attention to SMCC restricted to planar monotone circuits. Clearly, SMCC is in NP. Next, we show its NP-hardness. For that, we will use a reduction from PLANAR VERTEX COVER.

Theorem 1. SMCC *is NP-complete even restricted to planar circuits.*

Proof. It is easy to see that SMCC is in NP. In order to prove its NP-hardness, we present a reduction from PLANAR VERTEX COVER. First, consider the following preprocessing: Let (H, c') be an instance of PLANAR VERTEX COVER. By subdividing twice each edge of H, we obtain a graph G where each edge $e = (ab)$ of H is replaced by a P_4 $ab'a'b$, where a' and b' are new vertices. Notice that G is planar; H has a vertex cover of size c' if and only if G has a vertex cover of size $c = c' + |E(H)|$; and given a planar embedding of G, the boundary of any pair of adjacent faces of G contains at least three edges.

From a fixed planar embedding of the instance (G, c) of PLANAR VERTEX COVER, we proceed with the reduction. We will construct an instance (C, k) of SMCC where C is a planar monotone circuit, and k is the target size of the vertex cover. From the original structure of G, we apply the following:

1. Firstly, set $V(C) = V(G)$;
2. for each vertex $v_i \in V(G)$, create an input vertex v_i^{in}, assign $f(v_i) = \text{AND}$, and add a directed edge (v_i^{in}, v_i);
3. for each edge $e_i = (u, v) \in E(G)$, create a vertex $v_{e_i}^{cover}$ such that $f(v_{e_i}^{cover}) = \text{OR}$, and create the directed edges $(v, v_{e_i}^{cover})$ and $(u, v_{e_i}^{cover})$. This step guarantees that if $v_{e_i}^{cover}$ is in the succinct certification, then either v or u will also be on the certificate.

Notice that C is still planar. Now, preserving the planarity, we will ensure that every $v_{e_i}^{cover}$ is in any succinct certification of C as follows:

4. create an output vertex v_{out} such that $f(v_{out}) = \text{AND}$;
5. for each vertex $v_{e_i}^{cover}$ which are in the external face of G, create one directed edge from $v_{e_i}^{cover}$ to v_{out};

Let D_G be the dual graph of G, and denote by f_1 the vertex representing the external face of G. Let $\mathcal{T}_{D_G}$ be the spanning tree of D_G obtained from a breadth-first search of D_G rooted at f_1. In a top-down manner, according to a level-order traversal of $\mathcal{T}_{D_G}$, we visit each edge $e = (f_i, f_j)$ of $\mathcal{T}_{D_G}$, applying the following:

6. Let f_j be a child of f_i in $\mathcal{T}_{D_G}$;

By construction of G, it follows that the boundary between f_i and f_j contains at least three edges, at least one of which being between vertices a' and b' that do not exist in H;

Thus, create a vertex v_{f_j}, add edges from v_{f_j} to such a' and b'; and for each $v_{e_\ell}^{cover}$ in the face f_j that does not reach v_{out}, yet, add an edge from $v_{e_\ell}^{cover}$ to v_{f_j}; after that, if v_{f_j} has in-degree greater than 0, then set $f(v_{f_j}) = \mathtt{AND}$, otherwise v_{f_j} is an input vertex;

7. Finally, set $k = c + 2 \cdot |E(G)| + |V(\mathcal{T}_{D_G})| - 1$.

Given a vertex cover S of G with c vertices, without loss of generality, we can assume that S does not contain pairs of adjacent vertices that do not belong to $V(H)$. By setting 1 to the corresponding inputs of S in C, in exactly c edges flows 1 from vertices v_i^{in} to its out-neighbor v_i; from each v_i assigned with 1 flow positive values to each v_e^{cover} such that e is an out-edge of v_i. Since S is a vertex cover, each v_e^{cover} receives at least one positive value, which implies that every vertex v_{f_j} outputs 1, and v_{out} also outputs 1. Thus, C has a succinct certificate SC where all in-edges of v_{out} are in SC; each in-neighbor of v_{out} has as in-neighbor one vertex of S in SC; since the vertices representing faces and vertices of G have the label $\mathtt{AND}$, by construction, every v_e^{cover} is in SC and has exactly one out-edge in SC; Given that S does not contain pairs of adjacent vertices that do not belong to $V(H)$, each vertex v_{f_j} also has exactly one out-neighbor in SC; and as every v_e^{cover} is labeled $\mathtt{OR}$, one can construct SC in such a way that v_e^{cover} has as in-neighbor exactly one vertex in S. Thus, SC has size equal to $k = c + 2 \cdot |E(G)| + |V(\mathcal{T}_{D_G})| - 1$. (Namely, c in-edges of v_i^{in} vertices; one in-edge and one out-edge for each v_e^{cover}; one out-edge for each vertex v_{f_j}.)

Conversely, let SC be a succinct certificate of C with size equal to $k = c + 2 \cdot |E(G)| + |V(\mathcal{T}_{D_G})| - 1$. By construction, it is easy to see that any succinct certificate of C contains every v_e^{cover} vertex and has size at least $2 \cdot |E(G)| + |V(\mathcal{T}_{D_G})| - 1$. Therefore, SC has exactly c vertices of $V(G)$, which cover every edge of G. $\qquad\square$

3   Parameterized Complexity

In this section, we analyse the parameterized complexity of SMCC.

The W[P]-membership follows from a reduction of SMCC to WEIGHTED CIRCUIT SATISFIABILITY.

Lemma 1. SMCC(k) *is in W[P].*

Next, we prove the W[1]-hardness of SMCC(k) using a reduction from MULTICOLORED CLIQUE, a well-known W[1]-complete problem [6].

Theorem 2. SMCC(k) *is W[1]-hard.*

3.1   On the Treewidth of Monotone Circuits with Bounded Genus

In this section, we bound the treewidth of bounded genus circuits. The *win-win* approach applied in this section is based on the grid minor theorems proposed by Robertson and Seymour [15,16], see also [9].

First consider the following definitions.

A graph G has *genus* g if it can be drawn without crossings on a surface of genus g (a sphere with g handles), but not on a surface of genus $g - 1$. We refer the reader to [8] for more information on the genus of a graph. We consider the genus of a circuit as the genus of its underlying undirected graph.

Definition 7. *A* tree decomposition *of an undirected graph G is a pair $\mathcal{T} = (T, \{X_t\}_{t \in V(T)})$ such that T is a tree where each node t is assigned to a set of vertices $X_t \subseteq V(G)$, called* bags, *according to the following conditions:*

- $\bigcup_{t \in V(T)} X_t = V(G)$, *i.e. all vertices must be in one bag at least;*
- *For each $(u, v) \in E(G)$, there exist a node t such that the vertices $\{u, v\} \in X_t$;*
- *For each $v \in V(G)$, the set $T_v = t \in V(T) : v \in X_t$ spans a connected subtree of T.*

The *treewidth* $\mathrm{tw}(\mathcal{T})$ of a tree decomposition $\mathcal{T}$ is the size of the largest bag of T minus one. The treewidth of G is the minimum treewidth among all its possible tree decompositions.

Definition 8. *A graph H is a* minor *of a graph G if H can be constructed from G by deleting vertices or edges, and contracting edges.*

Definition 9. *A* grid $p \times q$, *denoted by $\boxplus_{p \times q}$ or $\boxplus_p$ when $p = q$, is a graph whose set of vertices is $V(G) = \{v_{ij} | (i,j) \in \{1, 2, \ldots, p\} \times \{1, 2, \ldots, q\}\}$ and there is an edge $(v_{ij}, v_{i'j'}) \in E(G)$ exactly if $|i' - i| = 1$ or $|j' - j| = 1$, but not both.*

Theorem 3 *(Excluded Grid Theorem [15]).* *Let t be a non-negative integer. Then every planar graph G of treewidth at least $9t/2$ contains $\boxplus_t$ as a minor.*

Definition 10. *For every face F of a planar embedding M, we define $d(F)$ to be the minimum value of r such that there is a sequence $F_0, F_1, \ldots, F_r$ of faces of M, where F_0 is the external face, $F = F_r$, and for $1 \le j \le r$ there is a vertex v incident with both F_{j-1} and F_j. The radius $\rho(M)$ of M is the minimum value r such that $\rho(F) \le r$ for all faces F of M. The radius of a planar graph is the minimum across all radii of its planar embeddings.*

From the Excluded Grid Theorem, it is easy to see that there is a connection between the radius of a planar graph and its treewidth. In [16], Robertson and Seymour presented a bound for the treewidth of a planar graph with respect to its radius.

Theorem 4 (Radius Theorem [16]). *If G is planar and has radius at most r, then its treewidth is at most $3r + 1$.*

Using Theorem 4 we are able to either solve SMCC(k) on planar circuits or output an equivalent instance C' with treewidth bounded by a function of k. First consider the following.

Lemma 2. *Let (C, k) be an instance of SMCC(k). There is an algorithm that in polynomial time either solves (C, k) or outputs an instance (C', k) of SMCC(k) having depth at most k, such that (C', k) is an yes-instance of SMCC(k) if and only if (C, k) is also an yes-instance.*

Proof. Let (C, k) be an instance for SMCC(k) such that C is a planar monotone circuit and k is a parameter. Firstly, we apply to C the following preprocessing steps to generate a graph C':

1. For each vertex v_j such that $f(v_j) = $ AND, if $|N^-_{v_j}| > k$, then v_j is deleted;
2. Delete every vertex which is at a distance greater than k from v_{out};
3. Delete all isolated vertex;
4. Delete all vertices whose in-degree became equal to 0; (the original inputs are not affected by this step)
5. Delete all AND-vertices that lost one of its in-neighbors;
6. Repeat steps 1 to 5 as long as possible.
7. If $C' = \emptyset$, then we conclude that (C, k) is a *no*-instance of SMCC(k).

It is easy to see that the rules described above are safe. Thus, after this preprocessing, if $C' \neq \emptyset$ then C' has only vertices at a distance at most k from v_{out}. □

Notice that the underlying undirected graph of the output C' has diameter at most $2k$, which implies that if it is planar, then it also has a radius at most $2k$, thus, by Theorem 4, it follows that the underlying undirected graph of C' has treewidth at most $6k + 1$. Next, we extend the previous reasoning for bounded genus graphs.

According to [10], for an edge $e = uv$ of a graph G, contracting e means removing the two vertices u and v from G, replacing them with a new vertex w, and for every vertex y in the neighborhood of v or u in G, adding in the new graph an edge wy whose multiplicity is the sum of the multiplicities of the edges of G between v and y and between u and y. If in the above definition we do not sum up multiplicities, and if the initial graph G is a simple graph, then we call the operation *simple contraction*, or for short *s-contraction*. Given a vertex-set $S \subseteq V(G)$ such that the subgraph of G induced by S, denoted $G[S]$, is connected, contracting S means contracting the edges between the vertices in S to obtain a single vertex at the end. We say that a graph H is an s-contraction of a graph G if H can be obtained after applying to G a (possibly empty) sequence of edge s-contractions.

The following is a construction presented in [7,10]. Consider an $(r \times r)$-grid. A corner vertex of the grid is a vertex of the grid of degree 2. By Γ_r we denote the graph obtained from the $(r \times r)$-grid as follows: construct first a graph called Γ'_r by triangulating all internal faces of the $(r \times r)$-grid such that all internal vertices of the grid are of degree 6, and all non-corner external vertices of the grid are of degree 4 (Γ_r' is unique up to isomorphism). Two of the corners of the initial grid have degree 2 in Γ_r'; let x be one of them. Now Γ_r obtained from Γ_r' by adding all the edges having x as an endpoint and a vertex of the external face of the grid that is not already a neighbor of x as the other endpoint. Observe again that Γ_r' is unique up to isomorphism. The following is a lemma from [10] implied from Lemma 6 in [7].

Lemma 3 (Lemma 4.5 in [10]). *Let G be a graph of genus g, and let r be any positive integer. If G excludes Γ_r as an s-contraction, then the treewidth of G is at most $(2r + 4) \cdot (g + 1)^{3/2}$.*

Lemma 4. *Let C' be the circuit obtained from Lemma 2. It holds that C' has treewidth at most $(4k + 10) \cdot (g + 1)^{3/2}$), where g is the genus of C'.*

Proof. First, notice that for each vertex u of a Γ_{2k+3} there is another vertex v such that the distance between u and v is at least $k + 1$. Now, suppose that C' has Γ_{2k+3} as an s-contraction, and let u be a vertex of a Γ_{2k+3} such that u is either v_{out} or a vertex obtained by contracting S containing v_{out}. Since there is a vertex v such that the distance between u and v is at least $k + 1$, it holds that C' does not have depth greater than k, which is a contradiction. Thus, by Lemma 3 we have that the treewidth of C' is at most $(4k + 10) \cdot (g + 1)^{3/2}$. □

3.2   Dynamic Programming on Treewidth

From Lemma 4, in order to solve SMCC(k) on bounded genus graphs, it is enough to present an FPT algorithm parameterized by the treewidth of C. For that, we use an extended nice tree decomposition [4].

Theorem 5. SMCC(k) *can be solved in time $2^{O(tw)} \cdot n$, where tw is the tree-width of the input.*

Proof. Let C be a planar monotone circuit and $\mathcal{T} = (T, \{X_t\}_{t \in V(T)})$ be an extended nice tree decomposition of C. For convenience, we add the vertex v_{out} to every bag of T; thus, the treewidth of $\mathcal{T}$ is increased by 1. The root bag X_r and the leaves are equal to $\{v_{out}\}$. This change ensures that for every bag, there exists at least one possible subsolution. It is worth to remember that all succinct certification necessarily contains v_{out}.

Another preprocessing must be made: The introduce edge nodes will be labeled according of Boolean functions of the head of the directed edge, thus, we have "*introduce edge of an* AND-*gate*" and "*introduce edge node of an* OR-*gate*". The same alteration is applied to forget nodes, i.e., we have "*forget node of* AND-*gate*" and "*forget node of* OR-*gate*". This separation of nodes help us to organize the subproblems according to the previous subsolutions already computed.

Let $\mathcal{T}_{X_t}$ be the subtree of $\mathcal{T}$ rooted by X_t and G_{X_t} be the graph/circuit having $\mathcal{T}_{X_t}$ as tree decomposition.

Each subproblem of the dynamic programming is represented by $c[t, X, \mathcal{B}]$, which denotes the minimum number of edges of a succinct subcircuit of G_{X_t}, where $X \subseteq X_t$ is the set of vertices of X_t in such a subcircuit, and $\mathcal{B}$ is a Boolean vector of size at most $|X|$ such that for each $v \in X$ with $f(v) = \text{OR}$ it is holds that if $\mathcal{B}[v] = 1$, then the OR-gate v has an in-edge in the subcircuit and $\mathcal{B}[v] = 0$ means that v does not yet have an out-edge in the subcircuit.

Note that since v_{out} belongs to every solution, we do not need to handle the connectivity issue, as this is a guaranteed property of any minimal solution. Therefore, the optimal solution can be found at $c[t, \{v_{out}\}, \mathcal{B}]$ where $\mathcal{B} = \emptyset$ if v_{out} is an AND-$gate$; otherwise $\mathcal{B}[v_{out}] = 1$. The recurrences are presented below.

Leaf node – Let t' be a leaf node, then $X_t = \{v_{out}\}$ which gives us two possibilities:

$$c[t, \emptyset, \emptyset] = +\infty \tag{1}$$

$$c[t, \{v_{out}\}, \emptyset] = 0 \tag{2}$$

Introduce vertex node – Let t be an introduce vertex node with exactly one child t' such that $X_t = X_{t'} \cup \{v\}$. Since no edge of v was introduced yet, v is isolated in G_{X_t}. The recurrence in Eq. (3) resumes the subproblems.

$$c[t, X, \mathcal{P}, \mathcal{B}] = \begin{cases} c[t', X \setminus \{v\}, \mathcal{B}], & \text{if } v \in X \\ c[t', X, \mathcal{B}], & \text{if } v \notin X \end{cases} \tag{3}$$

Introduce edge of an AND-$gate$ – Let t be a node that introduces the directed edge (u, v), where $f(v) = \text{AND}$ and let t' be the child of t. For each possible tuple $(t, X, \mathcal{B})$, we have three situations (See Eq. (4)):

1. If $v \in X$ and $u \in X$, then the edge (u, v) must be in the solution (increase the recurrence by 1);
2. If $v \notin X$, then a solution for t' is recovered;
3. Lastly, if $v \in X$ and $u \notin X$, then the edge (u, v) cannot be used, thus, this solution is invalid because v is an AND-gate.

$$c[t, X, \mathcal{B}] = \begin{cases} c[t', X, \mathcal{B}] + 1, & \text{if } v \in X \text{ and } u \in X \\ c[t', X, \mathcal{B}], & \text{if } v \notin X \\ +\infty & \text{if } v \in X \text{ and } u \notin X. \end{cases} \tag{4}$$

Introduce edge of an OR-$gate$ – Let t be a node that introduces the edge (u, v) where $f(v) = \text{OR}$ and let t' be the child of t. For each possible tuple $(t, X, \mathcal{B})$, we need check the following situations:

1. If $u \in X$, $v \in X$ and $\mathcal{B}[v] = 1$, then the edge (u, v) can be included in solution depending on the most advantageous conditions in t':
   - for a tuple of t' with $\mathcal{B}'[v] = 0$ and $\mathcal{B}'[w] = \mathcal{B}[w]$ $\forall w \neq v$; the OR-gate v was not satisfied, so we sum 1 to the result since we consider the use of (u, v) in the current stage.
   - for a tuple t' where $\mathcal{B}[v] = 1$; the OR-gate v has already been satisfied, i.e., it uses another edge.
2. Case $u \notin X$, $v \notin X$ or $\mathcal{B}[v] = 0$, the edge (u, v) can not be utilized in current solution; here we copy the solution of t' with the same condition.

$$c[t, X, \mathcal{B}] = \begin{cases} \min\{c[t', X, \mathcal{B}'] + 1, c[t', X, \mathcal{B}]\}, & \text{if } \{u, v\} \in X \text{ and } \mathcal{B}[v] = 1 \\ c[t', X, \mathcal{B}], & \text{if } u \notin X, v \notin X \text{ or } \mathcal{B}[v] = 0 \end{cases}$$

(5)

Forget node of an AND-*vertex* – Let t be a forget node and t' be its child such that $X_t = X_{t'} \backslash v$ and $f(v) = $ AND. In this case, we need choose the best of two possibilities: v is part of the solution; v is not a part of the current solution. These two situations are represented in Eq. (6).

$$c[t, X, \mathcal{B}] = \min\{c[t', X, \mathcal{B}], c[t', X \cup \{v\}, \mathcal{B}]\}$$

(6)

Forget node of an OR-*vertex* – Let t be a forget node and t' be its child such that $X_t = X_{t'} \backslash v$ and $f(v) = $ OR. We need the best of two possibilities:

1. v is part of the solution – in this case $\mathcal{B}'[v] = 1$ and $\mathcal{B}'[w] = \mathcal{B}[w] \ \forall w \neq v$; if $\mathcal{B}'[v] = 0$ the solution would be unfeasible.
2. If v is not a part of the current solution – in this case we recover the solution from t' with the similar conditions.

$$c[t, X, \mathcal{B}] = \min\left\{c[t', X, \mathcal{B}], c[t', X \cup \{v\}, \mathcal{B}']\right\}$$

(7)

Join node – Let t be a join node with two children t^1 and t^2. For tabulation of the join nodes, we need to encode the merging of two partial solutions: one originating from $G_{X_{t_1}}$ and another from $G_{X_{t_2}}$. When merging two partial solutions, we need check if some OR-gate has more than one in-edge. This can be done through a simple strategy: when we merge two solutions, two vectors $\mathcal{B}_1$ and $\mathcal{B}_2$ from t_1 and t_2, respectively, to form $\mathcal{B}$, we may assume that $\mathcal{B}[i] = \mathcal{B}_1[i] + \mathcal{B}_2[i]$ for any i. For each possible tuple $(t, X, \mathcal{B})$, we have:

$$c[t, X, \mathcal{B}] = \min_{\mathcal{B}_1, \mathcal{B}_2} \{c[t_1, X, \mathcal{B}_1] + c[t_2, X, \mathcal{B}_2]\}$$

(8)

Recall that every bag of $\mathcal{T}$ has at most $tw + 1$ vertices, each bag has at most 2^{tw+1} possible subsets X, and at most 2^{tw+1} possible Boolean vectors $\mathcal{B}$. Since each entry of the table can be computed in $2^{O(tw)}$ time, it holds that the algorithm performs in time $2^{O(tw)} \cdot n$. $\square$

Corollary 1. SMCC(k) *can be solved in time* $2^{O(k \cdot (g+1)^{3/2})} \cdot n^{O(1)}$, *where g is the genus of the input.*

Corollary 2. *Let $\mathcal{F}$ be either a class of graphs with the diameter-treewidth property or a class of graphs that does not contain every apex graph. Then* SMCC(k) *on monotone Boolean circuits whose underlying graph belongs to $\mathcal{F}$ can be solved in time $\alpha_{\mathcal{F}}(k) \cdot n^{O(1)}$, where $\alpha_{\mathcal{F}}$ is a function that depends only on the class $\mathcal{F}$.*

Theorem 6. SMCC(k) *on planar circuits does not admit a polynomial kernel, unless $NP \subseteq coNP/poly$.*

References

1. Barrington, D.A.M., Lu, C.-J., Miltersen, P.B., Skyum, S.: On monotone planar circuits. In: Proceedings of the Fourteenth Annual IEEE Conference on Computational Complexity, pp. 24–31 (1999)
2. Cai, L., Fellows, M., Juedes, D., Rosamond, F.: The complexity of polynomial-time approximation. Theory Comput. Syst. **41**(3), 459–477 (2007)
3. Creignou, N., Vollmer, H.: Parameterized complexity of weighted satisfiability problems: decision, enumeration, counting. Fundam. Inform. **136**(4), 297–316 (2015)
4. Cygan, M., et al.: Lower bounds for kernelization. In: Parameterized Algorithms, pp. 523–555. Springer, Cham (2015). https://doi.org/10.1007/978-3-319-21275-3_15
5. Downey, R.G., Fellows, M.R.: Parameterized Complexity. Springer, New York (2012)
6. Fellows, M.R., Hermelin, D., Rosamond, F.A., Vialette, S.: On the parameterized complexity of multiple-interval graph problems. Theoret. Comput. Sci. **410**(1), 53–61 (2009)
7. Fomin, F.V., Golovach, P., Thilikos, D.M.: Contraction obstructions for treewidth. J. Comb. Theor. Ser. B **101**(5), 302–314 (2011)
8. Gross, J.L., Tucker, T.W.: Topological Graph Theory. Courier Corporation (2001)
9. Gu, Q.P., Tamaki, H.: Improved bounds on the planar branchwidth with respect to the largest grid minor size. Algorithmica **64**(3), 416–453 (2012)
10. Kanj, I., Thilikos, D.M., Xia, G.: On the parameterized complexity of monotone and antimonotone weighted circuit satisfiability. Inf. Comput. **257**, 139–156 (2017)
11. Khanna, S., Motwani, R.: Towards a syntactic characterization of PTAS. In: Proceedings of the Twenty-Eighth Annual ACM Symposium on Theory of Computing, pp. 329–337 (1996)
12. Limaye, N., Mahajan, M., Sarma, J.M.: Upper bounds for monotone planar circuit value and variants. Comput. Complex. **18**(3), 377 (2009)
13. Marx, D.: Completely inapproximable monotone and antimonotone parameterized problems. J. Comput. Syst. Sci. **79**(1), 144–151 (2013)
14. Nilsson, N.J.: Problem-Solving Methods in Artificial Intelligence. McGraw-Hill Computer Science Series. McGraw-Hill, New York (1971)
15. Robertson, N., Seymour, P., Thomas, R.: Quickly excluding a planar graph. J. Comb. Theor. Ser. B **62**(2), 323–348 (1994)
16. Robertson, N., Seymour, P.D.: Graph minors. J. Comb. Theor. Ser. B **36**(1), 49–64 (1984)
17. Savage, J.E.: Planar circuit complexity and the performance of VLSI algorithms+. In: VLSI Systems and Computations, pp. 61–68. Springer, Heidelberg (1981)
18. Souza, U.S., Protti, F.: Tractability, hardness, and kernelization lower bound for and/or graph solution. Discrete Appl. Math. **232**, 125–133 (2017)
19. Souza, U.S., Protti, F., da Silva, M.D.: Revisiting the complexity of and/or graph solution. J. Comput. Syst. Sci. **79**(7), 1156–1163 (2013)
20. Szeider, S.: On fixed-parameter tractable parameterizations of SAT. In: Giunchiglia, E., Tacchella, A. (eds.) SAT 2003. LNCS, vol. 2919, pp. 188–202. Springer, Heidelberg (2004). https://doi.org/10.1007/978-3-540-24605-3_15
21. Turán, G.: On the complexity of planar boolean circuits. Comput. Complex. **5**(1), 24–42 (1995)
22. Uchizawa, K., Douglas, R., Maass, W.: On the computational power of threshold circuits with sparse activity. Neural Comput. **18**(12), 2994–3008 (2006)

On Measures of Space over Real and Complex Numbers

Om Prakash and B. V. Raghavendra Rao[✉]

Department of Computer Science and Engineering, IIT Madras, Chennai, India
bvrr@cse.iitm.ac.in

Abstract. Defining a notion of space in the real/complex model of computation introduced by Blum, Shub and Smale (BSS) is a challenging task. Though there were some attempts at defining a feasible notion of space over real/complex numbers, none of the measures seem to capture the notion of space in a satisfactory manner.

De Naurois [9] introduced the notion of weak space as a possible measure of space for capturing small space computations. Joglekar et. al. [11] exhibited limitations of the model over complex numbers.

It is important to explore various possibilities of defining space for computations over real/complex numbers to understand the difficulty of the problem. We study the feasibility of defining notions of space based on: 1) The unit cost model with a simultaneous time bound; 2) Size of an arithmetic circuit as a measure of space. We compare the space bounded complexity classes that can be defined based on these measures with the existing complexity classes.

Finally, we introduce the computational model of algebraic branching programs with select nodes and explore the relationship of the model with space bounded complexity classes based on circuit parameters.

1 Introduction

Numerical computation involves algebraic and comparison operations over real numbers. Any formalism for the foundations of numerical computation requires computational models that are capable of storing and performing operations on real numbers with infinite precision. The classical notions of computation developed by Church, Turing and others do not address computations with infinite precision. To overcome this difficulty, in 1989, Blum Shub and Smale [3] proposed a real analogue of the Turing machine, which is now referred to as the BSS model of real computation. A BSS machine can store an element from the underlying field with arbitrary precision in its cell. It can perform an algebraic operation on the contents of the cells or do a branch based on the outcome of a comparison operation. The decision problems accepted by BSS machines correspond to the union of semi-algebraic sets over the underlying field [2].

Assuming that each of the permissible operation requires unit time, Blum, Shub and Smale defined the real counterparts of the complexity classes P and NP denoted by $P_{\mathbb{R}}$ and $NP_{\mathbb{R}}$, respectively. Further, Blum, Cucker, Shub and Smale [3] developed the notion of reductions for the BSS model of computation, which

© Springer Nature Switzerland AG 2020
D. Kim et al. (Eds.): COCOON 2020, LNCS 12273, pp. 508–519, 2020.
https://doi.org/10.1007/978-3-030-58150-3_41

resulted in the discovery of $\mathsf{NP}_\mathbb{R}$ complete languages. For example, testing the feasibility of a system of quadratic equations is $\mathsf{NP}_\mathbb{R}$ complete under polynomial-time reductions [3]. See [2] for a detailed exposition on the topic.

Algebraic circuits (arithmetic circuits with comparison operations) are used to define real/complex analogues of parallel computation [2]. While the question of $\mathsf{P}_\mathbb{R}$ versus $\mathsf{NP}_\mathbb{R}$ is open, we do have some separation of complexity classes in the BSS model of computation. There are algebraic sets over $\mathbb{R}$ that can be computed in polynomial time, but cannot be computed in parallel poly-logarithmic time [6].

Though unit time per operation seems to be a natural choice of cost model for a mathematical formalization of real computation, it is far from real world constraints. In particular, this measure of complexity does not take into account size of the numbers that are obtained during the course of computation.

To address this issue, Koiran [12] introduced the notion of weak time for BSS computations. This allowed him to show that the set of all Boolean languages accepted by the weak BSS model in polynomial time is contained in P/poly.

Time complexity in the BSS model of computation is arguably well understood and the theory is somewhat analogous to the Boolean world. Soon after the introduction of the BSS model, Michaux [14] showed that everything decidable in the model can also be decided using only a constant number of cells. This rules out the possibility of considering the unit space as a useful notion of space. To overcome this limitation, the research community focused on algebraic circuit based complexity classes such as $\mathsf{NC}_\mathbb{R}^i$ and $\mathsf{PAR}_\mathbb{R}$ etc. While this has given us finer complexity classes, none of the classes except for $\mathsf{PAR}_\mathbb{R}$ have shown behavior similar to Boolean space bounded complexity classes.

To define a more realistic cost measure for space used by BSS machines, de Naurois [9] introduced the notion of weak space for real computation. This is motivated by Koiran's [12] notion of weak time. While the notion of weak space captured certain properties of space bounded computation such as a bound on the number of configurations in terms of space used, it was not powerful enough to decide problems that can be decided by constant-depth algebraic circuits. In fact, over the complex numbers, Joglekar et al. [11] showed that the hyper surface defined by the elementary symmetric polynomial of degree $n/2$ on n variables cannot be computed in polynomial weak space.

We explore the possibility of defining notions of space over the BSS model of computation using the notion of algebraic branching programs and circuit size.

Motivations: Though lack of a feasible notion of space is well documented in literature, apart from Michaux [14], which explains the failure of unit space model, reasons for the lack of other notions of space are not available in literature. Given the rich algebraic structure of polynomials, half spaces and varieties which are essential ingredients in the study of the BSS model of computation, one would expect to have deeper insights into resource bounded computation over real/complex numbers. Further, in the Boolean setting logspace bounded complexity classes have several different characterizations in terms of branching programs and circuits of bounded width [13,18]. Given this pretext, it is surprising that the investigation into reasons for lack of a notion of space over real computations did not get the attention it deserves.

It is important to understand the limitations of natural candidates for notions of space apart from the unit space model. One natural direction is to consider the inherent complexity of the polynomials that appear during the course of computation in a BSS machine as a measure of space. In this article, we look at the possibility of defining notions of space using various complexity measures for the polynomials that appear during the course of a BSS computation.

Further, for any possibility of having a notion of space that has properties similar to the one in the Boolean setting, it is important to have related computational models such as branching programs that characterize space bounded computation in the Boolean setting. Towards this, we develop a notion of branching programs for the BSS model of computation and relate the corresponding complexity classes with the existing classes.

Our Contributions: Although the simulation of arbitrary BSS machines accepting a set $L \subseteq \mathbb{R}^* = \bigcup_{n \geq 0} \mathbb{R}^n$ given by Michaux [14] involves only a constant number of cells, the time required could be exponential in the running time of the original machine. One possibility is to put a simultaneous restriction on time as well as the number of cells used. Taking cue from Boolean computation it is fair to expect a machine that uses at most s cells at any point of time during the computation to halt in $2^{O(s)}$ time. Note that this was considered by Cucker [7] in the context of polynomial space. We consider BSS machines with simultaneous space and time bound for small space computations. With the number of cells as notion of space and running time bounded by an exponential function of space, we observe that log-space bounded machines can accept sets accepted by $NC_{\mathbb{R}}^1$ (Theorem 1). However, it turns out that the Boolean part of log-space under this notion is powerful enough to contain P (Theorem 2). This makes the notion not very useful for defining analogues of small space complexity classes.

Our next attempt is using an implicit representation for the contents of the cell in a BSS machine. At any point of time during the execution, the content of any cell of a BSS machine can be viewed as an evaluation of a polynomial (or a rational function when division is allowed) at the given input. The definition of weak-space in [9] used the bit size required to represent the polynomial in explicit sparse form as the cost of each cell, sum of the costs taken over all cells being the cost of a configuration. A natural way to generalize this would be to use implicit circuit representation. We study the minimum size of an arithmetic circuit computing polynomials corresponding to a configuration as a notion of space. This notion has the desirable properties that when restricted to polynomial space the resulting complexity class is large enough to contain $P_{\mathbb{R}}$ and its boolean part is contained in $PSPACE$ (Theorems 3 and 4).

Algebraic branching programs (ABPs) play a vital role in algebraic complexity theory [16,17]. It may be noted that defining algebraic branching programs to capture real computation is not straightforward. In particular, a comparison operation depends on the actual input and it is not clear how to represent it as an edge label in the branching program. We introduce the notion of a select node and we propose algebraic branching programs with select nodes as a natural real-computation analogue of ABPs. We show that formulas with a small number of select nodes can be simulated by ABPs with select nodes (Theorem 5).

Finally, we consider the problem of depth reduction for algebraic formulas. We give efficient depth reduction for the case of formulas with a small number of select nodes or with bounded select depth (Theorem 6).

2   Preliminaries

We give necessary definitions and notations relating to the BSS model of real computation.

BSS Model: A BSS machine M over $\mathbb{F} \in \{\mathbb{R}, \mathbb{C}\}$ with machine constants α_1, $\alpha_2, \ldots, \alpha_k \in \mathbb{F}$, $k \geq 0$ and with admissible input $Y \subseteq \mathbb{F}^*$ is a random access machine having access to registers (called cells) and can execute three types of instructions: *Compute*: Perform algebraic operation $c_i \leftarrow c_j$ op c_k where op $\in \{+, \times, -\}$, and go to the next instruction. *Branch*: Perform test operation ≥ 0? (in the case where $\mathbb{F} = \mathbb{C}$, then the comparison would be $=$? 0) and branch to next instruction according to the result of the comparison. *Copy*: Store the content of one register into another, that is, $c_i \leftarrow c_j$ and go to the next instruction.

For the decision version of problems the *input-output* ($\phi_M : \mathbb{F}^* \to \mathbb{F}^*$) map is the characteristic function of the language accepted by the BSS machine M. For simplicity of exposition, we restrict ourselves to division-free computations. For a BSS machine M, let $L(M) = \{x \in Y \mid M \text{ accepts } x\}$. The running time of a BSS machine on an input $x \in \mathbb{R}^n$ is the number of operations it performs before halting. A BSS machine M is said to be t time bounded, if for any $x \in \mathbb{R}^*$, M runs for at most $t(|x|)$ time on input x of $|x|$ real numbers. For any time constructible function $t : \mathbb{N} \to \mathbb{N}$, let $\mathsf{DTIME}_\mathbb{F}(t)$ be the set of all subsets $L \subseteq \mathbb{F}^*$ that can be accepted by t-time bounded BSS machines. Let $\mathsf{P}_\mathbb{F}$ denote the set of all subsets of $\mathbb{F}^*$ accepted by polynomial-time bounded BSS machines, i.e., $\mathsf{P}_\mathbb{F} = \bigcup_{c \geq 0} \mathsf{DTIME}(n^c)$. For $L \subseteq \mathbb{F}^*$, let $\mathsf{BP}(L) = L \cap \{0, 1\}^*$, i.e., the Boolean part of L. For a BSS based complexity class $\mathcal{C}$, let $\mathsf{BP}(\mathcal{C}) = \{\mathsf{BP}(L) \mid L \in \mathcal{C}\}$.

Arithmetic Circuits and Algebraic Branching Programs: Let $\mathbb{F}$ be a field. An arithmetic circuit C over $\mathbb{F}$ is a directed acyclic graph where nodes of in-degree zero, called input gates, are labeled by an element in $X \cup \mathbb{F}$, where $X = \{x_1, \ldots, x_n\}$. Internal gates have in-degree two and are labeled by an operation in $\{+, -, \times\}$. Nodes of out-degree zero are called the output gates of the circuit. Every gate in C computes a unique polynomial in $\mathbb{F}[X]$. The set of polynomials computed at the output gates of the circuit is the set of outputs computed by C. An arithmetic formula is an arithmetic circuit where the underlying graph is a tree.

An Algebraic Branching Program ABP P is a directed acyclic graph with a source node s and a sink node t. The edges are labeled by elements from $X \cup \mathbb{F}$. For a s to t path ρ, the weight of ρ is the product of labels of edges in ρ. The polynomial computed by P is the sum of weights of all of the s to t paths in P.

The polynomial identity testing PIT problem is to test if the given arithmetic circuit computes the zero polynomial or not.

Proposition 1 [10,15,19]. PIT $\in$ coRP $\subseteq$ PSPACE.

Algebraic Circuits: An algebraic circuit is a directed acyclic graph having nodes (gates) of in-degree 0, 1 or 2. Gates with in-degree 0 are the input gates or constant gates and are labeled by input variables or constants from the underlying field, respectively. Nodes with in-degree 2 are the arithmetic gates and are labeled by symbols $\{+, -, \times\}$. Nodes with in-degree 1 are the select gates that are labeled ≥ 0?, when inputs to the circuit are from $\mathbb{R}$ or $=0$? for inputs coming from field of complex numbers $\mathbb{C}$. There is one designated select gate, output gate, with out-degree 0.

The value computed at gate g is defined recursively as in the case of arithmetic circuits. A select gate returns 0 if its input polynomial evaluates to a value less than 0, or 1 otherwise. The *size* of the algebraic circuit is the number of gates in it and *depth* is the maximum length of a path from output gate to input gate in the circuit. The *select depth* of an algebraic circuit is the maximum number of select gates in any root to leaf path in the circuit.

A set $L \subseteq \mathbb{F}^*$ is said to be accepted by an algebraic circuit family $(C_n)_{n \geq 0}$ if C_n computes the characteristic function of $L_n = L \cap \mathbb{F}^n$, for every n.

The parallel complexity class $\mathsf{NC}_\mathbb{F}$ for $\mathbb{F} \in \{\mathbb{R}, \mathbb{C}\}$ is defined as follows:

Definition 1 [2]. *For $i \geq 0$,*

$$\mathsf{NC}_\mathbb{F}^i \stackrel{\text{def}}{=} \left\{ L \subseteq \mathbb{F}^* \;\middle|\; \begin{array}{l} \textit{there is a log space uniform family } (C_n)_{n \geq 0} \textit{ of algebraic} \\ \textit{circuits, where} \\ C_n \textit{ is of size } n^c \textit{ for some constant } c \textit{ and of depth } O(\log^i n) \\ \textit{such that } L = \bigcup_{n \geq 0} L(C_n). \end{array} \right\}$$

The NC *hierarchy over $\mathbb{F}$ is defined as* $\mathsf{NC}_\mathbb{F} \stackrel{\text{def}}{=} \bigcup_{i \geq 1} \mathsf{NC}_\mathbb{F}^i$.

Unit Space and Weak Space: Let M be a BSS machine which runs in time $t(n)$, and $c_1, c_2, \ldots, c_t$ is its computation path on some input $x_1, x_2, \ldots, x_n$ where c_i's are configurations of M. Then $\mathsf{Size}(c)$ is the number of non-empty work tape cells in configuration c of M and unit space $\mathsf{USpace}(M, (x_1, x_2, \ldots, x_n))$ is the maximum of $\mathsf{Size}(c)$ over all configuration in the computation path of M on input $x_1, x_2, \ldots, x_n$, and $\mathsf{USpace}(M, n)$ is the maximum of $\mathsf{USpace}(M, (x_1, x_2 \ldots, x_n))$ over all input instances of length n on which M halts. Michaux [14] showed:

Proposition 2 [14]. *Let $L \subseteq \mathbb{R}^*$ be accepted by a BSS machine M. There a BSS machine M' such that M' accepts L in unit space $O(1)$.*

The result above makes unit space uninteresting for defining sub-linear space complexity classes. To overcome this, Naurois [9] proposed the notion of weak space for the BSS model. This definition was inspired by the notion of weak time introduced by Koiran [12]. We give a somewhat simplified description of the notion of weak space as presented in [11]. The *Weak-Size* of a polynomial $g \in \mathbb{Z}[x_1, x_2, \ldots, x_n]$ with integer coefficients is defined as the length of the binary encoding of the polynomial g using the sparse representation. Let $g = \sum_{m \in M} m$

where $M = \{m_1, \ldots, m_s\}$ is a set of monomials in the variables $\{x_1, \ldots, x_n\}$. For a monomial m, let $\mathsf{enc}(m)$ be a binary encoding of m. Then $\mathsf{Size}_w(g) = \sum_{i=1}^{s} |\mathsf{enc}(m_i)|$, where $|\mathsf{enc}(m_i)|$ is the number of bits in $\mathsf{enc}(m_i)$.

Remark 1. For simplicity of exposition, we do not consider any shift in variable indices which was included in the original definition by Naurois [9].

Definition 2. *Consider a BSS machine M with machine constants $\alpha_1, \ldots, \alpha_k \in \mathbb{F}$ running in time $t(n)$. Consider an input $x = (x_1, x_2, \ldots, x_n) \in \mathbb{F}^n$, $n \geq 0$. Let $c_1, c_2, \ldots, c_t$, where $t = t(n)$ be the sequence of configurations of M on x such that c_1 is the initial configuration and c_t is the final configuration. For $1 \leq i, j \leq t$, let $f_{ij} \in \mathbb{Z}[x_1, x_2, \ldots, x_n, y_1, \ldots, y_k]$ be the polynomial representing the content in the jth non-empty cell of the configuration c_i, i.e., the content of the jth cell is the value $f_{ij}(x_1, \ldots, x_n, \alpha_1, \ldots, \alpha_k)$. The polynomial f_{ij} is unique for deterministic computations. The weak space of the configuration c_i is defined as $\mathsf{WSpace}(M, c_i) = \sum_{j \in [l]} \mathsf{Size}_w(f_{i,j})$. The weak space of the machine M on input $x_1, x_2, \ldots, x_n$ is $\mathsf{WSpace}(M, (x_1, x_2, \ldots, x_n)) = \max_i \mathsf{WSpace}(M, c_i)$. The weak space of the machine M is the maximum taken over all inputs:*

$$\mathsf{WSpace}(M, n) = \max_{x_1, x_2, \ldots, x_n} \mathsf{WSpace}(M, (x_1, x_2, \ldots, x_n)).$$

$\mathsf{LOGSPACE_W}$ is defined to be the class of sets in $\mathbb{F}^*$ that can be accepted by BSS machines of weak space $O(\log n)$. Similarly, $\mathsf{PSPACE_W}$ denotes the class of sets that is accepted by BSS machines of polynomial weak space.

Remark 2. Any comparison between machine based complexity classes and circuit based complexity classes requires suitable notions of uniformity. For example, for polynomial size circuits, we assume that the circuit is P-uniform. For notions of uniformity, the reader is referred to [18].

3   On the Unit Cost Space Model with Time Bound

Proposition 2 does not give a good upper bound on the running time of the constant-cell machine. As far as we know, for simulating a t time bounded BSS machine with a constant number of cells, the running time required for the simulating machine can be as large as $2^{\mathsf{poly}(t)}$.

We look at computations where the number of cells and the running time are simultaneously bounded.

Cucker [7] had considered the BSS computation with a simultaneous restriction on time and space with a polynomial bound on space. We extend this to arbitrary time and space bound by defining complexity classes based on a simultaneous bound on the running time; as well as the number of cells used by the BSS machine before it halts. Proofs from this section are omitted due to space constraints.

Definition 3. *Let $\mathbb{F} \in \{\mathbb{C}, \mathbb{R}\}$ and $s : \mathbb{N} \to \mathbb{N}$ be any space constructible function and $t : \mathbb{N} \to \mathbb{N}$ be any time constructible function. Define*

$$\mathsf{SPACETIME}_{\mathbb{F}}(s, t) = \left\{ L \subseteq \mathbb{F}^* \ \middle| \ \begin{array}{l} \text{There is a BSS machine } M \text{ that accepts } L \\ \text{using at most } O(s) \text{ cells and time } O(t). \end{array} \right\}$$

Using a depth first evaluation of formulas, we get:

Theorem 1. *For any field* $\mathbb{F}$, $\mathsf{NC}^1_{\mathbb{F}} \subseteq \mathsf{SPACETIME}_{\mathbb{F}}(\log n, \mathrm{poly}(n))$.

Since the BSS machine is capable of storing an arbitrary real/complex number with infinite precision, even with a constant number of registers, a BSS machine can have the power of a polynomial-time-bounded TM.

Theorem 2. $\mathsf{P} \subseteq \mathsf{BP}(\mathsf{SPACETIME}_{\mathbb{R}}(O(1), \mathrm{poly}(n)))$.

Using the simulation given in the proof of Theorem 2, we can show that every polynomial space bounded TM can be simulated by a BSS machine using only a constant number of cells.

Corollary 1. $\mathsf{PSPACE} \subseteq \mathsf{BP}(\mathsf{SPACETIME}_{\mathbb{F}}(O(1), 2^{n^{O(1)}}) \subseteq \mathsf{PSPACE}_{\mathbb{F}}$ *where* $\mathbb{F} \in \{\mathbb{C}, \mathbb{R}\}$ *and* $\mathsf{PSPACE}_{\mathbb{F}}$ *is the BSS analogue of* PSPACE

Proof. The proof is similar to that of Theorem 2 except that a machine M accepting a language $L \in \mathsf{PSPACE}$ can run for exponential time.

4   Circuit Size as a Measure of Space

The notion of weak space given by Naurois [9] is based on the size of representation of a polynomial in the sum of product form. However, the arithmetic circuit model of computation gives us access to more intrinsic notions of complexity for polynomials. One possible avenue is to consider size measures on an arithmetic circuit representing the content of a cell in a BSS machine.

We study measures of space based on the size of arithmetic circuits computing the polynomials that arise during the course a computation in a BSS machine.

Definition 4. *Let M be a BSS machine with constants $\alpha_1, \ldots, \alpha_k$. Fix the input length to be n and let $x = (x_1, \ldots, x_n) \in \mathbb{F}^*$. Consider a configuration c on input x, with non-empty cells $e_1, \ldots, e_r$. For $1 \leq i \leq r$ let $f_i(x_1, \ldots, x_n, \alpha_1, \ldots, \alpha_k)$ be the polynomial representing the content of cell e_i in the configuration c. Define* $\mathsf{csize}(c)$ *as the minimum size of an arithmetic circuit computing $f_{e_1}, \ldots, f_{e_r}$ simultaneously, where the only constants used in the circuit are from $\{-1, 0, 1\}$. Then* $\mathsf{space}_{\mathsf{size}}(M, x)$ *of the machine M on a given input x is defined as the maximum* $\mathsf{csize}(c)$ *taken over all configurations of M on x. Finally, the cell size function for M is defined as* $\mathsf{csize}_M(n) \stackrel{\mathrm{def}}{=} \max_{x \in \mathbb{F}^n} \mathsf{space}_{\mathsf{size}}(M, x)$.

Based on the above notion, we define the following complexity classes:

Definition 5. *Let s be any space constructible function:*

$$\mathsf{SPACE}_{\mathsf{SIZE}}(s) \stackrel{\mathrm{def}}{=} \left\{ L \subseteq \mathbb{F}^* \;\middle|\; \begin{array}{l} \exists \text{ a BSS machine } M \text{ such that } L(M) = L, \text{ and} \\ \mathsf{csize}_M(n) = O(s(n)). \end{array} \right\}$$

$$\mathsf{LOGSPACE}_{\mathsf{SIZE}} \stackrel{\mathrm{def}}{=} \mathsf{SPACE}_{\mathsf{SIZE}}(\log n); \quad \mathsf{PSPACE}_{\mathsf{SIZE}} \stackrel{\mathrm{def}}{=} \bigcup_{i \geq 0} \mathsf{SPACE}_{\mathsf{SIZE}}(n^i).$$

Since sparse polynomials have small circuits, we have:

Observation 1. $\mathsf{LOGSPACE_W} \subseteq \mathsf{LOGSPACE_{SIZE}}$; $\mathsf{PSPACE_W} \subseteq \mathsf{PSPACE_{SIZE}}$.

For any $t \geq n$, the number of arithmetic circuits of size t over inputs $X = \{x_1, \ldots, x_n\}$ and constants $\{-1, 0, 1\}$ is at most $t^{O(t)}$. This immediately gives a bound on the total number of configurations in an s space bounded machine with the notion of space as above. As a consequence, we get:

Lemma 1. *For* $\mathbb{F} \in \{\mathbb{C}, \mathbb{R}\}$, $\mathsf{SPACE_{SIZE}}(t) \subseteq \mathsf{DTIME_{\mathbb{F}}}(2^{O(t(\log t + \log n))})$.

We observe that polynomial space under the above notion is powerful enough to capture polynomial time:

Theorem 3. *For* $\mathbb{F} \in \{\mathbb{R}, \mathbb{C}\}$, $\mathsf{P_{\mathbb{F}}} \subseteq \mathsf{PSPACE_{SIZE}}$.

In [11], it was shown that $\mathsf{PSPACE_W} \subset \mathsf{P_{\mathbb{C}}}$ over complex numbers. As an immediate corollary to Theorem 3, we have:

Corollary 2. *Over the field of complex numbers,* $\mathsf{PSPACE_W} \subset \mathsf{PSPACE_{SIZE}}$.

Finally, we obtain a PSPACE bound on the Boolean part of $\mathsf{PSPACE_{SIZE}}$.

Theorem 4. *Over the field of complex numbers,* $\mathsf{BP(PSPACE_{SIZE})} \subseteq \mathsf{PSPACE}$.

5   Algebraic Branching Programs with Select Nodes

The BSS model of computation can be viewed as a generalization of Valiant's algebraic model of computation where the intermediary values computed in the circuit can be compared and the output gate is a comparison gate. In an attempt to obtain a real-analogue of the well studied ABPs, we introduce the notion of algebraic branching programs with select nodes:

Definition 6. *An algebraic branching program over a field $\mathbb{F}$ with select nodes is a directed acyclic graph having one designated node of zero in-degree, called the source node, denoted by s and two nodes of zero out-degree called terminal nodes and denoted by t_{acc} and t_{rej}. Every node except the terminal nodes is labeled as either an algebraic node or a select node. Edges between any two algebraic nodes are labeled with either a variable or an element from $\mathbb{F}$. Every select node has in-degree one, out-degree two and is labeled by a comparison operation op which depends on the underlying field. For example, when $\mathbb{F} = \mathbb{R}$, op can be either $\leq$ or $=$. Whereas, for $\mathbb{C}$, op is treated as $=$.*

Notion of Acceptance in ABPs with Select Nodes: An algebraic branching program with select nodes can be viewed as a generalization of the classical algebraic branching program where the algebraic branching programs are connected via select node. Let P be an algebraic branching program with select nodes. Let s be the start node, t_{acc} and t_{rej} be the terminal nodes in P. Consider an input $x_1 = a_1, \cdots, x_n = a_n$ with $a_1, \ldots, a_n \in \mathbb{F}$. Let g_1 be a select node in P such that there is no select node in any of the paths from s to g_1 in P. Suppose g_1

corresponds to the comparison $\leq$. Let u and v be out-neighbors of g_1, and w be its in-neighbor. Let p_w be the polynomial computed at nodes w in P. The edge (g_1, u) is said to be *active* with respect to the input $a = (a_1, \ldots, a_n)$ if $p_u(a) \geq 0$ and is inactive otherwise. If (g_1, u) is inactive, then (g_1, v) is considered as active and vice-versa. For a select node g in P with out-neighbors u and v, in-neighbor w, suppose that for every select node along any s to w path their outgoing edges are marked as active or inactive. Let $[s, w]_{ac}$ denote the polynomial computed by the sub-program with s as the start node and w as the terminal node where all inactive edges are removed. If $[s, w]_{ac}(a) \geq 0$ then mark (g, u) as active and (g, v) as inactive, and vice-versa otherwise. This way, we have that for every select gate in P, one of its two outgoing edges is active and the other inactive. We say that P accepts the input $a = (a_1, \ldots, a_n)$ if there is a directed path from s to t_{acc} that does not contain any inactive edge.

For a branching program P, let L_P denote the set of inputs accepted by it, i.e., $L_P = \{(a_1, \ldots, a_n) \mid P \text{ accepts } (a_1, \ldots, a_n)\}$.

The resources such as size of an algebraic branching program with select nodes is defined in the same manner as for algebraic branching programs. Size of P is the number of nodes in P.

We define the following complexity classes based on ABPs with select nodes:

$$\mathsf{BP}_{\mathbb{F}} = \left\{ L \subseteq \mathbb{F}^* \;\middle|\; \begin{array}{l} \text{there is a log space uniform family } (P_n)_{n \geq 0} \text{ of ABPs} \\ \text{with select nodes where } P_n \text{ is of size } n^c \text{ for some con-} \\ \text{stant } c \text{ and } L = \bigcup_{n \geq 0} L(P_n). \end{array} \right\}$$

$$\mathsf{BWBP}_{\mathbb{F}} = \left\{ L \subseteq \mathbb{F}^* \;\middle|\; \begin{array}{l} \text{there is a log space uniform family } (P_n)_{n \geq 0} \text{ of ABPs} \\ \text{with select nodes where } P_n \text{ is of size } n^c \text{ and width } w \\ \text{for some constants } c \text{ and } w \text{ such that } L = \bigcup_{n \geq 0} L(P_n). \end{array} \right\}$$

It follows immediately that $\mathsf{BP}_{\mathbb{F}} \subseteq \mathsf{P}_{\mathbb{F}}$. By a simple divide-and-conquer construction we get:

Lemma 2. $\mathsf{BWBP}_{\mathbb{F}} \subseteq \mathsf{NC}^1_{\mathbb{F}}$.

By a straightforward series-parallel construction, we have

Lemma 3. $\mathsf{NC}^1_{\mathbb{F}} \subseteq \mathsf{BP}_{\mathbb{F}}$.

6   Algebraic Formulas

Definition 7. *An algebraic formula is a directed acyclic graph, having four types of nodes input node, select node, arithmetic node and output node, where each node has fan-out 1. Input node has fan-in zero and is labelled by the input variable, select node is the comparison gate having fan-in 3, one is the control input, other two inputs correspond to the possible output of the select gates based on the outcome of comparison test performed on control input. Arithmetic nodes are labelled by $\{+, \times, -\}$ and perform the arithmetic operation of addition and multiplication, output node is a select node whose other two inputs besides the control input are 0 and 1.*

We prove that languages accepted by a family of polynomial size algebraic formula having $\log n$ select gates can also be accepted by polynomial size constant-width algebraic-branching programs with select nodes.

Theorem 5. *Let $L \subseteq \mathbb{F}^*$ be a set accepted by a family $(F_n)_{n \geq 0}$ of algebraic formula such that F_n is of polynomial size, $O(\log n)$ depth and has at most $O(\log n)$ test gates. Then L can be accepted by a family of constant-width polynomial-size algebraic branching programs with select nodes.*

The proof involves guessing the values of the test gates in the formula, then compressing the resulting formula into an ABP using [1] and then carefully performing the verification.

The branching programs constructed in Theorem 5 can be seen as non-deterministic branching programs.

It is known that any polynomial computed by polynomial size arithmetic formulas can also be computed by formulas of logarithmic depth and polynomial size. We consider the problem of depth reduction for algebraic formulas.

The *select depth* of an algebraic formula is the maximum number of select gate in any path from root to leaf. We consider algebraic formulas where the top gate is a select gate of the form $s = (g, 1, 0)$, i.e., the output value is either 0 or 1. Let F be an algebraic formula with input variables $x_1, \ldots, x_n$. An input $a = (a_1, \ldots, a_n) \in \mathbb{F}^n$ is accepted by F, if the output of the final comparison gate on input a is 1. The class of sets accepted by families of formulas of polynomial size is denoted by $\mathsf{F}_\mathbb{F}$:

$$\mathsf{F}_\mathbb{F} = \left\{ L \subseteq \mathbb{F}^* \;\middle|\; \begin{array}{l} \text{there is a log space uniform family } (F_n)_{n \geq 0} \text{ of algebraic formulas where} \\ F_n \text{ is of size } n^c \text{ for some constant } c \text{ and } L = \\ \bigcup_{n \geq 0} L(F_n). \end{array} \right\}$$

$$\mathsf{F}\text{-}\mathsf{DEPTH}_\mathbb{F} = \left\{ L \subseteq \mathbb{F}^* \;\middle|\; \begin{array}{l} \text{there is a log space uniform family } (F_n)_{n \geq 0} \text{ of algebraic formulas where} \\ F_n \text{ is of size } n^c \text{ and depth } c \log n \text{ for some constant} \\ c \text{ and } L = \bigcup_{n \geq 0} L(F_n). \end{array} \right\}$$

We observe that circuits of logarithmic depth and polynomial size can be transformed to algebraic formulas:

Observation 2. $\mathsf{NC}^1_\mathbb{F}$ *is the same as the class of sets accepted by families of polynomial size algebraic formulas of logarithmic depth over $\mathbb{F}$.*

In the case of Boolean as well as Valiant's arithmetic model of computation, it is known that formulas of polynomials can be efficiently depth reduced to formulas of $O(\log n)$ depth and polynomial size. However, in the case of algebraic circuits with comparison gate, depth reduction is not known. We show depth reduction for the case of formulas with a small number of comparison gates.

Lemma 4. *Let $F = (F_n)_{n \geq 0}$ be a family of algebraic formulas, of size $s = s(n)$ and containing at most $\ell = \ell(n)$ comparison gates accepting a set L. Then* for every $n \geq 0$, there is an algebraic formula F'_n of size $2^\ell s^{O(1)}$ and depth $O(\log s + \log \ell)$ such that the family $F' = (F'_n)_{n \geq 0}$ accepts L. Moreover, if the family F is log-space uniform, then so is F'

Proof. A select gate s in the formula F_n is denoted by a triplet $s = (h, f, g)$. The output of s on a given input is denoted by η_s such that $\eta_s = f$ if $h \geq 0$ and $\eta_s = g$, otherwise. We do a depth-first search traversal of the formula F_n, let the select gate visited are in the order, $s_1, s_2, \ldots s_m$, where $m \leq \ell(n)$. For every $b \in \{0,1\}^n$, $F_n(b)$ is the formula obtained from F_n after replacing every select gate s_i with

$$\widehat{s}_i = \begin{cases} f_i & \text{if } b_i = 1 \\ g_i & \text{otherwise.} \end{cases}$$

Let $F(i, b)$ be the sub-formula of $F(b)$ rooted at select gate s_i and all other select gates $s_j \neq s_i$ in the sub-formula are replaced by $\widehat{s}_j$. Further, replace the select gate $s_i = (h_i, f_i, g_i)$ in formula $F(i, b)$ by $\tilde{s}_i = (h_i, 1, 0)$ such that

$$\tilde{s}_i = \begin{cases} 1 & \text{if } ((h_i \geq 0) \wedge (b_i = 1)) \vee ((h_i < 0) \wedge (b_i = 0)) \\ 0 & \text{otherwise.} \end{cases}$$

Let $\widehat{F}(i, b)$ denote the resulting formula. Let $\mathsf{VER}(b)$ be the verification formula, which verifies whether $b_i = 1$ if, and only if $h_i \geq 0$, for all i. In fact $\mathsf{VER}(b) = \prod_{i=1}^{\ell} \widehat{F}(i, b)$. Consider the formula $F'(b) = \sum_{b \in \{0,1\}^n} F(b) \times \mathsf{VER}(b)$, having one select gate at the output with a > 0? test. It is clear from the construction that, the formula $F'(b)$ accepts an input instance if and only if it is accepted by the formula F. Now since the formula $F'(b)$ has only one test gate at the top, we can depth reduce the resulting formula. The uniformity requirement follows from the fact the reachability in a forest can be done in logarithmic space [5]

Further, by a simple application of Brent's [4] depth reduction technique, we can show that formulas in which there are at most a constant number of select gates in any path from root to leaf can be efficiently depth reduced.

Theorem 6. *Let $L \subseteq \mathbb{F}^*$ be accepted by a family $F = (F_n)_{n \geq 0}$ polynomial size algebraic formulas such that F_n has constant select depth for every $n \geq 0$. Then L can be accepted by a family F' of algebraic formulas of polynomial size and depth $O(\log n)$. Moreover, if F is log-space uniform, so is F'.*

Conclusions. We have studied various notions of space for the BSS model of computation and discussed their limitations. We believe that it is worthwhile exploring the structure and power of ABPs with select nodes. In particular, a real analogue of Ben-Or and Cleve [1] will be interesting and might be helpful in the study of the class $\mathsf{a\text{-}NC}^1_{>}$ defined in [8].

Acknowledgments. The authors gratefully acknowledge anonymous reviewers of an earlier version of this article for their critical suggestions which helped in improving the presentation significantly.

References

1. Ben-Or, M., Cleve, R.: Computing algebraic formulas using a constant number of registers. SIAM J. Comput. **21**(1), 54–58 (1992)
2. Blum, L., Cucker, F., Shub, M., Smale, S.: Complexity and Real Computation. Springer, New York (1998). https://doi.org/10.1007/978-1-4612-0701-6
3. Blum, L., Shub, M., Smale, S.: On a theory of computation and complexity over the real numbers: NP-completeness, recursive functions and universal machines. Bull. AMS **21**(1), 1–46 (1989)
4. Brent, R.P.: The parallel evaluation of general arithmetic expressions. J. ACM **21**(2), 201–206 (1974)
5. Cook, S.A., McKenzie, P.: Problems complete for deterministic logarithmic space. J. Algorithms **8**(3), 385–394 (1987)
6. Cucker, F.: $P_r \neq NC_r$. J. Complex. **8**(3), 230–238 (1992)
7. Cucker, F.: On the complexity of quantifier elimination: the structural approach. Comput. J. **36**(5), 400–408 (1993)
8. Datta, S., Mahajan, M., Raghavendra Rao, B.V., Thomas, M., Vollmer, H.: Counting classes and the fine structure between NC^1 and L. Theor. Comput. Sci. **417**, 36–49 (2012)
9. Naurois, P.J.: A measure of space for computing over the reals. In: Beckmann, A., Berger, U., Löwe, B., Tucker, J.V. (eds.) CiE 2006. LNCS, vol. 3988, pp. 231–240. Springer, Heidelberg (2006). https://doi.org/10.1007/11780342_25
10. DeMillo, R.A., Lipton, R.J.: A probabilistic remark on algebraic program testing. Inf. Process. Lett. **7**(4), 193–195 (1978)
11. Joglekar, P.S., Rao, B.V.R., Sivakumar, S.: On weak-space complexity over complex numbers. In: Klasing, R., Zeitoun, M. (eds.) FCT 2017. LNCS, vol. 10472, pp. 298–311. Springer, Heidelberg (2017). https://doi.org/10.1007/978-3-662-55751-8_24
12. Koiran, P.: A weak version of the Blum, Shub, and Smale model. J. Comput. Syst. Sci. **54**(1), 177–189 (1997)
13. Meinel, C.: p-projection reducibility and the complexity classes $\mathscr{L}$ (nonuniform) and $N\mathscr{L}$ (nonuniform). In: Gruska, J., Rovan, B., Wiedermann, J. (eds.) MFCS 1986. LNCS, vol. 233, pp. 527–535. Springer, Heidelberg (1986). https://doi.org/10.1007/BFb0016279
14. Michaux, C.: Une remarque à propos des machines sur $\mathbb{R}$ introduites par Blum Shub et Smale. Comp. Rend. de l'Acad. des Sci. de Paris **309**(7), 435–437 (1989)
15. Schwartz, J.T.: Probabilistic algorithms for verification of polynomial identities. In: Ng, E.W. (ed.) Symbolic and Algebraic Computation. LNCS, vol. 72, pp. 200–215. Springer, Heidelberg (1979). https://doi.org/10.1007/3-540-09519-5_72
16. Shpilka, A., Yehudayoff, A.: Arithmetic circuits: a survey of recent results and open questions. FTTCS® **5**(3–4), 207–388 (2010)
17. Valiant, L.G.: The complexity of computing the permanent. Theor. Comput. Sci. **8**, 189–201 (1979)
18. Vollmer, H.: Introduction to Circuit Complexity: A Uniform Approach. Springer, Heidelberg (2003)
19. Zippel, R.: Probabilistic algorithms for sparse polynomials. In: Ng, E.W. (ed.) Symbolic and Algebraic Computation. LNCS, vol. 72, pp. 216–226. Springer, Heidelberg (1979). https://doi.org/10.1007/3-540-09519-5_73

Parallelized Maximization of Nonsubmodular Function Subject to a Cardinality Constraint

Hongxiang Zhang[1], Dachuan Xu[1], Longkun Guo[2(✉)], and Jingjing Tan[3]

[1] Department of Operations Research and Information Engineering, Beijing University of Technology, Beijing 100124, People's Republic of China
zhanghx010@emails.bjut.edu.cn, xudc@bjut.edu.cn
[2] Shandong Key Laboratory of Computer Networks, School of Computer Science and Technology, Shandong Computer Science Center, Qilu University of Technology (Shandong Academy of Sciences), Jinan 250353, People's Republic of China
longkun.guo@gmail.com
[3] School of Mathematics and Information Science, Weifang University, Weifang 261061, People's Republic of China
tanjingjing1108@163.com

Abstract. In the paper, we study the adaptivity of maximizing a monotone nonsubmodular function subject to a cardinality constraint. Adaptive approximation algorithm has been previously developed for the similar constrained maximization problem against submodular function, attaining an approximation ratio of $(1 - 1/e - \epsilon)$ and $O\left(\log n/\epsilon^2\right)$ rounds of adaptivity. For more general constraints, Chandra and Kent described parallel algorithms for approximately maximizing the multilinear relaxation of a monotone submodular function subject to either cardinality or packing constraints, achieving a near-optimal $(1 - 1/e - \epsilon)$-approximation in $O\left(\log^2 m \log n/\epsilon^4\right)$ rounds. We propose an Expand-Parallel-Greedy algorithm for the multilinear relaxation of a monotone and normalized set function subject to a cardinality constraint based on rounding the multilinear relaxation of the function. The algorithm achieves a ratio of $\left(1 - e^{-\gamma^2} - \epsilon\right)$, runs in $O\left(\log n/\epsilon^2\right)$ adaptive rounds and requires $O\left((n \log n/\epsilon^2)\right)$ queries, where γ is the Continuous generic submodularity ratio.

Keywords: Cardinality constraints · Parallel algorithm · Nonsubmodular · Multilinear relaxation

1 Introduction

The problem of maximizing a monotone set function over a k-cardinality constraint has broad applications in many scenarios, such as experiment design [4], sparse modeling [10], feature selection [15], graph inference [14], link recommendation [17]. Formally the problem can be described as follows:

$$\max \ f(S) \quad s.t \quad S \subseteq V, |S| \leq k, \qquad (P1)$$

© Springer Nature Switzerland AG 2020
D. Kim et al. (Eds.): COCOON 2020, LNCS 12273, pp. 520–531, 2020.
https://doi.org/10.1007/978-3-030-58150-3_42

where $V = \{v_1, ..., v_n\}$ is the ground set, $f : 2^N \rightarrow R_+$ is a monotone normalized set function.

$f(\cdot)$ is submodular if and only if it satisfies that $f(A \cup v) - f(A) \geq f(B \cup v) - f(B)$ for all $A \subseteq B \subseteq V$ and $v \in V$, where V is the ground set. In the case, we say the set function satisfies the diminishing property called submodularity and the problem is (relatively) well researched. The standard greedy algorithm is known as a theoretical performance guarantee for maximizing a submodular function, and nevertheless performs well empirically even when the objective function deviates from being submodular. For example, under a simple cardinality constraint, it is shown that the standard greedy algorithm deserves an approximation factor of $(1 - 1/e)$ [16,18]. This constant factor later has been further improved with respect to curvature [19], which is a property of a submodular function measuring how close is a submodular function to being modular [9].

However, there are many other important applications whose objective function is not submodular. An important class of such objectives are ς-weakly submodular functions, where ς is called submodularity ratio and characterizes how close the function is from being submodular. As first introduced in [10], it was shown that the approximation ratio of Greedy for (P1) attains $(1 - e^{-\varsigma})$, which degrades slowly as the submodularity ratio decreases. In [3], Bian et al. obtain the approximation guarantee of the form $\alpha^{-1}(1 - e^{-\alpha\varsigma})$, that further depends on the curvature α. In paper [13], Gong et al. propose a measurement γ' called generic submodularity ratio, which clearly characterizes how close a nonnegative increasing set function is to be submodular. Compared with submodularity ratio ς, γ' is more flexible in inequality applications, although both of them are actually derived from two different equivalent definitions of submodular functions. In fact, the min-marginal function is constructed from objective function with interpolation and decreasing property.

A recent line of work focused on developing distributed algorithms for submodular maximization problems in parallel models of computation. They focused on parallelizing sequential algorithms such as the greedy algorithm and its variants, aiming to achieve tradeoffs between the performance guarantee and resources including the number of rounds and the total amount of communication. Balkanski and Singer [2] recently initiated the study of adaptivity (or parallelism) with respect to constrained submodular function maximization subject to a cardinality constraint. Subsequent works individually developed by Balkanski et al. [1] and Ene and Nguyen [11] produced a near-optimal $(1 - 1/e - \epsilon)$-approximation in $O(\log n/\epsilon^2)$ rounds of adaptivity. For extending these results to more general constraints, Chandra and Kent [7] described parallel algorithms for approximately maximizing the multilinear relaxation of a monotone submodular function subject to packing constraints. Their algorithm achieves a near-optimal $(1 - 1/e - \epsilon)$-approximation in $O(\log^2 m \, \log n/\epsilon^4)$ rounds, where n is the cardinality of the ground set and m is the number of packing constraints.

1.1 Our Contribution

In this paper, we devise parallel algorithms for non-submodule maximization problems by solving the following multilinear relaxation in parallel:

$$\begin{aligned} \max \quad & F(x) \\ s.t. \quad & \langle 1, x \rangle \le k, \ x \in R_{\ge 0}^N \end{aligned} \qquad (P2),$$

where $F : [0,1]^N \to R_+$ is the multilinear extension of f [5].

The main result can be summarized as in the following theorem

Theorem 1. *For the multilinear relaxation of a monotone and normalized set function subject to a cardinality constraint, there is a parallel/adaptive algorithm which runs in $(O(\log n/\epsilon^2))$ adaptive rounds, consumes $O(n \log n/\epsilon^2)$ queries, and deserves a ratio of $((1 - e^{-\gamma^2}) - \epsilon)$ for any given parameter $\epsilon > 0$. Furthermore, by rounding a fractional solution of the multilinear relaxation, the algorithm eventually outputs a $\gamma((1 - e^{-\gamma^2}) - \epsilon)$-approximation solution for maximizing the nonsubmodular set function subject to a cardinality constraint.*

1.2 Organizations

The remainder of this paper is organized as follows. Section 2 provides some necessary preliminaries; Sect. 3 gives the main Expand-Parallel-Greedy algorithm and its analysis; Sect. 4 gives the rounding schemes and lastly Sect. 5 concludes our work.

2 Preliminaries

Let f be a nonnegative, monotone and normalized nonsubmodular set function. For any vectors $x, y \in [0,1]^N$, and a set of coordinates S, we say $x \le y$ if and only if $x_i \le y_i$ holds for any $i \in S$. Let $x \vee y$ be the coordinate-wise maximum of x and y, $x \wedge y$ be the coordinate-wise minimum, and $x \backslash y = x - x \wedge y$.

For a vector $x \in [0,1]^N$, and a set of coordinates S, we use $x \wedge S$ to denote the vector obtained from x by setting all coefficients not indexed by S to 0, and $x \backslash S = x - x \wedge S$ the vector obtained from x but setting all coordinates indexed by S to 0.

Definition 1. *Given a set function $f : 2^N \to R_+$, the multilinear extension of f, denoted F, extends f to the product space $[0,1]^N$ by interpreting each point $x \in [0,1]^N$ as an independent sample $S \subseteq N$ with sampling probabilities given by x, and taking the expectation of $f(S)$. Equivalently,*

$$F(x) = \sum_{S \subseteq N} \left(\prod_{i \in S} x_i \prod_{i \notin S} (1 - x_i) \right)$$

We extend F to the cone $R_{\geq 0}^N$ by truncation $F(x) = F(x \wedge 1)$, where $x \wedge 1$ takes the coordinate-wise minimum of x and the all-ones vector 1. Moreover, we write $F_y(x) = F(x \vee y) - F(y)$ which essentially generalizes the definition of marginal values to the continuous setting. Let $F'(x)$ be the gradient of F at x and $F_i'(x)$ denote the partial derivative of F with respect to i.

Lemma 1. *Let F be the multilinear extension of a set function f, $x \in [0,1]^N$. Then we have*

1) *(Multilinearty) For any $i \in N, F(x) = F(x \setminus i) + F_{x \setminus i}(i)$.*
2) *(Monotonicity) For any $i \in N, F_i'(x) = F_{x \setminus i}(i)$, if f is monotone, then F' is nonnegative, and F is monotone.*

In the work of [13], they proposed the definition of generic submodular ratio γ', for clearly characterizing how close a nonnegative increasing set function is to be submodular. Compared with submodularity ratio ς which proposed by Das and Kempe [10], γ' is more flexible in inequality applications. Next, we extend the definition to continuous situations.

Definition 2 *(Generic submodularity ratio). Given a ground set N and an increasing set function $f : 2^N \to R_+$, the generic submodularity ratio of f is the largest scalar γ' such that for any $S \subseteq T \subseteq N$ and any $j \in N \setminus T$, we have*

$$f_S(j) \geq \gamma' f_T(j).$$

Definition 3 *(Continuous generic submodularity ratio). Given any normalized set function f, the continuous generic submodular ratio is defined as the largest scalar $\gamma \in [0,1]$ subject to*

$$F_{x \setminus i}(i) \geq \gamma F_{y \setminus i}(i), \quad x \leq y.$$

Comparing the two submodularity ratio, the elements in the set S can be regarded as some coordinates in x, so we have $\gamma \leq \gamma'$ by comparing Definition 2 with Definition 3.

Evaluating F and F': The formula for $F(x)$ gives a natural random sampling algorithm to evaluate $F(x)$ in expectation. Often we need to evaluate $F(x)$ and $F'(x)$ to high accuracy. This issue has been addressed in prior work via standard Chernoff type concentration inequalities when f is non-negative.

Lemma 2 [6]. *Suppose $(F'(x))_i \in [0, M']$. Then with $r = O(p \log d / \epsilon^2)$ parallel evaluations of f, one can find an estimation Z of $(F'(x))_i$ such that*

$$P \left[|Z - (F'(x))_i| \geq \epsilon (F'(x))_i + \frac{\epsilon M'}{p} \right] \leq \frac{1}{d^3}.$$

Similarly, if $F(x) \in [0, M]$, then with $r = O(p \log d / \epsilon^2)$ parallel evaluations of f, one can find an estimated Z of $F(x)$ such that

$$P \left[|Z - F(x)| \geq \epsilon F(x) + \frac{\epsilon M}{p} \right] \leq \frac{1}{d^3}.$$

Algorithm 1. EPG: Expand-Parallel-Greedy(F, N, k, ϵ)

1: $x \leftarrow 0, \lambda \leftarrow OPT$
2: **while** $\langle x, 1 \rangle \leq k$ *and* $\lambda \geq e^{-\gamma^2} OPT$ **do**
3:     A. Let $M_\lambda = \{j \in N : F_j'(x) \geq \frac{(1-\epsilon)\lambda}{k}\}$
4:     B. Update $S_0 = M_\lambda$
5:     **while** S_{l-1} is not empty and $\langle x, 1 \rangle \leq k$ **do**
6:         a. choose δ maximal s.t.
7:             1). $F_x(x + \delta S_{l-1}) \geq \gamma^{1-l} \frac{(1-\epsilon)^2 \lambda \delta |S_{l-1}|}{k}$
8:             2). $\langle x + \delta S_{l-1}, 1 \rangle \leq k$
9:         b. $x \leftarrow x + \delta S_{l-1}$
10:         c. update $S_l = \{j \in N : F_j'(x) \geq \gamma^{-l} \frac{(1-\epsilon)\lambda}{k}\}$
11:     **end while**
12:     C. $\lambda \leftarrow (1 - \epsilon)\lambda$
13: **end while**
14: return x

The following algorithm and analysis were under the assumption that gradients of the multilinear extension F were easy to compute, i.e. could be computed by oracles. In fact, such oracles do exist for many real submodular functions of interest. Moreover, given oracle access to f, one can implement sufficiently accurate oracles to $F(x)$ and $F'(x)$ with $O(1)$ oracle calls to f but without increasing the depth.

3   The Greedy Algorithm and Its Analysis

3.1   Expand-Parallel-Greedy Algorithm

In this section, we shall describe our main algorithm. The key idea of our algorithm actually originated from the continuous-greedy algorithm proposed by Calinescu et al. in [5] which maximizes a submodular function within a cardinality constraint polytope through adding δe_j to x for a fixed and conservative step size $\delta > 0$. The algorithm was parallelized by Chekuri et al. [7] via incorporating two changes to the continuous-greedy algorithm: First, rather than increase x along the single best coordinate, identify all good coordinates with gradient values nearly as large as the best coordinate, and increase along all of these coordinates uniformly; Second, rather than increasing x along these coordinates by a fixed increment, they use a dynamical increment δ.

Although obtained via extending continuous-greedy algorithm [5] and the parallel-greedy algorithm of Chekuri et al. [7], our algorithm is different in sophisticated details. Due to the submodularity, the previous parallel-greedy algorithm can ensure the number of good coordinates decreases during iterations. However, when the function is nonsubmodular, the set of the best coordinate does not decrease during iterations, and hence the continuous-greedy algorithm and parallel-greedy algorithm are no longer feasible. In this paper, we overcome this difficulty by proposing the so-called Expand-Parallel-Greedy algorithm. In essential, our algorithm use a different definition of good coordinates with respect to the continuous generic submodularity ratio γ and gradient values, and actually increase along all of these coordinates uniformly.

The algorithm is briefly described as follows: The first part is to increase the good coordinates as much as possible when the threshold λ is given. The second part is to update our threshold λ carefully when x does not violate the constraints. The detailed layout of our algorithm is as formally in Algorithm 1.

3.2 Approximation Ratio

Lemma 3. *If the inner loop terminates after the m rounds, then any output value x satisfies $OPT - F(x) \leq \gamma^{-m-1}\lambda$.*

Proof. If z is an optimal solution, then we have

$$
\begin{aligned}
OPT - F(x) &\leq F_x(z) \\
&= F(x \vee z) - F(x) \\
&\leq \gamma^{-1}\langle F'(x, x \vee z - x)\rangle \\
&\leq \gamma^{-1}\langle F'(x, z)\rangle \\
&\leq \gamma^{-m-1}\frac{(1-\epsilon)\lambda}{k}\langle z, 1\rangle \\
&\leq \gamma^{-m-1}\lambda.
\end{aligned}
$$

Lemma 4. *If the inner loop terminates after the m rounds, the output x satisfies $F(x) \geq (1 - O(\epsilon))(1 - e^{-\gamma^2})OPT$.*

Proof. Let $t = \Sigma x_i$. From Lemma 1 and the choice of δ in Algorithm 1, we immediately have

$$
\begin{aligned}
F_x(x + \delta S_{m-1}) &\geq \frac{\gamma^{1-m}(1-\epsilon)^2\delta|S_{m-1}|}{k}\gamma^{1+m}(OPT - F(x)) \\
&\geq \frac{\gamma^2(1-\epsilon)^2\delta|S_{m-1}|}{k}(OPT - F(x)).
\end{aligned}
$$

Consequently,

$$
\frac{dF(x)}{dt} \geq \frac{\gamma^2(1-\epsilon)^2}{k}(OPT - F(x)).
$$

So we get

$$
F(x) \geq \left[1 - exp\left(-\gamma^2(1-\epsilon)\frac{2t}{k}\right)\right]OPT.
$$

Next, we analyze the above results in two cases:

1) If $t = \langle x, 1\rangle = k$ at the end of the algorithm, we have

$$
F(x) \geq (1 - O(\epsilon))(1 - e^{-\gamma^2})OPT.
$$

2) If $\lambda \leq e^{-\gamma^2}OPT$, we get

$$F(x) \geq (1 - \gamma^{-m-1}e^{-\gamma^2})OPT.$$

Combining 1) and 2) as above, we eventually have

$$F(x) \geq (1 - O(\epsilon))(1 - e^{-\gamma^2})OPT.$$

The analysis of Lemma 4 considers only the case that the set S is an empty set after the loop of the algorithm. How about the case when the set S is non-empty? Assuming that the corresponding solution of the previous update round of S is x', when the number of k elements are selected, the inner loop does not stop until S is an empty set, and the corresponding solutions are x^* and x'' respectively. Then we have

$$F(x') \geq (1 - O(\epsilon))(1 - e^{-\gamma^2})OPT, \ F(x'') \geq (1 - O(\epsilon))(1 - e^{-\gamma^2})OPT,$$

so

$$F(x^*) \geq (1 - O(\epsilon))(1 - e^{-\gamma^2})OPT.$$

3.3   Number of Iterations

Because the two inequalities in the sixth and seventh lines of the algorithm are possible to reach tight, so with the update of δ, there must be an inequality to be tight. When $(B.a.2))$ is tight, the algorithm will terminates, so we only need to analyze $(B.a.1))$.

Lemma 5. *If $F_x(x + \delta S) = \frac{\gamma^{1-l}(1-\epsilon)^2\lambda\delta|S|}{k}$, the loop at (B.a) iterates at most $O(\log n/\epsilon)$ times, and the total loop at most $O(\log n/\epsilon^2)$.*

Proof.

$$\frac{\gamma^{1-l}(1-\epsilon)^2\lambda\delta|S_{l-1}|}{k} = F_x(x + \delta S_{l-1})$$
$$\geq \gamma\langle F'(x + \delta S_{l-1}), \delta S_{l-1}\rangle$$
$$\geq \gamma\langle F'(x + \delta S_{l-1}), \delta S_l\rangle$$
$$\geq \frac{\gamma^{1-l}(1-\epsilon)\lambda\delta|S_l|}{k}$$

So, we have

$$|S_l| \leq (1 - \epsilon)|S_{l-1}|,$$

and the inner loop repeats at most $O(\log n/\epsilon)$ times.

Now, we continue to analyze Algorithm 1(C). Due to $\lambda \leftarrow (1 - \epsilon)\lambda$, the outside loop iterates for at most $O(1/\epsilon)$ times, and hence the total loop at most $O(\log n/\epsilon^2)$ times.

3.4   Oracle Queries

In Lemma 2, by setting $d = n$ and $p = n$ we can estimate $(F'(x))_i$ and $F(x)$ within a $(1 \pm \epsilon)$ multiplicative error, as well as an additive error of $\epsilon M'/n$ and $\epsilon M/n$ respectively [7]. From Algorithm 1, we find the number of oracle queries to F is at most $O(\log n/\epsilon^2)$, and oracle queries to F' at most $O(n \log n/\epsilon^2)$.

4   Rounding the Fractional Solution

In this section, we concentrate on rounding a fractional solution of (P2) to obtain a feasible solution of (P1). We shall first introduce basic definitions and depict the general idea of its construction, and then provide the approximation to complete the algorithm under the assumption as in [7] that $(1 - \epsilon, 1 - \epsilon)$-balanced CR scheme always exists.

Our algorithm solves the continuous relaxation and outputs a fractional solution x. To obtain an integer solution we need to round x. Several powerful and general rounding strategies have been developed over the years including pipage rounding, swap rounding, and contention resolution schemes [8]. However, most rounding strategies are not suitable in our scenario. E.g., pipage rounding technique is not applicable because it has strong requirement for submodularity. So we adopt contention resolution schemes to round solutions of the multilinear relaxation. Theorem 1 already gives an estimate of the value of the integer optimum solution. One interesting aspect of several of these rounding algorithms is the following:

Definition 4. *Let* $b, c \in [0, 1]$. *A* (b, c)-*balanced* CR *scheme* π *for* P_I *is a procedure that, for every* $x \in bP_I$ *and* $A \subseteq N$, *returns a random set* $\pi_x(A) \subseteq A \cap support(x)$ *and satisfies the following properties:*

(i) $\pi_x(A) \in I$ *with probability 1 for all* $A \subseteq N, x \in bP_I$, *and*
(ii) for all $i \in support(x), Pr[i \in \pi_x(R(x)) \,|\, i \in R(x)] \geq c$ *for all* $x \in bP_I$.

The rounding phase consists of a random $R(y)$ and a monotone CR scheme. We claim an expected performance ratio for the nonsubmodular maximization problem. Consider an increasing set function $f : 2^N \rightarrow R_+$ with generic submodularity ratio γ, and its multilinear extension $F : [0, 1]^N \rightarrow R_{\geq 0}$ on a cardinality constraint polytope $\{P_I = x \in [0, 1]^n : \sum_i x_i \leq k\}$.

We also restrict our attention to monotone functions. Let x be a feasible fractional solution to constraints of the form $\langle 1, x \rangle \leq k$. It's clear that the above constraint is satisfied by the following lemma.

Lemma 6 [8]. *Given a nonnegative* $m \times n$ *matrix* A *and nonnegative vector* d, *for a constant number of knapsack constraints* $Ax \leq d, x \in [0, 1]^n, (m = O(1))$, *by guessing and enumeration tricks, one can effectively get a* $(1 - \epsilon, 1 - \epsilon)$-*balanced* CR *scheme for any fixed* $\epsilon > 0$.

Algorithm 2 (b, c)-balanced CR scheme

1: Given parameters $b, c > 0$, let x^* be the fractional solution by EPG algorithm.
2: Let $R(x^*)$ be random set obtained by including each $i \in N$ independently with probability x_i^*.
3: Remove some elements from $R(bx^*)$, and ensure every element i appears in I with probability at least cx_i^*
4: return I

Lemma 7. *Let π be a bc-balanced CR scheme over P_I and $b, c \in [0, 1]$. For any fixed vector $y \in P_I$, we have $E_{R \leftarrow R(y), I \leftarrow \pi_y(R)}[f(I)] \geq bc\gamma' F(y)$.*

Here we give some technical outcomes about Min-Marginal Function, Distributive lattice and FKG inequality, which support the proof of Lemma 7.

Definition 5 *(Min-Marginal Function). Let $f : 2^N \to R$ be a set function. For any $S \subseteq N$ and any $j \in N$, we define the min-marginal function of f as follows*

$$L(S, j) = \min_{S' \subseteq S} f_{S'}(j)$$

where $f_{S'}(j) = f(S' \cup j) - f(S')$.

Lemma 8 [13]. *Let $f : 2^N \to R_+$ be an increasing set function with generic submodularity ratio γ'. For any $S \subseteq N$ and $j \in N$, denote by $L(S, j)$ the min-marginal function of f. We can show that (a) $\gamma' f_S(j) \leq L(S, j) \leq f_S(j)$, for any $S \subseteq N$ (interpolation property); (b) $L(S_1, j) \geq L(S_2, j)$, for any $S_1 \subseteq S_2 \subseteq N$ (decreasing property).*

Definition 6 *(FKG inequality [12]). Let X be a finite distributive lattice and μ be a nonnegative log supermodular function, that is, $\mu(x \wedge y)\mu(x \vee y) \geq \mu(x)\mu(y), \forall x, y \in X$. The FKG inequality says that for any two functions g and h with the same monotonicity on X, the following positive correlation inequality holds:*

$$\left(\sum_{x \in X} g(x)h(x)\mu(x) \right) \left(\sum_{x \in X} \mu(x) \right) \geq \left(\sum_{x \in X} g(x)\mu(x) \right) \left(\sum_{x \in X} h(x)\mu(x) \right).$$

Lemma 9 [13]. *Let $X = 2^N$ and $i \in N$. Let π be a CR scheme for P_I and $y \in P_I$. For any subset $R \subseteq N$ and any fixed element $i \in N$, define $g(R) = E_{I \leftarrow \pi_y(R)}[1_i \in I \mid R], h(R) = L(R, i), \mu(R) = Pr[R \mid i \in R]$, where $1_i \in I$ is an indicator that equals to 1 if $i \in I$ and 0 otherwise. We can show that*

$$\left(\sum_{R \in X} g(R)h(R)\mu(R) \right) \left(\sum_{R \in X} \mu(R) \right) \geq \left(\sum_{R \in X} g(R)\mu(R) \right) \left(\sum_{R \in X} h(R)\mu(R) \right).$$

Next, we prove Lemma 9. If π is a $bc-CR$ schemes with $b, c \in [0, 1]$, then for any $y \in P_I$, we have $E[f(\pi_y(R(y)))] \geq bc\gamma' F(y)$.

Proof. Let $R \leftarrow R(y)$ and $I \leftarrow \pi_y(R)$. Assume $R_i = R \cap \{1, ..., i\}$ and $I_i = I \cap \{1, ..., i\}$. For any fixed $i \in \{1, ..., n\}$, we have

$$
\begin{aligned}
&E_{R \leftarrow R(y), I \leftarrow \pi_y(R)}[f(I_i) - f(I_{i-1})] \\
&= E_{R \leftarrow R(y), I \leftarrow \pi_y(R)}[1_{i \in I} f_{I_{i-1}}(i)] \\
&= Pr[i \in R] \cdot E_{R \leftarrow R(y), I \leftarrow \pi_y(R)}[1_{i \in I} f_{I_{i-1}}(i) \mid i \in R] \\
&\geq Pr[i \in R] \cdot E_{R \leftarrow R(y), I \leftarrow \pi_y(R)}[1_{i \in I} L_{I_{i-1}}(i) \mid i \in R] \\
&\geq Pr[i \in R] \cdot E_{R \leftarrow R(y), I \leftarrow \pi_y(R)}[1_{i \in I} L_{R_{i-1}}(i) \mid i \in R] \\
&= Pr[i \in R] \cdot \left(\sum_R Pr[R \mid i \in R] \cdot E_{I \leftarrow \pi_y(R)}[1_{i \in I} \mid R] \cdot L(R_{i-1}, i) \right).
\end{aligned}
$$

Because $\sum_R Pr[R i \in R] = 1$, from Lemma 9, we have

$$
\sum_R Pr[R \mid i \in R] \cdot E_{I \leftarrow \pi_y(R)}[1_{i \in I} \mid R] \cdot L(R_{i-1}, i)
$$

$$
\geq \left(\sum_R Pr[R \mid i \in R] \cdot E_{I \leftarrow \pi_y(R)}[1_{i \in I} \mid R] \right) \cdot \left(\sum_R Pr[R \mid i \in R] \cdot L(R_{i-1}, i) \right)
$$

$$
= E_{R \leftarrow R(y)}[E_{I \leftarrow \pi_y(R)}[1_{i \in I} \mid R] \mid i \in R] \cdot E_{R \leftarrow R(y)}[L(R_{i-1}, i) \mid i \in R]
$$

$$
= E_{I \leftarrow \pi_y(R)}[1_{i \in I} \mid i \in R] \cdot E_{R \leftarrow R(y)}[L(R_{i-1}, i)].
$$

Then, we get

$$
\begin{aligned}
&E_{R \leftarrow R(y), I \leftarrow \pi_y(R)}[f(I_i) - f(I_{i-1})] \\
&\geq Pr[i \in R] \cdot E_{I \leftarrow \pi_y(R)}[1_{i \in I} \mid i \in R] \cdot E_{R \leftarrow R(y)}[L(R_{i-1}, i)] \\
&= Pr[i \in R] \cdot Pr[i \in I \mid i \in R] \cdot E_{R \leftarrow R(y)}[L(R_{i-1}, i)] \\
&\geq Pr[i \in R] \cdot b \cdot c \cdot E_{R \leftarrow R(y)}[L(R_{i-1}, i)] \\
&\geq b \cdot c \cdot \gamma' E_{R \leftarrow R(y)}[f_{R \cap [i-1]}(i)] \\
&= b \cdot c \cdot \gamma' E[f(R \cap [i]) - f(R \cap [i-1])].
\end{aligned}
$$

Therefore, we have

$$
\begin{aligned}
&E_{R \leftarrow R(y), I \leftarrow \pi_y(R)}[f(I)] \\
&= \sum_{i-1}^n E_{R \leftarrow R(y), I \leftarrow \pi_y(R)}[f(I_i) - f(I_{i-1})] \\
&\geq b \cdot c \cdot \gamma' \sum_{i-1}^n E_{R \leftarrow R(y)}[f(R_i) - f(R_{i-1})] \\
&\geq b \cdot c \cdot \gamma' E_{R \leftarrow R(y)}[f(R)]
\end{aligned}
$$

Combining Lemmas 5 and 6, we get a $\gamma'(1-\epsilon)$-approximate function value by using contention resolution schemes to convert a fractional solution of Multilinear relaxation Problem to a feasible solution of original Problem.

Recall that in Sect. 3, the continuous greedy method approximates (P2) within a factor of $(1 - O(\epsilon))(1 - e^{-\gamma^2})$. Then the contention resolution schemes converts a fractional solution of (P2) to a feasible solution of (P1) with $\gamma'(1-\epsilon)$-approximate function value. Assuming that continuous greedy algorithm returns a fractional solution $y \in P_I$ and the rounding process provides a discrete solution I, we eventually have

$$E[f(I)] \geq \gamma'(1 - O(\epsilon))(1 - e^{-\gamma^2})OPT \geq \gamma(1 - O(\epsilon))(1 - e^{-\gamma^2})OPT.$$

5 Conclusion

In this paper, we devised parallel algorithms to nonsubmodular maximization problems by first presenting a $((1 - e^{-\gamma^2}) - \epsilon)$-approximation to the multilinear relaxation of (P2) and then rounding a solution of the multilinear relaxation to obtain a $\gamma((1 - e^{-\gamma^2}) - \epsilon)$-approximation. In particular, when the continuous generic submodularity ratio is 1 (i.e. the function is submodular), our results coincide with the state-of-art result in [7]. Observing the approximate ratio $((1 - e^{-\gamma^2}) - \epsilon)$ depends on the choice of parameter δ, we are currently investigating a new update method for the parameter δ so as to improve the approximate ratio of our algorithm.

Acknowledgements. The first and second authors are supported by National Natural Science Foundation of China (Nos. 11871081, 11531014). The third author is supported by National Natural Science Foundation of China (No. 61772005).

References

1. Balkanski, E., Rubinstein, A., Singer, Y.: An exponential speedup in parallel running time for submodular maximization without loss in approximation. In: Proceedings of SODA, pp. 283–302 (2019)
2. Balkanski, E., Singer, Y.: The adaptive complexity of maximizing a submodular function. In: Proceedings of STOC, pp. 1138–1151 (2018)
3. Bian, A., Buhmann, M., Krause, A., Tschiatschek, S.: Guarantees for greedy maximization of non-submodular functions with applications. In: Proceedings of ICML, pp. 498–507 (2017)
4. Bouhtou, M., Stephane, G., Guillaume, S.: Submodularity and randomized rounding techniques for optimal experimental design. Electron. Notes Discrete Math. **36**, 679–686 (2010)
5. Calinescu, G., Chekuri, C., Pal, M.: Maximizing a monotone submodular function subject to a matroid constraint. SIAM J. Comput. **40**, 1740–1766 (2011)
6. Chekuri, C., Jayram, T.S., Vondrák, J.: On multiplicative weight updates for concave and submodular function maximization. In: Proceedings of CITCS, pp. 201–210 (2015)

7. Chekuri, C., Quanrud, K.: Submodular function maximization in parallel via the multilinear relaxation. In: Proceedings of SODA, pp. 303–322 (2019)
8. Chekuri, C., Vondrák, J., Zenklusen, R.: Submodular function maximization via the multilinear relaxation and contention resolution schemes. SIAM J. Comput. **43**, 1831–1879 (2014)
9. Conforti, M., Cornuéjols, G.: Submodular set functions, matroids and the greedy algorithm: tight worst-case bounds and some generalizations of the Rado-Edmonds theorem. Discrete Appl. Math. **7**, 251–274 (1984)
10. Das, A., Kempe, D.: Submodular meets spectral: greedy algorithms for subset selection, sparse approximation and dictionary selection. In: Proceedings of ICML, pp. 1057–1064 (2011)
11. Ene, A., Nguyễn, H.L.: Submodular maximization with nearly-optimal approximation and adaptivity in nearly-linear time. In: Proceedings of SODA, pp. 274–282 (2019)
12. Fortuin, C.M., Kasteleyn, P.W., Ginibre, J.: Correlation inequalities on some partially ordered sets. Commun. Math. Phys. **22**, 89–103 (1971)
13. Gong, S., Nong, Q., Liu, W., Fang, Q.: Parametric monotone function maximization with matroid constraints. J. Global Optim. **75**(3), 833–849 (2019). https://doi.org/10.1007/s10898-019-00800-2
14. Jegelka, S., Bilmes, J.: Submodularity beyond submodular energies: coupling edges in graph cuts. In: Proceedings of CVPR, pp. 1897–1904 (2011)
15. Liu, Y., Wei, K., Kirchhoff, K.: Submodular feature selection for high-dimensional acoustic score spaces. In: Proceedings of ICA, pp. 7184–7188 (2013)
16. Nemhauser, G.L., Wolsey, L.A., Fisher, M.L.: An analysis of approximations for maximizing submodular set functions-I. Math. Program. **14**, 265–294 (1978)
17. Parotsidis, N., Pitoura, E., Tsaparas, P.: Centrality-aware link recommendations. In: Proceedings of WSDM, pp. 503–512 (2016)
18. Vondrák, J.: Optimal approximation for the submodular welfare problem in the value oracle model. In: Proceedings of STOC, pp. 67–74 (2008)
19. Vondrák, J.: Submodularity and curvature: the optimal algorithm. Ann. Discrete Math. **2**, 65–74 (1978)

An Improved Bregman k-means++ Algorithm via Local Search

Xiaoyun Tian[1], Dachuan Xu[1], Longkun Guo[2(✉)], and Dan Wu[3]

[1] Department of Operations Research and Information Engineering, Beijing University of Technology, Beijing 100124, People's Republic of China
xiaoyun_txy@emails.bjut.edu.cn, xudc@bjut.edu.cn
[2] Shandong Key Laboratory of Computer Networks, School of Computer Science and Technology, Shandong Computer Science Center, Qilu University of Technology (Shandong Academy of Sciences), Jinan 250353, People's Republic of China
longkun.guo@gmail.com
[3] School of Mathematics and Statistics, Henan University of Science and Technology, Luoyang 471023, China
lywd2964@126.com

Abstract. In this paper, we study the Bregman k-means problem with respect to μ-similar Bregman divergences (μ-BKMP). Given an n-point set $\mathcal{S}$ and $k \leq n$, μ-BKMP is to find a center subset $C \subseteq \mathcal{S}$ with $|C| = k$ and separate the given set into k clusters accordingly, aiming to minimize the sum of μ-similar Bregman divergences of the points in $\mathcal{S}$ to their nearest centers. We propose a new variant of k-means++ by employing the local search scheme, and show the algorithm deserves a constant approximation guarantee.

Keywords: Seeding algorithm · Local search · k-means · μ-similar Bregman divergences

1 Introduction

The k-means problem is a classical NP-hard problem, whose roots can be traced back as far as the early 17th century. Formally, given a finite data points $\mathcal{S}$ in $\mathbb{R}^d$ and an integer k, the k-means problem is to choose k centers such that the sum of the squared distances from each point in $\mathcal{S}$ to its closest center attains minimum. In the past decades, k-means, as a basic "unsupervised" learning process, has been extensively studied in many fields within machine learning and theoretical computer science [10,11], such as data mining, data compression, picture segmentation, and pattern recognition.

With the explosive growth of stored data, a wide variety of dissimilarity measures are used for clustering, such as square Euclidean distance, Mahalanobis distance, Bregman divergences. In the context, it depends not only on the geometrical properties of Euclidean distance, such as symmetry and the triangle inequality, to describe the dissimilarity between data points.

© Springer Nature Switzerland AG 2020
D. Kim et al. (Eds.): COCOON 2020, LNCS 12273, pp. 532–541, 2020.
https://doi.org/10.1007/978-3-030-58150-3_43

To our knowledge, the family of Bregman divergences, which are frequently used in practice, were first proposed by Bregman to solve convex optimization problems in [7] and particularly the "Bregman distance" is coincided with the one defined in [8]. In addition, the family of Bregman divergences also applies to the context of clustering problems because of their combinatorial properties, and brings the Bregman k-means problem. In this paper, we mainly focus on using Bregman divergences as dissimilarity measurement.

In practice, the most celebrated heuristic for the k-means problem is Lloyd's algorithm [15], which initially choose k centers, and then repeats to improve the solution and clusters the data points to the nearest centers, until the partition and the center points become stable. Banerjee et al. [6] achieved breakthrough results via extending Lloyd's algorithm to the whole class of all Bregman divergences. The first $(1 + \varepsilon)$-approximation algorithm applicable to the Bregman k-median problem was proposed by Ackermann et al. [3], which is based on generalizing an earlier algorithm for the squared Euclidean distances in [13] with respect to a large number of Bregman divergences.

Although Lloyd's algorithm has high accuracy in practice, it does not possess a theoretical approximation guarantee. To obtain a performance guarantee, Arthur et al. developed the k-means++ seeding algorithm [4] that deserves $O(\log k)$-approximation by carefully choosing the first initial k centers with specified probability. In [2], Ackermann et al. generalized the k-means++ seeding approach as in [4] to the class of Bregman divergences. They showed how to construct a factor $O(\log k)$-approximation for the k-median problem with respect to a μ-similar Bregman divergence. It is known that the μ-similar Bregman divergence has some quasi-metric properties, such as triangle inequality and symmetry within a constant factor of $O(1/\mu)$. More recently, Lattanzi et al. developed a new variant of k-means++ seeding [14] based on the local search strategy. They showed their algorithm deserves a constant approximation guarantee and consumes $O(k \log \log k)$ rounds of local search.

Contribution. In this paper, we present an approximation algorithm for the μ-similar Bregman k-means problem (μ-BKMP) that uses an arbitrary μ-similar Bregman divergence as dissimilarity measure. Via combining k-means++ seeding and local search technique, we obtain a constant approximation for μ-BKMP, which is also a generalization of the k-means++ seeding approach via local search [14]. Formally, our main result can be summarized as follows:

Theorem 1.1. *If D_φ is a μ-similar Bregman divergence, $C \subseteq \mathbb{R}^d$ with $C = k$ is chosen at random according to D_φ, then we have $E[\text{cost}(\mathcal{S}, C)] \in O(opt_k)$ in expectation. The running time of the algorithm is $O(dnk^2 \log \log k)$.*

Organization. The remainder of the paper is organized as follows: Sect. 2 gives the notations and provides several lemmas related to μ-BKMP; Sect. 3 presents the algorithms based on local search techniques and then analyzes their performance guarantee; Sect. 4 provides all other proofs; Sect. 5 lastly concludes the paper. Due to the space constraints, the formal proofs are omitted and will be given in detail in the journal version.

2 Preliminaries and Notations

In this section, we formally define the k-means problem with respect to a Bregman divergence, as well as notations used in the paper. Let $\mathcal{S} = \{s_1, s_2, \cdots, s_n\}$ be a data points set in $\mathbb{R}^d$. For two points a, b in $\mathbb{R}^d$, the distance $D(a, b)$ is described as an arbitrary dissimilarity measure between them, where $D : \mathbb{X} \times \mathbb{X} \to \mathbb{R} \cup \infty$. Obviously, for a point a in $\mathbb{R}^d$ and a subset $C = \{c_1, c_2, \cdots, c_k\} \subseteq \mathcal{S}$, the distance $D(a, C) = \min_{c \in C} D(a, c)$ is characterized by the dissimilarity from point a towards the closest point from set C. Specifically, the total dissimilarity measurement of all points from $\mathcal{S}$ to their closest point from set C with respect to D is defined as $cost^D(\mathcal{S}, C) = \sum_{s_j \in \mathcal{S}} D(s_j, C)$, also written $\text{cost}(\mathcal{S}, C)$ in short. Specifically, $D(a, b) \geq 0$ and $D(a, b) = 0$ if and only if $a = b$.

Firstly, the classical k-means problem can be defined as follows. Given data points $\mathcal{S}$ and an integer k, we consider the squared Euclidean distance as a distance measure, the goal is to find a set C of k centers in $\mathbb{R}^d$ that minimize the sum of the squared distances from each point in $\mathcal{S}$ to its closest center, i.e. $\text{cost}(\mathcal{S}, C) = \sum_{j=1}^{n} \min_{i \in \{1, 2, \cdots, k\}} \| s_j - c_i \|^2$. The clusters are defined by assigning each point to their closest center.

In the following part, we will introduce an important subclass of the class of Bregman divergences among dissimilarity measures, namely μ-similar Bregman divergences [3]. To do this, we begin by introducing several related notions. Let D_φ denote a Bregman divergence which is defined with respect to a strictly convex function $\varphi : ri(\mathbb{X}) \to \mathbb{R}$ on the relative interior $ri(\mathbb{X})$ of convex domain $\mathcal{S} \in \mathbb{R}^d$. If φ also has continuous first-order partial derivatives on $ri(\mathbb{X})$, then it is called a (Bregman) generating function. Among the Bregman divergences, the class of Mahalanobis distances is closely related to the μ-similar Bregman divergences. For a symmetric positive definite matrix $A \in \mathbb{R}^{d \times d}$, Mahalanobis distances D_A is defined as $D_A(a, b) = (a - b)^\top A(a - b)$. Furthermore, for a positive constant $0 < \mu \leq 1$ if there exists the aforementioned A such that for the Mahalanobis distance D_A we have $\mu D_A(a, b) \leq D_\varphi(a, b) \leq D_A(a, b)$, then the Bregman divergences D_φ is called μ-similar Bregman divergences.

The paper focuses on primary concern is k-means with respect to a μ-similar Bregman divergence. Let D_φ be a μ-similar Bregman divergence, given a n-point set $\mathcal{S} \in \mathbb{R}^d$ and an integer k, the μ-BKMP is to find a set C of k points in $\mathbb{R}^d$, such that $\text{cost}(\mathcal{S}, C)$ is minimized. Apparently, each center implicitly defines a clustering, whereas objects in the same cluster should be similar to each other and objects in different clusters should be not.

In particular, a set S is called a feasible solution for μ-BKMP if it satisfies $F \in \mathbb{R}^d$ and $|S| = k$. For a feasible solution S, each point $s \in \mathcal{S}$ is assigned to one nearest center denoted by c_i, i.e., $c_i := \arg\min_{c \in C} D_\varphi(s, c)$. If the nearest center is not unique, then s is assigned to one of them arbitrarily. When the indices are not relevant, we will drop the index. For the sake of discussion, we refer to the set of optimal centers as O^* which can also be partitioned into k disjoint subsets $O_1^*, \cdots, O_k^*$ induced by the optimal centers. We refer to the cost of the optimal solution as opt_k, where $opt_k = \sum_{i=1}^{k} opt(O_i^*)$.

The centroid of $\mathcal{S}$ can be computed by $c(\mathcal{S}) = \frac{1}{n} \sum_{s_i \in \mathcal{S}} \mathcal{S}$. Note that $c(\mathcal{S})$ is the unique optimal 1-means of $\mathcal{S}$, akin to the dissimilarity measure as squared Euclidean distance. In this sense, μ-BKMP can be formally described mathematically as: $\text{cost}(\mathcal{S}, C) = \sum_{i=1}^{k} \sum_{s \in \mathcal{S}_i} D_\varphi(c(\mathcal{S}_i), s)$.

Furthermore, Banerjee et al. gave a crucial importance property of centroid point in [6].

Lemma 2.1. *Let D_φ be a μ-similar Bregman divergence on domain $\mathbb{X}$ and $\mathcal{S} \subseteq \mathbb{R}^d$ be a set of n-point. For all $s \in \mathcal{S}$, we have*

$$\text{cost}(\mathcal{S}, s) = \text{cost}(\mathcal{S}, c(\mathcal{S})) + nD_\varphi(c(\mathcal{S}), s)$$

It is well known that the dissimilarity measure as squared Euclidean distance satisfy the triangle inequality (i.e, there may exist $a, b, c \in \mathcal{S}$ with $D_{l_2^2}(a, c) > D_{l_2^2}(a, b) + D_{l_2^2}(b, c)$)and also symmetric. Unfortunately, it is not difficult to find that a μ-similar Bregman divergences does not obey the triangle inequality. As expected, Ackermann et al. [1] obtained that μ-similar Bergman divergences feature via the approximate metric properties in the following lemma.

Lemma 2.2. *Let D_φ be a μ-similar Bregman divergence on domain $\mathcal{S}$. For all $a, b, c \in \mathcal{S}$ we have*

$$D_\varphi(a, c) \leq 1/\mu D_\varphi(c, a)$$
$$D_\varphi(a, c) \leq 2/\mu D_\varphi(a, b) + 2/\mu D_\varphi(b, c)$$
$$D_\varphi(a, c) \leq 2/\mu D_\varphi(a, b) + 2/\mu D_\varphi(c, b)$$
$$D_\varphi(a, c) \leq 2/\mu D_\varphi(b, a) + 2/\mu D_\varphi(b, c)$$
$$D_\varphi(a, c) \leq 2/\mu D_\varphi(b, a) + 2/\mu D_\varphi(c, b),$$

where $0 \leq \mu \leq 1$.

From the above lemma, we know that μ-similar Bergman divergences are approximately symmetric within a factor of $O(1/\mu)$ and satisfy the triangle inequality within a factor of $O(1/\mu)$. The following lemma is also helpful for the analysis of our results generalizing the work in [9].

Lemma 2.3. *Let $\varepsilon > 0$, $a, b \in \mathbb{R}^d$ and $C \subseteq \mathbb{R}^d$ is a set of k centers. Then*

$$\mid \text{cost}(a, C) - \text{cost}(b, C) \mid \leq \frac{\varepsilon}{\mu} D_\varphi(a, C) + \frac{1}{\mu}(1 + 1/\varepsilon) D_\varphi(a, b).$$

Algorithm 1. BregMeans++ with local search

Input: A data point set $\mathcal{S} \subseteq \mathbb{R}^d$ with n points, integer k, M and $C = \phi$.
Output: An approximate Bregman k-means++ solution C for $\mathcal{S}$.
1: Sample the first center c_1 uniformly at random from $\mathcal{S}$ and set $C = C \cup c_1$.
2: **for** $i = 1$ to k **do**
3:     Sample the center $c_i = s' \in \mathcal{S}$ with probability $\frac{D_\varphi(s',C)}{\text{cost}(\mathcal{S},C)}$.
4:     $C \leftarrow C \cup c_i$.
5: **end for**
6: **for** $i = 1$ to N **do**
7:     Set $C := \text{LocalSearch}(\mathcal{S}, C)$.
8: **end for**

Algorithm 2. LocalSearch

Input: Data set $\mathcal{S}$ and center set C
Output: C
1: Sample the center $s' \in \mathcal{S}$ with probability $\frac{D_\varphi(s',C)}{\text{cost}(\mathcal{S},C)}$.
2: **if** $\exists\, c_i \in C$ s.t. $\text{cost}(\mathcal{S}, C \setminus c_i \cup s') < \text{cost}(\mathcal{S}, C)$ **then**
3:     Compute $(c_i) := \arg\min_{c_i \in C} \text{cost}(\mathcal{S}, C \setminus c_i \cup s')$.
4:     $C \leftarrow C \setminus c_i \cup s'$.
5: **else**
6:     $C \leftarrow C$.
7: **end if**

---

3   The μ-similar BregMeans++ Algorithm via Local Search

In this section, we mainly introduce the BregMeans++ algorithm based on local search for μ-BKMP, which is essentially k-means++ seeding combining with the local search strategy. We prove that the approach is also applicable to μ-similar Bregman k-means clusterings. The formal algorithm is presented in Algorithm 1.

The BregMeans++ algorithm starts with an empty solution C and choose the first center c_1 uniformly at random from $\mathcal{S}$. Recall that $\text{cost}(s', C)$ denotes the shortest distance from a data point $\mathcal{S}$ to the closest center we have already chosen. The remaining centers will be selected iteratively at random from $\mathcal{S}$ with a direction proportional to $\text{cost}(s', C)$, until the size of the initial clustering C attains k. If $|C| < k$, we add the chosen point to C; Otherwise the algorithm calls a local search subroutine(see Algorithm 2) to update the clustering by the single swap operation. The main idea of the local search method is based on improving the current solution iteratively until the clustering remains unchanged. The formal local search method is presented in Algorithm 2. If there exists a point $c_i \in C$ such that $\text{cost}(P, C \setminus c_i \cup s') < \text{cost}(P, C)$, we find from $\mathcal{S}$ a new point s' that reduces the cost function as much as possible and use it to replace c_i. For briefness, we denote such a single swap operation by $swap(c_i, s')$.

Our main result is that the expected approximation guarantee is $O(1)$. The main result of the paper attained by BregMeans++ with local search can be stated as below.

Theorem 3.1. *Let D_φ be a μ-similar Bregman divergence, $\mathcal{S} \subseteq \mathbb{R}^d$ be a set of n-point and C be the output of Algorithm 1. When using parameter $N \geq 100000k \log \log k$, Algorithm 1 runs in time $O(dnk^2 \log \log k)$, and produces μ-BKMP that satisfies $E[\text{cost}(\mathcal{S}, C)] \leq 516\text{cost}(\mathcal{S}, O^*)$, where O^* is the set of optimum centers.*

Proof (Sketch). Algorithm 1 is in fact k-means++ combining with $O(k \log \log k)$ rounds of local search. Before analyzing the running time of the whole algorithm, we shall focus on two crucial processes.

In the initial centers set sampling phase, that is performing the first for loop in Algorithm 1 repeatedly to construct a feasible solution. In every iteration, before we make a decision whether to add a new point to the set of current centers, we need to compute the distance from the new center to over all points in $\mathcal{S}$. If the new distance is smaller than the currently nearest center, add it to C. So we choose a new point at random according to D_φ and update the center set with probability proportional to $D_\varphi(s', C_i), i = 1, \cdots, k$. it means that for all $s' \in \mathcal{S}$, we have $\Pr[c_i = s' \mid c_1, \cdots, c_{i-1} \text{ already sampled}] = \frac{D_\varphi(s', C)}{\text{cost}(\mathcal{S}, C)}$. The sampling scheme is repeated until we have chosen such k points. Therefore, it can be done in linear time, to be more specific in $O(dn)$ time.

In the local search phase, we should decrease the cost function to an extreme by $swap(c_i, s')$ for each swap operation. In order to maintain a set of k centers, intuitively, the swap operation consists of insertions point and deletions of cluster centers. If there is no improving swap, we delete the sampled center. Therefore, it is necessary to calculate the change of swapping cost between the new center s' and the old center, i.e. $\text{cost}(P, C \setminus c_i \cup s')$. To guarantee the polynomial runtime, we require that all candidate centers be selected from $\mathcal{S}$. This requires to traverse over all clusters. Thus, a local search step requires $O(dkn)$ time in the worst case, which leads to an overall running time of $O(dnk^2 \log \log k)$. Furthermore, after $O(k \log \log k)$ iterations, our solution is expected a constant factor larger than the optimal solution.

Our general proof strategy is inspired by [12,14]. The details of proof will be given in the journal version.

4 Proof of the Main Result

In this section, we will introduce some definitions and notations to analyze the local search procedure which is starting from an initial feasible solution and is iteratively improved by single swaps. Given a feasible solution C and an optimal solution O^*, the optimal solution is apparently unique. Moreover, without loss of generality, we assume that $\mid S \mid = \mid O^* \mid = k$. For all $i, 1 \leq i \leq k$, the corresponding clustering and the k-partition are represented as $\mathcal{S}_i$ and O_i^*, respectively.

For each optimal center $o^* \in O^*$, we say that o^* is captured by a center in C, if c is the center closest to o^* among all centers in C. If $c \in C$ captures only one center $o^* \in O^*$, we consider a swap $swap(c, o^*)$. It means that we choose one center c to delete from the current set C, and select one point o^* to add to the current set of centers. Afterward, we reassign each point to its nearest center. If there are l such swaps, then there are $k - l$ elements left in C and in O^*. Some of the remaining elements of C may capture at least two centers of O^*. Also note that some centers in S do not capture any optimal centers in O^*.

We shall use the above information to analyze the swaps. Let E be the subset of indices of cluster centers from $C = \{c_1, \cdots, c_k\}$ that capture exactly one optimal cluster from O^*. It is easy to verify that the corresponding points can be used as a candidate center for this cluster. In this case, if $c_e (e \in E)$ is far away from the center of the optimal cluster, then we are likely to sample a point near the center with high probability. Meanwhile, we also need to assign all points in the cluster of c_e that are not in the captured optimal cluster to a different center without significantly increasing their contribution. The reassignment cost incurred in the context will be calculated as $R(c_e) = \text{cost}(\mathcal{S} \backslash O_e^*, C \backslash c_e) - \text{cost}(\mathcal{S} \backslash O_e^*, C)$.

Analogously, we call a center lonely when it is not captured by any optimal centers. The subset of all lonely centers in $\mathcal{S}$ is denoted by L. Let O_l^* be the cluster in the optimal solution captured by c_l. In this case, c_l can be moved to a different cluster. However, we instead sample a point from other clusters with high probability such that the reassignment cost is much less than the improvement for this cluster. The reassignment cost of c_l due to a swap is defined as $R(c_l) = \text{cost}(\mathcal{S}, C \backslash c_l) - \text{cost}(\mathcal{S}, C)$.

Furthermore, we can estimate the cost of the reassignment points through the following lemma:

Lemma 4.1. *For $m \in E \cup L$, we have*

$$R(c_m) = \frac{21}{100\mu^2} \text{cost}(\mathcal{S}_m, C) + \frac{24}{\mu^2} \text{cost}(\mathcal{S}_m, O^*).$$

The above lemma gives an upper bound for the reassignment, as the reassignment may not be optimal following the construction of the proof. Hence, we need to give a good bound on the reassignment cost with high probability. On one hand, for $e \in E$, we can replace e with any point near the optimal cluster center of the optimal cluster captured by e, which significantly increases the cost of the solution. Let $T = \{1, \cdots, k\} \backslash E$ be representing the index set of optimal cluster centers that were captured by centers. On the other, for $l \in L$, we focus on the centers $t \in T$ to remove an arbitrary center $l \in L$ and insert a new center close to one of the optimal centers of O_t^* for some $t \in T$, for the sake of improving the cost of the solution. We treat such clusters as good clusters and try to find the corresponding indexes. The precise definition of the concept is given as follows.

Definition 4.1 *(Good and Bad Center Indexes). A cluster center index $i \in \{1, \cdots, k\}$ is called good, if there exists a center index $e \in E$ such that*

$$\text{cost}(O_e^*, C) - R(c_e) - \frac{9}{\mu^2}\text{cost}(O_e^*, o_e^*) > \frac{1}{100k\mu^2}\text{cost}(\mathcal{S}, C),$$

or $T = \{1, \cdots, k\} \setminus E$ holds and there exists a center index $l \in L$ such that

$$\text{cost}(O_i^*, C) - R(c_l) - \frac{9}{\mu^2}\text{cost}(O_i^*, o_i^*) > \frac{1}{100k\mu^2}\text{cost}(\mathcal{S}, C).$$

Otherwise, the cluster center index is called bad.

Based on the above definition, we will calculate the cost of replacing an old point by a new sample point. It is not difficult to find the cost sum of good clusters is large and further show that sampling such a cluster with high probability. We still category all good clusters into two classes and calculate the total costs of good clusters individually.

Consider the case of $3\sum_{e \in E}\text{cost}(O_e, C) > \text{cost}(\mathcal{S}, C)$, where C is the set of center points corresponding to the current solution. Recall that for every $e \in E$ the optimal center is captured by c_e is c_e^*. For $e \in E$, by definition we can compute the gain of replacing c_e by a point close to the center of O_e^* and assigning all points in O_e^* to the new center. Without loss of generality, we abbreviate the facts e is a good or bad index in E as e_g or e_b, respectively.

Lemma 4.2. *For $e \in E$ and $0 < \mu \leq 1$, if $3\sum_{e \in E}\text{cost}(O_e^*, C) > \text{cost}(\mathcal{S}, C) > 500opt_k$, we have*

$$25\mu^2\sum_{e_g \in E}\text{cost}(O_{e_g}^*, C) \geq \text{cost}(\mathcal{S}, C),$$

where e_g is good index in E.

From the above lemma, we know that the total cost of good cluster is large. Nevertheless, we can further consider sampling points near the optimal center with high probability to get an approximation of the cost of the cluster.

Lemma 4.3. *Let $G \subseteq \mathbb{R}^d$ be a cluster and $C \subseteq \mathbb{R}^d$ be a set of k centers w.r.t the current solution, if $\text{cost}(G, C) \geq \delta\text{cost}(G, c(G))$, then*

$$\frac{\text{cost}(R, C)}{\text{cost}(G, c(G))} \geq \frac{\mu(\delta - 1)}{8}$$

where $\delta \geq 17$ and $R \subseteq G$ s.t. $D_\varphi(c(G), R) \leq 2\mu\frac{\text{cost}(G, c(G))}{|G|}$.

Next, consider the other case, $3\sum_{e \in E}\text{cost}(O_e, C) \leq \text{cost}(\mathcal{S}, C)$, where C is the set of center points corresponding to the current solution. Recall that $T = $

$\{1, \cdots, k\} \setminus E$, therefore $\sum_{t \in T} \text{cost}(O_t^*, C) \geq \frac{2}{3}\text{cost}(\mathcal{S}, C)$ holds. For $l \in L$, we can estimate the cost of removing l and inserting a new cluster center close to the center of O_i^* by considering a clustering that reassigns the points in O_i^* and assigns all points in O_i^* to the new center. In fact, we will prove the cost sum of good clusters is large in the lemma below. For any $t \in T$, we use t_g to denote the index t is good, and use t_b for otherwise.

Lemma 4.4. Let $T = \{1, \cdots, k\} \setminus E$, $t \in T$ and $0 < \mu \leq 1$, if $3 \sum_{e \in E} \text{cost}(O_e^*, C) \leq \text{cost}(\mathcal{S}, C)$ and $\text{cost}(\mathcal{S}, C) \geq 500opt_k$, we have

$$20\mu^2 \sum_{t_g \in T} \text{cost}(O_{e_g}^*, C) \geq \text{cost}(\mathcal{S}, C)$$

where t_g is good index in T.

Combining the above lemmas, we can eventually prove the following lemma, and then prove the main theorem.

Lemma 4.5. Let $\mathcal{S}$ be a set of points and $C \subseteq \mathcal{S}$ be the centers set with $\mid C \mid = k$ and $\text{cost}(\mathcal{S}, C) \geq 500opt_k$. Let $C' = LocalSearch(\mathcal{S}, C)$ then $\text{cost}(\mathcal{S}, C') \leq (1 - \frac{1}{100k\mu^2})\text{cost}(\mathcal{S}, C)$ with probability $\frac{1}{1000}$.

After the above analysis, we argue that the μ-similar BregMeans++ seeding algorithm via local search reduces the cost of the current solution by a $1 - \frac{1}{100k\mu^2}$ factor in every iteration with probability $\frac{1}{1000}$. That is, after $O(k \log \log k)$ iterations we can eventually obtain our main result.

5   Conclusions

In this paper, we devised a direct approximation algorithm for μ-BKMP by employing the local search scheme, achieving a constant approximation factor. The algorithm essentially generalized the previous k-means++ algorithm with local search due to Lattanzi and Sohler [14], which solved the k-means problem in squared Euclidean distance. The generalization observed that μ-similar Bergman divergences satisfy the triangle inequality within a factor of $O(1/\mu)$, which is different from the Euclidean distance measure. Challenges remains on μ-BKMP such as develop a direct algorithm with a smaller approximation ratio for the μ-BKMP. Moreover, it is an interesting problem to reduce the number of local search steps but meanwhile retain the approximation ratio.

Acknowledgements. The first and second authors are supported by National Natural Science Foundation of China (Nos. 11871081, 11531014). The third author is supported by National Natural Science Foundation of China (No. 61772005), and the fourth author is supported by National Natural Science Foundation of China (No. 11701150).

References

1. Ackermann, M.R.: Algorithms for the Bregman k-Median Problem. Doctoral Dissertation, Department of Computer Science, University of Paderborn (2009)
2. Ackermann, M.R., Blömer, J.: Coresets and approximate clustering for Bregman divergences. In: Proceedings of SODA, pp. 1088–1097 (2009)
3. Ackermann, M.R., Blömer, J., Sohler, C.: Clustering for metric and non-metric distance measures. ACM Trans. Algorithms **6**(4), 1–26 (2010)
4. Arthur, D., Vassilvitskii, S.: k-means++: the advantages of careful seeding. In: Proceedings of SODA, pp. 1027–1035 (2007)
5. Banerjee, A., Guo, X., Wang, H.: On the optimality of conditional expectation as a Bregman predictor. IEEE Trans. Inf. Theory **51**(7), 2664–2669 (2005)
6. Banerjee, A., Merugu, S., Dhillon, I.S., Ghosh, J.: Clustering with Bregman divergences. J. Mach. Learn. Res. **6**, 1705–1749 (2005)
7. Bregman, L.M.: The relaxation method of finding the common points of convex sets and its application to the solution of problems in convex programming. USSR Comput. Math. Math. Phys. **7**, 200–217 (1967)
8. Censor, Y., Lent, A.: An iterative rowaction method for interval convex programming. J. Optim. Theory Appl. **34**(3), 321–353 (1981)
9. Feldman, D., Schmidt, M., Sohler, C.: Turning big data into tiny data: constant-size coresets for k-means, PCA and projective clustering. arXiv preprint arXiv: 1807.04518 (2018)
10. Jain, A.K., Dubes, R.C.: Algorithms for Clustering Data. Prentice Hall, New Jersey (1988)
11. Jain, A.K., Murty, M.N., Flynn, P.J.: Data clustering: a review. ACM Comput. Surv. **31**, 264–323 (1999)
12. Kanungo, T., Mount, D.M., Netanyahu, N.S., Piatko, C.D., Silverman, R., Wu, A.Y.: A local search approximation algorithm for k-means clustering. In: Proceedings of SoCG, pp. 10–18 (2002)
13. Kumar, A., Sabharwal, Y., Sen, S.: A simple linear time $(1 + \varepsilon)$-approximation algorithm for k-means clustering in any dimensions. In: Proceedings of FOCS, pp. 454–462 (2004)
14. Lattanzi, S., Sohler, C.: A better k-means++ algorithm via local search. In: Proceedings of ICML, pp. 3662–3671 (2019)
15. Lloyd, S.: Least squares quantization in PCM. IEEE Trans. Inf. Theory **28**(2), 129–137 (1982)

Approximating Maximum Acyclic Matchings by Greedy and Local Search Strategies

Julien Baste, Maximilian Fürst, and Dieter Rautenbach[✉]

Institute of Optimization and Operations Research, Ulm University, Ulm, Germany
{julien.baste,maximilian.fuerst,dieter.rautenbach}@uni-ulm.de

Abstract. A matching M in a graph G is acyclic if the subgraph of G induced by the vertices that are incident to an edge in M is a forest. Even restricted to graphs of bounded maximum degree, the maximum acyclic matching problem is hard. We contribute efficient approximation algorithms for this problem, based on greedy and local search strategies, that have performance guarantees involving the maximum degree of the input graphs.

Keywords: Acyclic matching · Induced matching · Greedy algorithm · Local search

1 Introduction

We study efficient approximation algorithms for the following problem:

MAXIMUM ACYCLIC MATCHING
Instance: A graph G.
Task: Determine an acyclic matching in G of maximum size.

Our contributions are based on greedy and local search strategies and have performance guarantees that involve the maximum degree of the input graphs. Before we discuss our contributions and related results, we recall some terminology. We consider finite, simple, and undirected graphs. Let M be a matching in a graph G. The set of vertices of G incident to an edge in M is denoted by $V(M)$, and the subgraph of G induced by $V(M)$ is denoted by $G(M)$. If $G(M)$ is a forest, then M is an *acyclic* matching in G [10], and, if $G(M)$ is 1-regular, then M is an *induced* matching in G [21]. If $\nu(G)$, $\nu_{ac}(G)$, and $\nu_s(G)$ denote the maximum size of a matching, an acyclic matching, and an induced matching in G, respectively, then, since every induced matching is acyclic, we have

$$\nu(G) \geq \nu_{ac}(G) \geq \nu_s(G).$$

Funded by the Deutsche Forschungsgemeinschaft (DFG, German Research Foundation) - 388217545.

D. Kim et al. (Eds.): COCOON 2020, LNCS 12273, pp. 542–553, 2020.
https://doi.org/10.1007/978-3-030-58150-3_44

In contrast to the matching number $\nu(G)$, which is a well known classical tractable graph parameter, both, the acyclic matching number $\nu_{ac}(G)$ as well as the induced matching number $\nu_s(G)$ are computationally hard [10,21]. In fact, the problem to find a maximum induced matching in a given graph of order n does not allow an efficient approximation algorithm with approximation factor $n^{1/2-\epsilon}$ for every positive ϵ, unless P=NP [18]. Furthermore, Chalermsook et al. [4] showed that, unless NP=ZPP, for every $\epsilon > 0$ and every sufficiently large Δ, there is no approximation algorithm with approximation factor $\Delta^{1-\epsilon}$ for determining a maximum induced matching in bipartite graphs of maximum degree at most Δ. As the following observation [6] shows that the induced matching number and the acyclic matching number are within a factor of 2 from each other, the same hardness of approximation results hold for MAXIMUM ACYCLIC MATCHING.

Observation 1. $\nu_s(G) \geq \frac{\nu_{ac}(G)}{2}$ *for every graph* G.

Proof. If M is a maximum acyclic matching in G, then contracting each edge from M within the forest $G(M)$ yields a forest F of order $|M|$. If I is a maximum independent set in F, then $|I| \geq \frac{|M|}{2}$, and uncontracting the edges in I yields an induced matching of size $\frac{\nu_{ac}(G)}{2}$. $\qquad\square$

Altogether, it is unlikely that MAXIMUM ACYCLIC MATCHING allows efficient approximation algorithms with approximation factors that are considerably better than the maximum degree of the input graphs.

Approximating maximum induced matchings has been intensely studied for regular graphs and graphs of bounded maximum degree [1,5,9,11,15,17,20,22]. Currently, the best general results for the maximum induced matching problem are polynomial time approximation algorithms with approximation factors

- $0.75\Delta + 0.15$ for Δ-regular graphs [11], and
- $0.97995\Delta + 0.5$ for graphs of maximum degree at most Δ [1].

By Observation 1, these algorithms approximate MAXIMUM ACYCLIC MATCHING with factors that are twice as large. For the weighted version of maximum induced matching, Lin et al. [17] obtained an approximation factor of Δ for graphs of maximum degree at most Δ.

For MAXIMUM ACYCLIC MATCHING, some simple approximation algorithms are already known. Baste and Rautenbach [2] showed that one can find in polynomial time an acyclic matching of size at least $\frac{m}{\Delta^2}$ in a given graph of size m and maximum degree at most Δ. Fürst and Rautenbach [7] improved this to $\frac{m}{6}$ for connected subcubic graphs G of order at least 7. A simple edge counting yields the following upper bound.

Observation 2. *If G is a Δ-regular graph with m edges for some Δ at least 2, then* $\nu_{ac}(G) \leq \frac{m-1}{2(\Delta-1)}$.

Proof. If M is an acyclic matching, then $m(G(M)) \leq 2|M| - 1$. Since there are $2\Delta|M| - 2m(G(M))$ edges in G between $V(M)$ and $V(G) \setminus V(M)$, we obtain $m \geq 2\Delta|M| - 2m(G(M)) + m(G(M)) = 2\Delta|M| - m(G(M)) \geq 2\Delta|M| - 2|M| + 1$, which implies the stated upper bound. $\qquad\square$

Combining the above size guarantees from [2,7] with this upper bound yields polynomial time approximation algorithms for MAXIMUM ACYCLIC MATCHING with approximation factors

- $0.5\Delta + 0.5 + \frac{1}{2\Delta - 2}$ for Δ-regular graphs, and
- $\frac{3}{2}$ for cubic graphs.

Efficient exact algorithms for MAXIMUM ACYCLIC MATCHING are known only for certain graph classes; chain graphs and bipartite permutation graphs [19], P_5-free graphs and $2P_3$-free graphs [6,8], and chordal graphs [2]. Even graphs realizing extreme values are hard to recognize; while the equality $\nu(G) = \nu_s(G)$ can be decided efficiently for a given graph G [3,16], it is NP-complete to decide whether $\nu(G) = \nu_{ac}(G)$ for a given bipartite graph G of maximum degree at most 4 [8], that is, the two matching numbers behave differently in this respect. Lower bounds on the induced matching number have been studied in [12–15].

Our contributions in the present paper are efficient approximation algorithms for MAXIMUM ACYCLIC MATCHING in graphs of maximum degree at most Δ with the following performance guarantees:

- Approximation factor Δ (cf. Observation 3).
- Asymptotic approximation factor $\Delta - 1$ (cf. Corollary 1).
- Approximation factor $\frac{2(\Delta+1)}{3}$ (cf. Theorem 2).

The first two of these factors actually relate the size of the produced acyclic matching to the size of a maximum (not necessarily acyclic) matching.

Furthermore, combining greedy and local search strategies, we obtain an efficient algorithm that returns, for a given graph of order n, maximum degree at most Δ, and no isolated vertex, an acyclic matching of size at least

$$(1 - o(1))\frac{6n}{\Delta^2}.$$

Before we present our results in detail, we collect some more notation. Let G be a graph. The distance in G between two edges uv and xy of G is the minimum number of edges of a path in G between the two sets $\{u,v\}$ and $\{x,y\}$. In particular, the distance between two edges is 0 if and only if the edges are identical or adjacent. For an edge e of G, let $\delta_G(e)$ be the set of edges in $E(G)\backslash\{e\}$ that are adjacent to e, let $C_G(e)$ be the set of edges in $E(G) \backslash \{e\}$ that are at distance at most 1 to e, let $\delta_G[e] = \delta_G(e) \cup \{e\}$, and let $C_G[e] = C_G(e) \cup \{e\}$. For an integer Δ, let $[\Delta]$ be the set of positive integers that are at most Δ, and let $\mathcal{G}_\Delta$ be the set of graphs of maximum degree at most Δ.

2   Simple Greedy Algorithms

In this section we consider two greedy algorithms. The first algorithm ACM-COLOR greedily colors the edges of a maximum matching such that each color class is an acyclic matching, and returns the largest color class.

Observation 3. AcMColor *is a polynomial time approximation algorithm for* Maximum Acyclic Matching *in* $\mathcal{G}_\Delta$ *with approximation factor* Δ.

Proof. Since a maximum matching M for a given graph G can be determined efficiently, the statement follows immediately once we show that AcMColor determines a well defined function $f : M \to [\Delta]$ such that $f^{-1}(i)$ is an acyclic matching for each i in $[\Delta]$. Suppose, for a contradiction, that $f(e_i)$ is not well defined in line 4. This implies that there are at least two edges between e_i and each of the Δ sets $V\big(\{e_j : j \in [i-1] \text{ with } f(e_j) = k\}\big)$ for $k \in [\Delta]$. If $e_i = uv$, then this implies $d_G(u) + d_G(v) \geq 2\Delta + 2$, which is a contradiction. Hence, the function f is well defined. Since each of the sets $f^{-1}(i)$ is an acyclic matching by construction, and $\nu(G) \geq \nu_{ac}(G)$ the statement follows. $\qquad\square$

The proof of Observation 3 implies $\nu(G) \leq \Delta\nu_{ac}(G)$ for every graph G in $\mathcal{G}_\Delta$. Using Theorem 1, it is not difficult to show that $K_{\Delta,\Delta}$ is the only connected extremal graph for this inequality.

AcMColor
Input: A graph G from $\mathcal{G}_\Delta$.
Output: An acyclic matching in G.
1 **begin**
2   Determine a maximum matching $M = \{e_1, \ldots, e_\nu\}$ in G;
3   **for** $i = 1$ **to** ν **do**
4   Set $f(e_i)$ to the smallest k in $[\Delta]$ such that there is at most one edge between e_i and $V\big(\{e_j : j \in [i-1] \text{ with } f(e_j) = k\}\big)$;
5   **end**
6   **return** the largest of the sets $f^{-1}(1), \ldots, f^{-1}(\Delta)$;
7 **end**

Our second greedy algorithm AcMGreedy(G, M) is recursive, and iteratively selects edges from a given matching M in such a way as to minimize the number of edges between the selected edges and the rest of the graph G.

Theorem 1. *Let G be a graph of maximum degree at most Δ for some $\Delta \geq 3$, let M be a matching in G, and let* AcMGreedy *executed on the pair (G, M) return M_{ac}.*

(i) If $G(M)$ has no Δ-regular component, then $|M_{ac}| \geq \frac{|M|}{\Delta - 1}$.

(ii) If G is connected, then $|M_{ac}| \geq \frac{|M| - 1}{\Delta - 1}$.

Proof. (i) The proof is by induction on the number of recursive calls, say k, of AcMGreedy(G, M). Possibly replacing G with $G(M)$, we may assume that M is perfect. Since G has no Δ-regular component, some vertex in $V(M')$ has degree less than Δ in line 3 of AcMGreedy. Together with the fact that $G(M')$ is a tree, this implies that the number m of edges of G between $V(M')$ and $V(G) \setminus V(M')$ satisfies $m \leq \sum\limits_{u \in V(M')} d_G(u) - 2m(G(M')) \leq \big(2\Delta|M'| - 1\big) -$
$2(2|M'|-1) = 2(\Delta-2)|M'|+1$ throughout the entire execution of AcMGreedy.

By the condition for the **while** loop, every edge in M'' is joined to $V(M')$ by at least 2 edges in line 7, which implies $|M'| + |M''| \leq |M'| + \left\lfloor \frac{2(\Delta-2)|M'|+1}{2} \right\rfloor = (\Delta - 1)|M'|$.

If $k = 1$, then M''' in line 7 is empty, which implies $|M| = |M' \cup M''|$, and, hence, $|M'| \geq \frac{|M|}{\Delta-1}$. Since M' is an acyclic matching in G, this implies the base case of the induction. Now, let $k > 1$. Clearly, no component of $G(M''')$ is Δ-regular. By induction, it follows that $\textsc{AcMGreedy}\big(G(M'''), M'''\big)$ is an acyclic matching in $G(M''')$ of size at least $\frac{|M|-(|M'|+|M''|)}{\Delta-1}$. Since there are no edges between $V(M')$ and $V(M''')$, $\textsc{AcMGreedy}$ returns an acyclic matching in G in line 11 of size at least $|M'| + \frac{|M|-(|M'|+|M''|)}{\Delta-1} \geq \frac{|M'|+|M''|}{\Delta-1} + \frac{|M|-(|M'|+|M''|)}{\Delta-1} = \frac{|M|}{\Delta-1}$, which completes the proof of (i).

(ii) By (i), we may assume that M is perfect, and that G is Δ-regular. The upper bound on m, as determined within (i), worsens by 1, that is, we only have $m \leq 2(\Delta - 2)|M'| + 2$. This implies $|M'| + |M''| \leq |M'| + \left\lfloor \frac{2(\Delta-2)|M'|+2}{2} \right\rfloor = (\Delta - 1)|M'| + 1$. Since no component of $G(M''')$ is Δ-regular, we obtain, by (i), that $\textsc{AcMGreedy}$ returns an acyclic matching in G in line 11 of size at least $|M'| + \frac{|M|-(|M'|+|M''|)}{\Delta-1} \geq \frac{|M'|+|M''|-1}{\Delta-1} + \frac{|M|-(|M'|+|M''|)}{\Delta-1} = \frac{|M|-1}{\Delta-1}$.   □

$\textsc{AcMGreedy}(G, M)$
Input: A graph G and a matching M in G.
Output: An acyclic maximum in G that is a subset of M.

```
1  begin
2  |    Choose uv ∈ M minimizing d_G(u) + d_G(v);
3  |    M' ← {uv};
4  |    while ∃u'v' ∈ M \ M' : G(M' ∪ {u'v'}) is a tree do
5  |    |    M' ← M' ∪ {u'v'};
6  |    end
7  |    M'' ← ( ⋃_{u'v'∈M'} C_G(u'v') ) \ M';  M''' ← M \ (M' ∪ M'');
8  |    if M''' = ∅ then
9  |    |    return M';
10 |    else
11 |    |    return M'∪ AcMGreedy( G(M'''), M''' );
12 |    end
13 end
```

Combining a maximum matching algorithm with $\textsc{AcMGreedy}$ yields the following.

Corollary 1. Maximum Acyclic Matching *in* $\mathcal{G}_\Delta$ *has an efficient approximation algorithm with asymptotic approximation factor* $\Delta - 1$.

Theorem 1 implies the Brooks type inequality $\nu(G) \leq (\Delta - 1)\nu_{ac}(G) + 1$ for every graph G of maximum degree at most Δ. We conjecture that $K_{\Delta,\Delta}$ is the only extremal graph for this inequality. For $\Delta = 3$, this follows from the main result of [7]. If we restrict the acyclic matchings to subsets of some given maximum matching, then there are more extremal configurations, cf. Figure 1 for an example, which generalizes to larger maximum degrees.

Fig. 1. A graph G of maximum degree 3 that has a perfect matching M indicated by the dashed edges such that no acyclic matching in G that is a subset of M contains more than $\frac{|M|-1}{2}$ edges.

3   A Local Search Algorithm

In this section, we consider the following local search algorithm.

AcM-k-LocalSearch
Input: A graph G.
Output: An acyclic matching M in G.
begin
$\quad$ $M \leftarrow \emptyset$;
$\quad$ **while** *there is a set M_{in} of at most k edges in G and a subset M_{out} of* M *such that* $(M \setminus M_{\mathrm{out}}) \cup M_{\mathrm{in}}$ *is an acyclic matching in G that is larger than M* **do**
$\quad\quad$ $M \leftarrow (M \setminus M_{\mathrm{out}}) \cup M_{\mathrm{in}}$;
$\quad$ **end**
$\quad$ **return** M;
end

Note that the set M_{out} in each iteration of AcM-k-LocalSearch must be strictly smaller than M_{in}, which implies that AcM-k-LocalSearch has polynomial running time for fixed k. For large values of k, the behavior of AcM-k-LocalSearch is hard to analyze, but for $k = 3$, we can nicely exploit the tree structure.

Theorem 2. AcM-3-LocalSearch *is a polynomial time approximation algorithm for* Maximum Acyclic Matching *in* $\mathcal{G}_\Delta$ *with approximation factor* $\frac{2(\Delta+1)}{3}$.

Proof. As observed above, AcM-3-LocalSearch has polynomial running time, and we only need to establish the performance guarantee. Therefore, let G be a graph of maximum degree at most Δ, let M be the acyclic matching in G returned by AcM-3-LocalSearch, and let M^* be a maximum acyclic matching in G. For an edge e in M^*, let

$$f(e) = 2\big|\delta_G[e] \cap M\big| + |\{e' \in \delta_G(e) : \delta_G(e') \cap (M \setminus \delta_G[e]) \neq \emptyset\}|,$$

see Fig. 2 for an illustration. Let $f(M^*) = \sum_{e \in M^*} f(e)$.

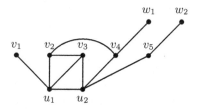

Fig. 2. We give the value of $f(u_1u_2)$ for different choices of M: If $M = \{v_4w_1\}$, then $f(u_1u_2) = 1$, if $M = \{u_1u_2\}$ or $M = \{v_2v_4\}$, then $f(u_1u_2) = 2$, if $M = \{u_1v_1, v_4w_1\}$ or $M = \{v_2v_3\}$, then $f(u_1u_2) = 3$, if $M = \{u_1v_1, u_2v_5, v_4w_1\}$ or $M = \{v_2v_3, v_4w_1, v_5w_2\}$, then $f(u_1u_2) = 5$.

Claim 1. $f(M^*) \leq 2\Delta|M|$.

Proof. We consider the contribution to $f(M^*)$ of each individual edge uv in M. Since M^* is a matching, we have $p \in \{0, 1, 2\}$ for $p = \big|\delta_G[uv] \cap M^*\big|$. If $p = 0$, then uv contributes 1 to each edge in M^* at distance exactly one to e. Since M^* is a matching, there are at most $|\delta_G(uv)|$ such edges, and, hence, the edge uv contributes at most $|\delta_G(uv)|$ to $f(M^*)$. If $p = 1$, then uv contributes 2 to $f(e)$, where e is the unique edge in $\delta_G[uv] \cap M^*$. Furthermore, the edge uv contributes 1 to each edge in M^* at distance exactly one to uv. Since there are at most $|\delta_G(uv)|$ such edges, the edge uv contributes at most $2 + |\delta_G(uv)|$ to $f(M^*)$. Finally, if $p = 2$, then $uv \notin M^*$, and u and v are incident to distinct edges in M^*, say e_u and e_v. The edge uv contributes 2 to $f(e_u)$ as well as to $f(e_v)$. Furthermore, the edge uv contributes 1 to each edge in M^* at distance exactly one to uv. In view of e_u and e_v, there are at most $|\delta_G(uv)| - 2$ such edges, and, hence, the edge uv contributes at most $2 + 2 + (|\delta_G(uv)| - 2)$ to $f(M^*)$. Altogether, the edge uv contributes at most $|\delta_G(uv)| + 2$ to $f(M^*)$. Since $|\delta_G(uv)| = d_G(u) + d_G(v) - 2 \leq 2\Delta - 2$, the claim follows. $\qquad\square$

If $f(e) \leq 1$ for some edge e in M^*, then $\delta_G[e]$ contains no edge from M, and there is at most one edge in G between e and $V(M)$. This implies the contradiction that $M \cup \{e\}$ is an acyclic matching in G. Therefore, we obtain that $f(e) \geq 2$ for every edge e in M^*, and, hence,

$$f(M^*) = \sum_{e \in M^*} f(e) \geq 2|M^*|. \tag{1}$$

Note that this inequality holds actually for every maximal acyclic matching, that is, for any output of ACM-1-LOCALSEARCH. Together with Claim 1 we obtain $|M| \geq \frac{|M^*|}{\Delta}$, that is, every maximal acyclic matching is within a factor of Δ from a maximum acyclic matching. In order to complete the proof, we bound the number of edges e in M^* with $f(e) = 2$. Therefore,

- let M_1^* be the set of edges e in M^* with $f(e) = 2$ and $|C_G[e] \cap M| = 1$, and
- let M_2^* be the set of the remaining edges e in $M^* \setminus M_1^*$ with $f(e) = 2$.

Since $|C_G[e] \cap M| \geq 1$ for every edge e in M^*, we have $|C_G[e] \cap M| \geq 2$ for every edge in M_2^*.

Claim 2. $|M_1^*| \leq |M|$.

Proof. Let the function $g : M_1^* \to M$ be such that $g(e)$ is the unique edge in $C_G[e] \cap M$ for every edge e in M_1^*. Suppose, for a contradiction, that g is not injective, that is, $g(e') = g(e'') = e$ for two distinct edges e' and e'' in M_1^* and some edge e in M. Note that e may coincide with e' or e''. Since $V(\{e', e''\})$ and $V(M \setminus \{e\})$ induce disjoint forests in G, and, by the definition of M_1^*, there is no edge in G between these two sets, it follows that $(M \setminus \{e\}) \cup \{e', e''\}$ is an acyclic matching in G, contradicting the choice of M. Hence, the function g is injective, which completes the proof. $\square$

Claim 3. $|M_2^*| \leq |M|$.

Proof. Let uv be an edge in M_2^*. If $\delta_G[uv]$ intersects M, then the definition of f and $f(uv) = 2$ imply that the set $C_G[uv]$ contains a unique element from M, that is, the edge uv would belong to M_1^*. Hence, the set $\delta_G[uv]$ contains no edge from M; in particular, the two sets M and M_2^* are disjoint. Similarly, it follows that no edge in M has both of its endpoints in $(N_G(u) \cup N_G(v)) \setminus \{u, v\}$. Altogether, it follows that there are exactly two edges, say e_1 and e_2, in $\delta_G[uv]$ such that e_i is adjacent to an edge f_i from M for $i \in \{1, 2\}$, both edges f_1 and f_2 belong to $C_G(uv) \setminus \delta_G[uv]$, and the two edges f_1 and f_2 are uniquely determined and distinct.

Let the multigraph H arise from the subgraph of G induced by $V(M \cup M_2^*)$ by contracting the edges in $M \cup M_2^*$. We consider $M \cup M_2^*$ to be the vertex set of H in the obvious way. The above observations easily imply that H has no parallel edges, that is, the graph H is simple. Let H' be the bipartite subgraph of H that arises by removing all edges of H that lie within either M or M_2^*, that is, the graph H' has the two partite sets M and M_2^*. By the above observations, every vertex of H' from M_2^* has exactly two neighbors in H'.

We now prove that every component of H' is either a C_4 or a tree.

Suppose, for a contradiction, that H' has a component K that is neither a C_4 nor a tree. First, we assume that K contains a cycle $e_1 f_1 e_2 f_2 \ldots e_k f_k e_1$ of length $2k$ at least 6 with $e_1, \ldots, e_k \in M_2^*$ and $f_1, \ldots, f_k \in M$, where we consider indices modulo k. If e_i is not adjacent to e_{i+1} in H, then $V(M \setminus \{f_i\})$ induces a forest in G, there is exactly one edge in G between $V(M \setminus \{f_i\})$ and each of e_i and e_{i+1}, and no edge in G between e_i and e_{i+1}. This implies that

$(M \setminus \{f_i\}) \cup \{e_i, e_{i+1}\}$ is an acyclic matching in G, contradicting the choice of M. Hence, e_i is adjacent to e_{i+1} in H for every i, which implies the contradiction that the subgraph of G induced by $V(\{e_1, \ldots, e_k\})$ contains a cycle. It follows that K contains a C_4 but is distinct from this C_4. Let $e_1 f_1 e_2 f_2 e_1$ with $e_1, e_2 \in M_2^*$ and $f_1, f_2 \in M$ be the C_4, and let f_1 have a neighbor e_3 in M_2^* distinct from e_1 and e_2. The sets $V(\{e_1, e_2, e_3\})$ and $V(M \setminus \{f_1, f_2\})$ induce disjoint forests in G, and there is at most one edge in G between these two sets. It follows that $(M \setminus \{f_1, f_2\}) \cup \{e_1, e_2, e_3\}$ is an acyclic matching in G, contradicting the choice of M. Altogether, it follows that every component of H' is either a C_4 or a tree. If H' has q components that are trees, then the number of edges of H' equals $2|M_2^*|$ as well as $n(H') - q = |M_2^*| + |M| - q$, which implies $|M_2^*| \leq |M|$. $\qquad \square$

Combining the three claims, we obtain

$$2(\Delta + 1)|M| = 2\Delta|M| + 2|M| \geq f(M^*) + |M_1^* \cup M_2^*| \geq 3|M^*|,$$

which completes the proof of Theorem 2. $\qquad \square$

Figure 3 shows that there is an instance for which the acyclic matching returned by AcM-3-LocalSearch is a factor of $(2\Delta - 3)/4$ away from the acyclic matching number. Note that AcM-3-LocalSearch may greedily pick the four dashed edges, and then output these four edges. On the other hand, taking one of the dashed edges together with all horizontal edges that are not one of the dashed edges nor adjacent to one of them yields a maximum acyclic matching of size $2(\Delta - 2) + 1 = 2\Delta - 3$. It would be very interesting to know the true approximation factor of AcM-3-LocalSearch.

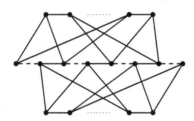

Fig. 3. An example where the output of AcM-3-LocalSearch is a factor of $(2\Delta - 3)/4$ away from the optimal solution.

4   Combining Greedy and Local Search

In this section we consider the recursive algorithm AcMExtend&Exchange that combines greedy and local search elements. Our goal is to show that this algorithm, executed on a graph G of order n, maximum degree at most Δ, and no isolated vertex, returns an acyclic matching in G of size at least

$$\frac{6n}{\Delta^2 + 12\Delta^{\frac{3}{2}}}. \tag{2}$$

In order to achieve this in an recursive/inductive way, AcMExtend&
Exchange chooses a non-empty acyclic matching M, constructs a *reduced graph*
G'_M from G by removing

- the set $N[M]$ of all vertices in $V(G)$ that have a neighbor in $V(M)$, and
- the set $I(M)$ of all isolated vertices in $G - N[M]$,

and returns $M \cup \text{AcMExtend\&Exchange}(G'_M)$.

> AcMExtend&Exchange(G)
> **Input:** A graph G.
> **Output:** An acyclic maximum M in G.
> 1 **begin**
> 2 | **if** $\Delta \leq 2$ **then**
> 3 | | **return** a maximum acyclic matching M;
> 4 | **end**
> 5 | $M \leftarrow \emptyset$;
> 6 | **if** $\exists uv \in E(G) : d_G(u) + d_G(v) \leq 2\sqrt{\Delta}$ **then**
> 7 | | Let $M = \{uv\}$ be such that $d_G(u) + d_G(v) \leq 2\sqrt{\Delta}$;
> 8 | | **return** $M \cup \text{AcMExtend\&Exchange}(G'_M)$;
> 9 | **end**
> 10 | **if** $S = \emptyset$, *where* $S := \{u \in V(G) : d_G(u) \leq \sqrt{\Delta}\}$ **then**
> 11 | | Let $M = \{uv\}$ be such that u has minimum degree in G;
> 12 | | **return** $M \cup \text{AcMExtend\&Exchange}(G'_M)$;
> 13 | **end**
> 14 | **if** $\max\{d_S(v) : v \in V(G)\} \notin [0.2\Delta, 0.8\Delta]$, *where* $d_S(v) := |N_G(v) \cap S|$
> | **then**
> 15 | | Choose a vertex v maximizing $d_S(v)$;
> 16 | | Choose a neighbor u of v minimizing $d_G(u)$;
> 17 | | $M \leftarrow \{uv\}$;
> 18 | | **return** $M \cup \text{AcMExtend\&Exchange}(G'_M)$;
> 19 | **end**
> 20 | **while** *there is a set M_{in} of at most 3 edges in G and a subset M_{out} of*
> | *M such that $M' = (M \setminus M_{\text{out}}) \cup M_{\text{in}}$ is a light $\circ K_1$-matching with*
> | *$w(M') > w(M)$* **do**
> 21 | | $M \leftarrow M'$, where M' is as in the **while**-condition;
> 22 | **end**
> 23 | **return** $M \cup \text{AcMExtend\&Exchange}(G'_M)$;
> 24 **end**

By construction, there are no edges between $V(M)$ and $V(G'_M)$, which implies
the correctness of AcMExtend&Exchange. In order to achieve the desired
guaranteed size (2) for the output, we show that the order of G'_M is not too
small. More precisely, we need to establish the inequality

$$|N[M]| + |I(M)| \leq \left(\frac{\Delta^2}{6} + 2\Delta^{\frac{3}{2}}\right)|M|. \tag{3}$$

In turn ACMEXTEND&EXCHANGE considers different ways of choosing M depending on properties of G. The most interesting and crucial choice leads to the notion of a *light* $\circ K_1$-*matching* defined as follows: Let S be the set of vertices of G of degree at most $\sqrt{\Delta}$, let N be the set of vertices that have a neighbor in S, and let $d_S(v) = |N_G(v) \cap S|$ for every vertex v in G. An acyclic matching M in G is a *light* $\circ K_1$-*matching* if

(i) M only contains edges with one endpoint in S,
(ii) every vertex in $V(M) \cap S$ has degree 1 in $G(M)$, and
(iii) every vertex v in $V(M) \cap N$ satisfies $d_S(v) \geq 0.2\Delta$.

The *weight* $w(M)$ of M is defined as $\sum\limits_{v \in V(M) \cap N} d_S(v)$.

The recursive steps within the **if**-statements in lines 2, 6, 10, and 14 ensure that $\Delta \geq 3$, $d_G(u) + d_G(v) > 2\sqrt{\Delta}$ for every edge uv of G, that S is non-empty, and that $\max\{d_S(v) : v \in V(G)\} \in [0.2\Delta, 0.8\Delta]$ in line 19, where we start the construction of a light $\circ K_1$-matching M, whose weight is maximized by local search exchanges. Since the weight is integral and polynomially bounded, there are only polynomially many iterations of the **while**-loop. Since G'_M always has strictly less vertices than G, the recursive depth is also polynomially bounded. Together, these two observations imply that ACMEX-TEND&EXCHANGE has polynomial running time. Therefore, in order to complete the proof of the following final result, omitted due to space restrictions, it suffices to verify condition (3) for each choice of M within ACMEXTEND&EXCHANGE.

Theorem 3. *Executed on a graph G of order n, maximum degree at most Δ, and no isolated vertex,* ACMEXTEND&EXCHANGE *returns in polynomial time an acyclic matching M in G with* $|M| \geq \frac{6n}{\Delta^2 + 12\Delta^{\frac{3}{2}}}$.

5   Conclusion

Our results suggest several interesting lines of further research. It would be very nice to obtain a tight analysis of ACM-3-LOCALSEARCH or to understand the performance of ACM-k-LOCALSEARCH for k larger than 3. The characterization of the extremal graphs for the Brooks type inequality $\nu(G) \leq (\Delta - 1)\nu_{ac}(G) + 1$ for G in $\mathcal{G}_\Delta$ is a nice graph theoretical problem. Finally, we believe that every graph G of order n, maximum degree at most Δ, and no isolated vertex has an acyclic matching of size at least $(1 - o(1))\frac{8n}{\Delta^2}$, which can be found efficiently.

References

1. Baste, J., Fürst, M., Rautenbach, D.: Linear programming based approximation for unweighted induced matchings – breaking the Δ barrier. arXiv:1812.05930
2. Baste, J., Rautenbach, D.: Degenerate matchings and edge colorings. Discret. Appl. Math. **239**, 38–44 (2018)
3. Cameron, K., Walker, T.: The graphs with maximum induced matching and maximum matching the same size. Discret. Math. **299**, 49–55 (2005)

4. Chalermsook, P., Laekhanukit, B., Nanongkai, D.: Independent set, induced matching, and pricing: connections and tight (subexponential time) approximation hardnesses. In: Proceedings of the 54th Annual Symposium on Foundations of Computer Science, FOCS '13, pp. 370–379 (2013)
5. Duckworth, W., Manlove, D.F., Zito, M.: On the approximability of the maximum induced matching problem. J. Discret. Algorithms **3**, 79–91 (2005)
6. Fürst, M.: Restricted matchings, Ph.D. thesis, Ulm University (2019)
7. Fürst, M., Rautenbach, D.: A lower bound on the acyclic matching number of subcubic graphs. Discret. Math. **341**, 2353–2358 (2018)
8. Fürst, M., Rautenbach, D.: On some hard and some tractable cases of the maximum acyclic matching problem. Ann. Oper. Res. **279**(1), 291–300 (2019). https://doi.org/10.1007/s10479-019-03311-1
9. Fürst, M., Leichter, M., Rautenbach, D.: Locally searching for large induced matchings. Theor. Comput. Sci. **720**, 64–72 (2018)
10. Goddard, W., Hedetniemi, S.M., Hedetniemi, S.T., Laskar, R.: Generalized subgraph-restricted matchings in graphs. Discret. Math. **293**, 129–138 (2005)
11. Ahuja, N., Baltz, A., Doerr, B., Přívětivý, A., Srivastav, A.: On the minimum load coloring problem. In: Erlebach, T., Persinao, G. (eds.) WAOA 2005. LNCS, vol. 3879, pp. 15–26. Springer, Heidelberg (2006). https://doi.org/10.1007/11671411_2
12. Henning, M.A., Rautenbach, D.: Induced matchings in subcubic graphs without short cycles. Discret. Math. **315**, 165–172 (2014)
13. Joos, F.: Induced matchings in graphs of bounded degree. SIAM J. Discret. Math. **30**, 1876–1882 (2016)
14. Joos, F.: Induced matchings in graphs of degree at most 4. SIAM J. Discret. Math. **30**, 154–165 (2016)
15. Joos, F., Rautenbach, D., Sasse, T.: Induced matchings in subcubic graphs. SIAM J. Discret. Math. **28**, 468–473 (2014)
16. Kobler, D., Rotics, U.: Finding Maximum induced matchings in subclasses of claw-free and P_5-free graphs, and in graphs with matching and induced matching of equal maximum size. Algorithmica **37**, 327–346 (2003)
17. Lin, M.C., Mestre, J., Vasiliev, S.: Approximating weighted induced matchings. Discret. Appl. Math. **243**, 304–310 (2018)
18. Orlovich, Y., Finke, G., Gordon, V., Zverovich, I.: Approximability results for the maximum and minimum maximal induced matching problems. Discret. Optim. **5**, 584–593 (2008)
19. Panda, B.S., Pradhan, D.: Acyclic matchings in subclasses of bipartite graphs. Discret. Math. Algorithms Appl. **4**, 1250050 (2012)
20. Rautenbach, D.: Two greedy consequences for maximum induced matchings. Theor. Comput. Sci. **602**, 32–38 (2015)
21. Stockmeyer, L.J., Vazirani, V.V.: NP-completeness of some generalizations of the maximum matching problem. Inf. Process. Lett. **15**, 14–19 (1982)
22. Zito, M.: Induced matchings in regular graphs and trees. In: Widmayer, P., Neyer, G., Eidenbenz, S. (eds.) WG 1999. LNCS, vol. 1665, pp. 89–101. Springer, Heidelberg (1999). https://doi.org/10.1007/3-540-46784-X_10

On the Complexity of Directed Intersection Representation of DAGs

Andrea Caucchiolo and Ferdinando Cicalese[(✉)] [iD]

Department of Computer Science, University of Verona, Verona, Italy
andrea.caucchiolo@studenti.univr.it, ferdinando.cicalese@univr.it
http://profs.scienze.univr.it/~cicalese/

Abstract. Motivated by the study of networks of web-pages generated by their information content, Kostochka et al. [ISIT 2019] introduced a novel notion of *directed intersection representation* of a (acyclic) directed graph and studied the problem of determining the *directed intersection number* of a digraph D, henceforth denoted by $DIN(D)$, defined as the minimum cardinality of a ground set $\mathcal{C}$ such that it is possible to assign to each vertex $v \in V(D)$ a subset $\varphi(v) \in \mathcal{C}$ such that $(u, v) \in E(D)$ if and only if the following two conditions hold: (i) $\varphi(v) \cap \varphi(u) \neq \emptyset$; (ii) $|\varphi(u)| < |\varphi(v)|$.

In this paper we show that determining $DIN(D)$ is NP-hard. We also show a 2-approximation algorithm for arborescences.

Keywords: Intersection number · Digraphs · NP-hardness · Approximation algorithms

1 Introduction

Every finite undirected graph can be represented by a family of finite sets associating each vertex to one of the sets of the family so that two vertices are adjacent if and only if their associated sets have non-empty intersection. In other words, every undirected graph is an *intersection graph* of finite sets. The *intersection number* of an undirected graph G, denoted $IN(G)$ is defined as the minimum cardinality of a set U such that G is the intersection graph of subsets of U. Erdős, Goodman and Posa [4] showed that the intersection number of a graph equals the minimum number of cliques needed to cover its edges, aka the size of a minimum edge clique cover of G. Determining the size of a minimum edge clique cover—and equivalently the intersection number—was proved to be NP-hard in [10] (see also [7]). By [8] both problems are not approximable within a factor of $|V|^\epsilon$ for some $\epsilon > 0$ unless $P = NP$. On the other hand, by the result of [5], it follows that computing the intersection number of a graph is fixed parameterized tractable (with respect to the intersection number as parameter).

Several analogues of the above concepts have been proposed for the case of directed graphs [1,2,9] that are based on the representation of a digraph by identifying each vertex v with a pair of subsets S_v, T_v of a ground set U, with

© Springer Nature Switzerland AG 2020
D. Kim et al. (Eds.): COCOON 2020, LNCS 12273, pp. 554–565, 2020.
https://doi.org/10.1007/978-3-030-58150-3_45

$(u, v) \in E$ if and only if $S_u \cap T_v \neq \emptyset$. In [2] a characterization is provided on the intersection number of a digraph, analogous to the one for undirected graphs given in [4].

Recently, motivated by the study of networks of web-pages generated by their information content, and cardinality dependent generative models of networks [3,11], Kostochka et al. [6] introduced a novel notion of *directed intersection representation* of a (acyclic) directed graph. In this model, an acyclic directed graph $D = (V(D), E(D))$ is represented by a family of subsets of a ground set $\mathcal{C}$ via an assignment $\varphi : V(D) \mapsto 2^{\mathcal{C}}$ such that $(u, v) \in E(D)$ if and only if $\varphi(u) \cap \varphi(v) \neq \emptyset$ and $|\varphi(u)| < |\varphi(v)|$.

The authors of [6] studied the problem of determining the corresponding notion of *directed intersection number* of a digraph D, denoted by $DIN(D)$ and defined as the minimum cardinality of a ground set $\mathcal{C}$ such that it is possible to assign to each vertex $v \in V(D)$ a subset $\varphi(v) \subseteq \mathcal{C}$ such that $(u, v) \in E(D)$ if and only if the following two conditions hold: (i) $\varphi(v) \cap \varphi(u) \neq \emptyset$; (ii) $|\varphi(u)| < |\varphi(v)|$.

The main results of [6] are about extremal values of $DIN(D)$ and precisely: (i) $DIN(D) \leq \frac{5n^2}{8} - \frac{3n}{4} + 1$ for every DAG D with n vertices; and (ii) for each n there exist DAGs D with n vertices with $DIN(D) \geq \frac{n^2}{2}$. These results, however, only bound the extremal approximation one can get in the worst possible case for a given size $n = |V(D)|$. Moreover, the tractability of the problem is left open. The authors limit themselves to observe that $DIN(D)$ is lower bounded by the length of the longest path in D, which is an easy problem on DAGs.

In this paper we show that determining $DIN(D)$ is in fact NP-hard. We also show a linear time 2-approximation algorithm for arborescences.

2   Notation and Basic Definitions

Given a DAG D, we use colouring as metaphor of intersection representation according to the definition of [6]. We say that $\varphi : V(D) \mapsto 2^{\mathcal{C}_\varphi}$ is a proper colouring (pc) of a DAG D if for each $u, v \in V(D)$ it holds that $(u, v) \in E(D)$ if and only if $\varphi(v) \cap \varphi(u) \neq \emptyset$ and $|\varphi(u)| < |\varphi(v)|$. We denote by $\Phi(D)$ the set of proper colourings of D. For a proper colouring φ, we denote by $|\varphi|$ the cardinality of the colour (ground) set $\mathcal{C}_\varphi$ and refer to $|\varphi| = |\mathcal{C}_\varphi|$ as the size of the colouring φ. We are interested in the problem of determining $DIN(D) = \min_{\varphi \in \Phi(D)} |\varphi|$.

For vertices u, v and colouring φ we will abuse notation and (whenever there is no risk of confusion) we will write $\varphi(u) < \varphi(v)$ (resp. $\varphi(u) \leq \varphi(v)$) to denote $|\varphi(u)| < |\varphi(v)|$ (resp. $|\varphi(u)| \leq |\varphi(v)|$). The notation $\varphi(u) = \varphi(v)$ (resp. $\varphi(u) \neq \varphi(v)$) will be reserved to indicate the set equality (resp. inequality).

For any integer $n \geq 1$ we shall use $[n]$ to denote the set $\{1, \ldots, n\}$.

3   The Hardness Proof

Let us consider the decision problems associated to the computation of the intersection number of an undirected graph and the computation of the directed intersection number of a DAG.

INTERSECTION NUMBER PROBLEM (INTNUMP)
Input: A graph $G = (V, E)$, and an integer bound k.
Question: Is $IN(G) \leq k$?

By the result in [4], showing that $IN(G) \leq V(G)^2/4$ for every G, we shall tacitly assume that for every instance of INTNUMP it holds that $k < n^2$.

DIRECTED INTERSECTION NUMBER PROBLEM (DIRINTNUMP)
Input: A directed acyclic graph $D = (V, E)$, and an integer bound k.
Question: Is $DIN(D) \leq k$?

In this section we are going to show that the computation of the directed intersection graph is NP-hard by providing a polynomial time reduction from INTNUMP to DIRINTNUMP.

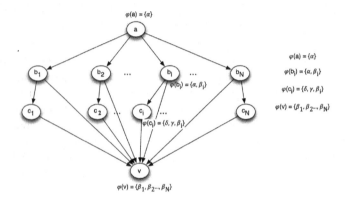

Fig. 1. An example of the gadget $\mathcal{V}_N$ which is used to fix the cardinality of the colour set of a vertex v. For $N > 3$, a proper colouring with $N+3$ colours $\{\alpha, \beta_1, \ldots, \beta_N, \gamma, \delta\}$ is: $\varphi(a) = \{\alpha\}, \varphi(b_i) = \{\alpha, \beta_i\}, \varphi(c_i) = \{\beta_i, \delta, \gamma\}$, and $\varphi(v) = \{\beta_1, \ldots, \beta_N\}$.

The Cardinality Gadget $\mathcal{V}_N$. As the main gadget of our reduction, we use several copies of a graph $\mathcal{V}_N$, that allows us to "force" the cardinality of the set of colours assigned to the vertices of the instance of the DIRINTNUMP problem.
Fix $N > 3$. Then, the set of vertices and edges of gadget $\mathcal{V}_N$ are as follows:

- $V(\mathcal{V}_N) = \{a, b_1, \ldots, b_N, c_1, \ldots, c_N, v\}$;
- $E(\mathcal{V}_N) = \{(a, b_i) \mid i = 1, \ldots N\} \cup \{(b_i, c_i) \mid i = 1, \ldots N\} \cup \{(b_i, v) \mid i = 1, \ldots N\} \cup \{(c_i, v) \mid i = 1, \ldots N\}$.

We start by collecting some useful properties on the *colourability* of this gadget. The structure of the gadget is exemplified in Fig. 1, where it is also shown that we can colour it with $N + 3$ colours (recall that, by definition, $N > 3$).
The following lemmas shows that $N + 3$ is also a lower bound on the number of colours necessary to properly colour $\mathcal{V}_N$.

Lemma 1. *For every proper colouring φ of $\mathcal{V}_N$ it holds that for each $i = 1, \ldots, N$, we have $\varphi(c_i) \setminus \cup_{j=1}^{i-1} \varphi(c_j) \neq \emptyset$.*

Proof. We argue by contradiction. Let i be the smallest value for which (contradicting the statement) it holds that $\varphi(c_i) \subseteq \bigcup_{j=1}^{i-1} \varphi(c_j)$.

Note that

$$\text{for each } j \neq k \text{ it holds that } \varphi(c_j) \not\subseteq \varphi(c_k). \tag{1}$$

For, otherwise, we would have $|\varphi(b_j)| < |\varphi(c_j)| \leq |\varphi(c_k)|$ and $\emptyset \neq \varphi(b_j) \cap \varphi(c_j) \subseteq \varphi(b_j) \cap \varphi(c_k)$, which is not possible because of the absence of an edge $b_j \to c_k$.

Under the hypothesis $\emptyset \neq \varphi(c_i) \subseteq \bigcup_{j=1}^{i-1} \varphi(c_j)$ we have that there are $j_1, \ldots, j_t \in \{1, \ldots, i-1\}$ such that for each $\ell = 1, \ldots, t$ we have $\varphi(c_i) \cap \varphi(c_{j_\ell}) \neq \emptyset$ and $\varphi(c_i) \subseteq \varphi(c_{j_1}) \cup \cdots \cup \varphi(c_{j_t})$. We have the following two possible cases:

1. For some ℓ it holds that $|\varphi(c_i)| \neq |\varphi(c_{j_\ell})|$. Hence, the difference in cardinality and the presence of non-empty intersection contradicts the absence of an edge between c_i and c_{j_ℓ}. So this case cannot happen.
2. For each $\ell = 1, \ldots, t$, it holds that $|\varphi(c_i)| = |\varphi(c_{j_\ell})|$. Hence, for each ℓ we have $|\varphi(b_i)| < |\varphi(c_i)| = |\varphi(c_{j_\ell})|$. Let $x \in (\varphi(b_i) \cap \varphi(c_i))$. Because of $\varphi(c_i) \subseteq \varphi(c_{j_1}) \cup \cdots \cup \varphi(c_{j_t})$ there is ℓ^* such that $x \in \varphi(c_{j_{\ell^*}})$. Hence $\varphi(b_i) \cap \varphi(c_{j_{\ell^*}}) \neq \emptyset$ which, together with the difference in cardinality contradicts the absence of the edge $b_i \to c_{j_{\ell^*}}$.

Since in both cases we reach a contradiction, the proof is complete. □

Lemma 2. *Every proper colouring of $\mathcal{V}_N$ uses at least $N + 3$ colours.*

Proof. Let φ be a proper colouring of $\mathcal{V}_N$. For each $i = 1, \ldots, N$, the existence of the path $a \to b_i \to c_i$, implies that $1 \leq \varphi(a) < \varphi(b_i) < \varphi(c_i)$, hence, in particular, we have $\varphi(c_1) \geq 3$. In addition, for each $i = 1, \ldots, N$, the fact that $\varphi(a) < \varphi(c_i)$ and the absence of an edge $a \to c_i$, we also have that $\varphi(a) \cap \varphi(c_i) = \emptyset$. Therefore, we have

$$|(\bigcup_{i=1}^N \varphi(c_i) \cup \varphi(a)| = |\bigcup_{i=1}^N \varphi(c_i)| + |\varphi(a)|. \tag{2}$$

Finally, using Lemma 1, we have

$$|\varphi(a) \cup (\bigcup_{i=1}^N \varphi(c_i))| = |\varphi(a)| + |\bigcup_{i=1}^N \varphi(c_i)| \geq 1 + |\bigcup_{i=1}^N \varphi(c_i)|$$

$$= 1 + |\varphi(c_1)| + \sum_{i=2}^N |\varphi(c_i) \setminus \bigcup_{j=1}^{i-1} \varphi(c_j)| \geq N + 3 \tag{3}$$

where the first equality follows from (2); the following inequality follows from $\varphi(a) \neq \emptyset$; the next equality follows by partitioning the union into distinct parts; the last inequality follows from $\varphi(c_1) \geq 3$ (proved above) and Lemma 1. □

We are now going to prove that in order to colour the gadget with $N + 3$ colours, it is necessary to colour the vertex v with at least N colours. We need to show some preliminary simple facts.

Fact 1. *If there exists i such that $|\varphi(b_i)| = 2$ then for each $j = 1, \ldots, N$ we have $|\varphi(b_j)| = 2$ and $\varphi(b_j) \cap \varphi(a) = \varphi(a)$.*

Proof. Since $2 = |\varphi(b_i)| > |\varphi(a)| > 0$, we have $|\varphi(a)| = 1$. Since for each j, it holds that $\emptyset \neq \varphi(a) \cap \varphi(b_j) \subseteq \varphi(a)$, we also have $\varphi(a) \cap \varphi(b_j) = \varphi(a)$. Therefore, for each $j \neq j'$ we have $\emptyset \neq \varphi(a) \subseteq \varphi(b_j) \cap \varphi(b_{j'})$, i.e., $\varphi(b_j)$ and $\varphi(b_{j'})$ have non-empty intersection. Hence we cannot have $|\varphi(b_j)| \neq |\varphi(b_{j'})|$, because otherwise the absence of an edge between b_j and $b_{j'}$ would imply that the colouring is not proper. □

Lemma 3. *If for some i it holds that $|\varphi(b_i)| = 2$ then $|\varphi(v)| \geq N$.*

Proof. By Fact 1, we have that for some colour x, it holds $\varphi(a) = \{x\}$ and for each $j = 1, \ldots, N$ we have $\varphi(b_j) = \{x, y_j\}$.

For each $j \neq j'$ we must have $y_j \neq y_{j'}$, for, otherwise, $\varphi(b_j) = \varphi(b_{j'})$ and, since the colouring is proper, this would contrast with the fact that we have an edge $b_{j'} \to c_{j'}$ but there is no edge $b_j \to c_{j'}$.

Since $\varphi(v)$ cannot contain x (for, otherwise, this would violate the absence of an edge from a to v), and $\varphi(v) \cap \varphi(b_j) \neq \emptyset$, we must have that for each j, $\varphi(v) \cap \varphi(b_j) = \{y_j\}$, and since these are all distinct colours, we have $|\varphi(v)| \geq N$.

The Path Gadget. The following lemma provides a lower bound on the number of colours necessary to properly colour a path $\mathcal{P} = s \to t_1 \to t_2 \to \cdots \to t_\ell$ (possibly part of a larger DAG, but, in this case, such that only the starting node is connected to the rest of the graph). The bound is given as a function of the length ℓ of the path and the cardinalities of a bipartition of the colouring $\varphi(s)$ into the colours that s shares with (possibly existing) nodes u such that $u \to s$ and the remaining colours of $\varphi(s)$.

Lemma 4. *Let ℓ be a positive integer. Let $\mathcal{P} = t_0 \to t_1 \to t_2 \to \cdots \to t_{2\ell}$ be a path in a DAG D such that for each $i = 1, \ldots, 2\ell$ the in-degree of t_i is equal to 1, and for each $i = 0, \ldots, \ell - 1$ the out-degree of t_i is equal to 1; and the out-degree of $t_{2\ell}$ is equal to 0.*

Fix a proper colouring φ for D. Let n_1 be the number of colours that t_0 shares with its in-neighbours; and n_2 be the number of remaining colours in $\varphi(t_0)$. Then, we have

$$\left| \left(\bigcup_{i=1}^{2\ell} \varphi(t_i) \right) \setminus \varphi(t_0) \right| \geq \ell(n_1 + n_2 + 1) + \ell^2.$$

Moreover, there is a colouring that attains this lower bound.

Proof. For each $i = 1, \ldots, 2\ell$ let $z_i = |\varphi(t_i) \cap \varphi(t_{i-1})|$ and $y_i = |\varphi(t_i) \setminus \varphi(t_{i-1})|$. For the sake of definiteness, let $z_0 = n_1$ and $y_0 = n_2$. It is not hard to see that for each $i = 1, \ldots, 2\ell$ it holds that $y_i + z_i > y_{i-1} + z_{i-1}$ (because of the edge $t_{i-1} \to t_i$) and $z_i \leq y_{i-1}$ (because of the absence of the edge $t_{i-2} \to t_i$). It follows that $y_i > z_{i-1}$. With this constraint, the minimum of $\sum_{i=1}^{2\ell} |\varphi(t_i)| = \sum_{i=1}^{2\ell} (z_i + y_i)$ is attained by setting, for each $j = 1, \ldots, \ell$ $y_{2j-1} = z_0 + j$ and $y_{2j} = y_0 + j$. Therefore, we have

$$\left| \left(\bigcup_{i=1}^{2\ell} \varphi(t_i) \right) \setminus \varphi(t_0) \right| \geq \sum_{j=1}^{\ell} (z_0 + j) + (y_0 + j) = \ell(z_0 + y_0 + 1) + \ell^2, \quad (4)$$

as desired. In addition, we can observe that the number of colours in the right hand side of (4) can be attained by setting $\varphi(t_i)$ to be the union of the y_{i-1} colours of $\varphi(t_{i-1})$ not used in any previous node and $z_{i-1} + 1$ new colours.

The Reduction. Let $(G = (V, E), k)$ be an instance of the INTERSECTION NUMBER (IN) problem. We define the instance (D, k') of DIRECTED INTER-SECTION NUMBER (DIN) problem, where D is the graph obtained from G as follows

1. fix an order on the vertices of G, let $v_1, \ldots, v_n$ be the vertices of G listed in the order fixed;
2. orient each edge (v_i, v_j) of G as $v_i \to v_j$ if and only if, $i < j$;
3. for each $i = 1, \ldots, n$ add a gadget $\mathcal{V}^{(i)} = \mathcal{V}_{N_i}$ to G with $N_i = i \cdot n^2$;
4. for each $i = 1, \ldots, n$, identify the vertex v_i with the vertex $v^{(i)}$ (the v vertex of the gadget $\mathcal{V}^{(i)}$;
5. add a path $\mathcal{P} = t_0 \to t_1 \to t_2 \to \cdots \to t_{2\ell}$ with ℓ a positive integer $> k + 4$;
6. for each $i = 1, \ldots, n$ and $j = 1, \ldots, N_i$, add an edge $c_j^{(i)} \to t_0$;
7. set $k' = k + \sum_{i=1}^n N_i + n + 4(\ell + 1) + \ell^2 + \ell$.

See Fig. 2 for a pictorial example of the transformation of the graph G into the DAG D.

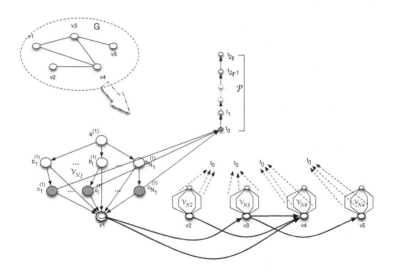

Fig. 2. An example of the reduction. The original graph G is on the top left of the figure. The vertices are arbitrarily sorted and edges directed accordingly. Edges and vertices of G are marked in bold in the resulting DAG D. Each vertex is extended by a $\mathcal{V}$-gadget and the c-vertices of this gadget are connected to the starting vertex of the path $\mathcal{P}$. For readability, this is explicitly drawn only for the first gadget on the left.

The direction $IN(G) \leq k \Rightarrow DIN(D) \leq k'$. We first show the "easy" direction of the reduction.

Theorem 1. *If $IN(G) \leq k$ then $DIN(D) \leq k'$.*

Proof. Let us assume that there is a set of colours $\mathcal{C}_G$ of cardinality k and a family $\mathcal{F} = \{S_v \subseteq \mathcal{C}_G | v \in V(G)\}$ such that $S_v \cap S_u \neq \emptyset$ if and only if $(u, v) \in E(G)$.

Let us define, for each $i = 1, \ldots, n$ a distinct set of $N_i + 1$ colours $\mathcal{C}^{(i)} = \{\alpha^{(i)}, \beta_1^{(i)}, \ldots, \beta_{N_i}^{(i)}\}$. Let $\mathcal{C}_\mathcal{P}$ be another distinct set of colours of cardinality $5\ell + \ell^2$. Let $\gamma, \delta, \gamma', \delta'$ be four additional distinct colours. Let $\mathcal{C}_D = \mathcal{C}_G \cup \bigcup_{i=1}^n \mathcal{C}^{(i)} \cup \mathcal{C}_\mathcal{P} \cup \{\gamma, \delta, \delta', \gamma'\}$. It is not hard to see that $|\mathcal{C}_D| = k'$.

For each $i = 1, \ldots, n$ we can use colours in $\tilde{\mathcal{C}}^{(i)} = \mathcal{C}^{(i)} \cup \{\delta, \gamma\}$ to properly colour the gadget $\mathcal{V}^{(i)}$, as shown in Fig. 1. In particular, this means to define the partial colouring φ' by setting

$$\varphi'(a^{(i)}) = \{\alpha^{(i)}\}, \text{ and } \varphi'(b_j^{(i)}) = \{\alpha^{(i)}, \beta_j^{(i)}\}, \varphi(c_j^{(i)}) = \{\beta_j^{(i)}, \delta, \gamma\}, \text{ for } j = 1, \ldots, N_i,$$

and assign N_i colours $\{\beta_1^{(i)}, \ldots, \beta_{N_i}^{(i)}\}$ to vertex $v_i = v^{(i)}$ i.e.,

$$\varphi'(v_i) = \{\beta_1^{(i)}, \ldots, \beta_{N_i}^{(i)}\}.$$

We now set $\varphi'(t_0) = \{\delta, \gamma, \delta', \gamma'\}$ and colour the remaining part of $\mathcal{P}$, i.e., vertices $t_1, \ldots, t_{2\ell}$ using the colours in $\mathcal{C}_\mathcal{P}$—this can be achieved by proceeding as in the proof of Lemma 4.

It is not hard to see that for each pair of vertices $u, u' \in V(D)$ such that they are not both vertices of $V(G)$ it holds that $u \to u' \in E(D)$ if and only if $\varphi'(u') \cap \varphi'(u) \neq \emptyset$ and $|\varphi'(u')| > |\varphi'(u)|$.

In order to take care of pairs of vertices both coming from $V(G)$ we extend φ' to a new colouring φ by setting $\varphi(u) = \varphi'(u)$ for each $u \notin V(G)$ and for each $i = 1, \ldots, n$ we set $\varphi(v_i) = \varphi'(v_i) \cup S_{v_i}$.

Recall that for each $i = 1, \ldots, n$ we have $|S_{v_i}| \leq |\mathcal{C}_G| = k < n^2$. It is not hard to see then, that for each $i = 1, \ldots, n$, we have

$$i \cdot n^2 < |\varphi(v_i)| = |S_{v_i}| + |\varphi'(v_i)| = |S_{v_i}| + N_i < n^2 + i \cdot n^2 = (i+1)n^2.$$

Therefore, for each $i < j$ we have $|\varphi(v_i)| < |\varphi(v_j)|$. Moreover, since $\varphi'(v_i) \cap \varphi'(v_j) = \emptyset$, it follows that $\varphi(v_i) \cap \varphi(v_j) \neq \emptyset$ if and only if $S_{v_i} \cap S_{v_j} \neq \emptyset$, i.e., if and only if $(v_i, v_j) \in E(G)$, and by construction (due to $i < j$) this is true if and only if $v_i \to v_j \in E(D)$, as desired. $\quad\square$

The direction $DIN(D) \leq k' \Rightarrow IN(G) \leq k$. We will need the following technical result, whose proof is deferred to the extendend version of the paper.

Lemma 5. *Let φ be a proper colouring of D. Then, it holds that*

$$\left| \bigcup_{i=1}^n \left(\varphi(a^{(i)}) \cup \bigcup_{j=1}^{N_i} \varphi(c_j^{(i)}) \right) \cup \varphi(t_0) \right| \geq n + 4 + \sum_{i=1}^n N_i.$$

Lemma 6. *Fix a colouring φ for the DAG D. If for some $i \in \{1, \ldots, n\}$ the vertex $v^{(i)}$ in $\mathcal{V}^{(i)}$ satisfies $|\varphi(v^{(i)})| < N_i$ then $|\varphi| > k'$.*

Proof. By Lemma 3, we have that there exists $j \in [N_i]$ such that $3 \leq |\varphi(b_j^{(i)})| \leq |\varphi(c_j^{(i)})| - 1 \leq |\varphi(t_0)| - 2$, hence $|\varphi(t_0)| \geq 5$. Then, by Lemma 4, with $(n_1 + n_2) = |\varphi(t_0)| \geq 5$, we have that

$$\left| \left(\bigcup_{i=1}^{2\ell} \varphi(t_i) \right) \setminus \varphi(t_0) \right| \geq 6\ell + \ell^2 > 5\ell + \ell^2 + k + 4, \tag{5}$$

where, in the last inequality we used $\ell > k + 4$.

We now observe that the colours used for the "private" vertices $(t_1, \ldots, t_{2\ell})$ of the path $\mathcal{P}$, i.e., $\bigcup_{j=1}^{2\ell} \varphi(t_j)$, cannot be used in the colouring of any vertex $a^{(i)}, b_j^{(i)}, c_j^{(i)}$. Since there is a path from each one of these vertices to any t_m, we have $\max\{|\varphi(a^{(i)})|, |\varphi(b_j^{(i)})|, |\varphi(c_j^{(i)})|\} \leq |\varphi(t_m)|$, for any i, j, m; hence, any non-empty intersection and the absence of an edge would imply that the colouring is not proper.

Therefore, we have

$$|\varphi| \geq \left| \left(\bigcup_{i=1}^{n} \varphi(a^{(i)}) \cup \bigcup_{j=1}^{N_i} \varphi(c_j^{(i)}) \right) \cup \left(\bigcup_{s=1}^{2\ell} \varphi(t_s) \right) \right| \tag{6}$$

$$= \left| \left(\bigcup_{i=1}^{n} \varphi(a^{(i)}) \cup \bigcup_{j=1}^{N_i} \varphi(c_j^{(i)}) \right) \cup \varphi(t_0) \right| + \left| \left(\bigcup_{s=1}^{2\ell} \varphi(t_s) \right) \setminus \varphi(t_0) \right| \tag{7}$$

$$> n + 4 + \sum_{i=1}^{n} N_i + 5\ell + \ell^2 + k + 4 > k', \tag{8}$$

where the last inequality follows by Lemma 5 and (5). $\qquad\square$

Theorem 2. *If $DIN(D) \leq k'$ then $IN(G) \leq k$.*

Proof. Assume we can color the DAG D (obtained from G via the above reduction) with k' colours. Then, for each $i = 1, \ldots, n$, and $j = 1, \ldots, N_i$ (by Lemma 6 and Lemma 4), we must have

$$|\varphi(t_0)| = 4, |\varphi(c_j^{(i)})| = 3, |\varphi(b_j^{(i)})| = 2, |\varphi(a^{(i)})| = 1. \tag{9}$$

To see this, first notice that the righthand sides of each equality is a lower bound on the quantity in the corresponding left hand side because of the path $a^{(i)} \to b_j^{(i)} \to c_j^{(i)} \to t_0$. Moreover, suppose that one of the equalities is not satisfied, hence it holds as a strict inequality ($>$). Then, because of the above path we have $|\varphi(t_0)| \geq 5$. By Lemma 4, with $n_1 + n_2 = |\varphi(t_0)| \geq 5$, proceeding like in (6)–(8), we have that the total number of colours would be

$$|\varphi| \geq n + 4 + \sum_{i=1}^{n} N_i + (|t_0| + 1)\ell + \ell^2 > n + 4 + \sum_{i=1}^{n} N_i + 5\ell + \ell^2 + k + 4 > k',$$

where the first strict inequality follows because of $\ell > k + 4$.

Since each a_i has a distinct out-neighborhood, we must have that there are distinct colours $\alpha_1, \ldots, \alpha_n$ such that $\varphi(a^{(i)}) = \{\alpha_i\}$. Analogously, it follows that, for each $i \in [n]$ and $j \in [N_i]$ there are distinct colours $\beta_j^{(i)}$ such that $\varphi(b_j^{(i)}) = \{\alpha_i, \beta_j^{(i)}\}$.

Also, we have $\varphi(v^{(i)}) \supseteq \{\beta_1^{(i)}, \ldots, \beta_{N_i}^{(i)}\}$.

Let $W^{(i)} = \varphi(v^{(i)}) \setminus \{\beta_1^{(i)}, \ldots, \beta_{N_i}^{(i)}\}$. Since for every graph G it holds that $IN(G) < n^2$, skipping trivialities we may assume that $k < n^2$. Therefore, under the standing hypothesis on the size of the colouring, because of Lemma 4 and Lemma 5, we have

$$| \cup_j W^{(j)}| \leq k' - \left(n + 4 + \sum_{i=1}^{n} N_i \right) - \left(\ell(n_1 + n_2 + 1) + \ell^2 \right) = k,$$

where the first bracket is the contribution from Lemma 5 and the second bracket is the contribution from Lemma 4. For the latter, we are using that $n_1 + n_2 = |\varphi(t_0)| = 4$, as argued above ($|\varphi(t_0)| \geq 5$ would imply $|\varphi| > k'$).

Then, we have

$$|W^{(i)}| \leq | \cup_j W^{(j)}| \leq k < n^2$$

These considerations, together with Lemma 6 imply that for each $i = 1, \ldots, n$, we have $N_i \leq |\varphi(v^{(i)})| \leq N_i + |W^{(i)}| < in^2 + n^2 = (i+1)n^2 = N_{i+1}$, hence, $|\varphi(v^{(i)})| < |\varphi(v^{(i+1)})|$.

Recall that for each $i \neq i'$, we have $\{\beta_1^{(i)}, \ldots, \beta_{N_i}^{(i)}\} \cap \{\beta_1^{(i')}, \ldots, \beta_{N_{i'}}^{(i')}\} = \emptyset$. Therefore, for each $i \neq i'$ such that $v_i \to v_{i'}$ (equivalently $(v_i, v_{i'}) \in E(G)$) it holds that $W^{(i)} \cap W^{(i+1)} = \varphi(v^{(i)}) \cap \varphi(v^{(i')}) \neq \emptyset$. Hence, G is the intersection graph of the family of sets $\{W^{(i)}\}_{i=1,\ldots,n}$ which is defined on the ground set of size k, i.e., $IN(G) \leq k$.

4   Approximation for Arborescences

In this section we present a simple linear time algorithm for computing a proper colouring for an arborescence graph. Recall that a directed graph T is an arborescence if there is a vertex r called the root such that for all other vertices v there is exactly one path from r to v. Alternatively, T is a directed rooted tree where all edges are directed in the direction away from the root.

Lemma 7. *Let T be an arborescence. Let ι be the number of internal vertices of T. Let κ be the set of levels of T with at least one leaf. Let h be the depth of T. Then, Algorithm 1 produces a colouring with $h(h-1)/2 + \iota + \kappa \leq h(h+1)/2 + \iota$ colours in linear time (plus the time to write down the sets of colours)*

Proof. For the time bound, it is enough to observe that all the quantities used by the algorithm can be defined during a constant number of traversals of the graph, hence in linear time in $|T|$.

Algorithm 1: Colouring Arborescences

Input: A non-empty arborescence graph T with root $r = root(T)$
Output: a proper colouring φ of T
Set $h \leftarrow$ depth of T and **for each** vertex v $level(v) \leftarrow$ level of vertex v (the root is on level 0);
for $\ell = 1, \ldots, h$ **do**
  Define a new set of colours for level ℓ: $C^{(\ell)} = \{a_1^{(\ell)}, \ldots, a_{\ell-1}^{(\ell)}\}$;
  if *there is at least one leaf on level i* **then**
    Define a new colour $\lambda(\ell)$;

for *each internal node v* **do**
  Define a new colour $c(v)$
Set $\varphi(root(T)) \leftarrow c(root(T))$;
for *each vertex $v \neq root(T)$* **do**
  if *v is not a leaf* **then**
    Set $\varphi(v) \leftarrow c(v) \cup C^{(level(v))} \cup c(parent(v))$
  else
    Set $\varphi(v) \leftarrow \lambda(level(v)) \cup C^{(level(v))} \cup c(parent(v))$

return φ

The algorithm uses: one colour per each internal vertex; one colour per each level with at least one leaf; and $\sum_{i=1}^{h}(i-1) = \sum_{i=1}^{h-1} i = \frac{h(h-1)}{2}$ colours for all the level sets $C^{(i)}$. In total the algorithm uses $\iota + h(h-1)/2 + \kappa \leq \iota + h(h+1)/2$, where the inequality holds because $\kappa \leq h$.

To see that the colouring φ is proper we observe that: (i) vertices on different levels have a different number of colours assigned; (ii) two vertices share a colour if and only if they are on the same level or they are in parent-child relationship.

Lemma 8. *Let T be an arborescence. Let ι be the number of internal vertices of T and h be the depth of T. Then, every proper colouring φ for T uses at least $\iota + \pi(h)$ colours, where $\pi(h) = \ell^2 + 1$ if $h = 2\ell$ and $\pi(h) = \ell^2 + \ell + 3$ if $h = 2\ell + 1$.*

Proof. Let us first consider the case where h is an even number, i.e., $h = 2\ell$ for some $\ell \in \mathbb{N}$ (we are tacitly skipping the trivial case where $h = 0$).

Let P be a root-to-leaf path in T of length h. By Lemma 4 (with $n_0 = 0$, $n_1 = 1$ and adding a single colour for $t_0 = root(T)$), we have that the number of colours used for the vertices of P in any proper colouring of T must satisfy $|\varphi(P)| \geq 1 + 2\ell + \ell^2$.

Let $v_1, v_2, \ldots, v_{\iota-2\ell}$ be all the internal vertices of T which are not on the path P and listed in DFS order from the root towards the leaves. We observe that

$$\varphi(v_i) \setminus \left(\varphi(P) \cup \bigcup_{j=1}^{i-1} \varphi(v_j) \right) \neq \emptyset. \tag{10}$$

To see this, note that there is a colour χ that $v = v_i$ shares with its child v_c. Moreover $|\varphi(v_c)| > |\varphi(v)|$. If there exists a vertex $u \in P \cup \bigcup_{j=1}^{i-1} \varphi(v_j)$ that shares colour χ then there are three possibilities: (i) $|\varphi(u)| \leq |\varphi(v)| < |\varphi(v_c)|$ hence there must be an edge $u \to v_c$ which is not possible since there are no vertices listed in DFS before v or on P that have an edge towards v_c (note that v_c cannot be not on P since v is not); (ii) $|\varphi(u)| > |\varphi(v)|$, hence there is an edge $v \to u$ which is also impossible since, no vertex listed in the DFS before v can be an out-neighbour of v and no vertex in P is a neighbour of v since v is not on P. Since in all cases we reach a contradiction the righthand side of (10) contains at least colour χ, which proves the inequality.

Therefore, we have

$$|\varphi| \geq |\varphi(P) \cup \varphi(\{v_1, \ldots, v_{\iota-2\ell}\})| = |\varphi(P)| + \sum_{j=1}^{\iota-2\ell} |\varphi(v_i) \setminus \left(\varphi(P) \cup \bigcup_{j=1}^{i-1} \varphi(v_j)\right)|$$

$$\geq \ell^2 + 2\ell + 1 + \iota - 2\ell = \ell^2 + \iota + 1 \qquad (11)$$

The case where h is odd, i.e. $h = 2\ell + 1$ can be dealt with in exactly the same way. In this case, by an immediate extension of Lemma 4 we have $|\varphi(P)| \geq \ell^2 + 3\ell + 2$. This together with the fact that P now contains $2\ell + 1$ internal vertices, gives us the claimed bound $|\varphi| \geq \ell^2 + \ell + 1 + \iota$.

Theorem 3. *Algorithm 1 guarantees approximation ≤ 2*

Proof. Let φ be the colouring produced by Algorithm 1 and φ^* be a proper colouring with the minimum possible number of colours.

Assume the number h of levels of T is an even number. Let $h = 2\ell$. Then, from Lemma 7 and Lemma 8 we have

$$\frac{|\varphi|}{|\varphi^*|} \leq \frac{h(h+1)/2 + \iota}{\ell^2 + \iota + 1} = \frac{2\ell(2\ell+1)/2 + \iota}{\ell^2 + \iota + 1} = \frac{2\ell^2 + \ell + \iota}{\ell^2 + \iota + 1} \leq 2,$$

where the last inequality follows from when $\iota > \ell - 2$, which is always verified by the internal vertices on the path P, which are at least 2ℓ.

Assume now that the number h of levels of T is an odd number, i.e., $h = 2\ell+1$. Then, from Lemma 7 and Lemma 8 we have

$$\frac{|\varphi|}{|\varphi^*|} \leq \frac{h(h+1)/2 + \iota}{\ell^2 + \ell + \iota + 1} = \frac{(\ell+1)(2\ell+1) + \iota}{\ell^2 + \ell + \iota + 1} = \frac{2\ell^2 + 3\ell + \iota + 1}{\ell^2 + \ell + \iota + 1} \leq 2,$$

where the last inequality follows when $\iota > \ell - 1$, which is always verified by the internal vertices on the path P, which are at least 2ℓ.

Remark 1. Note that the fuller the arborescence, the better the approximation, e.g., for any $\epsilon > 0$ if $\iota \geq \frac{1-\epsilon}{\epsilon}\ell^2 + \frac{\ell}{\epsilon}$ the approximation guarantee becomes $(1 + \epsilon)$.

In particular, with some more care in the analysis (and a refined lower bound) it is possible to show that the colouring output by the algorithm is optimal for the case of a T where the leaves are only on the last level. We defer this to the extended version of the paper.

5   Open Problems

Several natural and interesting questions are left open by our result. The first natural question regards the approximability and inapproximability of the problem for arbitrary DAGs. As mentioned in the introduction, the intersection number (for undirected graphs) is not approximable in polynomial time within a factor of $|V(G)|^\epsilon$ [8]. This result does not appear to carry over to the problem of computing DIN (through our reduction). Nor do the extremal results from [6] provide any approximation guarantee for arbitrary DAGs. For the special case of arborescences, we presented a 2-approximation algorithm. An exact polynomial time algorithm for arborescences appears to be already a challenging question. Another open question that arises from the comparison to the classical intersection number problem regards fixed parameterized tractability: is the problem FPT with respect to the value of $DIN(D)$?

References

1. Beineke, L.W., Zamfirescu, C.: Connection digraphs and second-order line digraphs. Discret. Math. **39**(3), 237–254 (1982)
2. Das, S., Sen, M.K., Roy, A.B., West, D.B.: Interval digraphs: an analogue of interval graphs. J. Graph Theor. **13**(2), 189–202 (1989)
3. Dau, H., Milenkovic, O.: Latent network features and overlapping community discovery via Boolean intersection representations. IEEE/ACM Trans. Netw. **25**(5), 3219–3234 (2017)
4. Erdős, P., Goodman, A.W., Pósa, L.: The representation of a graph by set intersections. Can. J. Math. **18**, 106–112 (1966)
5. Gramm, J., Guo, J., Hüffner, F., Niedermeier, R.: Data reduction and exact algorithms for clique cover. ACM J. Exp. Algorithm. **13** (2008)
6. Kostochka, A.V., Liu, X., Machado, R., Milenkovic, O.: Directed intersection representations and the information content of digraphs. In: IEEE International Symposium on Information Theory, ISIT 2019, Paris, France, 7–12 July 2019, pp. 1477–1481. IEEE (2019)
7. Kou, L.T., Stockmeyer, L.J., Wong, C.K.: Covering edges by cliques with regard to keyword conflicts and intersection graphs. Commun. ACM **21**(2), 135–139 (1978)
8. Lund, C., Yannakakis, M.: On the hardness of approximating minimization problems. J. ACM **41**(5), 960–981 (1994)
9. Maehara, H.: A digraph represented by a family of boxes or spheres. J. Graph Theor. **8**(3), 431–439 (1984)
10. Orlin, J.: Contentment in graph theory: covering graphs with cliques. Indagationes Math. (Proc.) **80**(5), 406–424 (1977)
11. Tsourakakis, C.: Provably fast inference of latent features from networks: with applications to learning social circles and multilabel classification. In: Proceedings of the 24th International Conference on World Wide Web, pp. 1111–1121 (2015)

On the Mystery of Negations in Circuits: Structure vs Power

Prashanth Amireddy, Sai Jayasurya, and Jayalal Sarma[⊠]

Indian Institute of Technology Madras, Chennai, India
jayalal@cse.iitm.ac.in

Abstract. Exploring further the power of negations in Boolean circuits, in this paper we study the effect of interdependency of negation gates in circuits in terms of computational power. As a starting point, we study the power of *independent* negations (where no negation feeds into another, even via other gates) in circuits and show the following results.

- The minimum number of independent negations required to compute a Boolean function is exactly characterized by the *decrease* of the function. We also provide an additional characterization by a generalization of orientation [9], which we call the *monotone orientation*.
- We define a new measure called the *thickness* of a Boolean function, and show that if f has thickness at most t and has a circuit of depth d, then f can be computed using $2^{\lceil \log(t+1) \rceil}$ (independent) negations in depth $d + O(\log n)$. When the function is monotone, we also show a parameterized version of this result, where the depth is expressed in terms of thickness and d. Our techniques include a natural generalization of the Karchmer-Widgerson games to include a *switch step*.
- For functions with thickness t, we show that the monotone and non-monotone circuit depths are related by the factor of thickness and an extra $O(\log n)$ additive factor. This generalizes the fact [16] that for slice functions, the monotone and non-monotone circuit depth complexities are related by an additive factor of $O(\log n)$.

To go further, we study the dependency between negations in the circuit by modeling the same using a *negation graph* with negation gates (and root) as vertices and directed edges representing pair of negation gates which feed into each other through a path which does not have negations. We associate a measure of *decrease capacity* with the negation graph, denoted $\mathsf{d}_{\max}$. We show the following results:

- For a negation graph N, $\mathsf{d}_{\max}(N)$ is the maximum decrease of any circuit which has this negation graph. Using this as a tool, we derive necessary conditions on the structure of negation graphs when the circuit is negation optimal.
- We show how to construct circuits for a function f, given a negation tree with decrease capacity at least $\frac{\mathsf{alt}(f)}{2}$. En route this result, we show that if f and g are two Boolean functions on n variables with $\mathsf{alt}(f) \leq \mathsf{alt}(g)$ and $f(0^n) = g(0^n)$, then any circuit for g can be used (with substitution of variables with monotone functions) to compute f without using any extra negation. This may be of independent interest.

© Springer Nature Switzerland AG 2020
D. Kim et al. (Eds.): COCOON 2020, LNCS 12273, pp. 566–577, 2020.
https://doi.org/10.1007/978-3-030-58150-3_46

1 Introduction

A central question in circuit complexity is to prove exponential size lower bounds for an explicit language in the class NP. Unfortunately, this task has evaded the attempts over decades, and the best known circuit size lower bounds for any explicit function is as small as $5n$. Noting that there are monotone function families (equivalently languages) which are NP-complete (like The CLIQUE function), a natural restricted question is to prove lower bounds for monotone circuits computing the CLIQUE function [1,13]. A similar success story in the setting of monotone circuits is in the context of depth lower bounds. In an attempt to separate the class P from NC^1, a line of research considered proving depth lower bounds against the perfect matching function (given a graph G, as the adjacency matrix, whether it has a perfect matching or not). An important tool that was introduced in this direction was the Karchmer-Wigderson games which exactly captured the depth of circuits computing a function. By proving strong lower bounds for the monotone variant of this game (which exactly captured the depth of monotone circuits), lower bounds for monotone circuits computing the reachability problem ($\Omega(\log^2 n)$ [8]) and perfect matching problem ($\Omega(n)$ [12]) were shown, where n is the number of vertices of the given graph.

To extend the success against monotone circuits to the general setting - a natural attempt is to study a measure of monotonicity of the circuit computing the function, and use it to prove lower bounds for non-monotone circuits, possibly even parameterized by the measure of non-monotonicity of the circuits. There are broadly two kinds of measures of non-monotonicity measures on circuit, one is syntactic on circuits. The most natural restriction on this is the number of negations used by the circuit. Power of negations in circuits has been a subject of study since the 1940s. Markov [10] proved that nearly $O(\log n)$ negations are sufficient to compute any Boolean function.[1] However, the size of the circuit can be exponential. In contrast, Morizumi [11] showed that in the case of formulas, $\lceil \frac{n}{2} \rceil$ negations are sufficient (and sometimes required) to compute a Boolean function on n variables. This showed that there is an exponential gap between the power of negations in the context of circuits and formulas. Fischer [4] showed that any function $f : \{0,1\}^n \rightarrow \{0,1\}$ that can be computed by circuits of size $\mathsf{poly}(n)$ can also be computed by circuits which $O(\log n)$ negations while retaining the circuit to be $\mathsf{poly}(n)$ size. This, in particular, implies that, to separate P from NP, it suffices to prove super-polynomial size lower bounds for circuits that use at most $O(\log n)$ negations. Closely following this, [2] proved a super-polynomial lower bound for circuits which use at most $\frac{1}{6} \log \log n$ negations. This is still the best known for general circuit size lower bound for a circuit with limited negations computing single bit output functions. For multioutput functions Jukna [5] has proved a super-polynomial size lower bound even when the number of negations is additively close to $O(\log n)$. For restricted depth scenario, Rossman

---

[1] The actual bound in [10] is stated in terms of the measure of non-monotonicity of a function called *decrease* (which we denote by $\mathsf{dec}(f)$) - see Sect. 2 for definition.

[14] showed that the whole of NC^1 cannot be computed by logarithmic depth polynomial size circuits with $\left(\frac{1}{2} - \epsilon\right) \log n$ negations for $\epsilon > 0$.

One of the strategies to interpolate between the general circuits and monotone circuits is to consider other measures of non-monotonicity of Boolean circuits. Several attempts has been made in this direction. Koroth and Sarma [9] considers *weight of the orientation*[2] of the functions computed at the individual gates as a measure of non-monotonicity of circuits. More recently, Jukna and Lingas [7] studied *negation-width* as a measure of non-monotonicity and proved circuit depth lower bounds limiting the same.

Our Results: Given the lack of further progress in lower bounds in terms of number of negations, it is natural to explore the interplay between negations and to see whether the way in which negation gates feed into each other affects the computational power. As noted earlier, the power of negation in Boolean circuits varies exponentially when (negation) gates are allowed to feed in to each other (through a series of gates). To understand this further, we study the dependency between negations. The simplest case to start with is when the negations do not feed into each other in a circuit (even indirectly via other gates). Such a circuit is said to have *independent negations*.

Power of Independent Negations: As a starting point, we show that restricting the negations to be independent (no negation feeds into another through series of gates)[3] makes the circuit as weak as a formula in terms of the decrease of the functions which they can compute.

Theorem 1. *For any Boolean function f, the independent negation complexity of f, denoted by $\mathcal{I}_\mathsf{d}(f)$ is exactly $\mathsf{dec}(f)$, where $\mathsf{dec}(f)$ denotes the decrease of f.*

The argument for the above Theorem is inspired by a result of Morizumi [11] who proved that $\mathsf{dec}(f)$ is exactly equal to the minimum number of negations that any formula computing a function f must contain (originally proved by [3]). We also generalize orientation [9] to obtain another characterization of $\mathcal{I}_\mathsf{d}(f)$.

Morizumi [11] also proved that any function which can be computed by formulas of depth d and size $\mathsf{poly}(n)$ can also be computed formulas that use at most $\lceil \frac{n}{2} \rceil$ negations with depth $d + O(\log n)$ and size $\mathsf{poly}(n)$.

We prove a similar statement for circuits with independent negations computing monotone functions. We parameterize it with the following new measure. The *thickness* of a (non-constant) function f is given as $\mathsf{t}(f) = \max_{x,y}(\mathsf{wt}(y) - \mathsf{wt}(x))$ where $x \in f^{-1}(1), y \in f^{-1}(0)$, and $\mathsf{wt}(x)$ denotes number of 1s in x . We show that:

Theorem 2. *If a Boolean function f of thickness t has a circuit of depth d, then f can also be computed by a circuit of depth $d + O(\log n)$ using $2^{\lceil \log(t+1) \rceil}$ independent negations.*

---

[2] Informally, this is the number of negations that any De-Morgan circuits requires, to compute the function.

[3] When the circuit is viewed as a graph, the negation gates represent an independent set.

As a tool to prove the above Theorem we define a modified version of the Karchmer-Wigderson games [8]. Karchmer and Wigderson considered two versions (monotone and non-monotone) of their communication game. They showed that the minimum cost of a non-monotone game ($\mathsf{KW}(f)$) for a function is equal to the minimum depth of a circuit computing it; and the minimum cost of a monotone game is equal to the minimum depth of a monotone circuit computing the function. Note that the versions relate to the case with unbounded negation gates and no negation gates respectively. Naturally we want a version of the game that controls the amount of negation gates in the circuit.

The simple generalization we define involves an intuitive *switch step* - which is allowed to Alice and Bob at any point in a protocol, it is allowed atmost once in a run of the protocol and if & after this is done, in order to complete the game, they need to find an index i such that $x_i = 0$ and $y_i = 1$. If there is no switch step used in a run of the protocol, then they have to find an i such that $x_i = 1$ and $y_i = 0$. Clearly, if this operation is allowed in an unrestricted way, then it is as powerful as the general version of the game. We study the version of the game where the total number of switch step operations in the communication tree is restricted to be at most k. We denote the communication required in this version of the game for the function f to be $\mathsf{SKW}^k(f)$ (which also includes the bit took for communicating if & when they switch). The following Lemma is very natural which forms our main tool to prove Theorem 2 stated earlier. *For every Boolean function f with decrease at least k, there is a circuit computing f which uses k independent negations with depth at most $\mathsf{SKW}^k(f)$.*
When the function f is monotone, we state below a parameterized (by the thickness of the function f) version of Theorem 2.

Theorem 3. *If a monotone Boolean function f of thickness t has a circuit of depth d, then for any $1 \leq k \leq \lceil \log(t+1) \rceil$, f can also be computed by a circuit of depth $d \lceil \frac{t}{2^k-1} \rceil + O(\log n)$ using only 2^k independent negations.*

Using the techniques developed en-route to the above Theorem we also show a relation between cost of monotone and non-monotone versions of the Karchmer-Wigderson games (denoted by $\mathsf{KW}(f)$ and $\mathsf{KW}^+(f)$ respectively) for a monotone function f, in terms of the thickness of f.

Theorem 4. *For any monotone function f having thickness t,*

$$\mathsf{KW}^+(f) \leq (t+1)\,\mathsf{KW}(f) + O(\log n).$$

Negation (Dependency) Graph: Theorem 1 indicates that the negations are more powerful when they feed into each other. To systematically study the structure of the dependency between negation gates in a circuit we introduce the *negation graph*: where the vertex set is the set of negation gates along with the root gate. A directed edge (u, v) indicates that there is a negation-free path between gates u and v in the circuit. Given a negation graph of a circuit, we associate a non-monotonicity measure with it, which we call the *decrease capacity* (denoted by $\mathsf{d}_{\max}$ defined in Sect. 5) of the negation graph (and hence the circuit). By adapting a lower bound argument due to [11], we show that:

Theorem 5. *If a circuit C computes a function f, then $\mathsf{dec}(f) \leq \mathsf{d}_{\max}(C)$.*

This gives us a useful tool to arrive at interesting structural properties of the negation gates in a circuit computing a given function. We use it to derive (Theorem 15) structural properties for negation optimal circuits. We use the measure to provide an alternative proof for a negation lower bound for circuits by Santha and Wilson [15]: If a Boolean function f of decrease k is computed by a circuit C of depth d, then the number of negations in C is at least $d(k^{1/d} - 1)$.

We also ask the question: Given a negation graph N and a function f, is it possible to design a circuit computing the f with the given negation dependency structure? We are able to answer this for negation graphs which are trees.

Theorem 6. *Given any function $f : \{0,1\}^n \to \{0,1\}$ with alternation k, for any negation tree N with $\mathsf{d}_{\max}(N) \geq k/2$, we can design a circuit C which computes function f and has negation graph N.*

En route the proof, we also prove the following: Let $f : \{0,1\}^n \to \{0,1\}$ and $g : \{0,1\}^m \to \{0,1\}$ be two functions such that $\mathsf{alt}(f) \leq \mathsf{alt}(g)$ and $f(0^m) = g(0^n)$. Then, any circuit for g can be used (with substitution of variables with monotone functions) to compute f without using any extra negations. This might be of independent interest.

2 Preliminaries

We now define basic notations and terms used in the paper. Unless explicitly mentioned, we deal with functions from $\{0,1\}^n$ to $\{0,1\}$. For definitions of circuit complexity classes, monotone functions and circuits we refer the reader to the textbook [6]. We deal with circuits whose $\vee$ and $\wedge$ gates have a fan-in of 2.

For any $x \in \{0,1\}^n$, we define weight of x, denoted by $\mathsf{wt}(x)$, as the number of 1s in the string x. Let $x, y \in \{0,1\}^n$ be two distinct strings and let s_i stand for the ith bit of a string s. We say $x \prec y$ iff $\forall i \in [n]$, $x_i \leq y_i$. A chain of inputs is defined as a sequence $\langle x^{(0)}, x^{(1)}, \ldots x^{(k)} \rangle$ where each $x^{(i)}$ is distinct and $i < j \implies x^{(i)} \prec x^{(j)}$. For a given Boolean function f and a chain $\mathcal{X} = \langle x^{(0)}, x^{(1)}, \ldots x^{(k)} \rangle$, the *decrease* of f along the chain is the number of indices i such that $f(x^{(i)}) = 1$ and $f(x^{(i+1)}) = 0$. The decrease of f, denoted by $\mathsf{dec}(f)$, is the maximum such decrease over all possible chains. Similarly, the *alternation* of f along a chain is the number of indices i such that $f(x^{(i)}) \neq f(x^{(i+1)})$. The alternation of f, denoted by $\mathsf{alt}(f)$, is the maximum alternation over all chains.

We quickly review the Karchmer-Wigderson game for functions defined by [8], and their relation to circuit depth complexity. The game is played between two players, Alice and Bob, who individually have infinite computational power and co-operate with each other. For a Boolean function f, Alice is given an input $x \in f^{-1}(1)$ (i.e, $f(x) = 1$) and Bob is given $y \in f^{-1}(0)$. Their aim is to communicate and find an index i such that $x_i \neq y_i$. The cost (sometimes called as complexity) of the game when Alice and Bob follow a given protocol is the number of bits communicated in the worst case. The cost of the game for a function f, denoted by $\mathsf{KW}(f)$, is the lowest possible cost of any valid protocol.

The protocol can also be viewed as a tree. The root of the tree is labelled with a matrix with rows from $f^{-1}(1)$ and columns from $f^{-1}(0)$. Whenever Alice speaks, we create two children node, one for the case she communicates 0 and other for the case she communicates 1. Since Alice has communicated, Bob will eliminate some possibilities for Alice's inputs and thus remove some rows of the matrix. Thus the matrix will be row-partitioned between the children nodes. We can construct children similarly when Bob speaks as well. The leaves of the tree correspond to the case when Alice and Bob have solved the game. So, the cost of the game can also be seen as the depth of the communication tree.

Karchmer and Wigderon studied a monotone variant of the game too where f is a monotone function and hence it is guaranteed that $\exists i \in [n]$ such that $x_i = 1$ and $y_i = 0$. The aim of this variant of the game is to output this index i. The cost of the game is defined similarly and is denoted by $\mathsf{KW}^+(f)$.

Karchmer and Wigderson [8] showed that the costs of these games for a function f are closely related to the minimum depth of non-monotone and monotone circuits that compute f. More formally, for a given Boolean function f, if the minimum depth of a (possibly non-monotone) circuit computing f is d, then $\mathsf{KW}(f) = d$. For a given monotone Boolean function f, if the minimum depth of a monotone circuit computing f is d_m, then $\mathsf{KW}^+(f) = d_m$. Exploring the weights of inputs and combining with some circuit theoretic ideas, we strengthen this to the following proposition (we defer the details to a full version of the paper).

Proposition 1. *The following five statements are equivalent for any monotone function $f : \{0,1\}^n \to \{0,1\}$.*

- *f has an $O(\log n)$ depth circuit.*
- *f has an $O(\log n)$ general KW game protocol.*
- *f has an $O(\log n)$ general KW game protocol in the case where Alice and Bob get inputs of equal weight.*
- *f has an $O(\log n)$ monotone KW game protocol in the case where Alice and Bob get inputs of equal weight.*
- *f has an $O(\log n)$ monotone KW game protocol in the case where weight of Alice's input is greater than or equal to weight of Bob's input.*

3   Power of Independent Negations

We begin our study by looking into circuits with only independent negations. We show that the minimum number of independent negations required to compute a given function is characterized by the decrease of the function.

For any Boolean function f, define the *independent negation complexity*, $\mathcal{I}_\mathsf{d}(f)$ to be the minimum number of negation gates that are required for any circuit computing the function f such that no negation gate feeds[4] in to another. We prove the following characterization. Due to lack of space, we defer the details to the full version.

---

[4] Not even through a series of gates.

Theorem 7. *For any Boolean function f, we have $\mathcal{I}_\mathsf{d}(f) = \mathsf{dec}(f)$.*

We now show that independent negation complexity is also characterized by a variant of *orientation* [9] which is a measure of non-monotonicity of a function considered in [9]. A function $f : \{0,1\}^n \to \{0,1\}$ is said to have *orientation* $\beta \in \{0,1\}^n$ if there is a monotone function $h : \{0,1\}^{2n} \to \{0,1\}$ such that: $\forall x \in \{0,1\}^n, f(x) = h(x, (x \oplus \beta))$. We generalize this in the following way.

Definition 1 (Monotone Orientation). *A function $f : \{0,1\}^n \to \{0,1\}$ is said to have* monotone orientation $\beta \in \{0,1\}^n$ *if there is a monotone function $h : \{0,1\}^{2n} \to \{0,1\}$ and a monotone function $g : \{0,1\}^n \to \{0,1\}^n$ such that : $\forall x \in \{0,1\}^n, f(x) = h(x, (g(x) \oplus \beta))$*

The *weight* of a monotone orientation β is defined as the number of 1s in the vector β. The monotone orientation weight of a function, $\mathsf{w}(f)$ is the minimum weight of a monotone orientation of f. Using basic properties of the definition, we show that the this measure is equivalent to independent negation complexity (see full version for a proof).

Theorem 8. *For any Boolean function $f : \{0,1\}^n \to \{0,1\}$, $\mathsf{w}(f) = \mathcal{I}_\mathsf{d}(f)$*

Now, we present a characterization for minimum depth of a formula with k independent negations computing a given function f. We have already seen the monotone and non-monotone (general) version of the Karchmer-Wigderson games. The monotone game corresponds to circuits in which there are no negation gates (that is, monotone circuits). The non-monotone game corresponds to general circuits where there can be any number of negations. Naturally, we would like to have an in-between version where we can control the number of negation gates in the circuit. To achieve this, we will modify the monotone version of the game by adding a *switch step*. Alice and Bob can, at any point in a protocol, choose[5] to switch. After the switch step, they are said to have played the game successfully if they find an index i such that $x_i = 0$ and $y_i = 1$.

We now define the Switch Karchmer-Wigderson (or SKW in short) game:

Definition 2 (Switch Karchmer-Wigderson Game). *Alice and Bob are given inputs from $f^{-1}(1)$ and $f^{-1}(0)$ respectively. They communicate between themselves and can at any point decide to perform the switch step. If the step was used, then they cannot use the step again. The aim of the game is to find, at the end of the game, an index i such that $x_i = 1 \neq y_i = 0$ if switch step was not used or $x_i = 0 \neq y_i = 1$ if the switch step was used*

Any protocol for the game can be seen as a communication tree [8]. We will also consider the switch step as an additional edge/level in the tree. The cost of a protocol is defined as the depth of the communication tree (number of bits

---

[5] Alice and Bob must both know that they are performing the operation. This can be inferred from the communication or can be indicated by one player by communicating with the other.

communicated + the number of switch steps (0 or 1) performed in the worst case). The cost of the game is the least cost of a valid protocol.

Clearly if this step is allowed in all cases we can play the game successfully as follows: Alice and Bob will play the general version of the game. After this they are guaranteed an index such that $x_i \neq y_i$. Now they can check if $x_i = 1$, if so, they are done. Otherwise they can perform the switch step and complete the game. This is similar to the non-monotone Karchmer-Wigderson game. If the step was not allowed, we arrive at the monotone Karchmer-Wigderson game.

We restrict the use of the switch step by allowing it only in a limited number of cases. We define it in a more concrete way as follows:

The switch step can be performed only at some k nodes in the communication tree, the nodes at which this is done is left to (the protocol)Alice and Bob. Let the said game be SKW^k and the cost of the game be $\mathsf{SKW}^k(f)$. We relate the cost of this game to the depth of a formula computing f with k independent negations. See full version for details.

Lemma 1. *For every Boolean function f with decrease at least k, there is a circuit (in fact a formula) computing f which uses k independent negations with depth at most $\mathsf{SKW}^k(f)$.*

4 Thickness and Independent Negation Complexity

We showed in Proposition 1 the effect of weights of the inputs in the complexity of Karchmer-Wigderson games. To exploit the full power of this restriction, we define a measure of complexity of a function which we call the *thickness*.

Definition 3 (Thickness). *Let $f : \{0,1\}^n \to \{0,1\}$ be a non-constant Boolean function. We define thickness of the f as $\mathsf{t}(f) = \max_{x,y}(\mathsf{wt}(y) - \mathsf{wt}(x))$ where $x \in f^{-1}(1), y \in f^{-1}(0)$.*

Indeed, $-1 \leq \mathsf{t}(f) \leq n$. The lower bound is achieved by threshold functions and the upper bound is achieved when $f(1^n) = 0$ and $f(0^n) = 1$.

Thickness and Independent Negations: We will now show that $\approx t$ independent negations are enough to compute a function with almost optimal depth.

Theorem 9. *If a Boolean function f of thickness t has a circuit of depth d, then f can also be computed by a circuit of depth $d + O(\log n)$ using $2^{\lceil \log(t+1) \rceil}$ independent negations.*

Proof. (Sketch) We provide a SKW protocol with the required properties. The main idea is for Alice and Bob to communicate and determine if $\mathsf{wt}(y) > \mathsf{wt}(x)$ and to perform the switch step if this is true. Generally this would take $O(\log n)$ bits of communication. However, since the thickness of f is t, to get $\mathsf{wt}(y) > \mathsf{wt}(x)$, $\mathsf{wt}(y)$ has only t possible values. We exploit this fact to reduce the initial communication required and in effect reduce the number of switch steps in the protocol.

We have seen what that we can compute f almost optimally if $2^{\lceil \log(t+1) \rceil} \approx t$ (thickness) number of negations are given. Note that all the negations are used as independent negations. A better bound may be possible if these negations are not used in that form. We defer the details of the proof to the full version.

Theorem 10. *If a Boolean function f of thickness t has a circuit of depth d, then f also has a circuit of depth $d + O(\log n)$ with only $\lceil \log(t+1) \rceil$ negations.*

A Parameterized Bound for Monotone Functions: We have seen that for a monotone function of thickness t; without using negations in a circuit, we can compute it within nearly t times the optimal depth. We have also seen that using nearly t independent negations, we can compute it with almost optimal depth. We will now see what can be done if fewer than t independent negations are allowed in the circuit. We defer the details to the full version.

Theorem 11. *If a monotone Boolean function f of thickness t has a circuit of depth d, then for any $1 \le k \le \lceil \log(t+1) \rceil$, f can also be computed by a circuit of depth $d\lceil \frac{t}{2^k - 1} \rceil + O(\log n)$ using only 2^k independent negations.*

Thickness and Karchmer-Wigderson Games for Monotone Functions: We now show that if a monotone function has low thickness, then negation gates are not very useful for computing it. We prove, by relating the complexity of the KW games to depth of circuits: $d \ge \frac{d_m - O(\log n)}{t+1}$, where d is the minimum depth of a (possibly non-monotone) circuit computing f and d_m is the minimum depth of a monotone circuit computing the function f of thickness t.

We remark a known special case of the theorem. A function f is said to be a *slice function* iff $\exists k$ such that $f(x) = 1$ if $\mathsf{wt}(x) > k$, $f(x) = 0$ if $\mathsf{wt}(x) < k$, and $f(x)$ is non-trivial for $\mathsf{wt}(x) = k$. Note that slice functions have thickness of 0. Thus, from the below Theorem, we may observe that for a slice function, the minimum depths of monotone and general circuits differ by $O(\log n)$.

Theorem 12. *For any monotone function $f : \{0,1\}^n \to \{0,1\}$ having a thickness t, $\mathsf{KW}^+(f) \le (t+1)\,\mathsf{KW}(f) + O(\log n)$.*

Proof. It suffices to show that given a circuit of depth d computing f, we can devise a protocol for the monotone KW game of cost $(t+1)d + c\log n$.

Recall that the setting of the monotone KW game is that there are two players Alice and Bob; Alice gets $x \in f^{-1}(1)$ and Bob gets $y \in f^{-1}(0)$. They have to find an index i such that $x_i = 1$ and $y_i = 0$ using minimum bits of communication.

We have a circuit of depth d computing f. We push down negations to the leaves of the circuit without increasing the depth using De Morgan's laws. From here on, we assume that negations are only at the input variables. Now they play the general KW game on the circuit with Alice communicating at $\wedge$ gates and Bob communicating at $\vee$ gates. They will move down through the circuit and reach a leaf literal. This will either be a variable or its negation. We are guaranteed that the literal evaluates to 1 for Alice and 0 for Bob. If the literal is positive, we have found an index where $x_i = 1$ and $y_i = 0$ and we are done.

If not, we have an index where $x_i = 0$ and $y_i = 1$. Alice sets the input bit x_i to 1. Let us call this new input x'. Since f is a monotone function and $x' > x$, $f(x') = 1$. Alice and Bob repeat playing the game, now on x' and y. Again they will end up in a literal evaluating to 1 for Alice and 0 for Bob. Note that the bits at which x is changed are now equal to those of y. Thus we cannot get those indices from the replay of the game. So, after each run of the game, they have either found the desired index, or the number of 1s in x has increased by 1.

They will repeat this process $t + 1$ times (unless the desired index is already obtained). Consider all the indices found in this process. Let the set of these indices be S. All the indices $i \in S$ satisfy $x_i = 0$ and $y_i = 1$. For any set $S \subseteq [n]$ we denote x_S as x restricted to the indices present in S. Thus $\mathsf{wt}(x_{\bar{S}}) = \mathsf{wt}(x)$ and $\mathsf{wt}(y_{\bar{S}}) = \mathsf{wt}(y) - (t + 1)$. Since the thickness of f is t and $x \in f^{-1}(1)$ and $\in f^{-1}(0)$, we have $\mathsf{wt}(x) \geq \mathsf{wt}(y) - t$. Thus $\mathsf{wt}(x_{\bar{S}}) = \mathsf{wt}(x) \geq \mathsf{wt}(y) - t \geq \mathsf{wt}(y_{\bar{S}}) + (t + 1) - t > \mathsf{wt}(y_{\bar{S}})$.

Now Alice will communicate $\mathsf{wt}(x_{\bar{S}})$ to Bob and they will consider the function $\mathsf{Th}_{\mathsf{wt}(x_{\bar{S}})}$. This function evaluates to 1 on $x_{\bar{S}}$ which is available for Alice at this point, and to 0 on $y_{\bar{S}}$ which is available for Bob. As any threshold function has a $O(\log n)$ depth monotone circuit, they can play the monotone game on such a circuit and find an index i such that the ith bit of $x_{\bar{S}}$ is 1 and that of $y_{\bar{S}}$ is 0. Since $i \notin S$, the ith bit of x is same as that of $x_{\bar{S}}$. Similar property holds for y and $y_{\bar{S}}$. Hence, $x_i = 1$ and $y_i = 0$ for the same i. This completes the protocol.

Cost of the protocol also follows from the description; in the worst case we would have played the general game $t+1$ times on the circuit computing f, after which we would have spent $O(\log n)$ bits due to the threshold circuit. Thus the cost is atmost $(t + 1)d + O(\log n)$. □

5   Negation Graph and Decrease Capacity

We have explored the power of independent negations. We also know that when we remove the restriction of independence, we exponentially increase their power. We now explore how the structure of the negation graph influences the decrease of the circuit. *Given a circuit, the negation graph contains the negation gates and the root gate[6] as vertices. There is an edge from a vertex g_1 to vertex g_2 iff the gate g_1 feeds into gate g_2 via a path which does not contain a negation gate.*

Definition 4 (Decrease Capacity of a Negation Graph). *Given a negation graph of a circuit, for every vertex v in the negation graph, we define the function $\mathsf{d}_{\max}(v)$ recursively (bottom-up) as follows: (1) Decrease capacity of a negation gate v with no incoming edges is $\mathsf{d}_{\max}(v) = 1$. (2) Decrease capacity of a negation gate v with incoming edges from vertex $v_1, \ldots v_k$ is: $\mathsf{d}_{\max}(v) = 1 + \sum_{i=1}^{k} \mathsf{d}_{\max}(v_i)$. (3) Decrease capacity of the root gate r is the sum of decrease capacities of all the vertices feeding into it. For a given negation graph N, we define $\mathsf{d}_{\max}(N) = \mathsf{d}_{\max}(r)$. The decrease capacity of a circuit C, denoted $\mathsf{d}_{\max}(C)$, is $\mathsf{d}_{\max}(N)$ where N is the underlying negation graph of the circuit.*

---

[6] If the root gate is a negation gate, add a dummy gate as a root gate.

To justify the word capacity, we will show that this measure is a bound on the decrease of a function computed by a given circuit.

Theorem 13. *If a circuit C computes a function f, then $\mathsf{dec}(f) \leq \mathsf{d}_{\max}(C)$.*

Proof. (*Sketch*) We present the main idea of the proof and defer the details to the full version. Morizumi [11] showed that for any negation gate g, across a given chain $\mathcal{X}$, the number of 0 to 1 transitions in the output of g can be bounded by the number of 1 to 0 transitions of negation gates that feed into g. We use this to arrive at an upper bound for the 1 to 0 transitions in the output of g.

Note that we in fact show something stronger: for any negation gate g, $\mathsf{d}_{\max}(g)$ is an upper bound on the decrease of the function computed at the gate.

We will show that given only the negation graph of a circuit C, $\mathsf{d}_{\max}(C)$ is the best upper bound obtainable if the negation graph is a *tree*. However, it is easy to see from the definition of decrease capacity of a negation tree is exactly the number of negation nodes.

Theorem 14. *Given a Negation Tree N with less than $\frac{n}{2}$ nodes, there is a circuit C with negation graph N computing a function with decrease $\mathsf{d}_{\max}(N)$.*

Necessary Conditions for Negation Optimal Circuits: We start by proving tight upper bounds on $\mathsf{d}_{\max}(C)$ for a circuit C in terms of the number of negations. Due to lack of space, we defer the proof of the following to the full version.

Theorem 15. *Any circuit C containing ℓ negations satisfies $\mathsf{d}_{\max}(C) \leq 2^{\ell} - 1$. Also the equality is achieved only when the undirected negation graph is a complete graph.*

Note that if C computes f, then $\mathsf{dec}(f) \leq \mathsf{d}_{\max}(C)$. Now if C has the minimum number of negations required to compute f (which is called the inversion complexity $I(f)$), the above Theorem gives $\mathsf{d}_{\max}(C) \leq 2^{I(f)} - 1$, and so $\mathsf{dec}(f) \leq 2^{I(f)} - 1$. This proves one side of Markov's Theorem [10].

Also, the equality condition shows that if a function f has decrease $\mathsf{dec}(f) = 2^{\ell} - 1$, then any circuit C containing ℓ negations and computing f will have a complete undirected negation graph. Note that ℓ is the minimum number of negations required to compute f. In addition, we can also conclude that if $2^{\ell} < \mathsf{dec}(f) \leq 2^{\ell+1} - 1$, then any circuit C computing f containing $\ell+1$ negations satisfies: Every negation gate in C either (1) feeds into another negation gate (via a negation free path) or (2) has a negation gate feeding into it. Alternatively, If N is the undirected negation graph of the circuit and r is the root gate vertex, $N \setminus r$ is connected.

We show that any function f can be computed using negation structure of any other given function g, as long as g has high enough alternation. We provide the detailed argument in the full version of the paper.

Theorem 16. *Let $f : \{0,1\}^n \to \{0,1\}$ and $g : \{0,1\}^m \to \{0,1\}$ be two functions such that $\mathsf{alt}(f) \leq \mathsf{alt}(g)$ and $f(0^m) = g(0^n)$. Then, any circuit for g can be used (with substitution of variables with monotone functions) to compute f without using any extra negation.*

By combining Theorem 16 and 14 we get Theorem 6 in the introduction.

Negation Lower Bound for Depth Limited Circuits: As yet another application of the notion of decrease capacity of the negation graph, we provide an alternate proof for a negation lower bound shown by Santha and Wilson [15].

Theorem 17. *If a Boolean function f of decrease k is computed by a circuit C of depth d, then the number of negations in C is at least $d(k^{1/d} - 1)$.*

References

1. Alon, N., Boppana, R.B.: The monotone circuit complexity of Boolean functions. Combinatorica **7**(1), 1–22 (1987)
2. Amano, K., Maruoka, A.: A superpolynomial lower bound for a circuit computing the clique function with at most $(1/6)$log log n negation gates. SIAM J. Comput. **35**(1), 201–216 (2005)
3. Nechiporuk, E.I.: On the complexity of schemes in some bases containing non-trivial elements with zero weights. Problemy Kibernetiki **8**, 123–160 (1962)
4. Fischer, M.J.: The complexity of negation-limited networks—a brief survey. In: Brakhage, H. (ed.) GI-Fachtagung 1975. LNCS, vol. 33, pp. 71–82. Springer, Heidelberg (1975). https://doi.org/10.1007/3-540-07407-4_9
5. Jukna, S.: On the minimum number of negations leading to super-polynomial savings. Inf. Process. Lett. **89**(2), 71–74 (2004)
6. Jukna, S.: Boolean Function Complexity. Advances and Frontiers. Springer, Heidelberg (2012). https://doi.org/10.1007/978-3-642-24508-4
7. Jukna, S., Lingas, A.: Lower bounds for demorgan circuits of bounded negation width. In: STACS (2019)
8. Karchmer, M., Wigderson, A.: Monotone circuits for connectivity require super-logarithmic depth. SIAM J. Discret. Math. **3**(2), 255–265 (1990)
9. Koroth, S., Sarma, J.: Depth lower bounds against circuits with sparse orientation. Fundam. Inf. **152**(2), 123–144 (2017)
10. Markov, A.A.: On the inversion complexity of a system of functions. J. ACM **5**(4), 331–334 (1958)
11. Morizumi, H.: Limiting negations in formulas. In: Albers, S., Marchetti-Spaccamela, A., Matias, Y., Nikoletseas, S., Thomas, W. (eds.) ICALP 2009. LNCS, vol. 5555, pp. 701–712. Springer, Heidelberg (2009). https://doi.org/10.1007/978-3-642-02927-1_58
12. Raz, R., Wigderson, A.: Monotone circuits for matching require linear depth. J. ACM **39**(3), 736–744 (1992)
13. Razborov, A.A.: Lower bounds for monotone complexity of some Boolean functions. Sov. Math. Doklady. **31**, 354–357 (1985)
14. Rossman, B.: Correlation bounds against monotone NC^1. In: Zuckerman, D. (ed.) 30th Conference on Computational Complexity, CCC 2015. LIPICS, vol. 33, pp. 392–411 (2015)
15. Santha, M., Wilson, C.: Limiting negations in constant depth circuits. SIAM J. Comput. **22**(2), 294–302 (1993)
16. Wegener, I.: On the complexity of slice functions. Theor. Comput. Sci. **38**, 55–68 (1985)

Even Better Fixed-Parameter Algorithms for Bicluster Editing

Manuel Lafond$^{(\boxtimes)}$

Université de Sherbrooke, Sherbrooke, Canada
manuel.lafond@USherbrooke.ca

Abstract. Given a bipartite graph G, the BICLUSTER EDITING problem asks for the minimum number of edges to insert or delete in G so that every connected component is a bicluster, i.e. a complete bipartite graph. This has applications in various areas such as social network analysis and bioinformatics. We study the parameterized complexity of the problem, the best published algorithm so far attaining a time of $O^*(3.24^k)$, with k the number of edges to edit. Using novel but intuitive ideas, we significantly improve this to an $O^*(2.695^k)$ time complexity.

Our algorithm has the advantage of being conceptually simple and does not require tedious case handling. Previous approaches were based on finding a forbidden induced subgraph (e.g. a P_4) and branching into several ways of eliminating such a subgraph. We take a departure from this local viewpoint, and instead solve conflicts globally. That is, we take two vertices that prevent the graph from containing only biclusters, and branch into the ways of resolving all the conflicts they are part of, at once. We hope that these ideas will allow simpler algorithms for other forbidden induced subgraph problems.

As a complementary result, we also show that BICLUSTER EDITING admits a problem kernel with $5k$ vertices.

1 Introduction

Partitioning data points into clusters, which are often interpreted as groups of similarity, is a fundamental task in computer science with several practical applications in areas such as social networks analysis and bioinformatics. Although many formulations of what constitutes a good clustering have been proposed (e.g. based on pairwise distances [8,13,17], modularity [19], random walks [22] or likelihood [14]), most approaches are based on the principle that a cluster should contain members that are similar to each other, and different from the members outside of the cluster. In a graph-theoretic setting, the ideal clustering should therefore consist of disjoint cliques.

In some applications, one has two classes of data points and only the relationships between classes are interesting. Clustering then takes the form of finding sub-groups in which the members of one class have similar relationships (e.g. groups of people who like the same movies). This can be modeled as a bipartite graph with two vertex sets V_1 and V_2, one for each class, and the goal is to

© Springer Nature Switzerland AG 2020
D. Kim et al. (Eds.): COCOON 2020, LNCS 12273, pp. 578–590, 2020.
https://doi.org/10.1007/978-3-030-58150-3_47

partition $V_1 \cup V_2$ into disjoint *biclusters*, which are complete bipartite graphs. This variant has several applications [18,27], for instance in the analysis of social interactions between groups [5], gene expression data [7], and phylogenetics (e.g. when comparing the left and right descendant of an ancestral species [2,16]).

In this work, we assume that bipartite graphs that do not consist of disjoint biclusters are due to erroneous edges and non-edges. In the BICLUSTER EDIT-ING problem, we ask whether a given bipartite graph G can be transformed into a set of disjoint biclusters by adding/removing at most k edges.

Related Work. The BICLUSTER EDITING problem is known to be NP-hard even on subcubic graphs [9] and on dense graphs [26]. By observing that graphs of disjoint biclusters coincide with bipartite P_4-free graphs, Protti et al. [21] first devised a simple $O^*(4^k)$ time algorithm that finds a P_4, and branches over the four possible ways to remove it (here, the O^* notation suppresses polynomial factors). They also show that BICLUSTER EDITING admits a kernel of $4k^2+6k$ vertices. In [12], the authors extend the branching algorithm to solve induced P_5's, if any—this leads to slightly more case handling but achieves an improved running time of $O^*(3.24^k)$. A kernel of size $4k$ is also proposed, but this turns out to be a slight inaccuracy (we provide a counter-example). An $O^*(2^{5\sqrt{pk}})$ algorithm is proposed in [9], where p is the number of desired biclusters. In terms of approximability, a factor 11 approximation algorithm is presented in [3] and is improved to a pivot-based, randomized factor 4 approximation in [1]. Owing to the practical applications of the problem, several heuristics and experiments have also been published [20,23–25].

A closely related problem is CLUSTER EDITING, where the given graph does not have to be bipartite and the goal is to attain a collection of disjoint cliques. To some extent, this problem seems inherently easier than its bipartite counterpart: CLUSTER EDITING is only known to be NP-hard on graphs of maximum degree 6 [15], it admits an $O^*(1.619^k)$ FPT algorithm [6] (obtained after a series of improvements [10,11]), and a 3-approximation approximation [4] (a 2.5-approximation is given in [28] if edit weights satisfy probability constraints).

Our Contributions. We provide an $O^*(2.695^k)$ time algorithm for BICLUSTER EDITING, a significant improvement over the best known bound of $O^*(3.24^k)$. To achieve this, we take a departure from the usual idea of branching over the ways to correct a forbidden induced subgraph. Instead of resolving such conflicts locally, we resolve these problems globally by finding two vertices that prevent the graph from containing only biclusters, and eliminating *every* conflict they are part of. More concretely, we apply a very intuitive but powerful idea. Given two vertices u and v with different but overlapping neighborhoods, we branch over two possibilities: either u and v belong to the same bicluster, or they do not. In the first case, we try every way to make their neighborhoods equal, and in the second, we try every way to make their neighborhoods non-intersecting.

This leads to a simpler algorithm, but also to less straightforward branching factors to analyze. In particular, our algorithm branches over a number of cases that is exponential in the number of modifications, but we characterize when it is worth it to do so (Lemma 3). We first show that this immediately leads to an $O^*(3.237^k)$ algorithm that is easier to implement than previously published approaches. The $O^*(2.695^k)$ time algorithm is obtained by only adding a special case to handle degree one vertices. Our algorithm therefore has the advantage of being very simple to comprehend and implement.

On another note, we also correct the inaccuracy of [12] concerning the $4k$ kernel size for BICLUSTER EDITING. We provide an example showing that the approach cannot achieve better than a $6k$ kernel. We then show that with an additional reduction rule, one can attain a $5k$ kernel size. The proof on the kernel size is based on a combinatorial charging argument.

Preliminary Notions. Given two sets A and B, we write $A \triangle B = (A \setminus B) \cup (B \setminus A)$ for the *symmetric difference* between A and B. Let G be a graph and let $v \in V(G)$. We write $N_G(v)$ for the set of neighbors of v and define $deg_G(v) = |N_G(v)|$. The G subscript may be dropped if it is clear from the context. For F a set of pairs of $V(G)$, we write $G - F$ for the graph $(V, E \setminus F)$. If $F = \{xy\}$ has a single element, we may write $G - xy$ instead of $G - \{xy\}$.

The vertex set $V(G)$ of a bipartite graph $G = (V_1 \cup V_2, E)$ has two disjoint subsets V_1 and V_2. For $X \subseteq V_i$, $i \in \{1, 2\}$, we define $N_G(X) = \bigcup_{x \in X} N_G(x)$. Two vertices $u, v \in V_i$, with $i \in \{1, 2\}$ are called *twins* if $N(u) = N(v)$. Note that twins form an equivalence relation. A *twin class* is an equivalence class, i.e. a maximal subset $X \subseteq V(G)$ such that x_1 and x_2 are twins for every $x_1, x_2 \in X$.

Given a bipartite graph $G = (V_1 \cup V_2, E)$ and subsets $X \subseteq V_1$ and $Y \subseteq V_2$, we say that $X \cup Y$ form a a *bicluster* if $N(x) = Y$ for all $x \in X$ and $N(y) = X$ for all $y \in Y$ (note that a single vertex is a bicluster). We say that G is a *bicluster graph* if each of its connected components is a bicluster. An *edge modification* is either the insertion of a non-existing edge, or the deletion of an existing edge.

The BICLUSTER EDITING problem asks, given a bipartite graph G, whether there exists a sequence of at most k edge modifications that transform G into a bicluster graph. We treat k as a parameter. A *solution* to a graph G is a graph $\mathcal{B}$ in which every connected component is a bicluster, and such that at most k modifications are needed to transform G into $\mathcal{B}$. We say that $\mathcal{B}$ is *optimal* if no other solution requires less modifications.

2   Reduction Rules and a $5k$ Problem Kernel

We provide three reduction rules based on those proposed in [12]. We use the notion of a *sister* of a vertex u. Let R be a twin class of G. Let $S = N(R)$ and $t \in N(S) \setminus R$. Then t is a *sister* of R if the two following conditions are satisfied:

- t does not have a twin in G;
- $N(t) = S \cup \{v\}$ for some vertex $v \in V(G) \setminus S$.

For any $u \in V(G)$, we say that t is a sister of u if t is a sister of the twin class containing u, see Fig. 1. We can now describe our reduction rules.

Rule 1: if a connected component X of G is a bicluster, remove X from G.

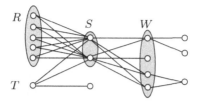

Fig. 1. R is a twin class, $S = N(R)$, T are the sisters of R (there is only one) and $W = N(S) \setminus (T \cup R)$. Note how the two bottom vertices of W are not sisters of R.

Rule 2: if there is a twin class R such that $|R| > |N(N(R)) \setminus R|$, then remove any vertex from R.

Rule 3: let R be a twin class, let T be the set of sisters of R, and let $W = N(N(R)) \setminus (R \cup T)$. If $|R| > |W|$ and $|T| \geq 1$, then choose any $t \in T$ and remove the edge between t and $N(t) \setminus N(R)$.

The idea of Rule 3 is that if removing a single edge from a T vertex would help it join a "large enough" twin-class, then we should do so. For instance in Fig. 1, according to Rule 3, we can remove the edge from the T vertex to the bottom degree 1 vertex, making the size of the R twin class larger.

Note that in [12], Rule 1 and Rule 2 were introduced and the authors suggested that they would lead to a kernel of size $4k$. However, the P_6 graph is a counter-example to this claim. Indeed, the P_6 admits a bicluster graph with $k = 1$, has $6k$ vertices, and Rule 1 and Rule 2 do not apply. It is plausible that Rule 1 and Rule 2 can lead to a $6k$ kernel, whereas Rule 3 allows us to reduce this to $5k$ (in particular, Rule 3 does reduce the P_6).

It is easy to see that Rule 1 is safe. Rule 2 was already shown to be safe in [12]. The proof was based on a result on twins that we restate here, as it will be useful later. Rule 3 can then be shown to be safe.

Lemma 1 ([12]). *There is an optimal solution $\mathcal{B}$ of G in which every pair of twins are in the same bicluster of $\mathcal{B}$.*

Lemma 2. *Let R be a twin class and let T be the set of sisters of R. Also let $S = N(R)$ and $W = N(S) \setminus (R \cup T)$. If $|R| > |W|$ and $|T| \geq 1$, then for any $t \in T$ there exists an optimal solution in which the edge between t and the vertex in $N(T) \setminus S$ is deleted.*

The proof of the latter is somewhat technical and we defer it to the full version. The main idea is that if some $t \in T$ keeps its edge to $N(t) \setminus S$ in some optimal solution, then we can modify this solution by forming a new bicluster with R, t, S and possibly other vertices but not $N(t) \setminus S$.

We now have enough ingredients to devise our small kernel. Here we only include the description of our charging scheme, which is perhaps the original portion of the proof. It also demonstrates why Rule 2 and Rule 3 are needed: it guarantees that $R \leq W$, which allows us to redirect the charge of every $r \in R$ to a distinct vertex in W.

Theorem 1. *Let G be a graph on which Rules 1, 2 and 3 do not apply. Then G has at most $5k$ vertices.*

Sketch of the proof. Let $\mathcal{B}$ be an optimal bicluster graph of G in which vertices in the same twin class of G belong to the same bicluster, which exists by Lemma 1. Let E_I be the set of inserted edges and let E_D be the set of deleted edges. Let X be the set of vertices of G that are incident to at least one edge of $E_I \cup E_D$, and let $\mathcal{R} = V \setminus X$ be the unaffected vertices of G. Let $\{R_1, \ldots, R_p\}$ be the partition of $\mathcal{R}$ into twin classes. For each R_i, let $S_i = N_G(R_i)$, let T_i be the sisters of R_i, and let $W_i = N_G(S_i) \setminus (T_i \cup R_i)$. Moreover, let B_i be the bicluster of $\mathcal{B}$ that R_i belongs to. Since for each $i \in [p]$, R_i is unmodified, we have $S_i \subseteq B_i$ and, since each $W_i \cup T_i$ vertex has a different neighborhood than the R_i vertices, we have $W_i \cup T_i \subseteq X$.

We argue that for $i \neq j$, we have $B_i \neq B_j$. This is because if R_i and R_j are both in the same part of the bipartition, say in V_1, then we would have $N_G(R_i) = N_G(R_j)$ and $R_i \cup R_j$ would be a larger twin class. If R_i and R_j are in different parts of the bipartition, then $R_i \cup R_j$ would form a connected component of G that is a bicluster, and should be removed according to Rule 1.

We want to bound the size of $V := V(G)$ by devising a charging scheme in which each vertex of V charges a total amount of 1 to edges of $E_I \cup E_D$. The idea is that every modified edge receives a charge of at most 5 in this scheme.

There are three rules that describe this charging scheme. C1 handles vertices of X, and C2, C3 handle vertices of $\mathcal{R}$.

C1. For each $x \in X$, let $E_x \subseteq E_I \cup E_D$ be the set of modified edges that are incident to x. Then x charges $1/|E_x|$ to each edge of E_x.

As for the $\mathcal{R}$ vertices, because our three rules do not apply, we have $|R_i| \leq |W_i|$ for each i. This is because if $|R_i| > |W_i|$, then if $|T_i| \geq 1$, Rule 3 applies, and if $T_i = \emptyset$, $W_i = N(N(R_i)) \setminus R_i$ and Rule 2 applies. Note that this is precisely where Rule 3 is needed. First map each vertex of R_i to a distinct vertex of W_i in an arbitrary manner using any injective function $f_i : R_i \to W_i$. Then denote $W_i^{in} = W_i \cap B_i$ and $W_i^{out} = W_i \setminus B_i$. Let $r \in R_i$ and let $w = f_i(r)$ be the vertex that r is mapped to. The charging scheme for r is described as follows.

C2. Suppose that $w \in W_i^{out}$. Let $S_w = N_G(w) \cap S_i$, noting that $|S_w| \geq 1$ and that each edge between w and S_w has been deleted. In that case, r charges $1/|S_w|$ to each edge between w and S_w.

C3. Suppose instead that $w \in W_i^{in}$. Then since w is not a sister of R, one of the following holds:
   (a) if w has a non-neighbor s in S_i, then ws was inserted, in which case r charge 1 to ws (if multiple choices of s arise, choose any).
   (b) If $S_i \subseteq N_G(w)$, then let $Z_w = N_G(w) \setminus S_i$, noting that $|Z_w| \geq 1$ and that each edge between w and Z_w has been deleted. In that case, r charges $1/|Z_w|$ to each edge between w and Z_w.

The total charge $c(e)$ of an edge e of $E_I \cup E_D$ is the sum of charges given to e by all the vertices of G. We claim that $c(e) \leq 5$. Since each vertex outputs a charge of 1, this allows us to establish that $|V| = \sum_{e \in E_I \cup E_D} c(e) \leq 5k$. We redirect the reader to the full version for the remaining details. The main idea is that any edge $e \in E_I \cup E_D$ can receive at most two charges from each of C1, C2, or C3, each charge is at most 1, and two of them must be at most $1/2$. □

We note that we do not know whether the $5k$ bound is tight, since we know of no example of a graph on which none of the rules apply, but that has size $5k$.

3   An $O^*(2.695^k)$ Branching Algorithm

We now present our main branching algorithm. We take two vertices $u, v \in V_i$, $i \in \{1, 2\}$ that are not twins but whose neighborhood intersects. Either u and v belong to the same bicluster, or they do not. If we fix the choice that u, v are in the same bicluster, we need to do something about $N(u) \triangle N(v)$, and we try every way of ensuring that u and v have the same neighbors. If we fix the choice that u, v are in different biclusters, we need to do something about $N(u) \cap N(v)$, and this time we ensure that u and v share no common neighbor. See Fig. 2.

```
 1  function biclusterize(G, k)
 2      if k < 0 then  Report "NO" and return
 3      Remove from G all bicluster connected components (Rule 1)
 4      if G has no vertex then  Report "YES" and return
 5      if G has maximum degree 2 then  Solve G in polynomial time
 6
 7      Let u, v ∈ V(G) such that N(u) ∩ N(v) ≠ ∅ and N(u)△N(v) ≠ ∅
 8      Let R_u be the twin class of u and R_v be the twin class of v
 9      /*Put u, v in the same bicluster*/
10      for each subset Z of N(u)△N(v) do
11          Obtain G' from G by:
                 inserting all missing edges between R_u ∪ R_v and Z and
                 deleting all edges between R_u ∪ R_v and (N(u)△N(v)) \ Z
12          Let h be the number of edges modified from G to G'
13          biclusterize(G', k − h)
14      end
15      /*Put u, v in different biclusters*/
16      for each subset Z of N(u) ∩ N(v) do
17          Obtain G' from G by:
                 deleting all edges between R_u and (N(u) ∩ N(v)) \ Z and
                 deleting all edges between R_v and Z
18          Let h be the number of edges modified from G to G'
19          biclusterize(G', k − h)
20      end
21      if some recursive call reported "YES" then report "YES"
22      else report "NO"
```

Algorithm 1: Main branching algorithm

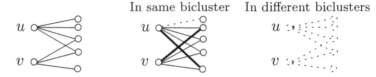

Fig. 2. Left: two vertices u, v and $N(u) \cup N(v)$. Middle: one of the 8 ways to branch into if u and v are in the same bicluster. Right: one of the 4 ways to branch into if u and v are in distinct biclusters. Dotted edges are deletions, fat edges are insertions.

The pseudo-code of this approach is presented in Algorithm 1. As we will show, it is sufficient to achieve time $O^*(3.237^k)$ with an easy analysis.

Importantly, we observe that $h \geq |N(u) \triangle N(v)|$ in the first case because each $z \in Z$ requires an insertion and each $z \notin Z$ requires a deletion. Similarly, $h \geq |N(u) \cap N(v)|$ in the second case, because each element requires a deletion.

Notice that even if Algorithm 1 might branch into an exponential number of cases, the larger the set of branching cases, the more k is reduced in each recursive call. It turns out to be more advantageous to have more cases: the larger $N(u) \cap N(v)$ and $N(u) \triangle N(v)$ are, the closer to an $O(2^k)$ algorithm we get. The graphs of small maximum degree are the most problematic.

To analyze this more formally, let $u, v \in V_i$ and let $c := |N(u) \cap N(v)|$ and $d := |N(u) \triangle N(v)|$ (c stands from 'common', d for 'different'). Then in the worst case, when $|R_u| = |R_v| = 1$, the number of recursive calls given by the recurrence

$$f(k) = 2^c f(k - c) + 2^d f(k - d),$$

whose characteristic polynomial is $a^k - 2^c a^{k-c} - 2^d a^{k-d}$. We will be interested in the worst possible combination of c and d, i.e. that lead to a polynomial with the maximum largest real root.

Definition 1. *Let f be a polynomial function. Then $lrr(f)$ denotes the largest real root of f.*

Let $c, d \geq 1$ be integers. We denote by $lrr(c, d)$ the largest real root of the polynomial function $f(a) = a^k - 2^c a^{k-c} - 2^d a^{k-d}$.

The intuition that higher c and d is better follows from the next technical lemma, which characterizes particular situations in which a characteristic polynomial is better than another. Roughly speaking, it says that if we can decrease k at the expense of creating more branching cases, it is advantageous if the additional number of cases increases exponentially in the amount decreased.

Although we will not need the full generality of the statement here, it might be of independent interest.

Lemma 3. *Let $k \in \mathbb{N}$, let $b > 1$ be a real and let $c, c_0, \dots, c_{k-1}$ be non-negative reals, with $0 < c \leq k$. Let*

$$f(a) = a^k - \sum_{j=0}^{k-1} c_j a^j - b^c a^{k-c}$$

be a polynomial. Moreover let $\epsilon > 0$ be a positive real, and let

$$f^*(a) = a^k - \sum_{j=0}^{k-1} c_j a^j - b^{c+\epsilon} a^{k-c-\epsilon}$$

Then $lrr(f^*) \le lrr(f)$.

Proof. We first claim that $f^*(a) \ge f(a)$ for all $a \ge b$. We prove this by contraposition, i.e. we assume that $f^*(a) < f(a)$ for some a, and deduce $a < b$. If $a \le 0$, then $a < b$, so suppose a is positive. Then

$$a^k - \sum_{j=0}^{k-1} c_j a^j - b^{c+\epsilon} a^{k-c-\epsilon} < a^k - \sum_{j=0}^{k-1} c_j a^j - b^c a^{k-c},$$

and thus $-b^{c+\epsilon} a^{k-c-\epsilon} < -b^c a^{k-c}$. Solving for a leads to $a^\epsilon < b^\epsilon$. Given that $a > 0$ and $b > 1$, this means that $a < b$, proving our claim by contraposition.

We next claim that $lrr(f) \ge b$. Note that for each a satisfying $0 \le a < b$, because the c_j's are non-negative, $f(a) \le a^k - b^c a^{k-c} = a^{k-c}(a^c - b^c)$. Still assuming that $0 \le a < b$, we have $a^c - b^c < 0$ and thus the roots of f cannot be in the interval $[0..b)$. Moreover, f is negative in this interval and, since the leading coefficient of f is positive, f is eventually positive for some $a \ge b$, and by the continuity of f, $f(a) = 0$ for some $a \ge b$. This implies $lrr(f) \ge b$.

Owing to its leading coefficient, we also know that f is positive for all $a > lrr(f)$. Since $f^*(a) \ge f(a)$ for all $a \ge b$ and $lrr(f) \ge b$, we know that f^* is also positive for all $a > lrr(f)$. Thus $f^*(a) > 0$ for all $a > lrr(f)$. Thus any real root of f^* must be equal or less than $lrr(f)$, proving the lemma. □

Corollary 1. *Let $c, d \ge 1$ be integers. Then $lrr(c, d) \ge lrr(c + 1, d)$ and $lrr(c, d) \ge lrr(c, d + 1)$.*

Proof. Recall that $lrr(c, d)$ is the largest real root of $f(a) = a^k - 2^c a^{k-c} - 2^d a^{k-d}$. Consider $lrr(c, d+1)$, the largest real root of $f^*(a) = a^k - 2^c a^{k-c} - 2^{d+1} a^{k-d-1}$. Using Lemma 3 and plugging in $b = 2$, $\epsilon = 1$, we see that $lrr(c, d+1) \le lrr(c, d)$. The proof is the same for $lrr(c + 1, d) \le lrr(c, d)$. □

We can then show that the simple algorithm above achieves a similar running time as that of [12]. The time complexity proof is based on the idea that, the worst case occurs when c and d are as small as possible. Since G contains a vertex of degree at least 3, the worst case is when we branch over u, v of degrees 3 and 1, which gives branching factor $lrr(1, 2) \simeq 3.237$.

Theorem 2. *Algorithm 1 is correct and runs in time $O^*(3.237^k)$.*

With a Little Bit More Work: An $O^*(2.695^k)$ Time Algorithm

One might notice that the worst case complexity of the algorithm is achieved when the maximum degree of G is low, since high degree vertices will lead to better branching factors. This complexity can be significantly improved by handling low degree vertices in an ad-hoc manner. In fact, only a slight modification of the algorithm is necessary. We only need to handle degree 1 vertices in a particular manner, to apply Rule 3 when possible, and to restrict ourselves to optimal solutions that favor deletions over insertions. These allow us to attain a time complexity of $O^*(2.695^k)$.

The latter point means the following: consider any vertex v and its degree $deg(v)$ in the original input graph. Then one option is to have v in its own bicluster and delete every edge incident to v. Therefore it is pointless to have more than $deg(v)$ modified edges with v an endpoint. Furthermore, if exactly $deg(v)$ modified edges contain v and some of them are insertions, we can always replace these by $deg(v)$ deletions without altering the optimality of the solution.

Lemma 4. *There exists an optimal solution of BICLUSTER EDITING for a graph G such that for any $v \in V(G)$, either $deg(v)$ modified edges contain v and they are all deletions, or at most $deg(v) - 1$ modified edges contain v.*

The modified algorithm remembers the original graph and checks that we meet the requirements of Lemma 4. The next step is to handle degree 1 vertices.

Lemma 5. *Let G be a graph on which Rule 1 does not apply, and suppose that G has a vertex of degree 1. Then it is possible to achieve a branching vector of $(1, 2, 3, 3, 4)$ and thus branching factor 2.066, or better.*

Proof. Assume that G has a vertex $u \in V_i$ with a single neighbor v, $i \in \{1, 2\}$. By Lemma 4, we may assume that either uv gets deleted, or that no modified edge contains u. Let R_u be the twin class that contains u. Let $W = N(v) \setminus R_u$, and observe that each $w \in W$ has degree at least 2 (otherwise, w would be in R_u). If W is empty, then $R_u \cup \{v\}$ forms a bicluster and Rule 1 applies, so suppose $W \neq \emptyset$. We consider three cases in the proof.

Case 1: W has a vertex of degree 2. In that case, the neighbors of w are v and some other vertex z. We can first branch into the situation where we delete uv and decrease k by 1. Otherwise, we fix uv. In that case, one can see that in any solution $\mathcal{B}$, w must be the endpoint of at least one modified edge. Indeed, if u and w are in the same bicluster in $\mathcal{B}$, then wz must be deleted (since we assume that uz is not inserted). If u and w are in different biclusters, then wv must be deleted (since uv is fixed). We argue that u and w can be assumed to be in the same bicluster. Suppose that in $\mathcal{B}$, u and w are in different biclusters. Notice that since no inserted edge contains u, the bicluster B that contains u and v satisfies $B \subseteq \{v\} \cup N(v)$. It follows that we can obtain an alternate solution $\mathcal{B}'$ by adding w into B. This requires deleting wz instead of wv. Thus, assuming that uv is fixed, there exists an optimal solution in which u and w are in the same bicluster. We can thus delete wz safely. We branch into two cases, each with one deletion. This gives branching vector $(1, 1)$ and branching factor 2.

In the remaining, we assume that every vertex of W has degree 3 or more.
Case 2: $|W| = 1$. Let w be the vertex of W, and observe that v only has neighbors $R_u \cup \{w\}$. We can either put u and w in the same bicluster or not. If u and w are in the same bicluster, we must delete the edges between w and $N(w) \setminus \{v\}$ since we forbid insertions that involve u. Since w has degree at least 3 or more, this decreases k by at least 2.

If u and w are not in the same bicluster, we can either delete uv or wv. We claim that we can branch on only deleting wv. Assume that in an optimal solution $\mathcal{B}$, u and v are not in the same bicluster and uv is deleted. We may assume that the bicluster B_u of $\mathcal{B}$ that contains u only contains u. Consider the solution $\mathcal{B}'$ obtained by removing v from its bicluster and adding v to B_u. This saves any inserted edge containing v, and saves the uv deletion. On the other hand, this requires deleting wv (but no other edge since $|W| = 1$). We save at least as many modifications as we create, so we may assume that wv is deleted. Thus we only branch in the case where wv is deleted, reducing k by 1.

The above cases lead to branching vector $(2, 1)$ or better, and thus to branching factor 1.619 or better.
Case 3: $|W| > 1$. Let $x, y \in W$. We branch into five scenarios that cover all ways of obtaining a solution[1]:

- delete uv and reduce k by 1;
- fix uv, and put u, x in the same bicluster. This requires deleting at least two edges incident to x (since it has degree 3 or more, and we forbid insertions with u). Once this is done, we consider two more cases:
  - put u, y in the same bicluster. This also requires deleting at least two edges incident to y. When we reach that case, we can decrease k by at least 4.
  - put u, y in different biclusters. This requires deleting yv, and we may decrease k by at least 3.
- fix uv, and put u, x in the different biclusters. This requires deleting xv. Once this is done, we consider two more cases:
  - put u, y in the same bicluster. This also requires deleting at least two edges incident to y. When we reach that case, we can decrease k by at least 3.
  - put u, y in different biclusters. This requires deleting yv, and we may decrease k by 2.

These five cases yield branching vector $(1, 2, 3, 3, 4)$, which has branching factor less than 2.066.   □

The rest of the time analysis is dedicated to show that if we get rid of vertices of degree one, we are able to achieve a much better branching factor. This part of the proof requires work but is elementary. The essential idea is that if G has minimum degree 5 or more, then any u, v pair that we branch on yields a low enough $lrr(c, d)$. We must deal with minimum degree 2, 3 and 4 on a case-by-case

---

[1] Notice that this could be divided into three cases: two of x, y are with u, only one of them is, or none. However, our division into five cases makes the recursion calls to make more explicit.

basis. Rule 3 is used in this analysis to handle difficult cases, e.g. when $d = 1$. The most important idea is that when running Algorithm 1, several recursive calls will create vertices of degree 1. When this happens, the next recursive call then allows us to use the branching vector of Lemma 5. Therefore, although $lrr(c, d)$ will be high if we branch on vertices u, v of small degree, the subcases that lead to graphs with a degree one vertex will counter-balance this with the low branching factor of Lemma 5.

Theorem 3. *BICLUSTER EDITING can be solved in time* $O^*(2.695^k)$.

Concluding Remarks. We conclude with some open ideas. First, one could check whether our approach could be improved by combining it with the half-edge ideas used in CLUSTER EDITING (see [6]). Second, we do not even know whether our $5k$ bound is tight, and we don't know the true complexity of Algorithm 1. In practice, its running time should be better than $O^*(2.695^k)$ if the input graph has high degree vertices. Moreover, we do not know whether our bound is tight even on graphs of maximum degree 2 or 3, and better analysis techniques might improve our complexity. We also note that Algorithm 1 could be implemented on the integer weighted Bipartite Clustering problem, where each deletion and each insertion has a positive integer cost. However, the extension that handles degree 1 vertices might not work on this problem: our analysis uses Rule 3 in the proof, which does not apply to integer weighted graphs.

References

1. Ailon, N., Avigdor-Elgrabli, N., Liberty, E., Van Zuylen, A.: Improved approximation algorithms for bipartite correlation clustering. SIAM J. Comput. **41**(5), 1110–1121 (2012)
2. Altenhoff, A.M., et al.: Oma standalone: orthology inference among public and custom genomes and transcriptomes. Genome Res. **29**(7), 1152–1163 (2019)
3. Amit, N.: The bicluster graph editing problem. Ph.D. thesis, Tel Aviv University (2004)
4. Bansal, N., Blum, A., Chawla, S.: Correlation clustering. Mach. Learn. **56**(1–3), 89–113 (2004)
5. Barber, M.J.: Modularity and community detection in bipartite networks. Phys. Rev. E **76**(6), 066102 (2007)
6. Böcker, S.: A golden ratio parameterized algorithm for cluster editing. J. Discret. Algorithms **16**, 79–89 (2012)
7. Cheng, Y., Church, G.M.: Biclustering of expression data. In: ISMB, vol. 8, pp. 93–103 (2000)
8. Dondi, R., Lafond, M.: On the tractability of covering a graph with 2-clubs. In: Gasieniec, L.A., Jansson, J., Levcopoulos, C. (eds.) FCT 2019. LNCS, vol. 11651, pp. 243–257. Springer, Cham (2019). https://doi.org/10.1007/978-3-030-25027-0_17

9. Drange, P.G., Reidl, F., Villaamil, F.S., Sikdar, S.: Fast biclustering by dual parameterization. arXiv preprint arXiv:1507.08158 (2015)
10. Gramm, J., Guo, J., Hüffner, F., Niedermeier, R.: Graph-modeled data clustering: fixed-parameter algorithms for clique generation. In: Petreschi, R., Persiano, G., Silvestri, R. (eds.) CIAC 2003. LNCS, vol. 2653, pp. 108–119. Springer, Heidelberg (2003). https://doi.org/10.1007/3-540-44849-7_17
11. Gramm, J., Guo, J., Hüffner, F., Niedermeier, R.: Automated generation of search tree algorithms for hard graph modification problems. Algorithmica 39(4), 321–347 (2004)
12. Guo, J., Hüffner, F., Komusiewicz, C., Zhang, Y.: Improved algorithms for bicluster editing. In: Agrawal, M., Du, D., Duan, Z., Li, A. (eds.) TAMC 2008. LNCS, vol. 4978, pp. 445–456. Springer, Heidelberg (2008). https://doi.org/10.1007/978-3-540-79228-4_39
13. Hartung, S., Komusiewicz, C., Nichterlein, A., Such ̀y, O.: On structural parameterizations for the 2-club problem. Discret. Appl. Math. 185, 79–92 (2015)
14. Karrer, B., Newman, M.E.: Stochastic blockmodels and community structure in networks. Phys. Rev. E 83(1), 016107 (2011)
15. Komusiewicz, C., Uhlmann, J.: Cluster editing with locally bounded modifications. Discret. Appl. Math. 160(15), 2259–2270 (2012)
16. Lafond, M., Meghdari Miardan, M., Sankoff, D.: Accurate prediction of orthologs in the presence of divergence after duplication. Bioinformatics 34(13), i366–i375 (2018)
17. Liu, H., Zhang, P., Zhu, D.: On editing graphs into 2-club clusters. In: Snoeyink, J., Lu, P., Su, K., Wang, L. (eds.) AAIM/FAW -2012. LNCS, vol. 7285, pp. 235–246. Springer, Heidelberg (2012). https://doi.org/10.1007/978-3-642-29700-7_22
18. Madeira, S.C., Oliveira, A.L.: Biclustering algorithms for biological data analysis: a survey. IEEE/ACM Trans. Comput. Biol. Bioinform. 1(1), 24–45 (2004)
19. Newman, M.E., Girvan, M.: Finding and evaluating community structure in networks. Phys. Rev. E 69(2), 026113 (2004)
20. Pinheiro, R.G., Martins, I.C., Protti, F., Ochi, L.S., Simonetti, L.G., Subramanian, A.: On solving manufacturing cell formation via bicluster editing. Eur. J. Oper. Res. 254(3), 769–779 (2016)
21. Protti, F., da Silva, M.D., Szwarcfiter, J.L.: Applying modular decomposition to parameterized bicluster editing. In: Bodlaender, H.L., Langston, M.A. (eds.) IWPEC 2006. LNCS, vol. 4169, pp. 1–12. Springer, Heidelberg (2006). https://doi.org/10.1007/11847250_1
22. Rosvall, M., Bergstrom, C.T.: Maps of random walks on complex networks reveal community structure. Proc. Nat. Acad. Sci. 105(4), 1118–1123 (2008)
23. de Sousa Filho, G.F., Lucidio dos Anjos, F.C., Ochi, L.S., Protti, F.: Hybrid metaheuristic for bicluster editing problem. Electron. Notes Discret. Math. 39, 35–42 (2012)
24. de Sousa Filho, G.F., Júnior, T.L.B., Cabral, L.A., Ochi, L.S., Protti, F.: New heuristics for the bicluster editing problem. Ann. Oper. Res. 258(2), 781–814 (2017)
25. Sun, P., Guo, J., Baumbach, J.: Biclue-exact and heuristic algorithms for weighted bi-cluster editing of biomedical data. BMC Proc. 7, S9 (2013). https://doi.org/10.1186/1753-6561-7-S7-S9

26. Sun, P., Guo, J., Baumbach, J.: Complexity of dense bicluster editing problems. In: Cai, Z., Zelikovsky, A., Bourgeois, A. (eds.) COCOON 2014. LNCS, vol. 8591, pp. 154–165. Springer, Cham (2014). https://doi.org/10.1007/978-3-319-08783-2_14
27. Tanay, A., Sharan, R., Shamir, R.: Biclustering algorithms: a survey. In: Handbook of Computational Molecular Biology, vol. 9, no. 1–20, pp. 122–124 (2005)
28. Van Zuylen, A., Williamson, D.P.: Deterministic pivoting algorithms for constrained ranking and clustering problems. Math. Oper. Res. **34**(3), 594–620 (2009)

Approximate Set Union via Approximate Randomization

Bin Fu[1], Pengfei Gu[1(✉)], and Yuming Zhao[2]

[1] Department of Computer Science, University of Texas Rio Grande Valley,
Edinburg, TX 78539, USA
{bin.fu,pengfei.gu01}@utrgv.edu
[2] School of Computer Science, Zhaoqing University, Zhaoqing 526061, Guangdong,
People's Republic of China
ymzhao@zqu.edu.cn

Abstract. We develop a randomized approximation algorithm for the size of set union problem $|A_1 \cup A_2 \cup \ldots \cup A_m|$, which is given a list of sets $A_1, \ldots, A_m$ with approximate set size m_i for A_i with $m_i \in ((1 - \beta_L)|A_i|, (1 + \beta_R)|A_i|)$, and biased random generators with probability $\mathrm{Prob}\,(x = \mathrm{RandomElement}(A_i)) \in \left[\frac{1-\alpha_L}{|A_i|}, \frac{1+\alpha_R}{|A_i|}\right]$ for each input set A_i and element $x \in A_i$, where $i = 1, 2, \ldots, m$ and $\alpha_L, \alpha_R, \beta_L, \beta_R \in (0, 1)$. The approximation ratio for $|A_1 \cup A_2 \cup \ldots \cup A_m|$ is in the range $[(1 - \epsilon)(1 - \alpha_L)(1 - \beta_L), (1 + \epsilon)(1 + \alpha_R)\,(1 + \beta_R)]$ for any $\epsilon \in (0, 1)$. The complexity of the algorithm is measured by both time complexity and round complexity. One round of the algorithm has non-adaptive accesses to those $\mathrm{RandomElement}(A_i)$ functions $1 \leq i \leq m$, and membership queries $(x \in A_i?)$ to input sets A_i with $1 \leq i \leq m$. Our algorithm gives an approximation scheme with $O(m \cdot (\log m)^7)$ running time and $O(\log m)$ rounds in contrast to the existing algorithm [18] that needs $\Omega(m)$ rounds in the worst case with $O((1+\epsilon)m/\epsilon^2)$ running time, where m is the number of sets. Our algorithm gives a flexible tradeoff with time complexity $O\left(m^{1+\xi}\right)$ and round complexity $O\left(\frac{1}{\xi}\right)$ for any $\xi \in (0, 1)$. Our algorithm runs sublinear in time under certain condition that each element in $A_1 \cup A_2 \cup \ldots \cup A_m$ belongs to m^a sets for any fixed $a > 0$, to our best knowledge, we have not seen any sublinear results about this problem.

Keywords: #P-hard · Randomized approximation · Lattice points · Rounds · Sublinear time

1 Introduction

Computing the cardinality of set union is a basic algorithmic problem that has a simple and natural definition. It is related to the following problem: given a list of sets $A_1, \ldots, A_m$ with set size $|A_i|$, and random generators $\mathrm{RandomElement}(A_i)$ for each input set A_i, where $i = 1, 2, \ldots, m$, the task

© Springer Nature Switzerland AG 2020
D. Kim et al. (Eds.): COCOON 2020, LNCS 12273, pp. 591–602, 2020.
https://doi.org/10.1007/978-3-030-58150-3_48

is to compute $|A_1 \cup A_2 \cup \ldots \cup A_m|$. This problem is #P-hard if each set contains 0, 1-lattice points of a high dimensional cube [20]. Karp, Luby, and Madras [18] developed a $(1+\epsilon)$-randomized approximation algorithm to improve the running time of approximating the number of distinct elements in the union $A_1 \cup \ldots \cup A_m$ to linear $O((1 + \epsilon)m/\epsilon^2)$ time. Their algorithm is based on the input that provides the exact size of each set and a uniform random element generator of each set. Bringmann and Friedrich [5] applied Karp, Luby, and Madras' algorithm in deriving an approximate algorithm for high dimensional geometric object with uniform random sampling. They also proved that it is #P-hard to compute the volume of the intersection of high dimensional boxes and showed that there is no polynomial time $2^{d^{1-\epsilon}}$-approximation unless NP = BPP. Of the algorithms mentioned above, some of them were based on random sampling, and some of them provided exact set sizes when approximating the cardinalities of multisets of data and some of them dealt with two multiple sets. However, in reality, it is really hard to have an uniform sampling or exact set size especially when dealing with high dimensional problems.

Motivation. The existing approximate set union algorithm [18] needs each input set having a uniform random generator. In order to have approximate set union algorithms with broad application, it is essential to have algorithms with biased random generator for each input set, and see how approximation ratio depends on the bias. In this paper, we propose a randomized approximation algorithm to approximate the size of set union problem by extending the model used in [18]. In our algorithm, each input set A_i is a black box that can provide its size $|A_i|$, generate a random element RandomElement(A_i) of A_i, and answer the membership query ($x \in A_i$?) in $O(1)$ time. Our algorithm can handle input sets that can generate random elements with bias with $\text{Prob}(x = \text{RandomElement}(A_i)) \in \left[\frac{1-\alpha_L}{|A_i|}, \frac{1+\alpha_R}{|A_i|}\right]$ for each input set A_i and approximate set size m_i for A_i with $m_i \in [(1 - \beta_L)|A_i|, (1 + \beta_R)|A_i|]$.

As the communication complexity is becoming important in distributed environment, data transmission among variant machines may be more time consuming than the computation inside a single machine. Our algorithm complexity is also measured by the number of rounds. The algorithm is allowed to make multiple membership queries and get random elements from the input sets in one round. Our algorithm makes adaptive accesses to input sets with multiple rounds. The round complexity is related a distributed computing complexity if input sets are stored in a distributed environment, and the number of rounds indicates the complexity of interactions between a central server, which runs the algorithm to approximate the size of set union, and clients, which save one set each.

Computation via bounded queries to another set has been well studied in the field of structural complexity theory. Polynomial time truth table reduction has a parallel way to access oracle with all queries to be provided in one round [6]. Polynomial time Turing reduction has a sequential way to access oracle by providing a query and receiving an answer in one round [7]. The constant-round truth table reduction (for example, see [10]) is between truth table reduction, and Turing reduction. Our algorithm is similar to a bounded round truth table reduction to input sets to approximate the size set union. Karp, Luby, and Madras [18]'s algorithm runs like a Turing reduction which has the number of adaptive queries proportional to the time.

Contributions. We have the following contributions to approximate the size of set union. 1. Our algorithm is based on a new approach that is different from that in [18]. 2. Our algorithm has constant number of rounds to access the input sets, which is contrast to the existing algorithm [18] that needs $\Omega(m)$ rounds in the worst case with m be the number of sets. This reduces an important complexity in a distributed environment where each set stays a different machine. 3. Our algorithm handles the approximate input set sizes and biased random sources. The existing algorithm [18] assumes uniform random source from each set. 4. Our algorithm runs in sublinear time when each element belongs to at least m^a sets for any fixed $a > 0$. We have not seen any sublinear results about this problem. 5. We show a tradeoff between the number of rounds, and the time complexity. Our algorithm takes $\log m$ rounds with time complexity $O\left(m(\log m)^7\right)$, and takes $O\left(\frac{1}{\xi}\right)$ rounds, with a time complexity $O\left(m^{1+\xi}\right)$ for any $\xi \in (0, 1)$. We still maintain the time complexity nearly linear time in the classical model. 6. We identify two additional parameters z_{min} and z_{max} that affect both the complexity of rounds and time, where z_{min} is the least number of sets that an element belongs to, and z_{max} is the largest number of sets that an element belongs to. 7. Our algorithm developed in the randomized model only accesses a small number of elements from the input sets. The algorithm developed in the streaming model algorithm accesses all the elements from the input sets. Therefore, our algorithm is incomparable with the results in the streaming model [1–4,8,9,11–14,16,17].

Organization. The rest of paper is organized as follows. In Sect. 2, we define the computational model and round complexity. Section 3 presents some theorems that play an important role in accuracy analysis. In Sect. 4, we give a randomized approximation algorithm to approximate the size of set union problem; time complexity and round complexity also be analyzed in Sect. 4. Section 5 summarizes the conclusions.

2   Computational Model and Complexity

In this section, we show our model of computation, and the definition of round complexity.

2.1   Model of Randomization

Definition 1. *Let A be a set of elements:*

1. *A α-biased random generator for set A is a generator that each element in A is generated with probability in the range $\left[\frac{1-\alpha}{|A|}, \frac{1+\alpha}{|A|}\right]$.*

2. *A (α_L, α_R)-biased random generator for set A is a generator that each element in A is generated with probability in the range $\left[\frac{1-\alpha_L}{|A|}, \frac{1+\alpha_R}{|A|}\right]$.*

Definition 2. *Let L be a list of sets $A_1, A_2, \ldots, A_m$ such that each supports the following operations:*

1. *The size of A_i has an approximation $m_i \in [(1 - \beta_L)|A_i|, (1 + \beta_R)|A_i|]$ for $i = 1, 2, \ldots, m$. Both $M = \sum_{i=1}^{m} m_i$ and m are part of the input.*
2. *Function* RandomElement(A_i) *returns a (α_L, α_R)-biased random element x from A_i for $i = 1, 2, \ldots, m$.*
3. *Function* query(x, A_i) *function returns 1 if $x \in A_i$, and 0 otherwise.*

Definition 3. *For a list L of sets $A_1, A_2, \ldots, A_m$ and real numbers $\alpha_L, \alpha_R, \beta_L, \beta_R \in (0, 1)$, it is called $((\alpha_L, \alpha_R), (\beta_L, \beta_R))$-list if each set A_i is associated with a number m_i with $(1 - \beta_L)|A_i| \leq m_i \leq (1 + \beta_R)|A_i|$ for $i = 1, 2, \ldots, m$, and the set A_i has a (α_L, α_R)-biased random generator* RandomElement(A_i).

Definition 4. *The model of randomized computation for our algorithm is defined below:*

1. *The input is a list L defined in Definition 2.*
2. *It allows all operations defined in Definition 2.*

2.2   Round and Round Complexity

The *round complexity* is the total number of rounds used in the algorithm. Our algorithm has several rounds to access input sets. At each round, the algorithm sends non-adaptive (i.e., parallel) requests to random generators, and membership queries, and receives the answers from them.

Our algorithm is considered as a client-server interaction. The algorithm is controlled by the server side, and each set is a client. In *one round*, the server asks some questions to clients which are selected.

The parameters m, ϵ, γ may be used to determine the time complexity and round complexity, where ϵ controls the accuracy of approximation, γ controls the failure probability, and m is the number of sets.

3   Preliminaries

During the accuracy analysis, Hoeffding Inequality [15] and Chernoff Bound [19] play an important role. They showed how the number of samples determines the accuracy of approximation.

Theorem 1. *Let $X_1, \ldots, X_m$ be m independent random 0-1 variables, where X_i takes 1 with probability at least p for $i = 1, \ldots, m$. Let $X = \sum_{i=1}^{m} X_i$, and $\mu = E[X]$. Then for any $\delta > 0$, $\Pr(X < (1 - \delta)pm) < e^{-\frac{1}{2}\delta^2 pm}$.*

Theorem 2. *Let $X_1, \ldots, X_m$ be m independent random 0-1 variables, where X_i takes 1 with probability at most p for $i = 1, \ldots, m$. Let $X = \sum_{i=1}^{m} X_i$. Then for any $\delta > 0$, $\Pr(X > (1 + \delta)pm) < \left[\frac{e^{\delta}}{(1+\delta)^{(1+\delta)}} \right]^{pm}$.*

Define $g_1(\delta) = e^{-\frac{1}{2}\delta^2}$, $g_2(\delta) = \frac{e^{\delta}}{(1+\delta)^{(1+\delta)}}$ and $g(\delta) = \max\left(g_1(\delta), g_2(\delta)\right)$. We give a bound for $g(\delta)$. First, we give a bound for $g_2(\delta) = \frac{e^{\delta}}{(1+\delta)^{(1+\delta)}}$. Let $u(x) = \frac{e^x}{(1+x)^{(1+x)}}$. We consider the case $x \in [0, 1]$. We have

$$\log u(x) = x - (1 + x)\log(1 + x) \le x - (1 + x)\left(x - \frac{x^2}{2}\right) \le -\frac{x^2}{6}.$$

Therefore,

$$u(x) \le e^{-\frac{x^2}{6}}$$

for all $x \in [0, 1]$. We let

$$g^*(x) = e^{-\frac{x^2}{6}}.$$

Hence, we have $g(\delta) \le g^*(\delta)$ for all $\delta \in [0, 1]$ as $g_1(\delta) = e^{-\frac{1}{2}\delta^2} \le e^{-\frac{1}{6}\delta^2}$.

A well known fact, called union bound, in probability theory is the inequality

$$\Pr(E_1 \cup E_2 \ldots \cup E_m) \le \Pr(E_1) + \Pr(E_2) + \ldots + \Pr(E_m),$$

where $E_1, E_2, \ldots, E_m$ are m events that may not be independent. In the analysis of our randomized algorithm, there are multiple events such that the failure from any of them may fail the entire algorithm. We often characterize the failure probability of each of those events, and use the above inequality to show that the whole algorithm has a small chance to fail after showing that each of them has a small chance to fail.

4   Algorithm Based on Adaptive Random Sampling

In this section, we develop a randomized algorithm for the size of set union when the approximate set sizes and biased random generators are given for the input sets. We give some definitions before the presentation of the algorithm. The algorithm developed in this section has an adaptive way to access the random generators from the input sets. All the random elements from input sets are generated in the beginning of the algorithm, and the number of random samples is known in the beginning of the algorithm. The results in this section show a tradeoff between the time complexity and the round complexity.

Definition 5. *Let $L = A_1, A_2, \ldots, A_m$ be a list of finite sets:*

1. *For an element x, define $T(x, L) = \left| \{i : 1 \le i \le m \text{ and } x \in A_i\} \right|.$*
2. *For an element x, and a subset H of indices with multiplicity of $\{1, 2, \ldots, m\}$, define $S(x, H) = \left| \{i : i \in H \text{ and } x \in A_i\} \right|.$*

3. *Define* $\text{minThickness}(L) = \min\{T(x, L) : x \in A_1 \cup A_2 \cup \ldots \cup A_m\}$.
4. *Define* $\text{maxThickness}(L) = \max\{T(x, L) : x \in A_1 \cup A_2 \cup \ldots \cup A_m\}$.
5. *Let W be a subset with multiplicity of $A_1 \cup \ldots \cup A_m$, define $F(W, h, s) =$*
   $\frac{s}{h} \sum\limits_{x \in W} \frac{1}{T(x,L)}$, *and* $F'(W) = \sum\limits_{x \in W} \frac{1}{T(x,L)} = \frac{h}{s} F(W, h, s)$, *where h and s are*
   real numbers.
6. *For a $\delta \in (0, 1)$, partition $A_1 \cup A_2 \cup \ldots \cup A_m$ into $A'_1, \ldots, A'_k$ such that*
   $A'_i = \{x : x \in A_1 \cup A_2 \cup \ldots \cup A_m \text{ and } T(x, L) \in [(1 + \delta)^{i-1}, (1 + \delta)^i)\}$ *where*
   $i = 1, 2, \ldots, k$. Define $v(\delta, z_1, z_2, L) = k$, which is the number of sets in the
   partition under the condition that $z_1 \leq T(x, L) \leq z_2$.

Remark: Our algorithm is based on random sampling, therefore, the random elements could be repeatedly chosen from the sets. For example, a subset H of indices with multiplicity of $\{1, 2, \ldots, m\}$ could be $\{3, 4, 4, 3, 5, \ldots, m\}$.

4.1   Overview of Algorithm

We give an overview of the algorithm. For a list L of input sets $A_1, \ldots, A_m$, each set A_i has an approximate size m_i and a random generator. It is easy to see that $|A_1 \cup A_2 \cup \ldots \cup A_m| = \sum\limits_{i=1}^{m} \sum\limits_{x \in A_i} \frac{1}{T(x,L)}$. In the first round, the algorithm approximates $\sum\limits_{i=1}^{m} \sum\limits_{x \in A_i} \frac{1}{T(x,L)}$ by $\frac{m_1 + \ldots + m_m}{|R_1|} \times \sum\limits_{x \in R_1} \frac{1}{T(x,L)}$ via generating a set of R_1 of sufficient random samples from the list of input sets. The algorithm has constant rounds to approximate the thickness $T(x, L)$ for each $x \in R_1$. In each round, the algorithm selects some number of subsets and check how frequently chosen (i.e., thickness) elements appear in the chosen subsets. Naturally, samples appearing in a large number of subsets would require small number of subsets to accurately approximate its thickness, and samples appearing in a small number of subsets would require large number of subsets to accurately approximate its thickness. As rounds proceed, the algorithm targets with decreasing thickness and samples more subsets. Finally, as the thickness $T(x, L)$ for every $x \in R_1$ have been approximated, $\frac{m_1 + \ldots + m_m}{|R_1|} \times \sum\limits_{x \in R_1} \frac{1}{T(x,L)}$ can be used to approximate $\sum\limits_{i=1}^{m} \sum\limits_{x \in A_i} \frac{1}{T(x,L)}$, which is equal to $|A_1 \cup A_2 \cup \ldots \cup A_m|$.

Example 1. Let L be a list of 10 sets $A_1, A_2, \ldots, A_{10}$, where $A_i = B_i \cup C$ with $|C| = 1000$ and $|B_i| = 100$ for $i = 1, 2, \ldots, 10$. In the beginning of the algorithm, we generate a set R_1 of $h_1 = 220$ random samples from list L, where 20 random samples with higher thickness $T(x, L)$ coming from C and 200 random samples with lower thickness $T(x, L)$ coming from B_i. At the first round, we only need to select sets A_1, A_3, and A_6 to approximate the thickness $T(x, L)$ of the 20 random samples locating at C. Then at the second round, we have to select all the sets $A_1, A_2, \ldots, A_{10}$, to approximate the thickness $T(x, L)$ of the 200 random samples coming from B_i (see Fig. 1).

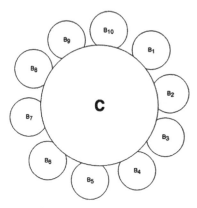

Fig. 1. Set union of ten sets.

4.2   Algorithm Description

Before giving the algorithm, we define an operation that selects a set of random elements from a list L of sets $A_1, \ldots, A_m$. We assume $m \geq 2$ throughout the paper.

Definition 6. *Let L be a list of m sets $A_1, \ldots, A_m$ with $m_i \in [(1 - \beta_L)|A_i|, (1 + \beta_R)|A_i|]$ and (α_L, α_R)-biased random generator* RandomElement(A_i) *for $i = 1, 2, \ldots, m$, and $M = m_1 + m_2 + \ldots + m_m$. A random choice of L is to get an element x via the following two steps:*

1. *With probability $\frac{m_i}{M}$, select a set A_i among $A_1, \ldots, A_m$.*
2. *Get an element x from set A_i via* RandomElement(A_i).

We give some definitions about the parameters and functions that affect our algorithm below. We assume that $\epsilon \in (0, 1)$ is used to control the accuracy of approximation, and $\gamma \in (0, 1)$ is used to control the failure probability. In the following algorithm, the two integer parameters z_{min} and z_{max} with $1 \leq z_{\min} \leq$ minThickness$(L) \leq$ maxThickness$(L) \leq z_{\max} \leq m$ can help speed up the computation. The algorithm is still correct if we use default case with $z_{min} = 1$ and $z_{max} = m$.

1. Function $f_1(.)$ is used to control the number of rounds of the algorithm. Its growth rate is mainly determined by the parameter c_1 that will be determined later:
$$f_1(m) = 8m^{c_1} \text{ with } c_1 \geq 0.$$

2. Function $f_2(.)$ determines the number of random samples from the input sets in the beginning of the algorithm, and $\delta = \frac{\epsilon}{432(\log m)}$:

$$
\begin{aligned}
f_2(m) = {} & \frac{m \, (\log m)^2}{z_{min} \epsilon^3} [26244 * (v \, (\delta, z_{\min}, z_{\max}, L) \\
& + \frac{\log \frac{m}{z_{min}}}{\log(1 + \delta)}) \log \left(\frac{54m^2 \log m}{\epsilon} \right) + 60466176 \log m * \log \left(\frac{12 \log m}{\gamma} \right)].
\end{aligned}
$$

3. Function $f_3(.)$ affects the number of random indices in the range $\{1, 2, \ldots, m\}$. Those random indices will be used to choose input sets to detect the approximate $T(x, L)$ for those random samples x:

$$f_3(m) = \frac{559872 * m^{c_1} * (\log m)^2}{\epsilon^2}$$

$$* [\log \left(\frac{24m (\log m)^3}{\gamma z_{min} \epsilon^3} \right)$$

$$+ \log(26244 * (v (\delta, z_{min}, z_{max}, L) + \frac{\log \frac{m}{z_{min}}}{\log(1 + \delta)}) \log \left(\frac{54m^2 \log m}{\epsilon} \right)$$

$$+ 60466176 * \log m * \log \left(\frac{12 \log m}{\gamma} \right))].$$

Algorithm 1. ApproximateUnion$(L, z_{min}, z_{max}, M, \gamma, \epsilon)$

Input : L is a list of m sets $A_1, A_2, \ldots, A_m$ with $m \geq 2$, $m_i \in [(1-\beta_L)|A_i|, (1+\beta_R)|A_i|]$ and (α_L, α_R)-biased random generator RandomElement(A_i) for $i = 1, 2, \ldots, m$, integers z_{min} and z_{max} with $1 \leq z_{min} \leq minThickness(L) \leq maxThickness(L) \leq z_{max} \leq m$, parameter $\gamma \in (0, 1)$ to control the failure probability, parameter $\epsilon \in (0, 1)$ to control the accuracy of approximation, and $M = m_1 + m_2 + \ldots + m_m$ as the sum of sizes of input sets.

Output : $sum \cdot M$.

1:      Initialize: $h_1 = f_5(m)$, currentThickness$_1 = z_{max}$, $s_1 = \frac{m}{currentThickness_1}$, $s_1' = 1$, and $sum = 0$
2:      Obtain a set R_1 of h_1 random choices of L (see definition 6)
3:      Let $i = 1$
4:      Round i
5:          Let $u_i = s_i \cdot f_6(m)$
6:          Select u_i random indices $H_i = \{k_1, \ldots, k_{u_i}\}$ from $\{1, 2, \ldots, m\}$
7:          Compute $S(x, H_i)$ for each $x \in R_i$
8:          Let V_i be the subset of R_i with elements x satisfying $S(x, H_i) \geq \frac{currentThickness_i}{2f_1(m) \cdot m} \cdot u_i$
9:          Let $sum = sum + s_i' \sum_{x \in V_i} \frac{u_i}{S(x, H_i)m}$
10:         Let $currentThickness_{i+1} = \frac{currentThickness_i}{f_1(m)}$
11:         Let $s_{i+1} = \frac{m}{currentThickness_{i+1}}$
12:         Let $h_{i+1} = \frac{h_1}{s_{i+1}}$
13:         If $(|R_i| - |V_i| < h_{i+1})$
14:         Then
15:         {
16:             Let $R_{i+1} = R_i - V_i$
17:             Let $a_i = 1$
18:         }

19:	Else
20:	{
21:	Let R_{i+1} be a set of random h_{i+1} samples from $R_i - V_i$
22:	Let $a_i = \frac{|R_i| - |V_i|}{h_{i+1}}$
23:	}
24:	Let $s'_{i+1} = s'_i \cdot a_i$
25:	Let $i = i + 1$
26:	If $(currentThickness_i < z_{min})$
27:	Return $sum \cdot M$ and terminate the algorithm
28:	Else
29:	Enter the next Round i

We let $M = m_1 + m_2 + \ldots + m_m$ and $z_{\min}$ be part of the input of the algorithm. It makes the algorithm be possible to run in a sublinear time when $z_{\min} \geq m^a$ for a fixed $a > 0$. Otherwise, the algorithm has to spend $\Omega(m)$ time to compute M.

4.3   Proof of Algorithm Performance

The accuracy and complexity of algorithm ApproximateUnion(.) will be proven in the following lemmas.

Lemma 1 gives an upper bound for the number of rounds for the algorithm. It shows how round complexity depends on z_{max}, z_{min} and constant c_1.

Lemma 1. *The number of rounds of the algorithm is* $O\left(\frac{\log\left(\frac{z_{max}}{z_{min}}\right)}{\log(8m^{c_1})}\right)$.

Lemma 2 shows that at round i, it can approximate $T(x, L)$ for all random samples with highest $T(x, L)$ in R_i. Those random elements with highest $T(x, L)$ will be removed in round i so that the algorithm will look for random elements with smaller $T(x, L)$ in the coming rounds.

Lemma 2. *After the execution of round i, with probability at least $1 - \gamma_2$, we have the following three statements:*

1. *Every element $x \in R_i$ with $T(x, L) \geq \frac{currentThickness_i}{4f_1(m)}$ has $S(x, H_i) \in \left[(1 - \epsilon_1)\frac{T(x,L)}{m}u_i, (1 + \epsilon_1)\frac{T(x,L)}{m}u_i\right]$.*
2. *Every element $x \in V_i$ with $T(x, L) \geq \frac{currentThickness_i}{f_1(m)}$, it satisfies the condition in line 8 of the algorithm.*
3. *Every element $x \in V_i$ with $T(x, L) < \frac{currentThickness_i}{4f_1(m)}$, it does not satisfy the condition in line 8 of the algorithm.*

Lemma 3. *Let x and y be positive real numbers with $1 \leq y$. Then we have:*

1. $1 - xy < (1 - x)^y$.
2. *If $xy < 1$, then $(1 + x)^y < 1 + 2xy$.*

3. *If $x_1, x_2 \in [0, 1)$, then $1 - x_1 - x_2 \leq (1 - x_1)(1 - x_2)$, and $(1 + x_1)(1 + x_2) \leq 1 + 2x_1 + x_2$.*

Lemma 4 shows that how to gradually approximate $F(R_1, h_1, 1)M$ via several rounds. It shows that the left random samples stored in R_{i+1} after round i is enough to approximate $F'(R_i - V_i)$.

Lemma 4. *Let y be the number of rounds. Let V_i be the set of elements removed from R_i in round i. Then we have the following facts:*

1. *With probability at least $1 - \gamma_2$, $a_i F'(R_{i+1}) \in [(1 - \epsilon_1)F' (R_i - V_i), (1 + \epsilon_1)F'(R_i - V_i)]$.*

2. *With probability at least $1 - 2y\gamma_2$, $\sum_{i=1}^{y} s_i' F'(V_i) \in [(1 - y\epsilon_1)S, (1 + 2y\epsilon_1)S]$,*
   where $S = F(R_1, h_1, 1)$.

Lemma 5 gives the time complexity of the algorithm. The running time depends on several parameters.

Lemma 5. *The algorithm ApproximateUnion(.) takes $O(\frac{m f_3(m)}{z_{\min}} \cdot \frac{\log \frac{z_{\max}}{z_{\min}}}{\log f_1(m)})$ time.*

We have Theorem 3 to show the performance of the algorithm. The algorithm is sublinear if minThickness$(L) \geq m^a$ for a fixed $a > 0$, and has a $z_{\min}$ with minThickness$(L) \geq z_{\min} \geq m^b$ for a positive fixed b (b may not be equal to a) to be part of input to the algorithm.

Theorem 3. *The algorithm ApproximateUnion(.) takes $O\left(\frac{\log\left(\frac{z_{max}}{z_{min}}\right)}{\log(8m^{c1})}\right)$ rounds and $O\left(\frac{m}{z_{\min}} \cdot \left(\frac{\log\left(\frac{z_{max}}{z_{min}}\right)}{\log(8m^{c1})}\right)(\log m)^6 poly(\epsilon, \gamma)\right)$ time such that with probability at least $1 - \gamma$, it gives*

$$sum \times M \in [(1 - \epsilon)(1 - \alpha_L)(1 - \beta_L) \times A, (1 + \epsilon)(1 + \alpha_R)(1 + \beta_R) \times A],$$

where $z_{\min}$ and $z_{\max}$ are parameters with $1 \leq z_{\min} \leq$ minThickness$(L) \leq$ maxThickness$(L) \leq z_{\max} \leq m$, and $A = |A_1 \cup \ldots \cup A_m|$.

Since $1 \leq z_{\min} \leq$ minThickness$(L) \leq$ maxThickness$(L) \leq z_{\max} \leq m$, we have the following Corollary 1. Its running time is almost linear in the classical model.

Corollary 1. *There is a $O\left(poly(\epsilon, \gamma) \cdot m \cdot (\log m)^7\right)$ time and $O(\log m)$ rounds algorithm for $|A_1 \cup A_2 \cup \ldots A_m|$ such that with probability at least $1 - \gamma$, it gives $sum \cdot M \in [(1 - \epsilon)(1 - \alpha_L)(1 - \beta_L) \times A, (1 + \epsilon)(1 + \alpha_R)(1 + \beta_R) \times A]$, where $A = |A_1 \cup \ldots \cup A_m|$.*

Corollary 2. *For each $\xi > 0$, there is a $O\left(poly\,(\epsilon, \gamma) \cdot m^{1+\xi}\right)$ time and $O\left(\frac{1}{\xi}\right)$ rounds algorithm for $|A_1 \cup A_2 \cup \ldots A_m|$ such that with probability at least $1 - \gamma$, it gives sum $\cdot M \in [(1 - \epsilon)(1 - \alpha_L)(1 - \beta_L) \times A, (1 + \epsilon)(1 + \alpha_R)(1 + \beta_R) \times A]$, where $A = |A_1 \cup \ldots \cup A_m|$.*

An interesting open problem is to find an $O(m)$ time and $O(\log m)$ rounds approximation scheme for $|A_1 \cup A_2 \cup \ldots A_m|$ with a similar accuracy performance as Corollary 1.

5 Conclusions

We introduce an almost linear bounded rounds randomized approximation algorithm for the size of set union problem $|A_1 \cup A_2 \cup \ldots \cup A_m|$, which given a list of sets $A_1, \ldots, A_m$ with approximate set size and biased random generators. The definition of round is introduced. We prove that our algorithm runs sublinear in time under certain condition. Due to the limitation of the pages, we refer the readers to https://arxiv.org/abs/1802.06204 for the full paper.

Acknowledgement. This research is supported in part by National Science Foundation Early Career Award 0845376, Bensten Fellowship of the University of Texas Rio Grande Valley, and National Natural Science Foundation of China 61772179.

References

1. Alon, N., Matias, Y., Szegedy, M.: The space complexity of approximating the frequency moments. In: Proceedings of the Twenty-Eighth Annual ACM Symposium on the Theory of Computing, Philadelphia, Pennsylvania, USA, 22–24 May 1996, pp. 20–29 (1996)
2. Bar-Yossef, Z., Jayram, T.S., Kumar, R., Sivakumar, D., Trevisan, L.: Counting distinct elements in a data stream. In: Rolim, J.D.P., Vadhan, S. (eds.) RANDOM 2002. LNCS, vol. 2483, pp. 1–10. Springer, Heidelberg (2002). https://doi.org/10.1007/3-540-45726-7_1
3. Bar-Yossef, Z., Kumar, R., Sivakumar, D.: Reductions in streaming algorithms, with an application to counting triangles in graphs. In: Proceedings of the Thirteenth Annual ACM-SIAM Symposium on Discrete Algorithms, 6–8 January 2002, San Francisco, CA, USA, pp. 623–632 (2002)
4. Blasiok, J.: Optimal streaming and tracking distinct elements with high probability. In: Proceedings of the Twenty-Ninth Annual ACM-SIAM Symposium on Discrete Algorithms, SODA 2018, New Orleans, LA, USA, 7–10 January 2018, pp. 2432–2448 (2018)
5. Bringmann, K., Friedrich, T.: Approximating the volume of unions and intersections of high-dimensional geometric objects. Comput. Geom. **43**(6–7), 601–610 (2010)
6. Buss, S.R., Hay, L.: On truth-table reducibility to SAT and the difference hierarchy over NP. In: Proceedings: Third Annual Structure in Complexity Theory Conference, Georgetown University, Washington, D. C., USA, 14–17 June 1988, pp. 224–233 (1988)

7. Cook, S.A.: The complexity of theorem-proving procedures. In: Proceedings of the 3rd Annual ACM Symposium on Theory of Computing, 3–5 May 1971, Shaker Heights, Ohio, USA, pp. 151–158 (1971)
8. Flajolet, P., Fusy, É., Gandoue, O., Meunier, F.: HyperLogLog: the analysis of a near-optimal cardinality estimation algorithm. In: 2007 Conference on Analysis of Algorithms, AofA 2007, pp. 127–146 (2007)
9. Flajolet, P., Martin, G.N.: Probabilistic counting algorithms for data base applications. J. Comput. Syst. Sci. **31**(2), 182–209 (1985)
10. Fortnow, L., Reingold, N.: PP is closed under truth-table reductions. In: Proceedings of the Sixth Annual Structure in Complexity Theory Conference, Chicago, Illinois, USA, June 30–July 3 1991, pp. 13–15 (1991)
11. Ganguly, S., Garofalakis, M.N., Rastogi, R.: Tracking set-expression cardinalities over continuous update streams. VLDB J. **13**(4), 354–369 (2004)
12. Gibbons, P.B.: Distinct sampling for highly-accurate answers to distinct values queries and event reports. In: VLDB 2001, Proceedings of 27th International Conference on Very Large Data Bases, 11–14 September 2001, Roma, Italy, pp. 541–550 (2001)
13. Gibbons, P.B., Tirthapura, S.: Estimating simple functions on the union of data streams. In: SPAA, pp. 281–291 (2001)
14. Haas, P.J., Naughton, J.F., Seshadri, S., Stokes, L.: Sampling-based estimation of the number of distinct values of an attribute. In: VLDB 1995, Proceedings of 21th International Conference on Very Large Data Bases, 11–15 September 1995, Zurich, Switzerland, pp. 311–322 (1995)
15. Hoeffding, W.: Probability inequalities for sums of bounded random variables. J. Am. Stat. Assoc. **58**(301), 13–30 (1963)
16. Huang, Z., Tai, W.M., Yi, K.: Tracking the frequency moments at all times. CoRR, abs/1412.1763 (2014)
17. Kane, D.M., Nelson, J., Woodruff, D.P.: An optimal algorithm for the distinct elements problem. In: Proceedings of the Twenty-Ninth ACM SIGMOD-SIGACT-SIGART Symposium on Principles of Database Systems, PODS 2010, 6–11 June 2010, Indianapolis, Indiana, USA, pp. 41–52 (2010)
18. Karp, R.M., Luby, M., Madras, N.: Monte-carlo approximation algorithms for enumeration problems. J. Algorithms **10**(3), 429–448 (1989)
19. Motwani, R., Raghavan, P.: Randomized Algorithms. Cambridge University Press, Cambridge (2000)
20. Valiant, L.G.: The complexity of computing the permanent. Theor. Comput. Sci. **8**, 189–201 (1979)

A Non-Extendibility Certificate for Submodularity and Applications

Umang Bhaskar$^{(\boxtimes)}$ and Gunjan Kumar

Tata Institute of Fundamental Research, Mumbai, India
{umang.bhaskar,gunjan.kumar}@tifr.res.in

Abstract. Can a function f defined on some domain $\mathcal{D}$ be extended to a submodular function on a larger domain $\mathcal{D}' \supset \mathcal{D}$? This is the problem of submodular partial function extension. In this work, we develop a new combinatorial certificate of nonextendibility called a square certificate. We then present two applications of our certificate: to submodular extension on lattices, and to property testing of submodularity.
  - For lattices, we define a new class of lattices called *pseudocyclic lattices* that strictly generalize modular lattices, and show that these are sublattice extendible, i.e., a partial function that is submodular on a sublattice is extendible to a submodular function on the lattice. We give an example to show that in general lattices this property does not hold.
  - For property testing, we show general lower bounds for a class of submodularity testers called proximity oblivious testers. One of our lower bounds is applicable to matroid rank functions as well, and is the first lower bound for this class of functions.

1 Introduction

Submodular functions are perhaps the most important functions in combinatorial optimization. They occur in many applications, including social networks, economics, and machine learning [6,7,10]. In economics, for example, they capture the common assumption of diminishing marginal returns for valuations. Many important functions such as coverage functions, matroid rank functions, and graph cut functions are submodular.

In this paper, we address the problem of extending a given partial function on a subset $\mathcal{D}$ of a lattice $\mathcal{L}$ to a submodular function on the lattice $\mathcal{L}$. A *partial function* consists of a subset $\mathcal{D} \subseteq \mathcal{L}$ and a function $h : \mathcal{D} \to \mathbb{R}$. The *partial function extension* problem is to determine if there exists a total function $f : \mathcal{L} \to \mathbb{R}$ satisfying a given property—in our case, submodularity—and that extends the partial function, i.e., $f(x) = h(x)$ for all x in $\mathcal{D}$. This problem is central to many areas such as property testing [13], computational learning theory [11] and revealed preference theory in economics [16].

In property testing, a function is given by an oracle, and the problem is to determine with high probability by querying the oracle whether the function satisfies a given property, or is far from it. For a function on $2^{[m]}$, the lattice of

© Springer Nature Switzerland AG 2020
D. Kim et al. (Eds.): COCOON 2020, LNCS 12273, pp. 603–614, 2020.
https://doi.org/10.1007/978-3-030-58150-3_49

subsets of $\{1, 2, \ldots, m\}$ ordered by containment, the function is (at least) ϵ-far if any function that satisfies the property differs from f on at least $\epsilon 2^m$ points. Earlier work studies property testing for submodular functions on $2^{[m]}$ and gives a combinatorial certificate for nonextendibility called a path certificate [13]. The existence of a path certificate for the partial function certifies that the partial function cannot be extended to a submodular function on the lattice.

Our first contribution is to give a different certificate of nonextendibility, called a *square certificate*. We give two applications of square certificates. We first apply square certificates to study submodular extendibility on general lattices. We are interested in classes of lattices that are sublattice extendible, i.e., for which a partial function that is submodular on a sublattice is always extendible to a submodular function on the lattice. Topkis studied this problem in an article on comparative statics, to understand when the solution to an optimization problem is a monotone function of an exogenous parameter [14]. He showed that modular lattices are sublattice extendible. We show that this property holds for a strictly larger class of lattices, which we call pseudocyclic lattices. We also give an example to show that general lattices are not sublattice extendible.

We note that apart from their applications in combinatorial optimization, there is also recent interest in submodular functions on lattices due to connections with the maximum constraint satisfaction problem, including product lattices [8] and diamonds [9]. Submodular functions on lattices are also studied in financial mathematics and supermodular games [12, 15].

Our second application of square certificates is to property testing of submodular functions on $2^{[m]}$. Partial function extension is a natural component of property testing, since testing algorithms[1] cleverly query some points and reject only if the values at the queried points cannot be extended to a function with the required property. For submodularity, a particular tester called a square tester repeatedly samples unit squares of the form $(A, A \cup \{i\}, A \cup \{j\}, A \cup \{i, j\})$, and rejects iff a unit square violates submodularlity [13]. The upper and lower bounds on the number of samples required are however quite distant, and the problem of property testing for submodularity remains wide open.

Preliminaries. We use $[m]$ for the set $\{1, 2, \ldots, m\}$. For a set C, 2^C is the power set of C.

Lattices. We restrict ourselves to finite lattices. A poset $(\mathcal{L}, \leq)$ is a binary relation $\leq$ on elements of $\mathcal{L}$, that satisfies for any $a, b, c \in \mathcal{L}$, $a \leq a$ (reflexivity), if $a \leq b$, $b \leq c$ then $a \leq c$ (transitivity), and if $a \leq b$, $b \leq a$ then $a = b$ (antisymmetry). Elements a and b are incomparable if neither $a \leq b$ nor $b \leq a$. Element c is an upper bound of a, b if $a \leq c$ and $b \leq c$. Similarly, d is a lower bound for a, b if $d \leq a$ and $d \leq b$. A lattice $\mathcal{L}$ is a poset in which any two elements a, b have a least upper bound (denoted $a \vee b$) and a greatest lower bound ($a \wedge b$). Hence if

---

[1] To be precise, this is true of one-sided testers, which must accept if a function satisfies the property.

c is an upper bound of a and b then $a \vee b \leq c$ and if d is an lower bound for a, b then $d \leq a \wedge b$.

We say a is covered by b (or b covers a) denoted by $a \prec b$ if $a \neq b$, $a \leq b$ and if $a \leq z \leq b$ then $z \in \{a, b\}$. We have $a \preceq b$ if either $a = b$ or $a \prec b$. Given $a \leq b$, a chain from a to b of length t is a sequence $a = z_0 \prec z_1 \cdots \prec z_t = b$. A lattice may have chains of different lengths from a to b.

Since lattices (in general, posets) are transitive, they can be described just by the covering relation $\prec$. They are pictorially represented by *Hasse diagrams* where elements are points on a plane and $a \prec b$ iff there is an upward line joining a and b.

A sublattice is a subset $\mathcal{L}' \subseteq \mathcal{L}$ that is closed under $\vee$ and $\wedge$. The lattice closure of a set $S \subseteq \mathcal{L}$ is the smallest sublattice containing all points in S.

A lattice $\mathcal{L}$ is modular if it does not contain a pentagon N_5 as a sublattice (see the full version or [5]). A lattice $\mathcal{L}$ is distributive if for all $x, y, z \in \mathcal{L}$, $x \wedge (y \vee z) = (x \wedge y) \vee (x \wedge z)$. Distributive lattices are isomorphic to the lattice $2^{\{[m]\}}$. We also refer to the latter as the hypercube.

Submodularity and Squares. A function $f : \mathcal{L} \to \mathbb{R}$ is submodular if $f(a) + f(b) \geq f(a \vee b) + f(a \wedge b)$ for all $a, b \in \mathcal{L}$. The quadruple $(a, b, a \vee b, a \wedge b)$ is called a square tuple. The square tuple is violated if $f(a) + f(b) < f(a \vee b) + f(a \wedge b)$. In case of the hypercube, the quadruple $(A, A \cup \{i\}, A \cup \{j\}, A \cup \{i, j\})$ for $A \subseteq [m]$, $i, j \notin A$ is called a unit square tuple.

Property Testing. Given a distance parameter $\epsilon \in (0, 1)$ (also called proximity), a function $f : 2^{[m]} \to \mathbb{R}$ is ϵ-far from submodular if at least ϵ fraction of the points must be changed to make the function submodular, i.e., $|\{S \subseteq [m] : f(S) \neq g(S)\}| \geq \epsilon 2^m$ for any submodular function g. A tester for submodular functions is a randomized algorithm that takes parameter ϵ and oracle access to a function $f : 2^{[m]} \to \mathbb{R}$ as input. The tester queries the oracle, accepts if f is submodular, and rejects with constant probability if f ϵ-far from submodular.

Many well-known and natural testers in the literature belong to a class of testers called *proximity oblivious testers* (POTs) [4]. Here, the testers have a *basic test* that is independent of ϵ. The tester uses the parameter ϵ only to determine the number of times a basic test is invoked. The tester rejects iff the value of points queried in a single basic test cannot belong to a function with the required property. For example, consider the celebrated BLR tester for linearity [1]. It repeats $O(1/\epsilon)$ times the basic test, which consists of randomly picking disjoint sets S, T, querying $f(S), f(T), f(S+T)$, and rejecting if $f(S+T) \neq f(S) + f(T)$. For the edge tester [3] for monotonicity testing, the basic test picks sets S and $S \cup \{j\}$ and rejects if $f(S) > f(S \cup \{j\})$. If the probability of rejecting when the function does not satisfy the property—the detection probability—of the basic test is $\rho(\epsilon)$ then the POT repeats the basic test $O(1/\rho(\epsilon))$ times.

Definition 1. ([4]) *A q-query POT with detection probability $\rho : (0, 1] \to (0, 1]$ for a property $\mathcal{P}$ is a randomized algorithm with oracle access to a function f that queries the oracle at q points, and (1) accepts if $f \in \mathcal{P}$, or (2) rejects with probability at least $\rho(\epsilon)$ if f is ϵ-far from the property $\mathcal{P}$.*

Thus the BLR tester is a 3-query POT with detection probability $\rho(\epsilon) = \epsilon$. Note that ϵ is not an input but a POT for $\mathcal{P}$ can be repeated $1/\rho(\epsilon)$ times to get a standard tester for $\mathcal{P}$. Since the number of repetitions of the basic test is the inverse of detection probability ρ, the upper bound for ρ is a lower bound on the number of queries the POT makes. To avoid confusion, our upper and lower bounds will always refer to the detection probability ρ of the basic test.

Our Contribution. A technical contribution of our work is the square certificate, which certifies nonextendibility of a given partial function. We view this as a significant contribution since it is a natural certificate based on multisets of squares. It is also useful in a variety of applications, as we demonstrate.

Sublattice Extendibility. We first show that general lattices are not sublattice extendible. We also give a novel but intuitive characterization of sublattice extendible lattices (Theorem 6). We then generalize Topkis' result for modular lattices, showing that a larger class of lattices, which we call pseudocyclic lattices, are sublattice extendible.

Theorem 1. *Modular lattices are pseudocyclic.*

Theorem 2. *Pseudocyclic lattices are sublattice extendible.*

Our proof depends on transforming one square certificate to another, using a graph-theoretic abstraction of a square certificate which we call a circuit graph.

Property Testing. Property testing for submodular functions is poorly understood. The square tester of Seshadhri and Vondrak [13] is a 4-query POT with detection probability at least $\Omega(\epsilon^{\sqrt{m}\log m})$. They also give a lower bound to show that the detection probability of the square tester cannot exceed $O(\epsilon^2)$. There is thus a large gap between lower and upper bounds, even for this tester.

The lower bound for Seshadhri and Vondrak (for the square tester) is shown by a family of functions defined on $2^{[m+2]}$. Each function f_{S^*} in the family is parametrized by a set $S^* \subseteq [m]$ of size $m/2$. We first show that for this lower bound instance, there is a significantly better tester than the square tester. In particular, there is a partial function consisting of just $O(m)$ points that is a square certificate for any function in the lower bound instance, and hence is not extendible to a submodular function. Thus a tester that queries these $O(m)$ sets and rejects iff the partial function so obtained is not extendible, will reject any function in the lower bound family described (and accept submodular functions).

Theorem 3. *There exists a family of sets $\mathcal{D} \subseteq 2^{[m+2]}$ with $|\mathcal{D}| = O(m)$ so that, for any function f_{S^*} in the family of functions in the lower bound instance of Seshadhri and Vondrak, the partial function $(S, f_{S^*}(S))_{S \in \mathcal{D}}$ is not extendible to a submodular function.*

The theorem suggests that instead of testing unit squares, a tester based on square certificates may be significantly more powerful.

We then show two lower bounds for testing submodularity on the hypercube. Our first lower bound also holds for matroid rank functions,[2] an important subclass of submodular functions. Testing matroid rank functions is mentioned as an open problem in [13], for which we provide the first non-trivial lower bound.

Theorem 4. *1. No $2^{o(m)}$-query POT for submodularity and matroid rank functions has detection probability $\rho(\epsilon) = \Omega(\epsilon^{1.2-c})$ for any constant $c > 0$.*
2. No constant query POT for submodularity has detection probability $\rho(\epsilon) = \omega(\epsilon^2)$.

The above theorem separates testing submodularity from other properties on the hypercube such as monotonicity, Lipschitzness, and unateness for which $O(m), O(m), O(m^{1.5})$ query POT exist respectively with optimal detection probability $\rho(\epsilon) = \Omega(\epsilon)$ [2,3][3]. Further, our second result generalises one of the main results of [13] which shows that the detection probability of the square tester (i.e., a particular 4-query POT) cannot exceed $\Omega(\epsilon^2)$.

We describe relevant related work and give all proofs in the full version.

2 Square Certificates

A partial function consists of a set of points $\mathcal{D} \subseteq \mathcal{L}$ and a function $h : \mathcal{D} \to \mathbb{R}$. The points in $\mathcal{D}$ are called *defined* points. In *partial function extension*, given a partial function h, the goal is to determine if there exists a submodular extension of h, i.e., a submodular function $f : \mathcal{L} \to \mathbb{R}$ such that $f(x) = h(x) \, \forall x \in \mathcal{D}$.

We define a combinatorial structure called a *square certificate* that certifies non-extendibility of a given partial function. To convey the intuition, we start with an example. Consider the lattice in Fig. 1a with partial function h defined on $\mathcal{D} = \{a, c, d, f, g, i\}$ that has value 1 at d and 0 at other points. If there is a submodular extension $s(\cdot)$ then (see Fig. 1b) $s(a) + s(e) \geq s(b) + s(d)$, $s(b) + s(i) \geq s(h) + s(c)$ and $s(h) + s(f) \geq s(e) + s(g)$. Summing, we get, $s(a) + s(i) + s(f) \geq s(c) + s(d) + s(g)$, or $h(a) + h(i) + h(f) \geq h(c) + h(d) + h(g)$ as s extends h. Therefore, $0 = h(a) + h(i) + h(f) < h(c) + h(d) + h(g) = 1$ is a certificate that h is not extendible. More precisely, the set of square tuples $\{(a, e, b, d), (b, i, h, c), (h, f, e, g)\}$ is a certificate of nonextendibility of h.

For a square tuple $(a, b, a \vee b, a \wedge b)$, the points a and b are called *middle points*, $a \vee b$ is the *top* point and $a \wedge b$ is the *bottom* point of this square. Points $a, b, a \vee b, a \wedge b$ are said to be *part* of this square. Given a *multiset of squares*, for a point $x \in \mathcal{L}$, define $m(x)$ to be the number of square tuples with x as a middle point, and $tb(x)$ to be the number of square tuples with x as a top or bottom point. A point x is *involved* if $m(x)$ or $tb(x)$ is > 0, i.e., it is a part of some square in the multiset. An involved point x is an *input point* if $m(x) > tb(x)$, an *intermediate point* if $m(x) = tb(x)$, and an *output point* if $m(x) < tb(x)$.

---

[2] A function $f : 2^{[m]} \to \mathbb{Z}_{\geq 0}$ is a matroid rank function if (i) $f(\emptyset) = 0$, (ii) $f(S \cup i) - f(S) \in \{0, 1\}$ for any S and $i \notin S$ and (iii) f is submodular.
[3] There exist constant query POTs with $\rho(\epsilon) = \epsilon/O(m), \epsilon/O(m), \epsilon/O(m^{1.5})$ respectively. These imply $O(m), O(m), O(m^{1.5})$-query POTs with $\rho(\epsilon) = \epsilon$.

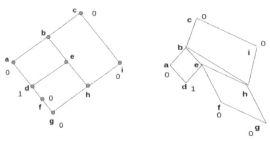

(a) A lattice that is not sub-lattice extendible

(b) A square certificate

Fig. 1. The function $h : \{a, c, d, f, g, i\} \rightarrow \{0, 1\}$ is submodular in the sublattice but not extendible to the whole lattice.

In the above example, points b, e, h have $tb(\cdot) = m(\cdot) = 1$, points c, d, g have $tb(\cdot) = 1$, $m(\cdot) = 0$, and points a, f, i have $tb(\cdot) = 0$, $m(\cdot) = 1$.

Square Certificates. Given a partial function $h : \mathcal{D} \rightarrow \mathbb{R}$, a *square certificate* is a multiset of squares satisfying the following properties.

(P1) If $x \in \mathcal{L}$ is an input or an output point, i.e., $m(x) \neq tb(x)$, then x must be in $\mathcal{D}$.

(P2) $\sum_{x \in \mathcal{D}} h(x) (tb(x) - m(x)) > 0$.

In the above example, a, i, f are input points and c, d, g are output points, and all of them are in $\mathcal{D}$. The intermediate points b, e, h are not required to be in $\mathcal{D}$.

Theorem 5. *Given a partial function $h : \mathcal{D} \rightarrow \mathbb{R}$, there exists a submodular function $f : \mathcal{L} \rightarrow \mathbb{R}$ such that $f(x) = h(x)$ for all $x \in \mathcal{D}$ iff there does not exist a square certificate.*

3   Sublattice Extendibility

We first give an example in Fig. 1a to show that not all lattices are sublattice extendible. One can check that $\{a, d, f, g, c, i\}$ is a sublattice. Consider a function on this sublattice with value 1 at d and 0 at other points. The function is clearly submodular within the sublattice, but is not extendible to the whole lattice as there is a square certificate shown in Fig. 1b and described earlier.

Topkis showed that modular lattices are sublattice extendible [14]. We give two main results. Firstly, we give a novel combinatorial characterization for sublattice extendible lattices (Theorem 6). Secondly, we define a strict generalization of modular lattices called *pseudocyclic* lattices, and show that these are sublattice extendible (Theorems 1, 2).

Characterizing Sublattice Extendibility. For the characterization of sublattice extendibility, we assume we are given a lattice $\mathcal{L}$ and a multiset of square tuples. For any $x \in \mathcal{L}$, define $m(x) - tb(x)$ to be the multiplicity of x. Two multisets of squares are *similar* if, for some $k \geq 1$ and for every $x \in \mathcal{L}$, the multiplicity of x in the first multiset is k times the multiplicity in the other. Note that by this definition, the set of input points and the set of output points are identical for both multisets, though the intermediate points may differ. This is because an intermediate point x in a multiset of squares has $m(x) - tb(x) = 0$. Hence x may be an intermediate point in one multiset, but may not be involved in the other multiset.[4] Further, a multiset of squares is *good* if all its involved points are in the lattice closure of the input and output points. The square certificate in Fig. 1b is not good as b, e, h are not in the lattice closure of $\{a, c, d, f, g, i\}$.

Theorem 6. *A lattice $\mathcal{L}$ is sublattice extendible iff for any multiset of squares there exists a similar and good multiset of squares.*

The proof of Theorem 2 only uses sufficiency of Theorem 6, that lattice $\mathcal{L}$ is sublattice extendible if for any multiset of squares there exists a good multiset for which the multiplicity $m(x) - tb(x)$ is identical for all $x \in \mathcal{L}$ (i.e., similar with $k = 1$). For a proof sketch of sufficiency, suppose a submodular function h on some sublattice $\mathcal{L}'$ is not extendible to a submodular function on the lattice $\mathcal{L}$. By Theorem 5, there exists a square certificate with input and output points in $\mathcal{L}'$ (because of (P1) as the set of defined points $\mathcal{D}$ is $\mathcal{L}'$). By assumption, there exists a good multiset of squares similar to the square certificate. This new multiset of square is thus another square certificate (this uses the similarity assumption) with all involved points in $\mathcal{L}'$ (this uses the good assumption). This contradicts that h is submodular on $\mathcal{L}'$.

Pseudocyclic Lattices. Here, we define pseudocyclic lattices and give some intuition for Theorems 1 and 2. Formal proofs are in the full version. Informally, a lattice is pseudocyclic if two multisets of squares on the lattice that have the same structure and the same input points, must have the same output points. In order to define the structure on multisets of squares, we will first define a graph-theoretic abstraction called a *circuit graph*, and describe the relation between square multisets and circuit graphs in terms of *satisfying functions*, that map vertices of the circuit graph to points in the multiset. We then formally define pseudocyclic lattices.

For the proof of Theorem 2, we will describe a process that converts a cyclic circuit graph into an acyclic one. This, combined with Tarski's fixed point theorem on lattices, will allow us to complete the proof. For the proof of Theorem 1, we will first present an alternate characterization of modular lattices. This characterization combined with the strong form of Tarski's fixed point theorem will be used to prove the result.

---

[4] E.g., in Fig. 1a, the multisets $\{(a, e, b, d), (d, h, e, g)\}$ and $\{(a, h, b, g)\}$ are similar (with $k = 1$).

Circuit Graphs. Theorems 1 and 2 require the transformation of one multiset of squares to another. For this transformation, we define an abstraction of a multiset of squares as a directed graph, which we call a *circuit graph*. This abstraction is useful in multiple ways, including to concretize the notion of a cycle in the multiset, and to define pseudocyclic lattices.

We define a multiset of squares to be *unit* if, for any $x \in \mathcal{L}$, $m(x), tb(x) \in \{0,1\}$, i.e., each point $x \in \mathcal{L}$ is in at most 2 squares, and further in at most 1 square as a middle point and at most 1 square as top or bottom point. It is easier to see the correspondence between circuit graphs and unit multisets. Informally, given a unit multiset of squares, the directed graph formed by drawing edges from a, b to both c and d for each square (a, b, c, d) in the multiset and labelling c by $\vee$ and d by $\wedge$ is a circuit graph. A formal definition is as follows.

Definition 2. *A circuit graph G is a directed graph consisting of input vertices (vertices with outdegree 2 and indegree 0), intermediate vertices (vertices with outdegree 2 and indegree 2) and output vertices (vertices with outdegree 0 and indegree 2) such that*

1. *All intermediate and output vertices are labelled by $\wedge$ or $\vee$.*
2. *If vertices v_1 and v_2 have an edge to a vertex v labelled by $\vee$ ($\wedge$) then v_1 and v_2 also have an edge to a vertex v' labelled by $\wedge$ ($\vee$).*

Figure 2b shows a circuit graph with u_1, u_2, u_3 as input vertices, z_1, z_2, z_3 as intermediate vertices and w_1, w_2, w_3 as output vertices. It follows immediately from the definition that for a circuit graph, the number of input vertices is equal to the number of output vertices. It can be seen that a circuit graph is a collection of *square subgraphs* where a square subgraph consists of 4 vertices (v_1, v_2, v_3, v_4) such that v_3 is labelled by $\vee$, v_4 is labelled by $\wedge$ and there are edges from v_1, v_2 to both v_3 and v_4. The above circuit graph consists of (u_1, z_3, z_1, w_3), (z_1, u_2, w_1, z_2) and (z_2, u_3, w_2, z_3) as square subgraphs. We further extend our existing nomenclature for multiset of squares to circuit graphs. Given a square subgraph (v_1, v_2, v_3, v_4), v_1 and v_2 are part of this square subgraph as middle vertices while v_3 and v_4 are part as top and bottom vertex respectively. For any vertex v, $m(v)$ and $tb(v)$ are the number of square subgraphs that v is part of as a middle vertex and a top or bottom vertex respectively. Thus $m(v) = 1$ and $tb(v) = 0$ for input vertices; $m(v) = 1$ and $tb(v) = 1$ for intermediate vertices and $m(v) = 0$ and $tb(v) = 1$ for output vertices.

The notion of a *satisfying function* formalizes the link between multiset of squares and circuit graphs.

Definition 3. *Given a circuit graph G and a lattice $\mathcal{L}$, a function $f : V(G) \to \mathcal{L}$ is called satisfying if $f(v_1) \vee f(v_2) = f(v_3)$ and $f(v_1) \wedge f(v_2) = f(v_4)$ for all square subgraphs (v_1, v_2, v_3, v_4) in G.*

Pseudocyclic Lattices. We now formally define pseudocyclic lattices. For clarity, we will reserve n for number of input (or output) vertices in the circuit graph G. We order the input and output vertices and denote them by $u_1, \ldots, u_n$ and $w_1, \ldots, w_n$ respectively.

Definition 4. *A lattice $\mathcal{L}$ is a pseudocyclic lattice if for any circuit graph G (with n input and output vertices), and any two satisfying functions $F, H :$ $V(G) \to \mathcal{L}$ with $F(u_i) = H(u_i) \ \forall i \in [n]$, it holds that $F(w_i) = H(w_i) \ \forall i \in [n]$.*

Thus to show a lattice not pseudocyclic we need to provide a circuit graph G and two satisfying functions F, G such that they have same values on input vertices but differ on at least one output vertex. We give an example of a lattice that is not pseudocyclic in Fig. 2.

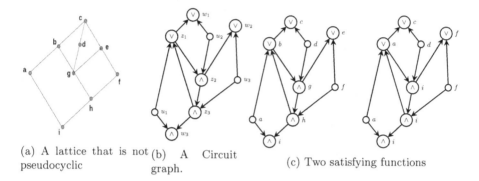

(a) A lattice that is not pseudocyclic

(b) A Circuit graph.

(c) Two satisfying functions

Fig. 2. The above lattice is not pseudocyclic as for the above circuit graph, there are two different satisfying functions with same value a, d, f on input vertices (u_1, u_2 and u_3 respectively) but different value on the output vertex w_2.

From Theorem 6, we want to show that given any multiset of squares that is not good in a pseudocyclic lattice, there exists a similar and good multiset of squares. Given the initial multiset of squares, we construct the circuit graph by an abstraction algorithm (see the full version). The algorithm gives a satisfying function $\mathcal{C}$ that maps vertices of the circuit graph to involved points in the multiset. However, for some vertex v, since the multiset is not good, $\mathcal{C}(v)$ may not be in the lattice closure of input points. Then we show existence of another satisfying function $\mathcal{C}'$ with the property that $\mathcal{C}'$ agrees with $\mathcal{C}$ on input vertices and additionally maps all vertices to lattice closure of input points. Since our lattice is pseudocyclic, $\mathcal{C}$ and $\mathcal{C}'$ must agree on output vertices as well. This will give us a similar and good multiset of squares and hence by Theorem 6 pseudocyclic lattices are sublattice extendible. One can see that the crux of this proof is the existence of $\mathcal{C}'$. Once the basic framework is developed, the existence of $\mathcal{C}'$ will be immediate by an application of Tarski's fixed point theorem.

For Theorem 1, at a high level, we first give an alternative characterization of modular lattices. Given a lattice $\mathcal{L}$ and $x \leq y \in \mathcal{L}$, we define the distance $d(x, y)$ between x and y to be the length of a chain of minimum length from x to y. Therefore $d(x, x) = 0$ and if $x \prec y$ then $d(x, y) = 1$. Define the function $F : \mathcal{L}^2 \to \mathcal{L}^2$ as $F(x, y) = (x \vee y, x \wedge y)$ for all $x, y \in \mathcal{L}$.

Proposition 1. *A lattice is modular iff for all x, x', y such that $x' \prec x$, it holds that $d(F(x', y), F(x, y)) = 1$.*

This characterization, combined with the strong form of Tarski's fixed point theorem—the non empty set of fixed points P form a complete lattice and hence have a minimum element—will give us our proof.

4   Property Testing

We here give a sketch of the proof of the first part of Theorem 4 here. The full proof of the theorem is given in the full version of the paper.

Proof sketch of Theorem 4 (1). We define a family of functions $\mathcal{F}$ from $2^{[m]}$ to $\mathbb{R}_{\geq 0}$ such that each function in $\mathcal{F}$ has distance $\epsilon = 2^{-5m/6}$ from submodularity and matroid rank. This family $\mathcal{F} = \{f_R \text{ s.t. } R \subseteq [m], |R| = m/2\}$ is parametrized by sets R of size $m/2$.

Fix a subset $R \subseteq [m]$ such that $|R| = m/2$. Let A_1, A_2, $A_3 \subseteq R$ be fixed sets such that $|A_i| = m/3$ for all $i = 1, 2, 3$ and $A_i \cup A_j = R$ for all $i \neq j$. Let $\mathcal{M}_i = \{S | A_i \subseteq S \subseteq R\}$ for $i = 1, 2, 3$. We note the following properties of the construction: (i) any two of A_1, A_2, A_3 fix the third, (ii) for sets $A'_i \in \mathcal{M}_i$, $A'_j \in \mathcal{M}_j$ with $i \neq j$, $A'_i \cup A'_j = R$, and (iii) $A_k \not\subseteq A'_i \cap A'_j$, for any $k = 1, 2, 3$.

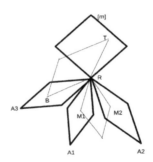

Fig. 3. At least one value in $\{M_1, M_2, M_1 \cap M_2, B, T, (T \setminus R) \cup B\}$ must be changed to make f submodular.

Since R is fixed, we drop the subscript from f_R. The function f is defined as:

$$f(S) = \begin{cases} |S| - 1 & \text{if } S \in \mathcal{M}_1 \text{ or } S \in \mathcal{M}_2, \\ |S| & \text{if } S \in 2^R \text{ but } S \notin \mathcal{M}_1, \mathcal{M}_2, \\ f(S \cap R) & \text{if } S \notin 2^R \text{ and } S \cap R \in \mathcal{M}_3 \\ f(S \cap R) + 1 & \text{if } S \notin 2^R \text{ and } S \cap R \notin \mathcal{M}_3 \end{cases}$$

Informally, if $S \in 2^R$, then $f(S)$ is $|S| - 1$ if it is a superset of A_1 or A_2, and $|S|$ otherwise. Otherwise, if $S = T \cup S'$ where $S' \subseteq R$ and $T \subseteq [m] \setminus R$, the value is $f(S')$ if $A_3 \subseteq S'$, and is $f(S') + 1$ otherwise.

For $i = 1, 2$, define the modified function f_i as $f_i(S) = f(S) + 1$ if $S \in \mathcal{M}_i \setminus R$, and $f_i(S) = f(S)$ otherwise. We show in the full version that the function $f_i(S)$ is a matroid rank function, for $i = 1, 2$. Note that the number of modifications required to change f into f_i is exactly $|\mathcal{M}_i \setminus R| = 2^{m/6} - 1$. Hence $\epsilon \leq 2^{-5m/6}$. Secondly, we show that this is tight: at least $2^{m/6} - 1$ points *must* be changed to make f submodular.

To show this, we construct $2^{m/6} - 1$ disjoint partial functions that each cannot be extended to a submodular function (see Fig. 3). Hence at least one point from each, i.e, total $2^{m/6} - 1$ points must be changed for f to be submodular. Each partial function consists of 6 points and will be shown to be not extendible by showing a square certificate consisting of 2 squares. The point R is not in any partial function, but will be in every square certificate, as a top point in one square and a middle square in another (thus R is an intermediate set in the square certificate, and need not be in the partial function).

The first square in each of the $2^{m/6} - 1$ square certificates consists of a set M_1 from $\mathcal{M}_1 \setminus R$, a set M_2 from $\mathcal{M}_2 \setminus R$, their union R and their intersection $M_1 \cap M_2$. We show in the full proof how to obtain $2^{m/6} - 1$ disjoint (apart from R) such squares. The second square in each of $2^{m/6} - 1$ square certificates consists of a set $B \in \mathcal{M}_3 \setminus R$ as a bottom point, a set $T \supset R$ as a top point, set R as a middle point, and the set $(T \setminus R) \cup B$ as the second middle point. Thus, the square obtained is $(R, (T \setminus R) \cup B, T, B)$. Again, we can obtain $2^{m/6} - 1$ disjoint (apart from R) such squares. We now construct $2^{m/6} - 1$ square certificates by selecting, for each square certificate, a unique square from the first set of squares and a unique square from the second set of squares. Let $(M_1, M_2, R, M_1 \cap M_2)$ and $(R, (T \setminus R) \cup B, T, B)$ be the squares selected. The partial function consists of the points $M_1, M_2, M_1 \cap M_2, (T \setminus R) \cup B, T$, and B (these are the defined points) and their values for the function f. The two squares described give a square certificate for this partial function, since all input and output sets are defined points, and $f(M_1) + f(M_2) + f((T \setminus R) \cup B) - f(T) - f(B) - f(M_1 \cap M_2) = -1$

Thus there are $2^{m/6} - 1$ disjoint partial functions, each of which cannot be extended to a submodular function. Hence the distance to submodularity (and matroid rank) is at least $\epsilon = 2^{-5m/6}$. From the earlier upper bound, this is exact.

By Yao's minmax principle, to bound the detection probability of a q-query POT, it suffices to bound the detection probability of a deterministic algorithm D (that queries q points) against a uniform distribution over functions in $\mathcal{F} = \{f_R \mid R \subseteq [m], |R| = m/2\}$. Let $\mathcal{Q}$ be the fixed set of points queried by D. Recall that the functions $f_i(S)$ are equal to $f(S)$ $(i = 1, 2)$ for all S not in $\mathcal{M}_i$, so $2^{[m]} \setminus \mathcal{M}_i$ can be extended to a matroid rank function (and hence a submodular function). Therefore, if D has to reject f_R then $\mathcal{Q}$ must contain[5] a set $S_1 \in \mathcal{M}_1$ and a set $S_2 \in \mathcal{M}_2$. That is, if D has to reject f_R then $\mathcal{Q}$ must contain sets S_1 and S_2 such that $S_1 \cup S_2 = R$. Therefore, if $|\mathcal{Q}| = 2^{o(m)}$ then the detection probability $|\mathcal{Q}|^2 / \binom{m}{m/2} = O(2^{o(m)}/2^m) \leq \epsilon^{1.2-c}$ for any constant $c > 0$.   □

---

[5] This is because we are dealing with one-sided testers. If a function has the property then the tester must accept the function.

Acknowledgements. Both authors acknowledge support from the Department of Atomic Energy, Government of India (project no. RTI4001). The first author is additionally supported by a Ramanujan Fellowship (SERB - SB/S2/RJN-055/2015) and an Early Career Research Award (SERB - ECR/2018/002766). The second author is additionally supported by a research fellowship from Tata Consultancy Services.

References

1. Blum, M., Luby, M., Rubinfeld, R.: Self-testing/correcting with applications to numerical problems. J. Comput. Syst. Sci. **47**(3), 549–595 (1993)
2. Chakrabarty, D., Seshadhri, C.: Optimal bounds for monotonicity and Lipschitz testing over hypercubes and hypergrids. In: STOC, pp. 419–428. ACM (2013)
3. Goldreich, O., Goldwasser, S., Lehman, E., Ron, D., Samorodnitsky, A.: Testing monotonicity. Combinatorica **20**(3), 301–337 (2000). https://doi.org/10.1007/s004930070011
4. Goldreich, O., Ron, D.: On proximity-oblivious testing. SIAM J. Comput. **40**(2), 534–566 (2011)
5. Grätzer, G.: Lattice Theory: Foundation. Springer, Heidelberg (2011). https://doi.org/10.1007/978-3-0348-0018-1
6. Kempe, D., Kleinberg, J.M., Tardos, É.: Maximizing the spread of influence through a social network. Theory of Computing **11**, 105–147 (2015)
7. Kolmogorov, V., Zabih, R.: What energy functions can be minimized via graph cuts? IEEE Trans. Pattern Anal. Mach. Intell. **26**(2), 147–159 (2004)
8. Krokhin, A., Larose, B.: Maximizing supermodular functions on product lattices, with application to maximum constraint satisfaction. SIAM J. Discret. Math. **22**(1), 312–328 (2008)
9. Kuivinen, F.: On the complexity of submodular function minimisation on diamonds. Discret. Optim. **8**(3), 459–477 (2011)
10. Lehmann, B., Lehmann, D.J., Nisan, N.: Combinatorial auctions with decreasing marginal utilities. Games Econ. Behav. **55**(2), 270–296 (2006)
11. Pitt, L., Valiant, L.G.: Computational limitations on learning from examples. J. ACM **35**(4), 965–984 (1988)
12. Promislow, S.D., Young, V.R.: Supermodular functions on finite lattices. Order **22**(4), 389–413 (2005). https://doi.org/10.1007/s11083-005-9026-5
13. Seshadhri, C., Vondrák, J.: Is submodularity testable? Algorithmica **69**(1), 1–25 (2014). https://doi.org/10.1007/s00453-012-9719-2
14. Topkis, D.M.: Minimizing a submodular function on a lattice. Oper. Res. **26**(2), 305–321 (1978)
15. Topkis, D.M.: Equilibrium points in nonzero-sum n-person submodular games. SIAM J. Control Optim. **17**(6), 773–787 (1979)
16. Varian, H.: Revealed preference. Samuelsonian economics and the twenty-first century, pp. 99–115 (2006)

Parameterized Complexity of MAXIMUM EDGE COLORABLE SUBGRAPH

Akanksha Agrawal[1], Madhumita Kundu[2], Abhishek Sahu[3], Saket Saurabh[3,4],
and Prafullkumar Tale[5(✉)]

[1] Ben Gurion University of the Negev, Be'er Sheva, Israel
agrawal@post.bgu.ac.il
[2] Indian Statistical Institute, Kolkata, India
kundumadhumita.134@gmail.com
[3] The Institute of Mathematical Sciences, HBNI, Chennai, India
{asahu,saket}@imsc.res.in
[4] University of Bergen, Bergen, Norway
[5] Max Planck Institute for Informatics, Saarland Informatics Campus,
Saarbrücken, Germany
prafullkumar.tale@mpi-inf.mpg.de

Abstract. A graph H is *p-edge colorable* if there is a coloring ψ : $E(H) \to \{1, 2, \ldots, p\}$, such that for distinct $uv, vw \in E(H)$, we have $\psi(uv) \neq \psi(vw)$. The MAXIMUM EDGE-COLORABLE SUBGRAPH problem takes as input a graph G and integers l and p, and the objective is to find a subgraph H of G and a p-edge-coloring of H, such that $|E(H)| \geq l$. We study the above problem from the viewpoint of Parameterized Complexity. We obtain FPT algorithms when parameterized by: (1) the vertex cover number of G, by using INTEGER LINEAR PROGRAMMING, and (2) l, a randomized algorithm via a reduction to RAINBOW MATCHING, and a deterministic algorithm by using color coding, and divide and color. With respect to the parameters $p + k$, where k is one of the following: (1) the solution size, l, (2) the vertex cover number of G, and (3) $l - \text{mm}(G)$, where $\text{mm}(G)$ is the size of a maximum matching in G; we show that the (decision version of the) problem admits a kernel with $\mathcal{O}(k \cdot p)$ vertices. Furthermore, we show that there is no kernel of size $\mathcal{O}(k^{1-\epsilon} \cdot f(p))$, for any $\epsilon > 0$ and computable function f, unless NP $\subseteq$ coNP/poly.

Akanksha Agrawal: Funded by the PBC Fellowship Program for Outstanding Post-Doctoral Researchers from China and India.
Saket Saurabh: Funded by the European Research Council (ERC) under the European Union's Horizon 2020 research and innovation programme (grant agreement No 819416), and Swarnajayanti Fellowship (No DST/SJF/MSA01/2017-18).

Prafullkumar Tale: Funded by the European Research Council (ERC) under the European Union's Horizon 2020 research and innovation programme under grant agreement SYSTEMATICGRAPH (No. 725978). Most parts of this work was completed when the author was a Senior Research Fellow at The Institute of Mathematical Sciences, HBNI, Chennai, India.

D. Kim et al. (Eds.): COCOON 2020, LNCS 12273, pp. 615–626, 2020.
https://doi.org/10.1007/978-3-030-58150-3_50

Keywords: Edge coloring · Kernelization · FPT algorithms · Kernel lower bound

1   Introduction

For a graph G, two (distinct) edges in $E(G)$ are *adjacent* if they share an endpoint. A p-edge coloring of G is a function $\psi : E(G) \rightarrow \{1, 2, \ldots, p\}$ such that adjacent edges receive different colors. One of the basic combinatorial optimization problems EDGE COLORING, where for the given graph G and an integer p, the objective is to find a p-edge coloring of G. EDGE COLORING is a very well studied problem in Graph Theory and Algorithm Design and we refer the readers to the survey by Cao et al. [3], the recent article by Grüttemeier et al. [11], and references with-in for various known results, conjectures, and practical importance of this problem.

The smallest integer p for which G is p-edge colorable is called its *chromatic index* and is denoted by $\chi'(G)$. The classical theorem of Vizing [18] states that $\chi'(G) \leq \Delta(G) + 1$, where $\Delta(G)$ is the maximum degree of a vertex in G. (Notice that by the definition of p-edge coloring, it follows that we require at least $\Delta(G)$ many colors to edge color G.) Holyer showed that deciding whether chromatic index of G is $\Delta(G)$ or $\Delta(G) + 1$ is NP-Hard even for cubic graphs [12]. Laven and Galil generalized this result to prove that the similar result holds for d-regular graphs, for $d \geq 3$ [15].

EDGE COLORING naturally leads to the question of finding the maximum number of edges in a given graph that can be colored with a given number of colors. This problem is called MAXIMUM EDGE COLORABLE SUBGRAPH which is formally defined below.

MAXIMUM EDGE COLORABLE SUBGRAPH
Input: A graph G and integers l, p
Output: A subgraph of G with at least l edges and its p-edge coloring or correctly conclude that no such subgraph exits.

Note that the classical polynomial time solvable problem, MAXIMUM MATCHING, is a special case of MAXIMUM EDGE COLORABLE SUBGRAPH (when $p = 1$). Feige et al. [8] showed that MAXIMUM EDGE COLORABLE SUBGRAPH is NP-hard even for $p = 2$. In the same paper, the authors presented a constant factor approximation algorithm for the problem and proved that for every fixed $p \geq 2$, there is $\epsilon > 0$, for which it is NP-hard to obtain a $(1 - \epsilon)$-approximation algorithm. Sinnamon presented a randomized algorithm for the problem [17]. To the best of knowledge, Aloisioa and Mkrtchyan were the first to study this problem from the viewpoint of Parameterized Complexity [1] (see Sect. 2 for definitions related to Parameterized Complexity). Aloisioa and Mkrtchyana proved that when $p = 2$, the problem is fixed-parameter tractable, with respect to various structural graph parameters like path-width, curving-width, and the dimension of cycle space. Grüttemeier et al. [11], very recently, obtained kernels, when the parameter is $p + k$, where k is one of the following: i) the number of edges that needs to be deleted from G, to obtain a graph with maximum degree at most $p - 1$,[1] and ii) the deletion set size to a graph whose connected components have at most p vertices. Galby et al. [10] proved that EDGE COLORING is fixed-parameter tractable when parameterized by the number of colors and the number of vertices having the maximum degree.

Our Contributions: Firstly, we consider MAXIMUM EDGE COLORABLE SUBGRAPH, parameterized by the vertex cover number, and we prove the following theorem.

Theorem 1. MAXIMUM EDGE COLORABLE SUBGRAPH, *parameterized by the vertex cover number of G, is* FPT.

We prove the above theorem, by designing an algorithm that, for the given instance, creates instances of ILP, and the resolves the ILP instance using the known algorithm [13,14]. Intuitively, for the instance (G, l, p), suppose (H, ϕ) is the solution that we are seeking for, and let X be a vertex cover of G. (We can compute X by the algorithm of Chen et al. [5].) We "guess" $H' = H[X]$ and $\phi' = \phi|_{E(H')}$. Once we have the above guess, we try to find the remaining edges (and their coloring), using ILP.

Next, we present two (different) FPT algorithms for MAXIMUM EDGE COLORABLE SUBGRAPH, when parameterized by the number of edges in the desired subgraph, l. More precisely, we prove following theorem.

Theorem 2 ($\star$[2]). *There exists a deterministic algorithm $\mathcal{A}$ and a randomized algorithm $\mathcal{B}$ with constant probability of success that solves* MAXIMUM EDGE COLORABLE SUBGRAPH. *For a given instance (G, l, p), Algorithms $\mathcal{A}$ and $\mathcal{B}$ terminate in time $\mathcal{O}^*(4^{l+o(l)})$ and $\mathcal{O}^*(2^l)$, respectively.*

We remark that in the above theorem, the Algorithms $\mathcal{A}$ and $\mathcal{B}$ use different sets of ideas. Algorithm $\mathcal{A}$, uses a combination of the technique [6] of color-coding [2] and divide and color. Algorithm $\mathcal{B}$ uses the algorithm to solve RAINBOW MATCHING as a black-box. We note that the improvement in the running time of Algorithm $\mathcal{B}$ comes at the cost of de-randomization, as we do not know how to de-randomize Algorithm $\mathcal{B}$.

Next we discuss our kernelization results. We show that (the decision version of) the problem admits a polynomial kernel, when parameteized by $p + k$, where k is one of the following: (a) the solution size, l, (b) the vertex cover number of G, and (c) $l - \mathrm{mm}(G)$, where $\mathrm{mm}(G)$ is the size of a maximum matching in G; admits a kernel with $\mathcal{O}(kp)$ vertices. We briefly discuss the choice of our third parameter. By the definition of edge coloring, each color class is a set of matching edges. Hence, we can find one such color class, in polynomial time [16], by computing a maximum matching in a given graph. In above guarantee parameterization theme, instead of parameterizing, say, by the solution size (l in this case), we look for some lower bound (which is the size of a maximum matching in G, for

---

[1] Recall that any graph with maximum degree at most $p - 1$, is p-edge colorable [18], and thus, this number is a measure of "distance-from-triviality".

[2] The proofs of results marked with $\star$ can be found in the full version.

our case) for the solution size, and use a more refined parameter $(l - mm(G))$. We prove the following theorem.

Theorem 3. MAXIMUM EDGE COLORABLE SUBGRAPH *admits a kernel with* $\mathcal{O}(kp)$ *vertices, for every* $k \in \{\ell, vc(G), l - mm(G)\}$.

We complement this kernelization result by proving that the dependency of k on the size of the kernel is optimal up-to a constant factor.

Theorem 4 $(\star)$. *For any* $k \in \{\ell, vc(G), l - mm(G)\}$, MAXIMUM EDGE COLORABLE SUBGRAPH *does not admit a compression of size* $\mathcal{O}(k^{1-\epsilon} \cdot f(p))$, *for any* $\epsilon > 0$ *and computable function* f, *unless* NP $\subseteq$ coNP$/poly$.

2   Preliminaries

For a positive integer n, we denote set $\{1, 2, \ldots, n\}$ by $[n]$. We work with simple undirected graphs. The vertex set and edge set of a graph G are denoted as $V(G)$ and $E(G)$, respectively. An edge between two vertices $u, v \in V(G)$ is denoted by uv. For an edge uv, u and v are called its *endpoints*. If there is an edge uv, vertices u, v are said to be *adjacent* to one another. Two edges are said to be *adjacent* if they share an endpoint. The *neighborhood* of a vertex v is a collection of vertices which are adjacent to v and it is represented as $N_G(v)$. The *degree* of vertex v, denoted by $\deg_G(v)$, is the size of its neighbourhood. For a graph G, $\Delta(G)$ denotes the maximum degree of vertices in G. The *closed neighborhood* of a vertex v, denoted by $N_G[v]$, is the subset $N_G(v) \cup \{v\}$. When the context of the graph is clear we drop the subscript. For set U, we define $N(U)$ as union of $N(v)$ for all vertices v in U. For two disjoint subsets $V_1, V_2 \subseteq V(G)$, $E(V_1, V_2)$ is set of edges where one endpoint is in V_1 and another is in V_2. An edge in the set $E(V_1, V_2)$ is said to be *going across* V_1, V_2. For an edge set E', $V(E')$ denotes the collection of endpoints of edges in E'. A graph H is said to be a *subgraph* of G if $V(H) \subseteq V(G)$ and $E(H) \subseteq E(G)$. In other words, any graph obtained from G by deleting vertices and/or edges is called a subgraph of G. For a vertex (resp. edge) subset $X \subset V(G)$ (resp. $\subset V(G)$), $G - X$ $(G - Y)$ denotes the graph obtained from G by deleting all vertices in X (resp. edges in Y). Moreover, by $G[X]$, we denote graph $G - (V(G) - X)$.

For a positive integer p, a p-edge coloring of a graph G is a function $\phi : E(G) \rightarrow \{1, 2, \ldots, p\}$ such that for every distinct $uv, wx \in E(G)$ s.t. $\{u, v\} \cap \{w, x\} \neq \emptyset$, we have $\phi(uv) \neq \phi(wx)$. The least positive integer p for which there exists a p-edge coloring of a graph G is called *edge chromatic number* of G and it is denoted by $\chi'(G)$.

Proposition 1 ([18] **Vizing**). *For any simple graph* G, $\Delta(G) \leq \chi'(G) \leq \Delta(G) + 1$.

For a coloring ϕ and for any i in $\{1, 2, \ldots, p\}$, the edge subset $\phi^{-1}(i)$ is called the ith *color class* of ϕ. Notice that by the definition of p-edge coloring, every color class is a matching in G.

For a graph G, a set of vertices W is called an *independent set* if no two vertices of W are adjacent with each other. A set $X \subseteq V(G)$ is a *vertex cover* of G if $G - S$ is an independent set. The size of a minimum vertex cover of graph is called its *vertex cover number* and it is denoted by $\mathsf{vc}(G)$. A *matching* of a graph G is a set of edges of G such that every edge shares no vertex with any other edge of *matching*. The size of maximum matching of a graph G is denoted by $\mathsf{mm}(G)$. It is easy to see that $\mathsf{mm}(G) \leq \mathsf{vc}(G) \leq 2 \cdot \mathsf{mm}(G)$.

Definition 1 (deg-1-modulator). *For a graph G, a set $X \subseteq V(G)$ is a deg-1-modulator of G, if the degree of each vertex in $G - X$ is at most 1.*

Expansion Lemma. Let t be a positive integer and G be a bipartite graph with vertex bipartition (P, Q). A set of edges $M \subseteq E(G)$ is called a *t-expansion of P into Q* if (i) every vertex of P is incident with exactly t edges of M, and (ii) the number of vertices in Q which are incident with at least one edge in M is exactly $t|P|$. We say that M *saturates* the end-points of its edges. Note that the set Q may contain vertices which are *not* saturated by M. We need the following generalization of Hall's Matching Theorem known as *expansion lemmas*:

Lemma 1 (See, for example, Lemma 2.18 **in** [7]**).** *Let t be a positive integer and G be a bipartite graph with vertex bipartition (P, Q) such that $|Q| \geq t|P|$ and there are no isolated vertices in Q. Then there exist nonempty vertex sets $P' \subseteq P$ and $Q' \subseteq Q$ such that (i) P' has a t-expansion into Q', and (ii) no vertex in Q' has a neighbour outside P'. Furthermore two such sets P' and Q' can be found in time polynomial in the size of G.*

Integer Linear Programming. The technical tool we use to prove that MAXIMUM EDGE COLORABLE SUBGRAPH is fixed-parameter tractable (defined in next sub-section) by the size of vertex cover is the fact that INTEGER LINEAR PROGRAMMING is fixed-parameter tractable when parameterized by the number of variables. An instance of INTEGER LINEAR PROGRAMMING consists of a matrix $A \in \mathbb{Z}^{m \times q}$, a vector $\bar{b} \in \mathbb{Z}^m$ and a vector $\bar{c} \in \mathbb{Z}^q$. The goal is to find a vector $\bar{x} \in \mathbb{Z}^q$ which satisfies $A\bar{x} \leq \bar{b}$ and minimizes the value of $\bar{c} \cdot \bar{x}$ (scalar product of $\bar{c}$ and $\bar{x}$). We assume that an input is given in binary and thus the size of the input instance or simply instance is the number of bits in its binary representation.

Proposition 2 ([13,14]**).** *An INTEGER LINEAR PROGRAMMING instance of size L with q variables can be solved using $\mathcal{O}(q^{2.5q+o(q)} \cdot (L + \log M_x) \cdot \log(M_x \cdot M_c))$ arithmetic operations and space polynomial in $L + \log M_x$, where M_x is an upper bound on the absolute value that a variable can take in a solution, and M_c is the largest absolute value of a coefficient in the vector $\bar{c}$.*

Parameterized Complexity. We refer readers to books [7,9] for basic definitions. We say a parameter k_2 is *larger* than a parameter k_1 if there exists a computable function $g(\cdot)$ such that $k_1 \leq g(k_2)$. In such case, we denote $k_1 \preceq k_2$ and say k_1 is *smaller* than k_2. If a problem if FPT parameterized by k_1 then it is also FPT parameterized by k_2. Moreover, if a problem admits a kernel of size $h(k_1)$ then it admits a kernel of size $h(g(k_2))$. For a graph G, let X be its minimum sized deg-1-modulator. By the definition of vertex cover, we have $|X| \leq vc(G)$. This implies $|X| \preceq vc(G)$. In the following observation, we argue that for "non-trivial" instances, $vc(G) \preceq l$ and $|X| \preceq l - mm(G)$.

Observation 21 ($\star$). *For a given instance* (G, l, p) *of* MAXIMUM EDGE COLORABLE SUBGRAPH, *in polynomial time, we can conclude that either* (G, l, p) *is a* YES *instance or* $vc(G) \preceq l$ *and* $|X| \preceq (l - mm(G))$, *where* X *is a minimum sized deg-1-modulator of* G.

3   **FPT** Algorithm Parameterized by the Vertex Cover Number of the Input

In this section, we consider the problem MAXIMUM EDGE COLORABLE SUBGRAPH, when parameterized the vertex cover number of the input graph, and our objective is to prove Theorem 1. Let (G, l, p) be an instance of the problem, where the graph G has n vertices. We assume that G has no isolated vertices as any such vertex is irrelevant for an edge coloring. We begin by computing a minimum sized vertex cover, X of G, in time $\mathcal{O}(2^{|X|} n |X|)$, using the algorithm of Chen et al. [4].

We begin by intuitively explaining the working of our algorithm. We assume an arbitrary (but fixed) ordering over vertices in G, and let $W = V(G) \setminus X$. Suppose that we are seeking for the subgraph H, of G, with at least ℓ edges and the coloring $\phi : E(H) \rightarrow \{1, 2, \dots, p\}$. We first "guess" the intersection of H with $G[X]$, i.e., the subgraph H' of $G[X]$, such that $V(H) \cap X = H'$ and $V(H) \cap E(G[X]) = H'$. (Actually, rather than guessing, we will go over all possible such H's, and do the steps, that we intuitively describe next.) Let $\phi' = \phi_{E(H')}$. Based on (H', ϕ'), we construct an instance of ILP, which will help us "extend" the partial solution (H', ϕ'), to the solution (if such an extended solution exists), for the instance (G, ℓ, p). Roughly speaking, the construction of the ILP relies on the following properties. Note that W is an independent set in G, and thus edges of the solution that do not belong to H', must have one endpoint in X and the other endpoint in W. Recall that H has the partition (given by ϕ) into (at most) p matchings, say, $M_1, M_2, \dots, M_{p'}$. The number of different neighborhoods in X, of vertices in W, is bounded by 2^k. This allows us to define a "type" for $M_i - E(H')$, based on the neighborhoods, in X, of the vertices appearing in $M_i - E(H')$. Once we have defined these types, we can create a variable $Y_{\mathbb{T}, \alpha}$, for each type $\mathbb{T}$ and color class α (in $\{0, 1, \dots, p'\}$). The special color 0 will be used for assigning all the edges that should be colored using the colors outside $\{1, 2, \dots, p'\}$ (and we will later see that it is enough to keep only one such color). We would like the variable $Y_{\mathbb{T}, \alpha}$ to store the number of matchings of type $\mathbb{T}$ that must be colored α. The above will heavily rely on the fact that each edge in H that does not belong to H', must be adjacent to a vertex in X, this in turn will facilitate in counting the number of edges in the matching (via the type, where the type will also encode the subset of vertices in X participating in the matching). Furthermore, only for $\alpha = 0$, the variable $Y_{\mathbb{T},\alpha}$ can store a value which is more than 1. Once we have the above variable set, by adding appropriate constraints, we will create an equivalent instance of ILP, corresponding to the pair (H', ϕ'). We will now move to the formal description of the algorithm.

For $S \subseteq X$, let $\Gamma(S)$ be the set of vertices in W whose neighborhood in G is exactly S, i.e., $\Gamma(S) := \{w \in W \mid N_G(w) = S\}$. We begin by defining a tuple, which will be a "type", and later we will relate a matching (between W and X), to a particular type.

Definition 2 (Type). A *type* $\mathbb{T} = \langle X' = \{x_1, x_2, \ldots, x_{|X'|}\}; S_1, S_2, \ldots, S_{|X|} \rangle$ is a $(|X| + 1)$ sized tuple where each entry is a subset of X and which satisfy following properties.

1. The first entry, X', is followed by $|X'|$ many entries which are non-empty subsets of X and the remaining $(|X| + 1 - |X'|)$ entries are empty sets.
2. Any non-empty set S of X appears at most $|\Gamma(S)|$ many times from the second entry onward in the tuple.
3. For every $i \in \{1, 2, \ldots, |X'|\}$, we have $x_i \in S_i$.

We note that the number of different types is at most $2^{|X|} \cdot 2^{|X|^2} \in 2^{\mathcal{O}(|X|^2)}$ and it can be enumerated in time $2^{\mathcal{O}(|X|^2)} \cdot n^{\mathcal{O}(1)}$. We need following an auxiliary function corresponding to a matching, which will be useful in defining the type for a matching. Let M be a matching across X, W (M has edges whose one endpoint is in X and the other endpoint is in W). Define $\tau_M : X \cap V(M) \to W \cap V(M)$, as $\tau_M(x) := w$ if xw is an edge in M. We drop the subscript M when the context is clear.

Definition 3 (Matching of type $\mathbb{T}$). A matching $M = \{x\tau(x) \mid x \in X \text{ and } \tau(x) \in W\}$, is of *type* $\mathbb{T} = \langle X'; S_1, S_2, \ldots, S_{|X|} \rangle$ if $V(M) \cap X = X'$ ($:= \{x_1, x_2, \ldots, x_{|X'|}\}$), and $S_j = N(\tau(x_j))$ for every j in $\{1, 2, \ldots, |X'|\}$.

We define some terms used in the sub-routine to construct an ILP instance. For a type $\mathbb{T} = \langle X'; S_1, S_2, \ldots, S_{|X|} \rangle$, we define $|\mathbb{T}| := |X'|$. Note that $|\mathbb{T}|$ is the number of edges in a matching of type $\mathbb{T}$. For a vertex $x \in X$ and a type $\mathbb{T} = \langle X'; S_1, S_2, \ldots, S_{|X|} \rangle$, value of `is_present`$(x, \mathbb{T})$ is 1 if $x \in X'$, and otherwise it is 0. For $w \in W$, define `false_twins`(w) as the number of vertices in W which have the same neighborhood as that of w. That is, `false_twins`$(w) = |\{\hat{w} \in W \mid N(w) = N(\hat{w})\}|$. For a vertex $w \in W$ and a type $\mathbb{T} = \langle X'; S_1, S_2, \ldots, S_{|X|} \rangle$, the value of `nr_nbr_present`$(w, \mathbb{T})$ denotes the number of different js in $\{1, 2, \ldots, |X'|\}$ for which $S_j = N(w)$. We remark that the values of all the functions defined above can be computed in (total) time bounded by $2^{\mathcal{O}(|X|^2)} \cdot n^{\mathcal{O}(1)}$.

Constructing ILP Instances. Recall that G is the input graph and X is a (minimum sized) vertex cover for G. Let $\mathfrak{T}$ be the set of all types. For every subgraph H' of $G[X]$, a (non-negative) integer $p_0 \leq p$, and a p_0-edge coloring

$\phi' : E(H') \rightarrow \{0, 1, 2, \ldots, p_0\}$, we create an instance $I_{(H', \phi')}$, of ILP as follows. Let $[p_0]' = \{0, 1, 2, \ldots, p_0\}$. Define a variable $Y_{\mathbb{T}, \alpha}$ for every type $\mathbb{T}$ and integer $\alpha \in [p_0]'$. (These variables will be allowed to take values from $\{0, 1, \ldots, p\}$). Intuitively speaking, for α in $[p_0]'$, the value assigned to $Y_{\mathbb{T}, \alpha}$ will indicates that there is a matching of type $\mathbb{T}$ which is assigned the color α. Moreover, for $\alpha = 0$, the value of $Y_{\mathbb{T}, 0}$ will indicate that there are $Y_{\mathbb{T}, 0}$ many matchings of type $\mathbb{T}$, each of which must be assigned a unique color which is strictly greater than p_0. Recall that for a type $\mathbb{T} \in \mathfrak{T}$, $|\mathbb{T}|$ is the number of edges in a matching of *type* $\mathbb{T}$. We next define our objective function, which (intuitively speaking) will maximize the number of edges in the solution.

$$\text{maximize} \sum_{\mathbb{T} \in \mathfrak{T}; \alpha \in [p_0]'} Y_{\mathbb{T}, \alpha} \cdot |\mathbb{T}|$$

We next discuss the set of constraints.

For every vertex x in X, we add the following constraint, which will ensure that x will be present in at most p matchings:

$$\sum_{\mathbb{T} \in \mathfrak{T}; \alpha \in [p_0]'} Y_{\mathbb{T}, \alpha} \cdot \texttt{is\_present}(x, \mathbb{T}) \leq p - \deg_{H'}(x). \qquad \text{(ConstSetI)}$$

For each $x \in X$, an edge $x\hat{x}$ incident on x in H', and $\mathbb{T} \in \mathfrak{T}$, we add the following constraint, which will ensure that no other edge incident on x and some vertex in W is assigned the color $\phi'(x\hat{x})$:

$$Y_{\mathbb{T}, \phi'(x\hat{x})} \cdot \texttt{is\_present}(x, \mathbb{T}) = 0. \qquad \text{(ConstSetII)}$$

We will next add the following constraint for each $w \in W$, which will help us in ensuring that w is present in at most p matchings:

$$\sum_{\mathbb{T} \in \mathfrak{T}; \alpha \in [p_0]'} Y_{\mathbb{T}, \alpha} \cdot \texttt{nr\_nbr\_present}(w, \mathbb{T}) \leq p \cdot \texttt{false\_twins}(w). \qquad \text{(ConstSetIII)}$$

Notice that for two vertices $w_1, w_2 \in W$, such that $N(w_1) = N(w_2)$, the above constraints corresponding to w_1 and w_2 is exactly the same (and we skip adding the same constraint twice).

When $\alpha \neq 0$, we want to ensure that at most one matching that is colored α. Thus, for $\alpha \in [p_0]$, add the constraint:

$$\sum_{\mathbb{T} \in \mathfrak{T}} Y_{\mathbb{T}, \alpha} \leq 1. \qquad \text{(ConstSetIV)}$$

Note that we want at most p color classes, which will be ensured by our final constraint as follows.

$$\sum_{\mathbb{T} \in \mathfrak{T}; \alpha \in [p_0]'} Y_{\mathbb{T}, \alpha} \leq p. \qquad \text{(ConstSetV)}$$

This completes the construction of the ILP instance of $I_{(H',\phi')}$.

Algorithm for Maximum Edge Colorable Subgraph: Consider the given instance (G, l, p) of MAXIMUM EDGE COLORABLE SUBGRAPH. The algorithm will either return a solution (H, ϕ) for the instance, or conclude that no such solution exists. We compute a minimum sized vertex cover, X of G, in time $\mathcal{O}(2^{|X|}n|X|)$, using the algorithm of Chen et al. [4]. For every subgraph H' of $G[X]$, a (non-negative) integer $p_0 \leq p$, and a p_0-edge coloring $\phi' : E(H') \to \{0, 1, 2, \ldots, p_0\}$, we create the instance $I_{(H',\phi')}$, and resolve it using Proposition 2. (In the above we only consider those $\phi' : E(H') \to \{0, 1, 2, \ldots, p_0\}$, where each of the color classes are non-empty.) If there exists a tuple (H', ϕ') for which the optimum value of the corresponding ILP instance is at least $(l - |E(H')|)$ then algorithm constructs a solution (H, ϕ) as specified in the proof of Lemma 3 and returns it as a solution. If there is no such tuple then the algorithm concludes that no solution exists for a given instance.

For a solution $(H, \phi : E(H) \to [p])$ for the instance (G, l, p), we say that (H, ϕ) is a good solution, if for some $p_0 \in [p]$, for each $e \in E(H) \cap E(G[X])$, we have $\phi(e) \in [p_0]$. Note that if (G, l, p) has a solution, then it also has a good solution. We argue the correctness of the algorithm in the following two lemmas.

Lemma 2. *If (G, l, p) has a good solution (H, ϕ) then the optimum value of the ILP instance $I_{(H',\phi')}$ is at least $(l - |E(H')|)$, where $H' = H[X]$ and $\phi' : E(H') \to \{1, 2, \ldots, p_0\}$, such that $\phi' = \phi|_{E(H')}$ and $p_0 = \max\{\phi(e) \mid e \in E(H) \cap E(G[X])\}$.*

Proof. Let $M_1, M_2, \ldots, M_p$ be the partition of edges in $E(H) \setminus E(H')$ according to the colors assigned to them by ϕ, and $\mathcal{M} = \{M_i \mid i \in [p]\} \setminus \{\emptyset\}$. Notice that each M_i is a matching, where the edges have one endpoint in X and the other endpoint in W. We create an assignment $\mathsf{asg} : \mathsf{Var}_{(H',\phi')} \to [p_0]'$, where $\mathsf{Var}_{(H',\phi')}$ is the set of variables in the instance $I_{(H',\phi')}$ as follows. Initialize $\mathsf{asg}(z) = 0$, for each $z \in \mathsf{Var}(I_{(H',\phi')})$. For $i \in [p]$, let $\mathbb{T}_i$ be the type of M_i and $p_i = \phi(e)$, where $e \in M_i$. For each $i \in [p]$, we do the following. If $p_i > p_0$, then increment $\mathsf{asg}(Y_{\mathbb{T}_i,0})$ by one, and otherwise increment value of $\mathsf{asg}(Y_{\mathbb{T}_i,p_i})$ by one. This completes the assignment of variables. Next we argue that asg satisfies all constraints in $I_{(H',\phi')}$ and the objective function evaluates to a value that is at least $(l - |E(H')|)$.

As there are at most p matchings, we have $\sum_{\mathbb{T} \in \mathfrak{T}; \alpha \in [p_0]'} Y_{\mathbb{T},\alpha} \leq p$, and thus, the constraint in ConstSetV is satisfied.

We will now argue that each constraint in ConstSetI is satisfied. To this end, consider a variable $x \in X$, and let $\mathsf{a}_x = \sum_{\mathbb{T} \in \mathfrak{T}; \alpha \in [p_0]'} \mathsf{asg}(Y_{\mathbb{T},\alpha}) \cdot \mathsf{is\_present}(x, \mathbb{T})$. Since H is p-edge colorable, $\deg_H(x) \leq \Delta(H) \leq p$. Hence, there are at most p edges incident on x in H (Proposition 1). For any $\mathbb{T} \in \mathfrak{T}$ and $\alpha \in [p_0]'$, if $\mathsf{asg}(Y_{\mathbb{T},\alpha}) \cdot \mathsf{is\_present}(x, \mathbb{T}) \neq 0$, then there are $\mathsf{asg}(Y_{\mathbb{T},\alpha})$ many matchings of type $\mathbb{T}$ in $\mathcal{M}$, each of which contains an edge incident on x. Moreover, each such matching contains a different edge incident on x. Since ϕ is a p-edge coloring of H, we have $\mathsf{a}_x + \deg_{H'}(x) = \deg_H(x) \leq p$. This implies that $\mathsf{a}_x = \sum_{\mathbb{T} \in \mathfrak{T}; \alpha \in [p_0]'} \mathsf{asg}(Y_{\mathbb{T},\alpha}) \cdot \mathsf{is\_present}(x, \mathbb{T}) \leq p - \deg_{H'}(x)$. Thus we conclude that all constraints in ConstSetI are satisfied.

Now we argue that all constraints in ConstSetII are satisfied. Consider $x \in X$, an edge $x\hat{x}$ incident on x in H', and $\mathbb{T} \in \mathfrak{T}$ such that $\texttt{is\_present}(x, \mathbb{T}) = 1$. Since $x\hat{x} \in E(H')$, there is no matching $M_i \in \mathcal{M}$, such that $p_i = \phi'(x\hat{x})$ and M contains an edge incident on x. Thus we can obtain that $\texttt{asg}(Y_{\mathbb{T},\phi'(x\hat{x})}) = 0$ (recall that $\texttt{is\_present}(x, \mathbb{T}) = 1$). From the above we can conclude that $\texttt{asg}(Y_{\mathbb{T},\phi'(x\hat{x})}) \cdot \texttt{is\_present}(x, \mathbb{T}) = 0$.

Next we argue that all constraints in ConstSetIII are satisfied. To this end, consider a (maximal) subset $W' = \{w_1, w_2, \ldots, w_r\} \subseteq W$, such that any two vertices in W' are false twins of each other. Notice that for each $j, j' \in [r]$, $\sum_{\mathbb{T} \in \mathfrak{T}; \alpha \in [p_0]'} Y_{\mathbb{T},\alpha} \cdot \texttt{nr\_nbr\_present}(w_j, \mathbb{T}) \le p \cdot \texttt{false\_twins}(w_j)$ is exactly the same as $\sum_{\mathbb{T} \in \mathfrak{T}; \alpha \in [p_0]'} Y_{\mathbb{T},\alpha} \cdot \texttt{nr\_nbr\_present}(w_j, \mathbb{T}) \le p \cdot \texttt{false\_twins}(w_{j'})$. Consider any $w \in W'$, $\mathbb{T} \in \mathfrak{T}$, and $\alpha \in [p_0]'$, such that we have $\texttt{asg}(Y_{\mathbb{T},\alpha}) \cdot \texttt{nr\_nbr\_present}(w, \mathbb{T}) \neq 0$. There are $\texttt{asg}(Y_{\mathbb{T},\alpha})$ many matchings in $\mathcal{M}$ each of which contains $\texttt{nr\_nbr\_present}(w, \mathbb{T})$ many edges incident vertices in W'. Hence $\sum_{\mathbb{T} \in \mathfrak{T}; \alpha \in [p_0]'} \texttt{asg}(Y_{\mathbb{T},\alpha}) \cdot \texttt{nr\_nbr\_present}(w_j, \mathbb{T})$ is the number of edges incident on W' in H. Note that $p \cdot \texttt{false\_twins}(w)$ is the maximum number of edges in H which can be incident on vertices in W'. Thus we can conclude that $\sum_{\mathbb{T} \in \mathfrak{T}; \alpha \in [p_0]'} \texttt{asg}(Y_{\mathbb{T},\alpha}) \cdot \texttt{nr\_nbr\_present}(w_j, \mathbb{T}) \le p \cdot \texttt{false\_twins}(w)$.

For any $\alpha \in [p_0]$, there is at most one matching in $\mathcal{M}$ whose edges are assigned the color α. This implies that $\sum_{\mathbb{T} \in \mathfrak{T}} \texttt{asg}(Y_{\mathbb{T},\alpha}) \le 1$. Hence all constraints in ConstSetIV are satisfied.

There are at least $(l - |E(H')|)$ many edges in $E(H) \setminus E(H')$ and each such edge has one endpoint in X and another in W. Every edge in matching contributes exactly one to the objective function. Thus we can obtain that $\sum_{\mathbb{T} \in \mathfrak{T}; \alpha \in [p_0]'} \texttt{asg}(Y_{\mathbb{T},\alpha}) \cdot |\mathbb{T}| \ge (l - |E(H')|)$. This concludes the proof. □

Lemma 3 ($\star$). *If there is (H', ϕ') for which the optimum value of the ILP instance $I_{(H',\phi')}$, is at least $(l - |E(H')|)$, then the* MAXIMUM EDGE COLORABLE SUBGRAPH *instance (G, l, p) admits a solution. Moreover, given* $\texttt{asg} : \texttt{Var}_{(H',\phi')} \to [p_0]'$, *where* $\texttt{Var}_{(H',\phi')}$, *we can be compute a solution (H, ϕ) for (G, l, p), in polynomial time.*

The proof of Theorem 1 follows from Lemma 2 and 3, and Proposition 2.

4   Kernelization Algorithm

In this section, we prove Theorem 3. To obtain our result, we show that MAXIMUM EDGE COLORABLE SUBGRAPH admits a polynomial kernel when parameterized by the number of colors and $|X|$, where X is a minimum sized deg-1-modulator. The above result, together with Observation 21, implies the proof of Theorem 3.

Consider an instance (G, p, l) of MAXIMUM EDGE COLORABLE SUBGRAPH. We assume that we are given a deg-1-modulator X of G (see Definition 1). We justify this assumption later and argue that one can find a deg-1-modulator which is close to a minimum sized deg-1-modulator in polynomial time. We start with the following simple reduction rule.

Reduction Rule 41. *If there exists a connected component C of $G - X$ such that no vertex of C is adjacent to a vertex in X, then delete all the vertices in C and reduce l by $|E(C)|$, i.e. return the instance $(G - V(C), l - |E(C)|, p)$.*

Lemma 4. *Reduction Rule 41 is safe and given X, it can be applied in polynomial time.*

Let (G, l, p) be the instance obtained by exhaustively applying Reduction Rule 41. This implies that every connected component of $G - X$ is adjacent to X. Let $\mathcal{C}$ be the set of connected components of $G - X$. We construct an auxiliary bipartite graph B, with vertex bipartition X and $\mathcal{C}$ (each $C \in \mathcal{C}$ corresponds to a vertex, say b_C of B). There exists edge $x b_C$ in B for $x \in X$ and $b_C \in \mathcal{C}$ if and only x is adjacent to at least one vertex in C in G. For $\mathcal{C}' \subseteq \mathcal{C}$ of connected components, $V(\mathcal{C}') \subseteq V(G)$ denotes the vertices in connected components in $\mathcal{C}'$ and $E(\mathcal{C}') \subseteq E(G)$ denotes the edges that have both endpoints in $V(\mathcal{C}')$. Since every connected component in $\mathcal{C}$ is adjacent to X, there are no isolated vertices in B. We thus apply the following rule which is based on the Expansion Lemma.

Reduction Rule 42. *If $|\mathcal{C}| \geq p|X|$ then apply Lemma 1 to find $X' \subseteq X$ and $\mathcal{C}' \subseteq \mathcal{C}$ such that (1) there exits a p-expansion from X' to $\mathcal{C}'$; and (2) no vertex in $\mathcal{C}'$ has a neighbour outside X'. Delete all the vertices in $X' \cup V(\mathcal{C}')$ from G and reduce l by $p|X'| + |E(\mathcal{C}')|$, i.e. return $(G - (X' \cup V(\mathcal{C}')), l - p|X'| - |E(\mathcal{C}')|, p)$.*

Lemma 5. *Reduction Rule 42 is safe and given set X, it can be applied in polynomial time.*

Next we argue that MAXIMUM EDGE COLORABLE SUBGRAPH admits a polynomial kernel when parameterized by size of the given deg-1-modulator.

Lemma 6. MAXIMUM EDGE COLORABLE SUBGRAPH *admits a kernel with $\mathcal{O}(|X|p)$ vertices, where X is a deg-1-modulator of G.*

Proof. (of Theorem 3) For an instance (G, l, p) of MAXIMUM EDGE COLORABLE SUBGRAPH the kernelization algorithm first uses Observation 21 to conclude that either (G, l, p) is a YES instance or $\mathsf{vc}(G) \preceq l$ and $|X_{opt}| \preceq (l - \mathsf{mm}(G))$, where X_{opt} is a minimum sized deg-1-modulator of G. In the first case, it returns a vacuously true instance of constant size. If it can not conclude that given instance is a YES instance then algorithm computes a deg-1-modulator, say X, of G using the simple 3-approximation algorithm: there exists a vertex u which is adjacent with two different vertices, say v_1, v_2 then algorithm adds u, v_1, v_2 to the solution. It keeps repeating this step until every vertex is of degree at most one. The algorithm uses the kernelization algorithm mentioned in Lemma 6 to compute a kernel of size $\mathcal{O}(p|X|)$.

The correctness of the algorithm follows from the correctness of Lemma 6. As X is obtained by using a 3-factor approximation algorithm, $|X| \leq 3|X_{opt}|$ and hence $|X| \preceq |X_{opt}|$. Since the algorithm was not able to conclude that (G, l, p) is a YES instance, by Observation 21, we have $|X_{opt}| \preceq \mathsf{vc}(G) \preceq l$ and

$|X_{opt}| \preceq l - \mathrm{mm}(G)$. This implies the number of vertices in the reduced instance is at most $\mathcal{O}(kp)$ where k is one of the parameters in the statement of the theorem. By Observation 21, Lemma 4 and Lemma 5, and the fact that every application of reduction rules reduces the number of vertices in the input graph, the algorithm terminates in polynomial time. $\square$

References

1. Aloisio, A., Mkrtchyan, V.: On the fixed-parameter tractability of the maximum 2-edge-colorable subgraph problem. arXiv preprint arXiv:1904.09246 (2019)
2. Alon, N., Yuster, R., Zwick, U.: Color coding. In: Kao, M. (ed.) Encyclopedia of Algorithms - 2008 Edition (2008)
3. Cao, Y., Chen, G., Jing, G., Stiebitz, M., Toft, B.: Graph edge coloring: a survey. Graphs Comb. **35**(1), 33–66 (2019). https://doi.org/10.1007/s00373-018-1986-5
4. Chen, J., Kanj, I.A., Xia, G.: Improved parameterized upper bounds for vertex cover. In: Královič, R., Urzyczyn, P. (eds.) MFCS 2006. LNCS, vol. 4162, pp. 238–249. Springer, Heidelberg (2006). https://doi.org/10.1007/11821069_21
5. Chen, J., Kanj, I.A., Xia, G.: Improved upper bounds for vertex cover. Theor. Comput. Sci. **411**(40–42), 3736–3756 (2010)
6. Chen, J., et al.: Randomized divide-and-conquer: improved path, matching, and packing algorithms. SIAM J. Comput. **38**(6), 2526–2547 (2009)
7. Cygan, M., et al.: Parameterized Algorithms. Springer, Heidelberg (2015). https://doi.org/10.1007/978-3-319-21275-3
8. Feige, U., Ofek, E., Wieder, U.: Approximating maximum edge coloring in multigraphs. In: Jansen, K., Leonardi, S., Vazirani, V. (eds.) APPROX 2002. LNCS, vol. 2462, pp. 108–121. Springer, Heidelberg (2002). https://doi.org/10.1007/3-540-45753-4_11
9. Fomin, F.V., Lokshtanov, D., Saurabh, S., Zehavi, M.: Kernelization: Theory of Parameterized Preprocessing. Cambridge University Press, Cambridge (2019)
10. Galby, E., Lima, P.T., Paulusma, D., Ries, B.: On the parameterized complexity of k-edge colouring. arXiv preprint arXiv:1901.01861 (2019)
11. Grüttemeier, N., Komusiewicz, C., Morawietz, N.: Maximum edge-colorable subgraph and strong triadic closure parameterized by distance to low-degree graphs. In: Scandinavian Symposium and Workshops on Algorithm Theory (2020, to appear)
12. Holyer, I.: The NP-completeness of edge-coloring. SIAM J. Comput. **10**(4), 718–720 (1981)
13. Kannan, R.: Minkowski's convex body theorem and integer programming. Math. Oper. Res. **12**(3), 415–440 (1987)
14. Lenstra Jr., H.W.: Integer programming with a fixed number of variables. Math. Oper. Res. **8**(4), 538–548 (1983)
15. Leven, D., Galil, Z.: NP completeness of finding the chromatic index of regular graphs. J. Algorithms **4**(1), 35–44 (1983)
16. Micali, S., Vazirani, V.V.: An $\mathcal{O}(\sqrt{|V|} \cdot |E|)$ algorithm for finding maximum matching in general graphs. In: 21st Annual Symposium on Foundations of Computer Science (sfcs 1980), pp. 17–27. IEEE (1980)
17. Sinnamon, C.: A randomized algorithm for edge-colouring graphs in $\mathcal{O}(m\sqrt{n})$ time. arXiv preprint arXiv:1907.03201 (2019)
18. Vizing, V.G.: On an estimate of the chromatic class of a p-graph. Discret Analiz **3**, 25–30 (1964)

Approximation Algorithms for the Lower-Bounded k-Median and Its Generalizations

Lu Han[1], Chunlin Hao[2], Chenchen Wu[3(✉)], and Zhenning Zhang[2]

[1] Academy of Mathematics and Systems Science, Chinese Academy of Sciences,
Beijing 100190, People's Republic of China
`hanlu@amss.ac.cn`
[2] Department of Operations Research and Information Engineering,
Beijing University of Technology, Beijing 100124, People's Republic of China
`{haochl,zhangzhenning}@bjut.edu.cn`
[3] College of Science, Tianjin University of Technology,
Tianjin 300384, People's Republic of China
`wu_chenchen_tjut@163.com`

Abstract. In this paper, we consider the lower-bounded k-median problem (LB k-median) that extends the classical k-median problem. In the LB k-median, a set of facilities, a set of clients and an integer k are given. Every facility has its own lower bound on the minimum number of clients that must be connected to the facility if it is opened. Every facility-client pair has its connection cost. We want to open at most k facilities and connect every client to some opened facility, such that the total connection cost is minimized.

As our main contribution, we study the LB k-median and present our main bi-criteria approximation algorithm, which, for any given constant $\alpha \in [0,1)$, outputs a solution that satisfies the lower bound constraints by a factor of α and has an approximation ratio of $\frac{1+\alpha}{1-\alpha}\rho$, where ρ is the state-of-art approximation ratio for the k-facility location problem (k-FL). Then, by extending the main algorithm to several general versions of the LB k-median, we show the versatility of our algorithm for the LB k-median. Last, through providing relationships between the constant α and the approximation ratios, we demonstrate the performances of all the algorithms for the LB k-median and its generalizations.

Keywords: k-median · Lower bounds · Approximation algorithm · Bi-criteria

1 Introduction

The uncapacitated facility location problem (UFL) has numerous applications in operations management and computer science. In this problem, we are given a set of facilities and a set of clients. Every facility has an associated opening cost, and every facility-client pair has an associated connection cost which is

© Springer Nature Switzerland AG 2020
D. Kim et al. (Eds.): COCOON 2020, LNCS 12273, pp. 627–639, 2020.
https://doi.org/10.1007/978-3-030-58150-3_51

proportional to the distance between the facility and client. The aim is to open some facilities and connect every client to an opened facility so as to minimize the total opening and connection cost. Since the UFL is a well-known NP-hard problem, researchers pay attention on designing approximation algorithms for it and its generalizations [3,8,10,12,15,16,18,19]. For a minimization problem, a λ-approximation algorithm is a polynomial time algorithm which can output a solution for any instance of the problem, such that the cost of the solution is within a factor of λ of the cost of an optimal solution. For the UFL, under the assumption that the connection costs are metric (i.e., the connection costs are non-negative, symmetric and satisfy the triangle inequality), Li [12] presents the current best 1.488-approximation algorithm and assume that P$\neq$NP Sviridenko [16] gives the 1.463-hardness of approximation.

However, in many real-life situations, the facility expects to be connected by a minimum number of clients for the profitable sake. In fact, the lower-bounded facility location problem (LBFL) characterizes these scenarios. Besides, the motivation of the lower bound constraints also comes from a data privacy perspective [1]. Compared with the UFL, in the LBFL, every facility is given an additional lower bound on the minimum number of clients that must be connected to the facility if it is opened. The goal is to find some facilities to open and connect every client to an opened facility without violating any lower bound constraints, such that the total opening as well as connection cost is minimized. The LBFL is introduced by Guha et al. [7] and Karger and Minkoff [11] simultaneously. Both give an $O(1)$-bi-criteria approximation algorithm that approximately subjects to the lower bound constraints. For the special case of the LBFL where the lower bound of every facility is the same, by reducing the LBFL to the capacitated facility location problem (CFL), Svitkina [17] proposes the first true 448-approximation algorithm. Later, Ahmadian and Swamy [2] improve the approximation ratio to 82.6. For the general case of the LBFL where every facility has its own lower bound, Li [13] also reduces the LBFL to the CFL and gives the breakthrough true approximation algorithm which has a ratio of 4000.

When every facility in the UFL does not have an opening cost and the aim becomes to find at most k facilities to open and connect every client to some opened facility so as to minimize the sum of connection costs, we get the classical k-median problem. The k-median is another well-studied NP-hard problem and has various generalizations. [3–6,9,10,14,18,19]. For the k-median, under the assumption that the connection costs are metric, Byrka et al. [5] present the state-of-art $(2.675 + \epsilon)$-approximation algorithm and assume that NP$\not\subseteq$DTIME$(n^{O(\log \log n)})$ Jain et al. [9] offer the 1.736-hardness of approximation. Despite the fact that many meaningful and interesting general versions of the k-median have been considered in the literatures, to the best of our knowledge, very little work concentrates on studying the k-median with lower bounds. This situation stimulates us to pay attention on the lower-bounded k-median problem (LB k-median). Compared with the k-median, the LB k-median has extra lower bound constraints which need to be respected.

In this paper, we study the LB k-median and its generalizations. First, inspired by the previous works of Guha et al. [7] and Karger and Minkoff [11] on the LBFL, we propose our main $O(1)$-bi-criteria approximation algorithm for the LB k-median, which satisfies the lower bound constraints by a factor of some given constant $\alpha \in [0,1)$ and has an approximation ratio of $\frac{1+\alpha}{1-\alpha}\rho$, where ρ is the current best approximation ratio for the k-facility location problem (k-FL). The key idea behind the main algorithm relies on an observation that constructing and solving a new instance of the k-FL instead of the original instance of the LB k-median can easily obtain a solution respects the cardinality constraint, and then trying to guarantee every facility is connected by a certain amount of clients can give us a bi-criteria solution. Second, we extend the main algorithm to several generalizations of the LB k-median, including the lower-bounded k-facility location problem (LB k-FL), the lower-bounded knapsack median problem (LB knapsack median) and the prize-collecting lower-bounded k-median problem (PLB k-median). The algorithms for these generalizations involve constructing and solving new instances of the k-FL, the knapsack facility location problem (knapsack FL) and the prize-collecting k-facility location problem (P k-FL), respectively. Last but not least, we give the relationships between the given constant α and the approximation ratios of all the algorithms to demonstrate their performances. Particularly, we show that our algorithm for the LB k-median can give a nice approximation ratio while violating the lower bound constraints within an acceptable range.

The remainder of our paper is structured as follows. Section 2 presents our main $O(1)$-bi-criteria approximation algorithm for the LB k-median. Section 3 extends the main algorithm to several general versions of the LB k-median. Section 4 demonstrates the performances of our algorithms. Due to space constraint, all proofs are removed but will further appear in a full version of this paper.

2   The Lower-Bounded k-median Problem

In this section, we present an $O(1)$-bi-criteria approximation algorithm for the LB k-median. Subsection 2.1 describes the LB k-median and the relevant k-FL along with their integer programs. Subsection 2.2 presents our main algorithm for the LB k-median and its analysis.

2.1   Preliminaries for the LB k-median

In the LB k-median, we are given a set of facilities $\mathcal{F}$, a set of clients $\mathcal{D}$ and an integer k. Every facility $i \in \mathcal{F}$ has an associated lower bound L_i on the minimum number of clients in $\mathcal{D}$ that must be connected to the facility if it is opened. Every facility-client pair (i,j), where $i \in \mathcal{F}$ and $j \in \mathcal{D}$, has an associated connection cost c_{ij} which is proportional to the distance between facility i and client j. Under the assumption that the connection costs are metric, the goal is to find at most k facilities to open and connect every client to some opened facility, such that the total connection cost is minimized.

The LB k-median can be formulated as the following integer program:

$$\min \sum_{i \in \mathcal{F}} \sum_{j \in \mathcal{D}} c_{ij} x_{ij} \tag{1}$$

$$\text{s. t.} \sum_{i \in \mathcal{F}} x_{ij} \geq 1, \qquad \forall j \in \mathcal{D}, \tag{2}$$

$$x_{ij} \leq y_i, \qquad \forall i \in \mathcal{F}, j \in \mathcal{D}, \tag{3}$$

$$\sum_{j \in \mathcal{D}} x_{ij} \geq L_i y_i, \qquad \forall i \in \mathcal{F}, \tag{4}$$

$$\sum_{i \in \mathcal{F}} y_i \leq k, \tag{5}$$

$$x_{ij} \in \{0, 1\}, \qquad \forall i \in \mathcal{F}, j \in \mathcal{D}, \tag{6}$$

$$y_i \in \{0, 1\}, \qquad \forall i \in \mathcal{F}. \tag{7}$$

In program (1–7), there are two types of variables ($\{x_{ij}\}_{i \in \mathcal{F}, j \in \mathcal{D}}$, $\{y_i\}_{i \in \mathcal{F}}$). The variable x_{ij} indicates whether client j is connected to facility i for any facility-client pair (i, j) where $i \in \mathcal{F}$ and $j \in \mathcal{D}$. The variable y_i indicates whether facility i is opened for any facility $i \in \mathcal{F}$. The objective function describes the total connection cost. The constraints (2) say that every client $j \in \mathcal{D}$ must be connected to some facility. The constraints (3) state that if a client j is connected to some facility $i \in \mathcal{F}$, then the facility must be opened. The constraints (4) guarantee that the lower bound of any opened facility cannot be violated. The constraint (5) shows that the number of opened facilities can not exceed k.

When every facility $i \in \mathcal{F}$ in the LB k-median has an associated opening cost f_i instead of the lower bound L_i and the aim becomes to find at most k facilities to open and connect every client to some opened facility so as to minimize the sum of opening costs as well as connection costs, we get the k-FL. By introducing the same variables ($\{x_{ij}\}_{i \in \mathcal{F}, j \in \mathcal{D}}$, $\{y_i\}_{i \in \mathcal{F}}$), as in the integer program (1–7), the k-FL can be formulated as the following integer program:

$$\min \sum_{i \in \mathcal{F}} f_i y_i + \sum_{i \in \mathcal{F}} \sum_{j \in \mathcal{D}} c_{ij} x_{ij} \tag{8}$$

$$\text{s. t.} \sum_{i \in \mathcal{F}} x_{ij} \geq 1, \qquad \forall j \in \mathcal{D}, \tag{9}$$

$$x_{ij} \leq y_i, \qquad \forall i \in \mathcal{F}, j \in \mathcal{D}, \tag{10}$$

$$\sum_{i \in \mathcal{F}} y_i \leq k, \tag{11}$$

$$x_{ij} \in \{0, 1\}, \qquad \forall i \in \mathcal{F}, j \in \mathcal{D}, \tag{12}$$

$$y_i \in \{0, 1\}, \qquad \forall i \in \mathcal{F}. \tag{13}$$

In program (8–13), the objective function consists of opening costs and connection costs.

Note that we have the following observation.

Lemma 1. *From program (1–7) and program (8–13), it is clear that with the same inputs of $\mathcal{F}$, $\mathcal{D}$ and k, any feasible solution for the LB k-median is also a feasible solution for the k-FL.*

2.2 Algorithm for the LB k-median

For the LB k-median, we propose a bi-criteria approximation algorithm, that, for any given constant $\alpha \in [0,1)$, outputs a solution in which every opened facility i is connected by at least αL_i clients and has a constant approximation ratio of $\frac{1+\alpha}{1-\alpha}\rho$, where ρ is the current best approximation ratio for the k-FL. Our main algorithm for the LB k-median consists of three steps. First of all, from the instance $\mathcal{IN}$ of the LB k-median, we construct a new instance $\mathcal{IN}'$ of the k-FL. Secondly, we apply existing approximation algorithm for the k-FL to solve the instance $\mathcal{IN}'$ and obtain a solution (S',σ') where S' is the set of opened facilities and $\sigma' : \mathcal{D} \to S'$ is the corresponding connections of clients in $\mathcal{D}$ to facilities in S'. Finally, we continually close some facility in S' and reconnect its clients to obtain a new solution (S,σ) which connects at least αL_i clients to every opened facility $i \in S$.

For any facility $i \in \mathcal{F}$, denote $\mathcal{D}_i$ as the set of closest L_i clients to it in $\mathcal{D}$. Now we are ready to present our main algorithm.

Algorithm 1

Step 1 Construct a new instance of the k-FL.
For the instance $\mathcal{IN} = (\mathcal{F}, \mathcal{D}, k, \{L_i\}_{i\in\mathcal{F}}, \{c_{ij}\}_{i\in\mathcal{F},j\in\mathcal{D}})$ of the LB k-median, pick a constant $\alpha \in [0,1)$, get rid of the lower bounds $\{L_i\}_{i\in\mathcal{F}}$ from $\mathcal{IN}$ and

$$\text{set } f_i := \frac{2\alpha}{1-\alpha} \sum_{j\in\mathcal{D}_i} c_{ij} \text{ for every } i \in \mathcal{F},$$

in order to obtain a new instance $\mathcal{IN}' = (\mathcal{F}, \mathcal{D}, k, \{f_i\}_{i\in\mathcal{F}}, \{c_{ij}\}_{i\in\mathcal{F},j\in\mathcal{D}})$ of the k-FL.
Step 2 Solve the instance of the k-FL.
Solve new instance $\mathcal{IN}'$ with the current best ρ-approximation algorithm for the k-FL (see [19]), where $\rho = 2 + \sqrt{3} + \epsilon$, and obtain a feasible solution (S',σ'), where S' is the set of opened facilities and $\sigma' : \mathcal{D} \to S'$ is a function that maps every client $j \in \mathcal{D}$ to the closest facility in S'. For any client $j \in \mathcal{D}$, let $\sigma'(j)$ denote its closest facility in S'.
Step 3 Construct a solution for the LB k-median.
  Step 3.1 Initialization.
  At the very beginning, set $S := S'$ and $\sigma(j) := \sigma'(j)$ for any $j \in \mathcal{D}$, define $l_i := |j \in \mathcal{D} : \sigma(j) = i|$ for any $i \in \mathcal{F}$ and $S_d := \{i \in S : l_i < \alpha L_i\}$.

Step 3.2 Close facilities and reconnect clients.
    While $S_d \neq \emptyset$ **do**
        *Arbitrarily choose some facility $i \in S_d$ and close it. For every client
        j with $\sigma(j) = i$, reconnect it to its closest facility i' in $S \setminus \{i\}$ and
        update $\sigma(j) := i'$. Update $S := S \setminus \{i\}$. Update l_i for any facility $i \in \mathcal{F}$
        and S_d.*
    Output *solution (S, σ).*

Algorithm 1 provides a solution (S, σ), where S is the set of opened facilities and $\sigma : \mathcal{D} \to S$ denotes the corresponding connections between clients in $\mathcal{D}$ and facilities in S, for the LB k-median. For any client $j \in \mathcal{D}$, let $\sigma(j)$ denote the facility which is connected by j in solution (S, σ).

The following theorem presents our main result for the LB k-median.

Theorem 1. *Algorithm 1 is a bi-criteria approximation algorithm for the LB k-median that produces a solution (S, σ), which connects at least αL_i clients to every opened facility $i \in S$, and has an approximation ratio of $\frac{1+\alpha}{1-\alpha}\rho$ where α is a given constant in interval $[0, 1)$ and ρ is the current best approximation ratio of $2 + \sqrt{3} + \epsilon$ for the k-FL.*

Because of Step 3.2 in Algorithm 1, it is not hard to see that

$$|j \in \mathcal{D} : \sigma(j) = i| = l_i \geq \alpha L_i \text{ for any } i \in S,$$

which means the solution (S, σ) connects at least αL_i clients to every opened facility $i \in S$. The remainder of this section will put focus on analyzing the approximation ratio of our algorithm for the LB k-median.

Suppose that (S^*, σ^*) is the optimal solution for the instance $\mathcal{IN}$ of the LB k-median, where S^* is the optimal set of opened facilities and $\sigma^* : \mathcal{D} \to S^*$ denotes the optimal corresponding connections. Let OPT_{lk} be the total cost of the solution (S^*, σ^*) for $\mathcal{IN}$, i.e., $OPT_{lk} = \sum_{j \in \mathcal{D}} c_{\sigma^*(j)j}$. For every client $j \in \mathcal{D}$, denote $\sigma^*(j)$ as the facility which is connected by j in solution (S^*, σ^*). In order to provide the approximation ratio of Algorithm 1, the following lemmas are essential.

Lemma 2. *The total cost of the solution (S', σ') for the instance $\mathcal{IN}'$ of the k-FL is within a factor of $\frac{1+\alpha}{1-\alpha}\rho$ of the total cost of the optimal solution (S^*, σ^*) for the instance $\mathcal{IN}$ of the LB k-median, i.e.,*

$$\sum_{i \in S'} f_i + \sum_{j \in \mathcal{D}} c_{\sigma'(j)j} \leq \frac{1+\alpha}{1-\alpha}\rho \cdot OPT_{lk},$$

where $\alpha \in [0, 1)$ and $\rho = 2 + \sqrt{3} + \epsilon$.

Lemma 3. *The total cost of the solution (S, σ) for the instance $\mathcal{IN}$ of the LB k-median is no more than the total cost of the solution (S', σ') for the instance $\mathcal{IN}'$ of the k-FL, i.e.,*

$$\sum_{j \in \mathcal{D}} c_{\sigma(j)j} \leq \sum_{i \in S'} f_i + \sum_{j \in \mathcal{D}} c_{\sigma'(j)j}.$$

Integrating Lemma 2 with Lemma 3 implies the approximation ratio of Algorithm 1.

3 Generalizations of the Lower-Bounded k-median Problem

In this section, by extending our main algorithm to several more general versions of the LB k-median, we show the versatility of Algorithm 1. Subsection 3.1, 3.2 and 3.3 present algorithms for the LB k-FL, LB knapsack median and PLB k-median through altering only the first step, the first two steps and all the steps in Algorithm 1, respectively.

3.1 The Lower-Bounded k-facility Location Problem

Compared with the LB k-median, in the LB k-FL, every facility $i \in \mathcal{F}$ is given an additional opening cost f_i. The aim is to open at most k facilities and connect every client to some opened facility, such that the total opening and connection cost is minimized.

The algorithm for the LB k-FL is obtained by only modifying the first step in Algorithm 1 slightly.

Algorithm 2

Step 1 Construct a new instance of the k-FL.
For the instance $\mathcal{IN} = (\mathcal{F}, \mathcal{D}, k, \{L_i\}_{i\in\mathcal{F}}, \{f_i\}_{i\in\mathcal{F}}, \{c_{ij}\}_{i\in\mathcal{F},j\in\mathcal{D}})$ of the LB k-FL, pick a constant $\alpha \in [0,1)$, get rid of the lower bounds $\{L_i\}_{i\in\mathcal{F}}$ from $\mathcal{IN}$ and

$$\text{set } f_i' := f_i + \frac{2\alpha}{1-\alpha}\sum_{j\in\mathcal{D}_i} c_{ij} \text{ for every } i \in \mathcal{F},$$

in order to obtain a new instance $\mathcal{IN}' = (\mathcal{F}, \mathcal{D}, k, \{f_i'\}_{i\in\mathcal{F}}, \{c_{ij}\}_{i\in\mathcal{F},j\in\mathcal{D}})$ of the k-FL.
Step 2 Solve the instance of the k-FL.
Same as Step 2 in Algorithm 1. Solve new instance $\mathcal{IN}'$ with the current best ρ-approximation algorithm for the k-FL (see [19]), where $\rho = 2 + \sqrt{3} + \epsilon$, and obtain a feasible solution (S', σ').
Step 3 Construct a solution for the LB k-FL.
Same as Step 3 in Algorithm 1. At the end of this step, output solution (S, σ).

The following theorem offers the result for the LB k-median.

Theorem 2. *Algorithm 2 is a bi-criteria approximation algorithm for the LB k-FL that produces a solution (S, σ), which connects at least αL_i clients to every opened facility $i \in S$, and has an approximation ratio of $\frac{1+\alpha}{1-\alpha}\rho$ where $\alpha \in [0,1)$ and $\rho = 2 + \sqrt{3} + \epsilon$.*

We skip the proof of this theorem since it is similar to the one for the LB k-median.

3.2   The Lower-Bounded Knapsack Median Problem

Compared with the LB k-median, in the LB knapsack median, the cardinality constraint is replaced with a knapsack constraint. More specifically, we are given some budget B instead of the integer k. Every facility $i \in \mathcal{F}$ has a weight w_i. We want to open a subset $S \subseteq \mathcal{F}$ of facilities which subjects to $\sum_{i \in S} w_i \leq B$, and connect every client to some opened facility, so as to minimize the total connection cost.

The algorithm for the LB knapsack median is offered by changing the first two steps in Algorithm 1.

Algorithm 3

Step 1 Construct a new instance of the knapsack FL.
For the instance $\mathcal{IN} = (\mathcal{F}, \mathcal{D}, B, \{L_i\}_{i \in \mathcal{F}}, \{w_i\}_{i \in \mathcal{F}}, \{c_{ij}\}_{i \in \mathcal{F}, j \in \mathcal{D}})$ of the LB knapsack median, pick a constant $\alpha \in [0, 1)$, get rid of the lower bounds $\{L_i\}_{i \in \mathcal{F}}$ from $\mathcal{IN}$ and

$$set\ f_i := \frac{2\alpha}{1 - \alpha} \sum_{j \in \mathcal{D}_i} c_{ij}\ for\ every\ i \in \mathcal{F},$$

in order to obtain instance $\mathcal{IN}' = (\mathcal{F}, \mathcal{D}, B, \{f_i\}_{i \in \mathcal{F}}, \{w_i\}_{i \in \mathcal{F}}, \{c_{ij}\}_{i \in \mathcal{F}, j \in \mathcal{D}})$ of the knapsack FL.

Step 2 Solve the instance of the knapsack FL.
Solve new instance $\mathcal{IN}'$ with the current best η-approximation algorithm for the knapsack FL (see [4]), where $\eta = 17.46 + \epsilon$, and obtain a feasible solution (S', σ').

Step 3 Construct a solution for the LB knapsack median.
Same as Step 3 in Algorithm 1. At the end of this step, output solution (S, σ).

The following theorem gives the result for the LB knapsack median.

Theorem 3. *Algorithm 3 is a bi-criteria approximation algorithm for the LB knapsack median that produces a solution (S, σ), which connects at least αL_i clients to every opened facility $i \in S$, and has an approximation ratio of $\frac{1+\alpha}{1-\alpha} \eta$ where $\alpha \in [0, 1)$ and $\eta = 17.46 + \epsilon$.*

We skip the proof of this theorem since it is analogous to the one for the LB k-median.

3.3   The Prize-Collecting Lower-Bounded k-median Problem

Compared with the LB k-median, in the PLB k-median, every client $j \in \mathcal{D}$ is given an additional penalty cost p_j. Our goal is to select at most k facilities to open, connect a portion of the clients and penalize the rest of them, so as to minimize the sum of opening, connection and penalty costs.

The algorithm for the PLB k-median is given by transforming all the steps in Algorithm 1.

Algorithm 4

Step 1 Construct a new instance of the P k-FL.
For the instance $\mathcal{IN} = (\mathcal{F}, \mathcal{D}, k, \{L_i\}_{i \in \mathcal{F}}, \{p_j\}_{j \in \mathcal{D}}, \{c_{ij}\}_{i \in \mathcal{F}, j \in \mathcal{D}})$ of the PLB k-median, pick a constant $\alpha \in [0, 1)$, get rid of the lower bounds $\{L_i\}_{i \in \mathcal{F}}$ from $\mathcal{IN}$ and

$$set \ f_i := \frac{1 + \alpha}{1 - \alpha} \sum_{j \in \mathcal{D}_i} c_{ij} \ for \ every \ i \in \mathcal{F},$$

in order to obtain instance $\mathcal{IN}' = (\mathcal{F}, \mathcal{D}, k, \{f_i\}_{i \in \mathcal{F}}, \{p_j\}_{j \in \mathcal{D}}, \{c_{ij}\}_{i \in \mathcal{F}, j \in \mathcal{D}})$ of the P k-FL.

Step 2 Solve the instance of the P k-FL.
Solve new instance $\mathcal{IN}'$ with the current best θ-approximation algorithm for the P k-FL (see [18]), where $\theta = 2 + \sqrt{3} + \epsilon$, and obtain a feasible solution (S', P', σ'), where S' is the set of opened facilities, P' is the set of penalized clients and $\sigma' : \mathcal{D} \setminus P' \to S'$ is a function that maps every client $j \in \mathcal{D} \setminus P'$ to the closest facility in S'. For any client $j \in \mathcal{D} \setminus P'$, let $\sigma'(j)$ denote its closest facility in S'. For any client $j \in P'$, define its $\sigma'(j) := i_p$ where i_p is a dummy facility for penalizing.

Step 3 Construct a solution for the PLB k-median.

Step 3.1 Initialization.
At the very beginning, set $S := S'$, $P := P'$ and $\sigma(j) := \sigma'(j)$ for any $j \in \mathcal{D}$, define $T_i := \{j \in \mathcal{D} : \sigma(j) = i\}$, $l_i := |T_i|$ and $P_i := \{j \in \mathcal{D} : j \in \mathcal{D}_i, \sigma(j) = i_p\}$ for any $i \in \mathcal{F}$. Define $S_d := \{i \in S : l_i < \alpha L_i\}$.

Step 3.2 Close facilities and reconnect clients.

While $S_d \neq \emptyset$ do
Arbitrarily choose some facility $i \in S_d$. There are two possible cases.

    Case 1. $|T_i| + |P_i| < \alpha L_i$.
In this case, close facility i. For every client $j \in T_i$, reconnect it to its closest facility $i' \in S \setminus \{i\}$ and update $\sigma(j) := i'$. Update $S := S \setminus \{i\}$. Update T_i, l_i for any facility $i \in \mathcal{F}$ and S_d.

    Case 2. $|T_i| + |P_i| \geq \alpha L_i$.
In this case, for every client $j \in P_i$, connect it to its closest facility $i' \in S$ and update $\sigma(j) := i'$. Update $P := P \setminus P_i$. Then, update P_i, T_i as well as l_i for any facility $i \in \mathcal{F}$, also update S_d.

Output *solution (S, P, σ).*

The following theorem provides the result for the PLB k-median.

Theorem 4. *Algorithm 4 is a bi-criteria approximation algorithm for the PLB k-median that produces a solution (S, P, σ), which connects at least αL_i clients to every opened facility $i \in S$, and has an approximation ratio of $\frac{2\theta}{1-\alpha}$ where $\alpha \in [0, 1)$ and $\theta = 2 + \sqrt{3} + \epsilon$.*

approximation ratio

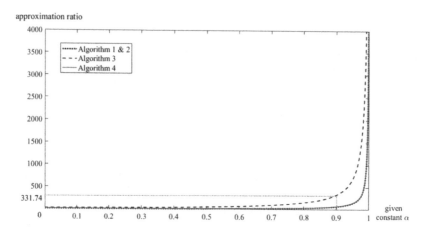

Fig. 1. Relationships between the constant α and approximation ratios.

The proof of this theorem is more intricate than the one for the LB k-median, since every client has an alternative decision in the PLB k-median, which is to be penalized. Suppose that (S^*, P^*, σ^*) is the optimal solution for the instance $\mathcal{IN}$ of the PLB k-median. Let OPT_{plk} be the total cost of the solution (S^*, P^*, σ^*) for the instance $\mathcal{IN}$. From Algorithm 4, it is clear that the solution (S, P, σ) connects at least αL_i clients to every opened facility $i \in S$. We need the following lemmas to achieve the approximation ratio of our algorithm for the PLB k-median.

Lemma 4. *The total cost of the solution (S', P', σ') for the instance $\mathcal{IN}'$ of the P k-FL is within a factor of $\frac{2\theta}{1-\alpha}$ of the total cost of the optimal solution (S^*, P^*, σ^*) for the instance $\mathcal{IN}$ of the PLB k-median, i.e.,*

$$\sum_{i \in S'} f_i + \sum_{j \in \mathcal{D} \setminus P'} c_{\sigma'(j)j} + \sum_{j \in P'} p_j \leq \frac{2\theta}{1-\alpha} \cdot OPT_{plk},$$

where $\alpha \in [0, 1)$ and $\theta = 2 + \sqrt{3} + \epsilon$.

Lemma 5. *The total cost of the solution (S, P, σ) for the instance $\mathcal{IN}$ of the PLB-k-median is no more than the total cost of the solution (S', P', σ') for the instance $\mathcal{IN}'$ of the P k-FL, i.e.,*

$$\sum_{j \in \mathcal{D} \setminus P} c_{\sigma(j)j} + \sum_{j \in P} p_j \leq \sum_{i \in S'} f_i + \sum_{j \in \mathcal{D} \setminus P'} c_{\sigma'(j)j} + \sum_{j \in P'} p_j.$$

Combining Lemma 4 and Lemma 5 implies the approximation ratio of Algorithm 4.

4 Performances Evaluation of the Algorithms

In this section, through providing the relationships between the given constant $\alpha \in [0, 1)$ and the approximation ratios, we demonstrate the performances of Algorithm 1–4.

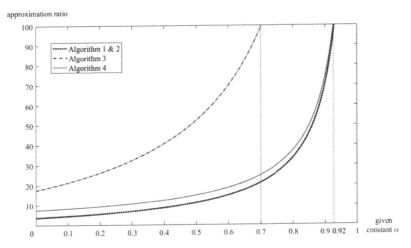

approximation ratio

Fig. 2. Relationships between the constant α and approximation ratios. Zoom in on approximation ratios smaller than 100.

It is worth mentioning that, combining the idea behind Algorithm 1 and the significant first true 4000-approximation algorithm of Li [13] for the LBFL, we strongly believe that there exists $O(1)$-approximation algorithm for the LB k-median which does not violate any lower bound. Unfortunately, the true approximation algorithm for the LB k-median cannot be practical, since the approximation ratio of it is likely no less than the one for the LBFL. Li [13] also states that even with more in-depth consideration, it is hard to reduce the approximation ratio for the LBFL to below 100 by using the same method.

Now, we want to demonstrate that our Algorithm 1 for the LB k-median can offer an obviously better approximation ratio while slightly violating the lower bound constraints. In Fig. 1, we show the relationships between constant $\alpha \in [0,1)$ and the approximation ratios of Algorithm 1–4. Note that the approximation ratios grow slowly and steadily at first, but after the constant α exceeds 0.9 the approximation ratios begin to increase in a steep way. From Fig. 1, it is clear that when $\alpha = 0.9$ (i.e., when the algorithm outputs a solution that 90% of the lower bound requirement of the opened facility is satisfied), the approximation ratio of Algorithm 1 for the LB k-median is significantly better than 4000. Figure 2 zooms in on approximation ratios smaller than 100. As we can see, when Algorithm 1 outputs a solution for the LB k-median with an approximation ratio of 100, the solution can satisfy the majority (i.e., more than 90%) of the lower bound requirement of any opened facility. In some real-world applications, it would be advisable to choose our algorithm, which has a preferable approximation ratio and violates the lower bound constraints within an acceptable range (i.e., violates no more than 10 % of the lower bound requirements).

Additionally, Fig. 1 and Fig. 2 show that Algorithm 2 performs as same as Algorithm 1 and Algorithm 4 is almost as well as Algorithm 1. Among our algorithms, Algorithm 3 has the worst performance. From Fig. 1, when $\alpha = 0.9$, the approximation ratio of Algorithm 3 for the LB knapsack median is visibly greater than the ratios of other algorithms. From Fig. 2, when Algorithm 3 outputs a solution with a ratio of 100, the solution can only guarantee to satisfy about 70% of the lower bound requirement of any opened facility.

Acknowledgement. The first author is supported by National Natural Science Foundation of China (No. 11531014). The second author is supported by National Natural Science Foundation of China (No. 11771003). The third author is supported by Natural Science Foundation of China (No. 11971349). The fourth author is supported by National Natural Science Foundation of China (No. 11871081) and the Science and Technology Program of Beijing Education Commission (No. KM201810005006).

References

1. Aggarwal, G., et al.: Achieving anonymity via clustering. ACM Trans. Algorithms **6**(3), 1–19 (2010)
2. Ahmadian, S., Swamy, C.: Improved approximation guarantees for lower-bounded facility Location. In: Erlebach, T., Persiano, G. (eds.) WAOA 2012. LNCS, vol. 7846, pp. 257–271. Springer, Heidelberg (2013). https://doi.org/10.1007/978-3-642-38016-7_21
3. Arya, V., Garg, N., Khandekar, R., Meyerson, A., Munagala, K., Pandit, V.: Local search heuristics for k-median and facility location problems. SIAM J. Comput. **33**(3), 544–562 (2004)
4. Byrka, J., Pensyl, T., Rybicki, B., Spoerhase, J., Srinivasan, A., Trinh, K.: An improved approximation algorithm for knapsack median using sparsification. Algorithmica **80**(4), 1093–1114 (2018). https://doi.org/10.1007/s00453-017-0294-4
5. Byrka, J., Pensyl, T., Rybicki, B., Srinivasan, A., Trinh, K.: An improved approximation for k-median, and positive correlation in budgeted optimization. ACM Trans. Algorithms **13**(2), 1–31 (2017)
6. Charikar, M., Guha, S., Tardos, É., Shmoys, D.B.: A constant-factor approximation algorithm for the k-median problem. J. Comput. Syst. Sci. **65**(1), 129–149 (2002)
7. Guha, S., Meyerson, A., Munagala, K.: Hierarchical placement and network design problems. In: Proceedings of the 41st Annual Symposium on Foundations of Computer Science, pp. 603–612 (2000)
8. Jain, K., Mahdian, M., Markakis, E., Saberi, E., Vazirani, V.V.: Greedy facility location algorithms analyzed using dual fitting with factor-revealing LP. J. ACM **50**(6), 795–824 (2003)
9. Jain, K., Mahdian, M., Saberi, A.: A new greedy approach for facility location problems. In: Proceedings of the 34th Annual ACM Symposium on Theory of Computing, pp. 731–740 (2002)
10. Jain, K., Vazirani, V.V.: Approximation algorithms for metric facility location and k-median problems using the primal-dual schema and Lagrangian relaxation. J. ACM **48**(2), 274–296 (2001)
11. Karger, D.R., Minkoff, M.: Building Steiner trees with incomplete global knowledge. In: Proceedings of the 41st Annual Symposium on Foundations of Computer Science, pp. 613–623 (2000)
12. Li, S.: A 1.488 approximation algorithm for the uncapacitated facility location problem. Inf. Comput. **222**, 45–58 (2013)

13. Li, S.: On facility location with general lower bounds. In: Proceedings of the 30th Annual ACM-SIAM Symposium on Discrete Algorithms, pp. 2279–2290 (2019)
14. Li, S., Svensson, O.: Approximating k-median via pseudo-approximation. SIAM J. Comput. **45**(2), 530–547 (2016)
15. Shmoys, D.B., Tardos, É., Aardal, K.I.: Approximation algorithms for facility location problems. In: Proceedings of the 29th Annual ACM symposium on Theory of Computing, pp. 265–274 (1997)
16. Sviridenko, M.: An improved approximation algorithm for the metric uncapacitated facility location problem. In: Cook, W.J., Schulz, A.S. (eds.) IPCO 2002. LNCS, vol. 2337, pp. 240–257. Springer, Heidelberg (2002). https://doi.org/10.1007/3-540-47867-1_18
17. Svitkina, Z.: Lower-bounded facility location. ACM Trans. Algorithms **6**(4) (2010). Article no. 69
18. Wang, Y., Xu, D., Du, D., Wu, C.: An approximation algorithm for k-facility location problem with linear penalties using local search scheme. J. Comb. Optim. **36**(1), 264–279 (2016). https://doi.org/10.1007/s10878-016-0080-2
19. Zhang, P.: A new approximation algorithm for the k-facility location problem. Theoret. Comput. Sci. **384**(1), 126–135 (2007)

A Survey for Conditional Diagnosability of Alternating Group Networks

Nai-Wen Chang and Sun-Yuan Hsieh[(✉)]

Department of Computer Science and Information Engineering, National Cheng
Kung University, No. 1, University Road, Tainan 70101, Taiwan
changnw@gmail.com, hsiehsy@mail.ncku.edu.tw

Abstract. Fault diagnosis of processors has played an essential role
when evaluating the reliability of multiprocessor systems. In many
novel multiprocessor systems, their diagnosability has been extensively
explored. Conditional diagnosability is a useful measure for evaluating
diagnosability by adding a further condition that all neighbors of every
node in the system do not fail at the same time. In this paper, we study
the conditional diagnosability of n-dimensional alternating group networks AN_n under the PMC model, and obtain the results $t_c(AN_4) = 5$,
and $t_c(AN_n) = 6n - 17$ for $n \geq 5$. In addition, for the isomorphism
property between AN_n and $S_{n,k}$ with $k = n - 2$, namely $(n, n - 2)$-star
graphs $S_{n,n-2}$, the above results can be extended to $S_{n,n-2}$, and we have
$t_c(S_{4,2}) = 5$ and $t_c(S_{n,n-2}) = 6n - 17$ for $n \geq 5$. It is worth noting that
the conditional diagnosability is about six times the degree of AN_n and
$S_{n,n-2}$, which is very different from general networks with a multiple of
four.

Keywords: Interconnection networks · Fault diagnosis · Conditional
diagnosability · PMC model · Alternating group networks · (n, k)-star
graphs · Fault tolerance · Multiprocessor systems

1 Introduction

As the very-large-scale integration (VLSI) technology grows rapidly, a multiprocessor system usually consists of hundreds or even thousands of processors
(nodes), some of which may fail when the system is running. This has spurred
our focus on the reliability issues of multiprocessor systems. As the number of
nodes in a multiprocessor system increases, diagnosing faulty nodes becomes
very important for parallel and reliable computing. The process of distinguishing faulty nodes from other fault-free nodes in a system is called *fault diagnosis*.
The *diagnosability* of a system refers to the maximum number of faulty nodes
the system can diagnose. Whenever a faulty node is diagnosed, it can be replaced
by a fault-free one to maintain the reliability of the system.

Supported by the Ministry of Science and Technology in Taiwan.

D. Kim et al. (Eds.): COCOON 2020, LNCS 12273, pp. 640–651, 2020.
https://doi.org/10.1007/978-3-030-58150-3_52

There are several diagnosis models proposed for measuring the diagnosability of a multiprocessor system. Among these models, the Preparata, Metze, and Chien's (PMC) model [20] and the Maeng and Malek's (MM) model [19] are best known and widely used. In the PMC model, a node is assumed to test the faulty/fault-free status of its neighboring nodes. A test result is called *reliable* (resp. *unreliable*) if the node enabling the test is fault-free (resp. faulty). A test for comparison in the MM model is performed by a node, chosen as a comparator. The comparator sends one same task as input to pairs of neighboring nodes. The neighboring nodes execute the received task and send back their responses to the comparator that then performs the comparison. For this purpose, the MM model is also called the *comparison diagnosis model*. The MM* model was first proposed by Maeng and Malek [11], which is a specialization of the MM model in which each node executes comparisons for every two neighboring nodes it is connected to.

Interconnection networks are often used to display the structure of multiprocessor systems. The n-dimensional hypercube, denoted by Q_n, and its variants are popular examples of interconnection networks. In 1987, Akers *et al.* [1,2] proposed the n-dimensional star graph, denoted by S_n, which is superior to Q_n in many ways such as lower node degree, smaller diameter, and a shorter average distance. In 1993, Jwo *et al.* [16] proposed the alternating group graph AG_n as an interconnection network topology for multiprocessor systems. AG_n has many nice properties including node transitivity, edge transitivity, strong hierarchy, maximal connectivity, and has small diameter and average distance [16,23]. Moreover, AG_n has many advantages over Q_n and S_n. In 1995, Chiang and Chen [9] proposed the (n, k)-star graph, denoted by $S_{n,k}$, as a generalization of S_n that keeps many attractive properties of S_n. In 1998, Ji [15] proposed a favorable topology structure of interconnection networks called alternating group network, denoted by AN_n, which improves AG_n and has many good properties such as that AN_n is Hamiltonian and has diameter $\left\lceil \frac{3(n-2)}{2} \right\rceil$.

In the classical measurement of the system-level diagnosis for multiprocessor systems, when all neighbors of a node v fail at the same time, it is impossible to determine whether v is faulty or fault-free. Then the diagnosability of a system is limited to be less than or equal to its minimum node degree. However, in some large-scale multiprocessor systems, the probability that all the neighbors of any node can fail at the same time is quite small. Therefore it is reasonable to make a assumption that all the neighbors of any node do not fail at the same time. Based on this assumption, Lai *et al.* [17] proposed the concept of *conditional diagnosability* and showed that the conditional diagnosability of an n-dimensional hypercube Q_n is $4n - 7$ for $n \geq 5$ under the PMC model. Numerous studies have contributed to the conditional diagnosability of multiprocessor systems under both the PMC and MM* models including hypercubes [14,17], alternating group graphs [12], star graphs [5,18], Cayley graphs [3,18], and (n, k)-star graphs [4,6,7,24], alternating group networks [7,25] (only in the MM* model). In this paper, we evaluate the conditional diagnosability for alternating group networks AN_n under the PMC model and show that $t_c(AN_4) = 5$, and

$t_c(AN_n) = 6n - 17$ for $n \geq 5$. Since Cheng *et al.* [8] have shown that AN_n is isomorphic to $(n, n-2)$-star graph $S_{n,n-2}$, our results can be extended to $S_{n,n-2}$ and obtain that $t_c(S_{4,2}) = 5$ and $t_c(S_{n,n-2}) = 6n - 17$ for $n \geq 5$.

The rest of the paper is organized as follows: Sect. 2 provides some necessary definitions and notations for system-level diagnosis. Section 3 introduces topological properties regarding both (n, k)-star graph $S_{n,k}$ and alternating group network AN_n. In Sect. 4, we evaluate the conditional diagnosability of AN_n and $S_{n,n-2}$. Finally, some conclusions are given in Sect. 5.

2   Preliminaries

An *undirected graph* (*graph* for short) $G = (V(G), E(G))$ is a pair consisting of a *node set* $V(G)$ and an *edge set* $E(G)$, where $V(G)$ is a finite set and $E(G)$ is a subset of $\{uv|$ u and v are distinct elements of $V(G)\}$. Throughout this paper, we consider simple and connected graphs.

Let $G = (V(G), E(G))$ be a graph and u be a node in G. The *neighborhood* of a node u in G, denoted by $N_G(u)$, is the set of all nodes adjacent to u in G. The cardinality $|N_G(u)|$ is called the *degree* of u in G, denoted by $deg_G(u)$. The *minimum degree* $\delta(G)$ equals $\min\{deg_G(u)| \ u \in V(G)\}$. A graph G is said to be *k-regular* if every node in G has the same degree k. For simplicity, we define $N_G(H) \equiv N_G(V(H))$, where H is a subgraph of G. For a node set T in a graph G, the notation $G \setminus T$ denotes the subgraph obtained by deleting all the nodes in T from G. For a subset of nodes $V' \subseteq V(G)$, the *neighborhood* of V' in G is defined as $N_G(V') = \{\bigcup_{u \in V'} N_G(u)\} \setminus V'$. The *components* of a graph G are its maximal connected subgraphs. A component is called a *singleton* if it is a single node.

The *connectivity* of a graph G, denoted by $\kappa(G)$, is the minimum number of nodes whose removal causes G to be disconnected or to have only one node. An *isomorphism* from a graph G to a graph H is a one-to-one and onto function $\pi : V(G) \to V(H)$ such that $(u, v) \in E(G)$ if and only if $(\pi(u), \pi(v)) \in E(H)$. We say "$G$ is *isomorphic* to H", written $G \cong H$, if there is an isomorphism from G to H. The *symmetric difference* of two sets F_1 and F_2 is defined as $F_1 \Delta F_2 = (F_1 \setminus F_2) \cup (F_2 \setminus F_1)$. For simplicity, we use $\langle n \rangle$ to denote the set $\{1, 2, \ldots, n\}$. Specifically, a *6-node-paw* is defined as a graph consisting of a 3-cycle with one node extending as a path of length 3.

A *multiprocessor system* is often modelled as an undirected graph $G = (V(G), E(G))$ whose nodes represent processors and edges represent communication links. Under the classical PMC model [20], adjacent nodes are capable of performing tests on each others. For adjacent nodes $u, v \in V(G)$, the ordered pair (u, v) represents the test performed by u on v. In this situation, u is called the *tester* and v is called the *tested node*. The outcome of a test (u, v) is 1 (resp. 0) if u evaluates v as faulty (resp. fault-free).

A *test assignment* for a system $G = (V(G), E(G))$ is a collection of tests (u, v) for some adjacent pairs of nodes. The collection of all test results is called a *syndrome*. Formally, a syndrome is a function $\sigma : L \to \{0, 1\}$. The set of faulty nodes in the system is called the *fault set*. This can be any subset of $V(G)$. The process of identifying all faulty nodes is called the *diagnosis* of the system. The maximum number of faulty nodes that the system G can guarantee to identify is called the *diagnosability* of G, written as $t(G)$.

For a given syndrome σ in a system G, a subset of nodes $F \subseteq V(G)$ is said to be *consistent* with syndrome σ if σ can be produced from the situation that, for any $(u, v) \in L$ such that for $u \in V(G) \setminus F$, $\sigma(u, v) = 1$ if $v \in F$; otherwise, $\sigma(u, v) = 0$. Because a faulty tester can lead to an unreliable result, a given fault set F may produce different syndromes. Let $\sigma(F)$ represent the set of all syndromes which could be produced if F is the fault set. Two distinct fault sets F_1 and F_2 in a system G are said to be *indistinguishable* if $\sigma(F_1) \cap \sigma(F_2) \neq \emptyset$; otherwise, they are said to be *distinguishable*.

Some known results regarding the definitions of a t-diagnosable system and related concepts are described below.

Definition 1 [20]. *A system of n nodes is t-diagnosable if all faulty nodes can be identified without replacement, provided that the number of faulty nodes presented does not exceed t.*

Lemma 1 [10]. *A system G is t-diagnosable if and only if for any two fault sets F_1 and F_2 in G satisfying $|F_1| \leq t$, $|F_2| \leq t$, and $F_1 \neq F_2$, there is at least one test from $V(G) \setminus (F_1 \cup F_2)$ to $F_1 \Delta F_2$.*

The following lemma comes directly from Lemma 1, which gives the necessary and sufficient condition for distinguishing two fault sets F_1 and F_2.

Lemma 2 [17]. *Let F_1 and F_2 be any two fault sets in a system G. Then, F_1 and F_2 are distinguishable if and only if there exists a node $u \in V(G) \setminus (F_1 \cup F_2)$ which is adjacent to a node $v \in F_1 \Delta F_2$.*

3   Properties of Alternating Group Networks and (n, k)-Star Graphs

In this section, we will introduce some useful properties of alternating group networks AN_n. Because AN_n is proven to be isomorphic to the well known interconnection network called (n, k)-star graph $S_{n,k}$ [8] by limiting $k = n - 2$, namely the $(n, n - 2)$-star graph $S_{n,n-2}$ and our main result will also applies to $S_{n,n-2}$, we first introduce several useful properties of $S_{n,k}$ and then apply these properties to AN_n.

3.1   Properties of $S_{n,k}$

This subsection is omitted due to page limit.

3.2   Properties of AN_n

The n-dimensional alternating group network AN_n [15] has node set consisting of all even permutations over $\{1, 2, \cdots, n\}$, where $n \geq 3$. Let $u = q_1 q_2 q_3 q_4 \cdots q_i \cdots q_n$ be any node in AN_n. For example, $u = 346152$, an even permutation over $\{1, 2, 3, 4, 5, 6\}$, is a node in AN_6, and we have $q_1 = 3, q_2 = 4, q_3 = 6, q_4 = 1, q_5 = 5$, and $q_6 = 2$. The edge adjacency about u is defined as follows:

1. u is adjacent to two nodes $v_1 = q_3 q_1 q_2 q_4 \cdots q_i \cdots q_n$ and $v_2 = q_2 q_3 q_1 q_4 \cdots q_i \cdots q_n$ through edges (called 3-*edges*) of dimension 3. The nodes v_1 and v_2 are called the 3-*neighbors* of u.
2. u is adjacent to the node $q_2 q_1 q_i q_4 \cdots q_3 \cdots q_n$, denoted by $(u)^i$, through an edge (also called i-*edge*) of dimension i, where $4 \leq i \leq n$ (i.e., swapping q_3 and q_i). The node $(u)^i$ is called the i-*neighbor* of u. In particular, u's n-neighbor $(u)^n$ is also called the *outgoing neighbor* of u.

Cheng *et al.* [8] give an important result for the isomorphism property between AN_n and $S_{n,n-2}$, which is written as the following lemma.

Lemma 3 [8].   *AN_n is isomorphic to $S_{n,n-2}$ for $n \geq 3$.*

According to Lemma 3 and the properties presented in Sect. 3.1, several useful properties of AN_n are given below. AN_n is $(n-1)$-regular and contains $\frac{n!}{(n-(n-2))!} = \frac{n!}{2}$ nodes.

We introduce two kinds of decomposition methods for AN_n. First, we use the same term *cluster* to denote a subgraph of AN_n induced by all the nodes having the same symbols in the last $(n-2) - 1 = n - 3$ positions, that is $q_4 q_5 \ldots q_n$. We then have the observations that (1) AN_n can be decomposed into node-disjoint clusters, and each node of AN_n belongs to a unique cluster, (2) each cluster in AN_n contains exactly $n - (n-2) + 1 = 3$ nodes, (3) any two nodes within the same cluster are adjacent, that is, each cluster in AN_n is isomorphic to a 3-cycle K_3, and (4) the edges within the same cluster are all 3-edges.

For the second kind of decomposition, let AN_n^i denote a subgraph of AN_n induced by all the nodes having the same symbol i in the last position n, i.e., $q_n = i$, where $n \geq 4$ and $1 \leq i \leq n$. AN_n can be decomposed along dimension n into n subgraphs $AN_n^1, AN_n^2, \cdots, AN_n^n$, and each subgraph AN_n^i is isomorphic to AN_{n-1}. The edges between two subgraphs AN_n^a and AN_n^b refer to the edge set $E^{a,b} = \{(u, v) | \ u = q_1 q_2 b q_4 \cdots q_{n-1} a \in V(AN_n^a)$, and $v = q_2 q_1 a q_4 \cdots q_{n-1} b \in V(AN_n^b)\}$. Here, we have $\left| E^{a,b} \right| = \frac{(n-2)!}{(n-(n-2))!} = \frac{(n-2)!}{2}$.

We generalize the above decomposition as follows. Let $AN_n^{j:i}$ denote the subgraph of AN_n induced by all the nodes having the same symbol i in the position j, i.e., $q_j = i$, where $4 \leq j \leq n$ and $1 \leq i \leq n$. AN_n can be decomposed along dimension j into n subgraphs $AN_n^{j:1}, AN_n^{j:2}, \ldots, AN_n^{j:i}, \ldots, AN_n^{j:n-1}, AN_n^{j:n}$.

Corollary 1. *Suppose that AN_n $(n \geq 4)$ is decomposed along dimension j into n subgraphs $AN_n^{j:1}$, $AN_n^{j:2}$, $\cdots$, $AN_n^{j:n}$, where $4 \leq j \leq n$. Then, each subgraph $AN_n^{j:i}$ is isomorphic to AN_{n-1} for $1 \leq i \leq n$.*

Corollary 2 [15]. *AN_n is $(n-1)$-connected, where $n \geq 4$.*

Corollary 3. *Let T be a set of nodes in AN_n with $|T| \leq 2n - 6$, where $n \geq 4$. Then, $AN_n \setminus T$ satisfies one of the following conditions.*

1. *$AN_n \setminus T$ is connected.*
2. *$AN_n \setminus T$ has two components, one of which is a singleton.*

The following lemma describes the outcome after deleting a certain set of nodes from AN_n.

Lemma 4 [25]. *Let T be a set of nodes in AN_n with $|T| \leq 3n-10$, where $n \geq 4$. Then, $AN_n \setminus T$ has a large component and some small components containing at most 2 nodes in total.*

Corollary 4. *Let (u,v) be any edge in AN_n, where $n \geq 3$. Then, we have*

$$|N_{AN_n}(\{u,v\})| = \begin{cases} 2n - 5 & \text{if } (u,v) \text{ is a 3-edge;} \\ 2n - 4 & \text{if } (u,v) \text{ is an } i\text{-edge,} \\ & \text{where } 4 \leq i \leq n. \end{cases}$$

Lemmas 5 and 6 show the property that AN_n cannot contain any 4-cycles and 5-cycles.

Lemma 5 [13,22]. *AN_n does not contain 4-cycles, where $n \geq 4$.*

Lemma 6 [13,22]. *AN_n does not contain 5-cycles, where $n \geq 4$.*

4   Conditional Diagnosability of Alternating Group Networks

An n-dimensional alternating group network AN_n contains $\binom{n!/2}{n-1}$ node subsets of size $n - 1$, among which only $\frac{n!}{2}$ node subsets contain all neighbors of some node. Since the ratio $\frac{n!}{2}/\binom{n!/2}{n-1}$ becomes relatively small as n grows sufficiently large, the probability of a fault set containing all the neighbors of some node is very low. For this reason, Somani and Agarwal [21] generalized the concept for system-level diagnosis. Moreover, by considering the situation that any fault set cannot contain all the neighbors of every node in a system, Lai et al. [17] proposed a new fault diagnosis strategy called *conditional diagnosability* for multiprocessor systems. We need to give some definitions formally. A set of faulty nods $F \subseteq V(G)$ is called a *conditional fault set* if $N_G(u) \nsubseteq F$ for every node $u \in V(G)$. Similar to Definition 1, the definition of a conditionally t-diagnosable system is given as follows.

Definition 2 [17]. A system G is *conditionally t-diagnosable* if any two conditional fault sets F_1 and F_2 in G satisfying $F_1 \neq F_2$, $|F_1| \leq t$, and $|F_2| \leq t$ are distinguishable.

An equivalent way of representing the above definition is given below, which will be utilized in our main theorem.

Lemma 7. *A system G is conditionally t-diagnosable if and only if for any two conditional fault sets F_1 and F_2 with $F_1 \neq F_2$ in G such that they are indistinguishable, it implies $|F_1| \geq t + 1$ or $|F_2| \geq t + 1$.*

The *conditional diagnosability* of G, written $t_c(G)$, is defined to be the maximum value of t such that G is conditionally t-diagnosable.

Before discussing conditional diagnosability, we need to have more observations regarding the neighborhood of a node in a system given two conditional fault sets F_1 and F_2 that are indistinguishable. Lai *et al.* [17] state this fact as the following lemma.

Lemma 8 [17]. *Suppose that two conditional fault sets F_1 and F_2 satisfying $F_1 \neq F_2$ are indistinguishable in a system G. Let $X = G \setminus (F_1 \cup F_2)$. Then, the following two properties hold:*

1. $|N_G(u) \cap V(X)| \geq 1$ for each $u \in V(X)$, and
2. $|N_G(v) \cap (F_1 \setminus F_2)| \geq 1$ and $|N_G(v) \cap (F_2 \setminus F_1)| \geq 1$ for each $v \in F_1 \Delta F_2$.

With Lemma 8, we establish the following important properties, which will be utilized in our main theorems.

Lemma 9. *Suppose that two conditional fault sets F_1 and F_2 satisfying $F_1 \neq F_2$ are indistinguishable in a system G. Then, $G \setminus (F_1 \cap F_2)$ has a component H with (1) $V(H) \subseteq F_1 \Delta F_2$ and (2) $\delta(H) \geq 2$. Moreover, if G contains neither 4-cycles nor 5-cycles, then we further have (i) H contains a 6-node-paw or P_8, (ii) $|H'| \geq 4$ or $|H''| \geq 4$ (i.e., $\max\{|H'|, |H''|\} \geq 4$), where $H' = V(H) \cap (F_1 \setminus F_2)$ and $H'' = V(H) \cap (F_2 \setminus F_1)$.*

Proof. The proof is omitted due to page limit.

4.1 Conditional Diagnosability of AN_4

This subsection is omitted due to page limit. The following is a list of lemmas introduced in this subsection.

Lemma 10. *The conditional diagnosability of AN_4 is at most 5, i.e., $t_c(AN_4) \leq 5$.*

Lemma 11. *AN_4 is 5-conditionally diagnosable.*

Theorem 1. *The conditional diagnosability of AN_4 under the PMC model is 5, i.e., $t_c(AN_4) = 5$.*

4.2   Conditional Diagnosability of AN_n for $n \geq 5$

Now consider the remaining case where $n \geq 5$. We first show that the conditional diagnosability of n-dimensional alternating group network AN_n does not exceed $6n-17$, i.e., $t_c(AN_n) \leq 6n-17$. Recall that each cluster in AN_n contains exactly 3 nodes. Let (u_1, v_1) be any 4-edge in AN_n, and u_2 and u_3 (resp. v_2 and v_3) be the two 3-neighbors of u_1 (resp. v_1). Let $V' = \{u_1, u_2, u_3, v_1, v_2, v_3\}$, $F_1 = \{u_1, v_1\} \cup N_{AN_n}(V')$, and $F_2 = \{u_2, u_3, v_2, v_3\} \cup N_{AN_n}(V')$. By actually observing the structure of AN_n, we can obtain that each node in F_1 (resp. F_2) has a neighbor outside F_1 (resp. F_2). Then, from definition, both F_1 and F_2 are conditional fault sets. Moreover, by Lemma 2, F_1 and F_2 are indistinguishable. Also, note that $|F_1 \setminus F_2| = |\{u_1, v_1\}| = 2$, $|F_2 \setminus F_1| = |\{u_2, u_3, v_2, v_3\}| = 4$, and $|F_1 \cap F_2| = |N_{AN_n}(V')| = 4 + 6 \cdot (n-4) = 6n - 20$, which implies $|F_1| = 2 + (6n-20) = 6n-18$ and $|F_2| = 4 + (6n-20) = 6n-16$. From Definition 2, AN_n is not conditionally $(6n-16)$-diagnosable, which implies $t_c(AN_n) \leq (6n-16) - 1 = 6n - 17$. An upper bound for $t_c(AN_n)$ is written below.

Lemma 12. $t_c(AN_n) \leq 6n - 17$, where $n \geq 5$.

Next, we derive a lower bound for the conditional diagnosability of AN_n. Suppose that two conditional fault sets F_1 and F_2 satisfying $F_1 \neq F_2$ are indistinguishable in AN_n for $n \geq 5$. We next show that $|F_1| \geq 6n - 16$ or $|F_2| \geq 6n - 16$.

Lemma 13. Suppose that two conditional fault sets F_1 and F_2 satisfying $F_1 \neq F_2$ are indistinguishable in AN_n for $n \geq 5$. Then, we have $|F_1| \geq 6n - 16$ or $|F_2| \geq 6n - 16$ (i.e., $\max\{|F_1|, |F_2|\} \geq 6n - 16$).

Proof. Let $T = F_1 \cap F_2$. By Lemmas 5, 6, and 9, $AN_n \setminus T$ has a component H with the following properties: (1) $V(H) \subseteq F_1 \Delta F_2$, (2) $\delta(H) \geq 2$, (3) H contains a 6-node-paw or P_8, which implies $|V(H)| \geq 6$, and (4) $|H'| \geq 4$ or $|H''| \geq 4$ (i.e., $\max\{|H'|, |H''|\} \geq 4$), where $H' = V(H) \cap (F_1 \setminus F_2)$ and $H'' = V(H) \cap (F_2 \setminus F_1)$, which implies $|F_1 \setminus F_2| \geq |H'| \geq 4$ or $|F_2 \setminus F_1| \geq |H''| \geq 4$. It suffices to prove $|T| + \max\{|H'|, |H''|\} \geq 6n-16$, which implies $\max\{|F_1|, |F_2|\} = \max\{|T| + |F_1 \setminus F_2|, |T| + |F_2 \setminus F_1|\} = |T| + \max\{|F_1 \setminus F_2|, |F_2 \setminus F_1|\} \geq |T| + \max\{|H'|, |H''|\} \geq 6n - 16$

If $|T| \geq 6n - 20$, then we have $|T| + \max\{|H'|, |H''|\} \geq (6n - 20) + 4 = 6n-16$, and the lemma holds immediately. In the remainder, we only consider the situation $|T| \leq 6n-21$. Note that because $|V(H)| \geq 6 > 3$, H contains two nodes, say u and v, which belong to different clusters. Suppose $[u]_j \neq [v]_j$ for some j with $4 \leq j \leq n$. By Corollary 1, we can decompose AN_n into n subgraphs AN_n^i for $i \in \langle n \rangle$ along dimension j such that u and v are in different subgraphs. Then, the nodes of H are distributed in at least two subgraphs. Denote $T_i = T \cap V(AN_n^i)$ for every $i \in \langle n \rangle$. For convenience, we classify all subgraphs into two categories by letting $A = \{i \mid |T_i| \leq 2n - 8\}$ and $B = \{i \mid |T_i| \geq 2n - 7\}$. Clearly, $|A| + |B| = n$. A subgraph AN_n^i is called an *A-subgraph* if $i \in A$; otherwise, it is called a *B-subgraph* (i.e., $i \in B$).

Because $|T| \leq 6n - 21$, we have $|B| \leq 3$ (i.e., there are at most three B-subgraphs), which implies $|A| \geq n - 3$, i.e., there are at least $n - 3(\geq 2)$

A-subgraphs. Otherwise, we have $|T| \geq 4(2n - 7) = 8n - 28 \geq 6n - 20 > |T|$, which leads to a contradiction. Note that in each A-subgraph AN_n^i (i.e., $i \in A$), $|T_i| \leq 2n - 8 = 2(n - 1) - 6$. By Corollary 3, $AN_n^i \setminus T_i$ has a large component, denoted by M_i, and up to one singleton. Let AN_n^a be an A-subgraph (i.e., $|T_a| \leq 2n - 8$), and M be the component of $AN_n \setminus T$ containing M_a, the large component of $AN_n^a \setminus T_a$. Before continuing the proof, we first give the following claim:

Claim. For every A-subgraph AN_n^i, the nodes of M_i are contained in M.

Proof of the claim: The proof is omitted due to page limit.

We continue the remaining part of the proof. According to the distribution of the nodes of H, we consider two cases:

Case 1: $V(H) \cap V(M) \neq \emptyset$.
Recall that both H and M are components of $AN_n \setminus T$. We conclude that H and M refer to the same component, i.e., $H = M$, which implies $|V(H)| = |V(M)|$. According to the size of n, we consider the following two cases:
Case 1.1: $n \geq 6$.
Recall that there are at least $n - 3 (\geq 2)$ A-subgraphs. By further utilizing Claim 4.2, we then have $|V(H)| = |V(M)| \geq (n - 3) \cdot \left[\frac{(n-1)!}{2} - ((2n - 8) + 1) \right] = (n-3) \cdot \left[\frac{(n-1)!}{2} - (2n - 7) \right] \geq 2 \cdot (6n - 16)$ for $n \geq 6$. Therefore, we conclude that $|T| + \max\{|H'|, |H''|\} \geq |T| + \left\lceil \frac{|V(H)|}{2} \right\rceil \geq 0 + \left\lceil \frac{2 \cdot (6n - 16)}{2} \right\rceil = 6n - 16$.
Case 1.2: $n = 5$.
In this case, we need $|T| + \max\{|H'|, |H''|\} \geq 6 \cdot 15 - 16 = 14$. Note that in each A-subgraph AN_5^i, $|T_i| \leq 2 \cdot 5 - 8 = 2 < (5 - 1) - 1$. By Corollary 2, $AN_5^i \setminus T_i$ is connected. Recall that there are at most three B-subgraphs. For the number of B-subgraphs, we consider the following two subcases.
Case 1.2.1: At most two B-subgraphs.
The proof of this subcase is omitted due to page limit.
Case 1.2.2: Exactly three B-subgraphs, say AN_5^α, AN_5^β, and AN_5^γ.
Note that there are $5 - 3 = 2$ A-subgraphs. Recall that AN_5^a is an A-subgraph. Let AN_5^b be the other A-subgraph. Since $|T_\alpha| \geq 2 \cdot 5 - 7 = 3$, $|T_\beta| \geq 2 \cdot 5 - 7 = 3$, $|T_\gamma| \geq 2 \cdot 5 - 7 = 3$ and $|T| \leq 6 \cdot 5 - 21 = 9$, we have $|T_\alpha| = |T_\beta| = |T_\gamma| = 3$ and $|T_a| = |T_b| = 0$, i.e., AN_5^a and AN_5^b are both fault-free. By Claim 4.2, M contains at least all nodes of AN_5^a and AN_5^b. Next, consider the outgoing neighbors of the nodes of AN_5^a and AN_5^b in AN_5^α, AN_5^β, and AN_5^γ. Since $|E^{\alpha,a}| + |E^{\alpha,b}| = 2 \cdot \frac{(5-2)!}{2} = 6$ and $|T_\alpha| = 3$, M contains at least $6 - 3 = 3$ nodes of $AN_5^\alpha \setminus T_\alpha$. Similarly, M also contains at least $6 - 3 = 3$ nodes of $AN_5^\beta \setminus T_\beta$ (resp. $AN_5^\gamma \setminus T_\gamma$). Accordingly, we obtain $|V(H)| = |V(M)| \geq 2 \cdot \frac{(5-1)!}{2} + 3 \cdot 3 = 24 + 9 = 33$. Therefore, we conclude that $|T| + \max\{|H'|, |H''|\} \geq |T| + \left\lceil \frac{|V(H)|}{2} \right\rceil \geq 0 + \left\lceil \frac{33}{2} \right\rceil = 17 \geq 14$.
Case 2: $V(H) \cap V(M) = \emptyset$.

By Claim 4.2, H cannot contain the nodes of M_i in every A-subgraph AN_n^i. Moreover, since $\delta(H) \geq 2$, H cannot contain any singletons among all A-subgraphs because every singleton has exactly one outgoing neighbor. So, the nodes of H cannot be distributed in any A-subgraphs, i,e., the nodes of H can be distributed in only B-subgraphs. Secondly, recall that (1) AN_n has been decomposed into n subgraphs along some dimension such that at least two subgraphs contain some nodes of H and (2) there are at most three B-subgraphs. Consequently, the nodes of H can be distributed in exactly two or three B-subgraphs. However, the latter case cannot occur. We explain this fact as the following claim:

Claim. The nodes of H cannot be distributed in exactly three B-subgraphs.

Proof of the claim: The proof of this claim is omitted due to page limit.

We continue the remaining part of the proof. By Claim 4.2, the nodes of H are distributed in exactly two B-subgraphs, say AN_n^α and AN_n^β. Note that $|T_\alpha| \geq 2n - 7$ and $|T_\beta| \geq 2n - 7$. Let (u_1, v_1) be an edge of H where u_1 is in $AN_n^\alpha \setminus T_\alpha$ and v_1 is in $AN_n^\beta \setminus T_\beta$. Also, because $\delta(H) \geq 2$, u_1 (resp. v_1) has a neighbor, say u_2 (resp. v_2), in $AN_n^\alpha \setminus T_\alpha$ (resp. $AN_n^\beta \setminus T_\beta$). Since $[u_1]_3 = \beta$ and $[u_1]_3 \neq [u_2]_3$, u_2's outgoing neighbor $(u_2)^n$ is not in AN_n^β, which causes $(u_2)^n \in T \setminus (T_\alpha \cup T_\beta)$. Similarly, u_2 has a neighbor u_3 ($\neq u_1$) in $AN_n^\alpha \setminus T_\alpha$, and u_3's outgoing neighbor $(u_3)^n$ is in $T \setminus (T_\alpha \cup T_\beta)$. With a similar manner, we also have that (1) v_2's outgoing neighbor $(v_2)^n \in T \setminus (T_\alpha \cup T_\beta)$, (2) v_2 has a neighbor v_3 ($\neq v_1$) in $AN_n^\beta \setminus T_\beta$, and (3) v_3's outgoing neighbor $(v_3)^n \in T \setminus (T_\alpha \cup T_\beta)$. Clearly, $(u_2)^n$, $(u_3)^n$, $(v_2)^n$, and $(v_3)^n$ are all distinct because each node has exactly one outgoing neighbor. Therefore, we have $|T \setminus (T_\alpha \cup T_\beta)| \geq |\{(u_2)^n, (u_3)^n, (v_2)^n, (v_3)^n\}| = 4$, which causes $|T_\alpha| + |T_\beta| = |T| - |T \setminus (T_\alpha \cup T_\beta)| \leq (6n - 21) - 4 = 6n - 25$.

Without loss of generality, assume $|T_\alpha| \leq |T_\beta|$. Then, we have $2|T_\alpha| \leq |T_\alpha| + |T_\beta| \leq 6n - 25$, which implies $|T_\alpha| \leq \lfloor \frac{6n-25}{2} \rfloor = 3n - 13 = 3(n-1) - 10$. By Lemma 4, $AN_n^\alpha \setminus T_\alpha$ has a large component M_α and up to some small components containing at most 2 nodes in total. This implies that u_1, u_2, and u_3 are all contained in M_α. Hence, H contains the nodes of M_α, and v_1, v_2, and v_3. So, we have $|V(H)| \geq |V(M_\alpha)| + |\{v_1, v_2, v_3\}| \geq \left[\frac{(n-1)!}{2} - (3n - 13) - 2 \right] + 3 = \frac{(n-1)!}{2} - 3n + 14 \geq 2 \cdot (2n - 6)$ for $n \geq 5$. Therefore, we obtain $|T| + \max\{|H'|, |H''|\} \geq |T| + \left\lceil \frac{|V(H)|}{2} \right\rceil = |T_\alpha| + |T_\beta| + |T \setminus (T_\alpha \cup T_\beta)| + \left\lceil \frac{|V(H)|}{2} \right\rceil \geq (2n - 7) + (2n - 7) + 4 + \left\lceil \frac{2(2n-6)}{2} \right\rceil = 6n - 16$.

Combining the above cases completes the proof.   □

We now express our main result as follows.

Theorem 2. $t_c(AN_n) = 6n - 17$ for $n \geq 5$.

Proof. We prove this theorem by combining both the upper and lower bounds of $t_c(AN_n)$. First, by Lemma 12, we have $t_c(AN_n) \leq 6n - 17$. Next, by Lemmas 7 and 13, AN_n is conditionally $(6n - 17)$-diagnosable, where $n \geq 5$, implying that $t_c(AN_n) \geq 6n - 17$, where $n \geq 5$. Therefore, the result holds.   □

Combined with Lemma 3, Theorems 1 and 2 can also be extended to $(n, n-2)$-star graphs $S_{n,n-2}$. We write them as the following corollary.

Corollary 5. $t_c(S_{4,2}) = 5$, and $t_c(S_{n,n-2}) = 6n - 17$ for $n \geq 5$

5   Conclusion

In this paper, we study the work for the conditional diagnosability of n-dimensional alternating networks AN_n under the PMC model. By investigating and utilizing the structural properties of AN_n and (n, k)-star graphs $S_{n,k}$, the conditional diagnosability of AN_n is determined to be (1) $t_c(AN_4) = 5$ and (2) $t_c(AN_n) = 6n - 17$ for $n \geq 5$. Also, because of the isomorphism property between AN_n and $S_{n,k}$ for $k = n - 2$, namely $(n, n - 2)$-star graphs $S_{n,n-2}$, the above results can also be extended to $S_{n,n-2}$. So, we further have (3) $t_c(S_{4,2}) = 5$ and (4) $t_c(S_{n,n-2}) = 6n - 17$. Compared with traditional fault diagnosis in which the diagnosability is limited by the system node degree, by introducing the concept of conditional diagnosability, the number of fault processors that the system can diagnose has increased significantly. These results illustrates the importance of conditional diagnosability in reliability analysis. It is worth noting that the conditional diagnosability of AN_n is about six times its degree, which is very different from general networks with a multiple of four. With our results, the problem for the conditional diagnosability of $S_{n,k}$ is completely solved.

References

1. Akers, S.B., Krishnamurthy, B.: A group-theoretic model for symmetric interconnection networks. IEEE Trans. Comput. **38**(4), 555–566 (1989)
2. Akers, S.B., Krishnamurthy, B., Harel, D.: The star graph: an attractive alternative to the n-cube. In: Proceedings of the International Conference on Parallel Processing, pp. 393–400 (1987)
3. Chang, N.W., Cheng, E., Hsieh, S.Y.: Conditional diagnosability of Cayley graphs generated by transposition trees under the PMC model. ACM Trans. Des. Autom. Electron. Syst. **20**(2) (2015). Article no. 20
4. Chang, N.W., Deng, W.H., Hsieh, S.Y.: Conditional diagnosability of (n, k)-star networks under the comparison diagnosis model. IEEE Trans. Reliab. **64**(1), 132–143 (2015)
5. Chang, N.W., Hsieh, S.Y.: Structural properties and conditional diagnosability of star graphs by using the PMC model. IEEE Trans. Parallel Distrib. Syst. **25**(11), 3002–3011 (2014)
6. Chang, N.W., Hsieh, S.Y.: Conditional diagnosability of (n, k)-star graphs under the PMC model. IEEE Trans. Dependable Secure Comput. **15**(2), 207–216 (2018)
7. Cheng, E., Lipták, L., Qiu, K., Shen, Z.: On deriving conditional diagnosability of interconnection networks. Inf. Process. Lett. **112**(17–18), 674–677 (2012)

8. Cheng, E., Qiu, K., Shen, Z.: A note on the alternating group network. J. Supercomput. **59**(1), 246–248 (2012). https://doi.org/10.1007/s11227-010-0434-y

9. Chiang, W.K., Chen, R.J.: The (n, k)-star graph: a generalized star graph. Inf. Process. Lett. **56**(5), 259–264 (1995)

10. Dahbura, A.T., Masson, G.M.: An $O(n^{2.5})$ fault identification algorithm for diagnosable systems. IEEE Trans. Comput. **C−33**(6), 486–492 (1984)

11. Duarte Jr., E.P., Ziwich, R.P., Albini, L.C.P.: A survey of comparison-based system-level diagnosis. ACM Comput. Surv. **43**(3) (2011). article no. 22

12. Hao, R.X., Feng, Y.Q., Zhou, J.X.: Conditional diagnosability of alternating group graphs. IEEE Trans. Comput. **62**(4), 827–831 (2013)

13. Hao, R.X., Zhou, J.X.: Characterize a kind of fault tolerance of alternating group network. Acta Mathematica Sinca Chinese Series **55**(6), 1055–1066 (2012)

14. Hsu, G.H., Chiang, C.F., Shih, L.M., Hsu, L.H., Tan, J.J.M.: Conditional diagnosability of hypercubes under the comparison diagnosis model. J. Syst. Architect. **55**(2), 140–146 (2009)

15. Ji, Y.: A class of Cayley networks based on the alternating groups. Adv. Math. (Chin.) **27**(4), 361–362 (1998)

16. Jwo, J.S., Lakshmivarahan, S., Dhall, S.K.: A new class of interconnection networks based on the alternating group. Networks **23**(4), 315–326 (1993)

17. Lai, P.L., Tan, J.J.M., Chang, C.P., Hsu, L.H.: Conditional diagnosability measures for large multiprocessor systems. IEEE Trans. Comput. **54**(2), 165–175 (2005)

18. Lin, C.K., Tan, J.J.M., Hsu, L.H., Cheng, E., Lipták, L.: Conditional diagnosability of Cayley graphs generated by transposition trees under the comparison diagnosis model. J. Interconnection Netw. **9**(1–2), 83–97 (2008)

19. Malek, M.: A comparison connection assignment for diagnosis of multiprocessor systems. In: Proceedings of the 7th International Symposium on Computer Architecture, pp. 31–35 (1980)

20. Preparata, F.P., Metze, G., Chien, R.T.: On the connection assignment problem of diagnosis systems. IEEE Trans. Electron. Comput. **16**(12), 848–854 (1967)

21. Somani, A.K., Agarwal, V.K., Avis, D.: A generalized theory for system level diagnosis. IEEE Trans. Comput. **C−36**(5), 538–546 (1987)

22. Wang, S., Yang, Y.: The 2-good-neighbor (2-extra) diagnosability of alternating group graph networks under the PMC model and MM* model. Appl. Math. Comput. **305**, 241–250 (2017)

23. Zhang, Z., Xiong, W., Yang, W.: A kind of conditional fault tolerance of alternating group graphs. Inf. Process. Lett. **110**(22), 998–1002 (2010)

24. Zhou, S.: The conditional fault diagnosability of (n, k)-star graphs. Appl. Math. Comput. **218**(19), 9742–9749 (2012)

25. Zhou, S., Xiao, W.: Conditional diagnosability of alternating group networks. Inf. Process. Lett. **110**(10), 403–409 (2010)

Fixed Parameter Tractability of Graph Deletion Problems over Data Streams

Arijit Bishnu[1(⊠)], Arijit Ghosh[1], Sudeshna Kolay[2], Gopinath Mishra[1], and Saket Saurabh[3]

[1] Indian Statistical Institute, Kolkata, India
arijit@isical.ac.in, arijitbishnu@gmail.com
[2] Indian Institute of Technology, Kharagpur, India
[3] The Institute of Mathematical Sciences, HBNI, Chennai, India

Abstract. The study of parameterized streaming complexity on graph problems was initiated by Fafianie et al. (MFCS'14) and Chitnis et al. (SODA'15 and SODA'16). In this work, we initiate a systematic study of parameterized streaming complexity of graph deletion problems – $\mathcal{F}$-SUBGRAPH DELETION, $\mathcal{F}$-MINOR DELETION in the four most well-studied streaming models: the EA (edge arrival), DEA (dynamic edge arrival), VA (vertex arrival) and AL (adjacency list) models. Our main conceptual contribution is to overcome the obstacles to efficient parameterized streaming algorithms by utilizing the power of parameterization. We focus on the vertex cover size K as the parameter for the parameterized graph deletion problems we consider. At the same time, most of the previous work in parameterized streaming complexity was restricted to the EA (edge arrival) or DEA (dynamic edge arrival) models. In this work, we consider the four most well-studied streaming models: the EA, DEA, VA (vertex arrival) and AL (adjacency list) models.

1 Introduction

In streaming algorithms, a graph is presented as a sequence of edges. For the upcoming discussion, $V(G)$ and $E(G)$ will denote the vertex and edge set, respectively of the graph G having n vertices. Based on the sequence in which the edges are revealed, streaming algorithms for graph problems are usually studied in the following models [8,16,19]: (i) EDGE ARRIVAL (EA) model: the stream consists of edges of G in an arbitrary order; (ii) DYNAMIC EDGE ARRIVAL (DEA) model: each element of the input stream is a pair (e, state), where $e \in E(G)$ and state $\in \{\text{insert}, \text{delete}\}$ describes whether e is being inserted into or deleted from the current graph; (iii) VERTEX ARRIVAL (VA) model: the vertices of $V(G)$ are exposed in an arbitrary order, after a vertex v is exposed, all the edges between v and neighbors of v that have already been exposed, are revealed one by one in an arbitrary order; (iv) ADJACENCY LIST (AL) model: the vertices of $V(G)$ are exposed in an arbitrary order and when a vertex v is exposed, all the edges that are incident to v are revealed one by one in an arbitrary order, and note that in this model each edge is exposed twice, once for each exposure of an endpoint.

D. Kim et al. (Eds.): COCOON 2020, LNCS 12273, pp. 652–663, 2020.
https://doi.org/10.1007/978-3-030-58150-3_53

The primary objective is to quickly answer some basic questions over the current state of the graph while storing only a small amount of information. There is a vast literature on graph streaming and we refer to the survey by McGregor [16] for more details. Algorithms that can access the sequence of edges of the input graph, p times in the same order, are defined as p-*pass streaming algorithms*. For simplicity, we refer to 1-pass streaming algorithms as *streaming algorithms*. The space used by a (p-pass) streaming algorithm, is defined as the *streaming complexity* of the algorithm. For *streaming algorithms*, it is the space complexity of the algorithm, or the *streaming complexity*, that is optimized.

Parameterized Complexity. The goal of parameterized complexity is to find ways of solving NP-hard problems by aiming to restrict the combinatorial explosion to a parameter that is hopefully much smaller than the input size. Formally, a *parameterization* of a problem is assigning an integer k to each input instance. A parameterized problem is said to be *fixed-parameter tractable (FPT)* if there is an algorithm that solves the problem in time $f(k) \cdot |I|^{O(1)}$, where $|I|$ is the size of the input and f is an arbitrary computable function depending only on the parameter k. There is a long list of NP-hard graph problems that are FPT under various parameterizations [10]. Given the definition of FPT for parameterized problems, it is desirable to expect an efficient algorithm for the corresponding parameterized streaming versions to allow $\mathcal{O}(f(k) \log^{O(1)} n)$ bits of space, where f is an arbitrary computable function of the parameter k.

There are several ways to formalize the parameterized streaming question. Some of these notions were formalized in the following two papers [5,6] and several results for VERTEX COVER and MAXIMUM MATCHING were presented there. Unfortunately, this relaxation to $\mathcal{O}(f(k) \log^{O(1)} n)$ bits of space does not buy us too many new results. Most of the problems for which parameterized streaming algorithms are known are "local problems". Other local problems like CLUSTER VERTEX DELETION (denoted as CVD) and TRIANGLE DELETION (denoted as TD) do not have positive results. Also, problems that require some global checking – such as FEEDBACK VERTEX SET (denoted as FVS), EVEN CYCLE TRANSVERSAL (denoted as ECT), ODD CYCLE TRANSVERSAL (denoted as OCT) etc. remain elusive (the formal definition of all such problems are in Appendix of [2]). In fact, one can show that, when edges of the graph arrive in an arbitrary order, using reductions from communication complexity all of the above problems will require $\Omega(n)$ space even if we allow a constant number of passes over the data stream [5].

The starting point of this paper is the above mentioned $\Omega(n)$ lower bounds on basic graph problems. We ask the most natural question – how do we deconstruct these intractability results? Possibly, look beyond the most well-studied parameter of *the size of the solution that we are seeking*.

What Parameters to Use? In parameterized complexity, after solution size and treewidth, arguably the most notable structural parameter is *vertex cover size* K [10,13]. For all the vertex deletion problems that we consider in this paper, a vertex cover is also a solution. Thus, the vertex cover size K is always larger than the solution size k for all the above problems. We do a study of vertex deletion problems from the view point of parameterized streaming in all known models. The main *conceptual* contribution of this paper is to use structural parameter in parameterized streaming algorithms.

What Problems to Study? We study the streaming complexity of parameterized versions of $\mathcal{F}$-SUBGRAPH DELETION and $\mathcal{F}$-MINOR DELETION. These problems are one of the most well studied ones in parametertized complexity and have led to development of the field. The parameters we consider in this paper are (i) the solution size k and (ii) the size K of the vertex cover of the input graph G. In $\mathcal{F}$-SUBGRAPH DELETION and $\mathcal{F}$-MINOR DELETION, the objective is to decide whether there exists $X \subset V(G)$ of size at most k such that $G \setminus X$ has no graphs in $\mathcal{F}$ as a subgraph, and has no graphs in $\mathcal{F}$ as a minor, respectively. $\mathcal{F}$-SUBGRAPH DELETION and $\mathcal{F}$-MINOR DELETION are interesting due to the following reasons. FEEDBACK VERTEX SET (FVS), EVEN CYCLE TRANSVERSAL (ECT), ODD CYCLE TRANSVERSAL (OCT) and TRIANGLE DELETION (TD) are special cases of $\mathcal{F}$-SUBGRAPH DELETION when $\mathcal{F} = \{C_3, C_4, C_5, \ldots\}$, $\mathcal{F} = \{C_3, C_5, \ldots\}$, $\mathcal{F} = \{C_4, C_6, \ldots\}$ and $\mathcal{F} = \{C_3\}$, respectively. FVS is also a special case of $\mathcal{F}$-MINOR DELETION when $\mathcal{F} = \{C_3\}$. For formal definitions of the problems, see Appendix of [2].

Related Work. Problems in class P have been extensively studied in streaming complexity in the last decade [16]. Recently, there has been a lot of interest in studying streaming complexity of NP-hard problems like HITTING SET, SET COVER, MAX CUT and MAX CSP [1,14,15]. Structural parameters have been considered to study MATCHING in streaming [3,5,9,11,17,18]. Fafianie and Kratsch [12] were the first to study parameterized streaming complexity of NP-hard problems like d-HITTING SET and EDGE DOMINATING SET in graphs. Chitnis *et al.* [5–7] developed a sampling technique to design efficient parameterized streaming algorithms for promised variants of VERTEX COVER, d-HITTING SET problem, b-MATCHING etc. They also proved lower bounds for problems like $\mathcal{G}$-FREE DELETION, $\mathcal{G}$-EDITING, CLUSTER VERTEX DELETION etc. [5]. Chitnis et al. [4] studied and defined different complexity classes for parameterized streaming problems.

Organisation of the Paper. Section 2 describes the interrelationship between the streaming models and our results. The algorithms for COMMON NEIGHBOR, $\mathcal{F}$-SUBGRAPH DELETION and $\mathcal{F}$-MINOR DELETION are given in Sect. 3. We skip the lower bound proofs that use reductions from communication complexity problems in this work; an interested reader is referred to [2].

2   Interrelation Between Models and Our Results

Streamability and Hardness. Let Π be a parameterized graph problem that takes as input a graph on n vertices and a parameter k. Let $f : \mathbb{N} \times \mathbb{N} \to \mathbb{R}$ be a *computable* function. For a model $\mathcal{M} \in \{\text{DEA}, \text{EA}, \text{VA}, \text{AL}\}$, whenever we say that *an algorithm $\mathcal{A}$ solves Π with complexity $f(n, k)$ in model $\mathcal{M}$*, we mean $\mathcal{A}$ is a randomized algorithm that for any input instance of Π in model $\mathcal{M}$ gives the correct output with probability $2/3$ and has streaming complexity $f(n, k)$.

Definition 1. A parameterized graph problem Π, that takes an n-vertex graph and a parameter k as input, is $\Omega(f)$ *p-pass hard* in the EDGE ARRIVAL model, or in short Π is (EA, f, p)-*hard*, if there does not exist any p-pass streaming algorithm of streaming complexity $\mathcal{O}(f(n, k))$ bits that can solve Π in model $\mathcal{M}$.

Analogously, (DEA, f, p)-*hard*, (VA, f, p)-*hard* and (AL, f, p)-*hard* are defined.

Definition 2. A graph problem Π, that takes an n-vertex graph and a parameter k as input, is $\mathcal{O}(f)$ *p-pass streamable* in EDGE ARRIVAL model, or in short Π is (EA, f, p)-*streamable* if there exists a p-pass streaming algorithm of streaming complexity $\mathcal{O}(f(n, k))$ words[1] that can solve Π in EDGE ARRIVAL model.

(DEA, f, p)-*streamable*, (VA, f, p)-*streamable* and (AL, f, p)-*streamable* are defined analogously. For simplicity, we refer to $(\mathcal{M}, f, 1)$-hard and $(\mathcal{M}, f, 1)$-streamable as $(\mathcal{M}, f)$-hard and $(\mathcal{M}, f)$-*streamable*, respectively, where $\mathcal{M} \in \{\text{DEA}, \text{EA}, \text{VA}, \text{AL}\}$.

Definition 3. Let $\mathcal{M}_1, \mathcal{M}_2 \in \{\text{DEA}, \text{EA}, \text{VA}, \text{AL}\}$ be two streaming models, $f : \mathbb{N} \times \mathbb{N} \to \mathbb{R}$ be a computable function, and $p \in \mathbb{N}$.

(i) If for any parameterized graph problem Π, $(\mathcal{M}_1, f, p)$-hardness of Π implies $(\mathcal{M}_2, f, p)$-hardness of Π, then we say $\mathcal{M}_1 \leq_h \mathcal{M}_2$.
(ii) If for any parameterized graph problem Π, $(\mathcal{M}_1, f, p)$-streamability of Π implies $(\mathcal{M}_2, f, p)$-streamability of Π, then we say $\mathcal{M}_1 \leq_s \mathcal{M}_2$.

Now, from Definitions 1, 2 and 3, we have the following Observation.

Observation 4. AL $\leq_h$ EA $\leq_h$ DEA; VA $\leq_h$ EA $\leq_h$ DEA; DEA $\leq_s$ EA $\leq_s$ VA; DEA $\leq_s$ EA $\leq_s$ AL.

This observation has the following implication. If we prove a lower (upper) bound result for some problem Π in model $\mathcal{M}$, then it also holds in any model $\mathcal{M}'$ such that $\mathcal{M} \leq_h \mathcal{M}'$ ($\mathcal{M} \leq_s \mathcal{M}'$). For example, if we prove a lower bound result in AL or VA model, it also holds in EA and DEA model; if we prove an upper bound result in DEA model, it also holds in EA, VA and AL model. In general, there is no direct connection between AL and VA. In AL and VA, the vertices are exposed in an arbitrary order. However, we can say the following when the vertices arrive in a fixed (known) order.

Observation 5. Let AL$'$(VA$'$) be the restricted version of AL (VA), where the vertices are exposed in a fixed (known) order. Then AL$' \leq_h$ VA$'$ and VA$' \leq_s$ AL$'$.

---

[1] It is usual in streaming that the lower bound results are in bits, and the upper bound results are in words.

Now, we remark the implication of the relation between different models discussed in this section to our results mentioned in Table 1.

Remark 1. In Table 1, the lower bound results in VA and AL hold even if we know the sequence in which vertices are exposed, and the upper bound results hold even if the vertices arrive in an arbitrary order. In general, the lower bound in the AL model for some problem Π does not imply the lower bound in the VA model for Π. However, our lower bound proofs in the AL model hold even if we know the order in which vertices are exposed. So, the lower bounds for FVS, ECT, OCT, presented in [2], in the AL model imply the lower bound in the VA model. By Observations 4 and 5, we will be done by showing a subset of the algorithmic and lower bound results mentioned in the Table 1.

Table 1. A summary of our results. "str." means streamable. The results marked with † in Table 1 are lower bound results of Chitnis et al. [5]. The other lower bound results are ours, some of them being improvements over the lower bound results of Chitnis et al. [5]. The full set of lower bound results are presented in [2]. Notice that the lower bound results depend only on n.

Problem	Parameter	AL model	VA model	EA/DEA model
$\mathcal{F}$-Subgraph Deletion	k	(AL, $n \log n$)-hard (AL, $n/p, p$)-hard	(VA, $n \log n$)-hard (VA, $n/p, p$)-hard	(EA, $n \log n$)-hard (EA, $n/p, p$)-hard†
	K	(AL, $\Delta(\mathcal{F}) \cdot K^{\Delta(\mathcal{F})+1}$)-str.* (Theorem 11)	(VA, $n/p, p$)-hard	(EA, $n/p, p$)-hard
$\mathcal{F}$-Minor Deletion	k	(AL, $n \log n$)-hard (AL, $n/p, p$)-hard	(VA, $n \log n$)-hard (VA, $n/p, p$)-hard	(EA, $n \log n$)-hard (EA, $n/p, p$)-hard
	K	(AL, $\Delta(\mathcal{F}) \cdot K^{\Delta(\mathcal{F})+1}$)-str.* (Theorem 14)	(VA, $n/p, p$)-hard	(EA, $n/p, p$)-hard

Our Results. Let a graph G and a non-negative integer k be the inputs to the graph problems we consider. Notice that for $\mathcal{F}$-Subgraph deletion and $\mathcal{F}$-Minor deletion, $K \geq k$. In particular, we obtain a range of streaming algorithms as well as lower bounds on streaming complexity for the problems we consider. The results of the paper are highlighted in Table 1 and the full range of results are highlighted in the Table in [2].

The highlight of our results are captured by the $\mathcal{F}$-Subgraph deletion and $\mathcal{F}$-Minor deletion. They are summarized below.

Theorem 6. ($\mathcal{F}$-Subgraph deletion *in the* AL *model*) *Parameterized by solution size* k, $\mathcal{F}$-Subgraph deletion *is* (AL, $\Omega(n \log n)$)-*hard. However, when parameterized by vertex cover* K, $\mathcal{F}$-Subgraph deletion *is* (AL, $\mathcal{O}\left(\Delta(\mathcal{F}) \cdot K^{\Delta(\mathcal{F})+1}\right)$)-*streamable. Here* $\Delta(\mathcal{F})$ *is the maximum degree of any graph in* $\mathcal{F}$.

The above Theorem is in contrast to results shown in [5]. First, we would like to point out that to the best of our knowledge this is the first set of results on hardness in the AL model. The results in [5] showed that $\mathcal{F}$-SUBGRAPH DELETION is $(\text{EA}, \Omega(n))$-hard. A hardness result in the AL model implies one in the EA model (Refer to Observation 4). Thus, our result (see the proofs of lower bounds of FVS, ECT, OCT in [2]) implies a stronger lower bound for $\mathcal{F}$-SUBGRAPH DELETION particularly in the EA model. On the positive side, we show that $\mathcal{F}$-SUBGRAPH DELETION parameterized by the vertex cover size K, is $\left(\text{AL}, \Delta(\mathcal{F}) \cdot K^{\Delta(\mathcal{F})+1}\right)$-streamable (Proof in Theorem 11).

Our hardness results are obtained from reductions from well-known problems in *communication complexity*. The problems we reduced from are INDEX_n, DISJ_n and PERM_n (refer to [2] for details). In order to obtain the algorithm, one of the main technical contributions of this paper is the introduction of the COMMON NEIGHBOR problem which plays a crucial role in designing streaming algorithms in this paper. We show that $\mathcal{F}$-SUBGRAPH DELETION and many of the other considered problems, like $\mathcal{F}$-MINOR DELETION parameterized by vertex cover size K, have a unifying structure that can be solved via COMMON NEIGHBOR, when the edges of the graph are arriving in the AL model. In COMMON NEIGH-BOR, the objective is to obtain a subgraph H of the input graph G such that the subgraph contains a maximal matching M of G. Also, for each pair of vertices $a, b \in V(M)^2$, the edge (a, b) is present in H if and only if $(a, b) \in E(G)$, and *enough*[3] common neighbors of all subsets of at most $\Delta(\mathcal{F})$ vertices of $V(M)$ are retained in H. Using structural properties of such a subgraph, called the *common neighbor subgraph*, we show that it is enough to solve $\mathcal{F}$-SUBGRAPH DELETION on the common neighbor subgraph. Similar algorithmic and lower bound results can be obtained for $\mathcal{F}$-MINOR DELETION. The following theorem can be proven using Theorem 14 in Sect. 3 and the lower bound results presented in [2] (see for example, the lower bound proofs of FVS, ECT, OCT in [2]).

Theorem 7. *Consider* $\mathcal{F}$-MINOR DELETION *in the* AL *model. Parameterized by solution size* k, $\mathcal{F}$-MINOR DELETION *is* $(\text{AL}, \Omega(n \log n))$-hard. *However, when parameterized by vertex cover* K, $\mathcal{F}$-MINOR DELETION *is* $\left(\text{AL}, \mathcal{O}\left(\Delta(\mathcal{F}) \cdot K^{\Delta(\mathcal{F})+1}\right)\right)$-streamable. *Here* $\Delta(\mathcal{F})$ *is the maximum degree of any graph in* $\mathcal{F}$.

General Notation. The set $\{1, \ldots, n\}$ is denoted as $[n]$. Without loss of generality, we assume that the number of vertices in the graph is n, which is a power of 2. Given an integer $i \in [n]$ and $r \in [\log_2 n]$, $\text{bit}(i, r)$ denotes the r-th bit in the bit expansion of i. The union of two graphs G_1 and G_2 with $V(G_1) = V(G_2)$, is $G_1 \cup G_2$, where $V(G_1 \cup G_2) = V(G_1) = V(G_2)$ and $E(G_1 \cup G_2) = E(G_1) \cup E(G_2)$. For $X \subseteq V(G)$, $G \setminus X$ is the subgraph of G induced by $V(G) \setminus X$. The degree of a vertex $u \in V(G)$, is denoted by $\deg_G(u)$. The maximum and average degrees of the vertices in G are denoted as $\Delta(G)$ and $\Delta_{av}(G)$, respectively. For a family of graphs $\mathcal{F}$, $\Delta(\mathcal{F}) = \max_{F \in \mathcal{F}} \Delta(F)$. A graph F is a *subgraph* of a graph G if

---

[2] $V(M)$ denotes the set of all vertices present in the matching M.

[3] By enough, we mean $\mathcal{O}(K)$ in this case.

$V(F) \subseteq V(G)$ and $E(F) \subseteq E(G)$ is the set of edges that can be formed only between vertices of $V(F)$. A graph F is said to be a *minor* of a graph G if F can be obtained from G by deleting edges and vertices and by contracting edges. The neighborhood of a vertex $v \in V(G)$ is denoted by $N_G(v)$. For $S \subseteq V(G)$, $N_G(S)$ denotes the set of vertices in $V(G) \setminus S$ that are *neighbors of every vertex in S*. A vertex $v \in N_G(S)$ is said to be a common neighbor of S in G. The size of any minimum vertex cover in G is denoted by $\mathrm{VC}(G)$. A cycle on the sequence of vertices $v_1, \ldots, v_n$ is denoted as $\mathcal{C}(v_1, \ldots, v_n)$. For a matching M in G, the vertices in the matching are denoted by $V(M)$. C_t denotes a cycle of length t. P_t denotes a path having t vertices. A graph G is said to a *cluster* graph if G is a disjoint union of cliques, that is, no three vertices of G can form an induced P_3.

3   Deterministic Algorithms in the AL Model

We can show that both $\mathcal{F}$-SUBGRAPH DELETION and $\mathcal{F}$-MINOR DELETION are $(\mathrm{AL}, n \log n)$-hard parameterized by solution size k (see the lower bound results for FVS, ECT and OCT in [2]) as because a lower bound on FEEDBACK VERTEX SET is also a lower bound for $\mathcal{F}$-SUBGRAPH DELETION (deletion of cycles as subgraphs) and $\mathcal{F}$-MINOR DELETION (deletion of 3-cycles as minors). This motivates us to study $\mathcal{F}$-SUBGRAPH DELETION and $\mathcal{F}$-MINOR DELETION when the vertex cover of the input graph is parameterized by K. In this Section, we show that $\mathcal{F}$-SUBGRAPH DELETION is $(\mathrm{AL}, \Delta(\mathcal{F}) \cdot K^{\Delta(\mathcal{F})+1})$-streamable when the vertex cover of the input graph is parameterized by K. This will imply that FVS, ECT, OCT and TD parameterized by vertex cover size K, are (AL, K^3)-streamable. Then we design an algorithm for $\mathcal{F}$-MINOR DELETION that is inspired by the algorithm.

For the algorithm for $\mathcal{F}$-SUBGRAPH DELETION, we define an auxiliary problem COMMON NEIGHBOR and a streaming algorithm for it. This works as a subroutine for our algorithm for $\mathcal{F}$-SUBGRAPH DELETION.

3.1   COMMON NEIGHBOR **Problem**

For a graph G and a parameter $\ell \in \mathbb{N}$, H will be called *a common neighbor subgraph* for G if

(i) $V(H) \subseteq V(G)$ such that H has no isolated vertex;
(ii) $E(H)$ contains the edges of a maximal matching M of G along with the edges where both the endpoints are from $V(M)$ such that
  - for all $S \subseteq V(M)$, with $|S| \leq d$, we have $|N_H(S) \setminus V(M)| = \min\{|N_G(S) \setminus V(M)|, \ell\}$. In other words, $E(H)$ contains edges to at most ℓ common neighbors of S in $N_G(S) \setminus V(M)$.

In simple words, a common neighbor subgraph H of G contains the subgraph of G induced by $V(M)$ as a subgraph of H for some maximal matching M in G. Also, for each subset S of at most d vertices in $V(M)$, H contains edges to *sufficient* common neighbors of S in G. The parameters $d \leq K$ and ℓ are referred to as the degree parameter and common neighbor parameter, respectively.

The COMMON NEIGHBOR problem is formally defined as follows. It takes as input a graph G with $\mathrm{VC}(G) \leq K$, degree parameter $d \leq K$ and common neighbor parameter ℓ and produces a common neighbor subgraph of G as the output. COMMON NEIGHBOR parameterized by vertex cover size K, has the following result.

Algorithm 1: COMMON NEIGHBOR

Input: A graph G, with $\mathrm{VC}(G) \leq K$, in the AL model, a degree parameter
     $d \leq K$, and a common neighbor parameter ℓ.
Output: A common neighbor subgraph H of G.

1 **begin**
2 | Initialize $M = \emptyset$ and $V(M) = \emptyset$, where M denotes the current maximal
    matching.
3 | Initialize a temporary storage $T = \emptyset$.
4 | **for** *(each vertex $u \in V(G)$ exposed in the stream)* **do**
5 | | **for** *(each $(u,x) \in E(G)$ in the stream)* **do**
6 | | | **if** *($u \notin V(M)$ and $x \notin V(M)$)* **then**
7 | | | | Add (u,x) to M and both u,x to $V(M)$.
8 | | | **if** *($x \in V(M)$)* **then**
9 | | | | Add (u,x) to T.
10 | |
11 | | **if** *(u is added to $V(M)$ during the exposure of u)* **then**
12 | | | Add all the edges present in T to $E(H)$.
13 | | **else**
14 | | | **for** *(each $S \subseteq V(M)$ such that $|S| \leq d$ and $(u,z) \in T \ \forall z \in S$)* **do**
15 | | | | **if** *($N_H(S)$ is less than ℓ)* **then**
16 | | | | | Add the edges $(u,z) \ \forall z \in S$ to $E(H)$.
17 | | |
18 | |
19 | | Reset T to $\emptyset$.
20 |
21 **end**

Lemma 8. COMMON NEIGHBOR, *with a commmon neighbor parameter ℓ and parameterized by vertex cover size K, is* $(\mathrm{AL}, K^2\ell)$-*streamable.*

Proof. We start our algorithm by initializing $M = \emptyset$ and construct a matching in G that is maximal under inclusion; See Algorithm 1. As $|\mathrm{VC}(G)| \leq K$, $|M| \leq K$. Recall that we are considering the AL model here. Let M_u and M'_u be the maximal matchings just before and after the exposure of the vertex u (including the processing of the edges adjacent to u), respectively. Note that, by construction these partial matchings M_u and M'_u are also maximal matchings in the subgraph exposed so far. The following Lemma will be useful for the proof.

Claim 9. *Let $u \in N_G(S) \setminus V(M)$ for some $S \subseteq V(M)$. Then $S \subseteq V(M_u)$, that is, u is exposed, after all the vertices in S are declared as vertices of $V(M)$.*

Proof. Observe that if there exists $x \in S$ such that $x \notin V(M_u)$, then after u is exposed, there exists $y \in N_G(u)$ such that (u, y) is present in M'_u. This implies $u \in V(M'_u) \subseteq V(M)$, which is a contradiction to $u \in N_G(S) \setminus V(M)$.   □

Now, we describe what our algorithm does when a vertex u is exposed. A complete pseudocode of our algorithm for COMMON NEIGHBOR is given in Algorithm 1. When a vertex u is exposed in the stream, we try to extend the maximal matching M_u. Also, we store all the edges of the form (u, x) such that $x \in V(M_u)$, in a temporary memory T. As $|M_u| \leq K$, we are storing at most $2K$ many edges in T. Now, there are the following possibilities.

- If $u \in V(M'_u)$, that is, either $u \in V(M_u)$ or the matching M_u is extended by one of the edges stored in T, then we add all the edges stored in T to $E(H)$.
- Otherwise, for each $S \subseteq V(M_u)$ such that $|S| \leq d$ and $S \subseteq N_G(u)$, we check whether the number of common neighbors of the vertices present in S, that are already stored, is less than ℓ. If yes, we add all the edges of the form (u, z) such that $z \in S$ to $E(H)$; else, we do nothing. Now, we reset T to $\emptyset$.

As $|M| \leq K$, $|V(M)| \leq 2K$. We are storing at most ℓ common neighbors for each $S \subseteq V(M)$ with $|S| \leq d$ and the number of edges having both the endpoints in M is at most $\mathcal{O}(K^2)$, the total amount of space used is at most $\mathcal{O}(K^d \ell)$.   □

We call our algorithm described in the proof of Lemma 8 and given in Algorithm 1, as $\mathcal{A}_{cn}$. The following structural Lemma of the common neighbor subgraph of G, obtained by algorithm $\mathcal{A}_{cn}$ is important for the design and analysis of streaming algorithms for $\mathcal{F}$-SUBGRAPH DELETION. The proof of this structural result is similar to that in [13].

Lemma 10. *Let G be a graph with $\mathrm{VC}(G) \leq K$ and let F be a connected graph with $\Delta(F) \leq d \leq K$. Let H be the common neighbor subgraph of G with degree parameter d and common neighbor parameter $(d+2)K$, obtained by running the algorithm $\mathcal{A}_{cn}$. Then the following holds in H: For any subset $X \subseteq V(H)$, where $|X| \leq K$, F is a subgraph of $G \setminus X$ if and only if F' is a subgraph of $H \setminus X$, such that F and F' are isomorphic.*

Proof. Let the common neighbor subgraph H, obtained by algorithm $\mathcal{A}_{cn}$, contain a maximal matching M of G. First, observe that since $\mathrm{VC}(G) \leq K$, the size of a subgraph F in G is at most dK. Now let us consider a subset $X \subseteq V(H)$ such that $|X| \leq K$. First, suppose that F' is a subgraph of $H \setminus X$ and F' is isomorphic to F. Then since H is a subgraph of G, F' is also a subgraph of $G \setminus X$. Therefore, $F = F'$ and we are done.

Conversely, suppose F is a subgraph of $G \setminus X$ that is not a subgraph in $H \setminus X$. We show that there is a subgraph F' of $H \setminus X$ such that F' is isomorphic to F. Consider an arbitrary ordering $\{e_1, e_2, \ldots, e_s\} \subseteq (E(G) \setminus E(H)) \cap E(F)$; note that $s \leq |E(F)|$. We describe an iterative subroutine that converts the subgraph F to

F' through s steps, or equivalently, through a sequence of isomorphic subgraphs $F_0, F_1, F_2, \ldots F_s$ in G such that $F_0 = F$ and $F_s = F'$.

Let us discuss the consequence of such an iterative routine. Just before the starting of step $i \in [s]$, we have the subgraph F_{i-1} such that F_{i-1} is isomorphic to F and the set of edges in $(E(G)\backslash E(H)) \cap E(F_{i-1})$ is a subset of $\{e_i, e_{i+1}, \ldots, e_s\}$. In step i, we convert the subgraph F_{i-1} into F_i such that F_{i-1} is isomorphic to F_i. Just after the step $i \in [s]$, we have the subgraph F_i such that F_i is isomorphic to F and the set of edges in $(E(G) \backslash E(H)) \cap E(F_i)$ is a subset of $\{e_{i+1}, e_{i+2}, \ldots, e_s\}$. In particular, in the end $F_s = F'$ is a subgraph both in G and H.

Now consider the instance just before step i. We show how we select the subgraph F_i from F_{i-1}. Let $e_i = (u, v)$. Note that $e_i \notin E(H)$. By the definition of the maximal matching M in G, it must be the case that $|\{u, v\} \cap V(M)| \geq 1$. From the construction of the common neighbor subgraph H, if both u and v are in $V(M)$, then $e_i = (u, v) \in E(H)$. So, exactly one of u and v is present in $V(M)$. Without loss of generality, let $u \in V(M)$. Observe that v is a common neighbor of $N_G(v)$ in G. Because of the maximality of M, each vertex in $N_G(v)$ is present in $V(M)$. Now, as $(u, v) \notin E(H)$, v is not a common neighbor of $N_G(v)$ in H. From the construction of the common neighbor subgraph, H contains $(d+2)K$ common neighbors of all the vertices present in $N_G(v)$. Of these common neighbors, at most $(d+1)K$ common neighbors can be vertices in $X \cup F_i$. Thus, there is a vertex v' that is a common neighbor of all the vertices present in $N_G(v)$ in H such that F_{i+1} is a subgraph that is isomorphic to F_i. Moreover, $(E(G) \backslash E(H)) \cap E(F_{i+1}) \subseteq \{e_{i+2}, e_{i+3} \ldots, e_s\}$. Thus, this leads to the fact that there is a subgraph F' in $H \backslash X$ that is isomorphic to the subgraph F in $G \backslash X$. $\qquad \square$

3.2 $\mathcal{F}$-SUBGRAPH DELETION and $\mathcal{F}$-MINOR DELETION

Our result on COMMON NEIGHBOR leads us to the following streamability result for $\mathcal{F}$-SUBGRAPH DELETION and $\mathcal{F}$-MINOR DELETION. We first discuss the result on $\mathcal{F}$-SUBGRAPH DELETION, which is stated in the following theorem.

Theorem 11. $\mathcal{F}$-SUBGRAPH DELETION *parameterized by vertex cover size K is* $(\mathrm{AL}, d \cdot K^{d+1})$-*streamable, where* $d = \Delta(\mathcal{F}) \leq K$.

Proof. Let (G, k, K) be an input for $\mathcal{F}$-SUBGRAPH DELETION, where G is the input graph, $k \leq K$ is the size of the solution of $\mathcal{F}$-SUBGRAPH DELETION, and the parameter K is at least $\mathrm{VC}(G)$.

Now, we describe the streaming algorithm for $\mathcal{F}$-SUBGRAPH DELETION. First, we run the COMMON NEIGHBOR streaming algorithm described in Lemma 8 (and given in Algorithm 1) with degree parameter d and common neighbor parameter $(d + 2)K$, and let the common neighbor subgraph obtained be H. We run a traditional FPT algorithm for $\mathcal{F}$-SUBGRAPH DELETION [10] on H and output YES if and only if the output on H is YES.

Let us argue the correctness of this algorithm. By Lemma 10, for any subset $X \subseteq V(H)$, where $|X| \leq K$, $F \in \mathcal{F}$ is a subgraph of $G \backslash X$ if and only if F', such that F' is isomorphic to F', is a subgraph of $H \setminus X$. In particular, let X be a k-sized vertex set of G. As mentioned before, $k \leq K$. Thus, by Lemma 10, X is a solution of $\mathcal{F}$-SUBGRAPH DELETION in H if and only if X is a solution of $\mathcal{F}$-SUBGRAPH DELETION in G. Therefore, we are done with the correctness of the streaming algorithm for $\mathcal{F}$-SUBGRAPH DELETION.

The streaming complexity of $\mathcal{F}$-SUBGRAPH DELETION is same as the streaming complexity for the algorithm $\mathcal{A}_{cn}$ from Lemma 8 with degree parameter $d = \Delta(\mathcal{F})$ and common neighbor parameter $(d+2)K$. Therefore, the streaming complexity of $\mathcal{F}$-SUBGRAPH DELETION is $\mathcal{O}(d \cdot K^{d+1})$. □

Corollary 12. FVS, ECT, OCT *and* TD *parameterized by vertex cover size K are* (AL, K^3)*-streamable due to deterministic algorithms.*

Finally, we describe a streaming algorithm for $\mathcal{F}$-MINOR DELETION that works similar to that of $\mathcal{F}$-SUBGRAPH DELETION due to the following proposition and the result is stated in Theorem 14.

Proposition 13 [13]. *Let G be a graph with F as a minor and $\mathrm{VC}(G) \leq K$. Then there exists a subgraph G^* of G that has F as a minor such that $\Delta(G^*) \leq \Delta(F)$ and $V(G^*) \leq V(F) + K(\Delta(F) + 1)$.*

Theorem 14. $\mathcal{F}$-MINOR DELETION *parameterized by vertex cover size K are* $(\mathrm{AL}, d \cdot K^{d+1})$*-streamable, where $d = \Delta(\mathcal{F}) \leq K$.*

Proof. Let (G, k, K) be an input for $\mathcal{F}$-MINOR DELETION, where G is the input graph, k is the size of the solution of $\mathcal{F}$-MINOR DELETION we are looking for, and the parameter K is such that $\mathrm{VC}(G) \leq K$. Note that, $k \leq K$.

Now, we describe the streaming algorithm for $\mathcal{F}$-MINOR DELETION. First, we run the COMMON NEIGHBOR streaming algorithm described in Lemma 8 with degree parameter d and common neighbor parameter $(d+2)K$, and let the common neighbor subgraph obtained be H. We run a traditional FPT algorithm for $\mathcal{F}$-MINOR DELETION [10] and output YES if and only if the output on H is YES.

Let us argue the correctness of this algorithm, that is, we prove the following for any $F \in \mathcal{F}$. $G \setminus X$ contains F as a minor if and only if $H \setminus X$ contains F' as a minor such that F and F' are isomorphic, where $X \subseteq V(G)$ is of size at most K. For the only if part, suppose $H \setminus X$ contains F' as a minor. Then since H is a subgraph of G, $G \setminus X$ contains F' as a minor. For the if part, let $G \setminus X$ contains F as a minor. By Proposition 13, $G \setminus X$ conatins a subgraph G^* such that G^* contains F as a minor and $\Delta(G^*) \leq \Delta(F)$. Now, Lemma 10 implies that $H \setminus X$ also contains a subgraph $\hat{G}^*$ that is isomorphic to G^*. Hence, $H \setminus X$ contains F' as a monor such that F' is isomorphic to F.

The streaming complexity of the streaming algorithm for $\mathcal{F}$-MINOR DELETION is same as the streaming complexity for the algorithm $\mathcal{A}_{cn}$ from Lemma 8 with degree parameter $d = \Delta(\mathcal{F})$ and common neighbor parameter $(d + 2)K$. Therefore, the streaming complexity for $\mathcal{F}$-MINOR DELETION is $\mathcal{O}(d \cdot K^{d+1})$. □

References

1. Assadi, S., Khanna, S., Li, Y.: Tight bounds for single-pass streaming complexity of the set cover problem. In: STOC, pp. 698–711 (2016)
2. Bishnu, A., Ghosh, A., Kolay, S., Mishra, G., Saurabh, S.: Fixed-parameter tractability of graph deletion problems over data streams. CoRR, abs/1906.05458 (2019)
3. Bury, M., et al.: Structural results on matching estimation with applications to streaming. Algorithmica **81**(1), 367–392 (2019)
4. Chitnis, R., Cormode, G.: Towards a theory of parameterized streaming algorithms. In: IPEC, vol. 148, pp. 7:1–7:15 (2019)
5. Chitnis, R., et al.: Kernelization via sampling with applications to finding matchings and related problems in dynamic graph streams. In: SODA, pp. 1326–1344 (2016)
6. Chitnis, R.H., Cormode, G., Esfandiari, H., Hajiaghayi, M., Monemizadeh, M.: Brief announcement: new streaming algorithms for parameterized maximal matching & beyond. In: SPAA, pp. 56–58 (2015)
7. Chitnis, R.H., Cormode, G., Hajiaghayi, M.T., Monemizadeh, M.: Parameterized streaming: maximal matching and vertex cover. In: SODA, pp. 1234–1251 (2015)
8. Cormode, G., Dark, J., Konrad, C.: Independent sets in vertex-arrival streams. In: ICALP, pp. 45:1–45:14 (2019)
9. Cormode, G., Jowhari, H., Monemizadeh, M., Muthukrishnan, S.: The sparse awakens: streaming algorithms for matching size estimation in sparse graphs. In: 25th Annual European Symposium on Algorithms, ESA 2017. LIPIcs, vol. 87, pp. 29:1–29:15 (2017)
10. Cygan, M., et al.: Parameterized Algorithms, 1st edn. Springer, Heidelberg (2015). https://doi.org/10.1007/978-3-319-21275-3
11. Esfandiari, H., Hajiaghayi, M., Liaghat, V., Monemizadeh, M., Onak, K.: Streaming algorithms for estimating the matching size in planar graphs and beyond. ACM Trans. Algorithms **14**(4), 1–23 (2018)
12. Fafianie, S., Kratsch, S.: Streaming kernelization. In: MFCS, pp. 275–286 (2014)
13. Fomin, F.V., Jansen, B.M.P., Pilipczuk, M.: Preprocessing subgraph and minor problems: When does a small vertex cover help? JCSS **80**(2), 468–495 (2014)
14. Guruswami, V., Velingker, A., Velusamy, S.: Streaming complexity of approximating max 2CSP and max acyclic subgraph. In: APPROX/RANDOM, pp. 8:1–8:19 (2017)
15. Kapralov, M., Khanna, S., Sudan, M., Velingker, A.: $1 + \omega(1)$ approximation to MAX-CUT requires linear space. In: SODA, pp. 1703–1722 (2017)
16. McGregor, A.: Graph stream algorithms: a survey. SIGMOD Rec. **43**(1), 9–20 (2014)
17. McGregor, A., Vorotnikova, S.: Planar matching in streams revisited. In: APPROX/RANDOM, Schloss Dagstuhl-Leibniz-Zentrum fuer Informatik (2016)
18. McGregor, A., Vorotnikova, S.: A simple, space-efficient, streaming algorithm for matchings in low arboricity graphs. In: SOSA (2018)
19. McGregor, A., Vorotnikova, S., Vu, H.T.: Better algorithms for counting triangles in data streams. In: PODS, pp. 401–411 (2016)

Mixing of Markov Chains
for Independent Sets on Chordal Graphs
with Bounded Separators

Ivona Bezáková[(✉)] and Wenbo Sun[(✉)]

Rochester Institute of Technology, Rochester, NY 14623, USA
ib@cs.rit.edu, ws3109@rit.edu

Abstract. We prove rapid mixing of well-known Markov chains for the hardcore model on a new graph class, the class of chordal graphs with a bound on minimal separator size. In the hardcore model, for a given graph G and a fugacity parameter $\lambda \in \mathbb{R}^+$, the goal is to produce an independent set S of G with probability proportional to $\lambda^{|S|}$. In general graphs and arbitrary λ, producing a sample from this distribution in polynomial time is provably difficult. However, natural Markov chains converge to the correct distribution for any graph, leading to the study of their mixing times for different graph classes. Rapid mixing for graphs of bounded degrees and a range of λs dependent on the maximum degree has attracted attention since the 1990s. Recent results showed rapid mixing for arbitrary λ and two other classes of graphs: graphs of bounded treewidth and graphs of bounded bipartite pathwidth. In this work, we extend these results by showing rapid mixing in a new graph class, class of chordal graphs with bounded minimal separators. Graphs in this class have no bound on the vertex degrees, the treewidth, or the bipartite pathwidth. Similar to the results dealing with bounded treewidth and with bounded bipartite pathwidth, we prove rapid mixing using the canonical paths technique. However, unlike in the previous works, we need to process the data using a non-linear, tree-like, approach.

1 Introduction

Independent sets, that is, sets of vertices in a graph without any edges between them, are heavily studied in computer science and other fields. Among their many applications is the hardcore model of a gas in statistical physics, where the goal is to sample independent sets of a given graph according to a specific probability distribution. In particular, for a given parameter (also known as fugacity) $\lambda \in \mathbb{R}^+$, the goal is to generate an independent set S with probability proportional to $\lambda^{|S|}$.

Markov chains have attracted attention as a sampling technique for the hardcore distribution since the late 1990s. The mixing time of a Markov chain is the time it takes to converge to its stationary distribution, and a Markov chain is said to be rapidly mixing if its mixing time is polynomial in the size of the input.

© Springer Nature Switzerland AG 2020
D. Kim et al. (Eds.): COCOON 2020, LNCS 12273, pp. 664–676, 2020.
https://doi.org/10.1007/978-3-030-58150-3_54

Luby and Vigoda [15] showed rapid mixing of a natural insert/delete chain (a single-site Glauber dynamics) for independent sets of triangle-free graphs with degree bound Δ and $\lambda < 2/(\Delta - 2)$, which was soon extended by Vigoda [23] to general graphs with degree bound Δ. Independently, Dyer and Greenhill [4] analyzed an insert/delete chain with an added drag transition, showing rapid mixing for the same graph class and range of λs. All these works used the coupling technique to obtain their mixing results.

Dyer, Frieze, and Jerrum [6] established a hardness result, showing that even for $\lambda = 1$, no Markov chain for sampling independent sets that changes only a "small" number (that is, a linear fraction) of vertices per step mixes rapidly for general graphs, even if the maximum degree is six. This was followed by an influential non-Markov-chain-based approach of Weitz [24] which leads to rapid mixing of the Glauber dynamics for subexponentially growing graphs with maximum degree Δ and $\lambda < \lambda_c := (\Delta - 1)^{\Delta-1}/(\Delta - 2)^{\Delta}$. Efthymiou et al. [7] used belief propagation to obtain rapid mixing for graphs with sufficiently large maximum degree and girth (that is, the length of the smallest cycle) $\geq$ 7, and $\lambda < \lambda_c$. Very recently, Anari, Liu, and Oveis Gharan [1] established rapid mixing for bounded degree graphs and $\lambda < \lambda_c$ using a new notion of spectral independence. We refer the reader to [1] for an overview of rapid mixing results for restricted graph classes with bounded degrees. On the complementary hardness side, assuming $NP \neq RP$, a celebrated result of Sly [20], together with [8,9,17,21], imply hardness of polynomial-time approximate sampling for bounded degree graphs and $\lambda > \lambda_c$.

Beyond graphs of bounded degrees, Bordewich and Kang [2] studied an insert/delete Markov chain (a multi-site Glauber dynamics) to sample vertex subsets, a generalization of the hardcore model, and proved that its mixing time is $n^{O(\text{tw})}$ for an arbitrary λ and n-vertex graphs of treewidth tw. Recently, generalizing work of Matthews [16] on claw-free graphs, Dyer, Greenhill, and Müller [5] introduced a new graph parameter, the bipartite pathwidth, obtaining a mixing time of $n^{O(p)}$ for the insert/delete chain for an arbitrary λ and graphs with bipartite pathwidth bounded by p. These works used the canonical paths technique [13] to prove rapid mixing.

We extend this line of work to another graph class, the class of chordal graphs with bounded minimum separator size. In particular, we obtain a mixing time of $O(n^{O(\log b)})$ for arbitrary λ and chordal graphs with minimal separators of size at most b (or, equivalently, bound b on the intersection size of any pair of maximal cliques). Graphs in this class have no bound on their degrees, treewidth, or bipartite pathwidth[1]. Chordal graphs, where each cycle of length at least four has a chord, are a widely studied graph class, playing an important role in many real-world applications such as inference in probabilistic graphical models [14].

We also use the canonical paths technique but we need to overcome the "nonlinearity" of our data. The technique relies on finding a Markov chain path (a

---

[1] This can be seen by taking a complete binary tree of $\sqrt{n}$ vertices, where each vertex is replaced by a clique of size $\sqrt{n}$, and each pair of adjacent cliques is connected by an edge.

666 I. Bezáková and W. Sun

canonical path) between every pair of states in such a way that no transition gets overloaded (congested). This is typically done by considering the symmetric difference of the two states (a pair of independent sets), gradually removing one vertex from the initial independent set while adding a vertex from the final independent set. If the symmetric difference induces a collection of paths in the original graph, we can "switch" each path from initial to final starting at one end-point of the path and gradually going to the other end-point, never violating the independent set property. Bounded bipartite pathwidth guarantees that the symmetric difference can be viewed as "wider" paths, as does bounded treewidth due to its relation to the (non-bipartite) pathwidth. However, for our graphs, the symmetric difference is tree-like, which leads to the need to recursively "switch" entire subtrees from initial to final before being able to process the root vertex from the final independent set. Due to this "tree-like" process we also need to overcome corresponding complications in the analysis of the congestion.

We note that if one is interested purely in sampling independent sets from the hardcore distribution on chordal graphs, just like for graphs of bounded treewidth, polynomial-time sampling algorithms exist: Okamoto, Uno, and Uehara [18] designed polynomial-time dynamic programming algorithms to count independent sets, maximum independent sets, and independent sets of fixed size on chordal graphs without any restrictions, which can then be used to sample independent sets from the hardcore distribution. In contrast, our work contributes to the understanding of the conditions under which the well-studied and easy-to-implement insert/delete(/drag) Glauber dynamics Markov chain mixes rapidly.

2   Preliminaries

For an undirected graph G, an *independent set* is a set of vertices $S \subseteq V(G)$ such that there is no edge $(u,v) \in E(G)$ with $u,v \in S$. Let Ω_G be the set of all independent sets of G. We study the problem of sampling independent sets from Ω_G, where the probability distribution is parameterized by a given constant $\lambda > 0$ as follows: A set $S \in \Omega_G$ is to be generated with probability $\pi(S) := \lambda^{|S|}/Z_G(\lambda)$, where the normalization factor $Z_G(\lambda) := \sum_{S \in \Omega_G} \lambda^{|S|}$ is known as the partition function.

We will use Markov chains to obtain a *fully polynomial almost uniform sampler (FPAUS)* from the target distribution π: For a given $\epsilon \in (0,1)$, we will produce a random element (a sample) from Ω_G chosen from a distribution μ that is ϵ-close to π. In particular, $d_{TV}(\mu,\pi) \leq \epsilon$, where $d_{TV}(\mu,\pi) := \sum_{S \in \Omega_G} |\mu(S) - \pi(S)|/2$ is the *total variation distance*. The sample will be provided in time polynomial in $|V(G)|$ and $\log(1/\epsilon)$.

Next we briefly review chordal graphs and Markov chains.

Chordal graphs

An undirected graph is *chordal* if every cycle of four or more vertices has a chord, that is, an edge that connects two vertices of the cycle but is not part of the cycle. For a nice treatment of chordal graphs, we refer the reader to [22]; in this section we briefly describe the concepts relevant to our work. Every chordal graph G has a *clique tree* T_G which satisfies the following conditions:

(i) T_G is a tree whose vertices are maximal cliques in G and
(ii) T_G has the *induced subtree property*: For every vertex $v \in V(G)$, the maximal cliques containing v form a subtree of T_G. We refer to this tree as the v-induced subtree $T_G(v)$.

In fact, this is a complete characterization of chordal graphs: such a clique tree exists if and only if G is chordal [3,10]. We note that in some literature the term "clique tree" refers only to the first condition above — in this text by a "clique tree" we mean a clique tree with the induced subtree property, that is, satisfying both conditions above. It follows that since an edge is a clique of size 2, it is a part of a maximal clique, and, therefore, for each edge $(u, v) \in E(G)$ there is a clique in $V(T_G)$ that contains both u and v. The existence of clique trees implies that the *treewidth* of a chordal graph is one less than the size of its largest clique, and, as such, chordal graphs can have unbounded treewidth.

In any graph, a *vertex separator* is a set of vertices whose removal leaves the remaining graph disconnected, and a separator is *minimal* if it has no subset that is also a separator. Suppose we root a clique tree T_G at an arbitrary clique $R \in V(T_G)$, denoting the rooted tree by T_G^R. Then, each clique $C \in T_G^R$ can be partitioned into a separator set $\mathrm{Sep}(C) = C \cap p(C)$ and a residual set $\mathrm{Res}(C) = C \setminus \mathrm{Sep}(C)$, where $p(C)$ denotes the parent clique of $C \neq R$ in T_G^R and $p(R) := \emptyset$. The induced subtree property implies the following theorem, see, for example [22]:

Theorem 1. *Let T_G^R be an R-rooted clique tree of a graph G.*

- *The separator sets $\mathrm{Sep}(C)$ where C ranges over all non-root cliques of T_G^R, are the minimal vertex separators of G.*
- *For each $v \in V(G)$, there is exactly one clique $C_v \in T_G^R$ that contains v in its residual set, that is, $v \in \mathrm{Res}(C_v)$. In particular, C_v is the root of the v-induced subtree $T_G(v)$ in T_G^R. (Therefore, the other cliques in $T_G(v)$ contain v in their separator sets.)*

In this work we assume, without loss of generality, that the given chordal graph G is connected. We also assume that there exists a constant $b \in \mathbb{N}^+$, which we refer to as the *separator bound*, that upper-bounds the size of every minimal separator of G.

Markov chains

In this section we briefly review Markov chains and the canonical paths technique for bounding their mixing times. For more details we refer the reader to, for example, [12]. A (finite discrete) *Markov chain* is a pair (P, Ω) where Ω denotes the state space and P is its transition matrix: a stochastic matrix of dimensions $|\Omega| \times |\Omega|$, indexed by elements from Ω, where $P(u, v)$ is the probability of transitioning from state $u \in \Omega$ to state $v \in \Omega$. The transition from one state to the next is also referred to as a *step* of the Markov chain. A distribution

π on Ω (viewed as a vector) is said to be *stationary* if $\pi P = \pi$. If a Markov chain is so-called ergodic, its stationary distribution is unique and it is the limiting distribution the Markov chain converges to as the number of its steps goes to infinity. In this work we deal with ergodic Markov chains and reserve the symbol π for the stationary distribution. For a start distribution μ on Ω, after t steps the chain is in distribution μP^t. For an ergodic chain, $\lim_{t\to\infty} \mu P^t = \pi$. For Markov chains with exponentially large state space the transition matrix is typically very sparse and not given explicitly but instead described implicitly by an algorithm that, for a current state, describes the random process of getting to the next state.

The *mixing time* of the Markov chain is the number of steps needed for the chain to get ϵ-close to its stationary distribution. For a start state $x \in \Omega$, let μ_x denote the distribution where $\mu_x(x) = 1$ and $\mu_x(y) = 0$ for every $y \in \Omega \setminus \{x\}$. Then, for a given $\epsilon \in (0,1)$, the mixing time $\tau_x(\epsilon)$ from the state x is the smallest t such that $d_{TV}(\mu_x P^t, \pi) \leq \epsilon$. Therefore, a polynomial mixing time for a polynomially-computable start state provides an FPAUS.

Canonical paths [13,19] is a technique for bounding the mixing time. The idea is to define, for every pair of states $x, y \in \Omega$, a path $\gamma_{x,y} = (x = z_0, \ldots, z_\ell = y)$ such that (z_i, z_{i+1}) are adjacent states in the Markov chain, that is, $P(z_i, z_{i+1}) > 0$. Let $\Gamma := \{\gamma_{xy} \mid x, y \in \Omega\}$ be the set of all canonical paths. The *congestion* through a transition $e = (u, v)$, where $P(u, v) > 0$, is

$$\varrho(\Gamma, e) := \frac{1}{\pi(u)P(u,v)} \sum_{x,y:\gamma_{xy} \text{ uses } e} \pi(x)\pi(y) |\gamma_{xy}| \tag{1}$$

where $|\gamma_{xy}|$ is the length of the path γ_{xy}. The overall congestion of the paths Γ is defined as $\varrho(\Gamma) := \max_{e=(u,v):P(u,v)>0} \varrho(\Gamma, e)$. The mixing time of the chain is bounded by $\tau_x(\epsilon) \leq \varrho(\Gamma)\left(\ln(\frac{1}{\pi(x)}) + \ln(\frac{1}{\epsilon})\right)$ [19].

3   Rapid Mixing for Chordal Graphs with Bounded Separators

Recall that we are given a graph G and a parameter $\lambda \in \mathbb{R}^+$. The most commonly used Markov chain for sampling independent sets is the Glauber dynamics (also known as the Luby-Vigoda chain or the insert/delete chain): Let S be the current independent set. Pick a random vertex $u \in V(G)$. If $u \in S$, remove it from S with probability dependent on λ to maintain the desired target distribution (this probability turns out to be $\frac{1}{1+\lambda}$). If $u \notin S$ and if none of its neighbors are in S, add it to S with probability $\frac{\lambda}{1+\lambda}$. Our polynomial mixing time results hold for the Glauber dynamics but in this work we prove mixing time bounds for a closely related Markov chain by Dyer and Greenhill [4].

The Dyer-Greenhill chain: Let $S \in \Omega_G$ be the current independent set. Pick a vertex u uniformly at random from $V(G)$. Then:

[Delete ↓:] If $u \in S$, remove it with probability $\frac{1}{1+\lambda}$.

[Insert ↑:] If $u \notin S$ and none of the neighbors of u are in S, add u with probability $\frac{\lambda}{1+\lambda}$.

[Drag ↔:] if $u \notin S$ and it has a unique neighbor $v \in S$, add u and remove v.

Let S' be the resulting independent set (if none of the above holds for u, let $S' = S$), which is the next state of the Markov chain. The chain is ergodic with the desired stationary distribution $\pi(S) = \frac{\lambda^{|S|}}{Z_G(\lambda)}$ [4].

3.1   Canonical Paths for Chordal Graphs

From now on we assume that G is a connected chordal graph with n vertices. We will define a canonical path between every pair of independent sets I ("initial") and F ("final") in G. As is often done in canonical paths construction, we will work only with vertices of $I \oplus F$, the symmetric difference of I and F: we will gradually remove vertices from $I \setminus F$ while adding vertices in $F \setminus I$. (Notice that vertices in $I \cap F$ do not neighbor $I \oplus F$, and hence we do not need to touch them.)

We first observe that the symmetric difference of two independent sets in a chordal graph forms an induced forest.

Lemma 1. *Let G be a chordal graph and let I and F be its two independent sets. Then, the subgraph of G induced by $I \oplus F$ is a forest.*

Proof. Let $H = G[I \oplus F]$ be the subgraph induced by $I \oplus F$. By contradiction, assume that H contains a cycle c. Since G is chordal and H is induced, c must have a chord in H, obtaining a shorter cycle. Applying this argument inductively, H contains a triangle which has a pair of adjacent vertices in I, or in F, a contradiction with $I, F \in \Omega_G$. $\qquad\square$

We assume that the vertices of G are labeled $1, \ldots, n$. Before defining our canonical paths, we fix a clique tree T_G corresponding to G and we root it at a vertex R (for example, let R be the clique that has vertex 1 in its residual set), obtaining T_G^R. For a vertex u in $V(G)$, let C_u be the clique of T_G^R that contains u in its residual set. We define the *depth* of u in T_G^R as $d(u) := d(C_u)$, where $d(C_u)$ is the depth of C_u in T_G^R (that is, $d(C_u)$ is the distance of C_u from the root R).

For a pair $I, F \in \Omega_G$, we define the canonical path from I to F as follows. By Lemma 1, each connected component of $G[I \oplus F]$, the subgraph of G induced by $I \oplus F$, is a tree. Since the connected components of $G[I \oplus F]$ form a partition of $I \oplus F$, we refer to the vertex sets of the connected components as components of $I \oplus F$. We process components in $I \oplus F$ in the ascending order of their smallest vertex. We first define a start vertex for each component: For a current component D, its *start vertex* $u_D \in I \oplus F$ is the vertex with the smallest depth. If there are multiple such vertices, we pick the smallest one.

We define the canonical way to convert the current component D from I to F as follows: We process D by doing depth-first search of $G[D]$ from its start vertex u_D, processing the children vertices of the current vertex in increasing order of the sizes of the subtrees associated with the children vertices. We break ties by processing smaller children first. Let u be the current vertex in the depth-first search. Then:

- If $u \in I$: If its parent has no other neighbors in the current independent set, we apply the drag transition $\leftrightarrow$ on u and its parent. Otherwise, we apply the delete transition $\downarrow$ on u.
- If $u \in F$: If u has no children, we apply the insert transition $\uparrow$ on u. Otherwise, we proceed to process the children of u.

In other words, we always remove an I-vertex before visiting its children, and we add an F-vertex (either by the insertion $\uparrow$ or by dragging $\leftrightarrow$) to the independent set after we process all its descendants. Clearly, the transitions for $u \in I$ maintain the current state as an independent set. Notice that an F-vertex is added after its I-children have been removed, and we have removed its I-parent prior to visiting this vertex; therefore, these transitions are also legal and maintain the current state as an independent set throughout the process.

3.2   Bounding the Congestion

Let $t = (S, S')$ be a transition for which we want to bound the congestion $\rho(\Gamma, t)$, see (1), the definition of which involves a sum through all canonical paths that use t. To bound this sum, one typically defines an "encoding" for each canonical path $\gamma_{I,F}$ through t. The goal for the encoding is to comprise of a state of Ω_G, and possibly some additional information chosen from a set of polynomial size.

Suppose $I, F \in \Omega_G$ are such that $\gamma_{I,F}$ uses t. Our encoding $\eta_{I,F}$ of $\gamma_{I,F}$ will consist of multiple parts. We start by defining its first part $\hat{\eta}_t(I, F)$, see Fig. 1:

- Let D be the component of $I \oplus F$ on which t is applied (that is, t inserts, deletes, or drags a vertex $u \in D$).
- Let $p_u = (u_D, \ldots, u)$ be the path from the start vertex u_D to u in $G[D]$.
- Let Q_{p_u} be the set of vertices in $p_u \setminus \{u\}$ that (a) have more than one child in the tree $G[D]$ rooted at u_D, and (b) their successor vertex on p_u is not their last child.
- Then, let

$$\hat{\eta}_t(I, F) = (I \oplus F \oplus (S \cup S')) \setminus Q_{p_u}. \tag{2}$$

Denote by $\mathrm{cp}(t) := \{(I, F) \mid t \in \gamma_{I,F}\}$ the set of pairs $(I, F) \in \Omega_G^2$ whose canonical path $\gamma_{I,F}$ uses transition t. Then we have the following lemma.

Lemma 2. *For a transition t and an independent set pair (I, F) such that $(I, F) \in \mathrm{cp}(t)$, $\hat{\eta}_t(I, F)$ is an independent set.*

Proof. Let S, S', u, and D be defined as above. Let $A = I \oplus F \oplus (S \cup S')$. Then by the definition of the canonical paths, components of $I \oplus F$ prior to D have been already processed, that is, for every such component D', the current state S (and S') contains vertices in $D' \cap F$. Likewise, every component D' after D is untouched, that is S (and S') contains vertices in $D' \cap I$. Thus, A,

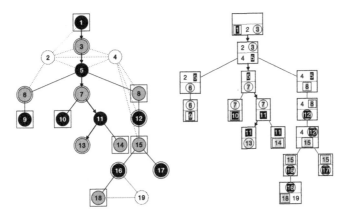

Fig. 1. On the canonical path from I to F: On the left is a chordal graph with 19 vertices. An initial and a final independent set I and F are shown in black and grey, respectively. Solid lines indicate the edges of the induced subgraph $G[I \oplus F]$, the other edges are dotted. $G[I \oplus F]$ is processed from vertex 1, the current transition t is adding $u = 13$, and the current independent set is shown in double circles. Path p_u is shown using arrows, $Q_{p_u} = \{5, 11\}$. Vertices in $\hat{\eta}_t(I, F)$ are squared. A corresponding clique tree is on the right, each clique represented by a rectangle with the separator set and the residual set at the top and bottom, respectively.

and therefore also $\hat{\eta}_t(I, F)$, contains the I-vertices in the processed components and the F-vertices in the untouched components. These I-vertices in A (and $\hat{\eta}_t(I, F)$) form an independent set since $I \in \Omega_G$, the same is true for the F-vertices. Moreover, if D' and D'' are two different components of $I \oplus F$ (that correspond to two different connected components of $G[I \oplus F]$), there is no edge in $G[I \oplus F]$ connecting D' and D''. Thus, so far, $A \setminus D$ forms an independent set, whose vertices do not neighbor D.

It remains to analyze D itself. The path p_u splits the tree $G[D]$ into processed parts and untouched parts. Then A agrees with I on the processed parts and it agrees with F on the untouched parts. If $v, v' \in D$ are adjacent and neither is on p_u, then v and v' cannot be both in A because these two vertices are either both in the processed or both in the untouched part of the tree. Therefore, for any two adjacent vertices in D that are both in A, at least one of them is on p_u. We will prove that it is sufficient to remove Q_{p_u} from A to make it an independent set.

Let v be a vertex in A and $v \in p_u \setminus Q_{p_u}$ (that is, v's last child in D is on p_u). Then, v must be in I because if v were in F, it would have been added to S (and therefore not be in A) by the drag transition $\leftrightarrow$ when processing v's last child. We will show that there is no neighbor v' of v in $A \setminus Q_{p_u}$, which will conclude our proof of $\hat{\eta}_t(I, F) = A \setminus Q_{p_u}$ being an independent set. Since $v \in I$, every neighbor of v in D is in F. We first consider v's neighbors on p_u: Let v_{parent} be the parent of v (if available) and v_{child} be the last child of v. Notice that $u \neq v$ because $u \in S \cup S'$ and, therefore, it is not in A. Thus, v_{child} exists.

We claim that a vertex v' is in $A \cap F \cap p_u$ if and only if it is in $Q_{p_u} \cap F$. This is because $v' \in A \cap F \cap p_u$ if and only if $v' \in F \cap p_u$ has not yet been added to S, which means that when we were processing the child v'' of v' on p_u, the transition over v'' was remove $\downarrow$ and thus v'' was not the last child of v', which is equivalent to $v' \in Q_{p_u} \cap F$. Therefore, for neighbor $v' \in \{v_{\text{parent}}, v_{\text{child}}\}$ of v we have $v' \in F$ and $v' \notin A \setminus Q_{p_u}$.

Finally, consider a neighbor v' of v in $A \setminus p_u$. Since v_{child} is the last child of v, we have that v' has been already processed. Since $v' \in F$, it has been already added to S. Therefore, $v' \notin A$, concluding the proof. $\qquad \square$

The following lemma bounds $|Q_{p_u}|$, the proof is omitted due to space constraints. A similar argument was made by Ge and Štefankovič [11].

Lemma 3. *Let $t = (S, S')$ be a transition, $(I, F) \in \text{cp}(t)$, and u, D, u_D, and Q_{p_u} be defined as above. Then, $|Q_{p_u}| \leq \log_2 n$.*

In our congestion bounds, we will view $I \oplus F$ through the lens of the clique tree T_G. The following observation follows directly from I and F being independent sets.

Observation. *Every clique in T_G can contain at most two vertices of $I \cup F$, and at most one vertex of I and at most one vertex of F.*

Next we relate components of $I \oplus F$ to subtrees of the rooted clique tree T_G^R. Recall that C_u refers to the clique in $V(T_G^R)$ that contains $u \in V(G)$ in its residual set, that is $u \in \text{Res}(C_u)$.

Lemma 4. *Let D be a component of $I \oplus F$ and let X be the subtree of T_G spanned by clique set $\{C_u \mid u \in D\}$. Let X^R be the corresponding rooted tree of X, with edge directions consistent with T_G^R. Then the following holds:*

(i) C_{u_D} is the root of X^R.
(ii) Let $v \in D$ and let $p = (u_D = u_0, \ldots, u_\ell = v)$ be the path from u_D to v in $G[D]$. Then the directed path p_C in X^R from C_{u_D} to C_v passes through $C_{u_0}, C_{u_1}, \ldots, C_{u_\ell}$ in this order. Moreover, C_{u_i}'s are all distinct, with a possible exception of $C_{u_0} = C_{u_1}$.

Proof. We begin by proving (i). By contradiction, assume that a clique vertex $R' \neq C_{u_D}$ is the root of X^R. Then there is a directed path p' from R' to C_{u_D} in X^R. Since $u_D \in D$ is the vertex of the smallest depth (which we defined as the depth of C_{u_D} in T_G^R), none of the cliques on the path p' contain a vertex in D in their residual set. Therefore, the only reason why R' would be included in X^R is that there is another vertex $w \in D$ such that the path from C_{u_D} to C_w in X goes through R'. Let p'' be the path from R' to C_w in X^R. Notice that p'' intersects p' only at R'. If u_D were of depth 0, we would have $C_{u_D} = R = R'$. Therefore, the depth of u_D, and thus also of w, is at least 1. Since both $u_D, w \in D$, there is a path from u_D to w in $G[D]$. Then, this path needs to pass through the separator set $\text{Sep}(C_{u_D})$, which means that $\text{Sep}(C_{u_D})$ contains a vertex $u' \in D$. But then

u' is in the parent clique of C_{u_D}, which would mean that u' has a smaller depth than u_D. This is a contradiction and, therefore, R' must be equal to C_{u_D}.

To prove (ii), we will use induction on the depth of v. For the base case, when v is of the same depth as u_D, we have two possibilities. If $v = u_D$, then $p = (u_D)$ and $p_C = (C_{u_D})$ and the statement holds. If $v \neq u_D$, since v and u_D are of the same depth and, by (i), C_{u_D} is the root of X^R, it follows that $C_v = C_{u_D}$. Then $p = (u_D, v)$ and $p_C = (C_{u_D})$ and the statement holds.

For the inductive claim, let v be of depth larger than u_D. If $\mathrm{Sep}(C_v)$ contains u_D, then $p = (u_D, v)$ and p_C starts at C_{u_D} and ends at C_v, so the statement holds. Otherwise, $\mathrm{Sep}(C_v)$ separates u_D from v. Therefore, there must be u_k, where $k \in \{1, \ldots, \ell - 1\}$, such that $u_k \in \mathrm{Sep}(C_v)$. We will show that $k = \ell - 1$, that is, $u_{\ell-1} \in \mathrm{Sep}(C_v)$. By contradiction, suppose that $k < \ell - 1$. By the observation on page 8, there are at most two vertices of D in C_v. Therefore, C_v contains u_k and v, and not $v_{\ell-1}$. But since u_k and v are in the same clique C_v, there is an edge between them. Therefore, $u_k, u_{k+1}, \ldots, u_{\ell-1}, u_\ell = v$ is a cycle, contradicting Lemma 1 which states that $G[D]$ is a tree. Thus, $k = \ell - 1$.

The subtree of X of cliques containing $u_{\ell-1}$ has its root $C_{u_{\ell-1}}$ at smaller depth than C_v, since this subtree contains C_v. Therefore, the path p_C needs to pass through $C_{u_{\ell-1}}$. Since the depth of $u_{\ell-1}$ is smaller than the depth of v, we may use the inductive hypothesis for $v' := u_{\ell-1}$. We get that the directed path p'_C in X^R from C_{u_D} to $C_{v'}$ passes through $C_{u_0}, C_{u_1}, \ldots, C_{u_{\ell-1}}$ in this order. Since p_C passes through $C_{v'}$, it is formed by extending p'_C to C_v. Therefore, p_C passes through $C_{u_0}, \ldots, C_{u_\ell}$ in this order. Moreover, $C_{u_{\ell-1}} \neq C_{u_\ell}$, finishing the proof. □

The following corollary characterizes the appearance of paths from $I \oplus F$ in T_G^R. The proof is omitted due to space constraints.

Corollary 1. *Let D be a component of $I \oplus F$, let $v \in D$, and let $p = (u_D = u_0, \ldots, u_\ell = v)$ be the path from u_D to v in $G[D]$. Then the following holds for the directed path $p_C = (C_{u_D} = C_0, \ldots, C_{\ell'} = C_v)$ in T_G^R from C_{u_D} to C_v:*

(i) *For every $i \in \{0, \ldots, \ell\}$, there exist j_i, k_i, $0 \leq j_i \leq k_i \leq \ell'$ such that the cliques on the path p_C that contain u_i are exactly cliques $C_{j_i}, C_{j_i+1}, \ldots, C_{k_i}$. Moreover, $u_i \in \mathrm{Res}(C_{j_i})$.*
(ii) *For every $i \in \{2, \ldots, \ell\}$, $u_{i-1} \in \mathrm{Sep}(C_{j_i})$.*

We are ready to define the encoding of the canonical path from I to F, passing through a transition $t = (S, S')$. Let $\mathbb{N}_b := \{1, \ldots, b\}$, where b is the separator bound of G. The encoding $\eta_t(I, F)$ consists of an independent set, a vertex, and a vector from $\mathbb{N}_b^{\lfloor \log n \rfloor}$:

$$\eta_t(I, F) := (\hat{\eta}_t(I, F), u_D, s_1, s_2, \ldots, s_{\lfloor \log n \rfloor}),$$

where the role of the vector s is to indicate the vertices of Q_{p_u} that were removed from $I \oplus F \oplus (S \cup S')$ during the construction of $\hat{\eta}_t(I, F)$, see (2). We define each s_x, $x \in \{1, \ldots, \lfloor \log n \rfloor\}$, as follows. We apply Corollary 1 to the path

$p = p_u = (u_D = u_0, \ldots, u_\ell = u)$. For each vertex $u_i \in Q_{p_u}$, we have that $u_i \in \mathrm{Sep}(C_{j_{i+1}})$ (notice that $u \notin Q_{p_u}$, thus j_{i+1} is always well-defined). Suppose we ordered Q_{p_u} in increasing order of distance from u. Let x be the position of u_i in this ordering, thus s_x will encode u_i. Since $|\mathrm{Sep}(C_{j_{i+1}})| \leq b$, we can specify u_i by its position in $\mathrm{Sep}(C_{j_{i+1}})$. Thus, s_x is such that u_i is the s_x-th smallest vertex in $\mathrm{Sep}(C_{j_{i+1}})$. Notice that we will need as many s_x's as is the size of Q_{p_u}, which is bounded by $\lfloor \log_2 n \rfloor$ by Lemma 3. For $x > |Q_{p_u}|$, we let $s_x = 1$.

Lemma 5. *Let t be a transition of the Markov chain. The above-described function $\eta_t : \mathrm{cp}(t) \to \Omega_G \times V \times \mathbb{N}_b^{\lfloor \log n \rfloor}$ is injective.*

Proof (Sketch due to space constraints). To prove the injectivity, we need to show that given a state $\hat{\eta}_t(I, F)$, a vertex u_D, a vector $(s_1, s_2, \ldots, s_{\lfloor \log n \rfloor})$, and the current transition $t = (S, S')$, we can uniquely recover the initial and final independent sets I and F.

Suppose we know $I \oplus F$. Then, due to the canonical order of processing the components, and also since we know S, we can reconstruct I and F.

It remains to recover $I \oplus F$. Notice that $I \oplus F = (\hat{\eta}_t(I, F) \oplus (S \cup S')) \cup Q_{p_u}$. Therefore, the only missing part in order to determine $I \oplus F$ is Q_{p_u}. Let $B = \hat{\eta}_t(I, F) \oplus (S \cup S')$. Since u_D is given and u is known from t, we can construct the path p_C from Corollary 1 applied to $p := p_u$. Notice that we do not yet have the path p_u constructed—if we did, we would get $I \oplus F$ as $B \cup p_u$ and we would not need to reconstruct Q_{p_u}—but, despite not having p_u, we can construct p_C uniquely just from u and u_D. Our next step will be to construct p_u.

Let $p_C = (C_{u_D} = C_0, \ldots, C_{\ell'} = C_u)$. We want to reconstruct $p_u = (u_D = u_0, u_1, \ldots, u_\ell = u)$. We know all the vertices in B and we have that $u \in C_u$. We will work our way backwards, reconstructing u_i for $i = \ell - 1, \ell - 2, \ldots, 1$. Suppose we know u_{i+1} and so far $x - 1$ vertices of Q_{p_u} have been reconstructed. We consider $C_{u_{i+1}}$. By Corollary 1(ii), we have that $u_i \in \mathrm{Sep}(C_{u_{i+1}})$. By the observation on page 8 we know that u_i and u_{i+1} are the only two vertices of $I \oplus F$ in $C_{u_{i+1}}$. Therefore, we start by checking if clique $C_{u_{i+1}}$ contains a vertex from B in its separator set. If yes, it must be u_i. If not, we will use s_x to recover u_i as the s_x-th smallest vertex in $\mathrm{Sep}(C_{u_{i+1}})$. This process uniquely determines p_u, and hence also $I \oplus F$, from which we obtain I and F.   □

Combining Lemmas 3 and 5 allows us to bound the congestion, which then leads to our mixing time bound. The proofs of the corresponding theorems are omitted for space reasons.

Theorem 2. *The congestion of the canonical paths defined above is bounded by $n^{(3+\log_2 b\lambda)}\bar{\lambda}$, where b is the separator bound of G and $\bar{\lambda} := \max\{1, \lambda\}$.*

Theorem 3. *Let G be a connected chordal graph with separator bound $b \in \mathbb{N}^+$, and let $\lambda \in \mathbb{R}^+$. If $\lambda < 1$, let $x = \emptyset$, otherwise, let x be a maximum independent set of G. The mixing time of the Dyer-Greenhill Markov chain from the start state x is $O(n^{(4+\log_2 b\lambda)})$.*

We remark that obtaining the start state x, a maximum independent set, is computable in polynomial time for chordal graphs. We conclude with a natural open problem, in addition to extending rapid mixing results to other graph classes: extending our results to arbitrary chordal graphs.

Acknowledgements. We thank the anonymous referees for their valuable feedback. Research supported in part by NSF grant DUE-1819546.

References

1. Anari, N., Liu, K., Gharan, S.O.: Spectral independence in high-dimensional expanders and applications to the hardcore model. In: Proceedings of the 52nd Annual ACM SIGACT Symposium on Theory of Computing (STOC). ACM (2020)
2. Bordewich, M., Kang, R.J.: Subset Glauber dynamics on graphs, hypergraphs and matroids of bounded tree-width. Electr. J. Comb. **21**(4), P4.19 (2014)
3. Buneman, P., et al.: A characterisation of rigid circuit graphs. Discrete Math. **9**(3), 205–212 (1974)
4. Dyer, M., Greenhill, C.: On Markov chains for independent sets. J. Algorithms **35**(1), 17–49 (2000)
5. Dyer, M., Greenhill, C., Müller, H.: Counting independent sets in graphs with bounded bipartite pathwidth. In: Sau, I., Thilikos, D.M. (eds.) WG 2019. LNCS, vol. 11789, pp. 298–310. Springer, Cham (2019). https://doi.org/10.1007/978-3-030-30786-8_23
6. Dyer, M.E., Frieze, A.M., Jerrum, M.: On counting independent sets in sparse graphs. SIAM J. Comput. **31**(5), 1527–1541 (2002)
7. Efthymiou, C., Hayes, T.P., Štefankovič, D., Vigoda, E., Yin, Y.: Convergence of MCMC and loopy BP in the tree uniqueness region for the hard-core model. SIAM J. Comput. **48**(2), 581–643 (2019)
8. Galanis, A., Ge, Q., Štefankovič, D., Vigoda, E., Yang, L.: Improved inapproximability results for counting independent sets in the hard-core model. Random Struct. Algorithms **45**(1), 78–110 (2014)
9. Galanis, A., Štefankovič, D., Vigoda, E.: Inapproximability of the partition function for the antiferromagnetic ising and hard-core models. Comb. Probab. Comput. **25**(4), 500–559 (2016)
10. Gavril, F.: The intersection graphs of subtrees in trees are exactly the chordal graphs. J. Comb. Theory Ser. B **16**(1), 47–56 (1974)
11. Ge, Q., Štefankovič, D.: A graph polynomial for independent sets of bipartite graphs. Comb. Probab. Comput. **21**(5), 695–714 (2012)
12. Jerrum, M.: Counting, Sampling and Integrating: Algorithms and Complexity. Birhäuser (2003)
13. Jerrum, M., Sinclair, A.: Approximating the permanent. SIAM J. Comput. **18**(6), 1149–1178 (1989)
14. Koller, D., Friedman, N.: Probabilistic Graphical Models: Principles and Techniques. MIT press, Cambridge (2009)
15. Luby, M., Vigoda, E.: Fast convergence of the Glauber dynamics for sampling independent sets. Random Struct. Algorithms **15**(3–4), 229–241 (1999)
16. Matthews, J.: Markov chains for sampling matchings. Ph.D. Thesis, University of Edinburgh (2008)

17. Mossel, E., Weitz, D., Wormald, N.: On the hardness of sampling independent sets beyond the tree threshold. Probab. Theory Rel. Fields **143**, 401–439 (2009)
18. Okamoto, Y., Uno, T., Uehara, R.: Linear-time counting algorithms for independent sets in chordal Graphs. In: Kratsch, D. (ed.) WG 2005. LNCS, vol. 3787, pp. 433–444. Springer, Heidelberg (2005). https://doi.org/10.1007/11604686_38
19. Sinclair, A.: Improved bounds for mixing rates of Markov chains and multicommodity flow. Comb. Prob. Comput. **1**(4), 351–370 (1992)
20. Sly, A.: Computational transition at the uniqueness threshold. In: 2010 IEEE 51st Annual Symposium on Foundations of Computer Science, pp. 287–296. IEEE (2010)
21. Sly, A., Sun, N.: Counting in two-spin models on d-regular graphs. Ann. Probab. **42**(6), 2383–2416 (2014)
22. Vandenberghe, L., Andersen, M.S., et al.: Chordal graphs and semidefinite optimization. Found. Trends ® Optim. **1**(4), 241–433 (2015)
23. Vigoda, E.: A note on the Glauber dynamics for sampling independent sets. Electr. J. Comb. **8**(1), R8 (2001)
24. Weitz, D.: Counting independent sets up to the tree threshold. In: Proceedings of the 38th Annual ACM symposium on Theory of Computing (STOC), pp. 140–149 (2006)

Author Index

Printed in the United States
By Bookmasters